*Huntington Library Publications*

# American Fiction

## 1876-1900

*A CONTRIBUTION TOWARD A BIBLIOGRAPHY*

BY

LYLE H. WRIGHT

THE HUNTINGTON LIBRARY

SAN MARINO, CALIFORNIA

1966

PRINTED IN U.S.A.
BY ANDERSON, RITCHIE & SIMON : LOS ANGELES

THIS WORK IS DEDICATED TO MY WIFE
*Marjorie E. Wright*
WHO HAS ALWAYS ENCOURAGED AND ASSISTED
ME IN MY ENDEAVORS THROUGHOUT THE YEARS

# CONTENTS

# PREFACE

THE purpose of this list is to record the fiction, within the framework of selection set forth below, written for adults by Americans and printed in the United States between 1876 and 1900. The few foreign-born authors who are included either considered the United States as their permanent home or wrote with coauthors who were American citizens. Anonymous works have been retained when it has not been determined whether they were of foreign or American authorship.

The scope of the work is similar to my preceding publications in this field, *American Fiction, 1774-1850* and *American Fiction, 1851-1875*. Included are novels, short stories, tall tales, allegories, tract-like tales, and fictitious biographies and travels.

I have intended to omit the same classifications of fiction as were omitted in the two works mentioned above: publications of the American Tract Society, Sunday school unions, and religious denominations; collections of anecdotes; juveniles, jestbooks, folklore, essays, and periodicals, including subscription series, which were classed as periodicals.

The basic rule of entry is to record only the first or earliest located edition printed in the United States. Exceptions are as follows: to list a subsequent edition when it contains new material other than an added preface or introduction (No. 108); to list a privately printed edition as well as the trade edition if it precedes the latter (Nos. 116, 117); to list in a note under the main entry republication of the novel with a changed title, providing it is not in a subscription series and appeared before 1901 (Nos. 42, 67); to list in a note under the main entry a variant imprint of an item issued simultaneously in a city other than that of the original publishers (Nos. 760, 5337). Usually the name of the local publisher was added to the imprint in these cases.

During the course of this compilation, I came across 195 subscription series, all of which are omitted herein. The frequency of their publications ranged from semi-weekly, such as Belford, Clarke & Company's "Household Library" at $30.00 per annum, to quarterly, such as Keppler & Schwarzmann's "Puck's Mulberry Series" at $2.00 per annum. Some of the publishers were modest in their output, such as Robert Bonner's Sons with the "Choice Series" and "Ledger Library"; Funk & Wagnalls with "Standard Library" and "Temperance Library"; Houghton, Mifflin with "Riverside Paper Series" and "Riverside Literature Series"; George Munro with "Calumet Series" and "Seaside Library"; and Ticknor & Co. with "Ticknor's Paper Series of Choice Reading." On the other hand, J. W. Lovell Co. had five series, F. Tennyson Neely seven, J. S. Ogilvie ten, and Street & Smith fifteen.

In 1879 the law defined mailable second-class matter as embracing newspapers and other periodical publications which were issued at stated intervals and as frequently as four times a year, bore a date of issue, and were numbered consecutively. Furthermore, such matter had to be issued from a known office of publication and be "formed of printed paper sheets, without board, cloth, leather, or other substantial binding, such as distinguish printed books for preservation from periodical publications."

Thousands of novels and other literary efforts, originals and reprints, were so published. The postmaster general in his annual report for the year ending June 30, 1891, said, "Books in packages of four pounds are carried at 8 cents a pound; but publishers of serials, so called, are able to ship their entire production from the Atlantic to the Pacific for 1 cent a pound." Further, "There are probably 50,000 tons of so-called serials passing through the post-offices every year at a penny a pound, causing a million of dollars per year to be added to the deficit."

More than one publisher issued titles simultaneously in paper-bound series and hard-cover edition. For example, Robert Bonner's Sons in 1892 published Harold Frederic's *The Return of the O'Mahony* (No. 2022) both in cloth and in the "Choice Series," and D. Appleton and Company in 1900 published Albert Lee's *The Gentleman Pensioner* (No. 3247) in cloth and in the subscription "Appleton's Town and Country Library, No. 279." In the latter case, the series name and number were retained on the title page of the cloth edition, though usually the subscription information required by law was found only on the front cover or spine of the paperbound editions. The problem, therefore, has been to find these hard-cover editions, and I am certain that there are a number yet to be found.

Not to be confused with subscription series are several series which were published at intervals but not by subscription. Others were not sold by subscription in their earlier numbers but were in later ones. For examples see Nos. 17, 18, 36, 125, and 176.

The most useful tool in screening out juveniles has been the *Publishers' Weekly*, particularly the monthly summary of publications by classes, which included "Fiction" and "Juvenile Books." Since college stories may be found in either class, all of them have been retained. Whenever I have been unable to determine the classification by contemporary advertisements or reviews, I have included the title. It must be emphasized that this list does not record all the fiction by each author herein entered, but only that which falls within the established scope.

## BIBLIOGRAPHICAL COMMENT

The list was compiled to serve as a guide to the books rather than as a complete bibliographical description of them. I have examined a large proportion of the items, but rarely have I examined multiple copies of a title. Consequently, variations between copies are seldom noted, and in only a few cases are distinguishing points of issues brought out. Copies are located in the fourteen libraries listed on page xix. Whenever no copy was found in any of these libraries, one is located in some other library that I visited (Nos. 11, 199) or acknowledgment is made of who supplied the information (Nos. 351, 482). If no copy is located, the source of information about the item is supplied (Nos. 14, 19, 228). The note "Listed PW, Jan. 14, 1899" (No. 19, for example) refers to the "Weekly Record of New Publications" in the *Publishers' Weekly*.

## MECHANICS OF COMPILATION

*Entries*  The books are entered under author's name when known, under unidentified pseudonym or initials, or under title. Square brackets around an entry indicate that the author's name is not on the title page.

*Titles*  Some titles are shortened, and authors' names and quotations appearing on the title pages are usually omitted. Omissions are indicated by ellipses. The abbreviation "pseud.," following a name that is on the title page as the author, is self-explanatory. To avoid the eccentricities of nineteenth-century printing, punctuation and capitalization are regularized.

*Imprints*  I have intended to list all the printers and publishers in the imprints, except that the "successors to" firm name is frequently dropped when not significant for identification of edition. Their addresses, if included, are also given whenever publication date had to be supplied. The "published by" so frequently found in an imprint is omitted.

*Dates*  Roman dates in the imprints are converted into Arabic. The date in the copyright notice, if any, is used for the undated books, providing it meets certain requirements. If the year given in the notice is within the publisher's years of occupation at the address from which the book was issued, it is accepted. The supplied date in the imprint is then preceded by the abbreviation "cop." and both are placed in square brackets. Occasionally the actual date of deposit at the Library of Congress for copyright purposes differs from the copyright date printed in the book. This is noted ("Deposited June 24, 1891") whenever I found a copyright copy (Nos. 38, 141, 185).

*Pagination*  Formal pagination is not supplied; the last numbered page of text is given, to afford an idea of the length of the contents, and unnumbered pages or leaves of text or colophon, if any, following this are recorded. When the text is printed in double columns, it is so noted. The sizes of books are not given. To designate a novel printed on machine-made paper as octavo or duodecimo has little significance. And to state that a page is seven inches tall when such a measurement has usually been derived from the examination of only one copy may be misleading.

*Illustrations*  The abbreviation "illus." is used to designate all types of illustrations within the book: plates, portraits, textual illustrations, and frontispieces, provided the latter are not alone. If a book contains only a frontispiece, it is noted by the abbreviation "front." Vignettes are not indicated or included in the abbreviation "illus."

*Notes*  The notes are for the most part self-explanatory. Books containing two or more stories usually have one of the three following notes: "Contents," which lists all the stories in the book; "Also contains," which lists all stories following the first (the first being used as the title of the book); "Contains," which lists only those stories that fall within the scope of this work.

*Annotations*  A note suggesting the topic of the novel or one of the subjects treated in it is frequently added. Under some entries the note refers to the locale and date or period when the title furnishes no clew. The annotations are based on cursory examination or heavy borrowing on my part from other sources, mainly the *Publishers' Weekly*.

*Cross References*  Cross references appear in the main body of the list. Only the main entries are numbered. When there are two or more stories by different authors in one book, all but the title story are analyzed, provided the authors' names are given. No attempt has been made to identify the anonymous stories.

### TITLE INDEX

The title index lists the titles in abbreviated form of all the main and analytical entries and the changed titles of new editions recorded in the notes under the original titles.

*August 1, 1964*                              LYLE H. WRIGHT

# ACKNOWLEDGMENTS

To compile a list such as the following can be accomplished only by the cooperation and interest of many people. This I have had from librarians, bibliographers, collectors, and antiquarian bookmen throughout the country. And I wish to express my sincere thanks to all who rendered assistance to the project.

To the Trustees of the Huntington Library, the Director, John E. Pomfret, and the Librarian, Robert O. Dougan, I am indebted for making it possible for me to work in several libraries from coast to coast. Miss Gwen Staniforth, formerly of the Reference Department, contributed much to this list, and Miss Mary Isabel Fry, Reference Librarian, has rendered invaluable assistance from the inception of the project. To Miss Mary Jane Bragg of the Publications Department my sincere thanks for an outstanding job of editing the manuscript.

To the following people who were responsible for having my preliminary list checked for locations, who answered interminable questions, or who gave personal assistance when I visited their libraries, I am most grateful:

Edward C. Carter II of the Athenaeum of Philadelphia.

Walter Muir Whitehill, Miss Margaret Hackett, and Mrs. Joan Spunt, of the Boston Athenaeum.

David A. Jonah, Mrs. Christine D. Hathaway, and Roger E. Stoddard, of the Brown University Library, and John R. Turner Ettlinger, formerly of that library.

Roland Baughman and Erle P. Kemp, of the Columbia University Libraries, Butler Division.

Robert H. Haynes and Miss Natalie B. Doyle, formerly of the Harvard College Library, and Richard A. Waswo, of the Houghton Library.

Frederick R. Goff and Roger J. Trienens, of the Library of Congress, and J. M. Edelstein, formerly of the Library of Congress.

Mrs. Mabel J. Erler and Richard Colles Johnson, of the Newberry Library, and Stanley Pargellis, formerly of that library.

Kermit Cudd and Mrs. Mary Key, of Ohio State University Libraries.

Robert Rosenthal, Helen McGregor, and J. Richard Phillips, of the University of Chicago Library.

Miss Norma Hovden, of the University of Minnesota Library.

Miss Neda M. Westlake, of the University of Pennsylvania Library.

William H. Runge and Neal B. Thornton, of the Alderman Library, University of Virginia. Neal Thornton checked C. Waller Barrett's books which are still in Mr. Barrett's New York office but ultimately will be transferred to the Barrett Room at the University of Virginia Library. Mrs. Katherine L. Mass, secretary to Mr. Barrett, was very helpful when I examined the New York collection.

Donald G. Wing and Robert J. Olson, of Yale University Library.

In addition, John Alden, of the Boston Public Library, and Lewis M. Stark, Mrs. Philomena C. Houlihan, and John D. Gordon, of the New York Public Library, made my visits to their libraries most worth while.

To my wife Marjorie, who has been involved in this project since its inception, I owe my deepest gratitude for her assistance on and interest in it.

The following also have contributed in one way or another to this work, and to them I wish to express my appreciation and thanks:

| | |
|---|---|
| Clifton Waller Barrett | Miss Evangeline Lynch |
| Jacob Blanck | George S. MacManus |
| Carey S. Bliss | Howard S. Mott |
| Mrs. Ann Bowden | Allan R. Ottley |
| George T. Goodspeed | Miss Ellen Shaffer |
| William A. Jackson | Clifford K. Shipton |
| William F. Kelleher | Ernest D. Starr |
| John S. Van E. Kohn | Ernest J. Wessen |

# KEY TO AUTHORS AND TITLES
# OF BOOKS REFERRED TO IN THE NOTES

**BAL**

Blanck, Jacob N., comp. *Bibliography of American Literature*. Vols. I-IV. New Haven, 1955-63.

**BANTA**

Banta, Richard E., comp. *Indiana Authors and Their Books, 1816-1916*. Crawfordsville, Ind., 1949.

**COYLE**

Coyle, William, ed. *Ohio Authors and Their Books*. Cleveland, Ohio [1962].

**HINKEL**

Hinkel, Edgar J., ed. *Bibliography of California Fiction*. Vol. I. Oakland, Calif., 1938.

**POWELL**

Powell, William S., ed. *North Carolina Fiction, 1734-1957*. Chapel Hill, 1958.

**PW**

*Publishers' Weekly*. New York, 1876-1900.

**D. E. THOMPSON**

Thompson, Donald E., comp. *A Bibliography of Louisiana Books and Pamphlets*. University, Ala., 1947.

**L. S. THOMPSON**

Thompson, Lawrence S., and Algernon D. Thompson. *The Kentucky Novel*. [Lexington, Ky., 1953.]

**TURNBULL**

Turnbull, Robert J. *Bibliography of South Carolina, 1563-1950*. Vol. IV. Charlottesville, Va. [1956].

**WILLIAMSON**

Williamson, Joseph. *A Bibliography of the State of Maine*. 2 vols. Portland, Me., 1896.

**WRIGHT I**

Wright, Lyle H. *American Fiction, 1774-1850*. Rev. ed. San Marino, Calif., 1948.

**WRIGHT II**

Wright, Lyle H. *American Fiction, 1851-1875*. San Marino, Calif., 1957.

# ABBREVIATIONS USED FOR LIBRARIES APPEARING IN THE CENSUS

**AP**

Athenaeum of Philadelphia, Philadelphia, Pennsylvania

**BA**

Boston Athenaeum, Boston, Massachusetts

**BU**

Brown University Library, Providence, Rhode Island

**CU**

Columbia University Library, New York, N.Y.

**H**

Harvard University Library, Cambridge, Massachusetts

**HEH**

Henry E. Huntington Library and Art Gallery, San Marino, California

**LC**

Library of Congress, Washington, D.C.

**N**

Newberry Library, Chicago, Illinois

**O**

Ohio State University Libraries, Columbus, Ohio

**UC**

University of Chicago Library, Chicago, Illinois

**UM**

University of Minnesota Library, Minneapolis, Minnesota

**UP**

University of Pennsylvania Library, Philadelphia, Pennsylvania

**UV**

University of Virginia Library, Charlottesville, Virginia

**UVB**

C. Waller Barrett Collection of the University of Virginia Library

**Y**

Yale University Library, New Haven, Connecticut

# BIBLIOGRAPHY

# American Fiction
## 1876-1900

A., C. E.   *See* Aiken, Clementine Edith

A., E. W.   *See* Allderdice, Elizabeth (Winslow)

1   A., Miss M. L.   Illma; or, Which Was Wife?   By Miss M. L. A.   New
    York: Cornwell & Johnson, 1881.   353 p.                                    LC
    New York state.

1a  ABBOT, ALICE IRVING.   Circumstantial Evidence . . .   New York: W. B.
    Smith & Co., Bond Street [cop. 1882].   358 p.                              LC

    ABBOTT, ANNE WALES.   Rex's Vacation.   *In* [H. L. Reed] *ed.*, "The City
    and the Sea" (1881), No. 4487.

2   ABBOTT, CHARLES CONRAD.   A Colonial Wooing . . .   Philadelphia: J. B.
    Lippincott Company, 1895.   241 p.        BA, CU, H, HEH, LC, O, UM, Y
    Quakers; Burlington County, New Jersey.

3   ———   The Hermit of Nottingham: A Novel . . .   Philadelphia: J. B.
    Lippincott Company, 1898.   332 p.        H, HEH, LC, O, UM, Y
    New Jersey.

4   ———   When the Century Was New: A Novel . . .   Philadelphia: J. B.
    Lippincott Company, 1897.   275 p.        H, HEH, LC, O, Y
    New Jersey.

5   ABBOTT, LAURA HUNSAKER.   Dan, the Tramp: A Story of To-Day . . .
    Chicago: Charles H. Kerr & Co., 1897.   150 p.                              CU
    Of Arizona interest.

6   ABBOTT, MARY PERKINS (IVES).   Alexia . . .   Chicago: A. C. McClurg
    and Company, 1889.   177 p.               AP, BA, H, HEH, LC, O, Y

7   ———   The Beverleys: A Story of Calcutta . . .   Chicago: A. C.
    McClurg and Company, 1890.   264 p.       AP, BA, H, HEH, O, UV, Y

    A'BECKET, JOHN J.   A Change of Temperature.   *In* Some Short Stories
    [cop. 1900], No. 5070.

    ———   The Song of the Comforter.   *In* Stories of Italy (1893), No.
    5278.

    ———   The Vigil of Fenton Barlowe.   *In* F. E. McKay, *ed.*, Vignettes
    [cop. 1890], No. 3523.

8 ABRAMS, ALBERT. Scattered Leaves from a Physician's Diary . . . St. Louis, Mo.: Fortnightly Press Co., 1900. 59 p., front.　　LC, UM

9 ────── Transactions of the Antiseptic Club . . . New York: E. B. Treat. Chicago: R. C. Treat. Boston: J. W. Adams & Co. New Orleans: N. D. McDonald. Cincinnati: John P. Hobart. San Francisco: Johnson & Emigh, 1895. 206 p., illus.　　CU, H, HEH, LC, O, UM, UP

10 ABROJAL, TULIS, *pseud.* An Index Finger . . . New York City: R. F. Fenno & Company, 1898. 382 p.　　CU, HEH, LC, UP
Of psychic phenomena.

11 ABY, JOSEPH C. The Tales of Rube Hoffenstein . . . New York: W. B. Smith & Co., Bond Street [cop. 1882]. 64 p.
Copy examined at New York Public Library.

12 ACKERMAN, A. W. The Price of Peace: A Story of the Times of Ahab, King of Israel . . . Chicago: A. C. McClurg and Company, 1894. 390 p.　　HEH, LC

13 ACKLAN, WILLIAM HAYES. Sterope . . . Washington: Gibson Bros., printers and bookbinders, 1892. 300 p.　　BU, CU, HEH, LC, Y
Ante bellum New Orleans.

14 ADAMS, CHARLES ABEL. An Ocean Special . . . New York: The author, 1900. 250 p., illus.
Information from LC card; no copy seen.

15 ADAMS, EVELYN. Is Marriage a Lottery? 16547 . . . New York: E. Adams, 1891. 131 p., illus.　　LC

16 ADAMS, FRANCIS ALEXANDRE. The Transgressors: Story of a Great Sin. A Political Novel of the Twentieth Century . . . Philadelphia: Independence Publishing Company [cop. 1900]. 345 p.　　H, HEH, LC, UC
Of the Pennsylvania coal fields.

17 [ADAMS, HENRY.] Democracy: An American Novel. New York: Henry Holt and Company, 1880. 374 p.
BA, BU, CU, H, HEH, LC, N, O, UC, UP, UVB, Y
At head of title: "Leisure-Hour Series—No. 112."
Politics and society in Washington, D.C.

18 [──────] Esther: A Novel. By Frances Snow Compton [pseud.]. New York: Henry Holt and Company, 1884. 302 p.
BA, BU, H, LC, UP, UV, Y
At head of title: "American Novel Series, No. 3."
Church life in New York City.

19 ADAMS, HENRY AUSTIN. Westchester: A Tale of the Revolution . . . St. Louis, Mo.: B. Herder, 1899. 264 p.
Listed PW, Jan. 14, 1899.

ADAMS, JACK, *pseud. See* Grigsby, Alcanoan O.

20 [ADAMS, JAMES ALONZO.] Colonel Hungerford's Daughter: Story of an American Girl. By Grapho [pseud.] . . . Chicago: Charles H. Kerr & Company, 1896. 304 p.
LC

21 ADAMS, MARY. An Honorable Surrender . . . New York: Charles Scribner's Sons, 1883. 323 p.
AP, BA, H, HEH, LC, O, Y
A New England village.

22 ADAMS, OSCAR FAY. The Archbishop's Unguarded Moment, and Other Stories . . . Boston: L. C. Page and Company (Incorporated), 1899. 270 p., front.
BA, CU, H, HEH, LC, O, UVB, Y
*Also contains:* The Evolution of a Bishop—Why the Bishop Left Rye Beach—The Trials of a Retired Bishop—A Night with William of Wykeham—The Discontented Bishop—The Serious Dilemma of the Bishop of Oklahoma.

———— A Night with William of Wykeham. *In* F. E. McKay, *ed.,* Vignettes [cop. 1890], No. 3523.
Later printed in No. 22.

23 ADAMS, WILLIAM TAYLOR. Living Too Fast; or, The Confessions of a Bank Officer . . . Boston: Lee and Shepard. New York: Charles T. Dillingham, 1876. 351 p., illus.
BU, CU, HEH, LC, O, UM, Y

ADDUMS, MOZIS, *pseud. See* Bagby, George William

24 ADE, GEORGE. Artie: A Story of the Streets and Town . . . Chicago: Herbert S. Stone & Co., 1896. 192, [1] p., 1 l., illus.
CU, HEH, LC, N, UC, UM, UP, UVB, Y

25 ———— Doc' Horne: A Story of the Streets and Town . . . Chicago and New York: Herbert S. Stone and Company, 1899. 292 p., 1 l., illus.
CU, H, HEH, N, UC, UM, UP, UVB

26 ———— Fables in Slang . . . Chicago & New York: Herbert S. Stone and Company, 1900. 201 p., 1 l., illus.
BU, CU, H, HEH, LC, N, O, UM, UP, UVB, Y
A collection of humorous stories.

———— The General Hatred of Mr. Darby. *In* Short Story Masterpieces (1900), No. 4931.

27 ———— More Fables . . . Chicago & New York: Herbert S. Stone and Company, 1900. 218 p., 1 l., illus.
BA, BU, CU, H, HEH, LC, N, O, UC, UM, UP, UVB, Y
HEH also has the tenth fable, "The Modern Fable of the Adult Girl," in "Syndicate Articles," a 6 p. prospectus issued by R. H. Russell, New York. This fable was to be released Sept. 30, 1900, as the first installment of a syndicated series.

28 ———— Pink Marsh: A Story of the Streets and Town . . . Chicago &
New York: Herbert S. Stone & Co., 1897. 196, [2] p., illus.
CU, H, HEH, LC, N, O, UM, UP, UVB, Y

———— Shiner's Love-Making in a Crowd. *In* Short Story Masterpieces (1900), No. 4931.

ADEE, ALVEY AUGUSTUS. The Life-Magnet. *In* Stories by American
Authors, VIII (1884), No. 5274.

ADELER, MAX, *pseud*. *See* Clark, Charles Heber

29 ADLER, CYRUS. Told in the Coffee-House: Turkish Tales . . . New
York: The Macmillan Company. London: Macmillan & Co., Ltd.,
1898. 174 p. BA, H, LC, O, Y
Allan Ramsay, jt. au.

30 [ADOLPH, ANNA.] Arqtiq: A Study of the Marvels at the North Pole.
[Oakland, Calif.: Carruth & Carruth, printers]; Published for the author,
1899. 80 p. LC

31 AFFERY, CHARLES. Misled: A Story of To-Day . . . New York: The
Minerva Publishing Company, 1889. 163 p. HEH

AFTEREM, GEORGE, *pseud*. *See* Williams, Harold

32 AGNEW, CORA. Peerless Cathleen; or, The Stolen Casket. An English
Society Story . . . New York: G. W. Carleton & Co.; Street & Smith,
New York Weekly, 1877. 440 p. HEH, Y
At head of title: " 'New York Weekly' Series, No. 2."

33 AGNUS, FELIX. A Woman of War, and Other Stories . . . Baltimore:
The American Job Printing Office, 1895. 180 p. HEH, LC
*Contents:* Noel of 1864–A Woman of War–The Gunner of "Lady Davis"–
A Sacred Trust.

34 [AIKEN, CLEMENTINE EDITH.] The Days We Live In: A Story of Society.
By C. E. A. . . . Boston: W. F. Brown & Company, 1876. 478 p., illus.
CU, HEH, LC, Y

AKERS, ELIZABETH. *See* Allen, Elizabeth Ann (Chase) Akers

35 ALBERT, BESSIE. How Bob and I Kept House: A Story of Chicago Hard
Times . . . New York: The Authors' Publishing Company, 27 Bond
Street [cop. 1880]. 65 p. LC

36 [ALCOTT, LOUISA MAY.] A Modern Mephistopheles. Boston: Roberts
Brothers, 1877. 290 p. BA, CU, H, HEH, LC, N, O, UC, UM, UP, UVB, Y
At head of title: "No Name Series."

37 ———— A Modern Mephistopheles, and A Whisper in the Dark . . .
Boston: Roberts Brothers, 1889. 350 p. AP, H, LC, O, Y

———— Transcendental Wild Oats. *In* [W. F. Gill] *ed.*, Laurel Leaves (1876), No. 2167.
Later printed in No. 3206.

ALDEN, MRS. G. R. *See* Alden, Isabella (Macdonald)

38 ALDEN, ISABELLA (MACDONALD). Aunt Hannah and Martha and John. By Pansy (Mrs. G. R. Alden) and Mrs. C. M. Livingston ... Boston: D. Lothrop Company, Washington Street opposite Bromfield [cop. 1890]. 432 p., illus.                                     HEH, LC, O, UM, Y
Deposited June 24, 1891.
Of a minister's life.

39 ———— By Way of the Wilderness ... Boston: Lothrop Publishing Company [cop. 1899]. 394 p., front.                          H, LC, Y
Mrs. C. M. Livingston, jt. au.

40 ———— John Remington, Martyr ... Boston: D. Lothrop Company, Washington Street opposite Bromfield [cop. 1892]. 417 p., illus.
                                                        HEH, LC, UC, Y
Mrs. C. M. Livingston, jt. au.
Of an outspoken minister.

41 ———— Missent: The Story of a Letter ... Boston: Lothrop Publishing Company, 1900. 175, [1] p., front.                       HEH, LC

ALDEN, JEAN FRANÇOIS, *pseud. See* Clemens, Samuel Langhorne

42 ALDEN, WILLIAM LIVINGSTON. Domestic Explosives, and Other Sixth Column Fancies ... New York: Lovell, Adam, Wesson & Company, 1877. 334 p., illus.                              CU, H, HEH, O, UM, Y

Also published as: *The Comic Liar: A Book Not Commonly Found in Sunday Schools.* New York: G. W. Carleton & Co. London: S. Low, Sons & Co., 1883.    H, UC, UM, Y

Also published as: *The Coming Girl: A Book Not Commonly Found in Sunday Schools.* New York: G. W. Carleton & Co. London: S. Low, Sons & Co., 1884. Information from LC card; no copy seen.

———— The Flying March. *In* I. Bacheller, *ed.*, Best Things from American Literature (1899), No. 195.

43 ———— Shooting Stars as Observed from the "Sixth Column" of the Times ... New York: G. P. Putnam's Sons, 1878. 224 p., illus.
                                          BU, CU, H, HEH, LC, N, O, UC, UM, Y

44 ———— Told by the Colonel ... New York: J. Selwin Tait & Sons [cop. 1893]. 176 p., illus.                        CU, HEH, LC, N, O, Y

45 ALDRICH, ANNE REEVE. The Feet of Love ... New York: Worthington & Co., 1890. 290 p., illus.                        AP, CU, HEH, LC, O, Y
"Gilead," Long Island.

46 ——— Gabriel Lusk . . . New York: Charles T. Dillingham & Co., 1894. 181 p.                                     HEH, Y

47 ——— A Village Ophelia . . . New York: G. W. Dillingham & Co., 1899. 188 p.                              CU, HEH, LC, UP, UVB
*Also contains:* A Story of the Vere de Vere—A Lamentable Comedy—An African Discovery—An Evening with Callender.

48 ALDRICH, THOMAS BAILEY. The Little Violinist . . . [Cambridge: University Press; John Wilson and Son]; Reprinted with the author's permission, and sold at the Fair of the Massachusetts Society for the Prevention of Cruelty to Children, 1880. 18 p.          H, HEH, UVB, Y
First separate printing; included in Nos. 49 and 50.

49 ——— Marjorie Daw, and Other Stories . . . Boston, New York: Houghton, Mifflin and Company. The Riverside Press, Cambridge, 1885. 287 p.                              H, HEH, LC, O, UC, Y
*Also contains:* Miss Mehetabel's Son—Our New Neighbors at Ponkapog—A Midnight Fantasy—Mademoiselle Olympe Zabriski—A Struggle for Life—Père Antoine's Date-Palm—Quite So—A Rivermouth Romance—The Little Violinist.

At head of title: "The Riverside Aldine Series."
Contains some of the same stories as Wright II, No. 36.

50 ——— A Midnight Fantasy, and The Little Violinist . . . Boston: James R. Osgood and Company, 1877. 96 p., illus.
                              CU, H, HEH, LC, N, O, UC, UM, UVB, Y
Both stories later included in No. 49; the latter printed separately, No. 48.

51 ——— Miss Mehetabel's Son . . . Boston: James R. Osgood and Company, 1877. 93 p., illus.                  H, HEH, N, UC, UVB, Y
*Also contains:* Père Antoine's Date-Palm.

Title story included in No. 49 and in Wright II, No. 36.

52 ——— The Queen of Sheba. Boston: James R. Osgood and Company, 1877. 270 p.          BU, CU, H, HEH, LC, N, O, UC, UP, UVB, Y
At head of title: "Thomas Bailey Aldrich."

53 ——— A Rivermouth Romance . . . Boston: James R. Osgood and Company, 1877. 94 p., illus.                  BU, H, N, UM, Y
First separate printing; included in No. 49 and in Wright II, No. 36.

54 ——— The Stillwater Tragedy . . . Boston: Houghton, Mifflin and Company. The Riverside Press, Cambridge, 1880. 324 p.
                              AP, BU, H, HEH, LC, N, O, UP, UVB, Y

55 ——— Two Bites at a Cherry, with Other Tales . . . Boston and New York: Houghton, Mifflin and Company. The Riverside Press, Cambridge, 1894. 269 p.     AP, BA, BU, CU, H, HEH, LC, N, O, UC, UP, UVB, Y

*Also contains:* "For Bravery on the Field of Battle"—The Chevalier de Resseguer—Goliath—My Cousin the Colonel—A Christmas Fantasy, with a Moral —Her Dying Words.

———— *jt. au. See* Oliphant, Margaret Oliphant (Wilson). The Second Son (1888), No. 4032.

56 [ALEXANDER, CHARLES WESLEY.] The Baby on the Door Step; or, A Rich, Jealous Woman's Revenge. How She Broke Up the Happy Home of Her Rival, and Her Terrible Punishment When Detected. Philadelphia, Pa.: The Old Franklin Publishing House, cop. 1886. 62 p., 1 l., illus.
HEH, LC
This is his *Bertha Barton* continued.

57 [————] Bertha Barton, the Boat Builder's Daughter: The Most Lucky High School Girl of This City, Who Rescued Sir George Gaunt during the Great Yacht Race between the Puritan and Genesta and Was Afterwards Married by Him ... Edited by Wellesley Bradshaw [pseud.]. Philadelphia: The Old Franklin Publishing House, cop. 1886. 46 p., 1 l., illus.
LC

58 [————] Only a Mill Girl! or, Vinnie Roche's Sad Fate. A True and Touching Account of "The Beauty of Glendale Silk Mill." How She Was Cruelly Betrayed by the Son of a Wealthy Mill Owner. Sent to America and Cast Adrift among Strangers! ... Philadelphia, Pa.: The Old Franklin Publishing House, cop., 1879. 30, [2] p., illus.
HEH

59 [————] Saved by Buffalo Bill during the Ghost Dances of the Wild Indians of Dakota ... Philadelphia, Pa.: The Old Franklin Publishing House, cop. 1891. 78 p., illus.
LC
At head of cover title: "Wellesley Bradshaw's [pseud.] Real Life Narratives."

60 ALEXANDER, MATILDA (GREATHOUSE). Going West; or, Homes for the Homeless. A Novel ... Indianapolis: Carlon & Hollenbeck, printers and binders, 1881. 258 p.
HEH, Y

61 ———— Worth Wins: A Novel ... St. Louis, Mo.: Commercial Printing Company, 1882. 250 p.
LC
Based on life of James Buchanan Eads, engineer and inventor.

62 ALEXANDER, SIGMUND BOWMAN. A Moral Blot: A Novel ... Boston: Arena Publishing Company, 1894. 233 p.
LC, Y
Boston.

63 ———— Ten of Us: Original Stories and Sketches ... Boston: Laughton, Macdonald & Co., 131 Tremont Street [cop. 1887]. 167 p., front.
H, HEH, LC
*Contents:* The Modern Mephistopheles—Behind the Scenes—Out of the Sea— Love and Creed—A Dual Life—Society vs. Societies—The Living Dead—The Talisman—The Mystery of Death—The Little Model.

64 ——— The Veiled Beyond: A Romance of the Adepts... New York: Cassell & Company, Limited, 104 & 106 Fourth Avenue [cop. 1888]. 276 p.                                      HEH, LC
Of reincarnation.

ALEXIS, *pseud.* *See* Leavitt, John McDowell

65 ALGATCHIE, *pseud.* Seen and Unseen: A Novel... New York: G. W. Carleton & Co. London: S. Low & Co., 1876. 309 p.
                                  CU, H, HEH, LC, UC, Y
Of spiritualism.

66 ALIUNDE; or, Love Ventures... New York: Charles P. Somerby, 1877. 226 p.                                       LC

67 ALL FOR HER; or, St. Jude's Assistant. A Novel. By * * * * ? ... New York: G. W. Carleton & Co. London: S. Low & Co., 1877. 429 p.
                                     H, HEH, LC

Also published as: *A Cruel Secret: A Novel.* New York: G. W. Carleton & Co. London: S. Low & Co., 1883.   LC

Of the murder of a clergyman.

68 ALL FOR HIM: A Novel. By * * * * ? Author of "All for Her"... New York: G. W. Carleton & Co. London: S. Low & Co., 1877. 376 p.                               BU, HEH, LC
Also published as: *Sweetheart and Wife: A Novel.* New York: G. W. Carleton & Co. London: S. Low, Son & Co., 1882.   LC

Of a murder; New York.

69 ALL ON ACCOUNT OF ELIZA: A Novel... New York: G. W. Carleton & Co. London: S. Low, Son & Co., 1881. 192 p.        HEH, LC

70 [ALLDERDICE, ELIZABETH (WINSLOW).] Heart's Delight: A Novel. By E. W. A.... New York: G. W. Carleton & Co. London: S. Low, Son & Co., 1879. 366 p.                                 HEH

71 ALLEN, ALFRED. The Heart of Don Vega... Westerly, R.I.: George G. Champlin, 1888. 156 p.                           CU, LC
Heart patient invents an electric heart; operation described.

72 [ALLEN, ELIZABETH ANN (CHASE) AKERS.] The Triangular Society: Leaves from the Life of a Portland Family. Portland [Me.]: Hoyt, Fogg & Donham, 1886. 381 p.       BA, BU, CU, HEH, N, O, Y

73 ALLEN, FRANK WALLER. My Ship's Aground... Chicago: The Blue Sky Press [1900]. [12] p., illus.                       HEH, N
125 copies printed.

74 [ALLEN, HENRY FRANCIS.] The Key of Industrial Co-operative Government. By Pruning Knife [pseud.]. St. Louis, Mo.: The author, 1886. 133 p., illus.                               LC, N
Social reforms.

75 [———] A Strange Voyage. A Revision of the Key of Industrial Co-
operative Government. An Interesting and Instructive Description of
Life on Planet Venus. By Pruning Knife [pseud.]. St. Louis, Mo.:
The Monitor Publishing Company, 1891. 226 p.     LC, Y
Extends the author's views expressed in previous book.

76 ALLEN, JAMES LANE. Aftermath: Part Second of "A Kentucky Cardinal"
... New York: Harper & Brothers, 1896. 135 p.
BA, CU, H, HEH, LC, N, O, UC, UM, UVB, Y

77 ——— The Choir Invisible... New York: The Macmillan Company.
London: Macmillan & Co., Ltd., 1897. 361 p.
AP, CU, H, HEH, LC, N, O, UC, UP, UV, Y
"The author published a few years ago a story entitled *John Gray* [No. 79].
Some of the material of that story has been used in the work herewith pub-
lished." Author's Note.

78 ——— Flute and Violin, and Other Kentucky Tales and Romances ...
New York: Harper & Brothers, 1891. 308 p., illus.
BA, BU, CU, H, HEH, LC, N, O, UC, UM, UP, UV, Y
*Also contains:* King Solomon of Kentucky—Two Gentlemen of Kentucky—
The White Cowl—Sister Dolorosa—Posthumous Fame.

79 ——— John Gray: A Kentucky Tale of the Olden Time... Philadel-
phia: J. B. Lippincott Company, 1893. 218 p., front.
BA, CU, H, HEH, N, O, UM, UP, UV, Y
Some of the material of this story later included in No. 77.

80 ——— A Kentucky Cardinal: A Story ... New York: Harper &
Brothers, 1895. 147 p., illus.     CU, H, HEH, LC, N, O, UP, UVB, Y

81 ——— The Reign of Law: A Tale of the Kentucky Hemp Fields ...
New York: The Macmillan Company. London: Macmillan & Co., Ltd.,
1900. 385 p., illus.     BA, BU, CU, H, HEH, LC, N, O, UC, UM, UP, UVB, Y

82 ——— Summer in Arcady: A Tale of Nature ... New York: Macmillan and Co. London: Macmillan & Co., Ltd., 1896. 170 p.
BA, H, HEH, LC, N, O, UC, UM, UVB, Y

83 ——— Two Gentlemen of Kentucky ... New York and London:
Harper & Brothers, 1899. 73 p., front.     CU, H, HEH, LC, N, UVB, Y
First separate printing; printed earlier in No. 78.

ALLEN, JOHN, *pseud. See* Clute, Oscar

ALLEN, JOHN W., *pseud. See* Lesley, J. Peter

84 [ALLEN, LINDA MARGUERITE SANGRÉE.] The Devil and I ... New York:
G. W. Dillingham, 1889. 322 p.     HEH, LC
Of Hypnotism.

85 [————] Florine; or, The Inner Life of One of the "Four Hundred" ...
New York: G. W. Dillingham, 1891.  326 p.  LC
In the form of a diary.

86 [————] Mignonnette: An Ideal Love Story.  By Sangrée [pseud.] ...
New York: G. W. Carleton & Co.  London: S. Low, Son & Co., 1885.
324 p.  HEH, LC

87 ALLEN, LUMAN.  Dane Walraven (A Tale of Old Boston) ...  Chicago:
Donohue, Henneberry & Co., 1892.  318 p., front.  LC

88 ———— Lucia Lascar: A Romance of Passion ...  Chicago: Donohue &
Henneberry, 1890.  329 p.  HEH

89 ALLEN, RICHARD.  Miss Eaton's Romance: A Story of the New Jersey
Shore ...  New York: Dodd, Mead and Company [cop. 1890].  300 p.
AP, HEH, LC, O

ALLEN, WILL, pseud.  See Dromgoole, Miss Will Allen

90 ALLERTON, JAMES MARTIN.  Hawk's Nest; or, The Last of the Cahoon-
shees.  A Tale of the Delaware Valley and Historical Romance of
1690 ...  Port Jervis, N.Y.: The Gazette Book & Job Print. [cop. 1892].
246, [6] p., illus.  CU, HEH, LC, UM

91 [ALLISON, CHARLES HENRY.]  Jones and Brown; or, Value and Waste. A
Novel.  By John Paul [pseud.].  [San Francisco: Allison, Neff & Co.,
cop. 1894.]  343 p.  CU, LC
LC has on file two letters from the publisher stating that Allison was the author.
"John Paul" pseud. used previously by Charles Henry Webb.

ALLSTON, MARGARET, pseud.  See Bergengren, Anna (Farquhar)

92 ALLYN, EUNICE GIBBS.  One Thousand Smiles . . .  [Dubuque, Iowa:
Press M. S. Hardie, cop. 1898.]  90 p.  LC
LC catalogues this as 2nd ed. rev.

93 [ALTGELD, EMMA (FORD).]  Sarah's Choice; or, The Norton Family ...
Chicago: Laird & Lee, cop. 1887.  189 p.  LC
Also published as: The Nortons.  Chicago: M. A. Donohue & Co., 407-429
Dearborn St. [cop. 1892].  191 p., illus.  N

94 ALTSHELER, JOSEPH ALEXANDER.  A Herald of the West: An American
Story of 1811-1815 ...  New York: D. Appleton and Company, 1898.
359 p.  CU, H, HEH, LC, O, UC, UM, UVB, Y
Attack on Washington, D.C., and the battle of New Orleans.

95 ———— The Hidden Mine ... New York: J. Selwin Tait & Sons, 65 Fifth Avenue [cop. 1896]. 273 p.  LC
California mining.

96 ———— In Circling Camps: A Romance of the Civil War ... New York: D. Appleton and Company, 1900. 419 p.  H, HEH, O, UVB

97 ———— In Hostile Red: A Romance of the Monmouth Campaign ... New York: Doubleday, Page and Company, 1900. 340 p.
H, HEH, O, UVB

98 ———— The Last Rebel ... Philadelphia & London: J. B. Lippincott Company, 1900. 219 p., illus.  HEH, LC, O
Of a Confederate colonel after the war.

99 ———— The Rainbow of Gold ... New York: Home Book Company [cop. 1896]. 228 p.
Listed PW, Apr. 18, 1896, with summary of story. LC has 1898 ed.
Across the plains to California.

100 ———— A Soldier of Manhattan and His Adventures at Ticonderoga and Quebec ... New York: D. Appleton and Company, 1897. 316 p.
HEH, O, UC, UP, UVB

101 ———— The Sun of Saratoga: A Romance of Burgoyne's Surrender ... New York: D. Appleton and Company, 1897. 313 p.  HEH, LC, O, UV, Y

102 AMERICAN COIN: A Novel ... By the Author of "Aristocracy." New York: D. Appleton and Company, 1889. 213 p.  HEH, O
Englishmen in search of fortunes in San Francisco.

103 [AMES, ELEANOR MARIA (EASTERBROOK).] Libra: An Astrological Romance. By Eleanor Kirk [pseud.]. Brooklyn: Eleanor Kirk, 696 Greene Avenue [cop. 1896]. 270 p.  CU, H, HEH, LC
P. 270, an irrelevant illus.

AMES, LUCIA TRUE. See Mead, Lucia True (Ames)

104 [ANDERSEN, MRS. MARY E.] The Merchant's Wife; or, He Blundered. A Political Romance of Our Own Day, and Other Miscellanies. By "A Looker-On Here in Vienna." Boston: Printed for the author, 1876. 124 p.  BU, CU, HEH, O
New York.

105 ANDERSON, C. H. Armour; or, What Are You Going to Do About It? ... New York: W. B. Smith & Co., Bond Street [cop. 1881]. 272 p., front.  AP, HEH, LC
American politics.

106 ANDERSON, CELIA. Jule Maghee's Anarchy ... Mobile, Ala., 1892. 188 p.  LC

107 ANDERSON, EDWARD. Camp Fire Stories: A Series of Sketches of the Union Army in the Southwest ... Chicago: Star Publishing Company, 1896. 222 p., illus. HEH, LC, N, UC, Y
*Contents:* The French Colonel—The Hospital Sheet—Tim Hickey and the Donkey—Irish Wit—Tim Hickey and the Flag—Raw Officers—The Devoted Major—The Sharpshooters—Boys—Jingle—Little Wes—Big Wes—Discomforts —Forrest and the Silver Pistol—Colonel Dick Mather's Leap—Pocahontas— Bravery—Quantrell—The Sabre Test—The New Generation—Sigel—Bummers —Captain Phil. Ritchie's Ride—Cannon Balls—Impressive Services—Jack Boswell—The Hospital Hymn—Little Piety—The Hospital Nurse—You'll Be Sorry for It Some Day—The Pay of Glory.

108 ———— ———— Chicago: Star Publishing Company [cop. 1900]. 274 p., illus. CU, H, HEH
This ed. adds: The Bugler—Aunt Ev—Caught Again—Sigel II—Colonel Nageley's Brevet—Courage in Battle—Muleteers—The Southern Dominie—The Northern Chaplain.

109 ANDERSON, MRS. FINLEY. A Woman with a Record: A Novel ... New York: G. W. Dillingham Co., 1896. 223 p. LC
High life in New York City.

ANDERSON, NELLIE V. *See* Gordon, Helen (Van Metre) Van-Anderson

110 ANDERSON, NEPHI. Added Upon: A Story ... Salt Lake City, Utah: Deseret News Publishing Company, 1898. 140 p. H, LC
Of the basic principles of Mormonism.

111 [ANDERSON, OLIVE SANTA LOUISE.] An American Girl and Her Four Years in a Boys' College. By Sola [pseud.]. New York: D. Appleton and Company, 1878. 269 p. BA, H, LC, UP

112 ———— Stories and Sketches. By Santa Louise Anderson ... [San Francisco? 1886.] 125 p. HEH
*Contents:* A Tale of Santa Barbara—The Californian Flea—An Opium Dream —The White Hart of the Sierras—Air Castles in California—Chickens—How I Found My Long Lost Brother—A Race for Life (Unfinished).
Hinkel states: "Author's works compiled by Elizabeth Curtis. Privately printed."

ANDERSON, WILLIAM H., *jt. au. See* [Stowers, W. H.] Appointed: An American Novel (1894), No. 5294.

113 ANDREWS, ELIZA FRANCES. A Family Secret: A Novel ... Philadelphia: J. B. Lippincott & Co., 1876. 213 p. Printed in double columns. CU, HEH, LC, O
The South at the end of the Civil War.

114 [————] A Mere Adventurer: A Novel. By Elzey Hay [pseud.] ... Philadelphia: J. B. Lippincott & Co., 1879. 174 p. Printed in double columns. HEH, LC, O

115 —— Prince Hal; or, The Romance of a Rich Young Man ... Philadelphia: J. B. Lippincott & Co., 1882. 350 p.     LC, O
The South, ante bellum.

116 ANDREWS, JESSIE AGNES. Eteocles: A Tale of Antioch ... New York: [A. D. F. Randolph and Co.], 1889. 135 p., front.     HEH, LC
100 copies printed.

117 —— —— First Edition, 10,000 Copies. New York: Lew Vanderpoole Publishing Company, 1890. 135 p.     H, HEH, O, UP, Y

117a —— The Narrow Way ... [N.p.], 1889. [13] p.     HEH

118 ANDREWS, SHANG. Chicago after Dark ... Author of "Cranky Ann," "Wicked Nell," "Irish Mollie, the Courtesan Queen" ... Chicago, 1882. 75 p., illus. Printed in double columns.     N

119 —— Wicked Nell, a Gay Girl of the Town ... Chicago, 1880. 73 p., illus. Printed in double columns.     N

120 [ANGELO] pseud. The Adventures of an Atom: Its Autobiography. By Itself ... New York: Hurst & Co., 122 Nassau Street [cop. 1880]. 416 p.     BU, CU, H, HEH, LC

121 —— pseud. The Dancing Imps of the Wine; or, Stories and Fables ... New York: Hurst & Co., 1880. 259 p., illus.     LC, UM, UP
Contains: The Silver Fairy—The Skeleton on the Wall—A Christmas Story—The Frog Jubilee of Animals—The Feast of Flowers—The Four Angels—The Haunted Castle.

122 —— pseud. Inexorable; or, The Wages of Sin ... New York: Hurst & Co., 122 Nassau Street [cop. 1881]. 335 p.     HEH, LC
Quotation at head of title.

123 ANTHONY, SARAH E. HOAG. True Love ... Boston: Reproduced in facsimile by the Photo-Electrotype Company, 1887. 1 p.l., [5]-24, [2] p., illus.     LC

124 ANTONA, ANNETTA HALLIDAY. Captives of Cupid: A Story of Old Detroit ... Detroit: John F. Eby & Company, 1896. 122 p.     LC

125 THE ARAB WIFE: A Romance of the Polynesian Seas. New York: D. Appleton and Company, 1878. 156 p.     LC, O, UVB
At head of title: "Appleton's New Handy-Volume Series."

ARCHER, WILLIAM W. Pendleton Neil of Rosalia. In [Mrs. K. P. Minor] comp., From Dixie (1893), No. 3756.

126 ARISTOCRACY: A Novel. New York: D. Appleton and Company, 1888. 257 p.     BA, CU, H, HEH
Satire on English society.

127 [Arkell, William J.] Napoleon Smith . . . New York: The Judge
Publishing Company, 1888. 202 p.  O
A. T. Worden, jt. au.
From the Civil War to the Franco-Prussian War.

128 [Armant, Fernand.] "Honni Soit Que Mal y Pense!" Nouvelle par
On-Sé-Kí [pseud.]. Nouvelle-Orléans: P. & E. Marchand, 1883. 73 p.
Listed in D. E. Thompson, No. 1783.

Armstrong, Elisa. See Bengough, Elisa (Armstrong)

129 Armstrong, Le Roy. An Indiana Man . . . Chicago, 1890. 218 p.
HEH, LC, N, UP
Indiana politics.

———— Sergeant Gore. In Stories of the Army (1893), No. 5280.

130 Armstrong, Mary Frances (Morgan). A Haunted House . . . New
York: Published for the Hampton Tract Committee, by G. P. Putnam's
Sons, 1879. 24 p.  H, HEH
At head of title: "Hampton Tracts for the People. Sanitary Series, No. V."

131 Armstrong, Minnie L. The Social Crime . . . New York: W. L. Allison
Company [cop. 1896]. 269 p.  LC
George N. Sceets, jt. au.
The workingman and the capitalist.

132 Armstrong, William. An American Nobleman: A Story of the Canaan
Wilderness . . . Chicago: F. J. Schulte & Company; the Ariel Press, No.
298 Dearborn Street [cop. 1892]. 277 p., illus.  CU, LC, UM
Deposited Nov. 26, 1892.
Of a Kentucky mountaineer.

133 ———— Cleopatra's Daughter: Romance of a Branch of Roses . . .
Boston: De Wolfe, Fiske & Co., 1889. 226 p.  HEH, LC, O

134 ———— Thekla: A Story of Viennese Musical Life . . . Philadelphia:
J. B. Lippincott Company, 1887. 239 p.  HEH, LC, O

135 Arnold, Alexander Streeter. Building to Win; or, Fortunes and Misfortunes. A Story of Life To-Day . . . Boston: James H. Earle, 1894.
402 p.  HEH, LC

136 ———— Henry Lovell: A Temperance Story for Old and Young . . .
Valley Falls, R.I.: Alex. S. Arnold, 1878. 196 p., illus.
BU, CU, H, HEH, LC

Arnold, Birch, pseud. See Bartlett, Alice Elinor (Bowen)

Arnold, George. Why Thomas Was Discharged. In Stories by American Authors, V (1884), No. 5271.

137 [ARNOLD, JOSEPHINE.] Bachelors and Butterflies: A Midsummer Diversion. By Allis Arnould [pseud.]. New York: W. B. Smith & Co., Bond Street [cop. 1882]. 194 p.  LC

ARNOULD, ALLIS, *pseud. See* Arnold, Josephine

ARP, BILL, *pseud. See* Smith, Charles Henry

138 ARRINGTON, ORA. Leona; or, Shadows and Sunbeams . . . Nashville, Tenn.: Published for the author by Wheeler, Marshall, & Bruce [cop. 1876]. 352 p.  HEH

139 ARTHUR, TIMOTHY SHAY. The Bar-Rooms at Brantley; or, The Great Hotel Speculation . . . Philadelphia: Porter & Coates, 822 Chestnut Street [cop. 1877]. 437 p., front.  CU, H, HEH, LC, O, UP, UVB, Y

140 ———— The Latimer Family; or, The Bottle and the Pledge, and Other Temperance Stories . . . Philadelphia: T. B. Peterson & Brothers, 1877. 182 p.

Information from National Union Catalogue; no copy seen.

141 ———— Saved as by Fire: A Story Illustrating How One of Nature's Noblemen Was Saved from the Demon Drink . . . Philadelphia, Boston, New York, Hartford, Cincinnati, St. Louis, Chicago, San Francisco, Kansas City, Atlanta: Cottage Library Publishing House [cop. 1881]. 391 p., illus.  LC, UM
Deposited Dec. 15, 1882.

142 ———— The Strike at Tivoli Mills and What Came of It . . . Philadelphia, Penna.: Garrigues Brothers, 1879. 147 p.  HEH, LC

143 ———— Strong Drink. The Curse and the Cure . . . Philadelphia, Cincinnati, Chicago, and Springfield, Mass.: Hubbard Brothers. St. Louis, Mo.: N. D. Thompson & Co. San Francisco, Cal.: A. L. Bancroft & Co. [cop. 1877]. 676 p., illus.  BU, CU, H, HEH, LC, UC, UM, UP, UVB, Y
Part II, "The Curse and the Cure," is nonfiction.

144 ———— The Wife's Engagement Ring . . . New York: National Temperance Society, 1877. 278 p., front.  LC

145 ———— Window Curtains . . . New York: J. S. Ogilvie and Company, 29 Rose Street [cop. 1880]. 281 p., front.  HEH, LC

146 ASHLEIGH, ROSE. His Other Wife: A Novel . . . New York: George W. Carleton & Co., 1881. 406 p.  CU

147 ASPINWALL, SHERMAN N. Garnered Sheaves: An Intensely Interesting Narration of the Good Deeds of a Young Lady of Wealth and Fashion . . . Grand Rapids, Mich.: W. W. Hart, book and job printer, 1886. 179 p.  HEH, LC
At head of title: "A Story with a Moral."

ASTER, RAY, *pseud.* *See* Leavitt, John McDowell

148 ASTOR, JOHN JACOB. A Journey in Other Worlds: A Romance of the Future ... New York: D. Appleton and Company, 1894. 476 p., illus.
AP, BA, BU, CU, H, HEH, LC, N, O, UM, UV, Y
Jupiter, Mars, Saturn; A.D. 2000.

149 ASTOR, WILLIAM WALDORF. Sforza: A Story of Milan ... New York: Charles Scribner's Sons, 1889. 282 p. AP, BA, CU, H, HEH, LC, UM, Y

150 —— Valentino: An Historical Romance of the Sixteenth Century in Italy ... New York: Charles Scribner's Sons, 1885. 325 p.
AP, BA, BU, CU, H, HEH, LC, N, O, UM, UP, UV, Y

151 AT WELLESLEY: Legenda for 1896 ... New York, London: G. P. Putnam's Sons; the Knickerbocker Press, 1896. 227 p. BA, HEH
*Contains:* A Question of Science, by S. V. Sherwood—Mental Telegraphy, by J. H. Batchelder—Reciprocal, by J. S. Parker—A Smile of Fortune, by S. V. Sherwood—At the First Floor Centre, by J. S. Parker—A Committee of Entertainment, by C. Park—A College Adhesion, by E. H. Young—The Claim of the Heathen, by S. V. Sherwood—An Experiment, by J. S. Parker and I. H. Fiske—Formerly of '96, by J. S. Parker.

152 ATHERTON, GERTRUDE FRANKLIN (HORN). American Wives and English Husbands: A Novel ... New York: Dodd, Mead and Company, 1898. 339 p. HEH, LC, O, UC, UP, UVB, Y

153 —— Before the Gringo Came ... New York: J. Selwin Tait & Sons, 65 Fifth Avenue [cop. 1894]. 306 p. BU, H, HEH, UVB, Y
*Contents:* Pearls of Loreto—The Ears of Twenty Americans—The Wash-Tub Mail—The Conquest of Doña Jacoba—A Ramble with Eulogia—Lukari's Story —La Perdida—Natalie Ivanhoff: A Memory of Fort Ross. MISSION TALES: The Vengeance of Padre Arroyo—The Bells of San Gabriel—When the Devil Was Well.

154 —— The Californians ... London and New York: John Lane, the Bodley Head, 1898. 351, [1] p. CU, HEH, N, O, UC, UP, Y
Colophon: "Printed for John Lane by John Wilson and Son, the University Press, Cambridge, U.S.A."

155 —— Los Cerritos: A Romance of the Modern Time ... New York: John W. Lovell Company, 150 Worth St., cor. Mission Place [cop. 1890]. 304 p. AP, BA, CU, H, HEH, LC, N, O, UM, UP, UVB, Y

156 —— A Daughter of the Vine ... London and New York: John Lane, the Bodley Head, 1899. 300 p., front. H, HEH, LC, O, UC, UVB, Y
Verso of title page: "University Press, Cambridge, U.S.A."

157 ——— The Doomswoman . . . New York: Tait, Sons & Company, Union Square [cop. 1893]. 263 p. AP, HEH, O, UVB, Y

158 ——— Hermia Suydam . . . New York, San Francisco, London, and Paris: The Current Literature Publishing Co. [cop. 1889]. 207 p.
CU, H, HEH, LC, N, O, UP, UVB, Y

159 ——— His Fortunate Grace . . . New York: D. Appleton and Company, 1897. 210 p. BA, H, HEH, LC, N, O, UC, UM, Y

160 ——— Patience Sparhawk and Her Times: A Novel . . . London and New York: John Lane, the Bodley Head, 1897. 488 p.
LC, N, O, UP, UVB, Y
Verso of title page: "University Press, John Wilson and Son, Cambridge, U.S.A."

161 ——— A Question of Time . . . New York: John W. Lovell Company, 150 Worth Street, cor. Mission Place [cop. 1891]. 250 p.
CU, UVB, Y
*Also contains:* Mrs. Pendleton's Four-in-Hand.

162 ——— Senator North . . . New York and London: John Lane, the Bodley Head, 1900. 367 p. BA, BU, HEH, LC, O, UM, UP, Y

163 [———] What Dreams May Come: A Romance. By Frank Lin [pseud.] . . . Chicago, New York, and San Francisco: Belford, Clarke and Co. [cop. 1888]. 192 p. CU, H, HEH, LC, N, O, UC, UP, UVB, Y

164 ——— A Whirl Asunder . . . New York and London: Frederick A. Stokes Company [cop. 1895]. 192 p., front. CU, HEH, LC, N, UP, UVB, Y
Deposited Aug. 19, 1895.

165 ATHEY, HENRY. With Gyves of Gold: A Novel . . . New York: G. W. Dillingham Co., 1898. 274 p. LC
A. Herbert Bowers, jt. au.
Of a reformer; St. Louis.

166 ATLANTIS, A. A., *pseud.* Mildred Brainridge; or, Passing through the "Vale of Tears" . . . Philadelphia: J. E. Potter and Company, 617 Sansom Street [cop. 1879]. 347 p. LC
Temperance novel.

167 ATWOOD, HORACE G. Avenged; or, Dick Thorne's Mistake . . . Jacksonville, Ill.: W. W. Barrett, 1877. 24 p. HEH

168 AUGUR, C. H. Half-True Tales: Stories Founded on Fiction . . . New York: Keppler & Schwarzmann, 1891. 203 p., illus.
BA, BU, H, HEH, UM
*Contents:* The Man Who Went a-Fishing—The Little Store around the Corner—The Man in the Box—At the Lonely Port—The Finding of the Finn—A Brief Account of Himself—The Style of Benjamin—A Night at McNaughton's

—Teacher—The Five Works of Art—A Fresh-Water Affair—The Switching of a Kicker—A Romance of the Forest—Cheviot's Downward Career—A Summer Morning—Mr. Stubb Penn, Humorist.

———— Mr. Wilkenning's Hobby. *In* Mavericks (1892), No. 3663.

———— The Story of Shiftless Smith. *In* Hanks: Assorted Yarns from Puck (1893), No. 2444.

169 AUGUSTIN, GEORGE. Romances of New Orleans . . . New Orleans: L. Graham & Son, 1891. 214 p. CU, LC
*Contains:* Yetta, the Nun—Lulette—Irreconcilable—The Creole Flower Girl—The Strangler of Congo Square—Iyala, the Dancer—The Death-Angel.

170 [AUGUSTIN, MARIE-JOSÉPHINE.] Le Macandal: Episode de l'Insurrection des Noirs a St. Domingue. Par Tante Marie [pseud.]. Nouvelle-Orleans: Imprimerie Geo. Müller, 1892. 112 p. BA, H, HEH, LC

171 AUSTIN, JANE (GOODWIN). Betty Alden, the First-Born Daughter of the Pilgrims . . . Boston and New York: Houghton, Mifflin and Company. The Riverside Press, Cambridge, 1891. 384 p.
BU, H, HEH, LC, O, UM, UP, UVB, Y

172 ———— David Alden's Daughter, and Other Stories of Colonial Times . . . Boston and New York: Houghton, Mifflin and Company. The Riverside Press, Cambridge, 1892. 316 p.
AP, BU, CU, H, HEH, LC, N, O, UC, UVB, Y
*Also contains:* The Wife of John Carver—Barbara Standish—William Bradford's Love Life—Nazareth Pitcher—Witch Hazel—The Freight of the Schooner Dolphin—Miss Betty's Pictures—The Love of John Mascarene—The Last of the Proud Pulsifers—The First and the Last—Wrecked and Rescued.

173 [————] The Desmond Hundred . . . Boston: James R. Osgood and Company, 1882. 330 p. CU, H, HEH, LC, N, O, UC, UVB, Y
At head of title: "Round-Robin Series."
Of religious interest; New England.

174 ———— Dr. LeBaron and His Daughters: A Story of the Old Colony . . . Boston and New York: Houghton, Mifflin and Company. The Riverside Press, Cambridge, 1890. 460 p. AP, BU, H, HEH, LC, UC, UM, UVB, Y

175 [————] Mrs. Beauchamp Brown . . . Boston: Roberts Brothers, 1880. 319 p. BA, CU, H, HEH, LC, O, UC, UV, Y
At head of title: "No Name Series."
On the coast of Maine.

176 [————] A Nameless Nobleman . . . Boston: James R. Osgood and Company, 1881. 369 p. CU, H, HEH, LC, O, UM, UP, UVB, Y
At head of title: "Round-Robin Series."
Plymouth, 1660's.

177 ———— Nantucket Scraps: Being the Experiences of an Off-Islander in Season and Out of Season, among a Passing People . . . Boston: James R. Osgood and Company, 1883. 354 p.

AP, BA, BU, CU, H, HEH, N, O, UVB, Y

———— Safe in Purgatory. *In* F. E. McKay, *ed.*, Vignettes [cop. 1890], No. 3523.

178 ———— Standish of Standish: A Story of the Pilgrims . . . Boston and New York: Houghton, Mifflin and Company. The Riverside Press, Cambridge, 1889. 422 p.

AP, H, HEH, O, UC, UM, UVB, Y

179 AUSTIN, JOHN OSBORNE. The Journal of William Jefferay, Gentleman. Born at Chiddingly, Old England . . . 1591; Died at Newport, New England . . . 1675 . . . A Diary That Might Have Been. Edited by John Osborne Austin . . . [Providence, R.I.: Press of E. L. Freeman & Sons], 1899. 189 p., front.

BU, CU, H, HEH, N, UC, Y

180 ———— More Seven Club Tales Found in Mr. Jefferay's Papers Marked: "Some Strange Relatings, Sent by Divers of Mine Acquaintance . . ." Edited by John Osborne Austin . . . [Newport, R.I.: Press of Newport Daily News, cop. 1900.] 101 p.

BU, HEH, LC, O, UM, Y

*Contents:* Mr. Ray's Tale: An Indian Legend of Block Island—Mr. Smith's Tale: A Nameless Guest at Narragansett—Mr. Willett's Tale: A Strange Lading at the Kennebec—Mr. Blackstone's Tale: Three Ghostly Appearings at Study Hill—Dr. Cranston's Tale: A Marvellous Cure at Newport—Mr. Baulstone's Tale: The First Caller to Mine Inn at Portsmouth—Mistress Porter's Tale: My Husbands and Other Trials.

181 AUSTIN, MAUDE MASON. 'Cension: A Sketch from Paso del Norte . . . New York: Harper & Brothers, 1896. 159 p., illus. HEH, LC, UC, UM, Y
On the Rio Grande.

AVARY, MYRTA LOCKETT. Romance of a Tin Roof and a Fire-Escape. *In* J. Hawthorne, One of Those Coincidences (1899), No. 2596.

182 AVERITT, WILLIAM. Stories and Poems of Western Texas . . . New York: John B. Alden, 1890. 123 p., front. BU, LC
*Contains:* Dead Man's Crossing—An Innocent Deception—A Ranger's Fortune —The Water-Spout Enois and Uela.

183 AVERY, M. A. Shadowed Perils: A Novel . . . New York: The Authors' Publishing Company, 1876. 260 p. LC

184 AVERY-STUTTLE, MRS. LILLA DALE. Making Home Happy . . . Battle Creek, Mich.; Chicago: Review & Herald Publishing Co., 1898. 206 p., illus.

Information from LC card; no copy seen.

185 ———— Making Home Peaceful: Sequel to "Making Home Happy" . . . Battle Creek, Michigan: Home Life Publishing Co., Limited [cop. 1899]. 232 p., illus. LC
Deposited Apr. 14, 1900.

186 AYLESWORTH, BARTON ORVILLE. "Thirteen," and Twelve Others from the Adirondacks and Elsewhere . . . St. Louis: Christian Publishing Company, 1892. 259 p.                                                          HEH
*Contains:* The Fairies at Au Sable Chasm—Maiden Rock—A Woman?—A Dream—Jim's Vict'ry—"Aunt Modgie"—A Double Revelation—A Christmas Story—Oduna—"Where There Is Life There Is Hope(?)"—A Soul's Resurrection.

B., C. R., *pseud.* *See* Hull, Charles

B., E. E. *See* Bower, Mrs. Ella E.

B., P. *See* Boynton, Percy Holmes

187 B. AND R. Helen Elwood, the Female Detective; or, A Celebrated Forger's Fate. By "B. and R." Chicago: Geo. W. Ogilvie, 230 Lake Street [cop. 1885]. 98 p., illus.                                   HEH, LC

188 BAARS, FRED D. The Story of the Seas: A Romance in Reality of a Sailor's Life . . . Arkadelphia, Ark.: Baars & Neeley [cop. 1896]. 265 p., illus.                                                                    LC
Verso of title page: "Burnham Print, 322 N. Third St., St. Louis."

189 BABCOCK, BERNIE (SMADE). The Daughter of a Republican . . . Chicago: The New Voice Press, 1900. 115, [1] p., illus.                    CU, LC, UV
Temperance tale.

190 ———— The Martyr: A Story of the Great Reform . . . Chicago: New Voice Press, 1900. 173 p., illus.                                           LC

191 [BABCOCK, JOHN MARTIN LUTHER.] The Dawning: A Novel . . . Boston: Lee and Shepard. New York: Charles T. Dillingham, 1886. 382 p.
                                                                     H, HEH, UC, Y
Social problems; Boston.

192 BABCOCK, WILLIAM HENRY. Cypress Beach . . . Washington, D.C.: Wm. H. Babcock, 1890. 178 p.                                              LC, Y
At head of title: "First American Edition."
Postwar South.

193 BACHE, RICHARD MEADE. Under the Palmetto in Peace and War . . . Philadelphia: Claxton, Remsen, & Haffelfinger, 1880. 106 p.            LC
South Carolina.

194 [BACHELDER, JOHN.] A.D. 2050. Electrical Development at Atlantis. By a Former Resident of "The Hub." San Francisco: The Bancroft Company, 1890. 83 p.                                                        HEH, LC, N

195 BACHELLER, IRVING, *ed.* Best Things from American Literature . . . New York: The Christian Herald, Louis Klopsch, proprietor, 1899. 416 p., illus. BU, CU, H, HEH, UP, UVB

*Contains:* The Sickle of Fire, by Charles Kelsey Gaines—The Sober, Industrious Poet and How He Fared at Easter-Time, by James L. Ford—The 'Jinin' Farms, by Eugene Field—A Tale of Mere Chance, by Stephen Crane—Captain Mallinger, by Harriet Prescott Spofford—John's Trial, by Philander Deming—The Flying March, by W. L. Alden—The Night before Thanksgiving, by Sarah Orne Jewett—The Decoy Despatch, by Clinton Ross—The Movement Cure for Rheumatism, by Robert J. Burdette—A Matter of Instinct, by Howard Fielding [i.e., Charles W. Hooke]—A New England Sunday, by Henry Ward Beecher—Rudgis and Grim, by Maurice Thompson—The Dog on the Roof, by Edward W. Townsend—The Night Elevator Man's Story, by E. W. Townsend—Double Head and Single Heart, by Elisabeth Pullen—A Romance of the City Room, by Elizabeth G. Jordan—Eunice and the Doll, by Mary E. Wilkins [Freeman]—Odin Moore's Confession: A Christmas Story, by Julian Hawthorne.

196 ———— Eben Holden: A Tale of the North Country . . . Boston: Lothrop Publishing Company [cop. 1900]. 432 p.

Upstate New York. AP, BU, CU, H, HEH, UC, UM, UVB, Y

197 ———— The Master of Silence: A Romance . . . New York: Charles L. Webster & Co., 1892. 176 p. CU, H, HEH, LC, UP, UVB, Y

———— The Night of a Thousand Years. *In* Short Story Masterpieces (1900), No. 4931.

198 BACHELLER, LOIS H. The Dabney Will . . . New York: Warner & Brownell, 1900. 232, [1] p. HEH, LC

*Also contains:* The Story of Lydia—Mrs. Minnie Puffer's Little Plan—A Superior Power—Out of a Dream—A Fashion in Grandmothers.

199 THE BACHELORS' SURRENDER. Boston: Loring, corner Bromfield and Washington Streets [cop. 1880]. 137 p.

Listed PW, Sept. 4, 1880; copy examined at Boston Public Library. On a California ranch.

200 [BACHMAN, MAURICE A.] Prejudice? A Novel. By Ovidius [pseud.] . . . New York: M. A. Bachman, 160 East 107th Street [cop. 1900]. 92 p., illus. LC

201 BACON, EDGAR MAYHEW. The Pocket Piece: Short Stories and Sketches by American Authors. First Series, No. 1 . . . New York: Walbridge & Co. [cop. 1891]. 128 p. HEH, LC

*Contents:* The Toddville Raffle—Zenas Smith's Ride to Roxbury—Squaring an Old Account—McRotty's Van—Uncle Sunday—The Historian of the Future.

202 BACON, EUGENIA (JONES). Lyddy: A Tale of the Old South . . . New York: Continental Publishing Co., 1898. 287 p. CU, HEH, LC, UC, UP, UV

203   BACON, JOSEPHINE DODGE (DASKAM). Smith College Stories. By Josephine Dodge Daskam. New York: Charles Scribner's Sons, 1900. 343 p.                                     BA, H, HEH, LC, O, UM, Y
Contents: The Emotions of a Sub-Guard—A Case of Interference—Miss Biddle of Bryn Mawr—Biscuits ex Machina—The Education of Elizabeth—A Family Affair—A Few Diversions—The Evolution of Evangeline—At Commencement—The End of It.

204   [BACON, MARY SCHELL (HOKE).] "I Will Ne'er Consent": A Novel. By Dolores Marbourg [pseud.]. New York: Robert Belford [cop. 1889]. 217 p.            HEH

———— jt. au. See Eggleston, G. C. Juggernaut (1891), No. 1730.

205   BADEAU, ADAM. Conspiracy: A Cuban Romance . . . New York: R. Worthington, 1885. 324 p.     AP, CU, H, HEH, LC, UC, UM, UP, UVB, Y

BADEN, FRANCES (HENSHAW). Other Stories. In E. D. E. N. Southworth, The Fatal Secret [cop. 1877], No. 5086; and E. D. E. N. Southworth, The Phantom Wedding [cop. 1878], No. 5097.

206   BADGER, ALFRED S. Christmas at the ABECS' . . . New York: National Temperance Society [cop. 1891]. 77 p., illus.     HEH

207   BADGER, HENRY. Bethlehem; or, Border Lands of Faith. A Historical Novel . . . New York: Benj. H. Tyrrel, 1895. 300 p., 1 l.     H
LC deposit copy, dated May 28, 1895, does not have an imprint and is without the "In Memoriam" leaf at end.

208   BAGBY, ALBERT MORRIS. "Miss Träumerei": A Weimar Idyl . . . New York: Published by the author, 1895. 292 p.     H, HEH, LC, Y
Deposited Mar. 4, 1895.
Also issued with imprint: Boston: Lamson, Wolffe and Company, 1895.   LC, O
Deposited May 22, 1895.

209   [BAGBY, GEORGE WILLIAM.] Meekins's Twinses: A Perduckshun uv Mozis Addums [pseud.] . . . Richmun, Fuhjinya: Mister Westun Jonsum & Kumpny, A Teen Sebenty 7 [1877]. Cover title, 16 p.     H, LC, UV
At head of cover title: "Price, a Quorter. . . ."
BAL 568 notes that 2nd ed. contains new material. Two copies located, including one at H.

210   [————] A Week in Hepsidam: Being the First and Only True Account of the Mountains, Men, Manners, and Morals Thereof . . . By Go. Wash. Meekins [pseud.] . . . Richmond: Geo. W. Gary, printer, 1879. 66 p.     HEH, UV

211   BAGNELL, N. D. Carl and Violet . . . New York: Hunt & Eaton. Cincinnati: Cranston & Stowe, 1890. 279 p.     LC

212 ——— Poky Clark: A Story of Virginia . . . New York: Hunt & Eaton. Cincinnati: Cranston & Stowe, 1890. 232 p.     HEH, LC

BAILEY, ALICE (WARD). Donald Grey (The Luck of a Good for Nothing), by A. B. Ward. *In* Short Stories from Outing [cop. 1895], No. 4930.

213 ——— Mark Heffron: A Novel . . . New York: Harper & Brothers, 1896. 354 p.     HEH, LC, O, Y
Of metaphysical interest.

——— A Medley of the Midway Plaisance, by A. B. Ward. *In* Short Stories from Outing [cop. 1895], No. 4930.

214 BAILEY, ANNA ELIZA (CLAY). My God! Whose Wife Am I? or, The Lost Heir. By Anna Eliza Clay. Chicago, 1879. 52 p.     LC

215 BAILEY, FRANCES STOUGHTON. Story and Song . . . Providence: Snow & Farnham, printers [cop. 1894]. 126 p., front.     BU, HEH, UM
*Contains:* Keturah Kiddle's Courtship—The Jordans and the Jordáns—An Equation of Errors—Mrs. Mulvaney's Sacrifice—A Mutiny on a Gold-Ship—The Lost Sheep—John Danforth's Derelicts—La Petite Gretchen—"One More to Bow to."

216 BAILEY, JAMES MONTGOMERY. The Danbury Boom! With a Full Account of Mrs. Cobleigh's Action Therein! Together with Many Other Interesting Phases in the Social and Domestic History of That Remarkable Village . . . Boston: Lee and Shepard. New York: Charles T. Dillingham, 1880. 317 p.     CU, HEH, LC, O, UC, UM, UP, UV, Y

217 ——— England from a Back-Window, with Views of Scotland and Ireland . . . Boston: Lee & Shepard. New York: Charles T. Dillingham, 1879. 475 p.     BA, BU, H, O, UM

218 ——— Mr. Phillips' Goneness . . . Boston: Lee and Shepard. New York: Charles T. Dillingham, 1879. 179 p.   CU, H, HEH, LC, O, UC, UP, Y
Of a country editor.

219 ——— They All Do It; or, Mr. Miggs of Danbury and His Neighbors . . . Boston: Lee and Shepard. New York: Charles T. Dillingham, 1877. 313 p., illus.     CU, HEH, LC, O, UM, UP, Y

220 BAILEY, NATHAN J. Johnsville in the Olden Time, and Other Stories . . . New York: Printed by Edward O. Jenkins' Sons, 1884. 255 p.
CU, H, HEH, LC, N, UM, Y
Twenty-eight stories with Fishkill, N.Y., the locale of the majority.

BAILEY, SADA. *See* Fowler, Sada (Bailey)

221 BAILY, THOMAS LOYD. Dr. Wallsten's Way . . . New York: National Temperance Society, 1889. 319 p., front.     HEH, LC
Temperance novel.

222 ———— An Entire Stranger . . . New York: Thomas Y. Crowell & Co., 40 East Fourteenth Street [cop. 1891]. 367 p., illus.    LC, Y
Of a schoolteacher.

223 ———— "Nat," the Coal-Miner's Boy; or, One Step at a Time . . . New York: National Temperance Society, 1890. 457 p., illus.    LC

224 ———— Only Me . . . Boston: D. Lothrop Company, Franklin and Hawley Streets [cop. 1887]. 296 p.    LC

225 ———— Possibilities . . . Boston: D. Lothrop Company, Franklin and Hawley Streets [cop. 1887]. 233 p.    HEH, LC
Schoolteacher introduces new methods of teaching.

226 BAINBRIDGE, WILLIAM F. Self-Giving: A Story of Christian Missions . . . Boston: D. Lothrop and Company, 30 and 32 Franklin Street [cop. 1883]. 521 p., front.    HEH, LC

BAINES, MINNIE W. See Miller, Minnie (Willis) Baines

227 BAKER, BETH. Mystery Evans . . . Boston: De Wolfe, Fiske & Co., 1890. 256 p.    BU, CU, HEH, LC, N
Boston, Montana Territory, Paris.

228 BAKER, EMMA EUGENE (HALL). The Master of L'Étrange. By Eugene Hall. Philadelphia: T. B. Peterson & Brothers [1886]. 346 p.
Powell, No. 17, locates five copies, including one in Duke University Library.

229 BAKER, FRANCES DAVIS. Uplands: A Novel . . . Buffalo, N.Y.: G. M. Hausauer, 1898. 116 p.    LC

230 BAKER, GEORGE AUGUSTUS. Mrs. Hephaestus, and Other Short Stories . . . New York: White, Stokes, & Allen, 1887. 211 p.
    AP, BA, BU, H, HEH, UC, UP, Y
*Also contains:* The Child of the Regiment—The Spirit of the Age—The Merman—The Invasion of Kleindorf—Labor Troubles on an Island.

231 [BAKER, HARRIETTE NEWELL (WOODS).] Out of the Depths; or, The Rector's Trial. By Mrs. Madeline Leslie [pseud.] . . . Boston: Ira Bradley & Co., 1879. 244 p., illus.
Copy examined at New York Public Library.

232 ———— Rebecca, the Jewess . . . 1879. 239 p., front.
Copy examined at New York Public Library; lacks title page.

233 [————] Ten Millions; or, Uncle Jacob's Legacy. By Mrs. Madeline Leslie [pseud.] . . . Boston: I. Bradley & Co. [cop. 1888]. 305 p., front.
    LC

234 [BAKER, JOSEPHINE R.] Calvin the Sinner . . . Boston: Henry Hoyt & Co., 1879. 347 p., front.    HEH

235 ———— Tom's Heathen . . . Boston: Henry Hoyt & Co., 1879. 233 p., front. HEH, LC

236 BAKER, JULIA KEIM (WETHERILL). Wings: A Novel. By Julie K. Wetherill . . . Philadelphia: J. B. Lippincott & Co., 1878. 274 p. HEH
Gulf coast, Louisiana.

237 BAKER, MARY MARSH. Ruby Dana: A Novel . . . New York: John B. Alden, 1890. 287 p. HEH, LC, Y

238 [BAKER, WILLIAM ELLIOTT SMITH.] The Battle of Coney Island; or, Free Trade Overthrown. A Scrap of History Written in 1900 . . . Philadelphia: J. A. Wagenseller, 1883. 116 p. BA, BU, CU, H, LC, O, UP

239 ———— The Widow Seymour: A Story for Youth and Age . . . Philadelphia, Pa.: J. A. Wagenseller, 1876. 632 p., illus. BA, HEH, LC, O
Philadelphia and New York.

240 [BAKER, WILLIAM MUMFORD.] Blessed Saint Certainty: A Story . . . Boston: Roberts Brothers, 1881. 445 p. BA, BU, CU, H, HEH, O, Y
Western trading post. Some of the characters first appeared in No. 243.

241 ———— Carter Quarterman: A Novel . . . New York: Harper & Brothers, 1876. 158 p., illus. Printed in double columns. H, HEH, LC, O
Life in the South following Jackson's administration.

242 [————] Colonel Dunwoddie, Millionaire: A Story of To-Day. New York: Harper & Brothers, 1878. 187 p. Printed in double columns.
H, LC, O, UV

243 [————] His Majesty, Myself . . . Boston: Roberts Brothers, 1880. 299 p. BA, BU, H, HEH, LC, N, O, UM, UV, Y
At head of title: "No Name Series."

244 [————] The Making of a Man . . . Boston: Roberts Brothers, 1884. 322 p. H, HEH, LC, O

245 ———— The Virginians in Texas: A Story for Young Folks and Old Young Folks . . . New York: Harper & Brothers, 1878. 169 p. Printed in double columns. AP, LC, O

246 ———— A Year Worth Living: A Story of a Place and of a People One Cannot Afford Not to Know . . . Boston: Lee and Shepard. New York: Charles T. Dillingham, 1878. 325 p. H, HEH, LC, N, O
Yellow fever; the South.

BAKETEL, HARRIE SHERIDAN. Out with the Tide. In H. J. Hapgood, ed., Echoes from Dartmouth (1895), No. 2446.

247 [BALCH, ELIZABETH.] An Author's Love: Being the Unpublished Letters of Prosper Mérimée's 'Inconnue.' New York: The Macmillan Company. London: Macmillan & Co., Ltd., 1900. 335 p., 2 l. H
The 1st ed. was published in London, 1889.

248 [———] Mustard Leaves; or, A Glimpse of London Society. By D.
T. S. [pseud.] . . . New York: Dodd, Mead & Company, 1885. 218 p.
H, HEH, LC, UV

249 ——— Zorah: A Love-Tale of Modern Egypt . . . Boston: Cupples
and Hurd, 1887. 287 p. AP, HEH, LC, O

250 BALCH, FREDERICK HOMER. The Bridge of the Gods: A Romance of
Indian Oregon . . . Chicago: A. C. McClurg and Company, 1890. 280
p. AP, CU, HEH, LC, N, UC, UP, UV, Y
Willamette Valley.

251 BALCH, WILLIAM STEVENS. A Peculiar People; or, Reality in Romance . . .
Chicago: Henry A. Sumner & Company, 1881. 452 p. BU, CU, HEH, LC
Mt. Lebanon.

252 [BALDWIN, MRS. A. E. COREY.] On the Battery; or, Mildred's Dishes.
A Story of New York City and Other Places . . . Published by the
Author. New York, 1879. 208 p., illus. LC

253 BALDWIN, EUGENE FRANCIS. Doctor Cavallo . . . Peoria, Illinois, 1895.
317 p. CU, H, HEH, LC, UVB, Y
Maurice Eisenberg, jt. au.
Of a doctor's practice and politics.

254 BALDWIN, MRS. H. Where Town and Country Meet: A Novel . . . New
York: Longmans, Green & Co., 1892. 300 p.
Listed PW, Feb. 13, 1892.

255 BALDY, ALICE MONTGOMERY. The Romance of a Spanish Nun . . . Philadelphia: J. B. Lippincott Company, 1891. 199 p. HEH, LC, O

256 BALESTIER, CHARLES WOLCOTT. The Average Woman . . . New York:
United States Book Company, 5 and 7 East Sixteenth Street. Chicago,
266 & 268 Wabash Ave. [cop. 1892]. 260 p. BA, H, HEH, UM, Y
Contains: Reffey—A Common Story—"Captain, My Captain!"

257 ——— Benefits Forgot . . . New York: D. Appleton and Company,
1894. 460 p. AP, BA, H, HEH, LC, N, O, UM, UV, Y
Colorado.

258 ——— A Victorious Defeat: A Romance . . . New York: Harper &
Brothers, 1886. 349 p., illus. AP, BA, HEH, LC, UV
Moravian life in Pennsylvania.

——— jt. au. See Kipling, R. The Naulahka (1892), No. 3150.

BALL, CAROLINE AUGUSTA (RUTLEDGE). See Fraser, Caroline Augusta
(Rutledge) Ball

259 DELETED.

260 BALL, WALTER SAVAGE, *ed.* Amherst Life: Selections from the Undergraduate Publications ... Amherst, [Mass.]: William Carpenter Howland, 1896. 139 p., illus. BU, H, HEH, UC, UM, UP, Y

261 BALLARD, ROBERT E. Myrtle Lawn: A Novel ... Philadelphia: T. B. Peterson & Brothers, 306 Chestnut Street [cop. 1879]. 288 p. HEH, LC
Life in Baltimore.

262 [BALLOU, CLARA E.] Ethelind. By "Carlottah" [pseud.] ... New York: J. S. Ogilvie & Company, 31 Rose Street [cop. 1885]. 179 p.
H, LC

263 [———] A Leaf in the Storm. By "Carlottah" [pseud.] ... New York: J. S. Ogilvie, 57 Rose Street. Chicago, 182 Wabash Avenue, cop. 1889. 123 p. LC

264 BANDELIER, ADOLF FRANCIS ALPHONSE. The Delight Makers ... New York: Dodd, Mead and Company [cop. 1890]. 490 p.
AP, CU, H, HEH, LC, N, O, UP, UVB, Y
Of the Pueblo Indians; New Mexico.

265 BANFIELD, AGNES HOUGHTON. Under Blue Skies, and Other Stories ... Philadelphia: Printed for the author by International Printing Co., 301 Chestnut Street [cop. 1900]. 268 p., front. HEH
*Also contains:* Jason and Matilda—Moonlight.

266 BANGS, CHARLOTTE REBECCA (WOGLOM). Wrongs to Right ... New York: H. B. Lounsbury, 1892. 82 p. LC

267 BANGS, JOHN KENDRICK. The Booming of Acre Hill, and Other Reminiscences of Urban and Suburban Life ... New York and London: Harper & Brothers, 1900. 265, [1] p., illus.
BA, BU, CU, H, HEH, LC, N, O, UM, UP, UVB, Y

268 ——— Coffee and Repartee ... New York: Harper & Brothers, 1893. 123 p., illus. BA, BU, CU, H, HEH, LC, N, O, UC, UM, UP, UVB, Y

269 ——— The Dreamers: A Club. Being a More or Less Faithful Account of the Literary Exercises of the First Regular Meeting of That Organization ... New York and London: Harper & Brothers, 1899. 246, [3] p., illus. BA, BU, CU, H, HEH, LC, N, O, UM, UP, UVB, Y

270 ——— The Enchanted Type-Writer ... New York and London: Harper & Brothers, 1899. 170, [1] p., illus.
BU, CU, H, HEH, LC, N, O, UC, UM, UP, UVB, Y

271 ——— Ghosts I Have Met, and Some Others ... New York and London: Harper & Brothers, 1898. 190, [1] p., illus.
BA, BU, CU, H, HEH, LC, N, O, UC, UM, UP, UVB, Y

272 —————— A House-Boat on the Styx: Being Some Account of the Divers Doings of the Associated Shades . . . New York: Harper & Brothers, 1896. 171 p., illus.     H, HEH, LC, N, O, UC, UP, UVB, Y

273 —————— The Idiot . . . New York: Harper & Brothers, 1895. 115 p., illus.     BA, BU, CU, H, HEH, LC, N, O, UC, UM, UP, UVB, Y

274 —————— The Idiot at Home . . . New York and London: Harper & Brothers, 1900. 313, [1] p., illus.     BA, BU, CU, H, HEH, LC, N, O, UC, UM, UP, UVB, Y

275 [——————] Mr. Bonaparte of Corsica. New York: Harper & Brothers, 1895. 265 p., illus.     CU, H, HEH, N, O, UM, UP, UVB, Y

276 [——————] New Waggings of Old Tales. By Two Wags . . . Boston: Ticknor and Company, 1888. 165 p., illus.     CU, H, HEH, LC, N, UC, UM, UP, UVB, Y

Tales by Bangs, poetry by Frank Dempster Sherman.

277 —————— Paste Jewels: Being Seven Tales of Domestic Woe . . . New York and London: Harper & Brothers, 1897. 202 p., front.     BU, CU, H, HEH, LC, N, O, UC, UM, UP, UVB, Y

*Contents:* The Emancipation of Thaddeus—Mrs. Bradley's Jewel—Unexpected Pomp at the Perkins's—An Object-Lesson—The Christmas Gifts of Thaddeus—A Strange Banquet—Jane.

278 —————— Peeps at People: Being Certain Papers from the Writings of Anne Warrington Witherup. Collected by John Kendrick Bangs . . . New York and London: Harper & Brothers, 1899. 184, [1] p., illus.     BU, CU, H, HEH, LC, N, O, UC, UM, UP, UVB, Y

279 —————— The Pursuit of the House-Boat: Being Some Further Account of the Divers Doings of the Associated Shades under the Leadership of Sherlock Holmes, Esq. . . . New York: Harper & Brothers, 1897. 204 p., illus.     BA, BU, CU, H, HEH, N, O, UM, UP, UVB, Y

*Also issued with imprint:* New York and London: Harper & Brothers, 1897.     CU, H, UM, UV

280 —————— A Rebellious Heroine: A Story . . . New York: Harper & Brothers, 1896. 225 p., illus.     BA, BU, CU, H, HEH, LC, N, O, UC, UM, UP, UVB, Y

281 [——————] Roger Camerden: A Strange Story. New York: George J. Coombes, 1887. 102 p.     BA, CU, H, HEH, LC, N, UC, UP, UVB, Y

282 —————— Three Weeks in Politics . . . New York: Harper and Brothers, 1894. 82 p., illus.     BA, BU, CU, H, HEH, LC, N, O, UC, UM, UP, UVB, Y

283 —————— Toppleton's Client; or, A Spirit in Exile . . . New York: Charles L. Webster & Company, 1893. 269 p.     BA, CU, H, HEH, LC, N, O, UC, UM, UP, UVB, Y

284 ——— The Water Ghost, and Others . . . New York: Harper & Brothers, 1894. 296 p., illus.     CU, H, HEH, LC, N, O, UC, UM, UP, UVB, Y
*Contents:* The Water Ghost of Harrowby Hall—The Spectre Cook of Bangletop—The Speck on the Lens—A Midnight Visitor—A Quicksilver Cassandra—The Ghost Club—A Psychical Prank—The Literary Remains of Thomas Bragdon.

285 BANKS, CHARLES EUGENE. In Hampton Roads: A Dramatic Romance . . . Chicago and New York: Rand, McNally & Company [cop. 1899]. 288 p., illus.     CU, H, HEH, LC, UC, UP, UVB
George Cram Cook, jt. au.
Of the "Merrimac" and the "Monitor."

286 BANKS, MARY ROSS. Bright Days in the Old Plantation Time . . . Boston: Lee and Shepard. New York: Charles T. Dillingham, 1882. 266 p., illus.     BA, CU, H, HEH, LC, O, UC, UV, Y
Georgia.

287 BARBE, WAITMAN. In the Virginias: Stories and Sketches . . . Akron, Ohio: Manufactured by the Werner Company, 1896. 184 p., illus.
    CU, H, HEH, UVB, Y
*Also contains:* The Preacher of the Three Churches—The King's Daughter—The Sketch Club Banquet—The Gypsy Trail—A Literary Atmosphere—His Last Campaign—A Tale of Fourth Street—Story of an Oil Strike—A Maiden of the Hills—The Artist's Story—In the Rue Royale—Martha—The Companions—Hafed Ben Hafed.

288 [BARBER, HARRIET BOOMER.] Drafted In: A Sequel to The Bread-Winners. A Social Study. By Faith Templeton [pseud.]. New York: Bliss Publishing Co., 235 Greenwich St. [cop. 1888]. 348 p.    HEH, N

289 [———] Wrecked, but Not Lost: A Novel. By Faith Templeton [pseud.] . . . Philadelphia: J. B. Lippincott & Co., 1880. 327 p.
    H, HEH, LC
Of a teacher, an author, and a farmer-soldier.

290 BARBOUR, MRS. ANNA MAYNARD. Told in the Rockies: A Pen Picture of the West . . . Chicago and New York: Rand, McNally & Company [cop. 1897]. 335 p.     LC, Y
Deposited Jan. 13, 1898.
At a mining camp.

BARBOUR, RALPH HENRY, *jt. au. See* Bickford, L. H. Phyllis in Bohemia (1897), No. 514.

BARBOUR, ROBERT F. *See* Rexdale, Robert

291 BARBOUR, SARAH G. Spiders and Rice Pudding . . . New York: The Authors' Publishing Company [cop. 1879]. 88 p.     LC
A love story.

292 [BARCLAY, MRS. CORNELIA S.] Mrs. Singleton. New York: The Authors' Publishing Company, Bond Street [cop. 1880]. 174 p.     LC

293 BARDEEN, CHARLES WILLIAM. Commissioner Hume: A Story of New York Schools . . . Syracuse, N.Y.: C. W. Bardeen, 1899. 210 p.

BU, H, HEH, LC, UC, UP

At head of title: "A Sequel to Roderick Hume, the Story of a New York Teacher."

294 ———— The Little Old Man; or, The School for Illiberal Mothers. 1893.
Mentioned in *Who Was Who in America*, Vol. I (Chicago, 1942).
Later ed. listed PW, Dec. 1, 1900: Syracuse, N.Y.: C. W. Bardeen, 1900. 70 p., illus.

295 ———— Roderick Hume: The Story of a New York Teacher . . . Syracuse, N.Y.: Davis, Bardeen & Co. New York: Baker, Pratt & Co., 1878. 295 p. BU, H, HEH, LC, UV, Y

BARKER, ELLEN (BLACKMAR) MAXWELL. *See* Maxwell, Ellen (Blackmar)

296 BARKER, LAURA EMILY (COOKE). Society Silhouettes: Collection of Short Stories . . . Cleveland: The Helman-Taylor Company, 1898. 271 p. LC, O
*Contents:* A Search for Sensations—The Senator's Wooing—Keeping Up Appearances—The Touch of Nature—Barbara's Emancipation—A Twentieth Century Romance.

297 BARKER, T. F. The Cross Road Store; or, The Evils of a Dramshop. The History of a Kentucky Village. A Novel. Founded on Facts . . . Lexington, Kentucky: E. D. Veach, printer, 1892. 165 p.
Listed in L. S. Thompson, p. 27, and in Willard R. Jillson, *Rare Kentucky Books* (Louisville, Ky., 1939), p. 162.

BARNACLE, *Captain, pseud.* *See* Newell, Charles Martin

BARNARD, CHARLES. Kate. *In* [W. J. Johnston] *comp.*, Lightning Flashes and Electric Dashes (1877), Nos. 3022, 3023.

298 ———— Knights of To-Day; or, Love and Science . . . New York: Charles Scribner's Sons, 1881. 256 p. AP, H, HEH, LC, O, Y
*Also contains:* A Sanitary Measure—Under High Pressure—Applied Science—Love and a Lantern—Put Yourself in Her Place—The Wreck of the Pioneer.

299 ———— Zegelda Romanief: A Story about Music . . . Boston: Musical Herald Company, 1880. 170 p., illus. HEH, Y

300 BARNARD, EDNA A. Maple Range . . . Chicago: Henry A. Sumner & Co., 1882. 444 p. BU, HEH, LC, UM, Y
At head of title: "A Frontier Romance."
Minnesota.

301 [BARNARD, J. HOWARD.] A Bright Idea and What Came of It. [San Francisco, 1891.] Cover title, 15 p. LC
A tale to promote the Occidental Fruit Company of San Francisco.

302 [————] How They Did It. [San Francisco, 1891.] Caption Title,
8 p.                                                            LC
To promote the Occidental Fruit Company.

303 [————] Over a Late Cigar. [San Francisco, 1891.] Caption title,
8 p.                                                            LC
To promote the Occidental Fruit Company.

304 BARNES, JAMES. A Princetonian: A Story of Undergraduate Life at the
College of New Jersey . . . New York, London: G. P. Putnam's Sons;
the Knickerbocker Press, 1896. 431 p., front.          H, HEH, O, Y

305 BARNES, WILLIS. Dame Fortune Smiled: The Doctor's Story . . . Boston:
Arena Publishing Company, 1896. 335 p.                          LC
The patients were New York millionaires.

306 BARNETT, EVELYN SCOTT (SNEAD). Mrs. Délire's Euchre Party, and
Other Tales . . . Franklin, Ohio: The Editor Publishing Co. [cop.
1895]. 96 p., front.                                        LC, UC
*Also contains:* A Wedding and a Half—Medjé—The Bursting of the Chrysalis.

307 BARNS, CHARLES EDWARD. Digby, Chess Professor . . . New York:
Fracker & Company, 1889. 152 p.                       CU, H, LC, O
New York life.

308 ———— A Disillusioned Occultist: A Drama-Novel . . . New York:
Willard Fracker & Company, 1889. 146 p.                  CU, LC, O
An East Indian story.

309 ———— A Portrait in Crimsons: A Drama-Novel . . . New York:
Fracker & Company, 1889. 195 p.                       AP, H, HEH, LC

310 ———— A Venetian Study in Black and White . . . New York: Willard
Fracker & Co., 1889. 172 p.                                 CU, LC

BARNUM, FRANCES COURTENAY (BAYLOR). *See* Baylor, Frances Courtenay

311 BARR, AMELIA EDITH (HUDDLESTON). The Beads of Tasmer . . . New
York: Robert Bonner's Sons [cop. 1891]. 395 p., illus.
                                               AP, H, HEH, N, O, UP

312 ———— Bernicia . . . New York: Dodd, Mead and Company, 1895.
306 p.                                     CU, H, HEH, LC, N, O, UM, Y
London, 18th century.

313 ———— Between Two Loves: A Tale of the West Riding . . . New
York: Dodd, Mead & Company [cop. 1889]. 311 p.            N, UP, Y
First published in the omitted "Harper's Handy Series," No. 102, 1886.

314 ———— A Border Shepherdess: A Romance of Eskdale . . . New York:
Dodd, Mead & Company [cop. 1887]. 325 p.
                              AP, CU, H, HEH, LC, N, O, UC, UM, UV, Y
Scotland, 1840's.

315 ———— The Bow of Orange Ribbon: A Romance of New York . . .
New York: Dodd, Mead and Company, 1886.   445 p.

AP, HEH, LC, N, UC, UVB, Y

Colonial period.

316 ———— Christopher, and Other Stories . . . New York: Phillips &
Hunt.   Cincinnati: Cranston & Stowe, 1888.   352 p.

AP, CU, H, HEH, LC, O, UV

*Also contains:* Crowther and Thirsk—The Master of Rushen—Rex Macarthy—
"Our Joe"—Jonathan Yeadon's Justification—Seed by the Wayside—The Heart
of Sam Naylor.

317 ———— A Daughter of Fife . . . New York: Dodd, Mead & Company,
1886.   335 p.   AP, CU, H, HEH, LC, O, UC, UV, Y

318 ———— Feet of Clay . . . New York: Dodd, Mead & Company [cop.
1889].   369 p.   AP, BU, H, HEH, LC, UC, UV
Deposited Jan. 16, 1889.   Second copy, deposited July 2, has front.

319 ———— The Flower of Gala Water: A Novel . . . New York: Robert
Bonner's Sons, 1894.   392 p., illus.   HEH

320 ———— Friend Olivia . . . New York: Dodd, Mead and Company
[cop. 1890].   455 p.   AP, CU, H, HEH, O, UC, UM, Y
Cromwell's England.

321 ———— Girls of a Feather: A Novel . . . New York: Robert Bonner's
Sons, 1893.   366 p., illus.   AP, H, HEH, O
Of a society doctor.

322 ———— The Hallam Succession: A Tale of Methodist Life in Two
Countries . . . New York: Phillips & Hunt.   Cincinnati: Cranston &
Stowe, 1885.   310 p.   H, HEH, LC
Deposited Feb. 6, 1885.

323 ———— The Household of McNeil . . . New York: Dodd, Mead and
Company [cop. 1890].   327 p.   AP, H, HEH, O, UC, UV, Y
Highlands of Scotland.

324 ———— I, Thou, and the Other One: A Love Story . . . New York:
Dodd, Mead and Company, 1898.   354 p., illus.   AP, H, HEH, LC, O, UVB, Y
England, 18th century.

325 ———— Jan Vedder's Wife . . . New York: Dodd, Mead & Company
[cop. 1885].   329 p.   AP, BU, H, HEH, LC, O, UC, UM, UP, UV, Y
Deposited Mar. 23, 1885.
Fishing village in the Shetland Islands.

34

326 ———— The King's Highway . . . New York: Dodd, Mead and Company, 1897. 371 p.  H, HEH, LC, O, UC, Y

327 ———— A Knight of the Nets . . . New York: Dodd, Mead and Company, 1896. 314 p.  BA, H, HEH, LC, O, UM, Y
Scotland.

328 ———— The Last of the Macallisters . . . New York: Dodd, Mead & Co. [cop. 1889]. 304 p.  AP, CU, O, UC, UV, Y
First published in the omitted "Harper's Handy Series," No. 58, 1886.

329 ———— The Lone House . . . New York: Dodd, Mead & Company [cop. 1893]. 235 p.  AP, BA, BU, H, HEH, LC, O, Y
Deposited Jan. 15, 1894.
Scotland.

330 ———— The Lost Silver of Briffault . . . New York: Phillips & Hunt. Cincinnati: Cranston & Stowe, 1885. 318 p.  AP, H, LC, Y
Texas.

331 ———— Love for an Hour Is Love Forever . . . New York: Dodd, Mead & Company [cop. 1891]. 306 p.  AP, BA, CU, HEH, LC, O, UP, Y
Deposited Apr. 20, 1892.
England.

332 ———— The Maid of Maiden Lane . . . New York: Dodd, Mead and Company, 1900. 338 p., illus.  AP, BA, BU, H, HEH, LC, N, O, UM, UV, Y
New York, 1891.

333 ———— Master of His Fate . . . New York: Dodd, Mead & Company [cop. 1888]. 293 p.  AP, BA, H, HEH, LC, O, UC, Y
Manchester and West Riding country.

334 ———— The Mate of the "Easter Bell," and Other Stories . . . New York: R. Bonner's Sons [cop. 1893]. 347 p., illus.
*Also contains:* The Harvest of Faith and Constancy—Consequences of a Mistake—Agnes Stirling—A Horse for a Wife—A Tale of Two Brothers—Romance of Two Pictures—The Story of a Wedding—A Discovered Life—The True Delzel—Earning One's Capital—A Brave Girl—Just As It Happened—The Druid's Moss—"I Meant No Harm"—The Hero of Saltham Pit—Only Jones—The "Blue Wesley Tea-Pot"—Not for Gold—One Pair of Gloves—A Dishonored Bill—The Belle of the Orkney Isles—Nap Fontaine's Duel—Tom Burleson's Love Affair—Davie's Shoulder-Straps—More Than Two at a Bargain—House-Wife and Wife—Only My Lord's Brother—The Gypsy Lady—The Saving of Eshold—"It's Guid to Be Honest and True."
Information from LC copy in the omitted "Choice Series." Evidence indicates this was also published outside the series.

335 ———— Mrs. Barr's Short Stories . . . New York: Robert Bonner's Sons, 1891. 335 p., illus.  HEH
*Contents:* Femmetia's Strange Experience—Marrying for Money—Out of Egypt—John Taggert's Trial—The Forsyth Will Case—Luck—Mary's Mar-

riage—"Only This Once"—A Southern Temper—A Man and His Own Way—
A Romance of Labor—A Faithful Woman—Kate Dalrymple—With Her Eyes
Open—James Macharg's Temper—"I Don't Care"—The Kennedys' Good For-
tune—Paid in His Own Coin—Roy of Airlie—The Udaler's Daughter—How
I Said "Yes"—Smitten with Remorse—Ike Brennan's Watch—"Sold for Naught"
—A Young Man Saved—"Anything for Peace"—The Good-for-Nothing—The
Parents' Mistake—The Ruined House—"For Better, for Worse."

336 ——— Paul and Christina . . . New York: Dodd, Mead and Company
[cop. 1887]. 227 p.          BA, CU, H, HEH, O, UC, UP, UV, Y

337 ——— The Preacher's Daughter: A Domestic Romance . . . Boston:
Bradley & Woodruff [cop. 1892]. 297 p., front.      AP, HEH, LC, O, Y

338 ——— Prisoners of Conscience . . . New York: The Century Co.,
1897. 240 p., illus.            H, HEH, LC, O, UM, UVB, Y
Shetland Islands.

339 ——— Remember the Alamo . . . New York: Dodd, Mead and Company [cop. 1888]. 431 p., front.    AP, BU, CU, H, HEH, N, O, UC, UM, UV, Y

340 ——— Romances and Realities: Tales of Truth and Fancy . . . New
York: J. B. Ford and Company, 1876. 432 p.         HEH, LC, Y
*Contains:* Content—Wisely, and Not Too Well—"Sold for Naught"—Every
Cross Bears Its Own Inscription—Seed and Fruit—The God of Our Idolatry—
The Sacrament of Poverty—The Law of Love—The Weakest Goes to the Wall
—A Faithful Woman—From Shore to Shore—Mary's Marriage—Not for Gold—
Agnes Stirling—Little Dime—Money at Interest—Thus Runs the World Away.

341 ——— A Rose of a Hundred Leaves: A Love-Story . . . New York:
Dodd, Mead and Company, 1891. 238 p., illus.
                     CU, H, HEH, LC, O, UV, Y

342 ——— Scottish Sketches . . . New York: Dodd, Mead and Company,
1895.
Listed PW, May 4, 1895.
First published by the American Tract Society, 1883.
New York Public Library has: New York: Dodd, Mead and Company, 1898.
320 p., front.
   *Contents:* Crawford's Sair Strait—James Blackie's Revenge—Facing His En-
emy—Andrew Cargill's Confession—One Wrong Step—Lile Davie.

343 ——— She Loved a Sailor . . . New York: Dodd, Mead & Company
[cop. 1891]. 459 p.           AP, H, HEH, O, UC, UV
New York during second term of Andrew Jackson.

344 ——— A Singer from the Sea . . . New York: Dodd, Mead & Company [cop. 1893]. 346 p.     AP, BA, BU, H, HEH, LC, O, UP, Y
On the Cornish coast.

345 ——— A Sister to Esau . . . New York: Dodd, Mead & Company
[cop. 1891]. 341 p.       AP, BA, BU, H, HEH, LC, O, UC
Scotland.

346 ———— The Squire of Sandal-Side: A Pastoral Romance . . . New York: Dodd, Mead and Company [cop. 1886]. 342 p.

AP, H, HEH, LC, O, UC, Y

Deposited May 28, 1887.
Scotland.

347 ———— Stories of Life and Love . . . New York: The Christian Herald, Louis Klopsch, proprietor [cop. 1897]. 320 p. HEH, LC
*Contains:* The Price She Paid—Old Maids—An Affair of the Heart—Every Cross Bears Its Own Inscription.

348 ———— Trinity Bells: A Tale of Old New York . . . New York: J. F. Taylor and Company, 1899. 278 p., illus. AP, BU, H, HEH, LC, O, Y

349 ———— Was It Right to Forgive? A Domestic Romance . . . Chicago and New York: Herbert S. Stone and Company, 1899. 294, [1] p.

BU, CU, HEH, LC, O, UVB, Y

New York.

350 ———— Winter Evening Tales . . . New York: The Christian Herald, Louis Klopsch, proprietor [cop. 1896]. 320 p. HEH, LC, Y
*Contents:* Cash: A Problem of Profit and Loss—Franz Müller's Wife—The Voice at Midnight—Six and Half-a-Dozen—The Story of David Morrison—Tom Duffan's Daughter—The Harvest of the Wind—The Seven Wise Men of Preston—Margaret Sinclair's Silent Money—Just What He Deserved—An Only Offer—Two Fair Deceivers—The Two Mr. Smiths—The Story of Mary Neil—The Heiress of Kurston Chace—Only This Once—Petralto's Love Story. Deposited Feb. 9, 1897.

BARR, ROBERT. The Type-Written Letter. *In* Tales from McClure's: Romance (1897), No. 5362.

351 BARRETT, JOHN PRESLEY. Iola; or, Facing the Truth . . . Raleigh, N.C.: Presses of Edwards, Broughton & Co., 1886. 220 p., front.
Information supplied by Florence Blakely of Duke University Library.

352 BARRETT, JONATHAN. How He Lost Her; or, True Love Never Runs Smooth . . . New York: G. W. Dillingham. London: S. Low, Son & Co., 1887. 512 p. HEH

353 BARRETT, WILSON. In Old New York: A Romance . . . Boston: L. C. Page and Company (Incorporated), 1900. 410 p., front.

CU, HEH, LC, O, UM

Elwyn Alfred Barron, jt. au., an American.

354 BARRON, ELWYN ALFRED. Manders: A Tale of Paris . . . Boston: L. C. Page and Company (Incorporated), 1899. 328 p., front.

HEH, LC, UC, UP, Y

———— jt. au. See Barrett, W. In Old New York (1900), No. 353.

355  BARROW, ELIZABETH N.  The Fortune of War: Being Portions of Many Letters and Journals Written . . . during . . . the Time of the Struggle for the Independence of the Colonies . . .  New York: Henry Holt and Company, 1900.  268 p.  CU, H, HEH, LC, O, Y

356  ——— The King's Rivals . . .  New York, London, and Bombay: Longmans, Green and Co., 1898.  365 p., front.  HEH, LC
Of Charles II.

357  BARRY, JOHN DANIEL.  The Intriguers: A Novel . . .  New York: D. Appleton and Company, 1896.  295 p.  BA, CU, H, HEH, LC, UV
Of social climbers.

358  ——— Mademoiselle Blanche: A Novel . . .  New York: Stone and Kimball, 1896.  330, [1] p.  H, HEH, O, Y

BARTLETT, A. JENNIE.  See Switzer, Jennie (Bartlett)

359  [BARTLETT, ALICE ELINOR (BOWEN).]  A New Aristocracy.  By "Birch Arnold" [pseud.] . . .  New York, Detroit: Bartlett Publishing Company, 1891.  316 p., front.  LC

360  ——— Until the Day Break: A Novel.  By Mrs. J. M. D. Bartlett . . .  Philadelphia: Porter and Coates, No. 822 Chestnut Street [cop. 1877].  373 p.  LC, O

361  BARTLETT, GEORGE HERBERT.  A Commercial Trip with an Uncommercial Ending . . .  New York, London: G. P. Putnam's Sons, 1884.  144 p.  HEH, LC, UM

362  ——— Water Tramps; or, The Cruise of the "Sea Bird" . . .  New York, London: G. P. Putnam's Sons; the Knickerbocker Press, 1895.  313 p., front.  BU, H, HEH, LC, O, Y

BARTLETT, MRS. J. M. D.  See Bartlett, Alice Elinor (Bowen)

363  BARTLETT, THEODORE.  Heart Stories . . .  New York and London: G. P. Putnam's Sons; the Knickerbocker Press, 1889.  67 p.  HEH
Contains: Lyddy—The Charity Ball—A Christmas Story.
Edited by Helen Bartlett Bridgman.

364  BARTLETT, WILLIAM CHAMBERS.  An Idyl of War-Times . . .  New York City: Lew Vanderpoole Publishing Company, 1890.  182 p.  CU, H, HEH, LC, N, UV, Y
Civil War novel.

——— A Major's Story.  In C. King, ed., The Colonel's Christmas Dinner (1890), No. 3098.
Later printed in No. 3099.

365  BARTON, CATHERINE JOSEPHINE (WIGGINTON).  Evangel Ahvallah; or, The White Spectrum.  A Novel Whose Incidents Are Linked Together by

38

a Chain of Metaphysical Deductions . . . Kansas City, Mo.: Illustrated and published by the author, 1895. 430 p., illus.     HEH, LC

366 [BARTON, SAMUEL] *broker*. Ask Her, Man! Ask Her! A Novel. By A. B. Roker [pseud.] . . . New York: G. W. Dillingham. London: S. Low, Son & Co., 1888. 381 p.     HEH, LC

367 BARTON, SAMUEL. The Battle of the Swash and the Capture of Canada . . . New York: Charles T. Dillingham, 718 and 720 Broadway [cop. 1888]. 131 p.     BU, HEH, LC, O, UM
Purporting to have been fought in 1890.

368 BARTON, WILLIAM ELEAZAR. A Hero in Homespun: A Tale of the Loyal South . . . Boston, New York, and London: Lamson, Wolffe and Company, 1897. 393 p., illus.     BA, BU, CU, H, HEH, LC, N, O, UM, UVB, Y
Civil War; Kentucky and Tennessee.

369 ———— Life in the Hills of Kentucky . . . Oberlin, O.: E. J. Goodrich, 1890. 295 p., illus.     CU, H, HEH, LC, N, O, UC, UM, Y
*Contents:* The Wind-Up of the Big Meetin' on No Bus'ness—Old Man Kline—The Poet of Fodderstack Mountain.

370 ———— Pine Knot: A Story of Kentucky Life . . . New York: D. Appleton and Company, 1900. 360 p., illus.     HEH, LC, O, UV
About 1860.

371 ———— Sim Galloway's Daughter-in-Law . . . Boston, Chicago: The Pilgrim Press [cop. 1897]. 112 p., illus.     HEH
Kentucky background.

372 ———— The Truth about the Trouble at Roundstone . . . Boston and Chicago: Pilgrim Press, 1897. 144 p., illus.     HEH

373 ———— The Wind-Up of the Big Meetin' on No Bus'ness . . . Oberlin, O.: Published for the author by the Oberlin News, 1887. 71 p.
    HEH, LC, UVB
At head of title: "A Tale of the Cumberland Mountains."
Later printed in No. 369.

BARZILLA, JACOB. *See* Rideout, Mrs. Jacob Barzilla

374 BASCOM, LEE. A God of Gotham: A Romance from the Life of a Well-Known Actress . . . New York: G. W. Dillingham, 1891. 277 p.     LC

375 BASKETT, JAMES NEWTON. As the Light Led . . . New York: The Macmillan Company. London: Macmillan & Co., Ltd., 1900. 392 p.
    AP, CU, H, HEH, LC, O, UM, Y
Northern Missouri in the late 1860's.

376 ———— "At You-All's House": A Missouri Nature Story . . . New York: The Macmillan Company. London: Macmillan & Co., Ltd., 1898. 346 p.     BA, CU, H, HEH, LC, O, Y

BASSETT, F. S.   How Rufus Came to Go to Sea.   *In* C. King, *ed.*, By Land and Sea (1891), No. 3092.
Later printed in No. 3099.

377   BASSETT, GEORGE.   Hippolyte, and Golden-Beak:   Two Stories... New York: Harper & Brothers, 1895.   227 p., illus.        BU, H, HEH, LC, O

378   BASSETT, MARY E. (STONE).   A Fair Plebeian.   By May E. Stone . . . Chicago: Henry A. Sumner and Company, 1883.   258 p.        HEH, LC, N
At head of title: "Hammock Series."

379   [————]   Jerusha's Jim.   New York: W. B. Smith & Co., Bond Street [cop. 1881].   96 p.        LC

380   ————   A Riddle of Luck.   By Mary E. Stone . . .   Philadelphia: J. B. Lippincott Company, 1893.   316 p.        HEH, LC
Aimed at too prolific authorship.

381   BATCHELDER, FANNIE.   Why Men Like Married Women . . .   New York: G. W. Dillingham, 1894.   214 p.
*Also contains:* Wigs on the Green—A Train Acquaintance—The Little Jaglantine—An International Episode—A Vestal Virgin—Sally and Her Midnight Visitor—Behind the Scenes of a New York Theatre—Why Women Marry Boys—Women in My Drawingroom—Two Amateurs—So the World Wags—Talent versus Beauty—Cherchez l'Homme—A Lost Illusion—What Is Repose? —The Story of a Programme.
Information from LC card; no copy seen.

BATCHELDER, J. H.   Mental Telegraphy.   *In* At Wellesley (1896), No. 151.

382   BATES, ARLO.   Albrecht . . .   Boston: Roberts Brothers, 1890.   265 p.
AP, BA, CU, H, HEH, LC, N, O, UC, UM, UVB, Y

383   ————   A Book o' Nine Tales . . .   Boston: Roberts Brothers, 1891. 332 p.        BA, CU, H, HEH, LC, N, O, UC, UM, UP, UVB, Y
*Contains:* A Strange Idyl—The Tuberose—Saucy Betty Mork—Jon Vantine— Mère Marchette—Barum West's Extravaganza—A Sketch in Umber—April's Lady—Delia Grimwet.

384   ————   In the Bundle of Time . . .   Boston: Roberts Brothers, 1893. 359 p.        CU, H, HEH, LC, O, UM, UVB, Y
*Contents:* The Witch of Harpswell—A Summer Comedy—A Political Dinner —An Amateur Photographer—The Man Who Committed Bigamy—An Amateur Rehearsal—In Mary Jane's House—An Afternoon Tea—The Tanjsar Tiger—Yes and No—The Chamber over the Gate—A Lesson in Natural History —One Class Day—A Fishing-Party—Franklin's Adventure—In the Jury-Room —Miss Jane—A Reading-Lesson—One Morning in Spring.

385   ————   A Lad's Love . . .   Boston: Roberts Brothers, 1887.   281 p.
AP, CU, H, HEH, LC, N, UP, Y
Campobello off the coast of Maine.

386   ——— Love in a Cloud: A Comedy in Filigree . . . Boston and New York: Houghton, Mifflin and Company. The Riverside Press, Cambridge, 1900. 291, [1] p.     BA, BU, CU, H, HEH, LC, N, O, UC, UP, UVB, Y

387   [———] Mr. Jacobs: A Tale of the Drummer, the Reporter, and the Prestidigitateur. Boston: W. B. Clarke & Carruth, 1883. 39 p.
    BA, CU, H, HEH, LC, N, O, UM, UVB, Y
Satire on F. M. Crawford's *Mr. Isaacs*, No. 1276.

388   ——— The Pagans . . . New York: Henry Holt and Company, 1884.
275 p.     AP, BA, BU, CU, HEH, LC, N, UVB, Y
At head of title: "American Novel Series, No. 2."
Bohemians in Boston.

389   [———] Patty's Perversities . . . Boston: James R. Osgood and Company, 1881. 308 p.     BA, CU, H, HEH, LC, N, UVB, Y
At head of title: "Round-Robin Series."
Of a New England village belle.

390   ——— The Philistines . . . Boston: Ticknor and Company, 1889.
442 p.     AP, BA, CU, H, HEH, LC, O, UM, Y
Boston life.

391   ——— The Puritans . . . Boston and New York: Houghton, Mifflin and Company. The Riverside Press, Cambridge, 1898. 424 p., 1 l.
    BA, CU, H, HEH, LC, N, O, UVB, Y
Of two clerical celibates; Boston.

392   ——— A Wheel of Fire . . . New York: Charles Scribner's Sons, 1885.
383 p.     AP, BA, BU, CU, H, LC, N, O, UC, Y
The fear of insanity.

393   [BATES, FANNY D.] My Sister Kitty: A Story of Election Day. Boston: Lee and Shepard. New York: Charles T. Dillingham, 1881. 232 p.
    H, LC
New England.

394   [———] Tatters: A Novel. By Beulah [pseud.] . . . Boston: Lee and Shepard, 1892. 311 p., front.     HEH
London.

395   [———] Zarailla: A Novel. By Beulah [pseud.] . . . New York: G. W. Dillingham, 1889. 323 p.     LC
From Italy to Brazil.

396   [BATES, HARRIET LEONORA (VOSE).] A Woodland Wooing. By Eleanor Putnam [pseud.]. Boston: Roberts Brothers, 1889. 289 p.
    BA, H, HEH, LC, N, O
Maine woods.

397   BATES, HARRIET TRUE. Two Men of the World: A Novel . . . New York: G. W. Dillingham, 1891. 344 p.     LC

398 BATES, JOSEPHINE (WHITE). A Blind Lead: The Story of a Mine . . .
Philadelphia: J. B. Lippincott Company, 1888. 250 p.   AP, CU, HEH, O
The "Colusa" mining camp in the Rocky Mountains.

399 ———— Bunch-Grass Stories. By Mrs. Lindon W. Bates . . . Philadelphia: J. B. Lippincott Company, 1895. 268 p.   H, HEH, LC, N
*Contents:* Resurrection on the Umpque—The Substitute—The Great Concern—Inspiration at the Cross-Roads—The Black Shell—Taken in at Oare's—
The Mavericks of the Trail—A Transferred Town.

400 ———— A Nameless Wrestler . . . Philadelphia: J. B. Lippincott Company, 1889. 215 p.   H, HEH, LC, O
Mining life in the Washington Territory.

BATES, KATHARINE LEE. An Impassable Gulf. Whither Thou Goest.
[Two stories.] *In* Stories from the Chap-Book (1896), No. 5277.

BATES, MRS. LINDON W. *See* Bates, Josephine (White)

401 BATES, MARGRET HOLMES (ERNSPERGER). The Chamber over the Gate.
By Margret Holmes [pseud.] . . . Indianapolis: Charles A. Bates, 1886.
559 p.   HEH, LC, O, UM
Domestic story; Indiana.

402 [————] Jasper Fairfax. By Margaret Holmes [pseud.] . . . New
York: R. F. Fenno & Company, 9 and 11 East 16th Street [cop. 1897].
319 p.   H, HEH, LC
Civil War novel.

403 [————] Manitou. By Margret Holmes [pseud.] . . . Indianapolis:
Carlon & Hollenbeck, printers and binders, 1881. 222 p.
CU, H, HEH, LC, N, Y
Indiana.

404 ———— Shylock's Daughter: A Novel . . . Chicago: Charles H. Kerr
& Company, 1894. 146 p., illus.   LC
Of politics.

405 BATES, MARTHA E. (CRAM). Along Traverse Shores . . . Traverse City,
Michigan: [Herald Office], 1891. 256 p., front.
Mrs. M. K. Buck, jt. au.
Information supplied by Mrs. Esther Loughin of Michigan State Library.

406 BATTERSHALL, FLETCHER WILLIAMS. A Daughter of This World . . .
New York: Dodd, Mead & Company, 1893. 382 p. AP, BU, CU, HEH, LC, O
From upstate New York to Europe.

407 ———— Mists: A Novel . . . New York: Dodd, Mead & Company,
1894. 338 p.   CU, HEH, LC, UM, Y
Coast of Maine.

408 BATTEY, CHARLES H. Tales and Sketches ... Providence: F. H. Townsend, printer, 1898. 98 p., illus. BU, HEH

*Contains:* Josiah—After Blackberries—Professor Bigidee's Researches—What the Chinese Mandarin Said—The Old Sun Dial—The Bank of Destiny.

409 BAUDER, EMMA POW (SMITH). Chrysolyte; or, The Journey to Light. By Mrs. Emma Pow Smith. San Francisco: Brunt & Co., printers and publishers, 1891. 234 p. HEH, LC

410 ———— Ruth and Marie: A Fascinating Story of the Nineteenth Century ... Chicago, Philadelphia, Stockton: Monarch Book Company, 1895. 363 p., illus. UM

LC deposit copy, dated Aug. 12, 1895, has imprint: Chicago, Ill.; Philadelphia, Pa.: American Bible House [n.d.].

HEH and Y have copies of later ed. without imprint on title page, [cop. 1895].

411 BAYLOR, FRANCES COURTENAY. Behind the Blue Ridge: A Homely Narrative ... Philadelphia: J. B. Lippincott Company, 1887. 313 p.

H, HEH, LC, O, UV, Y

Of Virginia mountaineers.

Author was born a Dawson, but mother resumed her maiden name of Baylor for herself and daughter. In 1896 Frances married G. S. Barnum but was soon widowed and apparently never wrote under the name Barnum.

412 ———— Claudia Hyde: A Novel ... Boston and New York: Houghton, Mifflin and Company. The Riverside Press, Cambridge, 1894. 442 p.

H, HEH, LC, N, O, UM, Y

An Englishman farms in Virginia.

413 ———— The Ladder of Fortune ... Boston and New York: Houghton, Mifflin and Company. The Riverside Press, Cambridge, 1899. 352, [1] p. CU, H, HEH, LC, O, UM, UV, Y

From California to Paris.

414 ———— On Both Sides: A Novel ... Philadelphia: J. B. Lippincott Company, 1886. 478 p. BU, H, HEH, LC, N, O, UV, Y

Social life in England and America.

415 ———— A Shocking Example, and Other Sketches ... Philadelphia: J. B. Lippincott Company, 1889. 364 p., front.

BU, CU, HEH, LC, N, O, UC, UM, UV, Y

*Also contains:* Craddock's Heldest—The Moral Policeman—In and Around a Despatch-Box—The Lost Voice—Table-Talk—Our Organist—In the Old Dominion—The Cold Punch Act—An Incident of English Railway Travel—Robert's Wife—Hidalgo, the Washington of Mexico—Aunt Sukey—The Drum-Major.

416 BAYNE, CHARLES JOSEPH. The Fall of Utopia ... Boston: Eastern Publishing Company, 61 Court Street [cop. 1900]. 190 p. BU, H, HEH, LC, N

417 BEACH, DAVID NELSON. How We Rose ... Boston: Roberts Brothers, 1895. 86, [2] p. H, LC

*Contents:* By Two and Two—Gautama and Jesus—About Some Mysteries—The Great Purpose.

418 BEACH, EDGAR RICE. Joshua Humble: A Tale of Old St. Louis . . . St. Louis: Edward R. Eddins & Co. [cop. 1899]. 328 p., front. HEH, LC, UM

419 ———— Stranded: A Story of the Garden City . . . Chicago: Donohue, Henneberry & Co., 1890. 348 p. HEH

420 [BEACH, REBECCA (GIBBONS).] The Puritan and the Quaker: A Story of Colonial Times . . . New York: G. P. Putnam's Sons, 1879. 393 p.
H, HEH, LC, O, Y

421 BEALE, CHARLES WILLING. The Ghost of Guir House . . . Cincinnati, Ohio: The Editor Publishing Co., 1897. 184 p., front. AP, LC

422 BEALE, MARIA (TAYLOR). Jack O'Doon: A Novel . . . New York: Henry Holt and Company, 1894. 277 p., front. H, HEH, LC, O
Carolina coast.

423 BEAN, FANNIE. Col. Judson of Alabama; or, A Southerner's Experience at the North . . . New York: United States Book Company, successors to John W. Lovell Company, 150 Worth Street [cop. 1892]. 197 p.
CU, H, HEH, LC

424 ———— Dr. Mortimer's Patient: A Novel . . . New York: G. W. Carleton & Co. London: S. Low & Co., 1878. 428 p., illus.
CU, HEH, LC, O

425 ———— Pudney and Walp . . . New York: John W. Lovell Company, 150 Worth Street [cop. 1891]. 328 p. HEH
At head of title: "Lovell's American Authors' Series, No. 40."
LC deposit copy, dated May 25, 1891, is in the omitted paper-cover ed.

426 ———— Ruth Marsh: A Story of the Aroostook . . . New York: United States Book Company, successors to John W. Lovell Company, 5 and 7 East Sixteenth St. [cop. 1892]. 166 p. HEH, LC

427 [BEAN, MRS. HELEN MARR.] The Widow Wyse: A Novel . . . Boston: Cupples, Upham and Company, 1885. 260 p. H, HEH, LC, Y
Alabama.

428 BEARD, DANIEL CARTER. Moonblight, and Six Feet of Romance . . . New York: Charles L. Webster and Company, 1892. 221 p., illus.
BU, CU, H, HEH, LC, UVB
Of social problems.

429 BEARD, OLIVER THOMAS. Bristling with Thorns . . . Detroit: The Detroit News Company, 1884. 424 p., illus. CU, HEH, LC, N, UVB
At head of title: "A Story of War and Reconstruction."

430 ———— Nadia, the Serf: A Novel . . . [Detroit, Mich.]: The Detroit News Company, cop. 1884. 48 p.
At head of title: "The American Story Library, No. 1."
Information from LC card; no copy seen.

BEARD, WOLCOTT LE CLÉAR. Francisco. *In* J. Hawthorne, One of Those Coincidences (1899), No. 2596.

431 ———— Sand and Cactus . . . New York: Charles Scribner's Sons, 1899. 337 p.                                                                HEH, LC, O, UP, Y
*Contents:* Bisnaga's Madeline—Specs—Rouge-et-Noir—Tizzard Castle—The Martyrdom of John the Baptist—Liver's Responsibility—Station 347+57.6—The Wind Wraith—The Salting of the Tio Juan—A Brother to St. James.

432 [BEASLEY, CHARLES OSCAR.] Those American R's: Rule, Ruin, Restoration. By One Who Has Been R'd . . . Philadelphia: Edward E. Wensley & Co., 1882. 335 p., front.                                     HEH, LC, O, UP
Reconstruction novel.

433 BEATTIE, HANS STEVENSON. Joshua Wray: A Novel . . . New York, Chicago: United States Book Company [cop. 1892]. 307 p.   HEH, LC, Y
Florida.

434 [————] Mike Moriarty, Alderman. By A. S. Phinx [pseud.] . . . New York: Columbia Publishing Co., 1894. 259 p.                     H, LC

435 BEATTY, JOHN. The Belle o' Becket's Lane: An American Novel . . . Philadelphia: J. B. Lippincott & Co., 1883. 330 p.        AP, HEH, LC, O
From a western town to Washington, D.C.

436 BEAULIEU: A Novel . . . Philadelphia: J. B. Lippincott & Co., 1881. 262 p.
                                                                                HEH
An English story.

437 BECH-MEYER, MRS. NICO. A Story from Pullmantown . . . Chicago: Charles H. Kerr & Company, 1894. 110 p., illus.              BU, H, LC, N
Labor and capital.

BECK, LEONORA. *See* Ellis, Leonora (Beck)

438 BECKETT, CHARLES HENRY. Who Is John Norman? . . . New York: Cassell & Company, Limited, 739 & 741 Broadway [cop. 1887]. 318 p.
                                                                            AP, CU, LC

439 [BECKMAN, EDWIN.] A Member of Congress: A Novel. By William Wentworth [pseud.] . . . New York: G. W. Dillingham Co., 1898. 243 p.
                                                                                LC
About laborers in a New Jersey sawmill.

440 [BECKWITH, ANNA LOUISE.] Constance Winter's Choice. Boston: A. K. Loring [cop. 1879]. 170 p.

Listed PW, Nov. 29, 1879.
LC has copy in the omitted Rand, McNally & Co.'s "Globe Library," 1891.
Of an actress.

BEECHER, HENRY WARD. A New England Sunday. *In* I. Bacheller, *ed.*, Best Things from American Literature (1899), No. 195.

BEERS, HENRY AUGUSTIN. Split Zephyr. *In* Stories by American Authors, VIII (1884), No. 5274.
Later printed in No. 441.

441 —— A Suburban Pastoral, and Other Tales . . . New York: Henry Holt and Company, 1894. 265 p., front.   BA, CU, H, HEH, LC, N, O, UVB, Y
*Also contains:* A Midwinter Night's Dream—A Comedy of Errors—Declaration of Independence—Split Zephyr—A Graveyard Idyl—Edric the Wild and the Witch Wife—The Wine-Flower.

442 BELDEN, JESSIE PERRY (VAN ZILE). Fate at the Door . . . Philadelphia: J. B. Lippincott Company, 1895. 240 p.   HEH, LC
New York society.

443 BELL, ALICE. Tangerines . . . Jacksonville, Fla.: The Vance-Garrett Press, 1894. 140 p.   LC

444 BELL, MRS. LENOX. Not to Be Won . . . New York: Norman L. Munro, 24 & 26 Vandewater St., cop. 1883. 317 p.   HEH

445 BELL, LILIAN LIDA. The Expatriates: A Novel . . . New York and London: Harper & Brothers, 1900. 431, [1] p.   H, HEH, LC, N, O, UV

446 —— From a Girl's Point of View . . . New York and London: Harper & Brothers, 1897. 192 p., front.   BA, BU, H, HEH, LC, O, UP, UV
*Contents:* The Untrained Man under Thirty-Five—The Philosophy of Clothes—Woman's Rights in Love—Men as Lovers—Love-Making as a Fine Art—Girls and Other Girls—On the Subject of Husbands—A Few Men Who Bore Us—The Self-Made Man—The Dyspeptic—The Too-Accurate Man—The Irresistible Man—And the Stupid Man—The New Woman.

447 —— The Instinct of Step-Fatherhood . . . New York and London: Harper & Brothers, 1898. 227, [1] p.   BU, CU, H, HEH, LC, O, UM, Y
*Also contains:* A Study in Hearts—The Heart of Brier Rose—Lizzie Lee's Separation—Mary Lou's Marryin'—The Strike at the "Billy Bowlegs"—A Woman of No Nerves.

448 —— A Little Sister to the Wilderness . . . Chicago: Stone & Kimball, 1895. 267 p., 1 l.   BA, CU, H, HEH, LC, N, O, UC, UV, Y
LC deposit copy, dated Apr. 6, 1895, has no colophon leaf and no date at end of preface.

449 —— The Love Affairs of an Old Maid . . . New York: Harper & Brothers, 1893. 188 p.   BA, BU, CU, HEH, O, UM, UV, Y

450 ———— The Under Side of Things: A Novel . . . New York: Harper & Brothers, 1896. 241 p., front.     BU, CU, HEH, LC, UC, UM, UV
Of West Point and Stockbridge, Pennsylvania.

451 BELLA STARR, THE BANDIT QUEEN; or, The Female Jesse James. A Full and Authentic History of the Dashing Female Highwayman, with Copious Extracts from Her Journal . . . New York: Richard K. Fox, 1889. Cover title, 64 p., illus.     Y

452 BELLAMY, CHARLES JOSEPH. The Breton Mills: A Romance . . . New York: G. P. Putnam's Sons, 1879. 454, [1] p.     AP, H, LC
Factory life.

453 ———— An Experiment in Marriage: A Romance . . . Albany, N.Y.: Albany Book Company, 1889. 286 p.     LC, Y
Utopian colony; California.

454 ———— A Moment of Madness: A Novel . . . New York: A. L. Burt [cop. 1888]. 235 p.     HEH, Y

455 ———— Were They Sinners? A Novel . . . Springfield, Mass.: Authors' Publishing Company, 1890. 219 p.     UVB

456 BELLAMY, EDWARD. The Blindman's World, and Other Stories . . . Boston and New York: Houghton, Mifflin and Company. The Riverside Press, Cambridge, 1898. 415, [1] p.
    BA, CU, H, HEH, LC, N, O, UC, UM, UP, UV, Y
*Also contains:* An Echo of Antietam—The Old Folks' Party—The Cold Snap—Two Days' Solitary Imprisonment—A Summer Evening's Dream—Potts's Painless Cure—A Love Story Reversed—Deserted—Hooking Watermelons—A Positive Romance—Lost—With the Eyes Shut—At Pinney's Ranch—To Whom This May Come.

457 ———— Dr. Heidenhoff's Process . . . New York: D. Appleton and Company, 1880. 140 p.     H, LC, N, O, UM, Y
At head of title: "Appletons' New Handy-Volume Series."

458 ———— The Duke of Stockbridge: A Romance of Shays' Rebellion . . . New York, Boston, Chicago: Silver, Burdett and Company, 1900. 371 p., illus.     BA, BU, CU, H, HEH, LC, N, O, UC, UM, UP, UV, Y
Copyright notice found in two lines and four; see BAL 970.

459 ———— Equality . . . New York: D. Appleton and Company, 1897. 412 p.     CU, H, HEH, LC, N, O, UP, UV, Y

460 ———— Looking Backward, 2000-1887 . . . Boston: Ticknor and Company, 1888. 470 p.     AP, BU, CU, H, HEH, N, O, UP, UV, Y
"Earliest printing has the imprint of J. J. Arakelyan on the copyright page." BAL 956.

———— Lost. *In* Stories by American Authors, VII (1884), No. 5273.

461 —— Miss Ludington's Sister: A Romance of Immortality . . .
Boston: James R. Osgood and Company, 1884. 260 p.
AP, BU, CU, H, HEH, LC, O, UM, UP, Y

462 [——] Six to One: A Nantucket Idyl. New York: G. P. Putnam's
Sons, 1878. 176 p., front. BA, CU, H, HEH, N, UC, UP, Y

463 [BELLAMY, ELIZABETH WHITFIELD (CROOM).] The Little Joanna: A
Novel. By Kamba Thorpe [pseud.]. New York: D. Appleton and
Company, 1876. 131 p. Printed in double columns. CU, HEH, LC

464 —— Old Man Gilbert . . . Chicago, New York, and San Francisco:
Belford, Clarke & Company [cop. 1888]. 115 p. AP, H, LC
In Tallahassee, Florida, 1857.

465 —— Penny Lancaster, Farmer . . . New York: Frank F. Lovell &
Company, 142 and 144 Worth Street [cop. 1889]. 314 p. HEH, LC
Georgia.

466 BELLEVILLE, BELLE. The Written Leaves: A Story of the New Year, and
Other Holiday Stories . . . Cincinnati: Robert Clarke & Co., 1892.
91 p. LC
*Also contains:* The Christmas Card—The Advent of the New Year—Cleopatra
in Hades.

467 BELLEW, FRANK. The Tramp, His Tricks, Tallies, and Tell-Tales, with
All His Signs . . . and Villainies Exposed. By an Ex-Tramp. Edited
by Frank Bellew . . . New York: Dick & Fitzgerald [cop. 1878]. 32 p.,
illus. Printed in double columns. BA, LC, O

468 BELLSMITH, HENRY WENTWORTH. Henry Cadavere: A Study of Life
and Work . . . New York: Commonwealth Company, 28 Lafayette
Place [cop. 1897]. 239 p., 2 l., [12] p. BU, HEH, UV

469 BELT, HARRIETT PENNAWELL. Marjorie Huntingdon: A Novel . . . Philadelphia: J. B. Lippincott & Co., 1884. 322 p. HEH, LC, O
Of a fashionable boarding school; New York.

470 —— A Mirage of Promise . . . Philadelphia: J. B. Lippincott Company, 1887. 354 p. CU, HEH, LC, UC

471 BENEDICT, FRANK LEE. Her Friend Laurence: A Novel . . . New York:
G. W. Carleton & Co., 1879. 408 p. CU, HEH, O, Y
Also published as: *Do I Love Her?* New York: G. W. Carleton & Co. Lon-
don: S. Low, Son & Co., 1882. LC
Italy.

472 —— A Late Remorse: A Novel . . . New York: G. W. Carleton &
Co. London: S. Low & Co., 1883. 417 p. AP, O

473 —— Madame: A Novel . . . New York: G. W. Carleton & Co. London: Samuel Tinsley, 1877. 484 p. HEH, LC, O

474 —— The Price She Paid: A Novel . . . Philadelphia: J. B. Lippincott & Co., 1883. 429 p. AP, H, HEH, O, UV
Farming, Lehigh Valley, Pennsylvania.

475 —— 'Twixt Hammer and Anvil: A Novel . . . Three Volumes in One. New York: G. W. Carleton & Co. London: Tinsley, 1876. 468 p. BA, HEH, LC, O
Also published as: Love's Warfare: A Novel. New York: G. W. Carleton & Co. London: S. Low & Co., 1884. LC

476 BENEDICT, GEORGE. Manager Bountiful's Buzz Saw; or, God's Way to Men . . . [Haverhill, Mass.: Chase Bros., printers, cop. 1893.] 23 p. LC

477 [BENEDICT, ROSWELL ALPHONZO.] Doubting Castle: A Religious Novelette. By John Smith [pseud.]. New York: John B. Alden, 1891. 246 p. LC

BENEFICE, pseud. See Worley, Frederick U.

478 BENGOUGH, ELISA (ARMSTRONG). The Teacup Club. By Eliza Armstrong. Chicago: Way and Williams, 1897. 307 p., 1 l. H, HEH, LC, N, UC, UM
Satire on woman's progress.

479 —— The Very Young Man and the Angel Child . . . New York: Dodge Publishing Company, One Hundred & Fifty Fifth Avenue [cop. 1900]. 239 p. LC
Of two "bachelor maids."

480 BENHAM, CHARLES. The Fourth Napoleon: A Romance . . . Chicago & New York: Herbert S. Stone & Co., 1897. 600 p., 1 l. HEH, LC, O, UM, Y

481 [BENHAM, GEORGE CHITTENDEN.] A Year of Wreck: A True Story. By a Victim. New York: Harper & Brothers, 1880. 472 p. BA, CU, H, HEH, LC, N, UC, UM, Y
Mississippi plantation; postwar.

482 BENHAM, HOWARD CURTISS. In After Years They Met: A Novel . . . Buffalo: G. M. Hausauer, 1898. 266 p.
Information supplied by Charles F. Gosnell of New York State Library.

483 —— Shipwrecks: A Romance of 1899 . . . Buffalo: G. M. Hausauer, printer, 1899. 217 p., front. HEH

484 [BENJAMIN, CHARLES A.] The Strike in the B—— Mill: A Study. Boston: Ticknor and Company, 1887. 362 p. O
At head of title: "Round-Robin Series."
Of employers and employees.

485  BENJAMIN, ELIZABETH DUNDAS (BEDELL).  Hilda and I: A Story of Three Loves ...  New York: G. W. Carleton & Co.  London: S. Low, Son & Co., 1880.  360 p.                                                                HEH

486  BENJAMIN, LEWIS.  Why Was It?  A Novel ...  Chicago, New York, and San Francisco: Belford, Clarke & Co. [cop. 1888].  257 p.
AP, LC, Y

BENJAMIN, PARK.  The End of New York. *In* Stories by American Authors, V (1884), No. 5271.

487  BENJAMIN, SAMUEL GREENE WHEELER.  Sea-Spray; or, Facts and Fancies of a Yachtsman ...  New York: Benjamin & Bell, 1887.  298 p.
AP, BA, H, LC

*Contents:* We Two on an Island—Evolution of the American Yacht—Stream Yachting in America—The Trans-Atlantic Railway—What Came of a Sea Picnic—A Cruise in a Pilot Boat—The Hidden Treasure—Out of the Depths—A Case of Circumstantial Evidence—Light-Houses of Old.

488  [BENNETT, MARY E.]  Jefferson Wildrider.  By Elizabeth Glover [pseud.].  New York: The Baker and Taylor Company, 5 and 7 East Sixteenth Street [cop. 1898].  313 p.                           HEH, LC, UC, UM
Of a New England family.

489  BENNETT, WILLIAM P.  The Sky-Sifter, the Great Chieftainess and "Medicine Woman" of the Mohawks: Remarkable Adventures and Experiences of Her White Foster Son ...  Scenes in Canada, in the States, on the Great Lakes, on the Plains, and in California ...  [Oakland, Calif.: Pacific Press Publishing Co., cop. 1892.]  302 p.
H, HEH, LC, N, UM

Author is not William Porter Bennett.

490  BENRIMO, ABRAHAM.  Vic: A Novel ...  New York: The Authors' Publishing Company, Bond Street [cop. 1879].  150 p.          LC

491  BENSON, BLACKWOOD KETCHUM.  Who Goes There?  The Story of a Spy in the Civil War ...  New York: The Macmillan Company. London: Macmillan & Co., Ltd., 1900.  485 p., illus.
H, HEH, LC, N, O, UM

492  BENSON, PERCIVAL R.  The Rev. John Henry: Incidents Which Deeply Concerned One Life, and Were Not Without Their Bearing Upon Others ...  New York: A. S. Barnes & Co., 1895.  188 p.          LC, Y

493  BENTLEY, CHARLES S.  The Fifth of November: A Romance of the Stuarts ...  Chicago and New York: Rand, McNally & Company [cop. 1898].  228 p.                                          HEH, LC, UM
Frank Kimball Scribner, jt. au.
The Gunpowder Plot; England.

494 BENTLEY, THOMAS. False Honor: A Novel . . . New York: Edward
Walker, 1879. 270 p.      HEH
An English story.

495 BENTON, KATE A. Geber: A Tale of the Reign of Harun al Raschid,
Khalif of Bagdad . . . New York: Frederick A. Stokes Company
[cop. 1900]. 487 p.      HEH, LC, O, UP

496 [BERGENGREN, ANNA (FARQUHAR).] Her Boston Experiences: A Picture
of Modern Boston Society and People. By Margaret Allston [pseud.]
. . . Boston: L. C. Page & Company (Incorporated), 1900. 208 p.,
illus.      BA, CU, H, HEH, LC, N, O, UM, Y

497 —— The Professor's Daughter. By Anna Farquhar. New York:
Doubleday & McClure Co., 1899. 324 p.      HEH, LC, Y
Seacoast village, Rhode Island.

498 —— A Singer's Heart. By Anna Farquhar . . . Boston: Roberts
Brothers, 1897. 159 p.      H, LC
Of a grand opera singer.

499 BERKELEY, AUGUST. A Modern Quixote; or, My Wife's Fool of a
Husband . . . Hartford, Conn.: American Publishing Company. San
Francisco: A. L. Bancroft & Company, 1884. 471 p., illus.
     HEH, LC, O, UC, UM, UP, Y

500 [BERNARD, MARY N.] Where the World Kneels: A Novel. By Christie
Steele [pseud.]. Culler, N.C.: W. C. Phillips, printer, 1893. 118 p.
     LC

501 BERRINGER, MRS. OSCAR. The New Virtue . . . New York: Edward
Arnold, 1896. 312 p.      AP, LC
At head of title: "Pioneer Series."

502 BERRY, ABEL B. The Last Penacook: A Tale of Provincial Times . . .
Boston: D. Lothrop and Company, Franklin and Hawley Streets [cop.
1887]. 180 p., illus.      HEH, LC, Y
Prior to the American Revolution.

503 BERRY, EDWARD PAYSON. Leah of Jerusalem: A Story of the Time of
Paul . . . New York: Anson D. F. Randolph & Company, 38 West
Twenty-Third Street [cop. 1890]. 388 p.      HEH, LC, O, UV, Y

504 —— Where the Tides Meet . . . Boston, Mass.: Arena Publishing
Company, 1893. 302 p.      HEH, LC, O, Y
New York.

505 BERRY, JOHN BENTON NATHANIEL. Maurice Burton; or, The Warp and
Weft of Fate . . . Baltimore: Printed by John Murphy & Co., 1882.
282 p.      HEH, LC

506 BERRY, MRS. MARY LEE. Philip Harum, the Nihilist Student . . . New York, St. Louis: I. H. Brown Publishing Company, 1892. 165 p.   LC

BERRY, VALERIE HAYS. Jane's Holiday. *In* Ten Notable Stories (1894), No. 5391.

507 BERTRON, MRS. OTTILIE. Edith: A Novel . . . New York: Jenkins & McCowan, 1887. 281 p.
Listed PW, Sept. 3, 1887.
Of banking and society.

BERTUCCIO, *pseud. See* Palmer, Charles T.

BESVAL, *pseud. See* Collins, Paul Valorous

508 BETTERSWORTH, ALEXANDER PITTS. John Smith, Democrat: His Two Days' Canvass (Sunday Included) for the Office of Mayor of the City of Bunkumville . . . Springfield, Ill.: Printed and bound by H. W. Rokker, 1877. 249 p.   HEH, O

509 [————] The Strange Ms. By ————, M.D. Springfield, Illinois: H. W. Rokker, printer and binder, 1883. 336 p.   LC

BETTS, CRAVEN LANGSTROTH, *jt. au. See* Eaton, A. W. Tales of a Garrison Town (1892), No. 1696.

BEULAH, *pseud. See* Bates, Fanny D.

BEVANS, NEILE, *pseud. See* Van Slingerland, Mrs. Nellie Bingham

510 BEY, ALEPH, *pseud.* That Eurasian . . . Chicago, New York: F. Tennyson Neely [cop. 1895]. 399 p.   CU, HEH, LC, O, UC, UV

511 BEYNON, MRS. MARIE EDITH. Saints, Sinners, and Queer People: Novelettes and Short Stories . . . New York: Authors' Publishing Association, 63 Fifth Avenue [cop. 1897]. 341 p., front.   LC
*Contents:* An Apostle of Hate—A Day in Castle Bohemia—Nanny—The Accused and a Pessimist—Two Men and a Madonna—The Old-Fashioned Preacher —Mrs. Chester—The Matrimonial Confidence Club.

512 BEYOND THE SUNRISE: Observations by Two Travellers. New York: John W. Lovell Company, 14 and 16 Vesey Street [cop. 1883]. 237 p.   HEH
Of clairvoyance and theosophy.

513 BICKFORD, LUTHER H. A Hopeless Case: The Remarkable Experience of an Unromantic Individual with a Romantic Name . . . Chicago: Charles H. Kerr & Company, 1889. 146 p.   LC
"As Edgar Fawcett had already published a novel under the title of *A Hopeless Case*, Mr. Bickford . . . consented to change his title. Hence the 2d ed. . . . is published as *Circumstances beyond Control*." PW, Sept. 21, 1889.

514 ——— Phyllis in Bohemia . . . Chicago and New York: Herbert S. Stone & Co., 1897. 233 p., illus.     H, HEH, LC, N, UVB, Y
Richard Stillman Powell (i.e., Ralph Henry Barbour), jt. au.

BICKNELL, FRANK MARTIN. Antaeus. *In* C. King, Rancho del Muerto [cop. 1895], No. 3109.

515 BIDDLE, ANTHONY JOSEPH DREXEL. A Dual Role, and Other Stories . . . Worcester, Mass.: The Warwick Book Publishing Company, 1894. 164 p., front.     LC, O
*Also contains:* At the Theatre—At the Ball—Which Wins?—The Life of an Ephemeron—Henri Blouchet—Brother Philander Wampus Washington's Discourse—Advice to a Newspaper Reporter—A Petition from Dwellers in Shantytown—Mrs. Mulhooney's Receiving Day.

516 ——— Shantytown Sketches . . . Philadelphia: Drexel Biddle, 1897. 64 p.     H, LC, UM
*Contents:* Mrs. Mulhooney's Receiving Day—O'Blather's Lecture on "Arnithology"—A Petition from Dwellers in Shantytown—Remember and Take Varning—Advice to a Newspaper Reporter—An Heiress—An Interrupted Debate on the Woman's Rights Question—Brother Winslow's Discourse on "De Modern People Am Exactly Laike de Ancients"—At the Theatre, from the Gallery Standpoint.

517 ——— Word for Word and Letter for Letter: A Biographical Romance . . . London: Gay & Bird. Philadelphia: Drexel Biddle, 1898. 207 p., illus.     BU, LC, O
Verso of title page: "Printed by Drexel Biddle, Philadelphia."

518 BIDWELL, JENNIE. There's Nothing in It . . . San Francisco: Henry Keller & Co., 1877. 221 p.     HEH, LC

519 BIEN, HERMAN M. Ben Beor: A Story of the Anti-Messiah in Two Divisions. Part I, Lunar Intaglios: The Man in the Moon, a Counterpart of Wallace's "Ben Hur." Part II, Historical Phantasmagoria: The Wandering Gentile, a Companion Romance to Sue's "Wandering Jew" . . . Baltimore: Isaac Friedenwald Co., 1891. 528 p.     CU, H, LC, UV, Y

520 BIERBOWER, AUSTIN. From Monkey to Man; or, Society in the Tertiary Age. A Story of the Missing Link, Showing the First Steps in Industry, Commerce, Government, Religion, and the Arts; with an Account of the Great Expedition from Cocoanut Hill and the Wars in Alligator Swamp . . . Chicago: Dibble Publishing Co., 1894. 231 p., illus.
    HEH, LC, UC

521 BIERCE, AMBROSE. Can Such Things Be? . . . New York: The Cassell Publishing Co., 31 East 17th St. [cop. 1893]. 320 p.
    BA, H, HEH, LC, UP, UV, Y

522 ——— Fantastic Fables . . . New York and London: G. P. Putnam's Sons; the Knickerbocker Press, 1899. 194 p.
    CU, H, HEH, LC, N, O, UC, UP, UVB, Y

523 ———— In the Midst of Life: Tales of Soldiers and Civilians . . . New York and London: G. P. Putnam's Sons; the Knickerbocker Press, 1898. 362 p.　　　　　　　　　　　　　　　　　CU, H, HEH, O, UP, UV

Contains same stories as No. 525, with the following additions: An Affair of Outposts—The Damned Thing—The Eyes of the Panther.

524 ———— The Monk and the Hangman's Daughter . . . Chicago: F. J. Schulte & Company, 1892. 166 p., illus.　　CU, H, HEH, LC, N, O, UP, UVB, Y

Gustav Adolph Danziger (i.e., Adolphe Danziger De Castro), jt. au.

525 ———— Tales of Soldiers and Civilians . . . San Francisco: E. L. G. Steele, 1891. 300 p.　　　　　　　　　BU, CU, H, HEH, LC, N, UP, UVB, Y

*Contents:* A Horseman in the Sky—An Occurrence at Owl Creek Bridge—Chickamauga—A Son of the Gods—One of the Missing—Killed at Resaca—The Affair at Coulter's Notch—A Tough Tussle—The Coup de Grace—Parker Adderson, Philosopher—A Watcher by the Dead—The Man and the Snake—A Holy Terror—The Suitable Surroundings—An Inhabitant of Carcosa—The Boarded Window—The Middle Toe of the Right Foot—Haita the Shepherd—An Heiress from Red Horse.

526 BIGELOW, EDITH EVELYN (JAFFRAY). Diplomatic Disenchantments: A Novel . . . New York: Harper & Brothers, 1895. 235 p.
　　　　　　　　　　　　　　　　　　　　BU, H, HEH, LC, O, Y

Of an American ambassador to Germany.

527 BILL, EDWARD LYMAN. The Last of the Danvers: The Story of a Fatalist . . . New York: Keynote Publishing Company, 3 East 14th Street [cop. 1894]. 173 p., illus.　　　　　　　　　　CU, LC

An expedition in the Northwest.

528 BINGHAM, JOEL FOOTE. The Twin Sisters of Martigny: A Story of Italian Life Forty Years Ago . . . Boston: Lee and Shepard, 1899. 390 p., illus.　　　　　　　　　　　　　　　　　　　H, HEH, Y

LC deposit copy, dated Aug. 10, 1898, does not have an imprint.

529 [BIRD, FREDERIC MAYER.] An Alien from the Commonwealth: The Romance of an Odd Young Man. By Robert Timsol [pseud.] . . . Boston: Cupples and Hurd; the Algonquin Press, 1889. 358 p., front.
　　　　　　　　　　　　　　　　　　　　CU, HEH, LC, O

530 [————] A Pessimist, in Theory and Practice. By Robert Timsol [pseud.]. New York: John B. Alden, 1888. 204 p.　　HEH, LC, UV

BISHOP, JULIA TRUITT. Old Clockwork. *In* Short Story Masterpieces (1900), No. 4931.

531 BISHOP, PUTNAM PETER. The Psychologist . . . New York and London: G. P. Putnam's Sons; the Knickerbocker Press, 1886. 354 p.
　　　　　　　　　　　　　　　　　　　　H, HEH, LC

Of business ventures.

532 BISHOP, R. F.   Camerton Slope: A Story of Mining Life . . .   Cincinnati: Cranston & Curts.   New York: Hunt & Eaton, 1893.   320 p., illus.

            CU, HEH, LC, UM

 Molly Maguires; Pennsylvania.

533 BISHOP, WILLIAM HENRY, 1843- .   The Garden of Eden, U.S.A.: A Very Possible Story . . .   Chicago: Charles H. Kerr & Company, 1895. 369 p.

                LC, Y

534 BISHOP, WILLIAM HENRY, 1847-1928.   The Brown Stone Boy, and Other Queer People . . .   New York: Cassell & Company, Limited, 104 & 106 Fourth Avenue [cop. 1888].   282 p.     H, LC, Y

 *Also contains:* A Little Dinner—Jerry and Clarinda—A Lunch at McArthur's—Near the Rose—Betwixt and Between—A Christmas Crime—A Domestic Menagerie.

535 ——— Choy Susan, and Other Stories . . .   Boston, New York: Houghton, Mifflin and Company.   The Riverside Press, Cambridge, 1885.   349 p.    AP, BA, CU, HEH, LC, N, O, UC, UVB, Y

 *Also contains:* The Battle of Bunkerloo—Deodand—Braxton's New Art—One of the Thirty Pieces—McIntyre's False Face—Miss Calderon's German.

536 ——— Detmold: A Romance . . .   Boston: Houghton, Osgood and Company.   The Riverside Press, Cambridge, 1879.   286 p.

          BA, H, HEH, LC, N, O, UP, UVB, Y

 An American architect in Europe.

537 ——— The Golden Justice . . .   Boston and New York: Houghton, Mifflin and Company.   The Riverside Press, Cambridge, 1887.   393 p.

        AP, BA, BU, CU, H, HEH, LC, N, O, UVB, Y

 Milwaukee.

538 ——— The House of a Merchant Prince: A Novel of New York . . .   Boston, New York: Houghton, Mifflin and Company.   The Riverside Press, Cambridge, 1883.   420 p.  AP, BA, CU, H, HEH, LC, N, O, UP, UVB, Y

 ——— One of the Thirty Pieces.   *In* Stories by American Authors, I (1884), No. 5267.

 Later printed in No. 535.

539 ——— A Pound of Cure: A Story of Monte Carlo . . .   New York: Charles Scribner's Sons, 1894.   200 p. BA, CU, H, HEH, LC, N, O, UP, UV, Y

540 [———] Sergeant Von; or, A Long Chase.   From the Diary of Inspector Byrnes.   By "Unknown" [pseud.].   New York: Cassell & Company, Limited, 104-106 Fourth Avenue [cop. 1889].   287 p.  LC

541 ——— Writing to Rosina . . .   New York: The Century Co., 1894. 117 p., illus.        BA, HEH, N, UVB, Y

 Love letters.

542 ———— The Yellow Snake: A Story of Treasure . . . New York: John
W. Lovell Company, 150 Worth Street [cop. 1891]. 274 p.

BA, CU, HEH, UVB, Y

Mexico.

BISLAND, ELIZABETH. *See* Wetmore, Elizabeth (Bisland)

543 BLACK, ALEXANDER. A Capital Courtship . . . New York: Charles
Scribner's Sons, 1897. 104 p., illus.     CU, H, HEH, LC, N, O, Y
Washington, D.C.

544 ———— The Girl and the Guardsman . . . New York: Charles Scribner's Sons, 1900. 212 p., illus.     HEH, LC, O
Philippine Islands.

———— The Last Pun. *In* The First Book of the Authors Club (1893),
No. 1868.

545 ———— Miss Jerry . . . New York: Charles Scribner's Sons, 1895.   121,
[1] p., 1 l., illus.     CU, HEH, LC, O, Y
New York.

546 ———— Modern Daughters: Conversations with Various American Girls
and One Man . . . New York: Charles Scribner's Sons, 1899.   212
p., illus.     H, LC, O, UM, UP, Y

547 BLACK, ANITA CIPRICO. Sketches in Prose and Verse . . . San Fran-
cisco: Press of H. S. Crocker Company, 1897. 50 p., front.   HEH, LC, Y
*Contains:* How He Conquered Fate—Who Was the Christian?—The Untold
Story of an Unsold Portrait—Lupé: A Tale of the Mission Dolores.

BLACK, H. T. Arrowatha. *In* J. J. Conway, *ed.*, Stories (1893), No.
1172.

BLACK, MARGARET HORTON (POTTER). *See* Potter, Margaret Horton

548 BLACK, MARGARET (SHAFER). Hadassah; or, Esther, Queen to Ahasuerus.
By Mrs. T. F. Black. Chicago: Laird & Lee [cop. 1895]. 277 p., front.
LC, UM, Y

549 [BLACK, ROBERT LEE.] The Deserter. By Herbert Shelton [pseud.].
Talladega, Ala.: Press of Our Mountain Home, 1900. 64 p.     LC
Of a Confederate soldier.

BLACK, MRS. T. F. *See* Black, Margaret (Shafer)

550 BLACK, WILLIAM. Green Pastures and Piccadilly: A Novel. By William
Black . . . in Conjunction with an American Writer. New York:
Harper & Brothers, 1878. 382 p.     AP, BU, CU, H, LC, UC, UP, UV, Y
American writer not identified.

551 BLACKALL, EMILY (LUCAS). Superior to Circumstances . . . Boston: D. Lothrop Company, Washington Street opposite Bromfield [cop. 1889]. 275 p., front. AP, LC, UC

552 ―――― Won and Not One . . . Philadelphia: J. B. Lippincott Company, 1891. 117 p., illus. LC
Tribulations of married couple of different denominations.

BLACKBURN, JEANNIE. See Moran, Jeannie Wormley (Blackburn)

553 BLACKBURN, MRS. MARGARET ELIZABETH. Katharine Conway . . . Buffalo: Charles W. Moulton, 1899. 270 p. LC

554 BLACKFAN, JOSEPHINE H. Between Two Worlds . . . New York: F. Tennyson Neely, 114 Fifth Avenue. Chicago, London [cop. 1899]. 355 p. H, HEH, LC
Southern California.

555 BLADEN, ELIZABETH SIMPSON. Curious Courtesy: A Sketch of Society in Philadelphia and Cape May . . . Philadelphia, 1900. 40 p.
Information supplied by Maxwell Whiteman of Dropsie College Library.

556 ―――― Eros Court: A Cape May Incident . . . Philadelphia: Spangler & Davis [187-?]. Cover title, 100 p.
Information supplied by William L. Purcell of Wistar Institute.

557 ―――― Family Bush . . . [Philadelphia: Spangler & Davis, 529 Commerce St.], 1888. 96 p.
Information supplied by R. N. Williams, 2nd, of Historical Society of Pennsylvania.

558 ―――― Romala: A Tale of Love in a Balloon . . . [Philadelphia]: Spangler [n.d.]. 43 p. UP

559 ―――― An Unpremeditated Heroine . . . Philadelphia [n.d.]. 96 p.
Information from National Union Catalogue; no copy seen.

560 [BLAIR, EDWARD TYLER.] Lloyd Lee: A Story of Yale. [New Haven: Privately printed, 1878.] 216 p. CU, Y

561 BLAIR, ELIZA (NELSON). Lisbeth Wilson, a Daughter of New Hampshire Hills . . . Boston: Lee and Shepard, 10 Milk Street [cop. 1895]. 374 p. HEH, LC, N, O, Y

562 [BLAISDELL, MRS. A. H.] Our Odyssey Club. By Agnes Gragg [pseud.]. Boston: D. Lothrop and Company, Franklin and Hawley Streets [cop. 1886]. 63, [1] p. LC, O

563 BLAISDELL, ELIJAH WHITTIER. The Hidden Record; or, The Old Sea Mystery. A Novel . . . Philadelphia: T. B. Peterson & Brothers, 306 Chestnut Street [cop. 1882]. 466 p. H, HEH, LC, UM
New York and Cuba.

564  BLAKE, LILLIE (DEVEREUX) UMSTED.  A Daring Experiment, and Other Stories . . . New York: Lovell, Coryell & Company, 5 and 7 East Sixteenth Street [cop. 1892]. 360 p., front.                     LC, O
*Also contains:* Miss Higgins's Niece—Jack Burns, Blacksmith—Miss Button's Candy Shop—Lost in the Ice—Ordeal by Fire—Postage Not Stated—A Romance of Lake George—Tessie's White Kitten—John Owen's Appeal—A Plain Country Gentleman—A Treasure Trove—Black Dave—Ten Years' Devotion— The Fair One with Silver Locks—That Mysterious Joe—A Stolen Baby—A Divided Republic.
Deposited Nov. 13, 1893.

565  BLAKELY, ELIZABETH SEAL.  Unto the Fourth Generation: One Solution of the Negro Problem . . . Cincinnati: H. H. Bevis, 1894.  125 p.
LC, UM

566  BLANCHARD, EVANGELINE B.  The Devil's Dream: A Temperance Story . . . New York, London: Funk & Wagnalls, 1889.  140 p.        BU, HEH, LC

567  BLAND, THOMAS AUGUSTUS.  Esau; or, The Banker's Victim . . . Washington, D.C.: Published by the author, 1892.  103 p.              CU
Political novel.

568  BLISS, EDGAR JANES.  The Peril of Oliver Sargent . . . New York: Charles L. Webster & Co., 1891.  177 p., front.        H, HEH, UM, UVB, Y
Patterned after Dr. Jekyll and Mr. Hyde.

BLODGETT, MABEL LOUISE (FULLER).  An Artistic Necessity, by Mabel Louise Fuller.  *In* F. E. McKay, *ed.*, Vignettes [cop. 1890], No. 3523.

569  ——— The Aspen Shade: A Romance . . . Boston: De Wolfe, Fiske & Co., 1889.  267 p.                                H, HEH, LC
From New York to Paris.

570  ——— At the Queen's Mercy . . . Boston, New York, and London: Lamson, Wolffe and Company, 1897.  261 p., illus.      H, HEH, LC, O, Y
African adventure story.

571  [BLOEDE, GERTRUDE.]  The Story of Two Lives.  By Stuart Sterne [pseud.].  New York: Cassell Publishing Company, 104 and 106 Fourth Avenue [cop. 1891].  302 p.                              LC, O, Y

572  BLOOMFIELD, WILL J.  Fay Banning . . . Chicago: Dibble Publishing Company, 1893.  304 p.                                    LC

573  BLOOMFIELD-MOORE, CLARA SOPHIA (JESSUP).  On Dangerous Ground; or, Agatha's Friendship.  A Romance of American Society . . . Philadelphia: Porter & Coates, No. 822 Chestnut Street [cop. 1876].  339 p.
H, HEH, LC, O, Y

574 BLOOMINGDALE, CHARLES. Mr., Miss, & Mrs.... Philadelphia & London: J. B. Lippincott Company, 1899. 272 p. HEH, LC, O
*Contents:* An Unfinished Tale—The First—Secrets—The King's Daughters' Musicale—The Man Who Reformed—An Unproductive Romance—The Man in the Case—Anita Cortez—Mrs. Rogers's Doll-Baby—The Wind-Up of Bohemia—An Every-Day Case—Bob Bates's Wedding—Randolph's Picture—Monteith's Romance—John Martin's Wife—Apple Blossoms—The Last Chapter —A Bunch of Violets—Bagley's Burglar—Number Five—Moonshine—The Bachelor Supper—The Class Dinner of '87.

575 BLOOR, MRS. N. A. Nothing; or, The Dream of My Life . . . Indianapolis: Carlon—Hollenbeck, printers, 1892. 201 p., front. Y

576 BLOSSOM, HENRY MARTYN. Checkers: A Hard-Luck Story . . . Chicago: Herbert S. Stone & Company, 1896. 239 p., 1 l. H, HEH, N, O, UV, Y
Of horse racing.

577 ——— The Documents in Evidence . . . St. Louis, Mo.: Buxton & Skinner, 1894. Cover title, 14 leaves. Y
Y cover title may be title page with paper covers lacking. O has complete copy with paper covers marked "3d Edition."
Facsimiles of purported letters and various newspaper clippings.

BLOT, THOMAS, *pseud.* *See* Simpson, William

578 BLUE, KATE LILLY. The Hand of Fate: A Romance of the Navy . . . Chicago: Charles H. Kerr and Company, 1895. 202 p. LC

579 BLUM, EDGAR C. Bertha Laycourt: A Novel . . . Philadelphia: J. B. Lippincott Company, 1889. 332 p. HEH, LC, UVB

580 ——— Satan's Realm . . . Chicago and New York: Rand, McNally & Company, 1899. 309 p. LC
An American newspaper man reports from Hell.

BLUM, PETER, *pseud.* *See* Miller, L. A.

BLUNT, MARIA. The Fate of the Georgiana. *In* Stories of the Sea (1893), No. 5282.

581 BOGART, CLARA LORING. Emily: A Tale of the Empire State . . . Ithaca, N.Y.: [Printed by Andrus Church], 1894. 245 p. LC

582 BOGGS, MARTHA FRYE. Jack Crews . . . New York: G. W. Dillingham Co., 1899. 273 p. HEH
Of railroad interest.

583 ——— A Romance of the New Virginia . . . Boston: Arena Publishing Company, 1896. 369 p. HEH, LC, UV
Also published as: *Margaret Steyne: A Romance of the New Virginia.* New York: G. W. Dillingham Co., 1899. LC

BOGGS, ROBERT, *pseud.* *See* Clark, Hugh A.

584 BOGY, LEWIS VITAL. A Cynic's Sacrifice: A Novel ... New York: G. W. Dillingham, 1893. 310 p.    LC

585 BOHAN, ELIZABETH BAKER. Un Americano: A Story of the Mission Days of California ... Los Angeles, Cal.: Los Angeles Printing Co., 1895. 44 p., illus.    LC
San Luis Rey Mission.

BOISGILBERT, EDMUND, *M.D., pseud.* *See* Donnelly, Ignatius Loyola

586 BOIT, ROBERT APTHORP. Eustis: A Novel ... Boston: James R. Osgood and Company, 1884. 360 p.    AP, BA, BU, H, HEH, LC, O
Postwar troubles in the South.

587 [BOLAND, LEWIS M.] For Better, for Worse. By J. Harlow Payne [pseud.] ... Seymour, Ind.: Emil E. Rettig, 1879. 120 p.    LC

588 BOLMER, W. B. The Time Is Coming ... New York: G. W. Dillingham Co., 1896. 282 p.    CU, LC
The return of Elijah.

589 BOLTON, SARAH (KNOWLES). A Country Idyl, and Other Stories ... New York, Boston: Thomas Y. Crowell & Company [cop. 1898]. 274 p., front.    CU, LC, O, Y
*Also contains:* The Second Time–Fifteen Thousand Dollars–The Ring of Gold–Four Letters–Rewarded–The Unopened Letter–Three College Students–The Twilight Hour Society–Slave Amy–Like Our Neighbors–Two at Once–The House Warming–Hannah and Joe–Burton Cone's Reason–Unsuitable–Playing with Hearts–Duty–Waify–The Black and Tan–The Christian Hunter–Love's Christmas Gift–An Unfortunate Sail–A New Kind of Wedding–Lost His Place–Struck It Rich–Food at the Door–How the Dog Tax Was Paid–The Story of Douglas.

590 ―――― Stories from Life ... New York: Thomas Y. Crowell & Co., No. 13 Astor Place [cop. 1886]. 361 p.    HEH, LC, UC, UM, UP, UV
*Contents:* The Girl in a Store–Miss Loveall's Experiment–A Friend at Court–Made Ready by Discipline–Afterwards–Duty Done–Not a Matter of Life and Death–Helpless Mrs. Jones–Could They Have Saved Him?–The Black Horses–A Judge or a Governor–Crazy Jason–The Rosewood Box–The Story of Jane–Our One Trial–Lost and Found–On a Side Street–Losing His Temper–Was It a Mistake?–Keeping the Faith–Very Select–The First Duty –The Minister's Wife–Two Christmas Days–Changing His Mind–Still the Work Goes On–A Woman's Purpose–Out of Their Set–Rickie's Christmas–Tested–Off the Right Track–Out of the Nest–Dr. Morton's Choice.

591 ―――― The Story of Douglas ... Cleveland, Ohio: [Thomas Y. Crowell & Company], 1898. [25] p.    H, HEH, LC, Y
First separate printing; included in No. 589.

592 BOND, LEWIS HAMILTON. One Year in Briartown . . . Cincinnati, O.: John Hamilton & Co., 1879. 245 p., illus.     HEH, LC, O Ohio.

593 [BONE, WILL, JR.] The "Impenetrable Mystery" of Zora Burns. Author's Copyright Edition. Chicago, 1888. 108 p., 1 l.    H, LC

594 BONNER, GERALDINE. Hard-Pan: A Story of Bonanza Fortunes . . . New York: The Century Co., 1900. 279 p.    CU, H, HEH, LC, O San Francisco.

———— The Philosophers. *In* Ten Notable Stories (1894), No. 5391.

BONNER, SHERWOOD, *pseud. See* McDowell, Katherine Sherwood (Bonner)

595 BONNY EAGLE. New York: Authors' Publishing Co., 1878. 121 p. Listed PW, Aug. 10, 1878.

596 BONSAL, STEPHEN. The Golden Horseshoe: Extracts from the Letters of Captain H. L. Herndon of the 21st U.S. Infantry, on Duty in the Philippine Islands, and Lieutenant Lawrence Gill, A.D.C. to the Military Governor of Puerto Rico . . . Edited by Stephen Bonsal . . . New York: The Macmillan Company. London: Macmillan & Co., Ltd., 1900. 316 p.    AP, CU, H, HEH, LC, O, Y Purportedly from actual letters with only the names changed.

597 BOOK, JOHN WILLIAM. Mollie's Mistake; or, Mixed Marriages . . . Cannelton, Ind.: The author, 1894. 135 p.    LC Opposes Catholics marrying Protestants.

598 THE BOOK OF ALGOONAH: Being a Concise Account of the History of the Early People of the Continent of America Known as Mound Builders . . . St. Louis, Mo.: Little & Becker, printers, 1884. 353 p.    H, HEH, LC, N, Y LC copy presented by Cyrus F. Newcomb, copyright holder. HEH copy has inscription: "This book was written by neighbor J. M. Hanks of Florence, Colo., and presented to F. A. Falkenburg by Dr. C. Q. Nelson of Canon City, Colo. Jan. 6, 1891."

599 BOOTH, BULKELEY. The Autocracy of Love: A Story . . . [New Britain, Conn.: Press of Herald Publishing Company, ca. 1890.] 40 p., front.    HEH Post Civil War.

600 [BOOTH, EMMA (SCARR).] Karan Kringle's Journal: Being Comical Episodes in an "Old Maid's Life." By Miss Karan Kringle (of Klodsville, Ohio) [pseud.] . . . Philadelphia: T. B. Peterson & Brothers, 306 Chestnut Street [cop. 1885]. 336 p., illus.    CU, HEH, LC, UC, UM

601 ———— A Wilful Heiress . . . Buffalo: Charles Wells Moulton, 1892. 230 p.    LC

602 BORING, CHARLES O. A Christmas Mystery . . . Chicago: The Forward
Movement Publishing Co., 1896. 32 p., illus.  LC

603 [BORNEMANN, MRS. MARY.] Madame Jane Junk and Joe: A Novel. By
Oraquill [pseud.]. San Francisco: A. L. Bancroft and Company, 1876.
539 p.  HEH, LC, Y
Of prison reform.

604 [BOSHER, KATE LEE (LANGLEY).] "Bobbie." By Kate Cairns [pseud.].
Richmond, Virginia: Presses of B. F. Johnson Publishing Co., 1899.
134 p., illus.  H, LC, UV
Of the Confederacy.

605 BOTELER, MATTIE M. The Conversion of Brian O'Dillon . . . Cincinnati,
Ohio: The Standard Publishing Co. [cop. 1896]. 253 p.  LC

606 ——— Shut In: A Story of the Silver Cross. And Other Stories . . .
Cincinnati, O.: The Standard Publishing Co. [cop. 1895]. 256 p.
*Also contains:* A Dollar and Costs—On Wings of Prayer—One of the King's
Sons—Angels Unawares—The Story of a Man.
Information supplied by Yeatman Anderson III of the Public Library of Cin-
cinnati.

607 BOTSFORD, EVA BELL. Lucky: A Tale of the Western Prairie . . . Buffalo:
The Peter Paul Book Company, 1895. 167 p.  LC, N

608 BOUTELL, HENRY SHERMAN. A Deserted Village . . . [Chicago]:
Chicago Literary Club, 1894. 63, [1] p., 1 l.  H, HEH, LC, N, Y
Colophon: "New York: The De Vinne Press."
215 copies privately printed.

609 BOUTELLE, CLARENCE MILES. The Man of Mt. Moriah: A Great Masonic
Serial . . . Revised, Introduced, and Indexed by John W. Brown . . .
[Chicago]: John W. Brown, cop. 1898. 298, viii, [28] p., illus.  LC, Y

610 ——— The Man Outside . . . New York: Pollard & Moss, 1888. 407
p., front.  HEH

611 BOUTON, JOHN BELL. The Enchanted: An Authentic Account of the
Strange Origin of the New Psychical Club . . . New York: Cassell
Publishing Company, 104 & 106 Fourth Avenue [cop. 1891]. 283 p.
HEH, LC

612 BOUVÉ, EDWARD TRACY. Centuries Apart . . . Boston: Little, Brown and
Company, 1894. 347 p., illus.  BA, H, HEH, O
English 16th and American 19th centuries meet.

613 BOUVÉ, PAULINE CARRINGTON (RUST). Their Shadows Before: A Story
of the Southampton Insurrection . . . Boston: Small, Maynard &
Company, 1899. 202 p.  H, HEH, LC, O, UV, Y

614 BOUVET, MARIE MARGUERITE. My Lady: A Story of Long Ago . . . Chicago: A. C. McClurg and Company, 1894. 284 p., illus.

HEH, LC, UV, Y

615 BOUVIER, CLARA. The Lily He Plucked: A Romance . . . New York, St. Louis: I. H. Brown & Company, 1891. 127 p. LC

616 BOWEN, GRACE GREENWOOD. Rosalys Harper; or, The Turn of the Wheel of Fortune . . . [N.p., n.d.] 91 p., illus. HEH
Preface signed: "Allentown, October, 1897."

617 BOWEN, HELEN M. A Daughter of Cuba . . . New York: The Merriam Company, 67 Fifth Avenue [cop. 1896]. 334 p. H, HEH

618 [BOWEN, WILLIAM ABRAHAM.] Chained Lightning. By Ike Philkins [pseud.], the Funny Man of the Austin (Texas) Statesman. New York: J. S. Ogilvie & Company, 31 Rose Street [cop. 1883]. 104 p., illus. CU, LC

619 [BOWER, MRS. ELLA E.] Leaves from a Bad Girl's Diary. By E. E. B. Chicago: Owens Publishing Company, 1884. 83 p. LC

BOWERS, A. HERBERT, jt. au. See Athey, H. With Gyves of Gold (1898), No. 165.

620 BOWERS, S. JAY. "Pleasure Promoter" . . . Chicago, 1888. 98 p. LC
Also published as: "Life Mirror." Chicago, 1889. 96 p. LC

621 BOWLES, JOHN. The Masked Prophet. One's Hidden Self. A Romance in Two Lives—Here and Hereafter . . . New York: Caxton Company [cop. 1895]. 190 p., illus. LC

622 ——— The Stormy Petrel: An Historical Romance . . . New York: A. Lovell & Co. London: Walter Scott [cop. 1892]. 349 p., front.

CU, HEH, LC

Deposited Mar. 20, 1893.
Ante bellum Kentucky.

623 BOWYER, EDITH M. (NICHOLL). Tales of Mountain and Mesa. By Edith M. Nicholl . . . Cincinnati: The Editor Publishing Co., 1899. 262 p.

CU, HEH, LC

New Mexico.

624 BOWYER, JAMES T. The Pollinctor . . . Richmond, Va.: J. W. Randolph & Co., 1895. 175 p. CU, HEH, UV
Civil War; Virginia.

625 ——— The Witch of Jamestown: A Story of Colonial Virginia . . . Richmond, Va.: J. W. Randolph & English, 1890. 151 p., front.

HEH, O, UV, Y

Boy, Mrs., *pseud.* *See* Griswold, Jane (Emmet)

Boyce, Neith. In a Garden. *In* Stories from the Chap-Book (1896), No. 5277.
Author's full name: Neith (Boyce) Hapgood.

———— The Sands of the Green River. *In* New Stories from the Chap-Book (1898), No. 3949.

626 Boyd, E. E. Quaint Folk of Haverly ... New York: Phillips & Hunt. Cincinnati: Walden & Stowe, 1882. 176 p., front.                   HEH

627 Boyd, John Edward. The Berkeley Heroine, and Other Stories. By Boyd, the Boss Baggage Buster of Beautiful Berkeley. Berkeley, Cal.: The Berkeley Printing Company, Odd Fellows' Building [1899?]. 96 p., front.                   HEH
*Contains:* The Capture of the Sultana—How We Fooled the Schoolmaster.

628 Boyd, Lucinda Joan (Rogers). The Sorrows of Nancy ... Richmond, Va.: O. E. Flanhart Printing Company, 1899. 95 p., illus.
                   BU, CU, H, HEH, LC, N, UC, UV, Y
Facts and fancies about Lincoln's mother woven into a story.

629 [Boyden, Emma.] Both Were Mistaken: A Novel. By Arline Dare [pseud.] ... New York: G. W. Dillingham, 1892. 287 p.          LC
Of a New York millionaire.

Boyesen, Hjalmar Hjorth. A Daring Fiction. *In* Stories by American Authors, X (1885), No. 5276.

630 [————] A Daughter of the Philistines. Boston: Roberts Brothers, 1883. 325 p.                   BA, CU, H, HEH, LC, O, UVB, Y
At head of title: "No Name Series."

631 ———— Falconberg ... New York: Charles Scribner's Sons, 1879. 287 p., illus.                   BA, BU, CU, H, HEH, LC, N, O, UC, UM, UP, UVB, Y

632 ———— The Golden Calf: A Novel ... Meadville, Penna.: Flood and Vincent; the Chautauqua-Century Press, 1892. 230 p.
                   BA, CU, UM, UVB, Y

633 ———— Ilka on the Hill-Top, and Other Stories ... New York: Charles Scribner's Sons, 1881. 240 p.          BA, BU, CU, H, HEH, LC, O, UVB, Y
*Also contains:* Annunciata—Under the Glacier—A Knight of Dannebrog—Mabel and I (A Philosophical Fairy Tale)—How Mr. Storm Met His Destiny.

634 ———— The Light of Her Countenance ... New York: D. Appleton and Company, 1889. 312 p.          AP, BA, CU, H, O, UM, UP, UVB

635 ———— The Mammon of Unrighteousness ... New York: John W. Lovell Company, 150 Worth St., cor. Mission Place [cop. 1891]. 386 p.
                   BA, O, UC, UM, UP, UVB

Author's name misspelled "Boyeson" on title page, which is conjugate of 7th leaf. At bottom of spine: "Lovell." These sheets were also bound up (rebound?) in 1896 or later with "American Publishers Corporation" at bottom of spine.

*Also issued with imprint:* New York: United States Book Company, successors to John W. Lovell Company, 150 Worth St., cor. Mission Place [cop. 1891]. CU, HEH, UV

> Author's name misspelled "Boyeson" on title page, which is conjugate of 7th leaf. At bottom of spine: "Lovell."

> LC deposit copy, dated July 21, 1892, has the United States Book Company imprint as above. Author's name correctly spelled "Boyesen" on title page. Frederick R. Goff of LC states: "Altho the copy has been rebound, the title leaf does not appear to be a conjugate of the 7th leaf."

*Also issued with imprint:* New York: Lovell, Coryell & Company, 43, 45, and 47 East Tenth Street [ca. 1892-93]. UV, Y

636 ——— Queen Titania . . . New York: Charles Scribner's Sons, 1881. 254 p.          BA, CU, H, HEH, LC, N, O, UVB, Y
*Also contains:* The Mountain's Face—A Dangerous Virtue.

637 ——— Social Strugglers: A Novel . . . New York: Charles Scribner's Sons, 1893. 299 p.          AP, BA, CU, H, HEH, LC, O, UP, UVB, Y

638 ——— Tales from Two Hemispheres . . . Boston: James R. Osgood and Company, 1877. 283 p., front.          BA, LC, O, UP, UVB, Y
*Contents:* The Man Who Lost His Name—The Story of an Outcast—A Good-for-Nothing—A Scientific Vagabond—Truls, the Nameless—Asathor's Vengeance.

639 ——— Vagabond Tales . . . Boston: D. Lothrop Company, Washington Street opposite Bromfield [cop. 1889]. 332 p.    BA, CU, HEH, LC, O, Y
*Contents:* Crooked John—A Child of the Age—Monk Tellenbach's Exile—A Disastrous Partnership—Liberty's Victim—A Perilous Incognito—Charity.

640 BOYLAN, GRACE (DUFFIE). If Tam O'Shanter'd Had a Wheel, and Other Poems and Sketches . . . New York: E. R. Herrick & Company, 70 Fifth Avenue [cop. 1898]. 222 p., illus.          BU, H, N
Contains same stories as No. 641, with the following additions: A Miracle of the Fishes—The Passing of Officedogski—Consider the Lilies—The Old Bugler—Sundown—A Son of Italy—White Organdy—A Baggage Reading—An Every Day Story—The Legend of the Moss Rose—Kelsey—Katie's Light Housekeeping—Keepin' Cump'ny—How Bud Brought in the Copy—Chiquita.

641 ——— The Old House, and Other Poems and Sketches . . . Chicago: Palmer & Co. New York: E. R. Herrick & Co. [cop. 1897]. 112 p., illus.

*Contains:* At the Refuge of Saint Sophia—Eph'rum's Matrimonial Surprises—Old "97"—Romance in the Irish Village—The Belle of the Block—Terry's Repentance—The Prison Gardener—Ishmael, the Exile—The Quest of Gudrun. Copy examined at New York Public Library.

642 BOYLE, VIRGINIA (FRAZER). Brockenburne: A Southern Auntie's War Tale . . . New York: E. R. Herrick & Company, 1897. 75 p., illus.
         BU, CU, H, HEH, LC, O, UC, UV, Y

643 —— Devil Tales . . . New York and London: Harper & Brothers, 1900. 210, [1] p., illus. H, HEH, LC, O, Y

*Contents:* Old Cinder Cat—"A Kingdom for Micajah"—The Devil's Little Fly—Asmodeus in the Quarters—The Taming of Jezrul—Dark er de Moon—The Other Maumer—Stolen Fire—The Black Cat—'Liza.

644 BOYLE, ZOLA M. A Master of Life . . . New York: G. W. Dillingham Co., 1900. 219 p., illus. LC

Of hypnosis.

BOYLSTON, PETER, *pseud. See* Curtis, George Ticknor

[BOYNTON, PERCY HOLMES.] The Proprieties, by B. P. *In* [F. L. Knowles] *ed.*, Cap and Gown in Prose (1900), No. 3182.

645 BRADFORD, WILLIAM. Rosebush; or, Life in California . . . New York: W. B. Smith & Co., Bond Street [cop. 1881]. 96 p. LC

646 —— Yesterdays in Paris: A Sketch from Real Life . . . New York: The Authors' Publishing Company, 27 Bond Street [cop. 1880]. 102 p. LC

647 BRADSHAW, MARGARET. My Heart Remembers How . . . Boston: James H. Earle, 178 Washington Street [cop. 1897]. 275 p., illus. BU, HEH, LC, Y

Deposited Aug. 12, 1898.

BRADSHAW, WELLESLEY, *pseud. See* Alexander, Charles Wesley

648 BRADSHAW, WILLIAM RICHARD. The Goddess of Atvatabar: Being the History of the Discovery of the Interior World and Conquest of Atvatabar . . . New York: J. F. Douthitt, 1892. 318 p., illus. CU, H, HEH, LC, UM

649 BRADY, CYRUS TOWNSEND. For Love of Country: A Story of Land and Sea in the Days of the Revolution . . . New York: Charles Scribner's Sons, 1898. 354 p. BA, CU, HEH, O, Y

650 —— For the Freedom of the Sea: A Romance of the War of 1812 . . . New York: Charles Scribner's Sons, 1899. 339 p., illus. AP, CU, H, HEH, LC, N, O, UV, Y

651 —— The Grip of Honor: A Story of Paul Jones and the American Revolution . . . New York: Charles Scribner's Sons, 1900. 246 p., illus. AP, CU, H, HEH, LC, N, O, UC, UM

652 BRADY, JASPER EWING. Tales of the Telegraph: The Story of a Telegrapher's Life and Adventures in Railroad, Commercial, and Military Work . . . New York: Doubleday & McClure Co., 1899. 272 p., illus. H, HEH, LC, O, UV, Y

653 BRAENDLE, ROSE ANNE. Only a Waif . . . New York: D. & J. Sadlier & Co., 1880. 230 p. HEH, Y
Of the stage.

BRAINARD, FREDERICK R. A Lady of Malta. *In* C. King, *ed.*, By Land and Sea (1891), No. 3092.
Later printed in No. 3099.

BRAINERD, THOMAS H., *pseud.* *See* Jarboe, Mary Halsey (Thomas)

654 BRAKE, JOSEPHINE WINFIELD. As It Happened: Being a Story in Three Books and Several Manners . . . Washington: The Neale Company, 1899. 253 p. LC
Also published as: *How It Happened: Being a Story in Three Books.* New York: The American News Company [cop. 1900]. 252 p., illus. HEH, LC, UV
Deposited June 5, 1900.

655 BRANCH, EDWARD PAYSON. Plain People: A Story of the Western Reserve . . . New York: The Publishers' Printing Co., 1892. 293 p.
H, HEH, LC, UM

656 BRANCH, HOMER P. Zeyna el Zegal, the Phantom Lady of the Villa Montinni: The Romance of a Haunted House . . . Mitchell, Ia.: Published by the author, 1890. 51 p. LC

657 BRANSCOM, ALEXANDER C. Mystic Romances of the Blue and the Grey: Masks of War, Commerce, and Society . . . New York: Mutual Publishing Company, 45, 47, 49, & 51 Rose Street [cop. 1883]. 324 p., illus.
Printed in double columns. CU, HEH, O

658 BRAZELTON, ETHEL MAUDE (COLSON). The Story of a Dream. By Ethel Maude Colson . . . Chicago: Charles H. Kerr & Company, 1896. 304 p. HEH, LC

BRAZZA, *Countess* DI. *See* Slocomb, Cora

659 BREARLEY, WILLIAM HENRY. Wanted, a Copyist . . . New York: The Cassell Publishing Co., 31 East 17th St. [cop. 1894]. 153 p. HEH, LC
At head of title: "The 'Unknown' Library."
Of newspaper publishing.

———— *jt. au.* *See* Kelley, A. S. King Washington (1898), No. 3062.

660 BRECKINRIDGE, JULIA. In Dead Earnest . . . New York: The Authors' Publishing Company, Bond Street [cop. 1878]. 239 p. LC
Philadelphia Quakers.

661 BREESE, W. W. Drifting: A Tale True to Life . . . Nashville, Tenn.: South Western Publishing House, 1879. Cover title, 367 p., illus.
LC, N

662 BRENNAN, JOHN. Erin Mor: The Story of Irish Republicanism . . . San
Francisco: P. M. Diers & Company, 1892. 272 p. HEH, LC, UM
Emigration of an Irishman to San Diego.

663 BREWER, CHARLES. Retribution at Last: A Mormon Tragedy of the
Rockies . . . Cincinnati: The Editor Publishing Co., 1899. 101 p.
HEH, LC, UM, Y

664 [BREWER, WILLIS.] The Children of Issachar . . . A Story of Wrongs
and Remedies . . . New York & London: G. P. Putnam's Sons; the
Knickerbocker Press, 1884. 297 p. CU, LC
Reconstruction in Alabama.

665 [———] supposed author. The Secret of Mankind: With Some
Singular Hints Gathered in the Elsewheres or After-Life, from Certain
Eminent Personages, as Also Some Brief Account of the Planet Mercury
and of Its Institutions . . . New York, London: G. P. Putnam's Sons;
the Knickerbocker Press, 1895. 417 p. BU, HEH, LC

666 BREWSTER, HENRY POMEROY. The Story of a Welsh Girl . . . [Roches-
ter, N.Y.], 1888. 71 p. Printed in double columns. LC

BRICKTOP, pseud. See Small, George G.

667 [BRIDGE, JAMES HOWARD.] A Fortnight in Heaven: An Unconventional
Romance. By Harold Brydges [pseud.]. New York: Henry Holt
and Company, 1886. 177 p. BU, H, Y

BRIDGES, MADELINE S., pseud. See De Vere, Mary Ainge

668 [BRIGGS, WILLIAM H. F.] The Career of the Stolen Boy, Charlie. By
Mrs. Caroline Oakley and Willie Fern [pseuds. of W. H. F. Briggs].
Oakland, Cal.: William H. Briggs, 1881. 197 p. HEH, LC, Y
Central California mining.

669 [BRIGHAM, HARRIET CONWAY.] The New Saint Cecilia . . . Detroit,
Mich.: Farrand & Votey, 1895. 32 p., illus. LC
A tale to sell Farrand & Votey pipe organs.

670 BRINE, MARY DOW (NORTHAM). Margaret Arnold's Christmas, and
Other Stories . . . New York: E. P. Dutton & Company, 1894. 322
p., illus. HEH, LC
Also contains: Mother's Visit—My One Little Talent—Their Experiment—
Grandpa, Mordaunt and I—Miss Betsey—The Blind Wife.

671 BRINKERHOFF, HENRY R. Nah-nee-ta: A Tale of the Navajos . . . Washington: J. H. Soulé & Co., 1886. 236 p. H, HEH, LC, N, Y
Arizona and New Mexico.

672 BRISCOE, GEORGE H. Angels of Commerce; or, Thirty Days with the
Drummers of Arkansas . . . New York: Press of the Publishers' Printing Co., 1891. 216 p. LC

BRISCOE, MARGARET SUTTON. *See* Hopkins, Margaret Sutton (Briscoe)

673 BRISTOL, ELIAS LEROY MACOMB. Before He Was Born; or, The Scarlet Arm ... [New York: M. J. Roth, printer, 1891.] 69 p.  LC

674 ——— What Would You Have Done? ... [New York: Press of John B. Watkins, cop. 1895.] 55 p.  LC

675 BRISTOW, G. O. Lost on Grand River ... Nowata, I.T.: Cherokee Air Publishing Company, 1900. 131 p.  LC
Of the "badmen."

676 BRODHEAD, EVA WILDER (McGLASSON). Bound in Shallows: A Novel ... New York: Harper & Brothers, 1897. 271 p., illus.  HEH, LC, O, Y
Lumbering in Kentucky.

677 ——— Diana's Livery. By Eva Wilder McGlasson. New York: Harper & Brothers, 1891. 286 p.  CU, HEH, LC, O, UC, UM
Shaker community life in Kentucky.

678 ——— An Earthly Paragon: A Novel ... New York: Harper & Brothers, 1892. 207 p., illus.  HEH, LC, Y
Lumbering in Kentucky.

679 ——— Ministers of Grace: A Novelette ... New York: Harper & Brothers, 1894. 141 p., illus.  HEH, LC, O, UC, UM, UV
A resort on the New Jersey coast.

680 ——— One of the Visconti: A Novelette ... New York: Charles Scribner's Sons, 1896. 194 p.  HEH, LC
Naples, Italy.

BRONSON, HOWARD, *M.D., pseud. See* McAndrew, William A.

680a BRONSON, THOMAS CURRY. Grace Baldwin; or, Schnell's Place ... Chicago: Franklin Printing and Publishing Company [cop. 1897]. 117 p., front.  HEH, LC
Temperance tale.

681 BROOKS, BYRON ALDEN. Earth Revisited ... Boston, Mass.: Arena Publishing Company, 1893. 318 p.  HEH, LC, O
Reincarnation.

682 ——— Those Children and Their Teachers: A Story of To-Day ... New York: G. P. Putnam's Sons, 1882. 272 p.  AP, HEH
Of the educational system.

683 BROOKS, ELBRIDGE STREETER. A Son of Issachar: A Romance of the Days of Messias ... New York, London: G. P. Putnam's Sons; the Knickerbocker Press, 1890. 293 p.  AP, BA, CU, H, HEH, O, UV, Y

684 ———— The Story of Miriam of Magdala, Sometimes Called the Magdalen ... New York: W. B. Perkins & Co., 1895. 66 p., illus.
HEH, Y

685 BROOKS, HENRY STANFORD. A Catastrophe in Bohemia, and Other Stories ... New York: Charles L. Webster & Company, 1893. 372 p., front.
CU, HEH, LC, O, UM, Y
*Also contains:* Doña Paula's Treasure—The Don in Pauper Alley—The Crazy Professor—The Arrival of the Magpie—A Scrap of Frontier History—An Unprofessional Money-Lender—La Tiburona—A Visit from an Esquimaux—A Chapter of Accidents—At Don Ignacio's—The Virgin of Pearls.

BROOKS, LILIAN, *jt. au. See* Camp, W. C. Drives and Puts (1899), No. 884.

BROOKS, NOAH. Lost in the Fog. *In* Stories by American Authors, IV (1884), No. 5270.

686 ———— Tales of the Maine Coast ... New York: Charles Scribner's Sons, 1894. 271 p.
BA, H, HEH, LC, O, UM, UP, Y
*Contents:* Pansy Pegg—The Apparition of Jo Murch—The Hereditary Barn— The Phantom Sailor—The Honor of a Family—The Waif of Nautilus Island— A Century Ago.

687 BROOKS, SARAH PEROT. In Divers Paths: Stories ... Hartford, Conn.: The Student Publishing Company, 1896. 242 p.
LC, O
*Contents:* Miss Morgan's Mission—An Identity Reclaimed—The Making and Unmaking of Fate—The Rejected Manuscript—From Within and Without— Nora—A Mistaken Diagnosis.

688 ———— In the Bivouac of Life ... Philadelphia, New York, London: Drexel Biddle, 1899. 300 p., front.
HEH, LC, O, UM
*Contents:* An Event at Krevlen—A Modern Unit—Dolorous Dolly—Evolution of Solitaire—A Novel Investment—Was She Christian or Pagan?—The Meeting of Minds—Ellen Willetts' Donation—Those Honest Eyes—Conflicting Logic.

689 BROOKS, SARAH (WARNER). My Fire Opal, and Other Tales ... Boston: Estes and Lauriat, 1896. 229 p.
CU, HEH, LC, UM, UVB, Y
*Also contains:* The Story of John Gravesend—A Bunch of Violets—A Disastrous Sleigh-Ride—Tuckered Out—A Prison Child—Escaped.

690 ———— Poverty Knob ... New York: A. Wessels Company, 1900. 207 p., 1 l.
CU, HEH, LC
*Also contains:* The Man on High Island—A Haunted Ruin—Captain White's Assistant—Ramon's—The Tramp from Bar Harbor—Flotsam of the Line Storm.

691 BROOME, ISAAC. "The Brother." Splendor and Woe ... Paterson, N.J.: J. A. Craig, printer and publisher, 1890. 288 p.
LC

692 BROSS, EDGAR CLIFTON. God's Pay Day: A Novel ... New York: G. W. Dillingham Co., 1898. 235 p.
HEH, LC
Of the degeneration of a man.

693 BROSS, WILLIAM. Legend of the Delaware: An Historical Sketch of Tom Quick. To Which Is Added The Winfield Family . . . Chicago: Knight & Leonard Co., printers, 1887. 195 p., illus.  CU, HEH, N, O, Y

694 BROUGHTON, RHODA. A Widower Indeed. By Rhoda Broughton and Elizabeth Bisland . . . New York: D. Appleton and Company, 1891. 228 p.  BA, O, Y
Elizabeth Bisland Wetmore an American.

695 BROWN, ABBY WHITNEY. Can She Atone? . . . Philadelphia: J. B. Lippincott & Co., 1880. 238 p.  H, LC
Social novel.

696 BROWN, ABRAM ENGLISH. Glimpses of Old New England Life: Legends of Old Bedford . . . Boston: R. H. Blodgett, printer, 30 Bromfield St. [cop. 1892]. 198, [1] p., illus.  BA, CU, H, HEH, N, Y

697 BROWN, ALICE. The Day of His Youth . . . Boston and New York: Houghton, Mifflin and Company. The Riverside Press, Cambridge, 1897. 143, [1] p.  BA, CU, H, HEH, LC, O, UC, UM, UP, UVB, Y

698 ——— Fools of Nature: A Novel . . . Boston: Ticknor and Company, 1887. 430 p.  BU, CU, H, HEH, LC, O, UC, Y
Of spiritualism.

699 ——— Meadow-Grass: Tales of New England Life . . . Boston: Copeland and Day, 1895. 315, [1] p.  BU, CU, H, HEH, N, O, UV, Y
Contents: Number Five—Farmer Eli's Vacation—After All—Told in the Poorhouse—Heman's Ma—Heartsease—Mis' Wadleigh's Guest—A Righteous Bargain—Joint Owners in Spain—At Sudleigh Fair—Bankrupt—Nancy Boyd's Last Sermon—Strollers in Tiverton.

700 [———] Stratford-by-the-Sea: A Novel. New York: Henry Holt and Company, 1884. 316 p.  BU, H, HEH, LC, O, Y
At head of title: "American Novel Series—No. 4."
A New England town.

701 ——— Tiverton Tales . . . Boston and New York: Houghton, Mifflin and Company. The Riverside Press, Cambridge, 1899. 339, [1] p.
BA, CU, H, HEH, LC, N, O, UC, UM, UP, Y
Contents: Dooryards—A March Wind—The Mortuary Chest—Horn-o'-the-Moon—A Stolen Festival—A Last Assembling—The Way of Peace—The Experience of Hannah Prime—Honey and Myrrh—A Second Marriage—The Flat-Iron Lot—The End of All Living.

702 BROWN, ALMEDIA MORTON. Diary of a Minister's Wife . . . New York: J. S. Ogilvie & Company, 31 Rose Street [cop. 1881]. 544 p., illus.
BU, H, HEH
Listed PW, Apr. 15, 1882.

BROWN, ANNA ROBESON. See Burr, Anna Robeson (Brown)

703 BROWN, ARTHUR ALADINE. Lumbering on the Cumberland: A Romance Taken from Life . . . Cincinnati: The Lumber Worker Company, 1887. 136 p., illus.     LC

704 [BROWN, MRS. C. R.] Ethel Dutton; or, Love's Triumph. By Mattie May [pseud.]. Boston: A. K. Loring, corner Bromfield and Washington Streets [cop. 1880]. 215 p.
Copy examined at Boston Public Library.
Of a fisherman and an heiress.

BROWN, CAROLINE, *pseud.* *See* Krout, Caroline Virginia

705 [BROWN, CARRIE L.] But Half a Heart. By Marie Oliver [pseud.] . . . Boston: D. Lothrop Company, Franklin and Hawley Streets [cop. 1885]. 434 p.     HEH, LC

706 BROWN, CLARA SPALDING. Life at Shut-In Valley, and Other Pacific Coast Tales . . . [Franklin, Ohio: The Editor Publishing Co., cop. 1895.] 188 p.     CU, H, HEH, LC, O, Y
*Also contains:* A Strike for Eight Hours–Hearts Are Trumps–A Mid-Day Call at Miner's Flat–The Mysterious Miss Aldeman–The School-Ma'am of Mineral Hill–The Trials of Jonathan Mollify–Reuben Hall's Christmas–Mrs. Brighton's Burglar–Through Night to Light–That Ugly Man–The Awakening.

707 BROWN, FRED H. One Dollar's Worth . . . [Chicago, cop. 1893.] 177 p., illus.
Information from LC card; no copy seen.

708 BROWN, FRED S. Strange Fancies: A Novel . . . Cincinnati, O.: Fred S. Brown, 1888. 217 p.     HEH, LC

709 BROWN, HELEN DAWES. A Civilian Attaché: A Story of a Frontier Army Post . . . New York: Charles Scribner's Sons, 1899. 161 p.
    CU, HEH, LC, O

710 ———— The Petrie Estate . . . Boston and New York: Houghton, Mifflin and Company. The Riverside Press, Cambridge, 1893. 316 p.
    BU, H, HEH, LC, O, UC, Y
New York.

711 ———— Two College Girls . . . Boston: Ticknor and Company, 1886. 325 p.     AP, BU, H, HEH, LC, O, UC

712 BROWN, HERBERT E. Betsey Jane on the New Woman . . . Chicago: Charles H. Kerr & Company, 1897. 271 p.     LC

713 BROWN, JAMES CABELL. Calabazas; or, Amusing Recollections of an Arizona "City" . . . San Francisco: Valleau & Peterson, printers and publishers, cop. 1892. 251 p., illus.     CU, H, HEH, N, Y

714 [BROWN, JAMES E.] Mose Skinner [pseud.], His Centennial Booke, in Which He Spans ye Hundred Years, and Everlastinglye Cuts Uppe Tantrums. Boston: The New England News Co., sole agents, 37 and 41 Court Street, cop. 1875. 46 p., illus.     BU, H, HEH, LC, UC, Y
Dedication dated "Jan., 1876."

715 [————] The Tribulations of an Office Seeker; or, The Doolittle Boom. By Mose Skinner [pseud.] . . . [Boston: New England News Co.], cop. 1885. 40 p.     LC

BROWN, JESSIE HUNTER. *See* Pounds, Jessie Hunter (Brown)

716 BROWN, JOSEPH M. Kennesaw's Bombardment; or, How the Sharp-shooters Woke Up the Batteries . . . Atlanta, Ga.: Record Publishing Company, 1890. 172, [1] p., illus.     HEH
Civil War.

717 BROWN, KATE CLARK. Beauty for Ashes . . . Boston: Arena Publishing Company, 1895. 120 p.     LC
Of reincarnation.

BROWN, KENNETH. Goodale's Revival. *In* Stories from the Harvard Advocate (1896), No. 5277a.

718 BROWN, L. MELYZIA. My Solomon: A Story of Modern New York . . . New York: Printed and published by W. L. Hyde & Co., 1879. 330 p.     HEH, LC

719 BROWN, L. Q. C. Kenneth Cameron . . . Philadelphia: T. B. Peterson & Brothers, 306 Chestnut Street [cop. 1888]. 349 p.     CU, HEH, O
Ante bellum New Orleans.

720 BROWN, MARY ELIZABETH ADAMS. Ellice Larrabee: A Tale of Olden Time . . . Cincinnati, O.: Elm Street Printing Co., 1889. 290 p., front.     LC, UC

721 [BROWN, S. A.] The Dissolution: A Projected Drama. By Ritter Dandelyon [pseud.]. New York: G. W. Dillingham, 1894. 219 p.     LC

722 [————] Rheingrafenstein: A Romance of the Eleventh Century. By Ritter Dandelyon [pseud.]. New York: G. W. Dillingham, 1893. 314 p.     LC

723 BROWN, SEBASTIAN. John Smith: A Journey along the High-Ways and By-Ways of Life . . . Baltimore: The Monumental Publishing Company, December, 1893. 268 p., front.     HEH, LC, UV, Y
Of a Philadelphia lawyer.

724 BROWN, STIRLING WILSON. In the Limestone Valley: Pen Pictures of Early Days in Western Wisconsin . . . [West Salem? Wis.], 1900. 214 p.     LC, UC

725 [BROWN, WALTER.] Mitylene: A Tale of New England and the Tropics. By "Mi Esposa e Yo." Being a Narration of the Personal Experiences of a Father, His Two Daughters, and Their Physician, Shipwrecked upon an Uninhabited Island of the Pacific . . . Chicago: Donohue and Henneberry, 1879. 347 p., illus.     HEH, LC, UV

UV has author's presentation copy: "Bishop Whipple with the kind regards of the authors Mr. and Mrs. Walter Brown, of Salerosse, Wisc."

726 BROWN, WALTER WIDEMAN. How the Victory Was Won: A Story . . . Nashville, Tennessee: Printed for the author, 1892. 94 p.     CU, LC

727 ——— Money Don' Make 'Ristercrats: A Story . . . Nashville, Tenn.: Printed for the author, 1893. 29 p.
Information from LC card; no copy seen.

728 BROWN, WILLIAM HORACE. The Slaves of Folly: A Narrative . . . Chicago and New York: Rand, McNally & Company, 1889. 322 p.  LC

BROWN, WILLIAM PERRY. Herne the Hunter. *In* C. King, Rancho del Muerto [cop. 1895], No. 3109.

729 ——— A Sea-Island Romance: A Story of South Carolina after the War . . . New York: John B. Alden, 1888. 161 p.     HEH, LC, N

730 BROWNE, MRS. LIDA BRIGGS. Words That Burn: A Romance . . . Utica, N.Y.: Daniel B. Briggs, 1900. 366 p., front.     HEH, LC, UM
English girl marries successful American businessman.

731 BROWNE, WALTER. "2894"; or, The Fossil Man. (A Mid-Winter Night's Dream.) . . . New York: G. W. Dillingham, 1894. 298 p.
Information from LC card; no copy seen.

732 BROWNE, WALTER SCOTT. Andrew Bentley; or, How He Retrieved His Honor. Story of the Civil War Founded on Facts . . . Camden, N.J.: A. C. Graw [cop. 1900]. 311 p., illus.     LC

733 BROWNELL, GERTRUDE (HALL). April's Sowing. [By] Gertrude Hall . . . New York: McClure, Phillips & Co., 1900. 282, [2] p., illus.     HEH, LC, O
From the Middle West to Vienna.

734 ——— Far from To-Day . . . Boston: Roberts Brothers, 1892. 291 p.     BA, BU, H, HEH, LC, Y
*Contents:* Tristiane–Sylvanus–The Sons of Philemon–Theodolind–Servirol–Shepherds.

735 ——— Foam of the Sea, and Other Tales . . . Boston: Roberts Brothers, 1895. 299 p.     H, HEH, LC, O, Y
*Also contains:* In Battlereagh House–Powers of Darkness–The Late Returning –The Wanderers–Garden Deadly.

736 ———— The Hundred, and Other Stories . . . New York and London: Harper & Brothers, 1898. 255, [1] p., illus.  CU, HEH, N, O, Y
*Also contains:* The Passing of Spring—Paula in Italy—Dorastus—Chloe, Chloris and Cytherea.

737 BROWNLEE, ALICE VIVIAN. The Affinities: A Novel . . . Atlanta, Ga.: The Constitution Publishing Co., 1890. 308 p., front.  HEH
Author's full name: Alice Vivian (Brownlee) Cole.

738 BRUCE, THOMAS. That Bruisin' Lad o' Greystone Lodge: A Novel . . . Author of "Cupid and Duty," "Historical Sketches of Roanoke," "Loveless Marriages" . . . Roanoke, Va.: The Bell Printing and Manufacturing Co., 1890. 154 p.  HEH, UV
North Carolina.

739 BRUNER, JANE WOODWORTH. Free Prisoners: A Story of California Life . . . Philadelphia: Claxton, Remsen, & Haffelfinger, 1877. 258 p.
CU, HEH, LC, UC
Grass Valley and Sacramento.

740 [BRUSH, CHRISTINE (CHAPLIN).] The Colonel's Opera Cloak. Boston: Roberts Brothers, 1879. 228 p.  BU, CU, H, HEH, N, O, UM, Y
At head of title: "No Name Series."
Of a southern family in the North.

741 ———— Inside Our Gate . . . Boston: Roberts Brothers, 1889. 304 p.
AP, H, HEH, LC, O, Y
A chronicle of home life.

742 [BRYAN, ELLA HOWARD.] Behind the Veil. Boston: Little, Brown and Company, 1899. 107 p.  HEH, LC, UM
Speculation on life after death.

743 BRYAN, MRS. EMMA LYON. 1860-1865: A Romance of the Valley of Virginia . . . [Harrisonburg, Va.: J. Taliaffero, cop. 1892.] 228 p.
H, HEH, LC, UV

744 BRYAN, MARY (EDWARDS). Manch . . . New York: D. Appleton and Company, 1880. 309 p.  H, LC, UV
Comanches; the West.

745 ———— Wild Work: The Story of the Red River Tragedy . . . New York: D. Appleton and Company, 1881. 410 p.  CU, H, HEH, LC, UM, Y
Reconstruction era in Louisiana.

746 BRYANSEN, JENNES, *pseud.* The Homesteader's Daughter: A Story of the Times. (Founded on Fact.) . . . New York, 1900. 158 p., front.  LC
Written in LC copy: "By Nathan Billstein, of Balt., Md."

747 BRYCE, LLOYD STEPHENS. A Dream of Conquest . . . Philadelphia: J. B. Lippincott Company [cop. 1889]. 80 p.  HEH
Conquest of the Atlantic seaboard by the Chinese fleet.

748 ———— Friends in Exile: A Tale of Diplomacy, Coronets, and Hearts ...
New York: Cassell Publishing Company, 104 & 106 Fourth Avenue
[cop. 1893]. 301 p. HEH, LC
Of a U.S. ambassador to France.

749 ———— Lady Blanche's Salon: A Story of Some Souls ... New York:
F. Tennyson Neely, 114 Fifth Avenue. Chicago, London [cop. 1899].
229 p. LC, Y
London.

750 ———— Paradise: A Novel ... New York, London: Funk & Wagnalls,
1887. 172 p. HEH, LC
Satire on a western city society.

751 ———— Romance of an Alter Ego ... New York, Washington, D.C.,
Chicago, London, Paris: Brentano's [cop. 1889]. 350 p.
AP, H, HEH, LC, O
Also published as: *An Extraordinary Experience; or, The Romance of an Alter
Ego.* New York: Brentano's, 1891. LC
Of mistaken identity.

BRYDGES, HAROLD, *pseud.* *See* Bridge, James Howard

752 BUCHANAN, FANNIE. The Lonely Trail: A Romance of Humboldt
County, Cal. ... Eureka, Cal. [cop. 1878]. Cover title, 42 p. Printed
in double columns. LC

BUCHANAN, RACHEL. *See* Longstreet, Rachel Abigail (Buchanan)

753 BUCK, FRANCIS TILLOU. A Fiancé on Trial ... New York: The Merriam
Company, 67 Fifth Avenue [cop. 1896]. 310 p. CU, HEH, LC

754 ———— A Man of Two Minds ... New York: The Merriam Company,
67 Fifth Avenue [cop. 1895]. 338 p., front. HEH, LC
Of a New Yorker in love with two women.

755 [BUCK, JAMES SMITH.] The Chronicles of the Land of Columbia, Com-
monly Called America. From the Landing of the Pilgrim Fathers, to
the Second Reign of Ulysses the I, a Period of Two Hundred and
Fifty-Two Years ... By the Prophet James [pseud.] ... Milwaukee,
Wis.: F. W. Stearns, 1876. 112, v, [2] p. Printed in double columns.
BU, H, LC, N, O, UC, UM, Y

BUCK, MRS. M. K., *jt. au.* *See* Bates, M. E. C. Along Traverse Shores
(1891), No. 405.

756 BUCKINGHAM, EMMA MAY. Parson Thorne's Trial: A Novel ... New
York: G. W. Carleton & Co. London: S. Low & Co., 1880. 364 p.
AP, LC

757 BUCKMAN, H. H. Merope; or, The Destruction of Atlantis . . . Jacksonville, Fla.: The DaCosta Printing and Publishing House, 1898. 123 p.

LC

758 [BUCKNER, ALICE MORRIS.] Towards the Gulf: A Romance of Louisiana . . . New York, London: Harper & Brothers, 1887. 315 p.

HEH, LC, O, Y

758a [BUCKNER, J. P.] The Hoosier Doctor: A Medicated Story. By Karl Kringle [pseud.] . . . Columbus, O.: Cott & Hann, book printers, 1881. 288 p.

HEH

759 BUEL, JAMES WILLIAM. The Border Outlaws: An Authentic and Thrilling History of the Most Noted Bandits of Ancient or Modern Times, the Younger Brothers, Jesse and Frank James, and Their Comrades in Crime . . . St. Louis, Mo.: Historical Publishing Company, 1881. 252 p., illus.

CU, HEH, LC, N, UC, UM, Y

Published with his *The Border Bandits: An Authentic and Thrilling History of the Noted Outlaws, Jesse and Frank James, and Their Bands of Highwaymen.* St. Louis, Mo.: Historical Publishing Company, 1881. 148 p., illus.
Also published as: *Jesse and Frank James and Their Comrades in Crime.* Baltimore: I. & M. Ottenheimer [n.d.]. 188 p., illus. Listed in Ramon F. Adams, *Six-Guns & Saddle Leather* (Norman, Okla. [1954]), No. 144; no copy seen.

760 ———— Heroes of the Plains; or, Lives and Wonderful Adventures of Wild Bill, Buffalo Bill, Kit Carson . . . and Other Celebrated Indian Fighters . . . Including a . . . History of Gen. Custer's Famous "Last Fight" . . . St. Louis, Mo.: Historical Publishing Co., 1881. 548 p., illus.

HEH

*Also issued with imprint:* San Francisco, Cal.: A. L. Bancroft & Co., 1881. Y

761 ———— Life and Marvelous Adventures of Wild Bill, the Scout . . . Chicago: Belford, Clarke & Co., 1880. 92, [1] p., illus.

LC, N

762 BUELL, MARY E. The Sixth Sense; or, Electricity. A Story for the Masses . . . Boston: Colby & Rich, 1891. 521 p.

HEH, LC, UP

763 [BUFFET, EDWARD PAYSON.] And Then Came Spring: A Story of Moods. By Garret Van Arkel [pseud.]. New York: E. R. Herrick & Company, 1899. 144 p.

LC

Of an artist.

764 BUFFINGTON, THOMAS PATRICK. Green Valley . . . New York: The Abbey Press, 114 Fifth Avenue [cop. 1900]. 151 p., port.

LC, N

765 BUGG, LELIA HARDIN. Orchids: A Novel . . . St. Louis, Mo.: B. Herder, 1894. 435 p.

LC

766 ———— The People of Our Parish: Being Chronicle and Comment of Katharine Fitzgerald, Pew-Holder in the Church of St. Paul the

Apostle. Edited by Lelia Hardin Bugg ... Boston: Marlier, Callanan & Company, 1900. 254 p.     H, HEH

767  ——— The Prodigal's Daughter, and Other Tales . . . New York, Cincinnati, Chicago: Benziger Brothers, 1898. 255 p.    H, LC, UVB
*Also contains:* Westgate's Past—At the Pension Roget—The Major.

BULL, CASE. *See* Bull, Jerome Case

BULL, JEROME CASE. A Difference in Clay. *In* F. E. McKay, *ed.*, Vignettes [cop. 1890], No. 3523.

——— In the Redwoods. A Streak of Crimson. [Two stories.] *In* Stories from the Harvard Advocate (1896), No. 5277a.

768  [BULL, KATHERINE THOMAS (JARBOE).] Aila. By Kate Thomas [pseud.]. San Francisco: William Doxey [cop. 1896]. 278 p.    CU, HEH
Early California.

769  BULLARD, PHEBE CONSALUS. Earl Stimson ... New York: The American News Company, 39 Chambers Street [cop. 1889]. 380 p.   HEH, LC

BULLION, *Judge, pseud. See* Heller, Levi D.

770  BULLOCK, CYNTHIA. A Cluster of Roses ... New York: Printed for the author by Styles & Cash, 1877. 228 p.    BU, CU, HEH, UV

771  BULLOCK, HARRIET OSGOOD (NOWLIN). On Shifting Sands: A Sketch from Real Life . . . Chicago: Donohue, Henneberry & Co., 407-429 Dearborn St. [cop. 1895]. 228 p., front.    HEH

772  BUMSTEAD, SAMUEL JOSIAH. The Riversons: A Novel ... New York: Welch, Fracker Company, 1890. 448 p., front.
    AP, CU, HEH, LC, O, UVB, Y
Wissahickon Valley, Pennsylvania.

773  BUNCE, OLIVER BELL. The Adventures of Timias Terrystone ... New York: D. Appleton and Company, 1885. 305 p.
    AP, CU, H, HEH, LC, O, Y
Of an artist.

774  ——— Bachelor Bluff, His Opinions, Sentiments, and Disputations . . . New York: D. Appleton and Company, 1881. 292 p.
    AP, BU, CU, H, HEH, LC, O, UP, Y

775  ——— The Story of Happinolande, and Other Legends . . . New York: D. Appleton and Company, 1889. 188 p.   AP, H, HEH, LC, O
*Also contains:* A Millionaire's Millions—The City Beautiful—John's Attic.

776  BUNNER, HENRY CUYLER. The Elephant's Love; or, Zenobia's Infidelity. Presented with the Compliments of C. I. Hood & Co., Proprietors of Hood's Sarsaparilla, Lowell, Mass. [N.p., 1891?] Cover title, 16 p.
    UVB

777 ———— Jersey Street and Jersey Lane: Urban and Suburban Sketches ... New York: Charles Scribner's Sons, 1896. 201 p., illus.

BA, BU, CU, H, HEH, LC, N, O, UC, UP, UVB, Y

*Contents:* Jersey and Mulberry—Tiemann's to Tubby Hook—The Bowery and Bohemia—The Story of a Path—The Lost Child—A Letter to Town.

———— A Letter and a Paragraph. *In* B. Matthews, In Partnership (1884), No. 3649.

Later printed in No. 778.

778 ———— Love in Old Cloathes, and Other Stories ... New York: Charles Scribner's Sons, 1896. 217 p., illus.

BA, CU, H, HEH, LC, N, O, UC, UM, UVB, Y

*Also contains:* A Letter and a Paragraph—"As One Having Authority"—Crazy Wife's Ship—French for a Fortnight—The Red Silk Handkerchief—Our Aromatic Uncle.

Title story printed earlier in Nos. 3649 and 5270.

779 ———— "Made in France": French Tales Retold with a United States Twist ... New York: Keppler & Schwarzmann, 1893. 207 p., illus.

BA, CU, H, HEH, LC, N, O, UC, UM, UP, UV, Y

*Contents:* By Way of Explanation—Tony—The Prize of Propriety—Dennis— The Minuet—A Pint's a Pound—A Capture—Uncle Atticus—The Pettibone 'Brolly—The Joke on M. Peptonneau—Father Dominick's Convert.

780 ———— The Midge ... New York: Charles Scribner's Sons, 1886. 235 p. AP, BA, BU, H, HEH, LC, N, O, UC, UM, UP, UVB, Y

Found with and without imprint of Grant & Faires on verso of title page.

781 ———— More "Short Sixes" ... New York: Keppler & Schwarzmann, 1894. 229 p., illus. BA, BU, CU, H, HEH, N, O, UC, UM, UP, UVB, Y

*Contents:* The Cumbersome Horse—Mr. Vincent Egg and the Wage of Sin— The Ghoollah—Cutwater of Seneca—Mr. Wick's Aunt—What Mrs. Fortescue Did—"The Man with the Pink Pants"—The Third Figure in the Cotillion— "Samantha Boom-de-ay"—My Dear Mrs. Billington.

———— The Recording Spook. *In* Mavericks (1892), No. 3663.

———— The Red Silk Handkerchief. *In* B. Matthews, In Partnership (1884), No. 3649.

Later printed in No. 778.

782 ———— The Runaway Browns: A Story of Small Stories ... New York: Keppler & Schwarzmann, 1892. 210, [1] p., illus.

BA, BU, CU, HEH, N, O, UC, UM, UP, UVB, Y

———— The Senator. *In* Hanks: Assorted Yarns from Puck (1893), No. 2444.

79

783 ———— "Short Sixes": Stories to Be Read While the Candle Burns . . . New York: Keppler & Schwarzmann, 1891. 232 p., illus.

AP, BA, BU, CU, H, HEH, LC, N, O, UC, UM, UP, UVB, Y

*Contents:* The Tenor—Col. Brereton's Aunty—A Round-Up—The Two Churches of 'Quawket—The Love-Letters of Smith—Zenobia's Infidelity—The Nine Cent-Girls—The Nice People—Mr. Copernicus and the Proletariat—Hector—A Sisterly Scheme—Zozo—An Old, Old Story.

For distinguishing points between 1st and 2nd states of 1st ed. see BAL 1913.

784 ———— The Story of a New York House . . . New York: Charles Scribner's Sons, 1887. 152 p., illus.

BA, CU, H, HEH, LC, N, O, UC, UM, UP, UVB, Y

785 ———— The Suburban Sage: Stray Notes and Comments on His Simple Life . . . New York: Keppler & Schwarzmann, 1896. 174 p., illus.

BU, CU, H, HEH, O, UC, UM, UP, UVB, Y

*Contents:* Mr. Chedby on a Regular Nuisance—Early Stages of the Bloomer Fever—The Suburban Horse—The Building Craze—Moving In—A Water-Color House—The Pointers—The Furnace—The Time-Table Test—The Society Church—The Suburbanite and His Golf—The Suburban Dog—The Newcomers—The First of It—The Sporting Scheme—The Evolution of the Suburbanite.

786 ———— A Woman of Honor . . . Boston: James R. Osgood and Company, 1883. 336 p.      BU, CU, H, HEH, LC, O, UC, UM, UP, UVB, Y

787 ———— Zadoc Pine, and Other Stories . . . New York: Charles Scribner's Sons, 1891. 256 p.      BA, CU, H, HEH, LC, N, O, UC, UM, UP, UVB, Y

*Contents:* The Zadoc Pine Labor Union—Natural Selections: A Romance of Chelsea Village and East Hampton Town—Casperl—A Second-Hand Story—Mrs. Tom's Spree—Squire Five-Fathom.

———— *jt. au.* *See* Matthews, B. The Documents in the Case. *In* B. Matthews, In Partnership (1884), No. 3649.

Later printed in Nos. 3659 and 5267.

———— *jt. au.* *See* Matthews, B. In Partnership (1884), No. 3649.

———— *jt. au.* *See* Matthews, B. The Seven Conversations of Dear Jones and Baby Van Rensselaer. *In* B. Matthews, In Partnership (1884), No. 3649.

Later printed in No. 3659.

BUNTLINE, NED, *pseud.* *See* Judson, Edward Zane Carroll

BUNYAN, E. T., *jt. au.* *See* Wagnar, H. The Street and the Flower (1883), No. 5710.

788 BURDETTE, ROBERT JONES. Chimes from a Jester's Bells . . . Part I, The Story of Rollo; Part II, Stories and Sketches . . . Indianapolis and Kansas City: The Bowen-Merrill Company, 1897. 268 p., illus.

BU, CU, H, HEH, LC, O, UM, UVB, Y

789 ———— Hawk-Eyes... New York: G. W. Carleton & Co., 1879. 319 p., illus.               BU, CU, HEH, LC, N, O, UC, UM, UVB, Y
Also published as: *Innach Garden, and Other Comic Sketches.* New York: G. W. Carleton & Co., 1886.   BU, CU

———— The Movement Cure for Rheumatism. *In* I. Bacheller, *ed.,* Best Things from American Literature (1899), No. 195.

790 ———— The Rise and Fall of the Mustache, and Other "Hawk-Eyetems" ... Burlington, Iowa: Burlington Publishing Company, 1877. 328 p., illus.           BU, CU, H, HEH, LC, N, O, UC, UM, UP, UVB, Y

791 ———— Schooners That Pass in the Dark . . . New York: G. W. Dillingham, 1894. 319 p., illus.            LC

792 [BURG, SWAN.] The Light of Eden; or, A Historical Narrative of the Barbarian Age. A Scientific Discovery . . . Seattle, Wash.: S. Burg, 1896. 192 p.          LC

793 BURGESS, GELETT. Vivette; or, The Memoirs of the Romance Association... Boston: Copeland and Day, 1897. 152 p., 2 maps.
                        BA, BU, CU, H, HEH, LC, N, O, UC, UM, UP, UVB, Y

794 BURGESS, MARIE LOUISE. Ave Maria . . . Boston: Press of the Monthly Review, 1895. 33 p., illus.           LC, Y

795 BURGWYN, COLLINSON PIERREPONT EDWARDS. The Huguenot Lovers: A Tale of the Old Dominion . . . Richmond, Va.: Published by the author, 1889. 219 p.         BU, H, HEH, LC, N, UC, UV, Y

796 [BURKE, R. R.] "Keep the Change": A Sketch of the Life of a News Agent with Details of Many Experiences on and off the Cars . . . Pittsburgh, Pa.: Commercial Printing & Publishing Co., 1895. 178 p., illus.          LC

797 BURKE, WILLIAM TALBOT. Pingleton; or, Queer People I Have Met. From the Notes of a New York Cicerone. Edited by Talbot Burke... New York: W. T. Burke & Co., 58 Warren Street [cop. 1886]. 156 p.          LC

798 BURMEISTER, MRS. KATE. "The Indian Maiden's Dream": A Novel . . . Kansas City, Mo.: Published by the author, 1895. 182 p.   LC

799 BURNETT, FRANCES ELIZA (HODGSON) TOWNSEND. Dolly: A Love Story . . . Philadelphia: Porter & Coates, 822 Chestnut Street [cop. 1877]. 319 p.          AP, BA, HEH, LC, O, UM, UVB, Y
Also published as: *Vagabondia: A Love Story.* Boston: James R. Osgood and Company, 1884. 392 p.   CU, HEH, UM

800 ———— The Drury Lane Boys' Club . . . Washington, D.C.: Press of "The Moon," 1892. 78 p.         BA, CU, H, HEH, LC, UVB, Y
800 copies printed by the author's son, Vivian Burnett.

801 ———— A Fair Barbarian ... Boston: James R. Osgood and Company, 1881. 258 p.      AP, BU, CU, H, HEH, N, O, UP, UVB, Y
Nevada girl mingles in English society.

802 ———— Haworth's ... New York: Charles Scribner's Sons, 1879. 374 p., illus.      BU, CU, H, HEH, N, O, UP, UVB, Y
Of Lancashire workers.

803 ———— His Grace of Osmonde: Being the Portions of That Nobleman's Life Omitted in the Relation of His Lady's Story Presented to the World of Fashion under the Title of a Lady of Quality ... New York: Charles Scribner's Sons, 1897. 465 p.
AP, BA, CU, H, HEH, LC, O, UP, UV, Y

804 ———— In Connection with the De Willoughby Claim ... New York: Charles Scribner's Sons, 1899. 445 p.
AP, BA, BU, CU, H, HEH, LC, N, O, UM, UVB, Y
North Carolina mountains.

805 ———— Jarl's Daughter, and Other Stories . . . Philadelphia: T. B. Peterson & Brothers, 306 Chestnut Street [cop. 1879]. 146 p.      LC, O, Y
*Also contains:* The Men Who Loved Elizabeth–Wanted, a Young Person.

806 ———— Jarl's Daughter, and Other Novelettes ... Philadelphia: T. B. Peterson & Brothers, 306 Chestnut Street [cop. 1882]. 180 p.
BA, CU, H, LC, Y
This ed. adds: Miss Vernon's Choice.

807 ———— Kathleen: A Love Story . . . Philadelphia: T. B. Peterson & Brothers, 306 Chestnut Street [cop. 1878]. 212 p.      LC, O, Y
Also published as: *Kathleen Mavourneen.* New York: Charles Scribner's Sons, 743 & 745 Broadway [cop. 1878]. 216 p.      AP, LC, Y

808 ———— A Lady of Quality: Being a Most Curious Hitherto Unknown History, as Related by Mr. Isaac Bickerstaff but Not Presented to the World of Fashion through the Pages of The Tatler ... New York: Charles Scribner's Sons, 1896. 363 p.
AP, BA, CU, H, HEH, LC, N, O, UC, UV, Y

809 ———— Lindsay's Luck ... New York: Charles Scribner's Sons, 743 & 745 Broadway [cop. 1878]. 154 p.      AP, HEH, LC, O, Y
At head of title: "Mrs. Burnett's Earlier Stories."

810 ———— Louisiana ... New York: Charles Scribner's Sons, 1880. 163 p., front.      BA, BU, CU, H, HEH, LC, N, O, UC, UM, UP, UVB, Y

811 ———— Miss Crespigny: A Love Story ... Philadelphia: T. B. Peterson & Brothers, 306 Chestnut Street [cop. 1878]. 252 p.      HEH, LC, O, UVB, Y

——— Miss Defarge. *In* J. Habberton, Brueton's Bayou (1888), No. 2344.

812 ——— The One I Knew the Best of All: A Memory of the Mind of a Child . . . New York: Charles Scribner's Sons, 1893. 325 p., illus.
AP, BA, CU, H, HEH, LC, O, UC, UVB, Y

813 ——— Pretty Polly Pemberton: A Love Story . . . Philadelphia: T. B. Peterson, 306 Chestnut Street [cop. 1877]. 248 p. H, HEH, LC, O, Y

814 ——— The Pretty Sister of José . . . New York: Charles Scribner's Sons, 1889. 127 p., illus.
AP, BA, BU, CU, H, HEH, LC, N, O, UC, UM, UP, UVB, Y

815 ——— A Quiet Life, and The Tide on the Moaning Bar . . . Philadelphia: T. B. Peterson & Brothers, 306 Chestnut Street [cop. 1878]. 230 p. BA, HEH, LC, O, Y

——— A Story of the Latin Quarter. *In* Stories by American Authors, III (1884), No. 5269.

816 ——— Surly Tim, and Other Stories . . . New York: Scribner, Armstrong & Co., 1877. 270 p. H, HEH, LC, O, UC, UVB, Y
*Also contains:* "Le Monsieur de la Petite Dame"—Smethurstses—One Day at Arle—Esmeralda—Mère Giraud's Little Daughter—Lodusky—"Seth."

817 ——— That Lass o' Lowrie's . . . New York: Scribner, Armstrong & Company, 1877. 269 p., illus. H, HEH, N, O, UC, UVB, Y
BAL 2033 notes three printings.

818 ——— "Theo": A Love Story . . . Philadelphia: T. B. Peterson & Brothers, 306 Chestnut Street [cop. 1877]. 232 p.
H, HEH, LC, N, O, UVB, Y

819 ——— Through One Administration . . . Boston: James R. Osgood and Company, 1883. 564 p. AP, H, HEH, N, O, UC, UP, UVB, Y

820 BURNHAM, CLARA LOUISE (ROOT). Dearly Bought: A Novel . . . Chicago: Henry A. Sumner & Company. Boston: Charles H. Whiting, 1884. 396 p., illus. AP, H, HEH, LC, N
At head of title: "Hammock Series."

821 ——— Dr. Latimer: A Story of Casco Bay . . . Boston and New York: Houghton, Mifflin and Company. The Riverside Press, Cambridge, 1893. 384 p. BA, BU, CU, H, HEH, LC, O, UM, Y

822 ——— A Great Love . . . Boston and New York: Houghton, Mifflin and Company. The Riverside Press, Cambridge, 1898. 309, [1] p.
CU, H, HEH, N, O, UM, Y

823 ———— Miss Archer Archer: A Novel . . . Boston and New York: Houghton, Mifflin and Company. The Riverside Press, Cambridge, 1897. 312 p.     BA, BU, CU, H, HEH, LC, O, UV, Y

824 ———— Miss Bagg's Secretary: A West Point Romance . . . Boston and New York: Houghton, Mifflin and Company. The Riverside Press, Cambridge, 1892. 424 p.     AP, BA, BU, CU, H, HEH, O, Y

825 ———— The Mistress of Beech Knoll: A Novel . . . Boston and New York: Houghton, Mifflin and Company. The Riverside Press, Cambridge, 1890. 413 p.     AP, BA, H, LC, O, UM

826 ———— Next Door . . . Boston: Ticknor and Company, 1886. 371 p.     AP, H, N, O, UM, UP

827 [————] "No Gentlemen" . . . Chicago: Henry A. Sumner & Company, 1881. 348 p.     HEH, UVB
White Mountains, New Hampshire.

828 ———— A Sane Lunatic . . . Chicago: Henry A. Sumner & Company, 1882. 325 p., front.     H, HEH, LC
At head of title: "Hammock Series."
New England life.

829 ———— Sweet Clover: A Romance of the White City . . . Boston and New York: Houghton, Mifflin and Company. The Riverside Press, Cambridge, 1894. 411 p.     BA, H, HEH, LC, N, O, UM
Columbian Exposition, Chicago.

830 [————] We, Von Arldens. By Edith Douglas [pseud.]. Chicago: Henry A. Sumner & Company, 1881. 487 p., illus.     HEH, LC

831 ———— A West Point Wooing, and Other Stories . . . Boston and New York: Houghton, Mifflin and Company. The Riverside Press, Cambridge, 1899. 305, [1] p.     CU, H, HEH, LC, O, Y
*Also contains:* Pursuer or Pursued? – A Cadet Camp Episode – A Franco-American – The Cadet Captain's Experiment – The New Organ – A Thanksgiving Revival – The Subjugation of Miss Blaine – A Mistake in Consonants – A Neutral Thanksgiving – Mary Annie – By a Minute – At Crest View.

832 ———— The Wise Woman: A Novel . . . Boston and New York: Houghton, Mifflin and Company. The Riverside Press, Cambridge, 1895. 430 p.     AP, BA, BU, CU, H, HEH, LC, N, O, UM, UP, UV, Y

833 ———— Young Maids and Old . . . Boston: Ticknor and Company, 1889. 404 p.     AP, CU, H, HEH, LC, O

834 BURNHAM, HAMPDEN. Adeline Gray: A Tale . . . [New York: Wynkoop & Hallenbeck, cop. 1894.] 155 p.     LC

835 BURR, ANNA ROBESON (BROWN). The Black Lamb. By Anna Robeson
Brown . . . Philadelphia: J. B. Lippincott Company, 1896. 322 p.
New York and London.                                    LC, O

836 ———— A Cosmopolitan Comedy . . . New York: D. Appleton and
Company, 1899. 304 p.               CU, HEH, LC, O, UC, UP
New England and Paris.

———— A Feline Fate. *In* Tales from McClure's: Romance (1897), No.
5362.

837 ———— The Immortal Garland: A Story of American Life . . . New
York: D. Appleton and Company, 1900. 324 p.       BU, HEH, LC, O
New York and New England.

838 ———— Sir Mark: A Tale of the First Capital . . . New York: D. Appleton and Company, 1896. 159 p.            H, HEH, LC, O, UC
Philadelphia.

839 BURR, ENOCH FITCH. Aleph, the Chaldean; or, The Messiah as Seen from
Alexandria . . . New York: Wilbur B. Ketcham, 2 Cooper Union
[cop. 1891]. 413 p.                  HEH, LC, O, UV, Y

840 ———— Dio, the Athenian; or, From Olympus to Calvary . . . New
York: Phillips & Hunt. Cincinnati: Hitchcock & Walden, 1880. 498
p., illus.                           BU, H, LC, UV

841 ———— Fabius, the Roman; or, How the Church Became Militant . . .
New York: The Baker & Taylor Company, 5 and 7 East Sixteenth
Street [cop. 1897]. 388 p.            BU, HEH, LC, UM

842 BURROUGHS, ELTON. College-Bred Ruth: A Romance of the Living . . .
New York: New York Recorder Linotype Print, 1895. 211 p.    LC

843 BURT, PITTS HARRISON. Regret of Spring: A Love Episode . . . New
York: G. W. Dillingham Co., 1898. 246 p., illus.      HEH, LC, Y
Of an elderly couple.

844 BURTON, FREDERICK RUSSELL. Shifting Sands . . . Chicago and New
York: Rand, McNally & Company [cop. 1898]. 259 p.     HEH, LC
Seaside resort.

845 [BURTON, MARIA AMPARO (RUIZ).] The Squatter and the Don: A Novel
Descriptive of Contemporary Occurrences in California. By C. Loyal
[pseud.]. San Francisco, 1885. 421 p.           LC, Y
*Also issued with imprint:* San Francisco: Samuel Carson & Co., 1885.   HEH

846 BUSCH, FRANC. The Jewess, Leonora: A Novel . . . New York: William
Paulding Caruthers, 1896. 222 p.             LC, Y
New York.

847 BUSH, CLARA ROXANA. Ninety-Nine Days . . . New York: Authors' Publishing Company [cop. 1879]. 162 p.     LC

848 BUTLER, WILLIAM ALLEN. Domesticus: A Tale of the Imperial City . . . New York: Charles Scribner's Sons, 1886. 281 p.
AP, BA, BU, CU, H, HEH, LC, N, O, UC, UM, UVB, Y
Mild criticism of social customs.

849 [————] Mrs. Limber's Raffle; or, A Church Fair and Its Victims. A Short Story. New York: D. Appleton and Company, 1876. 162 p.
BU, CU, H, HEH, LC, N, O, UM, UVB, Y

BUTT, FREDERICK S., *pseud. See* Irvine, F. K.

850 BUTTERWORTH, HEZEKIAH. In Old New England: The Romance of a Colonial Fireside . . . New York: D. Appleton and Company, 1895. 281 p.     CU, H, HEH, LC, O, Y
*Contents:* Pardon Ponder, Pedagogue—The Haunted Oven; or, A Regular Old-Fashioned Thanksgiving—Wych Hazel, the Jew—Captain Tut-Tut-Tuttle and the Miracle Clock—The Inn of the Good Woman—The Bewitched Clambake—The Miraculous Basket—No Room in the Inn; or, The Old Madhouse in the Orchard—Nix's Mate—Old "Bunker Hill"—Milo Mills's Fourth of July Poem—Husking Stories, Songs, and Fiddlers—King Philip's Last Hunt.

851 [————] Up from the Cape: A Plea for Republican Simplicity . . . Boston: Estes and Lauriat, 1883. 252 p., illus.
BU, CU, H, HEH, LC, N, O, UC

852 BYNNER, EDWIN LASSETTER. Agnes Surriage . . . Boston: Ticknor and Company, 1887. 418 p.     AP, BA, CU, H, HEH, N, O, UVB, Y
Colonial Boston.

853 ———— The Begum's Daughter . . . Boston: Little, Brown and Company, 1890. 473 p., illus.     AP, BA, CU, H, HEH, LC, N, O, UP, UVB, Y
New Amsterdam, late 17th century.

854 [————] Damen's Ghost . . . Boston: James R. Osgood and Company, 1881. 313 p.     BA, CU, H, HEH, N, O, UP, UVB, Y
At head of title: "Round-Robin Series."

855 [————] Nimport. Boston: Lockwood, Brooks and Company, 1877. 494 p.     BA, H, HEH, N, O, UP, UVB, Y
At head of title: "Wayside Series."

856 ———— Penelope's Suitors . . . Boston: Ticknor and Company, 1887. 68 p.     BA, BU, CU, H, HEH, N, O, UVB, Y
Colonial Massachusetts.

857 ———— Tritons: A Novel . . . Boston: Lockwood, Brooks and Company, 1878. 406 p.     BU, CU, H, HEH, LC, N, O, UP, UVB, Y
New York City life.

858 ——— Zachary Phips . . . Boston and New York: Houghton, Mifflin and Company. The Riverside Press, Cambridge, 1892. 512 p.

BA, BU, CU, H, HEH, N, O, UM, UP, UVB, Y

War of 1812 and Aaron Burr's western expedition.

——— *jt. au. See* Hale, L. P. An Uncloseted Skeleton [cop. 1888], No. 2394.

859 [BYRD, ELLA BILLINGSLEY.] Marston Hall: A Story Illustrative of Southern Life. By Beryl Carr [pseud.]. New York: G. W. Carleton & Co. London: S. Low, Son & Co., 1880. 389 p.   LC, N, O

860 [BYRN, MARCUS LAFAYETTE.] Ragged Edge Rambles. By David Rattlehead, M.D. [pseud.] . . . New York: M. L. Byrn, 49 Nassau Street [cop. 1882]. 165 p., illus.   LC

At head of title: "Rattlehead's Humorous Series, No. 4."
Deposited Mar. 10, 1883.

Also published as: *Frank Hall's Hard Hits in His Ragged Edge Rambles.* New York: Coast City Publishing Co. [cop. 1887]. Information from LC card; no copy seen.

861 [———] Vim and Ventures of Bolivar Hornet (the Alabama Doctor) with the Advice and Consent of David Rattlehead, M.D. [pseud.] . . . [New York]: Coast City Publishing Company, cop. 1886. 160 p., illus.   CU

At head of title: "Rattlehead's Humorous Series, No. 5."

862 [———] Wailings of a Wife Hunter; or, The Mishaps and the Hit-Haps of My Courtships. By David Rattlehead, M.D. [pseud.] . . . New York: M. L. Byrn, 49 Nassau Street [cop. 1882]. 170 p., illus.   LC
At head of title: "Rattlehead's Humorous Series, No. 3."
Deposited Nov. 4, 1882.

C———, E. *See* Custead, Elizabeth

C., P. H. *See* Cowan, Pamela H.

C., S. M. A. *See* Collins, S. M. A.

863 C., X. Q. Jones Himself; or, Coals of Fire. By X. Q. C. . . . Richmond: Whittet & Shepperson, 1887. 189 p.   HEH

864 ——— Who? Which? And What? A Story. By X. Q. C. Richmond, Va.: West, Johnston & Co., 1885. 77 p.   HEH

C. & C. *See* Cabot, Arthur Winslow

865 CABELL, ISA (CARRINGTON). Seen from the Saddle . . . New York: Harper & Brothers, 1893. 161 p., front.   CU, H, HEH, LC, UC, UV

866 CABLE, GEORGE WASHINGTON. Bonaventure: A Prose Pastoral of Acadian Louisiana ... New York: Charles Scribner's Sons, 1888. 314 p.

AP, BA, CU, H, HEH, LC, N, O, UC, UM, UP, UVB, Y

*Contents:* Carancro—Grande Pointe—Au Large.

867 —— Dr. Sevier ... Boston: James R. Osgood and Company, 1885. 473 p.

AP, H, HEH, LC, N, O, UC, UP, UVB, Y

868 —— The Grandissimes: A Story of Creole Life ... New York: Charles Scribner's Sons, 1880. 448 p.

AP, CU, H, HEH, N, O, UM, UP, UVB, Y

869 —— John March, Southerner ... New York: Charles Scribner's Sons, 1894. 513 p.

BA, CU, H, HEH, LC, N, O, UC, UM, UVB, Y

870 —— Madame Delphine ... New York: Charles Scribner's Sons, 1881. 125 p.

AP, BA, BU, CU, H, HEH, LC, N, O, UC, UM, UP, UVB, Y

871 —— Old Creole Days ... New York: Charles Scribner's Sons, 1879. 229 p.

BA, CU, H, HEH, N, O, UVB, Y

*Contents:* 'Sieur George—'Tite Poulette—Belles Demoiselles Plantation—Jean-Ah Poquelin—Madame Délicieuse—Café des Exilés—"Posson Jone'."

872 —— Strong Hearts ... New York: Charles Scribner's Sons, 1899. 214 p.

AP, BA, CU, H, HEH, N, O, UM, UP, UVB, Y

*Contents:* The Solitary—The Taxidermist—The Entomologist.

CABLE, JEROME, *pseud.* *See* Tippetts, Katherine (Bell)

873 [CABOT, ARTHUR WINSLOW.] Two Gentlemen of Gotham. By C. & C. New York: Cassell & Company, Limited, 739 & 741 Broadway [cop. 1887]. 344 p.

CU, H, HEH, LC, Y

Howard Coghill, jt. au.

874 CABOT, ELISABETH LYMAN. In Plain Air ... New York: Henry Holt and Company, 1897. 296 p.

H, HEH, LC, UM, Y

New England village life.

875 CAHAN, ABRAHAM. The Imported Bridegroom, and Other Stories of the New York Ghetto ... Boston and New York: Houghton, Mifflin and Company. The Riverside Press, Cambridge, 1898. 256 p., 1 l.

H, HEH, LC, O, UC, UM, UVB, Y

*Also contains:* A Providential Match—A Sweat-Shop Romance—Circumstances—A Ghetto Wedding.

876 —— Yekl: A Tale of the New York Ghetto ... New York: D. Appleton and Company, 1896. 190 p.

BA, CU, H, HEH, LC, N, O, UVB, Y

877 CAHILL, MABEL ESMONDE. Her Playthings, Men: A Novel ... New York: Russell Bros., printers, 1890. 242 p.

LC

CAIRNS, KATE, *pseud. See* Bosher, Kate Lee (Langley)

CALDER, ALMA. *See* Johnston, Alma (Calder)

878 CALDWELL, WILLIE WALKER. The Tie That Binds: A Story of the North and the South . . . Franklin, Ohio: The Editor Publishing Co., 1895. 111 p.         LC

CALHOUN, ALFRED ROCHEFORT. The Escape. *In* Tales from McClure's: War (1898), No. 5364.

879 CALL, WILLIAM T. Josh Hayseed in New York. Edited by Wm. T. Call (Sprouts) . . . New York: Excelsior Publishing House, 29 and 31 Beekman Street [cop. 1887]. 127 p., illus.     LC, Y

880 [CALLENDER, EDWARD BELCHER.] The Gigantic Meddler: A Tale Gathered from the Files of the Court of Uncommon Pleas . . . Boston, Massachusetts: The Blaxton Press, Pemberton Square [cop. 1900]. 187 p.       LC
Of laxity in granting injunctions.

881 [————] The Leg-Pullers; or, Politics as She Is Applied. A Tale of the Puritan Commonwealth. By One Who Has Been There. Boston, Mass.: Pemberton Square Publishing Co. [cop. 1895]. 201 p. BU, CU, LC

882 CAMERA, CARA, *pseud.* Sifting Matrimony . . . Philadelphia: T. B. Peterson & Brothers, 306 Chestnut Street [cop. 1890]. 313 p.     LC
Deposited Feb. 18, 1891.

883 [————] Society Rapids: High Life in Washington, Saratoga, and Bar Harbor. By "One in the Swim." Philadelphia: T. B. Peterson & Brothers, 306 Chestnut Street [cop. 1888]. 250 p.     HEH, LC, O, UM

884 CAMP, WALTER CHAUNCEY. Drives and Puts: A Book of Golf Stories . . . Boston: L. C. Page and Company (Incorporated), 1899. 243 p., front.
    BU, H, HEH, LC, N, UC, UM, Y
*Contents:* "Make or Break"—Sammy—The Great Professional—A Matter of Honour—The Second Lesson—One Off Two—Doing Something for His College—A Southern Gentleman—The Lady and the Cow—The Conversion of St. Ours—An Unknown Quantity.
Lilian Brooks, jt. au.

885 CAMPBELL, ALVIN. John Norton, M.D. . . . New York: W. B. Smith & Co., Bond Street [cop. 1882]. 79 p.     LC

886 CAMPBELL, FLORENCE M. "Jack's Afire"; or, The Burton Torch . . . Chicago: J. L. Regan Printing and Publishing Co., 226 to 230 Lake Street [cop. 1887]. 425 p.     HEH, LC

887 CAMPBELL, FLOY. Camp Arcady: The Story of Four Girls, and Some Others, Who "Kept House" in a New York "Flat" . . . Boston: Richard G. Badger & Co., 1900. 164 p., 1 l., illus.     CU, H, HEH, LC, O

888 [Campbell, Helen (Stuart).] His Grandmothers: A Summer Salad. New York: G. P. Putnam's Sons, 1877. 192 p., front. CU, H, HEH, LC, Y
The grandmothers take over the family.

889 —— Miss Melinda's Opportunity: A Story . . . Boston: Roberts Brothers, 1886. 217 p. AP, H, HEH, LC, O
Of working girls in New York.

890 —— Mrs. Herndon's Income: A Novel . . . Boston: Roberts Brothers, 1886. 534 p. AP, BU, H, HEH, LC, O

891 —— Roger Berkeley's Probation: A Story . . . Boston: Roberts Brothers, 1888. 183 p. AP, BA, BU, H, HEH, LC, O

892 —— Some Passages in the Practice of Dr. Martha Scarborough . . . Boston: Roberts Brothers, 1893. 180 p. HEH, LC, O, UM

893 —— Under Green Apple Boughs . . . New York: Fords, Howard, & Hulbert, 1882. 272 p., illus. AP, CU, H, HEH, LC, O, UM
At head of title: " 'Our Continent' Library."
New York and environs.

894 —— Unto the Third and Fourth Generation: A Study . . . New York: Fords, Howard, & Hulbert, 1880. 249 p. H, HEH, LC, O
Also published as: *Patty Pearsons' Boy; or, Unto the Third and Fourth Generation.* New York: Fords, Howard, & Hulbert [1881]. HEH

895 Campbell, Mary Bruce. The Secret Vow, and Life's Battle-Fields: Story and Essay . . . Philadelphia: Printed by J. B. Lippincott & Co., 1880. 47 p. LC

Campbell, Scott, *pseud.* *See* Davis, Frederick William

Canby, Henry Seidel. The Complete Athlete. A Fortunate Foursome. [Two stories.] *In* [F. L. Knowles] *ed.*, Cap and Gown in Prose (1900), No. 3182.

Canfield, Henry Spofford. An Idyll of Mesquiteland. When the Chance God Slept. [Two stories.] *In* Short Story Masterpieces (1900), No. 4931.

896 —— A Maid of the Frontier . . . Chicago and New York: Rand, McNally & Company [cop. 1898]. 219 p. HEH, LC, N
*Also contains:* State's Evidence—On a Christmas Morn—The Insult of an Ancestry—That Way Madness Lies—Tristam and Iseult—Told by the Deputy Sheriff—The Paint Horse of Seven Colors—How the Good Saint Came to Pancho.

897 CANN, MARION STUART. On Skidd's Branch: A Tale of the Kentucky Mountains . . . Scranton, Pa.: Printed at the Republican Job Rooms, 1884. 56 p.      CU, LC

898 CANTWELL, ANNIE F. S. A Little Love and Laughter . . . Coshocton, O.: Shaw & Company, 1886. 170 p.      HEH, LC

899 CAPERS, HENRY DICKSON. Belleview: A Story of the Past and of the Present . . . New York: E. J. Hale & Son, 1880. 165 p.      HEH
The South before and after the Civil War.

CAPRON, CARRIE M. *See* Coe, Caroline L. (Capron)

CARBOY, JOHN, *pseud. See* Harrington, John A.

900 CARDEN, W. THOMAS. A Year with Uncle Jack . . . Nashville, Tenn.: Printed for the author, 1897. 139 p.      LC

901 CAREW, RACHEL. Tangled: A Novel . . . Chicago: S. C. Griggs and Company, 1877. 218 p.      CU, H, HEH, LC, N, Y
Of an American at a Swiss spa.

902 CAREY, AIMEE. Heliotrope; or, The Soldier's Legacy. A Novel . . . Baltimore, 1884. 386 p.      HEH, LC, UV
Baltimore.

903 CAREY, ALICE V. Louisa Avondale; or, Two Southern Girls . . . New York: The Irving Co., 10 and 12 Vandewater Street [cop. 1894]. 144 p.      LC, O

904 CAREY, JOHN B. The Oddities of Short-Hand; or, The Coroner and His Friends . . . New York: Excelsior Publishing House [cop. 1891]. 270 p., illus.      BU, H, HEH, LC, N, Y

905 CAREY, MARY ELIZABETH. Alice O'Connor's Surrender . . . Boston: Angel Guardian Press, 1897. 149 p., illus.      LC
Catholic tale.

906 CARHART, JOHN WESLEY. Norma Trist; or, Pure Carbon. A Story of the Inversion of the Sexes . . . Austin, Texas: Eugene von Boeckman, printer, 1895. 255 p.      LC

907 ———— Under Palmetto and Pine . . . Cincinnati: The Editor Publishing Co., 1899. 228 p.      LC
*Contents:* The Worm in the Cotton Boll—Black Tulip—Crutch and Crown—Lynchers Foiled—Ned's Mascot—Malo Mori Quam Foedari—Benedicta's Trial—Benedicta's Fortune—Forbidden Fruit—Little Faggie—Legend of Mount Bonnell—The Story of Ianka—It Happened Thus—Under the Rose Bush—Might against Right—Sold His Birthright—Memory's Pictured Walls—His Ashes Were Still Warm—The Black Man's Burden—Complications Ended.

908 [CARLETON, HENRY GUY.] Lectures before the Thompson Street Poker Club. New York and London: White and Allen [cop. 1889]. 49 p., illus.        H, HEH, LC, UC, Y

909 [———] The South Fifth Avenue Poker Club . . . New York: M. J. Ivers & Co., 1888. 107 p., illus.       CU, LC

910 [———] The Thompson Street Poker Club, from "Life" . . . New York: White and Allen, 1888. 48 p., illus.      H, LC, UV

911 CARLETON, WILL. The Old Infant, and Similar Stories . . . New York: Harper & Brothers, 1896. 223 p.     BA, CU, HEH, N, O, UM, UVB, Y
*Also contains:* The Vestal Virgin—Lost, Two Young Ladies—The One-Ring Circus—The Christmas Car—A Business Flirtation—Oldbottle's Burglars.
To avoid confusion of authors of the same name see BAL under this author's full name, William McKendree Carleton.

CARLOTTAH, *pseud. See* Ballou, Clara E.

912 CARPENTER, EDITH. Your Money or Your Life: A Story . . . New York: Charles Scribner's Sons, 1896. 345 p.     HEH, LC, N, O, Y
A businessman moves West.

913 CARPENTER, EDMUND JANES. A Woman of Shawmut: A Romance of Colonial Times . . . Boston: Little, Brown and Company, 1891. 234 p., illus.     BU, CU, H, HEH, LC, N, O, UC, UM, Y

914 CARPENTER, ESTHER BERNON. South-County Neighbors . . . Boston: Roberts Brothers, 1887. 272 p.    AP, BA, CU, H, HEH, LC, UM, UP, Y
*Contents:* Sally of the South County—"When My Ship Comes In"—At a Sheep-Washing—Ailse Congdon—An Afternoon at Neighbor Northup's—From Hour to Hour in the Country Store—Evening Meeting at Uncle 'Sias's—Watching with the Sick—Jackson Dawley's Wife—Priscilla Gallaghan—L. C.

915 CARPENTER, FRANK DE YEAUX. Round about Rio . . . Chicago: Jansen, McClurg & Company, 1884. 415 p.     CU, N, O, UV, Y

CARPENTER, WILLIAM HENRY. The Southern Cross. *In* The First Book of the Authors Club (1893), No. 1868.

916 CARPER, MINNETTE SLAYBACK. The Dance of Death, and Other Stories . . . St. Louis, Mo.: Buxton & Skinner, 1894. 110 p., illus.     LC
*Also contains:* Miss Kemball—After the Storm—The Lady of the Gulf.

CARR, BERYL, *pseud. See* Byrd, Ella Billingsley

917 CARRET, ALICE DE. Flames and Ashes . . . New York: George W. Dillingham Co., 1898. 214 p.     LC
New England to Cuba.

918 [CARRINGTON, KATE.] Aschenbroedel. Boston: Roberts Brothers, 1882. 331 p.     H, HEH, LC, O, UM, UV, Y
At head of title: "No Name Series."
A New England village.

919  CARROLL, JOHN.  Leola: A Novel . . .  Philadelphia: J. B. Lippincott Company, 1888.  194 p.  AP, HEH, LC

920  [————]  St. Maur: An Earl's Wooing.  Philadelphia: T. B. Peterson & Brothers, 306 Chestnut Street [cop. 1879].  350 p.  LC

921  CARRUTH, FRED HAYDEN.  The Adventures of Jones . . .  New York: Harper & Brothers, 1895.  123 p., illus.  H, HEH, LC, O, UC, UM, Y
Tall tales.

922  ————  Mr. Milo Bush and Other Worthies: Their Recollections . . . New York and London: Harper & Brothers, 1899.  217, [1] p., illus.
BU, HEH, LC, O, UC, UM, UV

————  Old Hank and His Money.  *In* Short Story Masterpieces (1900), No. 4931.

923  ————  The Voyage of the Rattletrap . . .  New York: Harper & Brothers, 1897.  207 p., illus.  HEH, LC, N, UC, UM
Nebraska, Wyoming, and the Black Hills.

CARRUTH, HAYDEN.  *See* Carruth, Fred Hayden

CARRYL, CHARLES EDWARD.  Captain Black.  *In* Stories of the Sea (1893), No. 5282.
Later printed in No. 924.

924  ————  The River Syndicate, and Other Stories . . .  New York and London: Harper & Brothers, 1899.  296, [1] p., illus.
H, HEH, LC, N, O, UM, UV
*Also contains:* The Pasha Club—The House over the Way—Mrs. Porter's Paragon—The Asper Agency—The Colonel's Desk—Captain Black.

CARRYL, GUY WETMORE.  A Comedy.  *In* [F. L. Knowles] *ed.*, Cap and Gown in Prose (1900), No. 3182.

925  CARTER, JOHN HENTON.  The Impression Club: A Novel . . .  New York: Carter & Bro., 1899.  302 p., illus.  H, HEH, LC, Y
Wealthy group reformed their ways.

926  ————  The Man at the Wheel . . .  St. Louis: E. B. Carter, 1898.  187 p., illus.  CU, UV, Y
Steamboating on the Mississippi.

927  ————  Ozark Postoffice . . .  St. Louis: Carter & Bro., 1899.  271 p.  LC, N

928  ————  Thomas Rutherton: A Novel . . .  New York: H. C. Nixon, 117 Nassau St. [cop. 1890].  344 p., illus.  LC

929 CARTER, MARY NELSON. North Carolina Sketches: Phases of Life Where the Galax Grows ... Chicago: A. C. McClurg & Co., 1900. 313 p.

CU, H, HEH, LC, N, O, UC, Y

*Contents:* Mrs. Smith—Stepping Backwards—A Foggy Day—Mr. Timmins—Playing with Fire—Neighborly Gossip—Barter—The Course of True Love—Hiding Out—In Maria's Garden—The Summer Is Ended—A White Day—Now Is the Winter of Our Discontent—Sally—Old Times—Getting an Education—Like Other Children.

CARTER, RUTH, *pseud.* *See* Robertson, Sarah Franklin (Davis)

930 CARTER, SARAH NELSON. For Pity's Sake: A Story for the Times. Being Reminiscences of a Guest at a Country Inn ... Boston, Mass.: De Wolfe, Fiske & Company. Andover, Mass.: The Andover Press [cop. 1897]. 191 p., illus. BA, CU, H, LC, Y

*Also issued with imprint:* Andover, Mass.: The Andover Press [cop. 1897].

HEH

931 CARTERET, JOHN DUNLOE. A Fortune Hunter; or, The Old Stone Corral. A Tale of the Old Santa Fe Trail ... Cincinnati: Printed for the author, 1888. 290 p. CU, HEH, LC, N, O, UC, UM, UVB, Y

932 CARUS, PAUL. Truth in Fiction: Twelve Tales with a Moral ... Chicago: The Open-Court Publishing Co., 1893. 111 p.

BA, BU, H, HEH, UC, UP

*Contents:* The Chief's Daughter—After the Distribution of the Type—The Clock or the Watches—The Mysterious Beetle—The Highest Trump in Argument—The Philosopher's Martyrdom—The Convention of the Animals—The People by the Sea—The Dross Is Discarded but Nothing Is Lost—Charity—Capital and Labor—Ben-Midrash, the Gardener of Galilee.

CARY, GILLIE. *See* McCabe, Gillie (Cary)

933 CARY, JAMES. Halted between Two Opinions; or, A Madman's Confession. A Novel ... Birmingham [Ala.]: Press of Dispatch Printing Co., 1892. 300 p. LC

934 CASE, WILLIAM SCOVILLE. Forward House: A Romance ... New York: Charles Scribner's Sons, 1895. 149 p. AP, CU, HEH, LC, O, Y

Retired colonel invents an explosive.

935 CASH, CHARLES E. The Great Oriental and Trans-Continental Railroad: A Direct All-Rail Route from New Orleans, La., to St. Petersburg, Paris, and London, via the Behring Strait. Filled with Wit, Humor, Satire, and Philosophy ... Vicksburg, Miss.: The Commercial Herald Printing and Publishing House, 1896. 171 p. LC, N

936 CASH, MRS. M. I. Naaman, the Leper, and Princess Sarah, the Captive Maid ... Cincinnati: The Editor Publishing Co., 1899. 114 p. LC

CASKODEN, EDWIN, *pseud.* *See* Major, Charles

937 CASSEDY, FRANK H. The Milton Tragedy: A Novel . . . New York: G. W. Dillingham, 1891. 223 p. LC

938 CASSEL, A. J. It Isn't a Joke . . . [Spring City, Pa., cop. 1896.] Cover title, 16 p. LC

939 CASTLE, HENRY ANSON. The Army Mule, and Other War Sketches . . . Indianapolis and Kansas City: The Bowen-Merrill Company, 1898. 269 p., illus. CU, H, HEH, UM, UVB, Y
Contains: The Sutler—The Shelter-Tent—Dress Parade—The Boys in Blue Grown Gray.

———— "As You Like It." In J. J. Conway, ed., Stories (1893), No. 1172.

940 CATHER, GEORGE R. Dora's Device . . . Philadelphia: T. B. Peterson & Brothers, 306 Chestnut Street [cop. 1885]. 290 p. HEH, LC

941 CATHERWOOD, MARY (HARTWELL). The Chase of Saint-Castin, and Other Stories of the French in the New World . . . Boston and New York: Houghton, Mifflin and Company. The Riverside Press, Cambridge, 1894. 266 p. BA, CU, H, HEH, LC, N, O, UM, UP, UVB, Y
Also contains: The Beauport Loup-Garou—The Mill at Petit Cap—Wolfe's Cove—The Windigo—The Kidnaped Bride—Pontiac's Lookout.

942 ———— Craque-o'-Doom: A Story . . . Philadelphia: J. B. Lippincott & Co., 1881. 238 p., illus. H, LC, O, Y
Ohio.

943 ———— The Days of Jeanne d'Arc . . . New York: The Century Co., 1897. 278 p., front. BA, CU, H, HEH, LC, N, O, UC, UM, UP, UVB, Y

944 ———— The Lady of Fort St. John . . . Boston and New York: Houghton, Mifflin and Company. The Riverside Press, Cambridge, 1891. 284 p. AP, BA, BU, CU, H, HEH, LC, N, O, UC, UM, UP, UVB, Y
Acadia; 17th century.

945 ———— Mackinac and Lake Stories . . . New York and London: Harper & Brothers, 1899. 221, [1] p., illus. BA, CU, H, HEH, LC, N, O, UC, UVB, Y
Contents: Marianson—The Black Feather—The Cobbler in the Devil's Kitchen —The Skeleton on Round Island—The Penitent of Cross Village—The King of Beaver—Beaver Lights—A British Islander—The Cursed Patois—The Mothers of Honoré—The Blue Man—The Indian on the Trail.

946 ———— Old Kaskaskia . . . Boston and New York: Houghton, Mifflin and Company. The Riverside Press, Cambridge, 1893. 200 p. BA, CU, H, HEH, LC, N, O, UP, UVB, Y
Fur trading; Northwest Territory.

947 ———— The Queen of the Swamp, and Other Plain Americans . . . Boston and New York: Houghton, Mifflin and Company. The Riverside Press, Cambridge, 1899. 331, [1] p. BA, CU, H, HEH, LC, N, O, UC, UM, UVB, Y

*Contents:* Ohio: The Queen of the Swamp—The Stirring-Off—Sweetness—Serena—Rose Day. KENTUCKY: A Kentucky Princess. INDIANA: The Fairfield Poet—T'Férgore. ILLINOIS: Beetrus—The Bride of Arne Sandstrom—The Babe Jerome—The Calhoun Fiddler—A Man from the Spanish War.

948 ———— The Romance of Dollard . . . New York: The Century Co. [cop. 1889]. 206 p., illus.     AP, BU, CU, H, HEH, LC, N, O, UC, UP, UVB, Y
Early French settlements; Illinois.

949 ———— Spanish Peggy: A Story of Young Illinois . . . Chicago & New York: Herbert S. Stone & Co., 1899. 85 p., 1 l., illus.
BA, BU, CU, H, HEH, LC, N, O, UC, UM, UP, UVB, Y
Abraham Lincoln; Salem.

950 ———— The Spirit of an Illinois Town, and The Little Renault: Two Stories of Illinois at Different Periods . . . Boston and New York: Houghton, Mifflin and Company. The Riverside Press, Cambridge, 1897. 156 p., illus.     BA, CU, H, HEH, LC, N, O, UC, UP, UVB, Y

951 ———— The Story of Tonty . . . Chicago: A. C. McClurg and Company, 1890. 227 p., illus.     BA, CU, H, HEH, LC, N, O, UC, UM, UVB, Y
Based on the life of Henri de Tonty, aide to La Salle.

952 ———— The White Islander . . . New York: The Century Co., 1893. 164 p., illus.     BA, CU, H, HEH, LC, N, O, UC, UM, UVB, Y
French and Indian War.

953 CATLIN, HENRY GUY. Yellow Pine Basin: The Story of a Prospector . . . New York: George H. Richmond & Co., 1897. 214 p.
CU, H, HEH, LC, N, O, UM, Y
Idaho.

CAVAZZA, ELISABETH. *See* Pullen, Elisabeth (Jones) Cavazza

954 CAVENDISH, E. CECILLE. Popular Opinion . . . Meriden, Conn.: The Journal Publishing Co., 1898. 410 p., front.     LC

CAVENDISH, PAULINE BRADFORD (MACKIE) HOPKINS. *See* Hopkins, Pauline Bradford (Mackie)

955 CAWTHORNE, ELSIE M. Confessions of That Little English Girl; or, So Inexperienced . . . Chicago: The Fagan Publishing Company, cop. 1896. 180 p.     LC

956 CAYLOR, O. P. A Fated Promise: A Novel . . . New York: G. W. Dillingham, 1890. 310 p.     AP, LC
Of a young district attorney.

CEREAL, *pseud. See* Gibson, Louis Henry

Cervus, G. I., *pseud. See* Roe, William James

957 Chadwick, J. H. The Whole Truth: A Novel . . . New York: Cassell & Company, Limited, 739 & 741 Broadway [cop. 1887]. 305 p.
AP, HEH, LC

958 Chaffee, Frank. Bachelor Buttons . . . New York: Geo. M. Allen Company, 1892. 129 p.
HEH, LC, Y

959 Chamberlain, Henry Richardson. 6,000 Tons of Gold . . . Meadville, Pa.: Flood and Vincent; the Chautauqua-Century Press, 1894. 349 p.
AP, H, HEH, LC, O, Y
Risk to individuals or countries with too much money.

960 Chamberlain, Nathan Henry. The Sphinx in Aubrey Parish: A Novel . . . Boston: Cupples and Hurd; the Algonquin Press, 1889. 481 p., front.
AP, BA, HEH, LC, O

961 ——— What's the Matter? or, Our Tariff and Its Taxes . . . Boston: De Wolfe, Fiske & Co., 361 and 365 Washington Street [cop. 1890]. 268 p.
CU, H, HEH, LC, UC, Y
Grocery store discussion of free trade.

962 [Chamberlain, William Mellen.] Manuela Parédes. Boston: Roberts Brothers, 1881. 387 p.
BA, CU, H, HEH, LC, O, UV
At head of title: "No Name Series."
New York, Colorado, Mexico, etc.

Chambers, Julius. Exactly Zero. *In* The First Book of the Authors Club (1893), No. 1868.

963 ——— Lovers Four and Maidens Five: A Story of the Allegheny Mountains . . . Philadelphia: Porter & Coates, 1886. 155 p., illus.
HEH, LC, UC
Four copies examined, including author's presentation copy, dated Oct. 1886, at the Historical Society of Pennsylvania. All noted "25th thousand" on verso of title page.

964 ——— Missing: A Romance. Narrative of Capt. Austin Clark, of the Tramp Steamer "Caribas," Who, for Two Years, Was a Captive among the Savage People of the Seaweed Sea . . . New York, London: The Transatlantic Publishing Company, 1896. 182 p., front.
HEH, LC
At head of title: "In Sargasso."

965 [———] On a Margin . . . New York: Fords, Howard, & Hulbert, 1884. 416 p.
BA, H, HEH, LC, O, UP
Stock speculation.

966 Chambers, Robert William. Ashes of Empire: A Romance . . . New York: Frederick A. Stokes Company [cop. 1898]. 342 p.
CU, H, HEH, N, O, UC, UVB, Y
Siege of Paris; Franco-Prussian War.

967 ——— The Cambric Mask: A Romance ... New York: Frederick A. Stokes Company [cop. 1899]. 328 p.    BA, H, HEH, LC, O, UM, UVB, Y
Of a farm and the railroad.

968 ——— The Conspirators: A Romance ... New York and London: Harper & Brothers, 1900. 265, [1] p., illus.    H, HEH, N, O, UM, Y
Listed PW, Apr. 28, 1900. Advertised on p. 883 as having been published "ten days ago." LC has card for copy dated 1899, probably for copyright copy; not seen.

969 ——— The Haunts of Men ... New York: Frederick A. Stokes Company [cop. 1898]. 302 p.    CU, H, HEH, LC, O, UM, Y
Contents: The God of Battles—Pickets—An International Affair—Smith's Battery—Ambassador Extraordinary—Yo Espero—Collector of the Port—The Whisper—The Little Misery—Enter the Queen—Another Goodman—Envoi.
Deposited July 1, 1898.

970 [———] In the Quarter ... Chicago, New York: F. Tennyson Neely, 1894. 314 p., front.    N, UM, UVB, Y
A New Yorker studying art in Paris.

971 ——— A King and a Few Dukes: A Romance ... New York, London: G. P. Putnam's Sons; the Knickerbocker Press, 1896. 363 p.
BA, CU, H, HEH, N, O, UC, UM, UP, UVB, Y

972 ——— The King in Yellow ... Chicago, New York: F. Tennyson Neely, 1895. 316 p.    H, HEH, UC, UM, UP, UVB, Y
Contents: The Repairer of Reputations—The Mask—The Court of the Dragon —The Yellow Sign—The Demoiselle d'Ys—The Prophets' Paradise—The Street of the Four Winds—The Street of the First Shell—The Street of Our Lady of the Fields—Rue Barrée.

973 ——— Lorraine: A Romance ... New York and London: Harper & Brothers, 1898. 339 p.    BA, H, HEH, LC, O, UP, UVB, Y
Beginning of the Franco-Prussian War.

974 ——— The Maker of Moons ... New York, London: G. P. Putnam's Sons; the Knickerbocker Press, 1896. 401 p., front.
BA, CU, H, HEH, O, UM, UP, UVB, Y
Also contains: The Silent Land—The Black Water—In the Name of the Most High—The Boy's Sister—The Crime—A Pleasant Evening—The Man at the Next Table.
A 79 p. ed. of the title story was printed for copyright only and deposited Apr. 21, 1896. H also has a copy.

975 ——— The Mystery of Choice . . . New York: D. Appleton and Company, 1897. 288 p.    CU, H, HEH, N, O, UM, UVB, Y
Contents: The Purple Emperor—Pompe Funèbre—The Messenger—The White Shadow—Pasteur—A Matter of Interest—Envoi.

976 ——— Outsiders: An Outline . . . New York: Frederick A. Stokes Company [cop. 1899]. 301 p.    CU, HEH, N, O, UM, UVB, Y
Life in New York.

977 ——— The Red Republic: A Romance of the Commune . . . New York, London: G. P. Putnam's Sons; the Knickerbocker Press, 1895. 475 p.
Post Franco-Prussian War.                                                     CU, HEH, O, Y

CHAMPLIN, JOHN DENISON. The Fate of the Ninth Legion. *In* The First Book of the Authors Club (1893), No. 1868.

978 CHAMPNEY, MRS. EBEN FREEMONT. Love's Dream; or, Did He Mean to Wrong Her? . . . New York: J. S. Ogilvie Publishing Company, cop. 1900. 133 p., front.                                                           LC

979 CHAMPNEY, ELIZABETH (WILLIAMS). Bourbon Lilies: A Story of Artist Life . . . Boston: Lockwood, Brooks and Company, 1878. 388 p.
At head of title: "Wayside Series."                                   H, HEH, LC, O

——— A Crisis. *In* L. C. H. Langford, *comp.*, The Woman's Story (1889), No. 3206.

980 [———] Rosemary and Rue . . . Boston: James R. Osgood and Company, 1881. 292 p.                                                      H, HEH, LC, O
At head of title: "Round-Robin Series."
During the American Revolution.

CHAMPNEY, L. W. The Heartbreak Cameo. *In* Stories by American Authors, VI (1884), No. 5272.

981 CHANDLER, BESSIE. A Woman Who Failed, and Others . . . Boston: Roberts Brothers, 1893. 343 p.                                              H, HEH, LC
*Also contains:* A Silent Soul—Esther Godwin's Geese—Margaret's Romance—A Victim of Prejudice—The Middle Miss Tallman—A Thanksgiving Wedding—Miss Polly Atherton's Bell—Uncle Nathan's Ear-Trumpet—The Turning of the Worm.
Author's full name: Elizabeth Lowber (Chandler) Parker.

CHANDLER, MRS. G. W. *See* Chandler, Mrs. Izora Cecilia

982 CHANDLER, MRS. IZORA CECILIA. Anthè. By Mrs. G. W. Chandler . . . New York: Phillips & Hunt. Cincinnati: Cranston & Stowe, 1885. 272 p., illus.                                                                   HEH, LC
Of religious interest.

983 ——— A Dog of Constantinople . . . New York: Dodd, Mead and Company, 1896. 215 p., illus.                                               H, LC

984 ——— Elvira Hopkins of Tompkin's Corner . . . New York: Wilbur B. Ketcham, 7 and 9 West Eighteenth St. [cop. 1899]. 195 p. H, HEH, LC

985 CHANEY, JAMES M. Poliopolis and Polioland: A Trip to the North Pole . . . Kansas City, Mo.: J. M. Chaney, Jr., 1900. 172 p., front.         LC

CHANNING, GRACE ELLERY.  *See* Stetson, Grace Ellery (Channing)

CHANTLER, A. E.  How Orpheus Won.  *In* J. J. Conway, *ed.*, Stories (1893), No. 1172.

[CHAPLIN, HEMAN WHITE.]  Eli, by C. H. White [pseud.].  *In* Stories by American Authors, IX (1885), No. 5275.
Later printed in No. 986.

986  [————]  Five Hundred Dollars, and Other Stories of New England Life.  By C. H. W.  Boston: Little, Brown and Company, 1887.
305 p.                                    BA, CU, H, HEH, LC, N, O, UVB
*Also contains:* The Village Convict–Saint Patrick–Eli–By the Sea–In Madeira Place–The New Minister's Great Opportunity.

[————]  The Village Convict, by C. H. White [pseud.].  *In* Stories by American Authors, VI (1884), No. 5272.
Later printed in No. 986.

987  CHAPMAN, C. I. A.  Franklin's Oath: A Tale of Wyoming One Hundred Years Ago . . .  Pittston, Pa.: Hart, pr., Gazette Office, 1880.  110 p.
                                                            HEH, O, UC

CHAPMAN, JOHN ABNEY, *jt. au.*  *See* Mayer, O. B.  Mallodoce (1891), No. 3670.

988  CHAPMAN, SAMUEL E.  Doctor Jones' Picnic . . .  San Francisco: The Whitaker & Ray Co. [cop. 1898].  177 p.                    HEH, LC

989  [CHARLES, FRANCES (ASA).]  [Charley, and Other Stories.] [San Francisco? 1889.]  58 p.                                                HEH
*Also contains:* Through the Devil's Gate–The Love Story of Jesus and Refugio –Anita.
Author's prefatory note in lieu of title page, dated Sept. 12, 1889, states "I have decided to let *you* name it for me."

990  ————  Siftings from Poverty Flat: Short Stories . . .  San Francisco: The Californian Publishing Co., 1893.  96 p.               HEH, LC
*Contents:* We 'uns: A Tale of Vendetta–The Baby's Grandmother–Marah–Polly's Courtship–Elizabeth–Next in Order of Succession–In Memory.

991  [CHARLES, JAMES.]  Caddo; or, Cupid in the Gas Belt.  A Story from Real Life.  By Charles J. Wayne [pseud.] . . .  Richmond, Ind.: James Charles, 1889.  356 p., illus.                                        HEH, LC

992  DELETED.

993  [CHASE, CHARLES G.]  That Old Man and His Dream.  [Boston: Published by the author, cop. 1893.]  [26] p., illus.               BU, LC, Y
White Mountains, New Hampshire.

CHASE, E. O.  Wives for Two.  *In* [W. J. Johnston] *comp.*, Lightning Flashes and Electric Dashes (1877), Nos. 3022, 3023.

994  CHASE, HERBERT E.  A Double Life; or, Starr Cross.  An Hypnotic Romance . . .  New York: S. W. Green's Son, 1884.  301 p.

HEH, LC, Y

995  CHATFIELD-TAYLOR, HOBART CHATFIELD.  An American Peeress . . . Chicago: A. C. McClurg and Company, 1894.  293 p.

H, HEH, LC, N, O, UC, UV

Early Chicago and London society.

996  ———— The Idle Born: A Comedy of Manners . . .  Chicago: Herbert S. Stone and Company, 1900.  248 p., 1 l.

BU, CU, HEH, LC, N, UC, UM, Y

Reginald De Koven, jt. au.

997  ———— Two Women & a Fool . . .  Chicago: Stone & Kimball, 1895. 232 p., 1 l., illus.  CU, H, HEH, LC, N, UC, UM, UP

Theatrical life.

998  ———— The Vice of Fools . . .  Chicago & New York: Herbert S. Stone & Co., 1897.  310 p., 1 l., illus.  HEH, LC, N, UM, Y

Washington, D.C., society.

999  ———— With Edge Tools . . .  Chicago: A. C. McClurg and Company, 1891.  315 p.  HEH, LC, N, O, UM

Chicago and New York society.

CHAUNCEY, SHELTON, *pseud.*  *See* Nicholls, Charles Wilbur de Lyon

1000  CHAVANNES, ALBERT.  In Brighter Climes; or, Life in Socioland.  A Realistic Novel . . .  Knoxville, East Tennessee: Chavannes and Co., cop. 1895.  254 p.  HEH, N

1001  CHELLIS, MARY DWINELL.  All for Money . . .  New York: National Temperance Society, 1876.  362 p., front.  LC

Her stories which were considered of interest to both adults and young people are included; the "Fife and Drum Series" for younger readers is omitted.

1002  ———— The Attic Tenant . . .  New York: National Temperance Society, 1890.  306 p., front.  CU, LC

1003  ———— The Brewer's Fortune . . .  New York: National Temperance Society, 1877.  428 p., front.  HEH, LC

1004  ———— From Father to Son . . .  New York: National Temperance Society, 1879.  412 p., front.  LC

1005  ———— Miss Belinda's Friends . . .  New York: National Temperance Society, 1885.  349 p., front.  LC

1006 ——— Old Benches with New Props . . . New York: National Temperance Society, 1891. 321 p., front. LC

1007 ——— Our Homes . . . New York: National Temperance Society, 1881. 427 p., front. LC

1008 ——— Profit and Loss . . . New York: National Temperance Society, 1884. 387 p., front. HEH, LC

1009 ——— The Revere Estate . . . New York and Chicago: Fairbanks, Palmer & Company, 1883. 343 p., illus. LC

1010 ——— The Turning of the Wheel . . . New York: National Temperance Society, 1887. 342 p., front. LC

1011 ——— The Winning Side . . . New York: National Temperance Society, 1888. 323 p., front. LC

1012 CHENEY, EDNAH DOW (LITTLEHALE). Nora's Return: A Sequel to "The Doll's House" of Henry Ibsen . . . Boston: Lee and Shepard. New York: C. T. Dillingham, 1890. 64 p. BU, LC, UC, UP

1013 CHENEY, MRS. ELIZABETH. The King's Gold: A Story . . . New York: Eaton & Mains. Cincinnati: Jennings & Pye [cop. 1900]. 440 p. LC

1014 ——— The Lapidaries, and Aunt Deborah Hears "The Messiah" . . . New York: Eaton & Mains. Cincinnati: Jennings & Pye [cop. 1900]. 30 p. LC, UP, Y

1015 CHENEY, JOHN VANCE. The Old Doctor: A Romance of Queer Village . . . New York: D. Appleton and Company, 1885. 199 p. AP, BA, LC, N
Of clairvoyance.

1016 CHENEY, WALTER THOMAS. An Apocalypse of Life . . . Boston, Mass.: Arena Publishing Co., 1893. 312 p. H, HEH
Of life after death.

CHENEY, WILLIAM ATWELL. Miranda Higgins. *In* Short Stories by California Authors (1885), No. 4929.

CHESEBRO', CAROLINE. In Honor Bound. *In* C. C. Harrison, *ed.*, Short Stories (1893), No. 2514.

1017 CHESNUTT, CHARLES WADDELL. The Conjure Woman . . . Boston and New York: Houghton, Mifflin and Company. The Riverside Press, Cambridge, 1899. 229, [1] p. BA, BU, CU, H, HEH, LC, N, O, UP, UVB, Y
*Contents:* The Goophered Grapevine—Po' Sandy—Mars Jeems's Nightmare—The Conjurer's Revenge—Sis' Becky's Pickaninny—The Gray Wolf's Ha'nt—Hot-Foot Hannibal.

*Also issued with imprint:* Cambridge: Riverside Press, 1899. Information from LC card; no copy seen.
150 copies printed.

1018 ——— The House behind the Cedars . . . Boston and New York: Houghton, Mifflin and Company. The Riverside Press, Cambridge, 1900. 294 p.　　　　　H, HEH, LC, O, UM, UVB, Y
Of mixed marriages.

1019 ——— The Wife of His Youth, and Other Stories of the Color Line . . . Boston and New York: Houghton, Mifflin and Company. The Riverside Press, Cambridge, 1899. 323 p., illus.
　　　　　BA, BU, CU, H, LC, O, UC, UVB, Y
*Also contains:* Her Virginia Mammy—The Sheriff's Children—A Matter of Principle—Cicely's Dream—The Passing of Grandison—Uncle Wellington's Wives—The Bouquet—The Web of Circumstance.

1020 CHESTER, EVELYN. Miss Derrick: A Boston Society Girl's Diary . . . New York: G. W. Dillingham, 1894. 297 p.
Information from LC card; no copy seen.

1021 CHESTER, JOHN. Ruth, the Christian Scientist; or, The New Hygeia . . . Boston: H. H. Carter & Karrick, 1888. 343 p.　　　H, HEH, LC, Y

1022 CHILD, FRANK SAMUEL. A Colonial Witch: Being a Study of the Black Art in the Colony of Connecticut . . . New York: The Baker & Taylor Co. [cop. 1897]. 307 p.　　　CU, H, HEH, LC, UM, Y

1023 ——— Friend or Foe: A Tale of Connecticut during the War of 1812 . . . Boston and New York: Houghton, Mifflin and Company. The Riverside Press, Cambridge, 1900. 328 p., 1 l., illus.　　　CU, HEH, LC, Y

1024 ——— A Puritan Wooing: A Tale of the Great Awakening in New England . . . New York: The Baker and Taylor Company, 5 and 7 East Sixteenth Street [cop. 1898]. 305 p.　　　LC, O, Y

1025 ——— An Unknown Patriot: A Story of the Secret Service . . . Boston and New York: Houghton, Mifflin and Co. The Riverside Press, Cambridge, 1899. 396 p., 1 l., illus.　　　H, HEH, LC, O, UP

CHILD, LYDIA MARIA. Recollections of Ole Bull. *In* [W. F. Gill] *ed.*, Golden Treasures (1876), No. 2166.
Later printed in No. 2168.

1026 CHILDS, CARRIE GOLDSMITH. And the Sword Fell . . . Floral Park, N.Y.: Mayflower Publishing Co., 1895. 221 p., illus.　　　HEH, LC
A journal of married life.

1027 ——— Lost Lineage . . . Floral Park, N.Y.: Mayflower Publishing Co., 1897. 410 p.　　　HEH, LC

1028 [CHILDS, ELEANOR STUART (PATTERSON).] Averages: A Story of New York. By Eleanor Stuart [pseud.] ... New York: D. Appleton and Company, 1899. 410 p.     HEH, LC

1029 [———] Stonepastures. By Eleanor Stuart [pseud.]. New York: D. Appleton and Company, 1895. 178 p.     HEH, LC, O, Y
Of a female barber in a Pennsylvania mining town.

1030 CHILES, ROSA PENDLETON. Down among the Crackers ... Cincinnati: The Editor Publishing Co., 1900. 328 p.     HEH, LC, UM, Y

1031 CHIPMAN, DE WITT C. Beyond the Verge: Home of Ten Lost Tribes of Israel ... Boston: James H. Earle, 1896. 305 p., illus.     LC

1032 CHISHOLM, MRS. BELLE V. Stephen Lyle, Gentleman and Philanthropist ... Cincinnati: Cranston & Stowe. New York: Hunt & Eaton, 1891. 256 p.     HEH, O

1033 [CHITTENDEN, RICHARD HANDY.] The Knight of the Lily. By Philip May [pseud.] ... Brooklyn: Rome Brothers, printers, 1880. 7 p.     LC

1034 ——— Owls of the Always Open: A Novel ... Brooklyn: C. C. Whitney's Steam Print, 1883. 176 p.     LC

1035 [———] A Safe Investment. By Philip May [pseud.]. Brooklyn, 1879. Cover title, 10 p. Printed in double columns.     LC

CHOATE, LOWELL, pseud. See Hopkins, Mrs. Alice Kimball

1036 CHOPIN, KATE (O'FLAHERTY). At Fault: A Novel ... St. Louis: Nixon-Jones Printing Co., 1890. 218 p.     LC, UVB, Y

1037 ——— The Awakening ... Chicago & New York: Herbert S. Stone & Company, 1899. 303 p., 1 l.     BU, CU, H, HEH, LC, N, O, UC, UM, UVB, Y
Creole life and customs.

1038 ——— Bayou Folk ... Boston and New York: Houghton, Mifflin and Company. The Riverside Press, Cambridge, 1894. 313 p.
    BA, BU, CU, H, HEH, LC, O, UC, UM, UVB, Y
Contents: A No-Account Creole—In and Out of Old Natchitoches—In Sabine —A Very Fine Fiddle—Beyond the Bayou—Old Aunt Peggy—The Return of Alcibiade—A Rude Awakening—The Bênitous' Slave—Désirée's Baby—A Turkey Hunt—Madame Célestin's Divorce—Love on the Bon-Dieu—Loka— Boulôt and Boulotte—For Marse Chouchoute—A Visit to Avoyelles—A Wizard from Gettysburg—Ma'ame Pélagie—At the 'Cadian Ball—La Belle Zoraïde—A Gentleman of Bayou Têche—A Lady of Bayou St. John.

1039 ——— A Night in Acadie ... Chicago: Way & Williams, 1897. 416 p., front.     BU, CU, HEH, LC, N, O, UM, UVB, Y
Also contains: Athénaïse—After the Winter—Polydore—Regret—A Matter of Prejudice—Caline—A Dresden Lady in Dixie—Nég Créol—The Lilies—Azélie—

Mamouche—A Sentimental Soul—Dead Men's Shoes—At Chenière Caminada—
Odalie Misses Mass—Cavanelle—Tante Cat'rinette—A Respectable Woman—
Ripe Figs—Ozème's Holiday.

CHRISTIE, JOSEPH. The Volcanograph. *In* [W. J. Johnston] *comp.*,
Lightning Flashes and Electric Dashes (1877), Nos. 3022, 3023.

1040 CHUBBUCK, JUDSON. Shadowgraphs: A Novel . . . Proctor, Ill.: Published by the author. Chicago: Atwell & Goodall, printers [1896].
183 p.                                                                    LC
Illinois.

1041 CHURCH, SAMUEL HARDEN. Horatio Poldgers: A Story of To-Day . . .
New York: W. B. Smith & Co., Bond Street [cop. 1882]. 136 p.    LC

1042 ———— John Marmaduke: A Romance of the English Invasion of Ireland
in 1649 . . . New York and London: G. P. Putnam's Sons; the Knickerbocker Press, 1897. 328 p., illus.                     CU, HEH, LC, O, Y

CHURCHILL, LIDA ABBIE. Playing with Fire. *In* [W. J. Johnston] *comp.*,
Lightning Flashes and Electric Dashes (1877), Nos. 3022, 3023.

1043 CHURCHILL, WINSTON. The Celebrity: An Episode . . . New York: The
Macmillan Company. London: Macmillan & Co., Ltd., 1898. 302 p.
CU, H, HEH, N, O, UM, Y

1044 ———— Richard Carvel . . . New York: The Macmillan Company.
London: Macmillan & Co., Ltd., 1899. 538 p., illus.
CU, HEH, N, UC, UM, UVB, Y

1045 CLAFLIN, MARY BUCKLIN (DAVENPORT). Brampton Sketches: Old-Time
New England Life . . . New York: Thomas Y. Crowell & Co., 46
East Fourteenth Street [cop. 1890]. 158 p., illus.
AP, H, HEH, LC, O, UC, UM, Y

1046 ———— Real Happenings . . . New York: Thomas Y. Crowell & Co.,
46 East Fourteenth Street [cop. 1890]. 46 p.           AP, H, LC

1047 CLAGETT, SUE HARRY. Her Lovers: A Romance . . . Philadelphia: J. B.
Lippincott & Co., 1877. 366 p.                              HEH, O
Georgetown, D.C.

1048 CLAIBORNE, FERNARD. The Unfinished Tale; or, The Daughter of the
Mill. A Romance of Lake George . . . New York: W. L. Allison &
Son, 1881. 316 p.                                       CU, HEH, LC, Y

CLAPP, EVA KATHERINE. *See* Gibson, Eva Katherine (Clapp)

1049 CLARK, ARNOLD. Beneath the Dome . . . Chicago: The Schulte Publish-
ing Company, 1894. 361 p., front.                          LC, UP
At head of title: "A Posthumous Novel."
Political and social life in Michigan.

1050  [CLARK, CHARLES HEBER.] Elbow-Room: A Novel without a Plot. By
Max Adeler [pseud.] ... Philadelphia: J. M. Stoddart & Co. Chicago
and Cincinnati: A. G. Nettelton & Co. San Francisco, Cal.: A. Roman
& Co. [cop. 1876]. 384 p., illus.          BA, CU, HEH, N, O, UC, UM, UP, Y
H has copy which omits San Francisco part of imprint.
For later ed. credited to "Mark Twain" on title page see BAL 3654.

1051  [————] The Fortunate Island, and Other Stories. By Max Adeler
[pseud.] ... Boston: Lee & Shepard. New York: Charles T. Dillingham, 1882. 333 p., illus.          CU, HEH, LC, O, UC, UM, Y
*Also contains:* The City of Burlesque—An Old Fogy—Major Dunwoody's Leg
—Jinnie.

1052  [————] Random Shots. By Max Adeler [pseud.] ... Philadelphia:
J. M. Stoddart & Co., 1879. 326 p., illus.          CU, H, HEH, LC, N, O, UC, Y
*Contents:* The Tragedy of Thompson Dunbar—Mr. Skinner's Night in the
Underworld—Miss Hammer's Lovers—The Glee Club Tournament—How Jack
Forbes Was Avenged—Jerome Pinnickson's Mother-in-Law—Professor Quack-
enboss—Babies—The Shoals Lighthouse—Mr. Fisher's Bereavements—The Ad-
ventures of Abner Byng—Mr. Tooms, the Undertaker—Miss Wilmer's
Adventure.

1053  [CLARK, CHARLOTTE (MOON).] Baby Rue <Her Adventures and Mis-
adventures, Her Friends and Her Enemies>. Boston: Roberts
Brothers, 1881. 318 p.          BA, BU, H, HEH, LC, O
At head of title: "No Name Series."
Western frontier military life.

1054  [————] How She Came into Her Kingdom: A Romance . . . Chicago: Jansen, McClurg & Co., 1878. 337 p.          LC, N
Also published as: *A Daughter of the Gods; or, How She Came into Her
Kingdom. By Charles M. Clay [pseud.].* New York: White, Stokes, & Allen,
1883.   CU, HEH

1055  [————] The Modern Hagar: A Drama. By Charles M. Clay [pseud.]
. . . New York: George W. Harlan & Co., 1882. 2 vols. (369, 402 p.)
H, HEH, LC, UM
At head of title: "The Kaaterskill Series."
Continuation of *Baby Rue.*

1056  CLARK, FANNY BECKWITH. A Modern Experience . . . Cleveland: Privately printed by the author, 1897. 49 p.          LC

1057  CLARK, FELICIA (BUTTZ). The Cripple of Nuremberg . . . Cincinnati:
Jennings & Pye. New York: Eaton & Mains [cop. 1900]. 290 p., illus.
LC, UM
Protestants and Catholics; 16th century Germany.

1058 CLARK, FREDERICK THICKSTUN. In the Valley of Havilah . . . New
York: Frank F. Lovell & Company, 142-144 Worth Street [cop. 1890].
282 p.                                                        AP, HEH, LC, UC

1059 [———] A Mexican Girl. By Frederick Thickstun [pseud.]. Boston:
Ticknor and Company, 1888. 287 p.                          HEH, N, O
California border mining camp.

1060 ——— The Mistress of the Ranch: A Novel . . . New York: Harper
& Brothers, 1897. 357 p.                                   HEH, LC, O, Y
On the Rio Grande.

1061 ——— On Cloud Mountain: A Novel . . . New York: Harper &
Brothers, 1894. 230 p.                                     HEH, LC, O, UC, Y
Colorado.

1062 CLARK, HELEN F. The Lady of the Lily Feet, and Other Stories of
Chinatown . . . Philadelphia: The Griffith & Rowland Press, 1900.
125 p., illus.                                             H, LC, O, Y
*Also contains:* Mee Lee's Great Happiness—Joy Come—The Wedding Bells
That Rang for Ah Lon—"Who Cly?"—Ah Fay—Tai Mun.

CLARK, HENRY SCOTT, *pseud.* *See* Cox, Millard F.

1063 [CLARK, HUGH A.] After Many Years: A Novel. By Robert Boggs
[pseud.]. New York: The Authors' Publishing Company, Bond
Street [cop. 1880]. 462 p.                                 HEH, LC
Of art life.

1064 [———] A Stepdaughter of Israel. By Robert Boggs [pseud.]. New
York, London, Chicago: F. Tennyson Neely Co. [cop. 1900]. 281 p.
                                                           LC

1065 CLARK, IMOGEN. The Heresy of Parson Medlicott . . . New York:
Thomas Y. Crowell & Co. [cop. 1900]. 26 p.                H, LC, Y

1066 ——— The Las' Day . . . New York: Anson D. F. Randolph & Co.,
182 Fifth Avenue [cop. 1892]. 52 p., illus.               HEH, LC, UC
Of a married couple.

1067 ——— The Victory of Ezry Gardner . . . New York, Boston: Thomas
Y. Crowell & Company, 46 East 14th Street [cop. 1896]. 173 p., front.
                                                           H, HEH, LC
Nantucket.

1068 CLARK, J. FRED. The Society in Search of Truth; or, Stock Gambling in
San Francisco. A Novel, Published by the Author. Oakland, Cal.:
Pacific Press, printers, stereotypers and binders, 1878. 326 p.
                                                CU, H, HEH, LC, O, UC, UM, Y

1069 [CLARK, JOHN A.] A Young Disciple: A Novel. New York: W. B. Smith & Co., Bond Street [cop. 1882]. 441 p.    HEH, LC
Of teaching in district and Sunday schools.

1070 CLARK, KATE ELIZABETH. The Dominant Seventh: A Musical Story . . . New York: D. Appleton and Company, 1890. 164 p.
AP, BA, BU, CU, H, HEH, LC, O, Y

1071 CLARK, KATE (UPSON). White Butterflies, and Other Stories . . . New York: J. F. Taylor and Company, 1900. 283 p.    HEH, LC
*Also contains:* "Raldy"—The Charcoal Burners—Cupid and Minerva—The Case of Parson Hewlett—"For Looly"—Tomlin Dresser's Disappearance—Daffodils —"Solly"—Tid's Wife—"Ye Christmas Witch"—Direxia—Lyddy Washburn's Courtship.

1072 CLARK, MRS. MARY J. The Record of a Ministering Angel . . . Chicago and New York: Belford, Clarke & Co., 1885. 289 p.    LC, UC

1073 CLARK, SUSIE CHAMPNEY. Lorita, an Alaskan Maiden . . . Boston: Lee and Shepard, 1892. 171 p.    H, HEH, LC

1074 ——— Pilate's Query . . . Boston: Arena Publishing Company, 1895. 275 p.    H, LC

1074a [———] To Bear Witness! A Metaphysical Sketch. By Cecil St. Clair [pseud.] . . . Boston: H. H. Carter & Co., 1889. 180 p.  HEH, O
Of Christian Science; story ends in San Francisco.

CLARKE, A. STEWART. Jacob City. *In* J. Hawthorne, One of Those Coincidences (1899), No. 2596.

1075 CLARKE, HUGH ARCHIBALD. The "Scratch Club" . . . Philadelphia: The Poet-Lore Company, 223 S. 38th Street [cop. 1889]. 140 p.    UP
The record of the meetings of an imaginary group of musicians.

1076 CLARKE, JAMES FREEMAN. Deacon Herbert's Bible-Class . . . Boston: Geo. H. Ellis, 1890. 138 p.    H, LC

1077 CLARKE, O. P. The Colonel of the 10th Cavalry: A Story of the War . . . Utica, N.Y.: L. C. Childs & Son, printers and publishers, 1891. 175 p.
HEH, LC, N

1078 [CLARKE, REBECCA SOPHIA.] The Campion Diamonds. By Sophie May [pseud.]. Boston: Lee and Shepard, 1897. 53 p.    BU, HEH, LC

1079 [———] Drones' Honey. By Sophie May [pseud.] . . . Boston: Lee and Shepard. New York: Charles T. Dillingham, 1887. 281 p.
BU, CU, H, HEH, LC, O
PW, June 18, 1887, designated this as her "first novel." Most of her stories were for young people.

1080 [———] Her Friend's Lover. By Sophie May [pseud.]. Boston: Lee and Shepard, 1893. 281 p.    LC

1081 CLARKE, WILLIAM HORATIO. The Organist's Retrospect: An Autobiography of Ernest Onslow, Mus.D., Illustrating the Development of a Musical Artist . . . Reading, Mass., U.S.A.: E. T. Clarke [cop. 1896]. 227 p., front.

BA, LC

CLARKSON, L. *See* Whitelock, Louise (Clarkson)

CLAY, ANNA ELIZA. *See* Bailey, Anna Eliza (Clay)

CLAY, CHARLES M., *pseud. See* Clark, Charlotte (Moon)

CLAY, MRS. JOHN M. *See* Clay, Mrs. Josephine Russell

1082 CLAY, MRS. JOSEPHINE RUSSELL. Some Little of the Angel Still Left: A Novel. By Mrs. John M. Clay . . . Cincinnati: Robert Clarke & Co., 1893. 242 p.

HEH, LC

Crimean War; Paris.

1083 ———— Uncle Phil: A Novel . . . New York: F. Tennyson Neely, 114 Fifth Avenue. Chicago, London [cop. 1899]. 271 p.

HEH, N

California after the Civil War.

1084 CLAYTOR, GRAHAM. Pleasant Waters: A Story of Southern Life and Character . . . Philadelphia: J. B. Lippincott Company, 1888. 215 p.

HEH, LC, O

Post Civil War; Virginia.

1085 ———— Wheat and Tares: A Novel . . . Philadelphia: J. B. Lippincott Company, 1889. 273 p.

HEH, LC, O, UVB

The South from about 1852 to 1874.

1086 CLEARY, KATE (McPHELIM). Like a Gallant Lady . . . Chicago: Way and Williams, 1897. 292 p., 1 l.

HEH, LC, N, UM, Y

Nebraska farm life.

CLEMENS, SAMUEL LANGHORNE. [For the many bibliographical variations within the first editions listed below see BAL.]

1087 [————] The Adventures of Huckleberry Finn (Tom Sawyer's Comrade) . . . By Mark Twain [pseud.] . . . New York: Charles L. Webster and Company, 1885. 366 p., illus.

AP, BA, CU, H, HEH, LC, N, O, UC, UM, UVB, Y

1088 [————] The Adventures of Tom Sawyer. By Mark Twain [pseud.]. Hartford, Conn.; Chicago, Ill.; Cincinnati, Ohio: The American Publishing Company. San Francisco, Cal.: A. Roman & Co., 1876. 274, [1] p., illus.

BU, H, HEH, LC, N, UM, UP, UVB, Y

1089 [————] The American Claimant. By Mark Twain [pseud.]. New York: Charles L. Webster & Co., 1892. 277 p., illus.

AP, BA, BU, CU, H, HEH, LC, N, O, UC, UM, UP, UVB, Y

———— The Californian's Tale. *In* The First Book of the Authors Club (1893), No. 1868.

1090 [————] A Connecticut Yankee in King Arthur's Court. By Mark Twain [pseud.]. New York: Charles L. Webster & Company, 1889. 575 p., illus.  AP, BA, BU, H, HEH, LC, N, O, UM, UP, UVB, Y

1091 [————] Date 1601. Conversation as It Was by the Social Fireside, in the Time of the Tudors. [West Point, N.Y., 1882.] Caption title, 1 p.l., xi p.  H, HEH, UVB, Y

First authorized ed. According to BAL 3388 there were at least two earlier printings, possibly at Cleveland, Ohio, for Alexander Gunn, in 1880. Y has a copy of one printing and Princeton University Library of the other.

1092 [————] Life on the Mississippi. By Mark Twain [pseud.] . . . Boston: James R. Osgood and Company, 1883.  624 p., illus.
AP, BA, CU, H, HEH, LC, N, O, UC, UM, UP, UVB, Y

1093 [————] The Man That Corrupted Hadleyburg, and Other Stories and Essays. By Mark Twain [pseud.] . . . New York and London: Harper & Brothers, 1900.  398 p., illus.
AP, BA, CU, H, HEH, LC, O, UM, UP, UVB, Y

*Also contains:* My Début as a Literary Person—From the "London Times" of 1904—At the Appetite-Cure—My First Lie, and How I Got out of It—Is He Living or Is He Dead?—The Esquimau Maiden's Romance—How to Tell a Story—About Play-Acting—Concerning the Jews—Stirring Times in Austria—The Austrian Edison Keeping School Again—Travelling with a Reformer—Private History of the Jumping Frog Story—My Boyhood Dreams.

1094 [————] Merry Tales. By Mark Twain [pseud.]. New York: Charles L. Webster & Co., 1892.  209 p.
BA, BU, CU, H, HEH, LC, N, O, UC, UM, UP, UVB, Y

*Contents:* The Private History of a Campaign That Failed—The Invalid's Story —Luck—The Captain's Story—A Curious Experience—Mrs. McWilliams and the Lightning—Meisterschaft.

1095 [————] The £1,000,000 Bank-Note, and Other New Stories. By Mark Twain [pseud.]. New York: Charles L. Webster & Company, 1893.  260 p., front.  AP, BA, BU, CU, H, HEH, LC, N, O, UM, UP, UVB, Y
*Also contains:* Mental Telegraphy—A Cure for the Blues—The Enemy Conquered; or, Love Triumphant—About All Kinds of Ships—Playing Courier—The German Chicago—A Petition to the Queen of England—A Majestic Literary Fossil.

1096 [————] Personal Recollections of Joan of Arc. By the Sieur Louis de Conte [pseud.] . . . Freely Translated out of the Ancient French . . . by Jean François Alden [pseud.] . . . New York: Harper & Brothers, 1896.  461 p., illus.  AP, BA, CU, H, HEH, N, O, UC, UP, UVB, Y

1097 [————] The Prince and the Pauper: A Tale for Young People of All Ages. By Mark Twain [pseud.] . . . Boston: James R. Osgood and Company, 1882.  411 p., illus.
BU, CU, H, HEH, LC, N, O, UC, UP, UVB, Y

1098 [————] Punch, Brothers, Punch! and Other Sketches. By Mark Twain [pseud.]. New York: Slote, Woodman & Co. [cop. 1878]. 140 p.  CU, H, HEH, LC, N, O, UC, UM, UP, UVB, Y

*Also contains:* Speech on the Weather at the New England Society's Seventy-First Annual Dinner—Rogers—Map of Paris [with map]—Random Notes of an Idle Excursion—Speech at a Dinner of the Knights of St. Patrick—An Encounter with an Interviewer—The Loves of Alonzo Fitz Clarence, etc.—The Canvasser's Tale.

1099 [————] The Stolen White Elephant, etc. By Mark Twain [pseud.]. Boston: James R. Osgood and Company, 1882. 306 p.

AP, BA, CU, H, HEH, LC, N, O, UC, UM, UP, UVB, Y

*Also contains:* Some Rambling Notes of an Idle Excursion—The Facts Concerning the Recent Carnival of Crime in Connecticut—About Magnanimous-Incident Literature—Punch, Brothers, Punch—A Curious Experience—The Great Revolution in Pitcairn—Mrs. McWilliams and the Lightning—On the Decay of the Art of Lying—The Canvasser's Tale—An Encounter with an Interviewer—Paris Notes—Legend of Sagenfeld, in Germany—Speech on the Babies—Speech on the Weather—Concerning the American Language—Rogers—The Loves of Alonzo Fitz Clarence and Rosannah Ethelton.

1100 [————] Tom Sawyer Abroad. By Huck Finn. Edited by Mark Twain [pseud.] . . . New York: Charles L. Webster & Company, 1894. 219 p., illus.

AP, BU, CU, H, HEH, O, UC, UP, UVB, Y

1101 [————] Tom Sawyer Abroad; Tom Sawyer, Detective; and Other Stories . . . By Mark Twain [pseud.] . . . New York: Harper & Brothers, 1896. 410 p., illus.

HEH, UC, UP, UVB, Y

*Also contains:* The Stolen White Elephant—Some Rambling Notes of an Idle Excursion—The Facts Concerning the Recent Carnival of Crime in Connecticut—About Magnanimous-Incident Literature—Punch, Brothers, Punch—The Great Revolution in Pitcairn—On the Decay of the Art of Lying—The Canvasser's Tale—An Encounter with an Interviewer—Paris Notes—Legend of Sagenfeld, in Germany—Speech on the Babies—Speech on the Weather—Concerning the American Language—Rogers—The Loves of Alonzo Fitz Clarence and Rosannah Ethelton—Map of Paris [with map]—Letter Read at Dinner.

1102 ———— The Tragedy of Pudd'nhead Wilson, and The Comedy Those Extraordinary Twins . . . Hartford, Conn.: American Publishing Company, 1894. 432 p., illus.

BA, CU, H, HEH, LC, N, O, UC, UM, UP, UVB, Y

1103 ———— A Tramp Abroad . . . Hartford, Conn.: American Publishing Company. London: Chatto & Windus, 1880. 631 p., illus.

BU, CU, H, HEH, LC, N, O, UC, UM, UP, UVB, Y

1104 [————] A True Story, and The Recent Carnival of Crime. By Mark Twain [pseud.] . . . Boston: James R. Osgood and Company, 1877. 92 p., illus.

HEH, LC, UP, UVB, Y

CLEMENT, CLARA (ERSKINE). *See* Waters, Clara (Erskine) Clement

1105 CLEVELAND, CYNTHIA ELOISE. His Honor; or, Fate's Mysteries. A Thrilling Realistic Story of the United States Army . . . New York: The American News Company, 1889. 258 p., illus.

HEH, LC, Y

1106 [————] See-Saw; or, Civil Service in the Departments. By One of'm ... Detroit, Mich.: F. B. Dickerson & Co., 1887. 226 p.    LC, N

1107 [CLEVELAND, MAYHEW B.] From Boston, Mass., to Sodom, N.B., on a Bicycle. By Sam Hatchet [pseud.]. [Salem, Mass.], cop. 1887. 105 p., illus.    LC

1108 CLEVELAND, ROSE ELIZABETH. The Long Run ... Detroit, Mich.: F. B. Dickerson & Co., 1886. 146 p.    AP, CU, H, HEH, LC, O, UM, Y
    A socialite marries a scholar.

1109 CLEWS, JAMES BLANCHARD. Fortuna: A Story of Wall Street ... New York: J. S. Ogilvie Publishing Company, cop. 1898. 215 p.
    CU, H, HEH, O, Y

CLIFFORD, JOSEPHINE. See McCrackin, Josephine (Woempner) Clifford

1110 CLINGHAM, CLARICE IRENE. That Girl from Bogota: A Novel ... New York: The Home Publishing Company, 3 East Fourteenth Street [cop. 1896]. 262 p.    LC
    On the Hudson River.

1111 CLIPPINGER, JOHN ALBERT. Pedagogue of Widow's Gulch; or, The Adventures of a Pioneer School Teacher in a Secluded Vale in California, Where Married Men Could Not Live and Where Widows Did Not Die ... Sacramento: Robert Young, printer, 1876. 207 p.    HEH

1112 [————] Sam Johnson: The Experience and Observations of a Railroad Telegraph Operator. By Samson [pseud.]. New York: W. J. Johnston, 1878. 177 p.    LC, N, UV

1113 CLODFELTER, NOAH J. In Stony Places: A Story of the Mines in the Great Coal-Mining Region of Pennsylvania ... Philadelphia: T. B. Peterson & Brothers, 1892. 272 p.
    Listed PW, June 18, 1892.

1114 ———— Snatched from the Poor-House: A Young Girl's Life-History ... Philadelphia: T. B. Peterson & Brothers, 306 Chestnut Street [cop. 1888]. 272 p.    HEH, LC

1115 CLOSE, CHARLES WILLIAM. Occult Stories ... Bangor, Maine: C. W. Close, 124 Birch Street [cop. 1899]. 48 p.    LC
    Contents: A Curious Experience—One Thanksgiving—The Colonel's Story—We Shall Know Our Loved Ones—Hold On—Our Thoughts—Wait—Baby Bess.

CLOSSON, HENRY W. Chronicles of Carter Barracks. In C. King, ed., An Initial Experience (1894), No. 3105.

———— The Colonel's Story. In C. King, ed., The Colonel's Christmas Dinner (1890), No. 3098.
    Later printed in No. 3099.

1116 CLOUSTON, MRS. ADELLA OCTAVIA. A Title—Rejected: A Novel . . .
New York: G. W. Dillingham, 1894. 336 p. LC

1117 ——— What Would the World Think? A Novel . . . New York:
The Dodworth Publishing House, 108-110 East Fourth Street [cop.
1897]. 283 p. LC
New York society.

1118 [CLUTE, OSCAR.] The Blessed Bees. By John Allen [pseud.]. New
York: G. P. Putnam's Sons, 1878. 169 p. LC
Of beekeeping.

1119 COAKLEY, TIMOTHY WILFRED. Keef: A Life-Story in Nine Phases . . .
Boston: Charles E. Brown & Co., 1897. 151, [1] p., illus.
BU, CU, HEH, LC

1120 COALE, MRS. JAMES CAREY. The Cottage by the Sea . . . Baltimore:
John Murphy & Company, 1896. 186 p. LC
From Maine to Paris.

COANN, PEARL CLEMENT, jt. au. See Noble, A. L. Love and Shawl-
Straps (1894), No. 3977.

1121 COBB, SYLVANUS. The Gunmaker of Moscow; or, Vladimir the Monk . . .
New York: Robert Bonner's Sons, 1888. 196 p., front.
BU, H, HEH, O, UC, UP, UVB, Y
First ed. in book form.

1122 ——— The Painter of Parma; or, The Magic of a Masterpiece. An
Italian Story of Love, Mystery, and Adventure . . . New York: Cassell
& Company, Limited, 104-106 Fourth Avenue [cop. 1889]. 249 p.
HEH, LC, O
Deposited Feb. 26, 1889.

1123 COBBE, WILLIAM ROSSER. Doctor Judas: A Portrayal of the Opium
Habit . . . Chicago: S. C. Griggs and Company, 1895. 320 p.
LC, O, UC

COCHRAN, DE WITT KENNETH. The Reporter's Protege. In J. J. Conway, ed., Stories (1893), No. 1172.

1124 COCHRAN, KATHERINE MADISON. Posie; or, From Reveille to Retreat.
An Army Story. By Mrs. M. A. Cochran. Cincinnati: The Robert
Clarke Company, 1896. 194 p., illus. HEH

COCHRAN, MRS. M. A. See Cochran, Katherine Madison

1125 COCKE, JAMES R. Blind Leaders of the Blind: The Romance of a Blind
Lawyer . . . Boston: Lee and Shepard, 1896. 487 p., front.
H, HEH, LC, O
Boston.

1126 [COE, CAROLINE L. (CAPRON).] Me! July and August ... New York: G. W. Carleton & Co., 1877. 176 p., illus.     HEH, LC, O
Author also known as Mrs. Spencer Wallace Coe.

COE, MRS. SPENCER WALLACE. *See* Coe, Caroline L. (Capron)

1127 COEN, P. J. Evaline; or, Weighed and Not Wanting. A Catholic Tale ... New York: P. O'Shea, 45 Warren Street [n.d.]. 225 p.     HEH

1128 COFFIN, CHARLES CARLETON. Daughters of the Revolution and Their Times, 1769-1776: A Historical Romance ... Boston and New York: Houghton, Mifflin and Company. The Riverside Press, Cambridge, 1895. 387 p., illus.     AP, H, HEH, N, O, UM, UVB, Y

1128a [COFFIN, ROLAND FOLGER.] Archibald the Cat, and Other Sea Yarns. By the Old Sailor [pseud.] ... New York: The World, 1878. 60 p., illus. Printed in double columns.     HEH
*Also contains:* Pestilence on the Ocean—Game to the Very Last—Phantom Lights on Long Island Sound—The Great Sea-Sarpint—A Matrimonial Adventure—A Ride on an Ocean Steed—Born on the Ocean—The Cruise of the Polly Ann, of Gloucester—An Old-Time Mate—Discipline in the Olden Time—Absalom Boston—Quelling a Mutiny.

———— How Old Wiggins Wore Ship. *In* Stories by American Authors, IX (1885), No. 5275.

COGHILL, HOWARD, *jt. au. See* Cabot, A. W. Two Gentlemen of Gotham [cop. 1887], No. 873.

1129 COGSWELL, FREDERICK HULL. The Regicides: A Tale of Early Colonial Times ... New York: Colonial Publishing Co., 1896. 363, vi p.     CU, LC, N, Y
*Also issued with imprint:* New York: Baker and Taylor Co. [cop. 1896].     O, UV
Listed PW, Oct. 3, 1896.

1130 [COHEN, ALFRED J.] Conscience on Ice: A Story of the Stage. By Alan Dale [pseud.] ... Chicago: N. C. Smith Publishing Company [cop. 1892]. 275 p., front.     LC

1131 [————] An Eerie He and She. By Alan Dale [pseud.] ... New York: G. W. Dillingham, 1889. 366 p.     LC
Of marriage.

1132 [————] His Own Image: A Novel. By Alan Dale [pseud.] ... New York: G. W. Dillingham Co., 1899. 310 p.     HEH, LC, O
Of an actor.

1133 [————] Jonathan's Home. By Alan Dale [pseud.]. Boston: Doyle & Whittle, 1885. 204 p.     UC, UM

1134 [————] A Marriage below Zero: A Novel. By Alan Dale [pseud.] ...
New York: G. W. Dillingham, 1889. 319 p.                    HEH
London.

1135 [————] My Footlight Husband: A Story of the Stage. By Alan
Dale [pseud.] ... New York: Cleveland Publishing Company, 1893.
203 p.                                                      H

1136 [————] An Old Maid Kindled. By Alan Dale [pseud.] ... New
York: G. W. Dillingham, 1890. 345 p.                        LC

1137 [COHEN, DAVID SOLIS.] One Hundred Years a Republic: Our Show.
A Humorous Account of the International Exposition in Honor of the
Centennial Anniversary of American Independence ... By Daisy
Shortcut and 'Arry O'Pagus [pseuds.] ... Philadelphia: Claxton,
Remsen, & Haffelfinger, 1876. 82 p., illus. Printed in double columns.
                                                            H, O
At head of title: "1776. Fun. Humor. Burlesque. 1876."
H. B. Sommer, jt. au.

1138 COLBURN, FRONA EUNICE WAIT (SMITH). Yermah the Dorado. By
Frona Eunice Wait [pseud.] ... San Francisco: William Doxey, 1897.
350 p., front.                                              BU, LC
Of the city of a previous race located on site of San Francisco.

1139 COLBY, FREDERIC MYRON. The Daughter of Pharaoh: A Tale of the
Exodus ... New York: Phillips & Hunt. Cincinnati: Cranston &
Stowe, 1886. 436 p.                                         LC, N

1140 COLBY, MARY B. Deserted Jessie; or, A Girl without a Name ... New
York: U. D. Ward, 150 Nassau St. [cop. 1877]. 330 p., front.   LC

COLE, ALICE VIVIAN (BROWNLEE). See Brownlee, Alice Vivian

COLE, ASHLEY W., jt. au. See Davis, W. Shut the Gate (1889), No.
1446.

1141 [COLE, CORNELIUS.] California Three Hundred and Fifty Years Ago:
Manuelo's Narrative, Translated from the Portuguese, by a Pioneer.
San Francisco: Samuel Carson & Co. New York: C. T. Dillingham,
1888. 333 p., front.          BU, CU, H, HEH, LC, N, UC, UM, Y

1142 COLE, CYRUS. The Auroraphone: A Romance ... Chicago: Charles
H. Kerr & Company, 1890. 249 p.              HEH, LC, UC, UM
Of communication between Saturn and Earth.

1143 [COLE, WILLIAM MORSE.] An Old Man's Romance: A Tale Written
by Christopher Craigie [pseud.]. Boston: Copeland and Day, 1895.
215 p.                                      HEH, LC, O, UC, UV

1144 COLLINGWOOD, HERBERT WINSLOW. Andersonville Violets: A Story of Northern and Southern Life . . . Boston: Lee and Shepard. New York: Chas. T. Dillingham, 1889. 270 p.   CU, H, HEH, LC, N, O, UVB, Y
Post Civil War.

1145 [COLLINS, MRS. CLARA.] Rented, a Husband. By Voisin [pseud.]. New York: Cassell & Company, Limited, 104 & 106 Fourth Avenue [cop. 1889]. 299 p.   LC
New York.

1146 [COLLINS, CLARENCE B.] Tom and Joe, Two Farmer Boys in War and Peace and Love: A Louisiana Memory. Richmond, Va.: Everett Waddey, 1890. 259 p., front.   HEH, LC, UP, UVB

1147 COLLINS, MRS. JANE S. Free at Last . . . Pittsburgh: Press of Murdoch, Kerr & Co., 1896. 208 p., illus.   CU, HEH, LC
Temperance work among former slaves.

1148 [COLLINS, PAUL VALOROUS.] A Baton for a Heart: A Romance of American Student Life in Paris. By Besval [pseud.] . . . Chicago, New York: Rand, McNally & Company, 1888. 242 p., illus.   LC

1149 ———— A Country Romance . . . Milwaukee, Wis.: J. H. Yewdale & Sons Co., 1896. 138 p., illus.   HEH, LC, O
A story to promote the J. I. Case threshing machine.

1150 [COLLINS, ROBERT UPTON.] John Halsey, the Anti-Monopolist: A Novel. By Constant Reed [pseud.]. San Francisco: Geo. F. Neal & Co., 415 Montgomery Street [cop. 1884]. 151 p.
Information supplied by Allan R. Ottley of California State Library.
San Francisco politics in the 1870's.

1151 [COLLINS, S. M. A.] The Homestretch: A Novel. By S. M. A. C. New York: George W. Harlan, 1882. 230 p.   AP, CU, HEH
Of southern life.

COLSON, ETHEL MAUDE. *See* Brazelton, Ethel Maude (Colson)

1152 COLTER, HATTIE E. Medoline Selwyn's Work. By Mrs. J. J. Colter . . . Boston: I. Bradley & Co. [cop. 1889]. 395 p.   LC

COLTER, MRS. J. J. *See* Colter, Hattie E.

1153 COLTHARP, MRS. JEANNETTE DOWNES. Burrill Coleman, Colored: A Tale of the Cotton Fields . . . Franklin, Ohio: The Editor Publishing Company, 1896. 315 p.   LC

1154 COLTON, ARTHUR WILLIS. Bennie Ben Cree: Being the Story of His Adventure to Southward in the Year '62 . . . New York: Doubleday & McClure Co., 1900. 138 p.   HEH, LC, Y
North Carolina.

1155 COLVILLE, WILLIAM J. Dashed against the Rock: A Romance of the Coming Age ... Boston: Colby & Rich, 1894. 310 p.    HEH, UP
Includes brief description of Columbian Exposition, Chicago.
It has not been determined whether this is William Wilberforce Juvenal Colville, English author.

1156 COMER, CORNELIA ATWOOD (PRATT). A Book of Martyrs. By Cornelia Atwood Pratt. New York: Charles Scribner's Sons, 1896. 179 p.
CU, H, HEH, LC, UV, Y
Contents: Witherle's Freedom—Serene's Religious Experience: An Inland Story—An Instance of Chivalry—A Consuming Fire—An Unearned Reward —Hardesty's Cowardice—"The Honor of a Gentleman"—Rivals—At the End of the World.

1157 ——— The Daughter of a Stoic ... New York: Macmillan and Co. London: Macmillan & Co., Ltd., 1896. 179 p.    HEH, LC, UM

——— jt. au. See Slee, R. Dr. Berkeley's Discovery (1899), No. 4956.

1158 COMFORT, LUCY RANDALL. The Belle of Saratoga ... New York: George Munro, 84 Beekman Street [cop. 1876]. 93 p., illus. Printed in double columns.    HEH
Most of her stories were published in subscription series.

1159 COMFORT, WILL LEVINGTON. Trooper Tales: A Series of Sketches of the Real American Private Soldier ... New York: Street & Smith, 238 William Street [cop. 1899]. 248 p., front.    CU, HEH, LC, N, Y
Contents: The New Recruit in the Black Cavalry—The Silent Trooper—The Degeneration of Laddie—Toreador the Game One—The Wooing of Benito— Two Women and a Soldier—Red Brennan of the Seventh—A Soldier of Misfortune—Shadow and the Cherub—Back to San Anton'—The Voice in the Fourth Cell—The Good Which Was in Him—The Aberration of Private Brown—The Last Cell to the Right—The Fever's Fifth Man—The Story of a Cavalry Horse—A Soldier and a Man.

1160 COMMELIN, ANNA OLCOTT. Not in It ... New York: Fowler & Wells Co. London, E.C.: L. N. Fowler & Co. [cop. 1897]. 96 p.    HEH, LC, O
New York life.

COMPTON, FRANCES SNOW, pseud. See Adams, Henry

1161 CONE, JOHN ALBERT. A Musical Reformation ... New York: The Abbey Press, 114 Fifth Avenue. London, Montreal [cop. 1900]. 95 p.
LC
Also contains: "My Escape from Suicide"—A Strange Adoption—Mr. Brett's Excursion—A Spoiled Story—A Natural Conclusion—The New Minister—His "Week Off."

1162 THE CONFESSIONS OF A CONVICT. Edited by Julian Hawthorne ... Philadelphia: Rufus C. Hartranft, 1893. 288 p., illus.    AP, H, HEH, LC, UP
Purportedly by a former convict.

CONGER, HENRY RUTGERS, *jt. au. See* Lehman, H. H., *ed.* Williams Sketches (1898), No. 3269.

1163 CONKLIN, CARRIE. Lady Leonora; or, The Father's Curse. A Novel ... New York: G. W. Carleton & Co.; Street & Smith, New York Weekly, 1877. 344 p.                                                          HEH, Y
At head of title: "'New York Weekly' Series."

1164 CONNELLY, EMMA MARY. Tilting at Windmills: A Story of the Blue Grass Country . . . Boston: D. Lothrop Company, Franklin and Hawley Streets [cop. 1888]. 439 p., front.                       BA, LC, O, UC

1165 CONNERY, THOMAS BERNARD JOSEPH. In the Mafia's Clutches: Don Tiburcio. A Tale of New York and Mexico ... New York: The Minerva Publishing Company, 1891. 259 p.                              HEH

1166 CONOVER, JAMES FRANCIS. The Church Dramatic and Terpsichorean Association (Limited), Promoters of Novity: A Satire . . . Detroit: Raynor & Taylor, printers and binders, 1895. 67 p.              LC
At head of title: "Church Amusements."

CONSCIENCE, BLANCHE, *pseud. See* Cooper, Samuel Williams

CONTE, *Sieur* LOUIS DE, *pseud. See* Clemens, Samuel Langhorne

1167 CONVERSE, CLARENCE CONYERS. Mr. Isolate of Lonelyville . . . New York: R. H. Russell, 1899. 140 p., illus.                   CU, HEH, LC, UM, Y
A collection of humorous stories of events in "Lonelyville."

1168 CONVERSE, FLORENCE. The Burden of Christopher ... Boston and New York: Houghton, Mifflin and Company. The Riverside Press, Cambridge, 1900. 315, [1] p.                          CU, H, HEH, LC, N, O, Y
Of modern business life.

1169 ——— Diana Victrix: A Novel ... Boston and New York: Houghton, Mifflin and Company. The Riverside Press, Cambridge, 1897. 362 p., 1 l.                                                  BA, H, HEH, LC, O, UC
New Orleans; White Mountains, New Hampshire.

1170 CONVERSE, JAMES BOOTH. Uncle Sam's Bible; or, Bible Teachings about Politics . . . Chicago: The Schulte Publishing Company, 323-325 Dearborn Street [cop. 1899]. 230 p.                       HEH, LC

1171 CONWAY, CLARA L. Life's Promise to Pay: A Novel . . . Philadelphia: J. B. Lippincott & Co., 1876. 294 p.                       HEH, LC, O, UVB

CONWAY, JOHN JOSEPH. Old Holmes. *In* J. J. Conway, *ed.*, Stories (1893), No. 1172.

1172 ———— *ed.* Stories Told for Revenue Only. By the St. Paul Press Club . . . Published by the Club . . . St. Paul, 1893. 341 p., 1 l., illus.

HEH, UM

*Contains:* "As You Like It," by Hon. Henry A. Castle—How Orpheus Won, by Col. A. E. Chantler—A Mormon Convert, by Ruth Kimball—Mr. Wilkes of Harvard, by Harry W. Wack—Chinese White, by John Henderson Garnsey —Studies in the Occult, by Franklyn W. Lee—Old Holmes, by Rev. John J. Conway, A.M.—"Lib," by Mary Harriman Severance—Yannay, by Ed. A. Paradis—Our Twins, by Irving Todd—Private Potter, by J. S. Vandiver— Mario, by Luigi D. Ventura—Arrowatha, by H. T. Black—The Rev. Mr. Morrow, by Wm. Wettleson—A Psychological Effect, by F. A. Johnson—The Reporter's Protege, by De Witt Kenneth Cochran—Thornton's Redemption, by J. M. Hawks—Nell and I, by J. E. Gemmel, M.D.
Harry W. Wack (i.e., Henry Wellington Wack), jt. ed.

1173 CONWAY, KATHERINE ELEANOR. The Way of the World and Other Ways: A Story of Our Set . . . Boston: The Pilot Publishing Company, 1900. 251 p. HEH, LC

1174 CONWAY, MONCURE DANIEL. Pine and Palm: A Novel . . . New York: Henry Holt and Company, 1887. 348 p.

AP, BA, CU, H, HEH, LC, O, UV, Y

At head of title: "Leisure Hour Series—No. 207."
Of the North and South prior to the Civil War.

1175 ———— Prisons of Air . . . New York: John W. Lovell Company, 150 Worth Street, cor. Mission Place [cop. 1891]. 270 p.

AP, BU, CU, HEH, LC, O, UVB

At head of title: "Lovell's American Authors' Series, No. 35."

CONYNGHAM, DANE, *pseud.* See Curran, Mrs. L. P. M.

1176 CONYNGHAM, DAVID POWER. The O'Mahony, Chief of the Comeraghs: A Tale of the Rebellion of '98 . . . New York, Montreal: D. & J. Sadlier & Co., 1879. 268 p. HEH, LC
Irish rebellion.

1177 ———— Rose Parnell, the Flower of Avondale: A Tale of the Rebellion of '98 . . . New York: D. & J. Sadlier & Co., 1883. 429 p. LC

COOK, GEORGE CRAM, *jt. au.* See Banks, C. E. In Hampton Roads [cop. 1899], No. 285.

COOK, MRS. JAMES C. See Cook, Mary Louise (Redd)

1178 COOK, MARY LOUISE (REDD). A Woman's Perils; or, Driven from Home. By Mrs. James C. Cook (of Columbus, Georgia) . . . Philadelphia: T. B. Peterson & Brothers, 306 Chestnut Street [cop. 1882]. 498 p.

HEH, LC

COOK, WILLIAM WALLACE. The Romance of a Spotted Man. *In* Mavericks (1892), No. 3663.

Cooke, Grace (McGowan), *jt. au. See* McGowan, A. Return: A Story of the Sea Islands (1895), No. 3517.

1179 Cooke, John Esten. Canolles: The Fortunes of a Partisan of '81 . . . Detroit: E. B. Smith & Company, 1877. 313 p.
CU, H, HEH, LC, N, O, UC, UM, UP, UVB, Y

1180 [————] Fanchette. By One of Her Admirers . . . Boston: James R. Osgood and Company, 1883. 369 p. BA, CU, H, HEH, LC, O, UP, UVB, Y
At head of title: "Round-Robin Series."

1181 ———— The Maurice Mystery . . . New York: D. Appleton and Company, 1885. 245 p. BA, H, LC, O, UC, UM, UVB, Y
BAL 3764 notes this was later published as *Col. Ross of Piedmont.*

1182 ———— Mr. Grantley's Idea . . . New York: Harper & Brothers, 1879. 154 p. CU, H, LC, O, UVB, Y

1183 ———— My Lady Pokahontas: A True Relation of Virginia. Writ by Anas Todkill [pseud.], Puritan and Pilgrim. With Notes by John Esten Cooke. Boston, New York: Houghton, Mifflin and Company. The Riverside Press, Cambridge, 1885. 190 p.
AP, BA, BU, CU, H, HEH, LC, N, O, UC, UP, UVB, Y

1184 ———— Professor Pressensee, Materialist and Inventor: A Story . . . New York: Harper & Brothers, 1878. 133 p.
CU, H, HEH, LC, UP, UVB, Y

1185 ———— The Virginia Bohemians: A Novel . . . New York: Harper & Brothers, 1880. 233 p. Printed in double columns.
AP, BA, BU, CU, H, HEH, LC, UP, UVB, Y

1186 Cooke, Matilda Vance. The Zig-Zag Paths of Life: A Novel . . . Chicago: Charles H. Kerr and Company, 1895. 258 p. LC
Of a minister with an unsavory reputation in a western town.

1187 Cooke, Rose Terry. The Deacon's Week . . . New York & London: G. P. Putnam's Sons; the Knickerbocker Press, 1885. 22 p., illus.
H, HEH, N, Y
Also issued as a 34 p. ed. H, Y
First published by the Congregational Sunday School [1884?]; see BAL 3797.
Later printed in Nos. 1190 and 3206.

1188 ———— Huckleberries Gathered from New England Hills . . . Boston and New York: Houghton, Mifflin and Company. The Riverside Press, Cambridge, 1891. 343 p. BA, CU, H, HEH, LC, O, UM, UVB, Y
*Contents:* Grit—Mary Ann's Mind—Love—Old Miss Todd—An Old-Fashioned Thanksgiving—Hopson's Choice—Clary's Trial—A Double Thanksgiving—Home Again—How Celia Changed Her Mind—A Town Mouse and a Country Mouse.

1189 ——— Somebody's Neighbors . . . Boston: James R. Osgood and
Company, 1881. 421 p.    AP, CU, H, HEH, LC, N, O, UM, UVB, Y
*Contents:* Eben Jackson—Miss Lucinda—Dely's Cow—Squire Paine's Con-
version—Miss Beulah's Bonnet—Cal Culver and the Devil—Amandar—Polly
Mariner, Tailoress—Uncle Josh—Poll Jennings' Hair—Freedom Wheeler's Con-
troversy with Providence—Mrs. Flint's Married Experience.
For distinguishing points between 1st and 2nd states of 1st ed. see BAL 3784.

1190 ——— The Sphinx's Children, and Other People's . . . Boston: Tick-
nor and Company, 1886. 484 p.
AP, BA, H, HEH, LC, N, O, UM, UP, UVB, Y
*Also contains:* The Deacon's Week—A Black Silk—Jericho Jim—Lost on a
Railway—Doctor Parker's Patty—Doom and Dan—Some Account of Thomas
Tucker—The Forger's Bride—Too Late—My Thanksgiving—How She Found
Out—Ann Potter's Lesson—Aceldama Sparks; or, Old and New—Sallathiel
Bump's Stocking—Sally Parsons's Duty—A Hard Lesson—'Liab's First Christ-
mas.

1191 ——— Steadfast: The Story of a Saint and a Sinner . . . Boston:
Ticknor and Company, 1889. 426 p.
AP, BA, CU, H, HEH, LC, O, UC, UM, UP, UVB, Y

1192 COOLEY, ALICE (KINGSBURY). Asaph: An Historical Novel . . . New
York: United States Book Company, successors to John W. Lovell
Company, 142 to 150 Worth Street [cop. 1890]. 229 p.    HEH, LC, N, O
At head of title: "American Authors' Series, No. 33."

1193 COOLEY, ELLEN HODGES. The Boom of a Western City . . . Boston:
Lee and Shepard, 1897. 89 p.    BU, CU, HEH, LC, UC, UM, Y
Fargo, North Dakota.

1194 COOLEY, WILLIAM FORBES. Emmanuel: The Story of the Messiah . . .
New York: Dodd, Mead and Company, 1889. 546 p.    LC, O, UC

1195 COOLIDGE, ERWIN L. A Maine Girl: A Realistic Romance of Down
East . . . New York: G. W. Dillingham, 1892. 199 p.    LC

1196 [COOMBS, ANNE (SHELDON).] As Common Mortals: A Novel . . . New
York: Cassell & Company, Limited, 739 & 741 Broadway [cop. 1886].
404 p.    HEH, LC
"Goverick," i.e., Philadelphia.

1197 ——— A Game of Chance . . . New York: D. Appleton and Company, 1887. 245 p.    AP, HEH, LC, O, UC
Stock speculation; New York.

1198 ——— The Garden of Armida . . . New York: Cassell & Company,
Limited, 104 & 106 Fourth Avenue [cop. 1889]. 238 p.    AP, LC

COOPER, COLIN CAMPBELL, JR. Parthenope's Love. *In* The Septameron
(1888), No. 4867.

1199 [COOPER, MRS. JENNIE.] Those Orphans; or, The Trials of a Stepmother. Cleveland, Ohio: William W. Williams, 1883. 337 p., illus. LC

1200 COOPER, LOUISE BATTLES. Is This True? . . . San Francisco: Published by the author, 1893. 238 p. LC
On LC cover: "An Antithesis to the Kreutzer Sonata."

1201 [COOPER, SAMUEL WILLIAMS.] The Confessions of a Society Man. Edited by Miss Blanche Conscience [pseud.]. A Novel . . . New York and Chicago: Belford, Clarke & Co., 1887. 266 p., illus.
HEH, LC, O
Of sophisticated society.

——— Hazard. *In* The Septameron (1888), No. 4867.

1202 ——— Three Days: A Midsummer Love-Story . . . Philadelphia: J. B. Lippincott Company, 1889. 155 p., illus. HEH, O, UC
Atlantic seacoast resort.

1203 CORNELIUS, MARY ANN (MANN). Uncle Nathan's Farm: A Novel . . . Chicago: Laird & Lee, 1898. 318 p., illus. LC
Of religious tolerance.

1204 ——— The White Flame . . . Chicago: Stockham Publishing Co. [cop. 1900]. 402 p., front. HEH, LC
An occult story.

1205 CORNELL, LILLIAN. A Country Girl . . . New York: The Irving Company [cop. 1896]. 145 p. LC

1206 CORNISH, WILLIAM W. M. Behind Plastered Walls: A Novel . . . New York: G. W. Dillingham Co., 1896. 228 p. HEH, LC

CORNWALL, C. M., *pseud.* *See* Roe, Mary Abigail

1207 CORNWALLIS, KINAHAN. A Marvellous Coincidence; or, A Chain of Misadventures and Mysteries. An American Novel . . . New York: G. W. Dillingham, 1891. 325 p. LC
Also published as: *Two Strange Adventures; or, A Marvellous Coincidence.* New York: F. Tennyson Neely, 1897. LC

1208 CORWIN, CHARLES EDWARD. Onesimus, Christ's Freedman: A Tale of the Pauline Epistles . . . Chicago, New York, Toronto: Fleming H. Revell Company [cop. 1900]. 332 p., illus. LC, UC

1209 CORY, CHARLES BARNEY. Montezuma's Castle, and Other Weird Tales . . . New York: Ralph S. Mighill, 1899. 233 p., illus. H, HEH, N, UM
*Also contains:* The Amateur Championship—The Tragedy of the White Tanks—Too Close for Comfort—The Strange Powder of the Jou Jou Priests—An Aztec Mummy—A Lesson in Chemistry—An Interesting Ghost—The Mound of

Eternal Silence—The Story of a Bad Indian—A Queer Coincidence—The Story of an Insane Sailor—The Elixir of Life—The Voodoo Idol—An Arizona Episode —One Touch of Nature.

*Also issued with imprint:* Boston: [Press of Rockwell and Churchill] 1899. Copy examined at New York Public Library.

1210 [————] Southern Rambles: Florida. By Owen Nox [pseud.]. Boston: A. Williams & Company, 1881. 149 p., illus.    LC Humor.

CORYDON, *pseud.* See Jones, George F.

1211 CORYELL, ELEANOR HOOPER. Out of the Past . . . New York: Street & Smith, 238 William Street [cop. 1899]. 168 p.    HEH, LC, O

1212 COSTELLO, FRED H. The Sale of Mrs. Adral: A Novel . . . New York: G. W. Dillingham, 1889. 283 p.    LC It has not been determined whether this author is Frederick Hankerson Costello.

1213 COSTELLO, FREDERICK HANKERSON. Master Ardick, Buccaneer . . . New York: D. Appleton and Company, 1896. 311 p.    BA, H, HEH, O, UV, Y

1214 COTTMAN, GEORGE STREIBE. Four Hoosier Holiday Stories . . . Irvington, Ind.: G. S. Cottman, printer, 1891. 65 p.    HEH *Contents:* Sarah Jane Phipps Makes a Chris'mas—A Christmas Eve at Beeler's— A Great Thanksgiving Treat—Butler versus Purdue (A Thanksgiving Story).

1215 [COULSON, GEORGE JAMES ATKINSON.] The Clifton Picture: A Novel . . . Philadelphia: J. B. Lippincott & Co., 1878. 312 p.    HEH, LC, O, UVB

1216 [————] Flesh & Spirit: A Novel . . . New York: E. J. Hale & Son, 1876. 245 p.    H, HEH, LC, O

1217 [————] The Ghost of Redbrook: A Novel . . . Philadelphia: J. B. Lippincott & Co., 1879. 313 p.    H, HEH, LC, O

1218 COULTER, JAMES W. The Larger Faith: A Novel . . . Chicago: Charles H. Kerr & Company, 56 Fifth Avenue [cop. 1898]. 285 p.    HEH, LC Of religious interest; a ranch in New Mexico.

1219 COULTER, JOHN. Mr. Desmond, U.S.A. . . . Chicago: A. C. McClurg and Company, 1886. 244 p.    AP, HEH, O Army post at Fort Leavenworth, Kansas.

1220 COUNTRYMAN, ASA. A Tale of the Wyo. and Mo. Valley . . . [Great Bend, Kan.: Democrat Print, 1897.] 149 p., illus.    LC

1221 COURTNEY, MRS. LYDIA L. D. Pauline's Trial: A Novel . . . New York: G. W. Carleton & Co. London: S. Low & Co., 1877. 341 p.    HEH, LC

Coventry, John, *pseud.* *See* Palmer, John Williamson.

1222 [Coverdale, *Sir* Henry Standish] *pseud.* The Fall of the Great Republic. Boston: Roberts Brothers, 1885. 226 p.    CU, H, HEH, LC, O, UC, UP
Predicts fall of U.S. through socialism.

1223 Cowan, Frank. An American Story-Book: Short Stories from Studies of Life in Southwestern Pennsylvania . . . Greensburg, Pa., 1881. 390 p.
HEH, LC, O, Y

*Contents:* The Old Man of Beulah—The Coal King—The Railroad—The Grist-Mill—The Packsaddle Gap—The Fiddle-Faced Hog—The White Deer—The Steamboat—The Devil in a Coal-Bank—The Oil Derrick—The Ridger—The Erdspiegel—The Towscape—The Log Cabin—Yony Waffle—The Roadwagon—The Printer Tramp—The Coke Oven—The Red-Squirrels—The Cow-Doctor —The Blaze and the Block—The Bully Boy with the Glass Eye—Old Helgrimite —The Proof-Reader.

1224 ——— Revi-Lona: A Romance of Love in a Marvelous Land . . . [Greensburg, Pa., ca. 1890.] 247 p.    CU, HEH, UM, UP, Y
Of an inhabited warm oasis at the South Pole.

1225 Cowan, James. Daybreak: A Romance of an Old World . . . New York: George H. Richmond & Co., 1896. 399 p., illus. HEH, LC, UM, Y
A dream visit to Moon and Mars.

1226 Cowan, John Franklin. Endeavor Doin's Down to the Corners . . . Boston: D. Lothrop Company, 1893. 387 p., illus.    HEH, LC, UVB, Y
Of Christian Endeavorers.

1227 [Cowan, Pamela H.] Aimée's Marriage. By P. H. C. . . . Phila-delphia: W. H. Hirst. New York: J. L. Spicer, 1890. 534 p. LC, UM

1228 [Cowdrey, Robert H.] Foiled. By a Lawyer. A Story of Chicago. Chicago: Clark & Longley, printers, 1885. 337 p. BU, HEH, LC, N, O, UC

1229 ——— A Tramp in Society . . . Chicago: Francis J. Schulte & Com-pany, 1891. 290 p.    BU, LC
Of a labor organization.

1230 [Cowles, M. L.] Redbank: Life on a Southern Plantation . . . Boston, Mass.: Arena Publishing Company, 1893. 370 p.    HEH, UV, Y
Postwar Georgia.

1231 [Cowley, Mrs. Winifred Jennings.] Lorin Mooruck, and Other Indian Stories. By George Truman Kercheval [pseud.]. Boston: J. Stilman Smith & Co., 1888. 96, 27, 21 p.    H, HEH, LC, O, UP, Y
*Also contains:* Three Men of Wallowa—Samuel, an Arapahoe.

1232 Cox, Charlotte Crisman. Ione: A Sequel to "Vashti" . . . Boston: Eastern Publishing Company, 1900. 225 p.    LC

1233 Cox, George D. Run Down: A Psychological Novel . . . Philadelphia: T. B. Peterson & Brothers, 306 Chestnut Street [cop. 1888]. 242 p. Listed pw, Jan. 12, 1889.
New Orleans.

Cox, Isaac Joslin. His Decision. *In* H. J. Hapgood, *ed.*, Echoes from Dartmouth (1895), No. 2446.

1234 [Cox, Millard F.] The Legionaries. By Henry Scott Clark [pseud.]. A Story of the Great Raid . . . Indianapolis, Indiana: The Bowen-Merrill Company [cop. 1899]. 385 p., illus.          CU, HEH, UC, UV, Y
Of Morgan's cavalry.

1235 Coxe, Virginia Rosalie. The Embassy Ball . . . New York: F. Tennyson Neely, 114 Fifth Avenue. London, 96 Queen Street [cop. 1897]. 377 p., front.          BU, HEH, O
New York smart set.

1236 Coxey, Willard Douglas. A Hypnotic Crime, and Other Like True Tales: Being a Free Adaptation from the Minutes of the Society for Psychical Research . . . Maywood, Ill., 1896. 82 p.          LC
*Also contains:* His Evil Alter Ego—The Wraith of Paul Bleu—Prof. Dinkledonkie's Experiment—Bill Watson's Ghost.

1237 ———— The Other Woman's Husband: An Outline Sketch of To-Day . . . Maywood, Ill., 1896. 117 p.          LC

1238 ———— Tales by the Way: A Little Book of Odd Stories . . . Chicago, 1898. 75 p.          LC
*Contents:* The Village Coward—Col. Edgerly's Legacy—A Circus Episode—An Aboriginal Coquette—The Lost Creek Claim—A Masquerade.

1239 [Cozzens, Samuel Woodworth.] Nobody's Husband. Boston: Lee & Shepard. New York: Charles T. Dillingham, 1878. 258 p.          HEH
A bachelor's adventures on railroad and steamboat.

Crabtrie, N. Warrington, *pseud. See* James, Samuel Humphreys

1240 Cracraft, Louise Dudley. Between Me and Thee . . . Cleveland, Ohio: The Burrows Brothers Company, 1888. 227 p.          LC

Craddock, Charles Egbert, *pseud. See* Murfree, Mary Noailles

1241 Craddock, Florence Nightingale. The Soldier's Revenge; or, Roland and Wilfred . . . New York: The Abbey Press, 114 Fifth Avenue. London, Montreal [cop. 1900]. 208 p.          HEH, LC
Cadet life at West Point; 1861.

1242 Craig, Alexander. Ionia, Land of Wise Men and Fair Women . . . Chicago: E. A. Weeks Co., 1898. 301 p., illus.
Copy examined at New York Public Library.
A utopia in the Himalayas.

1243 CRAIG, B. F. The Rough Diamond . . . [Kansas City, Mo.: Ramsey, Millet, & Hudson, 1880.] 214 p., illus.   BU, CU, LC
Contains: The Story of a Hundred Years [of a Kentucky pioneer family].

CRAIGIE, CHRISTOPHER, pseud. See Cole, William Morse

1244 CRAIGIE, MARY E. John Anderson and I . . . Buffalo: Moulton, Wenborne and Company, 1888. 199 p.   LC
Utopian novel.

1245 CRAM, RALPH ADAMS. Black Spirits & White: A Book of Ghost Stories . . . Chicago: Stone & Kimball, 1895. 150, [1] p., 1 l.   BA, H, HEH, LC, O
Contents: No. 252 Rue M. le Prince—In Kropfsberg Keep—The White Villa—Sister Maddelena—Notre Dame des Eaux—The Dead Valley.
At head of title: "Carnation Series."

1246 [———] The Decadent: Being the Gospel of Inaction, Wherein Are Set Forth in Romance Form Certain Reflections Touching the Curious Characteristics of These Ultimate Years, and the Divers Causes Thereof. [Boston]: Privately printed for the author, 1893. 41, [1] p., front.
BA, CU, H, HEH, LC, UC, Y
125 copies printed.

1247 CRANE, CLARENCE. In the Next Generation, and Other Stories . . . Brooklyn: Franklin Printing Company, 1896. 40 p., front.   LC
Contains: The Evolution of a Poetaster—The Medium: A Spiritualistic-Detective Story—The Sun-Child.

1248 CRANE, JAMES LYONS. The Two Circuits: A Story of Illinois Life . . . Chicago: Jansen, McClurg & Co., 1877. 502 p., illus.   H, HEH, N, O, UC, Y

1249 CRANE, MRS. L. H. The Startled Sewing Society . . . New York and Chicago: Fleming H. Revell Company [cop. 1891]. 25 p.   LC

1250 CRANE, STEPHEN. Active Service: A Novel . . . New York: Frederick A. Stokes Company [cop. 1899]. 345 p.
BA, BU, CU, H, HEH, LC, N, O, UM, UP, UVB, Y
Greco-Turkish war.

1251 ——— George's Mother . . . New York, London: Edward Arnold, 1896. 177 p.   BA, CU, H, HEH, LC, N, O, UC, UM, UP, UVB, Y
New York slums.

1252 ——— The Little Regiment, and Other Episodes of the American Civil War . . . New York: D. Appleton and Company, 1896. 196 p.
BA, CU, H, HEH, LC, N, O, UC, UM, UP, UVB, Y
Also contains: Three Miraculous Soldiers—A Mystery of Heroism—An Indiana Campaign—A Gray Sleeve—The Veteran.

1253   [————] Maggie, a Girl of the Streets (A Story of New York). By Johnston Smith [pseud.] . . . [New York: Printed for the author, 1893.]  163 p.            CU, H, HEH, UP, UVB, Y
New York slum life.

1254   ———— ———— New York: D. Appleton and Company, 1896.  158 p.
                        BA, BU, CU, H, HEH, LC, N, O, UC, UP, UVB, Y
BAL 4075 notes two states of title page.

1255   ———— The Monster, and Other Stories . . .  New York and London: Harper & Brothers, 1899.  188, [1] p., illus.
                        BA, BU, CU, H, HEH, LC, N, O, UP, UVB, Y
*Also contains:* The Blue Hotel–His New Mittens.

1256   ———— The Open Boat, and Other Tales of Adventure . . .  New York: Doubleday & McClure Co., 1898.  336 p.
                        BA, CU, H, HEH, LC, N, O, UM, UP, UVB, Y
*Also contains:* A Man and Some Others–One Dash, Horses–Flanagan–The Bride Comes to Yellow Sky–The Wise Men–Death and the Child–The Five White Mice.

1257   ———— The Red Badge of Courage: An Episode of the American Civil War . . .  New York: D. Appleton and Company, 1895.  233 p.
                        AP, CU, HEH, LC, N, O, UP, UVB, Y

        ———— A Tale of Mere Chance. *In* I. Bacheller, *ed.,* Best Things from American Literature (1899), No. 195.

1258   ———— The Third Violet . . .  New York: D. Appleton and Company, 1897.  203 p.        BU, CU, H, HEH, LC, N, O, UC, UM, UP, UVB, Y
Bohemian life; New York.

1259   ———— Whilomville Stories . . .  New York and London: Harper & Brothers, 1900.  198, [1] p., illus.
                  AP, BU, CU, H, HEH, LC, N, O, UC, UM, UP, UVB, Y
*Contents:* The Angel Child–Lynx-Hunting–The Lover and the Telltale–"Showin' Off"–Making an Orator–Shame–The Carriage-Lamps–The Knife–The Stove–The Trial, Execution, and Burial of Homer Phelps–The Fight–The City Urchin and the Chaste Villagers–A Little Pilgrimage.

1260   ———— Wounds in the Rain: War Stories . . .  New York: Frederick A. Stokes Company [cop. 1900].  347 p.  BU, CU, HEH, LC, O, UP, UVB, Y
*Contents:* The Price of the Harness–The Lone Charge of William B. Perkins–The Clan of No-Name–God Rest Ye, Merry Gentlemen–The Revenge of the Adolphus–The Sergeant's Private Madhouse–Virtue in War–Marines Signalling under Fire at Guantanamo–This Majestic Lie–War Memories–The Second Generation.

1261   CRANE, WALTER BEVERLEY. Odd Tales . . .  New York, Chicago, and London: M. Witmark & Sons [cop. 1900].  106 p.         BU, LC
Thirteen fantasies reprinted from various periodicals.

1262  CRAWFORD, FRANCIS MARION.  Adam Johnstone's Son . . .  New York: Macmillan and Co.  London: Macmillan & Co., Ltd., 1896.  281 p., illus.

AP, CU, H, HEH, LC, O, UC, UP, UVB, Y

Verso of title page: "Norwood Press, J. S. Cushing & Co.–Berwick & Smith, Norwood, Mass., U.S.A."

The copyright issue at LC, deposited Feb. 28, 1895, is dated 1895 on title page.

1263  ———  An American Politician: A Novel . . .  Boston, New York: Houghton, Mifflin and Company.  The Riverside Press, Cambridge, 1885.  356 p.

AP, BU, H, HEH, LC, O, UC, UP, UVB, Y

1264  ———  Casa Braccio . . .  New York and London: Macmillan and Co., 1895.  2 vols. (334, 332 p.), illus.

AP, BA, CU, H, HEH, N, O, UC, UM(V.I), UP, UVB, Y

Verso of title page: "Norwood Press, J. S. Cushing & Co.–Berwick & Smith, Norwood, Mass., U.S.A."

The copyright issue at LC, deposited Sept. 19, 1894, is dated 1894 on title page.

1265  ———  The Children of the King: A Tale of Southern Italy . . .  New York and London: Macmillan and Co., 1893.  320 p.

AP, BA, BU, CU, H, HEH, LC, N, O, UC, UVB, Y

Verso of title page: "Typography by J. S. Cushing & Co., Boston, U.S.A. Presswork by Berwick & Smith, Boston, U.S.A."

1266  ———  A Cigarette-Maker's Romance . . .  New York and London: Macmillan and Co., 1893.  289 p.                                    UC

Verso of title page: "Norwich Press, J. S. Cushing & Co.–Berwick & Smith, Boston, Mass., U.S.A."

The 1st ed. published in U.S. (London and New York, 1890), BAL 4164, was printed in Edinburgh.

1267  ———  Corleone: A Tale of Sicily . . .  London: Macmillan and Co., Ltd.  New York: The Macmillan Company, 1897.  2 vols. (336, 341 p.)

AP, O, UC, UVB, Y

Printed in the U.S.; see BAL 4201.

Imprint of 1st U.S. ed.: New York: The Macmillan Company.  London: Macmillan & Co., Ltd., 1897.     CU, H, HEH, N, UVB, Y

The copyright issue at LC, deposited May 26, 1896, is dated 1896 on title page.

1268  ———  Doctor Claudius: A True Story . . .  New York and London: Macmillan and Co., 1893.  362 p.                                    HEH

Verso of title page: "New Uniform Edition . . . January, 1892; reprinted October, 1892."  The 1892 eds. not seen.

At bottom of p. 362: "Typography by J. S. Cushing & Co., Boston, U.S.A. Presswork by Berwick & Smith, Boston, U.S.A."

The 1st ed. published in the U.S. (New York, 1883), BAL 4132, was probably printed in Edinburgh.

1269  ———  Don Orsino . . .  New York and London: Macmillan and Co., 1892.  448 p.                 AP, CU, H, HEH, LC, N, O, UC, UP, UVB, Y

Verso of title page: "Typography by J. S. Cushing & Co., Boston.  Presswork by Berwick & Smith, Boston."

1270 ———— Greifenstein ... New York and London: Macmillan and Co., 1893. 385 p. LC, UC

Verso of title page: "First edition (3 vols. . . . .) March, 1889; reprinted June, 1889; 2d ed. (1 vol. . . .) December, 1889. Reprinted 1890, 1891, 1892." These eds. not printed in the U.S.

Also on verso of title page: "Norwood Press, J. S. Cushing & Co.–Berwick & Smith, Boston, Mass., U.S.A."

The 1st ed. published in the U.S. (London and New York, 1889), BAL 4156, was printed in Edinburgh.

1271 ———— In the Palace of the King: A Love Story of Old Madrid ... New York: The Macmillan Company. London: Macmillan & Co., Ltd., 1900. 367 p., illus. BA, H, HEH, LC, UP, UVB

Verso of title page: "Norwood Press, J. S. Cushing & Co.–Berwick & Smith, Norwood, Mass., U.S.A."

1272 ———— Katharine Lauderdale ... New York and London: Macmillan and Co., 1894. 2 vols. (332, 336 p.), illus.

AP, BA, BU, CU, H, HEH, LC, O, UC, UP, UVB, Y

Verso of title page: "Norwood Press, J. S. Cushing & Co.–Berwick & Smith, Boston, Mass., U.S.A."

1273 ———— Love in Idleness: A Tale of Bar Harbour ... New York and London: Macmillan and Co., 1894. 218 p., illus.

BA, CU, H, HEH, LC, N, O, UM, UP, UVB, Y

Verso of title page: "Norwood Press, J. S. Cushing & Co.–Berwick & Smith, Boston, Mass., U.S.A."

The copyright issue at LC, deposited May 9, 1894, collates 230 p. HEH also has a copy.

1274 ———— Marion Darche: A Story without Comment ... New York and London: Macmillan and Co., 1893. 309 p.

AP, BU, CU, H, HEH, LC, N, O, UC, UVB, Y

Verso of title page: "Norwood Press, J. S. Cushing & Co.–Berwick & Smith, Boston, Mass., U.S.A."

1275 ———— Marzio's Crucifix ... London and New York: Macmillan and Co., 1892. 250 p. HEH

Verso of title page: "Press of J. J. Little & Co., Astor Place, New York."

The 1st ed. published in the U.S. (London and New York, 1887), BAL 4150, was probably printed in Great Britain.

1276 ———— Mr. Isaacs: A Tale of Modern India ... New York and London: Macmillan and Co., 1892. 320 p. HEH

Verso of title page: "New Uniform Edition . . . Dec. 18, 1891. Reprinted October, 1892." These eds. not seen.

At bottom of p. 320: "Typography by J. S. Cushing & Co., Boston, U.S.A. Presswork by Berwick & Smith, Boston, U.S.A."

The 1st ed. published in the U.S. (New York, 1882), BAL 4130, was printed in Edinburgh.

There were New York, 1883, and London and New York, 1887, eds. also printed in Edinburgh. UM, however, has a New York, 1883, ed. without a "press" note.

1277 ——— Paul Patoff ... Boston and New York: Houghton, Mifflin and Company. The Riverside Press, Cambridge, 1887. 456 p.

AP, CU, H, HEH, LC, O, UC, UP, UVB, Y

1278 ——— Pietro Ghisleri ... New York and London: Macmillan & Co., 1893. 429 p. AP, BA, H, HEH, LC, N, O, UVB, Y

Verso of title page: "Norwood Press, J. S. Cushing & Co.–Berwick & Smith, Boston, Mass., U.S.A."

The copyright issue at LC, deposited Sept. 30, 1892, entitled *Laura Arden*, is dated 1892 on title page.

1279 ——— The Ralstons ... New York and London: Macmillan and Co., 1895. 2 vols. (340, 336 p.)

AP, BA, BU, CU, H, HEH, LC, N, O, UC, UM(V.1), UP, UVB, Y

Verso of title page: "Norwood Press, J. S. Cushing & Co.–Berwick & Smith, Boston, Mass., U.S.A."

Printed copyright notice dated 1893. BAL 4188 surmises that "the publishers deposited for copyright an advance printing dated 1894."

1280 ——— A Roman Singer ... Boston, New York: Houghton, Mifflin and Company. The Riverside Press, Cambridge, 1884. 378 p.

AP, H, HEH, N, O, UM, UVB, Y

1281 ——— A Rose of Yesteday ... New York: The Macmillan Company. London: Macmillan & Co., Ltd., 1897. 218 p.

AP, BA, BU, CU, H, HEH, LC, O, UC, UVB, Y

Verso of title page: "Norwood Press, J. S. Cushing & Co.–Berwick & Smith, Norwood, Mass., U.S.A."

1282 ——— Sant' Ilario ... New York and London: Macmillan and Co., 1893. 434 p. CU, H, HEH, LC, N

Verso of title page: "New Edition ... January, 1892. Reprinted December, 1892." The 1892 eds. not seen.

At bottom of p. 434: "Typography by J. S. Cushing & Co., Boston, U.S.A. Presswork by Berwick & Smith, Boston, U.S.A."

The 1st ed. published in the U.S. (London and New York, 1889), BAL 4158, was printed in Edinburgh.

1283 ——— Saracinesca ... New York: Macmillan and Co., 1893. 450 p.

H, HEH, Y

Verso of title page: "New Uniform Edition ... Aug. 6, 1891. Reprinted October, 1892." These eds. not seen.

At bottom of p. 450: "Typography by J. S. Cushing & Co., Boston. Presswork by Berwick & Smith, Boston."

The 1st ed. published in the U.S. (New York, 1887), BAL 4147, was printed in Edinburgh.

1284 ——— A Tale of a Lonely Parish ... New York and London: Macmillan and Co., 1893. 385 p. H, LC, Y

Verso of title page: "Norwood Press, J. S. Cushing & Co.–Berwick & Smith, Boston, Mass., U.S.A."

The 1st ed. published in the U.S. (London and New York, 1886), BAL 4143, was printed in Edinburgh.

1285 ———— Taquisara... New York: The Macmillan Company. London: Macmillan & Co., Ltd., 1896. 2 vols. (309, 317 p.)

AP, H, HEH, LC, N, O, UC, UVB

Verso of title page: "Norwood Press, J. S. Cushing & Co.–Berwick & Smith, Norwood, Mass., U.S.A."

The copyright issue at LC, deposited Feb. 7, 1895, is dated 1895 on title page.

1286 ———— The Three Fates ... London and New York: Macmillan and Co., 1892. 412 p.  AP, CU, H, HEH, N, O, UC, UP, UV, Y

At bottom of p. 412: "Typography by J. S. Cushing & Co., Boston, U.S.A. Presswork by Berwick & Smith, Boston, U.S.A."

1287 ———— To Leeward ... Boston, New York: Houghton, Mifflin and Company. The Riverside Press, Cambridge, 1884. 411 p.

AP, BU, CU, H, HEH, LC, UC, UVB, Y

1288 ———— The Upper Berth... New York, London: G. P. Putnam's Sons; the Knickerbocker Press, 1894. 145 p.

BA, BU, CU, H, HEH, LC, N, O, UC, UM, UP, UVB, Y

*Also contains:* By the Waters of Paradise.

At head of title: "F. Marion Crawford."

Title story previously published in Sir Henry Norman, *ed., The Broken Shaft* (New York, 1886); and "By the Waters of Paradise" in the same editor's *The Witching Time* (New York, 1887).

1289 ———— Via Crucis: A Romance of the Second Crusade ... New York: The Macmillan Company. London: Macmillan & Co., Ltd., 1899. 396 p., illus.  AP, BA, BU, H, HEH, LC, N, O, UC, UP, UVB, Y

Verso of title page: "Norwood Press, J. S. Cushing & Co.–Berwick & Smith, Norwood, Mass., U.S.A."

1290 ———— The Witch of Prague: A Fantastic Tale ... London and New York: Macmillan and Co., 1891. 435 p., illus.

AP, BU, CU, H, HEH, N, O, UVB, Y

Verso of title page: "Robert Drummond, electrotyper and printer, New York."

1291 ———— With the Immortals ... New York and London: Macmillan and Co., 1893. 312 p.  H, LC

Verso of title page: "1st ed. (2 vols.) June 1888 ... Reprinted 1891, 1892. New ed. reset Jan. 1893." The 1891 and 1892 eds. not seen.

Also on verso of title page: "Norwood Press, J. S. Cushing & Co.–Berwick & Smith, Boston, Mass., U.S.A."

The 1st ed. published in the U.S. (London and New York, 1888), BAL 4154, was printed in Edinburgh.

1292 ———— Zoroaster . . . London and New York: Macmillan and Co., 1892. 290 p.     LC

At bottom of p. 290: "Typography by J. S. Cushing & Co., Boston, U.S.A. Presswork by Berwick & Smith, Boston, U.S.A."

An 1893 ed. (CU, H, HEH, N) with same colophon has on verso of title page: "Set up and electrotyped November, 1891. Reprinted December, 1892." The 1891 ed. not seen.

The 1st ed. published in the U.S. (London and New York, 1885), BAL 4139, was printed in Edinburgh.

1293 CRAWFORD, THERON CLARK. The Disappearance Syndicate, and Senator Stanley's Story . . . New York: Charles B. Reed, 1894. 241 p., illus.     HEH, LC

*Also contains:* Napoleon Wolff and His Newspaper of the Future.

1294 ———— A Man and His Soul: An Occult Romance of Washington Life . . . New York: Charles B. Reed, 1894. 255 p., front.     CU, HEH, Y

1295 CREAMER, HANNAH GARDNER. The Household Myth . . . Boston: Charles H. Whiting, 1885. 155 p.     HEH

From the eastern seaboard to the Los Angeles vineyards.

CRICKET, *pseud. See* Gray, Clarence F.

1296 CRIDGE, ALFRED DENTON. Utopia; or, The History of an Extinct Planet . . . Oakland, Calif.: Winchester & Pew, printers, 1884. Cover title, 30 p. Printed in double columns.

Information from LC card; copy lacking front cover examined at Boston Public Library.

1297 CRIM, MARTHA JANE. Adventures of a Fair Rebel. By Matt Crim. New York: Charles L. Webster & Co., 1891. 323 p., front.     CU, HEH, LC

———— The Cross-Roads Ghost, by Matt Crim. In Ten Notable Stories (1894), No. 5391.

1298 ———— Elizabeth, Christian Scientist . . . New York: Charles L. Webster & Co., 1893. 350 p.     H, HEH, UC

H cover imprint: Chicago: F. M. Hawley Publishing Company, 87 Washington Street.

Georgia and New York.

1299 ———— In Beaver Cove and Elsewhere . . . New York: Charles L. Webster & Co., 1892. 346 p.     H, HEH, LC

*Also contains:* S'phiry Ann—An "Onfortunit Creetur"—Bet Crow—Silury—'Zek'l—Was It an Exceptional Case?—An Old-Time Love Story—How the Quarrel Ended—The Crucial Test—The Story of a Lilac Gown.

CRIM, MATT. *See* Crim, Martha Jane

CRINKLE, NYM, *pseud. See* Wheeler, Andrew Carpenter

1300  CRISP, CASSIUS.  An Enchanted Ghost, and Other Stories ...  New York:
Findlay Sackett, 1900.  165, [1] p., illus.
Contents: Paul Stoddard's Romance—An Enchanted Ghost—The Hunt for the
Golden Buck—Ruth—The Valley Tragedies.
Copy examined at New York Public Library.

1301  CRIST, MALEY BAINBRIDGE.  Patchwork: The Poems and Prose Sketches
...  Atlanta: The Martin & Hoyt Company; the Dixie Press, 1898.
238 p., illus.                                            BU, HEH, UV, Y
Contains: Romance of a Kentuckian in St. Augustine—Little Jean's Theft—
Number Fourteen—Catherine—The Experience of a Corpse—Love's First Con-
quest—A Confederate for a Day—The Two Hat Pins—How the Captain Found
His Servant—The Bridal Chamber of Florida's Silver Springs.

1302  CRISWELL, R. W.  Grandfather Lickshingle ...  New York: John W.
Lovell Company, 14 & 16 Vesey Street [cop. 1883].  208 p., illus.
                                                          HEH, LC, UM
Also contains: Astronomy for the Year—The Shorter Catechism.
Deposited Apr. 22, 1884.

1303  CRITTENDEN, EDWARD B.  The Entwined Lives of Miss Gabrielle Austin,
Daughter of the Late Rev. Ellis C. Austin, and of Redmond, the Outlaw,
Leader of the North Carolina "Moonshiners" ...  Philadelphia: Barclay
and Co., 21 North Seventh St. [cop. 1879].  80 p., illus.     H, HEH, LC
At head of title: "All Rights Reserved."

1304  [CROCKER, SAMUEL.]  That Island.  By Theodore Oceanic Islet [pseud.].
A Political Romance.  Kansas City, Mo.: Press of the Sidney F. Woody
Printing Co., cop. 1892.  156 p.                                LC
An allegory depicting industrial masses in America.

1305  CROFOOT, FREDERIC S.  Detroit Unveiled: A Graphic and Startling Revelation of the Mysteries of Michigan's Metropolis ...  Detroit: Sunday
World Print, 1887.  86 p., illus.                               LC

CROSBY, MARGARET.  An Islander.  *In* C. C. Harrison, *ed.*, Short Stories
(1893), No. 2514.
Printed earlier in No. 1306.

1306  ——— A Violin Obligato, and Other Stories ...  Boston: Roberts
Brothers, 1891.  321 p.                                   BA, LC, O, Y
Also contains: On the South Shore—An Islander—A Complete Misunderstand-
ing—The Copeland Collection—Last Chance Gulch—A Mad Englishman—Passages from the Journal of a Social Wreck—A Child of Light.

1307  CROWNINSHIELD, MARY (BRADFORD).  The Archbishop and the Lady.  By
Mrs. Schuyler Crowninshield ...  New York: McClure, Phillips & Co.,
1900.  458 p.                                         CU, H, HEH, LC, O
Paris society.

1308 ———— Latitude 19°: A Romance of the West Indies in the Year of Our Lord Eighteen Hundred and Twenty. Being a Faithful Account and True of the Painful Adventures of the Skipper, the Bo's'n, the Smith, the Mate, and Cynthia . . . New York: D. Appleton and Company, 1898. 418 p., illus.    BA, H, HEH, LC, O, UV

1309 ———— San Isidro . . . Chicago & New York: Herbert S. Stone & Company, 1900. 312 p., 1 l.    BA, HEH, LC, O, Y
Life and customs in Mexico.

1310 ———— Where the Trade-Wind Blows: West Indian Tales . . . New York: The Macmillan Company. London: Macmillan & Co., Ltd., 1898. 308 p.    CU, H, HEH, LC, O, UV
Contents: Candace–A Christmas Surprise–Paul Demarisi's Mortgage–Willie Baker's Good Sense–Jones's New Fin-Keel–Flandreau–The Value of a Banana Leaf–Anastasio's Revenge–Corndeau–Which of Three?–Plumero the Good –Paul's Orange Grove.

CROWNINSHIELD, MRS. SCHUYLER. See Crowninshield, Mary (Bradford)

1311 CROZIER, ROBERT HASKINS. Deep Waters; or, A Strange Story . . . St. Louis: Farris, Smith & Co., 919 Olive Street [cop. 1887]. 367 p.
LC, UM
Of Civil War interest.

1312 ———— Fiery Trials; or, A Story of an Infidel's Family . . . Memphis: Rogers & Co., printers, 1882. 527 p.    LC

1313 ———— Golden Rule: A Tale of Texas . . . Richmond, Virginia: Whittet & Shepperson, printers, 1900. 179 p.    HEH, LC

1314 ———— Hal Gilman; or, A Mississippi Story Substantially True . . . Sardis, Mississippi: W. H. Crockett & Co., 1883. 79 p.    LC
At head of title: " 'Mississippi Library' Number 1."

1315 [CRUGER, JULIE GRINNELL (STORROW).] A Diplomat's Diary. By Julien Gordon [pseud.]. Philadelphia: J. B. Lippincott Company, 1890. 233 p.    CU, H, HEH, LC, O, UV, Y
St. Petersburg.

1316 [————] Eat Not Thy Heart. By Julien Gordon [pseud.]. Chicago & New York: Herbert S. Stone & Co., 1897. 319 p., 1 l.
BA, H, HEH, LC, O, UV, Y
Of wealthy families on Long Island.

1317 [————] His Letters. By Julien Gordon [pseud.] . . . New York: Cassell Publishing Company, 104 & 106 Fourth Avenue [cop. 1892]. 280 p.    H, HEH, LC, O, Y
Love letters.

1318 [————] Marionettes. By Julien Gordon [pseud.] . . . New York: Cassell Publishing Company, 104 & 106 Fourth Avenue [cop. 1892]. 320 p.                                    BA, BU, H, HEH, LC, O, UV, Y

1319 [————] Poppaea. By Julien Gordon [pseud.] . . . Philadelphia: J. B. Lippincott Company, 1895. 320 p.          BA, H, HEH, LC, O, UV, Y "Smart set"; New York and Paris.

1320 [————] A Puritan Pagan: A Novel. By Julien Gordon [pseud.] . . . New York: D. Appleton and Company, 1891. 367 p.
BA, BU, CU, H, HEH, LC, N, O, UC, UV, Y
Society life; Washington, Newport, Paris.

[————] Redemption, by Julien Gordon [pseud.]. *In* Some Short Stories [cop. 1900], No. 5070.

1321 [————] A Successful Man. By Julien Gordon [pseud.] . . . Philadelphia: J. B. Lippincott Company, 1891. 184 p.      HEH, LC, O, UC, UP

1322 [————] Vampires. Mademoiselle Réséda. By Julien Gordon [pseud.] . . . Philadelphia: J. B. Lippincott Company, 1891. 299.
BA, CU, H, HEH, LC, O, UV

1323 [————] A Wedding, and Other Stories. By Julien Gordon [pseud.] . . . Philadelphia: J. B. Lippincott Company, 1896. 232 p.
BU, H, HEH, LC, O, UC
*Also contains:* The First Flight—Morning Mists—Conquered—Raking Straws— The Moujik.

1324 CRUGER, MARY. Brotherhood . . . Boston: D. Lothrop Company, Washington Street, opp. Bromfield [cop. 1891]. 306 p.      HEH, LC, Y

1325 ———— A Den of Thieves; or, The Lay-Reader of St. Mark's . . . New York, London: Funk & Wagnalls, 1886. 185 p.          AP, HEH, LC Temperance tale.

1326 ———— How She Did It; or, Comfort on $150 a Year . . . New York: D. Appleton and Company, 1888. 212 p., front.          H, LC, O

1327 ———— Hyperaesthesia: A Novel . . . New York: Fords, Howard, & Hulbert, 1886. 400 p.                              HEH, LC, N

1328 ———— The Vanderheyde Manor-House . . . New York: Worthington Company, 747 Broadway [cop. 1887]. 323 p.          H, LC, Y *Also published as: Harry Elliott, Cashier.* New York: Worthington Company, 747 Broadway [cop. 1887].    HEH

1329 CRUMPTON, M. NATALINE. The Silver Buckle: A Story of the Revolutionary Days . . . Philadelphia: Henry Altemus [cop. 1889]. 89 p., illus.                                          CU, H, HEH, LC

1330 CULLEN, CLARENCE LOUIS. Taking Chances . . . New York: G. W. Dillingham Company [cop. 1900]. 269 p.      H, HEH, LC, N, UC, UM, Y
A collection of stories on gambling.

1331 ———— Tales of the Ex-Tanks: A Book of Hard-Luck Stories . . . New York: Grosset & Dunlap, 1900.   392 p.      BU, H, HEH, LC, N, O, UM, UV, Y

1332 CULTER, MARY NANTZ (McCRAE). Four Roads to Happiness: A Story of Hoosier Life . . . Philadelphia: The Union Press, 1122 Chestnut Street [cop. 1900].   312 p., front.      LC

CUMMING, DUNCAN, pseud. See Cummings, George Duncan

1333 CUMMINGS, ARTHUR. The Fall of Kilman Kon . . . New York: G. W. Dillingham, 1889.   348 p.      HEH, LC
Americans in Europe.

1334 CUMMINGS, ARTHUR M. The Hercules Brand . . . New York: National Temperance Society, 1885.   447 p., front.      LC

CUMMINGS, EDWARD. The Appeal to Anne. In Stories from the Chap-Book (1896), No. 5277.

1335 [CUMMINGS, GEORGE DUNCAN.] A Change with the Seasons: A Novel. By Duncan Cumming [pseud.]. Dunsmuir, Cal.: The Dunsmuir Publishing Co., 1897.   171 p.      HEH, LC
Castle Crags, California.

CUMMINS, ELLA S., pseud. See Mighels, Ella Sterling (Clark)

1336 A CUNNING CULPRIT; or, A "Novel" Novel. A Composite Romance by Twenty Different Popular Writers. Chicago: The Hobart Publishing Company, 1895.   302 p.      LC

1337 CUNNINGHAM, MRS. B. SIM. For Honor's Sake . . . Philadelphia: J. B. Lippincott & Co., 1879.   281 p.      HEH, Y
New York society.

1338 ———— In Sancho Panza's Pit . . . Philadelphia: J. B. Lippincott & Co., 1883.   295 p.      AP, HEH

1339 CUNNINGHAM, G. CUNYNGHAM. Tales from the Land of Mañana . . . Cincinnati: The Editor Publishing Co., 1898.   241 p.      LC
Contents: In the Days of the Plague—The Ghost of the Count—An Incident—Dolores—Jumping Beans—The Love of Carita—Lupe, a Heathen—A Spider's Sting—The Ley de Fuga—An Unromantic Romance—Carmen—In the Role of Christ—Unclean—The Mummy of José—For a Sombrero de Fiesta.

1340 CURRAN, JOHN ELLIOTT. Miss Frances Merley: A Novel . . . Boston: Cupples and Hurd, 1888.   406 p.      AP, H, HEH, LC

1341 [CURRAN, MRS. L. P. M.] Eunice Quince: A New England Romance. By Dane Conyngham [pseud.]. New York: Lovell, Coryell & Company, 310-318 Sixth Avenue [cop. 1895]. 362 p.    HEH, LC, Y

CURRIE, FRANCES ISABEL. *See* Webb, Frances Isabel (Currie)

1342 CURRIER, CHARLES WARREN. Dimitrios and Irene; or, The Conquest of Constantinople. A Historical Romance . . . Baltimore: Gallery & McCann, 1894. 254 p., illus.    HEH, LC

1343 ———— The Rose of Alhama; or, The Conquest of Granada. An Episode of the Moorish Wars in Spain . . . New York: Christian Press Association Publishing Company, 1897. 198 p., illus.    LC

1344 CURRIER, EMMA C. Hubbub: A Story . . . New York: The Authors' Publishing Company, 27 Bond Street [cop. 1880]. 234 p.    LC, Y
West Indies.

1345 CURRY, ERASTUS S. The No-din': Romance, History, and Science of the Pre-Historic Races of America and Other Lands . . . Christy, Mo.: Published by the author, 1899. 335, II, V, p., illus.    LC

1346 CURRY, LILY. A Bohemian Tragedy . . . Philadelphia: T. B. Peterson & Brothers, 306 Chestnut Street [cop. 1886]. 256 p.    HEH, LC

1347 [CURTIS, CAROLINE GARDINER (CARY).] From Madge to Margaret. By Carroll Winchester [pseud.] . . . Boston: Lee and Shepard. New York: Charles T. Dillingham, 1880. 297 p.    BA, H, HEH, LC, O, Y
Development of a young married woman's character.

1348 [————] The Love of a Lifetime . . . Boston: Cupples, Upham and Company, 1884. 208 p.    BA, H, HEH, LC, O

1349 CURTIS, DAVID A. Queer Luck: Poker Stories from the New York Sun . . . New York: Brentano's, 1899. 235, [1] p.    H, HEH, LC, N, UVB, Y
*Contents:* Why He Quit the Game—Freeze-Out for a Life—A Gambler's Pistol Play—Queer Runs of Luck—Storms's Straight Flush—For a Senate Seat—The Bill Went Through—Poker for High Stakes—"Overland Jack"—His Last Sunday Game—Foss Stopped the Game—He Played for His Wife—The Club's Last Game.

1350 CURTIS, EMMA GHENT. The Administratrix . . . New York: John B. Alden, 1889. 373 p.    CU, LC

1351 ———— The Fate of a Fool . . . New York: John A. Berry & Company, 1888. 202 p.    HEH, LC
Of moral equality for the sexes.

1352 [CURTIS, GEORGE TICKNOR.] John Charáxes: A Tale of the Civil War in America. By Peter Boylston [pseud.]. Philadelphia: J. B. Lippincott Company, 1889. 289 p.    CU, H, HEH, LC, N, O, UC

CURTIS, WARDON ALLAN. Why the Reverend Edward Atkins Changed His Parish. *In* Hanks: Assorted Yarns from Puck (1893), No. 2444.

CUSHING, PAUL, *pseud. See* Wood-Seys, Roland Alexander

1353 [CUSTEAD, ELIZABETH.] Rose and Elza: Songs and Stories of Bygone Days in Fayette County and Elsewhere. By E. C——— . . . New York: Printed by Edward O. Jenkins' Sons [cop. 1882]. 596 p., front.
BU, HEH, LC
Deposited Aug. 25, 1884.

1354 CUTLER, HANNAH MARIA (CONANT) TRACY. Phillipia: A Woman's Question . . . Published by the Author. [Dwight, Ill.: C. L. Palmer Printing House, cop. 1886.] 183 p. HEH, LC, UC, Y

1355 CUTLER, JOHN ELWOOD. Every Man's Brother . . . [Sioux City, Ia., cop. 1891.] 220 p. LC
Deposited May 2, 1892.

1356 CUTLER, MARY C. Philip; or, What May Have Been. A Story of the First Century . . . New York: Thomas Y. Crowell & Co., 46 East Fourteenth Street [cop. 1890]. 237 p. AP, HEH, LC, O
New Testament scenes.

CUTTING, MARY STEWART (DOUBLEDAY). Fairy Gold. *In* Tales from McClure's: Humor (1897), No. 5361.

CZEIKA, *pseud. See* Furniss, Louise E.

D., M. A. *See* Denison, Mary (Andrews)

D., S. *See* Davieson, Sarah

D., S. E. *See* Douglas, Sarah E.

1357 DABNEY, JULIA PARKER. Little Daughter of the Sun . . . Boston: Roberts Brothers, 1896. 209 p., illus. H, HEH, O
Canary Islands about 1870.

1358 DABNEY, OWEN P. True Story of the Lost Shackle; or, Seven Years with the Indians . . . [Salem, Ore.: Capital Printing Co., cop. 1897.] 98 p., illus. BU, CU, LC, N, O, Y

1359 DABNEY, VIRGINIUS. Gold That Did Not Glitter: A Novel . . . Philadelphia: J. B. Lippincott Company, 1889. 254 p.
AP, CU, HEH, LC, N, O, UM, UV, Y
New York and Richmond.

——— A Mighty Hunter before the Lord. *In* C. King, Rancho del Muerto [cop. 1895], No. 3109.

1360 ——— The Story of Don Miff, as Told by His Friend John Bouche Whacker: A Symphony of Life. Edited by Virginius Dabney . . . Philadelphia: J. B. Lippincott Company, 1886. 492 p., illus.

AP, CU, H, HEH, O, UM, UP, UV

Virginia during the Civil War.

DAGGETT, MRS. CHARLES STEWART. *See* Daggett, Mary (Stewart)

1361 DAGGETT, MARY (STEWART). Mariposilla: A Novel. By Mrs. Charles Stewart Daggett. Chicago and New York: Rand, McNally & Company, 1895. 268 p. HEH, LC
San Gabriel Valley, California.

1362 DAGGETT, ROLLIN MALLORY. Braxton's Bar: A Tale of Pioneer Years in California . . . New York: G. W. Carleton & Co. London: S. Low, Son & Co., 1882. 453 p., illus. CU, H, HEH, LC, N
Mining.

1363 DAHLGREN, MADELEINE (VINTON). Chim, His Washington Winter . . . New York: Charles L. Webster & Co., 1892. 334 p., front. HEH, LC
Author's first name was Sarah.

1364 ——— Divorced: A Novel . . . Chicago and New York: Belford, Clarke & Co., 1887. 212 p. HEH, LC
Of too-easy divorce laws.

1365 ——— Lights and Shadows of a Life: A Novel . . . Boston: Ticknor and Company, 1887. 400 p. AP, CU, HEH, LC, N
Southern life; miscegenation.

1366 ——— The Lost Name: A Novelette . . . Boston: Ticknor and Company, 1886. 222 p. AP, CU, H, HEH, LC, O
Of the grandson of a French *émigré*.

1367 ——— The Secret Directory: A Romance of Hidden History . . . Philadelphia: H. L. Kilner & Co. [cop. 1896]. 330 p., illus. HEH, LC, UP
Of masonry.

1368 ——— A Washington Winter . . . Boston: James R. Osgood and Company, 1883. 247 p. AP, BA, H, HEH, LC, N, O, UC, UP, UVB, Y

1369 ——— The Woodley Lane Ghost, and Other Stories . . . Philadelphia: Drexel Biddle, 1899. 474 p., front. CU, HEH, O
*Also contains:* The Miser's Last Christmas—Who Was She?—My Dread Secret —The Amulet Ring—A Night's Adventure—A Sublime Sacrifice—A Reminiscence—Earth-Bound—The Fatal Boots—My First Patient—The Faithful Slave —A Murder Mystery—The Judge's Dream—Before the War—A Murillo—My Moufflon—Wilful Betty—How Not to Propose—The Trouble of a Double— His Plural Wives—The Poor Author—A Harmless Lunatic—Leap Year and Coincidence.

1370 DAIL, C. C. Willmoth the Wanderer; or, The Man from Saturn . . . [Atchison, Kan.: Haskell Printing Co., 1890.] 242 p., illus. HEH, LC Deposited Feb. 11, 1890.

1371 DAINTREY, LAURA. Actaeon . . . New York: The Empire City Publishing Company, 222 West 23rd Street [cop. 1892]. 280 p. LC Of New York's "four hundred."

1372 ———— The Arrows of Love . . . New York: G. W. Dillingham, 1893. 150 p. LC, N

1373 ———— Eros . . . Chicago, New York, and San Francisco: Belford, Clarke & Co. [cop. 1888]. 255 p. H, HEH, LC, Y Of the infidelity of a Wall Street broker's wife.

1374 ———— Fedor . . . New York: The Empire City Publishing Co. London: Sampson Low, Marston, Searle, and Rivington, Limited, 1889. 232 p. LC

1375 ———— Gold: A Novel . . . New York: G. W. Dillingham, 1893. 316 p. LC New York society.

1376 [————] Miss Varian of New York: A Newport and New York Society Novel. By ? New York: G. W. Dillingham, 1887. 372 p. LC

1377 DAKE, LAURA M. The Flight of the Shadow . . . Cincinnati, O.: The Editor Publishing Co., 1899. 128 p. LC Of the occult.

DALE, ALAN, pseud. See Cohen, Alfred J.

DALE, ANNAN, pseud. See Johnston, James Wesley

1378 DALLAS, MARY (KYLE). Adrietta; or, Her Grandfather's Heiress. A Novel . . . New York: Norman L. Munro, 1888. 220 p. H, LC

1379 ———— Billtry . . . New York: The Merriam Company, 67 Fifth Avenue [cop. 1895]. 133 p., illus. H, LC, Y

1380 ———— The Devil's Anvil . . . New York, Chicago, and San Francisco: Belford, Clarke and Company [cop. 1889]. 184 p. HEH Of an unhappy marriage.

1381 ———— The Grinder Papers: Being the Adventures of Miss Charity Grinder . . . While on a Visit to New York from the Country . . . New York: G. W. Carleton & Co.; Street & Smith, New York Weekly, 1877. 339 p., illus. CU, HEH, UC, UM, Y At head of title: " 'New York Weekly' Series."

1382 DALTON, EDITH LEVERETT. A Slight Romance . . . Boston: Damrell & Upham, 1896. 83 p.
H, LC

1383 DALY, JAMES. The Little Blind God on Rails: A Romaunt of the Gold Northwest . . . [Chicago: Rand, McNally & Co., cop. 1888.] 130 p., illus.
LC, Y
Of a trip on the Chicago & North-Western railroad.

1384 DAMON, SOPHIE M. (BUCKMAN). Old New-England Days: A Story of True Life . . . Boston: Cupples and Hurd, 1887. 434 p.
AP, CU, H, HEH, LC, O, Y

1385 DANA, FRANCIS. Leonora of the Yawmish: A Novel . . . New York: Harper & Brothers, 1897. 310 p.
HEH, LC, N, O, UC, UV, Y
Pacific Northwest.

1386 DANA, KATHARINE FLOYD. Our Phil, and Other Stories . . . Boston and New York: Houghton, Mifflin and Company. The Riverside Press, Cambridge, 1889. 147 p., illus.
AP, BA, CU, H, HEH, LC, N
Also contains: Aunt Rosy's Chest—Marty's Various Mercies.

1387 DANA, OLIVE E. Under Friendly Eaves . . . Augusta, Maine: Burleigh & Flynt, printers, 1894. 300 p.
HEH, LC

1388 DANDE, LEON, pseud. Blue Blood; or, White May and Black June . . . Boston: Henry L. Shepard & Co., 1877. 822 p., illus. CU, H, HEH, UC
Author may be A. F. Pillsbury, whose name is written on title page of a book-seller's copy.

DANDELYON, RITTER, pseud. See Brown, S. A.

DANFORTH, PARKE, pseud. See Talbot, Hannah Lincoln

1389 DANIEL, CHARLES S. AI: A Social Vision . . . Philadelphia: Miller Pub-lication Co., 1892. 296 p., 1 l.
AP, HEH, O, UP, Y
Utopian novel.

1390 DANIEL, ELOISE MATILDA. The Truth about It, and Other Sketches . . . St. Paul, Minn.: Dispatch Job Printing Company, 1897. 158 p. LC

1391 DANIELS, CORA LINN (MORRISON). As It Is to Be . . . Franklin, Mass.: Published by Cora Linn Daniels [cop. 1892]. 258 p., front. H, HEH, LC
Of spiritualism.

1392 ———— The Bronze Buddah: A Mystery . . . Boston: Little, Brown and Company, 1899. 295 p.
H, HEH, LC, O
New York.

1393 ———— Sardia: A Story of Love . . . Boston: Lee and Shepard. New York: Chas. T. Dillingham, 1891. 299 p.
HEH, N

1394 DANIELS, GERTRUDE POTTER. Halamar . . . Chicago, New York: George
M. Hill Company, 1900. 130 p. HEH, LC
Love story; New York.

1395 [DANIELS, MRS. IONE G.] A Social Conspiracy; or, Under the Ban. A
Novel. By Veen Iogo [pseud.] . . . [St. Paul: Geo. C. Pound, 1888.]
320 p., front. LC

DANZIGER, GUSTAV ADOLPH. *See* De Castro, Adolphe Danziger

1396 [D'APERY, HELEN (BURRELL).] A Fair Californian. By Olive Harper
[pseud.]. New York: The Minerva Publishing Company, 1889. 232 p.
HEH

DARE, ARLINE, *pseud. See* Boyden, Emma

1397 DARING DONALD McKAY; or, The Last War-Trail of the Modocs. The
Romance of the Life of Donald McKay, Government Scout, and Chief
of the Warm Spring Indians. Chicago: Rounds Brothers, printers and
engravers, 1881. 108 p., illus. HEH, LC, Y
On Y colored pictorial cover: "Second Edition."

1398 DARLING, MARY GREENLEAF. Gladys: A Romance . . . Boston: D. Lothrop Company, Franklin and Hawley Streets [cop. 1887]. 304 p.
H, HEH, LC, O, Y

Bar Harbor and Boston society.

1399 DARTON, ALICE WELDON (WASSERBACH). Hexandria. Written in the
Fond Hope of Pleasing My Dear Mother . . . Washington, D.C.: Path-
finder Publishing Company, 1894. 85 p., 1 l., front. LC
*Contains:* The Cause of It—The Professor's Skylarking—Death's Young—An
Easter King—A Quiver of Arrows—Rica's Eyes.

DASKAM, JOSEPHINE DODGE. *See* Bacon, Josephine Dodge (Daskam)

DAUGÉ, HENRI, *pseud. See* Hammond, Henrietta (Hardy)

1400 DAUGHTERS OF AESCULAPIUS: Stories Written by Alumnae and Students of
the Woman's Medical College of Pennsylvania, and Edited by a Committee Appointed by the Students' Association of the College. Philadelphia: George W. Jacobs & Co., 1897. 155 p., illus.
CU, HEH, LC, O, UC, UP

A collection of medical stories.

1401 DAVENPORT, BENJAMIN RUSH. Anglo-Saxons, Onward! A Romance of
the Future . . . Cleveland, Ohio, U.S.A.: Hubbell Publishing Company
[cop. 1898]. 279 p. LC

1402 DAVIDSON, MRS. DAN M. Alice Moon; or, A Brother's Crime . . . Detroit
Speaker Printing Company, 1898. 149 p., front. LC

Davies, Helen. *See* Tainter, Helen (Davies)

1403 [Davieson, Sarah.] The Seldens in Chicago: A Domestic Tale. By S. D. New York, Chicago, Washington, D.C., Paris: Brentanos, 1889. 189 p.
HEH, LC

1404 Davis, Arline E. The Romance of Guardamonte . . . New York: J. Selwin Tait & Sons, 65 Fifth Avenue [cop. 1896]. 136 p. LC
Of wealthy New Yorkers in Italy.

1405 Davis, Charles Belmont. The Borderland of Society . . . Chicago & New York: Herbert S. Stone & Co., 1898. 247 p., front.
H, HEH, LC, O, UC, UM, UP
*Contents:* The One Thing Needful—A Freak's Midsummer Night's Dream—La Gommeuse—Out of Her Class—A Friend of the Family—At a Café Chantant—The Story of His Life.

1406 Davis, Edith (Smith). Two, and Bits of Life . . . New York: Burr Printing House, 1888. 157 p. LC
*Also contains:* Sandy's Christmas—How Dick and Betty Were Educated—Harvest Home—Tot and Tim—Blossom's Message.

1407 ——— Whether White or Black, A Man . . . Chicago and New York, Toronto: Fleming H. Revell Company, 1898. 198, [1] p., illus. HEH, LC

1408 Davis, Ella Harding. Coranna: A Novel . . . St. Louis: Nixon-Jones Printing Co., 1890. 117 p. LC

1409 Davis, Ethel. When Love Is Done: A Novel . . . Boston: Estes and Lauriat, 1895. 301 p. H, HEH, LC, O, Y
In a New England town.

1410 Davis, Mrs. Frankie Parker. Kentucky Folks and Some Others . . . Cincinnati: The Editor Publishing Company, 1900. 233 p., illus.
BU, LC, UC

1411 [Davis, Frederick William.] Union Down: A Signal of Distress. By Scott Campbell [pseud.]. Boston: Arena Publishing Company, 1893. 368 p.
HEH, LC

1412 Davis, Garrett Morrow. Hugh Darnaby: A Story of Kentucky . . . Washington, D.C.: Gibson Bros., 1900. 253 p. LC, UC
Post Civil War.

1413 Davis, Harold McGill. The City of Endeavor: A Religious Novel Devoted to the Interests of Good Citizenship in the City of Brooklyn, N.Y. . . . Brooklyn, N.Y.: Collins & Day, printers, 1895. 98 p., front. LC

1414 Davis, Harriet Riddle. Gilbert Elgar's Son . . . New York, London: G. P. Putnam's Sons; the Knickerbocker Press, 1890. 450 p.
HEH, LC, N, O, UM, UV, Y
Of a Quaker family in Maryland.

1415 ———— In Sight of the Goddess: A Tale of Washington Life ... Philadelphia: J. B. Lippincott Company, 1896. 227 p., illus.   CU, HEH

1416 DAVIS, J. H.   The Possum Creek Poultry Club ... Chatham, N.Y.: The Fanciers' Review, 1895.   109 p., illus.   LC

1417 DAVIS, JOHN E.   Belleview: A Story of the South from 1860 to 1865 ... New York: John B. Alden, 1889.   349 p.   LC

1418 DAVIS, LEELA B.   Modern Argonaut ... San Francisco: Whitaker & Ray Co. [cop. 1896].   176 p.   HEH
Sacramento Valley.

1419 DAVIS, LEOPOLD.   Strange Occurrences ... Boston: Published for the author, 1877.   172 p.   H, HEH, LC
*Contents:* A Mystery Revealed—Two Souls Saved from Destruction—The Dead Killing the Living—How Near I Came to Seeing a Ghost—The Portrait of the Deceased—The Mysterious Call—A Detective's Story—Twenty Minutes between Life and Death—A Bad Omen—A Dream Realized—The Living Statue —Two Years in Darkness.

1420 DAVIS, MARTHA CAROLY.   The Refiner's Fire ... New York: J. Pott and Company, 1896.   303 p., front.   LC
How a widow educated two children.

1421 DAVIS, MRS. MARY DIUGUID.   She Waited Patiently ... Lynchburg, Va.: J. P. Bell Company, printers, 1900.   270 p.   LC, UV

1422 DAVIS, MARY EVELYN (MOORE).   An Elephant's Track, and Other Stories ... New York: Harper & Brothers, 1897.   276 p., illus.
CU, H, HEH, LC, O, UV

*Also contains:* A Snipe-Hunt—The Grovelling of Jinny Trimble—The Song of the Opal—At La Glorieuse—The Soul of Rose Dédé—A Miracle—At the Corner of Absinthe and Anisette—The Cloven Heart—A Heart-Leaf from Stony Creek Bottom—A Bamboula—Mr. Benjamin Franklin Gish's Ball—"The Centre Figger"—The "Zark"—The Love-Stranche.

1423 ———— The Queen's Garden ... Boston and New York: Houghton, Mifflin and Company.   The Riverside Press, Cambridge, 1900.   142 p., 1 l.   CU, H, HEH, LC, O, Y
Yellow fever epidemic in New Orleans.

1424 ———— Under the Man-Fig ... Boston and New York: Houghton, Mifflin and Company.   The Riverside Press, Cambridge, 1895.   323 p.
CU, HEH, LC, O
Civil War; Texas.

1425 ———— The Wire Cutters ... Boston and New York: Houghton, Mifflin and Company.   The Riverside Press, Cambridge, 1899.   373, [1] p.
CU, H, HEH, LC, O, UP, Y
Cattle ranges; Texas.

DAVIS, REBECCA (HARDING). Balacchi Brothers. *In* Stories by American Authors, I (1884), No. 5267.

1426 ——— Doctor Warrick's Daughters: A Novel ... New York: Harper & Brothers, 1896. 301 p., illus.

AP, BA, CU, H, HEH, LC, N, O, UC, UP, UVB, Y

1427 ——— Frances Waldeaux: A Novel . . . New York: Harper & Brothers, 1897. 207 p., illus. AP, CU, H, HEH, LC, N, O, UC, UP, UVB, Y

1428 ——— A Law unto Herself: A Novel ... Philadelphia: J. B. Lippincott & Co., 1878. 89 p. Printed in double columns. H, HEH, O, UP, UVB, Y

1429 ——— Silhouettes of American Life . . . New York: Charles Scribner's Sons, 1892. 280 p. BA, BU, CU, H, HEH, LC, N, O, UC, UM, UP, UVB, Y
*Contents:* At the Station—Tirar y Soult—Walhalla—The Doctor's Wife—Anne—An Ignoble Martyr—Across the Gulf—A Wayside Episode—Mademoiselle Joan—The End of the Vendetta—A Faded Leaf of History—The Yares of the Black Mountains—Marcia.

——— Tirar y Soult. *In* L. C. H. Langford, *comp.*, The Woman's Story (1889), No. 3206.
Later printed in Nos. 1429 and 5283.

1430 DAVIS, RICHARD HARDING. The Adventures of My Freshman: Sketches in Pen and Pencil . . . [Bethlehem, Pa.: Moravian Print, 1884.] 45 p., illus.
H, UVB, Y
*Contents:* Unappreciated Zeal—A Disciple of Theodore Hook's—Conway Maur as a Thespian—An Ass in Lion's Clothing—A Commencement Boomerang—A Midsummer Idyl.

1431 ——— Cinderella, and Other Stories . . . New York: Charles Scribner's Sons, 1896. 205 p., front.
AP, BA, BU, H, HEH, N, O, UC, UM, UVB, Y
*Also contains:* Miss Delamar's Understudy—The Editor's Story—An Assisted Emigrant—The Reporter Who Made Himself King.

1432 ——— Episodes in Van Bibber's Life . . . New York and London: Harper & Brothers, 1899. 98 p., front. CU, H, HEH, LC, Y
*Contents:* Her First Appearance—Van Bibber's Man-Servant—The Hungry Man Was Fed—Love Me, Love My Dog.
Contents printed earlier in No. 1439.

1433 ——— The Exiles, and Other Stories . . . New York: Harper & Brothers, 1894. 221 p., illus. AP, BA, H, HEH, LC, N, O, UC, UP, UVB, Y
*Also contains:* The Writing on the Wall—The Right of Way—His Bad Angel—The Boy Orator of Zepata City—The Romance in the Life of Hefty Burke—An Anonymous Letter.

1434 ——— Gallegher, and Other Stories . . . New York: Charles Scribner's Sons, 1891. 236 p.     AP, BA, CU, H, HEH, LC, N, O, UM, UVB, Y
*Also contains:* A Walk up the Avenue—My Disreputable Friend, Mr. Raegen—The Other Woman—The Trailer for Room No. 8—"There Were Ninety and Nine"—The Cynical Miss Catherwaight—Van Bibber and the Swan-Boats—Van Bibber's Burglar—Van Bibber as Best Man.

1435 ——— The King's Jackal . . . New York: Charles Scribner's Sons, 1898. 175 p., illus.     AP, BA, BU, CU, H, HEH, LC, N, O, UM, UVB, Y

1436 ——— The Lion and the Unicorn . . . New York: Charles Scribner's Sons, 1899. 204 p., illus.     BA, CU, H, HEH, LC, N, UP, UVB, Y
*Also contains:* On the Fever Ship—The Man with One Talent—The Vagrant—The Last Ride Together.

1437 ——— The Princess Aline . . . New York: Harper & Brothers, 1895. 163 p., illus.     AP, BA, BU, CU, H, HEH, O, UP, UVB, Y

1438 ——— Soldiers of Fortune . . . New York: Charles Scribner's Sons, 1897. 364 p., illus.     AP, H, HEH, O, UVB, Y

1439 ——— Van Bibber, and Others . . . New York: Harper & Brothers, 1892. 249 p., illus.     AP, CU, H, HEH, N, O, UC, UP, UVB, Y
*Contents:* Her First Appearance—Van Bibber's Man-Servant—The Hungry Man Was Fed—Van Bibber at the Races—An Experiment in Economy—Mr. Travers's First Hunt—Love Me, Love My Dog—Eleanore Cuyler—A Recruit at Christmas—A Patron of Art—Andy M'Gee's Chorus Girl—A Leander of the East River—How Hefty Burke Got Even—Outside the Prison—An Unfinished Story.

1440 [DAVIS, ROBERT S.] As It May Happen: A Story of American Life and Character. By Trebor [pseud.] . . . Philadelphia: Porter & Coates [cop. 1879, i.e., 1878.]. 416 p.     CU, H, HEH, LC, UC, UM, Y
LC copy has registration stamp dated 1878; printed copyright date of 1879 corrected in hand to 1878.

1441 DAVIS, SAMUEL POST. The Great Free-for-All . . . San Francisco: Golden Era Company, 1886.
Listed in Hinkel.

1442 ——— Short Stories . . . San Francisco, Cal.: Golden Era Company, 1886. 189, [1] p.     HEH
*Contains:* A Christmas Carol—Pine Nutmeg and Bass-Wood Hams—The Pocket-Miner—Miss Armstrong's Homicide—The Hermit of Treasure Peaks—A Carson Poker Incident—A Fair Exchange—Mark Haverly—The Reporter's Revenge—A Sage-Brush Chief—A Day with Bill Nye—The Parish Primaries—The Typographical Howitzer—A Stock Chapter—The Candidate's Diary—The Circus Advance Agent—The Quill Driver's Council.
BAL 3644 notes "The Typographical Howitzer" is by S. L. Clemens.

1443  DAVIS, VARINA ANNE JEFFERSON.  A Romance of Summer Seas: A Novel
      . . . New York and London: Harper & Brothers, 1898.  277, [1] p.
                                        BA, HEH, LC, N, O, UM, UV, Y

1444  ———— The Veiled Doctor: A Novel . . .  New York: Harper &
      Brothers, 1895.  220 p.        CU, H, HEH, LC, O, UC, UM, UVB, Y

1445  DAVIS, W. E.  Ziba Foote; or, "Foote's Grave Pond," And Other Stories,
      Being True Tales from the Short and Simple Annals of the Poor . . .
      [New Vienna, Ohio]: Published for the author, 1877.  241 p.
                                        N, O, UVB, Y
      *Also contains:* The Country Cousins—Ethel Hayes—Lillian Grey—Horace
      Stephens—Millbank.

1446  DAVIS, WASHINGTON.  Shut the Gate: An American Social Study.  A
      Novel . . . New York: The American News Company, 1889.  268 p.
                                                              LC
      Ashley W. Cole, jt. au.

1447  DAVIS, WILLIAM STEARNS.  A Friend of Caesar: A Tale of the Fall of the
      Roman Republic, Time, 50-47 B.C. . . . New York: The Macmillan
      Company.  London: Macmillan & Co., Ltd. 1900.  501 p.
                                        AP, H, HEH, O, UC, UM, UV, Y

      DAVISON, CHARLES STEWART.  How I Sent My Aunt to Baltimore.  *In*
      Stories of the Railway (1893), No. 5281.

1448  DAWS, MAUD.  Crankadom . . . Lincoln, Neb.: Jacob North & Co.,
      printers, 1895.  149 p.                                 LC

1449  DAWSON, EMMA FRANCES.  An Itinerant House, and Other Stories . . .
      San Francisco: William Doxey, 1897.  320 p., illus.
                                        BU, H, HEH, LC, UM, UV, Y
      *Also contains:* Singed Moths—A Stray Reveler—The Night before the Wed-
      ding—The Dramatic in My Destiny—A Gracious Visitation—A Sworn State-
      ment—"The Second Card Wins"—In Silver upon Purple—"Are the Dead
      Dead?"

1450  [DAY, ALBERT A.]  The Mysterious Beggar: A Novel Founded on Facts
      . . . New York: J. S. Ogilvie, 57 Rose Street [cop. 1891].  450 p., illus.
                                                              LC

1451  [DAY, MRS. MAIE DOVE.]  Virginia, Prehistoric and Antebellum.  [Dan-
      ville, Va.: Press of Dance Brothers Company, 1899.]  119 p.    LC, UV

1452  DEAN, FREDERIC ALVA.  The Heroines of Petoséga: A Novel . . .  New
      York: The Hawthorne Publishing Company, 1889.  283 p.  HEH, LC, UP
      Upper Michigan thirty centuries ago.

1453  DEAN, TERESA H.  Reveries of a Widow . . . New York: Town Topics
      Publishing Co., 1899.  238 p.                 HEH, LC, UM, Y

Dearborn, Laura, *pseud.* *See* Picton, Nina

Debby, *Aunt, pseud.* *See* Osborn, Mrs. Peter E.

De Castro, Adolphe Danziger, *jt. au.* *See* Bierce, A. The Monk and the Hangman's Daughter (1892), No. 524.

1454 [Decon, Thomas William.] The Experiences of an Englishman in Philadelphia Society. As Related by Himself and Set Down by Raconteur [pseud.]. [Philadelphia], cop. 1887. 32 p.    LC, O, Y

1455 De Cordova, Rafael. Mrs. Fizzlebury's New Girl: A Truly Domestic Story... New York: G. W. Carleton & Co., 1878. 160 p., illus.   LC
New York.

1456 De Cou, May Allis. Destiny: A Tale of the Mississippi... Cincinnati: The Editor Publishing Co., 1898. 305 p.    HEH

1457 De Forest, John William. The Bloody Chasm: A Novel... New York: D. Appleton and Company, 1881. 301 p.
AP, BA, BU, CU, HEH, LC, N, O, UC, UVB, Y
Also published as: *The Oddest of Courtships; or, The Bloody Chasm.* New York: D. Appleton and Company, 1882.   LC
Reconstruction; South Carolina.

——— The Brigade Commander. *In* Stories by American Authors, VIII (1884), No. 5274.

——— An Inspired Lobbyist. *In* Stories by American Authors, IV (1884), No. 5270.

1458 [———] Irene the Missionary. Boston: Roberts Brothers, 1879. 390 p.
BA, H, O, UVB, Y
Syria.

1459 [———] Justine's Lovers: A Novel. New York: Harper & Brothers, 1878. 135 p. Printed in double columns.   HEH, LC, UVB, Y
Washington, D.C.

1460 ——— A Lover's Revolt... New York, London, and Bombay: Longmans, Green and Co., 1898. 417 p., front.   BA, CU, H, LC, O, UM, UVB, Y
American Revolution.

——— A Strange Arrival. *In* [W. F. Gill] *ed.,* Laurel Leaves (1876), No. 2167.

1461 De Kay, Charles. The Bohemian: A Tragedy of Modern Life... New York: Charles Scribner's Sons, 743 & 745 Broadway [cop. 1878]. 107 p.
BU, H, HEH, LC, N, O, UP, UVB, Y
New York society.

———— Manmat'ha. *In* Stories by American Authors, X (1885), No. 5276.

1462 DE KOVEN, ANNA (FARWELL). A Sawdust Doll ... Chicago: Stone and Kimball, 1895. 237 p., 1 l.      BA, H, HEH, N, O, UC, UP, UV
Washington Square, New York, society.

DE KOVEN, REGINALD, *jt. au. See* Chatfield-Taylor, H. C. The Idle Born (1900), No. 996.

1463 DE KROYFT, SUSAN HELEN (ALDRICH). Mortara... Cambridge: Printed at the Riverside Press, 1887. 129 p.      LC
Written as a series of letters.

1464 DE LA HOUSSAYE, SIDONIE. Amis et Fortune . . . Bonnet Carré, La.: Imprimerie du Meschacébé, 1893. 558 p.      LC, Y
At head of title: "Roman Louisianais."
Deposited Mar. 12, 1894; printed copyright notice on title page dated 1892.

1465 ———— Pouponne et Balthazar: Nouvelle Acadienne . . . Nouvelle-Orleans: Librairie de l'Opinion, 1888. 217 p.      CU, LC, UM, UVB, Y

1466 DELAND, MARGARET WADE (CAMPBELL). Good for the Soul ... New York and London: Harper & Brothers, 1899. 86 p., front.
CU, H, HEH, LC, UC, UM, Y
First separate printing; printed earlier in No. 1469.

1467 ———— John Ward, Preacher... Boston and New York: Houghton, Mifflin and Company. The Riverside Press, Cambridge, 1888. 473 p.
AP, BA, CU, H, HEH, LC, O, UC, UM, UP, UV, Y
Of a strict Calvinist.

1468 ———— Mr. Tommy Dove, and Other Stories . . . Boston and New York: Houghton, Mifflin and Company. The Riverside Press, Cambridge, 1893. 280 p.      AP, BA, CU, H, HEH, LC, O, UC, UM, UP, Y
*Also contains:* The Face on the Wall—Elizabeth—At Whose Door?—A Fourth-Class Appointment.

1469 ———— Old Chester Tales . . . New York and London: Harper & Brothers, 1899. 359, [1] p., illus.      H, HEH, N, O, UV, Y
*Contents:* The Promises of Dorothea—Good for the Soul—Miss Maria—The Child's Mother—Justice and the Judge—Where the Laborers Are Few—Sally—The Unexpectedness of Mr. Horace Shields.

1470 ———— Philip and His Wife . . . Boston and New York: Houghton, Mifflin and Company. The Riverside Press, Cambridge, 1894. 438 p.
BA, CU, H, HEH, N, O, UC, UM, UP, UV, Y
Of the divorce question.

1471 —— Sidney ... Boston and New York: Houghton, Mifflin and Company. The Riverside Press, Cambridge, 1890. 429 p.
AP, BA, BU, CU, H, HEH, LC, N, O, UC, UM, UP, UVB, Y

1472 —— The Story of a Child ... Boston and New York: Houghton, Mifflin and Company. The Riverside Press, Cambridge, 1892. 226 p.
BA, BU, CU, H, HEH, LC, N, O, UC, UM, UP, Y

1473 —— The Wisdom of Fools ... Boston and New York: Houghton, Mifflin and Company, 1897. 248, p., 1 l.
AP, BA, CU, H, HEH, LC, O, UC, UM, UP, UV, Y
*Contents:* Where Ignorance Is Bliss, 't Is Folly to Be Wise—The House of Rimmon—Counting the Cost—The Law, or the Gospel?

1474 DE LEON, STUART. Bera; or, The C. and M. C. Railroad ... New York: The Authors' Publishing Company, Bond Street [cop. 1879]. 169 p.
LC

1475 DE LEON, THOMAS COOPER. Crag-Nest: A Romance of the Days of Sheridan's Ride ... Mobile, Ala.: The Gossip Printing Co., 1897. 220 p.
CU, LC, UM

1476 —— John Holden, Unionist: A Romance of the Days of Destruction and Reconstruction ... in Collaboration with Erwin Ledyard ... St. Paul: The Price-McGill Company, 455-473 Cedar Street [cop. 1893]. 338 p., illus.
BU, CU, N, O, UM, Y

1477 —— Juny; or, Only One Girl's Story. A Romance of the Society Crust—Upper and Under ... Mobile, Ala.: The Gossip Printing Company, 1890. 271 p.
LC
Also published as: *Juny; or, Only One Octoroon's Story. A Romance of the Society Crust.* St. Paul: The Price-McGill Company, 455-473 Cedar Street [1893]. 273 p., illus. HEH

1478 —— The Pride of the Mercers ... Philadelphia: J. B. Lippincott Company, 1898. 368 p.
LC
Post Civil War; Louisiana.

1479 —— The Puritan's Daughter <Sequel to "Creole and Puritan">. A Character Romance of Two Sections ... Mobile, Ala.: The Gossip Printing Company, 1891. 173 p.
HEH, LC, UM

1480 [——] The Rock or the Rye: An Understudy. After "The Quick or the Dead" ... Mobile: Gossip Printing Company, 1888. 34 p.
H, HEH, LC, UV

1481 [——] Schooners That Bump on the Bar: An Automatic Tow from "Ships That Pass in the Night" ... Mobile, Ala.: Gossip Printing Company, 1894. 79 p., illus.
LC

1482 [———] Society as I Have Foundered It; or, The Microscopic Metropolitan Menu-Manipulator Marvellously Money-Magnetized. By Cad
McBallastir [pseud.] ... Mobile, Ala.: The Gossip Printing Company,
1890. 73 p., illus.                                    CU, H, HEH, LC, UM, Y

1483 DE LESTRY, EDMOND LOUIS. Leaves from a Note Book: A Collection of
Miscellaneous Short Stories ... Special Limited Edition. St. Paul,
Minn., 1897. 72 p., front.                                            LC
*Contents:* The Story of a Ring—Alma: A Tale of Little Russia—The Tale of the
Singing River—A Christmas under Ground—The Sod House on the Plains—
The Walking Ghost Mine—How Dave Became a Millionaire—Sister Felicia.

DE LESTRY, LOUIS. *See* De Lestry, Edmond Louis

1484 DEMENT, ISAAC STRANGE. Baron Kinatas: A Tale of the Anti-Christ ...
Chicago: M. T. Need, 1894. 367 p.                                    LC

1485 DEMENT, RICHMOND SHEFFIELD. Ronbar: A Counterfeit Presentment
... New York: G. W. Dillingham, 1895. 257 p.                    LC, UM

1486 DEMETRAK, CHARLES. The Unfortunate Merchant and Experiences of
Drummers ... Berkeley, California: [World Publishing Co.], 1898.
103 p., illus.                                                      HEH

1487 DEMING, PHILANDER. Adirondack Stories ... Boston: Houghton, Os-
good and Company. The Riverside Press, Cambridge, 1880. 192 p.
                                    AP, BA, HEH, LC, N, O, UC, UM, UVB, Y
*Contents:* Lost—Lida Ann—John's Trial—Joe Baldwin—Willie—Benjamin
Jacques—Ike's Wife—An Adirondack Neighborhood.

——— John's Trial. *In* I. Bacheller, *ed.*, Best Things from American
Literature (1899), No. 195.
Printed earlier in No. 1487.

1488 ——— Tompkins, and Other Folks: Stories of the Hudson and the
Adirondacks ... Boston, New York: Houghton, Mifflin and Company.
The Riverside Press, Cambridge, 1885. 223 p.
                                    BA, BU, CU, H, HEH, LC, O, UM, UVB
*Also contains:* Rube Jones—Jacob's Insurance—Mr. Toby's Wedding Journey—
Hattie's Romance—The Court in Schoharie—An Adirondack Home.

1489 [DENISON, CHARLES WHEELER.] The Child-Hunters. By a Friend of
Italy ... Philadelphia: Claxton, Remsen, & Haffelfinger, 1877. 188 p.,
illus.                                                               LC

1490 DENISON, MARY (ANDREWS). Captain Molly: A Love Story ... Boston:
Lee and Shepard, 1897. 251 p.                              HEH, LC, O, Y
Of the Salvation Army; New York.

1491   [———]  Cracker Joe. Boston: Roberts Brothers, 1887.  322 p.
                                                           CU, HEH, LC, O
    At head of title: "No Name Series."
    Post Civil War; Florida.

1492   ———  Erin Go Bragh! . . . Washington, D.C.: Globe Printing and
    Publishing House, 1879.  354 p.                          LC

1493   ———  Ethel's Triumph: From Fifteen to Twenty-Five . . . Boston:
    Bradley & Woodruff [cop. 1890].  422 p., front.          HEH, LC

1494   ———  Grandmother Normandy . . . Boston: D. Lothrop and Com-
    pany [cop. 1882].  264 p.                           LC

1495   ———  His Triumph . . . Boston: Lee and Shepard. New York:
    Charles T. Dillingham, 1883.  248 p.         H, HEH, LC, Y
    Of the stage.

1496   ———  How She Helped Him . . . Boston: Ira Bradley & Co., 1889.
    212 p.                                         LC

1497   ———  If She Will She Will . . . Boston: Lee and Shepard. New
    York: Charles T. Dillingham, 1891.  351 p.         HEH

1498   [———]  Like a Gentleman. Boston: Lee and Shepard. New York:
    Charles T. Dillingham, 1882.  213 p.          HEH, LC

1499   [———]  Mr. Peter Crewitt . . . Boston: Lee and Shepard. New
    York: Charles T. Dillingham, 1878.  221 p.      HEH, LC, UVB

1500   ———  Old Slip Warehouse: A Novel . . . New York: Harper &
    Brothers, 1878.  145 p.  Printed in double columns.
                                           HEH, LC, O, UP, UV

1501   [———]  Rothmell . . . Boston: Lee and Shepard. New York:
    Charles T. Dillingham, 1878.  371 p.         H, HEH

1502   [———]  Sequel to Opposite the Jail; or, On Trial for His Life. By
    M. A. D. . . . Boston: Ira Bradley & Co., 162 Washington Street [cop.
    1883].  279 p., illus.                      HEH, LC
    For *Opposite the Jail* see Wright II, No. 731.

1503   [———]  Tell Your Wife. Boston: Lee & Shepard. New York:
    Charles T. Dillingham, 1886.  248 p.          HEH, LC

1504   [———]  That Husband of Mine. Boston: Lee and Shepard. New
    York: Charles T. Dillingham, 1877.  227 p.    BA, BU, CU, H, HEH, Y

1505   [———]  That Wife of Mine . . . Boston: Lee and Shepard. New
    York: Charles T. Dillingham, 1877.  228 p.
                                    BA, BU, CU, HEH, LC, N, O, UC, UVB

1506 [DENISON, THOMAS STEWART.] An Iron Crown: A Tale of the Great Republic ... Chicago: T. S. Denison [cop. 1885]. 560 p.
BU, HEH, LC, N, O, UC
Of the power of early railway monopolies.

1507 —— The Man Behind: A Novel ... Chicago: T. S. Denison, 163 Randolph Street [cop. 1888]. 311 p.                    O
The Southwest.

1508 —— My Invisible Partner ... Chicago and New York: Rand, McNally & Company [cop. 1898]. 231 p.                   LC
Mining; New Mexico.

1509 DENNIS, JAMES HOGARTH. Andrew: A Romance of Conesus Lake ... Rochester, N.Y.: Sunday Herald Printing Company, 1886. 165 p., illus.                                                          LC

1510 —— The Wooden Bottle ... Rochester, N.Y.: R. H. Dennis, 1887. 172 p., illus.                                            LC

1511 DENTON, LYMAN W. Under the Magnolias ... New York, London: Funk & Wagnalls, 1888. 317 p.                   LC, O, UM
To show the degradation of the southern Negro.

1512 DENTON, WILLIAM. Garrison in Heaven: A Dream ... Wellesley, Mass.: Denton Publishing Company, 1882. 45 p.           BU, HEH
LC has copy dated 1884 on title page and 1882 on cover.
William L. Garrison and Denton decide to reform Heaven.

1513 DERBY, ALECK. Ida Goldwin; or, The Perils of Fortune ... New York: Robert M. De Witt, 1876. 323 p.                 HEH, LC
New York.

DE SELINCOURT, ANNE DOUGLAS (SEDGWICK). See Sedgwick, Anne Douglas

1514 DESLONDE, MRS. MARIA DARRINGTON. John Maribel: A Novel ... New York: G. W. Carleton & Co. London: S. Low Co., 1877. 412 p.
Copy examined at New York Public Library.
Note on LC card: "Published in 1882 under title: My Heart's Content." Not found.

1515 DESPARD, MATILDA (PRATT). Kilrogan Cottage: A Novel ... New York: Harper & Brothers, 1878. 143 p. Printed in double columns.
AP, H, HEH, LC, O, UV

1516 DESSAR, LEO CHARLES. A Royal Enchantress: The Romance of the Last Queen of the Berbers ... New York: Continental Publishing Co., 1900. 350 p., illus.                                          HEH, LC, Y
Northern Africa, 7th century.

1517 DESSOMMES, GEORGE. Tante Cydette: Nouvelle Louisianaise . . . Nouvelle-Orléans: Imprimerie Franco-Américaine, 1888. 176 p.   Y

DE VALLIÉRE, GEORGE, *pseud. See* Duysters, George F.

[DE VERE, MARY AINGE.] Misther Handhrigan's Love Story, by Madeline S. Bridges [pseud.]. *In* Mavericks (1892), No. 3663.

[————] A Prairie Blossom, by Madeline S. Bridges [pseud.]. *In* Hanks: Assorted Yarns from Puck (1893), No. 2444.

1518 DEVEREUX, MARY. Betty Peach: A Tale of Colonial Days . . . Marblehead [Mass.]: Merrill H. Graves, 1896. 144 p.   HEH, LC
Author's full name: Mary Devereux Watson.

1519 ———— From Kingdom to Colony . . . Boston: Little, Brown and Company, 1899. 382 p., illus.   H, LC, O

DE VILLENEUVE, LOUIS, *pseud. See* Gibbons, Louise Elise

1520 DE VLIEGER, CON, JR. The Devil's Reception Room . . . Grand Haven, Mich.: Con De Vlieger, Jr. [cop. 1896]. 261 p., front.   LC

1521 DEVOORE, ANN. Oliver Iverson: His Adventures during Four Days and Nights in the City of New York in April of the Year 1890 . . . Chicago and New York: Herbert S. Stone and Company, 1899. 181 p., front.
CU, HEH, LC, N, UM, UVB, Y

———— The Whip-Hand. *In* Tales from McClure's: Romance (1897), No. 5362.

1522 DEWEY, BYRD SPILMAN. Bruno . . . Boston: Little, Brown and Company, 1899. 116 p.   HEH
Of a married couple and their dog.

1523 DE WITT, JULIA A. WOODHULL. Life's Battle Won . . . New York: Hunt & Eaton. Cincinnati: Cranston & Curts, 1893. 372 p., illus. LC
Of religious interest; Civil War background.

1524 DIAZ, ABBY (MORTON). Bybury to Beacon Street . . . Boston: D. Lothrop Company, Franklin and Hawley Streets [cop. 1887]. 276 p.
AP, BA, H, HEH, LC, O
Nearly all of her books were for young people.

DICK, HERBERT G., *pseud. See* Morgan, Carrie A.

1525 [DICKINSON, EDITH MAY.] So Runs the World Away: A Novel. By Ansley May [pseud. of E. M. Dickinson and Edward Ansley Stokes]. New York: G. W. Dillingham, 1891. 314 p.   LC
New England farm girl marries an Englishman and moves to London.

1526 DICKINSON, MRS. ELLEN E. The King's Daughters: A Fascinating Romance... Philadelphia: Hubbard Brothers, 1888. 275 p. LC
Also published as: *The King's Daughters: A Charming Story*. Philadelphia, Hubbard Brothers, 1888. CU, HEH
Of a woman's organization, The King's Daughters.

———— *jt. au.* See Dickinson, J. A Winter Picnic (1888), No. 1527.

1527 DICKINSON, J. A Winter Picnic: The Story of a Four Months' Outing in Nassau, Told in the Letters, Journals, and Talk of Four Picnicers. By J. and E. E. Dickinson and S. E. Dowd. New York: Henry Holt and Company, 1888, 265 p. AP, BA, H, HEH, LC, O, Y
At head of title: "Leisure Hour Series—No. 216."

1528 DICKINSON, MARY (LOWE). Among the Thorns: A Novel . . . New York: G. W. Carleton & Co. London: S. Low, Son & Co., 1880. 430 p.
H, HEH, LC, O, Y
North and South before the war.

1529 ———— Spring Blossoms: An Easter Story ... Philadelphia: Charles H. Banes, 1420 Chestnut St. [cop. 1895]. 54 p., illus. BU, LC

1530 ———— The Temptation of Katharine Gray . . . Philadelphia: A. J. Rowland, 1895. 380 p., front. H, HEH, LC
Of mother-love domination.

1531 DICKSON, CAPERS. John Ashton: A Story of the War between the States ... Atlanta, Ga.: The Foote & Davies Company, printers and binders, 1896. 279 p. CU, H, HEH, LC, UM, UV

1532 DICKSON, HARRIS. The Black Wolf's Breed: A Story of France in the Old World and the New, Happening in the Reign of Louis XIV ... Indianapolis: The Bowen-Merrill Company [cop. 1899]. 288 p., illus.
H, HEH, LC, O, UM, Y
DIDAMA, *pseud.* See White, Mrs. Betsey Ann

1533 DIDIER, CHARLES PEALE. The Exhibits in an Attachment Suit ... Baltimore: Press of Jno. H. Williams Company, 1896. 21 l. H, LC
Facsimiles of notes, telegrams, and newspaper clippings comprising a love story.

1534 ———— R. S. V. P.: A Novelette ... Baltimore: Williams & Wilkins Company [cop. 1897]. 34 p., illus. LC

1535 ———— Would Any Man? ... [Baltimore]: Williams & Wilkins Company, 1898. 169 p., illus. LC

DIDWIN, ISAAC, *pseud.* See Sturdy, William Allen

1536 DIEKENGA, INJE EILDERT. Between Times; or, Tales, Sketches, and Poems ... Boston: James H. Earle, 1882. 232 p. BU, LC
Contains: Beatrice Caramino–Dopps–Simeon Snuffly–The Old Cathedral–Ben Sickles–Sketches.

1537 ——— Daniel Poldertot: A Story Wherein Is Carefully Recorded the Interesting Adventures of Uncle Dan and His Faithful Friends, Mr. Robert Sturdy, Mr. Harry Cribbler, and Mr. Richard Doolittle ... Boston: J. H. Earle, 1882. 348 p., illus. HEH, LC
St. Louis.

1538 ——— Jasper Groales, and His Wonderful Journeys on Christmas Eve ... [Chicago: Goodman & Dickerson, cop. 1880.] Caption title, 24 p. Printed in triple columns. LC

1539 DIEUDONNÉ, FLORENCE (CARPENTER). Katherine: A Novel ... Washington, D.C.: W. J. Brewer [cop. 1898]. 214 p., illus. LC

1540 ——— Rondah; or, Thirty-Three Years in a Star ... Philadelphia: T. B. Peterson & Brothers, 306 Chestnut Street [cop. 1887]. 230 p. LC

1541 ——— Xartella ... Washington: Press of Gedney & Roberts [cop. 1891]. 28 p. LC

1542 ——— Zardec ... [Minneapolis]: Published by the author, 1885. 558 p., illus. HEH, LC

1543 DILLINGHAM, LUCY. The Missing Chord: A Novel ... New York: G. W. Dillingham, 1894. 206 p. CU, LC

1544 DILTZ, HANSON PENN. The Duchesse Undine; or, Slain by a Woman's Lie ... Philadelphia: T. B. Peterson & Brothers, 306 Chestnut Street [cop. 1883]. 454 p. LC, UC

1545 [DISOSWAY, ELLA TAYLOR.] The Grey Guest Chamber ... West New Brighton, S. I. [Staten Island]: Advance Steam Printing House, No. 72 Broadway [cop. 1888]. Cover title, 112 p. H, LC

1546 DITSON, LINA BARTLETT. The Soul and the Hammer: A Tale of Paris ... New York: Godfrey A. S. Wieners, 1900. 372 p. HEH, LC

DITTA, pseud. See Pengilly, Mrs. Ida E.

1547 DITTENHOEFER, MORTIMER A. A Dowie Elder ... Mansfield, Ohio: The News Printery, 1900. 63, [1] p., front. LC

1548 DIX, BURTON W. The Satin Tie: Being a Story of the Inner Life of the Civil War, Based upon Incidents Which Occurred during the Great Strife ... Carbondale, Pa., 1889. 406 p. HEH, LC

1549 DIX, EDWIN ASA. Deacon Bradbury: A Novel ... New York: The Century Co., 1900. 288 p.              H, HEH, LC, O, UV, Y
Religion in New England.

1550 DIX, GERTRUDE. The Girl from the Farm ... Boston: Roberts Bros. London: John Lane, 1895. 208 p.            BU, CU, LC, UC

1551 ———— The Image Breakers ... New York: Frederick A. Stokes Company [cop. 1900]. 392 p.           HEH, LC, O, UV
Of socialism.

1552 [DIXON, SAMUEL HOUSTON.] Robert Warren, the Texan Refugee: A Thrilling Story of the Lone Star State during the Late Civil War. Philadelphia: John E. Potter and Company, 617 Sansom Street [cop. 1879]. 568 p.            N, UV, Y
Sometime between 1880 and 1885 the same publisher reissued this with title: *Robert Warren, the Texan Refugee: A Thrilling Story of Field and Camp Life during the Late Civil War.* HEH, UC

1553 DOD, SAMUEL BAYARD. A Highland Chronicle ... New York: Dodd, Mead & Company, 1892. 290 p.           HEH, O, UV

1554 ———— A Hillside Parish ... New York: Dodd, Mead & Company, 1893. 269 p.          CU, HEH, LC
Clintonville, N.Y.

1555 ———— Stubble or Wheat? A Story of More Lives Than One ... New York: Anson D. F. Randolph & Company, 38 West Twenty-Third Street [cop. 1888]. 264 p.          HEH, LC, O
Of a Princeton graduate.

1556 DODD, ANNA BOWMAN (BLAKE). Glorinda: A Story ... Boston: Roberts Brothers, 1888. 293 p.         AP, BA, H, HEH, LC, O
Post Civil War; Kentucky.

1557 ———— The Republic of the Future; or, Socialism a Reality ... New York: Cassell & Company, Limited, 739 & 741 Broadway [cop. 1887]. 86 p.        BU, CU, H, N, O, UC, UM, UP, Y
New York 200 years hence.

1558 ———— Struthers, and The Comedy of the Masked Musicians ... New York: Lovell, Coryell & Company, 310-318 Sixth Avenue [cop. 1894]. 312 p.          HEH, LC, O

1559 DODGE, CHARLES RICHARDS. Louise and I: A Sea-Side Story ... New York: G. W. Carleton & Co. London: S. Low, Son & Co., 1879. 285 p.          HEH, LC

1560 [DODGE, LOUISE PRESTON.] A Question of Identity ... Boston: Roberts Brothers, 1887. 271 p.          HEH, LC, UV, Y
At head of title: "No Name Series."
Of twin sisters.

———— *jt. au. See* Preston, H. W. The Guardians (1888), No. 4377.

1561 [DODGE, MARY ABIGAIL.] First Love Is Best: A Sentimental Sketch. By Gail Hamilton [pseud.] . . . Boston: Estes and Lauriat, 1877. 305 p.
BA, CU, H, HEH, LC, O, UC, UM, UVB, Y

1562 DODGE, WALTER PHELPS. Three Greek Tales . . . New York: Geo. M. Allen Company, 1893. 173 p. HEH, UM, Y
*Contents:* Angelica and the Hermes—Marika—The Arrows of Heracles.

1563 DOE, WILLIAM D. Who Stole the Widow Snow's Thanksgiving Dinner? A Love Story . . . Belfast, Me.: Age Job Print, 1890. 16 p.
Listed in Williamson, No. 2879.

1564 DOGGETT, SOLON. Jumping Judas . . . Boston: B. B. Russell, 1896. 189 p., illus. LC
At head of title: "Solon Doggett's Novels."

1565 ———— Victims of Mammon . . . Boston: B. B. Russell, 1897. 184 p., front. HEH, LC
At head of title: "Solon Doggett's Novels."

1566 "DOING" NEW-YORK; or, Midnight Adventures of a D.D. . . . New York: Collin & Co., 1878. 62 p., illus. CU, H, LC

1567 [DOISSY, LOUISE.] A Business Venture in Los Angeles; or, A Christian Optimist. By Z. Z. [pseud.] . . . Cincinnati: The Robert Clarke Company, 1899. 243 p., illus. CU, HEH, LC

1568 DOLE, EDMUND PEARSON. Hiwa: A Tale of Ancient Hawaii . . . New York and London: Harper & Brothers, 1900. 107, [1] p.
BU, CU, H, HEH, LC, N, O, UM, Y

1569 ———— The Stand-By . . . New York: The Century Co., 1897. 228 p.
BU, CU, HEH, LC, O, Y
Temperance and prohibition.

1570 DOLE, NATHAN HASKELL. Not Angels Quite . . . Boston: Lee and Shepard, 1893. 327 p. H, HEH, LC, O

1571 ———— Omar, the Tentmaker: A Romance of Old Persia . . . Boston: L. C. Page and Company (Incorporated), 1899. 365 p., illus.
BA, H, HEH, LC, O, UC, Y

1572 ———— On the Point: A Summer Idyl . . . Boston: Joseph Knight Company, 1895. 252 p., illus. CU, H, HEH, LC, O, UC, UM, Y

DON JUAN, *pseud. See* Wheelock, John E.

1573 DONALDSON, A. L. A Millbrook Romance, and Other Tales . . . New York: Thomas Whittaker, 1893. 155 p. HEH, LC
*Also contains:* A Sound from the Past—The Story of a Picture—A Reverie—A Pair of Gloves—The Opal Ring—A Simple Story.

1574 DONALDSON, MARION C. Marguerite's Mistake: A Novel . . . Chicago: E. A. Weeks Company, 84 Wabash Ave. [cop. 1899]. 462 p., front.
HEH
Suburban college town, New York state.

1575 DONAVIN, SIMPSON K. Where Will This Path Lead! A Tale of a Summer Trip. Six Weeks at the Seaside and What It Led to. By S. K. Donovan. Norwalk, Ohio: The Laning Printing Company, 1898. 199 p. LC

1576 DONELSON, KATHARINE. Rodger Latimer's Mistake: A Novel . . . Chicago: Laird & Lee [cop. 1891]. 378 p. HEH, LC
He married the wrong woman.

1577 DONNELLY, ELEANOR CECILIA. The Fatal Diamonds . . . New York, Cincinnati, Chicago: Benziger Brothers, 1897. 73 p. HEH, LC

———— A Lost Prima Donna. *In* A Round Table of the Representative American Catholic Novelists (1897), No. 4703.

1578 ———— Storm-Bound: A Romance of Shell Beach . . . Philadelphia: H. L. Kilner & Co. [cop. 1898]. 218 p. HEH, LC, UV
New Jersey coast.

1579 [DONNELLY, IGNATIUS LOYOLA.] Caesar's Column: A Story of the Twentieth Century. By Edmund Boisgilbert, M.D. [pseud.] . . . Chicago: F. J. Schulte & Company [cop. 1890]. 367 p. CU, H, HEH, LC, O, Y
Socialism, 1988; New York.

1580 ———— Doctor Huguet: A Novel . . . Chicago: F. J. Schulte & Company, 298 Dearborn Street [cop. 1891]. 309 p.
AP, CU, HEH, LC, N, O, UC, UM, UVB, Y
Race problem in the South.

1581 ———— The Golden Bottle; or, The Story of Ephraim Benezet of Kansas . . . New York and St. Paul: D. D. Merrill Company, 1892. 313 p.
BU, CU, HEH, LC, N, O, UC, UM, UP, UVB, Y

1582 DONNELLY, JOSEPH GORDON. Jesus Delaney: A Novel . . . New York: The Macmillan Company. London: Macmillan & Co., Ltd., 1899. 331 p. CU, HEH, LC, N
Of a young Mexican converted to Protestantism.

DONOVAN, S. K. *See* Donavin, Simpson K.

1583 DOONER, PIERTON W. Last Days of the Republic ... San Francisco: Alta
California Publishing House, 1880. 258 p., illus.

CU, H, HEH, LC, UM, Y

Conquest of America by the Chinese.

1584 DORAN, JAMES. In the Depth of the First Degree: A Romance of the
Battle of Bull Run . . . Buffalo, New York: The Peter Paul Book
Company, 1898. 391 p.    LC
Of northern and southern secret service.

1585 —— Zanthon: A Novel ... San Francisco: The Bancroft Company,
1891. 539 p.    LC

1586 [DORR, DALTON.] The Sultan of Cathay: An Arabian Night's Entertainment. Philadelphia: J. E. Caldwell & Co., 902 Chestnut Street [cop.
1890]. [33] p., illus.    LC
Story advertises merchandise of publisher who is a jeweler and silversmith.

1587 DORR, JULIA CAROLINE (RIPLEY). In Kings' Houses: A Romance of the
Days of Queen Anne ... Boston: L. C. Page and Company (Incorporated), 1898. 372 p., illus.    AP, BU, H, HEH, LC, O, Y

—— Meg. In L. C. H. Langford, comp., The Woman's Story (1889),
No. 3206.

1588 DORR, LOUISE SNOW. The Mills of the Gods ... New York: A. S. Barnes
& Co., 1900. 369 p.    CU, LC, Y

1589 DORSET, MARIA. Bought or Won? A Story . . . Boston: James H.
Earle, 1896. 230 p., front.    HEH, LC

1590 DORSEY, ANNA HANSON (McKENNEY). Ada's Trust ... Baltimore, Md.,
New York: John Murphy Company [cop. 1887]. 244 p.    LC

1591 —— Adrift ... Baltimore: John Murphy & Co., 1887. 640 p.    LC

1592 —— 'Beth's Promise ... Baltimore: John Murphy & Co., 1887. 476
p.    LC

1593 —— The Fate of the Dane, and Other Stories ... Baltimore: John
Murphy & Co. [cop. 1888]. 58, 70, 113, 88 p.    HEH, LC
Contents: The Druid's Tower; or, The Fate of the Dane—The Story of a Brave
Girl—The Story of Manuel—The Mad Penitent of Todi.

1594 —— The Heiress of Carrigmona . . . Baltimore: John Murphy &
Co., 1887. 381 p.    LC

—— The Mad Penitent of Todi. In A Round Table of the Representative American Catholic Novelists (1897), No. 4703.
Printed earlier in No. 1593.

1595 ——— The Old House at Glenaran . . . Baltimore: John Murphy & Co., 1887. 408 p.     HEH, LC

1596 ——— Palms . . . Baltimore: John Murphy & Co., 1887. 569 p.     H, LC

1597 ——— Tangled Paths . . . New York, Montreal: D. & J. Sadlier & Co., 1879. 465 p.     LC

1598 ——— Warp and Woof . . . Baltimore: John Murphy & Co., 1887. 276 p.     LC

1599 ——— Zoé's Daughter . . . Baltimore: John Murphy & Co., 1888. 601 p.     LC, Y

DORSEY, ANNA VERNON. See Williams, Anna Vernon (Dorsey)

DORSEY, ELLA LORAINE. Speculum Justitiae. In A Round Table of the Representative American Catholic Novelists (1897), No. 4703.

1600 DORSEY, SARAH ANNE (ELLIS). Panola: A Tale of Louisiana . . . Philadelphia: T. B. Peterson & Brothers, 306 Chestnut Street [cop. 1877]. 261 p.     CU, HEH, LC, N, UC, UM, Y

DOTT, DOROTHY, pseud. See Smith, Mrs. Elvira V.

DOUBLE, LUKE, B.A., pseud. See Hyde, Thomas Alexander

1601 DOUBLEDAY, E. STILLMAN. Just Plain Folks: A Story of "Lost Opportunities" . . . Boston: Arena Publishing Company, 1894. 316 p.     LC
Of capital and labor.

1602 DOUGHTY, FRANCIS WORCESTER. Mirrikh; or, A Woman from Mars. A Tale of Occult Adventure . . . New York: The Burleigh & Johnston Company, 1892. 274 p., illus.     LC

1603 DOUGLAS, AMANDA MINNIE. Bethia Wray's New Name . . . Boston: Lee and Shepard, 1893. 405 p.     HEH, LC
Her "Sherburne Series," for the most part for teen-age girls, is omitted.

1604 ——— Drifted Asunder; or, The Tide of Fate . . . Boston: William F. Gill & Co., 1876. 393 p.     H, HEH, O, Y

1605 ——— Floyd Grandon's Honor . . . Boston: Lee and Shepard. New York: Charles T. Dillingham, 1884. 411 p.     H, HEH

1606 ——— Foes of Her Household . . . Boston: Lee and Shepard. New York: Charles T. Dillingham, 1887. 391 p.     HEH

1607 ——— The Fortunes of the Faradays . . . Boston: Lee and Shepard. New York: Charles T. Dillingham, 1888. 407 p.     H, HEH, LC, O

1608 ——— From Hand to Mouth . . . Boston: Lee and Shepard. New York: Charles T. Dillingham, 1878. 332 p.  BU, H, HEH, UV

1609 ——— The Heirs of Bradley House . . . Boston: Lee and Shepard, 1892. 431 p.  H, HEH, LC, O, UM

1610 ——— Her Place in the World . . . Boston: Lee and Shepard, 10 Milk Street [cop. 1897]. 355 p.  BU, HEH, LC, O

1611 ——— Hope Mills; or, Between Friend and Sweetheart . . . Boston: Lee and Shepard. New York: Charles T. Dillingham, 1880. 372 p.  H, HEH, LC, UM, Y
Of labor interest.

——— How One Man Was Saved. *In* [W. F. Gill] *ed.*, Golden Treasures (1876), No. 2166.
Later printed in No. 2168.

1612 ——— In the King's Country . . . Boston: Lee and Shepard, 1894. 300 p.  H, HEH, LC, O

1613 ——— In Wild Rose Time . . . Boston: Lee and Shepard, 1895. 299 p.  BU, HEH, LC, Y

1614 ——— Lost in a Great City . . . Boston: Lee and Shepard. New York: Charles T. Dillingham, 1881. 468 p.  AP, H, HEH, O

1615 ——— A Modern Adam and Eve in a Garden . . . Boston: Lee and Shepard. New York: Charles T. Dillingham, 1889. 411 p.  AP, H, HEH, LC, O, UM

1616 ——— Nelly Kinnard's Kingdom . . . Boston: Lee and Shepard. New York: Charles T. Dillingham, 1876. 352 p.  BA, CU, H, HEH, LC, O, Y

1617 ——— Osborne of Arrochar . . . Boston: Lee and Shepard. New York: Charles T. Dillingham, 1890. 449 p.  AP, H, HEH, LC, O, UM

1618 ——— Our Wedding Gifts . . . New York: The Authors' Publishing Company, Bond Street [cop. 1878]. 214 p.  LC

1619 ——— Out of the Wreck; or, Was It a Victory? . . . Boston: Lee and Shepard. New York: Charles T. Dillingham, 1885. 382 p.  H, HEH, LC, UV
Of a marriage.

1620 ——— A Woman's Inheritance . . . Boston: Lee and Shepard. New York: Charles T. Dillingham, 1886. 345 p.  H, Y

DOUGLAS, EDITH, *pseud.* *See* Burnham, Clara Louise (Root)

1621 DOUGLAS, L. G. Jeannette: A Venetian Memory . . . New York: Geo.
A. Leavitt, Jr., 1880. 128 p. o
*Also contains:* The Story the Old Letters Told–Psyche.
At head of title: "Odd Moment Series."

1622 DOUGLAS, MARK, *pseud.* Can Love Sin? . . . Philadelphia: T. B. Peterson
& Brothers, 306 Chestnut Street [cop. 1889]. 468 p. LC, UM
Of a U.S. Senator from Oregon.

DOUGLAS, PHILIP. The Men in the Ranks. *In* Tales from McClure's:
War (1898), No. 5364.

1623 [DOUGLAS, SARAH E.] Mahaly Sawyer; or, "Putting Yourself in Her
Place." By S. E. D. Boston: Cupples and Hurd, 1888. 328 p.
H, HEH, LC, UVB
Of "ladies and servant girls."

1624 DOUGLASS, MRS. AKEN. Beryl; or, The Silent Prompter. A Novel . . .
Chicago, Ill.: Scroll Publishing and Literary Syndicate, 1900. 296 p.
HEH

1625 DOUGLASS, MRS. R. DUN. A Romance at the Antipodes . . . New York
and London: G. P. Putnam's Sons; the Knickerbocker Press, 1890. 201
p. HEH, LC, O
Of a sea voyage to Australia.

1626 [DOW, JOY WHEELER.] Miss Polly Fairfax. New York: Printed at the
Printing House of P. F. McBreen, 1898. 71, [1] p. H, HEH, LC, O

1627 [———] Two Days. By W. Newport [pseud.] . . . New York:
Fords, Howard, & Hulbert [cop. 1882]. 73 p. LC

1628 DOWD, FREEMAN BENJAMIN. The Double Man: A Novel . . . Boston:
Arena Publishing Company, 1895. 303 p. LC
A Rosicrucian romance.

DOWD, S. E., *jt. au. See* Dickinson, J. A Winter Picnic (1888), No. 1527.

1629 DOWDEN, DARNALL. The Contrast: A Tale of Facts. Designed to Show
the Advantages of a Religious over an Irreligious Education in the
Family . . . Louisville: A. C. Caperton & Co., 1880. 240 p.
HEH, LC, UC

1630 DOWLING, GEORGE THOMAS. The Wreckers: A Social Study . . . Phila-
delphia: J. B. Lippincott Company, 1886. 400 p., illus.
BU, HEH, LC, UM
Of an Irishman who came to America.

1631 [DOWNS, SARAH ELIZABETH (FORBUSH).] Brownie's Triumph: A Novel. By Mrs. Georgie Sheldon [pseud.]. New York: G. W. Carleton & Co., 1880. 474 p.
Listed PW, Dec. 4, 1880.
LC has: New York: G. W. Dillingham. London: S. Low & Co., 1887.

1632 [————] Earle Wayne's Nobility: A Novel. By Mrs. Georgie Sheldon [pseud.] . . . New York: G. W. Carleton & Co.; Street & Smith, New York Weekly, 1882. 507 p.                    CU, HEH

1633 [————] The Forsaken Bride: A Novel. By Mrs. Georgie Sheldon [pseud.] . . . New York: G. W. Carleton & Co.; Street & Smith, New York Weekly, 1881. 456 p.                    HEH

1634 [————] Geoffrey's Victory; or, The Double Deception. By Mrs. Georgie Sheldon [pseud.] . . . New York: Street & Smith, 81 Fulton Street [cop. 1888]. 314 p.                    HEH
Probably printed in the late 1890's, the copyright date being the year of entry for the Street and Smith series.

1635 [————] Lost—A Pearle: A Novel. By Mrs. Georgie Sheldon [pseud.] . . . New York: G. W. Carleton & Co.; Street & Smith, New York Weekly, 1883. 540 p.                    HEH

1636 [————] Queen Bess; or, A Struggle for a Name. By Mrs. Georgie Sheldon [pseud.] . . . New York: Street & Smith, 238 William Street [cop. 1889]. 255 p.                    HEH
Probably printed in the late 1890's, the copyright date being the year of entry for the Street and Smith series.

1637 [————] Stella Rosevelt: A Novel. By Mrs. Georgie Sheldon [pseud.] . . . New York: G. W. Dillingham (successor to G. W. Carleton & Co.); Street & Smith, New York Weekly, 1886. 419 p.                    HEH, UP

1638 [————] A True Aristocrat: A Novel. By Mrs. Georgie Sheldon [pseud.] . . . New York: A. L. Burt [cop. 1889]. 350 p.                    BU, HEH
Probably printed in the late 1890's, the copyright date being the year of entry for the Street and Smith series.

1639 [————] Wedded by Fate; or, Sister Angela. By Mrs. Georgie Sheldon [pseud.] . . . New York: Dodd, Mead & Company [cop. 1892]. 421 p.                    HEH

1640 DOYLE, CHARLES WILLIAM. The Shadow of Quong Lung . . . Philadelphia & London: J. B. Lippincott Company, 1900. 267 p.
                    CU, HEH, LC, O, Y
Chinese quarter of San Francisco.

1641 ———— The Taming of the Jungle . . . Philadelphia & London: J. B. Lippincott Company, 1899. 200 p.                    H, HEH, LC, O, UM, UVB, Y

1642  DRAKE, JANET.  Wedding Bells Out of Tune, and The Devil's Wife (An Allegory) . . . New York: The Republic Press, 1898.  90 p.
BU, H, HEH
150 copies printed for the author.

1643  DRAKE, JEANIE.  In Old St. Stephen's: A Novel . . . New York: D. Appleton and Company, 1892.  232 p.  H, HEH, O
South Carolina, ante bellum.

1644  ———— The Metropolitans . . . New York: The Century Co., 1896.  267 p.  HEH, LC, O
New York society.

1645  DRAKE, SAMUEL ADAMS.  Captain Nelson: A Romance of Colonial Days . . . New York: Harper & Brothers, 1879.  172 p.  Printed in double columns.  AP, BA, H, HEH, O, UC, UM, UV
Boston, 1688.

1646  [DRAPER, JOHN SMITH.]  Shams; or, Uncle Ben's Experience with Hypocrites.  By Benjamin Morgan [pseud.] . . . Chicago, Ill.: The Lewis Publishing Company, 113 Adams St. [cop. 1887].  412 p., illus.  LC
Of a railroad trip from New York to California.

1647  DREISER, THEODORE.  Sister Carrie . . . New York: Doubleday, Page & Co., 1900.  557 p.  CU, H, HEH, LC, N, O, UP, UV, Y

1648  DREY, SYLVAN.  Lights and Shadows of the Soul: Collected Sketches and Stories . . . Baltimore: Cushing & Company, 1892.  91 p.  H, LC
*Contents:* The Drooping Rosebud—The Broken-Hearted Violinist—Why, Indeed!—Ross's Celebrated Statue of a Perfect Woman—The Poet and the Angel—Two Portraits of a Beautiful Girl—A Recollection—A Great Lunar Revelation—Two Love-Scenes—Stray Leaves from a Philosopher's Autobiography—Moonlight Musings.

1649  DROMGOOLE, MISS WILL ALLEN.  Cinch, and Other Stories: Tales of Tennessee . . . Boston: Dana Estes & Company, 1898.  362 p.
CU, H, HEH, LC, N, O
*Also contains:* The Leper of the Cumberlands—Old Hickory's Ball—A Scrap of College Lore—George Washington's "Bufday"—A Parable of Four Talents—Sweet 'Laases—A Grain of Gold—A Day in Asia—A Humble Advocate—Tappine.

1650  ———— The Heart of Old Hickory, and Other Stories of Tennessee . . . Boston, Mass.: The Arena Publishing Co. [cop. 1895].  208 p., illus.
LC, UM, UV
*Also contains:* Fiddling His Way to Fame—A Wonderful Experience Meeting—Who Broke Up de Meet'n?—Rags—Ole Logan's Courtship—The Heart of the Woods—Christmas Eve at the Corner Grocery.

1651 [————] The Sunny Side of the Cumberland: A Story of the Mountains. By Will Allen [pseud.]. Philadelphia: J. B. Lippincott Company, 1886. 438 p.                LC

1652 ———— The Valley Path . . . Boston: Estes and Lauriat, 1898. 268 p.
CU, H, HEH, LC
Tennessee life.

1653 DRYSDALE, WILLIAM. The Princess of Montserrat: A Strange Narrative of Adventure and Peril on Land and Sea . . . Albany, N.Y.: Albany Book Company, 1890. 238 p.                H, LC

1654 DU BOIS, CONSTANCE GODDARD. Columbus and Beatriz: A Novel . . . Chicago: A. C. McClurg and Company, 1892. 297 p.
H, HEH, LC, O, UC

1655 ———— Martha Corey: A Tale of the Salem Witchcraft . . . Chicago: A. C. McClurg and Company, 1890. 314 p.                H, HEH, LC, N, O

1656 ———— A Modern Pagan: A Novel . . . New York: The Merriam Company, 67 Fifth Avenue [cop. 1895]. 276 p.                CU, HEH, LC, O, Y

1657 ———— The Shield of the Fleur de Lis: A Novel . . . New York: The Merriam Company, 67 Fifth Ave. [cop. 1895]. 346 p.                HEH, O, UP
Lorraine, 15th century.

1658 ———— A Soul in Bronze: A Novel of Southern California . . . Chicago and New York: Herbert S. Stone and Company, 1900. 311, [1] p., 1 l.                CU, HEH, LC, O, UM, UVB, Y

1659 DuBois, LOUISE. Hilton Hall; or, A Thorn in the Flesh. A Novel . . . Salt Lake City, Utah: Geo. Q. Cannon & Sons Co., printers, 1898. 304 p.
H, HEH, LC

1660 DUFF, CONOVER. The Master-Knot, and "Another Story" . . . New York: Henry Holt and Company, 1895. 205 p., front.                HEH, LC, UP

1661 DUFF, MARY E. Star; or, Her Cross and Her Crown . . . Franklin, Ohio: The Editor Publishing Company, 1895. 304 p.                LC

1662 [DUFFELL, ANNIE.] In the Meshes: A Novel. By Christine McKenzie [pseud.] . . . Philadelphia: J. B. Lippincott & Co., 1878. 343 p.
HEH, UV

1663 DUGAN, JAMES. Doctor Dispachemquic: A Story of the Great Southern Plague of 1878 . . . New Orleans: Clark & Hofeline, printers and publishers, 1879. 198 p., illus. Printed in double columns.                HEH, LC

1664 DUGGER, SHEPHERD MONROE. The Balsam Groves of the Grandfather Mountain: A Tale of the Western North Carolina Mountains. To-

gether with Information Relating to the Section and Its Hotels, also a Table Showing the Height of Important Mountains . . . Banner Elk [N.C.]: Shepherd M. Dugger, 1892. 187 p., illus.     HEH, LC
Verso of title page: "Printed by J. B. Lippincott Company, Philadelphia."

DULAC, GEORGE, *pseud*. *See* Perkins, George

1665 DUMOND, ANNIE (HAMILTON) NELLES. Christlike—Save the Fallen . . . St. Louis: Published by the author, 1896. 307 p.     LC

1666 ———— The Hard Times: The Cause and the Remedy . . . St. Louis: Published by the author, 1522 Lucas Place [cop. 1895]. 318 p., front.
    H, LC
Temperance.

1667 DUMONT, JOSEPH. The False Heir of Martin Manor; or, Adroit Plotters of Crime for Money. (A Narrative That Occurred during the Rebellion.) By Mr. & Mrs. Joseph Dumont . . . Philadelphia, Pa.: Press of Charles L. Turner, 1885. 80 p.     LC

DUNBAR, ALICE. *See* Nelson, Alice Ruth (Moore) Dunbar

1668 DUNBAR, PAUL LAURENCE. Folks from Dixie . . . New York: Dodd, Mead and Company, 1898. 263 p., illus.
    BA, BU, CU, HEH, LC, N, O, UC, UP, UVB, Y
*Contents:* Anner 'Lizer's Stumblin' Block—The Ordeal at Mt. Hope—The Colonel's Awakening—The Trial Sermons on Bull-Skin—Jimsella—Mt. Pisgah's Christmas 'Possum—A Family Feud—Aunt Mandy's Investment—The Intervention of Peter—Nelse Hatton's Vengeance—At Shaft 11—The Deliberation of Mr. Dunkin.

1669 ———— The Love of Landry . . . New York: Dodd, Mead and Company, 1900. 200 p.     BA, BU, CU, H, HEH, LC, N, O, UC, UM, UP, UVB, Y
Colorado.

1670 ———— The Strength of Gideon, and Other Stories . . . New York: Dodd, Mead & Company, 1900. 362 p., illus.
    AP, BA, BU, CU, HEH, LC, N, O, UP, UVB, Y
*Also contains:* Mammy Peggy's Pride—Viney's Free Papers—The Fruitful Sleeping of the Rev. Elisha Edwards—The Ingrate—The Case of 'Ca'line—The Finish of Patsy Barnes—One Man's Fortunes—Jim's Probation—Uncle Simon's Sundays Out—Mr. Cornelius Johnson, Office-Seeker—An Old-Time Christmas —A Mess of Pottage—The Trustfulness of Polly—The Tragedy at Three Forks—The Finding of Zach—Johnsonham, Junior—The Faith Cure Man—A Council of State—Silas Jackson.

1671 ———— The Uncalled: A Novel . . . New York: Dodd, Mead and Company, 1898. 255 p.     BA, BU, CU, HEH, N, O, UC, UM, UP, UVB, Y
Small-town bigotry; Ohio.

1672 DUNBAR, MRS. VIRGINIA LYNDALL. A Cuban Amazon . . . Cincinnati, Ohio: The Editor Publishing Company, 1897. 295 p., front.  LC

1673 DUNCAN, FLORENCE I. My Intimate Friend: A Novel . . . Philadelphia: J. B. Lippincott & Co., 1878. 336 p.  H, HEH, LC, O
New York society.

1674 DUNCAN, NORMAN. The Soul of the Street: Correlated Stories of the New York Syrian Quarter . . . New York: McClure, Phillips & Company, 1900. 168 p.  HEH, LC, O, UP, Y
*Contents:* The Lamp of Liberty—In the Absence of Mrs. Halloran—The Greatest Player in All the World—For the Hand of Haleem—The Under-Shepherd—The Spirit of the Revolution.

1675 DUNHAM, CURTIS. The Casino Girl in London. By Herself. Edited by Curtis Dunham . . . New York: R. F. Fenno & Company, 1898. 270 p., illus.  H, HEH, LC, UM
Of an American theatrical company in England.

1676 DUNN, JULIA E. The Bewildering Widow: A Tale of Manhattan Beach . . . New York: W. B. Smith & Co., 27 Bond Street [cop. 1881]. 228 p.  LC
Coney Island.

1677 DUNN, MARTHA (BAKER). Memory Street: A Story of Life . . . Boston: L. C. Page and Company (Incorporated), 1900. 312 p., front.  HEH, LC, UM

1678 DUNN, N. J. The Vultures of Erin: A Tale of the Penal Laws . . . New York: P. J. Kenedy, 1886. 530 p., front.
Copy examined at Boston Public Library.

1679 [DUNNE, FINLEY PETER.] Mr. Dooley in Peace and in War . . . Boston: Small, Maynard & Company, 1898. 260 p.  BA, BU, CU, H, HEH, LC, N, O, UM, UVB, Y

1680 [———] Mr. Dooley in the Hearts of His Countrymen . . . Boston: Small, Maynard & Company, 1899. 285 p.  AP, BA, BU, CU, H, HEH, LC, O, UM, UP, UVB
Of copies examined, all listed on verso of title page three eds. of 10,000 copies each, Oct. 1899, "Before Publication."

1681 [———] Mr. Dooley's Philosophy . . . New York: R. H. Russell, 1900. 263 p., illus.  AP, BA, CU, H, HEH, LC, N, O, UC, UM, UP, UVB, Y
*Contents:* A Book Review—Americans Abroad—Servant Girl Problem—The Transvaal—War and War Makers—Under-Estimating the Enemy—The War Expert—Modern Explosives—The Boer Mission—The Chinese Situation—Minister Wu—The Future of China—Platform Making—President's Message—Polygamy—Public Fickleness—Kentucky Politics—Young Oratory—Public Gratitude—Marriage and Politics—Alcohol as Food—High Finance—The Paris Expo-

sition—Christian Journalism—The Admiral's Candidacy—Customs of Kentucky—A Society Scandal—Doings of Anarchists—Anglo-American Sports—Voices from the Tomb—The Negro Problem—The American Stage—Troubles of a Candidate—A Bachelor's Life—The Education of the Young—"L'Aiglon"—Casual Observations.

DUNNING, CHARLOTTE, *pseud.* *See* Wood, Charlotte Dunning

1682 [DUYSTERS, GEORGE F.] Opals from a Mexican Mine. By George De Vallière [pseud.]. New York: New Amsterdam Book Company, 1896. 285 p.                                                                                     H, LC
*Contents:* The Greatest of the Gods Is Quetzalcoatl—The Water Lady—The Mysterious Disappearance of Mrs. T. Tompkins Smith—The Vision of Don Juan on the Piedra de Los Angeles—Cosmopolitan Mexicana.

1683 ——— A Senator at Sea: A Story of Mine and Thine . . . New York: G. W. Dillingham, 1894. 165 p.                                                                 LC

DYAR, C. W., *jt. au. See* Montague, C. H. Written in Red [cop. 1890], No. 3798.

1684 DYE, EVA (EMERY). McLoughlin and Old Oregon: A Chronicle . . . Chicago: A. C. McClurg & Co., 1900. 381 p., illus.
                                                    BA, CU, HEH, LC, N, O, UC, UP

1685 DYER, ANNIE RUSSELL. The Touch of a Vanished Hand . . . Providence, R.I.: The American Book Exchange, 1897. 152, [1] p.       BU
Of spiritualism.

1686 DYSART, JOSEPH PATTERSON. Grace Porter: A Jewel Lost and Found . . . Milwaukee, Wis.: Published by the author [cop. 1899]. 213 p., illus.
                                                                                      LC

E., O. N., *pseud. See* Green, Mrs. Mary Josephine Armstrong

EAGAN, M. B., *pseud. See* Smith, Mary Pauline

1687 EARLE, ALICE (MORSE). In Old Narragansett: Romances and Realities . . . New York: Charles Scribner's Sons, 1898. 196 p.
                                              BA, BU, CU, H, HEH, LC, O, UM, UP, Y
*Contents:* A Narragansett Elopement—Narragansett Weavers—Where Three Towns Meet—Tuggie Bannock's Moonack—A Black Politician—The Witch Sheep—The Crusoes of the Noon-House—The Doctor's Pie-Plates—My Delft Apothecary Jars—The Dancing Turkey—Cuddy Monk's Ghost.

1688 EARLE, ANNE RICHARDSON. Her Great Ambition . . . Boston: Roberts Brothers, 1890. 307 p.                                                       HEH, UM, UV
Life of an aspiring artist.

1689 EARLE, MARY TRACY. The Man Who Worked for Collister . . . Boston: Copeland and Day, 1898. 284 p.                         CU, H, HEH, LC, N, O, UV, Y

*Also contains:* The Mask of the Lost Soul—The Race of the Little Ships, with Marguerite Tracy—The Governor's Prerogatives—The Mountain Gold—The Alarm Bell—The Hildreths' Wedding-Day—The Fig-Trees of Old Jourdé, with Marguerite Tracy—The Captor of Old Pontomoc—A Little Mountain Maid—The Great State of Johnsing—Aunt Clementine's Old Days—The Law and the Long Bone—Six Brave Soldiers—Mr. Willie's Wedding-Veil.

1690 ———— Through Old Rose Glasses, and Other Stories . . . Boston and New York: Houghton, Mifflin and Company. The Riverside Press, Cambridge, 1900. 209, [1] p.     CU, HEH, LC, UC
*Also contains:* The Tinkling Simlins—The First Mrs. Keener—Heartsease—The Shuttles of the Web—On the Night Train—Lawyer Money—The Beau of 'Harriette.

1691 ———— The Wonderful Wheel . . . New York: The Century Co., 1896. 152 p.     HEH, LC, O, UC
Louisiana Creoles.

EARLE, VICTORIA. *See* Matthews, Victoria (Earle)

1692 EAST, JOHN R. Theophilus Wallop: A Romantic History of a Country Neighborhood . . . New York: John B. Alden, 1890. 256 p.     LC, Y
Also published as: *Captain Wallop: A Romantic History of a Country Neighborhood.* New York: John B. Alden, 1890. 256 p., illus.   HEH

1693 EASTMAN, ANNIS FORD. Havé and Givé, and Other Parables . . . [Elmira, N.Y., cop. 1896.] Cover title, 47 p.     LC
*Also contains:* Flower Morals—Hide-the-Text—I See.

1694 EASTMAN, CHARLOTTE WHITNEY. The Evolution of Dodd's Sister: A Tragedy of Everyday Life . . . Chicago and New York: Rand, McNally & Company, 1897. 230 p.     HEH, UP, Y

1695 EASTON, MRS. C. F. "Considerations". . . New York: John B. Alden, 1894. 223 p., front.     LC

1696 EATON, ARTHUR WENTWORTH. Tales of a Garrison Town . . . New York and St. Paul: D. D. Merrill Company, 1892. 250 p., illus.     H, HEH, LC, Y
*Contents:* How Crossaway Betrayed His Friend—The Fall of the Darcys—The Story of Young Gilsby—An Increased Allowance—Simpson of the Slashers—How Grosvener Got His Church—Mrs. Buckingham's Revenge—The Reverend Washington Ham's Triumph—Court-Martialled—Too Truthful Spirits—The Corporal's Trousers—Touched with the Tar-Brush—Whigs and Tories—A Soldier's Funeral.
Craven Langstroth Betts, jt. au.

1697 [EATON, FRANCES U.] A Fearless Investigator. Chicago: A. C. McClurg and Company, 1896. 353 p.     HEH, LC
Of spiritualism.

1698  EATON, HARRY D.   The Emancipation of Silas Graves . . .   [New York, cop. 1895.]   Cover title, 15 p., illus.   LC

1699  EATON, IMOGENE.   Gwendolene Hope: A Tale of Gloucester . . .   Fall River, Mass.: J. H. Franklin & Co., printers, 1897.   236 p.   CU, HEH, Y

EDDY, JOHN.   A Dinner-Party.   *In* Stories by American Authors, II (1884), No. 5268.

1700  [EDES, ROBERT THAXTER.]   The Story of Rodman Heath; or, Mugwumps. By One of Them.   Boston: Arena Publishing Company, 1894.   328 p.
CU, HEH, LC, N
Of politics and the Civil War.

1701  EDMISTER, HENRY.   The Curse of Malvern . . .   Columbus, Ohio: Wm. G. Hubbard & Co., 1892.   295 p.   HEH, LC
Temperance novel.

1702  EDSON, MILAN C.   Solaris Farm: A Story of the Twentieth Century . . . Washington, D.C.: Published by the author; press work by Byron S. Adams, 1900.   447 p., front.   HEH, LC, UC, UM, Y
Of cooperative farming.

1703  EDWARDS, ALMUS HUGH.   Romance and Rome (Historical) . . .   New York: The Abbey Press, 114 Fifth Avenue [cop. 1900].   103 p., illus.
LC

1704  [EDWARDS, CHARLES.]   A Comic Journey to Washington . . .   By Joe Kosey [pseud.] . . .   [New York? cop. 1894.]   Cover title, 68 p., illus.
H, HEH, LC
Title continued on p. [i] reads: "Containing the Adventures of Rockland Co., the Pig and Rooster Pedestrian. . . ."
At head of cover title: "Price, Thirty Cents."

1705  ———  The New York Hooroarer: A Story of Newspaper Enterprise. Containing a Visit to the Infernal Regions and Return.   Second Edition . . .   New York: The Humboldt Publishing Co. [cop. 1894].   63 p., illus.   H, LC
Deposited Mar. 19, 1894.

1706  EDWARDS, ELISHA JAY.   Shad and Shed; or, The Remarkable Adventures of the Puritan Brothers . . .   Washington and New York: The United Service Publishing Company, 1889.   261 p., illus.   HEH, LC
U.S. colonies; late 17th century.

1707  EDWARDS, GEORGE WHARTON.   Break o'Day, and Other Stories . . .   New York: The Century Co., 1896.   163 p., illus.   HEH, LC, Y
*Contents:* A Watch and Chain—A Mole or Not—Manley—A Protégé—Pop's Yaller Fiddle—Break o'Day—A Matter of Will.

1708 ———— The Rivalries of Long and Short Codiac ... New York: The Century Co., 1895. 156 p., front. HEH, LC, UV

1709 EDWARDS, HARRY STILLWELL. His Defense, and Other Stories ... New York: The Century Co., 1899. 217 p., illus.

CU, H, HEH, LC, N, O, UC, UV, Y

*Also contains:* William Marsdal's Awakening—Isam and the Major—The Hard Trigger—Mas' Craffud's Freedom—The Woodhaven Goat—Captain Isam—The Gum Swamp Debate—Charley and the Possum.

1710 ———— The Marbeau Cousins ... Macon, Georgia: The J. W. Burke Company [cop. 1897]. 294 p. HEH, LC, N

1711 ———— Sons and Fathers ... Chicago and New York: Rand, McNally & Company, 1896. 349 p. BA, CU, H, HEH, LC, N, O, UM, UP, Y
Post Civil War; South.

1712 ———— Two Runaways, and Other Stories ... New York: The Century Co. [cop. 1889]. 246 p., illus. AP, BA, H, HEH, LC, N, O, UC, UM, Y
*Also contains:* Elder Brown's Backslide—An Idyl of "Sinkin' Mount'in"—"Ole Miss" and "Sweetheart"—Sister Todhunter's Heart—"De Valley an' de Shadder"—"Minc," a Plot—A Born Inventor—Tom's Strategy.

1713 EDWARDS, JAMES. True Love and Its Consequences ... Detroit, Mich.: Traynor's Publishing and Printing House, MDCCCXXXLI [i.e., 1881]. 200 p. LC

1714 EDWARDS, JAMES ALEXANDER. In the Court Circle: A Tale of Washington Life ... Washington, D.C.: [Columbian Publishing Company], 1895. 167 p. CU, LC

1715 EDWARDS, ROLLIN. Twice Defeated; or, The Story of a Dark Society in Two Countries ... Philadelphia: J. B. Lippincott & Co., 1877. 426 p. H, LC, O

1716 EGAN, LAVINIA HARTWELL. A Bundle of Fagots ... Franklin, Ohio: The Editor Publishing Co., 1895. 190 p., illus. LC
*Contents:* The Legend of the Rift—A Presidential Appointment—How Hank and His Folks Saw the Show—Snow-White—Thomas McTair and His Nancy—An Unbroken Bond—A Belated Springtime—At the Station—Neighbors—Another Valentine—Mexican Joe's Freedom—At the Turn of the Stair—Only a Tramp—The Wild Huntsman of Sequatchie Valley—Miss Pim's Party—A Break in the Levee.

1717 EGAN, MAURICE FRANCIS. The Disappearance of John Longworthy ... Notre Dame, Ind.: Office of the Ave Maria, 1890. 306 p.

CU, HEH, N, O, UC, UVB, Y

The Irish in New York.

———— How Perseus Became a Star. *In* Round Table of the Representative American Catholic Novelists (1897), No. 4703.

1718 ——— The Life around Us: A Collection of Stories . . . New York and Cincinnati: Fr. Pustet & Co. [cop. 1885]. 409 p.    CU, HEH, LC, Y
*Contents:* A Trági-Comedy—Lilies among Thorns—Philista—A Descendant of the Puritans—A Virginia Comedy—A Rosebud—Trifles—A Measureless Ill—John Nelson's Marriage—Among the "Olive Branches": The Story of a New York Boy—At the Gate of Death—The Financial Crash—A Story of To-Day—The Lisles—Inez—"A Sorrow's Crown of Sorrow"—Rose—The Jaws of Death—Carmel.

1719 ——— A Marriage of Reason . . . Baltimore: John Murphy & Co., 1893. 344 p.    HEH, LC

1720 ——— Short Stories . . . New York: Chas. Wildermann, 17 Barclay Street [cop. 1900]. 3 vols. in 1 (61, 64, 60 p.)    LC
*Contents:* King Solomon's Sentence—A Daughter of the Revolution—A Question of Divorce—The "New Hamlet"—The Income of Tommy Barton.

1721 ——— The Success of Patrick Desmond . . . Notre Dame, Ind.: Office of the "Ave Maria," 1893. 418 p.    HEH, LC, UM

1722 [———] That Girl of Mine . . . Philadelphia: T. B. Peterson & Brothers, 306 Chestnut Street [cop. 1877]. 294 p.    HEH, LC

1723 [———] That Lover of Mine: A Love Story . . . Philadelphia: T. B. Peterson & Brothers, 306 Chestnut Street [cop. 1877]. 248 p.
Listed PW, Nov. 3, 1877.

——— An Ungrateful Martyr. *In* The First Book of the Authors Club (1893), No. 1868.

1724 ——— The Vocation of Edward Conway . . . New York, Cincinnati, Chicago: Benziger Brothers, 1896. 322 p.    LC, UM

EGGLESTON, EDWARD. The Christmas Club. *In* [W. F. Gill] *ed.*, Laurel Leaves (1876), No. 2167.
Later printed in No. 1725.

1725 ——— Duffels . . . New York: D. Appleton and Company, 1893. 262 p.    BA, BU, CU, H, HEH, LC, O, UC, UVB, Y
*Contents:* Sister Tabea—The Redemptioner—A Basement Story—The Gunpowder Plot—The Story of a Valentine—Huldah, the Help—The New Cashier—Priscilla—Talking for Life—Periwinkle—The Christmas Club.

1726 ——— The Faith Doctor: A Story of New York . . . New York: D. Appleton and Company, 1891. 427 p.
AP, BU, CU, H, HEH, LC, N, O, UC, UM, UP, UVB, Y

1727 ——— The Graysons: A Story of Illinois . . . New York: The Century Co. [cop. 1887]. 362 p., illus.  BA, CU, H, HEH, LC, N, O, UC, UVB, Y
Deposited Sept. 24, 1888.

———— In Defense of the Dead. *In* The First Book of the Authors Club (1893), No. 1868.

———— Priscilla. *In* [W. F. Gill] *ed.*, Golden Treasures (1876), No. 2166.
Later printed in Nos. 1725 and 2168.

1728 ———— Roxy . . . New York: Charles Scribner's Sons, successors to Scribner, Armstrong & Co., 1878. 432 p., illus.
CU, H, HEH, N, O, UC, UVB, Y

1729 ———— Sister Tabea . . . Of This Edition One Hundred Copies Have Been Printed for Mrs. Eggleston. New York: D. Appleton and Company, 1896. 26 p.      LC
First separate printing; printed earlier in No. 1725.

1730 EGGLESTON, GEORGE CARY. Juggernaut: A Veiled Record. By George Cary Eggleston and Dolores Marbourg [pseud.]. New York: Fords, Howard, & Hulbert, 1891. 343 p.    BA, CU, HEH, LC, O, UC, UM, UVB, Y
Dolores Marbourg is pseud. of Mary Schell (Hoke) Bacon.

1731 ———— Southern Soldier Stories . . . New York: The Macmillan Company. London: Macmillan & Co., Ltd., 1898. 251 p., illus.
BA, CU, H, HEH, LC, N, O, UC, UVB, Y

1732 EHRMANN, MAX. A Farrago . . . Cambridge, Mass.: Co-operative Publishing Company, 1898. 220 p.      H, HEH, LC
*Contents:* The Blood of the Holy Cross—The Mystery of Love—Why Some Schoolmistresses Don't Marry—Mary—In the House of Contentment—At Commencement Time—A Few First Impressions of Harvard—Prose-Poetry and Symbolism.

1733 ———— The Mystery of Madeline Le Blanc . . . Cambridge, Mass.: The Co-operative Publishing Company [cop. 1900]. 107 p.      LC

1734 EILSHEMIUS, LOUIS MICHEL. Sweetbrier . . . New York, London, Montreal: The Abbey Press, 114 Fifth Avenue [cop. 1900]. 239 p., illus.
H, LC, Y

1735 ———— A Triple Flirtation . . . New York: The Abbey Press, 114 Fifth Avenue [cop. 1900]. 260 p., illus.      LC
*Also contains:* A Triumphant Dilemma—The Ways of Country Hotel Guests —Nancy, a Kentucky Sprite—A Railroad Smash Up—A Stroke of Providence —Charity—A Peculiar Person—Williamson's Story.

EISENBERG, MAURICE, *jt. au. See* Baldwin, E. F. Doctor Cavallo (1895), No. 253.

ELBON, BARBARA, *pseud. See* Halsted, Leonora B.

1736 [ELDER, MRS. D. H.] Mahetible Hopkins and her Travels. This Book Is Written by Mahetible Hopkins [pseud.] . . . Denver and Chicago: W. H. Lawrence & Company, 1884. 247 p., illus. H, LC, N, UM
Humorous adventures in Canada and the U.S.

ELEVE, *pseud. See* Stowe, Mrs. H. M.

1737 ELEVEN POSSIBLE CASES . . . New York: Cassell Publishing Company, 104 & 106 Fourth Avenue [cop. 1891]. 271 p. H, HEH, O, UM
*Contents:*The Only Girl at Overlook, by Franklin Fyles—A Thing That Glistened, by Frank R. Stockton—A Lion and a Lioness, by Joaquin Miller—A Head of Death, by Henry Harland—The Mystic Krewe, by Maurice Thompson—Strange Adventures of a Million Dollars, by Ingersoll Lockwood—A Lost Day, by Edgar Fawcett—A Tragedy of High Explosives, by Brainard Gardner Smith—The Bushwhacker's Gratitude, by Kirke Munroe—The End of All, by Nym Crinkle [i.e., Andrew C. Wheeler]—Shall He Marry Her? by Anna Katherine Green [Rohlfe].
"Shall He Marry Her?" included in No. 4660 as "Shall He Wed Her?"

ELI, *Hon.* BELL, *pseud. See* Smith, H. H.

ELIOT, ANNIE, *pseud. See* Trumbull, Annie Eliot

1738 ELISCU, EUGÉNIE R. Satan's Hoof and the Two Witches . . . Boston: Banner of Light Publishing Co., 1899. 79 p. LC

ELIVAS, KNARF, *pseud. See* Savile, Frank MacKenzie

1739 ELLERTON, EDWARD. A Fatal Resemblance: A Novel . . . New York: F. P. Lennon, 1885. 391 p. HEH

ELLIOTT, HENRY RUTHERFORD. After Business Hours. *In* The First Book of the Authors Club (1893), No. 1868.

1740 ——— The Bassett Claim . . . New York & London: G. P. Putnam's Sons; the Knickerbocker Press, 1884. 267 p. AP, CU, HEH, LC, O, Y
Life in Washington.

1741 ——— The Common Chord: A Story of the Ninth Ward . . . New York: Cassell & Company, Limited, 739 & 741 Broadway [cop. 1886]. 294 p. AP, CU, H, HEH, LC, Y
New York.

1742 ELLIOTT, MAUD (HOWE). Atalanta in the South: A Romance. By Maud Howe . . . Boston: Roberts Brothers, 1886. 345 p. BA, BU, CU, H, HEH, LC, O, UVB
New Orleans.

1743 ——— Honor: A Novel . . . St. Paul: The Price-McGill Company, 455-473 Cedar Street [cop. 1893]. 321 p., illus. CU, H, HEH, LC, O, UM

1744 [————] A Newport Aquarelle. Boston: Roberts Brothers, 1883.
250 p. BA, BU, CU, H, HEH, LC, N, O, Y

1745 ———— Phillida... New York: United States Book Company, successors to John W. Lovell Company, 150 Worth St. [cop. 1891]. 280 p.
CU, H, HEH

1746 ———— The San Rosario Ranch ... Boston: Roberts Brothers, 1884.
390 p. BA, CU, H, HEH, LC, N, O
California life and people.

1747 ELLIOTT, MRS. SARAH A. Days Long Ago: A Novelette ... Raleigh: Uzzell & Wiley, 1881. 57 p. HEH, LC

1748 ELLIOTT, MRS. SARAH BARNWELL. The Durket Sperret: A Novel . . .
New York: Henry Holt and Company, 1898. 222 p. BA, H, HEH, LC, O, Y
Also contains: An Idle Man.

1749 ———— The Felmeres: A Novel... New York: D. Appleton and Company, 1879. 357 p. CU, HEH, LC, Y

1750 ———— An Incident, and Other Happenings ... New York and London: Harper & Brothers, 1899. 272, [1] p., illus.
AP, BA, CU, H, HEH, LC, N, UM, UVB, Y
Also contains: Miss Maria's Revival—Faith and Faithfulness—An Ex-Brigadier
—Squire Kayley's Conclusions—Without the Courts—Mrs. Gollyshaw's Candy-
Stew—Baldy.

1751 ———— Jerry: A Novel ... New York: Henry Holt and Company,
1891. 473 p. AP, BA, CU, H, HEH, LC, O, Y
"Land and labor problems play a strong part in the story." PW, Apr. 11, 1891.

1752 ———— John Paget: A Novel... New York: Henry Holt and Company, 1893. 407 p. H, HEH, LC, O, Y
New York and Corpus Christi, Texas.

1753 ———— A Simple Heart... New York: John Ireland, 1887. 69 p.
HEH, LC
Pioneer town in Texas.

———— Some Data. In [Mrs. K. P. Minor] comp., From Dixie (1893),
No. 3756.

1754 ELLIS, ANNA C. Unforgiven ... St. Louis, Mo.: R. P. Studley & Co.,
printers, 1882. 258 p. LC

1755 ELLIS, JOHN BRECKENRIDGE. The Dread and Fear of Kings ... Chicago:
A. C. McClurg & Co., 1900. 360 p. HEH, LC

1756 —————— In the Days of Jehu . . . St. Louis: Christian Publishing Company, 1898. 189 p.       Y

1757 —————— King Saul . . . St. Louis: Christian Publishing Company, 1898. 281 p., illus.       Y

1758 —————— Shem: A Story of the Captivity . . . St. Louis: Christian Publishing Company, 1900. 299 p.       Y

1759 ELLIS, LEONORA (BECK). Star Heights, and Other Stories, Pastels, and Poems. By Leonora Beck. Atlanta, Ga.: The Foote & Davies Co., 1895. 240 p.       BU, LC
Contains: A Bridal on the Kaatskill—"Dolph's Ruverlation"—Lone—The Birthday Revery of a Rich Man's Wife—Three Old Maids.

1760 ELLISON, NINA E. Nadine: A Romance of Two Lives . . . Nashville, Tenn.: Gospel Advocate Publishing Co., 1897. 343 p., illus.   H, HEH, LC
From Kentucky to San Francisco and Alaska.

1761 ELLSWORTH, MRS. LOUISE C. Furono Amati: A Romance . . . New York: United States Book Company, 5 and 7 East Sixteenth Street. Chicago, 266 & 268 Wabash Ave. [cop. 1892]. 164 p.       LC
Deposited Dec. 20, 1892.

1762 [—————] A Little Worldling: A Novel. By Ellis Worth [pseud.] . . . New York: The American News Co., 1890. 320 p.       LC

ELLYSON, JOHN REGNAULT. The Primrose Dame. In New Stories from the Chap-Book (1898), No. 3949.

1763 ELMORE, MRS. A. "Billy's Mother" . . . New York: J. S. Ogilvie & Company, 31 Rose Street [cop. 1884]. 233 p., illus.       HEH, LC
Deposited Feb. 26, 1885.

1764 ELMORE, WESS, pseud? The Political Biography of the Hon. Sylvester MacFinnegan, a Man of High Renown . . . New York, Chicago, Washington: Brentano Bros., 1884. 65 p., illus.       HEH

ELSHEMUS, LOUIS MICHAEL. See Eilshemius, Louis Michel

1765 EMBREE, CHARLES FLEMING. A Dream of a Throne: The Story of a Mexican Revolt . . . Boston: Little, Brown and Company, 1900. 464 p., 1 l., illus.       AP, HEH, LC, O

1766 —————— For the Love of Tonita, & Other Tales of the Mesas . . . Chicago & New York: Herbert S. Stone & Co., 1897. 265 p., 1 l.       HEH, LC, Y
Also contains: A Compulsory Duel—The Driver of the Ocate—At the Passing of Sesca—The Race—Her Home-Coming—His Terrifying Nemesis—Cold Facts at the Tavern—The Absence of Narcisso.

1767 EMERSIE, JOHN. Allisto: A Romance . . . New York: John D. Williams, 24 West Fourteenth St. [cop. 1884]. 327 p.　　　　HEH
St. Paul, Minnesota.

1768 EMERSON, EDWIN. Pepys's Ghost: His Wanderings in Greater Gotham, His Adventures in the Spanish War, Together with His Minor Exploits in the Field of Love and Fashion with His Thoughts Thereon . . . Boston: Printed for Richard G. Badger & Co., 1900. 153, [1] p., 1 l.
BA, CU, H, HEH, LC, N, O, UM, UP, Y

1769 EMERSON, FLORENCE BROOKS. Vagaries . . . Boston: Small, Maynard & Company, 1900. 85 p.　　　　LC
*Contents:* The Fringe of War—The General's Parrot—The Goddess—Dinner in Bohemia—Possession—A Dream—In the Field—The Casino.

1770 [EMERSON, MARY S.] Among the Chosen. New York: Henry Holt and Company, 1884. 217 p.　　　　HEH, LC, N, UV, Y
At head of title: "American Novel Series—No. 5."

1771 EMERSON, WILLIS GEORGE. Winning Winds: A Novel . . . New York: G. W. Carleton & Co., 1885. 393 p.　　　　HEH, LC

1772 EMERY, SARAH ANNA. My Generation . . . Newburyport [Mass.]: Moses H. Sargent, 1893. 283 p. Printed in double columns.
BA, CU, H, HEH, LC, N, O, UV
Life in Massachusetts.

EMORY, A. M., *pseud. See* Watrous, Charles

EN QUAD, *pseud. See* Vernon, Thomas R.

1773 [ENGLISH, THOMAS DUNN.] Jacob Schuyler's Millions: A Novel. New York: D. Appleton and Company, 1886. 282 p.　　　　H, HEH, LC, Y
On the Hudson River.

ENRIQUE, ERRATIC, *pseud. See* Lukens, Henry Clay

ERIC, ALLAN, *pseud. See* Willis, Charles W.

1774 ERICHSEN, EMMA. The Waif; or, The Web of Life. A Novel . . . Atlanta, Ga.: Jas. P. Harrison & Co., state printers, 1883. 301 p.　　LC, N, O

1775 ERVIN, MABEL CLARE. As Told by the Typewriter Girl . . . New York: E. R. Herrick and Company, 70 Fifth Avenue [cop. 1898]. 245 p., illus.
HEH, LC, UC

ETHERIDGE, KELSIC, *pseud. See* Smith, William B.

EUFAULA, AULA, *pseud. See* Moore, Mrs. Aula

1776 [EVANS, ABIGAIL A.] Aunt Nabby, Her Rambles, Her Adventures, and Her Notions. By Mrs. Peleg Newsby [pseud.] ... Boston: Cupples and Hurd, 23 School Street; the Algonquin Press [cop. 1888]. 274 p., illus.
Copy examined at New York Public Library.

1777 EVANS, ELIZABETH EDSON (GIBSON). Laura, an American Girl ... Philadelphia: J. B. Lippincott & Co., 1884. 374 p.          LC, UM
On the Maine coast.

1778 EVANS, FLORENCE (WILKINSON). The Lady of the Flag-Flowers. By Florence Wilkinson. Chicago and New York: Herbert S. Stone and Company, 1899. 364 p., 1 l.          CU, LC, UC, Y
Tragic love story of a Huron maiden.

1779 EVERETT, EDITH TOWNSEND. A Duel with Destiny, and Other Stories ... Philadelphia: Drexel Biddle, 1898. 162 p., front.          HEH, LC
*Also contains:* A Very Curious Story—Miss Brown's Beat—The Way of the World—Diary of a Divorcee—Morley's Valentine—A Midsummer Memory—A Hero of the Wayside—Then and Now.

1780 EVERETT, HENRY LEXINGTON. The People's Program: The Twentieth Century Is Theirs ... A Romance of the Expectations of the Present Generation. New York: Workmen's Publishing Co. [cop. 1892]. 213 p.
BU, H, HEH, LC, N, UC
Labor propaganda.

1781 EVERTS, ORPHEUS. The Cliffords; or, "Almost Persuaded" ... Cincinnati: The Robert Clarke Company, 1898. 257 p.          LC

1782 ———— Giles & Co.; or, Views and Interviews Concerning Civilization ... Indianapolis: Bowen, Stewart & Co., 1878. 250 p.          CU, HEH

1783 EWELL, ALICE MAUDE. A White Guard to Satan: Being an Account of Mine Own Adventures and Observation in That Time of the Trouble in Virginia Now Called Bacon's Rebellion, Which Same Did Take Place in ... 1676, by Mistress Elizabeth Godstowe. Recovered by A. M. Ewell. Boston and New York: Houghton, Mifflin and Company. The Riverside Press, Cambridge, 1900. 187, [1] p. CU, HEH, LC, O, UC, UM, UP

EWELL, MARTHA LEWIS (BECKWITH). *See* Lewis, Martha Lewis (Beckwith) Ewell

1784 EWING, HUGH BOYLE. A Castle in the Air ... New York: Henry Holt and Company, 1888. 273 p.          AP, HEH, LC, O, UC, Y
At head of title: "Leisure Hour Series—No. 214."
Heirs seek nonexistent estate of New York property and gold in the banks of Amsterdam.

1785 EXPATRIATION: A Novel. By Author of "Aristocracy." New York: D. Appleton and Company, 1890. 307 p.     HEH, O
An American tries to imitate a titled Englishman.

FABER, CHRISTINE, *pseud. See* Smith, Mary E.

1786 FACTS. By a Woman. Oakland, Cal.: Pacific Press Publishing House, printers and binders, 1881. 356 p.     H, HEH, LC, N, UV, Y
Of a woman book canvasser in California.

1787 [FAGAN, T. A.] Uncle Jim, a Modern Roman. By Leon Sule [pseud.] ... Caldwell, Texas: E. P. Hutchings, 1893. 202 p.     LC

FAIRFAX, LINA REDWOOD. The Misfortunes of Bro' Thomas Wheatley. *In* Stories by American Authors, VI (1884), No. 5272.

1788 FAIRMAN, HENRY CLAY. The Third World: A Tale of Love and Strange Adventure ... Atlanta, Ga.: The Third World Publishing Co.; Press of C. P. Byrd, 1895.
Listed in exhibition pamphlet of the Atlanta Public Library, *Georgia, 1800-1900: A Series of Selections from the Georgiana Library of a Private Collector,* Ser. 3 (1954), No. 81.
LC has ed. with imprint: New York, London: The Transatlantic Publishing Company, 1896. 313 p. Printed copyright notice dated 1894 but copy deposited Dec. 20, 1895.

1789 FALKNER, WILLIAM C. The Little Brick Church: A Novel ... Philadelphia: J. B. Lippincott & Co., 1882. 429 p., front.     HEH
Before and during the American Revolution.

1790 ——— The White Rose of Memphis: A Novel ... New York: G. W. Carleton & Co. London: S. Low & Co., 1881. 531 p.     BU, CU, HEH, LC
Steamboat era, Mississippi River.

1791 FALL, MRS. ANNA CHRISTY. The Tragedy of a Widow's Third ... Boston: Irving P. Fox, 1898. 117 p., illus.     H, HEH, LC, Y
Illustrates injustice of Massachusetts inheritance laws.

1792 FALLS, ROSE C. Chenière Caminada; or, The Wind of Death. The Story of the Storm in Louisiana ... New Orleans: Hopkins Printing Office, 1893. 98 p., illus.     LC, Y

1793 FARLEY, JUDITH ELIZABETH. Don Lopez De Vere: A Romance ... Melvern, Kas.: A. & W. P. Ball Publishing Co. [cop. 1895]. 282 p.     LC

1794 FARLOW, KATE M. Silent Life and Silent Language; or, The Inner Life of a Mute in an Institution for the Deaf and Dumb ... Dayton, Ohio: Christian Publishing House Print, 1883. 221 p.     LC, UM

1795 FARMER, JAMES EUGENE. The Grand Mademoiselle: From the Memoirs of Charles-Alexandre, Comte de Lannoy, Premier Écuyer to the King, Louis XIV ... New York: Dodd, Mead & Company, 1899. 337 p.

HEH, LC, O

1796 ——— The Grenadier: A Story of the Empire ... New York: Dodd, Mead and Company, 1898. 328 p., front. BA, HEH, LC, O, Y

1797 FARMER, LYDIA (HOYT). Aunt Belindy's Points of View, and A Modern Mrs. Malaprop: Typical Character Sketches ... New York: The Merriam Company, 67 Fifth Avenue [cop. 1895]. 302 p., front.

AP, HEH, LC, UC

Author later married John Vickers Painter.

1798 ——— The Doom of the Holy City: Christ and Caesar ... New York: Anson D. F. Randolph and Company, 182 Fifth Avenue [cop. 1895]. 386 p. CU, HEH, LC, Y

1799 ——— A Knight of Faith ... New York: J. S. Ogilvie, 57 Rose Street. Chicago, 182 Wabash Avenue, cop. 1889. 288 p. BU, HEH, UC

1800 FARNELL, GEORGE. Rev. Josiah Hilton, the Apostle of the New Age ... Providence: Journal of Commerce Company, printers and publishers, 1898. 94 p. BU, LC, Y

FARNHAM, T. H. Jack Hilton's Love-Affair. *In* C. King, *ed.*, An Initial Experience (1894), No. 3105.

FARQUHAR, ANNA. *See* Bergengren, Anna (Farquhar)

1801 FARRAR, CHARLES ALDEN JOHN. From Lake to Lake; or, A Trip across Country. A Narrative of the Wilds of Maine ... Jamaica Plain, Mass.: Jamaica Publishing Co., 1887. 224 p., illus. H, HEH, LC, UP, Y

1802 FARRAR, IRENE. On the Rock: A Novel ... Atlanta, Georgia: Jas. P. Harrison Co., 1889. 291 p.
Information supplied by Eunice Coston, Georgia State Library.

1803 FARRARS, FRANCIS. Jim Cummings; or, The Crime of the 'Frisco Express ... Chicago: R. R. Publishing Co., 1887. 167 p., illus. HEH, LC, O
At head of title: "The Jesse James Detective Series."
This story was rewritten and published with "by Frank Pinkerton" on the title page (No. 4258). It is possible that Farrars was a pseudonym used by Pinkerton.

1804 FARRINGTON, JOSEPH J. The Uncrowned Prince; or, The Mystery of the Yellow Manse ... New York, 1900. 275 p. LC

FARRINGTON, MARGARET VERE. *See* Livingston, Margaret Vere (Farrington)

1805 FARRIS, JOHN H. Nearly Home; or, The Shelving Rock. A Story in Real
Life ... Springfield, Mo.: Casebeer & Copeland, printers, 1892. 194 p.,
front.                                                                    LC

1806 FARROW, JOHN PENDLETON. The Romantic Story of David Robertson,
among the Islands, off and on the Coast of Maine ... Belfast, Maine:
Press of Belfast Age Publishing Company, 1898. 283 p., 1 l., illus. H, LC

1806a FAWCETT, EDGAR. The Adopted Daughter ... Chicago and New York:
F. T. Neely [cop. 1892]. 262 p.                                            O
Many of his books were published in subscription series.

1807 ———— The Adventures of a Widow: A Novel ... Boston: James R.
Osgood and Company, 1884. 341 p.
                                    AP, CU, H, HEH, LC, N, O, UC, UM, UVB, Y

1808 ———— An Ambitious Woman: A Novel ... Boston, New York:
Houghton, Mifflin and Company. The Riverside Press, Cambridge, 1884.
444 p.                          AP, BA, BU, CU, H, HEH, LC, N, O, UC, UM, UVB, Y

1809 ———— American Push ... Chicago: F. J. Schulte & Company; the Ariel
Press, No. 298 Dearborn Street [cop. 1892]. 236 p.            N, UM, UVB, Y

———— A Comedy of Counterplots. In Short Stories from Outing [cop.
1895], No. 4930.

1810 ———— The Confessions of Claud: A Romance ... Boston: Ticknor
and Company, 1887. 395 p., front.    AP, BA, CU, HEH, LC, N, O, UC, UVB, Y

1811 ———— A Daughter of Silence: A Novel ... New York: Belford Company, 18-22 East 18th Street [cop. 1890]. 255 p.                        N, Y

1812 ———— A Demoralizing Marriage ... Philadelphia: J. B. Lippincott
Company, 1889. 205 p.                        AP, CU, HEH, LC, O, Y

1813 ———— Divided Lives: A Novel ... Chicago, New York, and San Francisco: Belford, Clarke & Co. [cop. 1888]. 250 p.    CU, HEH, O, UM, UVB, Y

———— Douglas Duane. In J. Hawthorne, Sinfire (1888), No. 2602.

1814 ———— Ellen Story: A Novel ... New York: E. J. Hale & Son, 1876.
234 p.                                              CU, H, LC, O, Y

1815 ———— The Evil That Men Do: A Novel ... New York: Belford Company, 18-22 East 18th Street [cop. 1889]. 339 p.          AP, CU, HEH, Y

1816 ———— Fabian Dimitry: A Novel ... Chicago and New York: Rand,
McNally & Company, 1890. 296 p.              CU, HEH, UM, UVB, Y

1817  ——— A Gentleman of Leisure: A Novel... Boston: Houghton, Mifflin and Company. The Riverside Press, Cambridge, 1881. 323 p.
BA, BU, H, HEH, N, O, UC, UM, UVB, Y

1818  ——— An Heir to Millions... Chicago: F. J. Schulte & Company; the Ariel Press, No. 298 Dearborn Street [cop. 1892]. 307 p. AP, O, UM, UVB

1819  ——— Her Fair Fame: A Novel... New York: Merrill & Baker, 1894. 220 p. CU, HEH, LC

1820  ——— A Hopeless Case... Boston: Houghton, Mifflin and Company. The Riverside Press, Cambridge, 1880. 275 p.
AP, BA, BU, H, HEH, LC, N, O, UC, UVB, Y

1821  ——— The House at High Bridge: A Novel... Boston: Ticknor and Company, 1887. 395 p. AP, BU, CU, H, HEH, LC, O, UM, Y

1822  ——— How a Husband Forgave: A Novel... New York: Belford Company, 18-22 East 18th Street [cop. 1890]. 228 p., illus. HEH, LC, UC

1823  ——— Loaded Dice: A Novel... New York: Tait, Sons & Company, Union Square [cop. 1891]. 288 p. CU, H, HEH, N, O, UVB, Y
Copyright notice in name of United States Book Co., which apparently never published the book. PW, Mar. 4, 1893, p. 412, notes "just issued" for the Tait ed.

 ——— A Lost Day. *In* Eleven Possible Cases [cop. 1891], No. 1737.

1824  ——— A Man's Will: A Novel... New York, London: Funk & Wagnalls, 1888. 308 p. AP, BA, CU, H, HEH, LC, N, O, UM, UP, UVB, Y

1825  ——— A Mild Barbarian: A Novel... New York: D. Appleton and Company, 1894. 272 p. BA, BU, CU, UM, UVB, Y

1826  ——— Miriam Balestier: A Novel... Chicago, New York, and San Francisco: Belford, Clarke & Company [cop. 1888]. 192 p.
AP, BA, CU, HEH, UM, Y

1827  ——— A New York Family: A Novel... New York: Cassell Publishing Company, 104 & 106 Fourth Avenue [cop. 1891]. 277 p., illus.
AP, BA, CU, H, HEH, LC, N, O, UM, UVB, Y

1828  ——— Olivia Delaplaine: A Novel... Boston: Ticknor and Company, 1888. 476 p. BA, CU, H, HEH, LC, N, O, UC, UM, UVB, Y

1829  ——— Outrageous Fortune: A Novel... Printed in Periodical Form as "A Martyr of Destiny." New York: The Concord Press; C. T. Dillingham & Co., agents, 1894. 431 p. HEH, LC

1830  ——— A Romance of Old New York... Philadelphia & London: J. B. Lippincott Company, 1897. 204 p. AP, BA, CU, H, HEH, LC, UC, UVB, Y

1831 ——— Rutherford ... New York, London: Funk & Wagnalls, 1884. 310 p.                                                                AP, CU, N, O, UVB

1832 ——— Social Silhouettes (Being the Impressions of Mr. Mark Manhattan). Edited by Edgar Fawcett ... Boston: Ticknor and Company, 1885. 368 p.                           AP, CU, H, HEH, LC, N, O, UC, UM, UVB, Y

1833 ——— Tinkling Cymbals: A Novel ... Boston: James R. Osgood and Company, 1884. 332 p.          AP, BU, CU, H, HEH, LC, N, O, UM, UVB, Y

1834 ——— Women Must Weep: A Novel ... Chicago: Laird & Lee [cop. 1891]. 331 p.                                                               CU, LC, O
At head of title: "The Library of Choice Fiction."
Deposited Jan. 22, 1892.

1835 [FEARING, LILIAN BLANCHE.] Asleep and Awake. By Raymond Russell [pseud.]. Chicago: Charles H. Kerr and Company, 1893. 199 p.   LC

1836 ——— Roberta: A Novel ... Chicago: Charles H. Kerr & Company, 1895. 424 p.                                                                        LC

1837 FEATHERSTONE, WILLIAM. It's a Way Love Has: A Novel ... New York: G. W. Dillingham. London: S. Low, Son & Co., 1887. 199 p. LC

1838 FELDSMITH, MRS. MATTIE DOHERTY. The Home on the Mountain ... Milwaukee: Press of the Evening Wisconsin Co., 1897. 106 p., illus.
                                                                                     LC, UVB

1839 FELLOWS, FEDORA. Delladine: A Story of a Heart of Pride. An Early Scene in the Scioto Valley ... Los Angeles: W. A. Vandercook, 1891. 128 p.                                                                      HEH

1840 FERGUSON, EMMA (HENRY). Courage and Loyalty: A Novel ... Cincinnati: The Editor Publishing Co., 1898. 195 p.              LC, UV

1841 FERGUSON, KATE LEE. Cliquot ... Philadelphia: T. B. Peterson & Brothers, 306 Chestnut Street [cop. 1889]. 152 p.                       LC
Horse racing in the South.

1842 FERGUSON, THOMPSON B. The Jayhawkers: A Tale of the Border War. Kansas in the Early Days ... Guthrie, Oklahoma: State Capital Printing Company, 1892. 415 p.                                           CU, LC

FERN, WILLIE, pseud. See Briggs, William H. F.

1843 FERNALD, CHESTER BAILEY. The Cat and the Cherub, and Other Stories ... New York: The Century Co., 1896. 250 p., front.
                                                           HEH, LC, N, O, UM, UVB, Y
*Also contains:* The Cruel Thousand Years—The Gentleman in the Barrel— The Man Who Lost His Head—The Pot of Frightful Doom—Chan Tow, the High-

rob—A Little Liberal—The Tragedy of Comedy—Enter the Earl of Tyne—The Spirit in the Pipe—The Parlous Wholeness of Ephraim.

1844 ——— The Original Papers, with a Portrait of the Lady. Edited by Chester Bailey Fernald. San Francisco: [Press of H. S. Crocker Company], 1892. 39 l., front.                                    CU, HEH, LC
On HEH paper cover: "Second Edition."

1845 FERRIS, MARY C. As a Man Lives ... Cincinnati, Ohio: The Editor Publishing Co., 1898. 175 p.                                    LC
Mining; California.

1846 FESSENDEN, LAURA (DAYTON). Bonnie Mackirby: An International Episode ... Chicago and New York: Rand, McNally & Company [cop. 1898]. 240 p.                                    HEH, LC, UC
Of an American heiress convicted of murdering her English husband.

1847 ——— A Colonial Dame: A Pen-Picture of Colonial Days and Ways ... Chicago and New York: Rand, McNally & Company [cop. 1897]. 116, 220 p.                                    HEH, LC, N, O, UC, UV, Y
Deposited Nov. 15, 1897.
With this was issued her *A Puritan Lover*, which has its own title page.
First published in the omitted "Globe Library," 1887.

1848 FIELD, ALICE DURAND. Palermo: A Christmas Story ... New York & London: G. P. Putnam's Sons; the Knickerbocker Press, 1885. 212 p., illus.                                    BU, H, HEH, UM, UP, Y

1849 [FIELD, CAROLINE C. (ALDEN).] Two Gentlemen of Boston: A Novel. Boston: Ticknor and Company, 1887. 481 p.                                    CU, HEH, LC, O

1850 [FIELD, CAROLINE LESLIE (WHITNEY).] High-Lights ... Boston and New York: Houghton, Mifflin and Company. The Riverside Press, Cambridge, 1886. 306 p.                                    BA, H, HEH, LC, O
Of music, literature, and the outdoors.

1851 FIELD, CHARLES KELLOGG. Stanford Stories: Tales of a Young University ... New York: Doubleday, Page & Company, 1900. 281 p., illus.
                                    BA, BU, CU, H, LC, O
*Contents:* A Midwinter Madness—Pocahontas, Freshman—His Uncle's Will—The Initiation of Dromio—The Substituted Full-Back—Two Pioneers and an Audience—For the Sake of Argument—An Alumni Dinner—Boggs' Election Feed—In the Dark Days—Crossroads—A Song-Cycle and a Puncture—One Commencement.
Will H. Irwin, jt. au.

FIELD, EDWARD. A Love-Chase. *In* C. King, *ed.*, By Land and Sea (1891), No. 3092.
Later printed in No. 3099.

———— The Senior Captain's Story. *In* C. King, *ed.*, The Colonel's Christmas Dinner (1890), No. 3098.
Later printed in No. 3099.

1852 FIELD, EUGENE. Florence Bardsley's Story: The Life and Death of a Remarkable Woman . . . Chicago: W. Irving Way, 1897. 59, [1] p., illus. BU, CU, H, HEH, LC, N, O, UC, UP, UVB, Y
175 copies printed.
A fictitious book review.

1853 ———— The Holy Cross, and Other Tales . . . Cambridge & Chicago: Stone & Kimball, 1893. 191 p., 1 l. BA, BU, CU, H, HEH, LC, N, O, UC, UV, Y
*Also contains:* The Rose and the Thrush—The Seal-Wife—Flail, Trask, and Bisland—The Touch in the Heart—Daniel and the Devil—Methuselah—Félice and Petit-Poulain—The River—Franz Abt—Mistress Merciless.
Census of copies does not distinguish between trade and limited eds.

1854 ———— ———— New York: Charles Scribner's Sons, 1896. 293 p.
H, HEH, O, UV
This ed. adds: The Platonic Bassoon—Hawaiian Folk Tales—Lute Baker and His Wife Em—Joel's Talk with Santa Claus—The Lonesome Little Shoe.

1855 ———— The House: An Episode in the Lives of Reuben Baker, Astronomer, and His Wife Alice . . . New York: Charles Scribner's Sons, 1896. 268 p. BA, BU, CU, H, HEH, LC, N, O, UC, UM, UVB, Y
Census of copies does not distinguish between trade and limited eds.

1856 ———— How One Friar Met the Devil and Two Pursued Him. Chicago: F. M. Morris [1900]. 37 p., 1 l. CU, HEH, N, O, UVB, Y
At head of title: "By Eugene Field."
300 copies printed.
Also published as: *The Temptation of the Friar Gonsol.* New York: Printed at the Cadmus Press, 1900. [17] p. 100 copies printed. CU, UC
Also published as: *The Temptation of Friar Gonsol: A Story of the Devil, Two Saints and a Booke.* Washington, D.C.: Woodward & Lothrop, 1900. 38 unnumbered l. 310 copies printed. BU, H, HEH, LC, O, UC, UM, UVB, Y

———— The 'Jinin' Farms. *In* I. Bacheller, *ed.*, Best Things from American Literature (1899), No. 195.
Printed earlier in No. 1858.

1857 ———— A Little Book of Profitable Tales . . . Chicago, 1889. 286 p., 1 l., illus. (music). BU, H, HEH, LC, N, UC, UVB, Y
*Contents:* The First Christmas Tree—The Symbol and the Saint—The Coming of the Prince—The Mouse and the Moonbeam—The Divell's Chrystmass —The Mountain and the Sea—The Robin and the Violet—The Oak-Tree and the Ivy—Margaret: A Pearl—The Springtime—Rodolph and His King—The Hampshire Hills—Ezra's Thanksgivin' Out West—Ludwig and Eloise—Fido's Little Friend—The Old Man—Bill, the Lokil Editor—The Little Yaller Baby —The Cyclopeedy—Dock Stebbins—The Fairies of Pesth.
Trade ed. published with imprint: New York: Charles Scribner's Sons, 1890.

1858 ——— Second Book of Tales. New York: Charles Scribner's Sons, 1896. 314 p., 1 l., front.    BU, CU, H, HEH, LC, N, O, UC, UM, UVB, Y
*Contents:* Humin Natur' on the Han'bul 'nd St. Jo—The Mother in Paradise—Mr. and Mrs. Blossom—Death and the Soldier—The 'Jinin' Farms—The Angel and the Flowers—The Child's Letter—The Singer Mother—The Two Wives —The Wooing of Miss Woppit—The Talisman—George's Birthday—Sweet-One-Darling and the Dream Fairies—Sweet-One-Darling and the Moon-Garden—Samuel Cowles and His Horse Royal—The Werewolf—A Marvellous Invention—The Story of Xanthippe—Baked Beans and Culture—Mlle. Prud'-homme's Book—The Demand for Condensed Music—Learning and Literature —"Die Walküre" und der Boomerangelungen—The Works of Sappho.
At head of title of special ed.: "The Writings in Prose and Verse of Eugene Field."
Census of copies does not distinguish between special and trade eds.

1859 ——— The Symbol and the Saint: A Christmas Tale . . . [Chicago? 1886.] Cover title, 11 l. (9 numbered) including covers, illus.
H, HEH, N, UVB, Y
A facsimile of Field's manuscript; later printed in No. 1857.

1860 FIELD, MRS. MARY HANNAH. The Evolution of Mrs. Thomas . . . [Boston]: Chautauqua Press, 1887. Cover title, 24 p.
Information supplied by John Saeger of Oberlin College Library.

1861 ——— Kate Thurston's Chautauqua Circles . . . Second Edition. Meadville, Penna.: Flood and Vincent, 1893. 227 p.    BU
San Benito, California.

1862 FIELD, ROSWELL MARTIN. In Sunflower Land: Stories of God's Own Country . . . Chicago: F. J. Schulte & Company, 1892. 257 p.
CU, HEH, LC, N, UC, UM, UP
*Contents:* The Old Crank—What Broke Up the Literary—He Played with Thomas—Tubbs of Kansas—How the Lord Remembered Curly—The Involuntary Marriage—Colonel Bollinger—The Deaf Ear—The Confession of a Crime—The Old Major's Story—Sweetheart—The Political Wanderings of Joseph Macon—The Distribution—The Awful Miss Boulder—The Luck of Silas Scott.

FIELDING, HOWARD, *pseud.* *See* Hooke, Charles Witherle

1863 [FILER, MRS. G.] From Out of the Shadows. Tried by Fire. By Gwinnie [pseud.]. [Detroit, Mich., cop. 1888.] Cover title, 199 p.    LC

1864 FINLEY, MARTHA. Signing the Contract and What It Cost . . . New York: Dodd, Mead & Company, 751 Broadway [cop. 1879]. 340 p.
BU, CU, H, HEH, LC
A mother gives up her child because of poverty.

1865 ——— The Thorn in the Nest . . . New York: Dodd, Mead & Company [cop. 1886]. 305 p.    HEH, LC, UC
Of insanity.

1866 ——— The Tragedy of Wild River Valley . . . New York: Dodd, Mead & Company [cop. 1893]. 231 p.　　　　HEH, LC, O
Northwest farming country.

1867 FIRESTONE, MAY ELIZABETH (COSTELLO). The Crucial Test . . . Chicago: A. Lincoln Firestone Co. [cop. 1899]. 232 p.　　　　LC

1868 THE FIRST BOOK OF THE AUTHORS CLUB. Liber Scriptorum . . . New York: Published by the Authors Club, 1893. 588, [4] p.
BU, H, HEH, LC, N, Y

*Contains:* The Last Pun, by Alexander Black—The Southern Cross, by William Henry Carpenter—Exactly Zero, by Julius Chambers—The Fate of the Ninth Legion, by John Denison Champlin—The Californian's Tale, by Samuel L. Clemens—An Ungrateful Martyr, by Maurice Francis Egan—In Defense of the Dead, by Edward Eggleston—After Business Hours, by Henry R. Elliot—Cordelia and the Moon, by Harold Frederic—Through the Great Siege, by Leonard Kip—Elsewhere, by George Parsons Lathrop—A Posthumous Letter of Adam's, by William H. McElroy—Fine del Opera, by Edwin Wilson Morse—A Cabalist Adrift, by Charles Ledyard Norton—The Lex Loci of the Hired Girl, by Edgar Wilson Nye—Held Up, by Bernard Francis O'Connor—M. Paul Berdon, by Duffield Osborne—The Star of the Folies Bergères, by Howard Seely—The Professor on "How to Train Our Wives and Children," by F. Hopkinson Smith—Pomona's Club, by Frank R. Stockton.
251 copies printed; each contribution signed by the author.

FISCHER, GRETE, *pseud. See* Schaefer, Konrad

FISH, WILLISTON. George Byers. *In* Hanks: Assorted Yarns from Puck (1893), No. 2444.

——— Recollections of a Busy Life. *In* Mavericks (1892), No. 3663.

1869 ——— Short Rations . . . New York and London: Harper & Brothers, 1899. 188, [1] p., illus.　　　　H, HEH, LC, O
From West Point to Fort Snelling, Minnesota.

1870 [———] Won at West Point: A Romance of the Hudson. By Fush [pseud.]. Chicago: Rand, McNally & Co., 1883. 297 p.
CU, H, HEH, LC, N

FISHER, F. C. *See* Tiernan, Frances Christine (Fisher)

1871 FISHER, FREDERICK VINING. The Transformation of Job: A Tale of the High Sierras . . . Elgin, Ill., and 36 Washington St., Chicago: David C. Cook Publishing Company [cop. 1900]. 96 p., illus. Printed in double columns.　　　　CU, H, HEH, LC, N, UM
*Also contains:* The Taking In of Martha Matilda, by Belle Kellogg Towne. Locale of title story is Yosemite Valley.

1872 FISHER, GEORGE P., JR. Out of the Woods: A Romance of Camp Life . . . Chicago: A. C. McClurg and Company, 1896. 270 p.     HEH, LC
Northern Michigan.

1873 FISHER, RORERT. The Reverend Green Willingwood; or, Life among the Clergy . . . New York: The Authors' Publishing Company, 1877. 266 p.     BU, LC, O, Y

1874 FISK, MAY ISABEL. The Repentant Magdalen, and Other Stories . . . New York: Zimmerman's, 1900. 178 p., front.     HEH, LC
*Also contains:* A Reconstructed Paradise—"Tatters"—From Out the Past—The Heart of a Woman—At Five o'Clock.
At head of title: "Zimmerman's Pocket Library."

1875 FISKE, AMOS KIDDER. Beyond the Bourn: Reports of a Traveller Returned from "The Undiscovered Country" . . . New York: Fords, Howard, & Hulbert, 1891. 222 p.     LC, O, Y

1876 ——— Midnight Talks at the Club . . . New York: Fords, Howard, & Hulbert, 1890. 298 p.     H, UV

FISKE, I. H., *jt. au.* See Parker, J. S. An Experiment. *In* At Wellesley (1896), No. 151.

1877 FISKE, MARY H. (FARNHAM). The Giddy Gusher Papers . . . Edited by Harrison Grey Fiske. New York: The New York Dramatic Mirror, 1889. 238 p.     H, HEH, LC, O, UM

1878 FISKE, STEPHEN RYDER. Holiday Stories . . . Boston: Benjamin R. Tucker, 1891. 208 p.     CU, H, LC, O
*Contents:* Paddy from Cork—The Sealskin Sacque—Summer Boarders—An American Ghost—The Unfortunate Heiress—Love on Instalments—Ten to Two—A Happy Escape—Over the Ferry.

FITCH. *See* Fitch, H. P.

FITCH, ANNA (MARISKA), *jt. au.* See Fitch, T. Better Days (1891), No. 1882.

FITCH, CLYDE. A Light Man. *In* F. E. McKay, *ed.*, Vignettes [cop. 1890], No. 3523.

1879 ——— The Smart Set: Correspondence and Conversations . . . Chicago & New York: Herbert S. Stone & Co., 1897. 201 p., 1 l.
    BU, CU, H, HEH, LC, O, UC, UP, UVB, Y
*Contents:* The Makeway Ball—The Plaintiff—The Summer—The Children—Maternity—A Letter of Introduction—Wagner, 1897—Art—Sorrow—The Theatre—The Opera—A Perfect Day—The Westington's Bohemian Dinner—The Gamblers.

1880 ———— Some Correspondence and Six Conversations . . . New York: Stone & Kimball, 1896. 149, [1] p., 1 l.

BA, CU, H, HEH, LC, O, UC, UP, UVB, Y

*Also Contains:* Two Letters and Two Telegrams—The Seven Daily Letters of a Sea Voyage—Two Letters and a Postal Card—Childhood—The Impressionist and the Widowed Lady: Six Conversations.

1881 FITCH, H. P. Through Shadow to Sunshine. [By] Fitch . . . Hastings, Nebraska: Gazette-Journal Company, 1885. 193 p. HEH, LC

1882 FITCH, THOMAS. Better Days; or, A Millionaire of To-morrow . . . San Francisco, Cal.: Better Days Publishing Co., 1891. 375 p. H, HEH
Anna M. Fitch, jt. au.
Coronado and San Francisco.

FITCH, WILLIAM CLYDE. *See* Fitch, Clyde

1883 FITZPORTER, JOHN L. My Vacation; or, The Millennium. A Novel . . . St. Louis, Mo., 1891. 154 p. LC

1884 FITZSIMON, E. A. The Joint Venture: A Tale in Two Lands . . . New York: James Sheehy. Baltimore, Washington, Boston, 1878. 327 p., illus. HEH, LC
Also published as: *Gerald Barry; or, The Joint Venture.* New York: J. Sheehy. Baltimore, Washington, Boston, 1881. LC
Attacks Protestant divorce laws.

1885 FIVE THOUSAND IN GOLD . . . Boston: Oliver Ellsworth & Co., general agents, 1878. 264 p. CU, HEH

1886 FLAACKE, MARIE. As Some Men Are . . . New York: The American News Company, 1890. 188 p. LC

1887 ———— How It Ended . . . New York: The Authors' Publishing Company, Bond Street [cop. 1879]. 103 p. LC

1888 FLAGG, EDMUND. De Molai, the Last of the Military Grand Masters of the Order of Templar Knights: A Romance of History . . . Philadelphia: T. B. Peterson & Brothers, 306 Chestnut Street [cop. 1888]. 378 p., front. CU, HEH, LC, O

1889 FLAGG, ELIZABETH E. Between Two Opinions; or, The Question of the Hour . . . Chicago: National Christian Association, 1885. 389 p.
H, HEH, LC, UC

1890 ———— Holden with Cords; or, The Power of the Secret Empire. A Faithful Representation in Story of the Evil Influence of Freemasonry . . . Chicago, Illinois: Ezra A. Cook, 1883. 384 p. H, HEH, LC, UC, Y

1891   FLAGG, WILLIAM JOSEPH.   Wall Street and the Woods; or, Woman the
       Stronger ...   New York: Baker & Taylor, 1885.   403 p.        AP, CU, Y
       Also published as: *Woman the Stronger*. Chicago, New York, and San
       Francisco: Belford, Clarke & Co. [1888].   HEH

1892   [FLANDERS, HENRY.]   The Adventures of a Virginian.   By Oliver Thurs-
       ton [pseud.].   Philadelphia: E. Claxton & Co., 1881.   127 p.
                                                          BU, HEH, LC, O, UC, UV, Y
       Early 19th century.

       FLANDRAU, CHARLES MACOMB.   The College Belle.   "Hollis Holworthy."
       [Two stories.]   *In* Stories from the Harvard Advocate (1896), No.
       5277a.

1893   ———   Harvard Episodes ...   Boston: Copeland and Day, 1897.   339
       p., 1 l.                           BA, CU, H, HEH, LC, N, O, UC, UM, UP, UVB, Y
       *Contents:* The Chance—The Serpent's Tooth—Wolcott the Magnificent—
       Wellington—Butterflies—A Dead Issue—The Class Day Idyl.

1894   FLATTERY, MAURICE DOUGLAS.   A Pair of Knaves and a Few Trumps: A
       Novel ...   New York: The Abbey Press, 114 Fifth Avenue [cop. 1900].
       310 p., illus.                                                       LC

1895   THE FLAW IN THE MARBLE . . .   New York and London: Frederick A.
       Stokes Company [cop. 1896].   240 p., illus.        BA, HEH, LC, UM, UV
       Artists' quarters, Paris.

1896   FLECKENSTEIN, ALFRED C.   The Prince of Gravas: A Story of the Past ...
       Philadelphia: George W. Jacobs & Co., 1898.   270 p., illus.   HEH, LC, Y

1897   FLEMING, ANDREW MAGNUS.   Captain Kiddle . . .   New York: John B.
       Alden, 1889.   306 p.                                           HEH, LC
       Sinbad-like adventures.

1898   FLEMING, AUGUSTIN.   The Sway of the Black ...   [Chicago]: The Lake-
       side Press, 1890.   219 p.                                          LC
       Reconstruction period in the South.

       FLEMING, GEORGE, *pseud.   See* Fletcher, Julia Constance

       FLEMING, GERALDINE.   Wild Margaret.   *In* Mrs. A. M. Miller, A Dread-
       ful Temptation [cop. 1883], No. 3727.

1899   FLEMING, MAY AGNES (EARLY).   The Actress' Daughter: A Novel . . .
       New York: G. W. Carleton & Co.   London: S. Low, Son & Co., 1886.
       394 p.                                                    H, HEH, UM, UV

1900   ———   Carried by Storm: A Novel ...   New York: G. W. Carleton &
       Co.   London: S. Low & Co., 1880.   400 p.               HEH, O, UM, Y
       In 1878, Street & Smith issued, with its own title page, the first three chapters

of *Carried by Storm* divided into eight chapters, to advertise the current serial in their *New York Weekly*. With it was bound "eight chapters" of Peter Hamilton Myer's *The Great Mogul*, also running as a serial. The latter apparently was never published in book form.     HEH, UVB

1901    ———— A Changed Heart: A Novel . . . New York: G. W. Carleton & Co. London: S. Low, Son & Co., 1881. 480 p.     HEH, O

1902    ———— Edith Percival: A Novel . . . New York: G. W. Dillingham, 1893. 330 p.
Information supplied by Harriet C. Jameson, University of Michigan Library.

1903    ———— The Heir of Charlton: A Novel . . . New York: G. W. Carleton & Co. London: S. Low & Co., 1879. 396 p.     HEH, O

1904    ———— Kate Danton; or, Captain Danton's Daughters. A Novel . . . New York: G. W. Carleton & Co. London: S. Low & Co., 1876. 436 p.     CU, H, HEH, LC, O, Y

1905    ———— Lost for a Woman: A Novel . . . New York: G. W. Carleton & Co. London: S. Low & Co., 1880. 456 p.     CU, H, HEH, LC, O

1906    ———— Maude Percy's Secret: A Novel . . . New York: G. W. Carleton & Co. London: S. Low & Co., 1884. 432 p.     CU, HEH, UM

1907    ———— The Midnight Queen: A Novel . . . New York: G. W. Dillingham, successor to G. W. Carleton & Co., 1888. 396 p.     HEH, O, UM

1908    ———— One Night's Mystery: A Novel . . . New York: G. W. Carleton & Co. London: S. Low & Co., 1876. 443 p.     H, HEH, O

1909    ———— Pride and Passion: A Novel . . . New York: G. W. Carleton & Co. London: S. Low, Son & Co., 1882. 416 p.     HEH, LC

1910    ———— The Secret Sorrow . . . New York: J. S. Ogilvie & Company, 25 Rose Street [1890?]. 341 p.     HEH
First published in the omitted "People's Library," June 25, 1881.

1911    ———— Sharing Her Crime: A Novel . . . New York: G. W. Carleton & Co. London: S. Low & Co., 1883. 384 p.     HEH, LC

1912    ———— Silent and True; or, A Little Queen. A Novel . . . New York: G. W. Carleton & Co. London: S. Low & Co., 1877. 460 p.     HEH, O

1913    ———— The Sisters of Torwood: A Novel . . . New York: G. W. Dillingham Co., 1898. 316 p.     HEH, LC

1914    ———— Wedded for Pique: A Novel . . . New York: G. W. Dillingham Co., 1897. 302 p.     LC, Y

1915 —— A Wife's Tragedy: A Novel ... New York: G. W. Carleton & Co. London: S. Low, Son & Co., 1881. 431 p.      CU, HEH, O

1916 —— A Wronged Wife: A Novel ... New York: G. W. Carleton & Co. London: S. Low & Co., 1883. 414 p.      HEH

FLEMMING, HARFORD, *pseud. See* McClellan, Harriet (Hare)

1917 FLETCHER, COYNE. The Bachelor's Baby ... New York: Clark & Zugalla, 1891. 220 p., illus.      HEH, LC

1918 —— Me and Chummy ... Washington, D.C.: Sterling Publishing Co., 1890. 266, [1] p.      LC

1919 [FLETCHER, JULIA CONSTANCE.] Andromeda: A Novel. By George Fleming [pseud.] ... Boston: Roberts Brothers, 1885. 377 p.      AP, BA, H, HEH, LC, O, UC

1920 [——] For Plain Women Only. By George Fleming [pseud.]. New York: The Merriam Co. London: John Lane, 1896. 202, [1] p.      LC, O, UM

1921 [——] The Head of Medusa. By George Fleming [pseud.] ... Boston: Roberts Brothers, 1880. 371 p.      AP, BA, H, HEH, LC, N, O, Y

1922 [——] Kismet ... Boston: Roberts Brothers, 1877. 338 p., illus.      CU, H, HEH, N, O, UM, UP
At head of title: "No Name Series."

1923 [——] Mirage ... Boston: Roberts Brothers, 1878. 346 p.      BA, BU, CU, H, HEH, LC, N, O, UM, UV, Y
At head of title: "No Name Series."

1924 [——] The Truth about Clement Ker ... Told by His Second Cousin, Geoffrey Ker, of London. By George Fleming [pseud.] ... Boston: Roberts Brothers, 1889. 317 p.      AP, BA, BU, H, HEH, O

1925 [——] Vestigia. By George Fleming [pseud.] ... Boston: Roberts Brothers, 1884. 288 p.      AP, H, HEH, LC, O, UM, UV, Y

1926 FLETCHER, ROBERT HOWE. A Blind Bargain: A Novel ... Chicago, New York, and San Francisco: Belford, Clarke & Co. London: Henry J. Drane [cop. 1889]. 316 p.      HEH

1927 —— The Johnstown Stage, and Other Stories ... New York: D. Appleton and Company, 1891. 252 p.      CU, HEH, UM
*Also contains:* Corner Lots: A Tale of a Boom—Gentleman Jack—Moses Cohen, the Jew—Cast Away: A Love Story—Between the Acts—Dick: A Naval Story—The Old Spanish Bedstead: A Ghost Story—The Mystery of a Studio.

FLETCHER, ROBERT HUNTINGTON. A Question of Ethics. *In* H. J. Hapgood, *ed.*, Echoes from Dartmouth (1895), No. 2446.

1928 FLINN, JOHN JOSEPH. The Mysterious Disappearance of Helen St. Vincent: A Story of the Vanished City . . . Chicago: Geo. K. Hazlitt & Co., 1895. 304 p., illus. LC

FLINT, ANNIE. Abraham's Mother. *In* Ten Notable Stories (1894), No. 5391.

1929 FLINT, JOSEPH FREDERICK. His Perpetual Adoration; or, The Captain's Old Diary . . . Boston: Arena Publishing Company, 1895. 228 p. LC, UM
Diary is of the Civil War.

1930 FLINT, SAM. On the Road to the Lake . . . Chicago: Charles H. Kerr & Company, 1895. 295 p., illus. LC

1931 FLISCH, JULIA A. Ashes of Hopes: A Novel . . . New York, London: Funk & Wagnalls, 1886. 556 p. HEH
Of three young women and their backgrounds.

1932 FLOOD, JOHN HEBER. The Great Seven–the Greater Nine: A Story for the People . . . Chicago, New York: W. B. Conkey [cop. 1897]. 162 p. LC, UM, UV

1933 FLORENCE, WILLIAM JERMYN. Florence Fables . . . Chicago, New York, and San Francisco: Belford, Clarke & Company [cop. 1888]. 246 p., front. HEH, UM, Y
*Contents:* Doctor Scaroni–Teelie's Grave–Fragelda's Gift–Snake Poison–The Log of the Zuyder-Zee–"Bertha Klein"–Santa Rosa–The Priest's Story–Tennessee Tom–Ernest Conti–"Dead-Shot Dan"–In Mid-Ocean–The Dead River–"Saucelito"–The Curtain-Man–Christmas at the Convent.

1934 FLOWER, SYDNEY. A Study in Hypnotism . . . Chicago: The Psychic Publishing Company, 1896. 226 p. LC, UM, Y

1935 FLOWERS, N. CLEONA. The End of a Skein: A Novel . . . Washington, D.C.: Hartman & Cadick, printers, 1896. 407 p., front. LC
Washington, D.C., social life.

1936 [FLOYD, JOHN G.] Talford: An Affair at the _____ Club in New York . . . New York: Funk & Wagnalls, 1885. 31 p. BU, LC, Y

FLOYD, MARGARET. Passages from the Journal of a Social Wreck. *In* Stories by American Authors, VII (1884), No. 5273.

1937 FLOYD, NICHOLAS JACKSON. Thorns in the Flesh <A Romance of the War and Ku-Klux Periods>. A Voice of Vindication from the South in Answer to "A Fool's Errand" and Other Slanders . . . Philadelphia,

Cincinnati, Chicago, New York, Boston, Kansas City: Hubbard Bros., 1884. 607 p., illus.     HEH, LC

FLYNT, JOSIAH, *pseud. See* Willard, Josiah Flynt

1938   FOGG, W. LE ROY. An Even Dozen: Short Stories . . . Manchester, N.H.: Printed by the John B. Clarke Company, 1897. 107 p.     HEH
*Contents:* Light of Gold—Teddy—May Blossom—Barnstormers—An Episode of the Plains—Ezeke, the Odd—Ike, Dad, and the Fiddle—His Guardian Angel —Fred's Friend—A Knock-Out—One Dark Night—Dorr, Jr., Says Good-by.

1939   FOLSOM, MONTGOMERY MORGAN. Scraps of Song and Southern Scenes . . . Atlanta, Georgia: Chas. P. Byrd, 1889. 199 p., illus.

                                      BU, HEH, N, UC, Y

FONDA, MARY ALICE (IVES) SEYMOUR. *See* Seymour, Mary Alice (Ives)

1940   FONTAINE, FRANCIS. Amanda, the Octoroon: A Novel . . . Atlanta, Georgia: Jas. P. Harrison & Co., printers (Franklin Publishing House), 1891. 2 p. l., [3]-42, 42a-42d, 43-60, 60a-60g, 61-96, 95-96, 96a-96d, 97-113 p.     HEH
Page 110 misnumbered 10.

1941   ——— Etowah: A Romance of the Confederacy . . . Atlanta, Georgia: Francis Fontaine, 1887. 522 [i.e., 524] p.     CU, HEH, LC, N, UP, UVB, Y
Misnumbering of p. 522 corrected during the printing.

1942   ——— The Modern Pariah: A Story of the South . . . Atlanta, Ga.: Francis Fontaine [cop. 1892]. 238 p.     CU, LC, UV, Y
Of the child of an octoroon.

1943   FOOTE, MARY (HALLOCK). The Chosen Valley . . . Boston and New York: Houghton, Mifflin and Company. The Riverside Press, Cambridge, 1892. 314 p.     AP, CU, HEH, LC, N, O, UC, UM, UP, UVB, Y
Idaho.

1944   ——— Coeur d'Alene . . . Boston and New York: Houghton, Mifflin and Company. The Riverside Press, Cambridge, 1894. 240 p.
                        BA, BU, CU, H, HEH, LC, O, UM, UVB, Y
Labor war between mining syndicate and union; Idaho.

1945   ——— The Cup of Trembling, and Other Stories . . . Boston and New York: Houghton, Mifflin and Company. The Riverside Press, Cambridge, 1895. 273 p.     BA, CU, H, HEH, LC, N, O, UC, UP, UVB, Y
*Also contains:* Maverick—On a Side-Track—The Trumpeter.

  ——— Friend Barton's Concern. *In* Stories by American Authors, IV (1884), No. 5270.
Later printed in No. 1946.

1946 ——— In Exile, and Other Stories ... Boston and New York: Houghton, Mifflin and Company. The Riverside Press, Cambridge, 1894. 253 p. AP, BA, CU, H, HEH, LC, N, O, UM, UVB, Y
*Also contains:* Friend Barton's "Concern"—The Story of the Alcázar—A Cloud on the Mountain—The Rapture of Hetty—The Watchman.

1947 ——— John Bodewin's Testimony ... Boston: Ticknor and Company, 1886. 344 p. AP, BA, CU, H, HEH, LC, O, Y
Mining in Arkansas.

1948 ——— The Last Assembly Ball, and The Fate of a Voice ... Boston and New York: Houghton, Mifflin and Company. The Riverside Press, Cambridge, 1889. 275 p. AP, BA, CU, H, HEH, LC, N, O, UM, UVB, Y

1949 ——— The Led-Horse Claim: A Romance of a Mining Camp ... Boston: James R. Osgood and Company, 1883. 279 p., illus. AP, BA, CU, H, HEH, LC, O, UM, UVB, Y
Colorado.

1950 ——— The Prodigal ... Boston and New York: Houghton, Mifflin and Company. The Riverside Press, Cambridge, 1900. 99, [1] p., illus. BA, CU, H, HEH, LC, O, UVB, Y

1951 FOR EACH OTHER: A Novel ... New York: G. W. Carleton & Co. London: S. Low & Co., 1878. 264 p. HEH
New York and Paris.

1952 FOR HER BABY'S SAKE; or, A Heroine in Real Life. A Full Detail of the Sufferings and Heart-Touching Life of Louise Porter, the Wealthy, Lovely Heiress, Who, Falling in Love with Robert Sommers, a Park Guard, Secretly Married Him, and Was at Once Disowned by Her Rich, Proud Parents ... Philadelphia, Pa.: The Old Franklin Publishing House, cop. 1880. 29 p., illus. LC
Copyrighted by Charles Wesley Alexander, who may be the author.

1953 FORAN, MARTIN AMBROSE. The Other Side: A Social Study Based on Fact ... Cleveland, Ohio: Ingham, Clarke & Co. Washington, D.C.: Gray & Clarkson, printers and publishers, 1886. 461 p., illus. HEH, LC, N, UV, Y

1954 FORD, DANIEL N. Born Again; or, The Romance of a Dual Life ... Falmouth, Mass.: Succanesset Press, Chas. Francis Adams, prop., 1893. 356 p. CU, LC

1955 FORD, HARRIET. Me an' Methuselar, and Other Episodes ... Buffalo: The Peter Paul Book Company, 1895. 84 p., front. BU, LC, UC
*Also contains:* At the Photographer's—Terra Incognita—Dr. Bean, Dentist—Between the Acts—The Matrimonial Manoeuvers of Major Musket—An American Girl at an English Dinner Party—A Young Maid and an Old Maid—A Fragment.
Author's full name: Harriet French (Ford) Morgan.

FORD, JAMES LAUREN. Aunt Mary's Obituary. *In* Mavericks (1892), No. 3663.

1956 ——— Bohemia Invaded, and Other Stories . . . New York and London: Frederick A. Stokes Company [cop. 1895]. 176 p., front.

H, HEH, LC, UP, Y

*Also contains:* Wedded Bliss—High Etiquette in Harlem—The Talent in the Napkin—A Dinner in Poverty Flat—The Better Element—The Squarer—The Joke That Failed—Dan Briordy's Gitaway Shadder—The Wardman's Wooing —The Change of the Luck—Mr. Synick's Anti-Bad-Break—Freaks and Kings.

——— The Career of a Society Actress. *In* Hanks: Assorted Yarns from Puck (1893), No. 2444.

1957 ——— Cupid and the Footlights . . . New York: Frederick A. Stokes Company, cop. 1899. [39] p., illus.

H, Y

Facsimiles of letters, telegrams, and newspaper clippings.

1958 ——— Dolly Dillenbeck. A Portrayal of Certain Phases of Metropolitan Life and Character . . . New York: George H. Richmond & Co., 1895. 392 p., illus.

AP, CU, H, HEH, LC, O, UM, UP, Y

Theatrical life; New York.

1959 ——— Hypnotic Tales and Other Tales . . . New York: Keppler & Schwarzmann, 1891. 220 p., illus.

H, LC, UVB, Y

*Contents:* The Landlord's Tale—The Fiddler's Tale—The Spiritualist's Tale—The Detective's Tale—The Boston Girl's Tale—The Representative Business Man's Tale—The Rich Presbyterian's Tale—The Genial's Tale—The Chaperon's Tale—The School-Boy's Tale. OTHER TALES: The Bunco-Steerer's Christmas—Aladdin—John Coppertug's Fall—The Assemblyman's Bridge—The Deserted House—Two Old Crones—'Lish' Pogram's Thanksgiving Hog—Beanville Journalism—The Stockbroker's Christmas Gift—In the "400" and Out—The Evolution of the Humorist—The Curiosities' Christmas—At the Chromo-Literary Reception—The Master Thief—An Undiplomatic Diary.

1960 ——— The Literary Shop, and Other Tales . . . New York: Geo. H. Richmond & Co., 1894. 298 p.

BU, CU, H, HEH, LC, UM, UP, UV, Y

*Contains:* The Poets' Strike—The Sober, Industrious Poet—The Two Brothers —The Story of the Young Man of Talent—The Society Reporter's Christmas—The Dying Gag—"Only a Type-Writer"—The Culture Bubble in Ourtown—Some Thoughts on the Construction and Preservation of Jokes.

1961 ——— ——— New York: The Chelsea Company [cop. 1899]. 360 p.

HEH, LC, UM

This ed. adds: McClure's Model Village for Literary Toilers—Arrival of the Scotch Authors at McClure's Literary Colony—The Canning of Perishable Literature—Literary Leaves by Manacled Hands—McClure's Birthday at Syndicate Village—Literature by Prison Contract Labor—Christmas Eve at the Syndicate Village.

——— The Sober, Industrious Poet and How He Fared at Easter-Time. *In* I. Bacheller, *ed.*, Best Things from American Literature (1899), No. 195.

1962 FORD, MARY HANFORD (FINNEY). Otto's Inspiration . . . Chicago: S. C.
Griggs & Company, 1895. 243 p.                   CU, HEH, LC
Of a musician.

1963 FORD, PAUL LEICESTER. The Great K. & A. Robbery . . . New York:
Dodd, Mead and Company, 1897. 200 p., front. Blue cloth.
                                    AP, CU, HEH, LC, N, O, UVB, Y
P. 164, last line: "talk in the presence of a lady!"
2nd printing has title: *The Great K. & A. Train-Robbery*. P. 164, last line,
as above.    UP, Y
3rd printing title same as 2nd. P. 164, last line: "lady!"    H, HEH, Y
BAL 6213 notes: "A reprint, dated 1897, has all the typographic features of the
Third Printing; bound in yellow . . . cloth."

1964     —— The Honorable Peter Stirling and What People Thought of
Him . . . New York: Henry Holt and Company, 1894.
                                      H, HEH, N, O, UVB, Y

1965      —— Janice Meredith: A Story of the American Revolution . . .
New York: Dodd, Mead and Company, 1899. 536 p., front.
                      AP, BU, CU, H, HEH, LC, N, O, UM, UP, UVB, Y
BAL 6224 notes five printings, the 1st with "five" on p. 57, line 14, the other
four with "four."

1966      —— The Story of an Untold Love . . . Boston and New York:
Houghton, Mifflin and Company. The Riverside Press, Cambridge,
1897. 348 p., 1 l.         BU, CU, H, HEH, LC, N, O, UVB, Y

1967      —— Tattle-Tales of Cupid . . . New York: Dodd, Mead and Com-
pany, 1898. 264 p.    BA, BU, CU, H, HEH, LC, N, O, UC, UM, UP, UVB, Y
*Contains:* His Version of It—A Warning to Lovers—"Sauce for the Goose"—
The Cortelyou Feud.

1968      —— Wanted—A Match Maker . . . New York: Dodd, Mead &
Company, 1900. 111 p., illus.   BA, BU, CU, H, HEH, LC, N, O, UC, UP, UVB, Y

1969 FORD, SALLIE (ROCHESTER). Ernest Quest; or, The Search for Truth . . .
New York: Sheldon & Company, 1878. 634 p.    CU, HEH, LC, O, UC

1970 FOREORDAINED: A Story of Heredity and of Special Parental Influences.
By an Observer. New York: Fowler & Wells & Co., 1886. 90 p.  LC
Information for prospective mothers.

FORFEX, *pseud.* *See* Morris, Bessie C.

1971 FORNEY, JOHN WIEN. The New Nobility: A Story of Europe and
America . . . New York: D. Appleton and Company, 1881. 395 p.
                                   AP, BU, CU, H, HEH, N, O, UVB, Y

1972  FOSDICK. GERTRUDE CHRISTIAN. Out of Bohemia: A Story of Paris Student-Life ... New York: George H. Richmond & Co., 1894. 236 p., illus.                                                                    H, HEH, LC

1973  FOSTER, CHARLES JAMES. The White Horse of Wootton: A Story of Love, Sport, and Adventure in the Midland Counties of England and on the Frontier of America ... Philadelphia: Porter & Coates, No. 822 Chestnut Street [cop. 1878]. 421 p.          BA, HEH, LC, N, O, UM, UV, Y

1974  FOSTER, DAVID SKAATS. Elinor Fenton: An Adirondack Story ... Philadelphia: J. B. Lippincott Company, 1893. 300 p.              AP, LC, O, Y

1975  ———— Prince Timoteo ... New York, London, Chicago: F. Tennyson Neely [cop. 1899]. 254 p.                                       HEH

1976  ———— Spanish Castles by the Rhine: A Triptychal Yarn . . . New York: Henry Holt and Company, 1897. 245 p., illus.        H, HEH, LC
       *Contents:* The Crisis in Oldendorf—The Six Dumb-Bells of Castle Schrecken-strohm—"The Man Who Looked Like the King."

1977  FOSTER, MRS. HARRIET TOWNSEND. The "Wind-Flower"; or, A Legend of the Ozarks ... Chicago: R. R. Donnelly & Sons, 1888. 411 p.
                                                                    HEH, LC, Y

1978  FOSTER, MARY FARRINGTON. Doty Dontcare: A Story of the Garden of the Antilles ... Boston: Estes & Lauriat, 1895. 187 p.    HEH, LC, O

       FOSTER, NATHANIEL LADD. An Incident in College Life. A Turkey Feather. [Two stories.] *In* H. J. Hapgood, *ed.*, Echoes from Dartmouth (1895), No. 2446.

1979  [FOSTER, THEODOSIA MARIA (TOLL).] Echoing and Re-Echoing. By Faye Huntington [pseud.] . . . Boston: D. Lothrop and Company, Franklin St., corner of Hawley [cop. 1878]. 309 p., front.        LC, UM
       Of two young college graduates.

1980  [————] His First Charge. By Faye Huntington [pseud.]. Boston: Lothrop Publishing Co. [cop. 1897]. 308 p., illus.            HEH, LC, UV
       Of a young minister.

1981  [————] Transformed. By Faye Huntington [pseud.]. New York: Thomas Y. Crowell & Co., 13 Astor Place [cop. 1886]. 341 p., illus.
       Copy examined at Boston Public Library.
       Of social work.

1982  FOULKE, WILLIAM DUDLEY. Maya: A Story of Yucatan ... New York and London: G. P. Putnam's Sons; the Knickerbocker Press, 1900. 219 p., illus.                                                     HEH, LC, UC

1983 FOWLER, HARRIET P. Our Smoking Husbands and What to Do with Them... New York: The Authors' Publishing Company, Bond Street [cop. 1879]. 47 p. LC

1984 FOWLER, SADA (BAILEY). Irene; or, The Road to Freedom. A Novel... Philadelphia: H. N. Fowler & Company, 1886. 608, [1] p. HEH, LC
Women's rights.

1985 ———— Irene: The Uncle Tom's Cabin of Social Slavery. A Thrilling Story of Facts. By Sada Bailey ... Philadelphia: Educational Union, 1879. Cover title, 64 p. LC
Part I. No more published.

1986 [FOWLES, MARY A.] A Hero's Last Days; or, Nepenthe ... Columbus, So. Ca.: W. J. Duffie. London: Trubner & Co., agents, 1883. 244 p. LC, O
The South.

1987 [FOX, MRS. EMILY.] Gemini. Boston: Roberts Brothers, 1878. 271 p. BA, BU, CU, H, HEH, O, UM, UV, Y
At head of title: "No Name Series."
New Hampshire prior to the Civil War.

1988 [————] Off the Rocks: A Novel. By Toler King [pseud.]. Chicago: Henry A. Sumner & Company, 1882. 414 p. HEH, N
At head of title: "Hammock Series."
Of a retired army officer; Ireland.

1989 [————] Rose O'Connor: A Story of the Day. By Toler King [pseud.]. Chicago: Chicago Legal News Co., 1880. 173 p.
Listed PW, Oct. 2, 1880.
British Museum has: Second Edition. Chicago: H. A. Sumner & Co., 1881.

1990 [FOX, HENRY CLAY.] The Adventures of a Philosopher, a Dun Mule, and a Brindle Dog. By an Indiana Man. Richmond, Ind.: M. Cullaton & Co., printers and publishers, 1888. 144 p. BU, LC, UM

1991 FOX, JOHN WILLIAM, JR. Crittenden: A Kentucky Story of Love and War... New York: Charles Scribner's Sons, 1900. 256 p. BA, CU, H, HEH, N, O, UP, UVB, Y
Spanish-American War.

1992 ———— A Cumberland Vendetta, and Other Stories ... New York: Harper & Brothers, 1896. 221 p., illus. H, HEH, LC, N, O, UM, UP, UVB, Y
Contents: A Mountain Europa–A Cumberland Vendetta–The Last Stetson– On Hell-fer-Sartain Creek.

1993 ———— "Hell fer Sartain," and Other Stories ... New York: Harper & Brothers, 1897. 118, [1] p. BA, CU, HEH, LC, N, O, UC, UP, UVB, Y

*Contents:* On Hell-fer-Sartain Creek—Through the Gap—A Trick o' Trade—Grayson's Baby—Courtin' on Cutshin—The Message in the Sand—The Senator's Last Trade—Preachin' on Kingdom-Come—The Passing of Abraham Shivers—A Purple Rhododendron.

1994 ———— The Kentuckians: A Novel . . . New York and London: Harper & Brothers, 1898. 227, [1] p., illus. BA, CU, H, HEH, N, O, UC, UP, UVB

1995 ———— A Mountain Europa . . . New York and London: Harper & Brothers, 1899. 191, [1] p., front. CU, H, HEH, LC, N, O, UC, UP, UVB, Y
First separate printing; printed earlier in No. 1992.

1996 FOX, MRS. NETTIE PEASE. Mysteries of the Border Land; or, The Conscious Side of Unconscious Life . . . Ottumwa, Iowa: D. M. & N. P. Fox, 1883. 536 p. LC
Spiritualism; narrative form.

1997 ———— The Phantom Form: Experiences in Earth and Spirit Life. A True Life History Communicated by a Spirit through the Trance Mediumship . . . Newton, Iowa: D. M. Fox, 1881. 169 p. LC, UVB

1998 [FOX, RICHARD KYLE.] Devil Anse; or, The Hatfield-McCoy Outlaws . . . [and] Trujillo; or, Bob Montclair, the Terror of Eldorado . . . New York: Richard K. Fox, 1889. 32, 28 p., illus. Printed in double columns. CU, LC

1999 [————] Rube Burrows' Raids: Historic Highwayman. Night Riders of the Ozarks; or, The Bald Knobbers of Missouri . . . New York: Richard K. Fox [cop. 1891]. 17, [4], 20-45, [2], 6-42 p., illus. Printed in double columns. CU, LC

FOX, WILLIAM HENRY. An Old Town Tale. *In* The Septameron (1888), No. 4867.

2000 FRANCE, LEWIS BROWNE. Mr. Dide, His Vacation in Colorado, and Other Sketches . . . New York: Bromfield and Company, 1890. 259 p., illus. CU, H, Y
*Also contains:* The Rivals of Basset Bar—The Owners of the Jack-Pot Lode—Called.

2001 ———— Mountain Trails and Parks in Colorado . . . Denver, Colorado: Chain, Hardy & Co., 1887. 224 p., illus. CU, H, LC, O, UV

2002 ———— Over the Old Trail: A Novel . . . Boston: Arena Publishing Company, 1895. 339 p. BU, HEH, LC, Y
Mining; Colorado.

2003 ———— Pine Valley . . . Denver, Col.: The Chain and Hardy Company [cop. 1891]. 38 p., illus. LC, UV, Y
*Contents:* One Winter at the Gray Eagle Mine—A Prayer for Baltimore Hatch.

2004 ——— ——— New York, Boston: Thomas Y. Crowell & Company [cop. 1897]. 138 p., illus.     HEH, LC, Y
This ed. adds: His Harvest—On His Honor—Finally Recognized—"And a Little Child Shall Lead Them."

2005 ——— Scraps . . . Denver, Colorado: The W. F. Robinson Printing Co., 1899. 44 p.     LC
*Also contains:* Friends—On the Fly.

2006 FRANCES, *pseud.* With the Church in an Early Day . . . Lamoni, Decatur Co., Iowa, 1891. 391 p., front.     Y
A narrative of the Mormons to 1844.

FRANCES, MARY, *pseud. See* Mason, Fanny Witherspoon

FRANCIS, MARY C. The Easter of La Mercedes. *In* J. Hawthorne, One of Those Coincidences (1899), No 2596.

2007 FRANK, HENRY. His Bold Experiment . . . New York: Twentieth Century, 1890.
Listed in Hinkel.
University of Illinois Library has copy with 279 p., lacking title page. Its catalogue card gives the date as 1892. Information supplied by T. E. Ratcliffe, Jr.

2008 ——— A Vision of the Invisible: An Allegory . . . New York, cop. 1898. 33 p.     HEH

2009 FRANKEL, A. H. In Gold We Trust . . . Philadelphia: William H. Pile's Sons, 1898. 332 p.     UP, Y
"The author through romance portrays the various phases of Ghetto Life in America." PW, July 23, 1898.

2009a FRASER, CAROLINE AUGUSTA (RUTLEDGE) BALL. Constance Beverley: A Tale of Southern Life in 1850 . . . Charleston, S.C.: Sunday Times Publishing House, 1879. Cover title, 96 p. Printed in double columns.     Y

2010 [FRAYSER, LOU H.] Then and Now; or, Hope's First School. By Zillah Raymond [pseud.]. Wilmington, N.C.: Jackson & Bell, 1883. 231 p.     LC
Powell, No. 194, locates nine additional copies.

2011 FRAZEE, THEO D. The Farmer's Niece: A Romance of the Mexican War . . . Newark, N.J.: The Heinz Printing Company, 1892. 232 p.     HEH, Y

FRÉCHETTE, ANNIE HOWELLS. How Cassie Saved the Spoons. *In* Tales from McClure's: Adventure (1897), No. 5360.

——— The Joneses' Telephone. *In* Tales from McClure's: Humor (1897), No 5361.

FREDERIC, HAROLD. Brother Sebastian's Friendship. *In* Stories by American Authors, VI (1884), No. 5272.

2012 —————— The Copperhead... New York: Charles Scribner's Sons, 1893. 197 p.  AP, BU, CU, H, HEH, LC, N, O, UC, UM, UP, UVB, Y Later printed in No. 2016.

—————— Cordelia and the Moon. *In* The First Book of the Authors Club (1893), No. 1868.

2013 —————— The Damnation of Theron Ware... Chicago: Stone & Kimball, 1896. 512 p., 1 l.  AP, CU, H, HEH, N, O, UC, UP, UVB, Y 2nd ed. adds to title *or Illumination*. Of Methodism.

2014 —————— The Deserter, and Other Stories. A Book of Two Wars... Boston: Lothrop Publishing Company [cop. 1898]. 401 p., illus.
BA, CU, H, HEH, LC, N, O, UC, UM, UP, UVB, Y
*Also contains:* A Day in the Wilderness—How Dickon Came By His Name —Where Avon into Severn Flows.

2015 —————— Gloria Mundi: A Novel... Chicago & New York: Herbert S. Stone & Company, 1898. 580 p., 1 l.
AP, BA, BU, CU, H, HEH, LC, N, O, UC, UM, UP, UVB, Y
Of English nobility.

2016 —————— In the Sixties... New York: Charles Scribner's Sons, 1897. 319 p.  CU, H, LC, O, UM, UVB, Y
*Contents:* The Copperhead—Marsena—The War Widow—The Eve of the Fourth—My Aunt Susan.

2017 —————— In the Valley... New York: Charles Scribner's Sons, 1890. 427 p., illus.  AP, H, HEH, LC, N, O, UC, UM, UP, UVB, Y French and Indian War; Mohawk Valley.

2018 —————— The Lawton Girl... New York: Charles Scribner's Sons, 1890. 472 p.  AP, BA, BU, CU, H, N, O, UC, UM, UP, UVB, Y Of a manufacturing town.

2019 —————— March Hares... New York: D. Appleton and Company, 1896. 281 p.  AP, BA, BU, CU, H, HEH, LC, N, O, UC, UM, UP, UVB, Y London.

2020 —————— The Market-Place... New York: Frederick A. Stokes Company [cop. 1899]. 401 p., illus.
AP, BA, BU, CU, H, HEH, LC, N, O, UC, UM, UP, UVB, Y
Deposited Apr. 28, 1899.

2021 —————— Marsena, and Other Stories of the Wartime... New York: Charles Scribner's Sons, 1894. 210 p.
AP, BA, CU, H, HEH, LC, N, O, UC, UM, UP, UVB, Y

*Also contains:* The War Widow—The Eve of the Fourth—My Aunt Susan. Contents later printed in No. 2016.

———— The Path of Murtogh. *In* Tales of Our Coast (1896), No. 5365.

2022 ———— The Return of the O'Mahony: A Novel ... New York: Robert Bonner's Sons, 1892. 334 p., illus.                    CU, UP, UVB

2023 ———— Seth's Brother's Wife: A Study of Life in the Greater New York ... New York: Charles Scribner's Sons, 1887. 405 p.
AP, BA, BU, CU, H, HEH, LC, N, O, UC, UM, UP, UVB, Y

2024 [FREELAND, MRS. CAROLINE J.] The Good Fight of Faith. By C. J. G. [pseud.]. New York: T. Y. Crowell [cop. 1876]. 276 p.            LC
Civil War novel.

2025 FREELEY, MARY BELLE. Fair to Look Upon ... Chicago: Morrill, Higgins & Co. [cop. 1892]. 180 p., illus.            HEH, LC, UC
*Contents:* The Story of Eve—The Abraham-Hagar Affair—Isaac's Wife—A Woman's Monument—Another of the Women of Old—All Naughty, but Fair—Story of Some Women and a Baby—Another of "The Mistakes of Moses"—Some Managing Women—Another Group of Them—The Famous Widow of Moab.

2026 [FREEMAN, MRS. A. M.] Altha ... Boston: B. B. Russell, 55 Cornhill. Philadelphia: Quaker City Publishing House. San Francisco: A. L. Bancroft & Co. Chicago: H. S. Beebe & Co. [cop. 1876]. 367 p., front.
CU, HEH, LC
LC copy has registration stamp dated 1877; printed copyright date of 1876 corrected in hand to 1877.

2027 ———— Somebody's Ned ... Chicago: S. C. Griggs and Company, 1879. 209 p.                    HEH, LC, N, UV, Y
Opposed to capital punishment.

FREEMAN, MARY ELEANOR (WILKINS). Eliza Sam, by Mary E. Wilkins. *In* Short Story Masterpieces (1900), No. 4931.

———— Eunice and the Doll. *In* I. Bacheller, *ed.*, Best Things from American Literature (1899), No. 195.

2028 ———— Evelina's Garden . . . New York and London: Harper & Brothers, 1899. 120 p., front.            CU, HEH, LC, N, O, Y
First separate printing; printed earlier in No. 2039.

———— Flora and Hannah. *In* Short Story Masterpieces (1900), No. 4931.

2029 ———— The Heart's Highway: A Romance of Virginia in the Seventeenth Century ... New York: Doubleday, Page & Co., 1900. 308 p., illus.                    BA, CU, H, HEH, LC, N, O, UC, UP, UVB, Y
For 1st ed. variations see BAL 6362.

2030 ——— A Humble Romance, and Other Stories . . . New York, London: Harper & Brothers, 1887. 436 p.

BU, H, HEH, LC, N, O, UC, UP, UVB, Y

*Also contains:* Two Old Lovers—A Symphony in Lavender—A Tardy Thanksgiving—A Modern Dragon—An Honest Soul—A Taste of Honey—Brakes and White Vi'lets—Robins and Hammers—On the Walpole Road—Old Lady Pingree—Cinnamon Roses—The Bar Light-House—A Lover of Flowers—A Far-Away Melody—A Moral Exigency—A Mistaken Charity—Gentian—An Object of Love—A Gatherer of Simples—An Independent Thinker—In Butterfly Time—An Unwilling Guest—A Souvenir—An Old Arithmetician—A Conflict Ended—A Patient Waiter—A Conquest of Humility.

2031 ——— The Jamesons . . . New York: Doubleday & McClure Company. Philadelphia: Curtis Publishing Company, 1899. 177 p., illus.

BA, BU, CU, H, HEH, LC, N, O, UM, UP, UVB, Y

*Also issued with imprint:* Philadelphia: Curtis Publishing Company. New York: Doubleday & McClure Co., 1899. HEH, UC

2032 ——— Jane Field: A Novel . . . New York: Harper & Brothers, 1893. 267 p., illus. BA, H, HEH, LC, N, O, UC, UM, UP, UVB, Y

2033 ——— Jerome, a Poor Man: A Novel . . . New York and London: Harper & Brothers, 1897. 506 p., illus.

BA, BU, H, HEH, LC, N, O, UC, UM, UP, UVB, Y

2034 ——— The Love of Parson Lord, and Other Stories . . . New York and London: Harper & Brothers, 1900. 232, [1] p., illus.

BA, BU, H, HEH, LC, N, O, UC, UM, UVB, Y

*Also contains:* The Tree of Knowledge—Catherine Carr—The Three Old Sisters and the Old Beau—One Good Time.

2035 ——— Madelon: A Novel . . . New York: Harper & Brothers, 1896. 376 p. BU, CU, H, HEH, N, O, UC, UM, UP, UVB, Y

2036 ——— A New England Nun, and Other Stories . . . New York: Harper & Brothers, 1891. 468 p., front.

BA, BU, CU, H, HEH, LC, N, O, UC, UM, UP, UVB, Y

*Also contains:* A Village Singer—A Gala Dress—The Twelfth Guest—Sister Liddy—Calla-Lilies and Hannah—A Wayfaring Couple—A Poetess—Christmas Jenny—A Pot of Gold—The Scent of the Roses—A Solitary—A Gentle Ghost—A Discovered Pearl—A Village Lear—Amanda and Love—Up Primrose Hill—A Stolen Christmas—Life Everlastin'—An Innocent Gamester—Louisa—A Church Mouse—A Kitchen Colonel—The Revolt of "Mother."

——— A New Year's Resolution. *In* Short Story Masterpieces (1900), No. 4931.

2037 ——— Pembroke: A Novel . . . New York: Harper & Brothers, 1894. 330 p., illus. CU, H, HEH, LC, N, O, UC, UM, UP, UVB, Y

2038 ———— The People of Our Neighborhood . . . Philadelphia: Curtis Publishing Company. New York: Doubleday & McClure Co. [cop. 1898]. 161 p., illus.     BA, BU, CU, H, HEH, LC, N, O, UC, UM, UP, UVB, Y

*Contents:* Timothy Sampson, the Wise Man—Little Margaret Snell, the Village Runaway—Cyrus Emmett, the Unlucky Man—Phebe Ann Little, the Neat Woman—Amanda Todd, the Friend of Cats—Lydia Wheelock, the Good Woman—A Quilting Bee in Our Village—The Stockwell's Apple-Paring Bee—The Christmas Sing in Our Village.

At head of title: "Ladies' Home Journal Library of Fiction."

2039 ———— Silence, and Other Stories . . . New York and London: Harper & Brothers, 1898.   279, [1] p., illus.

BA, BU, CU, H, HEH, LC, N, O, UC, UM, UP, UVB, Y

*Also contains:* The Buckley Lady—Evelina's Garden—A New England Prophet—The Little Maid at the Door—Lydia Hersey, of East Bridgewater.

2040 FREESE, JACOB R. Elizabeth's Mission (Faithful & True): A Parable of What Might Have Been, of What Was, and of What Will Be . . . Philadelphia: Crombargar & Co., 1882.   361 p., illus.     HEH, LC

At head of title: "Illustrated Edition.—Price $2."

New Jersey.

[FRENCH, ALICE.] Ambrose's Christmas Gift, by Octave Thanet [pseud.]. *In* Some Short Stories [cop. 1900], No. 5070.

[————] The Bishop's Vagabond, by Octave Thanet [pseud.]. *In* Stories by American Authors, VII (1884), No. 5273.

Later printed in No. 2045.

2041 [————] A Book of True Lovers. By Octave Thanet [pseud.]. Chicago: Way and Williams, 1897.   277, [1] p.

BA, CU, HEH, LC, N, O, UC, UM, UV, Y

*Contents:* The Strike at Glasscock's—The Judgment on Mrs. Swift—The Dilemma of Sir Guy the Neuter—The Court of Last Resort—Why Abbylonia Surrendered—The Ladder of Grief—The Captured Dream.

[————] By Uncomprehended Ways, by Octave Thanet [pseud.]. *In* Short Story Masterpieces (1900), No. 4931.

2042 [————] The Captured Dream, and Other Stories. By Octave Thanet [pseud.]. New York and London: Harper & Brothers, 1899.   128 p., illus.     CU, LC, N, O, UP, UV, Y

*Also contains:* His Duty—The Stout Miss Hopkins's Bicycle.

Title story printed earlier in No. 2041.

2043 [————] Expiation. By Octave Thanet [pseud.] . . . New York: Charles Scribner's Sons, 1890.   215 p., illus.

BA, BU, CU, H, LC, N, O, UP, UV, Y

[————] Half Devil, Half Child, by Octave Thanet [pseud.]. *In* Short Story Masterpieces (1900), No. 4931.

2044 [————] The Heart of Toil. By Octave Thanet [pseud.] ... New York: Charles Scribner's Sons, 1898. 215 p., illus.

BA, CU, H, HEH, LC, N, O, UC, UVB, Y

*Contents:* The Non-Combatant–The Way of an Election–The Moment of Clear Vision–Johnny's Job–The "Scab"–The Conscience of a Business Man.

2045 [————] Knitters in the Sun. By Octave Thanet [pseud.] ... Boston and New York: Houghton, Mifflin and Company. The Riverside Press, Cambridge, 1887. 352 p.     BA, CU, H, HEH, LC, N, O, UC, UM, UVB, Y

*Contents:* The Ogre of Ha Ha Bay–The Bishop's Vagabond–Mrs. Finlay's Elizabethan Chair–Father Quinnailon's Convert–A Communist's Wife–Schopenhauer on Lake Pepin–"Ma' Bowlin' "–Half a Curse–Whitsun Harp, Regulator.

[————] The Merry Thanksgiving of the Burglar and Plumber, by Octave Thanet [pseud.]. *In* Tales from McClure's: Humor (1897), No. 5361.

2046 [————] The Missionary Sheriff: Being Incidents in the Life of a Plain Man Who Tried to Do His Duty. By Octave Thanet [pseud.] ... New York: Harper & Brothers, 1897. 248 p., illus.

BA, CU, H, HEH, LC, N, O, UC, UM, UVB, Y

*Also contains:* The Cabinet Organ–His Duty–The Hypnotist–The Next Room–The Defeat of Amos Wickliff.

[————] The Old Partisan, by Octave Thanet [pseud.]. *In* Stories from the Chap-Book (1896), No. 5277.

2047 [————] Otto the Knight, and Other Trans-Mississippi Stories. By Octave Thanet [pseud.] ... Boston and New York: Houghton, Mifflin and Company. The Riverside Press, Cambridge, 1891. 348 p.

BA, BU, CU, H, HEH, LC, N, O, UC, UM, UP, UVB, Y

*Also contains:* The Conjured Kitchen–The First Mayor–Sist' Chaney's Black Silk–The Loaf of Peace–The Day of the Cyclone–Trusty No. 49–The Plumb Idiot–The Governor's Prerogative–The Mortgage on Jeffy.

2048 [————] A Slave to Duty, & Other Women. By Octave Thanet [pseud.]. Chicago & New York: Herbert S. Stone & Company, 1898. 221, [1] p.     BA, BU, CU, H, HEH, LC, N, O, UC, UM, UVB, Y

*Also contains:* A Colonial Dame–A Jealous Woman–A Problem in Honor –On the Blank Side of the Wall.

2049 [————] Stories of a Western Town. By Octave Thanet [pseud.] ... New York: Charles Scribner's Sons, 1893. 243 p., illus.

BA, CU, H, HEH, LC, N, O, UM, UP, UVB, Y

*Contents:* The Besetment of Kurt Lieders–The Face of Failure–Tommy and Thomas–Mother Emeritus–An Assisted Providence–Harry Lossing.

[————] Town Lot No. 1303, by Octave Thanet [pseud.]. *In* Tales from McClure's: The West (1897), No. 5363.

FRENCH, EDWARD. A Cigarette from Carcinto. *In* C. King, Rancho del Muerto [cop. 1895], No. 3109.

FRENCH, HARRY W. *See* French, Henry Willard

2050 FRENCH, HENRY WILLARD. Castle Foam; or, The Heir of Meerschaum. A Russian Story . . . Boston: Lee and Shepard. New York: Charles T. Dillingham, 1880. 371 p. H, HEH, Y

2051 ——— Ego: A Novel. By Harry W. French . . . Boston: Lee and Shepard. New York: Charles T. Dillingham, 1880. 258 p.
CU, H, HEH, LC, Y

2052 ——— Nuna, the Bramin Girl . . . Boston: Lee and Shepard. New York: Charles T. Dillingham, 1882. 322 p., illus. H, HEH

2053 ——— The Only One . . . Boston: Lee and Shepard. New York: Charles T. Dillingham, 1884. 314 p. HEH, LC, O, Y

2054 FRENCH, MINNIE REID. A Little Court of Yesterday . . . New York, London, Montreal: The Abbey Press, 114 Fifth Avenue [cop. 1900]. 230 p.
LC

FRENCH, W. E. P. The Lady in Rouge. *In* C. King, Rancho del Muerto [cop. 1895], No. 3109.
Author may be William Edward Pattison French.

2055 FRIEDMAN, ISAAC KAHN. The Lucky Number . . . Chicago: Way and Williams, 1896. 217 p., 1 l. H, HEH, LC, UC, UM, UP, Y
*Contents:* Chauvinism at Devereux's—Rouge et Noir—A Monger of Ballads—A Coat of One Color—A Pair of Eyes—The Magic Herb—The Return—The Flight of a Night-Hawk—A Fair Exchange—Aaron Pivansky's Picture.

2056 ——— Poor People: A Novel . . . Boston and New York: Houghton, Mifflin and Company. The Riverside Press, Cambridge, 1900. 244 p., 1 l. H, HEH, LC, O, UVB

2057 FRIEND, JAMES EDWARD. One Thousand Liars: A Political Romance . . . National City, California: Press of the Record Publishing Co., 1893. 147 p., illus. CU, HEH
San Diego politics.

2058 FRISBIE, FRANK DUNLAP. Number B, Sixty-Seven Million . . . Newton [Mass.]: The Circuit Press, 1900. 414 p. H, HEH, LC
*Also contains:* A Silent Witness—A School Teacher's Romance—The Story of a Ring—Joe—Corporal Tom.

2059 ——— Sir Tommy: A Chronicle of Six Events in His Life . . . Newton [Mass.]: The Circuit Press, 1899. 236, [1] p. HEH, LC
Of a man in society.

2060 DELETED.

2061 FRY, SUSANNA MARGARET DAVIDSON. A Paradise Valley Girl . . . Chicago: Woman's Temperance Publishing Association, 1899. 312 p., illus.
LC

2062 FRYE, JAMES ALBERT. Fables of Field and Staff . . . Boston: The Colonial Company, 1894. 211 p.                    BA, CU, H, HEH, LC
*Contents:* The March of the Forty Thieves—A Tale of Two Towers—One from the Veteran—Woodleigh, Q. M.—The Kerwick Cup—Officially Reported—Special Orders No. 49.

2063 ——— From Headquarters: Odd Tales Picked Up in the Volunteer Service . . . Boston: Estes and Lauriat, 1893. 211 p.       CU, H, HEH, LC
*Contents:* The Pluck of Captain Pender, C.S.N.—One Record on the Regimental Rolls—Our Horse "Acme"—From beyond the Pyramids—The Hymn That Helped—The Seventh Major—Concerning the Value of Sleep.

2064 FÜRST, HUGO. Iphigenia, a Modern Woman of Progress . . . Philadelphia: T. B. Peterson & Brothers, 306 Chestnut Street [cop. 1886]. 359 p. Copy examined at New York Public Library.

2065 FULLER, ANNA. A Literary Courtship under the Auspices of Pike's Peak . . . New York, London: G. P. Putnam's Sons; the Knickerbocker Press, 1893. 184 p., illus.                BA, H, HEH, LC, UC, UV, Y

2066 ——— One of the Pilgrims: A Bank Story . . . New York and London: G. P. Putnam's Sons; the Knickerbocker Press, 1898. 331 p.
BA, H, HEH, LC, N, O
The Pilgrim Savings Bank; New York.

2067 ——— Peak and Prairie: From a Colorado Sketch-Book . . . New York, London: G. P. Putnam's Sons; the Knickerbocker Press, 1894. 391 p., front.            BA, CU, H, HEH, LC, N, O, UC, UP, UV, Y
*Contents:* A Pilgrim in the Far West—Brian Boru—Jake Stanwood's Gal—At the Keith Ranch—The Rumpety Case—The Lame Gulch Professor—The Boss of the Wheel—Mr. Fetherbee's Adventure—An Amateur Gamble—A Rocky Mountain Shipwreck—A Stroke in the Game—The Blizzard Picnic —A Golden Vista.
1st issue make-up: title [i-ii]; Preface, iii-iv; Contents, v; dedication [vii].
2nd issue make-up: title [i-ii]; dedication [iii]; Preface, v-vi; Contents, vii. Census of copies does not distinguish between issues.

2068 ——— Pratt Portraits: Sketched in a New England Suburb . . . New York, London: G. P. Putnam's Sons; the Knickerbocker Press, 1892. 325 p.                    H, HEH, LC, N, O, UC, Y
*Contents:* Aunt Betsy's Photographs—Harriet—A Domestic Crisis—Ben's Wife —A Yankee Quixote—A New England Quack—A New England Conscience

—The Schoolmarm—A Valentine—Old Lady Pratt—Mary Anne—Well Matched —Uncle Bobby.

2069 ——— A Venetian June ... New York, London: G. P. Putnam's Sons; the Knickerbocker Press, 1896. 315 p., illus.

H, HEH, LC, N, O, UC, UM, UV, Y

Census of copies does not distinguish between trade and large-paper eds.

2070 FULLER, CAROLINE MACOMBER. Across the Campus: A Story of College Life ... New York: Charles Scribner's Sons, 1899. 441 p.

H, HEH, O, Y

2071 FULLER, EDWARD. The Complaining Millions of Men: A Novel ... New York: Harper & Brothers, 1893. 417 p. BA, CU, H, HEH, LC, O, UC, Y
Of socialism.

2072 ——— Fellow Travellers: A Story ... Boston: Cupples, Upham and Company, 1886. 341 p. AP, BA, HEH, LC

2073 ——— Forever and a Day: A Novel ... Philadelphia: J. B. Lippincott & Co., 1882. 306 p. AP, H, HEH

2074 FULLER, HECTOR. Roach & Co. Pirates, and Other Stories ... Indianapolis and Kansas City: The Bowen-Merrill Company, 1898. 236 p.

CU, HEH, LC, UP, Y

*Also contains:* The Strange Happenings in Tolly's Nullah—The Finding of the Ship—With the Sun Overhead—Gunga Hassim—The Third Mate of the Jumna—The Little Sisters of the Desolate—An Ocean Christmas—All's Well.

2075 FULLER, HENRY BLAKE. The Chatelaine of La Trinité ... New York: The Century Co., 1892. 176 p., illus.

BA, BU, CU, H, HEH, LC, N, O, UC, UM, UP, UVB, Y

2076 [———] The Chevalier of Pensieri-Vani, Together with Frequent References to the Prorege of Arcopia. By Stanton Page [pseud.]. Boston: J. G. Cupples Co. [cop. 1890]. 168 p.

BA, CU, H, HEH, N, O, UC, UVB, Y

4th ed., 1892, has author's name on title page.

2077 ——— The Cliff-Dwellers: A Novel ... New York: Harper & Brothers, 1893. 324 p., illus. BA, BU, CU, H, HEH, LC, N, O, UC, UM, UP, UVB, Y
Chicago life.

2078 ——— From the Other Side: Stories of Transatlantic Travel ... Boston and New York: Houghton, Mifflin and Company. The Riverside Press, Cambridge, 1898. 229, [1] p.

BA, BU, CU, HEH, LC, N, O, UC, UM, UP, UVB, Y

*Contents:* The Greatest of These—What Youth Can Do—The Pilgrim Sons —Pasquale's Picture.

2079 ———— The Last Refuge: A Sicilian Romance . . . Boston and New York: Houghton, Mifflin and Company. The Riverside Press, Cambridge, 1900. 284 p., 1 l.   BA, BU, CU, H, HEH, LC, N, O, UC, UM, UP, UVB, Y

2080 ———— With the Procession: A Novel . . . New York: Harper & Brothers, 1895. 336 p.   BA, BU, CU, H, HEH, LC, N, O, UC, UM, UP, UVB, Y
Business and social life; Chicago.

2081 FULLER, HULBERT. God's Rebel . . . Chicago: Regan Printing House, 1899. 373 p.   HEH, LC, UC

2082 ———— Vivian of Virginia: Being the Memoirs of Our First Rebellion . . . Boston, New York, and London: Lamson, Wolffe and Company, 1897. 377 p., illus.   CU, HEH, O, UM, UV, Y

FULLER, MABEL LOUISE. See Blodgett, Mabel Louise (Fuller)

2083 [FULLERTON, GEORGE H.] Persis: A Tale of the White Mountains. By Rambler [pseud.]. New York: Authors' Publishing Co. [cop. 1879]. 129 p.
Listed PW, Dec. 20, 1879.

2084 FULTON, CHANDOS. A Society Star; or, She Would Be an Actress. A Novel . . . New York: G. W. Dillingham, successor to G. W. Carleton & Co. London: S. Low, Son & Co., 1888. 240 p.   HEH

2085 FURMAN, LUCY S. Stories of a Sanctified Town . . . New York: The Century Co., 1896. 230 p.   H, HEH, LC, O, UC, Y
Contents: Brother Rolly's Drawback—Kate Negley's Leadings—An Experience on the Dress Line—Mary Alice's Emancipation—The Ararat Cactus Company—The Cub Run Outpouring—The Band at Smithsboro—A Special Providence—A Shiftless Man—The Grissoms—The Floating Bethel—A Sanctified Girl.

2086 [FURNISS, LOUISE E.] An Operetta in Profile. By Czeika [pseud.]. Boston: Ticknor and Company, 1887. 265 p.   BA, BU, CU, HEH, LC, N, UP
Of an effort to raise money for the church.

FUSH, pseud. See Fish, Williston

FYLES, FRANKLIN. The Only Girl at Overlook. In Eleven Possible Cases [cop. 1891], No. 1737.

G., C. J., pseud. See Freeland, Mrs. Caroline J.

2087 G., F. E. The Darling of an Empire. By F. E. G. New York: G. W. Dillingham. London: S. Low, Sons & Co., 1887. 282 p.   O

2088 G., M. A. Jeanne: The Story of a Fresh Air Child. By M. A. G. . . . Albany, N.Y.: Press of Brandon Printing Company, 1893. 50 p., front.   LC

GADE, JOHN ALLYNE. Notre Dame de Paris. On a Paris Omnibus. [Two stories.] *In* Stories from the Harvard Advocate (1896), No. 5277a.

GAGE, CHARLES S. Mr. Bixby's Christmas Visitor. *In* Stories by American Authors, IX (1885), No. 5275.

GAINES, CHARLES KELSEY. The Sickle of Fire. *In* I. Bacheller, *ed.*, Best Things from American Literature (1899), No. 195.

2089 GALLAGHER, GEORGE WASHINGTON. One Man's Struggle ... New York, London: Funk & Wagnalls, 1890. 169 p.   H, HEH, LC, UM
Temperance tale.

2090 GALLAGHER, JAMES NESTOR. Timothy Winebruiser: A Narrative in Prose and Verse ... [San Antonio, Tex.]: San Antonio Light Print, 1886. 148 p.   LC

GALLAHER, GRACE MARGARET. An Alien. *In* [F. L. Knowles] *ed.*, Cap and Gown in Prose (1900), No. 3182.

2091 —— Vassar Stories ... Boston: Richard G. Badger & Co., 1900. 269 p., 1 l., illus.   BA, HEH, LC, O
*Contents:* In the Matter of Room-Mates—The Moulders of Public Opinion —Her Position—A Sense of Obligation—Neither a Lender nor a Borrower Be—The Clan—At the First Game—On Baccalaureate Sunday.

2091a GALLAHER, JOHN. The McAllisters on the Tariff ... Boston: William H. Brine, 1893. 27 p.   HEH

2092 [GALLOWAY, JAMES M.] John Harvey: A Tale of the Twentieth Century. By Anon Moore [pseud.]. Chicago: Charles H. Kerr & Company, 1897. 407 p.   CU, H, LC
A utopia in the Missouri Valley.

GALLY, JAMES WELLESLEY. Quartz. *In* Short Stories by California Authors (1885), No. 4929.

2093 —— Sand, and Big Jack Small ... Chicago: Belford, Clarke & Co., 1880. 243 p., illus.   HEH
Locale of "Sand" is San Francisco.

2094 GARD, ANSON ALBERT. My Friend Bill: Many Stories Told in the Telling of One ... New York City: The Emerson Press, 149 Broadway [cop. 1900]. 336 p., illus.   HEH, LC

2095 GARDENER, HELEN HAMILTON. Is This Your Son, My Lord? A Novel ... Boston, Mass.: Arena Publishing Company, 1890. 257 p., front.   HEH, LC, Y

Of the double standard.

Author's maiden name was Alice Chenoweth; she adopted the name Helen H. Gardener.

2096 ———— Pray You, Sir, Whose Daughter? . . . Boston, Mass.: Arena Publishing Company, 1892. 183 p.      H, UM, UV
The New York, R. F. Fenno & Co. [cop. 1892], ed. was published no earlier than 1897.
Advocates political and intellectual freedom for women.

2097 ———— Pushed by Unseen Hands . . . New York: Commonwealth Company, 121 Fourth Avenue [cop. 1892]. 303 [i.e., 283] p., front.   Y

2098 ———— A Thoughtless Yes . . . New York: Belford Company, 18-22 East 18th Street [cop. 1890]. 231 p.      HEH
*Contents:* A Splendid Judge of a Woman—The Lady of the Club—Under Protest—For the Prosecution—A Rusty Link in the Chain—The Boler House of Mystery—The Time-Lock of Our Ancestors—Florence Campbell's Fate—My Patient's Story.

2099 ———— An Unofficial Patriot . . . Boston: Arena Publishing Company, 1894. 351 p., front.      BU, CU, H, HEH, LC
A belated antislavery novel.

———— Why Judge Dutton Resigned. *In* Short Story Masterpieces (1900), No. 4931.

2100 GARDINER, ALFRED PAUL. A Drummer's Parlor Stories . . . New York: A. P. Gardiner, 1898. 107 p., illus.      HEH, N

2101 ———— The House of Cariboo, and Other Tales from Arcadia . . . New York: A. P. Gardiner, 1900. 218 p., illus.      HEH
*Contents:* The Archipelago—Along the Front—The House of Cariboo—The Growing Maskinonge.

GARDINER, WILLIAM RAY. The Museme with the Silver Heart. *In* Short Story Masterpieces (1900), No. 4931.

GARDNER, ALFRED AUGUSTUS. Fidèle. Rev. Dr. Black. [Two stories.] *In* Short Stories from Outing [cop. 1895], No. 4930.

———— Viola. *In* Stories from the Harvard Advocate (1896), No. 5277a.

2102 GARDNER, CELIA EMMELINE. Seraph—or Mortal? A Romance . . . New York: G. W. Dillingham, 1890. 430 p.      HEH, LC

2103 ———— Terrace Roses: A Romance . . . New York: G. W. Carleton & Co. London: S. Low & Co., 1878. 394 p.      LC

2104 ———— A Woman's Wiles: "An Ower True Tale" . . . New York: G. W. Carleton & Co. London: S. Low & Co., 1876. 452 p.      HEH

2105 ——— Won Under Protest: A Romance ... New York: G. W. Dillingham Co., 1896. 286 p.                                          HEH, LC

2106 GARDNER, ETTA M. The Old Graham Place ... New York, London, Montreal: The Abbey Press [cop. 1900]. 55 p.                       LC
New Hampshire.

2107 GARDNER, FULTON. Checkered Lights: A Novel ... Chicago: Laird & Lee, cop. 1887. 175 p., illus.                                LC

2108 GARDNER, S. A. Outwitted at Last: A Novel ... New York: G. W. Carleton & Co. London: S. Low & Co., 1878. 360 p.            HEH
Of a bank robbery.

2109 GARDNER, MRS. SARAH M. H. The Fortunes of Margaret Weld ... Boston: Arena Publishing Company, 1894. 233 p.              H, HEH, LC
Of the relationship of the sexes.

2110 ——— Quaker Idyls ... New York: Henry Holt and Company, 1894. 223 p., front.                                   HEH, LC, O, UV, Y
Contents: Twelfth Street Meeting—A Quaker Wedding—Two Gentlewomen —Our Little Neighbors—Pamelia Tewksbury's Courtship—Some Ante-Bellum Letters from a Quaker Girl—Uncle Joseph—My Grandame's Secret.

2111 GARDNER, WILLIAM HENRY. The Curious Case of General Delaney Smythe ... New York, London, Montreal: The Abbey Press, 114 Fifth Avenue [cop. 1900]. 204 p., illus.                                LC
Deposited Dec. 22, 1900.

2112 GARLAND, HAMLIN. The Eagle's Heart ... New York: D. Appleton and Company, 1900. 369 p.          CU, H, HEH, N, O, UC, UM, UVB, Y
Life on the midwest plains.

2113 ——— Jason Edwards, an Average Man ... Boston: Arena Publishing Company, 1892. 213 p.      BA, CU, H, HEH, N, O, UC, UM, UP, UVB, Y
Of a workingman.

2114 ——— A Little Norsk; or, Ol' Pap's Flaxen ... New York: D. Appleton and Company, 1892. 157 p.
BA, BU, CU, H, HEH, LC, N, O, UC, UM, UP, UVB, Y
Of a Dakota farm girl.

2115 ——— Main-Travelled Roads: Six Mississippi Valley Stories ... Boston, Mass.: Arena Publishing Company, 1891. 260 p.
CU, H, HEH, LC, N, O, UM, UVB, Y
Contents: A Branch-Road—Up the Coulé—Among the Corn-Rows—The Return of a Private—Under the Lion's Paw—Mrs. Ripley's Trip.

2116 ——— ——— New York: The Macmillan Company. London: Macmillan & Co., Ltd., 1899. 299 p.          LC, UM, UP, UVB, Y
This ed. adds: The Creamery Man—A Day's Pleasure—Uncle Ethan Ripley.

2117 —————— A Member of the Third House: A Dramatic Story . . . Chicago: F. J. Schulte & Company; the Ariel Press, 298 Dearborn Street [cop. 1892]. 239 p., front.  BA, CU, HEH, LC, N, O, UC, UP, UVB, Y
Of political warfare.

2118 —————— Prairie Folks . . . Chicago: F. J. Schulte & Company, 1893. 255 p.  CU, H, HEH, N, O, UVB, Y
Contents: Uncle Ethan's Speculation—The Test of Elder Pill—William Bacon's Hired Man—Sim Burns's Wife—Saturday Night on the Farm—Village Cronies—Drifting Crane—Old Daddy Deering—The Sociable at Dudley's.

2119 —————— Rose of Dutcher's Coolly . . . Chicago: Stone & Kimball, 1895. 403 p., 1 l.  CU, H, HEH, LC, N, O, UC, UP, UVB, Y
Country girl goes to Chicago.

2120 —————— The Spirit of Sweetwater . . . Philadelphia: Curtis Publishing Company. New York: Doubleday & McClure Co. [cop. 1898]. 100 p., illus.  CU, H, HEH, LC, N, O, UC, UM, UP, UVB, Y
At head of title: "Ladies' Home Journal Library of Fiction."
Colorado.

2121 —————— A Spoil of Office: A Story of the Modern West . . . Boston, Mass.: Arena Publishing Company, 1892. 385 p., front.
CU, HEH, LC, N, O, UC, UP, UVB, Y

2122 —————— The Trail of the Goldseekers: A Record of Travel in Prose and Verse . . . New York: The Macmillan Company. London: Macmillan & Co., Ltd., 1899. 264 p.  BU, CU, H, HEH, LC, N, O, UM, UP, UVB, Y
Based on his trip to the Yukon; much of the material is from his diary which is in HEH.

2123 —————— Wayside Courtships . . . New York: D. Appleton and Company, 1897. 281 p.  BA, CU, H, HEH, LC, N, O, UC, UP, UVB, Y
Contents: At the Beginning—A Preacher's Love Story—A Meeting in the Foothills—A Stop-Over at Tyre—An Alien in the Pines—The Owner of the Mill Farm—Of Those Who Seek—Before the Low Green Door—Upon Impulse—The End of Love Is Love of Love.

2124 GARLAND, RUFUS CUMMINS. Zaléa: A Psychological Episode and Tale of Love . . . Washington: The Neale Company, 1900. 146 p.  HEH, LC
Detective story; Washington, D.C.

2125 GARLAND, WILL A. The Broken Locket . . . New York: G. W. Dillingham Co., 1899. 316 p.  LC
Deposited Aug. 14, 1899.
Of Kentucky and Washington, D.C., political life.

2126 —————— Matthew Doyle . . . New York: G. W. Dillingham Co., 1900. 282 p.  LC
Of lynch law; a southern town.

2127 GARNER, LOUIS. An Unmistakable Flirtation . . . New York: G. W. Carleton & Co., 1879. 256 p. AP, LC

2128 GARNER, MRS. ZELOTA F. Sex in Sin . . . Battle Creek, Mich.: Gage, De Vos & Company, 1884. 385 p., illus. HEH
Temperance novel.

GARNSEY, JOHN HENDERSON. Chinese White. *In* J. J. Conway, *ed.*, Stories (1893), No. 1172.

2129 GARRIGUES, MRS. ADÉLE M. Summer Boarders . . . New York: The Authors' Publishing Company, 27 Bond Street [cop. 1880]. 188 p., front. HEH, LC
Of a country boardinghouse.

GARRISON, LLOYD McKIM. Phryne: A Phantasy. *In* Stories from the Harvard Advocate (1896), No. 5277a.

2130 GARRISON, WENDELL PHILLIPS. The New Gulliver . . . Jamaica, Queensborough, New York: The Marion Press, 1898. 50 p., 1 l. BU, H, HEH, LC, Y
Verso of last leaf of some copies: "One hundred and twenty copies printed on the Marion Press . . . ."

2131 GARVER, WILLIAM LINCOLN. Brother of the Third Degree . . . Boston: Arena Publishing Company, 1894. 377 p. LC
Of Rosicrucian interest.

2132 GASH, ABRAM DALE. The False Star: A Tale of the Occident . . . Chicago: W. B. Conkey Company, 1899. 578 p., front. BU, H, HEH, LC
Anti-Mormon; Utah.

2133 [GASTON, HENRY A.] Mars Revealed; or, Seven Days in the Spirit World, Containing an Account of the Spirit's Trip to Mars, and His Return to Earth. What He Saw and Heard on Mars . . . By a Spirit Yet in the Flesh. San Francisco: Published for the writer, by A. L. Bancroft & Co., 1880. 208 p. HEH, LC

2134 [GATCHELL, CHARLES.] Haschisch: A Novel. By Thorold King [pseud.]. Chicago: A. C. McClurg & Company, 1886. 314 p. HEH, LC
"Haschisch" was used to expose the murderer.

2135 ——— What a Woman Did . . . Chicago: Era Publishing Company, 1900. 337 p., illus.
Information supplied by Helen D. Baird, of St. Benedict's College Library, Atchison, Kansas.

2136 GATES, LOU. A Hell and Heaven to Even Up . . . Atlanta, 1897.
Ella M. Thornton, comp., *Finding-List of Books . . . Relating to Georgia* (Atlanta, Ga., 1928), locates a copy in Georgia State Library, Atlanta.

2137 GATEWOOD, JULIA GREENLEAF (HOWARD). Wedded Unwooed: A Novel
... New York: G. W. Dillingham, 1892. 517 p.          LC, Y

2138 GAY, EVA. A Tale of the Twin Cities: Lights and Shadows of the Street
Car Strike in Minneapolis and St. Paul, Minnesota, Beginning April 11,
1889... Minneapolis, 1889. 84 p., illus.          LC, UM, Y

2139 GAYARRÉ, CHARLES ÉTIENNE ARTHUR. Aubert Dubayet; or, The Two Sister Republics ... Boston: James R. Osgood and Company, 1882. 479
p., front.          AP, BA, CU, H, HEH, LC, O, UC, UP, UVB, Y
Historical romance of American and French revolutions.

2140 GAYLER, CHARLES. Fritz, the Emigrant: A Story of New York Life.
Founded upon Mr. Gayler's Drama of "Fritz" ... New York: Frank
Leslie's Publishing House, 1876. 89 p., front. Printed in double col-
umns.          BU, HEH, LC

2141 ――― Montague; or, The Belle of the Matinee ... New York: Frank
Leslie's Publishing House, 1877. 90 p., illus. Printed in double col-
umns.          HEH
At head of title: "Popular Library Series."

2142 GAYMAN, HORACE. The Pretty Stenographer; or, The State of Arboria
under Prohibition and Female Suffrage ... New York: Published for
the author, 1889. 272 p.
Listed PW, May 18, 1889.

2143 [GAZZAM, ANNA READING.] A Sketch in the Ideal: A Romance. Philadelphia: J. B. Lippincott Company, 1891. 194 p., illus.          LC

2144 GEDNEY, FREDERICK G. Shenandoah; or, The Horizon's Bar. A Story of
the War ... New York: J. S. Ogilvie, 57 Rose Street, cop. 1890. 241 p.
                                                                   Y

2145 GEISSLER, LUDWIG A. Looking Beyond ... A Sequel to "Looking Backward" by Edward Bellamy, and an Answer to "Looking Further Forward" by Richard Michaelis ... New Orleans: L. Graham & Son,
printers, 1891. 134 p.          LC

GEMMEL, J. E. Nell and I. In J. J. Conway, ed., Stories (1893), No 1172.

GENONE, HUDOR, pseud. See Roe, William James

2146 GEPPERT, DORA (HIGBEE). In "God's Country": A Southern Romance.
By D. Higbee ... New York: American Publishers Corporation, 310-
318 Sixth Avenue [cop. 1897]. 243 p.          H, HEH, UC, Y
First published in the omitted "Belford American Novel Series," No. 218,
1890.
Kentucky bluegrass country.

2147 ———— "Un ze Studio": An Idyl of the Housetops . . . Atlanta, Ga.: The Franklin Printing and Publishing Co., Geo. W. Harrison, state printer, 1895. 60 p. LC

2148 GESTEFELD, URSULA NEWELL. The Leprosy of Miriam . . . New York: The Gestefeld Library & Publishing Co., 1894. 265 p. LC

2149 ———— The Woman Who Dares . . . New York: Lovell, Gestefeld & Company, 125 East Twenty-Third Street [cop. 1892]. 358 p. H, LC

2150 GIBBONS, LOUISE ELISE. Janet; or, The Christmas Stockings . . . New York: The Knickerbocker Press, 1899. 40 p. BU
Little girl dies in canal.
Not a juvenile.

2151 [————] Truth: A Novel. By Louis de Villeneuve [pseud.]. New York: Published by the author, 1894. 369 p. HEH, LC
HEH copy autographed by author.

2152 GIBSON, EVA KATHERINE (CLAPP). A Dark Secret. By Eva Katherine Clapp. Chicago: Laird & Lee, 1889. 178 p., front.
Information from National Union Catalogue; no copy seen.

2153 [————] Her Bright Future . . . Chicago: Henry A. Sumner and Company, 1880. 309 p. CU, HEH, LC

2154 ———— A Lucky Mishap: A Novel . . . Chicago: Belford, Clarke & Co., 1883. 276 p. HEH, LC
Kansas and Colorado.

2155 [————] A Woman's Triumph: A True Story of Western Life. Chicago: A. H. Andrews & Co., 1885. 80 p. LC

2156 [GIBSON, LOUIS HENRY.] A Romance of the Milling Revolutions; or, The History of a Typical Modern Mill. By "Cereal" [pseud.]. Kansas City, Mo.: Clifford F. Hall, 1886. 109 p., 2 diag. LC, UV

2157 GIELOW, MARTHA (SAWYER). Mammy's Reminiscences, and Other Sketches . . . New York: A. S. Barnes and Company, 1898. 109 p., illus. BU, CU, HEH, LC, UV, Y
*Contains:* Ca'line's Weddin'—How Brer' Simon Got 'Erligion—How Sis' Viney Went Home to Glory—"De Pianner Juett"—Seein' Sperrits—Dat Time Honey Got Los'—Plantation Nursery Scene.

2158 GIFFORD, PHILIP A. The Quaker Schoolmarm . . . New York: The Mershon Company [cop. 1898]. 134 p., illus. LC

2159 GILBERT, FRANK M. Plunkett's Troubles . . . New York: W. B. Smith & Co., 27 Bond Street [cop. 1882]. 155 p., illus. LC

2160 [GILBERT, MRS. R. L.] Thump's Client. By Charles D. Knight [pseud.] ... New York: The Authors' Publishing Company, 27 Bond Street [cop. 1880]. 505 p.
H, HEH, LC, O

2161 GILCHRIST, ANNIE (SOMERS). Harcourt; or, A Soul Illumined ... Philadelphia: J. B. Lippincott Company, 1886. 490 p.
LC

2162 ———— Rosehurst; or, The Step-Daughter. A Novel ... Philadelphia: J. B. Lippincott & Co., 1884. 292 p.
LC

2163 [GILCHRIST, MRS. ROSETTA LUCE.] Apples of Sodom: A Story of Mormon Life. Cleveland: William W. Williams, 1883. 322 p.
HEH, LC
HEH copy has printed author slip, bound in, preceding title page.
Anti-Mormon novel.

2164 [GILDER, JEANNETTE LEONARD.] Taken by Siege: A Novel. Philadelphia: J. B. Lippincott & Company, 1887. 294 p.
HEH, LC, N
Of journalists and New York society.

GILES, ELLA A. *See* Ruddy, Ella Augusta (Giles)

GILFILLAN, LILLIAN. Uncle Duke's "B'ar" Story. *In* C. King, Rancho del Muerto [cop. 1895], No. 3109.

2165 [GILL, J. THOMPSON.] Within and Without: A Philosophical, Lego-Ethical, and Religious Romance in Four Parts. Part 1, Helen Ray's Narrative; Part 2, The Moody Revival of 1876; Part 3, The Unfinished Conflict; Part 4, Truth and the Law Triumphant. Chicago: J. Thompson Gill, manager, C. & B. Publishing Co., 1887. 318 p.
LC, UM

2166 [GILL, WILLIAM FEARING] ed. Golden Treasures of Poetry, Romance, and Art ... Boston: William F. Gill and Company, 1876. 360 p., illus.
BU, H, LC
*Contains:* Priscilla, by Edward Eggleston—Recollections of Ole Bull, by L. Maria Child—Going Somewhere, by M. Quad [i.e., Charles B. Lewis]—How One Man Was Saved, by Amanda M. Douglass.

2167 [————] ed. Laurel Leaves: Original Poems, Stories, and Essays ... Boston: William F. Gill and Company, 1876. 446 p., illus.
BA, BU, H, HEH, LC, N, UC, UM, UVB, Y
*Contains:* A Moonlight Wreck, by Harriet Prescott Spofford—Woe unto the Pitcher, by Louise Chandler Moulton—Transcendental Wild Oats, by Louisa M. Alcott—A Strange Arrival, by J. W. De Forrest [i.e., De Forest]—The Christmas Club: A Ghost Story, by Edward Eggleston.

2168 ———— ed. Papyrus Leaves: Poems, Stories, and Essays ... New York: R. Worthington, 1880. 403 p., illus.
CU, H, LC, UC, Y
*Contains:* Rougegorge, by Harriet Prescott Spofford—Recollections of Old Bull, by L. Maria Child—The Too Soon Dead, by G. P. Lathrop—Priscilla, by Edward Eggleston—My Friend Moses, by John Habberton—How One Man Was Saved, by Amanda M. Douglass.

2169 GILLETTE, WILLIAM HOOKER. A Legal Wreck ... New York: Rockwood Publishing Co., 1888. 288 p. BU, H, HEH, Y
Of the law.

2170 GILLIAM, CHARLES FREDERICK. Love and Medicine: A Novel ... Washington, D. C.: Gray & Clarkson, 1886. 390 p. LC
Southern Ohio.

2171 GILLIAM, EDWARD WINSLOW. Paul Beaumont ... Baltimore: Press of the Sun Printing Office, 1899. 486 p. CU, HEH, LC
A defense of orthodoxy.

2172 ———— 1791: A Tale of San Domingo ... Baltimore: John Murphy & Co., 1890. 308 p. CU, HEH, LC, Y

2173 ———— Thomas Ruffin ... Baltimore: Nichols, Killam, & Maffitt, 1896. 335 p. HEH, LC, Y
Ante bellum South.

2174 GILLMAN, HENRY. Hassan, a Fellah: A Romance of Palestine ... Boston: Little, Brown and Company, 1898. 597 p. H, HEH, LC, O, UP, UVB, Y

2175 GILLMAN, NATHANIEL ISAIAH. Circumstantial Affection: A Realistic Romance of the New York Ghetto ... New York and London: F. Tennyson Neely Co. [cop. 1900]. 119 p., illus. LC, Y
Deposited Nov. 19, 1900.

2176 GILMAN, BRADLEY. The Parsonage Porch: Seven Stories from a Clergyman's Note-Book ... Boston: Little, Brown and Company, 1900. 250 p. H, HEH, LC, O, UM, UP, Y
Contents: A Misunderstood Dog—My Old Silk Hat—A Frankenstein Family—Here Endeth the First Lesson—Willis the Dreamer—Wanted: A Young Minister—The Rival Undertakers.

2177 GILMAN, CHARLOTTE (PERKINS) STETSON. The Yellow Wall Paper. By Charlotte Perkins Stetson. Boston: Small, Maynard & Company, 1899. 55 p. BA, HEH, LC, O, UVB, Y
Wallpaper drives a woman insane.

2178 GILMAN, SAMUEL C. The Story of a Western Claim: A Tale of How Two Boys Solved the Indian Question ... Philadelphia: J. B. Lippincott Company, 1893. 201 p. CU, LC

2179 GILMAN, MRS. STELLA LUCILE. That Dakota Girl ... New York: United States Book Company, 5 and 7 East Sixteenth Street. Chicago, 266 & 268 Wabash Ave. [cop. 1892]. 240 p. H, HEH, LC

GILMAN, WENONA, pseud. See Schoeffel, Florence Blackburn (White)

GILMER, ELIZABETH M. The Miracle of Love. *In* Short Story Masterpieces (1900), No. 4931.

2180 GILMORE, JAMES ROBERTS. The Last of the Thorndikes... New York: The People's Publishing Company, 1889. 304 p.    CU, HEH, N, Y

2181 GILMORE, MINNIE L. A Son of Esau ... New York: Lovell, Coryell & Company, 43, 45, and 47 East Tenth Street [cop. 1892]. 353 p., front.
HEH, LC, UM, UVB
Society in "Newfield," Colorado.

2182 ———— The Woman Who Stood Between . . . New York: Lovell, Coryell & Company, 43, 45, and 47 East Tenth Street [cop. 1892]. 155 p.    HEH, O, UVB
Of an anarchist.

GIPSY, *pseud. See* Sherman, Miss Frankie B.

2183 [GIVINS, ROBERT CARTWRIGHT.] Land Poor: A Chicago Parable. By Snivig C. Trebor [pseud.]. Chicago, 1884. 117 p., front.    LC

2184 [————] The Millionaire Tramp. By Snivig C. Trebor [pseud.] ... Chicago: Cook County Review, 1886. 181 p., front.    LC

2185 ———— The Rich Man's Fool: A Novel ... Chicago: Laird & Lee, 1890. 431 p., illus.    LC, N
At head of title: "The Library of Choice Fiction."

2186 [————] The Unwritten Will: A Romance. By Snivig C. Trebor [pseud.] ... Chicago: Rhodes & McClure Publishing Company, 1886. 214 p.    HEH

2187 GLADDEN, WASHINGTON. The Cosmopolis City Club ... New York: The Century Company, 1893. 135 p.    CU, HEH, N, O, UC, UM, UP, Y

2188 GLASCOCK, MARY WILLIS (WALL). Dare ... San Francisco: The California Publishing Company, 1882. 293 p.    HEH, LC
San Francisco.

———— Liz. *In* Short Stories by California Authors (1885), No. 4929.

2189 [GLASGOW, MISS CARY.] A Successful Failure: An Outline ... Richmond, Va.: West, Johnston & Co., 1883. 68 p.    LC

2190 [GLASGOW, ELLEN ANDERSON GHOLSON.] The Descendant: A Novel ... New York: Harper & Brothers, 1897. 276 p.
BU, CU, H, HEH, N, O, UP, UV, Y
*Also issued with imprint:* New York and London: Harper & Brothers, 1897.
HEH, UV

2191 —— Phases of an Inferior Planet ... New York and London: Harper & Brothers, 1898. 324, [1] p.

BU, CU, H, HEH, LC, N, O, UC, UM, UP, UVB, Y

New York.

2192 —— The Voice of the People ... New York: Doubleday, Page & Co., 1900. 444 p. BU, H, HEH, N, O, UC, UM, UP, UV, Y

Reconstruction period; Virginia.

2193 GLASIER, JESSIE C. Gaining the Heights ... Cincinnati: Standard Publishing Company, 1890. 242 p. LC

2194 [GLASS, MAXIMILLIAN.] Van Alden, Jr.; or, A New York Gentleman. By Maximillian [pseud.]. [Newark, N.J., cop. 1891.] 220 p. LC

Deposited Apr. 6, 1892.

2195 GLEASON, ADELE. The Georgia Belle ... New York: Charles Francis, printer, 1895. 218, [1] p., front. HEH

2196 GLENNON, M. J. Boomville: A Tale of Western Minnesota ... Minneapolis: L. Kimball Printing Co., 1891. 131 p. LC, UM

GLENWOOD, IDA, *pseud. See* Gorton, Mrs. Cynthia M. R.

GLOVER, ELIZABETH, *pseud. See* Bennett, Mary E.

2197 GOFF, GEORGE PAUL. Johnny Quickstep's Whaling Voyage ... San Francisco, Cal., 1894. 240 p. HEH, LC

2198 —— Nick Baba's Last Drink, and Other Sketches ... Lancaster, Penna.: Inquirer Printing and Publishing Company, 1879. 84 p., illus.
LC

*Also contains:* Trip to Currituck—Haunted Island—Legend of Berkeley Springs.

2199 [GOFF, HARRIET NEWELL (KNEELAND).] Other Fools and Their Doings; or, Life among the Freedmen. By One Who Has Seen It. New York: J. S. Ogilvie & Company, 29 Rose Street [cop. 1880]. 234 p., illus.

CU, HEH, LC, N, UM

Of Negro massacres in South Carolina.

2200 —— Was It an Inheritance; or, Nannie Grant. A Narrative ... Philadelphia: Claxton, Remsen, & Haffelfinger, 1876. 352 p., illus.

H, HEH, LC

GOLDEN LIGHT, *pseud. See* Hicks, William Watkin

2201 GOLDSBOROUGH, EDMUND KENNEDY. Ole Mars an' Ole Miss ... Washington, D.C.: National Publishing Co., 1900. 219 p., illus. BU, HEH, LC, UV

GOLDSMITH, CHRISTABEL, *pseud. See* Smith, Fannie N.

2202　GOOCH, FANI PUSEY. Miss Mordeck's Father . . . New York: Dodd, Mead & Company [cop. 1890]. 288 p.　AP, HEH, LC, O, UC
Of a dual personality and existence.

2203　GOODHUE, JAMES M. Struck a Lead: An Historical Tale of the Upper Lead Region . . . Chicago: Jameson & Morse, 1883. 115 p.　H, LC
Wisconsin-Illinois border.

2204　GOODLOE, ABBIE CARTER. College Girls . . . New York: Charles Scribner's Sons, 1895. 288 p., illus.　BU, H, HEH, N, O, UP, Y
Contents: A Photograph—An Aquarelle—"La Belle Hélène"—As Told by Her —A Short Career—An Episode—Her Decision—Revenge—The College Beauty —A Telephoned Telegram—"Miss Rose"—A Short Study in Evolution—The Genius of Bowlder Bluff—Time and Tide.

2205　GOODWIN, CHARLES CARROLL. The Comstock Club . . . Salt Lake City, Utah: Tribune Printing Company, 1891. 288 p., illus.
CU, H, HEH, LC, N, UM, UC, Y
California and Nevada mining.

2206　——— The Wedge of Gold . . . Salt Lake City, Utah: Tribune Job Printing Company, 1893. 283 p.　CU, H, HEH, N, UC, Y
Relates to the Comstock lode.

2207　GOODWIN, CHARLES JAQUES. The Rose and the Thorn: A Tale of Modern Life . . . New York, Chicago, London: The Neely Company [cop. 1900]. 302 p.　LC
Boston.

GOODWIN, MRS. H. B.　See Talcott, Hannah Elizabeth (Bradbury) Goodwin

2208　[GOODWIN, HENRY LEAVITT.] Clare Duval: A Novel. By Clement Wilkes [pseud.]. New York: G. W. Dillingham Company [cop. 1900]. 316 p.　LC

2209　[———] Sidney Forrester. By Clement Wilkes [pseud.]. New York: H. W. Hagemann, 1895. 351 p.　LC

GOODWIN, JAMES S. Internecine Comparison. In Mavericks (1892), No. 3663.

2210　GOODWIN, MAUD (WILDER). Flint, His Faults, His Friendships, and His Fortunes . . . Boston: Little, Brown and Company, 1897. 362 p.
BA, CU, H, HEH, LC, N, O, UVB, Y
From a seashore resort to New York.

2211　——— The Head of a Hundred: Being an Account of Certain Passages in the Life of Humphrey Huntoon, Esqr., Sometyme an Officer in the Colony of Virginia. Edited by Maud Wilder Goodwin . . . Boston:

Little, Brown & Comp'y, 1895. 225 p. BA, CU, H, HEH, LC, N, O, UM, UV, Y
Of the arrival of maids at James City, about 1622, to be married, and of the massacre.

2212 ——— White Aprons: A Romance of Bacon's Rebellion, Virginia, 1676 ... Boston: Little, Brown and Co., 1896. 339 p.
BA, BU, H, HEH, LC, UV, Y

GOOLSBY, C. V., *jt. au. See* [Miller, L. A.] The Life of a Tramp (1894), No. 3743.

GORDON, ARMISTEAD CHURCHILL. Flandroe's Mogul. *In* Stories of the Railway (1893), No. 5281.

2213 GORDON, C. I. The Bankrupt's Son: A Tale of the Panic of '73 ... Denver, Colo.: G. M. Collier, printer, 1892. 263 p. CU, LC

2214 [GORDON, EMMA E.] Cousin John's Extravagant Wife: A Story. Brattleboro, Vt.: C. M. Colburn & Co., druggists [188-?]. Cover title, 32 p., illus. HEH
Caption title includes "By Emily Hayes" [pseud.].
The tale, written to sell Diamond dyes, occupies first 12 p.

2215 GORDON, HELEN (VAN METRE) VAN-ANDERSON. It Is Possible: A Story of Life. By Helen Van-Anderson. Chicago: New Era Publishing Co., 1891. 342 p. HEH, LC

2216 ——— The Journal of a Live Woman ... Boston, Mass.: Geo. H. Wright, 1895. 164 p. BU, LC

2217 ——— The Right Knock: A Story. By Nellie V. Anderson ... Chicago: Published by the author, 1889. 307 p. HEH, LC, N, UC
Of Christian Science.

2218 GORDON, HENRI. Alva Vine; or, Art Versus Duty ... New York: The American News Company, 39 & 41 Chambers Street [cop. 1880]. 233 p., illus. H, LC
Of a woman who thinks for herself.

GORDON, JULIEN, *pseud. See* Cruger, Julie Grinnell (Storrow)

2219 GORDON, NANCY MCKAY. Her Bungalow: An Atlantian Memory ... Chicago: Hermetic Publishing Co., 1898. 238 p. LC

2220 GORRELL, JOSEPH R. Sins Absolved: A Romance. War, Religion, and Love ... Des Moines: Kenyon Printing and Mfs. Co., 1895. 272 p.
Information supplied by Frederick L. Arnold of Princeton University Library.

2221 [GORTON, MRS. CYNTHIA M. R.] Lily Pearl and the Mistress of Rosedale. By Ida Glenwood [pseud.] . . . Edited by Major Joseph Kirkland. Chicago: Dibble Publishing Co., 1892. 458 p., illus.     BU, HEH, LC

2222 GOSEWISCH, WALTER R. Memoirs of Student Life in Germany and Vacation Trips in the Tyrol, Switzerland, and Austria . . . Los Angeles, Cal.: John H. Train, 1898. 282 p., illus.     HEH, LC

2223 GOSS, CHARLES FREDERIC. The Redemption of David Corson . . . Indianapolis: The Bowen-Merrill Company [cop. 1900]. 418 p.
BU, H, HEH, LC, O, UM, UV

2224 GOULD, ANTHONY. A Woman of Sorek . . . New York: The American News Company, 39 Chambers Street [cop. 1889]. 257 p.     HEH, LC
"Story belongs to the sensational, unhealthy class of fiction misnamed 'realistic'." PW, Aug. 3, 1889.

2225 [GOULD, MRS. JENNIE W.] Truth Is Stranger Than Fiction. By Zelma Hope [pseud.]. [Port Henry, N.Y.?]: W. Lansing & Son, 1891. 86 p.
HEH, LC, UM
"A Port Henry vs. California story." P. [5].

GRAGG, AGNES, *pseud. See* Blaisdell, Mrs. A. H.

2226 GRAHAM, ANDREW JACKSON. The Lost Document: A Story of the Northwest . . . Minneapolis, Minn.: Printed by F. F. Hennig [1888?]. 80 p., 1 l., illus.     HEH, LC, UM, Y

2227 [GRAHAM, EDWIN BROWN.] In the Coils; or, The Coming Conflict. By "A Fanatic." Philadelphia: A. T. McDill, 1882. 352 p.     HEH, LC
Anti-Masonic.

2228 GRAHAM, MARGARET (COLLIER). Stories of the Foot-Hills . . . Boston and New York: Houghton, Mifflin and Company. The Riverside Press, Cambridge, 1895. 262 p.     BA, CU, H, HEH, LC, O, UC, UM, UP, Y
*Contents:* The Withrow Water Right—Alex Randall's Conversion—Idy—The Complicity of Enoch Embody—Em—Colonel Bob Jarvis—Brice.

2229 GRAHAM, MARIE. A Devout Bluebeard . . . New York: The Abbey Press, 114 Fifth Avenue [cop. 1900]. 300 p., front.     LC, UC
Deposited Dec. 13, 1900.

GRANDGENT, CHARLES HALL. An Indian Legend. *In* Stories from the Harvard Advocate (1896), No. 5277a.

GRANICE, ROWENA. *See* Steele, Rowena (Granice)

2230 GRANT, ROBERT. The Art of Living . . . New York: Charles Scribner's Sons, 1895. 353 p.     AP, BA, CU, H, HEH, LC, O, UC, UP, UVB, Y

*Contents:* Income—The Dwelling—House-Furnishing and the Commissariat —Education—Occupation—The Use of Time—The Summer Problem—The Case of Man—The Case of Woman—The Conduct of Life.
In narrative form.

2231 ———— An Average Man ... Boston: James R. Osgood and Company, 1884. 300 p.             AP, BA, CU, H, HEH, LC, N, O, UC, UM, UP, UVB
New York.

2232 ———— The Bachelor's Christmas, and Other Stories ... New York: Charles Scribner's Sons, 1895. 309 p., illus.
                                  BA, H, HEH, LC, O, UC, UM, UP, UVB, Y
*Also contains:* An Eye for an Eye—In Fly-Time—Richard and Robin—The Matrimonial Tontine Benefit Association—By Hook or Crook.

2233 ———— The Carletons: A Novel ... New York: Robert Bonner's Sons, 1891. 309 p., illus.                   AP, CU, HEH, UC

2234 ———— The Confessions of a Frivolous Girl: A Story of Fashionable Life ... Boston: A. Williams and Co. New York: Brentano's Literary Emporium, 1880. 220 p.        AP, BU, CU, H, HEH, N, O, UP, UVB, Y

2235 [————] Face to Face ... New York: Charles Scribner's Sons, 1886. 396 p.                          BA, H, HEH, LC, N, O
Of capital and labor.

2236 ———— The King's Men: A Tale of To-Morrow ... New York: Charles Scribner's Sons, 1884. 270 p.
                        BA, BU, CU, H, HEH, LC, N, O, UC, UM, UP, UVB, Y
John Boyle O'Reilly, J. S. of Dale (i.e., Frederic Jesup Stimson), and John T. Wheelwright, jt. aus.
England 200 years hence.

2237 ———— The Knave of Hearts: A Fairy Story ... Boston: Ticknor and Company, 1886. 198 p., illus.     AP, BA, BU, CU, H, HEH, LC, N, O, UVB

2238 ———— Mrs. Harold Stagg: A Novel ... New York: Robert Bonner's Sons [cop. 1891]. 240 p., illus.      BA, CU, H, HEH, N, UVB
First published in the omitted "Choice Series" and "Ledger Library."
Social satire.

2239 ———— Opinions of a Philosopher ... New York: Charles Scribner's Sons, 1893. 224 p., illus.     AP, BA, CU, H, HEH, LC, O, UP, UVB, Y

2240 ———— The Reflections of a Married Man ... New York: Charles Scribner's Sons, 1892. 165 p.     AP, BA, CU, H, LC, O, UC, UP, UV, Y

2241 ———— A Romantic Young Lady ... Boston: Ticknor and Company, 1886. 354 p.         AP, BA, CU, H, HEH, LC, N, O, UP, UVB
Of the daughter of a millionaire.

2242 ——— Unleavened Bread ... New York: Charles Scribner's Sons, 1900. 431 p.          AP, BA, BU, H, HEH, LC, N, O, UC, UM, UP, UVB, Y
Of an ambitious woman.

2243 GRANVILLE, AUSTYN. The Fallen Race ... New York and Chicago: F. T. Neely [cop. 1892]. 352 p., illus.          CU, HEH, O
Probably first published in the omitted "Neely's Library of Choice Literature," Vol. I, No. 15, 1892.

GRAPHO, pseud. See Adams, James Alonzo

2244 [GRAY, CLARENCE F.] Ancilla DeMontes; or, One Summer. With a Key. By the Cricket [pseud.]. [San Francisco]: Published by the author, 1885. 135 p.          LC

2245 GRAY, DAVID. Gallops ... New York: The Century Co., 1898. 226 p., front.          HEH, O
Contents: The Parish of St. Thomas Equinus–Braybrooke's Double-Event Steeplechase–How the Fence-Breakers' League Was "Stumped"–The Ride of His Life–The "Transfigured Pair"–The Popularity of Tompkins–Chalmers's Gold Piece–The Bishop's Missionary Meeting–His First Race–Carty Carteret's Sister.

2246 [GRAY, ISA E.] Marjory Graham: A Novel ... New York: G. P. Putnam's Sons, 1882. 200 p.          LC

2247 GRAY, PATRICK LEOPOLD. The Book of Ruth: A Novel ... Bendena, Kansas: Published by the author, 1892. 219 p.          LC

GRAYDON, WILLIAM MURRAY. An Inherited Debt. In F. E. McKay, ed., Vignettes [cop. 1890], No. 3523.

2248 GRAYSON, PAULINE. Pyrrha: A Story of Two Crimes ... New York: The American News Company, 1889. 196 p.          LC

2249 THE GREAT WRONGS OF THE SHOP GIRLS: The Life and Persecutions of Miss Beatrice Claflin, Daughter of the Late Claflin, Founder of the Well-Known New York Firm of Claflin & Co., from a Narrative Furnished by the Ladies Philanthropical Society. How Miss Claflin Became the White Slave in the Gilded Dry Goods Palace of a Merchant Prince ... Philadelphia: Barclay & Co., No. 21 North Seventh Street [cop. 1879]. 64 p., illus.          LC

GREEN, ANNA KATHARINE. See Rohlfs, Anna Katharine (Green)

2250 GREEN, MRS. M. A. Life of Martha Robbison; or, The Mysterious Will. A True Story ... Greeley, Colorado: John C. Lee, Colorado Sun Book Rooms, 1880. 85 p.          Y

2251 [GREEN, MISS M. P.] The Fight for Dominion: A Romance of Our First War with Spain. By Gay Parker [pseud.] ... New York: E. R. Herrick & Company, 70 Fifth Avenue [cop. 1899]. 316 p., illus.          HEH, LC

2252 [GREEN, MRS. MARY JOSEPHINE ARMSTRONG.] A Sketch for Mothers. By O. N. E. [pseud.] . . . Colusa [Calif.]: Addington & Green, printers, 1878. 33 p.
At head of title: "I Will Multiply Thy Sorrows."
Library of University of California, Los Angeles, has a copy.

2253 GREEN, MASON ARNOLD. Bitterwood: A Novel . . . New York: G. W. Carleton & Co. London: S. Low & Co., 1878. 288 p.    HEH, LC
New York state.

2254 [GREEN, WARREN.] A Blue-Grass Thoroughbred: A Novel. By Tom Johnson [pseud.]. Chicago, New York, and San Francisco: Belford, Clarke & Co. London: Henry J. Drane [cop. 1889]. 216 p.    HEH

GREEN, WILLIAM SEMPLE. Mea Culpa. *In* Short Stories by California Authors (1885), No. 4929.

2255 ——— Sacrifice; or, The Living Dead . . . Colusa [Calif.]: Addington & Green, 1882. 225 p.    HEH, LC

2256 GREENE, AELLA. Culminations: A Novel . . . [Springfield, Mass.: Clark W. Bryan & Co., printers], 1892. 142 p.    BU, CU, HEH, LC, Y

2257 ——— John Peters: A Novel . . . [Springfield, Mass.: Clark W. Bryan & Company, electrotypers, printers, and binders], 1890. 2 vols. (227, 204 p.)    BU, CU, H(V. I), HEH(V. I), LC
Vol. I deposited Jan. 25; Vol. II, Oct. 22, 1890.

GREENE, BELLE C. *See* Greene, Isabel Catherine (Colton)

2258 GREENE, ISABEL CATHERINE (COLTON). Adventures of an Old Maid. By Aunt Ruth. Belle C. Greene . . . New York: J. S. Ogilvie and Company, 31 Rose Street [cop. 1886]. 183 p., illus.    HEH, UM

2259 ——— Mr. and Mrs. Hannibal Hawkins . . . New York: American Publishers Corporation, 310-318 Sixth Avenue [cop. 1897]. 219 p., illus.    LC, UM

2260 ——— A New England Conscience . . . New York & London: G .P. Putnam's Sons; the Knickerbocker Press, 1885. 196 p.    HEH, LC, UVB
New England Methodists.

2261 ——— A New England Idyl . . . Boston: D. Lothrop and Company, Franklin and Hawley Streets [cop. 1886]. 222 p.    HEH, LC
Of Vermont farmers.

2262 GREENE, JOHN O. The Ke Whonkus People . . . [Indianapolis, Ind.: Vincent Publishing Company, 1893.] 426 p.    CU, HEH, LC
Imprint from 2nd leaf, which also has the title: "A Story of the North Pole Country." Printed copyright notice on 1st leaf dated Sept. 29, 1890, but LC copy deposited Aug. 17, 1893.

2263  GREENE, NANCI LEWIS. Nance: A Story of Kentucky Feuds . . . Chicago, New York: F. T. Neely [cop. 1893]. 257 p.                    O

2264  [GREENE, SARAH PRATT (MCLEAN).] Cape Cod Folks: A Novel. . . Boston: A. Williams & Company, 1881. 327, [1] p., front.
BA, BU, CU, H, HEH, N, Y
Story first appeared with actual names of Cape Cod people. In later eds. these were changed to fictitious names.

2265  [————] Lastchance Junction, Far, Far West: A Novel . . . Boston: Cupples and Hurd; the Algonquin Press, 1889. 258 p.
BA, BU, CU, HEH, LC, O
Of a refuge of fugitives from justice.

2266  ———— Leon Pontifex . . . Boston: De Wolfe, Fiske & Co., 361 and 365 Washington Street [cop. 1890]. 232 p.                    CU, H, HEH, LC, O
Of a minister.

2267  ———— The Moral Imbeciles . . . New York and London: Harper & Brothers, 1898. 237 p.                    BU, CU, H, HEH, LC, N, O, UM, Y

2268  ———— Some Other Folks. By Sarah Pratt McLean . . . Boston: Cupples, Upham and Company, 1884. 287 p.                    BA, H, HEH, LC, O, UM
Contents: Santa Maria—"A Career"—The Singular Vote of Aut Tilbox—Sam Sperry's Pension.

2269  ———— Stuart and Bamboo: A Novel . . . New York and London: Harper & Brothers, 1897. 276 p.                    CU, H, HEH, LC, N, O, UV, Y
Nova Scotia.

2270  ———— Towhead: The Story of a Girl . . . Boston: A. Williams and Company, 1883. 303 p., front.                    BA, CU, H, HEH, O, UC, Y

2271  ———— Vesty of the Basins: A Novel . . . New York: Harper & Brothers, 1892. 271 p.                    BU, CU, HEH, LC, N, O
Fishing village on the Maine coast.

GREENFELLOW, BOB, pseud. See Rullmann, John D.

2272  GREENLEAF, ELIZABETH. The Working Ten of the King's Daughters . . . New York: E. P. Dutton & Company, 1888. 114 p.                    LC, UC
Of the effort to build a church in a western town.

2273  GREENLEE, W. M. "Spes" in the Shadow of the Alhambra; or, The Last of the Moorish Kings . . . Knoxville, Tenn.: S. B. Newman & Co., 1893. 537 p., front.                    HEH, LC

2274  [GREENOUGH, MRS. FRANCES BOOTT.] Annals of Brookdale, a New-England Village . . . Philadelphia: J. B. Lippincott & Co., 1881. 243 p.
HEH, LC, UM

2275 GREENSWORD, MATHIAS P. Twenty Years in the Tropics . . . Poughkeep-sie, N.Y.: W. F. Boshart, book and job printer, 1887. 191 p., front. LC

GREENWOOD, GRACE, *pseud*. *See* Lippincott, Sara Jane (Clarke)

2276 GREEY, EDWARD. A Captive of Love: Founded upon Bakin's Japanese Romance, Kumono Tayema Ama Yo No Tsuki (The Moon Shining through a Cloud-Rift on a Rainy Night) . . . Boston: Lee and Shepard. New York: Charles T. Dillingham, 1886. 280 p., illus.

AP, BA, CU, H, HEH, LC, UM, UP, Y

2277 GREGG, HORTENSE GARDNER. Jac and Gill; or, A Sister's Fidelity. A Novel . . . Norway, Me.: Advertiser Book Print, 1898. 94 p. HEH, LC

2278 GREGORY, PAULINE. Living and Loving; or, Ideal Letters about Life . . . Memphis: S. C. Toof & Co., printers, 1884. 266 p. LC, UC, Y
Printed copyright notice dated 1877, but copy not deposited until June 10, 1884.

2279 GRENDEL, M. R. Contrasts . . . New York: G. P. Putnam's Sons, 1881. 392 p. HEH, LC, O
Society in North and South.

GREY, WILLIAM, *pseud*. *See* White, William Francis

2280 [GRIFFEN, ANNIE M.] All Wrong: A Leaf from a Drama. Philadelphia: J. B. Lippincott & Co., 1877. 136 p. HEH, LC

GRIFFIN, ELLEN M. *See* Hoey, Ellen Mary (Griffin)

2281 GRIFFIN, JOHN A. Leola . . . [Troy, N.Y.]: Published by the author [cop. 1890]. 93 p. LC
Deposited Feb. 20, 1890.

2282 GRIFFIN, LA ROY FREESE. The Abduction of Princess Chriemhild: A Ro-mance . . . New York: Robert Lewis Weed Company. London: Gay and Bird [cop. 1898]. 295 p. LC

2283 GRIFFIS, WILLIAM ELLIOT. The Pathfinders of the Revolution: A Story of the Great March into the Wilderness and Lake Region of New York in 1779 . . . Boston and Chicago: W. A. Wilde Company [cop. 1900]. 316 p., illus. LC, Y

2284 GRIFFITH, BENJAMIN LEASE CROZER. By the Light of the Fire: A Collec-tion of Short Stories . . . Philadelphia: The Penn Publishing Company, 1896. 273 p., illus. HEH, LC
*Contents:* The Ribbon of Gold—For Home, for Freedom, Fatherland—For Her Sake—The Man from Nowhere—Dad's Little Feller—The Phases of the Honeymoon.

2285 GRIFFITH, W. C. Gifts Without Graces; or, Life at Powhatan ... Hagerstown [Md.]: The Morning News Print, 1895. 316 p., front.   HEH

2286 GRIGGS, SUTTON ELBERT. Imperium in Imperio ... Cincinnati: The Editor Publishing Co., 1899. 265 p.
Copy examined at Boston Public Library.
Texas was to become a Negro republic.

2287 [GRIGSBY, ALCANOAN O.] Nequa; or, The Problem of the Ages. By Jack Adams [pseud.] ... Topeka, Kansas: Equity Publishing Company, 1900. 387 p.   BU
"Equity Library Series," Vol. I.
Utopian novel.

2288 GRIMSHAW, ROBERT. Fifty Years Hence; or, What May Be in 1943. A Prophecy Based on Scientific Deductions by an Improved Graphical Method ... New York: Practical Publishing Co., 1892. 89 p.
Copy examined at New York Public Library.

2289 GRINNELL, ELIZABETH (PRATT). John and I and the Church ... New York, Chicago, Toronto: Fleming H. Revell Company, 1897. 205 p., illus.   LC

2290 GRINNELL, MORTON. An Eclipse of Memory: A Novel ... New York: Frederick A. Stokes Company [cop. 1899]. 254 p.   CU, HEH, LC, Y
Of a female "Enoch Arden."

2291 GRISMER, JOSEPH RHODE. 'Way Down East: A Romance of New England Life ... Founded on the Phenomenally Successful Play of the Same Title by Lottie Blair Parker. New York: J. S. Ogilvie Publishing Company, 57 Rose Street [cop. 1900]. 190 p., illus.   BU, H, HEH, N

2292 GRISWOLD, FRANCES IRENE (BURGE) SMITH. Miss Bent; or, At His Footstool. By Mrs. F. Burge Smith ... New York: Thomas Whittaker, 1881. 256 p.
Copy examined at New York Public Library.

2293 [GRISWOLD, JANE (EMMET).] The Lost Wedding-Ring. By Mrs. Winter and Mrs. Boy [pseuds. of Jane Griswold]. New York and London: G. P. Putnam's Sons; the Knickerbocker Press, 1887. 171 p.
HEH, LC, UP, UV
Causes of "post-matrimonial unhappiness" discussed.

2294 [GRISWOLD, LORENZO.] Priest and Puritan. New York, Chicago, Washington, London, Paris: Brentano's [cop. 1889]. 192 p.   LC

2295 GRISWOLD, SARAH ELIZABETH. Out of Law into Gospel; or, God in Man ... Chicago, Ill.: F. M. Harley Publishing Co., 1893. 129 p.   LC

GROVER, EDWIN OSGOOD. Thetford Sketches. *In* H. J. Hapgood, *ed.*, Echoes from Dartmouth (1895), No. 2446.

2296 [GRUMBINE, JESSE CHARLES FREMONT.] Lethe: A Novel. By May Wright [pseud.]. Cincinnati, Ohio: Knight & Co., steam printing works, 1883. 111 p.                                                                LC

2297 GUERNSEY, LUCY ELLEN. The Chevalier's Daughter: Being One of the Stanton Corbet Chronicles ... New York: Thomas Whittaker, 1880. 473 p.                                                                           LC, UP
Her stories were considered of interest to both adults and young people and are included.

2298 —— The Foster Sisters; or, Lucy Corbet's Chronicle ... New York: Thomas Whittaker, 1882. 519 p.                                                O

2299 —— The Hidden Treasure: A Tale of Troublous Times ... New York: Thomas Whittaker, 1890. 339 p., front.                    HEH, LC, O
Of a copy of the Wickliffe Bible.

2300 —— Loveday's History: A Tale of Many Changes ... New York: Thomas Whittaker, 1885. 366 p.                                       HEH, LC

2301 —— Oldham; or, Beside All Waters ... New York: Thomas Whittaker, 1886 370 p., illus.                                                   LC

2302 —— Through Unknown Ways; or, The Journal-Books of Mrs. Dorathea Studley ... New York: Thomas Whittaker, 1886. 406 p.  HEH

2303 GUILFORD, LUCINDA THAYER. Margaret's Plighted Troth ... Cleveland, O.: W. M. Bayne Printing Company, 1899. 174 p.                   LC

2304 GUINEY, LOUISE IMOGEN. Lovers' Saint Ruth's, and Three Other Tales. ... Boston: Copeland and Day, 1895. 123, [1] p.
                        BA, BU, CU, H, HEH, LC, N, O, UM, UP, UVB, Y
*Also contains:* Our Lady of the Union—An Event on the River—The Provider.
Census of copies does not distinguish between limited and trade eds.

2305 GUIREY, GEORGE. Deacon Cranky, the Old Sinner ... New York: The Authors' Publishing Company, Bond Street [cop. 1878]. 333 p.
                                                                       BU, HEH, LC
Of church fairs and choir troubles.

2306 GUNNISON, CHARLES ANDREW. The Beautiful Eyes of Ysidria ... [San Francisco: Press of Commercial Publishing Co., 34 California St., 1894.] 55 p.                                                                        HEH, Y
Spanish-California days.

2307 —————— The Butler's Story . . . [San Francisco: Press of Commercial Publishing Company, 34 California Street, cop. 1890.] 39 p. H, HEH, LC Deposited Jan. 14, 1891.

2308 —————— Fuji-No-Yama . . . [San Francisco: Press of Commercial Publishing Company, 34 California Street, 1893.] 116 p. H, HEH

2309 —————— In Macao . . . [San Francisco: Press of Commercial Publishing Co., 34 California St., 1892.] 39, [1] p. BU, HEH

2310 —————— In the San Benito Hills . . . [San Francisco: Press of Commercial Publishing Co., 34 California St., 1891.] 44, [1] p. BU, HEH, Y
*Contains:* The Mystery of the Red Horse Inn—Bobby Taylor's wife.

2311 [—————] A Napa Christchild, and Benicia's Letters. [San Francisco: Press of Commercial Publishing Company, 1896.] 74 p. HEH

2312 [—————] Though Given in Vain, The Mysterious Egg, and A Berkshire Story. [San Francisco: Press of Commercial Publishing Company, cop. 1889.] 71 p. H, LC
Deposited Dec. 16, 1889.

2313 GUNSAULUS, FRANK WAKELEY. Monk and Knight: An Historical Study in Fiction . . . Chicago: A. C. McClurg and Company, 1891. 2 vols. (365, 342 p.) BU, HEH, LC, N, O, UC, UM, Y
Census of copies does not distinguish between limited and trade eds.

GUNTER, ARCHIBALD CLAVERING. [Evidence at hand indicates that most of his stories listed below were first issued in cloth or paper covers and then reissued in paper covers in the omitted "Welcome Series."]

2314 —————— Adrienne de Portalis: A Novel ... New York: The Home Publishing Company [cop. 1900]. 309 p.
Copy examined at New York Public Library.
Advertised PW, Mar. 10, 1900, p. 491: publisher "will very shortly issue" in cloth and paper.
LC deposit copy, dated Mar. 24, 1900, is in the omitted "Welcome Series."

2315 [—————] The Adventures of a Naval Officer: A Narrative. By Lieut. Warneford [pseud.]. New York: The Home Publishing Company [cop. 1898]. 219 p., illus. LC
Deposited July 11, 1898.

2316 —————— Baron Montez of Panama and Paris: A Novel ... New York: The Home Publishing Company, 1893. 266 p.
H, HEH, LC, N, O, UP, UVB, Y

2317 —————— Billy Hamilton: A Novel ... New York: The Home Publishing Company, 3 East Fourteenth Street [cop. 1898]. 317 p. CU, H, LC
From invasion of Maryland by Stonewall Jackson to the death of Lincoln.

2318 —— Bob Covington: A Novel . . . New York: Home Publishing Company, 3 East Fourteenth Street [cop. 1897]. 313 p.   H, HEH, O
New Orleans.

2319 —— Don Balasco of Key West: A Novel . . . New York: The Home Publishing Co., 3 East Fourteenth Street [cop. 1896]. 259 p.
HEH, LC, O, UC
Deposited Jan. 16, 1897.

2320 —— The Fighting Troubadour: A Novel . . . New York: The Home Publishing Company [cop. 1899]. 271 p.   O, Y

2321 —— The First of the English: A Novel . . . New York: The Home Publishing Co., 3 East Fourteenth Street [cop. 1894]. 271 p.   LC, O
Deposited Feb. 28, 1895.

2322 —— A Florida Enchantment: A Novel . . . New York: The Home Publishing Company, 1892. 260 p.   CU, H, HEH, LC, N, UM
Fergus Redmond, jt. au.

2323 —— Her Senator: A Novel . . . New York: The Home Publishing Co., 3 East Fourteenth Street [cop. 1896]. 261 p.   CU, H, LC, N, O, Y
Deposited Mar. 20, 1896.

2324 —— Jack Curzon: Being a Portion of the Records of the Managing Clerk of Martin, Thompson & Co., English Merchants Doing Business in Hong Kong, Manila, Cebu and the Straits Settlements. A Novel . . . New York: The Home Publishing Company, 3 East Fourteenth Street [cop. 1898]. 330, ix p.   HEH, O
LC deposit copy, dated Dec. 21, 1898, is in the omitted "Welcome Series."

2325 —— The King's Stockbroker: The Sequel to "A Princess of Paris." A Novel . . . New York: The Home Publishing Co., 1894. 283 p.
CU, HEH, N, Y

2326 —— The Ladies' Juggernaut: A Novel . . . New York: The Home Publishing Co., 1895. 243 p., illus.   HEH, LC, Y

2327 —— M. S. Bradford, Special: A Marvelous Story of the Day . . . New York: The Home Publishing Company [cop. 1899]. 289 p.   HEH

2328 —— Miss Dividends: A Novel . . . New York: The Home Publishing Company, 1892. 276 p.   H, HEH, O, UVB, Y

2329 —— Miss Nobody of Nowhere: A Novel . . . New York: The Home Publishing Company, 1890. 294 p.   AP, BA, H, HEH, O

2330 —— Mr. Barnes of New York: A Novel . . . New York: Deshler, Welch, & Company, 1887. 250 p.   AP, CU, HEH, LC, N, UVB

*Also issued with imprint:* New York: The Home Publishing Company, 1887.
BA, BU, H, O, UVB, Y

2331 ———— Mr. Potter of Texas: A Novel... New York: The Home Publishing Company, 1888. 278 p. AP, BA, BU, HEH, LC, N, O, UC, UM, UVB, Y

2332 ———— The Power of Woman ... New York: The Home Publishing Co. [cop. 1897]. 2 vols. (317, 318 p.) HEH(pt. II), O
Part I, Susan Turnbull; Part II, Ballyho Bey (The Sequel . . .).

2333 ———— The Princess of Copper: A Novel ... New York: The Home Publishing Company [cop. 1900]. 283 p., illus. CU, HEH, O
LC deposit copy, dated June 12, 1900, is in the omitted "Welcome Series."

2334 ———— A Princess of Paris: A Novel ... New York: The Home Publishing Co., 1894. 283 p. O, N, UM, Y

2335 ———— Tangled Flags: A Novel... New York: The Home Publishing Company [cop. 1900]. 282 p. BU, HEH, O
LC deposit copy, dated Oct. 12, 1900, is in the omitted "Welcome Series."

2336 ———— That Frenchman: A Novel ... New York: The Home Publishing Company, 1889. 365 p. (36 lines of text to the page).
LC, UM, UVB, Y
Deposited May 23, 1889.
In PW, May 4, 1889, p. 630, publisher announced postponement of publication until May 10, "owing to the extraordinary size of the first edition."
PW, June 8, 1889, lists a 299 p. ed. CU, H, HEH, O
Has 43 lines of text to the page.

GUNTER, ESTHER LISBETH (BURNS), *jt. au.* *See* Savage, R. H. His Cuban Sweetheart [cop. 1895], No. 4780.

2337 GUY AVERALL: A Patriotic Sketch. As Written by a Private Soldier of the U.S. Army. Philadelphia: E. Claxton & Company, 1881. 429 p.
HEH, LC

GWINNIE, *pseud.* *See* Filer, Mrs. G.

2338 GWYN, MRS. LAURA. Wanita: A Novel ... Charleston, S.C.: Walker, Evans, & Cogswell, printers, 1880. 198 p. CU, LC

H., A. K. *See* Hopkins, Mrs. Alice Kimball

2339 H., C. J. Miss Percie of Clifden. By C. J. H. Privately Printed. Philadelphia: Claxton, Remsen, & Haffelfinger, 1876. 178 p. HEH
Northumberland, England.

H., E. M. *See* Heaton, Ellen Marvin

H., J. B.   *See* Hope, James Barron

H., K. E.   *See* Harriman, Karl Edwin

H., S. E.   *See* Heald, Mrs. Sarah E.

H., W. P.   *See* Hoxie, Walter Palmer

2340   HAAS, CAROLINE HOOK.  A White Slave of the North; or, Lucy Manchester.  A Romance of Real Life ...  Atlanta, Ga.: The Foote & Davies Company, 1895.  352 p.                                    HEH

2341   HABBERTON, JOHN.  All He Knew: A Story ...  Meadville, Penna.: Flood
and Vincent; the Chautauqua-Century Press, 1890.  197 p.
                                          HEH, LC, N, UM, UP, UVB
Of a converted ex-convict.

2342   [———]  The Barton Experiment ...  New York: G. P. Putnam's Sons,
1877.  202 p.                  BA, CU, H, HEH, LC, O, UM, UP, UV, Y
Of temperance.

2343   ———  The Bowsham Puzzle: A Novel ...  New York: Funk & Wagnalls, 1884.  222 p.                            CU, HEH, LC, O
*Also contains:* My Friend Moses.

2344   ———  Brueton's Bayou.  By John Habberton.  Miss Defarge.  By F.
Hodgson Burnett.  Philadelphia: J. B. Lippincott Company, 1888.  209
p.                                CU, H, HEH, LC, UM, UC, Y

2345   ———  The Chautauquans ...  New York: Robert Bonner's Sons, 1891.
351 p., front.                                                 O

2346   ———  Couldn't Say No ...  New York: Belford Company, 18-22 East
18th Street [cop. 1889].  229 p.                          H, HEH
LC deposit copy, dated Feb. 13, 1890, is in the omitted "Household Library,"
Vol. IV, No. 43.

2347   ———  Country Luck . . .  Philadelphia: J. B. Lippincott Company,
1887.  260 p.                        AP, HEH, LC, O, UC, Y

2348   ———  The Crew of the "Sam Weller" ...  New York: G. P. Putnam's
Sons, 1878.  161 p., front.                  CU, H, HEH, LC, O, Y
Of a flatboat.

2349   [———]  Helen's Babies, with Some Account of Their Ways, Innocent,
Crafty, Angelic, Impish, Witching and Repulsive.  Also, a Partial Record of Their Actions during Ten Days of Their Existence.  By Their
Latest Victim.  Boston: Loring, cor. Bromfield & Washington Streets
[cop. 1876].  206 p.          BA, BU, CU, H, HEH, LC, N, O, UC, UP, UV, Y

2350   [————]  The Jericho Road: A Story of Western Life . . . Chicago: Jansen, McClurg & Co., 1877.  222 p.     BU, H, HEH, LC, N, O, UC, UV, Y

2351   [————]  Just One Day . . . New York: George R. Lockwood, 1879. 172 p.                                      LC, Y
Also published as: *Mrs. Mayburn's Twins, with Her Trials in the Morning, Noon, Afternoon, and Evening of Just One Day.* Philadelphia: T. B. Peterson & Brothers [cop. 1882].  188 p.   LC

2352   ————  A Lucky Lover . . . Boston: Bradley & Woodruff [cop. 1892]. 306 p.                                 H, HEH, LC, O, UM, Y

  ————  My Friend Moses. *In* W. F. Gill, *ed.*, Papyrus Leaves (1880), No. 2168.
Later printed in No. 2343.

2353   [————]  Other People's Children: Containing a Veracious Account of the Management of Helen's Babies by a Lady Who Knew Just How the Children of Other People Should be Trained . . . New York: G. P. Putnam's Sons, 1877.  303 p., front.    CU, H, HEH, LC, O, UC, UM, UP, Y
Also published as: *Budge and Toddie, Their Haps and Mishaps.* New York: G. P. Putnam's Sons [1877].  Information from H catalogue card; not found.

2354   [————]  The Scripture Club of Valley Rest; or, Sketches of Everybody's Neighbours . . . New York: G. P. Putnam's Sons, 1877.  188 p., front.                    BU, CU, H, HEH, LC, O, UC, UM, UP, UVB, Y

2355   ————  Some Folks. By John Habberton . . . Sold Only by Subscription. New York: Derby Brothers, 1877.  6 p. l., [9]-502 p., illus.  8 13/16 x 5 3/4 in.                     BU, H, HEH, LC, O, UC, Y
*Contents:* The Schoolteacher at Bottle Flat—Jim Hockson's Revenge—Making His Mark—Codago—The Last Pike at Jagger's Bend—First Prayer at Hanney's—The New Sheriff of Bunker County—Major Martt's Friend—Buffle—Mattelette's Section—A Story of Ten Mile Gulch—Captain Sam's Change—Miss Fewne's Last Conquest—Markson's House—Grump's Pet—Wardelow's Boy [omitted in table of contents]—Tom Chafflin's Luck—Old Twitchett's Treasure—Blizzer's Wife—A Boarding-House Romance—Retiring from Business—The Hardhack Mistake—The Carmi Chums—Little Guzzy—A Romance of Happy Rest—Two Powerful Arguments—Mr. Putchett's Love—The Meanest Man at Blugsey's—Deacon Barker's Conversion—Joe Gatter's Life Insurance—The Temperance Meeting at Blackley—Jude—A Love of a Cottage—The Bleighton Rivals—Budge and Toddie at Aunt Alice's—Sailing Up Stream—Free Speech.
At head of title: "There's as much difference in 'some folks' as anybody."
HEH copy has full-page author's autograph note dated May 30, 1901. It reads in part: "This collection of short stories was published without my permission, for the sufficient reason that I had no permission to give, the tales having been sold, years before, to the newspaper publisher who made the book for the Messrs. Derby. One of the tales—'A Story of Ten-Mile Gulch'—was not written by me."

Also published as: *Little Guzzy, and Other Stories. By the Author of "Helen's Babies." With Illustrations.* New York: G. W. Carleton & Co. London: S. Low, Son & Co., 1878. 2 p.l., [7]-384 p., illus. 7⅜ x 5⅛ in.    LC

This ed. transposes "Little Guzzy" to the beginning of the collection and omits four p.l., "A Story of Ten Mile Gulch," and the last three stories. Rearrangement of the plates of *Some Folks* necessitated repagination.

Also published as: *Little Guzzy, and Other Stories. By the Author of "Helen's Babies." With Illustrations.* New York: G. W. Carleton & Co. London: S. Low, Son & Co., 1878. 2 p.l., [9]-402 p., illus. 7⅛ x 5⅛ in.    HEH, O

This ed. is from same plates and in same order as *Some Folks*, but it omits four p.l. and the last five stories.

Also published as: *Stirring Stories for Winter Evenings. With Numerous Illustrations.* New York: G. W. Carleton & Co., 1879. 2 p.l., [9]-402 p., illus. 7⅛ x 5 in.    HEH

Except for title page, this ed. identical to 402 p. ed. of *Little Guzzy* above.

Also published as: *Romance of California Life, Illustrated by Pacific Slope Stories, Thrilling, Pathetic, and Humorous. By the Author of Helen's Babies.* San Francisco: James T. White & Co., 1879. 4 p.l., 502 p., illus. 8¾ x 5⅞ in.    H, HEH

Except for title page and omission of half title and leaf of "Introduction," this ed. is identical to *Some Folks*.

The New York, 1880, ed. adds author's name to title page and includes the "Introduction."

2356 —— Trif and Trixy ... A Story of a Dreadfully Delightful Little Girl and Her Adoring and Tormented Parents, Relations, and Friends. Philadelphia: Henry Altemus, 1897. 241 p.    H, HEH, LC, O, UC, UM, Y

—— Where Love Was Blind. *In* Short Story Masterpieces (1900), No. 4931.

2357 —— The Worst Boy in Town ... New York: G. P. Putnam's Sons, 1880. 214 p., illus.    BA, BU, H, LC, N, O, UC, UM, Y

HADERMANN, JEANNETTE R. *See* Walworth, Jeannette Ritchie (Hadermann)

2358 DELETED.

2359 DELETED.

2360 HADSELLE, MRS. CELIA ANTOINETTE CHAPMAN. Scraps: New and Old ... Pittsfield, Mass.: Press of the Sun Printing Company, 1900. 141 p., front.    BU, HEH

*Contains:* Uncle Moses' Stratagem.

The remaining "prose numbers" are "narratives of facts—proper names excepted." Introductory remarks.

2361 HAGAN, FRANCIS J. A Mountain Exile: The Story of a Kentucky Feud ... Cincinnati, O.: Press of S. Rosenthal & Co., 1899. 251 p., illus.    HEH

2362 HAGEMAN, SAMUEL MILLER. Once: A Novel . . . New York: W. B. Smith & Co., 27 Bond Street [cop. 1881]. 217 p.     HEH, LC
Princeton, New Jersey.

2363 HAINS, THORNTON JENKINS. Captain Gore's Courtship: His Narrative of the Affair of the Clipper "Conemaugh" and Loss of the "Countess of Warwick" . . . Philadelphia: J. B. Lippincott Company, 1896. 233 p., illus.     HEH, LC, O, UC, Y

2364 ———— Mr. Trunnell, Mate of the Ship Pirate . . . Boston: Lothrop Publishing Company, 1900. 324 p., front.     H, HEH, LC, O

2365 ———— Richard Judkins' Wooing: A Tale of Virginia in the Revolution . . . New York and London: F. Tennyson Neely, 1898. 266 p.  LC

2366 ———— Tales of the South Seas . . . Portland, Maine: Brown Thurston Company, 1894. 274 p.     LC, O
*Contents:* My Pirate—The Albatross—Johnnie—Genus Carcharodon—The Ghost on the Cammerdown—On the St. Paul's Rock—Bos'n Jim—Catching a Whale—In the Huascar's Turret—Mr. Garnett's Narrative—Hard Lines—Murphy—John Thompson—Loa—The Pompero of the River Plate—Timber Noggins—Three Men from Manilla—The Richard III—David—Kit—Lieut. Soakum, U.S.N.—A Race 'round the Horn—The Missing Ship.

2367 ———— The Wind-Jammers . . . Philadelphia & London: J. B. Lippincott Company, 1899. 273 p.     H, HEH, LC, O

2368 ———— The Wreck of the Conemaugh: Being a Record of Some Events Set Down from the Notes of an English Baronet during the American War with Spain . . . Philadelphia & London: J. B. Lippincott Company, 1900. 252 p.     BA, HEH, LC, O

2369 HALDANE, WINIFRED AGNES. A Chord from a Violin . . . Chicago: Laird & Lee [cop. 1896]. 164 p., front.     HEH
Autobiography of a rare old violin.

2370 HALE, EDWARD EVERETT. Aunt Caroline's Present . . . Boston: J. Stilman Smith & Co. [cop. 1895]. 36 p.     CU, HEH, UC
At head of title: "Tell It Again."
Later printed in No. 2391.
*Also issued with imprint:* Boston: Lend a Hand Society [cop. 1895].  H, HEH, O, UVB

2371 ———— Back to Back: A Story of To-Day . . . New York: Harper & Brothers, 1878. 98 p.     BU
Rewritten as: *How They Lived in Hampton: A Study of Practical Christianity Applied in the Manufacture of Woollens.* Boston: J. S. Smith & Co. [cop. 1888]. 281 p.  LC, UVB

2372 ———— The Brick Moon, and Other Stories . . . Boston: Little, Brown and Company, 1899. 369 p., front.     BA, H, N, O, UM

*Also contains:* Crusoe in New York—Bread on the Waters—The Lost Palace—99 Linwood Street—Ideals—Thanksgiving at the Polls—The Survivor's Story.

2373 ———— Christmas in Narragansett . . . New York, London: Funk & Wagnalls, 1884. 293 p. AP, BA, BU, CU, H, HEH, LC, O, UVB, Y
*Contents:* Ann Hutchinson's Exile—The Governor's Dinner—One Cent—The Happy Island—Cromwell's Statue—The Ballad of Ben Franklin at the Inn—The Return Message—The Survivor's Story—Pilchards—Law and Gospel—Colonel Ingham's Journey—East and West—The Three Anniversaries—The Cottage on the Viminal—Next His Hand—Dick's Christmas—The Palatine.

2374 ———— Col. Clipsham's Calendar . . . Boston: J. Stilman Smith & Co. [cop. 1895]. 51 p. CU, H, HEH
At head of title: "Tell It Again."
Later printed in No. 2391.
*Also issued with imprint:* Boston: Lend a Hand Society [cop. 1895]. H, O

2375 ———— Crusoe in New York, and Other Tales . . . Boston: Roberts Brothers, 1880. 259 p. AP, BA, BU, CU, H, HEH, LC, N, O, UC, UM, UP, Y
*Also contains:* Alif-Laila—A Civil Servant—Nicolette and Aucassin—The Lost Palace—The Western Ginevra—Max Keesler's Horse-Car—The Modern Psyche.

2376 ———— Daily Bread: A Story of the Snow Blockade . . . Boston: J. Stilman Smith & Company, 1888. 44 p. BU, CU, Y
Printed earlier in Wright II, No. 1055.

2377 ———— East and West: A Story of New-Born Ohio . . . New York: Cassell Publishing Company, 104 & 106 Fourth Avenue [cop. 1892]. 267 p. CU, H, HEH, LC, N, O, UC, Y

2378 ———— The Fortunes of Rachel . . . New York: Funk & Wagnalls, 1884. 221 p. AP, BA, CU, O

2379 ———— G. T. T.; or, The Wonderful Adventures of a Pullman . . . Boston: Roberts Brothers, 1877. 221 p. BA, BU, CU, H, HEH, N, O, UC, UM

2380 ———— Hands Off . . . Boston: J. Stilman Smith & Co. [cop. 1895]. 39 p. O
At head of title: "Tell It Again."

2381 ———— If Jesus Came to Boston . . . Boston: J. Stilman Smith & Co., 3 Hamilton Place [cop. 1894]. 45 p. BA, H, O, UC, UVB, Y
*Also issued with imprint:* Boston: Lamson, Wolffe and Company, 1895. BA, H, HEH, O

2382 ———— Mr. Tangier's Vacations: A Novel . . . Boston: Roberts Brothers, 1888. 303 p. BA, CU, H, HEH, N, O, UC, UM, UVB, Y

2383 —————— My Double & How He Undid Me ... Boston, New York: Lamson, Wolffe & Co., 1895. 50 p., front.     CU, H, HEH, O, UV, Y
1000 copies printed.
Printed earlier in Wright II, Nos. 155 and 1053.

2384 —————— My Friend the Boss: A Story of To-Day ... Boston: J. Stilman Smith & Company, 1888. 191 p. BA, CU, H, HEH, LC, O, UC, UP, UV, Y

2385 —————— The New Harry and Lucy: A Story of Boston in the Summer of 1891 ... Boston: Roberts Brothers, 1892. 321 p., illus.
    BA, BU, CU, H, HEH, N, O, UC, UM, UV, Y
Lucretia P. Hale, jt. au.

2386 —————— One Good Turn: A Story ... Boston: J. Stilman Smith & Co. [cop. 1893]. 37 p.     CU, HEH, Y
At head of cover title: "Tell It Again."
Later printed in No. 2391.
*Also issued with imprint:* Boston: Lend a Hand Society [cop. 1893].   H

2387 —————— Our Christmas in a Palace: A Traveller's Story ... New York: Funk & Wagnalls, 1883. 268 p.     BA, CU, H, HEH, O, UC, UP, UVB, Y

2388 —————— Philip Nolan's Friends: A Story of the Change of Western Empire ... New York: Scribner, Armstrong and Company, 1877. 395 p., illus.     BA, CU, H, HEH, N, O, UVB, Y

2389 —————— A Safe Deposit ... Boston: J. Stilman Smith & Co. [cop. 1895]. 43 p.     BA, HEH, Y
At head of title: "Tell It Again."

2390 —————— Susan's Escort ... Boston: J. Stilman Smith & Co. [cop. 1895]. 53 p.     LC, N, O, UP, Y
At head of title: "Tell It Again."
Later printed in No. 2391.
*Also issued with imprint:* Boston: Lend a Hand Society [cop. 1895].   H, HEH, Y

2391 —————— Susan's Escort, and Others ... New York: Harper & Brothers, 1897. 416 p., illus.     AP, BA, CU, H, HEH, LC, O, UVB
*Also contains:* One Good Turn—The Minister's Black Veil—Aunt Caroline's Present—Colonel Clipsham's Calendar—Bread on the Waters—General Glover's True Story—Both Their Houses—Colonel Ingham's Journey—A New Arabian Night—Only a Fly—John Rich and Lucy Poor—From Generation to Generation—Mrs. De Laix's Indecision—King Charles's Shilling—From Making to Baking—The First Grain Market—Pharaoh's Harvest.
*Also issued with imprint:* New York and London: Harper & Brothers, 1897.
O

2392 —————— Sybil Knox; or, Home Again. A Story of To-Day ... New York: Cassell Publishing Company, 104 & 106 Fourth Avenue [cop. 1892]. 321 p.     BA, BU, CU, H, HEH, LC, O, UC, UVB, Y

2393 HALE, EDWIN W. Random Skits. By Ned Hale . . . Cleveland, O.: The Brooks Company, printers and binders, 1896. 62 p., illus. LC

[HALE, LUCRETIA PEABODY.] The Spider's Eye. *In* Stories by American Authors, III (1884), No. 5269.

2394 ―――― An Uncloseted Skeleton . . . Boston: Ticknor and Company, 211 Tremont Street [cop. 1888]. 100 p. CU, H, HEH, LC, N, UVB, Y
Deposited Apr. 2, 1888.
Edwin Lassetter Bynner, jt. au.

―――― jt. au. *See* Hale, E. E. The New Harry and Lucy (1892), No. 2385.

HALE, NED. *See* Hale, Edwin W.

2395 HALE, ROBERT BEVERLY. Six Stories and Some Verses . . . Boston: J. M. Bowles [cop. 1896]. 188, [3] p., illus. BA, BU, H, LC, Y
*Contains:* A Philosopher with an Eye for Beauty—Too Much of a Bad Thing —The Two Sides of a Promise—Antaeus in Love—A Middle-Aged Woman— Untaught by Experience.
Deposited Dec. 12, 1896.

2396 HALL, ALICE C. Miss Leighton's Perplexities: A Love Story . . . New York: Fords, Howard, & Hulbert, 1882. 379 p. AP, LC, O

2397 HALL, ARTHUR DUDLEY. Anselma; or, In Spite of All. Adapted from the French . . . Based upon the Famous Play of the Same Name, by Victorien Sardou. Chicago: Rand, McNally & Co., 1886. 256 p. LC

2398 ―――― La Tosca: A Novel . . . Founded on the Famous Play of the Same Name, by Victorien Sardou. Chicago: Rand, McNally & Company, 1888. 223 p., illus. UC

2399 HALL, CARA OAKEY. Sweet Bells Jangled: A Dramatic Love Tale . . . New York: American News Company, 1876. 130 p. Printed in double columns. HEH, LC
At head of title: "Library of Select Novels."

2400 HALL, CHARLES WINSLOW. Cartagena; or, The Lost Brigade. A Story of Heroism in the British War with Spain, 1740-1742 . . . Boston, New York, and London: Lamson, Wolffe and Company, 1898. 574 p., illus.
CU, HEH, LC, N, O

HALL, EUGENE. *See* Baker, Emma Eugene (Hall)

2401 HALL, GEORGE FRANKLIN. A Study in Bloomers; or, The Model New Woman. A Novel . . . Chicago, Philadelphia, Stockton: American Bible House, 1895. 272 p., illus. H, HEH
Wisconsin.

HALL, GERTRUDE. *See* Brownell, Gertrude (Hall)

2402 HALL, GRANVILLE DAVISSON. Daughter of the Elm: A Tale of Western Virginia before the War ... Chicago: Mayer & Miller, printers and publishers, 1899. 326 p. CU, HEH, LC

2403 HALL, MARY LUCY. Preparation: A Novel ... New York: J. S. Ogilvie and Company, 31 Rose Street. Syracuse: Charles Robler [cop. 1883]. 284 p. LC

2404 HALL, RUTH. The Black Gown ... Boston and New York: Houghton, Mifflin and Company. The Riverside Press, Cambridge, 1900. 318 p.
H, HEH, LC, O, Y
French and Indian War; Albany.

2405 HALL, THOMAS WINTHROP. An Experimental Wooing ... New York: E. R. Herrick & Company, 70 Fifth Avenue [cop. 1898]. 180 p. HEH, LC

2406 ———— The Little Lady, Some Other People, and Myself ... New York: E. R. Herrick & Company, 70 Fifth Avenue [cop. 1898]. 222 p., illus. CU, HEH, UM, UVB

2407 ———— Tales ... New York: Frederick A. Stokes Company [1899]. 310 p. H, LC, UP, UV
Deposited Apr. 10, 1899.

2408 HALLOWELL, ALICE. Forgetmenot; or, Sunshine in Affliction. A Story from Life ... Washington, D. C.: Gibson Bros., 1893. 255 p., front.
LC

2409 HALPIN, WILL R. Juan Pico ... New York: Robert Lewis Weed Company [cop. 1899]. 272 p., illus. H, HEH, LC, O
Southern California.

2410 [HALSEY, HARLAN PAGE.] The Confessions of an Imp: A Narrative. New York: J. E. Rhodes & Co., 20 Cliff St. [cop. 1887]. 143 p. LC
Cover title: "The Autobiography of a Barrel of Bourbon. By 'Old Sleuth' [pseud.]."
Many of his stories appeared in subscription series only.

2411 [————] Gipsy Blair, the Western Detective ... By Judson R. Taylor [pseud.] ... New York: International Book Company, 310-318 Sixth Avenue [189-?]. 141 p. HEH
First published in the omitted "People's Library," No. 216, 1882.

2412 [————] Macon Moore, the Southern Detective. By Judson R. Taylor [pseud.] ... New York: J. S. Ogilvie & Company, 25 Rose Street [cop. 1881]. 161 p., illus. HEH

2413 [———] Phil Scott, the Indian Detective: A Tale of Startling Mysteries. By Judson R. Taylor [pseud.]. New York: J. S. Ogilvie & Co.
[1882]. 136 p.
Listed PW, June 17, 1882.

HALSTEAD, ADA L., *pseud. See* Newhall, Mrs. Laura Eugenia

2414 [HALSTED, LEONORA B.] Bethesda. By Barbara Elbon [pseud.]. New
York: Macmillan & Co., 1884. 313 p.                    BU, HEH, LC, O

2415 HAMBLEN, HERBERT ELLIOTT. The General Manager's Story: Old-Time
Reminiscences of Railroading in the United States ... New York: The
Macmillan Company. London: Macmillan & Co., Ltd., 1898. 311 p.,
illus.                                        BA, HEH, N, O, UC, Y

2416 HAMILTON, ALICE KING. Mildred's Cadet; or, Hearts and Bell-Buttons.
An Idyl of West Point ... Philadelphia: T. B. Peterson & Brothers,
306 Chestnut Street [cop. 1881]. 302 p.                       LC

2417 ——— One of the Duanes: A Novel ... Philadelphia: J. B. Lippincott
Company, 1885. 317 p.              AP, BU, CU, H, HEH, LC, O, UC, Y
Navy yard life; Pensacola.

——— White Lilies. *In* C. King, *ed.*, Captain Dreams (1895), No. 3097.

2418 HAMILTON, ARTHUR WARREN. Scrabble of the Fairchilds ... Boston:
James H. Earle, 178 Washington Street [cop. 1896]. 301 p., front. LC

HAMILTON, MRS. C. V. *See* Jamison, Cecilia Viets (Dakin) Hamilton

HAMILTON, GAIL, *pseud. See* Dodge, Mary Abigail

2419 HAMILTON, GEORGE W. Kit Caffrey's Grit: A Story of Texas ... Cincinnati, O.: The Standard Publishing Company [cop. 1895]. 233 p.,
illus.                                                        LC
Deposited Mar. 7, 1896.

2420 ——— Tom Croly's Word ... Cincinnati: The Standard Publishing
Company [cop. 1893]. 238 p., illus.                           LC
Deposited Mar. 3, 1893.

2421 HAMILTON, KATE WATERMAN. The Parson's Proxy ... Boston and New
York: Houghton, Mifflin and Company. The Riverside Press, Cam-
bridge, 1896. 303 p.                        BU, H, HEH, LC, O, Y
Railroad band substitutes for the minister.

2422 [———] Rachel's Share of the Road ... Boston: James R. Osgood
and Company, 1882. 331 p.                        BA, H, HEH, LC
At head of title: "Round-Robin Series."
Of railroad interest.

2423 HAMILTON, LOUISE FRANCES PAINE. Romance of Graylock Manor . . . Chicago and New York: Rand, McNally & Company [cop. 1899]. 242 p.                                                             HEH, LC
Civil War novel.

2424 HAMILTON, SAMUEL A. The Vengeance of the Mob: A Tale of the Florida Pines . . . New York: The Abbey Press, 114 Fifth Avenue [cop. 1900]. 206 p., front.                                              CU
Lynch law; Florida.

HAMILTON, W. H. A Strange Wound. *In* C. King, *ed.*, Captain Dreams (1895), No. 3097.

2425 HAMLEN, GEORGIANNA. Our Hotel . . . Boston, 1888. 132 p.          LC

2426 HAMLIN, MYRA LOUISA (SAWYER). A Politician's Daughter . . . New York: D. Appleton and Company, 1886. 231 p.
AP, CU, H, HEH, LC, N, O, UV, Y

HAMMOND, CLEMENT MILTON, *jt. au. See* Montague, C. H. The Doctor's Mistake (1888), No. 3795.

2427 [HAMMOND, HENRIETTA (HARDY).] A Fair Philosopher. By Henri Daugé [pseud.] . . . New York: George W. Harlan & Co., 1882. 296 p.                                                            H, HEH, LC, O
At head of title: "The Kaaterskill Series."
Of a woman writer.

2428 [———] The Georgians. Boston: James R. Osgood and Company, 1881. 322 p.                                    BA, BU, H, HEH, LC, UM, UP
At head of title: "Round-Robin Series."
Georgia social life after the war.

2429 HAMMOND, WILLIAM ALEXANDER. Doctor Grattan: A Novel . . . New York: D. Appleton and Company, 1885. 417 p.
AP, BA, CU, H, HEH, LC, O, UV, Y
Central New York.

2430 ——— Lal: A Novel . . . New York: D. Appleton and Company, 1884. 466 p.                          AP, BU, CU, H, HEH, LC, N, O
Of lawless men in Colorado.

2431 ——— Mr. Oldmixon: A Novel . . . New York: D. Appleton and Company, 1885. 456 p.                      AP, BA, CU, H, HEH, LC, O, Y
Of an eccentric.

2432 ——— On the Susquehanna: A Novel . . . New York: D. Appleton and Company, 1887. 412 p.              AP, BA, BU, CU, HEH, LC, N, O, Y
Of the "Susquehanna Iron-Works."

2433 ———— The Son of Perdition . . . Chicago & New York: Herbert S. Stone & Company, 1898. 494 p.  BA, H, HEH, UC, Y
Of Judas Iscariot.

2434 ———— A Strong-Minded Woman; or, Two Years After . . . New York: D. Appleton and Company, 1885. 503 p.  AP, BA, HEH, LC, O, UV
Sequel to *Lal*.

2435 ———— Tales of Eccentric Life . . . New York: D. Appleton and Company, 1886. 209 p.  AP, BA, LC, O, UM
*Contents:* The Mystery of Mrs. Brown—Mr. St. Arnaud—A Candidate for Bedlam—The Golden Lock—An Incident in Dr. Temple's Career—A Madness Most Discreet—The Black Camel—Bill Hedden's Gal—Priscilla—Miss Remmington's Bonnet.
Clara Hammond Lanza, jt. au.

HAMPTON, MRS. WADE, JR. She Who Listened. *In* Short Story Masterpieces (1900), No. 4931.

2436 HANCOCK, ANSON URIEL. The Genius of Galilee: An Historical Novel . . . Chicago: Charles H. Kerr & Company, 1891. 507 p.  LC

2437 ———— John Auburntop, Novelist: His Development in the Atmosphere of a Fresh-Water College . . . Chicago: Charles H. Kerr & Company, 1891. 275 p., front.  BU, HEH, LC, UM, Y
Story begins at the University of Nebraska.

2438 ———— Silhouettes from Life on the Prairie, in the Backwoods . . . Chicago: Charles H. Kerr & Company, 1893. 158, [1] p.  UM

2439 HANCOCK, ARTHUR. Her Pastor's Victim . . . Chicago: Scroll Publishing Co., 1900. 60 p., front.
Information from LC card; no copy seen.

2440 [HANDY, MRS. JOHN.] Clip Her Wing or Let Her Soar: A Novel. By a Lady of Louisiana. New York: G. W. Dillingham, 1889. 383 p.  HEH, LC, Y

2441 [HANIFIN, JOHN M.] The Blind Men and the Devil. By Phineas [pseud.]. Boston: Lee and Shepard. New York: Charles T. Dillingham, 1891. 219 p.  LC

2442 HANKS, BEULAH DOWNEY. For the Honor of a Child . . . New York: Continental Publishing Co., 1899. 219 p.  HEH, LC, O

2443 HANKS, STEDMAN WRIGHT. The Crystal River Turned Upon the Black Valley Railroad and Black Valley Country: A Temperance Allegory . . . New Edition . . . Boston: D. Lothrop and Company, Franklin St., cor. of Hawley [cop. 1879]. 213 p., illus.  H, HEH, LC, UM
"This book has grown out of the tract called 'The Black Valley Road.' " Preface.

2444 HANKS: Assorted Yarns from Puck ... New York: Keppler & Schwarzmann, 1893. 175 p., illus. HEH, UM

*Contents:* The Senator, by H. C. Bunner—A Prairie Blossom, by Madeline S.
Bridges [i.e., Mary Ainge De Vere]—The Jigs of Abner Peabody, by C. S.
Montgomery—The Career of a Society Actress, by J. L. Ford—The Story of
Shiftless Smith, by C. H. Augur—A Fin de Siécle Genie; or, Arabian Nights
up to Date, by W. J. Henderson—The Mosquitoville Club, by R. K. Munkit-
trick—The Story of William, by H. L. Wilson—His Lucky Night, by Harry
Romaine—Foiled Again; or, The Banker's Vengeance, by Tudor Jenks—Van
Gibber and the Street-Car, by Robert B. Peattie—Suing for Damages, by G.
H. Jessop—Why the Reverend Edward Atkins Changed His Parish, by War-
don Allan Curtis—Willy and the Missionary, by H. G. Paine—A Slave to
Fancy, by Flavel S. Mines—George Byers, by Williston Fish.

2445 HANSHEW, THOMAS W. Young Mrs. Charnleigh: A Novel ... New
York: G. W. Carleton & Co., 1883. 317 p. HEH, LC

2446 HAPGOOD, HERBERT JACKSON, *ed.* Echoes from Dartmouth: A Collection
of Poems, Stories, and Historical Sketches ... Hanover, N.H., 1895.
151 p., illus. BU, CU, H, HEH, O, UM, Y

*Contains:* Clarkson, Right Guard, by Harlan Colby Pearson—In Senior Days,
by H. C. Pearson—Out with the Tide, by Harrie Sheridan Baketel—Thetford
Sketches, by Edwin Osgood Grover—With the Dawning, by H. C. Pearson
—His Decision, by Isaac Joslin Cox—The Undecided Bet, by Burpee Caldwell
Taylor—A Turkey Feather, by Nathaniel Ladd Foster—Pledging a Freshman,
by Charles Nicholas McCall—A Question of Ethics, by Robert Huntington
Fletcher—An Experience with the Rho Kap's, by B. C. Taylor—An Incident
in College Life, by N. L. Foster.
Craven Laycock, jt. ed.

HAPGOOD, NEITH (BOYCE). *See* Boyce, Neith

HARBEN, WILLIAM NATHANIEL. A Cohutta Valley Shooting Match. *In*
C. King, Rancho del Muerto [cop. 1895], No. 3109.

2447 —— The Land of the Changing Sun ... New York: The Merriam
Company, 67 Fifth Avenue [cop. 1894]. 233 p., front. BA, H, HEH, LC, Y
Utopian novel.

2448 —— A Mute Confessor: The Romance of a Southern Town. A
Novel ... Boston: Arena Publishing Co., 1892. 192 p., front.
Listed PW, Aug. 26, 1893.

2449 —— Northern Georgia Sketches ... Chicago: A. C. McClurg & Co.,
1900. 305 p. CU, H, HEH, LC, N, UM, UV, Y

*Contents:* A Humble Abolitionist—The Whipping of Uncle Henry—A Filial
Impulse—The Sale of Uncle Rustus—The Convict's Return—A Rural Visitor
—Jim Trundle's Crisis—The Courage of Ericson—The Heresy of Abner Cali-
han—The Tender Link.

2450 HARBERT, ELIZABETH MORRISSON (BOYNTON). "Amore" ... New York:
Lovell, Gestefeld & Co., 125 East 23d Street [cop. 1892]. 278 p. HEH, LC

Deposited Nov. 2, 1892.
*Also issued with imprint:* Chicago, Ill.: New Era Publishing Co. [cop. 1892].
H, LC
Of a minister and his wife.

HARDENBROOK, MRS. L. E. L.   The Strange Case of Esther Atkins.   *In* J.
Hawthorne, One of Those Coincidences (1899), No. 2596.

2451   HARDING, JOHN WILLIAM.   An Art Failure: A Story of the Latin Quarter
as It Is . . .   New York, Chicago: F. Tennyson Neely, 1896.   209 p.,
illus.                                                                      HEH, LC

2452   HARDING, MARIE VIRGINIA.   The Soul of Lady Agnes . . .   New York:
G. W. Dillingham, 1889.   204 p.                                               LC

2453   HARDY, ALBERT H.   The Maid of Bethany: A Study of the Christ . . .
Author's Edition.   Springfield, Mass., 1889.   33 p.                          LC

2454   HARDY, ARTHUR SHERBURNE.   But Yet a Woman: A Novel . . .   Boston,
New York: Houghton, Mifflin and Company.   The Riverside Press,
Cambridge, 1883.   348 p.      AP, BA, BU, CU, H, HEH, O, UC, UM, UP, UVB, Y
France.

2455   ——— Passe Rose . . .   Boston and New York: Houghton, Mifflin and
Company.   The Riverside Press, Cambridge, 1889.   361 p.
                                    AP, CU, H, HEH, LC, N, O, UM, UP, UVB, Y
Europe during the reign of Charlemagne.

2456   ——— The Wind of Destiny . . .   Boston and New York: Houghton,
Mifflin and Company.   The Riverside Press, Cambridge, 1886.   307 p.
                                    AP, BA, BU, CU, H, HEH, LC, N, O, UC, UM, UP, UVB, Y

2457   HARFIELD, G. EUGENE.   An Oriental Constellation: A Romantic Page of
Hidden History in the Barbaric Age . . .   Richmond, Va.: Hewlett &
Pierce, 1888.   172 p., 2 l., illus.                                         HEH, LC

2458   HARGIS, THOMAS F.   A Patriot's Strategy . . .   Louisville, Ky.: Chas. T.
Dearing, 1895.   291 p.                                        HEH, LC, UC, UM
Civil War novel.

2459   HARLAN, CALEB.   The Fate of Marcel . . .   Philadelphia: J. B. Lippincott
& Co., 1883.   262 p.                                     CU, H, HEH, LC, O, UV, Y
Delaware.

2460   [HARLAND, HENRY.]   As It Was Written: A Jewish Musician's Story.
By Sidney Luska [pseud.] . . .   New York: Cassell & Company, Lim-
ited, 739 & 741 Broadway [cop. 1885].   253 p.
                                    AP, BA, BU, CU, H, HEH, LC, N, O, UP, UVB, Y
New York.

2461 ———— The Cardinal's Snuff-Box . . . London & New York: John Lane, 1900. 319 p.   AP, BU, CU, HEH, LC, UC, UM, UVB
Verso of title page: "University Press, John Wilson and Son, Cambridge, U.S.A."

2462 ———— Grandison Mather; or, An Account of the Fortunes of Mr. and Mrs. Thomas Gardiner . . . New York: Cassell & Company, Limited, 104-106 Fourth Avenue [cop. 1889]. 387 p.
AP, BA, CU, H, HEH, LC, N, UP, UVB, Y
Literary life; New York.

2463 ———— Gray Roses . . . Boston: Roberts Bros. London: John Lane, 1895. 208 p.   CU, HEH, LC, N, O, UP, Y
*Contents:* The Bohemian Girl—Mercedes—A Broken Looking-Glass—The Reward of Virtue—A Re-Incarnation—Flower o' the Quince—When I Am King—A Responsibility—Castles near Spain.

———— A Head of Death. *In* Eleven Possible Cases [cop. 1891], No. 1737.

2464 ———— A Latin-Quarter Courtship, and Other Stories . . . New York: Cassell & Company, Limited, 104-106 Fourth Avenue [cop. 1889]. 269 p.
AP, BA, H, HEH, O, UVB
*Also contains:* Mr. Sonnenschein's Inheritance—Lilith—Mrs. Ormizon's Dinner Party.

2465 ———— Mademoiselle Miss. To Which Is Added: The Funeral March of a Marionette, The Prodigal Father, A Sleeveless Errand, A Light Sovereign . . . New York: Lovell, Coryell & Company, 1893. 192 p.
CU, HEH, LC, UP, UVB, Y

2466 ———— Mea Culpa: A Woman's Last Word . . . New York: John W. Lovell Company, 150 Worth Street, corner Mission Place [cop. 1891]. 347 p.   BA, H, HEH, LC, O, UVB
Bohemian Paris.

2467 [————] Mrs. Peixada. By Sidney Luska [pseud.] . . . New York: Cassell & Company, Limited, 739 & 741 Broadway [cop. 1886]. 317 p.
AP, CU, H, HEH, LC, N, O, UP, UVB, Y
New York.

2468 ———— Two Voices . . . New York: Cassell & Company, Limited, 104-106 Fourth Avenue [cop. 1890]. 106 p.   AP, BA, H, HEH, LC, O
*Contents:* Dies Irae—De Profundis.

2469 ———— Two Women or One? From the Mss. of Dr. Leonard Benary . . . New York: Cassell Publishing Company, 104 & 106 Fourth Avenue [cop. 1890]. 199 p.   AP, H, HEH, UVB

2470 [————] The Yoke of the Thorah. By Sidney Luska [pseud.] . . . New York: Cassell & Company, Limited, 739 & 741 Broadway [cop.

1887]. 320 p.           AP, BA, H, HEH, LC, O, UVB, Y
Love story of a Jewish painter and a Gentile; New York.

HARLAND, MARION, *pseud*. *See* Terhune, Mary Virginia (Hawes)

2471  HARLOW, WILLIAM BURT. Aunt Elvira Abroad . . . New York: J. S.
Ogilvie Publishing Company, 1898. 63 p., front.     H
New Englander visits England.

2472  HARMON, S. L. Ptocowa: A Strange, Sad Story of Fifteen Years in Dixie
as Told in a Single Night . . . Rochester, N. Y.: Publishing House of
John P. Smith, 1887. 267 p., front.     HEH
Of the Ku Klux Klan.

2473  HARPER, ELLA ADELAIDE. A Face in a Crowd, and Other Stories . . . New
York: Privately printed, 1893. 353 p.     HEH, LC
*Also contains:* At Farmlands–Christmas at Hillside–A New Year Wish–My
Little Neighbor–Somebody's Sunbeam–Snow in the Country–His First,
Last Love–Hugh's Destiny–Kate's Ring–Their Reconciliation–Dorothy–
Mr. Dick–Pine Villa–Uncle Guy's Christmas Present–Margaret's Friend–
Silver Falls–One June Day–Daisy's Whim.

2474  HARPER, ELLA JEANNETTE. Our Thanksgiving . . . Indianapolis: Carlon
& Hollenbeck, 1893. 16 p., front.     LC

2475  HARPER, FRANCES ELLEN (WATKINS). Iola Leroy; or, Shadows Uplifted
. . . Philadelphia, Pa.: Garrigues Brothers, 1892. 282 p., front.
    CU, HEH, O
Of the Negroes during and after the Civil War.

2476  HARPER, HARRY. File No. 115; or, A Man of Steel . . . New York: J. S.
Ogilvie and Company, cop. 1886. 149 p., illus.     LC
Detective story; New York.

2477  HARPER, LIZZIE (ST. JOHN). St. Peter's Bride . . . New York: G. W.
Carleton & Co. London: S. Low & Co., 1878. 279 p.     HEH, O, Y

2478  HARPER, MARGARET. Clouds and Sunshine . . . Philadelphia: J. B. Lippincott Company, 1890. 177 p.     LC

HARPER, OLIVE, *pseud*. *See* D'Apery, Helen (Burrell)

2479  [HARRELL, JOHN MORTIMER.] The Hot Springs Doctor: Seven Storiettes
. . . By "An Old Habitué" [pseud.]. [Hammond, Ind.: W. M. Con-
key Co., cop. 1899.] 213 p., illus.     LC, UC
Deposited Oct. 3, 1899.

[HARRIMAN, KARL EDWIN.] A Very Young Man, by K. E. H. *In* [F. L.
Knowles] *ed*., Cap and Gown in Prose (1900), No. 3182.

2480 HARRINGTON, FRANK. A Dixie Gentleman: A Novel . . . Indianapolis:
The Syndicate Press, 1895. 293 p.                                    LC
Copyrighted by William F. Harrington.

2480a [HARRINGTON, JOHN A.] Beanwhacker's Trouble; or, Not a Bit Like
His Uncle. A Sequel to "Just Like His Uncle." By John Carboy
[pseud.] . . . New York: J. B. Collin, 1881. 37 p., illus. Printed in
double columns.                                                     HEH

2481 [————] Blue Glass: A Sure Cure for the Blues. By John Carboy
[pseud.] . . . New York: J. B. Collin & Co., 1877. 59 p., illus.    HEH

2482 ———— Bounced; or, The Adventures of an Unlucky Man . . . New
York: J. B. Collin & Co. [1876?]. 64 p., illus.
From advertisement in his *Blue Glass*.

2483 [————] The Strange Woman. By John Carboy [pseud.] . . . New
York: Collin & Small, 1876. 100 p., illus.                          CU

2484 HARRIS, FRANK. Elder Conklin, and Other Stories . . . New York and
London: Macmillan and Co., 1894. 277 p.   BA, CU, H, HEH, LC, O, UVB, Y
*Also contains:* The Sheriff and His Partner—A Modern Idyll—Eatin' Crow—
The Best Man in Garotte—Gulmore, the Boss.

HARRIS, GARRARD. The Atonement. *In* Short Story Masterpieces (1900),
No. 4931.

HARRIS, JOEL CHANDLER. Aunt Fountain's Prisoner. *In* Stories of the
South (1893), No. 5283.
Printed earlier in No. 2487.

2485 ———— Balaam and His Master, and Other Sketches and Stories . . .
Boston and New York: Houghton, Mifflin and Company. The River-
side Press, Cambridge, 1891. 293 p.   BA, CU, H, HEH, N, O, UC, UM, UVB, Y
*Also contains:* A Conscript's Christmas—Ananias—Where's Duncan?—Mom
Bi—The Old Bascom Place.

2486 ———— The Chronicles of Aunt Minervy Ann . . . New York: Charles
Scribner's Sons, 1899. 210 p., illus.   BA, CU, H, HEH, LC, N, O, UC, UVB, Y

2487 ———— Free Joe, and Other Georgian Sketches . . . New York: Charles
Scribner's Sons, 1887. 236 p.   AP, BA, CU, H, HEH, N, O, UC, UVB, Y
*Also contains:* Little Compton—Aunt Fountain's Prisoner—Trouble on Lost
Mountain—Azalia.

2488 ———— Mingo, and Other Sketches in Black and White . . . Boston:
James R. Osgood and Company, 1884. 273 p.
AP, BA, CU, HEH, N, O, UC, UM, UVB, Y
*Also contains:* At Teague Poteet's: A Sketch of the Hog Mountain Range—
Blue Dave—A Piece of Land.

2489 ——— On the Plantation: A Story of a Georgia Boy's Adventures during the War ... New York: D. Appleton and Company, 1892. 233 p.,
illus. AP, BA, BU, CU, H, HEH, LC, N, O, UC, UM, UP, UVB, Y

2490 ——— On the Wing of Occasions: Being the Authorized Version of
Certain Curious Episodes of the Late Civil War, Including the Hitherto
Suppressed Narrative of the Kidnapping of President Lincoln ... New
York: Doubleday, Page & Co., 1900. 310 p., illus.
BA, BU, CU, H, HEH, LC, N, O, UC, UM, UP, UVB, Y
*Contents:* Why the Confederacy Failed—In the Order of Providence—The
Troubles of Martin Coy—The Kidnapping of President Lincoln—The Whims
of Captain McCarthy.

2491 ——— Sister Jane, Her Friends and Acquaintances: A Narrative of
Certain Events and Episodes Transcribed from the Papers of the Late
William Wornum ... Boston and New York: Houghton, Mifflin and
Company. The Riverside Press, Cambridge, 1896. 363 p.
BU, CU, H, HEH, N, O, UC, UM, UVB, Y

2492 ——— Tales of the Home Folks in Peace and War ... Boston and
New York: Houghton, Mifflin and Company. The Riverside Press,
Cambridge, 1898. 417, [1] p., illus.
AP, BA, CU, H, HEH, LC, N, O, UC, UP, UVB, Y
*Contents:* How Whalebone Caused a Wedding—The Colonel's "Nigger Dog"
—A Run of Luck—The Late Mr. Watkins of Georgia—A Belle of St. Valerien
—The Comedy of War—A Bold Deserter—A Baby in the Siege—The Baby's
Fortune—An Ambuscade—The Cause of the Difficulty—The Baby's Christmas.

2493 HARRIS, LEE O. The Man Who Tramps: A Story of To-Day ... In-
dianapolis: Douglass & Carlon, 1878. 304 p. LC, O
*Also contains:* Indiana—June—The Reapers—An Autumn Reverie—Forty
Years Old.

2494 HARRIS, MIRIAM (COLES). A Chit of Sixteen, and Other Stories ... New
York: G. W. Dillingham, successor to G. W. Carleton & Co., 1892.
180 p. LC
*Also contains:* In an Omnibus—The Black Wind of March.

2495 ——— Happy-Go-Lucky: A Novel ... New York: G. W. Carleton
& Co. London: S. Low, Son & Co., 1881. 420 p. HEH, N, O, UM

2496 [———] Missy: A Novel ... New York: G. W. Carleton & Co. London: S. Low, Son & Co., 1880. 412 p. BA, CU, H, HEH, O, Y

2497 [———] Phoebe: A Novel ... Boston, New York: Houghton, Mifflin
and Company. The Riverside Press, Cambridge, 1884. 332 p.
BU, CU, H, HEH, LC, O, UV, Y

2498 ——— An Utter Failure: A Novel ... New York: D. Appleton and
Company, 1891. 334 p. BU, CU, H, HEH, LC, O, UC, Y

2499 HARRIS, WALTER BUTLER. Pioneer Life in California ... Stockton, California: D. H. Berdine & Co., printers, 1884. 98 p.     HEH
Of gambling and drinking at the mines.

2500 HARRIS, WILLIAM SHULER. Mr. World and Miss Church Goer; or, The Secret Service of Satan. An Allegory ... Cleona, Pa.; G. Holzapfel, 1900. 307 p., illus.     LC

HARRISON, MRS. BURTON. *See* Harrison, Constance (Cary)

2501 [HARRISON, CONSTANCE (CARY).] The Anglomaniacs ... New York: Cassell Publishing Company, 104 & 106 Fourth Avenue [cop. 1890]. 296 p.     BA, BU, CU, H, HEH, N, O, UVB, Y
Satire on American worship of all things English.

2502 ——— A Bachelor Maid. By Mrs. Burton Harrison ... New York: The Century Co., 1894. 224 p., illus.
    BA, CU, H, HEH, LC, N, O, UC, UM, UVB, Y
New York society.

2503 ——— Bar Harbor Days ... New York: Harper & Brothers, 1887. 181, [1] p., illus.     BA, BU, CU, H, HEH, LC, N, O, UC, UM, UVB, Y

2504 ——— Belhaven Tales. Crow's Nest. Una and King David ... New York: The Century Co., 1892. 212 p., illus.
    BA, BU, CU, H, HEH, N, O, UM, UVB, Y
*Also contains:* When the Century Came In—Penelope's Swains—Monsieur Alcibiade—Gay's Romance.

2505 ——— The Carcellini Emerald, with Other Tales ... Chicago and New York: Herbert S. Stone and Company, 1899. 314 p., 1 l., illus.
    BA, CU, HEH, LC, O, UP, UVB, Y
*Also contains:* An Author's Reading and Its Consequences—Leander of Betsy's Pride—The Three Misses Benedict at Yale—A Girl of the Period—The Stolen Stradivarius—Wanted: A Chaperon.

2506 ——— The Circle of a Century ... New York: The Century Co., 1899. 225 p.     BA, CU, H, HEH, LC, N, O, UM, UV, Y
Part I, In Old New York; Part II, In New York of To-Day.

2507 ——— A Daughter of the South, and Shorter Stories ... New York: Cassell Publishing Company, 104 & 106 Fourth Avenue [cop. 1892]. 281 p.     BA, CU, H, HEH, LC, N, O, UM, UVB, Y
*Also contains:* A Thorn in His Cushion—Mr. Clendenning Piper—Jenny, the Débutante—Wife's Love—A Harp Unstrung—A Suit Decided.

2508 ——— An Edelweiss of the Sierras, Golden-Rod, and Other Tales ... New York: Harper & Brothers, 1892. 209 p.
    BA, CU, H, HEH, LC, N, O, UM, UV, Y
*Also contains:* Under the Convent Wall—Cherrycote—The Shattered Violin—A House Built upon the Sand—On a Hill-Top.

2509 ———— An Errant Wooing . . . New York: The Century Co., 1895. 258 p., illus.      BA, CU, HEH, LC, N, UC, UP, UVB, Y

2510 ———— Flower de Hundred: The Story of a Virginia Plantation . . . New York: Cassell Publishing Company, 104 & 106 Fourth Avenue [cop. 1890]. 301 p.      BA, BU, CU, H, HEH, LC, N, O, UM, UVB, Y

2511 [————] Golden-Rod: An Idyl of Mount Desert. New York: Harper & Brothers, 1880. 115 p.      BA, H, HEH, LC, UV, Y
Later printed in No. 2508.

2512 ———— Good Americans . . . New York: The Century Co., 1898. 220 p., front.      BA, BU, CU, HEH, LC, N, O, UV, Y

2513 ———— The Merry Maid of Arcady, His Lordship, and Other Stories . . . Boston, London, New York: Lamson, Wolffe and Company, 1897. 348 p., illus.      BA, CU, H, HEH, LC, N, O, UVB, Y
*Also contains:* Worrosquoyacke—Leaves from the Diary of Ruth Marchmont, Spinster—Thirteen at Table—At a Winter House-Party—The Secret of San Juan—"The Stranger within Thy Gate"—His Lordship.
Census of copies does not distinguish between eds. on thick paper or thin.

———— Monsieur Alcibiade. *In* C. C. Harrison, *ed.*, Short Stories (1893), No. 2514.
Printed earlier in No. 2504.

2514 ———— *ed.* Short Stories . . . New York: Harper & Brothers, 1893. 220 p.      CU, HEH, LC, N, O, UC, Y
*Contents:* My Own Story, by Elizabeth Dean [i.e., Drew] Barstow Stoddard —In Honor Bound, by Caroline Chesebro—An Islander, by Margaret Crosby —A Speakin' Ghost, by Mrs. Annie Trumbull Slosson—Monsieur Alcibiade, by Constance Cary Harrison.

2515 ———— A Son of the Old Dominion . . . Boston, New York, and London: Lamson, Wolffe and Company, 1897. 355 p.      BA, CU, H, HEH, N, O, UM, UP, UVB, Y

2516 [————] The Story of Helen Troy . . . New York: Harper & Brothers, 1881. 202 p.      CU, H, HEH, LC, N, UV, Y

2517 ———— Sweet Bells Out of Tune . . . New York: The Century Co., 1893. 231 p., illus.      BA, CU, H, HEH, LC, N, O, UP, UVB, Y

2518 ———— A Triple Entanglement . . . Philadelphia: J. B. Lippincott Company, 1899. 272 p., illus.      CU, HEH, LC, N, O, UV, Y

2519 ———— A Virginia Cousin & Bar Harbor Tales . . . Boston and New York: Lamson, Wolffe and Co., 1895. 202 p., front.      BA, CU, H, HEH, LC, N, O, UVB, Y
*Also contains:* Out of Season—On Frenchman's Bay.

2520 HARRISON, JAMES ALBERT. Autrefois: Tales of Old New Orleans and Elsewhere... New York: Cassell & Company, Limited, 104-106 Fourth Avenue [cop. 1888]. 295 p.                                      AP, BA, HEH, LC, UV
*Contents:* Aunt Annette—The Story of Carlito Jacmel—Soeur Agathe—The Hall of Tiger-Skins—The Story of an Urn—Sieu' Cayétane—The Episode of Père Benachi—Old Mamzel—Man Cribiche's Meditations—Izzét and Esmé—Piti-Josi-Ba'tiste.

HARRISON, LEWIS, *pseud. See* Watson, Lewis H.

2521 HARRISON, LOUIS REEVES. Rothermal: A Story of a Lost Identity . . . New York: The American News Company [cop. 1890]. 281 p.     LC

2522 [HARSHA, WILLIAM JUSTIN.] Ploughed Under: The Story of an Indian Chief, Told by Himself. With an Introduction by Inshta Theamba (Bright Eyes). New York: Fords, Howard, & Hulbert, 1881. 268 p.
                                               BA, CU, H, HEH, N, UV, Y
Bright Eyes is pseud. of Susette (La Flesche) Tibbles.

2523 HART, EDWIN KIRKMAN. The Sleeping Sentinel of Valley Forge: A Romance of the Revolution . . . Philadelphia, 1897. 37, [1] p., illus.
                                               CU, HEH, LC, UVB

2524 HART, FRED H. The Sazerac Lying Club: A Nevada Book... San Francisco: Henry Keller & Co., 1878. 240, [1] p., illus. CU, H, HEH, UC, UM, Y
*Contents:* Origin of the Sazerac Lying Club—"Uncle John"—"Old Dad"—"Stub"—Some Lies and Otherwise—Frontier Sketches—Life in a Mining Town—Indians and Chinese.

2525 HART, THOMAS W. Robert Sanders; or, Light Out of Darkness. A Romance of Greenville and of the Pee Dee Section of South Carolina . . . New York: The Irving Co., 1897. 279 p.                      LC

2526 HARTE, BRET. The Argonauts of North Liberty . . . Boston and New York: Houghton, Mifflin and Company. The Riverside Press, Cambridge, 1888. 206 p.   AP, BA, BU, CU, H, HEH, LC, N, O, UC, UM, UP, UVB, Y

2527 ———— Barker's Luck, and Other Stories . . . Boston and New York: Houghton, Mifflin and Company. The Riverside Press, Cambridge, 1896. 265 p.       BA, CU, H, HEH, LC, N, O, UC, UP, UVB
*Also contains:* A Yellow Dog—A Mother of Five—Bulger's Reputation—In the Tules—A Convert of the Mission—The Indiscretion of Elsbeth—The Devotion of Enriquez.

2528 ———— The Bell-Ringer of Angel's, and Other Stories . . . Boston and New York: Houghton, Mifflin and Company. The Riverside Press, Cambridge, 1894. 334 p.  AP, BA, CU, H, HEH, LC, N, O, UC, UM, UP, UVB, Y
*Also contains:* Johnnyboy—Young Robin Gray—The Sheriff of Siskyou—A Rose of Glenbogie—The Mystery of the Hacienda—Chu Chu—My First Book.

2529 —————— By Shore and Sedge ... Boston, New York: Houghton, Mifflin and Company. The Riverside Press, Cambridge, 1885. 260 p.

AP, BA, BU, CU, H, HEH, LC, N, O, UC, UM, UP, UVB, Y

*Contents:* An Apostle of the Tules—Sarah Walker—A Ship of '49.

2530 —————— Clarence ... Boston and New York: Houghton, Mifflin and Company. The Riverside Press, Cambridge, 1895. 270 p.

AP, BA, BU, CU, H, HEH, LC, N, O, UC, UP, UVB, Y

2531 —————— Colonel Starbottle's Client, and Some Other People ... Boston and New York: Houghton, Mifflin and Company. The Riverside Press, Cambridge, 1892. 283 p.

AP, BA, CU, H, HEH, LC, N, UC, UM, UP, UVB, Y

*Also contains:* The Postmistress of Laurel Run—A Night at "Hays"—Johnson's "Old Woman"—The New Assistant at Pine Clearing School—In a Pioneer Restaurant—A Treasure of the Galleon—Out of a Pioneer's Trunk—The Ghosts of Stuckeley.

2532 —————— Cressy ... Boston and New York: Houghton, Mifflin and Company. The Riverside Press, Cambridge, 1889. 290 p.

AP, BA, BU, CU, H, HEH, LC, N, O, UVB, Y

2533 —————— The Crusade of the Excelsior ... Boston and New York: Houghton, Mifflin and Company. The Riverside Press, Cambridge, 1887. 250 p., illus.    AP, BU, CU, H, HEH, LC, N, O, UC, UM, UP, UVB, Y

2534 —————— Drift from Two Shores ... Boston: Houghton, Osgood and Company. The Riverside Press, Cambridge, 1878. 266 p.

BA, BU, CU, H, HEH, LC, N, O, UM, UP, UVB, Y

*Contents:* The Man on the Beach—Two Saints of the Foot-Hills—Jinny—Roger Catron's Friend—Who Was My Quiet Friend?—A Ghost of the Sierras—The Hoodlum Band (A Condensed Novel)—The Man Whose Yoke Was Not Easy—My Friend, the Tramp—The Man from Solano—The Office Seeker—A Sleeping-Car Experience—Five o'Clock in the Morning—With the Entrées.

2535 —————— A First Family of Tasajara ... Boston and New York: Houghton, Mifflin and Company. The Riverside Press, Cambridge, 1892. 301 p.    AP, BA, CU, H, HEH, LC, O, UC, UM, UP, UVB, Y

2536 —————— Flip, and Found at Blazing Star ... Boston, New York: Houghton, Mifflin and Company. The Riverside Press, Cambridge, 1882. 192 p.    AP, BA, BU, CU, H, HEH, LC, N, O, UC, UM, UP, UVB, Y
Later printed in No. 2538.

2537 —————— From Sand Hill to Pine ... Boston and New York: Houghton, Mifflin and Company. The Riverside Press, Cambridge, 1900. 327, [1] p.    AP, BA, CU, H, HEH, LC, N, O, UC, UM, UP, UVB, Y

*Contents:* A Niece of "Snapshot Harry's"—A Treasure of the Redwoods—A Belle of Cañada City—What Happened at the Fonda—A Jack and Jill of the Sierras—Mr. Bilson's Housekeeper.

2538 ——— Frontier Stories ... Boston and New York: Houghton, Mifflin and Company. The Riverside Press, Cambridge, 1887. 452 p.

HEH, UVB, Y

*Contents:* Flip: A California Romance—Found at Blazing Star—In the Carquinez Woods—At the Mission of San Carmel—A Blue-Grass Penelope—Left Out on Lone Star Mountain—A Ship of '49.

2539 ——— Gabriel Conroy ... Hartford, Conn.: American Publishing Company, 1876. 466, [1] p., illus. BA, CU, H, HEH, LC, N, O, UM, UP, UVB, Y

2540 ——— The Heritage of Dedlow Marsh, and Other Tales ... Boston and New York: Houghton, Mifflin and Company. The Riverside Press, Cambridge, 1889. 259 p. AP, CU, H, HEH, LC, N, O, UP, UVB, Y

*Also contains:* A Knight-Errant of the Foot-Hills—A Secret of Telegraph Hill —Captain Jim's Friend.

2541 ——— In a Hollow of the Hills ... Boston and New York: Houghton, Mifflin and Company. The Riverside Press, Cambridge, 1895. 210 p.

CU, H, HEH, LC, N, O, UC, UP, UVB, Y

2542 ——— In the Carquinez Woods ... Boston, New York: Houghton, Mifflin and Company. The Riverside Press, Cambridge, 1884. 241 p.

BA, BU, CU, H, HEH, LC, N, O, UC, UP, UVB, Y

Later printed in No. 2538.

2543 ——— Maruja ... Boston and New York: Houghton, Mifflin and Company. The Riverside Press, Cambridge, 1885. 271 p.

AP, BA, CU, H, HEH, LC, N, O, UC, UP, UVB, Y

2544 ——— A Millionaire of Rough-and-Ready, and Devil's Ford ... Boston and New York: Houghton, Mifflin and Company. The Riverside Press, Cambridge, 1887. 299 p.

AP, BU, H, HEH, LC, N, O, UC, UM, UP, UVB, Y

2545 ——— Mr. Jack Hamlin's Mediation, and Other Stories ... Boston and New York: Houghton, Mifflin and Company. The Riverside Press, Cambridge, 1899. 289, [1] p.

BA, CU, H, HEH, LC, N, O, UC, UM, UP, UVB, Y

*Also contains:* The Man at the Semaphore—An Esmeralda of Rocky Cañon —Dick Spindler's Family Christmas—When the Waters Were Up at "Jules" —The Boom in the "Calaveras Clarion"—The Secret of Sobriente's Well— Liberty Jones's Discovery.

2546 ——— On the Frontier ... Boston, New York: Houghton, Mifflin and Company. The Riverside Press, Cambridge, 1884. 288 p.

AP, BA, BU, CU, H, HEH, LC, N, O, UC, UM, UP, UVB, Y

*Contents:* At the Mission of San Carmel—A Blue Grass Penelope—Left Out on Lone Star Mountain.

Contents later included in No. 2538.

2547 ———— A Phyllis of the Sierras, and A Drift from Redwood Camp . . . Boston and New York: Houghton, Mifflin and Company. The Riverside Press, Cambridge, 1888. 215 p.

AP, BU, CU, H, HEH, LC, N, O, UC, UP, UVB, Y

2548 ———— A Protégée of Jack Hamlin's, and Other Stories . . . Boston and New York: Houghton, Mifflin and Company. The Riverside Press, Cambridge, 1894. 292 p.

AP, BA, CU, H, HEH, LC, N, O, UC, UM, UP, UVB, Y

*Also contains:* An Ingénue of the Sierras—The Reformation of James Reddy —The Heir of the McHulishes—An Episode of West Woodlands—The Home-Coming of Jim Wilkes.

2549 ———— Sally Dows, and Other Stories . . . Boston and New York: Houghton, Mifflin and Company. The Riverside Press, Cambridge, 1893. 299 p. AP, CU, H, HEH, LC, N, O, UC, UM, UP, UVB, Y

*Also contains:* The Conspiracy of Mrs. Bunker—The Transformation of Buckeye Camp—Their Uncle from California.

2550 ———— A Sappho of Green Springs, and Other Stories . . . Boston and New York: Houghton, Mifflin and Company. The Riverside Press, Cambridge, 1891. 294 p. AP, BU, CU, H, HEH, LC, N, O, UC, UM, UP, UVB, Y

*Also contains:* The Chatelaine of Burnt Ridge—Through the Santa Clara Wheat—A Maecenas of the Pacific Slope.

2551 ———— Snow-Bound at Eagle's . . . Boston and New York: Houghton, Mifflin and Company. The Riverside Press, Cambridge, 1886. 213 p.

AP, BA, BU, CU, H, HEH, LC, N, O, UC, UP, UVB, Y

2552 ———— Stories in Light and Shadow . . . Boston and New York: Houghton, Mifflin and Company. The Riverside Press, Cambridge, 1898. 304 p., 1 l. BA, CU, H, HEH, LC, N, O, UC, UP, UVB, Y

*Contents:* "Unser Karl"—Uncle Jim and Uncle Billy—See Yup—The Desborough Connections—Salomy Jane's Kiss—The Man and the Mountain—The Passing of Enriquez.

2553 ———— The Story of a Mine . . . Boston: James R. Osgood & Company, late Ticknor & Fields, and Fields, Osgood & Co., 1878. 172 p.

AP, BA, CU, H, HEH, LC, N, O, UM, UP, Y

2554 ———— Susy: A Story of the Plains . . . Boston and New York: Houghton, Mifflin and Company. The Riverside Press, Cambridge, 1893. 264 p. AP, BA, CU, H, HEH, LC, N, O, UC, UP, UVB, Y

2555 ———— Tales of Trail and Town . . . Boston and New York: Houghton, Mifflin and Company. The Riverside Press, Cambridge, 1898. 348 p., 1 l. BA, CU, H, HEH, LC, N, O, UC, UM, UP, UVB, Y

*Contents:* The Ancestors of Peter Atherly—Two Americans—The Judgment of Bolinas Plain—The Strange Experience of Alkali Dick—A Night on the Divide—The Youngest Prospector in Calaveras—A Tale of Three Truants.

2556 ——— Thankful Blossom: A Romance of the Jerseys, 1779 . . . Boston: James R. Osgood and Company, late Ticknor & Fields, and Fields, Osgood & Co., 1877. 158 p., illus.

AP, BA, BU, CU, H, HEH, LC, N, O, UC, UP, UVB, Y

2557 ——— Three Partners; or, The Big Strike on Heavy Tree Hill . . . Boston and New York: Houghton, Mifflin and Company. The Riverside Press, Cambridge, 1897. 342 p.

AP, BA, CU, H, HEH, LC, N, O, UC, UM, UP, UVB, Y

2558 ——— The Twins of Table Mountain, and Other Stories . . . Boston: Houghton, Osgood and Company. The Riverside Press, Cambridge, 1879. 249 p. CU, H, HEH, LC, O, UM, UP, UVB, Y
*Also contains:* An Heiress of Red Dog—The Great Deadwood Mystery—A Legend of Sammtstadt—Views from a German Spion.

2559 ——— A Waif of the Plains . . . Boston and New York: Houghton, Mifflin and Company. The Riverside Press, Cambridge, 1890. 231 p.

AP, BA, BU, CU, H, HEH, LC, N, UC, UM, UP, UVB, Y

2560 ——— A Ward of the Golden Gate . . . Boston and New York: Houghton, Mifflin and Company. The Riverside Press, Cambridge, 1890. 249 p. AP, CU, H, HEH, LC, N, O, UC, UM, UP, UVB, Y

2561 HARTOUGH, MRS. S. M. The Curse of Mill Valley . . . New York: National Temperance Society, 1877. 326 p., front.
Listed PW, Dec. 1, 1877.

2562 [HARTT, IRENE WIDDEMER.] Another Man's Wife. New York: G. W. Carleton & Co., 1877. 350 p.
Listed PW, Nov. 17, 1877.

2563 [HARTWELL, LOLA G.] Told by a Photo. Limited to 12 copies. [St. Louis, Mo., cop. 1898.] [12] p. LC
Deposited Apr. 7, 1898.

2564 HARVEY, GEORGE COCKBURN. The Light That Lies . . . Philadelphia: J. B. Lippincott Company, 1896. 163 p., illus. LC
Of several flirtations.

HARVEY, JAMES CLARENCE, *jt. au. See* Wilson, T. B. After Many Days [cop. 1892], No. 6022.

——— *jt. au. See* Lanza, C. H. Scarabaeus [cop 1892], No. 3211.

2565 HARVEY, MINNIE L. Louisa Van Benthusen: A Novel . . . Philadelphia: W. H. Thompson, 1882. 297 p. HEH, LC, Y
New York society.

2566 HARVEY, WILLIAM HOPE. A Tale of Two Nations . . . Chicago: Coin Publishing Company, cop. 1894. 302 p.   CU, HEH
On free coinage of silver.

2567 HASSAUREK, FRIEDRICH. The Secret of the Andes: A Romance . . . Cincinnati: Robert Clarke & Co., 1879. 466 p.  BA, BU, H, HEH, LC, O, UV, Y

HASTA, *pseud. See* Spear, Anne B.

HASTINGS, ELIZABETH, *pseud. See* Sherwood, Margaret (Pollock)

2568 HASTINGS, FRANK WARREN. Wed to a Lunatic: A Wild, Weird Yarn of Love, and Some Other Things, Delivered in the Form of Hash for the Benefit of Tired Readers . . . St. Johnsbury, Vt.: L. W. Rowell, publisher and printer, 1896. 135, [1] p.   HEH, LC

2569 [HATCH, DAVID PATTERSON.] El Reshid: A Novel . . . Los Angeles, Cal.: B. R. Baumgardt & Co., 1899. 438 p.   H, HEH, LC

2570 HATCH, MARY R. (PLATT). The Bank Tragedy: A Novel . . . New York: Welch, Fracker Company, 1890. 427 p., front.  AP, HEH, LC, O, Y
Detective story.

2571 —— The Strange Disappearance of Eugene Comstocks . . . New York: G. W. Dillingham Company, 1895. 307 p.   LC
Detective story; Maine.

2572 —— The Upland Mystery: A Tragedy of New England . . . Chicago: Laird & Lee, cop. 1887. 172 p., front.   LC, Y
Deposited Aug. 15, 1887.

HATCHET, SAM, *pseud. See* Cleveland, Mayhew B.

2573 HATCHETT, MAMIE LAMKIN. Myra: A Novel . . . Richmond, Va.: J. W. Randolph & English, 1884. 249 p.   LC, UV

2574 [HAVEN, J.] The Adventures of Frank Friendless and Elder Webber; or, The Pirate's Ghost. Philadelphia [Salem, N.J.: Standard Print], 1878. 86 p.   LC

2575 HAW, MARY JANE. The Beechwood Tragedy: A Tale of the Chickahominy . . . Richmond, Va.: J. W. Randolph & English, 1889. 241 p.   HEH, LC, UVB
An enlargement of *The Rivals* (1864), Wright II, No. 1131.

2576 [HAWKINS, THOMAS HAYDEN.] Drifting. By Vigilans [pseud.]. Denver: The Chain & Hardy Co., 1892. 313 p.   LC
Sometimes attributed to M. N. Patrick.
Of a New York doctor.

HAWKS, J. M. Thornton's Redemption. *In* J. J. Conway, *ed.*, Stories (1893), No. 1172.

2577 HAWTHORNE, JULIAN. An American Penman: From the Diary of Inspector Byrnes . . . New York: Cassell & Company, 739 & 741 Broadway [cop. 1887]. 280 p.                    O

2578 ——— Another's Crime: From the Diary of Inspector Byrnes . . . New York: Cassell & Company, Limited, 104 & 106 Fourth Avenue [cop. 1888]. 242 p.                    AP, CU, H, HEH, LC, O

2579 ——— Archibald Malmaison . . . New York: Funk & Wagnalls, 1884. 126 p.                    H, O, Y
Of psychic phenomena.

2580 ——— Beatrix Randolph: A Story . . . Boston: James R. Osgood and Company, 1884. 280 p., illus.    AP, BA, CU, H, HEH, LC, N, O, UC, UP, UV, Y
Of an opera star.

2581 ——— Constance, and Calbot's Rival: Tales . . . New York: D. Appleton and Company, 1889. 227 p.    AP, BA, CU, HEH, LC, O, UVB

2582 ——— David Poindexter's Disappearance, and Other Tales . . . New York: D. Appleton and Company, 1888. 210 p.    AP, H, HEH, O, UVB, Y
*Also contains:* Ken's Mystery—"When Half-Gods Go, the Gods Arrive"— "Set Not Thy Foot on Graves"—My Friend Paton.

2583 ——— A Dream and a Forgetting . . . Chicago, New York, and San Francisco: Belford, Clarke & Co. [cop. 1888]. 209 p.    AP, H, HEH, LC, O, Y

2584 ——— Dust: A Novel . . . New York: Fords, Howards, & Hulbert, 1883. 402 p., illus.    AP, BA, CU, H, HEH, N, O, UVB, Y
At head of title: " 'Our Continent' Library."

2585 ——— A Fool of Nature . . . New York: Charles Scribner's Sons, 1896. 287 p.    AP, BU, CU, H, HEH, LC, O, UC, UM, UP, UVB, Y

2586 ——— Fortune's Fool . . . Boston: James R. Osgood and Company, 1883. 470 p.    AP, BA, CU, H, HEH, LC, N, O, UVB, Y

2587 ——— Garth: A Novel . . . New York: D. Appleton and Company, 1877. 291 p. Printed in double columns.    BA, BU, CU, H, O, UC, UV, Y

2588 ——— The Golden Fleece: A Romance . . . Philadelphia: J. B. Lippincott Company, 1896. 193 p., illus.    CU, LC
Southern California.

2589 ——— The Great Bank Robbery: From the Diary of Inspector Byrnes . . . New York: Cassell & Company, Limited, 739 & 741 Broadway [cop. 1887]. 235 p.    AP, CU, HEH, LC, O, Y

2590 ———— John Parmelee's Curse . . . New York: Cassell & Company, Limited, 739 & 741 Broadway [cop. 1886]. 270 p.

AP, BA, BU, CU, HEH, LC, N, O, UVB, Y

Of the opium habit.

2591 ———— Kildhurm's Oak . . . New York: A. L. Burt [cop. 1888]. 219 p.

CU, HEH, N, UVB

Probably first published in the omitted "Manhattan Series," 1889.

2592 ———— Love Is a Spirit: A Novel . . . New York: Harper & Brothers, 1896. 200 p. AP, BA, CU, H, HEH, LC, N, UM, UVB, Y

West Indies.

2593 ———— Love—or a Name: A Story . . . Boston: Ticknor and Company, 1885. 304 p. AP, BA, CU, H, HEH, LC, N, O, UVB, Y

New York politics.

2594 ———— Mrs. Gainsborough's Diamonds: A Story . . . New York: D. Appleton and Company, 1878. 117 p. LC, Y

At head of title: "Appleton's New Handy-Volume Series."

2595 ———— Noble Blood . . . New York: D. Appleton and Company, 1885. 214 p. AP, BA, H, LC, N, Y

———— Odin Moore's Confession: A Christmas Story. *In* I. Bacheller, *ed.*, Best Things from American Literature (1899), No. 195.

2596 ———— One of Those Coincidences, and Ten Other Stories . . . New York and London: Funk & Wagnalls Company, 1899. 315 p., illus.

CU, HEH, LC, N

*Contains:* Francisco, by Wolcott Le Clear Beard—John Merrill's Experiment in Palmistry, by Florence M. Kingsley—The Strange Case of Esther Atkins, by Mrs. L. E. L. Hardenbrook—Jacob City, by A. Stewart Clarke—Selma the Soprano, by Mabel Wagnalls—At the End of His Rope, by Florence M. Kingsley—The Easter of La Mercedes, by Mary C. Francis—Romance of a Tin Roof and a Fire-Escape, by Myrta L. Avary.

2597 ———— Pauline . . . New York: United States Book Company, 150 Worth St., cor. Mission Place [cop. 1890]. 280 p. AP, LC, O

*Also contains:* Ellice Quentin—The Countess's Ruby.

At head of title: "American Authors' Series, No. 25."

2598 ———— Prince Saroni's Wife, and The Pearl-Shell Necklace . . . New York, London: Funk & Wagnalls, 1884. 117 p. AP, CU, H, HEH, N, O, UP

2599 ———— The Professor's Sister: A Romance . . . Chicago, New York, and San Francisco: Belford, Clarke & Co. [cop. 1888]. 180 p.

AP, BU, CU, HEH, LC, O, Y

Of the occult.

2600 ———— Sebastian Strome: A Novel ... New York: D. Appleton and Company, 1880. 195 p. Printed in double columns.

AP, BA, CU, H, HEH, LC, O, UM, UP, UVB, Y

"Psychological study of a young English divinity student." PW, Jan. 10, 1880.

2601 ———— Section 558; or, The Fatal Letter. From the Diary of Inspector Byrnes ... New York: Cassell & Company, Limited, 104 & 106 Fourth Avenue [cop. 1888]. 246 p.    AP, CU, HEH, LC, N, O, UV, Y

2602 ———— Sinfire. By Julian Hawthorne. Douglas Duane. By Edgar Fawcett. Philadelphia: J. B. Lippincott Company, 1888. 239 p.    CU

2603 ———— Six Cent Sam's ... St. Paul: The Price-McGill Company, 455-473 Cedar Street [cop. 1893]. 332, [1] p., illus.

AP, CU, HEH, LC, O, UM, UV, Y

Contents: Mr. Dunton's Invention—Greaves' Disappearance—Raxworthy's Treasure—The John North Mystery—A Model Murder—The Symposium.

2604 ———— A Tragic Mystery: From the Diary of Inspector Byrnes ... New York: Cassell & Company, Limited, 739 & 741 Broadway [cop. 1887]. 269 p.    AP, BA, BU, CU, H, LC, O, UM, UVB, Y

2605 ———— The Trial of Gideon, and Countess Almara's Murder ... New York, London: Funk & Wagnalls, 1886. 96 p.    LC, N, O, UM, Y

2606 HAWTHORNE, NATHANIEL. Doctor Grimshawe's Secret: A Romance ... Edited with Preface and Notes by Julian Hawthorne. Boston: James R. Osgood and Company, 1883. 368 p., illus.

AP, BU, CU, H, HEH, LC, N, O, UM, UP, UVB, Y

Census of copies does not distinguish between trade and large-paper eds.

2607 ———— The Dolliver Romance, and Other Pieces ... Boston: James R. Osgood and Company, 1876. 213 p.    BU, CU, H, HEH, LC, N, O, UP, UVB, Y

For contents see Wallace H. Cathcart, Bibliography of the Works of Nathaniel Hawthorne (Cleveland, Ohio, 1905), pp. 58-59.

HAY, ELZEY, pseud. See Andrews, Eliza Frances

2608 [HAY, JOHN MILTON.] The Bread-Winners: A Social Study. New York: Harper & Brothers, 1884. 319 p.

BA, BU, CU, H, HEH, LC, N, O, UC, UP, UVB, Y

Found with and without "The End" on p. 319.

HAYES, AUGUSTUS ALLEN. The Denver Express. In Stories by American Authors, VI (1884), No. 5272.

2609 ———— The Jesuit's Ring: A Romance of Mount Desert ... New York: Charles Scribner's Sons, 1887. 306 p.

AP, BA, CU, H, HEH, LC, N, O, UM, Y

HAYES, EMILY, *pseud.* *See* Gordon, Emma E.

HAYES, HENRY, *pseud.* *See* Kirk, Ellen Warner (Olney)

2610 HAYES, JEFF W. Tales of the Sierras ... Portland, Oregon: F. W. Baltes
and Company, 1900. 136 p., illus.                    HEH, LC, O, UM, Y
Contents: The Throckmortons–Sun Lee's Courtship–The Hermit of Telegraph Hill–Carrying the War into China–Whiskey Flat–Lost Opportunities
–"Pass Me Not"–Welcoming the President–"What's Atin' You"–Pioneer
and Modern Telegraphy–Billy McGinniss' Wake–A Messenger Boy's Trip
to London–A Piute Detective–Across the Sierras–Digging Wells by Telephone–Enterprise in Emergency–Some Reminiscences–A Youthful Don
Quixote–Oysters Cause Wire Trouble–The Carson Canning Company–
Bran Again–Col. Dickey's Paper Weight–The Cowboy Dispatcher.

HAYES, LAURA, *jt. au.* *See* Yandell, E. Three Girls in a Flat [cop. 1892],
Nos. 6146, 6147.

2611 HAYNES, EMORY JAMES. Dollars and Duty . . . New York: Ward &
Drummond, 1887. 458 p.                                      HEH
Business or the ministry.

2612 ——— The Fairest of Three: A Tale of American life ... New York:
American News Co., 1883. 196 p.
Listed PW, Jan. 12, 1884.

2613 ——— A Farm-House Cobweb: A Novel ... New York: Harper &
Brothers, 1895. 261 p.                              H, HEH, LC, O, Y
Vermont.

2614 ——— None Such? There Will Yet Be Thousands ... Boston: The
North Publishing Co., 1893. 331 p.                  H, HEH, LC, O, Y
Of a millionaire's philanthropic plan.

2615 ——— A Wedding in War-Time ... Boston: James H. Earle, 1889.
414 p.                                                       O
Civil War era.

2616 HAYS, MRS. HELEN. Aspirations . . . New York: Thomas Whittaker,
1886. 331 p.                                    AP, HEH, LC, O, UM
Also published as: *An Unexpected Legacy; or, Aspirations.* New York:
Thomas Whittaker, 1887. Listed PW, Oct. 22, 1887.

2617 HAYWARD, C. F. R. The Mentons. Was It a Crime? ... Chicago: R. R.
Donnelley & Sons, 1887. 157 p., illus.                       LC

2618 [HEALD, MRS. SARAH E.] The Eagle's Plume: A Story of the Early Days
of Vermont. By S. E. H. Philadelphia: Sunshine Publishing Company, 1890. 112 p., front.                               H, HEH, O

2619 HEARD, J. E. Revoked Vengeance: A Novel. By J. E. Heard, M.D., of Baltimore, Md. Baltimore: Press of John Cox's Sons, 1886. 304 p. HEH

HEARD, JOHN, JR. A Charge for France. *In* Stories of the Army (1893), No. 5280.

2620 HEARN, LAFCADIO. Chita: A Memory of Last Island . . . New York: Harper & Brothers, 1889. 204 p.
AP, BU, CU, H, HEH, LC, N, O, UC, UP, UVB, Y

2621 ——— Youma: The Story of a West-Indian Slave . . . New York: Harper & Brothers, 1890. 193 p., front. AP, CU, HEH, LC, N, O, UC, UVB, Y

2622 [HEATON, ELLEN MARVIN.] The Octagon Club: A Character Study. By E. M. H. . . . New York: G. P. Putnam's Sons, 1880. 284 p. LC

2623 HEATON, JOHN LANGDON. The Book of Lies . . . New York: The Morse Company, 1896. 175 p., illus. CU, LC

2624 HEAVEN, LOUISE (PALMER). Chata and Chinita: A Novel . . . Boston: Roberts Brothers, 1889. 475 p. AP, H, HEH, LC, O, UP, Y
Mexico.

HECKEL, GEORGE B., *jt. au. See* Wall, G. A. Jacob Valmont (1889), No. 5719.

2625 HEDDEN, WILLIAM D. Sunshine among the Clouds; or, The Macdonalds. A Story of Trust on Trial . . . New York: U. D. Ward, 150 Nassau St. [cop. 1877]. 347 p., illus. CU, HEH, LC
Scotland and Canada.

2626 HEERMANS, FORBES. Thirteen Stories of the Far West . . . Syracuse, N.Y.: C. W. Bardeen, 1887. 263 p. BA, H, HEH, LC, N, O, Y
*Contents:* Shingles—The Widow of the Late Smith—Alanascar and His Uncle —The Ascent of Uncompahgre—The Descent of Uncompahgre—Buried under an Avalanche—The Wedding at Puerta da Luna—On Watch with the Night Herd—Don Quixote de Santa Rosa—The Assayer's Story—The Log of a Landsman—Molokai: Death's Valley—The Home of Everlasting Fire.

2627 [HELLER, LEVI D.] Victims of Marriage . . . By Judge Bullion [pseud.]. Columbus, Ohio: The Heller Publishing Co., 1890. 306 p. LC
Marriage impedes the progress of women.

2628 HELLER, ROBLEY E. The Free Soil Prophet of the Verdigris . . . [To-peka, Kan., cop. 1894.] 316 p. HEH, LC, Y

2629 HELM, FLORA. Between Two Forces: A Record of a Theory and a Passion . . . Boston: Arena Publishing Company, 1894. 238 p. LC
Touches upon labor problems.

2630  HELMBOLD, MASSON PELL. Althea St. John: A Tale . . . New York: Brentano Bros., 1886. 89 p.         H

HEMENWAY, CRABTREE, *pseud*. *See* Hemenway, Myles

2631  [HEMENWAY, MYLES.] Doomsday. By Crabtree Hemenway [pseud.]. Boston: Copeland and Day, 1898. 128 p., 1 l.     CU, H, LC, UP, Y
Later printed in No. 2632.
Of a prophet involved in a romance.

2632  ———— Passengers. Doomsday. April . . . Boston: Small, Maynard and Company, 1900. 290 p., 1 l.     H, LC

2633  HENDERSON, ISAAC. Agatha Page: A Parable . . . Boston: Ticknor and Company, 1888. 413 p., front.     BA, H, HEH, LC, O
Italy.

2634  ———— The Prelate: A Novel . . . Boston: Ticknor and Company, 1886. 350 p.     AP, BA, BU, H, HEH, LC, N, O
Of Americans in Rome.

2635  HENDERSON, MRS. S. E. Jelard . . . Logansport, Ind.: Longwell & Cummings, 1892. 554 p.     LC
Kentucky.

HENDERSON, WILLIAM JAMES. A Fin de Siécle Genie. *In* Hanks: Assorted Yarns from Puck (1893), No. 2444.

———— A Modern Hans Sachs. *In* Mavericks (1892), No. 3663.

2636  HENNESSY, ROLAND BURKE. Tales of the Heart . . . New York: Meyer Brothers & Co., 1897. 126 p.     BU, HEH, LC

2637  HENRY, ARTHUR. Nicholas Blood, Candidate . . . New York: Oliver Dodd, Judge Building [cop. 1890]. 200 p.     HEH, UP, UVB
Political campaign between white and Negro in Memphis.

2638  ———— A Princess of Arcady . . . New York: Doubleday, Page & Co., 1900. 307 p.     BU, CU, HEH, LC, UP, Y
According to Vrest Orton, *Dreiserana* (New York, 1929), p. 13, Theodore Dreiser wrote the last chapter.

HENRY, EDGAR, *pseud*. *See* Tourgee, Albion Winegar

HENSEL, OCTAVIA, *pseud*. *See* Seymour, Mary Alice (Ives)

2639  HEPWORTH, GEORGE HUGHES. Brown Studies; or, Camp Fires and Morals . . . New York: E. P. Dutton & Company, 1895. 332 p., illus.     HEH, O, Y
Adirondacks.

2640 ———— !!! By George H. Hepworth ... New York: Harper & Brothers, 1881. 196 p.       HEH, O, UM, Y
Of the occult.

2641 ———— The Farmer and the Lord . . . New York: E. P. Dutton and Company, 1896. 238 p.       BU, CU, H, HEH, LC, UC, Y

2642 [————] Hiram Golf's Religion; or, The "Shoemaker by the Grace of God." New York: E. P. Dutton & Company, 1893. 127 p., front.
      CU, H, LC

2643 ———— The Queerest Man Alive, and Other Stories . . . New York: R. F. Fenno & Company, 9 and 11 East 16th Street [cop. 1897]. 271 p.
      HEH, LC, Y
*Also contains:* Yegor's Portrait—A Little Mouse—For Tom's Sake—The Flirt —Klang and Klung.

2644 ———— They Met in Heaven ... New York: E. P. Dutton & Company, 1894. 209 p.       H, LC

2645 HER CRIME ... Boston: Roberts Brothers, 1882. 284 p.
      BA, CU, H, HEH, LC, N, O, UV
At head of title: "No Name Series."
New York society.

2646 HER MISTAKE: A Novel. New York: George W. Dillingham, 1892. 360 p.
Listed PW, Apr. 16, 1892.

2647 HERBERT, WILL, *pseud.* Not His Daughter: An American Novel . . . Philadelphia: T. B. Peterson & Brothers, 306 Chestnut Street [cop. 1886]. 284 p.       LC
"Author said to be a prominent member of the Baltimore bar." PW, May 8, 1886.

2648 THE HERMIT OF THE LAKE; or, The Island Princess. A Story of Lake Memphremagog and the Southwest. Presented by the Connecticut Valley & Passumpsic Railroads, Season of 1886. [New York: Liberty Printing Co., 1886?] 32 p., illus.       BA, H, HEH, N

2649 [HERN, HENRY] *pseud.* Rev. Waldo Messaros' Fall and Miss Ryler's Suicide at Niagara Falls: To Which Is Added, the History of Her Sister's Sad Life and Death ... Philadelphia, Pa.: The Old Franklin Publishing House [1886]. 14, 3-46 p., illus.       LC

2650 [————] *pseud.* A Stepmother's Victim: A True Narrative of the Sufferings, Trials, and Perils of the Lovely Daughter of Daniel Stuart, Esq., the New York Millionaire, at the Hands of His Second Wife, Who After His Death Cruelly Persecuted Her . . . Philadelphia, Pa.: The Old Franklin Publishing House, cop. 1885. 62 p., illus.       LC

2651 HERRICK, ROBERT. The Gospel of Freedom ... New York: The Macmillan Company. London: Macmillan & Co., Ltd., 1898. 287 p.

BA, CU, H, HEH, LC, N, UC, UM, UP, UV, Y

2652 ———— Literary Love-Letters, and Other Stories ... New York: Charles Scribner's Sons, 1897. 245 p. BA, CU, HEH, LC, N, O, UC, Y

*Also contains:* A Question in Art—Mare Morto—The Price of Romance—A Rejected Titian—Payment in Full—A Prothalamion.

2653 ———— Love's Dilemmas ... Chicago: H. S. Stone & Company, 1898. 193 p., 1 l. BA, CU, H, HEH, N, O, UC, UP, Y

*Contents:* Mute—A Temporary Infidelity—Miss Atherton's Mission—A Pension Love Story—A Marriage by Proxy—The Psychological Moment.

2654 ———— The Man Who Wins ... New York: Charles Scribner's Sons, 1897. 125 p. BA, CU, H, HEH, LC, N, O, UC, Y

2655 ———— The Web of Life ... New York: The Macmillan Company. London: Macmillan & Co., Ltd., 1900. 356 p.

BA, CU, H, HEH, LC, N, O, UC, UP, Y

2656 HERVEY, SARA E. The Esty Family ... Onset, Mass.: Published by the author, 1889. 276 p. H, HEH, LC, UP, Y

Of a woman doctor; New York.

2657 HEWITT, R. BEAUMONT. Life of Robert Whitman; or, The Man Who Sold His Wife ... N. O. [New Orleans]: Meine & Weihing, printers, cop. 1895. 15 pts.

Alabama University Library has Part I: cover title, 78 p. Information supplied by Vivien M. Lawson.

2658 HEYWOOD, D. HERBERT. Twentieth Century: A Prophecy of the Coming Age ... Boston: F. B. Heywood, 2000 [cop. 1889]. 48 p., illus. LC

Prospectus of a book that was to run to about 550 p.; deposited Apr. 4, 1890.

HIBBARD, GEORGE ABIAH. As the Sparks Fly Upward. *In* Stories of the Railway (1893), No. 5281.

Printed earlier in No. 2659.

———— The End of the Beginning. *In* Stories of New York (1893), No 5279.

Printed earlier in No. 2659.

2659 ———— The Governor, and Other Stories ... New York: Charles Scribner's Sons, 1892. 292 p. BA, BU, CU, H, HEH, LC, N, O, UM, UVB, Y

*Also contains:* A Deedless Drama—"As the Sparks Fly Upward"—A Matter of Fact—A Fresh-Water Romance—The End of the Beginning.

2660 ———— Iduna, and Other Stories ... New York: Harper & Brothers, 1891. 296 p. H, HEH, LC, O, Y

*Also contains:* The Woman in the Case—Papoose—"Would Dick Do That?" —"The Dragoness"—In Maiden Meditation.

2661 ——— Nowadays, and Other Stories . . . New York: Harper & Brothers, 1893. 268 p., illus.  AP, CU, H, HEH, LC, N, O, UM, UVB, Y
*Also contains:* "There's Nothing Half So Sweet in Life"—"A Mad World, My Masters"—"Guilty Sir Guy"—In the Midst of Life—A Flirt.

2662 HICKS, HENRY S. Christmas-Eve in a Light-House; or, A Batch of Old Stories Re-told . . . New York: The American News Company [cop. 1877]. 100 p.  LC

2663 [HICKS, WILLIAM WATKIN.] Angels' Visits to My Farm in Florida. By Golden Light [pseud.] . . . New York: United States Book Company, successors to John W. Lovell Company, 142 to 150 Worth Street [cop. 1892]. 283 p.  H, HEH, LC

HIGBEE, DORA. *See* Geppert, Dora (Higbee)

2664 HIGGINSON, ELIZABETH CHANNING. Life in a Country Village in War Times: A Story . . . Brattleboro, Vt.: Frank E. Housh & Co., 1887. 29 p.  H

2665 HIGGINSON, ELLA RHOADS. The Flower That Grew in the Sand, and Other Stories . . . Seattle: The Calvert Company, 1896. 256 p.
HEH, LC, Y
*Also contains:* The Isle of Lepers—The Takin' In of Old Mis' Lane—The Maneuvering of Mrs. Sybert—A Point of Knuckling-Down—The Cuttin'-Out of Bart Winn—Zarelda—In the Bitter Root Mountains—Patience Appleby's Confessing-Up—The Mother of "Pills"—Mrs. Risley's Christmas Dinner.

2666 ——— A Forest Orchid, and Other Stories . . . New York: The Macmillan Company. London: Macmillan & Co., Ltd., 1897. 242 p.
H, HEH, LC
*Also contains:* 'Mandy's Organ—The Lord's Prayer Drinkin' Glass—Euphemy—The Pity of It—Belindy's One Beau—Mis' Bunnels's Funeral—A Passion-Flower of the West—The Arnspiker Chickens—The Light That Came to Abraham.

2667 ——— From the Land of the Snow-Pearls: Tales from Puget Sound . . . New York: The Macmillan Company. London: Macmillan & Co., Ltd., 1897. 268 p.  H, HEH, LC, O
Contains same stories as No. 2665 with two stories, "Esther's 'Fourth'" and "The Blow-Out at Jenkins's Grocery," added and one, "The Isle of Lepers," omitted.

——— A Point of Knucklin' Down. *In* Tales from McClure's: The West (1897), No. 5363.
Printed earlier in No. 2665 and included in No. 2667.

2668 HIGGINSON, SARAH JANE (HATFIELD). The Bedouin Girl . . . New York: J. Selwin Tait & Sons, 65 Fifth Avenue [cop. 1894]. 347 p., illus.
AP, BU, HEH, LC, O
Deposited Mar. 6, 1894.

2669 ——— A Princess of Java: A Tale of the Far East . . . Boston and New York: Houghton, Mifflin and Company. The Riverside Press, Cambridge, 1887. 426 p.      AP, H, HEH, LC, O, UP, Y

2670 HIGGINSON, THOMAS WENTWORTH. The Monarch of Dreams . . . Boston: Lee and Shepard, 1887. 52 p.    BA, BU, CU, H, HEH, LC, N, O, UVB, Y

2671 HIGHAM, MRS. MARY R. Agatha Lee's Inheritance . . . New York: Anson D. F. Randolph & Company, 900 Broadway, cor. 20th Street [cop. 1878]. 208 p.      LC

2672 ——— The Other House . . . New York: Anson D. F. Randolph & Company, 900 Broadway, cor. 20th Street [cop. 1878]. 252 p.   LC, O

2673 HILDRETH, HARRY DEAN. Wauneta: An Indian Story of Happiness as a Mental Condition . . . Chicago: Donohue, Henneberry & Co., 407-425 Dearborn St. [cop. 1894]. 182 p., front.
Information supplied by Mrs. Frances J. Brewer of Detroit Public Library.

2674 HILL, BEVERIDGE. "The Story of a Cañon" . . . Boston, Mass.: Arena Publishing Company, 1895. 452 p.      HEH, LC
Silver mining; Colorado.

2675 HILL, FREDERICK TREVOR. The Case and Exceptions: Stories of Counsel and Clients . . . New York: Frederick A. Stokes Company [cop. 1900]. 241 p.      CU, H, HEH, LC, N, O, UM, UV, Y
Contents: Outside the Record—In the Matter of Bateman—The Finding of Fact—A Conclusion of Law—The Burden of Proof—In His Own Behalf—His Honour—An Abstract Story—By Way of Counterclaim—In the Name of the People—The Latest Decision—The Distant Drum.

2676 HILL, JOHN ALEXANDER. Jim Skeevers' Object Lessons on Railroading for Railroaders . . . New York: Press of Railway & Locomotive Engineering, 1899. 159 p.      H, UV

2677 ——— Stories of the Railroad . . . New York: Doubleday & McClure Co., 1899. 297 p., illus.      CU, H, HEH, LC, UV, Y
Contents: An Engineer's Christmas Story—The Clean Man and the Dirty Angels—Jim Wainwright's Kid—A Peg-Legged Romance—My Lady of the Eyes—Some Freaks of Fate—Mormon Joe, the Robber—A Midsummer Night's Trip—The Polar Zone.

2678 HILLES, LEWIS BAKER. Chickens Come Home to Roost: A Novel . . . New York: Isaac H. Blanchard Co. [cop. 1899] 307 p., illus.    CU, Y
Of horse racing.

2679 HILLHOUSE, MANSFIELD LOVELL. Iola, the Senator's Daughter: A Story of Ancient Rome (about 24 B.C.) . . . New York, London: G. P. Putnam's Sons; the Knickerbocker Press, 1894. 501 p.      HEH, LC, UP

2680 HILLYER, SHALER GRANBY. The Marable Family: A Novel . . . Philadelphia: J. B. Lippincott & Co., 1879. 404 p.     H, HEH, LC, UV

HIMMEL, ERNST VON, *pseud.* *See* Petersilea, Carlyle

HINCKLEY, WILLIAM. A Very Strange Case. *In* Short Stories from Outing [cop. 1895], No. 4930.

2681 HINMAN, WALTER FISK. Corporal Si Klegg and His "Pard": How They
Lived and Talked and What They Did and Suffered, While Fighting
for the Flag . . . Cleveland, Ohio: The Williams Publishing Company,
1887. 706 p., illus.     BA, CU, H, HEH, N, UC, Y

2682 HINMAN, WALTER N. Under the Maples: A Story of Village Life . . .
Chicago, New York, San Francisco: Belford, Clarke & Co., 1888. 299 p.
New York state.     HEH, LC

2683 HIS DEAR LITTLE WIFE. Philadelphia: J. M. Stoddart & Co., 1878. 176 p.
Listed PW, June 22, 1878.

2684 HIS WAY TO GREATNESS. Philadelphia: E. Claxton & Company, 1881.
100 p.     LC
Lawyer becomes a senator at the expense of many women.

2685 DELETED.

2686 HOBART, GEORGE VERE. D. Dinkelspiel, His Gonversationings . . . New
York: New Amsterdam Book Company, 1900. 231 p., illus.
BU, H, HEH, LC, O, UC, UM

HODDER, ALFRED, *jt. au. See* [Willard, J. F.] The Powers That Prey
(1900), No. 5979.

2687 [HOES, ROBERT R.] Two Broken Hearts. New York: G. P. Putnam's
Sons, 1885. 77 p.
Information supplied by Charles H. Burkman of Princeton University Li-
brary.

2688 HOEY, ELLEN MARY (GRIFFIN). Moll Pitcher's Prophecies; or, The
American Sibyl. By Mrs. Ellen M. Griffin. Boston, Mass.: The East-
burn Press, 1895. 170 p., illus.     H, LC

2689 HOFF, J. WALLACE. Seven Strange Stories: A Little Life, a Little Metaphysics, a Little Love . . . Trenton [N.J.]: The Brandt Press, 1894.
108 p.     HEH, LC, Y
*Contents:* Felix Mondet–Daphne–Frontier Service in '49–And This Is Love
–Baffling a Conspiracy–Little Nell–Metempsychosis.

2690 —— Some Strange Stories: A Little Life, a Little Metaphysics, a Little Love ... Somerville, N.J.: Press of the Unionist-Gazette, 1895. 131 p. LC
Contains same stories as No. 2689, with the following additions: The Spirit Avenger—The Power of Conscience—A Story's Mission—A Man's Experience—The Octopus Syndicate.

2691 HOFFMAN, MRS. MARY JANE. Aunt Olive, Her Hidden Past ... New York: Peter O'Shea, 1882. 414 p.
Listed PW, July 8, 1882.

2692 [——] The King's Daughters; or, The Heiress and the Outcast ... New York: Norman L. Munro, 1889. 278 p. LC

2693 HOFMAN, FREDERICK B. The Trouble of Living Alone: A Novel ... Boston: Arena Publishing Company, 1894. 263 p. LC

2694 HOGBIN, ALFRED C. Elsa: A Romance ... Philadelphia: J. B. Lippincott & Co., 1879. 413 p. LC

2695 HOLBROOK, AMELIA WEED. One of the McIntyres ... Chicago: W. B. Conkey Company, 1896. 58 p., illus. HEH

2696 —— "Whiz": A Story of the Mines ... Chicago: Laird & Lee [cop. 1898]. 283 p., illus.
Listed PW, May 7, 1898.

2697 HOLBROOK, ELIZABETH. Old 'Kaskia Days: A Novel ... Chicago: The Schulte Publishing Company, 1893. 295 p., illus. HEH, LC, N

2698 HOLBROOK, RICHARD THAYER. Boys and Men: A Story of Life at Yale ... New York: Charles Scribner's Sons, 1900. 278 p. H, HEH, O, UP, UVB, Y

2699 HOLCOMBE, WILLIAM HENRY. A Mystery of New Orleans Solved by New Methods ... Philadelphia: J. B. Lippincott Company, 1890. 332 p. H, HEH, LC, O, UM

2700 [HOLDEN, E. GOODMAN.] A Famous Victory ... Chicago: Jansen, McClurg & Company, 1880. 368 p. HEH, LC, N, Y
Satirical political novel.

2701 HOLFORD, CASTELLO N. Aristopia: A Romance History of the New World ... Boston: Arena Publishing Company, 1895. 234 p. LC, UM

2702 HOLLAND, MRS. ANNIE JEFFERSON. The Refugees: A Sequel to "Uncle Tom's Cabin" ... Austin, Texas: Published for the author, 1892. 179 p. HEH, LC, UM, UP

2703 [HOLLAND, JANE JANSEN.] Jane Jansen: A Story of a Woman's Heritage in the Heart of Appalachia ... Writer's Proof Edition, Limited to

Twenty-Seven Copies. Greenesburgh, Pennsylvania: The Oliver Publishing House, 1895. 328 p. LC, Y

2704 HOLLAND, JOSIAH GILBERT. Nicholas Minturn: A Study in a Story . . . New York: Scribner, Armstrong & Co., 1877. 418 p., illus.

BU, CU, H, HEH, N, O, UC, UM, UP, UV, Y

2705 HOLLAND, M. The Love Adventures of Lola Mortz . . . Chicago: M. Holland [cop. 1897]. 16 p., illus. LC

2706 —— Love and Passion . . . Chicago: M. Holland [cop. 1897]. 16 p., illus. LC

Also published as: *Grace's Confession.* Chicago: M. Holland [cop. 1897]. LC

2707 HOLLANDS, HULDA THEODATE (ST. BERNARD). Marfa: A Story of the Opium Smugglers of the St. Clair River . . . Detroit, 1889. 145 p., illus. LC

HOLLEY, MARIETTA. Fourth of July in Jonesville. *In* L. C. H. Langford, *comp.,* The Woman's Story (1889), No. 3206.

2708 [——] Josiah Allen's Wife [pseud.] as a P. A. and P. I.: Samantha at the Centennial. Designed as a Bright and Shining Light, to Pierce the Fogs of Error and Injustice That Surround Society and Josiah . . . Hartford, Conn.: American Publishing Company, 1877. 580 p., illus.

BU, CU, H, HEH, LC, UV

2709 [——] Josiah's Alarm, and Abel Perry's Funeral. By Josiah Allen's Wife [pseud.] . . . Philadelphia: J. B. Lippincott Company, 1895. 85 p., illus.

Copy examined at New York Public Library.

2710 [——] Miss Jones' Quilting. By Josiah Allen's Wife [pseud.] . . . and Other Stories . . . New York: International Book Company, 17 and 19 Waverley Place [ca. 1892]. 206, 118 p., illus. HEH, UP

*Also contains:* Fitzquisite's New Year's Calls—Fitzquisite Marries a Fortune —Fitzquisite Receives Calls—Fitzquisite Settles in Life—B. Umber, Artist— Mrs. Fogy's Table-Talk—Perdita [with separate pagination].

First 206 p. first published in the omitted Ogilvie's "Fireside Series," 1887.

2711 —— Miss Richards' Boy, and Other Stories . . . Hartford, Conn.: American Publishing Company, 1883. 410 p., illus.

H, HEH, O, UC, UM, UV, Y

*Also contains:* The Outcast—The Deserted Wives—Mrs. Wingate's Charity —Faith Winslow—True unto Death—Cecil Vail—The Dorcas Society—Belinda, Caroline, and Henrietta—Little Christie's Will—John's Wife—The Plain Miss Page—Miss Higgins' Man—Kate's Wedding Gift—Kitty Ross—A Woman's Heart—Katy Avenal.

2712 ———— My Wayward Pardner; or, My Trials with Josiah, America, the Widow Bump, and Etcetery ... Hartford, Conn.: American Publishing Company, 1880. 490 p., illus.      CU, H, HEH, LC, O

2713 ———— Samantha among the Brethren ... New York, London: Funk & Wagnalls, 1890. 437 p., illus.      AP, CU, H, HEH, LC, N, O, UM, UP, UV, Y

2714 ———— Samantha at Saratoga; or, "Flirtin' with Fashion" ... Sold by Subscription Only. Philadelphia: Hubbard Brothers, 1887. 3 p. l., 7-583 p., illus.      CU, H, HEH, N, O, UM, UP, UV, Y
LC deposit copy, dated July 23, 1887, has imprint: Philadelphia, Boston, Cincinnati, Kansas City: Hubbard Bros. San Francisco: History Co. [cop. 1887]. 3 p.l., v-xvii, 19-561 p., illus. Text the same but p.l.'s reset; other minor variations.

2715 ———— Samantha at the World's Fair ... New York, London, and Toronto: Funk & Wagnalls Company, 1893. 694 p., illus.
     BU, CU, H, LC, N, O, UC, UM, Y

2716 ———— Samantha in Europe ... New York, London, and Toronto: Funk & Wagnalls Company, 1896. 714 p., illus.
     CU, H, HEH, LC, N, O, UC, UM, UV, Y

2717 ———— Samantha on the Race Problem ... New York: Dodd, Mead & Company [cop. 1892]. 387 p., illus.      CU, HEH, LC
Deposited Oct. 18, 1892.
Also published as: *Samantha among the Colored Folks: "My Ideas on the Race Problem"* ... New York: Dodd, Mead & Company, 1894.   H, HEH, LC, O, UM, UP, UV, Y

2718 ———— Sweet Cicely; or, Josiah Allen as a Politician ... New York, London: Funk & Wagnalls, 1885. 381 p., illus.
     AP, H, HEH, LC, O, UC, UM, Y

2719 [————] The Widder Doodle's Courtship, and Other Sketches. By Josiah Allen's Wife [pseud.] ... New York: J. S. Ogilvie Publishing Company, 57 Rose Street [cop. 1890]. 120 p., illus.      CU, LC, UC
*Also contains:* A Pleasure Exertion—How We Took in Summer Boarders—The Sufferens of Nathan Spooner—The Widder Doodle as a Comforter—Betsy Bobbit: Her Poem—Deacon Slimpsey's Mournful Forebordings—Borrowing "Peterson"—Melankton Spicer'ses Wife—How the Bamberses Borrowed Josiah.

2720 HOLLISTER, GIDEON HIRAM. Kinley Hollow: A Novel ... New York: Henry Holt and Company, 1882. 379 p.
     AP, BA, BU, H, HEH, LC, O, UC, UVB, Y
At head of title: "Leisure Hour Series—No. 138."

2721 [HOLLOWAY, MRS. ANNA.] Kate Comerford; or, Sketches of Garrison Life. By Teresa A. Thornet [pseud.]. Philadelphia: J. B. Lippincott & Co., 1881. 252 p.      HEH, LC
Texas, 1850's.

2722 HOLLOWAY, CHARLOTTE MOLYNEUX. A Story of Five . . . New York: E. P. Dutton & Company, 1890. 447 p., illus.    HEH, O, UVB

HOLLOWAY, LAURA C. *See* Langford, Laura (Carter) Holloway

HOLLOWAY, WILLIAM. The Making of Monsieur Lescarbot's Ballad. *In* Stories from Chap-Book (1896), No. 5277.

HOLM, SAXE, *pseud. See* Jackson, Helen Maria (Fiske) Hunt

2723 HOLMES, JOHN. Magdalen: A Romance of the Social Crusade . . . Washington: Columbia Publishing Co., 1897. 128 p.
Listed in Wilhelmus Bogart Bryan, *Bibliography of the District of Columbia* (Washington, 1900), p. 88.

HOLMES, JOHN, 1812-1899. A Cambridge Robinson Crusoe. *In* [H. L. Reed] *ed.,* "The City and the Sea" (1881), No. 4487.

HOLMES, MRS. M. E. [See BAL, Vol. IV, p. 231, for discussion about this author. The two titles listed below are the only ones found to date published outside the omitted "Pastime Series."]

2724 ———— Her Fatal Sin . . . Author of "A Woman's Love," "The Redmount Tragedy" . . . Chicago: Laird & Lee, 286 S. Water St., cor. Lake, cop. 1886. 185 p., illus.    UM
At head of title: "A Sparkling American Novel."

2725 ———— The Tragedy of Redmount . . . Chicago: Laird & Lee, 286 S. Water St., cor. Lake, cop. 1886. 230 p., illus.    HEH

HOLMES, MARGRET, *pseud. See* Bates, Margret Holmes (Ernsperger)

HOLMES, MARY JANE (HAWES). Adam Floyd. *In* L. C. H. Langford, *comp.,* The Woman's Story (1889), No. 3206.

2726 ———— Bessie's Fortune: A Novel . . . New York: G. W. Carleton & Co. London: S. Low, Son & Co., 1886. 453 p.    HEH

2727 ———— Chateau d'Or, Norah, and Kitty Craig . . . New York: G. W. Carleton & Co. London: S. Low & Co., 1880. 389 p.
   HEH, N, O, UC, UP, UVB, Y

2728 ———— Christmas Stories . . . New York: G. W. Carleton & Co. London: S. Low, Son & Co., 1885. 372 p., front.    CU, H, HEH, LC, Y

2729 ———— Daisy Thornton, and Jessie Graham . . . New York: G. W. Carleton & Co. London: S. Low & Co., 1878. 377 p.
   CU, H, HEH, LC, N, O, UC, UM, UVB, Y

2730 ——— Doctor Hathern's Daughters: A Story of Virginia, in Four Parts ... New York: G. W. Dillingham, successor to G. W. Carleton & Co., 1895. 471 p.            H, HEH, N, O, UC, UVB, Y

2731 ——— Edith Lyle: A Novel ... New York: G. W. Carleton & Co. London: S. Low & Co., 1876. 420 p.     CU, H, HEH, O, UC, UP, UVB, Y

2732 ——— Forrest House: A Novel ... New York: G. W. Carleton & Co., 1879. 394 p.           H, HEH, O, UVB

2733 ——— Gretchen: A Novel ... New York: G. W. Dillingham, successor to G. W. Carleton & Co. London: S. Low, Son & Co., 1887. 452 p.                    CU, H, HEH, O, Y

2734 ——— Madeline: A Novel ... New York: G. W. Carleton & Co. London: S. Low, Son & Co., 1881. 374 p.             CU, HEH, N, O, UC, UM, UP, UVB, Y

2735 ——— Marguerite: A Novel ... New York: G. W. Dillingham, successor to G. W. Carleton & Co., 1891. 473 p.     H, HEH, O

2736 ——— Mildred: A Novel ... New York: G. W. Carleton & Co. London: S. Low & Co., 1877. 324 p.     H, HEH, O, UP, UVB, Y

2737 ——— Mrs. Hallam's Companion, and The Spring Farm, and Other Tales ... New York: G. W. Dillingham, 1896. 437 p.                CU, H, HEH, LC, O, UM
*Also contains:* The Hepburn Line–Mildred's Ambition.

2738 ——— Paul Ralston: A Novel ... New York: G. W. Dillingham Co., 1897. 393 p.       CU, HEH, LC, N, UM, UP, UVB, Y

2739 ——— Queenie Hetherton: A Novel ... New York: G. W. Carleton & Co. London: S. Low & Co., 1883. 454 p.    CU, HEH, N, O, UC, UVB, Y

2740 ——— The Tracy Diamonds ... New York: G. W. Dillingham Co., 1899. 390 p.          HEH, N, O, UVB, Y

2741 HOLMES, MRS. MARY JOHNSON. Ashes: A Society Novel ... New York: Hurst & Co., 1890. 294 p.
Information from LC card; no copy seen.

2742 ——— A Fair Puritan: A New England Tale ... New York: Hurst and Company, 1891. 202 p.
Information from LC card; no copy seen.

2743 ——— The House of Five Gables ... New York: Hurst and Company, 1892. 187 p., front.
Information from LC card; no copy seen.

2744 HOLMES, OLIVER WENDELL. A Mortal Antipathy: First Opening of the New Portfolio . . . Boston and New York: Houghton, Mifflin and Company. The Riverside Press, Cambridge, 1885. 307 p.

AP, BU, H, HEH, LC, N, O, UC, UM, UP, UVB, Y

2745 [HOLMES, THOMAS J.] The Adventures of Ferdinand Tomasso. By Lehmos [pseud.]. New York: The Irving Co., 1894. 155 p.    LC, N
Written in a series of letters; Mexico, 16th century.

2746 HOLT, TILBURY. Miss Beck: A Novel . . . New York: G. W. Carleton & Co. London: S. Low, Son & Co., 1882. 401 p.    AP, HEH, LC

2747 HOOD, MRS. EMMA NELSON. Bob Dean; or, "Our Other Boarder" . . . Philadelphia: E. Claxton & Company. Austin, Texas: A. K. Hawkes, 1882. 379 p.    HEH, LC, N, UV
Texas from the time of the Republic to the close of the Civil War.

2748 HOOD, MRS. FRANCES HAMILTON. Maud Mansfield: A Novel . . . Macon, Georgia: J. W. Burke & Company, 1876. 278 p.    LC
The South in the early days of the Civil War.

2749 HOOD, WILLIAM I. Betsy Gaskins (Dimicrat), Wife of Jobe Gaskins (Republican); or, Uncle Tom's Cabin up to Date . . . Chicago: The Schulte Publishing Company; the Ariel Press, 323 and 325 Dearborn Street [cop. 1897]. 407 p., illus.    HEH, LC, UC

2750 HOOGSTRAAT, MOREE E. VON. Where the Sage and Cactus Grow . . . Chicago, Ill.: Scroll Publishing Company, 1900. 243 p., illus.    LC
Mojave Desert mining.

2751 [HOOKE, CHARLES WITHERLE.] Automatic Bridget, and Other Humorous Sketches. By Howard Fielding [pseud.]. New York: The Manhattan Therapeutic Company [cop. 1889]. 32 p., illus.    LC
*Also contains:* Light on Theosophy—A New York Alderman—We Try a City Flat—My Wife's Superstitions—The Adventures of a Super.
Published as an advertisement for Cascarria.

2751a [———] Col. Evans from Kentucky, and Other Humorous Sketches. By Howard Fielding [pseud.]. New York: The Manhattan Therapeutic Company, cop. 1889. 32 p., illus.
*Also contains:* The Automatic Bridget—My Wife's Superstitions—A New York Alderman—The Adventures of a Super.
Published as an advertisement for Cascarria.

[———] A Matter of Instinct, by Howard Fielding [pseud.]. *In* I. Bacheller, *ed.*, Best Things from American Literature (1899), No. 195.

2752 [———] The Mind Cure, and Other Humorous Sketches. By Howard Fielding [pseud.] . . . New York: The Manhattan Therapeutic Company, cop. 1888. 31, [1] p., illus.    HEH

*Also contains:* Working Pension Claims— Christmas Down East—A Sawdust Tragedy—She Knew It Was Going to Thunder.
Published as an advertisement for Cascarria.

[———] A Passage in the Life of an Honest Man, by Howard Fielding [pseud.]. *In* Short Story Masterpieces (1900), No. 4931.

2753 HOOPER, CYRUS LAURON. A Cloverdale Skeleton ... New York: John B. Alden, 1889. 170 p.                                                    LC

2754 [HOOPER, LUCY HAMILTON (JONES).] Those Pretty St. George Girls: A Society Novel ... Philadelphia: T. B. Peterson & Brothers, 306 Chestnut Street [cop. 1883]. 346 p.                           H, HEH, LC
English and Continental society.

2755 [———] The Tsar's Window ... Boston: Roberts Brothers, 1881. 272 p.                                        BA, H, HEH, LC, O, UP, UV
At head of title: "No Name Series."
Americans in St. Petersburg's social circles.

2756 ——— Under the Tricolor; or, The American Colony in Paris. A Novel ... Philadelphia, London: J. B. Lippincott & Co., 1880. 244 p.
AP, BU, CU, H, HEH, LC, O, UC, Y

2757 HOOVER, FRANCIS TROUT. Enemies in the Rear; or, A Golden Circle Squared. A Story of Southeastern Pennsylvania in the Time of Our Civil War ... Boston: Arena Publishing Company, 1895. 604 p.
HEH, LC, UP, UVB
Of the Knights of the Golden Circle.

2758 HOPE, ANDREW J. The Ghost of Pumptown: A Christmas Story ... New York, 1899. 44, [1] p.                                           HEH

2759 HOPE, ERNEST. A Day of Reckoning; or, She Rode a Bicycle ... Chicago: Scroll Publishing Company, 1900. 115 p.           HEH, LC
From Cincinnati to Chicago.

2760 [HOPE, JAMES BARRON.] Under the Empire; or, The Story of Madelon. By J. B. H. Norfolk, Va.: James B. Hope & Co., 1878. 216 p.   LC, N, UV

2761 HOPE, JANEY B. Stories and Papers ... [Norfolk, Va.: Printed at the Norfolk Landmark, 188-?] 64 p. Printed in double columns.
HEH, LC, O, UV
*Contains:* My Protegee; or, From San Francisco to Naples—A Christmas Charity and What Came of It—The Blunder of a Near-Sighted Man.

HOPE, ZELMA, *pseud. See* Gould, Mrs. Jennie W.

2762 [HOPKINS, MRS. ALICE KIMBALL.] A Daughter of the Druids. By A. K. H. Boston, 1892. 297, [1] p., 1 l., illus.                       LC

2763 [————] The Romance of a Letter. By Lowell Choate [pseud.]. Boston: D. Lothrop Company, Franklin and Hawley Streets [cop. 1887]. 356 p.     BU, H, LC

2764 HOPKINS, ALPHONSO ALVA. Sinner and Saint: A Story of the Woman's Crusade. A Novel . . . Boston: D. Lothrop and Company, 30 and 32 Franklin Street [cop. 1881]. 336 p.     LC, UM, Y
Temperance novel.

HOPKINS, JEUNE. *See* Hopkins, Squire D.

2765 HOPKINS, LIVINGSTON. A Comic History of the United States . . . New York: G. W. Carleton & Co., 1876. 223 p., illus.     H, O, UP, Y
At head of title: "The matter on the opposite page may be freely translated as follows."
*Also issued with imprint:* New York: American Book Exchange, 1876.   LC

HOPKINS, MAHETIBLE, *pseud. See* Elder, Mrs. D. H.

2766 HOPKINS, MARGARET SUTTON (BRISCOE). Jimty, and Others. By Margaret Sutton Briscoe . . . New York and London: Harper & Brothers, 1898. 325, [1] p., illus.     CU, HEH, LC, UC, Y
*Also contains:* The Price of Peace–An Echo–The Christmas Mummers–Concealed Weapons–Annie Tousey's Little Game–Princess I-Would-I-Wot-Not–It Is the Custom–Salt of the Earth–A Goose-Chase–An Entomological Wooing–The Quarter Loaf.

2767 ———— Links in a Chain . . . New York: Dodd, Mead and Company, 1893. 227 p.     BU, HEH, LC

2768 ———— "Perchance to Dream," and Other Stories . . . New York: Dodd, Mead and Company, 1892. 280 p.     HEH, LC, Y
*Also contains:* How the Spirit Moved Cynthia–A Chip–The Gentleman-in-Plush–A Tea-Leaf–Ned–"Through a Glass Darkly"–The Old Peninsula House–Fifteen County Rock–A Legacy–Thomas Bates's Covenant–Miss Chesilia McCarthy–"Die, Which I Won't."

2769 ———— The Sixth Sense, and Other Stories . . . New York and London: Harper & Brothers, 1899. 273, [1] p., illus.     CU, HEH, LC, O, Y
*Also contains:* Uncle Elijah's Corner Cupboard–An I.O.U.–A Will and a Way–Of Her Own Household–Apples of Gold–Matilda's Address-Book–A Temple of Solomon–This Mortal Coil.

2770 HOPKINS, MARK. The World's Verdict: A Novel . . . Boston: Ticknor and Company, 1888. 355 p.     AP, BA, H, HEH, LC, Y
Americans in the international society set.

2771 HOPKINS, PAULINE BRADFORD (MACKIE). A Georgian Actress. By Pauline Bradford Mackie . . . Boston: L. C. Page & Company (Incorporated), 1900. 296 p., illus.     HEH, LC, O, UC
Author's full name: Pauline Bradford (Mackie) Hopkins Cavendish.
Of the time of George III.

2772 ——— Ye Lyttle Salem Maide: A Story of Witchcraft . . . Boston, New York, and London: Lamson, Wolffe and Company, 1898.   321 p., illus.   HEH, LC, O, UC, Y

2773 ——— Mademoiselle de Berny: A Story of Valley Forge . . . Boston, New York, and London: Lamson, Wolffe and Company, 1897.   272 p., illus.   HEH, LC, Y

2774 HOPKINS, PAULINE ELIZABETH.  Contending Forces: A Romance Illustrative of Negro Life North and South . . . Boston: The Colored Co-operative Publishing Co., 1900.   402 p., illus.   CU, H, LC

2775 HOPKINS, SQUIRE D.  The Mysterious Hunter; or, The Last of the Aztecs. By Vic St. L. (Jeune Hopkins) . . . Chicago: The Jeune Hopkins Company [cop. 1892].   293 p., illus.   HEH, LC

2776 HOPPIN, AUGUSTUS.  A Fashionable Sufferer; or, Chapters from Life's Comedy . . . Boston, New York: Houghton, Mifflin and Company. The Riverside Press, Cambridge, 1883.   246 p., illus.
AP, BA, BU, H, HEH, LC, O, UM, Y

2777 HOPPIN, EMILY HOWLAND.  From Out of the Past: The Story of a Meeting in Touraine . . . New York: Dodd, Mead & Company [cop. 1893].   238 p.   BA, H, HEH, LC, O, Y
Deposited Apr. 29, 1893.

2778 ——— Under the Corsican . . . New York: J. Selwin Tait and Sons, 65 Fifth Avenue [cop. 1894].   333 p.   BA, LC, Y
Deposited Dec. 21, 1894.

2779 HORNADAY, WILLIAM TEMPLE.  The Man Who Became a Savage: A Story of Our Own Times . . . Buffalo, N.Y.: The Peter Paul Book Co., 1896.   413 p., illus.   HEH, LC, N, UM, UV, Y
A New Yorker went to Borneo.

2780 HORNER, FREDERICK.  The Seal of Love: A Tale of Four Chapters . . . San Francisco: T. R. Tilley, printer and binder, 1887.   24 p.
Information supplied by Kenneth J. Carpenter, University of California Library, Berkeley.

2781 HORTON, ELLIS.  The Hoosier Practitioner; or, Medicine on the Wabash . . . Indianapolis: T. A. Randall & Co., printers [cop. 1888].   166 p.   CU, LC

2782 HORTON, GEORGE.  Constantine: A Tale of Greece under King Otho . . . Chicago: Way and Williams, 1897.   232 p., 1 l.   HEH

2783 ——— A Fair Brigand . . . Chicago and New York: Herbert S. Stone and Company, 1899.   330 p., 1 l., illus.   HEH, LC, UP

2784 [HOSEA, LUCY (KLINCK) RICE.] Eastward; or, A Buddhist Lover. A Novel . . . Boston: J. G. Cupples Co. [cop. 1890]. 267 p.    H, LC

2785 HOSMER, GEORGE WASHINGTON. "As We Went Marching On": A Story of the War . . . New York: Harper & Brothers, 1885. 310 p.
AP, CU, HEH, LC, N, O, UM, UVB, Y

2786 HOSMER, JAMES KENDALL. How Thankful Was Bewitched . . . New York, London: G. P. Putnam's Sons; the Knickerbocker Press, 1894. 299 p.    CU, H, HEH, O
Invasion of Massachusetts during Queen Anne's War.

2787 HOTCHKISS, CHAUNCEY CRAFTS. A Colonial Free-Lance . . . New York: D. Appleton and Company, 1897. 312 p.    BU, CU, HEH, LC, O, UP, UV, Y

2788 ———— In Defiance of the King: A Romance of the American Revolution . . . New York: D. Appleton and Company, 1895. 334 p.
BU, CU, HEH, LC, O, UM, UV, Y

2789 HOTCHKISS, LOUISE SARAH. Their Own Wedding . . . Boston: George H. Ellis, 1900. 115 p.    LC
Americans abroad.

2790 HOUGH, EMERSON. The Girl at the Halfway House: A Story of the Plains . . . New York: D. Appleton and Company, 1900. 371 p.
BA, CU, H, HEH, N, O, UM, UVB, Y

2791 HOUK, ELIZA PHILLIPS (THRUSTON). The Lamarks; or, Marriageable Women . . . Cincinnati: Robert Clarke & Co., 1889. 290 p.    LC

2792 HOUSE, EDWARD HOWARD. Yone Santo, a Child of Japan . . . Chicago, New York, and San Francisco: Belford, Clarke and Co. [cop. 1888]. 285 p.    BA, H, HEH, Y
HEH has author's presentation copy dated "Jan. 31, 1889."

HOUSSAYE, SIDONIE DE LA. See De La Houssaye, Sidonie.

2793 HOUSTON, A. C. Hugh Harrison (A Mulatto) . . . Richmond, Va.: J. W. Randolph & English, 1890. 67 p.    H, HEH, UV, Y
Cover imprint of H and HEH has date 1891.

HOVORRÈ, M. AUBURRÉ, pseud. See Howard, Albert Waldo

How, LOUIS. Little Sister: A Love Story. In Stories from the Harvard Advocate (1896), No. 5277a.

2794 ———— The Penitentes of San Rafael: A Tale of the San Luis Valley . . . Indianapolis: The Bowen-Merrill Company [cop. 1900]. 381 p.
CU, H, HEH, LC, UM
New Mexico.

———— *jt. au. See* Mott, L. W. Mr. Thaddeus Almanac's Scientific Proposal. An Unconventional Detective Story. [Two stories.] *In* Stories from the Harvard Advocate (1896), No. 5277a.

2795 How Is Your Man? or, The Sharks of Sharksville. Realities of the Graveyard Insurance System. Boston: Lee and Shepard. New York: Charles T. Dillingham, 1882. 130 p., illus.                    LC, O

2796 [Howard, Albert Waldo.] The Milltillionaire. By M. Auburré Hovorrè [pseud.]. [Boston, 1895?] 30 p.                              LC
Depicts the world as one utopia.

Howard, Blanche Willis. *See* Teuffel, Blanche Willis (Howard) von

2797 Howard, James H. W. Bond and Free: A True Tale of Slave Times ... Harrisburg [Pa.]: Edwin K. Myers, printer and binder, 1886. 280 p.
HEH, LC, N, O, UC, UM, UV, Y

2798 Howe, Cora E. The Pilgrim's Christmas ... Sandy Creek, N.Y.: News Book Print, 1899. 52 p., illus.                              LC

2799 Howe, Edgar Watson. A Man Story ... Boston: Ticknor and Company, 1889. 380 p.          AP, CU, H, HEH, LC, N, O, UC, UP, UVB, Y
Of a man with two wives.

2800 ———— A Moonlight Boy ... Boston: Ticknor and Company, 1886. 342 p., front.          AP, BA, H, HEH, LC, UC, UP, Y

2801 ———— The Mystery of the Locks ... Boston: James R. Osgood and Company, 1885. 293 p.     AP, BA, CU, H, HEH, LC, N, O, UC, UM, UP, UVB, Y

2802 ———— The Story of a Country Town ... Atchison, Kas.: Howe & Co., 1883. 226 p., illus.          BU, CU, H, HEH, LC, N, O, UC, UP, UVB, Y
Early life in Missouri.

2803 Howe, Edward Everett. The Chronicles of Break o' Day ... Boston: Arena Publishing Company, 1894. 342 p.                    HEH, LC
Michigan.

2804 Howe, Elizabeth. Hazleburgh: A Romance ... New York: W. B. Smith & Co., Bond Street [cop. 1883]. 207 p.                    HEH

Howe, George. The Last Slave-Ship. *In* Stories of the Sea (1893), No. 5282.

[Howe, Julia Ward] *attrib. au.* In War-Time; or, Only a Woman's Shoe. *In* [Mrs. J. Lodge] *ed.*, A Week away from Time (1887), No. 3382.

Howe, Maud. *See* Elliott, Maud (Howe)

2805 HOWE, MURRAY. Stable Conversation . . . Chicago: The Horse Review Company, 1900. 262 p., illus. LC, UC

2806 HOWE, SUSAN HOWARD (JEWETT). Kate Ford's Family . . . Cincinnati: The Editor Publishing Co., 1899. 184 p. HEH, LC

2807 HOWELL, GEORGE ROGERS. Noah's Log Book: How Two Americans Blasted the Ice on Mt. Ararat and Found Noah's Ark and Some Curious Relics . . . New York and London: F. Tennyson Neely, 1898. 345 p.
H, Y

2808 HOWELL, JEANNE M. A Common Mistake . . . New York, St. Paul: The Merriam Company [1894]. 290 p. LC
First published in the omitted "Golden Library," No. 3, 1892.

2809 HOWELLS, WILLIAM DEAN. Annie Kilburn: A Novel . . . New York: Harper & Brothers, 1889. 331 p. BU, H, HEH, LC, N, O, UM, UP, UVB, Y
Howells' works in dialogue form are omitted here as being drama rather than fiction.

2810 ———— April Hopes . . . New York: Harper & Brothers, 1888. 484 p.
AP, BA, BU, CU, H, HEH, LC, N, O, UC, UM, UP, UVB, Y

2811 ———— The Coast of Bohemia: A Novel . . . New York: Harper & Brothers, 1893. 340 p., illus.
AP, BA, BU, H, HEH, LC, N, O, UC, UM, UP, UVB, Y

2812 ———— The Day of Their Wedding: A Novel . . . New York: Harper & Brothers, 1896. 158 p., illus.
AP, BA, BU, CU, H, HEH, LC, N, O, UC, UM, UP, UVB, Y

2813 ———— A Day's Pleasure . . . Boston: James R. Osgood and Company, 1876. 91 p., illus. BA, BU, CU, H, HEH, LC, N, O, UM, UP, UVB, Y
Reprinted from his *Suburban Sketches* (1871), which is for the most part a collection of essays.

2814 ———— A Day's Pleasure, and Other Sketches . . . Boston: Houghton, Mifflin and Company. The Riverside Press, Cambridge, 1881. 240 p., illus. LC, O, UC, UVB
*Contains:* Buying a Horse.
At head of title: "Modern Classics."

2815 ———— Doctor Breen's Practice: A Novel . . . Boston: James R. Osgood and Company, 1881. 272 p.
BA, BU, CU, H, HEH, LC, N, O, UM, UP, UVB, Y

2816 ———— A Fearful Responsibility, and Other Stories . . . Boston: James R. Osgood and Company, 1881. 255 p.
AP, BA, BU, CU, H, HEH, LC, N, O, UC, UP, UVB, Y
*Also contains:* At the Sign of the Savage—Tonelli's Marriage.

2817 ———— A Hazard of New Fortunes: A Novel . . . New York: Harper & Brothers, 1890. 2 vols. (332, 332 p.) CU, H, HEH, LC, N, O, UC, UP
Published earlier in 171 p. ed. in the omitted "Franklin Square Library, New Series," No. 661, Nov. 1889.

2818 ———— An Imperative Duty: A Novel . . . New York: Harper & Brothers, 1892. 150 p. AP, BA, BU, CU, H, HEH, LC, N, O, UC, UM, UP, UVB, Y

2819 ———— Indian Summer . . . Boston: Ticknor and Company, 1886. 395 p. AP, BA, BU, H, HEH, LC, N, UP, UVB, Y

2820 ———— The Lady of the Aroostook . . . Boston: Houghton, Osgood and Company. The Riverside Press, Cambridge, 1879. 326 p.
BA, BU, CU, H, HEH, LC, N, O, UC, UM, UP, UVB, Y

2821 ———— The Landlord at Lion's Head: A Novel . . . New York: Harper & Brothers, 1897. 461 p., illus.
AP, BA, BU, CU, H, HEH, LC, N, O, UP, UVB, Y

2822 ———— The Minister's Charge; or, The Apprenticeship of Lemuel Barker . . . Boston: Ticknor and Company, 1887. 463 p.
AP, BA, CU, H, HEH, LC, N, O, UP, UVB, Y

2823 ———— A Modern Instance: A Novel . . . Boston: James R. Osgood and Company, 1882. 514 p. AP, BA, BU, H, HEH, LC, N, O, UP, UVB, Y

2824 ———— Niagara Revisited . . . Chicago: D. Dalziel [1884?]. 12 p.
CU, H, HEH, N, UVB, Y
See BAL 9615 for detailed description.

2825 ———— An Open-Eyed Conspiracy: An Idyl of Saratoga . . . New York and London: Harper & Brothers, 1897. 181 p.
AP, BA, BU, CU, H, HEH, LC, N, O, UC, UM, UP, UVB, Y

2826 ———— A Parting and a Meeting: Story . . . New York: Harper & Brothers, 1896. 98, [1] p., illus.
BA, BU, CU, H, HEH, LC, N, O, UC, UM, UP, UVB, Y

2827 ———— The Quality of Mercy: A Novel . . . New York: Harper & Brothers, 1892. 474 p. AP, BA, BU, CU, H, HEH, LC, N, UC, UM, UP, UVB, Y

2828 ———— Ragged Lady: A Novel . . . New York and London: Harper & Brothers, 1899. 357 p., illus.
AP, BU, CU, H, HEH, LC, N, O, UC, UM, UP, UVB, Y

2829 ———— The Rise of Silas Lapham . . . Boston: Ticknor and Company, 1885. 515 p. BU, H, HEH, LC, N, O, UM, Y

2830 ———— The Shadow of a Dream: A Story . . . New York: Harper & Brothers, 1890. 218 p. AP, BA, BU, H, HEH, LC, N, O, UM, UP, UVB, Y

2831 —— The Story of a Play: A Novel . . . New York and London: Harper & Brothers, 1898. 312 p.

AP, BA, BU, CU, H, HEH, LC, N, O, UC, UM, UP, UVB, Y

2832 —— Their Silver Wedding Journey . . . New York and London: Harper & Brothers, 1899. 2 vols. (400, [1], 463, [1] p.), illus.

BA, BU, CU, H, HEH, LC, N, O, UM, UP, UVB, Y

2833 —— A Traveler from Altruria: Romance . . . New York: Harper & Brothers, 1894. 318 p. AP, BU, H, HEH, LC, N, O, UC, UP, UVB, Y

2834 —— The Undiscovered Country . . . Boston: Houghton, Mifflin and Company. The Riverside Press, Cambridge, 1880. 419 p.

AP, BA, BU, CU, H, HEH, LC, N, O, UC, UM, UP, UVB, Y

2835 —— A Woman's Reason: A Novel . . . Boston: James R. Osgood and Company, 1883. 466 p. AP, BU, CU, H, HEH, LC, N, O, UC, UP, UVB, Y

2836 —— The World of Chance: A Novel . . . New York: Harper & Brothers, 1893. 375 p. BA, BU, CU, H, HEH, LC, N, O, UC, UM, UP, UVB, Y

2837 [HOXIE, WALTER PALMER.] Eugenia, a Friend's Victim: A Tale of Italy. By Alton Hurlba [pseud.] (W. P. H.) . . . New York: The Welles Publishing Company, 695 Broadway [cop. 1888]. 214 p. LC
At head of title: "The Elite Library."
Of mesmerism.

2838 HUBARD, SUE W. "As Thyself!" A Novel . . . Philadelphia: J. B. Lippincott & Co., 1881. 280 p. LC, O

2839 HUBBARD, ELBERT. Forbes of Harvard . . . Boston: Arena Publishing Company, 1894. 328 p. H, HEH, UC, UP, UVB, Y
Written in a series of letters.

2840 —— No Enemy (but Himself) . . . New York, London: G. P. Putnam's Sons; the Knickerbocker Press, 1894. 283 p., illus.

CU, HEH, LC, UVB, Y

2841 —— One Day: A Tale of the Prairies . . . Boston: Arena Publishing Co., 1893. 103 p. H, HEH, UVB, Y

2842 —— This Is the Story of the Legacy . . . East Aurora, N.Y.: Printed at the Roycroft Printing Shop, 1896. 448 p., 1 l., front. HEH, LC, Y
Some copies bound in 1 vol., some in 2.
Of a "Professor Wilson" of Harvard.

2843 —— Time and Chance: A Romance and a History. Being the Story of the Life of a Man . . . East Aurora, N.Y., U.S.A.: Done into a book by the Roycrofters at the Roycroft Shop, 1899. 2 vols. (582 p., 1 l.), illus. CU, H, HEH, LC, UC, UP, UVB, Y
Of John Brown.

2844 HUBBELL, WALTER. The Curse of Marriage: A True Story of Domestic Life . . . New York: The American News Company, 1888. 218 p., illus. LC

2845 ——— The Great Amherst Mystery: A True Narrative of the Supernatural . . . New York, Chicago, Paris: Brentano's, 1888. 168 p.
HEH, LC

2846 HUCKER, ANNIE M. Nearly Lost: A Novel . . . New York: G. W. Dillingham, 1890. 255 p. LC

2847 HUDSON, MARY WORRELL (SMITH). Esther the Gentile . . . Topeka, Kansas: Geo. W. Crane & Co., printers and binders, 1888. 167 p.
H, HEH, LC, Y

Anti Mormon novel.

2848 HUDSON, WILLIAM CADWALADER. An American Cavalier: A Novel . . . New York: The Cassell Publishing Co., 31 East 17th St. [cop. 1897]. 374 p. H, HEH

2849 [———] The Diamond Button: Whose Was It? A Tale from the Diary of a Lawyer and the Note-Book of a Reporter. By Barclay North [pseud.]. New York: Cassell & Company, Limited, 104 & 106 Fourth Avenue [cop. 1889]. 247 p. HEH, LC, O

2850 ——— The Dugdale Millions: A Novel . . . New York: Cassell Publishing Company, 104 & 106 Fourth Avenue [cop. 1891]. 319 p. HEH, O

2851 ——— The Man with a Thumb . . . New York: Cassell Publishing Company, 104 & 106 Fourth Avenue [cop. 1891]. 266 p.
AP, BA, HEH, LC, O, UM

2852 ——— On the Rack: A Novel . . . New York: Cassell Publishing Company, 104 & 106 Fourth Avenue [cop. 1891]. 283 p. AP, HEH, O

2853 ——— Should She Have Left Him? . . . New York: The Cassell Publishing Co., 31 East 17th St. [cop. 1894]. 273 p. HEH, LC

2854 ——— Vivier of Vivier, Longman & Company, Bankers: A Novel . . . New York: Cassell Publishing Company, 104 & 106 Fourth Avenue [cop. 1890]. 280 p. AP, HEH, LC, O

2855 HUDSPETH, ROSA. In the Market Places: A Few Chapters Concerning Carolyn Anselm's Journalistic Career . . . Omaha, Neb.: Douglas Printing Co., 1900. 145, [1] p. LC

2856 ——— The Juggernaut of the Moderns: A Novel . . . Boston: Arena Publishing Company, 1896. 327 p. HEH, LC

Of the double standard; Black Hills of Dakota.

2857  HUGHES, HARRY.  Katharine Barry: A Novel . . . New York: G. W. Dillingham Co., 1900.  270 p.  HEH, LC
Of psychic and religious interest.

2858  HUGHES, MRS. REGINALD.  Sybil Trevyllian . . . New York: Ward & Drummond, 711 Broadway [cop. 1892].  411 p.  LC, O, UC

2859  [HULL, CHARLES.]  Redeemed: A Novel.  By C. R. B. [pseud.] . . . New York: G. W. Dillingham, 1894.  272 p.  LC
Crime and intrigue; New York.

2860  HULSEY, AUGUSTUS JENNINGS.  Philip . . . [and] Warp and Woof: A Story of Life's Checkered Scenes . . . Atlanta, Ga.: V. P. Sisson, 1879.  191 p.
Information supplied by Florence Blakely of Duke University Library.

2861  HUME, ETTA LOUIS.  Etalee: A Novel.  [By] Etta Louis Hume, Columbia, Boone Co., Mo.  St. Louis: Chancy R. Barns, 1879.  288 p.  HEH, N

2862  HUME, ROBERT W.  My Lodger's Legacy; or, The History of a Recluse . . . New York, London: Funk & Wagnalls, 1886.  186 p.  HEH
Also contains: The Powers of Woman.

2863  HUMPHREY, FRANK POPE.  A New England Cactus, and Other Tales . . . New York: Cassell Publishing Company, 104 & 106 Fourth Avenue [cop. 1892].  188 p.  H, HEH, LC, O
Also contains: A Car of Love—The Courageous Action of Lucia Richmond—A Middle-Aged Comedy—A Belated Letter—Olive—A High Ideal.
At head of title: "The 'Unknown' Library."

2864  HUMPHREY, MRS. FRANK POPE.  Phoebe Tilson . . . Chicago and New York: Rand, McNally & Company [cop. 1898].  251 p.  HEH, LC, UM, Y
New England village life.

2865  HUMPHREY, MARY A. (VANCE).  The Squatter Sovereign; or, Kansas in the '50's. A Life Picture of the Early Settlement of the Debatable Ground.  A Story, Founded upon Memorable and Historical Events . . . Chicago, Ill.: Coburn & Newman Publishing Co., 1883.  354 p., illus.  CU, H, HEH, LC, N, UC, UM, Y

HUNGERFORD, MARY (CHURCHILL), jt. au.  See [Young, V. C.] Philip (1898), No. 6167.

2866  HUNT, GEORGE DILLWYN.  Albert Merton, the Farm Hand: A Domestic Story of Life among Working People . . . Published by the Author. Salem, Ohio: The Thos. J. Walton Job Printing House, 1893.  79 p., illus.  LC

2867  HUNT, JULIA MORRELL. A Woman's Talent, and Other Stories . . . Boston: De Wolfe, Fiske & Co., 361 and 365 Washington Street [cop. 1891]. 323 p.    HEH
*Also contains:* Paul—A Modern Actress—The Heroine of a Picture—Friendship? A Sketch—The Lost Jewel—A Strange Choice.

2868  [HUNTINGTON, EDWARD STANTON.] Dreams of the Dead. By Edward Stanton [pseud.] . . . Boston: Lee and Shepard, 1892. 268 p.
BA, BU, H, UP

HUNTINGTON, FAYE, *pseud.* *See* Foster, Theodosia Maria (Toll)

2869  HUNTINGTON, MRS. MARY H. The Strange Envelope; or, Twice Married. A Novel . . . New York: The American News Co., cop. 1893. 252 p.    LC
Florida.

2870  HUNTLEY, FLORENCE (CHANCE). The Dream Child . . . Boston, Mass.: Arena Publishing Co., 1892. 229 p.    HEH
Of the spirit world.

2871  HUNTLEY, STANLEY. Mr. and Mrs. Spoopendyke . . . New York: W. B. Smith & Co., Bond Street [cop. 1881]. 145 p. (41 chapters.) BU, HEH, LC
The 156 p. ed. contains 44 chapters.    H, HEH, UC
The 193 p. ed. contains 57 chapters.    CU, Y

2872  HURD, GRACE MARGUERITE. The Bennett Twins . . . New York: The Macmillan Company. London: Macmillan & Co., Ltd., 1900. 313 p.
H, HEH, LC, N, O
In a New York studio.

HURLBA, ALTON, *pseud.* *See* Hoxie, Walter Palmer

2873  HURLBUT, ELLA CHILDS. Mrs. Clift-Crosby's Niece . . . New York: Tait, Sons & Company, 1893. 178 p.    LC
New York.

2874  HUSBAND-HUNTERS; or, Matrimony and Misery. The Experience of a Philadelphia Polygamist with Ten Wives . . . Philadelphia: Barclay & Co., No. 21 North Seventh Street [cop. 1877]. 110 p., illus.    LC

HUSE, CAROLYN E. The Old "Academic." *In* C. King, *ed.*, By Land and Sea (1891), No. 3092.
Later printed in No. 3099.

2875  HUTSON, CHARLES WOODWARD. The Story of Beryl . . . New York: John B. Alden, 1888. 151 p.    HEH, LC
Ante bellum South.

2876  HYDE, EMILY. The Way . . . Baltimore: John Murphy & Co., 1888. 191 p.    LC

2877 HYDE, MILES GOODYEAR. The Girl from Mexico, and Other Stories and Sketches... New York: Isaac H. Blanchard Co. [cop. 1900]. 184 p. Y
*Also contains:* The Confessions of Terence McManus—Dora Willoughby's Latest Engagement—A Call on Dr. Sam Johnson.

2878 [HYDE, THOMAS ALEXANDER.] Won by a Bicycle; or, A Race for a Wife. By Luke Double, B. A. [pseud.]. Boston, Mass.: Greater Boston Publishing Co., 1895. 191 p. HEH, LC

I., J. T. *See* Irving, John Treat

IGNOTA, *pseud. See* MacKenzie, Adelheid (Zwissler)

2879 IKE, *pseud.* The Girl from Oshkosh... Chicago: E. A. Weeks & Company, 521-531 Wabash Ave. [cop. 1896]. 159 p., illus. HEH
Wisconsin.

2880 ILMEN, HARAS, *pseud.* Jack o' Hearts; or, Her Protégé... New York: Lowe & Company, printers, 1880. 193 p. BU, HEH

2881 I'M OFF! Sense and Nonsense for Summer Reading. New York: The American News Company. Philadelphia: The Central News Agency, 1884. 96 p., illus. LC
On LC paper cover: "Second Edition."

INGERSOLL, ERNEST. Bear's-Head Brooch. *In* C. King, Rancho del Muerto [cop. 1895], No. 3109.

2882 INGERSOLL, JUSTINE. Chronicles of Teapot Town... New Haven, Connecticut, 1895. 37 p. H, HEH, LC

2883 [INGRAHAM, MRS. ELLEN M.] Bond and Free: A Tale of the South. By Grace Lintner [pseud.]... Indianapolis: Carlon & Hollenbeck, printers and binders, 1882. 288 p., illus. H, N, UP, Y

2884 INMAN, HENRY. A Pioneer from Kentucky: An Idyl of the Raton Range... Topeka, Kansas: Crane & Company, 1898. 160 p., front.
CU, HEH, LC, N, UP, UV, Y

INNSLY, OWEN, *pseud. See* Jennison, Lucy White

IOGO, VEEN, *pseud. See* Daniels, Mrs. Ione G.

2885 IRELAND, HOWARD. A Green Mariner: A Landsman's Account of a Deep-Sea Voyage... Philadelphia and London: J. B. Lippincott Company, 1900. 262 p., illus. LC, O
An American's trip on a British ship.

2886 IRELAND, MARY ELIZA (HAINES). What I Told Dorcas: A Story for Mission Workers... New York: E. P. Dutton and Company, 1895. 354 p., illus. LC, UC

2887 [IRVINE, F. K.] Hialdo: A Novel. Sequel to Senorita Margarita. By Frederick S. Butt [pseud.] . . . Logansport, Ind.: Olympic Publishing Co., 1892. 268 p., illus.                                    LC

2888 [———] Labienus. By Frederick S. Butt [pseud.] . . . A Passionate Romance of Old Rome . . . Logansport, Ind.: Olympic Publishing Company, 1893. 204 p., illus.                            LC

2889 [IRVING, JOHN TREAT.] The Van Gelder Papers, and Other Sketches. Edited by J. T. I. New York & London: G. P. Putnam's Sons; the Knickerbocker Press, 1887. 316 p.           CU, H, HEH, LC, UP, UVB, Y
Contents: Teunis Van Gelder–Nick Wanzer's Adventure–Derrick Van Dam–Ralph Craft–Zadoc Town–Rulif Van Pelt–Obed Groot–Harry Blake –John Munro–A Visit of St. Nicholas–Little Sharpshins.

2890 IRWIN, HARVEY SAMUEL. Helena . . . New York: G. W. Dillingham Co., 1899. 278 p.                                              HEH, LC, UC
Several law cases contained in the plot.

IRWIN, WILLIAM HENRY, jt. au. See Field, C. K. Stanford Stories (1900), No. 1851.

2891 ISAACS, ABRAM SAMUEL. Stories from the Rabbis . . . New York: Charles L. Webster & Company, 1893. 201 p.              BA, H, HEH, LC, UV
Contents: The Faust of the Talmud–The Wooing of the Princess–The Rip Van Winkle of the Talmud–Rabbinical Romance–The Shepherd's Wife– The Repentant Rabbi–The Inheritance–Elijah in the Legends– When Solomon Was King–Rabbinical Humor–The Munchausen of the Talmud–The Rabbi's Dream–The Gift That Blessed–In the Sweat of Thy Brow–A Four-Leaved Clover–The Expiation–A String of Pearls.

ISLET, THEODORE OCEANIC, pseud. See Crocker, Samuel

2892 JACKMAN, ABI S. Fatima: A Dream of Passion . . . Watertown, N. Y. [cop. 1889]. 146 p.                                        CU, HEH, LC

2893 ——— In the Arms of Love . . . New York: Pollard Publishing Co., 1891. 128, 38 p.                                              LC
The 38 p. at end advertise publisher's Her Private Character.

2894 ——— A Silver Ray . . . Chicago: R. R. Donnelley & Sons, 1885. 272 p., front.                                                  LC

2895 JACKSON, AMBROSE LESTER. When Shiloh Came . . . New York: J. S. Ogilvie Publishing Company, 57 Rose Street [cop. 1899]. 295 p., illus.                                                      LC

A religious fantasy.

2896 [JACKSON, EDWARD PAYSON.] A Demigod: A Novel . . . New York: Harper & Brothers, 1887. 337 p.           BA, BU, HEH, LC, N, O, UV
Greece.

2897 JACKSON, GEORGE ANSON. The Son of a Prophet . . . Boston and New York: Houghton, Mifflin and Company. The Riverside Press, Cambridge, 1893. 394 p.                                      H, HEH, LC, O, Y

2898 JACKSON, HELEN MARIA (FISKE) HUNT. Between Whiles . . . Boston: Roberts Brothers, 1887. 304 p.          CU, H, HEH, LC, N, O, UC, UP, Y
     *Contents:* The Inn of the Golden Pear—The Mystery of Wilhelm Rütter—Little Bel's Supplement—The Captain of the "Heather Bell"—Dandy Steve—The Prince's Little Sweetheart.

2899 [————] Hetty's Strange History . . . Boston: Roberts Brothers, 1877. 291 p.                    BA, CU, H, HEH, LC, N, O, UC, UM, UP, UVB, Y
     At head of title: "No Name Series."

2900 [————] Mercy Philbrick's Choice. Boston: Roberts Brothers, 1876. 296 p.                   BA, BU, CU, H, HEH, LC, N, O, UC, UM, UP, UVB, Y
     At head of title: "No Name Series."

2901 ———— Ramona: A Story . . . Boston: Roberts Brothers, 1884. 490 p.
                              BA, CU, H, HEH, LC, N, O, UC, UVB, Y

2902 [————] Saxe Holm's [pseud.] Stories. Second Series. New York: Charles Scribner's Sons, 1878. 384 p.          CU, H, HEH, LC, O, Y
     *Contents:* A Four-Leaved Clover—Farmer Bassett's Romance—My Tourmaline—Joe Hale's Red Stockings—Susan Lawton's Escape.
     For "First Series" see Wright II, No. 1332.

2903 ———— Zeph: A Posthumous Story . . . Boston: Roberts Brothers, 1885. 253 p.          BA, BU, CU, H, HEH, N, O, UC, UM, UP, UVB, Y

2904 JACKSON, MARY E. The Spy of Osawatomie; or, The Mysterious Companions of Old John Brown . . . St. Louis, Mo.: W. S. Bryan, 1881. 439 p., illus.                          CU, H, HEH, LC, N, O, UM

2905 JACOB, CARRYE SILVEY. Love Can Conquer Pride . . . Nashville, Tenn.: The University Press, 1893. 110 p.                              LC

2906 JACOBI, MARY (PUTNAM). Found and Lost . . . New York, London: G. P. Putnam's Sons; the Knickerbocker Press, 1894. 139 p.
                                        H, HEH, LC, UC, UV
     *Also contains:* A Sermon at Notre-Dame; or, Religion under the Second Empire.
     At head of title: "Mary Putnam Jacobi."

     ———— A Martyr to Science. *In* Stories by American Authors, II (1884), No. 5268.

2907 JACOBUS, RUSSELL P. An Escape from Philistia: A Novel . . . Boston: J. G. Cupples Company, 250 Boylston Street [cop. 1893]. 204 p., 1 l.
                                        H, HEH, LC, O

2908  JAEGER, CARL.  Verana: A Tale of Border Life . . .  New York: The Abbey Press, 114 Fifth Avenue. London, Montreal [cop. 1900].  101, [1] p.                                                                    H, HEH

JAMES, *Prophet, pseud.  See* Buck, James Smith

2909  JAMES, HENRY.  The American . . .  Boston: James R. Osgood and Company, late Ticknor & Fields, and Fields, Osgood & Co., 1877.  473 p.
BA, CU, HEH, LC, N, O, UM, UP, UVB, Y

2910  ———  The Author of Beltraffio.  Pandora.  Georgina's Reasons.  The Path of Duty.  Four Meetings.  Boston: James R. Osgood and Company, 1885.  362 p.      AP, BA, BU, CU, H, HEH, LC, N, O, UC, UM, UVB, Y
At head of title: "Henry James."

2911  ———  The Awkward Age: A Novel . . .  New York and London: Harper & Brothers, 1899.  456, [1] p.
AP, BA, BU, CU, H, HEH, LC, N, O, UC, UM, UP, UVB, Y

2912  ———  A Bundle of Letters . . .  Boston: Loring, corner Bromfield & Washington Streets [1880].  64 p.
BA, BU, CU, H, HEH, LC, N, O, UC, UM, UP, UVB, Y
First separate printing; included in No. 2915.
BA copy received Nov. 6, 1880.

2913  ———  Confidence . . .  Boston: Houghton, Osgood and Company.  The Riverside Press, Cambridge, 1880.  347 p.
BA, BU, CU, H, HEH, LC, O, UC, UM, UP, UVB, Y

2914  ———  Daisy Miller: A Study . . .  New York: Harper & Brothers, 1879.  116 p.                        CU, H, HEH, LC, N, UC, UP, UVB, Y

2915  ———  The Diary of a Man of Fifty, and A Bundle of Letters . . .  New York: Harper & Brothers, 1880.  135 p.
BU, CU, H, HEH, LC, N, UC, UM, UP, UVB, Y

2916  ———  Embarrassments . . .  New York: The Macmillan Company.  London: Macmillan & Co., Ltd., 1896.  320 p.
BA, CU, H, HEH, LC, N, O, UM, UP, UVB, Y
*Contents:* The Figure in the Carpet—Glasses—The Next Time—The Way It Came.

2917  ———  The Europeans: A Sketch . . .  Boston: Houghton, Osgood and Company.  The Riverside Press, Cambridge, 1879.  281 p.
H, HEH, LC, N, O, UC, UM, UP, UVB, Y

2918  ———  In the Cage . . .  Chicago & New York: Herbert S. Stone & Company, 1898.  229 p., 1 l.    BA, BU, CU, H, HEH, LC, N, O, UC, UM, UP, UVB, Y

2919  ———  An International Episode . . .  New York: Harper & Brothers, 1879.  136 p.                          H, HEH, LC, N, O, UVB, Y

2920 —— John Delavoy . . . New York: The Macmillan Company. London: Macmillan & Co., Ltd., 1897. 74 p.               LC, UVB, Y
Later printed in No. 2928.

2921 —— The Lesson of the Master. The Marriages. The Pupil. Brooksmith. The Solution. Sir Edmund Orme . . . New York and London: Macmillan and Co., 1892. 302 p.
AP, BA, CU, H, HEH, LC, N, O, UM, UP, UVB, Y

—— A Light Man. *In* Stories by American Authors, V (1884), No. 5271.

2922 —— The Other House . . . New York: The Macmillan Company. London: Macmillan & Co., Ltd., 1896. 388 p.
AP, BU, CU, H, HEH, LC, N, O, UC, UM, UP, UVB, Y

2923 —— The Portrait of a Lady . . . Boston, New York: Houghton, Mifflin and Company. The Riverside Press, Cambridge, 1882. 520 p.
AP, BU, CU, H, HEH, LC, N, O, UC, UP, UVB, Y

2924 —— The Private Life. Lord Beaupré. The Visits . . . New York: Harper & Brothers, 1893. 232 p.
AP, BA, CU, H, HEH, LC, N, O, UC, UP, UVB, Y

2925 —— The Real Thing, and Other Tales . . . New York and London: Macmillan and Co., 1893. 275 p.
AP, BA, BU, CU, H, HEH, LC, N, O, UC, UM, UP, UVB, Y
*Also contains:* Sir Dominick Ferrand—Nona Vincent—The Chaperon—Greville Fane.

2926 —— Roderick Hudson . . . Boston: James R. Osgood and Company, late Ticknor & Fields, and Fields, Osgood & Co., 1876. 482 p.
CU, H, HEH, LC, N, UC, UP, UVB, Y

2927 —— The Siege of London, The Pension Beaurepas, and The Point of View . . . Boston: James R. Osgood and Company, 1883. 294 p.
AP, CU, H, HEH, LC, N, O, UC, UM, UVB, Y

2928 —— The Soft Side . . . New York: The Macmillan Company. London: Macmillan & Co., Ltd., 1900. 326 p.
AP, BU, CU, H, HEH, LC, N, O, UC, UM, UP, UVB, Y
*Contents:* The Great Good Place—'Europe'—Paste—The Real Right Thing—The Great Condition—The Tree of Knowledge—The Abasement of the Northmores—The Given Case—John Delavoy—The Third Person—Maud-Evelyn—Miss Gunton of Poughkeepsie.

2929 —— The Spoils of Poynton . . . Boston and New York: Houghton, Mifflin and Company. The Riverside Press, Cambridge, 1897. 323 p.
AP, BA, BU, CU, HEH, LC, N, O, UC, UM, UP, UVB, Y

2930 ———— Tales of Three Cities. Boston: James R. Osgood and Company, 1884. 359 p.     BA, CU, H, HEH, LC, N, O, UC, UP, UVB, Y
*Contents:* The Impressions of a Cousin—Lady Barberina—A New England Winter.
At head of title: "Henry James."

2931 ———— Terminations. The Death of the Lion. The Coxon Fund. The Middle Years. The Altar of the Dead ... New York: Harper & Brothers, 1895. 242 p.     BA, CU, H, HEH, LC, N, O, UC, UP, UVB, Y

2932 ———— The Tragic Muse ... Boston and New York: Houghton, Mifflin and Company. The Riverside Press, Cambridge, 1890. 2 vols. (882 p.)     AP, BA, CU, H, HEH, LC, O, UC, UM, UP, UVB, Y

2933 ———— The Two Magics. The Turn of the Screw. Covering End ... New York: The Macmillan Company. London: Macmillan & Co., Ltd., 1898. 393 p.     CU, HEH, LC, N, UC, UM, UP, UVB, Y

2934 ———— Washington Square ... New York: Harper & Brothers, 1881. 266 p., illus.     AP, BA, BU, CU, H, HEH, LC, O, UC, UM, UP, UVB, Y

2935 ———— Watch and Ward ... Boston: Houghton, Osgood and Company. The Riverside Press, Cambridge, 1878. 219 p.
AP, BA, BU, CU, H, HEH, LC, N, O, UC, UM, UP, UVB, Y

2936 ———— What Maisie Knew ... Chicago & New York: Herbert Stone & Co., 1897. 470 p., 1 l.     AP, CU, H, HEH, LC, N, O, UC, UM, UP, UVB, Y

2937 ———— The Wheel of Time. Collaboration. Owen Wingrave ... New York: Harper & Brothers, 1893. 220 p.
AP, BA, BU, CU, H, HEH, LC, N, O, UC, UM, UP, UVB, Y

2938 JAMES, PAUL. What Became of Eugene Ridgewood? A Novel ... New York: G. W. Carleton & Co. London: S. Low, Son & Co., 1883. 368 p.     HEH, LC, Y

2939 [JAMES, SAMUEL HUMPHREYS.] A Prince of Good Fellows: A Picture from Life ... Edited by N. Warrington Crabtrie [pseud.]. New York: The American News Co. [cop. 1890]. 208 p.     LC, UV
Postwar cotton plantations.

2940 [————] A Woman of New Orleans. By a Man o' the Town. [New Orleans?] 1899. 238 p.
Listed in D. E. Thompson, No. 1909.

2941 JAMISON, CECILIA VIETS (DAKIN) HAMILTON. The Lily of San Miniato: A Story of Florence. By Mrs. C. V. Hamilton ... New York: G. W. Carleton & Co. London: Smith, Elder & Co., 1878. 390 p.
H, HEH, LC, O
Of a hunchback and his protégé.

2942 —— My Bonnie Lass . . . Boston: Estes and Lauriat, 301 Washington Street [cop. 1877]. 131 p. Printed in double columns.

HEH, LC, O, UV

2943 —— The Story of an Enthusiast. Told by Himself . . . Boston: Ticknor and Company, 1888. 466 p.     H, HEH, LC, O
Of an artist.

2944 JANEWAY, J. B. H. "His Love for Helen". . . New York: G. W. Dillingham, 1893. 314 p.     LC
Cowboys; Colorado and Kansas.

2945 JANNEY, LUCY N. Alton-Thorpe: A Novel . . . Philadelphia: J. B. Lippincott & Co., 1880. 242 p.     H, HEH, LC, O

2946 JANVIER, THOMAS ALLIBONE. The Aztec Treasure-House: A Romance of Contemporaneous Antiquity . . . New York: Harper & Brothers, 1890. 446 p., illus.     AP, BA, CU, H, HEH, N, UC, UP, UVB, Y

2947 —— Color Studies . . . New York: Charles Scribner's Sons, 1885. 227 p.     AP, BU, CU, H, HEH, LC, N, O, UC, UVB, Y
*Contents:* Rose Madder—Jaune d'Antimoine—Orpiment & Gamboge—Roberson's Medium.

2948 —— Color Studies, and A Mexican Campaign . . . New York: Charles Scribner's Sons, 1891. 391 p.     BA, CU, H, HEH, LC, O, UP, UVB, Y
First four stories from same plates as the 1885 ed., No. 2947.

2949 —— In the Sargasso Sea: A Novel . . . New York and London: Harper & Brothers, 1898. 292, [1] p.
AP, BA, CU, HEH, LC, N, O, UC, UM, UP, UVB, Y

—— Pancha. *In* Stories by American Authors, X (1885), No. 5276. Later printed in No. 2951.

2950 —— The Passing of Thomas. In the St. Peter's Set. At the Grand Hôtel du Paradis. The Fish of Monsieur Quissard. Le Bon Oncle d'Amérique . . . New York and London: Harper & Brothers, 1900. 180, [1] p., illus.     AP, CU, H, HEH, LC, N, O, UP, UVB, Y

2951 —— Stories of Old New Spain . . . New York: D. Appleton and Company, 1891. 326 p., front.     AP, BA, BU, CU, HEH, UVB, Y
*Contents:* San Antonio of the Gardens—Niñita—Pancha: A Story of Monterey—The Town of the Holy Children—The Flower of Death—A Mexican Night—La Mina de los Padres—Saint Mary of the Angels—The Legend of Padre José.

2952 —— The Uncle of an Angel, and Other Stories . . . New York: Harper and Brothers, 1891. 287 p., illus.
BA, CU, H, HEH, LC, N, O, UC, UM, UP, UVB, Y

*Also contains:* A Border Ruffian–Our Pirate Hoard–A Temporary Dead-Lock–For the Honor of France–A Romance of Tompkins Square–An Idyl of the East Side.

2953 [JARBOE, MARY HALSEY (THOMAS).] "Go Forth and Find." By Thomas H. Brainerd [pseud.] . . . New York: The Cassell Publishing Co., 31 East 17th St. [cop. 1895]. 239 p.         HEH, LC
At head of title: "The 'Unknown' Library."
Santa Cruz and Monterey, California.

2954 [———] Robert Atterbury: A Study of Love and Life. By Thomas H. Brainerd [pseud.] . . . New York: The Cassell Publishing Co., 31 East 17th St. [cop. 1896]. 284 p.         LC
At head of title: "The 'Unknown' Library."

2955 JARROLD, ERNEST. Mickey Finn Idylls . . . New York: Doubleday & Mc-Clure Co., 1899. 281 p.         BU, HEH, LC, UM

——— *jt. au. See* McCann, J. E. Odds and Ends [cop. 1891], No. 3460.

JAY, W. L. M., *pseud. See* Woodruff, Julia Louisa Matilda (Curtiss)

2956 JEFFREY, ROSA (GRIFFITH) VERTNER JOHNSON. Marah: A Novel . . . Philadelphia: J. B. Lippincott & Co., 1884. 241 p.         CU, HEH, LC
From Narragansett Bay to Mississippi.

2957 [JELLEY, SYMMES M.] Shadowed to Europe: A Chicago Detective on Two Continents. By "Le Jemlys" [pseud.] . . . Chicago and New York: Belford, Clarke & Co., 1885. 357 p., illus.     HEH, LC, N, UM

2958 JENKENS, C. A. The Story of Pot Hooks; or, Society as Seen by a Back-woods Philosopher . . . St. Louis, Mo.: C. R. Barns Publishing Co. Cleveland, O.: Harris, Barns & Co., 1892. 378 p., illus.    HEH
Author may be Charles Augustus Jenkens.

2959 JENKINS, KATHARINE. Stories . . . Baltimore: John Murphy & Co., 1892. 195 p.         HEH, LC
*Contents:* Was It a Lost Day?—The New Postmaster—The Whim of a Nobleman—After Many Years—What the Beach Birds Know—Aunt Sarah's Wedding Boots—Hilda—The Bridal Bouquet—The Light Blue Tea Gown—The Lullaby—The Iron Cross—The Prize Chrysanthemums—The Afterglow.

2960 [JENKINS, WALTER L.] Madrine Doucet: A Romance. By Maj. Walter Leigh [pseud.] . . . Weymouth, Mass.: Weymouth and Braintree Publishing Co., 1899. 297 p.         CU, HEH, LC
The South after the Civil War.

2961 [———] A Romance of the Old Cave Mill: A Study in Ethics. By Maj. Walter Leigh [pseud.]. Hyannis, Mass.: F. B. & F. P. Goss, 1897. 272 p.         CU, HEH, LC
Kentucky bluegrass country.

JENKS, TUDOR. A Drawn Battle. *In* Mavericks (1892), No 3663.

——— Foiled Again. *In* Hanks: Assorted Yarns from Puck (1893), No. 2444.

JENNESS, ANNIE. *See* Miller, Annie (Jenness)

2962 JENNINGS, JOHN JOSEPH. Widow Magoogin ... New York: G. W. Dillingham Co., 1900. 364 p.  HEH, LC, UM

2963 JENNINGS, MARY ELIZABETH. Asa of Bethlehem and His Household. B.C. IV–A.D. XXX ... New York: Anson D. F. Randolph and Company, 1895. 268 p.  LC, Y

2964 ——— The Brave Little Maid of Goldau ... New York: Anson D. F. Randolph & Company (Incorporated), 182 Fifth Avenue [cop. 1892]. 39 p., illus.  LC

2965 [JENNISON, LUCY WHITE.] Penelope's Web: An Episode of Sorrento. By Owen Innsly [pseud.] ... Boston: J. G. Cupples Co. [cop. 1890]. 330 p.  H, LC, O

JEPSON, RING, *pseud. See* Latham, Henry Jepson

2966 JEROME, FERRIS. High-Water-Mark: A Novel ... Philadelphia: J. B. Lippincott & Co., 1879. 385 p.  HEH, LC, O
Life in a western prairie town.

2967 JEROME, THOMAS JEFFERSON. Ku-Klux Klan No. 40: A Novel ... Raleigh, N.C.: Edwards & Broughton, printers and binders, 1895. 259 p.
H, LC, N, UC, UM, Y

2968 JESSE JAMES: The Life and Daring Adventures of This Bold Highwayman and Bank Robber and His No Less Celebrated Brother, Frank James. Together with the Thrilling Exploits of the Younger Boys. Written by ***** (One Who Dare Not Now Disclose His Identity). The Only Book Containing the Romantic Life of Jesse James and His Pretty Wife, Who Clung to Him to the Last! Philadelphia, Pa.: Barclay & Co., 21 North Seventh Street [cop. 1882]. 96 p., illus.  HEH, Y

JESSOP, GEORGE HENRY. Biddy's Dream. *In* Mavericks (1892), No. 3663.

——— Dreams Go by Contraries. *In* Tales from McClure's: Adventure (1897), No. 5360.

2969 ——— Gerald Ffrench's Friends ... New York: Longmans, Green & Co., 1889. 240 p.  AP, BA, BU, CU, H, HEH, O
*Contents:* The Rise and Fall of the "Irish Aigle"—A Dissolving View of Carrick Meagher—At the Town of the Queen of the Angels—An Old Man from the Old Country—The Last of the Costellos—Under the Redwood Tree.

2970 ———— Judge Lynch: A Romance of the California Vineyards... Chicago, New York, and San Francisco: Belford, Clarke & Co. London: Henry J. Drane [cop. 1889]. 232 p. CU, HEH

———— Suing for Damages. *In* Hanks: Assorted Yarns from Puck (1893), No. 2444.

———— *jt. au. See* Matthews, B. One Story Is Good Till Another Is Told. *In* B. Matthews, With My Friends (1891), No. 3659.

———— *jt. au. See* Matthews, B. A Tale of Twenty-Five Hours (1892), No. 3656.

2971 JEWELL, MRS. A. IRENE. Muriel Sterling: A Tale of the African Veldt... New York: International Book and Publishing Company, 1900. 296 p., front. HEH, LC, O

2972 JEWETT, SARAH ORNE. Country By-Ways... Boston: Houghton, Mifflin and Company. The Riverside Press, Cambridge, 1881. 249 p.
AP, BA, BU, CU, H, HEH, LC, N, O, UC, UM, UVB, Y
*Contents:* River Driftwood—Andrew's Fortune—An October Ride—From a Mournful Villager—An Autumn Holiday—A Winter Drive—Good Luck: A Girl's Story—Miss Becky's Pilgrimage.

2973 ———— A Country Doctor... Boston, New York: Houghton, Mifflin and Company. The Riverside Press, Cambridge, 1884. 351 p.
CU, H, HEH, N, O, UC, UM, UP, UVB, Y

2974 ———— The Country of the Pointed Firs ... Boston and New York: Houghton, Mifflin and Company. The Riverside Press, Cambridge, 1896. 213 p. AP, CU, H, HEH, LC, N, O, UM, UVB, Y

2975 ———— Deephaven ... Boston: James R. Osgood and Company, late Ticknor & Fields, and Fields, Osgood & Co., 1877. 255 p.
BA, CU, H, HEH, LC, N, O, UP, UVB

2976 ———— The King of Folly Island, and Other People ... Boston and New York: Houghton, Mifflin and Company. The Riverside Press, Cambridge, 1888. 339 p. AP, BU, CU, H, HEH, LC, N, O, UC, UP, UVB, Y
*Also contains:* The Courting of Sister Wisby—The Landscape Chamber—Law Lane—Miss Peck's Promotion—Miss Tempy's Watchers—A Village Shop—Mère Pochette.

2977 ———— The Life of Nancy ... Boston and New York: Houghton, Mifflin and Company. The Riverside Press, Cambridge, 1895. 322 p.
AP, BA, CU, H, HEH, LC, N, O, UC, UP, UVB, Y
*Also contains:* Fame's Little Day—A War Debt—The Hiltons' Holiday—The Only Rose—A Second Spring—Little French Mary—The Guests of Mrs. Timms—A Neighbor's Landmark—All My Sad Captains.

2978 ———— A Marsh Island . . . Boston, New York: Houghton, Mifflin and Company. The Riverside Press, Cambridge, 1885. 292 p.

AP, BU, CU, H, HEH, LC, N, O, UC, UP, UVB, Y

2979 ———— The Mate of the Daylight, and Friends Ashore . . . Boston, New York: Houghton, Mifflin and Company. The Riverside Press, Cambridge, 1884. 254 p.     AP, BA, CU, H, HEH, LC, N, O, UC, UP, UVB

*Also contains:* A Landless Farmer—A New Parishioner—An Only Son—Miss Debby's Neighbors—Tom's Husband—The Confession of a House-Breaker—A Little Traveler.

2980 ———— A Native of Winby, and Other Tales . . . Boston and New York: Houghton, Mifflin and Company. The Riverside Press, Cambridge, 1893. 309 p.     AP, CU, H, HEH, LC, N, O, UM, UP, UVB, Y

*Also contains:* Decoration Day—Jim's Little Woman—The Failure of David Berry—The Passing of Sister Barsett—Miss Esther's Guest—The Flight of Betsey Lane—Between Mass and Vespers—A Little Captive Maid.

———— The Night before Thanksgiving. *In* I. Bachellor, *ed.*, Best Things from American Literature (1899), No. 195.

Also included in No. 2982.

2981 ———— Old Friends and New . . . Boston: Houghton, Osgood and Company. The Riverside Press, Cambridge, 1879. 269 p.

AP, CU, H, HEH, LC, N, UC, UP, UVB, Y

*Contents:* A Lost Lover—A Sorrowful Guest—A Late Supper—Mr. Bruce—Miss Sydney's Flowers—Lady Ferry—A Bit of Shore Life.

2982 ———— The Queen's Twin, and Other Stories . . . Boston and New York: Houghton, Mifflin and Company. The Riverside Press, Cambridge, 1899. 232 p., 1 l.     AP, BA, CU, H, HEH, LC, N, O, UP, UV, Y

*Also contains:* A Dunnet Shepherdess—Where's Nora?—Bold Words at the Bridge—Martha's Lady—The Coon Dog—Aunt Cynthy Dallett—The Night before Thanksgiving.

2983 ———— Strangers and Wayfarers . . . Boston and New York: Houghton, Mifflin and Company. The Riverside Press, Cambridge, 1890. 279 p.     AP, CU, H, LC, N, O, UM, UP, UVB, Y

*Contents:* A Winter Courtship—The Mistress of Sydenham Plantation—The Town Poor—The Quest of Mr. Teaby—The Luck of the Bogans—Fair Day—Going to Shrewsbury—The Taking of the Captain Ball—By the Morning Boat—In Dark New England Days—The White Rose Road.

2984 ———— Tales of New England . . . Boston and New York: Houghton, Mifflin and Company. The Riverside Press, Cambridge, 1890. 276 p.

AP, H, HEH, N, O, UP, UVB, Y

*Contents:* Miss Tempy's Watchers—The Dulham Ladies—An Only Son—Marsh Rosemary—A White Heron—Law Lane—A Lost Lover—The Courting of Sister Wisby.

At head of title: "The Riverside Aldine Series."

2985 ———— A White Heron, and Other Stories ... Boston and New York: Houghton, Mifflin and Company. The Riverside Press, Cambridge, 1886. 254 p.          AP, BA, BU, H, HEH, LC, N, O, UC, UM, UP, UVB, Y
*Also contains:* The Gray Man—Farmer Finch—Marsh Rosemary—The Dulham Ladies—A Business Man—Mary and Martha—The News from Petersham —The Two Browns.
Title story later printed in No. 2984.

2986 JINKS, JONATHAN, *pseud.* A Cure for the Blues ... Philadelphia, 1878. 213 p., front.          LC

JOANNA, *pseud. See* McCornick, Mrs. Joanna

2987 JOHN, *Captain* DUM, *pseud.* The Autobituary of a West Pointer, Written at the Request of George Washington, General Chewflicket, and Some Foreign Gentlemen ... New York: Metropolitan Publishing Co., cop. 1882. 72 p., illus.          HEH

2988 JOHNES, WINIFRED WALLACE (TINKER). Memoirs of a Little Girl ... New York & London: The Transatlantic Publishing Co., 1896. 255 p.          LC
In a Michigan logging camp.

2989 ———— Miss Gwynne, Bachelor: A Novel ... New York: G. W. Dillingham, 1894. 285 p.          LC
Art students in New York.

2990 JOHNS, ANNIE E. Cooleemee: A Tale of Southern Life ... Leaksville, Rockingham County, N.C.: Leaksville Gazette Print, 1882. Cover title, 225 p.          LC
Civil War.

2991 JOHNSON, ELIZABETH WINTHROP. Orchard Folk: Two California Stories ... New York: Continental Publishing Company, 1898. 316 p.          HEH, LC, UV
*Contents:* The Delicians—Silvela of Dulzura.

2992 ———— Two Loyal Lovers: A Romance ... New York: Frederick A. Stokes Company, 1890. 381 p.          HEH, LC
Civil War.

2993 [————] Yesterday: An American Novel. New York: Henry Holt and Company, 1882. 300 p.          HEH, LC, Y
At head of title: "Leisure Hour Series—No. 137."
Of an actor's life.

2994 JOHNSON, EVELYN KIMBALL. An Errand Girl: A Romance of New York Life ... New York: G. W. Dillingham, successor to G. W. Carleton & Co., 1889. 341 p.          HEH, LC

2995 ———— Tangles Unravelled . . . A Realistic Melodrama, Spiced with Comedy. New York: J. S. Ogilvie & Company, 31 Rose Street [cop. 1884]. 263 p.                                        BU, CU, HEH, LC

JOHNSON, F. A. A Psychological Effect. *In* J. J. Conway, *ed.*, Stories (1893), No. 1172.
Author may be Frank Amos Johnson.

2996 JOHNSON, MRS. F. BARRETT. Rocks and Romance: A Story . . . New York: J. S. Ogilvie, 57 Rose Street. Chicago, 79 Wabash Avenue [cop. 1889]. 300 p., illus.                                CU, H, HEH, LC, N, UM
Vermont.

2997 JOHNSON, HARRY M. Edith: A Story of Chinatown . . . Boston: Arena Publishing Co., 1895. 84 p.                                   HEH, LC
San Francisco.

2998 JOHNSON, HELEN LOUISE (KENDRICK). Raleigh Westgate; or, Epimenides in Maine. A Romance . . . New York: D. Appleton and Company, 1889. 259 p.                                       HEH

2998a [JOHNSON, HOMER URI.] The Great Co-Partnership, and Other Papers. By Obed [pseud.] . . . Cleveland: Ingham, Clarke & Co., 1879. 197, [2] p., illus.                                     HEH
Verso of title page: "Buffalo, N.Y.: A. C. VanDuzee, engraver. Erie, Pa.: Jno. M. Glazier, printer, 1879."
Humorous account of the Centennial Exhibition, Philadelphia, 1876.

2999 JOHNSON, LILLIAN (HARTMAN). Christmas Thorns . . . Durango, Colorado, cop. 1895. 23 p.                                       LC
Deposited Jan. 27, 1896.

3000 JOHNSON, MRS. MARY KELLOGG. Mac: A Dog's True Story . . . Boston: H. H. Carter & Company, 1895. 126 p., illus.                                  LC

3001 JOHNSON, P. DEMAREST. Claudius, the Cowboy of Ramapo Valley: A Story of Revolutionary Times in Southern New York . . . Middletown, N.Y.: Slauson & Boyd, press steam print, 1894. 206 p.    CU, H, LC, UM, Y

3002 JOHNSON, STANLEY EDWARDS. The Temper Cure . . . New York: The Abbey Press, 114 Fifth Avenue [cop. 1900]. 62 p.                   LC
Deposited Nov. 30, 1900.

JOHNSON, TOM, *pseud. See* Green, Warren

3003 JOHNSON, VIRGINIA WALES. An English "Daisy Miller" . . . Boston: Estes and Lauriat, 1882. 67 p.         AP, BA, H, HEH, LC, O, UP, UV, Y

3004 ———— The Fainalls of Tipton . . . New York: Charles Scribner's Sons, 1884. 482 p.                                AP, H, HEH, LC, O

3005 [————] A Foreign Marriage; or, Buying a Title. A Novel. New York: Harper & Brothers, 1880. 197 p. Printed in double columns.

H, HEH, LC

———— The Image of San Donato. *In* Stories by American Authors, VII (1884), No. 5273.

3006 ———— Miss Nancy's Pilgrimage: A Story of Travel . . . New York: Harper & Brothers, 1876. 136 p.  HEH, LC, O, UC, UP

3007 JOHNSON, WILLIAM HENRY. King or Knave, Which Wins? An Old Tale of Huguenot Days. Edited by William Henry Johnson. Boston: Little, Brown and Company, 1899. 343 p., illus.  BA, HEH, LC, N, O, Y

3008 ———— The King's Henchman: A Chronicle of the Sixteenth Century. Brought to Light and Edited by William Henry Johnson. Boston: Little, Brown and Company, 1898. 293 p.  BA, H, HEH, LC, O, UP, Y

3009 JOHNSTON, ALMA (CALDER). Miriam's Heritage: A Story of the Delaware River. By Alma Calder. New York: Harper & Brothers, 1878. 175 p. Printed in double columns.  BU, CU, HEH, LC

D. E. Thompson, No. 1914, lists this book wtih "Rush Ellis [pseud.]" on title page.

3010 JOHNSTON, ELIZABETH BRYANT. Christmas in Kentucky, 1862 . . . Washington, D.C.: Gibson Bros., printers and bookbinders, 1892. 24 p., illus.

LC

3011 [JOHNSTON, JAMES WESLEY.] Dwellers in Gotham: A Romance of New York. By Annan Dale [pseud.]. New York: Eaton & Mains. Cincinnati: Curts & Jennings, 1898. 392 p.  H, HEH, LC

3012 JOHNSTON, MARY. Prisoners of Hope: A Tale of Colonial Virginia . . . Boston and New York: Houghton, Mifflin and Company. The Riverside Press, Cambridge, 1898. 378 p., 1 l., front.  H, HEH, LC, N, O, UVB, Y

3013 ———— To Have and to Hold . . . Boston and New York: Houghton, Mifflin and Company. The Riverside Press, Cambridge, 1900. 403, [1] p., illus.  AP, BA, BU, CU, H, HEH, LC, N, O, UM, UP, UVB, Y

3014 JOHNSTON, RICHARD MALCOLM. Mr. Absalom Billingslea, and Other Georgia Folk . . . New York: Harper & Brothers, 1888. 414 p., illus.  AP, BA, BU, CU, H, HEH, N, O, UC, UM, UVB, Y

*Contents:* A Critical Accident to Mr. Absalom Billingslea—The Brief Embarrassment of Mr. Iverson Blount—Rev. Rainford Gunn and the Arab Chief—Martha Reid's Lovers—The Suicidal Tendencies of Mr. Ephrodtus Twilley—Dr. Hinson's Degree—The Meditations of Mr. Archie Kittrell—The Rivalries of Mr. Toby Gillam—The Hotel Experience of Mr. Pink Fluker—The Wimpy Adoptions—The Stubblefield Contingents—Historic Doubts of Riley Hood—Mr. Thomas Chiver's Boarder—Moll and Virgil.

3015 ———— Mr. Billy Downs and His Likes . . . New York: Charles L. Webster & Co., 1892. 232 p., front.

BA, CU, H, HEH, LC, N, O, UC, UP, UVB, Y

*Contents:* A Bachelor's Counselings—Parting from Sailor—Two Administrations—Almost a Wedding in Dooly District—Something in a Name—The Townses and Their Cousins.

Half title: "Fiction, Fact, and Fancy Series. Edited by Arthur Stedman."

3016 ———— Mr. Fortner's Marital Claims, and Other Stories . . . New York: D. Appleton and Company, 1892. 182 p.

BA, CU, H, HEH, LC, N, UC, UM, UP, UVB, Y

*Also contains:* Old Gus Lawson—An Adventure of Mr. Joel Bozzle—A Moccasin among the Hobbys—A Surprise to Mr. Thompson Byers.

3017 ———— Old Mark Langston: A Tale of Duke's Creek . . . New York: Harper & Brothers, 1884. 338 p.

AP, H, HEH, LC, N, O, UC, UM, UP, UVB, Y

3018 ———— Old Times in Middle Georgia . . . New York: The Macmillan Company. London: Macmillan & Co., Ltd., 1897. 249 p.

BA, H, HEH, LC, O, UC, UM, UP, UVB, Y

*Contents:* Mr. Eben Bull's Investments—Mr. Cummin's Relinquishment—Mr. Pate's Only Infirmity—Shadowy Foes—Their Cousin Lethy—Old Lady Lazenberry—Our Witch—Weasels on a Debauch—Ephe—A Case of Spite—Mr. Pea Nearly Nonplussed—Lost—Mutual Schoolmasters—Miss Clisby's Romance—Ishmael.

3019 ———— Pearce Amerson's Will . . . Chicago: Way and Williams, 1898. 275 p., 1 l., illus.

CU, H, HEH, LC, N, O, UC, UVB, Y

3020 ———— The Primes and Their Neighbors: Ten Tales of Middle Georgia . . . New York: D. Appleton and Company, 1891. 310 p., illus.

BA, CU, H, HEH, N, O, UC, UM, UP, UVB, Y

*Contents:* The Durance of Mr. Dickerson Prime—The Combustion of Jim Rakestraw—The Self-Protection of Mr. Littleberry Roach—The Humors of Jacky Bundle—The Experiment of Miss Sally Cash—Travis and Major Jonathan Wilby—New Discipline at Rock Spring—Mr. Joseph Pate and His People—Mr. Gibble Colt's Ducks—The Pursuit of the Martyns.

3021 ———— Widow Guthrie: A Novel . . . New York: D. Appleton and Company, 1890. 309 p., illus.

AP, BA, CU, H, HEH, LC, N, O, UC, UM, UP, UVB, Y

3021a JOHNSTON, W. CAIRNS. Beyond the Ether: A Speculative and Original Story . . . Andover, Maine: W. C. Johnston, 1896. 86 p.     HEH

JOHNSTON, WILLIAM JOHN. A Centennial-Telegraphic Romance. *In* [W. J. Johnston] *comp.,* Lightning Flashes and Electric Dashes (1877), Nos. 3022, 3023.

3022 [———] *comp.* Lightning Flashes and Electric Dashes: A Volume of Choice Telegraphic Literature, Humor, Fun, Wit, & Wisdom. Contributed to by All the Principal Writers in the Ranks of Telegraphic Literature ... New York: W. J. Johnston, 1877. 141 p., illus. Printed in double columns.          CU, HEH, Y
*Contains:* The Volcanograph, by Joseph Christie—A Leaf of Autobiography, by W. P. Phillips—The Telegraph Dispatch, by J. D. Reid—Wives for Two; or, Joe's Little Joke, by E. O. Chase—Kate, by Charles Barnard—A Perilous Christmas Courtship, by J. M. Maclachlan—Playing with Fire, by L. A. Churchill—The Vow of the Six Telegraph Operators, by G. W. Russell—A Centennial-Telegraphic Romance, by W. J. Johnston—Into the Jaws of Death, by H. Van Hoevenbergh.

3023 ——— ——— New York: W. J. Johnston, 1877. 189 p., illus.    LC
This ed. adds: Wooing by Wire, by Miss J. J. Schofield.

JONATHAN, *Brother, D.D., pseud.* *See* Pierce, Zerelda F.

JONES, *Major, pseud.* *See* Thompson, William Tappan

3024 JONES, ALICE ILGENFRITZ. Beatrice of Bayou Têche ... Chicago: A. C. McClurg and Company, 1895. 386 p.        H, HEH, LC, O, Y
Ante bellum New Orleans.

3025 ——— The Chevalier de St. Denis ... Chicago: A. C. McClurg and Company, 1900. 387 p.        H, HEH, LC, Y
Louisiana, early 18th century.

3026 JONES, CHARLES HENRY. Davault's Mills: A Novel ... Philadelphia: J. B. Lippincott & Co., 1876. 424 p.        CU, H, HEH, LC, O

3027 JONES, ERASMUS W. Gold, Tinsel, and Trash: Stories of Country and City ... New York: Hunt & Eaton. Cincinnati: Cranston & Stowe, 1890. 319 p.        HEH, LC
*Also contains:* Sharp Words on Old Flintrock Circuit—The Man with the Ruffled Shirt; or, My First Week on L——— Charge—John's Wife's Brother: A Thanksgiving Story—The Conspiracy: A Story of the Medes and Persians—Sunny Memories of Conference Chums—"I Took You with Guile"—The Great Revival at Tonville.

3028 ——— Llangobaith: A Story of North Wales ... Utica, N.Y.: Thomas J. Griffiths, 1886. 363 p.        H, HEH, LC, Y

3029 [JONES, GEORGE F.] Polly's Scheme. By Corydon [pseud.]. Boston: D. Lothrop and Company, 32 Franklin Street [cop. 1882]. 207 p.    LC
Of a summer boardinghouse.

3030 JONES, IRA LAFAYETTE. Beoni the Sphinx: A Novel ... [N.p., cop. 1898.] 160 p.        HEH, LC
Deposited June 18, 1898.
Of temperance interest.

3031 JONES, J. MCHENRY. Hearts of Gold: A Novel ... Wheeling [W.Va.]: Daily Intelligencer Steam Job Press, 1896. 299 p.     HEH
Reconstruction era.

3032 [JONES, L. L.] Oberlin and Eastern School Life ... Warren, Ohio: The Trumbull Ptg. Co., 1889. 361 p.     HEH
Author may be Lewis Linus Jones.

3033 JONES, M. P. Rebekah: A Tale of Three Cities ... New York: John B. Alden, 1889. 319 p.     LC, Y
Caesar's Rome.

3034 JONES, RANDOLPH. The Buccaneers: A Historical Novel of the Times of William III and Louis XIV ... New York: The Authors' Publishing Company, 1878. 551 p.     HEH, LC, UC

3035 JONES, SAMUEL ARTHUR. The Porcelain Painter's Son: A Fantasy ... Philadelphia: Boericke & Tafel, 1898. 126 p.     H, LC

3036 JONES, VICTORINE CLARISSE (JACQUET). Miss Hogg, the American Heiress: A Novel ... New York: G. W. Dillingham Co., 1900. 583 p.     HEH, LC
An American girl in London.

3037 JORDAN, DAVID STARR. Matka and Kotik: A Tale of the Mist-Islands ... San Francisco: The Whitaker & Ray Company (Incorporated), 1897. 68, [1] p., illus.     BU, HEH, LC, UP
Of fur seals.

3038 —— The Story of the Innumerable Company ... [Palo Alto, Calif.]: Stanford University Press, 1895. 38, [1] p.     BU, H, HEH
An allegory.

3039 DELETED.

JORDAN, ELIZABETH GARVER. A Romance of the City Room. *In* I. Bacheller, *ed.*, Best Things from American Literature (1899), No. 195.
Printed earlier in No. 3040.

3040 —— Tales of the City Room ... New York: Charles Scribner's Sons, 1898. 232 p.     BA, CU, H, HEH, LC, N, O, UM
*Contents:* Ruth Herrick's Assignment—The Love Affair of Chesterfield, Jr. —At the Close of the Second Day—The Wife of the Candidate—Mrs. Ogilvie's Local Color—From the Hand of Dolorita—The Passing of Hope Abbott—A Point of Ethics—A Romance of the City Room—Miss Van Dyke's Best Story.

3041 JORDAN, KATE. A Circle in the Sand ... Boston, New York, and London: Lamson, Wolffe and Company, 1898. 303 p.     CU, HEH, LC, Y
Of a newspaper woman.
Author married Frederick M. Vermilye.

3042 —————— The Other House: A Study of Human Nature ... New York: Lovell, Coryell & Company, 43, 45, and 47 East Tenth Street [cop. 1892]. 183 p., illus. LC, UC

—————— A Rose of the Mire. *In* Ten Notable Stories (1894), No. 5391.

3043 A JORUM IDYL. [Philadelphia: Craig, Finley & Co., steam-power printers and lithographers]; Printed for private circulation only, 1884. 142 p.
HEH, LC
Chapters are by various authors identified in the text by initials only. Former owner of HEH copy penciled in some of the last names.

JOSIAH ALLEN'S WIFE, *pseud. See* Holley, Marietta

JOSLYN, EARL. The Mistress of the Foundry. *In* Tales from McClure's: Adventure (1897), No. 5360.

3044 JUDAH, MRS. MARY JAMESON. Down Our Way: Stories of Southern and Western Character ... Chicago: Way & Williams [cop. 1897]. 266 p., 1 l. HEH, LC, UC, UM, Y
*Contents:* A Visible Sign—The End of Society—An Adventure of a Lady of Quality—A Part of the New South—A Conflict of Rights—The Morningstar Elopement—The Wife of a Carpenter—A Gentlewoman—The Blue Blazers.

3045 —————— The Outcomings of Addisonville: A Story ... Indianapolis, 1892.
May Louise Shipp, jt. au.
Listed in Banta, p. 173.

3046 [JUDSON, EDWARD ZANE CARROLL.] Buffalo Bill and His Adventures in the West. By Ned Buntline [pseud.] ... New York: J. S. Ogilvie Publishing Company, 57 Rose Street, cop. 1886. 314 p.
CU, H, HEH, UM, Y
Published earlier in the omitted "People's Library," 1881, with title: *Buffalo Bill, the King of Border Men.*

3047 JULIAN, EMAIL. John Dale: The American Story ... San Francisco: Alta Printing House, 1876. 30 p.
Information supplied by Kenneth J. Carpenter, University of California Library, Berkeley, from copy in Bancroft Library.

3048 JULIAN, HARRY, *pseud?* Love Ventures: A Novel with an Affidavit ... New York: The Truth Seeker Company, 28 Lafayette Place [cop. 1888]. 226 p., illus. LC
Copyrighted by Charles P. Somerby; deposited Sept. 12, 1888.

JUNIOUS, JUNIOR, *pseud. See* Wells, Samuel E.

3049 JUSTICE, MAIBELLE HEICKS (MONROE). Love Affairs of a Worldly Man ... Chicago, New York: F. Tennyson Neely, 1894. 311 p. LC
New York.

3050 [KANE, ALICE L.] Echoes from the Spirit World. Topeka, Kansas: Crane & Company, printers, 1899. 142 p., 1 l., illus. BU, LC

3051 KANE, EDWARD CHARLES. A Gentleman Born . . . New York: G. W. Dillingham Co., 1900. 340 p.
Listed PW, June 30, 1900.

3052 KANE, JAMES JOHNSON. Adift on the Black Wild Tide . . . Philadelphia: J. B. Lippincott & Co., 1879. 80 p. H, LC, O, UV

3053 ———— Ilian; or, The Curse of the Old South Church of Boston. A Psychological Tale of the Late Civil War . . . Philadelphia, London: J. B. Lippincott Company, 1888. 368 p., illus.
AP, CU, H, HEH, LC, N, O, UM, UVB

3054 KATZENBERGER, FRANCES ISABELLE. He Would Have Me Be Brave: A Story Taken from Life . . . Dayton, Ohio: Press of the Groneweg Printing Company, 1893. 395 p., front. LC

3055 ———— The Three Verdicts: A Story . . . Cincinnati: The Editor Publishing Co., 1898. 251 p. LC

3056 KAUFFMAN, CATHERINE. As Nature Prompts: A Novelette . . . Cleveland, O.: The Cleveland Printing & Publishing Co., 1891. 261 p. HEH
Ohio.

3057 KAVEN, EDWARD THOMAS. From Clouds to Sunshine; or, The Evolution of a Soul . . . New York: The Abbey Press, 114 Fifth Avenue [cop. 1900]. 182 p. LC, UV

3058 KEENAN, HENRY FRANCIS. The Aliens: A Novel . . . New York: D. Appleton and Company, 1886. 453 p. AP, BA, H, HEH, LC, O
Irish immigrants; New York state.

3059 ———— The Iron Game: A Tale of the War . . . New York: D. Appleton and Company, 1891. 405 p. AP, CU, HEH, N, UV, Y
Civil War.

3060 [————] The Money-Makers: A Social Parable . . . New York: D. Appleton and Company, 1885. 337 p.
BA, BU, CU, H, HEH, LC, N, O, UM, UVB, Y
Social and political life; New York and Washington.

3061 ———— Trajan: The History of a Sentimental Young Man, with Some Episodes in the Comedy of Many Lives' Error. A Novel . . . New York: Cassell & Company, Limited, 1885. 642 p.
AP, BA, CU, H, HEH, LC, O, UM, UP, Y
Preceding the Commune of Paris.

KEITH, ALYN YATES, *pseud*. *See* Morris, Eugenia Laura (Tuttle)

KELLER, MARTHA CAROLYNE. *See* Miller, Martha Carolyne (Keller)

3062 KELLEY, ADELAIDE (SKEEL). King Washington: A Romance of the Hudson Highlands. By Adelaide Skeel & William H. Brearley. Philadelphia: J. B. Lippincott Company, 1898. 307 p., illus.

BA, CU, H, HEH, LC, N, O, Y

3063 —— My Three Legged Story Teller . . . Philadelphia: R. C. Hartranft, 1892. 203 p. CU, H, LC, UP, Y

*Contents:* A Christmas Card—Christmas Developments—At St. Cross—The Latent Image—Mrs. Santa Claus—A Sea Change—The Lady of Shalott's Negatives—On a Film—Mascot—England through an American Lens—Without His Camera—A Scarecrow's Shadow—A Photographic Correspondence—The Solution—The Impossible She—A Midsummer Flash—Her Anchor to Windward—Out of Focus—Bright Shadows of Long Island—A Copyrighted Shadow—Historic Homes—Outlines from the Log of "The Happy"—Photographing Yesterday.

3064 KELLEY, EMMA DUNHAM. Megda . . . Boston: James H. Earle, 1891. 394 p., front. HEH, LC
Of religious interest.

3065 KELLEY, JAMES DOUGLAS JERROLD. A Desperate Chance . . . New York: Charles Scribner's Sons, 1886. 233 p. H, HEH, LC, O
Detective story.

3066 KELLOGG, MARGARET AUGUSTA. Leo Dayne: A Novel . . . Boston: James H. West Company, 1899. 508 p., illus. H, HEH, LC, UV
Social conditions of wage earners in New England.

3067 KELLY, FLORENCE (FINCH). Frances: A Story for Men and Women . . . New York: Sanfred & Company, 1889. 221 p. LC

3068 —— On the Inside . . . New York: Sanfred & Company, 1890. 238 p. LC
"Not recommended for sale. A Novel of New York Life." PW, Feb. 22, 1890.

3069 —— With Hoops of Steel . . . Indianapolis: The Bowen-Merrill Company [cop. 1900]. 342 p., illus. LC, O
Of three rugged ranchmen.

3070 [KELLY, MARY R.] Hannah Hawkins and Her Neighbor. [Groveland, N.Y.?]: Published for the author, 1879. 200 p. CU, LC

3071 KELLY, TEAGUE M. Mucca Scob; or, Threads of Pre-Historic and Present History Concatenated . . . Oakland, California: Published for the author, 1885. 144 p. HEH, LC

3072 KELSON, JOHN H. Seth's Work Is Done; or, The Phantom of the Belfry . . . Salt Lake City: Jos. Hyrum Parry, 1883. 80 p. H, LC
At head of title: "A New Year's Prize Story."

3073 KEMBLE, FRANCES ANNE. Far Away and Long Ago . . . New York: Henry Holt and Company, 1889. 260 p.
AP, BA, CU, H, HEH, LC, O, UC, UVB, Y
At head of title: "Leisure Hour Series—No. 225."

KENNEDY, WALKER. Between the Acts. *In* Short Story Masterpieces (1900), No. 4931.

3074 ——— In the Dwellings of Silence: A Romance of Russia . . . New York: Dodd, Mead & Company, 1893. 283 p. H, HEH, LC, O

3075 ——— Javan Ben Seir: A Story of Olden Israel . . . New York: Frederick A. Stokes Company [cop. 1898]. 291 p. LC

KENNEY, MINNIE E. *See* Paull, Minnie E. (Kenney)

3076 KENT, JAMES. The Johnson Manor: A Tale of Olden Time in New York . . . New York: G. P. Putnam's Sons, 1877. 304 p.
CU, HEH, LC, O, UVB, Y

3077 ——— Sibyl Spencer . . . New York: G. P. Putnam's Sons, 1878. 309 p. LC, O

3078 KENT, WINNIFRED. Sell Not Thyself: A Novel . . . Chicago: Laird & Lee [cop. 1893]. 207 p., illus. HEH, LC
Deposited Feb. 5, 1894.
Of a marriage which was a business proposition.

KENYON, ELLEN E. *See* Warner, Ellen E. (Kenyon)

3079 KEPLINGER, MRS. E. M. Bernice: A Novel . . . New Orleans: S. M. Haight, 1878. 405 p. LC, N
Ante bellum South.

KERCHEVAL, GEORGE TRUMAN, *pseud. See* Cowley, Mrs. Winifred Jennings

KERR, *pseud. See* Pinnix, Hannah Courtney (Baxter)

3080 KERR, ALVAH MILTON. Trean; or, The Mormon's Daughter. A Romantic Story of Life among the Latter-Day Saints . . . Chicago, New York, and San Francisco: Belford, Clarke & Company. London: H. J. Drane [cop. 1889]. 184 p. H, HEH

3081 KERR, ARTEMUS P. The Lost Tribes and the Land of Nod: An Original Natural Gas Story . . . Indianapolis: Press of the Indiana Newspaper Union, 1897. 73 p., illus. Printed in double columns. LC

3082 KESTER, PAUL. Tales of the Real Gypsy . . . New York: Doubleday and McClure Co., 1897. 312 p. BA, HEH, LC, O, UVB

*Contains:* A Rommany Guldo—The House of the Gorgio—Mrs. Cooper's Later Adventures—Mrs. Hearne's Chavies—A Tale of the Roads—My Lady of Egypt.

KETCHUM, ARTHUR. Founded on Fact. *In* [F. L. Knowles] *ed.*, Cap and Gown in Prose (1900), No. 3182.

———— *jt. au. See* Lehman, H. H., *ed.* Williams Sketches (1898), No. 3269.

KEYES, EDWARD L. The Maid of the Hills. *In* C. King, *ed.*, By Land and Sea (1891), No. 3092.
Later printed in No. 3099.

———— The Quartermaster's Story. *In* C. King, *ed.*, The Colonel's Christmas Dinner (1890), No. 3098.
Later printed in No. 3099.

3082a [KEYES, HERVEY.] The Forest King; or, The Wild Hunter of the Adaca. A Tale of the Seventeenth Century. New York: Wheat & Cornett, printers, 1878. 63 p.     HEH
Valley of the Mohawk, New York.

3083 KEYSER, HARRIETTE A. On the Borderland: A Novel . . . New York: G. P. Putnam's Sons, 1882. 249 p.     LC, Y
On sanity.

3084 ———— Thorns in Your Sides . . . New York, London: G. P. Putnam's Sons, 1884. 238 p.     AP, H, LC
Of the Irish in New York.

3085 KEYSER, LEANDER SYLVESTER. The Only Way Out . . . New York: Anson D. F. Randolph & Company, 38 West Twenty-Third Street [cop. 1888]. 325 p.     HEH, LC
Of religious interest.

3086 KILBY, L. CLAY. Vernon Lonsdale . . . Philadelphia: Published for the author by J. B. Lippincott & Co., 1876. 269 p.     HEH, LC, UV
Civil War; Virginia.

KILMER, GEORGE L. A Raid on the Wires. *In* Tales from McClure's: War (1898), No. 5364.

3087 [KIMBALL, ANNIE LYDIA (McPHAIL.)] At Daybreak: A Novel. By A. Stirling [pseud.]. Boston: James R. Osgood and Company, 1884. 316 p.     BU, H, HEH, LC, O, UC

KIMBALL, RUTH. A Mormon Convert. *In* J. J. Conway, *ed.*, Stories (1893), No. 1172.

3088 KING, ALBERT BARNES. Memorable Voyages of Rebel and Victory . . .
Boston: James H. Earle, 1895. 248 p., front. LC

KING, ANNA (EICHBERG). *See* Lane, Anna (Eichberg) King

3089 KING, BASIL. Griselda . . . Chicago: Herbert S. Stone and Company,
1900. 333 p., 1 l. CU, H, HEH, LC, Y
Author's full name: William Benjamin Basil King.

KING, CHARLES. The Adjutant's Story. *In* C. King, *ed.*, The Colonel's
Christmas Dinner (1890), No. 3098.
Later printed in No. 3099.

———— Alouette's Warning. *In* Short Story Masterpieces (1900), No.
4931.

3090 ———— An Army Wife . . . New York: F. Tennyson Neely, 1896.
278 p., illus. BA, H, HEH, LC, N, O, UC, UM, UVB, Y
For additional information about King's novels see Charles E. Dornbusch,
*Charles King, American Army Novelist: A Bibliography* . . . (Cornwallville,
N.Y., 1963).

3091 ———— Between the Lines: A Story of the War . . . New York: Harper & Brothers, 1889. 312 p., illus. AP, H, HEH, N, O, UC, UM, UV, Y

3092 ———— *ed.* By Land and Sea . . . Philadelphia: L. R. Hamersly & Co.,
1891. 198, [2] p. BU, H, HEH, O, UVB
*Contents:* The Warlock Fight, by Lieutenant John P. Wisser—Tamba (A
Story of the Sea), by Captain H. D. Smith—The Story of Wobberts, by
Captain Charles King—The Ruse of the Yankee Captain, by a Rear-Admiral
in the Navy—A Love-Chase, by Captain Edward Field—A Lady of Malta,
by Ensign F. R. Brainard—The Maid of the Hills, by Edward L. Keyes—Did
It Pay? by Captain Henry Romeyn—How Rufus Came to Go to Sea, by
Lieutenant F. S. Bassett—The Old "Academic" (A Story of West Point), by
Carolyn E. Huse.
Contents from "List of Contributors" at end.

3093 ———— Cadet Days: A Story of West Point . . . New York: Harper &
Brothers, 1894. 293 p., illus. BA, H, HEH, O, UC, UVB, Y

3094 ———— Campaigning with Crook, and Stories of Army Life . . . New
York: Harper & Brothers, 1890. 295 p., illus.
CU, H, HEH, N, O, UC, UM, Y
*Contains:* Captain Santa Claus—The Mystery of 'Mahbin Mill—Plodder's
Promotion.
"Campaigning with Crook" is a factual account, first published in 1880; the
other contents are fiction.

3095 ———— Captain Blake . . . Philadelphia: J. B. Lippincott Company,
1891. 495 p., illus. AP, BA, CU, H, HEH, LC, O, UC, UVB, Y

3096 ——— Captain Close, and Sergeant Croesus: Two Novels . . . Philadelphia: J. B. Lippincott Company, 1895. 245 p.

BU, CU, H, HEH, LC, UC, UVB

3097 ——— *ed.* Captain Dreams, and Other Stories . . . Philadelphia: J. B. Lippincott Company, 1895. 210 p.

BA, CU, H, HEH, LC, N, O, UC, UM, UVB, Y

*Also contains:* The Ebb-Tide, by Lieutenant A. H. Sydenham——White Lilies, by Alice King Hamilton—A Strange Wound, by Lieutenant W. H. Hamilton—The Story of Alcatraz, by Lieutenant A. H. Sydenham—The Other Fellow, by R. Monckton-Dene—Buttons, by Captain J. G. Leefe.

3098 ——— *ed.* The Colonel's Christmas Dinner . . . Philadelphia: L. R. Hamersly & Co., 1890. 182, [2] p.      AP, H, HEH, N, O, Y

*Contents:* Introduction, by Capt. Chas. King—The Adjutant's Story, by Capt. C. King—The Senior Lieutenant's Story, by Lieut. Thos. H. Wilson—The Senior Captain's Story, by Capt. Edward Field—The Captain's Story, by Capt. Henry Romeyn—The Colonel's Daughter's Story, by Caroline F. Little—A Major's Story, by Capt. W. C. Bartlett—The Quartermaster's Story, by Edward L. Key[e]s—The Major's Story, by Major Wm. H. Powell—A Guest's Story, by Alice King Livingston—The Colonel's Story, by Col. H. W. Closson. Contents from "List of Contributors" at end.

3099 ——— *ed.* The Colonel's Christmas Dinner, and Other Stories . . . Philadelphia: J. B. Lippincott Company, 1892. 182 p., 1 l., 5-198 p.

BU, CU, LC, UC

A reissue of Nos. 3092 and 3098.

3100 ——— The Colonel's Daughter; or, Winning His Spurs . . . Philadelphia: J. B. Lippincott & Co., 1883. 440 p.      AP, H, HEH, LC, O, UVB, Y

3101 ——— The Deserter, and From the Ranks: Two Novels . . . Philadelphia: J. B. Lippincott Company, 1888. 324 p.      AP, BA, HEH, UC, Y

3102 ——— Foes in Ambush . . . Philadelphia: J. B. Lippincott Company, 1893. 263 p.      BA, BU, CU, H, HEH, LC, O, UC, UVB, Y

3103 ——— A Garrison Tangle . . . New York: F. Tennyson Neely, 1896. 280 p.      BA, BU, H, HEH, LC, N, O, UC, UM, UVB, Y

3104 ——— The General's Double: A Story of the Army of the Potomac . . . Philadelphia: J. B. Lippincott Company, 1898. 466 p., illus.

BA, H, HEH, LC, N, O, UC, Y

——— The Guidon of the Grays. *In* Short Story Masterpieces (1900), No. 4931.

3105 ——— *ed.* An Initial Experience, and Other Stories . . . Philadelphia: J. B. Lippincott Company, 1894. 254 p. AP, H, HEH, O, UC, UM, UVB, Y

*Also contains:* In the "Never Never Country," by R. Monckton-Dene—The Siren of Three-Mile Bend, by R. Monckton-Dene—The Lost Pine Mine, by

Alvin Sydenham—Private Jones of the Eighth, by R. Monckton-Dene—Jack Hilton's Love-Affair, by T. H. Farnham—Wauna, the Witch-Maiden, by A. Sydenham—Conyngham Foxe and the Charity Ball, by A. Sydenham—The Soldier's Aid Society, by Caroline Frances Little—A Pitiful Surrender, by John P. Wisser—The Story of a Recruit, by D. Robinson—Chronicles of Carter Barracks, by H. W. Closson.

———— Introduction. *In* C. King, *ed.*, The Colonel's Christmas Dinner (1890), No. 3098.
Later printed in No. 3099.

3106 ———— Kitty's Conquest . . . Philadelphia: J. B. Lippincott & Co., 1884.
302 p.                                                                      AP, H, LC, N, O

3107 ———— "Laramie"; or, The Queen of Bedlam. A Story of the Sioux War of 1876 . . . Philadelphia: J. B. Lippincott Company, 1889. 277 p.
AP, BA, H, HEH, LC, N, O, UC, UVB, Y
2nd issue omits "A Story of Frontier Army Life" from caption on p. 5. Census of copies does not distinguish between issues.

3108 ———— Marion's Faith: A Sequel to The Colonel's Daughter . . . Philadelphia: J. B. Lippincott Company, 1886. 446 p.
AP, BU, H, HEH, O, UM, UP, UVB, Y

3109 ———— Rancho del Muerto . . . and Other Stories from Outing . . . New York and London: The Outing Publishing Company [cop. 1895]. 190, 185 p., illus.                                                          HEH, Y
*Also contains:* PART I: A Mighty Hunter before the Lord, by Virginius Dabney—A Cohutta Valley Shooting Match, by Will N. Harben—Moeran's Moose, by Ed. W. Sandys—The Mystery of a Christmas Hunt, by Talbot Torrance—Herne the Hunter, by William Perry Brown—Uncle Duke's "B'ar" Story, by Lillian Gilfillan—A Cigarette from Carcinto, by Edward French. PART II: Antaeus, by Frank M. Bicknell—Which Miss Charteris? by C. G. Rodgers—Bear's-Head Brooch, by Ernest Ingersoll—Miss Gwynne's Burglar, by Violet E. Mitchell—The Lady in Rouge, by W. E. P. French—The Breaking of Winter, by Patience Stapleton—Cynthy's Joe, by Clara Sprague Ross.
Part I first published in the omitted "Outing Library," Vol. I, No. 3, Dec. 1894.

3110 ———— Ray's Recruit . . . Philadelphia: J. B. Lippincott Company, 1898. 249 p., illus.                                                  BA, H, HEH, LC, N, O, Y

———— The Sheridan Romance. *In* Short Story Masterpieces (1900), No. 4931.

3111 ———— A Soldier's Secret: A Story of the Sioux War of 1890; and An Army Portia. Two Novels . . . Philadelphia: J. B. Lippincott Company, 1893. 293 p.                                                         BU, H, HEH, O, UC, UVB

3112 ———— Starlight Ranch, and Other Stories of Army Life on the Frontier . . . Philadelphia: J. B. Lippincott Company, 1890. 260 p.
AP, BA, BU, CU, H, HEH, N, O, UC, UM, UP, UVB, Y

*Also contains:* Well Won; or, From the Plains to "The Point"—From "The Point" to the Plains—The Worst Man in the Troop—Van.

3113  ———  The Story of Fort Frayne . . . Chicago, New York: F. Tennyson Neely [cop. 1895]. 310 p., front.  AP, H, HEH, LC, N, UC, UVB, Y
Later published as *Fort Frayne* but not until after 1900 in the U.S.

———  The Story of Wobberts. *In* C. King, *ed.*, By Land and Sea (1891), No. 3092.
Later printed in No. 3099.

3114  ———  Sunset Pass; or, Running the Gauntlet through Apache Land . . . New York: John W. Lovell Company, 150 Worth St., cor. Mission Place [cop. 1890]. 202, [1] p., illus.  AP, BA, H, HEH, UC, UVB
At head of title: "American Authors' Series, No. 11."

3115  ———  A Tame Surrender: A Story of the Chicago Strike . . . Philadelphia: J. B. Lippincott Company, 1896. 277 p., illus.
BA, H, HEH, LC, N, O, UC, UVB, Y

3116  ———  A Trooper Galahad . . . Philadelphia: J. B. Lippincott Company, 1899. 257 p., front.  BA, BU, CU, HEH, LC, N, O, UC, UVB, Y

3117  ———  Trooper Ross and Signal Butte . . . Philadelphia: J. B. Lippincott Company, 1896. 297 p., illus.  H, HEH, LC, N, O, UC, UM, UVB, Y

3118  ———  Trumpeter Fred: A Story of the Plains . . . New York, Chicago: F. Tennyson Neely, 1896. 201 p., illus.
BA, H, HEH, LC, N, O, UC, UM, UP, UVB, Y

3119  ———  Two Soldiers, and Dunraven Ranch: Two Novels . . . Philadelphia: J. B. Lippincott Co., 1891. 263 p.  BU, UC

3120  ———  Under Fire . . . Philadelphia: J. B. Lippincott Company, 1895. 511 p., illus.  AP, BA, CU, H, HEH, O, UC, UM, UVB, Y

3121  ———  A War-Time Wooing: A Story . . . New York: Harper & Brothers, 1888. 195 p., illus.  AP, CU, H, HEH, LC, N, O, UC, UM, UVB, Y

3122  ———  Waring's Peril . . . Philadelphia: J. B. Lippincott Company, 1894. 230 p.  AP, BA, BU, CU, H, HEH, N, O, UC, UVB

———  A West Point Parallel. *In* E. von Wildenbrüch, Noble Blood (1896), No. 5968.

3123  KING, EDWARD SMITH. The Gentle Savage . . . Boston: James R. Osgood and Company, 1883. 444 p.  AP, BA, CU, H, HEH, LC, O, Y

3124  ———  The Golden Spike: Fantasie in Prose . . . Boston: Ticknor and Company, 1886. 407 p.  AP, BA, CU, H, HEH, LC, O, Y
Completion of the Northern Pacific Railway.

3125 ———— Joseph Zalmonah: A Novel . . . Boston: Lee and Shepard, 1893. 365 p.    HEH, LC
Slums of New York.

3126 KING, ELISHA STERLING. The Wild Rose of Cherokee; or, Nancy Ward, "The Pocahontas of the West." A Story of the Early Exploration, Occupancy, and Settlement of the State of Tennessee. A Romance, Founded on and Interwoven with History . . . Nashville: University Press, 1895. 119 p.    LC

3127 KING, MRS. FRANKIE FALING. Mark Maynard's Wife . . . Philadelphia: T. B. Peterson & Brothers, 306 Chestnut Street [cop. 1885]. 294 p.   LC
Chicago.

KING, GEORGIANA GODDARD. In the Afternoon Car. *In* [F. L. Knowles] *ed.*, Cap and Gown in Prose (1900), No. 3182.

3128 KING, GRACE ELIZABETH. Balcony Stories . . . New York: The Century Co., 1893. 245 p., illus.   BA, CU, H, HEH, LC, N, O, UM, UP, UVB, Y
*Contents:* The Balcony—A Drama of Three—La Grande Demoiselle—Mimi's Marriage—The Miracle Chapel—The Story of a Day—Anne Marie and Jeanne Marie—A Crippled Hope—"One of Us"—The Little Convent Girl—Grandmother's Grandmother—The Old Lady's Restoration—A Delicate Affair—Pupasse.

3129 ———— Monsieur Motte . . . New York: A. C. Armstrong and Son, 1888. 327 p.   AP, BA, CU, H, HEH, LC, O, UC, UM, UP, UVB, Y
*Also contains:* The Drama of an Evening—Marriage of Marie Modeste.

3130 ———— Tales of a Time and Place . . . New York: Harper & Brothers, 1892. 303 p.   CU, H, HEH, LC, O, UM, UP, UVB, Y
*Contents:* Bayou l'Ombre—Bonne Maman—Madrilène; or, The Festival of the Dead—The Christmas Story of a Little Church.

3131 KING, PAULINE. Alida Craig . . . New York: George H. Richmond & Co., 1896. 289 p., illus.   BA, HEH, LC, O
An art studio; New York.

KING, THOROLD, *pseud.* *See* Gatchell, Charles

KING, TOLER, *pseud.* *See* Fox, Mrs. Emily

KING, WILLIAM BENJAMIN BASIL. *See* King, Basil

3132 KING, WILLIAM HARVEY. My Smoking-Room Companions . . . New York: Thomas Whittaker, 2 and 3 Bible House [cop. 1899]. 221 p., illus.   BU, CU, HEH, LC
Of an ocean voyage.

3133 KINGSBURY, ELIZABETH. Tale of an Amateur Adventuress: The Autobiography of Esther Gray. Abridged and Edited by Elizabeth Kingsbury. Cincinnati, Ohio: The Editor Publishing Co., 1898. 199 p.   LC

3134 KINGSBURY, J. W.  Mountain Rambles . . .  New York: W. B. Smith & Co., [cop. 1881].  135 p.  LC
Deposited May 19, 1881.

3135 KINGSLEY, ADELAIDE DELIA (NICHOLS).  Heart or Purse: A Story of To-Day . . .  Chicago: S. P. Rounds, Jr., & Co., 1887.  322 p., illus.  LC

KINGSLEY, FLORENCE (MORSE).  At the End of His Rope.  *In* J. Hawthorne, One of Those Coincidences (1899), No. 2596.

3136 ———— The Cross Triumphant . . .  Philadelphia: Henry Altemus, 1899.  364 p.  BU, LC, O, Y

———— John Merrill's Experiment in Palmistry.  *In* J. Hawthorne, One of Those Coincidences (1899), No. 2596.

3137 ———— Paul, a Herald of the Cross . . .  Philadelphia: Henry Altemus, 1897.  450 p.  LC, O, Y

3138 ———— Prisoners of the Sea: A Romance of the Seventeenth Century . . .  Philadelphia: David McKay, 1897.  480 p.  H, HEH, LC

3139 ———— Stephen, a Soldier of the Cross . . .  Philadelphia: Henry Altemus, 1896.  369 p., front.  BU, HEH, LC, O, UV

3140 ———— Titus, a Comrade of the Cross . . .  Chicago: David C. Cook Publishing Company, 1895.  280 p., illus.  BU, HEH, LC, O, UM

KINGSTON, MAY, *pseud.*  *See* Lane, Sarah

3141 KINKEAD, ELEANOR TALBOT.  Florida Alexander, a Kentucky Girl . . .  Chicago: A. C. McClurg and Company, 1898.  276 p.  LC, UC

3142 ———— Young Greer of Kentucky: A Novel . . .  Chicago and New York: Rand, McNally & Company, 1895.  332 p.  LC

3143 KINKEAD, JAMES H.  Hoosier Odd Fellows: A Story of Indiana . . .  Cincinnati: J. H. Kinkead & Company, 1877.  96 p.  Printed in double columns.  LC

3144 ———— No Money: An Odd Fellows' Story . . .  Cincinnati: J. H. Kinkead & Co., 1876.  104 p.  Printed in double columns.  LC

3145 KINSELLA, FRANK.  The Degeneration of Dorothy: A Novel . . .  New York: G. W. Dillingham Co., 1899.  320 p.  HEH, LC, UP, Y
"A highly improbable story about the discovery of the transfusion of blood, full of details totally unsuitable for fiction."  PW, Dec. 16, 1899.

KIP, LEONARD.  "————mas Has Come."  *In* Stories by American Authors, IX (1885), No. 5275.

3146 ———— Hannibal's Man, and Other Tales: The Argus Christmas Stories . . . Albany: The Argus Company, printers, 1878. 371 p.

BA, HEH, LC, N, UM, Y

*Also contains:* In Three Heads—The Ghosts at Grantley—The Secret of Apollonius Septrio—Prior Polycarp's Portrait—St. Nicholas and the Gnome. For earlier printing of title story see Wright II, No. 1484.

3147 ———— Nestlenook: A Tale . . . New York: G. P. Putnam's Sons, 1880. 315 p. CU, HEH, LC, N

———— Through the Great Siege. *In* The First Book of the Authors Club (1893), No. 1868.

3148 ———— Under the Bells: A Romance . . . New York: G. P. Putnam's Sons, 1879. 307 p. AP, HEH, LC, Y

3149 KIP, WILLIAM FARGO. Would You Have Left Her? . . . New York & London: G. P. Putnam's Sons; the Knickerbocker Press, 1888. 295 p.

HEH, LC, O, Y

3150 KIPLING, RUDYARD. The Naulahka: A Story of West and East . . . New York and London: Macmillan and Co., 1892. 379 p.

AP, H, HEH, LC, UC, Y

Charles Wolcott Balestier, jt. au., an American.

3151 KIRBY, LOUIS PAUL. Agnes: A Story of the Streets. A Realistic Novel . . . Chicago: Laird & Lee, 1890. 218 p., illus.

Listed PW, May 31, 1890.

KIRK, ELEANOR, *pseud.* See Ames, Eleanor Maria (Easterbrook)

3152 [KIRK, ELLEN WARNER (OLNEY).] Better Times Stories . . . Boston: Ticknor and Company, 1889. 400 p. AP, H, HEH, LC

*Also contains:* One Too Many—The Tragedy at Dale Farm—The Story of a Silk Dress—A Bohemian—Miss Ruth—A Pair of Silk Stockings—Aux Sérieux —The Young Doctor—The Widow's Mite.

3153 ———— Ciphers . . . Boston and New York: Houghton, Mifflin and Company. The Riverside Press, Cambridge, 1891. 311 p.

AP, CU, H, HEH, LC, N, O, UM, Y

3154 [————] Clare and Bébé: A Novel . . . Philadelphia: J. B. Lippincott & Co., 1879. 302 p. H, HEH, LC

3155 [————] A Daughter of Eve . . . Boston: Ticknor and Company, 1889. 447 p. AP, CU, H, HEH, LC, N, UM

3156 [————] Fairy Gold: A Novel . . . Philadelphia: J. B. Lippincott & Co., 1883. 114 p., illus. Printed in double columns. H, HEH, LC, Y

3157 [———] His Heart's Desire: A Novel ... Philadelphia: J. B. Lippincott & Co., 1878. 417 p. H, O, UP

3158 [———] A Lesson in Love ... Boston: James R. Osgood and Company, 1881. 318 p. AP, BA, H, HEH, LC, O, UP
At head of title: "Round-Robin Series."

3159 ——— Love in Idleness: A Summer Story ... Philadelphia: J. B. Lippincott & Co., 1877. 131 p. Printed in double columns. LC

3160 ——— A Midsummer Madness ... Boston: James R. Osgood and
Company, 1884. 395 p. AP, H, HEH, LC, O, Y

3161 [———] Queen Money ... Boston: Ticknor and Company, 1888.
513 p. AP, BA, CU, H, HEH, LC, O, UC, UP, UVB

3162 ——— The Revolt of a Daughter ... Boston and New York: Houghton, Mifflin and Company. The Riverside Press, Cambridge, 1897.
338 p., 1 l. BA, H, HEH, LC, O, Y

3163 ——— A Revolutionary Love-Story, and The High Steeple of St.
Chrysostom's ... Chicago & New York: Herbert S. Stone & Company,
1898. 255 p. BA, H, HEH, LC, O, UC, UP, Y

3164 [———] Sons and Daughters ... Boston: Ticknor and Company,
1887. 473 p. AP, BA, CU, H, HEH, O, UVB

3165 ——— The Story of Lawrence Garthe ... Boston and New York:
Houghton, Mifflin and Company. The Riverside Press, Cambridge,
1894. 435 p. AP, CU, H, HEH, LC, N, O, UP, UVB, Y

3166 [———] The Story of Margaret Kent: A Novel. By Henry Hayes
[pseud.] ... Boston: Ticknor and Company, 1886. 444 p.
AP, H, HEH, LC, O, UM, Y

3167 ——— Through Winding Ways: A Novel ... Philadelphia: J. B. Lippincott & Co., 1880. 263 p. Printed in double columns. HEH, LC, O

3168 ——— Walford ... Boston and New York: Houghton, Mifflin and
Company. The Riverside Press, Cambridge, 1890. 432 p.
AP, BU, H, HEH, LC, N, UVB, Y

3169 KIRK, HYLAND CLARE. The Revolt of the Brutes: A Fantasy of the Chicago Fair ... New York: Charles T. Dillingham, 1893. 123 p., illus. LC

3170 ——— When Age Grows Young: A Romance ... New York: Charles
T. Dillingham, 718 & 720 Broadway [cop. 1888]. 281 p. AP, HEH, LC

3171 KIRKHAM, CHARLES J. Sally Cavanagh; or, The Untenanted Graves. A
Tale of Tipperary ... New York: Peter O'Shea, 1882. 265 p.
Listed PW, July 8, 1882.

3172 KIRKLAND, JOSEPH. The Captain of Company K . . . Chicago: Dibble Publishing Company, 1891. 351 p., illus.

CU, H, HEH, LC, N, O, UC, UM, UP, UVB, Y

At head of title: "'Detroit Free-Press' Competition, First-Prize Story." Civil War story.

3173 ———— The McVeys (An Episode) . . . Boston and New York: Houghton, Mifflin and Company. The Riverside Press, Cambridge, 1888. 468 p. BA, BU, CU, H, HEH, LC, N, O, UC, UM, UP, UVB, Y

Pioneer life in the West.

———— The Surgeon's Miracle. *In* Tales from McClure's: The West (1897), No. 5363.

3174 ———— Zury, the Meanest Man in Spring County: A Novel of Western Life . . . Boston and New York: Houghton, Mifflin and Company. The Riverside Press, Cambridge, 1887. 538 p., front.

AP, CU, H, HEH, LC, N, O, UC, UM, UP, UVB, Y

3175 KIRKMAN, MARSHALL MONROE. The Romance of Gilbert Holmes: An Historical Novel . . . Chicago, New York, London: The World Railway Publishing Company, 1900. 425 p., 1 l., illus.

BU, HEH, LC, N, O, UM, Y

3176 KIRWAN, THOMAS. In Fetters: The Man or the Priest? . . . Boston: De Wolfe, Fiske & Co., 1893. 272 p. HEH, LC

At head of title: "An Unconventional Novel."

3177 KISER, SAMUEL ELLSWORTH. Georgie . . . Boston: Small, Maynard & Company, 1900. 225 p., illus. HEH, LC, O, UM, Y

KITCHEL, EVA PAINE, *jt. au. See* Wood, F. H. Warp and Woof (1890), No. 6061.

3178 KNAPP, ADELINE. One Thousand Dollars a Day: Studies in Practical Economics . . . Boston, Mass.: The Arena Publishing Company, 1894. 132 p. CU, HEH, LC

*Also contains:* The Sick Man—The Discontented Machine—Getting Ahead —The Earth Slept.

3179 KNAPP, MARY CLAY. Whose Soul Have I Now? A Novel . . . Boston: Arena Publishing Company, 1896. 242 p. LC

KNIFE, PRUNING, *pseud. See* Allen, Henry Francis

KNIGHT, CHARLES D., *pseud. See* Gilbert, Mrs. R. L.

KNOBLAUCH, EDWARD GUSTAVUS. The Moody Man. *In* Stories from the Harvard Advocate (1896), No. 5277a.

3180 KNOWLES, ARCHIBALD CAMPBELL. Balsam Boughs: Being Adirondack and Other Stories . . . Philadelphia: Porter & Coates, 1893. 200 p., illus.

HEH, LC, O, UP

*Contents:* The Signor—Old Grumps—Little Tim's Christmas—Love Victorious—A Romance of Eden—The Lake of the Broken Heart—Her Mistake—Lost in the Indian Pass—A Mountain Ramble—A Jolly Good Time—A Mother's Love—I'm Going Home—The Guide's Story—Balsam Boughs.

3181 —————— Joscelyn Vernon: A Story of the Days of King Charles the First . . . Philadelphia: George W. Jacobs & Co., 1898. 140 p. LC, O, UP

3182 [KNOWLES, FREDERIC LAWRENCE] *ed.* Cap and Gown in Prose: Short Sketches Selected from Undergraduate Periodicals of Recent Years. Edited by R. L. Paget [pseud.] . . . Boston: L. C. Page & Company (Incorporated), 1900. 298 p. BU, H, HEH, N, Y

*Contains:* A Very Young Man, by K. E. H. [i.e., Karl Edwin Harriman]—In the Afternoon Car, by Georgiana Goddard King—The Complete Athlete, by Henry Seidel Canby—The Proprieties, by P. B. [i.e., Percy Holmes Boynton]—Old Man, by Leonard Robbins—An Alien, by Grace Margaret Gallaher—A Fortunate Foursome, by Henry Seidel Canby—Poor Little Reginald, by Percival Henry Truman—A Comedy, by Guy Wetmore Carryl—Founded on Fact, by Arthur Ketchum.

Of the more than 60 contributors to this collection, the above have been selected because they are recognized by standard biographical dictionaries or are included in this bibliography for other stories.

3183 [KNOWLES, JAMES O.] Rockton: A Story of Spring-Time Recreations. By Kel Snow, Esq. [pseud.]. Cincinnati: Cranston & Stowe. New York: Hunt & Eaton, 1891. 280 p. CU, HEH, LC

3184 KNOWLTON, J. A. Origin . . . Boston: The Eastern Publishing Company, 1900. 339 p., illus. HEH

Of the beginning of man.

3185 —————— Txleama: A Tale of Ancient Mexico . . . Boston: J. G. Cupples Company, 250 Boylston Street [cop. 1892]. 199 p. LC, N, Y

3186 KNOX, ADELINE (TRAFTON). Dorothy's Experience. By Adeline Trafton . . . Boston: Lee and Shepard. New York: Chas. T. Dillingham [cop. 1890]. 211 p. LC

Of religious interest.

3187 —————— His Inheritance . . . Boston: Lee and Shepard. New York: Charles T. Dillingham, 1878. 428 p. BA, CU, H, HEH, LC, O, UC, Y

An army post on the Arkansas before the Civil War.

KNOX, JOHN ARMOY, *jt. au. See* Sweet, A. E. On a Mexican Mustang (1883), No. 5337; *and* Sketches from "Texas Siftings" (1882), No. 5338.

3188 KOEHLER, GEORGE. Nick Putzel; or, Arthur Gurney's Ruin. A Narrative Showing . . . the Art of Political Wire Pulling and Especially Ex-

posing the Resistless Power of the Bar-Room and Beer-Saloon... Philadelphia; Springfield, Mass.; Chicago, Ill.; Cincinnati, O.; Atlanta, Ga.: Hubbard Bros. St. Louis, Mo.: N. D. Thompson & Co. Kansas City, Mo.: T. Prothero. San Francisco, Cal.: A. L. Bancroft & Co. [1881]. 308 p., illus.            HEH, LC, N, UC
Deposited Jan. 8, 1881.

3189 KOPPKE, GEORGENIA JOSEPHINE LUKE. Bows of White Ribbon: A Romance of the Spanish-American War... Chicago: Woman's Temperance Publishing Association [cop. 1899]. 265 p., illus.      LC, UM
Deposited Dec. 20, 1899.

KOSEY, JOE, *pseud. See* Edwards, Charles

3190 [KOUNS, NATHAN CHAPMAN.] Arius the Libyan: An Idyl of the Primitive Church. New York: D. Appleton and Company, 1884. 398 p.
           H, HEH, LC, O, UC, UP, UVB, Y

3191 ——— Dorcas, the Daughter of Faustina... New York: Fords, Howard, & Hulbert, 1884. 255 p., illus.      AP, CU, H, HEH, LC, O

3192 KOUNTZ, WILLIAM J. Billy Baxter's Letters... Harmarville, Pa.: Duquesne Distributing Co. [cop. 1899]. 90 p., 1 l., illus.
           BA, H, HEH, LC, UC, UM, UP
*Contents:* Out Hunting—One Night—In Society—In Love—In New York—Johnny Black's Girl.
*Also issued with imprint:* Harmarville, Pa.: Red Raven Corporation [cop. 1899].    HEH, UV

3193 [KRAUSÉ, LYDA FARRINGTON.] Fortune's Boats. By Barbara Yechton [pseud.]... Boston and New York: Houghton, Mifflin and Company. The Riverside Press, Cambridge, 1900. 357, [1] p.     H, HEH, LC, Y
Majority of her books were for girls.

KRINGLE, KARAN, *pseud. See* Booth, Emma (Scarr)

KRINGLE, KARL, *pseud. See* Buckner, J. P.

3194 [KROUT, CAROLINE VIRGINIA.] Knights in Fustian: A War Time Story of Indiana. By Caroline Brown [pseud.]... Boston and New York: Houghton, Mifflin and Company. The Riverside Press, Cambridge, 1900. 279, [1] p.     BU, CU, H, HEH, LC, O, UM, Y

3195 KUTCH, ARCHIE. Young Sleuthe's Victory; or, A Detective's Adventure... Chicago: Geo. W. Ogilvie, 230 Lake Street [cop. 1885]. 125 p., front.     LC

3196 KYLE, RUBY BERYL. Paul St. Paul, a Son of the People: A Novel... Buffalo: Charles Wells Moulton, 1895. 248 p.     LC

L., E. G. *See* Lindsey, E. G.

L., KATIE. *See* Lennan, Katie.

3197 LAMB, MARY ELIZABETH (JORDAN). The Mystery of Walderstein: A Story from the Life of Two Prussian Officers ... Chicago: Donohue, Henneberry & Co., cop. 1894. 194 p., front.    LC

LAMB-GRÉVY, *pseud. See* Mitchell, George Depui

3198 LAMBOURNE, ALFRED. Jo: A Christmas Tale of the Wasatch ... Chicago: Belford–Clarke Co., 1891. 73 p.    Y

3199 LANCASTER, ALBERT EDMUND. "All's Dross but Love": A Strange Record of Two Reincarnated Souls. Republished from the Christmas Number of the New York Morning Journal, December 16th, 1888 ... New York: John W. Lovell Company, 14 and 16 Vesey Street [cop. 1889]. 64 p.    AP, BA, HEH, LC, UC

———— *jt. au See* Vincent, F. The Lady of Cawnpore (1891), No. 5696.

3200 LANDIS, CHARLES KLINE. Carabajal, the Jew: A Legend of Monterey, Mexico ... Vineland, N.J., cop. 1894. 27 p. Printed in double columns.    LC, Y

3201 LANE, ANNA (EICHBERG) KING. Brown's Retreat, and Other Stories. By Anna Eichberg King ... Boston: Roberts Brothers, 1893. 303 p.
BA, CU, H, HEH, LC, O, UM, UVB
*Also contains:* Odelia Blynn–The Heart Story of Miss Jack–"Father"–The Story of Agee Sang Long–John Sterling's Courtship–The Professor of Dollingen–A Trifle of Information–Mr. Carmichael's Conversion–Jacinth–A Freak of Fate–Monsieur Pampalon's Repentance–A Legend of Old New York.

3202 ———— Kitwyk Stories ... New York: The Century Co., 1895. 319 p., illus.    BA, H, HEH, LC, O, Y
*Contents:* The Courting of Juffrouw van Loo–The Factions of Kitwyk–The Singular Cleverness of Toby van Loo–The Violoncello of Juffrouw Rozenboom–Juffrouw van Steen–The Wild Huntsmen of Kitwyk–The Blighting of Mynheer van Steen–The Burgomaster's Sofa–Josselin–A Tragedy of Kitwyk–A Romance of Kitwyk–The Story of Lesken.

3203 [LANE, MARY E. (BRADLEY).] Mizora: A Prophecy. A Mss. Found among the Private Papers of the Princess Vera Zarovitch [pseud.]. Being a True and Faithful Account of Her Journey to the Interior of the Earth ... New York: G. W. Dillingham, 1890. 312 p.    LC

3204 [LANE, SARAH.] Phoebe Skiddy's Theology. By May Kingston [pseud.]. Boston: Howard Gannett, 1883. 449 p.    HEH, LC

3205 [————] That Wonderful Cousin Sarah, and Her Receipts. By May Kingston [pseud.]. Boston: Howard Gannett, 1883. 116 p.    HEH

3206 LANGFORD, LAURA (CARTER) HOLLOWAY, *comp.* The Woman's Story as Told by Twenty American Women ... [compiled by] Laura C. Holloway ... New York: John B. Alden, 1889. 541 p., illus.

HEH, LC, O, UM, UV

*Contents:* Uncle Lot, by Harriet Beecher Stowe—Old Madame, by Harriet Prescott Spofford—Tirar y Soult, by Rebecca Harding Davis—Tom Foster's Wife, by Edna Dean Proctor—Fourth of July in Jonesville, by Marietta Holley—Dorothy, by Nora Perry—The Trial of Beryl, by Augusta Evans Wilson—"Nan," by Louise Chandler Moulton—A Memorable Murder, by Celia Thaxter—A Cup of Cold Water, by Sara J. Lippincott—An Evening's Adventure, by Abba Gould Woolson—Adam Floyd, by Mary J. Holmes— My Borrowing Neighbor, by Margaret E. Sangster—The Girls' Sketching Camp, by Olive Thorne Miller [i.e., Harriet M. Miller]—A Crisis, by Elizabeth W. Champney—Meg, by Julia C. R. Dorr—A Confederate Idyl, by Marion Harland [i.e., Mary V. H. Terhune]—Transcendental Wild Oats, by Louisa Mary Alcott—Dave's Wife, by Ella Wheeler Wilcox—The Deacon's Week, by Rose Terry Cooke.

3206a LANGHORNE, MAURICE. An-As-Tar-Ta; or, A Trip to Ould Nick's Land ... It Is Historical, Political, Allegorical, and Metaphorical ... Washington, D.C.: M. Langhorne, cop. 1879. Cover title, 82 p. HEH

3207 LANZA, CLARA (HAMMOND). Basil Morton's Transgression: A Novel ... New York: Press of the Minerva Publishing Company, 10 West 23d Street [cop. 1889]. 275 p. AP, HEH

3208 ———— Horace Everett: A Novel ... New York: G. W. Dillingham Co., 1897. 275 p. HEH, LC, UV

3209 ———— Mr. Perkins' Daughter ... New York: G. P. Putnam's Sons, 1881. 535 p., front. AP, CU, HEH, LC, O
Of "periodical amnesia."

3210 ———— A Righteous Apostate ... New York: G. P. Putnam's Sons, 1883. 423 p. HEH, LC, O
Santa Fe, New Mexico.

3211 ———— Scarabaeus: The Story of an African Beetle ... New York: Lovell, Coryell & Company, 43, 45, and 47 East Tenth Street [cop. 1892]. 283 p. HEH, LC, O
James Clarence Harvey, jt. au.

3212 ———— Tit for Tat: A Teutonic Adventure ... New York: G. P. Putnam's Sons, 1880. 190 p. HEH, LC, O

———— *jt. au.* See Hammond, W. A. Tales of Eccentric Life (1886), No. 2435.

3213 LARNED, AUGUSTA. Village Photographs ... New York: Henry Holt and Company, 1887. 474 p. BA, HEH, LC, O, UM, Y

3214 LARNED, WALTER CRANSTON. Arnaud's Master-Piece: A Romance of the Pyrenees ... New York: Charles Scribner's Sons, 1897. 213 p., 1 l.
H, HEH, LC, N, O, UC, Y

3215 ———— Rembrandt: A Romance of Holland ... New York: Charles Scribner's Sons, 1898. 400 p., illus. H, HEH, LC, N, O, UC, Y

3216 LA SELLE, E. P. A True Virginian ... Petersburg, Va.: Presses of Fenn & Owen, 1893. 196 p.
Information supplied by Florence Blakely of Duke University Library.

3217 [LA SELLE, EVELYN.] The Black Sheep. By Qui [pseud.] ... Raleigh, N.C.: Edwards & Broughton, 1895. 347 p. LC

3218 [LATHAM, HENRY JEPSON.] Among the Mormons: How an American and an Englishman Went to Salt Lake City and Married Seven Wives Apiece. Their Lively Experience ... By Ring Jepson [pseud.]. San Francisco: The San Francisco News Company, 1879. 115 p.
CU, H, HEH, LC, Y
Each divorced their seven at $10 per wife.

3219 [LATHROP, GEORGE PARSONS.] Afterglow. Boston: Roberts Brothers, 1877. 316 p. BA, CU, H, HEH, LC, O, UV, Y
At head of title: "No Name Series."
Americans in Dresden.

3220 ———— An Echo of Passion ... Boston, New York: Houghton, Mifflin and Company. The Riverside Press, Cambridge, 1882. 230 p.
AP, BA, CU, H, HEH, LC, N, O, UVB, Y
Summer resort near Boston.

———— Elsewhere. In The First Book of the Authors Club (1893), No. 1868.

3221 ———— Gold of Pleasure ... Philadelphia: J. B. Lippincott Company, 1892. 140 p., front. CU, N

3222 ———— In the Distance: A Novel ... Boston: James R. Osgood and Company, 1882. 374 p. AP, BA, BU, CU, H, HEH, LC, N, O, UVB, Y
New Hampshire.

3223 ———— Newport ... New York: Charles Scribner's Sons, 1884. 297 p.
AP, BA, BU, CU, H, HEH, LC, N, O, UC, UP, UVB, Y

3224 ———— Somebody Else ... Boston: Roberts Brothers, 1878. 342 p.
AP, BU, CU, H, HEH, LC, N, O, UP, UVB, Y
———— The Too Soon Dead. In W. F. Gill, ed., Papyrus Leaves (1880), No. 2168.

3225 ──────── True, and Other Stories... New York, London: Funk & Wagnalls, 1884. 270 p. AP, CU, H, HEH, Y
*Also contains:* Major Barrington's Marriage—"Bad Peppers"—Three Bridges —In Each Other's Shoes.

──────── Two Purse-Companions. *In* Stories by American Authors, III (1884), No. 5269.

3226 ──────── Two Sides of a Story ... New York: Brentano's, 1900. 238 p. HEH, O
*Also contains:* Oley Grow's Daughter—Captain Billy—Mrs. Winterrowd's Musicale—"Unfinished"—March and April—"Raising Cain"—In a Market-Wagon.
First published in the omitted Cassell's "Sunshine Series of Choice Fiction," Vol. I, No. 33, 1889. Deposited July 12, 1889.

3227 ──────── Would You Kill Him? A Novel ... New York: Harper & Brothers, 1890. 384 p. AP, BA, CU, HEH, LC, N, O

3228 [LATIMER, ELIZABETH (WORMELEY).] My Wife and My Wife's Sister. Boston: Roberts Brothers, 1881. 319 p. H, HEH, LC, O, UV
At head of title: "No Name Series."

3229 [────────] Princess Amélie: A Fragment of Autobiography. Boston: Roberts Brothers, 1883. 322 p. H, HEH, LC, O, UV
At head of title: "No Name Series."

3230 [────────] Salvage ... Boston: Roberts Brothers, 1880. 293 p. BU, CU, H, HEH, LC, O, UM, UV, Y
At head of title: "No Name Series."
Of divorce and marriage.

3231 [LAWRENCE, ELIZABETH.] A Heroic Sinner and the Pilgrim Spinster: A Romance. By Gorham Silva [pseud.]. Albany, N.Y.: The Granite Publishing Company, 1893. 256 p. LC
Of the Salvation Army.

3232 [────────] The Worm That Ceased to Turn. By Gorham Silva [pseud.] ... New York: J. S. Ogilvie Publishing Company, 57 Rose Street [cop. 1895]. 140 p. H

3233 LAWRENCE, FRED WALLACE. Transmission ... Cincinnati: The Editor Publishing Co., 1900. 304 p. LC, Y

3234 LAWSON, MINNIE. Money to Loan on All Collaterals: A Tale of the Times ... Detroit, Mich.: Excelsior Publishing Company [cop. 1895]. 160 p.
Information supplied by John Saeger of Oberlin College Library.

3235 LEACH, BAILEY KAY. Soulless Saints: A Strange Revelation . . . Chicago: American Publishing Company [cop. 1892]. 253 p., illus.  LC
Deposited Jan. 14, 1893.

3236 LEAHY, WILLIAM AUGUSTINE. The Incendiary: A Story of Mystery . . . Chicago and New York: Rand, McNally & Company, 1897. 412 p.
CU, HEH, UP, UV, Y

3237 LEAMON, MRS. SARAH CANNON. A Minister's Probation . . . Nashville, Tenn.: Barbee & Smith, 1899. 276 p.  LC

3238 ——— Taught by Experience . . . Cincinnati, Ohio: Press of Curts & Jennings [cop. 1900]. 106 p.  LC
On an Ohio farm.

LEARNED, WALTER. Old Jonesy. *In* Mavericks (1892), No. 3663.

3239 [LEAVITT, JOHN MCDOWELL.] Alicia: A Tale of the American Navy. By Alexis [pseud.]. New York: Bonnell, Silver and Company, 1898. 257 p.  LC

3240 [———] Americans in Rome; or, Paul Errington and His Struggles. A Novel. By Ray Aster [pseud.]. New York: James R. Barnett & Company, 1886. 308 p.  HEH, LC

3241 ——— Kings of Capital and Knights of Labor, for the People . . . New York, Cincinnati, St. Louis: John S. Willey Publishing Co. [cop. 1885]. 613 p., illus.  CU, HEH, UC, UM, Y
" . . . only Fiction can reach certain monstrous evils in our American Society." Preface.

3242 ——— Paul Errington and Our Scarlet Prince: A Book for the American People . . . . New York, Chicago, Toronto: Fleming H. Revell Company [cop. 1894]. 286 p.  H, LC

3243 LE CATO, NATHANIEL JAMES WALTER. Tom Burton; or, The Days of '61 . . . Chicago, New York, and San Francisco: Belford, Clarke & Company [cop. 1888]. 235 p.  HEH, LC

LECKY, WALTER, *pseud. See* McDermott, William A.

3244 LE CONTE, CAROLINE EATON. The Statue in the Air . . . New York: The Macmillan Company. London: Macmillan & Co., Ltd., 1897. 120 p.
LC, UC

3245 LEDOUX, ALBERT REID. Princess Anne: A Story of the Dismal Swamp. And Other Sketches . . . New York: The Looker-On Publishing Co., 1896. 132 p., illus.  HEH, LC, UV, Y
*Also contains:* A Hackle in the Nesse—On a Bee-Line—An Anxious Moment.

LEDYARD, ERWIN, *jt. au. See* De Leon, T. C. John Holden, Unionist [cop. 1893], No. 1476.

3246 LEE, ADDIE McGRATH. Playing 'Possum, and Other Pine Wood Stories . . . Baton Rouge: Printed at the Truth Book and Job Office, 1895. 129 p.                                                                                      LC
*Also contains:* The Shiftless Simpsons—Uncle Dan's Divining Rod—Mr. Podsen's Letter—Mending Mandy.

3247 LEE, ALBERT, 1858-  The Gentleman Pensioner: A Romance of the Year 1569 . . . New York: D. Appleton and Company, 1900.   351 p.
                                                                          CU, H, HEH, LC, O, Y
At head of title: "Appleton's Town and Country Library, No. 279."

3248 ———— The Key of the Holy House: A Romance of Old Antwerp . . . New York: D. Appleton and Company, 1899.   315 p.
                                                                          HEH, LC, O, UP, UV

3249 ———— King Stork of the Netherlands: A Romance of the Early Days of the Dutch Republic . . . New York: D. Appleton and Company, 1900.   315 p.                                                          HEH, LC, O, Y

3250 LEE, ALBERT, 1868-1946. Four for a Fortune: A Tale . . . New York and London: Harper & Brothers, 1898.   268, [1] p., illus.
                                                                          H, HEH, LC, N, O, Y
Of a treasure hunt in Newfoundland.

3251 ———— He, She, & They: Being a Faithful Record of the Woful Enjoyments and Joyful Woes of Him & Her . . . New York and London: Harper & Brothers, 1899.   140, [1] p., illus.          CU, H, HEH, LC
A married couple's conversations about their social position.

LEE, BARTON, *pseud. See* Lewis, William H.

LEE, FRANKLYN WARNER. The Ghost at White Bear. *In* Short Stories from Outing [cop. 1895], No. 4930.

3252 ———— A Shred of Lace . . . St. Paul, Minn.: The Price-McGill Publishing Co., 1891.   317 p.                                          LC

———— Studies in the Occult. *In* J. J. Conway, *ed.*, Stories (1893), No. 1172.

3253 LEE, GEORGE HYDE. Kith and Kin . . . Washington: The Neale Company, 1900.   174 p.                                          HEH, LC
Official life; Washington, D.C., and New York.

3254 ———— What Was His Duty? . . . Washington: The Neale Company, 1900.   221 p.                                          HEH, LC

3255 LEE, J. F. Octavia the Octoroon . . . New York: The Abbey Press, 114 Fifth Avenue. London, Montreal [cop. 1900]. 115 p. HEH, LC, UM Civil War period; Alabama.

3256 LEE, MARGARET. Divorce; or, Faithful and Unfaithful . . . New York: Frank F. Lovell & Company, 142 and 144 Worth Street [cop. 1889]. 411 p. AP, H
First published in the omitted "Lovell's Library," No. 25, 1883.

3257 ——— Lorimer and Wife: A Novel . . . New York: George W. Harlan, 1881. 295 p. HEH, LC

3258 ——— The Story of a Story . . . New York: Ward & Drummond, 1884. 319 p. CU, LC

3259 LEE, MARY CATHERINE (JENKINS). In the Cheering-Up Business . . . Boston and New York: Houghton, Mifflin and Company. The Riverside Press, Cambridge, 1891. 322 p. HEH, LC, N, O, UM, Y

3260 ——— An Island Plant: A Nantucket Story . . . Nantucket [Mass.]: Goldenrod Literary and Debating Society, 1896. 82 p., illus.
H, HEH, LC, Y

3261 ——— A Quaker Girl of Nantucket . . . Boston and New York: Houghton, Mifflin and Company. The Riverside Press, Cambridge, 1889. 320 p. BA, HEH, LC, O, UM, Y

3262 ——— A Soulless Singer . . . Boston and New York: Houghton, Mifflin and Company. The Riverside Press, Cambridge, 1895. 272 p.
BA, H, HEH, LC, O

3263 LEE, MARY HOLLAND. Margaret Salisbury . . . Boston: Arena Publishing Company, 1894. 349 p. HEH
Of psychic powers and hypnotism.

LEE, MINNIE MARY, pseud. See Wood, Julia Amanda (Sargent)

LEEFE, JOHN G. Buttons. In C. King, ed., Captain Dreams (1895), No. 3097.

LEFEVRE, EDWIN. On the Brink. In Stories from the Chap-Book (1896), No. 5277.

——— The Unsullied Brow of the Viceroy. In New Stories from the Chap-Book (1898), No. 3949.

3264 LEFFINGWELL, ALSOP. The Mystery of Bar Harbor: A Melo-Dramatic Romance of France and Mt. Desert . . . New York: G. W. Dillingham. London: S. Low, Son & Co., 1887. 207 p. CU, HEH

3265 LEFFINGWELL, WILLIAM BRUCE. Manulito; or, A Strange Friendship . . .
Philadelphia: J. B. Lippincott Company, 1892. 320 p.     HEH, LC, O

3266 LEGATE, ROSA BOTTOMS. Magnolia Blooms . . . Evansville, Ind.: The
Keller Printing Co., 1896. 262 p.     LC
Kentucky.

3267 LEGGETT, F. W. Ethel's Perplexity . . . New York: W. B. Smith & Co.,
27 Bond Street [cop. 1881]. 93 p.     LC
A New York lawyer's office.

3268 LEGGETT, MORTIMER DORMER. A Dream of a Modest Prophet . . . Philadelphia: J. B. Lippincott Co., 1890. 207 p.     CU, HEH, O
Of a visit to Mars.

3269 LEHMAN, HERBERT HENRY, ed. Williams Sketches. By Arthur Ketch-
um, Percival H. Truman, Henry R. Conger. Edited by Herbert H.
Lehman, Isaac H. Vrooman, Jr. First Edition. Williamstown, Mass.,
1898. 327 p.     HEH, LC, Y
Verso of title page: "Albany, N.Y.: James B. Lyon, Printer."
Contains twelve unsigned stories.

LEHMOS, pseud. See Holmes, Thomas J.

3270 LEIGH, LEOTI. Nonie . . . [Cincinnati: The Editor Publishing Company,
cop. 1899.] 306 p., illus.     LC
Deposited June 10, 1899.
Post Civil War South.

3271 LEIGH, ROSE ANNA. Marguerite; or, A Wild Flower . . . Dallas, Texas:
The Showalter-Lincoln Co., cop. 1893. 56 p.     LC
Deposited Mar. 4, 1895.

LEIGH, Major WALTER, pseud. See Jenkins, Walter L.

3272 [LEISHER, J. J.] The Decline and Fall of Samuel Sawbones, M.D., on the
Klondike. By His Next Best Friend. New York, Chicago, London:
The Neely Company [cop. 1900]. 197 p., illus.     H, LC
Deposited Dec. 15, 1900.
Y has copy with places of publication Chicago, New York.

LE JEMLYS, pseud. See Jelley, Symmes M.

LELAND, ANTHONY. The Saving of Jim Moseby. In New Stories from
the Chap-Book (1898), No. 3949.

———— "When the King Comes In." A Woman's Life. [Two stories.] In Stories from the Chap-Book (1896), No. 5277.

3273 LELAND, SAMUEL PHELPS. Peculiar People ... Cleveland, Ohio: Aust & Clark, 1891. 152 p. LC

3274 LEMARS, CLAYTON. The Confessions of an American Citizen ... Chicago: The Schulte Publishing Company, 323-325 Dearborn Street [cop. 1898]. 194 p. LC, UC, Y
Of an unscrupulous politician.

3275 LEMON, JOEL BUNYAN. Elijah the Prophet: A Dream of the Christ ... New York, Chicago, Toronto: Fleming H. Revell Company [cop. 1899]. 282 p. HEH, LC

3276 [LENNAN, KATIE.] Elmwood; or, The Withered Arm. By Katie L. Baltimore: Kelly, Piet & Co., 1876. 233 p. LC

LENORE, *pseud. See* Rowland, K. Alice

LEON, MITA, *pseud. See* Rivenback, Mrs. Robert W.

3277 LEONARD, MARY HALL. A Code of Honor ... Cincinnati, Ohio: The Editor Publishing Company, 1897. 116 p. BA
A college story.

3278 ——— A Discovered Country ... Cincinnati: The Editor Publishing Co., 1900. 167 p. LC

3279 LEONHART, RUDOLPH. Atonement; or, Fallen and Risen ... Canton, Ohio: Roller Printing Co., 1895. 266 p., front. HEH, LC

3280 ——— The Children of the Outlaw: A Story of the Middle Ages ... Pittsburgh: Stevenson, Foster & Co., 1879. 408 p., illus. HEH, LC

3281 ——— Either, or ... Canton, Ohio: Roller Printing Co., printers, 1893. 408 p., front. HEH, LC, Y
Socialistic novel.

3282 ——— The Treasure of Montezuma ... Canton, Ohio: Cassidy, book and job printer, 1888. 279 p., illus. HEH, Y

3283 ——— The Wild Rose of the Beaver, and Tononqua, the Pride of the Wyandots: Two Border Tales of the 18th Century ... Akron, Ohio: Printed and bound by Werner & Lohmann [cop. 1886]. 373 p. LC, Y
For earlier printing of title story see Wright II, No. 1537a.

3284 LE ROW, CAROLINE BIGELOW. A Fortunate Failure ... Boston: D. Lothrop and Company, 32 Franklin Street [cop. 1882]. 280 p., illus. BU, HEH, LC
Of a New Hampshire farm girl.

LEROY, *pseud. See* Stoner, Leroy

3285 LESESNE, MARY RICHARDSON. Torpedoes; or, Dynamite in Society. A Story Founded on Fact ... Galveston, Texas: Press of Shaw & Blaylock, 1883. 351 p.     Y
Powell, No. 320, locates two additional copies.

3286 [LESLEY, J. PETER.] Paul Dreifuss, His Holiday Abroad. By John W. Allen [pseud.]. Boston: George H. Ellis, 1882. 266 p.     H, O

LESLIE, MADELINE, *pseud.* *See* Baker, Harriette Newell (Woods)

3287 LESTER, CHARLES. A Dangerous Mission: A Story of the Philippines ... Cincinnati: The Editor Publishing Co., 1900. 196 p.     LC

3288 LEWIS, ALFRED HENRY. Sandburrs ... New York: Frederick A. Stokes Company [cop. 1900]. 318 p., illus.     CU, HEH, N, O, UC, UP, Y
Fifty-one stories of the East Side of New York.

3289 ———— Wolfville ... New York: Frederick A. Stokes Company [cop. 1897]. 337 p., illus.     BU, CU, H, HEH, O, UC, UV, Y
Of the range, cowboys, and gunmen; Arizona.

3290 [LEWIS, CHARLES BERTRAND.] Brother Gardner's Lime-Kiln Club: Being the Regular Proceedings of the Regular Club for the Last Three Years ... By M. Quad [pseud.] and Brother Gardner ... Chicago: Belford, Clarke & Co., 1882. 300 p., illus.     BU, CU, H, HEH, N, O, UC, UV, Y

[————] Going Somewhere, by M. Quad [pseud.]. *In* [W. F. Gill] *ed.*, Golden Treasures (1876), No. 2166.

3291 ———— Mr. and Mrs. Bowser and Their Varied Experiences ... New York: J. S. Ogilvie Publishing Company, 57 Rose Street [cop. 1899]. 1 p. l., [13]-131 p.     H

3292 ———— ———— New York: J. S. Ogilvie Publishing Company, 57 Rose Street [cop. 1899]. 2 p.l., [vii]-x, [13]-321 p.     LC, UM
It would appear that this is a reprint of Nos. 3291 and 3294 with an "Author's Preface," table of contents, and twelve new sketches added.

3293 ———— Sawed-off Sketches: Humorous and Pathetic ... New York: G. W. Carleton & Co. London: S. Low & Co., 1884. 324 p., illus.
    CU, O, UC, UM, UP

3294 [————] Trials and Troubles of the Bowser Family. By M. Quad [pseud.]. New York: J. S. Ogilvie Publishing Company, 57 Rose Street [cop. 1899]. 1 p.l., [137-254] p., illus.     H
It would appear that this was intended as part two of No. 3291.

3295 LEWIS, HARRIET NEWELL (O'BRIEN). Amber the Adopted ... New York: J. S. Ogilvie & Co., 1880. 392 p.     CU
All of her titles listed are posthumous eds. which were previously published in subscription series or periodicals.

3296 ———— The Bailiff's Scheme: A Novel . . . New York: Robert Bonner's Sons [cop. 1889]. 436 p., front.  HEH, LC
Deposited Dec. 21, 1889.

3297 ———— Her Double Life: A Novel . . . New York: Robert Bonner's Sons; the American News Company [cop. 1888]. 500 p., front.  HEH

3298 ———— Lady Kildare: A Novel . . . New York: Robert Bonner's Sons [cop. 1889]. 402 p., front.  HEH, Y

3299 ———— Neva's Three Lovers: A Novel . . . New York: Robert Bonner's Sons [cop. 1892]. 504 p., illus.  HEH

3300 ———— The Old Life's Shadows: A Novel . . . New York: Robert Bonner's Sons, 1890.
Listed PW, July 12, 1890.

3301 ———— Sundered Hearts . . . New York: Robert Bonner's Sons [1890]. 394 p., front.
Listed PW, Mar. 8, 1890.

3302 LEWIS, JULIUS A. A Prince of the Blood: A Novel . . . New York: [Trow Directory Printing and Bookbinding Company], 1898. 259 p.  HEH, LC
Of the search for descendants of Charles Edward, the Young Pretender.

3303 [LEWIS, MARTHA LEWIS (BECKWITH) EWELL.] Blue Ribbons . . . New Haven, Conn.: The Protective Publishing Company, 1882. 387 p.  LC

3304 ———— The Harvest of Years. By M. L. B. Ewell. New York: G. P. Putnam's Sons, 1880. 327 p.  BU, LC, Y

3305 ———— Lorette; or, The Work of an Honest Heart . . . New Haven, Conn.: J. H. Benham, 1876. 260 p.  LC

3306 LEWIS, MRS. MARTHA WILLIAMS. Twice Tried; or, Asa Warren's Metal . . . Philadelphia: The Silver-Line Publishing Co. [cop. 1899]. 161 p., front.  LC, O

3307 ———— The Wife's Vow . . . Philadelphia: W. S. Fortescue & Co., 819 Arch St. [cop. 1895]. 237 p., front.  LC, O
Deposited Apr. 13, 1896.

3308 LEWIS, WILLIAM ALBERT. The Greatest Crime in the World . . . [Baltimore: The American Job Printing Office, cop. 1895.] 156 p., front.  LC, Y
Deposited Mar. 5, 1895.

3309 [————] High Life in Washington: A Romance of Life. By a Public Man. Chicago: The Bow Knot Publishing Co., 1895. 314 p.
Information from LC card; no copy seen.

3310 [————] A Widow's Predicament: A Novelette. By One of Her Own Sex... Washington, D.C.: The writer [1891]. Cover title, 26 p.
Information from LC card; no copy seen.

3311 [LEWIS, WILLIAM H.] Thomas Hard, Priest. By Barton Lee [pseud.]. New York: Anson D. F. Randolph & Company, 38 West Twenty-Third Street [cop. 1889]. 64 p.     HEH, LC
Of a marriage between a High-Church Episcopalian and a Congregationalist.

3312 LIBBEY, LAURA JEAN. The Alphabet of Love: A Thrilling Romance ... New York: Norman L. Munro, 1892. 224 p.     LC

3313 ———— The Beautiful Coquette; or, The Love That Won Her. The Most Intense Love Story Ever Written ... New York: Norman L. Munro, 1892. 256 p.     HEH, LC

3314 ———— The Crime of Hallow-e'en; or, The Heiress of Graystone Hall. A Thrilling Love Story ... New York: Norman L. Munro, 1891. 216 p.
Information from LC card; no copy seen.

3315 ———— Daisy Gordon's Folly; or, The World Lost for Love's Sake ... New York: Norman L. Munro, 1892. 204 p.     LC

3316 ———— Dora Miller; or, A Young Girl's Love and Pride ... New York: Norman L. Munro, 1892. 218 p.     LC

3317 ———— The Flirtations of a Beauty; or, A Summer's Romance at Newport ... New York: Norman L. Munro, 1890. 234 p., illus.     LC, UVB

3318 ———— Florabell's Lover; or, Rival Belles. A Novel ... New York: Robert Bonner's Sons, 1892. 357 p., illus.     HEH

3319 ———— A Forbidden Marriage; or, Love with a Handsome Spendthrift. A Novel ... New York: The American News Company, 1888. 212 p., front.     LC

3320 ———— He Loved but Was Lured Away ... New York: The American News Company, 1891.
From advertisement in her *Olive's Courtship*.

3321 ———— Ione: A Broken Love Dream. A Novel ... New York: Robert Bonner's Sons, 1890. 256 p., illus.
Listed PW, July 12, 1890.
LC has copy in the omitted "Choice Series," No. 17.

3322 ———— Little Leafy, the Cloakmaker's Beautiful Daughter: A Romantic Story of a Lovely Working-Girl in the City of New York ... New York: Norman L. Munro, 1891. 237 p.     LC

3323 ——— Little Ruby's Rival Lovers; or, A Cruel Revenge . . . New York: Norman L. Munro, 1892. 192 p.
Information from LC card; no copy seen.

3324 ——— Lovers Once but Strangers Now; or, The Strange Romance of Miss Beatrice Reamer. A Novel . . . New York: The American News Co., 1890. 172 p.
Information from LC card; no copy seen.

3325 ——— Lyndall's Temptation; or, Blinded by Love. A Story of Fashionable Life at Lenox . . . New York: Norman L. Munro, 1892. 218 p.
LC

3326 ——— A Mad Betrothal; or, Nadine's Vow. A Novel . . . New York: Robert Bonner's Sons [cop. 1890]. 431 p., front.
HEH

3327 ——— A Master Workman's Oath; or, Coralie the Unfortunate. A Love Story Portraying the Life, Romance, and Strange Fate of a Beautiful New York Working-Girl . . . New York: Norman L. Munro, 1892. 223 p.
HEH

3328 ——— Miss Middleton's Lover; or, Parted on Their Bridal Tour. A Novel . . . New York: The American News Company, 1888. 212 p., front.
HEH, LC, Y

3329 ——— Olive's Courtship: A Novel . . . New York: The American News Company, 1892. 192 p.
HEH
At head of title: " 'Lovers Once, but Strangers Now.' . . ."
This may be No. 3324.

3330 ——— Only a Mechanic's Daughter: A Charming Love Story of Love and Passion . . . New York: Norman L. Munro, 1892. 192 p.
Information from LC card; no copy seen.

3331 ——— Parted by Fate; or, The Mystery of Black-Tor Lighthouse . . . New York: Robert Bonner's Sons, 1890. 283 p., illus.
Recorded PW, Sept. 27, 1890, p. 329.
LC has copy in the omitted "Popular Series."

3332 ——— Pretty Freda's Lovers; or, Married by Mistake. A Thrilling Romance of a Beautiful Young Schoolgirl . . . New York: Norman L. Munro, 1889. 233 p.
HEH

3333 ——— That Pretty Young Girl: A Novel . . . New York: The American News Company, 1889. 191 p.
HEH

3334 ——— We Parted at the Altar: A Novel . . . New York: Robert Bonner's Sons, 1892. 345 p., illus.
HEH

3335 ——— When Lovely Maiden Stoops to Folly; or, "When Lovely Woman Stoops to Folly." A Novel ... New York: The American News Company, cop. 1896. 192 p.
Information from LC card; no copy seen.

3336 ——— Willful Gaynell; or, The Little Beauty of the Passaic Cotton Mills. A Romantic Story of the Life and Love of a Lovely Working Girl ... New York: Norman L. Munro, 1890. 249 p., illus.     HEH

3337 LIBBY, HERBERT CARLYLE, *ed.* Colby Stories as Told by Colby Men of the Classes 1832 to 1902 ... Concord, N.H.: The Rumford Press, 1900. 238 p., illus.     BU, H, HEH, UM, Y
Stories unsigned; frontispiece made up of pictures of 15 of the contributors.

3337a THE LIFE OF ANSON BUNKER, "the Bloody Hand." The Perpetrator of No Less Than Fifteen Cold-Blooded Murders, Among Which Were the Great Nathan Murder of New York City, and Those of His Three Wives ... Philadelphia: Barclay & Co., 21 North Seventh Street [cop. 1886]. 95 p., illus.     HEH
At head of title: "A Great Number of Mysterious Murders Revealed."

3338 LIGHTNER, ADNA H. (CORNELL). Shadow and Sunshine ... Cincinnati, O.: Wrightson & Company, 1884. 187 p.     LC

3339 ——— A Wayside Violet ... Cincinnati, O.: Wrightson & Co., 1885. 125 p.     HEH

3340 LIGHTON, WILLIAM RHEEM. Sons of Strength: A Romance of the Kansas Border Wars ... New York: Doubleday & McClure Co., 1899. 242 p.     CU, HEH, LC, UC, Y

3341 LILLIE, LUCY CECIL (WHITE). Prudence: A Story of Aesthetic London ... New York: Harper & Brothers, 1882. 177 p., illus.     AP, BA, CU, HEH, LC, N, O, UC, Y
Majority of her books were for girls.

3342 ——— Roslyn's Trust: A Novel ... New York: A. L. Burt [cop. 1889]. 256 p.     LC, O
Deposited May 10, 1889.

LIN, FRANK, *pseud. See* Atherton, Gertrude Franklin (Horn)

3343 LINCOLN, JEANIE THOMAS (GOULD). Her Washington Season ... Boston: James R. Osgood and Company, 1884. 207 p.     BA, CU, H, HEH, LC, O, UV

3344 ——— A Pretty Tory: Being a Romance of Partisan Warfare during the War of Independence in the Provinces of Georgia and South Carolina, Relating to Mistress Geraldine Moncriffe ... Boston and New York: Houghton, Mifflin and Company. The Riverside Press, Cambridge, 1899. 268 p., 1 l., illus.     CU, HEH, LC, O

3345 ——— An Unwilling Maid: Being the History of Certain Episodes during the American Revolution in the Early Life of Mistress Betty Yorke, Born Wolcott . . . Boston and New York: Houghton, Mifflin and Company. The Riverside Press, Cambridge, 1897. 263, [1] p., illus.

BA, BU, CU, HEH, LC, O, UV

3346 LINCOLN, RIXFORD JOSEPH. Poems and Short Stories . . . New Orleans: Dalton Williams, 1900. 95 p., illus.                                HEH, Y

*Contains:* Grande Terre: A Story of the Sea—The Artist and His Picture—Wenonah: An Indian Tale—The Romance of an Old Man—Her First Ball—Blanche de-la-Vigne—The Missing Will—The Little Rag-Picker's Christmas—A Carnival Story.

3347 ——— A Tale of Pagan Rome: A Story . . . New Orleans: Philippe's Printery, 1900. 38 p.

Information supplied by Dorothy M. Black of University of Illinois Library.

3348 LINDSAY, BATTERMAN. Derelicts of Destiny . . . New York, Chicago, London: The Neely Company [cop. 1900]. 76 p.                    LC

*Contents:* Abandoned—My Great Aunt's Wedding—An Aboriginal Episode—Kwelth-Elite, the Proud Slave—The Vanishing City of Tamalpais—Squaw Charley.

Deposited Nov. 8, 1900.

3349 LINDSAY, J. T. French Exiles of Louisiana . . . New York: W. B. Smith & Co., Bond Street [cop. 1881]. 240 p., illus.                 H, HEH, LC, N

During the Napoleonic Wars.

3350 [LINDSEY, E. G.] Marie; or, Fort Beauharnois. An Historic Tale of Early Days in the Northwest. By E. G. L. . . . Minneapolis, Minn.: A. C. Bausman, printer and publisher, cop. 1893. 176 p., 1 l., iv p., illus.

LC, UM

3351 LINDSEY, WILLIAM. At Start and Finish . . . Boston: Small, Maynard & Company, 1899. 256 p.                                      CU, H, LC, UP

*Contents:* Old England and New England—My First for Money—The Hollow Hammer—His Name Is Mud—How Kitty Queered the "Mile"—Atherton's Last "Half"—The Charge of the Heavy Brigade—A Virginia Jumper—And Every One a Winner.

3352 ——— Cinder-Path Tales . . . Boston: Copeland and Day, 1896. 210 p., 1 l.                                      BA, BU, H, HEH, LC, N, UM, UVB, Y

*Contents:* My First for Money—The Hollow Hammer—How Kitty Queered the "Mile"—Paddy the Leaper's Probation—Atherton's Last "Half"—A Virginia Jumper—And Every One a Winner.

3353 LINTHICUM, RICHARD. A Book of Rocky Mountain Tales (Souvenir Edition) . . . [Denver, Colo.: W. F. Robinson & Co., printers, 1892.] 158 p., illus.                                      CU, HEH, UM, Y

*Contents:* Chased by a Creditor—Love Making of "Chihuahua" Brown—"Diablo"—A Picture of Spring—"Texas Joe"—The Round-Up—Maverick Bill

—A Great Sensation—The Case of "Lone Jack"—Wrecked by Amateurs—De Shudgment of der Court—Two Tenderfeet—I Cannot Sing the New Songs —An Artificial Clam—My First Assignment—Alma—A Study in Red.

LINTNER, GRACE, *pseud.* *See* Ingraham, Mrs. Ellen M.

LIPPINCOTT, SARA JANE (CLARKE). A Cup of Cold Water. *In* L. C. H. Langford, *comp.*, The Woman's Story (1889), No. 3206.

3354 [————] Stories and Sketches. By Grace Greenwood [pseud.] . . . New York: Tait, Sons & Company, Union Square [cop. 1892]. 219 p.

H, HEH, LC

*Contains:* Two Sermons on One Text—Two Saints Not in the Calendar— Running Away with a Balloon—How Malcolm Cam' Hame—A Night of Years.

3355 [————] Stories for Home-Folks, Young and Old. By Grace Greenwood [pseud.]. New York: John B. Alden, 1884. 185 p. LC

3356 LITCHFIELD, GRACE DENIO. Criss-Cross . . . New York & London: G. P. Putnam's Sons; the Knickerbocker Press, 1885. 256 p.

BA, BU, H, HEH, LC, O

3357 ———— A Hard-Won Victory . . . New York and London: G. P. Putnam's Sons; the Knickerbocker Press, 1888. 384 p. H, HEH, LC, O New York.

3358 ———— In the Crucible . . . New York, London: G. P. Putnam's Sons; the Knickerbocker Press, 1897. 344 p. H, HEH, LC Washington society.

3359 ———— The Knight of the Black Forest . . . New York & London: G. P. Putnam's Sons; the Knickerbocker Press, 1885. 169 p., illus.

BA, HEH, LC, O

Americans in Europe.

3360 ———— Little Venice, and Other Stories . . . New York and London: G. P. Putnam's Sons; the Knickerbocker Press, 1890. 298 p., front.

H, HEH, LC, O

*Also contains:* Selina's Singular Marriage—Myrtle—One Chapter—An American Flirtation—La Rochefoucauld's Saying—Hilary's Husband—The Price I Paid for a Set of Ruskin.

3361 ———— The Moving Finger Writes . . . New York and London: G. P. Putnam's Sons, 1900. 265 p. CU, H, HEH, LC, O, UV Of a poet.

3362 ———— Only an Incident . . . New York, London: G. P. Putnam's Sons, 1883. 226 p. CU, HEH, LC, O, Y New York state.

3363 LITSEY, EDWIN CARLILE. The Princess of Gramfalon . . . Cincinnati:
The Editor Publishing Co., 1898. 323 p.     LC

LITTLE, CAROLINE FRANCES. The Colonel's Daughter's Story. *In* C. King,
*ed.*, The Colonel's Christmas Dinner (1890), No. 3098.
Later printed in No. 3099.

———— The Soldier's Aid Society. *In* C. King, *ed.*, An Initial Experience (1894), No. 3105.

3364 LIVERMORE, MARY ASHTON (RICE). Thirty Years Too Late: A True
Story. And One in a Thousand . . . Boston: Lockwood, Brooks &
Co. [1878]. 96 p., illus.     H, LC
Listed PW, Jan. 12, 1878.

LIVINGSTON, ALICE KING. A Guest's Story. *In* C. King, *ed.*, The Colonel's Christmas Dinner (1890), No. 3098.
Later printed in No. 3099.

3365 LIVINGSTON, Mrs. C. M. Susan's Sheaves, and Other Stories . . . New
York: National Temperance Society, 1887. 364 p., front.     LC
*Also contains:* Mrs. Dale's Diamonds—Where He Found Her—Their Christmas Presents—Topknot—John Trent's Discoveries—That Cellar Door—Books
and Bread—Who Is to Blame?—Mrs. Raynor's New Nurse-Maid.

———— *jt. au. See* Alden, I. M. Aunt Hannah and Martha and John
[cop. 1890], No. 38; By Way of the Wilderness [cop. 1899], No. 39;
*and* John Remington, Martyr [cop. 1892], No. 40.

3366 LIVINGSTON, MARGARET VERE (FARRINGTON). Fra Lippo Lippi: A Romance. By Margaret Vere Farrington . . . New York, London: G. P.
Putnam's Sons; the Knickerbocker Press, 1890. 225 p., illus.
    CU, HEH, LC, UV, Y

LLOYD, DAVID D. Poor Ogla-Moga. *In* Stories by American Authors,
III (1884), No. 5269.

3367 LLOYD, FRANCIS BARTOW. Sketches of Country Life: Humor, Wisdom,
and Pathos from the "Sage of Rocky Creek" . . . Birmingham, Ala.:
Press of Roberts & Son, 1898. 300 p., illus.     HEH, UM, UV, Y

3368 LLOYD, JOHN URI. Etidorhpa; or, The End of Earth. The Strange
History of a Mysterious Being and the Account of a Remarkable Journey . . . Cincinnati: John Uri Lloyd, cop. 1895. 376 p., illus.
    CU, LC, N, O, UC, UVB, Y

3369 ———— The Right Side of the Car . . . Boston: Richard G. Badger &
Company, 1897. 59 p., 1 l., illus.     CU, H, HEH, LC, N, O, UC, UM, UVB, Y
On the Northern Pacific Railway.

3370 ———— Stringtown on the Pike: A Tale of Northernmost Kentucky . . . New York: Dodd, Mead and Company, 1900. 414 p., illus.

CU, H, HEH, LC, N, O, UM, UP, UVB, Y

3371 LLOYD, NELSON McALLISTER. The Chronic Loafer . . . New York: J. F. Taylor & Company, 1900. 254 p. BA, H, HEH, LC, N, O, UM
Stories told around the stove in a central Pennsylvania store.

3372 LOCKE, DAVID ROSS. The Demagogue: A Political Novel . . . Boston: Lee and Shepard. New York: Charles T. Dillingham, 1891. 465 p.

BU, CU, HEH, LC, N, O, UC, UM, UP, UVB, Y

3373 [————] The Democratic John Bunyan: Being Eleven Dreams. By Rev. Petroleum V. Nasby [pseud.] . . . Toledo, Ohio: Toledo Blade Company, 1880. 24 p., illus. LC, UM, UP, Y

3374 ———— The Diary of an Office Seeker: Being a Record of the Experience of Thomas Jefferson Watkins (Who Wanted an Office, and Labored for One, but Didn't Get It) . . . Edited by D. R. Locke . . . Toledo, Ohio: Blade Company, 1881. 31 p. LC

3375 ———— Nasby in Exile; or, Six Months of Travel . . . Toledo and Boston: Locke Publishing Company, 1882. 672 p., illus.

BA, BU, CU, H, HEH, LC, N, O, UC, UM, UP, UVB, Y

3376 ———— The Nasby Letters: Being the Original Nasby Letters as Written during His Lifetime . . . Toledo, Ohio: The Toledo Blade Co. [cop. 1893]. 510 p., front. CU, H, N, UM, UVB

3377 ———— A Paper City . . . Boston: Lee and Shepard. New York: Charles T. Dillingham, 1879. 431 p.

BA, CU, H, HEH, LC, N, O, UC, UM, UVB, Y

3378 LOCKWOOD, INGERSOLL. 1900; or, The Last President . . . New York: The American News Company, cop. 1896. 48 p. CU, H, LC, Y

———— Strange Adventures of a Million Dollars. In Eleven Possible Cases [cop. 1891], No. 1737.

3379 [LOCKWOOD, MELANCTHON CLARENCE.] The New Minister. By Kenneth Paul [pseud.]. New York: A. S. Barnes & Company [cop. 1893]. 342 p. HEH, Y

3380 [LOCKWOOD, WILLIAM LEWIS.] The Lord or the Doctor? A Story. By Lock Wood [pseud.]. [Brooklyn, N.Y., cop. 1892.] 200 p. LC

3381 LODGE, HARRIET (NEWELL). A Bit of Finesse: A Story of Fifty Years Ago . . . Indianapolis: The Bowen-Merrill Company, 1894. 104 p.

HEH, LC

[LODGE, MRS. JAMES.] The Voice. *In* [Mrs. J. Lodge] *ed.*, A Week away from Time (1887), No. 3382.

3382 [————] *ed.* A Week away from Time. Boston: Roberts Brothers, 1887. 349 p.   BA, BU, CU, HEH, LC, N, O, UC, Y
*Contains:* The Lawyer's Story [by Mrs. E. E. Pratt, attrib. au.]—The Palace of the Closed Window [by Owen Wister, attrib. au.]—The Voice [by Mrs. James Lodge]—In War-Time; or, Only a Woman's Shoe [by Julia Ward Howe, attrib. au.]—Happiness [by Mrs. Henry Whitman, attrib. au.].
The above attributions are from PW, Sept. 3, 1887, p. 252, except the one to Julia Ward Howe. The latter name is supplied from the HEH annotated copy.

3383 LOGAN, ALGERNON SYDNEY. Amy Warren: A Tale of the Bay Shore . . . New York: G. W. Dillingham Co., 1900. 370 p.   AP, HEH, LC, O, Y

3384 ————— Not on the Chart: A Novel of To-Day . . . New York: G. W. Dillingham Co., 1899. 277 p., illus.   HEH, LC, O, UV, Y

3385 LOGAN, BELLE V. Her Shattered Idol . . . Chicago: W. B. Conkey Company [cop. 1893]. 250 p., front.   HEH
First published in the omitted "Midland Series," Vol. I, No. 38, 1893.

3386 LONDON, JACK. The Son of the Wolf: Tales of the Far North . . . Boston and New York: Houghton, Mifflin and Company. The Riverside Press, Cambridge, 1900. 251, [1] p., front.   BA, CU, H, HEH, LC, N, O, UM, UP, UV, Y
*Contents:* The White Silence—The Son of the Wolf—The Men of Forty-Mile—In a Far Country—To the Man on Trail—The Priestly Prerogative—The Wisdom of the Trail—The Wife of a King—An Odyssey of the North.

3387 LONG, FRANK CARLETON. The Lady of the Lens: A Novel . . . Chicago: L. E. Crandall & Co., 1891. 287 p., illus.   LC

3388 LONG, JOHN LUTHER. The Fox-Woman . . . Philadelphia & London: J. B. Lippincott Company, 1900. 308 p., front.   BA, HEH, LC

3389 ————— Madame Butterfly. Purple Eyes. A Gentleman of Japan. Kito. Glory . . . New York: The Century Co., 1898. 224 p., front.   BA, HEH, LC, UP, UV, Y

3390 ————— Miss Cherry-Blossom of Tôkyô . . . Philadelphia: J. B. Lippincott Company, 1895. 364 p.   AP, LC

3391 LONG, LILY AUGUSTA. Apprentices to Destiny . . . New York: Merrill & Baker, 74 5th Ave. [cop. 1893]. 348 p.   HEH, LC, O, UC, UM

3392 ————— A Squire of Low Degree . . . New York: D. Appleton and Company, 1890. 316 p.   AP, HEH, UM

3393 LONGSTREET, RACHEL ABIGAIL (BUCHANAN). A Debutante in New York Society: Her Illusions and What Became of Them. By Rachel Buchanan. New York: D. Appleton and Company, 1888. 363 p.   H, LC, O

3394 LONGWORTH, NICHOLAS. The Marquis and the Moon: A Story . . . Cincinnati: Robert Clarke & Co., 1889. 39 p.    HEH, LC, O

3395 ——— Silas Jackson's Wrongs: A Romance of Anderson's Ferry . . . Cincinnati: Robert Clarke & Co., 1889. 123 p.    HEH
Civil War background.

LOOKER, O. N., *pseud.* See Urner, Nathan Dane

3396 LOOMIS, CHARLES BATTELL. The Four-Masted Cat-Boat, and Other Truthful Tales . . . New York: The Century Co., 1899. 241 p., illus.
   CU, H, HEH, LC, UM, Y
A collection of short stories and sketches.

3397 LOOTA, *pseud.* Montresor: An English-American Love Story, 1854-1894 . . . New York: F. Tennyson Neely, 1897. 238 p., front.  CU, H, HEH, Y

3398 LORD, MRS. MARY N. Mary Milton; or, The Conquests of Grace. A Brief Account of the Life . . . of a Humble Servant of Christ . . . Claremont, N.H.: Printed by the Claremont Manufacturing Company, 1876. 236 p.    BU, LC

3399 THE LOST DISPATCH. Galesburg, Ill.: Galesburg Printing and Publishing Company, 1889. 115 p.    CU, HEH, LC
Civil War novel.

3400 LOTH, MORITZ. On a Higher Plane . . . Cincinnati: The Monitor Company [cop. 1899]. 175 p.    LC

3401 [LOTHROP, HARRIET MULFORD (STONE).] How Tom and Dorothy Made and Kept a Christian Home. By Margaret Sidney [pseud.]. Boston: D. Lothrop Company, Franklin and Hawley Streets [cop. 1888]. 163 p., illus.    LC
For young married couples.

3402 [———] The Judges' Cave: Being a Romance of the New Haven Colony in the Days of the Regicides. By Margaret Sidney [pseud.] . . . Boston: Lothrop Publishing Company [cop. 1900]. 410 p., front.
   H, HEH, LC, UM, Y

3403 [———] The Pettibone Name: A New England Story. By Margaret Sidney [pseud.] . . . Boston: Lothrop and Company, 32 Franklin Street [cop. 1882]. 315 p.    CU, H, HEH, LC

LOUGHBOROUGH, JEAN, *jt. au.* See Yandell, E. Three Girls in a Flat [cop. 1892], Nos. 6146, 6147.

3404 LOUGHEAD, FLORA (HAINES) APPONYI. The Abandoned Claim . . . Boston and New York: Houghton, Mifflin and Company. The Riverside Press, Cambridge, 1891. 330 p.    HEH, N, O, Y
Farming in California.

3405 ——— The Black Curtain . . . Boston and New York: Houghton, Mifflin and Company. The Riverside Press, Cambridge, 1898. 369, [1] p.                                          H, HEH, LC, N, O
Of an artist and a singer in the foothills of the Sierra.

3406 ——— The Man Who Was Guilty . . . Boston and New York: Houghton, Mifflin and Company. The Riverside Press, Cambridge, 1886. 398 p.                                          AP, CU, HEH, O
San Francisco.

3407 LOUISIANA, *pseud.* "Blue and Gray"; or, Two Oaths and Three Warnings . . . New Orleans: [Press of L. Graham & Son], 1885. 169 p.
Information supplied by Evangeline Lynch of Louisiana State University Library.

3408 LOVE, MARGARET (BROWN). Tom Huston's Transformation . . . New York: F. Tennyson Neely, 1899. 92 p.
Listed PW, June 10, 1899.
LC has: Second Edition. New York: F. Tennyson Neely, 114 Fifth Avenue. London, Montreal [cop. 1899]. 92 p., front. Deposited Dec. 24, 1900.

3409 LOVE, WILLIAM EWING. Graven on the Tables . . . Boston: L. C. Page & Company, 1900. 32 p.                                          LC
According to preface author had a few copies privately printed prior to publication.

3410 LOVE AND DEATH IN A BARN; or, The Sad, Sorrowful Life of Beautiful Kate Harrington . . . in Philadelphia. Philadelphia, Pa.: The Old Franklin Publishing House, cop. 1876. 30 p., 1 l., illus.                                          HEH, UP, Y

3410a ——— Philadelphia, Pa.: The Old Franklin Publishing House, cop. 1876. 30 p., 2 l., [3]-30 p., 1 l., illus.                                          HEH
This ed. adds: "Bertha Barton; or, The Coney Island Mystery." Paged separately.

3411 LOVELACE, KATIE R. Rosamond Howard . . . New York: The Authors' Publishing Company, Bond Street [cop. 1878]. 112 p.                                          HEH, LC

3412 [LOWELL, FRANCIS CABOT.] Simply a Love Story. By Philip Orne [pseud.]. Boston: Cupples, Upham and Company, 1885. 387 p. LC, N
New England fishing village.

3413 LOWELL, PRUDENCE. The Millionaire's Wife: A Story of New England Society Life . . . Philadelphia: T. B. Peterson & Brothers, 306 Chestnut Street [cop. 1890]. 400 p.                                          LC

3414 LOWELL, ROBERT TRAILL SPENCE. A Story or Two from an Old Dutch Town . . . Boston: Roberts Brothers, 1878. 322 p.
                                          AP, BA, BU, CU, H, HEH, LC, O, UM, UVB, Y
*Contains:* Abram Van Zandt, the Man in the Picture–Mr. Schermerhorn's Marriage and Widowhood–Master Vorhagen's Wife.

3415 LOWELL, WALTER M. S. Against the Tide . . . Albany, New York: Leonard Publishing Company, 1892. 102 p., illus.    LC
Of the Salvation Army.

3416 LOWREY, OLIVER. A Runaway Couple: A Story of New York Society . . . New York and London: F. Tennyson Neely, 1898. 454 p.    HEH, LC

LOYAL, C., *pseud. See* Burton, Maria Amparo (Ruiz)

3417 LUBIN, DAVID. Let There Be Light: The Story of a Workingmen's Club. Its Search for the Causes of Poverty and Social Inequality, Its Discussions and Its Plan for the Amelioration of Existing Evils . . . New York and London: G. P. Putnam's Sons; the Knickerbocker Press, 1900. 526 p.    CU, HEH, LC, O, UC, UM, Y

3418 LUCAS, DANIEL R. Paul Darst; or, A Conflict between Love and Infidelity . . . Oskaloosa, Iowa: Central Book Concern, 1877. 206 p.    LC

3419 LUDLOW, JAMES MEEKER. The Baritone's Parish; or, "All Things to All Men" . . . New York, Chicago, Toronto: Fleming H. Revell Company, 1896. 40 p., front.    HEH, LC, Y

3420 ———— The Captain of the Janizaries: A Story of the Times of Scanderbeg and the Fall of Constantinople . . . New York: Dodd, Mead & Company, 1886. 404 p.    AP, BA, CU, H, HEH, LC, UVB

3421 ———— A King of Tyre: A Tale of the Times of Ezra and Nehemiah . . . New York: Harper & Brothers, 1891. 298 p.
CU, H, HEH, LC, O, UC, UM, UV

3422 ———— My Saint John . . . New York: Funk & Wagnalls, 1883. 44 p.    LC
Also published as: "*A Man for A' That*"; *or, My Saint John.* New York and Chicago: Revell, 1900. Listed PW, July 21, 1900.

3423 ———— That Angelic Woman: A Story . . . New York: Harper & Brothers, 1892. 149 p.    HEH, LC, O, UC, UM

3424 LUDLUM, JEAN KATE. Barclay's Daughter . . . New York: National Temperance Society, 1893. 314 p., front.    LC

3425 ———— John Winthrop's Defeat: A Novel . . . New York: Robert Bonner's Sons, 1891. 287 p., illus.    CU, HEH

3426 ———— Lida Campbell; or, Drama of a Life. A Novel . . . New York: Robert Bonner's Sons, 1892. 351 p.    LC

3427 ———— Under a Cloud: A Novel . . . New York: Robert Bonner's Sons, 1891. 300 p.
Advertised PW, May 30, 1891, back cover.
LC has copy in the omitted "Choice Series," No. 40.

3428 ———— Under Oath: An Adirondack Story . . . New York: Robert Bonner's Sons [cop. 1890]. 337 p., illus.      HEH, Y

LÜDERS, CHARLES HENRY. The Lost Elixir. *In* The Septameron (1888), No. 4867.

3429 LUFSEY, ROBERT EDGAR. Zeldee, the Devil's Daughter . . . Salisbury, N.C.: Bridgers & Lufsey [cop. 1898]. 138 p.      LC

3430 [LUKENS, HENRY CLAY.] Jets and Flashes. By Erratic Enrique [pseud.] . . . New York: John W. Lovell Company, 14 and 16 Vesey Street [cop. 1883]. 200 p., illus.      BU, H, LC, UM

3431 LULL, DE LOS. Father Solon; or, The Helper Helped . . . New York: Wilbur B. Ketcham, 71 Bible House [cop. 1888]. 367, [1] p.      HEH Of Mormon interest.

3432 LUMMIS, CHARLES FLETCHER. The Enchanted Burro: Stories of New Mexico and South America . . . Chicago: Way and Williams, 1897. 277, [1] p., illus.      BA, H, HEH, LC, O, Y
*Also contains:* The Mummy-Miner—A Boy of the Andes—A Daughter of the Misti—The Witch Deer—Felipe's Sugaring-off—Andrés, the Arriero—Our Yellow Slave—The Peak of Gold—Pablo's Deer Hunt—Candelária's Curse—The Habit of the Fraile—The Great Magician—The Balsa Boy of Lake Titicaca.

3433 ———— The Gold Fish of Gran Chimú . . . Boston and New York: Lamson, Wolffe and Company, 1896. 126 p., illus.
     CU, HEH, LC, UM, UVB, Y

3434 ———— The King of the Broncos, and Other Stories of New Mexico . . . New York: Charles Scribner's Sons, 1897. 254 p., illus.      BA, HEH, LC
*Also contains:* Bogged Down—The Bite of the Pichu-cuate—Poh-hlaik, the Cave-Boy—The Jawbone Telegraph—A Penitente Flower-Pot—Bravo's Day Off—Bonifacio's Horse-Thief—Green's Bear-Trap—My Smallest Sitter—Our Worst Snake—Kelley's Ground-Sluice—The Old Sharpe—My Friend Will.

3435 ———— A New Mexico David, and Other Stories and Sketches of the Southwest . . . New York: Charles Scribner's Sons, 1891. 217 p., illus.
     BA, BU, CU, H, HEH, LC, N, UM, Y
*Also contains:* How I Lost My Shadow—'Quito's Nugget—The Enchanted Mesa—A Pueblo Rabbit-Hunt—Pablo Apodaca's Bear—The Box S Round-Up —The Comanche's Revenge—In the Pueblo Alto—Little Lolita—Three Live Witches—How to Throw the Lasso—"Old Surely"—The Gallo Race—On the Pay-Streak—The Mircale of San Felipe—A New Old Game—A New Mexican Hero.

LUNDT, DOROTHY. Dikkon's Dog. *In* Tales from McClure's: The West (1897), No. 5363.

3436 LUSH, CHARLES KEELER. The Federal Judge: A Novel ... Boston and New York: Houghton, Mifflin and Company. The Riverside Press, Cambridge, 1897. 355, [1] p.     AP, CU, H, HEH, LC, O, UV
Of a judge and a railroad tycoon.

LUSKA, SIDNEY, *pseud.* *See* Harland, Henry

3437 LUTE, *Uncle, pseud.* Paul Hart; or, The Love of His Life ... Philadelphia: T. B. Peterson & Brothers, 306 Chestnut Street [cop. 1881]. 420 p.     HEH
Of a self-made man; New York.

3438 LUTHER, MARK LEE. The Favor of Princes ... New York: The Macmillan Company: London: Macmillan & Co., Ltd., 1899. 259 p.
    H, HEH, LC, O
Louis XV and Madame Pompadour.

3439 LUTZ, ELLEN A. One Woman's Story; or, The Chronicles of a Quiet Life as Told in Dorothea's Diary ... Cincinnati: Cranston & Curts. New York: Hunt & Eaton, 1895. 300 p., illus.     LC

3440 LYDSTON, GEORGE FRANK. Over the Hookah: The Tales of a Talkative Doctor ... Chicago: Fred Klein Company, 1896. 618 p., illus.
    HEH, N, UC, UP

LYKKEJAEGER, HANS, *pseud.* *See* Smith, Andrew Madsen

3441 [LYNCH, HARRIET LOUISE (HUSTED).] A Little Game with Destiny. By Marie St. Felix [pseud.] ... New York: Nocton & Co., 1892. 152 p.
    H

3442 [———] Patricia: A Sequel to "Two Bad Brown Eyes." By Marie St. Félix [pseud.] ... New York: The Merriam Company, 67 Fifth Avenue [cop. 1895]. 290 p.     LC
Of an unhappy marriage and suicide.

3443 [———] Two Bad Brown Eyes. By Marie St. Félix [pseud.]. New York: The Merriam Company [cop. 1894]. 245 p.
Information from LC card; no copy seen.

LYNCH, LAWRENCE L., *pseud.* *See* Van Deventer, Emma Murdoch

3444 LYNCH, VIRGINIA. Dr. Tom Gardner: A Story from Life ... New York, Chicago, London: F. Tennyson Neely Co. [cop. 1900]. 80 p.
    LC

3445 LYNDE, FRANCIS. The Helpers ... Boston and New York: Houghton, Mifflin and Company. The Riverside Press, Cambridge, 1899. 420 p., 1 l.     HEH, O
Denver and the outlying mining towns.

3446 ——— A Private Chivalry: A Novel . . . New York: D. Appleton and
Company, 1900. 332 p.                                    HEH, LC, N, O
Of railroads.

3447 ——— A Romance in Transit . . . New York: Charles Scribner's Sons,
1897. 227 p.                                             HEH, LC, O, Y
On the Colorado and Utah train out of Chicago.

3448 LYON, ANNE BOZEMAN. "No Saint": A Novel . . . Louisville: John P.
Morton and Company, printers [cop. 1890]. 165 p.             LC

3449 LYON, SIDNEY, *pseud.* For a Mess of Pottage . . . Philadelphia: J. B.
Lippincott Company, 1890. 414 p.                         AP, LC, O
"Said to be written by a Southern lady." PW, May 31, 1890.

M., A. S. *See* McNeill, Nevada

M., L. H. *See* Morehouse, Linden H.

M., M. A. *See* Macdonald, Mrs. M. A.

3450 MABIE, HAMILTON WRIGHT. In the Forest of Arden . . . New York:
Dodd, Mead and Company, 1898. 124 p., illus.   CU, HEH, LC, UC, UP, Y

3451 MABILLE UNMASKED; or, The Wickedest Place in the World . . . A Lurid
Panorama of the Night Life of Paris. By the Author of "Paris by Gas-
light." New York: Richard K. Fox [cop. 1882]. 56 p., illus.     LC
Deposited May 14, 1883.
Publisher may be the author.

3452 MC., J. The Witch-Woman's Revenge; or, The Golden Secret of the
"Oswego." By J. Mc. Oswego, N.Y.: R. J. Oliphant, book and job
printer, 1882. 16 p.                                         HEH
An Indian tale to promote the sale of Austen's Oswego Bitters.

3453 MCAFEE, NELLY NICHOL (MARSHALL). A Criminal through Love: A
Novel . . . Louisville, Ky.: The Gilbert & Mallory Publishing Company, 1882. 540 p.                                           UC

3454 ——— Passion; or, Bartered and Sold . . . Louisville, 1876.
Listed in *Library of Southern Literature*, Vol. XV (New Orleans [1910]),
p. 289.

3455 [MCANDREW, WILLIAM A.] Silhouette: A Tale of Minnetonka. Being
an Account of a Peculiar Case by Howard Bronson, M.D. [pseud.].
Edited with Notes by W. J. D. Ann Arbor, Michigan: The Register
Publishing Company, 1891. 24, [2] p., illus.                 LC
To advertise the Great Northern Railway.

3456 MACARTHUR, ADELLA R. "That Romanist": A Novel . . . Boston: Arena
Publishing Company, 1896. 364 p.                         CU, LC
Courtship of a Protestant and a Catholic.

McBALLASTIR, CAD, *pseud. See* De Leon, Thomas Cooper

3457 McCABE, GILLIE (CARY). Uncle Jerry's Platform, and Other Christmas Stories. By Gillie Cary. Boston: Arena Publishing Co., 1895. 56 p., illus.
*Also contains:* Pops—A Daughter of the Revolution.
Listed PW, Jan. 18, 1896.
UV has: Richmond: Everett Waddey Co., 1897.

3458 McCABE, JAMES DABNEY. The Night Express . . . Philadelphia: J. M. Stoddart & Co., 1879. 153 p.                                                LC
From Philadelphia to New York.

3459 M'CALEB, THOMAS. Anthony Melgrave . . . New York, London: G. P. Putnam's Sons; the Knickerbocker Press, 1892. 203 p.        HEH, LC, O
Washington, D.C., and Virginia.

McCALL, CHARLES NICHOLAS. Pledging a Freshman. *In* H. J. Hapgood, *ed.,* Echoes from Dartmouth (1895), No. 2446.

3460 McCANN, JOHN ERNEST. Odds and Ends . . . New York: The Alliance Publishing Company [cop. 1891]. 99, [1] p.                    BU, HEH
Ernest Jarrold, jt. au.

3461 McCANN, WALTER E. In the Middle of the Night: A Novel . . . Baltimore, Md.: Gallery & McCann, 1895. 256 p.                        HEH, LC

3462 McCARDELL, ROY LARCOM. "The Wage Slaves of New York" . . . New York: G. W. Dillingham Co., 1899. 196 p., illus.                    H, LC

3463 McCARTHY, CARLTON. Our Distinguished Fellow-Citizen . . . Richmond: J. L. Hill Printing Company, 1890. 169 p., illus.        HEH, LC
Deposited May 21, 1890.
Former liquor store owner becomes a member of the legislature.

3464 MacCARTHY, MRS. EMMA W. Assemblyman John; or, His Wife's Ambition . . . Chicago and New York: Belford, Clarke & Co., 1889. 134 p.
Listed PW, Aug. 3, 1889.

3465 ——— Congressman John and His Wife's Satisfaction: A Novel . . . New York: G. W. Dillingham, 1891. 283 p.                        LC

3466 McCARTNEY, MRS. CATHERINE ROBERTSON. The Hero of the Ages: A Story of the Nazarene . . . New York, Chicago, Toronto: Fleming H. Revell Company [cop. 1896]. 240 p.                                LC

3467 McCHESNEY, DORA GREENWELL. Beatrix Infelix: A Summer Tragedy in Rome . . . New York: John Lane [1898]. 193 p.
Listed PW, Dec. 3, 1898.

3468 ──── Miriam Cromwell, Royalist: A Romance of the Great Rebellion ... Chicago: Way & Williams, 1897. 429 p.  HEH
The English rebellion.

3469 [MACCHETTA, BLANCHE ROOSEVELT (TUCKER).] Marked "In Haste": A Story of To-Day ... New York: Trow's Printing and Bookbinding Co., 1883. 362 p.  HEH, UVB, Y
Of Americans in Paris during the 1870's.

3470 [────] Stage-Struck; or, She Would Be an Opera-Singer. By Blanche Roosevelt [pseud.] ... New York: Fords, Howard, & Hulbert. London: Sampson Low & Co., 1884. 521 p.  H, LC, UC
Of European voice training.

MCCLELLAN, MRS. GEORGE. *See* McClellan, Harriet (Hare)

3471 MCCLELLAN, HARRIET (HARE). Broken Chords Crossed by the Echo of a False Note. By Mrs. George McClellan ... Philadelphia: J. B. Lippincott Company, 1893. 373 p.  AP, HEH, LC, O
Of an actress.

3472 [────] A Carpet Knight: A Novel. By Harford Flemming [pseud.] ... Boston, New York: Houghton, Mifflin and Company. The Riverside Press, Cambridge, 1885. 436 p.  AP, CU, H, HEH, LC, N
Philadelphia society.

3473 [────] Cupid and the Sphinx. By Harford Flemming [pseud.]. New York: G. P. Putnam's Sons, 1878. 434 p.  AP, HEH, LC
Egypt.

MCCLELLAND, MARY GREENWAY. Alison Stewart. *In* [Mrs. K. P. Minor] *comp.*, From Dixie (1893), No. 3756.

3474 ──── Broadoaks ... St. Paul: The Price-McGill Company, 455-473 Cedar Street [cop. 1893]. 268 p., front.  O, UV
Virginia life.

3475 ──── Burkett's Lock ... New York: Cassell & Company, Limited, 104-106 Fourth Avenue [cop. 1888]. 279 p.  HEH, O
A canal story.

3476 ──── Jean Monteith ... New York: Henry Holt and Company, 1887. 252 p.  AP, H, HEH, LC, O, UM, UV
At head of title: "Leisure Hour Series—No. 204."
Northern Alabama.

3477 ──── Madame Silva ... New York: Cassell & Company, Limited, 104-106 Fourth Avenue [cop. 1888]. 320 p.  AP, BA, HEH, LC
*Also contains:* The Ghost of Dred Power.

3478 —— Mammy Mystic . . . New York: The Merriam Company, 67
Fifth Avenue [cop. 1895]. 242 p., front. HEH, LC, UV
Miscegenation; New Orleans.

3479 —— Manitou Island . . . New York: Henry Holt and Company,
1892. 294 p. HEH, LC, O, UM, UV, Y
Swamps of South Carolina.

3480 —— Oblivion: An Episode . . . New York: Henry Holt and Com-
pany, 1885. 290 p. AP, BA, H, HEH, LC, O, UV, Y
At head of title: "Leisure Hours Series—No. 175."
Of amnesia.

3481 —— The Old Post-Road . . . New York: The Merriam Company,
67 Fifth Avenue [cop. 1894]. 163 p., front. HEH, LC, O, UV, Y
Maryland, early 19th century.

3482 —— Princess . . . New York: Henry Holt and Company, 1886. 297
p. AP, BA, H, HEH, LC, O, UC, UM
At head of title: "Leisure Hour Series—No. 194."
Post Civil War Virginia

3483 —— St. John's Wooing: A Story . . . New York: Harper & Brothers,
1895. 175 p., illus. H, HEH, LC, O, UC, Y

3484 McCONNELL, ANNIE BLISS. Half Married: Agamé Gamé . . . Philadelphia: J. B. Lippincott Company, 1887. 311 p. AP, HEH, LC, O
From a frontier army post to New York.

3485 McCOOK, HENRY CHRISTOPHER. The Latimers: A Tale of the Western
Insurrection of 1794 . . . Philadelphia: George W. Jacobs & Co., 1898.
593 p., front. AP, CU, HEH, LC, O, UC, UP, Y
Whisky Insurrection.

3486 [McCORNICK, MRS. JOANNA.] By Hudson's Banks: A Novel. By Joanna
[pseud.]. San Francisco: The Bancroft Company, 1889. 392 p. LC

3487 McCOWAN, ARCHIBALD. The Billionaire: A Peep into the Future . . .
New York: Printed by Jenkins & McCowan, 1900. 79 p. HEH, N

3488 [——] Christ the Socialist . . . Boston: Arena Publishing Company,
1894. 357 p. LC

3489 [McCOY, JOHN.] A Prophetic Romance: Mars to Earth . . . Boston:
Arena Publishing Co., 1896. 283 p. LC

3490 McCRACKIN, JOSEPHINE (WOEMPNER) CLIFFORD. "Another Juanita," and
Other Stories. By Josephine Clifford. Buffalo: Charles Wells Moulton, 1893. 295 p. H, HEH

*Also contains:* Camp Life in Arizona—San Xavier del Bac—Crossing the Rio Grande—An Episode of Fort Desolation—Toby—Flight! A Sequel to Toby—A Miner from Arizona—That Ranch of His—The Story of a Garden—St. Mary's—Modern Monterey.

3491 ———— Overland Tales . . . Philadelphia: Claxton, Remsen, & Haffelfinger, 1877. 383 p.     H, HEH, LC, Y

*Contents:* La Graciosa—Juanita—Hetty's Heroism—A Woman's Treachery—The Gentleman from Siskiyou—Something about My Pets—Poker-Jim—The Tragedy at Mohawk Station—Lone Linden—Manuela—The Romance of Gila Bend—A Lady in Camp—The Golden Lamb—It Occurred at Tucson—A Bit of "Early California"—Her Name Was Sylvia—Crossing the Arizona Deserts—Down among the Dead Letters—Marching with a Command—To Texas and by the Way—My First Experience in New Mexico.

*Also issued with imprint:* San Francisco: A. Roman & Co., 1877.     H, HEH

3492 McCRAY, FLORINE THAYER. Environment: A Story of Modern Society . . . New York, London: Funk & Wagnalls, 1887. 404 p.     HEH, LC, O
New York.

3493 [————] Wheels and Whims: An Etching . . . Boston: Cupples, Upham & Company, 1884. 288 p., illus.     HEH, LC
Esther Louise Smith, jt. au.
Of a cycling trip through Connecticut.

McDERMOTT, WILLIAM A. Gilliman Ogley, by Walter Lecky [pseud.]. *In* A Round Table of the Representative American Catholic Novelists (1897), No. 4703.

3494 [————] Mr. Billy Buttons: A Novel. By Walter Lecky [pseud.]. New York, Cincinnati, Chicago: Benziger Brothers, 1896. 274 p.     LC
In the Adirondacks.

3495 [————] Père Monnier's Ward: A Novel. By Walter Lecky [pseud.] . . . New York, Cincinnati, Chicago: Benziger Brothers, 1898. 304 p.
    LC

3496 McDONALD, FRANK J. Gail Donner . . . [St. Albans, Vt., cop. 1895.] Cover title, 346 p.     LC

3497 [MACDONALD, MRS. M. A.] Deacon Hackmetack. By M. A. M. Philadelphia: Treager & Lamb, 1888. 170 p.     LC
Temperance novel.

3498 McDONALD, ROBERT. In the Reign of Boris: A Tale of Carpathia . . . New York: Frank A. Munsey, 1897. 284 p.     CU, HEH
Of an American newspaperman.

3499 ———— A Princess and a Woman: A Romance of Carpathia . . . New York: Frank A. Munsey, 1897. 252 p.     HEH, LC, UV

3500 [McDougall, Ella L. (Randall).] From Side Streets and Boulevards:
A Collection of Chicago Stories. By Preserved Wheeler [pseud.].
Chicago: R. R. Donnelley & Sons Company, printers, 1893. 352 p.
HEH, LC, N
*Contains:* A Vagabond for a Year—All on a Christmas Eve—A Piece of Land.

3501 [————] Hennessey, of Lake County. By Preserved Wheeler [pseud.].
Antioch, Illinois: Burke & Storms, 1894. 50 p., illus. LC

3502 [————] One Schoolma'am Less. By Preserved Wheeler [pseud.].
Chicago: R. R. Donnelley & Sons Co., printers, 1895. 217 p., illus. LC

3503 McDougall, Walter Hugh. The Hidden City ... New York: Cassell
Publishing Company, 104 & 106 Fourth Avenue [cop. 1891]. 321 p.,
illus. LC
Deposited Oct. 14, 1891.

McDowell, Henry B. The Marquis of Aguayo. *In* Short Stories by
California Authors (1885), No. 4929.

3504 [McDowell, Katherine Sherwood (Bonner).] Dialect Tales. By
Sherwood Bonner [pseud.] ... New York: Harper & Brothers, 1883.
187 p., illus. BA, CU, H, HEH, LC, N, O, UC, UM, UV, Y
*Contents:* The Gentlemen of Sarsar—On the Nine-Mile—Hieronymus Pop
and the Baby—Sister Weeden's Prayer—Aunt Anniky's Teeth—Dr. Jex's Pre-
dicament—In Aunt Mely's Cabin—The Case of Eliza Bleylock—The Bran
Dance at the Apple Settlement—Lame Jerry—Jack and the Mountain Pink.
Her *Suwanee River Tales* (1884) is a juvenile.

3505 [————] Like unto Like: A Novel. By Sherwood Bonner [pseud.].
New York: Harper & Brothers, 1878. 169 p. Printed in double col-
umns. BA, H, HEH, LC, O, UVB
Reconstruction period; Mississippi.

3506 Mace, Richard. The First Families: A Tale of North and South ...
New York: Frank A. Munsey, 1897. 249 p. CU, HEH, LC, UV, Y

3507 McElroy, John. Decline and Fall of the American Republic: Confessions of a Repentant Politician. A Story of Fifty Years Hence: Time
A.D. 1930 ... [Toledo, Ohio: Toledo Blade Co., cop. 1880.] Caption
title, 16 p. Printed in double columns. LC
His humorous "Si Kleg" stories were published in a subscription series.

3508 ———— The Red Acorn: A Novel ... Chicago: Henry A. Sumner &
Company, 1883. 322 p. BU, CU, HEH, N, UM
At head of title: "The Acorn Series."
Civil War novel.

3509 McElroy, Lucy (Cleaver). Answered: A Romance of the Silent Years
... Franklin, Ohio: The Editor Publishing Company, 1896. 80 p. LC
A fantasy concerning the life of Buddha.

3510 McELROY, WILLIAM HENRY. Matthew Middlemas's Experiment . . .
New York: Anson D. F. Randolph & Company, 38 West Twenty-Third
Street [cop. 1888]. 32 p.
Copy examined at New York Public Library.
Of how a minister reformed a town.

——— A Posthumous Letter of Adam's. *In* The First Book of the
Authors Club (1893), No. 1868.

McENERY, RUTH. *See* Stuart, Ruth (McEnery)

3511 MACFARLANE, MARGARET RUSSELL. The Magic of a Voice: A Novel . . .
New York: Cassell & Company, Limited, 739 & 741 Broadway [cop.
1886]. 285 p.                    AP, BA, H, HEH, LC, O, UM, UP
Life in Germany.

3512 ——— Odds Against Her . . . New York: Cassell & Company, Limited,
104-106 Fourth Avenue [cop. 1888]. 249 p.                    AP, LC

3513 MACGAHAN, MRS. BARBARA. Xenis Repninà: A Story of the Russia of To-
Day . . . New York, London, Glasgow, and Manchester: George Rout-
ledge & Sons, Limited [cop. 1890]. 295 p.                    AP, BA, LC, O

3514 McGEHEE, MRS. JUNIUS. Glen Mary: A Catholic Novel . . . Baltimore:
John Murphy & Co., 1887. 198 p.                    CU, LC

McGLASSON, EVA WILDER. *See* Brodhead, Eva Wilder (McGlasson)

3515 McGLOIN, FRANK. Norodom, King of Cambodia: A Romance of the
East . . . New York: D. Appleton and Company, 1882. 327 p.
BU, HEH, LC, O, Y

3516 McGOVERN, JOHN. Daniel Trentworthy: A Tale of the Great Fire of
Chicago . . . Chicago, New York: Rand, McNally & Company, 1889.
281 p., illus.                    LC, N, UC

3517 McGOWAN, ALICE. Return: A Story of the Sea Islands . . . Boston: L. C.
Page and Company (Incorporated), 1895. 544 p.
Grace McGowan Cooke, jt. au.
Listed in Turnbull, Vol. IV, p. 344.

——— The Rustlers. *In* Ten Notable Stories (1894), No. 5391.

3518 MACGRATH, HAROLD. Arms and the Woman: A Romance . . . New
York: Doubleday & McClure Co., 1899. 329 p.                    H, HEH, O
Of a German princess in London.

3519 MACGREGOR, ANNIE LYNDSAY. "Bound, Not Blessed" . . . New York:
G. W. Dillingham, 1892. 226 p.                    LC
Of an unhappy marriage.

McGUZZLER, STEWARD, *pseud. See* Thompson, Alfred

3519a McIntosh, Burr William. Football and Love: A Story of the Yale-Princeton Game of '94 . . . New York, London: The Transatlantic Publishing Co., 1895. 58 p., illus. HEH

Mack, John, Jr. The "Paper" Sport. *In* Stories from the Harvard Advocate (1896), No. 5277a.

McKay, Mrs. Alfred Almond. *See* McKay, Mrs. Annie E.

3520 McKay, Mrs. Annie E. Easter-Lilies. By Mrs. A. A. McKay. A Quaint Little Story, an Easter Offering. Buffalo: The Peter Paul Book Company, 1896. 18 p. LC

3521 ———— A Latter Day Saint. By Mrs. Alfred Almond McKay . . . New York, Chicago, Toronto: Fleming H. Revell Company [cop. 1893]. 279 p. LC

3522 McKay, Donald. The Dynamite Ship . . . New York: Manhattan Publishing House, 1888. 209 p., illus. AP, HEH, LC
Of an attack on London.

McKay, Frederic Edward. An Interrupted Finesse. *In* F. E. McKay, ed., Vignettes [cop. 1890], No. 3523.

3523 ———— ed. Vignettes: Real and Ideal. Stories by American Authors . . . Boston: De Wolfe, Fiske & Co., 361 and 365 Washington Street [cop. 1890]. 288 p. BA, CU, H, HEH, LC, O, UM
*Contents:* A Light Man, by William Clyde Fitch—The Untold Word, by F. C. de Sumichrast—An Artistic Necessity, by Mabel Louise Fuller [Blodgett] —Madame Clerc, by Edward Irenaeus Stevenson—A Choice, by Emma V. Sheridan—A Difference in Clay, by Jerome Case Bull—A Night with William of Wykeham, by Oscar Fay Adams—Safe in Purgatory, by Jane G. Austin —A Quarter Past Six, by Matthew White, Jr.—An Inherited Debt, by William Murray Graydon—The Vigil of Fenton Barlowe, by John J. A'Becket— The Face of Abel, by William D. Moffat—The Return, by Algernon Tassin —At Sûk Wady Barada, by Clinton Scollard—An Interrupted Finesse, by Frederic Edward McKay.

McKay, James T. A Leap in the Dark. Two Modern Prodigals. [Two stories.] *In* Tales from McClure's: Adventure (1897), No. 5360.

———— Stella Grayland. *In* Stories by American Authors, VII (1884), No. 5273.

3524 MacKay, William R. The Skein of Life . . . Philadelphia: J. B. Lippincott Company, 1897. 260 p., illus. LC, UC
*Contents:* The Reverend Erasmus—Simon Smith—Kit—A Brilliant Adventure—The Mexican or the Tiger—The Mystery of Hampton—Cap'n Johnsin of Bermuda—A Close Shave—The Reverend Mr. Higginton's Prize Story.

3525 [MacKenzie, Adelheid (Zwissler).] His Sweetheart. By Ignota [pseud.]. Philadelphia: James A. Moore, 1877. 229 p. HEH, LC, O

McKenzie, Christine, *pseud.* *See* Duffell, Annie

3526 McKey, Ada Jean. Silopaen: A Novel ... Chicago: A. J. Palmer & Co., 1888. 62, 137, 31 p., illus.
Listed PW, May 11, 1889.
Of Ireland and America.

Mackey, Thomas J. The Bravest Deed of the War. An Incident of Gettysburg. [Two stories.] *In* Tales from McClure's: War (1898), No. 5364.

Mackie, Pauline Bradford. *See* Hopkins, Pauline Bradford (Mackie)

3527 Mackin, Mrs. Marie. The Mystery of the Marbletons: A Romance of Reality ... New York: The Abbey Press, 114 Fifth Avenue [cop. 1900]. 165 p.                                                    LC, UM
Deposited Dec. 13, 1900.

3528 [Mackintosh, D. B.] The Life and Adventures of Roderick Douglas. Boston: Charles H. Whiting, 1886. 265 p.                                    LC

3529 McKnight, Charles. Simon Girty: "The White Savage" ... A Romance of the Border ... Philadelphia, Chicago, St. Louis, and Cincinnati: J. C. McCurdy & Co. [cop. 1880]. 393 p., illus.                  UC

3530 Mackubin, Ellen. The King of the Town ... Boston and New York: Houghton, Mifflin and Company. The Riverside Press, Cambridge, 1898. 152 p., 1 l.                      HEH, LC, O, UC, UM, UV
Army life, Fort Ludlow, Montana.

Maclachlan, J. M. A Perilous Christmas Courtship. *In* [W. J. Johnston] *comp.*, Lightning Flashes and Electric Dashes (1877), Nos. 3022, 3023.

3531 McLandburgh, Florence. The Automaton Ear, and Other Sketches ... Chicago: Jansen, McClurg & Co., 1876. 282 p.                      HEH, LC
*Also contains:* The Paths of the Sea—Reinhart, the German—Silver Islet—Boydell, the Stroller—The Death-Watch—The Man at the Crib—Prof. Kellermann's Funeral—The Feverfew—Old Simlin, the Moulder—The Anthem of Judea.

3532 McLane, Hiram H. Irene Viesca: A Tale of the Magee Expedition in the Gauchipin War in Texas, A.D. 1812-13 ... San Antonio, Texas: San Antonio Printing Company, printers and binders, 1886. 548 p., illus.                                            CU, H, HEH, N, Y

3533 McLaren, James Henry. Calvin Paxton's Patmos ... Chicago, Ill.: The Pilgrim Press, 1898. 56 p.                                            LC

3534 McLaughlin, Nathan Monroe. The Last Man: A Novel . . . Washington: The Neale Company, 1900. 221 p.  HEH, LC, UM
A Civil War love story.

3535 Maclay, Arthur Collins. Mito Yashiki: A Tale of Old Japan. Being a Feudal Romance Descriptive of the Decline of the Shogunate . . . New York & London: G. P. Putnam's Sons; the Knickerbocker Press, 1889. 456 p.  AP, CU, H, HEH, LC, O, UM, Y

3536 Maclean, Clara Victoria (Dargan). Light o' Love . . . New York: Worthington Company, 1891. 259 p., illus.  HEH, O

McLean, Sally Pratt. See Greene, Sarah Pratt (McLean)

3537 McLeod, Clara Nevada. Then, and Not 'til Then: A Novel . . . New York: Authors' Publishing Association, 65 Fifth Avenue [cop. 1897]. 215 p.  LC

3538 McLoughlin, Maurice Edmund. The Gowanusians: Humorous Sketches of Every-Day Life among Plain People . . . New York: Edmunds Publishing Company, 1894. 205 p., illus.  LC

3539 McMahon, Patrick Justin. Philip; or, The Mollie's Secret. A Tale of the Coal Regions . . . Philadelphia: H. L. Kilner & Co. [cop. 1891]. 578 p.  LC
Deposited Dec. 31, 1891.
Molly Maguires; Pennsylvania.

3540 McMartin, Donald. A Leap into the Future; or, How Things Will Be. A Romance of the Year 2000 . . . Albany, N.Y.: Weed, Parsons & Company, printers, 1890. 202 p.  LC
On cover: "A Sequel to Looking Backward."

3541 McMichael, William. Konneautt Lake: A Story of Early Times in North-Western Pennsylvania . . . New York: W. B. Smith & Co., Bond Street [cop. 1882]. 256 p.  LC, O, UM
Deposited Nov. 29, 1882.

3542 ——— The Minister's Daughter . . . New York: W. B. Smith & Co., Bond Street [cop. 1881]. 299 p.  LC
Deposited Oct. 1, 1881.

3543 McMillan, William F. Zelda . . . St. Paul, Minn.: McMillan Publishing Co., 1895. 440 p.  LC
St. Paul, Minnesota.

3544 McMinn, Edwin. Nemorama the Nautchnee: A Story of India . . . New York: Hunt & Eaton. Cincinnati: Cranston & Stowe, 1890. 291 p., illus.  CU, LC, N, O, Y

3545 ———— Thrilling Scenes in the Persian Kingdom: The Story of a Scribe ... New York: Hunt & Eaton. Cincinnati: Cranston & Curts, 1892. 323 p.                                                                                              LC, UP

3546 [McNAUGHTON, JAMES.] The Anti-Biled Shirt Club. New York: The Authors' Publishing Company, 1878. 121 p.                                    LC
Experiences of a group of gentlemen in the Maine woods.

3547 McNEILL, CORA. "Mizzoura" ... Minneapolis: Mizzoura Publishing Company, 1898. 391 p., illus.                                                   LC
Missouri after the Civil War.

3548 [McNEILL, NEVADA.] The Banker and the Typewriter. New York: G. W. Dillingham, 1895. 302 p.                                                      LC
New York.

3549 [————] The Disagreeable Man: A Novel. By A. S. M. New York: G. W. Dillingham, 1895. 189 p.                                                      LC

3550 [————] A Marriage above Zero: A Novel. By Nevada [pseud.]. New York: G. W. Dillingham, 1894. 288 p.
Information from LC card; no copy seen.

3551 [————] La Nouvelle Femme. By A. S. M. .... New York: G. W. Dillingham, 1896. 288 p., illus.                                                    LC

3552 [————] The Red Rose of Savannah: A Novel. By A. S. M. New York: G. W. Dillingham, cop. 1894. 276 p.                                            LC
Heroine deserted after a false marriage ceremony.

3553 [————] Rob Rockafellow: A Boston Society Man's Diary. By A. Mann [pseud.]. New York: G. W. Dillingham, 1894. 176 p.                            LC

3554 [————] The Yellow Rose of New Orleans: A Novel. By A. S. M. New York: G. W. Dillingham, 1895. 246 p.                                           LC

3555 McNEILL, ORANGE. A Jesuit of To-Day ... New York: J. Selwin Tait & Sons, 65 Fifth Avenue [cop. 1895]. 146 p., illus.        HEH, LC, UM, Y

3556 [MACNIE, JOHN.] The Diothas; or, A Far Look Ahead. By Ismar Thiusen [pseud.]. New York: G. P. Putnam's Sons, 1883. 358 p.
                                                                                           CU, N, UP, Y
Also published as: *A Far Look Ahead; or, The Diothas.* New York: G. P. Putnam's Sons; the Knickerbocker Press, 1890.   HEH
Of the 96th century.

3557 McNUTT, CYRUS F. Broken Lives ... Chicago: T. S. Denison, 163 Randolph Street [cop. 1888]. 188 p.                                             LC

3558 —— —— Second Edition ... Terre Haute, Ind.: Moore & Mc-
Nutt, 1896. 245 p., illus.                                        LC
*Also contains:* Circumstantial Evidence—Will Murder Out?—A Judgment of
Death Arrested.

3559 MACON, JOHN ALFRED. Uncle Gabe Tucker; or, Reflection, Song, and
Sentiment in the Quarters ... Philadelphia: J. B. Lippincott & Co.,
1883. 181 p., front.                          BU, LC, N, UC, UM, Y

MCPHERSON, MISS, *pseud.* *See* Pinckney, Susanna Shulride Hayne

3560 MCROBERTS, WALTER. Rounding Cape Horn, and Other Sea Stories ...
Peoria, Ill.: H. S. Hill Printing Company, 1895. 293 p., illus.     LC
*Contents:* The Life-Savers—Thanksgiving on the Dicky Bird—My Brazilian
Adventure—Bringing in a Derelict—The Monomaniac—Crossing the Line—
Missing—A Dangerous Cargo—The Parson's Text—Rounding Cape Horn.

3561 MACSHERRY, HOWARD. Chums: A Satirical Sketch ... Jersey City, N.J.:
Charles S. Clarke, Jr. [cop. 1878]. 127 p.                  HEH, LC

3562 MCVICKAR, HENRY GOELET. The Purple Light of Love ... New York:
D. Appleton and Company, 1894. 176 p.                       HEH, LC
Fashionable life; New York and Newport.

3563 MCVITTIE, JOSEPH. Vagor; or, Vicissitudes of a Vagabond ... Albion,
N.Y.: A. M. Eddy, book and job printer, 1891. 336 p.             LC

3564 MADDUX, BERTON J. The Veil Withdrawn: A Novel ... New York:
G. W. Dillingham Co., 1900. 266 p.                          HEH, LC
Detective story.

3565 MADEIRA, F. V. B. Justice Will Win; or, The Trials and Final Triumphs
of Arthur Steele ... Philadelphia: Printed by Sherman & Co., 1883.
214 p.                                                 H, HEH, LC

3566 MADISON, MARIE. The Witch: A Novel ... New Haven, Conn.: New
Haven Publishing Company, 1891. 131 p., illus.                   LC
Colonial period.

3567 MAG: A Story of To-Day. New York: Harper & Brothers, 1878. 122 p.
Printed in double columns.                         BA, BU, CU, LC, UV

3568 MAGIE, L. B. My Sister Marion ... New York: Tibbals Book Company, 26 Warren Street [cop. 1892]. 407 p., illus.              LC
A New England village.

3569 [MAGRUDER, JULIA.] Across the Chasm. New York: Charles Scribner's
Sons, 1885. 310 p.                            H, HEH, LC, O, UP, UV
Washington social scene.

3570 ——— At Anchor, and Honored in the Breach: Two Novels ... Philadelphia: J. B. Lippincott Company, 1891. 233 p.                    HEH

3571 ——— A Beautiful Alien ... Boston: Richard G. Badger & Co., 1900.
223 p., 1 l., front.                              H, HEH, LC, O, UP, UV

3572 ——— Dead Selves ... Philadelphia: J. B. Lippincott Company, 1898.
260 p.                                           BA, HEH, O, UV, Y

3573 ——— A Heaven-Kissing Hill ... Chicago and New York: Herbert S.
Stone and Company, 1899. 159 p., front.          HEH, LC, UV, Y
Of a poor artist.

3574 ——— A Magnificent Plebeian ... New York: Harper & Brothers,
1888. 228 p.                                     AP, H, HEH, LC, O, UV

3575 ——— A Manifest Destiny ... New York and London: Harper &
Brothers, 1900. 225, [1] p., illus.              HEH, LC, N, O, UV

3576 ——— Miss Ayr of Virginia, & Other Stories ... Chicago: Herbert S.
Stone & Co., 1896. 395 p., 1 l.                  HEH, LC, O, Y
*Also contains:* A New Thing under the Sun—The Thirst and the Draught—
A Bartered Birthright—His Heart's Desire—The Masked Singer—The Story
of an Old Soul—Once More.

3577 ——— The Princess Sonia ... New York: The Century Co., 1895.
225 p., illus.                      AP, BA, BU, H, HEH, LC, N, O, UC, UV

3578 ——— A Realized Ideal ... Chicago & New York: Herbert S. Stone &
Company, 1898. 135 p.                   H, HEH, LC, N, O, UC, UV, Y
Of the ideal wife.

3579 ——— Struan ... Boston: Richard G. Badger & Co., 1899. 330 p.
                                                 HEH, LC, O, UV
Of a musician and a singer; New York.

3580 ——— The Violet ... New York, London, and Bombay: Longmans,
Green and Co., 1896. 210 p., illus.              HEH, LC, O, UV, Y
Fashionable life; New York.

3581 MAGUIRE, DON. The American Adventurer ... New York: Trow's
Printing and Bookbinding Co., 1879. 307 p.       H, HEH, LC
From the South to California mining towns.

3582 MAHER, WILLIAM H. Drum Taps: Leaves from the Diary of a Commercial Traveler ... Toledo, O.: The Toledo Book Company, 1890. 120 p.
                                                 LC

3583 ——— A Man of Samples: Something about the Men He Met "on the
Road" ... Toledo, O.: Toledo Book Company, 1887. 160 p.   H, LC, O

3584 MAHONY, MARY G. Marmaduke Denver, and Other Stories . . . San Francisco: Women's Co-operative Printing Office, 1887. 119 p. HEH
*Also contains:* Only a Tramp—A Sweet Singer—A Broken Heart.

3585 MAITLAND, CHRISTAL V. A Woman's Web: A Novel . . . New York: G. W. Carleton & Co.; Street & Smith, New York Weekly, 1884. 419 p. CU, HEH, UM, Y
*Also contains:* The Beautiful Icicle.

3586 [MAITLAND, JAMES.] Suppressed Sensations; or, Leaves from the Note Book of a Chicago Reporter . . . Chicago: Rand, McNally & Co., 1879. 254 p., illus. N
*Contents:* A Mysterious Murder—The Romance of a Tramp—The Carnival's Victim—The Story of a Waif—The Tell-Tale Skull—Janet and Jamie—The Witness from the Dead—Fanny Mordaunt's Love—The Man with the Comical Hat—True Love and False Friendship—"Pizun Jack" of Texas—Gloria: A Tale of Four Cities—Lord Ullin's Daughter.
Purportedly factual.

3587 MAITLAND, ROY. One Little Indian . . . New York: The Authors' Publishing Company, Bond Street [cop. 1879]. 134 p. LC
Listed PW, Mar. 20, 1880.

3588 [MAJOR, CHARLES.] When Knighthood Was in Flower; or, The Love Story of Charles Brandon and Mary Tudor, the King's Sister, and Happening in the Reign of His August Majesty, King Henry VIII . . . By Edwin Caskoden [pseud.]. Indianapolis and Kansas City: The Bowen-Merrill Company, 1898. 249 p., illus. CU, H, HEH, N, UC, UV, Y
Printed copyright notice dated 1897.
2nd issue has author's name on title page.

3589 MAKEEVER, JOHN L. The Wandering Jew: A Tale of the Ten Lost Tribes of Israel . . . Osceola, Nebr.: E. A. Walrath, 1891. 137, [5] p., front. LC

3590 MALCOLM, DAVID. A Fiend Incarnate . . . New York: J. Selwin Tait & Sons, 65 Fifth Avenue [cop. 1895]. 213 p. LC

3591 ——— Fifty Thousand Dollars Ransom: A Novel . . . New York: J. Selwin Tait & Sons, 1896. 227 p. HEH, LC

3592 MALLOW, MARSH, *pseud.* The Woman Did It . . . Chicago: Stereotyped and printed by the Chicago Legal News Company, 1879. 323 p. N

3593 MALONE, WALTER. The Coming of the King . . . Philadelphia: J. B. Lippincott Company, 1897. 174 p. CU, LC
*Also contains:* Manuscript Found on Mount Mitchell—The Judgment Day of the Moon—Foreclosing the Mortgage—A Preacher's Love Story—A Guardian and a Ward—Two Women—The Two Friends.

3594 MAN ABROAD: A Yarn of Some Other Century . . . New York: G. W. Dillingham. London: S. Low, Son & Co., 1887. 114 p.     LC

3595 MANLEY, R. M. The Queen of Ecuador: A Novel . . . New York: The H. W. Hagemann Publishing Company, 1894. 331 p., illus.     HEH

3596 ——— Some Children of Adam . . . New York: Worthington Company, 1892. 310 p., front.     CU, HEH

3597 MANLY, MRS. ANGIE STEWART. Hit and Miss: A Story of Real Life . . . Chicago: J. L. Regan & Co., printers and binders, 1883. 428 p.
     HEH, LC, N
Also published as: *Secrets of a Dark Plot in New York Society.* Chicago: Rhodes & McClure Publishing Co., 1893. 428 p., illus.     HEH
Also published as: *Kidnapped; or, Secrets of a Great Mystery.* Chicago: Rhodes & McClure Pub. Co., 1899.     HEH

MANN, A., *pseud. See* McNeill, Nevada

3598 MANN, FLORIAN ALEXANDER. Story of the Huguenots: A Sixteenth Century Narrative . . . St. Augustine, Fla.: Mann & Mann, 1898. 197 p.
     BU, CU, H, LC
At head of title: "Florida Historical Tales."
Deposited Mar. 6, 1899; printed copyright notice dated 1897.

3599 MANN, MARY TYLER (PEABODY). Juanita: A Romance of Real Life in Cuba Fifty Years Ago . . . Boston: D. Lothrop Company, Franklin and Hawley Streets [cop. 1887]. 436 p.     BA, H, HEH, N, O, UVB, Y

MANN, RUFUS, *pseud. See* Shaler, Sophia Penn (Page)

3600 MANNIX, MARY ELLEN. Chronicles of "The Little Sisters" . . . Notre Dame, Indiana: The Ave Maria [cop. 1899]. 378 p.     LC

3601 "A MAN'S A MAN FOR A' THAT" . . . New York: G. P. Putnam's Sons, 1879. 390 p.     BU, HEH, LC, Y
Of an American family in Rome.

MARBOURG, DOLORES, *pseud. See* Bacon, Mary Schell (Hoke)

MARCHMONT, JOHN, *pseud. See* Means, Mrs. Celina E.

3602 MAREAN, BEATRICE. The Tragedies of Oak Hurst: A Florida Romance . . . Chicago: Donohue, Henneberry & Co., 1891. 401 p., illus.     HEH

3603 ——— Won at Last: A Novel . . . Chicago: Donohue, Henneberry & Co., 1892. 342 p., front.     LC
Memphis, Tennessee.

MARIE, *Tante, pseud. See* Augustin, Marie-Joséphine

3604 MARK TWAIN'S LIBRARY OF HUMOR ... New York: Charles L. Webster & Company, 1888. 707 p., illus.    BU, CU, HEH, N, O, UC, UM, UP, UVB, Y
Comprises short stories, sketches, fables, excerpts from longer works, and poetry, by fifty-five authors.
Edited by William D. Howells.
BAL 1982 notes two states.

3605 MARKELL, CHARLES FREDERICK. Ypiranga: A Love Tale of the Brazils ... Baltimore: Printed by John Murphy & Co., 1897. 228 p.    HEH, LC, UM, UV

3606 MARKOE, ELLIS. My Lady's Heart: A Sketch ... Boston: Roberts Brothers, 1896. 178 p.    HEH, LC
Of a Belgian artist.

3607 MARR, KATE THYSON. Bound by the Law ... New York: G. W. Dillingham Co., 1898. 362 p.    HEH, LC
Of a worthless husband.

3608 ———— Confessions of a Grass Widow: A Novel ... New York, Chicago, London: F. Tennyson Neely Co. [cop. 1900]. 301 p., illus.    LC
Deposited Jan. 5, 1900.

3609 MARRIED ABOVE HER: A Society Romance. By a Lady of New York ... Philadelphia: T. B. Peterson & Brothers, 306 Chestnut Street [cop. 1884]. 566 p.    HEH
Country girl marries a city man.

3610 MARSH, CHARLES LEONARD. A Gentleman Juror ... Chicago and New York: Rand, McNally & Co., 1899. 319 p.    HEH, LC, Y
A juror proves a convicted man innocent.

3611 ———— Opening the Oyster: A Story of Adventure ... Chicago: A. C. McClurg and Company, 1889. 361 p., illus.    AP, HEH, LC, N, O, UM, Y
Two men and their travels; partly in California.

3612 [MARSH, GEORGE COOK.] Lakeside Cottage ... Boston: James H. Earle, publisher, 1894. 280 p.    H, HEH, LC
Temperance novel.

3613 MARSHALL, B. Silver Lining Series, Number Two ... San Francisco: William Doxey, 1894. 149 p., illus.    HEH, LC
*Contains:* Story of a Watch—The Contraband.
At head of title: "Author's Edition."
Binder's title: "Story of a Watch, and Other Sketches."

MARSHALL, DABNEY. The Escape. *In* New Stories from the Chap-Book (1898), No. 3949.

3614 MARSHALL, LUTHER. Thomas Boobig: A Complete Enough Account of His Life and Singular Disappearance. Narration of His Scribe . . . Boston: Lee and Shepard, 10 Milk Street [cop. 1895]. 349 p., front.
HEH, LC, N, UP
Science fiction.

MARSHALL, NELLY NICHOL. *See* McAfee, Nelly Nichol (Marshall)

3615 MARTIN, AMARALA (ARTER). A Feather's Weight: A Story of Mystery . . . New York: The Abbey Press, 114 Fifth Avenue. London, Montreal [cop. 1900]. 131 p.
LC
Registered Nov. 30, 1900, but LC copies not received until Jan. 22, 1901.

3616 ———— Our Uncle and Aunt . . . New York & London: G. P. Putnam's Sons; the Knickerbocker Press, 1888. 223 p.
HEH, LC, O, UC, Y

3617 MARTIN, CAROLINE. The Blue Ridge Mystery: A Novel . . . New York: Robert Lewis Weed Company [cop. 1897]. 373 p.
HEH
Murder mystery.

3618 MARTIN, DÉSIRÉE. Les Veillées d'une Soeur; ou, Le Destin d'un Brin de Mousse . . . Nouvelle-Orléans: Imprimerie Cosmopolite, 1877. 230 p.
LC, Y

3619 MARTIN, ELIZABETH GILBERT (DAVIS). Whom God Hath Joined: A Novel . . . New York: Henry Holt and Company, 1886. 387 p.
AP, BA, H, HEH, LC, O, Y
At head of title: "Leisure Hour Series—No. 189."

3620 MARTIN, ELLEN. The Feet of Clay: A Novel . . . New York: Brown & Derby, 1882. 343 p.
BU, CU, H, HEH, LC
Civil War novel.

3621 MARTIN, HELEN (REIMENSNYDER). The Elusive Hildegarde: A Novel . . . New York: R. F. Fenno & Company, 1900. 328 p.
H, HEH, LC, O, UP
Charleston, South Carolina.

3622 [————] Warren Hyde . . . New York: R. F. Fenno & Company, 9 and 11 East 16th Street [cop. 1897]. 346 p.
HEH, LC, O
Hyde is the owner of a woolen mill in Winchester, Pa.

3623 MARTIN, JAMES M. Which Way, Sirs, the Better? A Story of Our Toilers . . . Boston: Arena Publishing Company, 1895. 215 p.
LC
Of a strike in the Pennsylvania coal mines.

3624 MARVIN, EULA. Beset on Every Side: A Novel . . . Rahway, N.J.: W. L. Mershon & Co., 1879. 100 p. Printed in double columns.
HEH

3625 MASON, BENJAMIN FRANKLIN. Scientific Prospecting, and Other Short Stories . . . [Oakland, Calif.? 189-?] Cover title, pp. [52]-111.
This apparently incomplete book examined at New York Public Library.

3626 ———— Through War to Peace . . . [Oakland, Calif.: Pacific Publishing Co.]; Published for the author, 1891. 113 p., front.    HEH, LC
Civil War story.

3627 ———— The Village Mystery; or, The Spectres of St. Argyle . . . New York: Whiting, 1887.
Listed in Hinkel.

3628 MASON, CAROLINE (ATWATER). The Minister of Carthage . . . Philadelphia: Curtis Publishing Company. New York: Doubleday & McClure Co., 1899. 150 p., illus.    HEH, LC, UC
At head of title: "Ladies' Home Journal Library of Fiction."
Arraignment of clergymen who seek self-aggrandisement.

3629 ———— A Minister of the World . . . New York: A. D. F. Randolph and Co., 182 Fifth Avenue [cop. 1895]. 154 p., illus.    LC, O
Deposited June 6, 1895.
Of a fashionable New York pastorate.

3630 ———— A Wind Flower: A Novel . . . Philadelphia: A. J. Rowland, 1420 Chestnut Street [cop. 1899]. 282 p., front.    HEH, LC, O
Of a Quaker and a priest.

3631 ———— A Woman of Yesterday . . . New York: Doubleday, Page & Co., 1900. 367 p.    HEH, LC, O, Y
Of a utopian settlement.

3632 MASON, MRS. EVELEEN LAURA. An Episode in the Doings of the Dualized . . . Brookline, Mass.: Eveleen Laura Mason, 1898. 117 p.    H, LC
Verso of title page: "Boston: Press of Fish & Libby."

3633 ———— Hiero-Salem: The Vision of Peace. A Fiction Founded on Ideals Which Are Grounded in the Real . . . Boston: J. G. Cupples Company [cop. 1889]. 508 p., illus.    BU, H, HEH, LC, UP, Y
On the improvement of the human race.

3634 [MASON, FANNY WITHERSPOON.] Daddy Dave. By Mary Frances [pseud.]. New York: Funk & Wagnalls, 1886. 116 p.    CU, LC
Relationship between slave and master during and after the Civil War.

3635 MASON, MRS. JAMES. All about Edith . . . Troy, N.Y.: H. B. Nims & Company, 1878. 232 p.    HEH

3636 [MASON, JAMES FREDERICK.] Cupid's Game with Hearts: A Tale as Told by Documents . . . San Francisco: Dodge Book and Stationery Co. [cop. 1897]. 18 l., illus.    BU, H, LC
Made up of facsimiles of letters, clippings, etc.

3637 MASON, MARY MURDOCH. Mae Madden ... Chicago: Jansen, McClurg & Co., 1876. 192 p.     BU, CU, H, HEH, LC, N, O, UC, UM, UP, Y
An American family in Rome.

3638 MASTERSON, KATE. The Dobleys . . . New York: G. W. Dillingham Company [cop. 1900]. 311 p.     HEH, LC, UM, UV
First published as a series of Sunday stories in the New York *Sun*.

3639 MATHER, FRED. In the Louisiana Lowlands: A Sketch of Plantation Life, Fishing, and Camping Just after the Civil War, and Other Tales . . . New York: Forest and Stream Publishing Co., 1900. 321 p., illus.
    CU, H, LC, Y

3640 MATHEWS, AMELIE VERONIQUE (PETIT) CHILD. Plural Marriage: The Heart-History of Adèle Hersch. By Veronique Petit. Ithaca, N.Y.: E. D. Norton, 1885. 99 p.     LC

3641 [MATHEWS, FRANCES AYMAR.] His Way and Her Will: A Novel. By A. X. [pseud.]. Chicago, New York, and San Francisco: Belford, Clarke & Co., 1888. 235 p.     LC

3642 ——— A Married Man: A Novel ... Chicago and New York: Rand, McNally & Company [cop. 1899]. 331 p.     HEH, LC, O
Paris.

3643 ——— The New Yorkers, and Other People ... New York: Godfrey A. S. Wieners, 1900. 436 p.     H, LC, UC
*Also contains:* In Clinton Place—The Foreigner—Two of a Kind and the Joker—The Empress of an Hour—When the Tzar Is Crowned—The Spirit Traveller—The Lost Year—The Prisoner of the Steen—The Cat's Eye.

3644 MATSON, NEHEMIAH. Raconter: Four Romantic Stories Relating to Pioneer Life, Scenes in Foreign Countries, Religious Fanaticism, Love, Murder ... Chicago: Geo. K. Hazlitt & Co., printers, 1882. 219 p., illus.     LC, N, UM

3645 MATTHEWS, BRANDER. The Action and the Word: A Novel of New York ... New York and London: Harper & Brothers, 1900. 261 p., illus.     AP, BU, H, HEH, LC, N, O, UM, UP, UV, Y

——— Chesterfield's Postal-Cards to His Son. *In* Mavericks (1892), No. 3663.

3646 ——— A Confident To-Morrow: A Novel of New York ... New York and London: Harper & Brothers, 1900. 300 p., illus.
    AP, CU, H, HEH, LC, N, O, UC, UVB, Y

——— The Documents in the Case, with H. C. Bunner. *In* B. Matthews, In Partnership (1884), No. 3649.
Later printed in Nos. 3659 and 5267.

———— Edged Tools, with W. H. Pollock. *In* B. Matthews, With My Friends (1891), No. 3659.

3647 ———— A Family Tree, and Other Stories ... New York: Longmans, Green & Co., 1889. 236 p.      AP, BA, CU, H, HEH, LC, N, O, UC, UVB, Y
*Also contains:* Memories—Idle Notes of an Uneventful Voyage—On the Battle-Field—Scherzi & Skizzen.

3648 ———— His Father's Son: A Novel of New York ... New York: Harper & Brothers, 1896. 248 p., illus.      CU, H, HEH, O, UC, UM, UVB, Y
The copyright issue at LC, deposited July 10, 1895, is dated 1895 on title page.

3649 ———— In Partnership: Studies in Story-Telling. By Brander Matthews and H. C. Bunner. New York: Charles Scribner's Sons, 1884. 210 p.
AP, BA, BU, CU, H, HEH, LC, N, O, Y
*Contents:* The Documents in the Case, by Brander Matthews and H. C. Bunner—Venetian Glass, by B. Matthews—The Red Silk Handkerchief, by H. C. Bunner—The Seven Conversations of Dear Jones and Baby Van Rensselaer, by B. Matthews and H. C. Bunner—The Rival Ghosts, by B. Matthews—A Letter and a Paragraph, by H. C. Bunner—Playing a Part, by B. Matthews—Love in Old Cloathes, by H. C. Bunner.

3650 ———— In the Vestibule Limited ... New York: Harper and Brothers, 1892. 93 p., illus.      BA, CU, H, HEH, LC, N, O, UC, UM, UP, UVB

3651 ———— The Last Meeting: A Story ... New York: Charles Scribner's Sons, 1885. 268 p., illus.      AP, BA, CU, H, HEH, LC, N, O, UVB, Y

———— Mated by Magic, with W. H. Pollock. *In* B. Matthews, With My Friends (1891), No. 3659.

———— Memories. *In* Stories of the Army (1893), No. 5280.
Printed earlier in No. 3647.

———— One Story Is Good Till Another Is Told, with G. H. Jessop. *In* B. Matthews, With My Friends (1891), No. 3659.

3652 ———— Outlines in Local Color ... New York and London: Harper & Brothers, 1898. 240 p., illus.      BA, CU, H, HEH, LC, N, O, UC, UM, UV, Y
*Contents:* An Interview with Miss Marlenspuyk—A Letter of Farewell—A Glimpse of the Under World—A Wall Street Wooing—A Spring Flood in Broadway—The Vigil of McDowell Sutro—An Irrepressible Conflict—The Solo Orchestra—The Rehearsal of the New Play—A Candle in the Plate—Men and Women and Horses—In the Watches of the Night.

———— Playing a Part. *In* his In Partnership (1884), No. 3649.

———— The Rival Ghosts. *In* his In Partnership (1884), No. 3649.
Later printed in No. 3657.

3653 —————— The Royal Marine: An Idyl of Narragansett Pier . . . New York: Harper & Brothers, 1894. 144 p., illus.

BA, BU, CU, H, HEH, LC, N, O, UC, UM, UVB, Y

3654 —————— A Secret of the Sea, &c. . . . New York: Charles Scribner's Sons, 1886. 220 p. AP, BA, CU, H, HEH, LC, N, O, UM, UVB, Y

*Also contains:* 'Love at First Sight'—Brief, as Woman's Love—Perchance to Dream—Perturbed Spirits—Esther Feverel.

—————— The Seven Conversations of Dear Jones and Baby Van Rensselaer, with H. C. Brunner. *In* B. Matthews, In Partnership (1884), No. 3649.
Later printed in No. 3659.

3655 —————— The Story of a Story, and Other Stories . . . New York: Harper & Brothers, 1893. 234 p., illus. BA, CU, H, HEH, LC, N, O, UM, UVB, Y

*Also contains:* A Cameo and a Pastel—Two Letters—The New Member of the Club—Etelka Talmeyr: A Tale of Three.

3656 —————— A Tale of Twenty-Five Hours . . . New York: D. Appleton and Company, 1892. 189 p. BA, CU, H, HEH, LC, N, O, UC, UP, UVB, Y
George H. Jessop, jt. au.

3657 —————— Tales of Fantasy and Fact . . . New York: Harper & Brothers, 1896. 216 p., front. BA, BU, CU, H, HEH, LC, O, UM, UVB, Y

*Contents:* A Primer of Imaginary Geography—The Kinetoscope of Time—The Dream-Gown of the Japanese Ambassador—The Rival Ghosts—Sixteen Years without a Birthday—The Twinkling of an Eye—A Confidential Postscript.

—————— Three Wishes, with F. Anstey [i.e., T. A. Guthrie]. *In* B. Matthews, With My Friends (1891), No. 3659.

—————— Venetian Glass. *In* his In Partnership (1884), No. 3649.
Later included in No. 5269.

3658 —————— Vignettes of Manhattan . . . New York: Harper & Brothers, 1894. 180 p., illus. AP, BA, BU, CU, H, HEH, LC, N, O, UC, UM, UVB, Y

*Contents:* In the Little Church Down the Street—The Twenty-Ninth of February—At a Private View—Spring in a Side Street—A Decoration-Day Revery—In Search of Local Color—Before the Break of Day—A Midsummer Midnight—A Vista in Central Park—The Speech of the Evening—A Thanksgiving-Day Dinner—In the Midst of Life.

3659 —————— With My Friends: Tales Told in Partnership . . . New York: Longmans, Green & Co., 1891. 284 p.

AP, BA, CU, H, HEH, LC, N, O, UP, UVB, Y

*Contents:* The Documents in the Case, with H. C. Bunner—Seven Conversations of Dear Jones and Baby Van Rensselaer, with H. C. Bunner—Edged Tools: A Tale in Two Chapters, with Walter Herries Pollock—Mated by

Magic: A Story with a Postscript, with W. H. Pollock—One Story Is Good Till Another Is Told, with George H. Jessop—Three Wishes, with F. Anstey [pseud. of English writer Thomas Anstey Guthrie].

MATTHEWS, BRINSLEY, *pseud. See* Pearson, William Simpson

MATTHEWS, JAMES BRANDER. *See* Matthews, Brander

3660 MATTHEWS, SUE FROMAN. A Beggar's Story . . . New York, Chicago, Toronto: Fleming H. Revell Company [cop. 1894]. 114 p.  LC

3661 ——— Sic Vita Est (Such Is Life) . . . New York: G. W. Dillingham Co., 1896. 301 p.  LC

3662 MATTHEWS, VICTORIA (EARLE). Aunt Lindy: A Story Founded on Real Life. By Victoria Earle . . . New York, 1893. 16 p.  LC

3663 MAVERICKS: Short Stories Rounded Up. By Puck's Authors . . . New York: Keppler & Schwarzmann, 1892. 199 p., illus.  HEH, UC, Y
*Contents:* A Modern Hans Sachs, by W. J. Henderson—Chesterfield's Postal-Cards to His Son, by Brander Matthews—Misther Handhrigan's Love Story, by Madeline S. Bridges [i.e., Mary Ainge De Vere]—Old Jonesy, by Walter Learned—The Romance of a Spotted Man, by William Wallace Cook—Recollections of a Busy Life, by Williston Fish—The Wight That Quailed, by Kate W. Rider—Biddy's Dream, by George H. Jessop—True Love's Triumph, by H. L. Wilson—Aunt Mary's Obituary, by James L. Ford—Internecine Comparison, by James S. Goodwin—A Drawn Battle, by Tudor Jenks—The Magic City, by "Sidney" [pseud.]—Mr. Wilkenning's Hobby, by C. H. Augur—The Cashier and the Burglar, by Thomas Wharton—A Timely Hint, by Harry Romaine—A Brilliant Idea, by Flavel S. Mines—The Man with the Black Crape Mask, by R. K. Munkittrick—The Recording Spook, by H. C. Bunner.

MAXIMILLIAN, *pseud. See* Glass, Maximillian

3664 MAXWELL, ELLEN (BLACKMAR). The Bishop's Conversion . . . New York: Hunt & Eaton. Cincinnati: Cranston & Curts, 1892. 384 p., illus.
LC, Y
To refute false impressions of missionaries in India.

3665 ——— Three Old Maids in Hawaii . . . New York: Eaton & Mains. Cincinnati: Curts & Jennings, 1896. 394 p., illus.  BA, H, HEH, LC, Y

3666 ——— The Way of Fire . . . New York: Dodd, Mead and Company, 1897. 244 p.  BA, HEH, LC, O
Of India's half-castes.

MAY, ANSLEY, *pseud. See* Dickinson, Edith May

MAY, MATTIE, *pseud. See* Brown, Mrs. C. R.

MAY, PHILIP, *pseud. See* Chittenden, Richard Handy

MAY, SOPHIE, *pseud. See* Clarke, Rebecca Sophia

3667 [MAY, THOMAS P.] The Earl of Mayfield: A Novel ... Philadelphia: T. B. Peterson & Brothers, 306 Chestnut Street [cop. 1879]. 438 p.
HEH, LC
Civil War and after.

3668 —— Illan Yenrutt: A Romance ... New Orleans: Printed at the New Orleans Democrat Office, 1880. Cover title, 90 p. Printed in double columns. LC

3669 —— A Prince of Breffny ... Philadelphia: T. B. Peterson & Brothers, 306 Chestnut Street [cop. 1881]. 428 p. HEH, LC, UVB
Deposited Oct. 6, 1881.
Also published as: *Lady Edith; or, Alton Towers.* Philadelphia: T. B. Peterson & Brothers [cop. 1882]. LC
Deposited Mar. 27, 1882.

3670 MAYER, ORLANDO B. Mallodoce, the Briton: His Wanderings from Druidism to Christianity ... Richmond, Va.: Everett Waddey Co., 1891. 110 p. LC
John A. Chapman, jt. au.

3671 MAYNARD, CORA. The Letter and the Spirit ... New York: Stokes, 1898. 330 p. CU, HEH, LC
New York society.

3672 —— Some Modern Heretics: A Novel ... Boston: Roberts Bros., 1896. 382 p. CU, HEH, LC, UVB

3673 MAYO, JOSEPH. Woodbourne: A Novel of the Revolutionary Period in Virginia and Maryland. In Two Parts ... Baltimore: The Baltimore Publishing Company, 1884. 224, 138, [1] p. HEH, LC

3674 MEAD, LEON. The Bow-Legged Ghost, and Other Stories: A Book of Humorous Sketches... New York; Akron, Ohio; Chicago: The Werner Company [cop. 1899]. 581 p., front. CU, HEH, LC, O, UM
*Contains:* When Ezra Sang First Bass—The Woman in Yellow—An Assumed Weakness—"Revels of the Muses"—The Belle of the Dinner—The Rise of Regan—Mrs. Tubbs's Manoeuvres—A Parlor-Car Romance—A Telling Speech —The Great Sparrow Dispute—"Brooms"—The Bearded Wife—Montressor —Mrs. Beveridge's Adventure—A Poet's Passion—The Story of Four Carrier Pigeons—A Living Tombstone—The Mind Children.

3675 MEAD, LUCIA TRUE (AMES). Memoirs of a Millionaire. By Lucia True Ames ... Boston and New York: Houghton, Mifflin and Company. The Riverside Press, Cambridge, 1889. 325 p. BA, H, HEH, LC, N, O
The Boston millionaire was a woman philanthropist.

MEAD, WILLIAM LEON. *See* Mead, Leon

3676 [MEANS, MRS. CELINA E.] Thirty-Four Years: An American Story of Southern Life. By John Marchmont [pseud.] ... Philadelphia: Claxton, Remsen & Haffelfinger, 1878. 336 p.                    LC, O, UV
Of the Ku Klux Klan.

3677 MEANY, J. L. The Lovers; or, Cupid in Ireland ... [Havana, Ill.: Democrat Power Printing House], cop. 1891. 104 p.                    LC

3678 MEARS, MARY MARTHA. Emma Lou—Her Book ... New York: Henry Holt and Company, 1896. 277 p.                    H, LC, O, Y

3679 MECRACKEN, SARA L. Elsie Ainslie, a Victim of Social Wrong ... Springfield, Mass.: Star Publishing Co., cop. 1885. 108 p.                    HEH, LC

3680 [MEDICI, CHARLES DE.] Two Lunatics: A Remarkable Story by One of Them ... New York: The Oxford Publishing Co., 1889. 157 p.    HEH

3681 [MEEKER, MRS. NELLIE J.] Beverly Osgood; or, When the Great City Is Awake. A Novel. By Jane Valentine [pseud.] ... New York: G. W. Dillingham, 1900. 335 p.                    LC
New York.

3682 [———] The Old Stone House. By Jane Valentine [pseud.] ... St. Louis: The St. Louis News Company, 1883. 241 p.          HEH, LC, Y

3683 [———] Time's Scythe. By Jane Valentine [pseud.] ... New York: Cassell & Company, Limited, 104-106 Fourth Avenue [cop. 1889]. 209 p.                    LC

MEEKINS, GO. WASH., *pseud. See* Bagby, George William

MEEKINS, LYNN ROBY. On the Woodbrook Accommodation. *In* Short Story Masterpieces (1900), No. 4931.

3684 ——— The Robb's Island Wreck, and Other Stories ... Chicago and Cambridge: Stone and Kimball, 1894. 182 p., 1 l.
CU, H, HEH, LC, N, O, UC, Y
*Also contains:* Two Booms—In the Early Christmas Morning—The Colonel's Call—The Nomination—The Opening Gun—The Election—A New Deal.

3685 ——— Some of Our People ... Baltimore: Williams & Wilkins Company, 1898. 196 p., 1 l., front.                    H, HEH, LC, UV

3686 MEISSNER, SOPHIE (RADFORD) DE. A Tcherkesse Prince ... Boston: De Wolfe, Fiske & Co., 361 and 365 Washington Street [cop. 1892]. 305 p.
HEH, LC

3687 [———] The Terrace of Mon Désir: A Novel of Russian Life. Boston: Cupples, Upham and Company [cop. 1886]. 241 p.        LC, UP

3688 MELOY, WILLIAM T. Lucile Vernon; or, The Church at Lansington . . .
Chicago, New York: Fleming H. Revell [1890]. 208 p.　　HEH
First published by the United Presbyterian Board, 1881.

3689 [MENDENHALL, BENONI.] Married the Wrong Man: A True and Wonderful Story . . . [Dallas City, Ill., cop. 1893.] 146 p.　　LC
Deposited Jan. 20, 1893.

3690 MERCIER, ALFRED. La Fille du Prêtre . . . Nouvelle-Orléans: Imprimerie
Cosmopolite, 1877. 3 vols. (135, 107, 156 p.)　　H

3691 ────── L'Habitation Saint-Ybars; ou, Maitres et Esclaves en Louisiane.
Récit Social . . . Nouvelle-Orléans: Imprimerie Franco-Américaine,
Eugène Antoine, propriétaire, 1881. 234 p.　　LC, N, UV, Y
Ante bellum Louisiana.

3692 ────── Johnelle. Nouvelle-Orléans: Eugène Antoine, 1891. 221 p.　LC

3693 ────── Lidia . . . Nouvelle-Orléans: Imprimerie Franco-Américaine
d'Eugène Antoine, 1887. 102 p., 1 l.　　LC

3694 MEREDITH, HARRY. King Alcohol: A Romance of the Keeley Institute
. . . New York, 1893. 153 p.　　LC

3695 MEREDITH, KATHERINE MARY CHEEVER. Drumsticks . . . A Little Story
of a Sinner and a Child. New York, London: The Transatlantic Publishing Company, 1895. 192 p.　　HEH, LC

3696 ────── Green Gates: An Analysis of Foolishness . . . New York: D.
Appleton and Company, 1896. 257 p.　　HEH, LC, O
New York fashionable life.

3697 [──────] Sketches from Truth. By Johanna Staats [pseud.]. New
York: Press of Nocton & Company, 1892. 211 p., illus.　　LC
Contents: The Waltz from Nanon–Written on a Roseleaf–A Glass of Mar-
aschino–A Mirrored Fantasy–The Red Mouse–A Chromatic Effect–My
Friend the Cat–The Story of a Chump–The Innocent Guilty–Jim Cuff, Ras-
cal–A Rich Pauper–A Dilettante's Baby–Jack of Hearts–A Modern Guin-
evere.

3698 MEREDITH, WILLIAM TUCKEY. Not of Her Father's Race . . . New York:
Cassell Publishing Company, 104 & 106 Fourth Avenue [cop. 1890].
291 p.　　AP, LC, O, Y
Miscegenation.

3699 MEREDITH, Y. B. Point Prominence: The History of a Church . . . Cincinnati: Walden & Stowe, 1883. 226 p., illus.　　LC

MERINGTON, MARGUERITE. A Matter of Course. In Some Short Stories
[cop. 1900], No. 5070.

3700 MERIWETHER, ELIZABETH (AVERY). Black and White: A Novel... New York: E. J. Hale & Son, 1883. 250 p. LC

3701 ——— The Master of Red Leaf: A Tale ... First American from the London Edition. New York: E. J. Hale & Son, 1880. 277 p.
AP, HEH, LC, O
Post Civil War Louisiana.

3702 MERIWETHER, LEE. A Lord's Courtship: A Novel ... Chicago: Laird & Lee [cop. 1900]. 288 p., illus. HEH, LC
Wealthy Americans in Europe.

3703 [———] Miss Chunk: A Tale of the Times. St. Louis, Mo.: Walter Vrooman [1897]. 247 p. HEH
Of labor and politics.

3704 MERRILL, ALBERT ADAMS. The Great Awakening: The Story of the Twenty-Second Century ... Boston: George Book Publishing Co., 1899. 345 p., front. H, HEH, LC, Y

3705 [MERRILL, JAMES MILFORD.] Forced Apart; or, Exiled by Fate. By Morris Redwing [pseud.]. Chicago: Laird & Lee, cop. 1886. 166 p., illus. Y

3706 [———] Tracked to Death; or, Eagle Gray, the Western Detective. By Morris Redwing [pseud.] ... Chicago: Laird & Lee, cop. 1886. 197 p., front. HEH

3707 MERRON, ELEANOR. As the Wind Blows: A Novel... New York: Lovell, Coryell & Company, 310-318 Sixth Avenue [cop. 1895]. 330 p., front. HEH, LC

3708 MERWIN, SAMUEL. The Short Line War. By Merwin-Webster. New York: The Macmillan Company. London: Macmillan & Co., Ltd., 1899. 334 p. BA, CU, H, HEH, LC, N, O, UV
Henry Kitchell Webster, jt. au.
Of railroads.

3709 METCALF, W. H. A Summer in Oldport Harbor: A Novel ... Philadelphia: J. B. Lippincott Company, 1887. 285 p.
AP, BU, CU, HEH, LC, O, Y

3710 METCALFE, JAMES STETSON. Mythology for Moderns ... New York: Life Publishing Company, 1899. 117 p., illus. BU, H, UM, Y

3711 [MEYER, ANNIE (NATHAN).] Helen Brent, M.D.: A Social Study. New York: Cassell Publishing Company, 104 & 106 Fourth Avenue [cop. 1892]. 196 p. BA, HEH, LC, O, UC

3712 [MEYER, GEORGE HOMER.] Almiranté: A Romance of Old-Time California. By "A Native." San Francisco: W. M. Hinton & Co., 1890. 115 p. LC

3713 MEYER, LUCY JANE (RIDER). Deaconess Stories . . . Chicago: Hope Publishing Co., 84 Wabash Avenue [cop. 1900]. 253 p., illus.    LC

3714 MEYERS, ROBERT CORNELIUS V. The Colonel's Christmas Morning, and Other Stories . . . Philadelphia: Franklin Book Co., 1900. 340 p., illus.
                                                                                    LC

3715 ———— Miss Margery's Roses: A Love Story . . . Philadelphia: T. B. Peterson & Brothers, 306 Chestnut Street [cop. 1879]. 256 p.    LC

3716 MEYNARDIE, FLORELLA. Amy Oakly; or, The Reign of the Carpet-Bagger. A Story . . . Charleston, S.C.: Walker, Evans, & Cogswell, printers, 1879. 249 p.    LC, O
South Carolina.

3717 MICHAELIS, RICHARD C. Looking Forward . . . An Answer to Looking Backward, by Edward Bellamy. [Chicago and New York: Rand, McNally & Company], cop. 1890. 123 p.    CU, H, N

3718 MICHAELS, JANIE CHASE. A Natural Sequence: A Story of Phoenix, Arizona . . . Bangor, Maine: Charles H. Glass & Company, 1895. 151 p.
                                                                                    HEH

3719 MICHELS, NICHOLAS. The Godhood of Man . . . His Religious, Political, and Economic Development and the Sources of Social Inequality. By Nicolai Mikalowich. Chicago, U.S.A.: Published by the author, 1899. 150 p.    LC
Note on LC card: "A sociological work in narrative and conversational style, representing the working classes as victims of church and state."

3720 ———— Numa's Vision: An Allegory . . . Chicago: Nicholas Michels [cop. 1899]. 173 p.    BU, H, LC, UC

3721 [MICHELS, ELLA STERLING (CLARK).] The Little Mountain Princess, a Sierra Snow-Plant. By Ella S. Cummins [pseud.]. Boston: Loring publishers, corner Bromfield and Washington Streets [cop. 1880]. 230 p.    HEH
California and Mexico.

[————] Portrait of a California Girl, by Ella Sterling Cummins [pseud.]. *In* Short Stories by California Authors (1885), No. 4929.

3722 MICHELS, PHILIP VERRILL. Nella, the Heart of the Army: A Novel . . . New York: R. F. Fenno & Company. London: John Macqueen [cop. 1900]. 395 p.    LC

MIKALOWICH, NICOLAI. *See* Michels, Nicholas

3723 MILDRED, E. W. The Ghost-House; or, The Story of Rose Lichen . . . [New York: A. D. F. Randolph & Co.], 1893. 65 p., illus. BU, HEH, LC, Y
Florida.

3724 MILES, AUSTIN. About My Father's Business ... New York: The Mershon Company [cop. 1900]. 265 p.      LC
Of the church.

3725 MILLARD, BAILEY. A Pretty Bandit ... New York: The Eskdale Press, 1 Madison Avenue [cop. 1897]. 264 p.      HEH, LC
*Contains:* The Girl Reporter—All for a Mormon Girl—A Notch in a Principality—A Struggle wtih Insomnia—The "Bar L" Brand—'Lish of Alkali Flat —Horse-in-the-Water—Perfectly Legal—Kate of the Desert—Athletic Miss Brown—The Brakebeam Rider—On the Caliente Trail—Lolita—The Making of Her.
Deposited May 1, 1897.
Also published as: *She of the West.* New York: Continental Publishing Co. [1899]. Listed PW, Feb. 18, 1899.

MILLARD, FRANK BAILEY. *See* Millard, Bailey

3726 [MILLARD, MRS. SARAH M.] M. of B. Council Bluffs, Iowa: Printed by S. M. Millard [cop. 1893]. 51 p.      LC

3727 MILLER, MRS. ALEXANDER McVEIGH. A Dreadful Temptation ... New York: International Book Company, 3, 4, 5, and 6 Mission Place [cop. 1883]. 285 p.      HEH
*Also contains:* Wild Margaret, by Geraldine Fleming.
Majority of Mrs. Miller's novels were published in subscription series.

3728 ——— Nina's Peril: A Novel ... New York: G. W. Dillingham. London: S. Low, Son & Co., 1887. 368 p.      UVB

3729 MILLER, ANNIE (JENNESS). Barbara Thayer, Her Glorious Career: A Novel. By Annie Jenness. Boston: Lee and Shepard. New York: Charles T. Dillingham, 1884. 180 p.      H, HEH, LC, O, Y

3730 ——— The Philosopher of Driftwood: A Novel. By Mrs. Jenness Miller. Washington, D.C.: Jenness Miller Publications, 1897. 323 p., front.      CU, HEH, LC

3731 MILLER, BELLE M. Veni! Vidi! ———? ... Columbus, O.: Hann & Adair [cop. 1888]. 186 p.      LC
Deposited Dec. 15, 1888, by Julia A. Miller, author's sister.

MILLER, CINCINNATUS HINER. *See* Miller, Joaquin

3732 MILLER, EMILY CLARK (HUNTINGTON). The Parish of Fair Haven ... Chicago: The Union Book Concern, 1876. 30 p.      LC

3733 MILLER, GEORGE ERNEST. Luxilla: A Romance ... [Mobile, Ala.], cop. 1885. 54 p.      LC

3734 ——— Mobilia: A Novel ... [Mobile, Ala.], cop. 1886. 137 p.   HEH, LC

3735 [MILLER, GEORGE NOYES.] The Strike of a Sex: A Novel. By ? New York: G. W. Dillingham, 1890. 235 p. LC

3736 MILLER, GUSTAVUS HINDMAN. Is Marriage a Failure? . . . Chattanooga, Tenn.: Republican Printing Co., 1892. 292 p. LC
At head of title: "Copyrighted 1892 by Gus Miller."

MILLER, HARRIET (MANN). The Girls' Sketching Camp, by Olive Thorne Miller [pseud.]. *In* L. C. H. Langford, *comp.*, The Woman's Story (1889), No. 3206.

MILLER, MRS. JENNESS. *See* Miller, Annie (Jenness)

3737 MILLER, JOAQUIN. The Building of the City Beautiful . . . Cambridge & Chicago: Stone & Kimball, 1893. 196 p., 1 l.
BU, H, HEH, LC, N, UC, UP, UVB, Y
Utopian romance.

3738 ———— The Destruction of Gotham . . . New York, London: Funk & Wagnalls, 1886. 214 p.
AP, BA, BU, CU, H, HEH, LC, N, O, UC, UM, UP, UVB, Y

3739 ———— First Fam'lies of the Sierras . . . Chicago: Jansen, McClurg & Co., 1876. 258 p.     BA, BU, CU, H, HEH, LC, N, O, UC, UM, UVB, Y
Also published as: *The Danites in the Sierras.* Chicago: Jansen, McClurg & Company, 1881. 258 p.     BA, BU, H, HEH, LC, N
The later ed. cuts back chap. xvii from p. 156 to p. 154 and supplies a new chap. xviii, "The Magdalene Samaritans," for the one previously entitled "Blood."

3740 ———— '49: The Gold-Seeker of the Sierras . . . New York, London: Funk & Wagnalls, 1884. 148 p.     AP, BA, CU, N, UC, Y
Also published in the omitted "Standard Library," No. 123, Sept. 8, 1884.

———— A Lion and a Lioness. *In* Eleven Possible Cases [cop. 1891], No. 1737.

3741 ———— The One Fair Woman . . . Three Volumes in One. New York: G. W. Carleton & Co. London: Chapman & Hall, 1876. 548 p.
BA, BU, CU, H, HEH, LC, N, O, UC, UM, UP, UVB, Y

3742 ———— Shadows of Shasta . . . Chicago: Jansen, McClurg & Company, 1881. 184 p.     BA, BU, CU, H, HEH, LC, N, O, UC, UM, UP, UVB, Y

3743 [MILLER, L. A.] The Life of a Tramp and a Trip through Hell. By Peter Blum [pseud. of L. A. Miller and C. V. Goolsby] . . . Jacksonville, Fla.: C. S. Warnock & Co., 1894. 146 p. LC
Copyright notice at head of title.

3744 MILLER, MRS. LUCY HENRY. Ash-Wednesday; or, Society's Ban. A Long Story of One Chapter . . . Richmond, Va.: Patrick Keenan, book publisher and printer, 1882. 102 p.     HEH, UV
Catholic story; South.

3745 MILLER, MARTHA CAROLYNE (KELLER). The Fair Enchantress; or, How She Won Men's Hearts. By Miss M. C. Keller . . . Philadelphia: T. B. Peterson & Brothers, 306 Chestnut Street [cop. 1883]. 330 p.    UM
New Orleans.

3746 MILLER, MINNIE (WILLIS) BAINES. His Cousin, the Doctor: A Story. By Minnie Willis Baines . . . Cincinnati: Cranston & Stowe. New York: Hunt & Eaton, 1891. 198 p.     LC
Attacks Christian Science.

3747 —— Mrs. Cherry's Sister; or, Christian Science at Fairfax. By Minnie W. Baines-Miller . . . Cincinnati: Jennings & Pye. New York: Eaton & Mains [cop. 1900]. 355 p.     HEH, LC

3748 —— The Silent Land: A Study . . . Cincinnati: Cranston & Stowe. New York: Hunt & Eaton, 1890. 164 p.     LC, UC

MILLER, OLIVE THORNE, pseud. See Miller, Harriet (Mann)

3749 MILLER, SALLIE BRANCH. "Zeph": A Novel . . . Lynchburg, Va.: J. P. Bell Company, 1889. 184 p.     LC

3750 MILLER, WILLIAM AMOS. The Sovereign Guide: A Tale of Eden . . . Los Angeles, California: Geo. Rice & Sons, 1898. 130 p., front. HEH, LC
California.

3751 MILLET, FRANCIS DAVIS. A Capillary Crime, and Other Stories . . . New York: Harper & Brothers, 1892. 284 p., illus.   BA, BU, H, LC, Y
Also contains: A Faded Scapular—Yatil—Tedesco's Rubina—Medusa's Head —The Fourth Waits—The Bush.

—— Yatil. In Stories by American Authors, V (1884), No. 5271. Later printed in No. 3751.

3752 MILLS, ESTELLA J. Storm-Swept; or, Saved to Serve . . . Boston: James H. Earle, 1896. 334 p., front.     HEH, O
The copyright issue at LC, deposited Feb. 22, 1897, is dated 1897 on title page.

3753 MILLS, S. M. Palm Branches . . . [Sandusky, Ohio: Register Steam Press], 1878. 128 p.     UC, Y

3754 MILLS, WILLIS. Scarlet or White? . . . New York: Authors' Publishing Association, 114 Fifth Avenue [cop. 1897]. 172 p.     LC
Of a fallen woman.

3755 MILNE, FRANCES MARGARET (TENER). Heliotrope: A San Francisco Idyl Twenty-Five Years Ago. And Other Sketches ... San Francisco: The Star Publishing Company, 1897. 124 p.    HEH
*Also contains:* A May Basket—"Home, Sweet Home"—Her Neighbor—Broken Promises.

MINES, FLAVEL SCOTT. A Brilliant Idea. *In* Mavericks (1892), No. 3663.

———— A Slave to Fancy. *In* Hanks: Assorted Yarns from Puck (1893), No. 2444.

3756 [MINOR, MRS. KATE PLEASANTS] *comp.* From Dixie: Original Articles Contributed by Southern Writers for Publication as a Souvenir of the Memorial Bazaar for the Benefit of the Monument to the Private Soldiers and Sailors of the Confederacy ... Richmond, Va.: West, Johnston & Co., 1893. 167 p.    CU, H, HEH, LC, N, UV, Y
*Contains:* Alison Stewart, by M. G. McClelland—Pendleton Neil of Rosalia, by William W. Archer—Miss Isabella, by N. B. Winston—Some Data, by Sarah Barnwell Elliott.

3757 MINOR, THOMAS CHALMERS. Athothis: A Satire on Modern Medicine ... Cincinnati: Robert Clarke & Co., 1887. 194 p.    BA, CU, HEH, O, UM, UV

3758 [————] Her Ladyship ... Cincinnati: Peter G. Thomson, 1880. 217 p.    BA, LC, N, O

3759 [MINOT, RORERT SEDGWICK.] The Dead Speak. Boston: Alfred Mudge & Son, printers, 1881. 64 p.    LC

3760 MINTON, MAURICE M. Country Lanes and City Pavements: A Realistic Story of Metropolitan Life ... New York: Circulated through the American News Company, Chambers Street [cop. 1894]. 416 p., illus.    HEH

3761 MR. GHIM'S DREAM. New York: G. W. Carleton & Co. London: S. Low & Co., 1878. 258 p.    HEH, LC, O

3762 MRS. DRUSE'S CASE, and Maggie Houghtaling. An Innocent Woman Hanged. The Truth Revealed at Last. A Startling Confession. Dying Innocent to Save Those She Loved. Philadelphia, Pa.: The Old Franklin Publishing House, cop. 1887. 62 p., 1 l., illus.    HEH

3763 MITCHEL, FREDERIC AUGUSTUS. Chattanooga: A Romance of the American Civil War ... [New York]: The American News Company [cop. 1891]. 229 p.    HEH, LC

3764 ———— Chickamauga: A Romance of the American Civil War ... New York: The Star Book Company [cop. 1892]. 289 p.    N, UM

3765 ———— Sweet Revenge: A Romance of the Civil War ... New York: Harper & Brothers, 1897. 248 p.    CU, HEH, LC, O

3766 [————] The Twenty Million Ransom: A Story of the Future. New York: "The Journalist," 1890. 198 p., map. LC

MITCHELL, E. P. The Ablest Man in the World. *In* Stories by American Authors, X (1885), No. 5276.

———— The Tachypomp. *In* Stories by American Authors, V (1884), No. 5271.

3767 [MITCHELL, GEORGE DEPUI.] "1999": An Historical Romance. By the Joint Editors, Lamb-Grévy [pseud. of G. D. Mitchell and Hugh Carlyle Young]. Wellsboro, Pa.: Republican Advocate Print, 1887. 30, [1] p., illus. LC

3768 MITCHELL, JOHN AMES. Amos Judd ... New York: Charles Scribner's Sons, 1895. 199 p. BA, H, HEH, LC, N, UM, UVB, Y

3769 ———— Gloria Victis ... New York: Charles Scribner's Sons, 1897. 269 p. BA, CU, H, HEH, LC, N, O, UM, UVB, Y

3770 ———— The Last American: A Fragment from the Journal of Khan-Li, Prince of Dimph-Yoo-Chur and Admiral in the Persian Navy. Edited by J. A. Mitchell. New York: Frederick A. Stokes & Brother, 1889. 78 p., 1 l., illus. H, HEH, LC, N, UC, UP, UV, Y

3771 ———— Life's Fairy Tales ... New York: Frederick A. Stokes Company, 1892. 117 p., illus. CU, HEH, LC, N, UM, UP, Y
*Contents:* The Drowsy Village—The Fairy Bishop—Uncle Rody—The Westwind and the Pine—Stillabel—The Wedding That Wasn't—The Pious Nobleman and the Blind Horse—The Belle and the Seal—The Lover, the Twelve Hornets, and the Enchanted Garden of Zpek—Why the Ocean Is Colder at Some Places Than at Others—The Average Dog and the Usual Man—The Luckless Prince—The Adventures of Two Criminals—The Dissolute Beetle —The Enchanted Portrait.

3772 ———— That First Affair, and Other Sketches ... New York: Charles Scribner's Sons, 1896. 177 p., illus.
BA, CU, H, HEH, LC, N, O, UM, UP, UVB, Y
*Also contains:* Mrs. Lofter's Ride—Two Portraits—The Man Who Vanished —A Bachelor's Supper.

3773 MITCHELL, JOHN WILLIAM. On the Mesa ... Washington: Will A. Page, 1897. 28, [1] p., 2 l. LC
225 copies printed.

3774 MITCHELL, LAISDELL. Colonel ... Philadelphia: A. J. Rowland, 1896. 203 p., illus. HEH, LC
Post Civil War South.

3775 MITCHELL, LANGDON ELWYN. Love in the Backwoods ... New York: Harper & Brothers, 1897. 249 p., illus. BA, CU, HEH, LC, O
*Contents:* Two Mormons from Muddlety—Alfred's Wife.

3776 MITCHELL, SILAS WEIR. The Adventures of François, Foundling, Thief, Juggler, and Fencing-Master during the French Revolution ... New York: The Century Co., 1898. 321 p., illus.
AP, BU, CU, H, HEH, N, O, UC, UP, UVB, Y

3777 ——— The Autobiography of a Quack, and The Case of George Dedlow ... New York: The Century Co., 1900. 149 p., illus.
AP, BA, BU, CU, H, HEH, LC, N, O, UC, UM, UVB, Y

3778 ——— Characteristics ... New York: The Century Co., 1892. 307 p.
H, HEH, LC, N, O, UVB, Y

3779 ——— Dr. North and His Friends ... New York: The Century Co., 1900. 499 p. AP, BA, H, HEH, LC, N, O, UP, UVB, Y

3780 ——— Far in the Forest: A Story ... Philadelphia: J. B. Lippincott Company, 1889. 298 p. AP, BA, BU, HEH, LC, N, O, UVB, Y
LC has copy of 302 p. ed. published New York: The Century Co., 1898; adds a new chapter.

3781 ——— Hephzibah Guinness, Thee and You, and A Draft on the Bank of Spain ... Philadelphia: J. B. Lippincott & Co., 1880. 199 p.
AP, BA, CU, HEH, LC, N, O, UC, UM, UP, UVB, Y

3782 ——— Hugh Wynne, Free Quaker, Sometime Brevet Lieutenant-Colonel on the Staff of His Excellency General Washington ... New York: The Century Co., 1897. 2 vols. (306, 261 p.), fronts.
AP, BA, CU, H, HEH, LC, N, O, UC, UM, UP, UVB

3783 ——— In War Time ... Boston, New York: Houghton, Mifflin and Company. The Riverside Press, Cambridge, 1885. 423 p.
AP, H, HEH, LC, N, O, UVB, Y

3784 ——— A Madeira Party ... New York: The Century Co., 1895. 165 p., front. BA, H, HEH, LC, N, O, UVB, Y
*Also contains:* A Little More Burgundy.

3785 ——— Roland Blake ... Boston and New York: Houghton, Mifflin and Company. The Riverside Press, Cambridge, 1886. 379 p.
AP, CU, H, HEH, LC, N, O, UM, UP, UVB
Civil War novel.

3786 ——— When All the Woods Are Green: A Novel ... New York: The Century Co., 1894. 419 p., front. AP, BA, HEH, LC, N, O, UM, UP, UVB, Y

MITCHELL, VIOLET E. Miss Gwynne's Burglar. *In* C. King, Rancho del Muerto [cop. 1895], No. 3109.

3787 MITCHELL, WALTER. Two Strings to His Bow . . . Boston and New York: Houghton, Mifflin and Company. The Riverside Press, Cambridge, 1894. 278 p.                    H, HEH, LC, O, Y
Of a clergyman.

3788 MITCHELL, WILLIS. The Inhabitants of Mars, Their Manners and Advancement in Civilization and Their Opinion of Us . . . Malden [Mass.]: C. E. Spofford & Co., 1895.  178 p., front.                    LC

3789 MIZE, W. H.  Gold, Grace, and Glory: A Story of Religious Life among the Wealthy Classes of the West and South . . . New York: G. W. Dillingham, 1896.  431 p.                    LC, UC

MOFFAT, WILLIAM DAVID. The Face of Abel. *In* F. E. McKay, *ed.*, Vignettes [cop. 1890], No. 3523.

3790 MOFFETT, CLEVELAND LANGSTON.  True Detective Stories from the Archives of the Pinkertons . . .  New York: Doubleday & McClure Co., 1897.  250 p.                    BA, H, LC
*Contents:* The Northampton Bank Robbery—The Susquehanna Express Robbery—The Pollock Diamond Robbery—The Rock Island Express—The Destruction of the Renos—The American Exchange Bank Robbery.

3791 THE MONARCH PHILANTHROPIST.  San Francisco: Cubery & Company, steam book and job printers, 1892.  Cover title, 22 p.                    HEH, LC, Y
At head of title: "The manuscript of this California Romance was found near the docks of San Francisco. . . ."
A veiled attack on Senator Leland Stanford.

MONCKTON-DENE, R.  In the "Never Never Country." Private Jones of the Eighth.  The Siren of Three-Mile Bend.  [Three stories.]  *In* C. King, *ed.*, An Initial Experience (1894), No. 3105.

——— The Other Fellow.  *In* C. King, *ed.*, Captain Dreams (1895), No. 3097.

3792 MONROE, ANNE SHANNON.  Eugene Norton: A Tale of the Sagebrush Land . . .  Chicago and New York: Rand, McNally & Company [cop. 1900].  291 p.                    LC

3793 MONROE, HARRIET (EARHART).  Past Thirty . . .  Published for the Author.  Philadelphia, No. 42 North Ninth Street, 1879.  168 p.
                    H, HEH, LC, UV, Y

3794 MONTAGUE, CHARLES HOWARD.  The Countess Muta: A Novel . . .  New York: Belford Company, 18-22 East 18th Street [cop. 1889].  244 p.
                    AP, BA

3795 ——— The Doctor's Mistake; or, What Myrta Saw. An Experiment with Life. A Novel ... Boston: Thomas Downey, Jr., & Co., 1888. 146 p., illus. LC
Clement Milton Hammond, jt. au.

3796 ——— The Romance of the Lilies ... Boston: W. I. Harris & Co., 1886. 214 p. LC
Maine.

3797 ——— Two Strokes of the Bell: A Strange Story ... Boston: W. I. Harris & Co., 1886. 185 p. H, HEH, LC, Y
Of amnesia.

3798 ——— Written in Red; or, The Conspiracy in the North Case. (A Story of Boston.) ... New York: Cassell Publishing Company, 104 & 106 Fourth Avenue [cop. 1890]. 335 p. AP, BA, HEH, LC, O
C. W. Dyar, jt. au.

3799 MONTAGUE, MURRAY. A Modern Tragedy ... Hartford: S. W. Barrows & Co., 1891. 192 p. HEH, LC, UM

3800 [MONTEITH, JOHN.] Parson Brooks, a Plumb Powerful Hard-Shell: A Story of Humble Southern Life. St. Louis: O. H. P. Applegate, 1884. 115 p. LC
Of Ozark people.

3801 [MONTGOMERY, A. B.] The Making of a Millionaire. By Himself. A True Story ... New York: G. W. Dillingham, 1898. 219 p., illus. LC

MONTGOMERY, C. S. The Jigs of Abner Peabody. In Hanks: Assorted Yarns from Puck (1893), No. 2444.

3802 [MONTI, LUIGI.] Adventures of a Consul Abroad. By Samuel Sampleton [pseud.] ... Boston: Lee and Shepard. New York: Charles T. Dillingham, 1878. 270 p. BA, H, LC, O, Y
A consul attempts to live on his income.

3803 [———] Leone ... Boston: James R. Osgood and Company, 1882. 370 p. BA, H, HEH, LC, O
At head of title: "Round-Robin Series."
Of an American girl studying art in Italy.

3804 MOODEY, MARTHA LIVINGSTON. Alan Thorne ... Boston: D. Lothrop Company, Washington Street opposite Bromfield [cop. 1889]. 367 p. AP, BU, HEH, LC, O, UM

3805 ——— The Tragedy of Brinkwater: A Novel ... New York: Cassell & Company, Limited, 739 & 741 Broadway [cop. 1887]. 238 p. AP, HEH, LC, O

3806 MOODY, EDWIN F. Bob Rutherford and His Wife: An Historical Romance ... Louisville, Ky.: Printed for the author by John P. Morton & Company, 1888. 212 p.  HEH, LC, Y
During the Texas Revolution.

3807 MOONEY, JAMES. A Millionaire's Folly; or, The Beautiful Unknown. A Sensational Tale of Criminal Life ... New York, Chicago: J. S. Ogilvie, 1888. 236 p., front.  LC

3808 ——— The Trail of the Barrow; or, The Brother's Revenge ... New York, Chicago: J. S. Ogilvie & Company, 1888. 216 p., front.  LC

MOORE, ANON, *pseud*. *See* Galloway, James M.

3809 [MOORE, MRS. AULA.] A King's Heart: An American Fairy Story. By Aula Eufaula [pseud.]. [Houston, Texas], cop. 1894. Cover title, 19 p.  LC

3810 MOORE, B. P. Endura; or, Three Generations. A New England Romance ... San Francisco: Golden Era Company, 1885. 296 p., illus.  CU, HEH, LC

MOORE, CLARA SOPHIA (JESSUP). *See* Bloomfield-Moore, Clara Sophia (Jessup)

3811 MOORE, DAVID ALBERT. How She Won Him; or, The Bride of Charming Valley ... Philadelphia: T. B. Peterson & Brothers, 306 Chestnut Street [cop. 1879]. 330 p.  LC
From Charming Valley, Pennsylvania, to the California gold fields.

3812 MOORE, DUDLEY WINTHROP. Time's Ungentle Tide ... New York: The American News Company, 1876. 108 p. Printed in double columns.  HEH, LC
At head of title: "Library of Select Novels."

3813 MOORE, H. H. Ida Norton; or, Life at Chautauqua ... Jameston, N.Y.: M. Bailey. Fair Point: Chautauqua Press, 1878. 293 p.  LC

3814 MOORE, HOMER H. Sickness as a Profession: How Practiced by an Expert and Why Abandoned ... New York: Phillips & Hunt. Cincinnati: Cranston & Stowe, 1889. 291 p.  LC

3815 MOORE, JOHN TROTWOOD. Songs and Stories from Tennessee ... Chicago: John C. Bauer, 1897. 247, [3] p.  BU, CU, H, HEH, LC, UM, UV
*Contains:* Ole Mistis—A Cavalry Drill in Old Tennessee—Miss Kitty's Fun'ral—The Wolf Hunt on Big Bigby—Gray Gamma—Yesterday—The Mule Race at Ashwood—The Tennessee Girl and the Pacing Mare—"Dick"—Nora—The Spelling Match at Big Sandy—How the Bishop Broke the Record—How Robert J. Broke the Record—How Old Wash Sold the Filly—How Ole Wash Captured a Gun—Br'er Washington's Arraignment.

3816 MOORE, JOHN WHEELER. The Heirs of St. Kilda: A Story of the Southern Past... Raleigh: Edwards, Broughton & Co., 1881. 493 p.   H, UC
North Carolina.

3817 [MOORE, M. LOUISE.] Al-Modad; or, Life Scenes beyond the Polar Circumflex. A Religio-Scientific Solution of the Problems of Present and Future Life. By an Untrammeled Free-Thinker... Shell Bank, Cameron Parish, La.: M. Louise Moore & M. Beauchamp, 1892. Cover title, 220 p.   LC

3818 MOORE, SUSAN TEACKLE. Ryle's Open Gate... Boston and New York: Houghton, Mifflin and Company. The Riverside Press, Cambridge, 1891. 256 p.   BU, H, HEH, LC, O, Y
Village life on Long Island.

3819 MOOREHEAD, WARREN KING. Wanneta, the Sioux... New York: Dodd, Mead and Company [cop. 1890]. 285 p., illus.   CU, LC, N, O, UM

3820 MORAN, JEANNIE WORMLEY (BLACKRURN). Miss Washington of Virginia: A Semi-Centennial Love-Story. By Jeannie Blackburn. Richmond, Va.: Published by the author, 1889. 77 p.   HEH, LC

3821 MORAN, W. H. W. From School-Room to Bar: A Novel... Philadelphia: J. B. Lippincott Company, 1892. 304 p.   LC, O, UV
Of a postwar Virginian striking out on his own.

3822 MORE, ENOCH ANSON. Out of the Past... Boston: Arena Publishing Company, 1895. 248, [1] p.   LC

3823 MOREHOUSE, MRS. JULIA HUNT. Her Own Way... Albany, N.Y.: D. R. Niver, 1885. 445 p., illus.   HEH
*Also issued with imprint:* New York: Ward & Drummond, 1885. Listed PW, Feb. 20, 1886.

3824 [MOREHOUSE, LINDEN H.] Biscuits and Dried Beef: A Panacea. By L. H. M.... Milwaukee: The Young Churchman Co., 1894. 76 p.   LC

3825 MORETTE, EDGAR. The Sturgis Wager: A Detective Story... New York: Frederick A. Stokes Company [cop. 1899]. 260 p.
BU, H, HEH, O, UP
New York.

3826 [MORFORD, HENRY.] The Spur of Monmouth; or, Washington in Arms. A Historical and Centennial Romance of the Revolution... By an Ex-Pension Agent. Philadelphia: Claxton, Remsen, & Haffelfinger, 1876. 480 p.   CU, HEH, LC, N, UP, UVB, Y

MORGAN, BENJAMIN, *pseud. See* Draper, John Smith

3827 [MORGAN, CARRIE A.] Mistaken Paths: A Novel. By Herbert G. Dick [pseud.]. Philadelphia: J. B. Lippincott Company, 1887. 321 p. HEH, LC

3828 [———] Sounding Brass: A Novel. By Herbert G. Dick [pseud.] . . . New York: The American News Company, 39 Chambers Street [cop. 1889]. 182 p. HEH, LC
Of a society woman.

3829 MORGAN, EMILY MALBONE. The Flight of the "Swallow" . . . New York: Anson D. F. Randolph & Company (Incorporated), 182 Fifth Avenue [cop. 1894]. 108 p., illus. BU, HEH, LC, UM, Y
Of a French refugee.

3830 ——— A Lady of the Olden Time . . . Hartford, Conn.: Belknap & Warfield [cop. 1896]. 87 p. HEH, N, UP
Fictitious biography of Lady Alice Fenwick, wife of colonial governor of Fort Saybrook.

3831 ——— Madonnas of the Smoke; or, Our "Mary's Meadow" . . . New York: Anson D. F. Randolph & Company (Incorporated), 182 Fifth Avenue [cop. 1893]. 38 p. LC, Y
Of working girls.

3832 ——— A Poppy Garden . . . Hartford: Belknap & Warfield, 1892. 54 p. HEH, LC

3833 ——— Prior Rahere's Rose . . . [New Haven, cop. 1892.] 31 p. HEH
Of a London waif.

3834 MORGAN, GEORGE. John Littlejohn of J.: Being in Particular an Account of His Remarkable Entanglement with the King's Intrigues against General Washington . . . Philadelphia: J. B. Lippincott Company, 1897. 281 p. H, HEH, LC, O, UP, UV
Valley Forge.

MORGAN, HARRIET FRENCH (FORD). See Ford, Harriet

3835 MORGAN, HENRY. Boston Inside Out! Sins of a Great City! A Story of Real Life . . . Boston: Shawmut Publishing Company, 1880. 480 p. CU, H, LC, N, O
Of vice and corruption in Boston.

3836 ——— ——— Twentieth Thousand, Revised and Enlarged. Seven Chapters Added . . . Boston: Shawmut Publishing Company, 1880. 524, [8] p., front. H, HEH

3837 ——— The Fallen Priest: Story Founded on Fact. Key and Sequel to "Boston Inside Out" . . . Third Edition, Eleven Extra Chapters. Boston: Shawmut Publishing Company, cop. 1883. 434, 76, 8, [ix]-xxiv, [4] p. LC, UC

3838   MORGAN, SALLIE B.  Tahoe; or, Life in California.  A Romance . . . Atlanta, Ga.: Jas. P. Harrison & Co., 1881.  245 p.    CU, HEH, LC, N, UV

3839   [MORRIS, BESSIE C.]  The Lost Key; or, The Mysterious Box.  By Forfex et Hasta [pseuds.] . . . Philadelphia: Grant, Faires, & Rodgers, printers, 1879.  81 p.    LC
Anne B. Spear, jt. au.

3840   MORRIS, CLARA.  A Silent Singer . . . New York: Brentano's, 1899.  308 p., 1 l.    CU, H, HEH, LC, O, Y
*Also contains:* An Old Hulk—The Gentleman Who Was Going to Die—Old Myra's Waiting—"In Paris, Suddenly ———"—Two Buds—The Ambition of MacIlhenny—John Hickey: Coachman—Black Watch—Dinah—Life's Aftermath.

3841   [MORRIS, EUGENIA LAURA (TUTTLE).]  Aunt Billy, and Other Sketches. By Alyn Yates Keith [pseud.] . . . Boston: Lee and Shepard, 1896. 139 p.    BA, HEH, LC, UC, Y
*Also contains:* A Limited Angel—A Wayside Character—A Day of Days—Miss Hetty—A Desultory Club.

3842   [———]  A Hilltop Summer.  By Alyn Yates Keith [pseud.] . . . Boston: Lee and Shepard, 10 Milk Street [cop. 1894].  110 p., illus.    H, HEH, LC, Y
*Contents:* Rachel and Jesse—Jess's Money—A Little World—Cap'n Saul—The Widow Pease—A Hot Sunday—Hilltop's Desolation—A New Friend—The Last of Hilltop.

3843   [———]  A Spinster's Leaflets: Wherein Is Written the History of Her "Doorstep Baby," a Fancy Which in Time Became a Fact and Changed a Life.  By Alyn Yates Keith [pseud.].  Boston: Lee and Shepard, 1894. 137 p., illus.    H, HEH, LC, Y

MORRIS, HARRISON SMITH.  A Symphony.  *In* The Septameron (1888), No. 4867.

3844   MORRIS, HENRY O.  Waiting for the Signal: A Novel . . . Chicago: The Schulte Publishing Co. [cop. 1897].  407 p., illus.    H, HEH, LC, UM
Deposited July 2, 1898.
Socialistic view of the wrongs of labor.

3845   MORRIS, RAMSAY.  Crucify Her!  A Story of <u>Now</u> . . . New York: The Eclectic Publishing Co., 309 Broadway [cop. 1888].  476 p.    LC

3846   [MORRISON, ABRAHAM CRESSY.]  Damon and Pythias: A Souvenir to the Knights of Pythias of the World.  [Milwaukee: King, Fowle & Co., printers and engravers, cop. 1890.]  29 p., illus.    BA, LC
At head of title: "A Story."
Souvenir, compliments Pabst Brewing Co.

3847 MORRISON, HENRY CLAY. The Two Lawyers: A Story for the Times ... Eighth Thousand. Louisville, Ky.: The Pentecostal Pub. Co., 1898. 240 p. HEH

3848 MORRISON, MARY GRAY. The Sea-Farers: A Romance of a New England Coast Town ... New York: Doubleday, Page & Co., 1900. 326 p.
H, HEH, LC, O, Y

3849 MORRISON, WILLIAM A. Josh Canzy's Experience: What He Saw and What Use He Made of It ... Boston: The Barta Press, 1897. 170 p. LC
Boston business.

3850 MORROW, WILLIAM CHAMBERS. The Ape, the Idiot, & Other People ... Philadelphia: J. B. Lippincott Company, 1897. 291 p. AP, HEH, LC
Contents: The Resurrection of Little Wang Tai—The Hero of the Plague —His Unconquerable Enemy—The Permanent Stiletto—Over an Absinthe Bottle—The Inmate of the Dungeon—A Game of Honor—Treacherous Velasco—An Uncommon View of It—A Story Told by the Sea—The Monster-Maker—An Original Revenge—Two Singular Men—The Faithful Amulet.

3851 ——— Blood-Money ... San Francisco: F. J. Walker & Co., 1882. 237 p. HEH, LC
San Joaquin Valley, California.

3852 ——— A Man, His Mark: A Romance ... Philadelphia & London: J. B. Lippincott Company, 1900. 249 p., front. H, HEH, LC
Mt. Shasta.

3853 MORSE, CLARA FRANCES. Blush Roses: A Novel ... New York: Harper & Brothers, 1878. 135 p. Printed in double columns. LC, O

MORSE, EDWIN WILSON. Fine del Opera. In The First Book of the Authors Club (1893), No. 1868.

3854 MORSE, LUCY (GIBBONS). Rachel Stanwood: A Story of the Middle of the Nineteenth Century ... Boston and New York: Houghton, Mifflin and Company. The Riverside Press, Cambridge, 1893. 441 p.
BA, H, HEH, O
Of antislavery activity.

3855 [MORSE, PAUL.] Should Women Vote? ... By a Bachelor. New York: Paul Morse, 1895. 180 p. LC, O

3856 MORTIMER, CHARLES. Captain Antle, the Sailor's Friend ... Boston: Damrell & Upham, 1898. 184 p. H, LC

MORTIMER, GRACE, pseud. See Stuart, Miss M. B.

3857 MORTON, A. J. Beyond the Palaeocrystic Sea; or, The Legend of Halfjord ... Chicago: Privately printed, 1895. 264 p., 1 l. H, LC, N, UM

3858 MORTON, FRANK. Self-Accused ... New York: G. W. Dillingham, 1893. 304 p., front.    LC
From Alabama to Hawaii and the Sandwich Islands.

3859 MORTON, MARY A. Abbie Saunders: A Story of Pioneer Days in Minnesota ... Fresno, Cal.: Published for the author, 1892. 294 p., front.
CU, HEH, N, UM, Y

3860 MORTON, OREN FREDERIC. Under the Cottonwoods: A Sketch of Life on a Prairie Homestead ... Morgantown, W.Va.: The Acme Publishing Company, 1900. 318 p., illus.    CU, HEH, LC

3861 MORTON, S. S. At the Dawning: A Novel ... Philadelphia: Keystone Publishing Co., 1890. 262 p.    AP, LC, O
At head of title: "Library of American Fiction."

3862 MOTT, EDWARD HAROLD. The Black Homer of Jimtown ... New York: Grosset & Dunlap, 1900. 286 p.    H, HEH, LC, O, UC, UM, UV, Y
*Contents:* The Rise and Fall of Absalom—The Man from Caloosa-Hatchee—A Plague of Egypt—Persecuted Sandy Bunn—Polite Simson Cowlip—Poor Bear's Bad Brother—The Selfish Gobbler—A Vanished Heap of Gold—The Jug of Live-Forever Water—Saved by the Man in the Moon—One-Eye Pete Neaffie's Parrot—Scornful Sue and Lean Lucinda—King Bip—The Bones of Bozar Bunn—The Cranky Crane—Little Davy—Headless Ghost That Walked with a Crutch—Snuffy Sam's Kingdom.
Verso of title page: "These sketches originally appeared in the columns of The New York Sun."

3863 ———— The Old Settler and His Tales of Sugar Swamp ... Chicago, New York, and San Francisco: Belford, Clarke & Co. London: J. H. Drane, 1889. 213 p.    HEH, N, UC
*Contents:* The Widow Wiggs and Betsey Fassett—Honey McGonigle's Feast—Peleg Brings Bad Luck—Education on Lost Crow Barren—What the Wild Waves Said—Little Blue Lightning—The Wogglybob of Sugar Swamp—The Old Settler in Hard Luck—Billy Cripp's Good Luck—The Flying Bear of Sugar Swamp—Opportune Dominie Ripper—Jabez Sugarbone's Fate—Nate Tankelbun—The McAllister Twins—The Tale of Snuffy Snyder's Boots—Old-Time Sport in Sugar Swamp—Job Streeter's Start in Life—Katydids and Eternal Vigilance—Bijer Davis's Lost Bear.

3864 ———— The Old Settler, the Squire, and Little Peleg ... New York: United States Book Company, 310-318 Sixth Avenue [cop. 1895]. 302 p., illus.    BU, HEH, UM, Y
*Contents:* Contributing to the Heathen—The Tushwobbler and Its Friend, the Bibsnook—His Mother's Narrow Escape—Redtail, the Ripper—The Case of Smedgeley vs. Smedgeley—Old Mrs. Hagencruft—Pretty Nearly a Rumpus—Cousin Keturah Ann Pepperwell—Potiphar Jump's Great Shot—Aunt Polly and the New Doctor—Shadrack Bobentiff's Buckskin Breeches—The Unfailing Sign of Yellow-Leg Chickens—The Gingerbread Heart—His First Christmas—The Widow Pudgecrack Clearing—Why Bill Fiddler Missed the Stone Frolic—Jeptha Plum's Boy Joe—Bamsmuzzlegigged by Circumstances—Maria Tells a Story—The Twin Uncles—Hiram Wuncut, Victim of Circumstances—Jerry Bilflinger's Bald Head—The Old Stingo from San Domingo—The Sugar Swamp Snake-Bite Cure—Andy Blink's Oath.

3865 ———— Pike County Folks ... New York: John W. Lovell Company, 14 and 16 Vesey Street [cop. 1883]. 278 p., illus.   CU, HEH, N

*Contents:* His Wife's Relations—A Very Cold Day—"Don't Spile the Skin!" —A Horticultural Experiment—Obstinate Widder White—"Hoopers"—Jerry and Mag's Wedding—The Sheriff's Christmas Story—Wig. Macomber's Heartstrings—The Intelligent Steer—"Pizen Injins"—Panama and Keturah—Jerry Whiting's Conversion—Soggy Spooner's Dicker—Squire Billins's Pet Pickerel —Marier Dishbelter—On a Roarin' Fresh—A Tough Customer—The Old Settler and the Squire—In '54, When Eggs Were Eggs—Uncle Eph and the Roman Candles—Uncle Billy and the Coon—Small Game Reminiscences— The Old Settler on Truth—Wonderful Quinine—Constable Steve's Levy— Agriculture and Panthers—Chris Litts's Spotted Calf—A Mink's Gratitude— The Old Settler Despondent—"We've All Got 'Em!"

3866 ———— Robby Walton's Christmas Eve ... New York: Hackett, Carhart & Co., 1886. 33 p., illus.   LC

MOTT, LUTHER WRIGHT. Mr. Thaddeus Almanac's Scientific Proposal. An Unconventional Detective Story. [Two stories.] *In* Stories from the Harvard Advocate (1896), No. 5277a.
Louis How, jt. au.

3867 MOULTON, LOUISE (CHANDLER). Miss Eyre from Boston, and Others ... Boston: Roberts Brothers, 1889. 339 p.
  AP, BA, BU, CU, H, HEH, LC, N, O, UVB, Y

*Also contains:* John Jay's Long Journey—The Perils of a Studio—On the Stroke of the Clock—Nan: A New England Love-Story—For Pastime—A Clod of the Valley—A Story of Planchette—Riching versus Providence—The Haunted Inn—His Uncle's Memory—Woe unto the Pitcher—Dr. Huger's Intention—Did He Forget Her?

———— "Nan." *In* L. C. H. Langford, *comp.*, The Woman's Story (1889), No. 3206.
Also included in No. 3867.

———— When She Was Thirty. *In* Tales from McClure's: Romance (1897), No. 5362.

———— Woe unto the Pitcher. *In* [W. F. Gill] *ed.*, Laurel Leaves (1876), No. 2167.
Later printed in No. 3867.

3868 MOUTON, EUGENIE. Josephine Joseph: Texas Sketches ... Cincinnati: The Editor Publishing Co., 1900. 234 p.   LC

3869 MUIR, OLIVE BEATRICE. Thy Name Is Woman: A Novel ... New York: G. W. Dillingham, 1894. 320 p.   LC

3870 ———— With Malice toward None ... Chicago and New York: Rand, McNally & Company [cop. 1900]. 342 p., illus.   H, LC, O
Of an actress.

3871 MULHERN, DONALD S. Donald Stephenson's Reminiscences: A True Story
... Pittsburgh: Wm. G. Johnston & Co., printers and stationers, 1891.
246 p. CU, HEH, LC

3872 MUMFORD, GURDON SALTONSTALL. An Island God: A Tale of the First
Kamehameha ... New York: Printed for the author, 1897. 141 p.
H, HEH, LC, N
First King of Hawaii.

3873 [MUNDAY, JOHN WILLIAM.] The Lost Canyon of the Toltecs: An Ac-
count of Strange Adventures in Central America. By Charles Sumner
Seeley [pseud.]. Chicago: A. C. McClurg and Company, 1893. 275 p.
H, N, UM

3874 [————] The Spanish Galleon: Being an Account of a Search for
Sunken Treasure in the Caribbean Sea. By Charles Sumner Seeley
[pseud.]. Chicago: A. C. McClurg and Company, 1891. 290 p.
BA, CU, H, HEH

3875 MUNDO, OTO E. The Recovered Continent: A Tale of the Chinese Invasion ... Columbus, Ohio: The Harper-Osgood Co., 1898. 331 p.,
illus. HEH, LC, O
Story opens in 1874 and ends in 1926.

3876 MUNFORD, GEORGE WYTHE. The Two Parsons, Cupid's Sports, The
Dream, and The Jewels of Virginia ... Richmond: J. D. K. Sleight,
1884. 593 p. CU, HEH, O, UVB, Y

3877 MUNKITTRICK, RICHARD KENDALL. Farming ... New York: Harper &
Brothers, 1891. [102] p., illus. H, HEH, LC, N, O, UC, UM, UP, UV
Of a city man trying to farm.

———— The Man with the Black Crape Mask. In Mavericks (1892),
No. 3663.

———— The Mosquitoville Club. In Hanks: Assorted Yarns from Puck
(1893), No. 2444.

3878 ———— Some New Jersey Arabian Nights ... New York: Keppler &
Schwarzmann, 1892. 170 p., illus. CU, HEH, UC, UM

3879 MUNN, B. T. La Petite Belle; or, The Life of an Adventurer. A Novel
... A Life Is Not Fully Rounded Out Till Its Close. Skaneateles,
N.Y., 1877. 368 p., front. HEH, LC, Y
At bottom of p. 368: "End of Volume I." No more published.

3880 MUNN, CHARLES CLARK. Pocket Island: A Story of Country Life in New
England ... New York: The Abbey Press, 114 Fifth Avenue [cop.
1900]. 185 p., illus. HEH, N, UM

3881 —— Uncle Terry: A Story of the Maine Coast ... Boston: Lee and Shepard, 1900. 365 p., illus.    CU, H, HEH, LC, N, O, UM, Y

MUNROE, KIRK. The Bushwhacker's Gratitude. *In* Eleven Possible Cases [cop 1891], No. 1737.

3882 MUNSEY, FRANK ANDREW. Derringforth ... New York: Frank A. Munsey & Company, 1894. 2 vols. (503, [1] p.)    BU, HEH, LC, Y
Majority of his books were for boys.

3883 —— A Tragedy of Errors ... New York: Frank A. Munsey & Company, 1889. 444 p., illus.    AP, HEH, N, UM, Y
A Yale graduate becomes a publisher.

3883a THE MURDER OF THE GEOGLES and Lynching of the Fiend Snyder ... Philadelphia: Barclay & Co., 21 North Seventh Street [cop. 1881]. 44, 9-36 p., illus.    HEH
Book included because of a separately paged story, "Startling and Thrilling Extracts from the Journal of Henry Madison," following the above account.

3884 MURDOCK, W. N. Third Hand High: A Novel ... Boston: Lee and Shepard, 1893. 254 p.    HEH, LC
A New England farmer inherits a million dollars.

3885 MURFREE, FANNY NOAILLES DICKINSON. Felicia: A Novel ... Boston and New York: Houghton, Mifflin and Company. The Riverside Press, Cambridge, 1891. 358 p.    BA, H, HEH, LC, O, Y
Of stage life; South.

3886 [MURFREE, MARY NOAILLES.] The Bushwhackers, & Other Stories. By Charles Egbert Craddock [pseud.] ... Chicago & New York: Herbert S. Stone & Company, 1899. 312 p., 1 l.
    BA, CU, H, HEH, LC, N, O, UC, UM, UP, UV, Y
*Also contains:* The Panther of Jolton's Ridge—The Exploit of Choolah, the Chickasaw.

3887 [——] The Despot of Broomsedge Cove. By Charles Egbert Craddock [pseud.] ... Boston and New York: Houghton, Mifflin and Company. The Riverside Press, Cambridge, 1889. 490 p.
    BA, CU, H, HEH, LC, N, O, UC, UM, Y

3888 [——] His Vanished Star. By Charles Egbert Craddock [pseud.]. Boston and New York: Houghton, Mifflin and Company. The Riverside Press, Cambridge, 1894. 394 p.
    BA, BU, CU, H, HEH, LC, N, O, UC, UM, UP, UV, Y
Of Tennessee moonshine.

3889 [——] In the Clouds. By Charles Egbert Craddock [pseud.] ... Boston and New York: Houghton, Mifflin and Company. The Riverside Press, Cambridge, 1887. 452 p.
    BA, CU, H, HEH, LC, N, O, UC, UM, UP, UV, Y

3890 [————] In the "Stranger People's" Country: A Novel. By Charles Egbert Craddock [pseud.] . . . New York: Harper & Brothers, 1891. 360 p., illus.　　　　　BA, CU, H, HEH, LC, N, O, UC, UP, UV, Y
A prehistoric race in Tennessee.

3891 [————] In the Tennessee Mountains. By Charles Egbert Craddock [pseud.]. Boston, New York: Houghton, Mifflin and Company. The Riverside Press, Cambridge, 1884. 322 p.
　　　　　BA, CU, H, HEH, LC, N, O, UC, UM, UP, UV, Y
*Contents:* Drifting down Lost Creek—A-Playin' of Old Sledge at the Settlemint—The Star in the Valley—Electioneerin' on Big Injun Mounting—The Romance of Sunrise Rock—The Dancin' Party at Harrison's Cove—Over on the T'other Mounting—The "Harnt" That Walks Chilhowee.

3892 [————] The Juggler. By Charles Egbert Craddock [pseud.]. Boston and New York: Houghton, Mifflin and Company. The Riverside Press, Cambridge, 1897. 405, [1] p.
　　　　　BA, BU, CU, H, HEH, LC, N, O, UC, UM, UV, Y
Tennessee mountains.

3893 [————] The Mystery of Witch-Face Mountain, and Other Stories. By Charles Egbert Craddock [pseud.]. Boston and New York: Houghton, Mifflin and Company. The Riverside Press, Cambridge, 1895. 279 p.　　　　　BA, BU, CU, H, HEH, N, O, UC, UV, Y
*Also contains:* Taking the Blue Ribbon at the County Fair—The Casting Vote.

3894 [————] The Phantoms of the Foot-Bridge, and Other Stories. By Charles Egbert Craddock [pseud.] . . . New York: Harper & Brothers, 1895. 353 p., illus.　　　　　BA, CU, H, HEH, LC, N, O, UC, UP, Y
*Also contains:* His "Day in Court"—'Way Down in Lonesome Cove—The Moonshiners at HoHo-Hebee Falls—The Riddle of the Rocks.

3895 [————] The Prophet of the Great Smoky Mountains. By Charles Egbert Craddock [pseud.]. Boston and New York: Houghton, Mifflin and Company. The Riverside Press, Cambridge, 1885. 308 p.
　　　　　BA, BU, CU, H, HEH, O, UC, UM, UP, UV, Y

3896 [————] The Story of Keedon Bluffs. By Charles Egbert Craddock [pseud.] . . . Boston and New York: Houghton, Mifflin and Company. The Riverside Press, Cambridge, 1888. 257 p.
　　　　　BA, CU, H, HEH, LC, O, UM, UP, UV, Y

3897 [————] The Story of Old Fort Loudon. By Charles Egbert Craddock [pseud.] . . . New York: The Macmillan Company. London: Macmillan & Co., Ltd., 1899. 409 p., illus.　BA, H, HEH, LC, O, UC, UM, Y
French and Indian war.

3898 [————] Where the Battle Was Fought: A Novel. By Charles Egbert Craddock [pseud.] . . . Boston: James R. Osgood and Company, 1884. 423 p.　　　　　BA, CU, HEH, O, UVB
Reconstruction; South.

3899 MURPHY, DAVID. Old Moneypenny's . . . Cleveland: Cleveland Plain Dealer Print, 1900. 147 p., front.    LC New York.

3900 MURRAY, CHARLES THEODORE. Sub Rosâ: A Novel . . . New York: G. W. Carleton & Co. London: S. Low & Co., 1880. 419 p.   HEH, LC, O, Y

3901 MURRAY, ELIZABETH. A Story of the Strike: Scenes in City Life . . . New York: The Authors' Publishing Company [cop. 1877]. 125 p.
Copy examined at New York Public Library.
Publisher's notice in book: "Though three editions of this work sold in a few weeks under the title 'Why Don't Fido Eat Candy?' it is not a juvenile." No copy found.

3902 MURRAY, FRANK F. The Middle Ten . . . Titusville, Pa.: The World Publishing Company, 1895. 119 p.    LC

3903 MURRAY, THOMAS. Tom and Sylvia; or, How to Live in Style on Twenty-Five Hundred a Year . . . New York: Evening Post Job Print [cop. 1890]. 87, [1] p., illus.    LC
This New Jersey couple could not do it.

3904 MURRAY, WILLIAM HENRY HARRISON. Adirondack Tales . . . Boston: The Golden Rule Publishing Co., 1877. 459 p., illus.
BA, CU, H, HEH, N, O, UM, UV, Y
Contents: The Story That the Keg Told Me—The Story of the Man Who Didn't Know Much—Sketches.

3905 ———— Cones for the Camp Fire . . . Boston: De Wolfe, Fiske & Co., 361 and 365 Washington St. [cop. 1891]. 189 p.   BU, H, HEH, O, UM, Y
Sketches previously published in author's earlier works.

3906 ———— Daylight Land: The Experiences, Incidents, and Adventures, Humorous and Otherwise, Which Befel Judge John Doe . . . and Divers Others, in Their Parlor-Car Excursion over Prairie and Mountain . . . Boston: Cupples and Hurd, 1888. 338 p., illus.
CU, H, HEH, LC, N, O, UM, UVB, Y

3907 ———— The Doom of Mamelons: A Legend of the Saguenay . . . Philadelphia: Hubbard Brothers, 1888. 136 p.   H, HEH, LC, UP, UVB, Y
Later printed in No. 3912 as "Mamelons."

3908 ———— Holiday Tales: Christmas in the Adirondacks . . . [Springfield, Mass.: Press of Springfield Printing and Binding Company], cop. 1897. 113 p., illus.   CU, H, HEH, LC, N, UC, UVB, Y
Contents: How John Norton the Trapper Kept His Christmas—John Norton's Vagabond.
Deposited Nov. 7, 1898.

3909 —— How Deacon Tubman and Parson Whitney Kept New Year's, and Other Stories ... St. Johnsbury, Vt.: Caledonia County Publishing Company, 1887. 196 p., illus. HEH, LC, UC, UM, UVB
*Also contains:* The Old Beggar's Dog—The Ball—Who Was He?
Title story later condensed and printed in No. 3915. "The Ball" is chap. iv of "The Story of the Man Who Didn't Know Much" in No. 3904.

3910 —— How John Norton the Trapper Kept His Christmas ... [St. Johnsbury, Vt.: The Republican Print.]; Author's Publication, cop. 1885. 99 p. HEH, UVB, Y
Later printed in No. 3908.

3911 —— John Norton's Thanksgiving Party, and Other Stories ... Boston: De Wolfe, Fiske & Co., 361 and 365 Washington Street [cop. 1886]. 231 p., front. HEH, LC, N, Y
*Also contains:* Henry Herbert's Thanksgiving—A Strange Visitor—The Shadow on the Wall—Was It Suicide?—The Old Beggar's Dog—Who Was He?
Deposited July 11, 1891.

3912 —— Mamelons, and Ungava: A Legend of the Saguenay ... Boston: De Wolfe, Fiske & Co., 365 Washington Street [cop. 1890]. 190, 204 p. AP, BU, CU, H, HEH, LC, UM, Y
First story published originally as *The Doom of Mamelons* (1888), No. 3907.

3913 —— The Mystery of the Woods, and The Man Who Missed It ... Boston: De Wolfe, Fiske & Co., 361 and 365 Washington Street [cop. 1891]. 460 p. CU, H, LC, O
Deposited July 11, 1891.

3914 —— The Story That the Keg Told Me, and The Story of the Man Who Didn't Know Much ... Boston: Cupples and Hurd; the Algonquin Press [cop. 1889]. 454 p., front. AP, H, LC, O, UV
Deposited May 3, 1889.
Both stories printed earlier in No. 3904.

3915 —— Three Stories: The Busted Ex-Texan, How Deacon Tubman and Parson Whitney Celebrated New Years, The Leaf of Red Rose [verse] ... [Boston: Electrotyped and printed by C. W. Calkins & Co., 52 Purchase Street, cop. 1889.] 112 p., illus. LC
Deposited Sept. 17, 1889.
Second story is condensed version of title story of No. 3909.
HEH copy adds "The 'World' Typewriter," pp. [113]-125, part of it written and signed by Murray. Leaf of advertisements preceding title page lists 11 of Murray's works published by Cupples & Hurd; verso of back cover has stamp: "Compliments of Typewriter Department, Pope Mfg. Co., Boston, Mass."
Also published as: *The Busted Ex-Texan, and Other Stories.* Boston: De Wolfe, Fiske & Co., 1890. 112 p., illus. BU, HEH, O, Y

3916 MUSICK, JOHN ROY. Braddock: A Story of the French and Indian Wars . . . New York, London, and Toronto: Funk & Wagnalls Company, 1893. 470 p., illus. CU, HEH, LC

3917 ———— A Century Too Soon: A Story of Bacon's Rebellion . . . New York, London, and Toronto: Funk & Wagnalls Company, 1893. 402 p., illus. CU, HEH, O, UV, Y

3918 ———— Columbia: A Story of the Discovery of America . . . New York, London, and Toronto: Funk & Wagnalls Company, 1892. 354 p., illus. H

First published in the omitted Worthington's "International Library," No. 19, 1891.

3919 ———— Cuba Libre: A Story of the Hispano-American War . . . New York and London: Funk & Wagnalls Company, 1900. 454 p., illus. Information from LC card; no copy seen.

3920 ———— Estevan: A Story of the Spanish Conquests . . . New York, London, and Toronto: Funk & Wagnalls Company, 1892. 399 p., illus. HEH, LC

3921 ———— Humbled Pride: A Story of the Mexican War . . . New York, London, and Toronto: Funk & Wagnalls Company, 1893. 462 p., illus. HEH, LC

H, O have copies of 467 p. ed. with "Chronology" added.

3922 ———— Independence: A Story of the Revolution . . . New York, London, and Toronto: Funk & Wagnalls Company, 1893. 456 p., illus. LC

3923 ———— The Pilgrims: A Story of Massachusetts . . . New York, London, and Toronto: Funk & Wagnalls Company, 1893. 368 p., illus. HEH, LC, O

3924 ———— Pocahontas: A Story of Virginia . . . New York, London, and Toronto: Funk & Wagnalls Company, 1893. 366 p., illus. BU, LC, UV

3925 ———— Saint Augustine: A Story of the Huguenots in America . . . New York, London, and Toronto: Funk & Wagnalls Company, 1892. 319 p., illus. HEH, LC, N

3926 ———— Sustained Honor: A Story of the War of 1812 . . . New York, London, and Toronto: Funk & Wagnalls Company, 1893. 451 p., illus. HEH, LC, O

3927 ———— Union: A Story of the Great Rebellion . . . New York, London, and Toronto: Funk & Wagnalls Company, 1894. 505 p., illus. BU, LC

HEH has copy of 526 p. ed. with "Chronology" added.

3928 ———— The Witch of Salem; or, Credulity Run Mad . . . New York, London, and Toronto: Funk & Wagnalls Company, 1893. 389 p., illus. CU, HEH, LC, UM

3929 MY INTIMATE ENEMY: A Story. Philadelphia: Claxton, Remsen, & Haffelfinger, 1878. 176 p.     LC

3930 MY MOTHER-IN-LAW ... Boston: Lockwood, Brooks and Company, 1877. 159 p.     BA, CU, HEH, O

3931 MYERS, GEORGE L. Aboard "The American Duchess" ... New York & London: G. P. Putnam's Sons; the Knickerbocker Press, 1900. 341 p.     H, HEH, LC, Y
"G. P. Putnam's Sons made the startling discovery, shortly after they had published ... the novel ... that it was in reality identical with *The Queen of Night*, a novel written by Headon Hill [i.e., Francis E. Grainger, an English author], and published some years ago in London [1896], save that the scene of action had been changed to New York." PW, Feb. 17, 1900, p. 361.

3932 THE MYSTERIOUS CRIME at the Burleigh Mansion, North Reading, Mass.: Being the Wonderful Career of Mrs. Jane Burleigh ... A True and Complete Account of Which Is Now for the First Time Published, although Strenuous Efforts Were Made to Suppress It. Philadelphia: Barclay & Co., 21 North Seventh Street [cop. 1887]. 78 p., illus.   HEH
At head of title: "A Remarkable and Romantic History of Love and Treachery."
"To the Reader" signed "Francis Tracey, Editor."

3933 NADAL, EHRMAN SYME. Notes of a Professional Exile ... New York: The Century Co., 1895. 164 p., front.     H, O, UM, Y
Life at an imaginary European spa.

3934 NARD, RAY, *pseud.* Rita; or, Sin's Harvest ... New York: George W. Dillingham, 1895. 313 p.
Listed PW, Mar. 16, 1895.

3935 NARRATIVE OF JOHN TRUST. Translated from His MSS ... Alexandria, Va.: J. Marriott Hill & Co., steam book and job printers, 1883. Cover title, 42 p.     HEH
At head of cover title: "Truth Is Stranger Than Fiction."

NASBY, PETROLEUM V., *pseud.* See Locke, David Ross

3936 NASH, WILLARD GLOVER. A Century of Gossip; or, The Real and the Seeming ... Chicago: W. B. Keen, Cooke & Co., 1876. 334 p., illus.     CU, HEH, LC, N, Y
At head of title: "New England Life."

3937 NAYLOR, JAMES BALL. Under Mad Anthony's Banner ... Columbus, Ohio: Ohio State Journal Co., 1899. 177 p., front.     O

3938 NEEDHAM, ELIZABETH ANNABLE. Mrs. Whilling's Faith Cure. By Mrs. Geo. C. Needham. Boston: Bradley & Woodruff, 234 and 236 Congress [cop. 1891]. 146 p.     LC
Deposited June 5, 1891.
Anti Christian Science.

NEEDHAM, MRS. GEORGE C.  *See* Needham, Elizabeth Annable

3939 NEEDHAM, GEORGE CARTER. Father Flynn . . . New York: James A. O'Connor, 72 Bible House [cop. 1890]. 123 p.  LC
Deposited Mar. 10, 1890.

3940 NEEDHAM, WILLIAM P. The House of Graydon: A Novel . . . Richmond, Indiana: M. Cullaton & Co., printers and binders, 1888. 270 p.
LC

NEFF, ELIZABETH (HYER). A Strange Story: The Lost Years. *In* Tales from McClure's: Adventure (1897), No. 5360.

3941 NELSON, ALICE RUTH (MOORE) DUNBAR. The Goodness of St. Rocque, and Other Stories. By Alice Dunbar. New York: Dodd, Mead and Company, 1899. 224 p.  H, HEH, LC, O, UP
*Also contains:* Tony's Wife—The Fisherman of Pass Christian—M'sieu Fortier's Violin—By the Bayou St. John—When the Bayou Overflows—Mr. Baptiste—A Carnival Jangle—Little Miss Sophie—Sister Josepha—The Praline Woman—Odalie—La Juanita—Titee.

3942 NELSON, HENRY LOOMIS. John Rantoul . . . Boston: James R. Osgood and Company, 1885. 347 p.  AP, BA, H, HEH, LC, O

3943 NELSON, MRS. R. E. Dorance . . . New York: John B. Alden, 1889. 223 p.
LC
Ante bellum Virginia.

3944 NELSON, ROBERTA BERESFORD. Once upon a Time: Stories . . . Franklin, Ohio: The Editor Publishing Co., 1895. 225 p.  LC
*Contents:* A Woman and a Cynic—Champagne Corks.

3945 NELSON, WILLIAM. Isabel: A Tale of the Mexican Banditti . . . [Paterson, N.J.?]: Privately printed, 1884. 16 p.  CU, LC, Y
25 copies printed.

NEMO, OMEN, *pseud.*  *See* Rehm, Warren S.

NERO, *pseud.*  *See* Wells, Samuel E.

NEVADA, *pseud.*  *See* McNeill, Nevada

3946 NEVILLE, CONSTANCE MAUD. Behind the Arras: A Novel . . . San Francisco: A. L. Bancroft and Company, 1877. 251 p.  LC

3947 NEW, CATHERINE (McLAEN). A Woman Reigns . . . Indianapolis: The Bowen-Merrill Co., 1896. 112 p.  HEH, LC, Y
*Also contains:* The Fate of a Fatalist.

3948  THE NEW SCHOOLMA'AM; or, A Summer in North Sparta. Boston: Lor-
ing, corner of Broomfield and Washington Streets [cop. 1877].  140 p.
H, HEH
Rich schoolteacher marries penniless artist.

3949  NEW STORIES FROM THE CHAP-BOOK: Being a Miscellany of Curious and
Interesting Tales . . . Chicago, New York: Herbert S. Stone & Com-
pany, 1898.  260 p., 1 l.                        HEH, N, UM, UV, Y
*Contents:* The Sands of the Green River, by Neith Boyce—The Unsullied
Brow of the Viceroy, by Edwin Lefevre—The Saving of Jim Moseby, by
Anthony Leland—The Escape, by Dabney Marshall—Dick, by Marie Louise
Pool—The Primrose Dame, by John Regnault Ellyson—When His Majesty
Nicholas Came to England, by Clinton Ross—At "The Temple of Unending
Peace," by Alfred Dwight Sheffield—The Tumbrils, by Nathaniel Stephen-
son—Gil Horne's Bergonzi, by Maurice Thompson—Her Last Love, by
Clarence Wellford—A Little Boy of Dreams, by Beatrice Witte—The Wolf
in Sheep's Clothing, by Edith Franklin Wyatt.
Second series. For first series see No. 5277.

3950  NEWBERRY, FANNIE E.  The Impress of a Gentlewoman . . . Boston:
Bradley & Woodruff [cop. 1891].  397 p., illus.            BU, LC, O
In a western mining town.

3951  NEWCOMB, SIMON.  His Wisdom the Defender: A Story . . . New York
and London: Harper & Brothers, 1900.  328, [1] p., front.
HEH, O, UM, Y
Of an airship attaining an altitude of 70 miles and traveling 90 miles per
minute.

3952  NEWELL, CHARLES MARTIN.  The Isle of Palms: Adventures While Wreck-
ing for Gold, Encounter with a Mad Whale, Battle with a Devil-Fish,
and Capture of a Mermaid . . . Boston: De Wolfe, Fiske & Co., 1888.
460 p., illus.                                AP, H, HEH, LC, Y
At head of title: "The Fleetwing Series."

3953  ——— Kalani of Oahu: An Historical Romance of Hawaii . . . Boston:
Published by the author, 1881.  415 p., front.  BA, BU, CU, H, HEH, LC, O, Y

3954  ——— Kaméhaméha, the Conquering King: The Mystery of His Birth,
Loves, and Conquests. A Romance of Hawáii . . . New York & Lon-
don: G. P. Putnam's Sons; the Knickerbocker Press, 1885.  399 p., illus.
AP, BA, H, HEH, LC, O, UM

3955  [———] Leaves from an Old Log: Péhe Nú-e, the Tiger Whale of the
Pacific. By Captain Barnacle [pseud.] . . . Boston: D. Lothrop and
Company, 1877.  112 p., illus.                        H, LC, Y

3956  ——— The Voyage of the Fleetwing: A Narrative of Love, Wreck, and
Whaling Adventures . . . Boston: De Wolfe, Fiske & Co., 365 Wash-
ington Street [cop. 1886].  443 p., illus.            H, HEH, LC, O, Y
Deposited Dec. 15, 1887.

3957 ———— The Wreck of the Greyhound; or, The Romantic Love of the Earl's Daughter... Boston: De Wolfe, Fiske & Co., 1889.   446 p., illus.

HEH, LC, O

At head of title: "The Fleetwing Series."

3958 NEWELL, ROBERT HENRY.  There Was Once a Man: A Story ...   New York: Fords, Howard, & Hulbert for Our Continent Publishing Co., 1884.   526 p., illus.     CU, H, HEH, LC, N, O, UM, UP, UV, Y

At head of title: "'Our Continent' Library."

3959 [NEWHALL, MRS. LAURA EUGENIA.]   Adopted; or, The Serpent Bracelet. A Novel.  By Ada L. Halstead [pseud.].  San Francisco, Cal.: Golden Era Co., 1886.   308 p.     CU, HEH, LC

3960 [————]  The Bride of Infelice: A Novel.  By Ada L. Halstead [pseud.] ...  [San Francisco: The Bancroft Company, 1892.]   318 p., front.   LC

Deposited June 24, 1892.

HEH has copy which notes on 2nd p. l.: "Issued from the Press of the San Francisco Printing Co., 411 Market Street, 1893."

3961 [————]  The Death Trust: A Novel.  By Ada L. Halstead [pseud.] ...  Boston and San Francisco: Published by the author, 1889.   318 p.

HEH, O

NEWPORT, W., pseud.  See Dow, Joy Wheeler

NEWSBY, MRS. PELEG, pseud.  See Evans, Mrs. Abigail A.

3962 NEWTON, D'RENCE.  Mysterious Mr. Sawyer . . .  Philadelphia: Published by "Artisans Chat," 1888.   64 p.     LC

3963 [NEWTON, EMMA (MESSEREAU).]  Boscobel: A Novel . . .  New York: W. B. Smith & Co., Bond Street [cop. 1881].   242 p.     LC

Life at Florida winter resorts.

3964 NEWTON, WATSON JAMES.  Cupid and Creeds . . .  Washington: The Neale Company, 1900.   191 p.     HEH

LC deposit copy, dated Apr. 23, 1900, does not have date on title page.

3965 NEWTON, WILLIAM WILBERFORCE.  Philip Mac Gregor . . .  Hartford, Conn.: The Student Publishing Company, 1895.   338 p., illus.

BU, HEH, LC, N, O, UP

3966 [————]  The Priest and the Man; or, Abelard and Heloisa.  A Novel ...  Boston: Cupples, Upham & Co., 1883.   548 p., illus.

AP, BA, BU, H, HEH, LC, O, UP

2nd ed. gives author's name on title page.

3967 NICHOLAS, ANNA.  An Idyl of the Wabash, and Other Stories ...  Indianapolis and Kansas City: The Bowen-Merrill Company, 1899.   256 p.

HEH, LC, UM, Y

*Also contains:* At a Way Station—Mrs. Brooks's Change of Heart—An Abiding Love—A Farmhouse Drama—The Solution of a Text—An Occult Experience—An Itinerant Pair—A Movement in Art—The Quickening of a Soul.

NICHOLAS, GRIFFITH A., *pseud. See* Worthington, Elizabeth Strong

NICHOLL, EDITH M. *See* Bowyer, Edith M. (Nicholl)

3968 NICHOLLS, CHARLES WILBUR DE LYON. The Décadents: A Story of Blackwell's Island and Newport . . . New York: J. S. Ogilvie Publishing Company, 57 Rose Street, cop. 1899. 172 p., front. BU, HEH, LC, UM, Y

3969 [————] The Greek Madonna. By Shelton Chauncey [pseud.]. New York: G. W. Dillingham, 1894. 315 p. HEH, LC

3970 NIELD, THOMAS. Pat's Palace: A Story of Our Country's Curse . . . Indianapolis: William F. Clark, 1892. 201 p. HEH, LC

3971 NISWONGER, CHARLES ELLIOT. The Isle of Feminine . . . Little Rock [Ark.]: Press of Brown Printing Company [cop. 1893]. 160 p. LC
Deposited Dec. 26, 1893.
A utopia.

3972 [NITSCH, HELEN ALICE (MATTHEWS).] Gentle Breadwinners: The Story of One of Them. By Catherine Owen [pseud.] . . . Boston and New York: Houghton, Mifflin and Company. The Riverside Press, Cambridge, 1888. 186 p. AP, BA, H, HEH, LC, O, UC, UM
New York.

3973 [————] Molly Bishop's Family. By Catherine Owen [pseud.] . . . Boston and New York: Houghton, Mifflin and Company. The Riverside Press, Cambridge, 1888. 270 p. CU, H, HEH, LC, O, UC
Of housekeeping and recipes.

3974 NIXON, J[AMES?] LEROY. The Lowly Nazarene: A Story of Christ . . . New York: J. S. Ogilvie Publishing Company, 57 Rose Street [cop. 1897]. 308 p. LC
Deposited May 27, 1897.

NIXON, MARY F. *See* Roulet, Mary F. (Nixon)

3975 NOBLE, ANNETTE LUCILLE. Eunice Lathrop, Spinster . . . New York: G. P. Putnam's Sons, 1882. 322 p. H, HEH, LC, O, Y

3976 ————— In a Country Town . . . New York: National Temperance Society, 1890. 385 p., front. HEH
Of the opium habit.

3977 ————— Love and Shawl-Straps . . . New York, London: G. P. Putnam's Sons; the Knickerbocker Press, 1894. 291 p. LC
Pearl Clement Coann, jt. au.
Of travel abroad.

3978 ——— The Parsonage Secret ... New York: James B. Dunn, 1898. 152 p. LC

3979 ——— The Professor's Dilemma ... New York, London: G. P. Putnam's Sons; the Knickerbocker Press, 1897. 316 p.   H, HEH, LC, O, UC
A professor of psychology in love with two women.

3980 ——— Uncle Jack's Executors ... New York: G. P. Putnam's Sons, 1880. 303 p.   AP, BU, H, HEH, LC, O

3981 [NOBLE, LUCRETIA GRAY.]   A Reverend Idol: A Novel.   Boston: James R. Osgood and Company, 1882.   450 p.   AP, BA, BU, CU, HEH, N, O, UVB, Y
A minister vacations at Cape Cod.

3982 NOBODY, A, *pseud.*   Nobody Knows; or, Facts That Are Not Fictions, in the Life of an Unknown ...   New York, London: Funk & Wagnalls, 1888.   290 p.   BU, HEH
*Who Was Who in America,* Vol. I (Chicago, 1942), credits a *Nobody Knows,* 1889, to William Eddy Barns.
Of current social problems.

3983 NOEL, HENRY TAYLOR.   Brysonia: A Story of the Newest South ...   Boston: Arena Publishing Company, 1896.   340 p.   HEH, LC
Of a freed slave.

3984 NOLAN, MARY.   Biddy Finnigan's Botheration; or, That Romp of a Girl ...   St. Louis, Mo.: Ev. E. Carreras, 1884.   272 p., illus.   LC

3985 NORMAN, CYRIL.   The Mermaid Dance ...   Chicago: Brown & Co. [cop. 1897].   264 p.   LC

3986 ——— Rondo ...   New York: G. W. Dillingham Co.   London: Gay and Bird, 1898.   261 p., illus.   HEH, LC
Metropolitan life; London, New York, San Francisco.

3987 NORR, WILLIAM.   Stories of Chinatown: Sketches from Life in the Chinese Colony of Mott, Pell, and Doyers Streets ...   New York: W. Norr [1892].   83 p., illus.   CU
*Contents:* The Romance of "Chuck" Connors—Mrs. Morrissey's Present—A Romance of Pell Street—'Round the Opium Lamp—A Chinatown Tragedy—The Pearl of Chinatown.

3988 NORRIS, FRANK.   Blix ...   New York: Doubleday & McClure Co., 1899. 339 p.   CU, H, HEH, LC, N, O, UP, UVB, Y
San Francisco.

3989 ——— Mc Teague: A Story of San Francisco ...   New York: Doubleday & McClure Co., 1899.   442 p.   BA, CU, H, HEH, LC, N, O, UP, UVB, Y

3990 ——— A Man's Woman . . . New York: Doubleday & McClure Co., 1900. 286 p. CU, H, HEH, LC, N, O, UC, UM, UP, UVB, Y

3991 ——— Moran of the Lady Letty: A Story of Adventure off the California Coast . . . New York: Doubleday & McClure Co., 1898. 293 p.
BU, CU, H, HEH, LC, N, O, UP, UVB, Y

3992 NORRIS, MARY HARRIOTT. A Damsel of the Eighteenth Century; or, Cicely's Choice . . . New York: Phillips & Hunt. Cincinnati: Cranston & Stowe, 1889. 275 p. LC, O
London.

3993 ——— Dorothy Delafield . . . New York: Phillips & Hunt. Cincinnati: Cranston & Stowe, 1886. 430 p. HEH, LC

3994 ——— The Gray House of the Quarries . . . Boston, New York, and London: Lamson, Wolffe and Company, 1898. 498 p., front.
HEH, LC, O
On the Hudson

3995 ——— Lakewood: A Story of To-Day . . . New York and London: Frederick A. Stokes Company [cop. 1895]. 331 p., illus.
H, HEH, LC, O, UV, Y

NORTH, BARCLAY, *pseud.* *See* Hudson, William Cadwalader

3996 NORTH, FRANKLIN H. The Awakening of Noahville . . . New York: New York Publishing Co., 1898. 383 p., illus. CU, HEH
Of a lost kingdom on the North American continent.

NORTH, LEIGH, *pseud.* *See* Phelps, Elizabeth Steward (Natt)

NORTON, CHARLES LEDYARD. A Cabalist Adrift. *In* The First Book of the Authors Club (1893), No. 1868.

3997 NORTON, FRANCES MARIE (GUITEAU). The Stalwarts; or, Who Were to Blame. A Novel, Portraying Fifty Years of American History . . . Chicago: Frances Marie Norton, 1888. 311 p., front. H, LC, N, Y
American politics.

3998 NORTON, FRANK HENRY. The Days of Daniel Boone: A Romance of "The Dark and Bloody Ground" . . . New York: The American News Company [cop. 1883]. 406 p., illus. BU, H, HEH, LC, UC
Deposited Nov. 1, 1883.

3999 NORWOOD, THOMAS MANSON. Plutocracy; or, American White Slavery. A Politico-Social Novel . . . New York: The American News Company, 1888. 431 p., front. H, N, UC, UM, Y
Verso of title page: "Press of J. J. Little & Co., Astor Place, New York."
*Also issued with imprint:* New York: Metropolitan Pub. Co.; the American News Company, 1888. CU, HEH, LC, O, UVB
No "press" note on verso of title page.

NOTT, CHARLES COOPER, JR. The Letter of Credit. *In* Short Stories from Outing [cop. 1895], No. 4930.

———— The Tale of a Goblin Horse. *In* Stories of the Army (1893), No. 5280.

NOX, OWEN, *pseud*. *See* Cory, Charles Barney

4000 NOYES, STEPHEN W., *pseud?* Thrice Falsely Accused; or, Two Sides of a Story . . . [New York? 1889?] 242 p.                                      HEH
Purportedly a true story of an Indian mistaken for a Negro.

4001 NUNN, LOTTIE. Ada Greenwood; or, Rescue the Perishing . . . Cincinnati, Ohio, 1878. 200 p., illus.                                              HEH

4002 NYE, EDGAR WILSON. Baled Hay: A Drier Book Than Walt Whitman's "Leaves o' Grass". . . New York and Chicago: Belford, Clarke & Co., 1884. 320 p., illus.                          CU, H, LC, N, O, UC, UM, UVB, Y

4003 ———— Bill Nye and Boomerang; or, The Tale of a Meek-Eyed Mule . . . Chicago: Belford, Clarke & Co., 1881. 286 p., illus.
BU, CU, H, HEH, N, O, UC, UM, UVB

4004 ———— Bill Nye's Chestnuts Old and New . . . Chicago, New York, and San Francisco: Belford, Clarke & Co., 1888. 286 p., illus.      HEH, LC
*Also issued with imprint:* Chicago and New York: Belford, Clarke & Co., 1888.
H, UM

4005 ———— Bill Nye's Cordwood . . . Chicago: Rhodes & McClure Publishing Co., 1887. 161 p., illus.                            H, N, UC, UM, Y

4006 ———— Bill Nye's History of England from the Druids to the Reign of Henry VIII . . . Philadelphia: J. B. Lippincott Company, 1896. 195, [18] p., illus.                              BU, CU, H, HEH, LC, O, UC, UM, Y

4007 ———— Bill Nye's History of the United States . . . Philadelphia: J. B. Lippincott Co. [cop. 1894]. 329 p., illus.          CU, H, HEH, N, UC, UV

4008 DELETED.

4009 ———— Bill Nye's Thinks . . . Chicago, New York, San Francisco: The Dearborn Publishing Co., 1888. 181 p.                        LC, N, UM

4010 ———— Forty Liars, and Other Lies. By Bill Nye . . . Chicago: Belford, Clarke & Co. St. Louis: Belford & Clarke Publishing Co., 1882. 264 p., illus.                          CU, H, HEH, LC, N, UVB, Y

4011 ———— A Guest at the Ludlow, and Other Stories . . . Indianapolis and Kansas City: The Bowen-Merrill Company, 1897. 272 p., illus.
BU, H, HEH, LC, O, UC, UVB, Y

——— The Lex Loci of the Hired Girl. *In* The First Book of the Authors Club (1893), No. 1868.

4012 ——— Nye and Riley's Railway Guide ... Chicago, New York, San Francisco: The Dearborn Publishing Company, 1888. 203 p., illus.

BA, CU, H, HEH, LC, UC, UM, UP, Y

James Whitcomb Riley, jt. au.

4013 ——— Remarks by Bill Nye ... Chicago: A. E. Davis & Company, 1887. 504 p., illus. H, HEH, LC

*Also issued with imprint:* San Francisco: A. L. Bancroft & Co., 1887. HEH

O., T. W., *pseud.* *See* Young, Virginia C.

OAKLEY, MRS. CAROLINE, *pseud.* *See* Briggs, William H. F.

4014 OAKLEY, HESTER CALDWELL. As Having Nothing ... New York & London: G. P. Putnam's Sons; the Knickerbocker Press, 1898. 330 p.

HEH, LC, O

Of a book illustrator, a publisher, and a novelist.

OAKS, *pseud.* *See* Wetmore, Mai M.

OAKUM, JOHN, *pseud.* *See* Phillips, Walter Polk

OBED, *pseud.* *See* Johnson, Homer Uri

4015 OBERHOLTZER, ELLIS PAXSON. The New Man: A Chronicle of the Modern Time ... Philadelphia: The Levytype Company, 1897. 487 p.

CU, H, LC, O, UVB

4016 OBERHOLTZER, SARA LOUISE (VICKERS). Hope's Heart Bells: A Romance ... Philadelphia: J. B. Lippincott & Co., 1884. 282 p. LC, O, UP

Of a Quaker family.

4017 O'BRIEN, DILLON. Frank Blake ... St. Paul: The Pioneer-Press Company, 1876. 270 p. HEH, LC, N, UM, Y

Ireland.

4018 ——— Widow Melville's Boarding House ... St. Paul: The Pioneer Press Print, 1881. 64 p. LC

Western locale.

4019 O'BRIEN, FITZ-JAMES. The Diamond Lens, with Other Stories ... New York: Charles Scribner's Sons, 1885. 337 p. AP, BA, O, UC, Y

Contains same stories as No. 4020. Title story printed earlier in Wright II, No. 155.

4020 ——— The Poems and Stories . . . Collected and Edited . . . by William Winter. Boston: James R. Osgood and Company, 1881. 485 p., illus.  BA, CU, H, HEH, LC, UC, UM, UP, UV, Y

*Contains:* The Diamond Lens—The Wondersmith—Tommatoo—Mother of Pearl—The Bohemian—The Lost Room—The Pot of Tulips—The Golden Ingot—My Wife's Tempter—What Was It?—Duke Humphrey's Dinner—Milly Dove—The Dragon Fang.

4021 O'BRIEN, MARGARET E.  Judith, the Daughter of Judas: A Tale . . . Philadelphia: J. B. Lippincott Company, 1891. 248 p.  LC, O, Y

4022 [O'CONNOR, BARRY.]  Turf-Fire Stories and Fairy Tales of Ireland . . . New York: P. J. Kenedy, 1891. 405 p., illus.  H

O'CONNOR, BERNARD FRANCIS.  Held Up. *In* The First Book of the Authors Club (1893), No. 1868.

4023 O'CONNOR, WILLIAM DOUGLAS.  Three Tales: The Ghost, The Brazen Android, The Carpenter . . . Boston and New York: Houghton, Mifflin and Company. The Riverside Press, Cambridge, 1892. 320 p.

BA, BU, CU, H, HEH, LC, N, UC, UM, UP, UVB, Y

For earlier printing of "The Ghost" see Wright II, No. 1813.

4024 ODELL, SAMUEL W.  Delilah: A Sequel to "Samson" . . . Cincinnati: Cranston & Curts. New York: Hunt & Eaton [cop. 1891]. 207 p., front.  HEH, Y

4025 ——— Samson: An Historical Romance . . . Cincinnati: Jennings & Pye. New York: Eaton & Mains [1891]. 284 p., front.  Y

4026 O'DONNELL, JESSIE FREMONT.  A Soul from Pudge's Corners: A Novel . . . New York: G. W. Dillingham, 1892. 312 p.

Listed PW, Sept. 3, 1892.

4027 OLD FATHER TIME: A Christmas Dream. By a Reporter. Boston: Alfred Mudge & Son, printers, 1884. 21 p.

Copy examined at New York Public Library.

AN OLD HABITUÉ, *pseud. See* Harrell, John Mortimer

OLD SAILOR, *pseud. See* Coffin, Roland Folger

OLD SLEUTH, *pseud. See* Halsey, Harlan Page

4028 OLDBOY, OLIVER, *pseud.* George Bailey: A Tale of New York Mercantile Life . . . New York: Harper & Brothers, 1880. 288 p.  AP, H, HEH, LC, Y

4029 OLDHAM, HENRY.  The Man from Texas: A Western Romance . . . Philadelphia: T. B. Peterson & Brothers, 306 Chestnut Street [cop. 1884]. 442 p.  LC

Guerrilla warfare along the Kansas-Missouri border.

4030 OLERICH, HENRY. A Cityless and Countryless World: An Outline of Practical Co-operative Individualism . . . Holstein, Iowa: Gilmore & Olerich [cop. 1893]. 447 p., illus.      H, HEH, N, UC, UM
Of social conditions on Mars.

4031 OLIN, ALLEN H. The Old Frame School-House; or, Surmounting the Barrier . . . Muncie, Ind.: The Daily Herald, 1899. 71 p., illus.      LC

4032 OLIPHANT, MARGARET OLIPHANT (WILSON). The Second Son: A Novel . . . Boston and New York: Houghton, Mifflin and Company. The Riverside Press, Cambridge, 1888. 524 p.
     AP, BA, CU, H, HEH, LC, N, O, UC, UM, UP, UVB, Y
Thomas Bailey Aldrich, jt. au., an American.

OLIVER, MARIE, *pseud.* See Brown, Carrie L.

OLNEY, ELLEN W. See Kirk, Ellen Warner (Olney)

4033 O'NEILL, JAMES. Garrison Tales from Tonquin . . . Boston: Copeland and Day, 1895. 184 p., 1 l.      BA, CU, H, HEH, LC, N, UC, Y
*Contents:* Roebke—Père Loraine—Homesickness—Slovatski—A Spiritual Combat—The Story of Youp-Youp—Eckermann and Tannemeyer—The Cooly—"Le Buif"—A Dream—De Perier—The Worst of the Bargain—The Pagoda.

ON-SÉ-KÍ, *pseud.* See Armant, Fernand

O'PAGUS, 'ARRY, *pseud.* See Sommer, H. B.

4034 THE OPEN SECRET. By a Priest. Boston: Arena Publishing Co., 1893. 61, [1] p.      UC, Y
Message from Mars sets forth destiny of mankind.

ORAQUILL, *pseud.* See Bornemann, Mrs. Mary

4035 ORCUTT, HARRIET E. The Empire of the Invisibles . . . New York: The Metaphysical Publishing Co., 1899. 80 p.      CU, HEH, LC, UP
Life after death.

4036 ORD, MRS. AUGUSTA L. Agatha . . . New York: W. B. Smith & Co., Bond Street [cop. 1882]. 74 p.      LC

4037 O'REILLY, AUGUSTINE J. Alvira, the Heroine of Vesuvius: A Remarkable Sensation of the Seventeenth Century. Founded on Facts Recorded in the Acts of Canonization of St. Francis of Jerome . . . New York, Montreal: D. & J. Sadlier & Co., 1877. 220 p.      HEH, LC

4038 [———] Strange Memories: Death-Bed Scenes, Extraordinary Conversions, Incidents of Travel, etc. . . . New York, Montreal: D. & J. Sadlier & Co., 1880. 387 p.      LC

4039 O'REILLY, BERNARD. The Two Brides: A Tale ... New York: G. W. Carleton & Co. London: S. Low, Son & Co., 1879. 411 p. CU, HEH, LC, Y
Civil War.

4040 O'REILLY, JOHN BOYLE. Moondyne: A Story from the Under-World ... Boston: The Pilot Publishing Company, 1879. 327 p.
BA, H, HEH, LC, N, O, UP

——— jt. au. See Grant, R. The King's Men (1884), No. 2236.

ORLEANIAN, pseud. See Wharton, Edward Clifton

4041 ORMAR, JAMES ALLAN. William Wakefield: A Tale of the West ... Minneapolis, Minn.: Tribune Printing Company, 1899. 256 p., illus.
HEH, LC, UM, Y
Minnesota.

4042 ORMEROD, MRS. MAUD W. Madam Paradox: A Novel ... New York, Philadelphia, London: Drexel Biddle [cop. 1899]. 176 p., front. LC

ORNE, PHILIP, pseud. See Lowell, Francis Cabot

4043 [OSBORN, MRS. PETER E.] The Danbury Fair. By Aunt Debby [pseud.]. Danbury, Conn.: The Danbury Medical Printing Co., 1894. 165 p.
HEH, LC

4044 [OSBORNE, MRS. D. C.] Under Golden Skies; or, In the New Eldorado. A Story of Southern Life by a Southern Author ... Raleigh, N. C.: Edwards & Broughton, printers and binders, 1898. 485 p. HEH, LC, UVB
"Introductory" signed Howard A. Banks.
North Carolina.

OSBORNE, DUFFIELD. M. Paul Berdon. In The First Book of the Authors Club (1893), No. 1868.

4045 ——— The Secret of the Crater (A Mountain Moloch) ... New York and London: G. P. Putnam's Sons; the Knickerbocker Press, 1900. 312 p. LC
An imaginary island in the South Pacific.

4046 ——— The Spell of Ashtaroth ... New York: Charles Scribner's Sons, 1888. 234 p. AP, BA, BU, H, HEH, LC, O, UP, Y
Of the siege of Jericho.

4047 OSBOURNE, LLOYD. The Queen versus Billy, and Other Stories ... New York: Charles Scribner's Sons, 1900. 309 p. H, HEH, LC, O, UP, Y
Also contains: The Beautiful Man of Pingalap—The Dust of Defeat—The Happiest Day of His Life—Father Zosimus—Frenchy's Last Job—The Devil's White Man—The Phantom City—Amatua's Sailor.

———— *jt. au.* *See* Stevenson, R. L. The Ebb Tide (1894), No. 5197; The Wrecker (1892), No. 5198; *and* The Wrong Box (1899), No. 5199.

4048 OSGOOD, IRENE (DE BELLOT). The Shadow of Desire . . . New York: The Cleveland Publishing Company, 1893. 282 p.        HEH, LC, O, UVB

4049 OSTRANDER, FANNIE E. When Hearts Are True: A Novel . . . Chicago: Laird & Lee [cop. 1897]. 251 p., illus.
Listed PW, Feb. 20, 1897.

4050 OTT, EDWARD AMHERST. Philip Gerard, an Individual . . . Des Moines, Ia.: Drake University, College of Oratory and English [cop. 1899]. 334 p.        LC

4051 OTTOLENGUI, RODRIGUES. An Artist in Crime . . . New York, London: G. P. Putnam's Sons; the Knickerbocker Press, 1892. 281 p.        H, UP
Detective story.

4052 ———— A Conflict of Evidence . . . New York, London: G. P. Putnam's Sons; the Knickerbocker Press [cop. 1893]. 347 p.        CU, HEH, LC, O, UP
Deposited June 15, 1893.
Detective story; New Hampshire.

4053 ———— The Crime of the Century . . . New York, London: G. P. Putnam's Sons; the Knickerbocker Press, 1896. 349 p.        HEH, LC, O, UP

4054 ———— Final Proof; or, The Value of Evidence . . . New York and London: G. P. Putnam's Sons; the Knickerbocker Press, 1898. 390 p.
HEH, LC

4055 ———— A Modern Wizard . . . New York, London: G. P. Putnam's Sons; the Knickerbocker Press, 1894. 434 p.        AP, H, HEH, LC, O, Y
Of hypnotism; New York.

4056 OUR GREAT INDIAN WAR: The Miraculous Lives of Mustang Bill (Mr. Wm. Rhodes Decker) and Miss Marion Fannin. The Brave Indian Fighter among the Hostile Sioux. The Custer Expedition Massacre . . . Philadelphia: Barclay & Co., No. 21 North Seventh Street [cop. 1876]. 78 p., 1 l., illus.        LC, N, Y
Deposited Jan. 23, 1877.

4057 OUT OF TOWN . . . New York: Harper & Brothers, 1896. 235 p., illus.
BA, BU, HEH, LC
*Also contains:* A Question of Identity—A Little Music—The Railroad Humorist—Moments with Mechanics—Village Theatricals—The Professor—The Lawn-Tennis Match—The Naphtha Launch—The Wedding.

4058 OVERBAUGH, DE WITT CLINTON. The Hermit of the Catskills: A Tale of the American Revolution . . . New York: G. W. Dillingham Company, 1900. 223 p., front.        HEH, LC

OVIDIUS, *pseud.* *See* Bachman, Maurice A.

OWANDA, *pseud.* *See* Robinson, Edgar Williams

OWEN, CATHERINE, *pseud.* *See* Nitsch, Helen Alice (Matthews)

4059 OWEN, GEORGE WASHINGTON. Out of the Cage: An O'er True Tale . . . New York: G. W. Carleton & Co. London: S. Low & Co., 1877. 279 p.

BU, HEH, LC

OWL, EUGENE, *pseud.* *See* Pilgrim, Thomas

P., G. H. *See* Putnam, George Haven

4060 PACHECO, MARY. The New Don Quixote . . . New York: The Abbey Press, 114 Fifth Avenue. London, Montreal [cop. 1900]. 241 p.

HEH, LC, N

Arizona and England.

PADDOCK, MRS. A. G. *See* Paddock, Mrs. Cornelia

4061 PADDOCK, MRS. CORNELIA. The Fate of Madame La Tour: A Tale of Great Salt Lake. By Mrs. A. G. Paddock. New York: Fords, Howard, & Hulbert, 1881. 352 p.    AP, H, HEH, LC, N, O, UC, UM, Y
2nd issue, also with 1881 on title page, adds "The Remedy," pp. [353]-361, dated at end "Feb. 9th, 1882."    HEH, O
3rd issue changes date on title page to 1882.    BU, HEH, N, UV

4062 ———— In the Toils; or, Martyrs of the Latter Days . . . Chicago: Dixon & Shepard, 1879. 301 p.    H, HEH, LC, O, UM, Y

4063 PADDOCK, MARY FRANCES. Only Acorns . . . Boston: James H. Earle, 178 Washington Street [cop. 1899]. 43 p.    LC
*Contents:* The Mystery of Ivy Castle—Grandma's Christmas Story—The Lightning's Mission—Is Cupid Ever Defeated?—How Bessie Went to the Picnic.

4064 PAGE, ELIZA (JAQUITH). Only a Waif: The Romance of an Earthquake . . . St. Louis: Lewis E. Kline, 1109 Olive Street [cop. 1890]. 295 p., front.    LC
To encourage adoption.

PAGE, STANTON, *pseud.* *See* Fuller, Henry Blake

4065 PAGE, THOMAS MANNING. Bohemian Life; or, The Autobiography of a Tramp . . . St. Louis, 1884. 451 p., illus.    LC
*Also issued with imprint:* San Francisco, Cal.: J. Dewing & Co., 1884.    HEH

4066 PAGE, THOMAS NELSON. The Burial of the Guns . . . New York: Charles Scribner's Sons, 1894. 258 p.    BA, CU, H, HEH, LC, N, O, UC, UP, UVB, Y
*Contents:* My Cousin Fanny—The Burial of the Guns—The Gray Jacket of "No. 4"—Miss Dangerlie's Roses—How the Captain Made Christmas—Little Darby.

4067 —————— Elsket, and Other Stories . . . New York: Charles Scribner's Sons, 1891. 208 p.  BA, H, HEH, LC, N, O, UC, UP, UVB, Y
*Also contains:* "George Washington's" Last Duel—P'laski's Tunament—"Run to Seed"—"A Soldier of the Empire."

4068 —————— In Ole Virginia; or, Marse Chan, and Other Stories . . . New York: Charles Scribner's Sons, 1887. 230 p.  HEH, LC, N, O, UC, UP, UVB, Y
*Contents:* Marse Chan: A Tale of Old Virginia—"Unc' Edinburg's Drowndin'": A Plantation Echo—Meh Lady: A Story of the War—Ole 'Stracted—"No Haid Pawn"—Polly: A Christmas Recollection.

4069 —————— Marse Chan: A Tale of Old Virginia . . . New York: Charles Scribner's Sons, 1892. 53 p., illus.  BA, CU, H, HEH, LC, N, UC, UV, Y
First separate printing; printed earlier in Nos. 4068 and 5275.

4070 —————— Meh Lady: A Story of the War . . . New York: Charles Scribner's Sons, 1893. 70 p., illus.  BA, HEH, N, UC, UVB, Y
First separate printing; printed earlier in No. 4068.

—————— No Haid Pawn. *In* Stories of the South (1893), No. 5283.
Printed earlier in No. 4068.

4071 —————— The Old Gentleman of the Black Stock . . . New York: Charles Scribner's Sons, 1897. 137 p.  BA, H, HEH, LC, N, O, UP, UVB, Y

4072 —————— On Newfound River . . . New York: Charles Scribner's Sons, 1891. 240 p.  CU, H, HEH, LC, N, O, UC, UP, UVB, Y

4073 —————— Pastime Stories . . . New York: Harper & Brothers, 1894. 220 p., illus.  BA, CU, H, HEH, LC, N, O, UP, UVB, Y
*Contents:* Old Sue—How Jinny Eased Her Mind—Isrul's Bargain—The True Story of the Surrender of the Marquis Cornwallis—When Little Mordecai Was at the Bar—Charlie Whittler's Christmas Party—How Relius "Bossed the Ranch"—The Prosecution of Mrs. Dullet—One from Four—The Danger of Being Too Thorough—Uncle Jack's Views of Geography—Billington's Valentine—She Had on Her Geranium Leaves—A Story of Charles Harris—He Would Have Gotten a Lawyer—How Andrew Carried the Precinct—"Rasmus"—Her Sympathetic Editor—He Knew What Was Due to the Court —Her Great-Grandmother's Ghost—Rachel's Lovers—John's Wedding Suit —When the Colonel Was a Duellist.

4074 —————— Polly: A Christmas Recollection . . . New York: Charles Scribner's Sons, 1894. 49 p., illus.  BA, CU, H, HEH, LC, N, UC, UVB, Y
First separate printing; printed earlier in No. 4068.

4075 —————— Red Rock: A Chronicle of Reconstruction . . . New York: Charles Scribner's Sons, 1898. 584 p., illus.
AP, CU, H, HEH, LC, N, O, UC, UVB, Y

—————— Run to Seed. *In* Stories of the Railway (1893), No. 5281.
Printed earlier in No. 4067.

4076 —— Unc' Edinburg: A Plantation Echo . . . New York: Charles Scribner's Sons, 1895. 53 p., illus.     BA, CU, H, HEH, LC, N, O, UP, UV, Y
First separate printing; printed earlier in No. 4068.

PAGET, R. L., *pseud.*  *See* Knowles, Frederic Lawrence

4077 PAIGE, MRS. SIMON B.  A Lovely Girl's Fetters: A Spicy Novel . . . New York: The American News Company, 1884.  191 p.     LC
Of an unhappy marriage.

4078 PAINE, ALBERT BIGELOW.  The Bread Line: A Story of a Paper . . . New York: The Century Co., 1900.  228 p., front.  CU, H, HEH, LC, N, O, UM, Y

—— A Glimpse of Bohemia. *In* Short Story Masterpieces (1900), No. 4931.

4079 —— Mystery of Evelin Delorme: A Hypnotic Story . . . Boston: Arena Publishing Co., 1894.  129 p.     BU, HEH, LC, O, UM, Y

PAINE, HENRY GALLUP.  Their Lives and Letters. *In* Short Story Masterpieces (1900), No. 4931.

—— Willy and the Missionary. *In* Hanks: Assorted Yarns from Puck (1893), No. 2444.

PAINTER, LYDIA (HOYT) FARMER. *See* Farmer, Lydia (Hoyt)

4080 A PALACE-PRISON; or, The Past and the Present . . . New York: Fords, Howard, & Hulbert, 1884.  347 p.     H, HEH, LC, Y
Of an insane asylum.

4081 PALIER, EMILE A.  Social Sinners . . . New York: The Abbey Press, 114 Fifth Avenue [cop. 1900].  229 p.     LC, UP

4082 [PALMER, CHARLES T.]  A Fool's Effort: An Echo of Civic Administrations. By "Bertuccio" [pseud.].  Chicago: Barnard & Gunthorp, law printers, 1891.  82 p.     LC
Critical of law enforcement.

4083 PALMER, FANNY (PURDY).  A Dead Level, and Other Episodes . . . Buffalo: Charles Wells Moulton, 1892.  270 p.     BU, Y
*Also contains:* Meeta—Matt's Lovers—Outside the Pale—The Story of a Singer —April and August—A Woman—The Story of a Scapegrace—Doctor Waldemar's Title—Arnold's Creed.

4084 [PALMER, JOHN WILLIAMSON.]  After His Kind. By John Coventry [pseud.] . . . New York: Henry Holt and Company, 1886.  324 p., illus.     BA, BU, HEH, LC, Y
At head of title: "Leisure Hour Series—No. 184."

4085 PALMER, JULIUS AUBOINEAU. One Voyage and Its Consequences . . . Boston: D. Lothrop Company, Washington Street opposite Bromfield [cop. 1889]. 365 p.                                         BA, CU, H, HEH, LC, O

PALMER, LYNDE, *pseud.* *See* Peebles, Mary Louise (Parmelee)

4086 PALMER, MARY TOWLE. The Doctor of Deane . . . Boston: D. Lothrop Company, Franklin and Hawley Streets [cop. 1888]. 293 p., front.
AP, H, HEH, LC, O

4087 PANGBORN, FREDERIC WERDEN. Alice; or, The Wages of Sin. A Novel . . . New York: Charles T. Dillingham, 1883. 119 p.      AP, LC, UVB, Y

PARADIS, EDOUARD A. Yannay. *In* J. J. Conway, *ed.*, Stories (1893), No. 1172.

4088 PARISH, GRANT. Décolleté Washington: A National Satire . . . Baltimore, Md.: Press of John Cox's Sons [cop. 1892]. 125 p.
Copy examined at New York Public Library.

4089 ———— A Senator's Crime . . . [Washington, D. C.: Grant Parish Publishing Co., 1892.] 243 p., illus.                                      LC

4090 PARISH, JULIA ROYCE. Bud, Blossom, Fruit: A Story . . . Dedicated to Busy Women . . . Detroit, Mich.: J. C. Chilton Publishing Company, 1886. 286 p.                                                         LC

4091 ———— Diadama Van Dyne . . . [and] Thistledown. [Bay City, Mich.: J. P. Lambert], cop. 1899. 80 p.                            LC

PARK, C. A Committee of Entertainment. *In* At Wellesley (1896), No. 151.

4092 PARKER, AGNES. The Real Madeleine Pollard: A Diary of Ten Weeks' Association with the Plaintiff in the Famous Breckinridge-Pollard Suit . . . New York: G. W. Dillingham, 1894. 336 p.                    LC
Fictionalized account of breach of promise suit in Lexington, Kentucky.

4093 PARKER, CLARA. An Eventful Night: A Comedy of a Western Mining Town . . . New York: Doubleday & McClure Co., 1900. 152 p.
HEH, LC, O, Y

PARKER, ELIZABETH LOWBER (CHANDLER). *See* Chandler, Bessie

PARKER, GAY, *pseud.* *See* Green, Miss M. P.

PARKER, J. S. At the First Floor Centre. An Experiment, with I. H. Fiske. Formerly of '96. Reciprocal. [Four stories.] *In* At Wellesley (1896), No. 151.

4094 PARKER, JANE (MARSH). The Midnight Cry: A Novel . . . New York: Dodd, Mead & Company [cop. 1886]. 298 p.     CU, HEH, LC, O
Genesee, New York.

4095 [PARKER, Jo. A.] The Kansas Man Abroad: Tales of the Plains. By a Traveling Man. Lagrange, Ky.: Jo. A. Parker, 1889. 43 p.     LC

4096 PARKER, MARIA HILDRETH. The Country Home; or, Events of a Season . . . Lowell, Mass.: Citizen Newspaper Co., printers, 1894. 203 p.
HEH, LC

4097 ———— Halworth Hill: A Novel . . . [Lowell, Mass.: Stone, Bacheller, & Livingston, printers, 1881?] 198 p.     HEH
HEH has author's presentation copy dated "Oct. 29, '81."

4098 PARKER, MARY MONCURE. A Fair Maid of Florida . . . A Story of the Spanish Possession of the Floridas in the Eighteenth Century. Chicago, 1898. 104 p.     HEH, LC

4099 PARKINS, W. H. How I Escaped: A Novel . . . Edited by Archibald Clavering Gunter . . . New York: The Home Publishing Company, 1889. 180 p.     AP, H, HEH, LC, N, O, Y
Civil War novel.

4100 PARKS, L. K. With British and Braves: Story of the War of 1812 . . . Cincinnati: Curts & Jennings. New York: Eaton & Mains [cop. 1898]. 301 p., illus.     LC, O, UM

4101 [PARKS, MARY WONDERLY.] The New Reveries of a Bachelor; or, Bob, Belle, and That Mule. A Meadowgrass Idyl. By Timothy Toodles, Bachelor [pseud.] . . . Baltimore: Printed by John B. Piet [cop. 1881]. 99 p., illus.     LC

4102 PARMELE, MARY (PLATT). Answered in the Negative . . . New York: Parmele & Chaffee, 52 East 23d Street [cop. 1892]. 203 p.     LC, O
Also contains: Ariel; or, The Author's World.

4103 PARMER, ENRIQUE. Maple Hall Mystery: A Romance . . . New York: The Authors' Publishing Company, 27 Bond Street [cop. 1880]. 109 p.
LC

4104 PARSONS, CAROLINE. A Girl's Confessional, and Other Stories . . . Boston: Eastern Publishing Company, 61 Court Street [cop. 1899]. 264 p.
HEH, LC, O
Also contains: Women of Putney—Thomas Warren, Cupid vs. Theory—Zilpah Treat's Confession—Miss Bremen—The Chalk Line—A Squirrel Island Love Story— Mrs. Weir's Case—The First Meeting of a Browning Club—Cleones: A Story of the Fifteenth Century.

4105　PARSONS, CORNELIA MITCHELL.　A Secret of the Sea . . .　New York: J. S. Ogilvie Publishing Company, 57 Rose Street [cop. 1896].　135 p.
HEH, LC, Y
On the disappearance of Theodosia Burr.

4106　[PARSONS, JULIA (WARTH).]　Dorothy Thorn of Thornton.　By Julian Warth [pseud.] . . .　Boston: D. Lothrop & Company, Franklin and Hawley Streets [cop. 1887].　276 p.　AP, H, LC
North shore of Long Island.

4107　[————]　The Full Stature of a Man: A Life Story.　By Julian Warth [pseud.].　Boston: D. Lothrop and Company, Franklin and Hawley Streets [cop. 1886].　300 p.　BU, H, HEH, LC
Also published as: *John Greenleaf, Minister*.　Boston: D. Lothrop Company [cop. 1888].　LC

4108　PARTRIDGE, WILLIAM ORDWAY.　The Angel of Clay . . .　New York & London: G. P. Putnam's Sons; the Knickerbocker Press, 1900.　213 p., illus.　H, HEH, LC, O

4109　PATCH, KATE (WHITING).　Middleway: Tales of a New England Village . . .　Boston: Copeland and Day, 1897.　227 p., 1 l.　CU, H, HEH, LC, N, O, Y
*Contents:* Tilda's Wedding Present—David's Fortune—Miss Thankful's Love Affair—A Morning with Miss Postmistress—Mr. Trueworthy's Mission—The Minister's Vacation—Dr. Gerry's Birthday—"Not a Sparrow Falleth"—A Winter Wedding.

PATRICK, M. N.　*See* Hawkins, Thomas Hayden.　Drifting (1892), No. 2576.

4110　PATTERSON, J. T.　What Next? or, The Honest Thief . . .　[Lexington, Ky.: Transylvania Printing Co., 1899.]　499 p., front.　HEH
Life in Kentucky before the Civil War.

4111　PATTESON, CAMM.　The Young Bachelor.　With an Appendix Containing an Essay on "The Destiny of the Negro in America" . . .　Lynchburg, Va.: Printed for the author by J. P. Bell Company, 1900.　119 p., front.　UV
The South during and after the Civil War.

PAUL, JOHN, *pseud.　See* Allison, Charles Henry

PAUL, KENNETH, *pseud.　See* Lockwood, Melancthon Clarence

4112　PAUL, MRS. MARJORIE.　The Passing of Alix: A Novel . . .　Boston: Arena Publishing Company, 1895.　266 p.　LC
Fashionable set in New York and Paris.

4113　PAUL DOUGLASS; or, There Is That Within Which Passeth Show.　A Story.　Philadelphia: J. L. Sibole & Co., 1877.　96 p.　HEH

4114 PAULL, MINNIE E. (KENNEY). Gypsie. By Minnie E. Kenney. New York: G. P. Putnam's Sons, 1882. 313 p.  o
Majority of her books were juveniles.

4115 PAXTON, HENRY MIDDLETON. The Man with the Lantern . . . Boston: Banner of Light Publishing Co., 1898. 111 p., illus.  HEH, LC

4116 PAYNE, ALICE HUNTLEY. The Rage of the Age: A Story . . . New York: Oscar Dryer, 1883. 260 p.  HEH, LC

PAYNE, J. HARLOW, *pseud. See* Boland, Lewis M.

4117 PAYNE, ODESSA (STRICKLAND). Psyche: A Novel . . . Atlanta, Georgia: Jas. P. Harrison & Co., printers and publishers, 1885. 287 p.  HEH
The South.

4118 PAYNE, WILL. Jerry, the Dreamer: A Novel . . . New York: Harper & Brothers, 1896. 299 p.  CU, HEH, LC, N, O, UC, UVB, Y
Of a newspaperman in Chicago.

4119 —— The Money Captain . . . Chicago & New York: Herbert S. Stone & Company, 1898. 323 p.  HEH, LC, N, UC, UM, UP, Y
A Chicago gas company scandal.

4120 PAYNTER, MARY MONCURE. Caleb, the Irrepressible . . . Chicago: Henry A. Sumner & Company, 1883. 267 p.  CU, HEH, LC
At head of title: "Hammock Series."
Southern romance before and during the Civil War.

4121 —— The Little Lass . . . Chicago, Ill.: H. M. Paynter, Jr., 1886. 192 p.  LC

4122 PAYSON, EDWARD. Doctor Tom . . . Boston: Lee and Shepard. Portland, Me.: Dresser, McLellan & Co., 1877. 395 p.  H, HEH, LC, UM

4123 PAYSON, WILLIAM FARQUHAR. The Copy-Maker . . . New York: New Amsterdam Book Company, 156 Fifth Avenue [cop. 1897]. 192 p., illus.  CU, HEH, LC, N, O, UP
Newspaper story; New York.

4124 —— The Title-Mongers . . . New York: Dodd, Mead and Company, 1898. 333 p.  H, HEH, LC, UM
Newport social season.

4125 PEAKE, ELMORE ELLIOTT. The Darlingtons . . . New York: McClure, Phillips & Co., 1900. 416 p.  AP, H, HEH, LC, O
Of a railroad family.

4126 PEALE, MARGARET. In the Time of the Cherry Viewing: An Episode in Japan . . . New York and London: G. P. Putnam's Sons; the Knickerbocker Press, 1889. 127 p.  AP, H, LC, O

4127 PEARSON, CHARLES H. The Wiltons of Grand Prairie . . . New York: J. Selwin Tait & Sons, 65 Fifth Avenue [cop. 1896]. 276 p.    HEH, LC
Deposited Jan. 2, 1897.

4128 PEARSON, EMILY (CLEMENS). Madonna Hall: The Story of Our Country's Peril . . . Boston: James H. Earle, 1890. 478 p.    HEH, LC, N

4129 PEARSON, FREDERICK W. A Forced Marriage: A Novel . . . New York: J. S. Ogilvie, 1890. 176 p.
Listed PW, Dec. 27, 1890.
LC has copy in the omitted "Sunnyside Series," No. 11, 1891.

4130 ——— Miñon: A Tale of Love and Intrigue . . . New York: The Welles Publishing Company, 645 Broadway [cop. 1888]. 135 p.    LC

PEARSON, HARLAN COLBY. Clarkson, Right Guard. In Senior Days. With the Dawning. [Three stories.] *In* H. J. Hapgood, *ed.*, Echoes from Dartmouth (1895), No. 2446.

4131 PEARSON, HENRY CLEMENS. Her Opportunity . . . Boston: James H. Earle, 1888. 462 p.    BU, HEH, Y
Society and slums; New York.

4132 ——— His Opportunity . . . Boston: James H. Earle, 1886. 447 p.
CU, HEH, LC, O, Y
Of steelworkers.

4133 [PEARSON, WILLIAM SIMPSON.] MΩNON OY; or, Well-Nigh Reconstructed. A Political Novel. By Brinsley Matthews [pseud.] . . . New York: E. J. Hale & Son, 1882. 279 p.    HEH, LC, Y

4134 PEASE, VERNE SETH. In the Wake of War: A Tale of the South under Carpet-Bagger Administrations . . . Chicago, New York: George M. Hill Company, 1900. 440 p.    CU, H, HEH, UM, UV, Y

4135 PEATTIE, ELIA (WILKINSON). A Mountain Woman . . . Chicago: Way & Williams, 1896. 251 p.    BA, CU, H, HEH, LC, N, O, UM, Y
*Also contains:* Jim Lancy's Waterloo—The Three Johns—A Resuscitation—Two Pioneers—Up the Gulch—A Michigan Man—A Lady of Yesterday.

——— Old Majah Chaffee. *In* Short Story Masterpieces (1900), No. 4931.

4136 ——— Pippins and Cheese: Being the Relation of How a Number of Persons Ate a Number of Dinners at Various Times and Places . . . Chicago: Way and Williams, 1897. 282 p., 1 l.    HEH, LC, N, O, UP
*Contents:* Dinner for Two—The Price of a Dinner—At Luncheon—The Princess Dines—The Stop Gap—Covers for Twelve—A Diminuendo—The Blood Apple—A Mess of Pottage.

4137 ——— The Shape of Fear, and Other Ghostly Tales . . . New York: The Macmillan Company. London: Macmillan & Co., Ltd., 1898. 175 p.                                    H, HEH, LC, O, UP
*Also contains:* On the Northern Ice—Their Dear Little Ghost—A Spectral Collie—The House That Was Not—Story of an Obstinate Corpse—A Child of the Rain—The Room of the Evil Thought—Story of the Vanishing Patient—The Piano Next Door—An Astral Onion—From the Loom of the Dead—A Grammatical Ghost.

PEATTIE, ROBERT BURNS. Van Gibber and the Street-Car. *In* Hanks: Assorted Yarns from Puck (1893), No. 2444.

4138 PECK, BRADFORD. The World a Department Store: A Story of Life under a Coöperative System . . . Lewiston, Maine: Bradford Peck. Boston, 564 Washington Street [cop. 1900]. 311 p., illus.
                                    BU, CU, H, HEH, LC, N, O, UC, UM, Y
Deposited Apr. 3, 1900.
A cooperative city in 1925.

4139 PECK, GEORGE WILBUR. The Grocery Man and Peck's Bad Boy: Being a Continuation of Peck's Bad Boy and His Pa . . . Chicago and New York: Belford, Clarke & Co., 1883. 240 p., illus.     CU, H, HEH, N
At head of title: "Peck's Bad Boy, No. 2."

4140 [———] How Private Geo. W. Peck Put Down the Rebellion; or, The Funny Experiences of a Raw Recruit . . . Chicago and New York: Belford, Clarke & Co., 1887. 316 p., illus.     CU, H, HEH, N, O, UC, UM

4141 ——— Mirth for the Million: Peck's Compendium of Fun, Comprising the Immortal Deeds of Peck's Bad Boy and His Pa, and All the Choice Gems of Wit . . . from the Prolific Pen of George W. Peck . . . Edited by Elmo. Chicago: Belford, Clarke & Co., 1883. 540 p., illus.     LC
Elmo is pseud. of Thomas W. Handford.

4142 ——— Peck's Bad Boy and His Pa . . . Chicago: Belford, Clarke & Co., 1883. 196 p., illus.                    H, HEH, LC, N, UC

4143 ——— ——— Chicago: C. B. Beach & Co., 1883. 256 p., illus.   HEH
This ed. adds chaps. xxxvii-xxxix.

4144 ——— Peck's Boss Book . . . Chicago and New York: Belford, Clarke & Co., 1884. 252 p., illus.                CU, H, HEH, LC, N, UC

4145 ——— Peck's Irish Friend, Phelan Geoheagan . . . Chicago and New York: Belford, Clarke & Co., 1888. 205 p., illus.     LC, UVB, Y

4146 ——— Peck's Sunshine: Being a Collection of Articles Written for Peck's Sun, Milwaukee, Wis. . . . Chicago: Belford, Clarke & Co. St. Louis: Belford & Clarke Publishing Co., 1882. 296 p., illus.
                                    CU, H, HEH, LC, UM, Y

4147 —— Peck's Uncle Ike and the Red Headed Boy ... Chicago: Alexander Belford & Co., 1899. 217 p., illus. CU, HEH, N, UC, UV

4148 —— Sunbeams ... Humor, Sarcasm, and Sense ... Chicago: Jamieson-Higgins Co., 1900. 220 p., illus. LC, UM

4149 PECK, WALLACE. The Golden Age of Patents: A Parody on Yankee Inventiveness ... New York: Frederick A. Stokes & Brothers, 1888. 55 p. BU, H, HEH, LC, O, UC, Y

4150 —— The Memoirs of a Counterfeit Dollar ... [N.p.], cop. 1888. [28] p., illus. LC
Text and pages in the shape of a silver dollar.

4151 —— A Stitch in Time Saves the Nine ... [New York], cop. 1888. [24] p., illus. LC
Leaves are circular in shape.

4152 —— The Story of a Train of Cars: A Tale of Travel ... New York: Authors' Publishing Association, 114 Fifth Avenue [cop. 1895]. 70 p., illus. LC, UV
Deposited Dec. 9, 1896.
Of a private train.

4153 —— The Story of the Puritans: A Go-as-You Please History (Part Fact, Part Fiction) from the First Leeway Voyage of the Mayflower down to the Close of the Doughnut Dynasty ... St. Johnsbury [Vt.]: Charles T. Walter, 1889. 90 p., illus. HEH, LC, UM

4154 PECK, WILLIAM HENRY. The Stone-Cutter of Lisbon: A Novel ... New York: Robert Bonner's Sons [cop. 1889]. 436 p., front. CU, H, HEH, Y

4155 [PEEBLES, MARY LOUISE (PARMELEE).] Jeannette's Cisterns. By Lynde Palmer [pseud.] ... Troy, N. Y.: H. B. Nims & Co., 1881. 281 p. HEH, LC, Y

4156 [——] A Question of Honour. By Lynde Palmer [pseud.] ... New York: Dodd, Mead & Company [cop. 1893]. 315 p. LC, O
Deposited Aug. 18, 1890.

4157 [——] Where Honour Leads. By Lynde Palmer [pseud.] ... New York: Dodd, Mead & Company [cop. 1894]. 363 p. BU, HEH, LC, O
Deposited Oct. 15, 1894.

4158 PEEKE, MARGARET BLOODGOOD (PECK). Born of Flame: A Rosicrucian Story ... Philadelphia: J. B. Lippincott Company, 1892. 299 p. BU, LC, O, UC

4159 —— Zenia, the Vestal; or, The Problem of Vibrations ... Boston, Mass.: Arena Publishing Company, 1893. 355 p. BU, HEH, LC
Of occult laws.

4160 PEIRCE, ARTHUR C.  A Man from Corpus Christi; or, The Adventures of Two Bird Hunters and a Dog in Texan Bogs ... New York: Forest and Stream Publishing Company, 1894.  257 p., illus.  LC, N

4161 PELLETREAU, CHARLES.  Sylvester Romaine: A Novel ... New York: James Pott & Co., 1892.  255 p.  HEH, LC, Y
Newlyweds separated by shipwreck.

4162 PEMBERTON, CAROLINE H.  Stephen the Black ... Philadelphia: George W. Jacobs & Co., 103-105 South Fifteenth Street [cop. 1899].  282 p.  CU, HEH, LC, UP, Y
Thirty years after slavery.

4163 ——— Your Little Brother James ... Philadelphia: George W. Jacobs & Co., 1896.  132 p., illus.  H, LC, O
*Also issued with imprint:* Stamford, N.Y.: The Recorder Book Press, 1896. 93 p.  BU
Order of printing not determined.

4164 PEMBERTON, JEANNETTE.  Buffeting ... New York: Dodd, Mead & Company [cop. 1892].  239 p.  HEH
Of a governess.

4165 PENDLETON, EDMUND.  A Complication in Hearts: A Novel ... New York: The Home Publishing Company, 1893.  244 p.  LC, UVB, Y
Washington, D.C.

4166 ——— A Conventional Bohemian ... New York: D. Appleton and Company, 1886.  372 p.  AP, BA, H, HEH, LC, O, UV, Y
Of two women travelers.

4167 ——— One Woman's Way: A Novel ... New York: D. Appleton and Company, 1891.  345 p.  BA, HEH, O

4168 ——— A Virginia Inheritance: A Novel ... New York: D. Appleton and Company, 1888.  303 p.  AP, BA, H, HEH, LC, O, UM, UV
Virginia and New York City society contrasted.

4169 PENDLETON, LOUIS BEAUREGARD.  Bewitched: A Tale ... New York: Cassell & Company, Limited, 104-106 Fourth Avenue [cop. 1888]. 288 p.  AP, HEH, Y
*Also contains:* Ariadne in the Wire-Grass—The Story of Black Dan.

4170 ——— Carita: A Cuban Romance ... Boston, New York, and London: Lamson, Wolffe and Company, 1898.  247 p.  CU, HEH, LC, O, Y

4171 ——— Corona of the Nantahalas: A Romance ... New York: The Merriam Company, 67 Fifth Avenue [cop. 1895].  199 p., front.  HEH, LC
North Carolina mountains.

4172 ——— In the Wire-Grass: A Novel ... New York: D. Appleton and Company, 1899. 245 p. BA, HEH, Y

4173 ——— The Sons of Ham: A Tale of the New South ... Boston: Roberts Brothers, 1895. 328 p. HEH, LC, O, UM
Maintains color line must remain.

4174 ——— The Wedding Garment: A Tale of the Life to Come ... Boston: Roberts Brothers, 1894. 246 p. BA, H, HEH, LC

4175 PENDLETON, MARK PIERCE. Andy Dodge: The History of a Scapegrace ... Boston: Lee and Shepard, 1900. 255 p., front. HEH, LC
Of newspapers and politics.

4176 PENFIELD, RICHARD. Luelle: A Southern Romance ... Philadelphia: E. Claxton & Company, 1884. 349 p. LC
North Georgia gold fields.

4177 [PENGILLY, MRS. IDA E.] The Minister's Daughter, and Other Stories. By Ditta [pseud.] ... [Manitowoc, Wis., cop. 1896.] 153 p. LC
*Also contains:* Alone and Forsaken—The Witch of Castleton—Two Blighted Lives—Fickle Fortune.

PENN, RACHEL, *pseud.* *See* Willard, Caroline McCoy (White)

4178 PENNINGTON, JEANNE GILLESPIE. Some Marked Passages, and Other Stories ... New York: Fords, Howard, and Hulbert, 1898. 219 p.
HEH, LC, O, UVB
*Contents:* Where the Road Forked—A Codicil—The Necessary Voice—The Darkest Hour—At Eventide—"Renzy"—Miss Zenobia's Experiment—A Fragment of Life—Chrystenah.

PENNOT, *Rev.* PETER, *pseud.* *See* Round, William Marshall Fitts

4179 PERKINS, ANNIE STEVENS. Appointed Paths ... Boston: James H. Earle, 1896. 201 p., front. HEH, LC

4180 PERKINS, FREDERIC BEECHER. Devil-Puzzlers, and Other Studies ... New York: G. P. Putnam's Sons, 1877. 215 p., front. BA, H, HEH, LC, O, UM, Y
*Also contains:* The Man-ufactory—Childhood: A Study—The Compensation Office—My Forenoon with the Baby.
Title story printed earlier in Wright II, No. 2457.

4181 ——— My Three Conversations with Miss Chester ... New York: G. P. Putnam's Sons, 1877. 86 p. LC

4182 [PERKINS, GEORGE.] Before the Dawn: A Story of Paris and the Jacquerie. By George Dulac [pseud.]. New York and London: G. P. Putnam's Sons, 1888. 307 p. AP, LC, O

4183 PERKINS, PEPPERMINT, *pseud.* The Familiar Letters of Peppermint Perkins [pseud.] . . . Boston: Ticknor and Company, 1886. 411 p., illus.

BU, H, HEH, LC, O, UC, UM, UP

"'Peppermint Perkins' is said to be the nom de plume of a young society lady of Boston." PW, May 22, 1886, p. 645.

4184 PERKINS, SARAH MARIA (CLINTON). Helen; or, Will She Save Him? . . . New York: Funk & Wagnalls, 1886. 138 p.                LC

Temperance tale.

4185 [PERLEY, MRS. T. E.] From Timber to Town: Down in Egypt. By an Early Settler. Chicago: A. C. McClurg and Company, 1891. 287 p.

H, HEH, LC, N, Y

Illinois frontier.

4186 PERRIGO, G. A. The Man and the Woman . . . Atlanta, Ga.: American Publishing & Engraving Co., 1895. 208 p.                HEH, LC

An American marries an Englishwoman.

4187 [PERRIN, RAYMOND ST. JAMES.] The Student's Dream. Published for the Author. Chicago: Jensen, McClurg & Company, 1881. 97 p.

BU, CU, H, LC

Printed on one side of each leaf.
Metaphysical.

4188 PERROW, GEORGE L. The Hoosier Editor: A Tale of Indiana Life . . . Indianapolis: Tilford & Carlon, printers, 1877. 223, [1] p.

H, HEH, LC, N, O, UC, UM, Y

4189 PERRY, A. T. A Windfall . . . New York: The Authors' Publishing Company, 27 Bond Street [cop. 1880]. 262 p.                HEH, LC

4190 PERRY, ALICE. Esther Pennefather: A Novel . . . New York: Harper & Brothers, 1878. 175 p. Printed in double columns.    CU, HEH, LC, O

4191 ———— More Ways Than One . . . Boston: D. Lothrop and Company, Franklin St., corner of Hawley [cop. 1879]. 484 p., illus.  CU, HEH, LC, O

4192 ———— The Schoolmaster's Trial; or, Old School and New . . . New York: Charles Scribner's Sons, 1881. 185 p.      AP, H, HEH, LC

Schoolmaster acquitted on grounds that certain abuses were due to faulty system.

4193 PERRY, BLISS. The Broughton House . . . New York: Charles Scribner's Sons, 1890. 366 p.          AP, BA, BU, H, HEH, LC, O, UC, UM, Y

New England summer resort.

———— The Commonest Possible Story. *In* Stories of New York (1893), No. 5279.

Later printed in No. 4196.

4194 ———— The Plated City ... New York: Charles Scribner's Sons, 1895. 397 p.    BA, H, HEH, LC, O, Y
A Connecticut industrial city.

4195 ———— The Powers at Play ... New York: Charles Scribner's Sons, 1899. 286 p.    BA, H, HEH, LC, O, UM, UVB, Y
*Contents:* His Word of Honor–In the Rip–By the Committee–Madame Annalena–The Incident of the British Ambassador–The Fish-Warden of Madrid–Jepson's Third Adjective–The White Blackbird.

4196 ———— Salem Kittredge, and Other Stories ... New York: Charles Scribner's Sons, 1894. 291 p.    BA, CU, H, HEH, LC, N, O, UM, Y
*Also contains:* The Czar's Diamond–By the Ill–Lombardy Poplars–The Phenix–The Commonest Possible Story–An Incorrigible Poet–Number Three–At Sesenheim.

4197 PERRY, NORA. A Book of Love Stories ... Boston: James R. Osgood and Company, 1881. 309 p.    AP, BA, CU, H, HEH, LC, O, UVB
*Contents:* Dolly–Dick Halliday's Wife–Laura and Her Hero–Christine–Mr. and Mrs. Meyer–The Charmer Charmed–After Five Years–John Eccleston's Thanksgiving–An Heiress–Margaret Freyer's Heart.

———— Dorothy. *In* L. C. H. Langford, *comp.,* The Woman's Story (1889), No. 3206.

4198 ———— For a Woman: A Novel ... Boston: Ticknor and Company, 1886. 181 p.    BA, H, HEH, LC, O
Story partly laid at and around Moosehead Lake, Maine.

4199 ———— The Tragedy of the Unexpected, and Other Stories ... Boston: Houghton, Mifflin and Company. The Riverside Press, Cambridge, 1880. 294 p.    AP, BA, BU, CU, HEH, O, UV, Y
*Also contains:* Mrs. Stanhope's Last Lodger–A Foolish Girl–Our Ice Man–In the Red Room–"My Nannie O"–In a Street Car–Mrs. F.'s Waiting-Maid–The Ribbon of Honor.

4200 PETERS, JOHN A. Two Odd Girls; or, Douglas Rock's Secret ... New York: G. W. Dillingham Co., 1898. 529 p.    LC
Sharon Springs, New York.

4201 [PETERS, WILLIAM ANDREW.] Human Natur'. By Joel Sloper [pseud.] ... New York: Knickerbocker Book Co., 1885. 208 p., illus.    H, HEH, LC

4202 PETERSEN, MARCUS. A Modern Despotism: A True Story of American Political Life in 1893 ... Buffalo, N.Y.: Charles Wells Moulton, 1894. 312 p.    LC, UC

4203 [PETERSILEA, CARLYLE.] The Discovered Country. By Ernst von Himmel [pseud.]. Boston: Ernst von Himmel Publishing Company, Hotel Boyleston [cop. 1889]. 234 p.    BU, H, LC, UM

4204 —— Mary Anne Carew: Wife, Mother, Spirit, Angel . . . Boston: Colby & Rich, 1893. 252 p.        HEH, LC

4205 [——] Oceanides: A Psychical Novel. By Ernst von Himmel [pseud.] . . . Boston: E. von Himmel Publishing Co., Hotel Boyleston [cop. 1890]. 418 p.        LC

4206 PETERSON, BELLE. A Beautiful Bird without a Name; or, A True Kentucky Girl . . . Louisville: Courier-Journal Job Printing Company, 1883. 328 p.        HEH, LC, UC, Y

4207 [PETERSON, HENRY.] Bessie's Six Lovers: A Summer Idyl. Philadelphia: T. B. Peterson & Brothers [1877].
Listed PW, Oct. 27 and Nov. 3, 1877.
Later ed. listed PW, July 9, 1887.

4208 PETERSON, MATTIE J. Little Pansy: A Novel . . . Wilmington [N.C.]: Messenger Steam Job Print, 1890. 54 p.
Information supplied by Harry Bergholz of University of North Carolina Library.

PETIT, VERONIQUE. See Mathews, Amelie Veronique (Petit) Child

4209 PEX, pseud. Nicholas Nickleton: A California Christmas Story . . . San Francisco: S. F. News Company, 1876. 68 p., illus.
Copy examined at New York Public Library.

4210 PEYTON, JOHN LEWIS. Tom Swindel; or, The Adventures of a Boomer . . . Staunton, Va.: George L. Bolen, 1893. 136 p.   H, HEH, LC, UC, UV, Y
Of Virginia real estate booms.

PHELON, MIRA M., jt. au. See Phelon, W. P. Three Sevens (1889), No. 4211.

4211 PHELON, WILLIAM P. Three Sevens: A Story of Ancient Initiations. By the Phelons . . . Chicago, Ill.: The Hermetic Publishing Company, 1889. 271 p.        CU, LC
Mira M. Phelon, jt. au.

4212 —— A Witch of the Nineteenth Century . . . Chicago, Ill.: The Hermetic Publishing Company, 1893. 149 p.        LC

4213 PHELPS, CHARLES EDWARD DAVIS. The Bailiff of Tewkesbury. By C. E. D. Phelps and Leigh North [pseud.] . . . Chicago: A. C. McClurg & Company, 1893. 199 p., illus.     CU, H, HEH, LC, UM
Leigh North is pseud. of Elizabeth Steward (Natt) Phelps.

4214 [PHELPS, ELIZABETH STEWARD (NATT).] Allendale's Choice: A Village Chronicle. By Leigh North [pseud.]. Milwaukee, Wis.: The Young Churchman Co., 1895. 181 p.        LC
Of the selection of a rector.

———— *jt. au.* *See* Phelps, C. E. D. The Bailiff of Tewkesbury (1893), No. 4213.

PHELPS, ELIZABETH STUART. *See* Ward, Elizabeth Stuart (Phelps)

4215 PHIL JOHNSON'S LIFE ON THE PLAINS. Chicago: Rhodes & McClure Publishing Company, 1888. 358 p., illus. Y

4216 PHILIP MOORE, THE SCULPTOR: A Temperance Story ... New York: Hunt and Eaton. Cincinnati: Cranston & Curts [1880?]. 186 p., front. HEH

4217 PHILIPS, MELVILLE. The Devil's Hat: A Sketch in Oil ... Boston: Ticknor and Company, 1887. 328 p. AP, CU, HEH, LC, Y

4218 ———— Snap: A Novel ... Philadelphia: Harper & Brothers, 1881. 183 p. LC

PHILKINS, IKE, *pseud.* *See* Bowen, William Abraham

4219 PHILLIPS, BARNET. Burning Their Ships ... New York: Harper & Brothers, 1879. 120 p. BA, BU, H, HEH, UV
Of a married couple.

4220 ———— A Struggle: A Story in Four Parts ... New York: D. Appleton and Company, 1878. 171 p. BA, H, LC, O, UP
At head of title: "Appletons' New Handy-Volume Series."

4221 PHILLIPS, EPHRAIM. Lost in the Adirondacks! Triumphs of a Southern Beauty. A Tale of Love at Piseco! A Faithful Lover's Tragic End! "Truth Stranger Than Fiction." Adventure in "Forest and Stream" ... Schenectady, N.Y.: Chas. Burrows printer, 1890. 60, [1] p. HEH, UP

4222 PHILLIPS, LUDERN MERRISS. Miskel: A Novel ... Franklin, Ohio: The Editor Publishing Co., 1895. 266 p. LC

4223 PHILLIPS, SAMUEL LOUIS. Prince Como II. An Heiress Abroad... New York: The American News Company, 1893. 269 p. LC
From western U.S. mines to Paris.

4224 PHILLIPS, WALDORF HENRY. Who Is Your Wife? A Complex Conundrum Colloquially Considered ... New York: E. J. Hale & Son, 1880. 126 p. LC
Humorous treatment in story form of divorce.

PHILLIPS, WALTER POLK. A Leaf of Autobiography. *In* [W. J. Johnston] *comp.*, Lightning Flashes and Electric Dashes (1877), Nos. 3022, 3023.

4225 ———— My Debut in Journalism, and Other Odd Happenings... New York: The International Telegram Co. [cop. 1892]. 201 p., illus. LC

*Also contains:* An Agreeable Saunterer—Miss Britton's Romance—An Evening Reverie—Esther Romaine—An Old Man's Exegesis—Agnes Leigh—Stage Coaching—Old George Wentworth.

4226 [————] Oakum Pickings: A Collection of Stories, Sketches and Paragraphs... By John Oakum [pseud.]... New York: W. J. Johnston, 1876. 176 p., front. CU, HEH, LC, N, UC, UP, Y

*Contains:* Love and Lightning—Old Jim Lawless—Thomas Johnson—Little Tip McClosky—Stage Coaching—Posie Van Dusen—Block Island—Bad Medicine—The Bloodless Onslaught—Cap. De Costa—Uncle Daniel—Summer Recreation—The Blue and the Gray—An Autumn Episode—An Old Man's Exegesis—Departed Days.

HEH has a 188 p. printing, also dated 1876, which inserts the story "Statistics" between "An Old Man's Exegesis" and "Departed Days."

4227 ———— Sketches Old and New; Together with an Address, Entitled "From Franklin to Edison"... New York: George Munro's Sons, 17 to 27 Vandewater Street [cop. 1897]. 200 p., front. H, HEH

*Contains:* Old Jim Lawless—Posie Van Dusen—Little Tip McCloskey—An Autumn Episode—Cap De Costa—Old George Wentworth—Patsy Flannagan —Narcissa—An Agreeable Saunterer—Pop Donaldson—Bif.

PHINEAS, *pseud.* *See* Hanifin, John M.

PHINX, A. S., *pseud.* *See* Beattie, Hans Stevenson

4228 PHIPPS, MRS. SARAH E. Violet Gray; or, From Ambition to Success... New York, London: Funk & Wagnalls, 1889. 288 p., illus. LC

4229 PIATT, DONN. The Lone Grave of the Shenandoah, and Other Tales... Chicago, New York, and San Francisco: Belford, Clarke & Co., 1888. 156 p. CU, HEH, LC, N, O, UP, UVB, Y

*Also contains:* Peter Pepperton's Fourth o' July Triumph—Luny Len—Handled Goods—Aunt Hetty—Mr. Bardolph Bottles—About Love and Law—Old Shack—The Sales-Lady of the City—Montezuma Hawkins, Reformer—The Wharf-Rat—The Female Clerk at Washington—The Great Dynamite Scare— A Story about Bears.

4230 ———— The Reverend Melancthon Poundex: A Novel... Chicago: Robert J. Belford, 1893. 366 p., illus. HEH

4231 PICARD, GEORGE HENRY. A Matter of Taste: A Novel... New York: White, Stokes, & Allen, 1884. 220 p., illus. H, HEH, LC, O

Americans in Italy.

4232 ———— A Mission Flower: An American Novel... New York: White, Stokes, & Allen, 1885. 342 p. HEH, LC, O

On the U.S.-Mexican border.

4233 — Old Boniface: A Novel ... New York: White, Stokes, & Allen, 1886. 279 p. AP, HEH, LC, O
London.

4234 PICKARD, WILLIAM LOWNDES. Under the War Flags of 1861: A Romance of the South ... Louisville, Ky.: Chas. T. Dearing, 1895. 372 p. LC, UV

4235 PICKETT, ANITA (TRUEMAN). Anton's Angels: A Romance. By Anita Trueman ... New York: The Alliance Publishing Co., 1900. 131 p.
 LC

PICKETT, MRS. GEORGE E. *See* Pickett, La Salle (Corbell)

PICKETT, LA SALLE (CORBELL). As the Curtain Fell. The Rose of Hell. By Mrs. Gen. George E. Pickett. [Two stories.] *In* Short Story Masterpieces (1900), No. 4931.

4236 — Kunnoo Sperits, and Others ... Washington: The Neale Co., 1900. 174 p., illus. H, HEH, LC
*Contents:* In de Miz—Marse Tom's Kunnoo Sperits—De Marikle er Twinzes—'Storical Juels.

4237 — Yule Log ... Washington: The Neale Co., 1900. 164 p., illus.
 H, HEH, LC
*Also contains:* De Ole Ox Kyart—Wuz Santa Claus a Nigger Dat Year?—De Bridegroom—Mammy Borry—A Christmas Vista.

4238 [PICTON, NINA.] At the Threshold. By Laura Dearborn [pseud.] ... New York: Cassell Publishing Company, 104 & 106 Fourth Avenue [cop. 1893]. 144 p. HEH, LC
At head of title: "The 'Unknown' Library."

4239 [PICTON, THOMAS.] The Count's Niece; or, The Veteran of Marengo. An Historical Tale of the Napoleonic Empire. By Paul Preston, Esq. [pseud.]. New York: Pollard & Moss, 1888. 117 p. HEH
At head of title: "The $1,000 Prize Story."

4240 PIDGIN, CHARLES FELTON. Quincy Adams Sawyer and Mason's Corner Folks: A Novel. A Picture of New England Home Life ... Boston: C. M. Clark Publishing Company, 1900. 586 p., front., map.
 H, HEH, LC, O, Y

PIER, ARTHUR STANWOOD. For Unknown Reasons. *In* Stories from the Harvard Advocate (1896), No. 5277a

4241 — The Pedagogues: A Story of the Harvard Summer School ... Boston: Small, Maynard & Company, 1899. 287 p.
 BA, H, HEH, LC, O, UM, UP, Y
Of a Harvard instructor.

4242    Pierce, Gilbert Ashville.   A Dangerous Woman: Being the Experience of the Hon. John Billings, M.C. . . .    Chicago: R. R. Donnelley & Sons, printers, 1884.   505 p., illus.            N, UVB
Washington, D.C.

4243    ———— Peggy, a Country Heroine . . .    Chicago: Donnelley, Lloyd & Co., 1883.   50 p.
Information from LC card; no copy seen.

4244    ———— Zachariah, the Congressman: A Tale of American Society . . . Chicago: Donnelley, Gassette, & Lloyd, 1880.   440 p., front.
                        CU, HEH, LC, N, O, UC, UM, UVB, Y

4245    Pierce, Lucy France.   The White Devil of Verde: A Story of the West . . .   New York: G. W. Dillingham Co., 1898.   236 p.        HEH, LC
Mining.

4246    Pierce, Squier Littell.   Di: A Story . . .    Philadelphia: J. B. Lippincott Company, 1891.   318 p., illus.                         HEH, O
On the Miami Canal, Minnesota.

4247    ———— Stolen Steps: A Story . . .    Philadelphia: J. B. Lippincott Company, 1892.   189 p., front.                  HEH, LC, UC
Minnesota.

4248    [Pierce, Zerelda F.]   The Church Republic: A Romance of Methodism. By Brother Jonathan, D.D. [pseud.] . . .   New York: Wilbur B. Ketcham, 2 Cooper Union [cop. 1892].   433 p.            HEH, LC

4249    Pierson, A. C.   The White Church . . .    Cincinnati: Standard Publishing Co., 1887.   252 p.                        HEH, LC, O
Of a business boom in a small village.

4250    Pierson, Ernest De Lancey.   The Black Ball: A Fantastic Romance . . . Chicago, New York, and San Francisco: Belford, Clarke & Company. London: H. J. Drane [cop. 1889].   223 p.          AP, HEH
New York.

4251    ———— A Slave of Circumstances: A Story of New York . . .   Chicago, New York, & San Francisco: Belford, Clarke & Co. [cop. 1888].   195 p.
                        AP, HEH, LC, O

4252    ———— A Vagabond's Honor: A Romance . . .   New York: Belford Co. [cop. 1889].   217 p.
Listed PW, Feb. 22, 1890.

4253    Pike, Louise.   Southern Echoes . . .    Boston: Eastern Publishing Company, 1900.   131 p.                    CU, HEH, LC, UM, Y
Contents: A Prank of Hymen—Clarissa's Maw—The Revolt of Amos—Tobit's Call—A Game of Craps—Tempe's Venture—He Knew the Mistress—A No 'Count Nigger—Big Ben—Two Gourds of Fat—Ephiram's Bold Stroke—A Hoodoed Seven.

4254 [PILGRIM, THOMAS.] Old Nick's Camp-Meetin': A Narration of Occurrences Thereat, in Which M. Satan Did Not Take a Hand, but Other People Did—Several in Fact. By Eugene Owl [pseud.] ... New York: The Authors' Publishing Company, Bond Street [cop. 1880]. 224 p. LC

4255 [PINCKNEY, SUSANNA SHULRIDE HAYNE.] Douglas, Tender and True. By Miss McPherson [pseud.]. St. Louis: Nixon-Jones Printing Co., 1892. 210 p.                                                                LC
Civil War novel.

4256 PINER, HOWELL LAKE. Ruth: A Romance of the Civil War ... Van Alstyne, Texas: Leader Publishing House, 1895. 172 p.         LC

4257 PINKERTON, A. FRANK. Dyke Darrel, the Railroad Detective; or, The Crime of the Midnight Express ... Chicago: Laird & Lee, cop. 1886. 155 p., illus.                                                        UM, UP, UV

4258 ——— Jim Cummings; or, The Great Adams Express Robbery ... By Frank Pinkerton ... Chicago: Laird & Lee, 286 S. Water St., cop. 1887. 162 p., illus.                                                              Y
Y copy bound in original cloth.
This is virtually the same story, some passages word for word, as No. 1803; illus. differ except the front. If Farrars is not a pseudonym of Pinkerton's, the above work is a plagiarism.

4259 PINKERTON, ALLAN. Bank-Robbers and the Detectives ... New York: G. W. Carleton & Co. London: S. Low, Son & Co., 1883. 339 p., illus.
                                                        CU, HEH, LC, O, UM, UVB
*Also contains:* A Modern Eugene Aram—The Old Coin Dealer—Early Illinois Justice—A Sham Prince.

4260 ——— Bucholz and the Detectives ... New York: G. W. Carleton & Co., 1880. 341 p., illus.                          CU, HEH, LC, N, UVB

4261 ——— The Burglar's Fate and the Detectives ... New York: G. W. Carleton & Co. London: S. Low, Son & Co., 1884. 344 p., illus.
                                                                         HEH, UVB

4262 ——— Criminal Reminiscences and Detective Sketches ... New York: G. W. Carleton & Co. London: S. Low, Son & Co., 1879. 324 p., illus.
                                                              BA, CU, H, LC, UVB

4263 ——— A Double Life and the Detectives ... New York: G. W. Carleton & Co. London: S. Low, Son & Co., 1884. 360 p., illus.     CU, HEH
*Also contains:* From the Bank to the Prison—A Clever Express Robbery—Fragment of Highland History.

4264 ——— The Gypsies and the Detectives ... New York: G. W. Carleton & Co. London: S. Low, Son & Co., 1879. 330 p., illus.         N

4265 ———— Mississippi Outlaws and the Detectives. Don Pedro and the Detectives. Poisoner and the Detectives ... New York: G. W. Carleton & Co. London: S. Low & Co., 1879. 377 p., illus.  CU, LC, N, UC

4266 ———— The Model Town and the Detectives. Byron as a Detective ... New York: G. W. Carleton & Co. London: S. Low & Co., 1876. 288 p., illus.  HEH, N, O, UVB

4267 ———— The Molly Maguires and the Detectives ... New York: G. W. Carleton Co. London: S. Low & Co. Chicago: Dustin, Gilman & Co. Phila.: H. W. Kelley. Boston: Geo. M. Smith & Co. San Francisco: A. Roman & Co., 1877. 552 p., illus.  BU, H, N, O

4268 ———— The Rail-Road Forger and the Detectives ... New York: G. W. Carleton & Co., 1881. 364 p., illus.  CU, H, LC, O, UM, UVB

4269 ———— The Spiritualists and the Detectives ... New York: G. W. Carleton & Co. London: S. Low & Co., 1877. 354 p., illus.
. CU, HEH, LC, N, O, UM, UVB, Y

4270 [PINKERTON, COLIN MCKENZIE.] Buckeye-Hawkeye School-Master; or, The Life of Carl Mackenzie. Dedicated to the School-Teachers of America. By One of the Teachers. Chicago: W. W. Knowles & Co., 1891. 176 p., front.  LC, Y

PINKERTON, FRANK. *See* Pinkerton, A. Frank

4271 [PINNIX, HANNAH COURTNEY (BAXTER).] A Watch-Key: A Novel. By Kerr [pseud.] ... Raleigh [N.C.]: Edwards & Broughton, 1889. 291 p.
LC

PIXLEY, FRANK, *jt. au. See* Read, O. The Carpetbagger [cop. 1899], No. 4461.

4272 PLACE, FREDERICK RORERT. Blind Bob: A Matter-of-Fact Romance ... Rochester, N.Y.: Union and Advertiser Co., 1897. 253, [1] p., front.
LC

4273 PLATT, CHARLES MALCOLM. How Old Man Corn Held Possession ... New York: Current Literature Publishing Co., 1894. 8 p.
Powell, No. 480, locates a copy in Pack Memorial Public Library, Asheville, North Carolina.

4274 PLATT, WILLIAM HENRY. Judith Carson; or, Which Was the Heiress? ... Rochester, N.Y.: E. R. Andrews, 1887. 266 p.  LC, UM

4275 PLYMPTON, ALMIRA GEORGE. A Bud of Promise: A Story for Ambitious Parents ... Boston: Roberts Brothers, 1895. 93 p.  LC, UC

4276 ——— A Willing Transgressor, and Other Stories... Boston: Roberts Brothers, 1897. 244 p.     HEH, LC
*Also contains:* The Scandal of Scarborough—A Case of Conscience—A Question in Ethics—Hardly Guilty—A Strange Bargain.

4277 POLLARD, PERCIVAL. Cape of Storms: A Novel ... Chicago: The Echo, 1895. 216 p.     HEH, LC, N, O
Of an artist.

4278 ——— Dreams of To-Day ... Chicago: Way and Williams, 1897. 264 p., 1 l., front.     CU, HEH, LC, UC
*Contents:* The Dream of a Kiss—The Dream of a Failure—The Dream of Circumstances—The Dream of an Agreement—Dropping the Curtain—The Dream of Two Ambitions—A Dream of Amber—The Crumbling of a Castle—Sister to Violets—For a Jest's Sake—A Dance in Dream-Land—The Dream Palace—The White City's Dream.

POLLOCK, WALTER HERRIES, *jt. au. See* Matthews, B. Edged Tools. Mated by Magic. [Two stories.] *In* B. Matthews, With My Friends (1891), No. 3659.

4279 POOL, MARIA LOUISE. Against Human Nature: A Novel... New York: Harper & Brothers, 1895. 361 p.     BA, CU, HEH, LC, O, UV, Y
North Carolina mountains.

4280 ——— Boss and Other Dogs ... New York: Stone & Kimball, 1896. 134 p., 1 l.     CU, H, LC, Y

4281 ——— Dally ... New York: Harper & Brothers, 1891. 280 p.     BA, H, HEH, LC, O, Y
North Carolina mountain people.

——— Dick. *In* New Stories from the Chap-Book (1898), No. 3949.

4282 ——— Friendship and Folly: A Novel ... Boston: L. C. Page and Company (Incorporated), 1898. 302 p., illus.     BA, HEH, LC, O, UV, Y
New England girl revolts against custom.

4283 ——— A Golden Sorrow ... Chicago & New York: Herbert S. Stone Company, 1898. 441 p.     BA, H, HEH, LC, O, UM, Y
St. Augustine, Florida.

4284 ——— In a Dike Shanty ... Chicago: Stone & Kimball, 1896. 231 p., 1 l.     BU, CU, H, HEH, LC, N, O, UM, Y

4285 ——— In Buncombe County ... Chicago: Herbert S. Stone & Company, 1896. 295 p., 1 l.     BA, BU, CU, H, HEH, LC, N, O, UC, UM, Y
North Carolina mountains.

4286 ——— In the First Person: A Novel ... New York: Harper & Brothers, 1896. 315 p.     CU, HEH, N, O

4287 ——— Katharine North: A Novel ... New York: Harper & Brothers, 1893. 312 p.     BA, BU, H, HEH, LC, O, Y

——— Mandany's Fool. *In* Stories from the Chap-Book (1896), No. 5277.

4288 ——— The Meloon Farm: A Novel ... New York and London: Harper & Brothers, 1900. 400, [1] p., illus.     HEH, LC, O, UC, UM, Y
New England.

4289 ——— Mrs. Gerald: A Novel ... New York: Harper & Brothers, 1896. 339 p., illus.     CU, H, HEH, LC, N, O, Y

4290 ——— Mrs. Keats Bradford: A Novel ... New York: Harper & Brothers, 1892. 309 p.     BA, BU, H, HEH, LC, O, UM, Y

4291 ——— Out of Step: A Novel ... New York: Harper & Brothers, 1894. 300 p.     BA, H, HEH, LC, O, UM, Y

4292 ——— The Red-Bridge Neighborhood: A Novel ... New York and London: Harper & Brothers, 1898. 369 p., illus.
    BA, CU, H, HEH, LC, N, O, Y
Village in the foothills of North Carolina.

4293 ——— Roweny in Boston: A Novel ... New York: Harper & Brothers, 1892. 348 p.     BA, CU, H, HEH, LC, N, O, Y

4294 ——— Sand 'n' Bushes ... Chicago & New York: Herbert S. Stone & Company, 1899. 364, [1] p., 1 l.
    BA, BU, CU, H, HEH, LC, N, O, UC, UM, UV, Y
Two women ride horseback from Boston to Cape Cod.

4295 ——— Tenting at Stony Beach ... Boston and New York: Houghton, Mifflin and Company. The Riverside Press, Cambridge, 1888. 235 p.
    AP, BA, CU, H, HEH, LC, O, Y
Cape Cod.

4296 ——— The Two Salomes: A Novel ... New York: Harper & Brothers, 1893. 372 p.     BA, H, HEH, LC, O, Y

4297 ——— Vacation in a Buggy ... New York and London: G. P. Putnam's Sons; the Knickerbocker Press, 1887. 156 p., front.
    AP, BU, CU, H, HEH, LC, Y

4298 ——— A Widower & Some Spinsters: Short Stories ... Chicago & New York: Herbert S. Stone & Company, 1899. 326 p., 1 l., illus.
    BA, CU, HEH, LC, N, O, UV, Y
*Also contains:* Miss Candish's Christmas Boy—One of Wealthy's Husbands—Miss Kibby's Lovers—Mehitable—The Hen-Man—Mehitable's Romance—A Snowy Thanksgiving—Mr. Marsh's Rebellion—Malina's Clock—"Getting Cast"—Summer Boarders.

4299 POOLE, MARY BELLE. Down Fate's Walk: A Modern Society Novel . . . [New Orleans, La.: Men and Masters Magazine], 1896. 204 p., illus. Information supplied by Frederick L. Arnold of Princeton University Library.

4300 ———— What the Years Brought: A Novelette . . . New Orleans: Current Topic Publishing House, 1894. 60 p.
Listed in Lizzie C. McVoy and Ruth B. Campbell, *A Bibliography of Fiction by Louisianians* [Baton Rouge, La., 1935], p. 60.

4301 POOR, AGNES BLAKE. Boston Neighbours in Town and Out . . . New York and London: G. P. Putnam's Sons; the Knickerbocker Press, 1898. 321 p., front.     BA, CU, H, HEH, LC, N, O, Y
*Contents:* Our Tolstoi Club—A Little Fool—Why I Married Eleanor—The Story of a Wall-Flower—Poor Mr. Ponsonby—Modern Vengeance—Three Cups of Tea—The Tramp's Wedding.

4302 ———— Brothers and Strangers . . . Boston: Roberts Brothers, 1893. 321 p.     BA, H, HEH, LC, O, Y

4303 POOR THEOPHILUS AND THE CITY OF FIN. New York: The Authors' Publishing Company, Bond Street [cop. 1878]. 99 p.     LC

4304 POPE, GUSTAVUS W. Journey to Mars: The Wonderful World, Its Beauty and Splendor, Its Mighty Races and Kingdoms, Its Final Doom . . . New York: G. W. Dillingham, 1894. 543 p.     HEH, LC
At head of title: "Romances of the Planets, No. 1."

4305 ———— Journey to Venus: The Primeval World, Its Wonderful Creations and Gigantic Monsters . . . Boston: Arena Publishing Co., 1895. 499 p., illus.     CU, LC
At head of title: "Romances of the Planets, No. 2."

4306 POPE, MARION (MANVILLE). Up the Matterhorn in a Boat . . . New York: The Century Co., 1897. 199 p., illus.     HEH, LC, O, UM, UVB
The boat is attached to a balloon.

4307 PORCH, HESTER EDWARDS An Ideal Fanatic . . . Chicago: Henry A. Sumner & Company, 1883. 325 p.     HEH, LC, UC
A New England village.

PORTER, MRS. A. E. *See* Porter, Lydia Ann (Emerson)

4308 PORTER, DAVID DIXON. Adventures of Harry Marline; or, Notes from an American Midshipman's Lucky Bag . . . New York: D. Appleton and Company, 1885. 378 p., illus.     AP, BU, H, HEH, LC, N, O, UP, UV, Y

4309 ———— Allan Dare and Robert le Diable: A Romance . . . New York: D. Appleton and Company, 1885. 876 p., illus.     AP, BA, BU, CU, H, HEH, LC, O, UM, UP, Y
Some copies bound in 1 vol., some in 2. Published originally in 9 parts; 1st pt. listed PW, Oct. 4, 1884, and 9th pt. listed Jan. 17, 1885.

4310 ———— Arthur Merton: A Romance . . . New York: D. Appleton and
Company, 1889. 328 p. AP, BA, LC

4311 PORTER, DELIA LYMAN. The Blues Cure, and Other Stories . . . New
York: Anson D. F. Randolph & Company, 182 Fifth Avenue [cop.
1892]. 15, 14, 14, 13, 18 p. BU, LC, Y
*Also contains:* Pull Out the Plug—Hospital for Broken Resolutions—The
Measuring-Rod—My Possible Self.
Advertised PW, Jan. 28, 1893, p. 231. The stories could be had as separates
or bound together in cloth.

4312 PORTER, JAMES A. A Prince of Anahuac: A Histori-Traditional Story
Antedating the Aztec Empire . . . Galion, Ohio: The Crawford Company. Cincinnati: Press of C. J. Krehbiel & Co., 248-250 Walnut Street
[cop. 1894]. 378 p., front. CU, HEH

4313 [PORTER, LINN BOYD.] A Black Adonis. By Albert Ross [pseud.]. New
York: G. W. Dillingham, 1895. 318 p.
Listed PW, July 20, 1895.

4314 [————] The Garston Bigamy. By Albert Ross [pseud.] . . . New
York: G. W. Dillingham, 1892. 332 p. LC

4315 [————] Her Husband's Friend. By Albert Ross [pseud.] . . . New
York: G. W. Dillingham, 1891. 361 p. LC

4316 [————] His Foster Sister. By Albert Ross [pseud.] . . . New York:
G. W. Dillingham, 1896. 303 p.
Listed PW, Jan. 16, 1897.

4317 [————] His Private Character. By Albert Ross [pseud.] . . . New
York: G. W. Dillingham, 1889. 366 p. LC
"Story of sin and scandal . . . (Not recommended for sale.)" PW, Aug. 3,
1889.

4318 [————] In Stella's Shadow. By Albert Ross [pseud.]. New York:
G. W. Dillingham, 1890. 350 p. UV

4319 [————] Love at Seventy. By Albert Ross [pseud.] . . . New York:
G. W. Dillingham, 1894. 311 p. LC

4320 [————] Moulding a Maiden. By Albert Ross [pseud.]. New York:
G. W. Dillingham, 1891. 364 p. UV

4321 [————] The Naked Truth. By Albert Ross [pseud.] . . . New York:
G. W. Dillingham Co., cop. 1899. 275 p. H

4322 [————] A New Sensation. By Albert Ross [pseud.] . . . New York:
G. W. Dillingham Co., cop. 1898. 309 p. H, Y

4323 [————] An Original Sinner. By Albert Ross [pseud.] . . . New York: G. W. Dillingham, 1893. 348 p.
Information from LC card; no copy seen.

4324 [————] Out of Wedlock. By Albert Ross [pseud.]. New York: G. W. Dillingham, 1894. 311 p.
Listed PW, Jan. 19, 1895.

4325 [————] Speaking of Ellen. By Albert Ross [pseud.] . . . New York: G. W. Dillingham, 1890. 345 p.     LC

4326 [————] Stranger Than Fiction. By Albert Ross [pseud.] . . . New York: G. W. Dillingham Co., 1900. 328 p.     HEH

4327 [————] A Sugar Princess. By Albert Ross [pseud.]. New York: G. W. Dillingham Co. [cop. 1900]. 320 p.
Listed PW, July 28, 1900.

4328 ———— That Gay Deceiver . . . New York: G. W. Dillingham Co., 1899. 306 p.     LC

4329 [————] Their Marriage Bond. By Albert Ross [pseud.] . . . New York: G. W. Dillingham Co., cop. 1897. 288 p.
Copy examined at New York Public Library.

4330 [————] Thou Shalt Not . . . New York: G. W. Dillingham, 1889. 366 p.     H, HEH

4331 [————] Thy Neighbor's Wife. By Albert Ross [pseud.] . . . New York: G. W. Dillingham, 1892. 316 p.     HEH, LC

4332 [————] Why I'm Single. By Albert Ross [pseud.]. New York: G. W. Dillingham, 1892. 360 p.
Information from LC card; no copy seen.

4333 ———— Young Fawcett's Mabel . . . New York: G. W. Dillingham Co., cop. 1895. 312 p.
Copy examined at New York Public Library.

4334 [————] Young Miss Giddy. By Albert Ross [pseud.] . . . New York: G. W. Dillingham, 1893. 343 p.     LC

4335 PORTER, LYDIA ANN (EMERSON). Cousin Polly's Gold Mine: A Novel. By Mrs. A. E. Porter. New York: Harper & Brothers, 1878. 109 p.
Printed in double columns.     HEH, LC, O

4336 PORTER, MRS. MEL-INDA JENNIE. Frankincense; or, The Bride of Clairemont . . . New York: G. W. Dillingham, successor to G. W. Carleton & Co. London: S. Low, Son & Co., 1887. 180 p.     HEH, LC

4337   PORTER, ROSE.   Charity, Sweet Charity ...   New York: Anson D. F. Randolph & Company, 900 Broadway [cop. 1880].  242 p.     HEH, LC

4338   ————   Christmas Evergreens ...   New York: Anson D. F. Randolph & Company, 900 Boadway [cop. 1876].  63 p.     HEH, LC, Y

4339   ————   A Daughter of Israel ...   New York: E. P. Dutton & Company, 1899.  212 p., 1 l.     LC, O, Y

4340   ————   Driftings from Mid-Ocean: Character Studies. A Sequel to Summer Drift-Wood and The Winter Fire ...   New York: Anson D. F. Randolph & Company, 38 West Twenty-Third Street [cop. 1889]. 308 p.     LC, O, UC
For *Summer Drift-Wood* and *The Winter Fire* see Wright II, Nos. 1939 and 1941.

4341   ————   Honoria; or, The Gospel of a Life ...   New York: Anson D. F. Randolph & Company, 900 Broadway [cop. 1885].  279 p.   HEH, LC, O, Y

4342   ————   In the Mist ...   New York: Anson D. F. Randolph & Company, 900 Broadway [cop. 1879].  287 p.     CU, HEH, LC, N, O, UM

4343   ————   A Modern Saint Christopher; or, The Brothers ...   New York: Anson D. F. Randolph & Company, 38 West Twenty-Third Street [cop. 1887].  231 p.     HEH, LC, O, UC

4344   ————   My Son's Wife ...   New York: Anson D. F. Randolph & Co., 182 Fifth Avenue [cop. 1895].  215 p.     HEH, LC, Y

4345   ————   One of the Sweet Old Chapters: A Fragment ...   New York, Chicago, Toronto: Fleming H. Revell Company, 1896.  48 p., front.     HEH, LC, UV, Y

4346   ————   Our Saints: A Family Story ...   New York: Anson D. F. Randolph & Company, 900 Broadway [cop. 1881].  264 p.     HEH, LC, Y

4347   ————   Saint Martin's Summer; or, The Romance of the Cliff ...   New York and Chicago: Fleming H. Revell Company [cop. 1891].  263 p.     UC, UM, UV, Y

4348   ————   A Song and a Sigh ...   New York: Anson D. F. Randolph & Company, 900 Broadway [cop. 1877].  273 p.     HEH, LC, O, Y

4349   ————   The Story of a Flower, and Other Fragments Twice Gathered ...   New York: Anson D. F. Randolph & Company, 900 Broadway [cop. 1883].  297 p.     HEH, LC, UC

4350   POST, CHARLES CYREL.   Congressman Swanson ...   Chicago: Charles H. Sergel & Company [cop. 1891].  358 p.
Copy examined at New York Public Library.

4351 ———— Driven from Sea to Sea; or, Just a Campin' . . . Chicago: J. E. Downey & Co., 1884. 334 p., illus. LC, UC

HEH has copy of 333 p. ed. partially reset; omits some illus. and adds others. One of many comments on the book at the end is dated Jan. 31, 1885.

4352 ———— From the Wabash to the Rio Grande and Oklahoma: A Novel, with Characters True to Life . . . Chicago: Rhodes & McClure Publishing Company, 1886. 358 p. HEH

Also published anonymously as: *Ten Years a Cowboy*. Chicago: Rhodes & McClure Publishing Company, 1888. 471 p., illus. o
The first 23 chaps., to p. 358, are from the 1886 plates; pp. 359-471 has heading "The Plains" and consists of factual material.
Also published as: *Ten Years a Cowboy. By Tex Bender, the Cowboy Fiddler*. Chicago: Rhodes & McClure Publishing Company, 1890. o
Collation same as the 1888 ed.
Also published as: *Ten Years a Cowboy. By C. C. Post. Addenda by Tex Bender, the Cowboy Fiddler*. Chicago: Rhodes & McClure Publishing Company, 1892. UV
Collation same as the 1888 ed.

4353 POST, MARTIN. The Riverton Minister . . . Atlanta, Ga.: American Publishing and Engraving Co., 1897. 354 p. H, LC, Y

4354 POST, MRS. MARY A. Poverty Hollow: A True Story . . . Brooklyn, N. Y.: T. B. Ventres, bookseller and stationer, 1887. 59 p. H, LC, UV, Y

4355 POST, MELVILLE DAVISSON. The Man of Last Resort; or, The Clients of Randolph Mason . . . New York and London: G. P. Putnam's Sons, 1897. 284 p. N, O, UV

*Contents:* The Governor's Machine—Mrs. Van Varton—Once in Jeopardy—The Grazier—The Rule against Carper.

4356 ———— The Strange Schemes of Randolph Mason . . . New York and London: G. P. Putnam's Sons, 1896. 280 p. N, O, UV, Y

*Contents:* The Corpus Delicti—Two Plungers of Manhattan—Woodford's Partner—The Error of William Van Broom—The Men of the Jimmy—The Sheriff of Gullmore—The Animus Furandi.

4357 POST, WALDRON KINTZING. Harvard Stories: Sketches of the Undergraduate . . . New York, London: G. P. Putnam's Sons; the Knickerbocker Press, 1893. 312 p. BA, CU, H, HEH, LC, N, O, UC, Y

*Contents:* Jack Rattleton Goes to Springfield and Back—The Waking Nightmare of Hollis Holworthy—The Plot against Bullam—The Dog Blathers—A Howard and Harvard Evening—The Harvard Legion at Philippi—In the Early Sixties—Little Helping Hands—A Rambling Discussion and an Adventure, Perhaps Unconnected—Serious Situations in Burleigh's Rooms—A Harvard-Yale Episode—The Day of Reckoning—Class Day—How River's Luck Turned.

4358 ———— Smith Brunt: A Story of the Old Navy . . . New York & London: G. P. Putnam's Sons; the Knickerbocker Press, 1899. 459 p., illus. H, HEH, LC, O

4359 POSTGATE, JOHN W. The Strange Case of Henry Toplass and Capt. Shiers ... Chicago: Homewood Publishing Company [cop. 1893]. 208 p.

HEH

4360 ―――― Two Women in Black: The Marvelous Career of a Noted Forger ... Chicago and New York: Belford, Clarke & Co., 1886. 288 p., illus.

HEH, LC

4361 ―――― A Woman's Devotion; or, The Mixed Marriage. A Story of the Rival Detectives. An American Novel Founded on Facts ... Chicago: Rand, McNally & Co. [cop. 1886]. 270 p.

Listed PW, Apr. 24, 1886.

4362 [POTTER, MARGARET HORTON.] A Social Lion. By Robert Dolly Williams [pseud.]. Chicago: R. R. Donnelley & Sons Co., 1899. 432 p., 1 l., front.

LC, N

Author later married John D. Black.

4363 ―――― Uncanonized: A Romance of English Monachism ... Chicago: A. C. McClurg & Co., 1900. 495 p., front.

H, HEH, LC, N, O

4364 POUNDS, JESSIE HUNTER (BROWN). The Ironclad Pledge: A Story of Christian Endeavor. By Jessie H. Brown ... Cincinnati: Standard Publishing Company, 1890. 187 p.

LC

4365 ―――― Norman Macdonald ... Cincinnati: Standard Publishing Co., 1887. 217 p.

LC

4366 ―――― Roderick Wayne ... Cincinnati: Standard Publishing Company, 1889. 213 p.

LC

4367 ―――― A Woman's Doing ... Cincinnati: Standard Publishing Company, 1887. 198 p.

LC

4368 POWELL, ELLA MARY. Clio, a Child of Fate ... Atlanta, Ga.: Jas. P. Harrison & Co., printers, 1889. 122 p.

HEH, LC

4369 ―――― Winona: A Story of To-Day ... New York: A. Lovell & Co. [cop. 1891]. 223 p.

LC

4370 ―――― Women Who Laugh ... New York, London: The Transatlantic Publishing Company, 1895. 186 p., front.

LC

POWELL, RICHARD STILLMAN, *pseud*. *See* Barbour, Ralph Henry

4371 POWELL, TALLULAH MATTESON. An English Girl in America ... Chicago, New York: F. T. Neely [cop. 1892]. 137 p.

N

POWELL, WILLIAM H. The Major's Story. *In* C. King, *ed*., The Colonel's Christmas Dinner (1890), No. 3098.

Later printed in No. 3099.

4372 PRATT, ADA A. M. Widow Jones' Monopoly, and Other Stories . . .
New York: A. D. F. Randolph Company, 91 and 93 Fifth Avenue [cop.
1896]. 174 p.                                              CU, HEH, LC, Y
*Also contains:* Little Poozel's All-Wool—The Quest of Billy, Sammy, and
Phrony—Pore Paw—The Little Sister of South Kensington—At Mammy
Turnipseed's—Miss Madge Black.

PRATT, CORNELIA ATWOOD. *See* Comer, Cornelia Atwood (Pratt)

[PRATT, MRS. E. E.] *attrib. au.* The Lawyer's Story. *In* [Mrs. J. Lodge]
ed., A Week away from Time (1887), No. 3382.

4373 [PRENTICE, DWIGHT S.] Revelations in Politics: A Story Illustrating
Thirty Years of American Political History. National Prosperity and
Adversity the Result of Law . . . [Findlay, Ohio: Populist Publishing
Co.], cop. 1895. 138 p.                                            LC

4374 PRENTISS, ELIZABETH (PAYSON). Avis Benson; or, Mine and Thine.
With Other Sketches . . . New York: Anson D. F. Randolph & Company, 900 Broadway [cop. 1879]. 273 p., illus.        HEH, LC, UC, Y
*Contents:* Mine and Thine—Such as I Have—Homeward Bound—Taking for
Granted—Why Satan Trembles—Having Nothing, yet Having All—Success
and Defeat—On the Banks of the River of Life—A Model Servant—Playing
with Sunbeams—Saved from His Friends.

4375 ———— Gentleman Jim . . . New York: Anson D. F. Randolph & Company, 900 Broadway [cop. 1878]. 76 p., front.            HEH, LC, Y

4376 ———— Pemaquid: A Story of Old Times in New England . . . New
York: Anson D. F. Randolph & Company, 900 Broadway [cop. 1877].
370 p., illus.                     BA CU, H, HEH, LC, O, UC, UM, UV, Y

PRESCOTT, HARRIET ELIZABETH. *See* Spofford, Harriet Elizabeth (Prescott)

4377 [PRESTON, HARRIET WATERS.] The Guardians . . . Boston and New
York: Houghton, Mifflin and Company. The Riverside Press, Cam-
bridge, 1888. 412 p.                               AP, H, HEH, LC, O
Louise Preston Dodge, jt. au.
Of hereditary traits.

4378 [————] Is That All? Boston: Roberts Brothers, 1876. 244 p.
                                     BA, CU, H, HEH, LC, O, UM, UVB
At head of title: "No Name Series."
New England social life.

4379 ———— A Year in Eden . . . Boston: Roberts Brothers, 1887. 420 p.
                                         AP, BA, H, HEH, LC, O

4380 PRESTON, MARGARET (JUNKIN). Aunt Dorothy: An Old Virginia Planta-
tion-Story . . . New York: Anson D. F. Randolph and Co., 38 West
Twenty-Third Street [cop. 1890]. 92 p., illus.      CU, HEH, LC, N, UV

PRESTON, PAUL, *Esq., pseud.* *See* Picton, Thomas

4381 PREWITT, EMMA YOUNG. Karlene Hoy; or, In Need of a Guide and Guard ... Philadelphia: Printed by J. B. Lippincott Company, 1889. 253 p.                                                                                    HEH, LC
A romance that began in Tennessee.

4382 PRICE, B. F. Him and Them; or, The Ideal Man ... Elkton, Md.: The Elkton Appeal Press, 1899. 206 p.                                                          UVB

4383 PRICE, ELLA BROWN. The Major's Love; or, The Sequel of a Crime ... Philadelphia: T. B. Peterson & Brothers, 306 Chestnut Street [cop. 1888]. 179 p.                                                                            HEH, LC
Western Missouri.

4384 PRICE, T. BUCHANAN. Snap: The Ox-Train Era. Early Troubles of Border Trade ... New York: W. B. Smith & Co., Bond Street [cop. 1881]. 320 p., front.                                          CU, H, HEH, LC, N, UM, Y

4385 PRICHARD, SARAH JOHNSON. The Only Woman in the Town, and Other Tales of the American Revolution ... Waterbury, Conn.: Melicent Porter Chapter, Daughters of the American Revolution, 1898. 199, [1] p., illus.                                                              HEH, LC, N, Y
*Also contains:* A Windham Lamb in Boston Town—How One Boy Helped the British Troops Out of Boston in 1776—Pussy Dean's Beacon Fire—David Bushnell and His American Turtle—The Birthday of Our Nation—The Overthrow of the Statue of King George—Sleet and Snow—Patty Rutter, the Quaker Doll Who Slept in Independence Hall—Becca Blackstone's Turkeys at Valley Forge—How Two Little Stockings Saved Fort Safety—A Day and a Night in the Old Porter House.

PRIME, *Lord, Esq., pseud.* *See* Reynolds, Walter Doty

4386 PRINCE, HELEN CHOATE (PRATT). At the Sign of the Silver Crescent ... Boston and New York: Houghton, Mifflin and Company. The Riverside Press, Cambridge, 1898. 382 p., 1 l.          CU, H, HEH, LC, N, O, UP, UV

4387 ———— The Story of Christine Rochefort ... Boston and New York: Houghton, Mifflin and Company. The Riverside Press, Cambridge, 1895. 313 p.                                        BA, CU, H, HEH, LC, N, O
Labor and capital; France.

4388 ———— A Transatlantic Chatelaine ... Boston and New York: Houghton, Mifflin and Company. The Riverside Press, Cambridge, 1897. 465 p.                                        BA, H, HEH, LC, O, UV, Y

4389 THE PRINCESS DAPHNE: A Novel ... Chicago, New York, and San Francisco: Belford, Clarke & Co., 1888. 260 p.                                    HEH
Bohemian life in New York and London.

PROCTOR, EDNA DEAN. Tom Foster's Wife. *In* L. C. H. Langford, *comp.,* The Woman's Story (1889), No. 3206.

4390 [PROUDFIT, DAVID LAW.]   The Man from the West: A Novel Descriptive
of Adventures from the Chaparral to Wall Street.   By a Wall Street
Man.   New York: William H. Davis, 1892.   245 p.          HEH
Published earlier in the omitted "Echo Series," 1889.

PRUNING KNIFE, *pseud.*   *See* Allen, Henry Francis

4391 PRYER, CHARLES.   Reminiscences of an Old Westchester Homestead . . .
New York and London: G. P. Putnam's Sons; the Knickerbocker
Press, 1897.   174 p., illus.          BA, CU, H, LC, N, UM, Y
*Contents:* Marvellous Tales of Nicholas the Hunter—Wonderful and Mysterious Tales of James the Fearless—A Queer Old House—A Noted Musician
—The Battle of Davenport's Neck—The Wood Famine—The Treasure Hunters—Tales of the Old Homestead.

4392 PULITZER, WALTER.   That Duel at the Chateau Barsanac . . .   New York
and London: Funk & Wagnalls Company, 1899.   120 p., illus.
H, HEH, LC, N, O

4393 PULLEN, ELISABETH (JONES) CAVAZZA.   Don Finimondone: Calabrian
Sketches.   By Elisabeth Cavazza.   New York: Charles L. Webster &
Co., 1892.   179 p., front.          BA, H, HEH, LC, O, UM
*Also contains:* A Calabrian Penelope—The Story of Cirillo—The Tree of the
Bride—A Trumpet Call—Princess Humming-Bird.

———— Double Head and Single Heart.   *In* I. Bacheller, *ed.,* Best
Things from American Literature (1899), No. 195.

PUNTAGORDA, *General, pseud.*   *See* Trabue, Isaac Hodgen

4394 A PURE SOULED LIAR.   Chicago: Charles H. Kerr & Company, 1888.   191
p.          HEH, LC
Of art students in Boston.

4395 PURVIS, T. T.   Hagar, the Singing Maiden, with Other Stories and
Rhymes . . .   Philadelphia: Walton & Co., 1881.   288 p.          BU, H, UP

4396 [PUSEY, PENNOCK.]   Ebba Borjeson: A True Love Story of the Olden
Time.   By Hampden Vaughn [pseud.] . . .   [Wilmington, Del.: Costa
Print, cop. 1894.]   596 p.          HEH, LC, O, UM, Y

PUTNAM, ELEANOR, *pseud.*   *See* Bates, Harriet Leonora (Vose)

4397 [PUTNAM, GEORGE HAVEN.]   The Artificial Mother: A Marital Fantasy.
By G. H. P. . . .   New York, London: G. P. Putnam's Sons; the Knickerbocker Press, 1894.   31 p., illus.          BA, LC, Y

4398 PUTNAM, GEORGE ISRAEL.   In Blue Uniform: An Army Novel . . .   New
York: Charles Scribner's Sons, 1893.   279 p.
BU, CU, H, HEH, LC, O, UM, UV

4399 ——— On the Offensive: An Army Story . . . New York: Charles Scribner's Sons, 1894. 297 p. CU, H, HEH, LC, N, O

4400 PUTNAM, SAMUEL PORTER. Golden Throne: A Romance . . . Boston, Mass.: George Chainey, 51 Fort Avenue [n.d.]. 153 p. Printed in double columns. HEH
HEH copy has owner's name and is dated "July '86."

4401 ——— Waifs and Wanderings: A Novel . . . New York: The Truth Seeker Company, 33 Clinton Place [cop. 1884]. 192 p. CU, HEH, LC
Deposited May 8, 1885.

4402 PYLE, HOWARD. A Modern Aladdin; or, The Wonderful Adventures of Oliver Munier. An Extravaganza in Four Acts . . . New York: Harper & Brothers, 1892. 205 p., illus. BA, BU, CU, H, HEH, LC, N, O, UM, UP, UVB, Y

4403 ——— The Price of Blood: An Extravaganza of New York Life in 1807 . . . Boston: Richard G. Badger & Co., 1899. 98 p., 1 l., illus. BA, BU, CU, H, HEH, LC, N, O, UM, UP, UVB, Y

4404 ——— The Rose of Paradise: Being a Detailed Account of Certain Adventures That Happened to Captain John Mackra, in Connection with the Famous Pirate, Edward England, in the Year 1720 . . . New York: Harper & Brothers, 1888. 231 p., illus. AP, BA, BU, H, HEH, LC, O, UVB, Y

4405 ——— Within the Capes . . . New York: Charles Scribner's Sons, 1885. 266 p. AP, BA, HEH, LC, O, UVB

QUAD, M., pseud. See Lewis, Charles Bertrand

4406 [QUEEN, Sister MARY XAVIER.] Wonders Will Never Cease, and Other Stories. By S. M. X. . . . Baltimore, Md.: Gallery & McCann, 1898. 104 p., front. LC
Also contains: Agnes Martinez—Marie Teutonne—The Haunted Hollow—The Old Bachelor's Cats.

QUI, pseud. See La Selle, Evelyn

4407 QUIGG, LEMUEL ELY. Tin-Types Taken in the Streets of New York: A Series of Stories and Sketches Portraying Many Singular Phases of Metropolitan Life . . . New York: Cassell Publishing Company, 104 & 106 Fourth Avenue [cop. 1890]. 297 p., illus. CU, H, HEH, LC, N, O, UP

4408 QUINCY, EDMUND. The Haunted Adjutant, and Other Stories . . . Edited by His Son, Edmund Quincy. Boston: Ticknor and Company, 1885. 366 p., front. AP, BA, CU, H, HEH, LC, N, O, UM, UVB, Y
Contents: An Octogenary—The Haunted Adjutant—Lewis Herbert—Two Nights in St. Domingo—Phoebe Mallory—Old Houses—Dinah Rollins.

4409 QUINCY, JOSIAH PHILLIPS. The Peckster Professorship: An Episode in the History of Psychical Research ... Boston and New York: Houghton, Mifflin and Company. The Riverside Press, Cambridge, 1888. 310 p. AP, BA, CU, H, HEH, LC, N, O, UC, Y

4410 [QUINCY, SAMUEL MILLER.] The Man Who Was Not a Colonel. By a High Private. Boston: Loring, cor. Bromfield and Washington Streets [cop. 1877]. 191 p. CU, HEH, O, UC
A citizen masquerades as an army officer.

4411 QUINN, ARTHUR HOBSON. Pennsylvania Stories ... Philadelphia: The Penn Publishing Company, 1899. 259 p., illus. BA, CU, H, HEH, LC, O, UC, UM, UP, Y
Contents: The Last Five Yards—On the Top of the Old Grand-Stand—The Conversion of Warren Forbes—A Page to Fill—The Lost Election—The Second Act—Harrington's Cousin—For Pennsylvania's Honor—When the College Was Young.

QUONDAM, pseud. See Stevens, Charles McClellan

R., G. S. See Richards, George S.

R., L. KING. See Rodenberger, Lizzie King

R., R. F. See Reed, Francis R.

RACONTEUR, pseud. See Decon, Thomas William

RAE, pseud. See Stiles, W. L., Jr.

4412 RAFFENSPERGER, MRS. ANNA FRANCES. Patience Preston, M.D. . . . Boston: D. Lothrop Company, Franklin and Hawley Streets [cop. 1887]. 327 p. HEH, LC, O

4413 RAGSDALE, LULAH. A Shadow's Shadow ... Philadelphia: J. B. Lippincott Company, 1893. 237 p. LC

4414 [RAHM, IDA.] Miss Nancy ... Philadelphia: David McKay, 1884. 254 p. AP, HEH, LC, UP, Y
Philadelphia society.

RAIMOND, C. E., pseud. See Robins, Elizabeth

4415 RALPH, JULIAN. Alone in China, and Other Stories ... New York: Harper & Brothers, 1897. 282 p., illus. BA, HEH, O, UV, Y
Contents: House-Boating in China—Alone in China—Plumblossom Beebe's Adventures—The Story of Miss Pi—The "Boss" of Ling-Foo—Little Fairy's Constancy—The Lover-Letters of Superfine Gold.

4416 ———— An Angel in a Web ... New York and London: Harper & Brothers, 1899. 238, [1] p., illus. H, HEH, N, O

4417 —— People We Pass: Stories of Life among the Masses of New York City ... New York: Harper & Brothers, 1896. 209 p., illus.

AP, BA, CU, HEH, LC, N, O, Y

*Contents:* The Line-Man's Wedding—The Mother Song—Love in the Big Barracks—A Day of the Pinochle Club—Cordelia's Night of Romance—Dutch Kitty's White Slippers—Petey Burke and His Pupil—Low Dutch and High.

4418 —— The Prince of Georgia, and Other Tales ... New York and London: Harper & Brothers, 1899. 161, [1] p., illus.

AP, HEH, LC, O, UM, Y

*Also contains:* When the Clouds Fell Down—A Dandy at His Best—The Sad Fate of a New Woman—Mrs. Ruppert's Christmas—My Borrowed Torpedo-Boat—Bruce's Mighty Weakness.

4419 RALPH, SEM. A Virginia Belle ... New York: W. B. Smith & Co. [cop. 1881]. 131 p.
Information from LC card; no copy seen.

RAMBLER, *pseud.* *See* Fullerton, George H.

RAMSAY, ALLAN, *jt. au.* *See* Adler, C. Told in the Coffee-House (1898), No. 29.

4420 RAMSEY, MILTON WORTH. Six Thousand Years Hence ... Minneapolis: [Press of Alfred Roper], 1891. 239 p.            LC
Visits to other planets.

4421 RANCEVAU, EDGAR H. A Knight of the Key; or, A Romance Amid Dots and Dashes ... Vinton, Iowa: The Telegraphers' Pub. Co., 1893. 153 p.            LC

4422 RAND, EDWARD AUGUSTUS. After the Freshet ... Boston: D. Lothrop and Company, 32 Franklin Street [cop. 1882]. 423 p.            LC

4423 —— Behind Manhattan Gables: A Story of New Amsterdam, 1663-1664 ... New York: Thomas Whittaker, 1896. 382 p., illus.  H, HEH, LC

4424 —— The Down East Master's First School ... Boston: D. Lothrop Company, Washington Street opposite Bromfield [cop. 1892]. 473 p., illus.            HEH, LC, Y

4425 —— Two College Boys; or, The Old Man of the Mountain ... New York: Thomas Whittaker, 2 and 3 Bible House [cop. 1895]. 166 p., illus.            H, LC

4426 RAND, JOSEPHINE. Sardis and the Spirit-Guest: The Story of a Dream ... New York: E. P. Dutton & Company, 1897. 65 p.            LC, UV

4427 RAND, KATHARINE E. The Childhood of an Affinity ... Boston: Arena Publishing Co., 1893. 304 p.            HEH

RANDALL, THERESA M. The Flagelante's Sin. *In* Short Stories from Outing [cop. 1895], No. 4930.

4428 RANDLE, FREDERICK ALANSON. Idwymon: A Story of Napoleonic Complications, Orleans and Bourbonic Entanglements. A Romance of the Pyrenees ... King's River Cañon and Yosemite Valley, California, and Yellowstone ... New York: G. W. Dillingham, 1895. 412 p. HEH, LC

4429 ———— Imgar: A Story of India ... Hillsboro, Illinois, 1889. 61 p. LC
LC has copy of 128 p. ed. published New York: John B. Alden, 1890; same story reset in larger type.

4430 RANKIN, GEORGE CAMERON. Border Canucks, Our Friendly Relations: A Novel ... Detroit, Mich.: G. C. Rankin, 1890. 305 p. LC

4431 RANKIN, ROLAND OSWELL. The Girl from Paris; or, The Scene Painter's Fancy. A Novel ... New York: The Associated Authors, 1894. 264 p. LC

4432 RAPP, VIRGINIA. The Blacksmith's Daughter: A Novel ... Vicksburg, Miss.: Press of the Commercial Herald [cop. 1890]. 224 p. LC

RATHBONE, CORNELIA KATE. A Pastel. *In* Ten Notable Stories (1894), No. 5391.

4433 RATHBORNE, ST. GEORGE HENRY. A Chase for a Bride: A Romance of the Philippines ... New York: Street & Smith [1899]. 337 p.
Information from LC card; no copy seen.
Majority of his adult fiction was published in subscription series.

4434 ———— Doctor Jack: A Novel ... New York: Street & Smith, 29 Rose Street [1899]. 299 p., illus. HEH, N
First published in the omitted "Primrose Series," 1890.

4435 ———— The Fair Maid of Fez: A Novel ... New York: Home Book Company [cop. 1895]. 248 p., front. Y

4436 ———— Miss Fairfax of Virginia: A Romance of Love and Adventure under the Palmettos ... New York: Street & Smith, 238 William Street [cop. 1899]. 289 p. HEH, LC, UV
Deposited Sept. 26, 1899.

4437 ———— A Sailor's Sweetheart; or, Fighting for Love and Country ... New York: Street and Smith [1900]. 284 p.
Listed PW, Aug. 25, 1900.

RATTLEHEAD, DAVID, *M.D., pseud.* See Byrn, Marcus Lafayette

4438 RAVENEL, HARRIOTT HORRY (RUTLEDGE). Ashurst; or, The Days That Are Not. The Prize Story of the Charleston Weekly News ... Charleston, S.C.: The News & Courier Book Presses, 1879. 57 p.
Listed in Turnbull, Vol. IV, p. 101.
Author also known as Mrs. St. Julien Ravenel.

Ravenel, Mrs. St. Julien.  *See* Ravenel, Harriott Horry (Rutledge)

4439  Rawson, Abel M.  The Junior Partners . . .  San Francisco: J. Stuart & Company, 1891.  409 p., 1 l., illus.                              HEH, LC, Y
Temperance novel.

4440  ———  Seraltha . . .  New York and San Francisco: The Authors' Association, 1893.  388 p.                                         LC
San Francisco.

4441  Ray, Anna Chapin.  Each Life Unfulfilled . . .  Boston: Little, Brown and Company, 1899.  257 p.                                H, HEH, LC, O
Of a singer and an author; New York.

4442  Ray, Mrs. Maude Massey.  Lillian and Lucile: A Novel . . .  Atlanta, Ga.: The Franklin Printing and Publishing Co., 1899.  425 p.     LC

4443  Raymond, Emma Frances Harmon.  A Romance of New Meadows . . .  Lewiston, Maine: Press of Lewiston Journal Co., 1900.  236 p., front.
                                                                        HEH, LC, Y
Maine.

4444  Raymond, Frances.  Maylou . . .  New York: G. W. Dillingham Co. London: Sampson, Low, Marston & Co., Limited, 1898.  248 p.      LC
Of a woman with many lovers.

4445  [Raymond, George Lansing.]  Modern Fishers of Men among the Various Sexes, Sects, and Sets of Chartville Church and Community.  New York: D. Appleton and Company, 1879.  179 p.                  LC

Raymond, Grace, *pseud.*  *See* Stillman, Annie Raymond

4446  Raymond, James F.  The Lost Colony . . .  Philadelphia: T. B. Peterson & Brothers, 306 Chestnut Street [cop. 1891].  413 p.      LC, UM
A desert island.

4447  Raymond, Ross.  No Laggards We . . .  New York: George W. Harlan, 1881.  192 p.                                              HEH, LC, N, O
Newport social life.

4448  Raymond, Rossiter Worthington.  Camp and Cabin: Sketches of Life and Travel in the West . . .  New York: Fords, Howard, & Hulbert, 1880.  243 p., front.                     BA, CU, H, HEH, LC, N, O, UM, Y
*Contents:* Thanksgiving Joe—Agamemnon—Widow Baker—Wonders of the Yellowstone—The Ice-Caves of Washington Territory—The Ascent of Gray's Peak.

4449  Raymond, Walter Marion.  Citronaloes: A Novel . . .  Richmond, Va.: J. W. Randolph & English, 1888.  158 p.                     HEH, LC

4450 ——— Condemn Her Not; or, Virgil Wayt's Temptation . . . Richmond, Va.: T. J. Starke & Sons, 1887. 67 p.
Information supplied by Milton C. Russell of Virginia State Library.

4451 ——— Two Men and Some Women . . . New York: The Abbey Press, 114 Fifth Avenue. London, Montreal [cop. 1900]. 160 p., port.
LC
Deposited Dec. 12, 1900.

RAYMOND, ZILLAH, *pseud.* *See* Frayser, Lou H.

4452 RAYNE, MRS. MARTHA LOUISE. Against Fate: A True Story . . . Chicago: W. B. Keen, Cooke & Co., 1876. 251 p., illus. CU, HEH, O, UVB

4453 ——— Fallen among Thieves. A Summer Tour . . . New York: G. W. Carleton & Co. London: S. Low, Son & Co., 1879. 315 p., map.
HEH, LC, N, UVB
Caption title of 2nd story: "The Romance of a Summer Tour."

4454 ——— Her Desperate Victory . . . Chicago and New York: Belford, Clarke & Co., 1886. 242 p., illus. HEH, UM, Y

4455 RAYNER, EMMA. Free to Serve: A Tale of Colonial New York . . . Boston: Copeland and Day, 1897. 434 p., 1 l. BA, CU, H, HEH, LC, O, UM

4456 ——— In Castle & Colony . . . Chicago and New York: Herbert S. Stone and Company, 1899. 467 p., 1 l.
BA, BU, H, HEH, LC, O, UC, UM, UV, Y

4457 ——— Visiting the Sin: A Tale of Mountain Life in Kentucky and Tennessee . . . Boston: Small, Maynard & Company, 1900. 448 p.
H, HEH, LC, N, O

READ, EMILY, *jt. au.* *See* Reeves, M. C. L. Old Martin Boscawen's Jest (1878), No. 4501; *and* Pilot Fortune (1885), No. 4502.

READ, OPIE. [Read's publications have presented problems that have not been herein satisfactorily resolved. Some titles appeared in papercover subscription series prior to separate publication in hard covers, others appeared simultaneously in the two formats, and still others appeared first in hard covers.]

4458 ——— An Arkansas Planter . . . Chicago and New York: Rand, McNally & Company [cop. 1896]. 315 p., illus.
CU, H, HEH, O, UC, UM, UVB, Y

4459 ——— Bolanyo: A Novel . . . Chicago: Way & Williams, 1897. 309 p., 1 l., front. HEH, LC, N, O, UC, UM
Laid in Mississippi.

4460 ——— The Captain's Romance; or, Tales of the Backwoods . . . New York, Chicago: F. Tennyson Neely [cop. 1896]. 319 p.  BU, HEH, O, UC
*Contents:* Miss Madam—A Backwoods Sunday—The History of the Watch—Old Luxton's Wolf—Shelling Pease—A Young Man's Advice—The Professor—Old Brothers—Old John—An Old Woman's Dream—Interviewed a Corpse—Montgomery Peel—The Captain's Romance—An Historic Shell—Old Rachel—Her Inspiration—The Mill Boys—A Chicago Man—Withered Joe—In the Cumberland Mountains—The Wildcat Circuit—Old Bill's Recital—Five Years—A Strange Experience—A Marine Farm House—The Radish King—Brought the Money—Zozi—Dan Miters—Clem, the Outlaw.
Published first as *Miss Madam* in the omitted "Neely's Library of Choice Fiction," Vol. II, No. 3, 1893, and later with the above title in the omitted "Neely's Popular Library," No. 54, 1896.

4461 ——— The Carpetbagger: A Novel . . . Chicago: Laird & Lee [cop. 1899]. 305 p., illus.  CU, H, HEH, LC, N, UC, UM, UVB, Y
Deposited Sept. 4, 1899.
Frank Pixley, jt. au.

4462 ——— The Colossus . . . Chicago: F. J. Schulte & Co., 298 Dearborn Street [1893]. 254 p.  N, UM

4463 ——— Emmett Bonlore . . . Chicago: F. J. Schulte & Company, 298 Dearborn Street [cop. 1891]. 371 p.  HEH, LC
Deposited Nov. 27, 1891.
Arkansas.

4464 ——— In the Alamo . . . Chicago and New York: Rand, McNally & Company [cop. 1900]. 367 p., front.  CU, HEH, LC, N, O, UC, UM, UVB, Y
Deposited Oct. 18, 1900.

4465 ——— The Jucklins: A Novel . . . Chicago: Laird & Lee [cop. 1896]. 291 p., illus.  LC, UC
1st ed. has eight titles after author's name on title page.
Deposited Feb. 3, 1896.
Of a family on the North Carolina-Tennessee border.

4466 ——— Judge Elbridge . . . Chicago and New York: Rand, McNally & Co., 1899. 295 p., illus.  CU, H, HEH, LC, N, UC, UM, UVB, Y
Gambling in Chicago.

4467 ——— A Kentucky Colonel . . . Chicago: F. J. Schulte & Company, 1890. 342 p.  HEH, LC, N, UC, UVB, Y

4468 ——— Len Gansett . . . Boston: Ticknor and Company, 1888. 383 p.  AP, CU, HEH, LC, N, UM, Y
In the Southwest.

4469 ——— Mrs. Annie Green: A Romance . . . Chicago and New York: Rand, McNally & Company [cop. 1889]. 236 p.  HEH, N, O, UM
The omitted "Globe Library" ed. listed PW, Dec. 21, 1889.

4470 ——— My Young Master: A Novel . . . Chicago: Laird & Lee [cop. 1896]. 305 p., illus.                    HEH, UM

At head of title: "Opie Read's Select Works."

Listed PW, Nov. 7, 1896.

Story told by a slave; Kentucky.

4471 ——— "Odd Folks" . . . New York: F. Tennyson Neely, 114 Fifth Avenue, 1897. 207 p.            BU, H, HEH, UC, UM

Contents: The Superintendent's Example—The Brick Office—The Greek God Barber—Ugly Rachel—The Moon in the Picture—His Sixteen-Eighty-Nine—Big Hep and Little Lady—An Ivory Smile—Old Jobley—Old Billy—Swinging in the Dusk—A Memorable Meal—A Dead March—An Imperious Court—His Special—At the Spring—Not for Three Hundred Thousand—Her Sweet Dream.

4472 ——— Old Ebenezer . . . Chicago: Laird & Lee [cop. 1897]. 345 p., illus.                 H, HEH, LC, N, UC

At head of title: "Opie Read's Select Works."

Deposited Sept. 29, 1897.

UM has copy without note at head of title.

A Vermonter goes South.

4473 ——— On the Suwanee River: A Romance . . . Chicago: Laird & Lee [cop. 1895]. 254 p., illus.             H, UC, UM, Y

At head of title: "Opie Read's Select Works."

The omitted "Pastime Series" ed. listed PW, Aug. 31, 1895.

——— The Princess Yepti. In Short Story Masterpieces (1900), No. 4931.

4474 ——— Selected Stories . . . Chicago: F. J. Schulte & Company, 298 Dearborn Street [cop. 1891]. 199 p.                 LC

Contents: Big Bill and Little Bill—The Same Pistol—A Coat Like Proctor's—An Arkansas Hanging—"Run Along, Now!"—There Was a Fool—The Road to the Mire—Sun Dust—No Mo' Widders—A "Scab"—Little Diser—Big Lige—He Was a Bronson—He Was Amusing—John and Jack—The Tear in the Cup. Deposited Nov. 2, 1891.

4475 ——— The Tear in the Cup, and Other Stories . . . Chicago: Laird & Lee [cop. 1894]. 235 p., illus.               HEH, UM

Contains same stories as No. 4474, with the following additions: In the Cypress View Neighborhood—Drawing the Color Line—Running Down His Business —A Careful Man.

4476 ——— A Tennessee Judge: A Novel . . . Chicago: Laird & Lee [cop. 1893]. 325 p., illus.            HEH, N, UC, UM, UV, Y

4477 ——— Twenty Good Stories . . . New York: J. S. Ogilvie, 57 Rose Street, cop. 1891. 89 p., illus.                 LC

H has copy in the omitted "Sunnyside Series," 192 p. Listed PW, July 25, 1891.

4478 ——— Up Terrapin River . . . Chicago and New York: Rand, Mc-Nally & Company, 1889. 226 p., front.      H, HEH, N, UC

*Also contains:* Behind a Bugler—In the Cumberland Mountains—A Commercial Rip-Snorter—His Friend Flanders—Hendricks Knew It—Wearing Out the Carpet—A Bridegroom—Dave Summers—The Captain's Romance—Old Tildy.

Issued simultaneously in cloth binding and paper covers, the latter in the omitted "Rialto Series," No. 13.

Later issues, in cloth bindings, with and without illus., do not have date on title page. Copyright date is 1888.

4479 ——— The Waters of Caney Fork: A Romance of Tennessee . . . Chicago and New York: Rand, McNally & Company [cop. 1898]. 287 p.
CU, H, HEH, LC, N, O, UC, UM, UVB, Y
Deposited Apr. 18, 1898.

——— When Tom's Luck Changed. *In* Short Story Masterpieces (1900), No. 4931.

4480 ——— The Wives of the Prophet: A Novel . . . Chicago: Laird & Lee [1894]. 287 p., illus.      CU, HEH, N, UM
In a Tennessee valley.

4481 ——— A Yankee from the West: A Novel . . . Chicago and New York: Rand, McNally & Company [cop. 1898]. 277 p.
CU, H, HEH, LC, N, UC, UM, UVB, Y
Deposited Nov. 28, 1898.

4482 REDD, REBECCA FERGUS. The Brierfield Tragedy . . . New York: John W. Lovell Company, 1883. 312 p.      HEH
Of a murder.

REDMOND, FERGUS, *jt. au. See* Gunter, A. C. A Florida Enchantment (1892), No. 2322.

REDWING, MORRIS, *pseud. See* Merrill, James Milford

4483 REED, CARMAN. The Knights of the Silver Star . . . New York: Guild Publishing Concern, 57 Rose Street, cop. 1897. 249 p.      HEH
Civil War novel.

REED, CONSTANT, *pseud. See* Collins, Robert Upton

4484 REED, FANNIE KIMBALL. A Chopin Nocturne, and Other Sketches . . . Cleveland: Privately printed for the author, 1900. 110 p.      LC
200 copies printed.

4485 REED, MRS. FLORIDA PRESLEY. Vesta; or, The Hidden Cross . . . Atlanta, Ga.: The Foote & Davies Co., printers & binders, 1894. 232 p.      LC
Civil War novel.

4486 [REED, FRANCIS R.] Experience of a New York Clerk. By R. F. R. New York: F. R. Reed, 1877. Cover title, 125 p.     LC
*Also contains:* The Gored Huntsman.

4487 [REED, HELEN LEAH] *ed.* "The City and the Sea," with Other Cambridge Contributions, in Aid of the Hospital Fund . . . Cambridge: John Wilson and Son; University Press, 1881. 192 p., illus.
    BA, BU, CU, H, HEH, LC, UC, UM, UP, Y
*Contains:* A Cambridge Robinson Crusoe, by John Holmes—Rex's Vacation, by Anne W. Abbott.

4488 ——— Miss Theodora: A West End Story . . . Boston: Richard G. Badger & Co., 1898. 250 p., illus.     BA, BU, H, HEH, LC, N, O, Y
Boston life.

4489 REED, ISAAC GEORGE. From Heaven to New York; or, The Good Hearts and the Brown Stone Fronts. A Fact Founded on a Fancy . . . New York: Murray Hill Publishing Company, 1876. 114 p.     HEH, LC
Of industrial and social life.

4490 REED, MYRTLE. Later Love Letters of a Musician . . . New York and London: G. P. Putnam's Sons; the Knickerbocker Press, 1900. 165 p., illus.     CU, HEH, LC, O

4491 ——— Love Letters of a Musician . . . New York and London: G. P. Putnam's Sons; the Knickerbocker Press, 1899. 170 p., illus.
    CU, HEH, UV
An 1898 limited ed. was mentioned in PW, Sept. 30, 1899, p. 474. No copy seen.

4492 REED, VERNER ZEVOLA. Adobeland Stories . . . Boston: Richard G. Badger & Co., 1899. 179 p.     CU, H, HEH, LC, O
*Contents:* Antonio Salcido's Story—Santa Beatriz—The Tale of Burnt-Foot Maiden—Luz—An Indian's Revenge—At the Pu-yé Cliffs—The Law of Seh-Now-Wuff.

4493 ——— Lo-To-Kah . . . New York and London: Continental Publishing Company, 1897. 229, [1] p., illus.     CU, HEH, LC, N, O, UP, Y
*Contents:* Lo-To-Kah, the Uncivilized—The Witch of Rancho Soledad—Lo-To-Kah and the Golden Woman—Lo-To-Kah and the Witch—The Death of Lo-To-Kah—The Vision of the Witch.

4494 ——— Tales of the Sun-Land . . . New York and London: Continental Publishing Co., 1897. 250 p., illus.     HEH, LC, O
*Contents:* An Enchanted Night—The Carib Queen—The Herald of the Great White Christ—The Last Man of a Nation—In the Caverns of Ulo—Lost Pueblo—A Civilized Heathen—The Bruja Bonita.

4495 REEDER, A. P. Around the Golden Deep: A Romance of the Sierras . . . San Francisco: Samuel Carson and Company. Boston: Cupples and Hurd, 1888. 495 p.     HEH, UV

*Also issued with imprint:* Boston: Cupples and Hurd. San Francisco: Samuel Carson & Co., 1888.   CU, LC
Copyrighted by Samuel Carson & Co.; deposited Feb. 4, 1889.

4496  REESE, ALICE.  Hurrah for America: A Tale of Welsh Life . . .  Dayton, Ohio: Press of the U. B. Publishing House, 1898.  204 p.          HEH, O
Welsh-American life; southern Wisconsin.

4497  REESE, CARA.  "And She Got All That!"  Woman's Sphere in Life's Battle . . .  New York, Chicago, Toronto: Fleming H. Revell Company, 1897.  176 p., illus.                                             LC
Of a mill hand.

4498  REEVES, ARTHUR MIDDLETON.  Jan: A Short Story . . .  Chicago, 1892. 31 p.                                                                              N

4499  REEVES, MRS. E. M.  Under the Stars and Stripes . . .  Castalia, S. Dak.: Published by the author, 1891.  545 p., illus.                 LC, UM

4500  REEVES, MARIAN CALHOUN LEGARÉ.  A Little Maid of Acadie . . .  New York: D. Appleton and Company, 1888.  180 p.          HEH, LC, O
Author's full name: Marian Calhoun Legaré (Reeves) Rodney.

4501  ———  Old Martin Boscawen's Jest.  By Marian C. L. Reeves . . . and Emily Read . . .  New York: D. Appleton and Company, 1878.  98 p. Printed in double columns.                                         LC, O

4502  ———  Pilot Fortune.  By Marian C. L. Reeves and Emily Read . . . Boston, New York: Houghton, Mifflin and Company.  The Riverside Press, Cambridge, 1885.  340 p.          AP, BA, H, HEH, LC, O, Y
In a Nova Scotia fishing village.

4503  [REHM, WARREN S.]  The Practical City: A Future City Romance; or, A Study in Environment.  By Omen Nemo [pseud.].  Lancaster, Pa.: The Lancaster County Magazine, [1898].  35 p., front.          LC
Deposited Aug. 5, 1898.

REID, CHRISTIAN, *pseud.*  *See* Tiernan, Frances Christine (Fisher)

REID, JAMES D.  The Telegraph Dispatch.  *In* [W. J. Johnston] *comp.,* Lightning Flashes and Electric Dashes (1877), Nos. 3022, 3023.

4504  REIFSNIDER, ANNA CYRENE (PORTER).  Between Two Worlds . . .  By Mrs. Calvin Kryder Reifsnider . . .  St. Louis: The Anna C. Reifsnider Book Company, 1897.  292 p., illus.                                    LC

4505  ———  Ruby Gladstone; or, A Return to Earth . . .  St. Louis: The Anna C. Reifsnider Book Company, 1893.
Advertised PW, May 27, 1893, p. 823, as "Ready July 1"; summary of plot.

4506 ———— Unforgiven. Second Edition . . . St. Louis, Mo.: The Anna C. Reifsnider Book Co. [cop. 1893]. 271 p., illus.
At head of title: "The Happy Hour Library."
Copy examined at New York Public Library.

REIFSNIDER, MRS. CALVIN KRYDER. *See* Reifsnider, Anna Cyrene (Porter)

4507 [REILLY, BERNARD JAMES.] Passing Shadows: A Novel. By Anthony Yorke [pseud.]. New York, Cincinnati, Chicago: Benziger Brothers, 1897. 301 p. LC
Of a New York family.

REIMENSNYDER, HELEN. *See* Martin, Helen (Reimensnyder)

4508 REIMERS, JOHANNES. Unto the Heights of Simplicity . . . Boston: L. C. Page & Company (Incorporated), 1900. 288 p. CU, HEH, LC
Central California mountains.

4509 REMINGTON, EUGENE. The Victim of the Mysterious Mark; or, The Magic Mirror. A Tale of the Times . . . Lowell, Mass.: Published at [Wheeler & Son's], 88 and 90 Central Street, 1880. Cover title, 23 p.
HEH
Published to advertise Wheeler & Son's, one-price clothiers.

4510 REMINGTON, FREDERIC. Crooked Trails . . . New York and London: Harper & Brothers, 1898. 150 p., 1 l., illus.
BA, CU, H, HEH, LC, O, UP, UV, Y
*Contents:* How the Law Got into the Chaparral—The Blue Quail of the Cactus—A Sergeant of the Orphan Troop—The Spirit of Mahonqui—The Essentials at Fort Adobe—Massai's Crooked Trail—Joshua Goodenough's Old Letter—Cracker Cowboys of Florida—The Strange Days That Came to Jimmie Friday—The Soledad Girls.

4511 ———— Men with the Bark On . . . New York and London: Harper & Brothers, 1900. 208, [1] p., illus. CU, HEH, LC, O, UC, UM, UP, UV, Y
*Contents:* The War Dreams—The Bowels of a Battle-Ship—The Honor of the Troop—A Sketch by MacNeil—The Story of the Dry Leaves—A Failure of Justice—Sorrows of Don Tomas Pidal, Reconcentrado—When a Document Is Official—The White Forest—They Bore a Hand—The Trouble Brothers: Bill and the Wolf—With the Fifth Corps.

4512 ———— Stories of Peace and War . . . New York and London: Harper & Brothers, 1899. 98 p., illus. CU, H, HEH, LC, N, O, UM, UP, UV, Y
*Contents:* The Strange Days That Came to Jimmie Friday—Joshua Goodenough's Old Letter—Chasing a Major-General.

4513 ———— Sundown Leflare . . . New York and London: Harper & Brothers, 1899. 114, [1] p., illus. BA, CU, H, HEH, LC, O, UC, UM, UP, Y

*Contents:* The Great Medicine—Horse (An Indian Myth of the Thunder)—How Order No. 6 Went Through (As Told by Sundown Leflare)—Sundown Leflare's Warm Spot—Sundown Leflare's Money—Sundown's Higher Self.

4514 RENÉ, JOSEPH ADELARD. Wanderings of French Ed, and Other Stories ... New York: Wright & Company [cop. 1899]. 172 p., front.  LC

*Also contains:* Her Great Sorrow—A Writer's Confession—A Strange Suicide—White Eagle's Love—Chemist Beaumont's Life-Fluid—Romance of the Woods—Half an Hour in Heaven—A Snake Story—A Sad Case—Weeping Rock—The Stolen Soul—The Story of Many—"Doc" Benson. Deposited Dec. 27, 1899.

4515 RENO, ITTI (KINNEY). An Exceptional Case: A Novel ... Philadelphia: J. B. Lippincott Company, 1891. 181 p.  BA, HEH, LC, O

Heroine aspires to paint.

4516 [——] Miss Breckenridge, a Daughter of Dixie. By a Nashville Pen ... Philadelphia: J. B. Lippincott Company, 1890. 203 p.  AP, HEH, LC

4517 RENO, JAMES J. Fairway and Folly ... Kansas City, Mo.: Ramsey, Millett, & Hudson, printers, binders, etc., 1881. 585 p., illus.  LC

4518 RENSINK, MRS. J. W. The World's Fairest; or, True Hearts at Home ... Chicago: Published for the author by Donohue, Henneberry & Co. [cop. 1893]. 408 p., illus.  HEH

4519 REXDALE, ROBERT. Saved by the Sword: A Novel ... Boston: Winthrop Publishing Company, 1889. 226 p.  LC

According to LC, author's name was changed from Robert F. Barbour by court action.

4520 REXFORD, EBEN EUGENE. What the Christmas Brought Her ... [Chicago]: The John Church Company, cop. 1894. Cover title, [16] p., illus.  LC

A story to advertise the Everett piano.

4521 REYNOLDS, BEATRICE. The Match-Maker ... Philadelphia: T. B. Peterson & Brothers, 1878. 300 p.

Listed PW, Apr. 27, 1878.

4522 REYNOLDS, CUYLER. Janet: A Character Study ... Albany, N.Y.: James B. Lyon, 1889. 219 p.  LC

4523 REYNOLDS, D. A. Wolverton; or, The Modern Arena ... Chicago and New York: Rand, McNally & Company, 1891. 391 p.  HEH, LC

To teach the need of religious faith.

4524 [REYNOLDS, WALTER DOTY.] Mr. Jonnemacher's Machine: The Port to Which We Drifted. By Lord Prime, Esq. [pseud.], Librarian to the State Library of Pennsylvania. A.D. MMXVI ... Philadelphia: Knickerbocker Book Company [cop. 1898]. 255 p., illus.  HEH, LC, UVB

By the year 2016, U.S. government owned and ran everything.

4525 RHODES, WILLIAM HENRY. Caxton's Book: A Collection of Essays, Poems, Tales, and Sketches . . . San Francisco: A. L. Bancroft and Company, 1876. 300 p.                    BU, CU, HEH, LC, UM, Y
*Contains:* The Case of Summerfield—The Deserted Schoolhouse—Phases in the Life of John Pollixfen—The Aztec Princess—Legends of Lake Bigler—The Telescopic Eye—The Earth's Hot Center—Whitherward—A Pair of Myths—The Two Georges—The Summerfield Case.

RHONE, MRS. D. L. *See* Rhone, Rosamond (Dodson)

4526 RHONE, ROSAMOND (DODSON). Among the Dunes. By Mrs. D. L. Rhone . . . New York and London: F. Tennyson Neely, 1897. 396 p.
HEH, UM

4527 RICE, THOMAS CARY. Doom of Washakim: A Chapter in King Philip's War . . . Worcester, Mass.: J. S. Wesby and Sons, 1899. 305, [1] p.
BU, HEH, LC, Y

4528 RICH, BENJAMIN ERASTUS. Mr. Durant of Salt Lake City, "That Mormon" . . . Salt Lake City: George Q. Cannon & Sons Co., printers, 1893. 320 p., front.                    BU, CU, H, HEH, LC, O, Y
Of a Mormon missionary in Tennessee.

4529 RICHARDS, E. J. Two Dreams; or, '62 and '90. By a Comrade of the Late War . . . Henderson, N.Y., cop. 1890. Cover title, 15 p.          LC

4530 [RICHARDS, GEORGE S.] The Widow and the Farm: A Lancaster County Romance. [By] G. S. R. Lancaster, Pa.: The New Era Printing House, 1890. 151 p.                    HEH, O, UVB

4531 RICHARDS, LAURA ELIZABETH (HOWE). Love and Rocks . . . Boston: Estes and Lauriat, 1898. 180 p., front.          BA, CU, H, HEH, LC, O
Majority of her books were for young people.

4532 RICHARDS, LYSANDER SALMON. Breaking Up; or, The Birth, Development, and Death of the Earth and Its Satellite in Story . . . Boston: J. E. Farwell & Co., printers, 1896. 247 p.          H, HEH, LC, Y

4533 [RICHARDSON, CHARLES FRANCIS.] The End of the Beginning. Boston: Little, Brown and Company, 1896. 326 p.          CU, HEH, LC, O, Y
Of a bookshop and teaching.

4534 RICHARDSON, LEANDER PEASE. Lord Dunmersey, His Recollections and Moral Reflections by Himself. Edited by Leander Richardson. New York: John Delay, 1889. 215 p.          H, LC

4535 RICHARDSON, WARREN. Dr. Zell and the Princess Charlotte. An Autobiographical Relation of Adventures in the Life of a Distinguished Modern Necromancer, Seer and Theosophist . . . New York: L. Kabis and Company, 1892. 342 p.          H, HEH, LC

4536  RICHBERG, ELOISE O. RANDALL.  Bunker Hill to Chicago: A Story . . . Chicago: The Dibble Publishing Company, 1893.  151 p., front.  LC, N

4537  RICHMOND, ALMON BENSON.  A Hawk in an Eagle's Nest . . .  [N.p.], 1881.  575 p.  HEH, LC

4538  RIDDLE, ALBERT GALLATIN.  Ansel's Cave: A Story of Early Life in the Western Reserve . . .  Cleveland: The Burrows Brothers Company, 1893.  249 p.  BA, H, HEH, LC, N, O, UM, Y

4539  [———]  Castle Gregory: A Story of the Western Reserve Woods in the Olden Times . . .  Cleveland, Ohio: Leader Printing Company, 1884.  99 p.  Printed in double columns.  H, LC

4540  ———  The House of Ross, and Other Tales . . .  Boston: Hall & Whiting, 1881.  448 p.  BA, LC, UM
Also contains: The Stowes of Auburn—Lu Pettengill's Punishment—Edith Grover—Monson.

4541  ———  The Tory's Daughter: A Romance of the North-West, 1812-1813 . . .  New York & London: G. P. Putnam's Sons; the Knickerbocker Press, 1888.  385 p.  CU, HEH, LC, N, O, UM, UVB, Y

4542  RIDDLE, WILLIAM.  Nicholas Comenius; or, Ye Pennsylvania Schoolmaster of ye Olden Time . . .  Lancaster [Pa.]: Wickersham Printing Company, 1897.  469 p., illus.  BU, CU, H, HEH, LC, UM, UP, Y

4543  RIDEING, WILLIAM HENRY.  The Captured Cunarder: An Episode of the Atlantic . . .  Boston: Copeland and Day, 1896.  104, [1] p., 1 l.  CU, H, HEH, UVB, Y

4544  ———  A Little Upstart: A Novel . . .  Boston: Cupples, Upham and Company, 1885.  284 p.  AP, H, HEH, O, UVB, Y
Literary Boston.

4545  RIDENBAUGH, MRS. MARY YOUNG.  Enola; or, Her Fatal Mistake . . .  St. Louis: Published for the author by Woodward & Tiernan, printers and binders, 1886.  296 p., illus.  H, LC, N
Civil War background; Kentucky.

4546  [RIDEOUT, MRS. JACOB BARZILLA.]  She Beats the Devil.  Los Angeles, Cal.: Charles W. Palm Co., 1898.  330 p., illus.
Information from LC card, which notes "Copyright by J. Barzilla Rideout, Whittier, Calif.," and enters book under Jacob Barzilla. No copy seen.

RIDER, KATE W.  The Wight That Quailed.  In Mavericks (1892), No. 3663.

RIDGEWAY, ALGERNON, pseud.  See Wood, Anna Cogswell

4546a RIFFE, PETER B.  Celeste, and Other Sketches . . .  Lebanon, Ky.: Printed at the Standard Office, 1876.  179 p.  HEH

> *Also contains:* First Protracted Meeting Ever Held in Liberty, Kentucky—A Chapter from Real Life Forty-Seven Years Ago—"Love's Young Dream" on the Banks of Green River—A Court Scene in Casey in the Olden Time. John Winston Coleman, *A Bibliography of Kentucky History* (Lexington, Ky., 1949), No. 1513, locates two additional copies.

4547 RIIS, JACOB AUGUST.  Nibsy's Christmas . . .  New York: Charles Scribner's Sons, 1893.  52 p., illus.  H, LC, O, UC

> *Also contains:* What the Christmas Sun Saw in the Tenements—Skippy of Scrabble Alley.

4548 ———— Out of Mulberry Street: Stories of Tenement Life in New York City . . .  New York: The Century Co., 1898.  269 p., front.

BA, BU, CU, H, HEH, LC, N, UC, UM, Y

4549 RILEY, JAMES WHITCOMB.  The Boss Girl: A Christmas Story.  And Other Sketches . . .  Indianapolis: The Bowen-Merrill Co., 1886.  263 p.

BU, CU, HEH, LC, N, UC, UM, UV

> *Contains:* An Adjustable Lunatic—Tod—A Remarkable Man—A Nest-Egg —Tale of a Spider—Where Is Mary Alice Smith?—Eccentric Mr. Clark—"The Boy from Zeeny"—The Old Man.
> At head of title: "Character Sketches."
> Also published as: *Sketches in Prose and Occasional Verses.* Indianapolis: The Bowen-Merrill Co., 1891.  BU, HEH, LC, UV, Y
> Title of first story changed from "The Boss Girl" to "Jamesy."

4550 ———— Pipes o' Pan at Zekesbury . . .  Indianapolis: Bowen-Merrill Co., 1889.  245 p.  BU, CU, H, HEH, UC, UVB, Y

> *Contains:* At Zekesbury—Mrs. Miller—An Old Settler's Story—A Wild Irishman—The Gilded Roll.

———— *jt. au.  See* Nye, E. W.  Nye and Riley's Railway Guide (1888), No. 4012.

4551 [RINGGOLD, JACOB.]  Lord Jacquelin Burkney, the Whitechapel Terror. By "Rodissi" [pseud.].  New York: [Anton Publishing Co.], 1889. 152 p.  LC

4552 RISLEY, RICHARD VOORHEES.  Men's Tragedies . . .  New York: The Macmillan Company.  London: Macmillan & Co., Ltd., 1899.  303 p.

H, HEH, LC, O

4553 ———— The Sledge . . .  Boston: Richard G. Badger & Co. [cop. 1900]. 209 p.  LC

> Deposited Apr. 12, 1900.
> Of a Russian priest on the Baltic.

4554 RITTER, JOHN P.  The Man Who Dared . . .  A Historical Romance of the Time of Robespierre . . .  New York: G. W. Dillingham Company, 1899.  284 p., illus.  H, HEH, LC

4555 RIVAL CHARMS: A Novel . . . New York: G. W. Carleton & Co. London: S. Low & Co., 1884. 202, 236 p.     HEH
"A Spanish Story," with caption title only, occupies last 236 p.

4556 RIVENBACK, MRS. ROBERT W. Pauline; or, The Girl of Piney Dell. By Mita Leon [pseud.]. Wilmington [N.C.]: S. G. Hall, 1883. 149 p. Powell, No. 510, locates a copy in University of North Carolina Library.

4557 RIVERS, GEORGE ROBERT RUSSELL. Captain Shays: A Populist of 1786 . . . Boston: Little, Brown and Co., 1897. 358 p.
BA, CU, H, HEH, LC, N, O, UM, UP, UVB, Y

4558 ———— The Count's Snuff-Box: A Romance of Washington and Buzzard's Bay during the War of 1812 . . . Boston: Little, Brown and Company, 1898. 283 p., illus.     CU, H, HEH, LC, O, UM, Y

4559 ———— The Governor's Garden: A Relation of Some Passages in the Life of His Excellency, Thomas Hutchinson, Sometime Captain-General and Governor-in-Chief of His Majesty's Province of Massachusetts Bay . . . Boston: Joseph Knight Company, 1896. 259 p., 1 l., illus.
BA, BU, CU, H, HEH, LC, O

RIVES, AMÉLIE. *See* Troubetzkoy, Amélie (Rives) Chanler

4560 RIVES, HALLIE ERMINIE. As the Hart Panteth . . . New York: G. W. Dillingham Co., 1898. 237 p.     H, HEH, LC, UC
Of music and platonic love.
Author later married Post Wheeler.

4561 ———— A Fool in Spots . . . Saint Louis: Woodward and Tiernan Printing Company, 1894. 234 p.
Listed in L. S. Thompson, p. 98.

4562 ———— A Furnace of Earth . . . New York: The Camelot Company, 1900. 224 p.     CU, H, HEH, LC, N, O, UC, UM, UP, UV, Y

4563 ———— The Singing Wire, and Other Stories . . . Clarksville, Tenn.: W. P. Titus, agt., printer, and binder, 1892. 98 p.     LC
*Also contains:* A Gift of the Sea—The Sculptor of Dreams—A False Crown—Under the Palms.

4564 ROBBINS, CHARLES HENRY. The Gam: Being a Group of Whaling Stories . . . New Bedford: H. S. Hutchinson & Company, 1899. 203 p., illus.     BA, BU, H, HEH, LC, O, UM, UP, UV

ROBBINS, LEONARD HARMAN. Old Man. *In* [F. L. Knowles] *ed.*, Cap and Gown in Prose (1900), No. 3182.

4565 ROBERTS, CHARLES HUMPHREY. "Down the O-hi-o" . . . Chicago: A. C. McClurg and Company, 1891. 313 p.     H, HEH, LC, O, UM, Y

4566 ROBERTS, CLARA (LEMORE). A Covenant with the Dead: A Novel . . . Philadelphia: J. B. Lippincott Company, 1892. 395 p.    LC

4567 [RORERTS, MRS. ELIZABETH S.] A Holiday Book: Sketches of Men, Women, and Things. Founded on Truth . . . [By] E. S. Streebor [pseud.]. New York: E. Scott, printer, 1890. 188 p.    LC

4567a ROBERTS, ELLEN. One of Earth's Daughters . . . Boston: Arena Publishing Co., 1893. 316 p.    HEH
Boston.

4568 ROBERTS, J. W. Looking Within: The Misleading Tendencies of "Looking Backward" Made Manifest . . . New York: A. S. Barnes & Company, 1893. 279 p.    BU, CU, H, HEH, UC, Y
Projected to the year 2000.

4569 [ROBERTS, MAGGIE.] Ambition; or, The Launch of a Skiff upon the Sea of Life. By Eiggam Strebor [pseud.]. New York: Published for the author by Lange, Little & Co., 1876. 224 p., illus.    HEH, LC
New York.

4570 [————] Gem of Youth; or, Fireside Tales. By Eiggam Strebor [pseud.] . . . New York: Published for the author by Lange, Little & Co., 1876. 255 p., illus.    LC

4571 ROBERTS, RALPH. Delivered from Afar; or, Hopes Realized in Dakota . . . New York: Phillips & Hunt. Cincinnati: Cranston & Stowe, 1885. 428 p.    H, LC
New York family moves to Dakota Territory.

4572 ROBERTSHAW, JAMES. Merivale; or, Phases of Southern Life . . . New York: G. W. Dillingham Co., 1898. 245 p.    HEH, LC
Of a man wrongly accused of murder.

4573 ———— Volney Randolph: A Novel . . . New York: G. W. Dillingham, 1893. 293 p.    LC

4574 ROBERTSON, ESTHER. The World Well Lost . . . New York, Cincinnati, Chicago: Benziger Brothers, 1898. 182 p.    LC

ROBERTSON, HARRISON. How the Derby Was Won. *In* Stories of the South (1893), No. 5283.

4575 ———— "If I Were a Man": The Story of a New-Southerner . . . New York: Charles Scribner's Sons, 1899. 190 p.    HEH, LC, UC
Politics in Kentucky.

4576 ———— Red Blood and Blue . . . New York: Charles Scribner's Sons, 1900. 324 p.    HEH, LC, O, UC, Y
Tennessee.

4577 ROBERTSON, MORGAN. Futility ... New York: M. F. Mansfield, 22 East
Sixteenth Street [cop. 1898]. 145 p.       HEH, LC, UVB, Y
Of the "Titan," a nonsinkable ship carrying about 3,000 passengers, which
sank in April.

4578 ———— Spun-Yarn: Sea Stories ... New York and London: Harper
& Brothers, 1898. 214, [1] p., illus.       BA, H, HEH, O, UC, UVB
*Contents:* The Slumber of a Soul: A Tale of a Mate and a Cook—The Sur-
vival of the Fittest—A Creature of Circumstance—The Derelict "Neptune"
—Honor among Thieves.

4579 ———— "Where Angels Fear to Tread," and Other Tales of the Sea ...
New York: The Century Co., 1899. 302 p., front.    H, HEH, O, UVB, Y
*Also contains:* The Brain of the Battle-ship—The Wigwag Message—The
Trade-Wind—Salvage—Between the Millstones—The Battle of the Monsters
—From the Royal-Yard Down—Needs Must When the Devil Drives—When
Greek Meets Greek—Primordial.

———— A Yarn without a Moral. *In* Tales from McClure's: Humor
(1897), No. 5361.

4580 [ROBERTSON, SARAH FRANKLIN (DAVIS).] Errors; or, The Rightful Master. A Novel. By Ruth Carter [pseud.]. New York: G. W. Carleton & Co. London: S. Low, Son & Co., 1879. 347 p.       LC
On a Georgia plantation; Civil War.

4581 [ROBINS, ELIZABETH.] The Fatal Gift of Beauty, and Other Stories. By
C. E. Raimond [pseud.] ... Chicago: Herbert S. Stone & Co., 1896.
248, [1] p., 1 l.       H, HEH, LC, UM
*Also contains:* The Portman Memoirs—Below the Salt—Confessions of a Cruel
Mistress—Vroni.

4582 [————] George Mandeville's Husband. By C. E. Raimond [pseud.].
New York: D. Appleton and Company, 1894. 219 p.    H, LC, O, UM

4583 [————] The New Moon. By C. E. Raimond [pseud.] ... New
York: D. Appleton and Company, 1895. 213 p.       HEH, LC, O

4584 [————] The Open Question: A Tale of Two Temperaments. By
C. E. Raimond [pseud.] ... New York and London: Harper & Brothers, 1899. 523 p.       CU, LC, N
2nd issue drops last page number and adds one paragraph.    HEH, UV
3rd issue is same as 2nd except author's name appears on title page.    H, HEH,
LC, O, Y

ROBINSON, D[ANIEL?]. The Story of a Recruit. *In* C. King, *ed.*, An
Initial Experience (1894), No. 3105.

4585 [ROBINSON, EDGAR WILLIAMS.] Only a Tramp. By Owanda [pseud.]
... New York: The Authors' Publishing Company, Bond Street [cop.
1878]. 212 p.       LC
LC copy has registration stamp dated 1879.

4586 ROBINSON, EDITH. Penhallow Tales . . . Boston: Copeland and Day, 1896. 184 p.                    CU, H, HEH, LC, N, O, UP, Y

*Contents:* Penhallow—A Mental Princess—A Return to Nature—The Tenth of September—Marm Phoebe's Fortune—The Satyr's Head—The Portrait by Hunt.

4587 ROBINSON, EDWARD A. The Disk: A Tale of Two Passions. By Robinson and Wall. Boston: Cupples, Upham and Company, 1884. 204 p.

AP, CU, HEH, LC, N

George A. Wall, jt. au.

Fantasy.

4588 ROBINSON, HERBERT B. Chester: A Novel . . . Chicago, New York: W. B. Conkey Company [cop. 1898]. 145 p.                    HEH

Chicago.

4589 ROBINSON, JOHN BUNYAN. The Serpent of Sugar Creek Colony: A Temperance Narrative of Pioneer Life in Ohio . . . Philadelphia, Pa.: G. W. Johnson, printer, 1885. 128 p., illus.                    HEH, Y

4590 ROBINSON, MARGARET BLAKE. Souls in Pawn: A Story of New York Life . . . New York, Chicago, Toronto: Fleming H. Revell Company [cop. 1900]. 308 p.                    CU, LC

4591 ROBINSON, NUGENT. Better Than Gold . . . Notre Dame, Indiana: "Ave Maria" Press [cop. 1885]. 80 p.                    H, LC

4592 ROBINSON, ROWLAND EVANS. Danvis Folks . . . Boston and New York: Houghton, Mifflin and Company. The Riverside Press, Cambridge, 1894. 349 p.                    BA, CU, H, HEH, LC, N, UVB, Y

Rural Vermont in the 1840's.

4593 ———— A Danvis Pioneer: A Story of One of Ethan Allen's Green Mountain Boys . . . Boston and New York: Houghton, Mifflin and Company. The Riverside Press, Cambridge, 1900. 214 p., 1 l.

CU, H, HEH, LC, N, O, UC, UP, UVB, Y

4594 ———— A Hero of Ticonderoga . . . Burlington, Vt.: Hobart J. Shanley & Co., 1898. 187 p., front.                    BU, CU, H, HEH, LC, N, UC, UP, UVB, Y

4595 ———— In the Green Wood . . . Burlington, Vt.: Hobart J. Shanley & Co., 1899. 163 p.                    HEH, LC, UP, UVB, Y

American Revolution; Vermont.

4596 ———— Sam Lovel's Camps: Uncle Lisha's Friends under Bark and Canvas. A Sequel to Uncle Lisha's Shop . . . New York: Forest and Stream Publishing Co., 1889. 253 p.                    BU, CU, HEH, LC, N, UVB, Y

*Contents:* The camp on the Slang—The Camp on the Lake.

4597 ———— Uncle Lisha's Outing . . . Boston and New York: Houghton, Mifflin and Company. The Riverside Press, Cambridge, 1897. 308 p., 1 l. BA, CU, H, HEH, LC, N, O, UP, UVB, Y

4598 ———— Uncle Lisha's Shop: Life in a Corner of Yankeeland . . . New York: Forest and Stream Publishing Co., 1887. 187 p.
BU, CU, H, HEH, LC, N, UVB, Y

4599 [ROBINSON, STEPHEN T.] The Shadow of the War: A Story of the South in Reconstruction Times. Chicago: Jansen, McClurg & Company, 1884. 378 p. CU, H, HEH, LC, N, UM, UV, Y
South Carolina.

4600 ROBINSON, W. A. His Way and Hers . . . Cincinnati: Cranston & Curts. New York: Hunt & Eaton, 1895. 149 p. LC
Of a married couple's struggle with poverty.

4601 ROCHE, JAMES JEFFREY. Her Majesty the King: A Romance of the Harem . . . Boston: Richard G. Badger & Co., 1899. 163 p., illus.
HEH, N, UV, Y

4602 ROCKWOOD, CAROLINE WASHBURN. An Adirondack Romance . . . New York: New Amsterdam Book Company, 156 Fifth Avenue [cop. 1897]. 181 p., illus. CU, LC, O, UP, Y

4603 ———— An East Florida Romance . . . New York: New Amsterdam Book Company, 156 Fifth Avenue [cop. 1897]. 258 p., illus. LC, O

4604 ———— In Biscayne Bay . . . New York: Dodd, Mead and Company, 1891. 286 p., illus. H, HEH, LC, O, Y

4605 ———— A Masque of Honor: A Saratoga Romance . . . New York, London: Funk & Wagnalls, 1889. 167 p. HEH, LC, Y
Also published as: *A Saratoga Romance; or, A Mask of Honor.* New York, London: Funk & Wagnalls, 1889. o has copy with "Twelfth Edition" on title page.

ROCKWOOD, HARRY, *pseud. See* Young, Ernest A.

4606 [RODENBERGER, LIZZIE KING.] Vesta Vane: A Novel. By "L. King R." New York: G. W. Carleton & Co. London: S. Low & Co., 1878. 360 p.
LC
Entry from New York Public Library.

RODGERS, C. G. Which Miss Charteris? *In* C. King, Rancho del Muerto [cop. 1895], No. 3109.

RODISSI, *pseud. See* Ringgold, Jacob

4607 RODNEY, GEORGE BRYDGES. In Buff and Blue: Being Certain Portions from the Diary of Richard Hilton, Gentleman, of Haslet's Regiment of Delaware Foot in Our Ever Glorious War of Independence . . . Boston: Little, Brown and Company, 1897. 206 p.

CU, HEH, LC, N, O, UVB, Y

RODNEY, MARIAN CALHOUN LEGARÉ (REEVES). *See* Reeves, Marian Calhoun Legaré

4608 ROE, AZEL STEVENS. True Love Rewarded: A Tale . . . New York: G. W. Carleton & Co. London: S. Low & Co., 1877. 306 p. HEH, LC

4609 ROE, EDWARD PAYSON. A Day of Fate . . . New York: Dodd, Mead & Company [cop. 1880]. 450 p. BU, H, HEH, N, O, UM, UP, UVB, Y

4610 ———— The Earth Trembled . . . New York: Dodd, Mead and Company, 1887. 452 p. CU, H, HEH, N, O, Y
From bombardment of Fort Sumter to earthquake of 1886.

4611 ———— A Face Illumined . . . New York: Dodd, Mead & Company, 751 Broadway [cop. 1878]. 658 p. BU, H, HEH, LC, N, O, UC, UM, UVB, Y
Hotel on the Hudson.

4612 ———— Found, yet Lost . . . New York: Dodd, Mead & Company [cop. 1888]. 222 p. HEH, UVB

4613 ———— He Fell in Love with His Wife . . . New York: Dodd, Mead and Company [cop. 1886]. 359 p., front. BU, CU, HEH, O, Y
Later ed. contains 333 p.

4614 ———— His Sombre Rivals . . . New York: Dodd, Mead & Company [cop. 1883]. 487 p. BA, BU, CU, H, HEH, LC, N, O, UC, UM, UVB, Y
Civil War novel.

4615 ———— The Hornets' Nest: A Story of Love and War . . . New York: Dodd, Mead & Company, 1887. 157 p. O

4616 ———— A Knight of the Nineteenth Century . . . New York: Dodd, Mead & Company, 1877. 582 p. CU, H, HEH, LC, N, O, UC, UM, UVB, Y

4617 ———— "Miss Lou" . . . New York: Dodd, Mead and Company, 1888. 368 p. AP, BU, CU, H, HEH, LC, N, O, UC, UM, UVB, Y
Virginia at the end of the Civil War.

4618 ———— Nature's Serial Story . . . New York: Harper & Brothers, 1885. 430 p., illus. BA, H, HEH, LC, N, UVB, Y

4619 ———— Near to Nature's Heart . . . New York: Dodd, Mead & Company, 751 Broadway [cop. 1876]. 556 p.
BA, BU, CU, H, HEH, LC, N, O, UM, UVB, Y
Deposited Oct. 2, 1876.
Hudson highlands during the Revolution.

4620 ——— An Original Belle ... New York: Dodd, Mead and Company [cop. 1885]. 533 p.     AP, BU, CU, H, HEH, O, UC, UM, UVB, Y Civil War novel.

4621 ——— Taken Alive, and Other Stories. With an Autobiography ... New York: Dodd, Mead and Company [cop. 1889]. 375 p., front.     AP, BU, O, UM

Contents: "A Native Author Called Roe"—Taken Alive—Found yet Lost—Queen of Spades—An Unexpected Result—A Christmas-Eve Suit—Three Thanksgiving Kisses—Susie Rolliffe's Christmas—Jeff's Treasure—Caught on the Ebb-Tide—Christmas Eve in War Times—A Brave Little Quakeress.

Verso of title page: "Copyright, 1883, 1889, by Dodd, Mead and Company. Copyright, 1888, by J. B. Lippincott & Co."

Also on verso of title page: "University Press, John Wilson and Son, Cambridge."

BU copy drops "press" note.

Five of these stories later reprinted under title: A Brave Little Quakeress, and Other Stories. New York: Dodd, Mead & Company [cop. 1892]. 214 p. HEH

4622 ——— An Unexpected Result, and Other Stories ... New York: Dodd, Mead & Company [cop. 1883]. 134 p.   AP, HEH, LC, N, O, UVB, Y

Also contains: Christmas Eve in War Times—Three Thanksgiving Kisses. Later printed in No. 4621.

4623 ——— Without a Home ... New York: Dodd, Mead & Company [cop. 1881]. 560 p.     BU, H, HEH, N, O, UM, UVB

Later issue has "No. 755 Broadway" in imprint.

4624 ——— A Young Girl's Wooing ... New York: Dodd, Mead & Company [cop. 1884]. 482 p.     BU, CU, H, HEH, N, O, UVB

Later ed. contains 340 p.

4625 ROE, EDWARD REYNOLDS. Belteshazzar: A Romance of Babylon ... Chicago: Donohue, Henneberry & Co., 1890. 267 p.     CU, LC, UM

4626 ——— Brought to Bay ... Boston: Estes and Lauriat, 1882. 285 p.     HEH, LC, O, Y

On the Wabash and Mississippi rivers.

4627 ——— Dr. Caldwell; or, The Trail of the Serpent ... Chicago: Laird & Lee, cop. 1889. 251 p., front.     HEH

4628 ——— The Gray and the Blue: A Story Founded on Incidents Connected with the War for the Union ... Chicago: Rand, McNally & Co., 1884. 292 p.     CU, LC

4629 [ROE, MARY ABIGAIL.] Free, yet Forging Their Own Chains. By C. M. Cornwall [pseud.]. New York: Dodd, Mead & Company, 751 Broadway [cop. 1876]. 378 p.     HEH, N, O, UM, Y

Coal region of Pennsylvania.

4630 ——— A Long Search ... New York: Dodd, Mead & Company [cop. 1885]. 391 p. AP, HEH, LC
Deposited Dec. 19, 1885.

4631 [ROE, WILLIAM JAMES.] Bellona's Husband: A Romance. By Hudor Genone [pseud.] ... Philadelphia: J. B. Lippincott Company, 1887. 332 p. AP, BA, O
From New York to Mars.

4632 [———] Cut: A Story of West Point. By G. I. Cervus [pseud.]. Philadelphia: J. B. Lippincott Company, 1886. 286 p. AP

4633 [———] Inquirendo Island. By Hudor Genone [pseud.]. New York & London: G. P. Putnam's Sons; the Knickerbocker Press, 1886. 347 p. AP, CU, HEH, LC, O, UP, Y
Attacks outward display of religion and superstition.

4634 [———] The Last Tenet Imposed upon the Khan of Tomathoz. By Hudor Genone [pseud.] ... Chicago: Charles H. Kerr and Company, 1892. 165 p., illus. BU, LC

4635 [———] A Model Wife: A Novel. By G. I. Cervus [pseud.] ... Philadelphia: J. B. Lippincott Company, 1885. 343 p. AP, LC, O
New York.

4636 [———] "White Feathers": A Novel. By G. I. Cervus [pseud.]. Philadelphia: J. B. Lippincott & Co., 1885. 313 p. HEH, LC, O
Of a coward.

4637 ROGERS, ANNA (ALEXANDER). Sweethearts and Wives: Stories of Life in the Navy ... New York: Charles Scribner's Sons, 1899. 220 p. HEH, LC, O
*Also contains:* Mutiny on the Flag-Ship—The Commodore's Chair—From Three to Six, Dancing—War and Peace—Marjory and the Captain—Amma-San—Reconstruction Days.

4638 ROGERS, FRANK D. Reveries of an Undertaker ... [Clayton, N.Y., cop. 1899.] 118 p., port. LC
Deposited May 24, 1899.

4639 ROGERS, JOHN RANKIN. The Graftons; or, Looking Forward. A Story of Pioneer Life. By S. L. Rogers. Chicago: Milton George Publishing House, 1893. 115 p. Printed in double columns. HEH, LC
Also published as: *Looking Forward; or, The Story of an American Farm. By John R. Rogers.* [Olympia, Wash.]: Spike Publishing Company, 1898. 325 p., illus. HEH, LC

4640 ROGERS, LEBBEUS HARDING. The Kite Trust (A Romance of Wealth) ... New York City: Kite Trust Publishing Company, 75 Maiden Lane [cop. 1900]. 475 p., front. HEH, O, UM, Y

4641 ROGERS, ROBERT CAMERON. Old Dorset: Chronicles of a New York Countryside ... New York and London: G. P. Putnam's Sons, 1897. 209 p.                                        BU, H, HEH, LC, N, UC, UM
*Contents:* A Dorset Prodigal—The Denison Vendue—Madam Callander—The Expiation of Ezra Spicer—The Case of Pinkney Tolliver—The Last of the Old Church.

4642 ——— Will o' the Wasp: A Sea Yarn of the War of '12. Edited by Henry Lawrence, U.S.N., and Now Brought before the Public for the First Time by Robert Cameron Rogers. New York and London: G. P. Putnam's Sons, 1896. 269 p., front.                      CU, H, HEH, N, Y

ROGERS, S. L. *See* Rogers, John Rankin

4643 ROGERS, SARA BULKLEY. Ezra Hardman, M. A., of Wayback College, and Other Stories ... New York: Dodge Publishing Company, 150 Fifth Avenue [cop. 1900]. 209 p., illus.                                        LC
*Also contains:* The Light of Circumstance—Silva Graham Kimberton—The Giant's Strength—The Crime of Lois Baxter—In Poverty Row—The Chevalier d'Artois—Her Son—Poison Flowers.
Deposited Apr. 10, 1900.

4644 ROGERS, THOMAS H. Nehalem: A Story of the Pacific, A.D. 1700 ... McMinnville, Oregon: H. L. Heath [cop. 1898]. 182 p., illus.      Y

4645 ROHLFS, ANNA KATHARINE (GREEN). Agatha Webb. By Anna Katharine Green ... New York & London: G. P. Putnam's Sons; the Knickerbocker Press, 1899. 360 p.              BA, BU, CU, HEH, LC, N, O, UP, Y

4646 ——— Behind Closed Doors ... New York & London: G. P. Putnam's Sons; the Knickerbocker Press, 1888. 523 p.              CU, HEH, O, Y

4647 ——— The Circular Study ... New York: McClure, Phillips & Co., 1900. 289 p.              BA, CU, H, HEH, LC, O, UM, UP, Y

4648 ——— Cynthia Wakeham's Money ... New York, London: G. P. Putnam's Sons; the Knickerbocker Press, 1892. 336 p., front.
CU, H, HEH, LC, O, Y

4649 ——— A Difficult Problem, The Staircase at the Heart's Delight, and Other Stories ... New York: The F. M. Lupton Publishing Company, 1900. 344 p.              CU, H, HEH, LC, N, O, UM, UP, Y
*Also contains:* The Gray Madam—The Bronze Hand—Midnight in Beauchamp Row—The Staircase at the Heart's Delight—The Hermit of——Street.

4650 ——— The Doctor, His Wife, and the Clock ... New York, London: G. P. Putnam's Sons; the Knickerbocker Press, 1895. 131 p., front.
BA, CU, H, HEH, N, O, UC, UP, Y
At head of title: "Anna Katharine Green."

4651 ———— Doctor Izard ... New York, London: G. P. Putnam's Sons; the Knickerbocker Press, 1895. 268 p., front. BA, HEH, LC, O, UP, Y

4652 ———— The Forsaken Inn: A Novel ... New York: Robert Bonner's Sons [cop. 1890]. 346 p., illus. BA, H, HEH, LC, O, UM, UP, Y Deposited Apr. 9, 1890.

4653 ———— Hand and Ring ... New York, London: G. P. Putnam's Sons, 1883. 608 p., illus. BA, H, HEH, N, O, UM, UP, Y

4654 ———— The Leavenworth Case: A Lawyer's Story ... New York: G. P. Putnam's Sons, 1878. 475 p., illus. BA, CU, H, HEH, O, UV, Y

4655 ———— Lost Man's Lane: A Second Episode in the Life of Amelia Butterworth ... New York & London: G. P. Putnam's Sons; the Knickerbocker Press, 1898. 403 p. BA, CU, H, HEH, LC, O, UP, Y

4656 ———— Marked "Personal" ... New York, London: G. P. Putnam's Sons; the Knickerbocker Press, 1893. 415 p. CU, H, HEH, LC, N, O, UM, UP, Y

4657 ———— A Matter of Millions: A Novel ... New York: Robert Bonner's Sons, 1890. 482 p., illus. BA, H, HEH, O, UP, Y

4658 ———— The Mill Mystery ... New York & London: G. P. Putnam's Sons; the Knickerbocker Press, 1886. 389 p. BA, CU, H, HEH, O, UM, Y

4659 ———— Miss Hurd, an Enigma ... New York, London: G. P. Putnam's Sons; the Knickerbocker Press, 1894. 357 p. BA, CU, LC, N, O

4660 ———— The Old Stone House, and Other Stories ... New York, London: G. P. Putnam's Sons; the Knickerbocker Press, 1891. 202 p. CU, H, HEH, LC, O, UP, Y
*Also contains:* A Memorable Night—The Black Cross—A Mysterious Case—Shall He Wed Her?

4661 ———— 7 to 12: A Detective Story ... New York and London: G. P. Putnam's Sons; the Knickerbocker Press, 1887. 114 p., illus. BA, H, HEH, LC, O
*Also contains:* One Hour More.

———— Shall He Marry Her? *In* Eleven Possible Cases [cop. 1891], No. 1737.
Included in No. 4660 as "Shall He Wed Her?"

4662 ———— A Strange Disappearance ... New York: G. P. Putnam's Sons, 1880. 280 p. H, HEH, LC, N, UP, Y

4663 ———— The Sword of Damocles: A Story of New York Life ... New York: G. P. Putnam's Sons, 1881. 540, [1] p. CU, H, HEH, O, UM, UP, UV, Y

4664 ——— That Affair Next Door ... New York, London: G. P. Putnam's Sons; the Knickerbocker Press, 1897. 399 p.

CU, HEH, O, UC, UM, UV, Y

4665 ——— X Y Z: A Detective Story ... New York: G. P. Putnam's Sons, 1883. 97 p.

CU, H, HEH, LC, UP, Y

ROKER, A. B., *pseud. See* Barton, Samuel, *broker*

4666 ROLAND, MRS. ALICE KATE. Rosalind Morton; or, The Mystery of Ivy Crown. A Kentucky Story ... Louisville, Ky.: Chas T. Dearing, 1898. 434 p.

LC, UC

4667 ROLLIN, HORACE JUDSON. Yetta Ségal ... New York: G. W. Dillingham Co., 1898. 174 p.

HEH, LC, Y

Of race blending.

4668 ROLLINS, ALICE MARLAND (WELLINGTON). The Story of a Ranch ... New York: Cassell & Company, Limited, 739 & 741 Broadway [cop. 1885]. 190 p.

AP, BA, BU, CU, H, HEH, LC, O

Kansas.

4669 ——— The Three Tetons: A Story of the Yellowstone ... New York: Cassell & Company, Limited, 739 & 741 Broadway [cop. 1887]. 219 p.

AP, BA, H, HEH, LC, O, Y

4670 ——— Uncle Tom's Tenement: A Novel ... Boston: The William E. Smythe Company, 1888. 468 p.

BA, H, HEH, O, UM, Y

New York.

4671 ROLLINS, CLARA HARRIOT (SHERWOOD). A Burne-Jones Head, and Other Sketches ... New York: Lovell, Coryell & Company, 1894. 164 p., front.

H, LC, UV

*Also contains:* Kismet—Human Sunshine—Aunt Charlotte—A Chance Shot —A Case in Point.

4672 ——— Threads of Life ... Boston, New York, and London: Lamson, Wolffe and Company, 1897. 204 p.

BA, H, HEH, LC, O

4673 ROLLINS, FRANK WEST. Break o' Day Tales ... Boston: Joseph Knight Company, 1894. 204 p.

BA, H, HEH

*Contents:* Miss Stillings—The Steam Interlude—Joining the Cavalry—The Bishop's Fifth—The Magic Flask.

4674 ——— The Lady of the Violets ... Boston: Lee & Shepard, 1897. 238 p.

BU, HEH

Of two successful women speculators in Wall Street.

ROMAINE, HARRY. His Lucky Night. *In* Hanks: Assorted Yarns from Puck (1893), No. 2444.

———— A Timely Hint. *In* Mavericks (1892), No. 3663.

4675 A ROMANCE OF THE WHITE MOUNTAINS. [New York: The Spectator Company, cop. 1896.] Cover title, [16] p., illus.                    LC
Deposited Sept. 17, 1896.

ROMEYN, HENRY. The Captain's Story. *In* C. King, *ed.*, The Colonel's Christmas Dinner (1890), No. 3098.
Later printed in No. 3099.

———— Did It Pay? *In* C. King, *ed.*, By Land and Sea (1891), No. 3092.
Later printed in No. 3099.

4676 ROMIG, HENRY HORACE. Another Bob; or, What Father and Mother Sparenot, Uncle Ham and Auntie Hephzibah, and Others Had to Say . . . Milton, Pa.: The Milton Printing Co., 1899.   108 p.                    LC

4677 ROOD, HENRY EDWARD. The Company Doctor: An American Story . . . New York: The Merriam Company, 67 Fifth Avenue [cop. 1895].   259 p.                    CU, HEH, LC, N, O, Y
For restricted immigration.

ROOSEVELT, BLANCHE, *pseud.* *See* Macchetta, Blanche Roosevelt (Tucker)

4678 ROOSEVELT, ROBERT BARNWELL. Love and Luck: The Story of a Summer's Loitering on the Great South Bay . . . New York: Harper & Brothers, 1886.   350 p.                    AP, BA, CU, H, HEH, LC, O, UVB, Y
Long Island.

ROSCOE, DEANE, *pseud.* *See* Yates, Frederic B.

4679 ROSE, DUNCAN. Madeline; or, A Commencement Proposal and What Came of It. A Love Story . . . Fayetteville [N.C.]: Cape Fear Press [cop. 1898].   158 p.
Information supplied by Harry Bergholz of University of North Carolina Library.

4680 ROSEBOOM, JANE. The Starless Crown: A Story . . . Lansing, Mich.: Launt Thompson, printer and binder, 1889.   377 p., illus.                    HEH, LC

4681 ROSEBORO', VIOLA. Old Ways and New: Stories . . . New York: The Century Co., 1892.   216 p., illus.                    CU, HEH, LC, O
*Contents:* The Clown and the Missionary—Bentley's System—A Jest of Fate —The Last Marchbanks—The Reign of Reason—Nannie's Career—The Force of Example—Rudolph—The Village Alien—The Girl and the Problem.

ROSEN, LEW, *pseud.* *See* Rosenthal, Lewis

4682 [ROSENTHAL, LEWIS.] Grisette: A Tale of Paris and New York. By Lew Rosen [pseud.]. New York: John Delay, 1889.   221 p.                    LC, UP

4683 ROSEWATER, FRANK. '96: A Romance of Utopia. Presenting a Solution of the Labor Problem, a New God, and a New Religion . . . Omaha, Neb.: The Utopia Company, 1894. 268 p.      CU, LC, N, Y

Ross, ALBERT, *pseud. See* Porter, Linn Boyd

Ross, CLARA SPRAGUE. Cynthy's Joe. *In* C. King, Rancho del Muerto [cop. 1895], No. 3109.

———— Pastelle. *In* Short Stories from Outing [cop. 1895], No. 4930.

4684 Ross, CLINTON. The Adventures of Three Worthies . . . New York, London: G. P. Putnam's Sons; the Knickerbocker Press, 1891. 162 p.
     BA, CU, HEH, LC, Y

4685 ———— Bobbie McDuff . . . Boston: L. C. Page and Company (Incorporated), 1898. 258 p., illus.      CU, HEH, LC, O, UC

4686 ———— Chalmette: The History of the Adventures & Love Affairs of Captain Robe before & during the Battle of New Orleans. Written by Himself . . . Philadelphia & London: J. B. Lippincott Company, 1898. 264 p., front.      HEH, LC, O, UM, Y

———— The Decoy Despatch. *In* I. Bacheller, *ed.*, Best Things from American Literature (1899), No. 195.

4687 ———— The Gallery of a Random Collector . . . New York and London: G. P. Putnam's Sons; the Knickerbocker Press, 1888. 310 p.
     HEH, LC, Y
*Contents:* A Door Swings Open—In New Spain—The Man in the Frayed Frock-Coat—Colonel Bludlow's Idea—The Gentleman and the Dryad—The Trainer Cap'n—An Adventure of Felix Latoon—The Young Woman in Shabby Black—The Diary of a Sentimental Fortune-Hunter—A November Night—Now: A Sentimental Comedy—The Silver Mug at Frangipini's.

4688 ———— Improbable Tales . . . New York, London: G. P. Putnam's Sons; the Knickerbocker Press, 1892. 256 p.      CU, H, HEH, LC, Y
*Contents:* The Pretender—The Peace of the Hills—After the Play of "The Rivals."

4689 ———— The Meddling Hussy: Being Fourteen Tales Retold . . . New York: Stone and Kimball, 1897. 400 p., 1 l., illus.      CU, H, HEH, LC, Y
Part I, Tales of American Wars; Part II, Tales of Personages; Part III, Tales of the New Road; Part IV, A Tale of an India Mystery, and A Tale of the Ghost of the Stretching Moor.

4690 ———— The Puppet . . . New York: Stone & Kimball, 1896. 183 p., 1 l.      H, HEH, LC, N, O, Y

4691 ———— The Scarlet Coat . . . New York: Stone & Kimball, 1896. 309, [1] p., 1 l.      CU, H, HEH, LC, N, O, UP, UVB, Y
Siege of Yorktown.

4692 ———— The Silent Workman: A Story . . . New York & London: G. P. Putnam's Sons; the Knickerbocker Press, 1886. 131 p. HEH, LC

4693 ———— The Speculator . . . New York, London: G. P. Putnam's Sons; the Knickerbocker Press, 1891. 125 p. HEH, LC, O, UP, UV, Y

4694 ———— A Trooper of the Empress . . . New York: D. Appleton and Company, 1898. 224 p. HEH, LC, O
South Africa.

4695 ———— Two Soldiers and a Politician . . . New York and London: G. P. Putnam's Sons; the Knickerbocker Press, 1893. 139 p.
H, HEH, LC, Y
Contents: On Imaginary Portraits—Wolfe—The First Lord Fenwold—Talleyrand.

———— The Way to Constantinople. In Stories from the Chap-Book (1896), No. 5277.

———— When His Majesty Nicholas Came to England. In New Stories from the Chap-Book (1898), No. 3949.

4696 ———— Zuleka: Being the History of an Adventure in the Life of an American Gentleman, with Some Account of the Recent Disturbances in Dorola . . . Boston, New York, and London: Lamson, Wolffe and Company, 1897. 222 p. CU, H, HEH, LC, N, O, UM, Y

4697 Rossiter, William Sidney. An Accidental Romance, and Other Stories . . . New York: The Republic Press, 1895. 185 p., illus. H, HEH, LC, UM
Also contains: A Common Sense Cupid—The Auction Bottle—An Unauthenticated Serpent—The Twice Told Life of Thomas Dart.

4698 Roulet, Mary F. (Nixon). God, the King, My Brother. By Mary F. Nixon . . . Boston: L. C. Page & Company, 1900. 296 p., front. LC, Y

4699 ———— A Harp of Many Chords . . . St. Louis, Freiburg, Strasburg, Munich, Vienna: B. Herder [cop. 1899]. 232 p. LC

4700 ———— Lasca, and Other Stories . . . Saint Louis: B. Herder. Freiburg, Baden; Strasburg, Alsace; Munich, Bavaria; Vienna, Austria [cop. 1898]. 190 p. HEH
Also contains: The Quality of Mercy—To Forgive Divine—The Black-Horse Clock of the Señor Valdez—The Goldsmith's Madonna—The Señorita Americana—Our Lady's Soldier—For Cuba?—Pepita—On the Way to Madrid—What Babette Saw at Tiverney—Il Signor' Dottore—The Edgerton's Maid.

4701 [Round, William Marshall Fitts.] Achsah: A New England Life-Study. By Rev. Peter Pennot [pseud.]. Boston: Lee & Shepard, 1876. 368 p., illus. BA, H, HEH, LC, N, O, UVB, Y

4702 ——— Rosecroft: A Story of Common Places and Common People . . . Boston: Lee and Shepard. New York: Charles T. Dillingham, 1881. 357 p. CU, H, HEH, LC, O, Y

4703 A ROUND TABLE OF THE REPRESENTATIVE AMERICAN CATHOLIC NOVELISTS, at Which Is Served a Feast of Excellent Stories . . . New York, Cincinnati, Chicago: Benziger Brothers, 1897. 353 p., illus.

H, HEH, LC, N, O, Y

*Contains:* A Lost Prima Donna, by Eleanor C. Donnelly—The Mad Penitent of Todi, by Anna Hanson Dorsey—Speculum Justitiae, by Ella Loraine Dorsey—How Perseus Became a Star, by Maurice Francis Egan—Gilliman Ogley, by Walter Lecky [i.e., William A. McDermott]—In the Quebrada, by Christian Reid [i.e., Frances C. F. Tiernan]—The Baron of Cherubusco, by John Talbot Smith—Joe of Lahaina, by Charles Warren Stoddard.

4704 ROUNDY, ALICE MIRIAM. A Race with a Hurricane, and Other Stories . . . New York: The Abbey Press, 114 Fifth Avenue. London, Montreal [cop. 1900]. 101 p. LC

*Also contains:* The Double-Barreled Basket—"The Great Father John"—Romantic Adventures of a Fox Terrier—The Don Silvestro Choir-Book. Deposited Dec. 27, 1900.

4705 ROWE, HENRIETTA (GOULD). Queenshithe . . . Buffalo: Charles Wells Moulton, 1895. 184 p. HEH, LC, UV

4706 ——— Re-Told Tales of the Hills and Shores of Maine . . . Bangor, Me.: D. Bugbee & Co., 1892. 357 p., illus. HEH, LC, N, O, UC, Y

*Contains:* Pretty Patty Parton: A Tale of the Revolution—A College Girl—The Eagle in the Sea-Bird's Nest—Church Mice—Marjorie's Knight—Stuffing the Thanksgiving Turkey—Tempest in a Teapot—Betsey—Puck in the Pulpit—Sugaring Off.

4707 [ROWLAND, K. ALICE.] Fickle Fate. By Lenore [pseud.] . . . Birmingham, Ala.: Roberts & Son, printers, 1892. 249 p. LC

4708 ROWLEY, MARY S. Marion; or, The Dawning Light . . . Philadelphia: Printed by J. B. Lippincott Company, 1888. 244 p., front. LC

4709 ROYAL, MATTHEW J. The Isle of the Virgins: A Romance . . . Buffalo, N.Y.: The Wenborne-Sumner Co., 1899. 328 p., illus.

Information from LC card; no copy seen.

4710 ROYCE, JOSIAH. The Feud of Oakfield Creek: A Novel of California Life . . . Boston and New York: Houghton, Mifflin and Company. The Riverside Press, Cambridge, 1887. 483 p.

AP, BA, BU, CU, H, HEH, LC, N, O, UC, UP, UVB, Y

4711 RUBEN, EDWARD. The Path to Fame . . . New York: O. Lauckner, 1887. 342 p. HEH

A New York art studio.

4712 RUDD, MRS. JEAN PORTER. Bas' Theres: A Narrative-Drama of Tirol . . . Norwich, Conn.: The Bulletin Press, 1897. 103 p. LC

4713 —— The Tower of the Old Schloss . . . New York, London: G. P. Putnam's Sons; the Knickerbocker Press, 1896. 277 p. LC Austria.

4714 RUDDY, ELLA AUGUSTA (GILES). Maiden Rachel . . . Madison, Wis.: David Atwood. Chicago: Jansen, McClurg and Company, 1879. 319 p. UVB, Y

4715 —— Out from the Shadows; or, Trial and Triumph. By Ella A. Giles . . . Madison, Wis.: Atwood & Culver. Chicago: Jansen, McClurg and Company, 1876. 317 p. H, HEH, LC

4716 [RULLMANN, JOHN D.] Bob Greenfellow's [pseud.] Sketches. San Antonio, Tex.: Johnson Bros. Ptg. Co. [cop. 1892]. 284 p. LC, Y
Contents: "A Bet"—"My Mascot"—"A Deer Hunt"—"My First Oration"—Our Most Unlucky Day on the Farm—The Tariff Question—A Duck Hunt—Ignis Fatuus—Must Have a Wife Again—Love and Politics—Dwellers in Celestial Spheres.

4717 RUMBOUGH, GEORGE P. C. From Dust to Ashes: A Romance of the Confederacy . . . Little Rock, Arkansas: The Brown Printing Company, 1895. 193 p., illus. CU, LC, UV

4718 RUNAWAY GIRLS AND THEIR STARTLING ADVENTURES: True Narratives of Actual Occurrences. With Real Names of Many Young Women Who Imbibed Romantic Notions of Life through Reading Sensational Novels in a Class of Highly Injurious Weekly Story Papers and Left Their Homes . . . Philadelphia: Barclay & Co., 21 North Seventh Street [cop. 1878]. 64 p., illus. HEH, LC

4719 RUNYAN, NICHOLAS PATTERSON. A Quaker Scout . . . New York: The Abbey Press, 114 Fifth Avenue. London, Montreal [cop. 1900]. 277 p., front. HEH, LC
Deposited Nov. 30, 1900.
Civil War novel.

4720 RUSSELL, ADDISON PEALE. Sub-Coelum: A Sky-Built Human World . . . Boston and New York: Houghton, Mifflin and Company. The Riverside Press, Cambridge, 1893. 267 p. BA, CU, H, HEH, UC, UM, Y

4721 RUSSELL, CHARLES, WELLS. The Fall of Damascus: An Historical Novel . . . Boston: Lee & Shepard. New York: Charles T. Dillingham, 1878. 287 p. BU, CU, HEH, LC, O, UV

4722 RUSSELL, ERNEST E. The Reason Why: A Story of Fact and Fiction . . . New York: Ernest E. Russell, 1896. 365 p. CU, LC
Of agnosticism.

RUSSELL, FOX. Over a Cigar. *In* Short Stories from Outing [cop. 1895], No. 4930.

4723 RUSSELL, FRANCES E. A Quaint Spinster . . . Boston: Roberts Brothers, 1895. 119 p. HEH, LC
She endowed a home for spinsters.

RUSSELL, G. W. The Vow of the Six Telegraph Operators. *In* [W. J. Johnston] *comp.*, Lightning Flashes and Electric Dashes (1877), Nos. 3022, 3023.

RUSSELL, RAYMOND, *pseud. See* Fearing, Lilian Blanche

4724 RYALS, JOHN VINCENT. Yankee Doodle Dixie; or, Love the Light of Life. An Historical Romance, Illustrative of Life and Love in an Old Virginia Country Home . . . Richmond, Va.: Everett Waddey Co., stationers and printers, 1890. 532 p. CU, HEH, LC, UV

4725 RYAN, MARAH ELLIS (MARTIN). The Bondwoman . . . Chicago and New York: Rand, McNally & Company, 1899. 403 p., front.
HEH, LC, O, UM, UV, Y
Slave girl is a spy for the Union army.

4726 —— A Chance Child, Comrades, Hendrex and Margotte, and Persephone: Being Four Tales . . . Chicago and New York: Rand, McNally & Company, 1896. 263 p. HEH, LC, O, Y

4727 —— A Flower of France: A Story of Old Louisiana . . . Chicago: Rand, McNally & Company, 1894. 327 p.
BA, BU, HEH, LC, N, O, UM, UV, Y

4728 —— In Love's Domains: A Trilogy . . . Chicago and New York: Rand, McNally & Company [cop. 1889]. 317 p. H, UC
Probably first published in the omitted "Rialto Series," 1890.

4729 —— Merze: The Story of an Actress . . . Chicago and New York: Rand, McNally & Company, 1889. 313 p., illus. LC, O, UV

4730 —— A Pagan of the Alleghanies . . . Chicago and New York: Rand, McNally & Company [cop. 1891]. 297 p. CU, HEH, O, UV, Y

4731 —— Squaw Élouise . . . Chicago and New York: Rand, McNally & Company [cop. 1892]. 240 p. H, HEH, UM
Early settlements along the Columbia River.

4732 —— Told in the Hills: A Novel . . . Chicago and New York: Rand, McNally & Company, 1891. 362 p., front. LC, N, UC
Montana and Idaho.

4733 RYDER, JOHN W. John Crow: A Novel Founded on Facts . . . York, Pa.: P. Anstadt & Sons, 1900. 138 p. LC

4734 RYER, WILLIAM. Jaccardin . . . New York: G. W. Dillingham Company [cop. 1900]. 364 p.    LC
Of a wealthy man interested in charity.

S., D. S.  *See* Sherwin, Mrs. D. S.

S., D. T., *pseud.*  *See* Balch, Elizabeth

S., E. A. B.  *See* Shackelford, Miss E. A. B.

S., E. B.  *See* Swan, Eliza B.

S., J., OF DALE.  *See* Stimson, Frederic Jesup

S., M. E. W.  *See* Sherwood, Mary Elizabeth (Wilson)

S., N. L.  *See* Smith, Nina Larre

4735 THE SAD CASE OF MRS. KATE SOUTHERN! The Beautiful, Virtuous Georgia Wife, Who, Being Maddened to Insanity by the Outrageous Taunts of a Bad Woman Who Had Enticed Her Husband Away, Killed Her . . . She Was Arrested . . . and Sentenced to Be Hung . . . Philadelphia, Pa.: The Old Franklin Publishing House, cop. 1878.  31, [1] p., illus.    HEH, LC

4736 ———— Philadelphia, Pa.: The Old Franklin Publishing House, cop. 1878.  60, [4] p., illus.    HEH
This ed. adds new material about the case and about Georgia penitentiaries.

4737 SAGE, WILLIAM. Robert Tournay: A Romance of the French Revolution . . . Boston and New York: Houghton, Mifflin and Company. The Riverside Press, Cambridge, 1900.  372 p., illus.
BA, CU, H, HEH, LC, N, O, UP, UV, Y

4738 SAIN, CHARLES MACKNIGHT. An Expectant Heir to Millions: A Novel . . . New York: Robert Lewis Weed Co. [cop. 1897].  241 p.
Listed PW, July 24, 1897.

4739 ST. CLAIR, A. H. Western Lies and Quaint Conceits: A Collection of Original Stories in Chapters Told in Style Similar to "Peck's Bad Boy" . . . St. Louis, Mo.: I. H. Brown, 1892.  150 p.
Listed PW, Feb. 13, 1892.

ST. CLAIR, CECIL, *pseud.*  *See* Clark, Susie Champney

4740 DELETED.

ST. FÉLIX, MARIE, *pseud.*  *See* Lynch, Harriet Louise (Husted)

4741 SALE, MRS. LOUISE MONTGOMERY. The Saddest of All Is Loving . . . New York: The Authors' Publishing Company, Bond Street [cop. 1880].  252 p.    LC

4742 SALISBURY, HENRY BARNARD. Miss Worden's Hero: A Novel . . . New York: G. W. Dillingham, 1890. 149 p.    LC
Of labor interest; New York.

4743 SALTER, MARY J. A Friend in Need . . . Boston: Wright and Potter Printing Company, 1887. 120 p.    CU, UV

4744 ———— The Lost Receipt; or, Frustrated Designs . . . Boston: Wright & Potter Printing Company, 1879. 95 p.    BU, CU, HEH

4745 ———— ———— Boston: Wright & Potter Printing Company, 1881. 95 p., 102 p., 1 l., front.    HEH
With this was issued her "*All That Glitters Is Not Gold*," which has its own title page.

4746 SALTUS, EDGAR EVERSTON. Eden: An Episode. . . Chicago, New York, and San Francisco: Belford, Clarke & Company [cop. 1888]. 187 p.
AP, BU, CU, H, HEH, LC, N, O, UC, UM, UP, UVB, Y

4747 ———— Enthralled: A Story of International Life Setting Forth the Curious Circumstances Concerning Lord Cloden and Oswald Quain . . . London, Paris, Melbourne: The Tudor Press; the American News Company, 1894. [224] p.    BU, CU, HEH, LC, O, Y
Verso of title page: "Press of J. J. Little & Co., Astor Place, New York." Deposited Mar. 2, 1894.
LC second copy of this title, also deposited Mar. 2, 1894, has imprint: London: J. R. Osgood, McIlvaine & Co., 1894. Verso of title page has same "press" note, reset.

4748 ———— Imperial Purple . . . Chicago: Morrill, Higgins & Co., 1892. 234 p.    CU, H, HEH, N, UC, UM, UVB, Y
Rome at the time of Caesar.

4749 ———— Mary Magdalen: A Chronicle . . . New York: Belford Company, 860 Broadway, Union Square, corner Seventeenth Street [cop. 1891]. 254 p.    BU, CU, N, UC

4750 ———— Mr. Incoul's Misadventure: A Novel . . . New York: Benjamin & Bell, 1887. 216 p.   AP, BU, CU, H, HEH, LC, N, O, UC, UM, UP, UVB, Y

4751 ———— The Pace That Kills: A Chronicle . . . Chicago, New York, and San Francisco: Belford, Clarke & Company. London: H. J. Drane [cop. 1889]. 202 p.    AP, BU, CU, HEH, N, UP, UVB, Y

4752 ———— A Transaction in Hearts: An Episode . . . New York, Chicago, and San Francisco: Belford, Clarke & Co. [cop. 1889]. 188 p.
HEH, N, UP, Y

4753 ——— A Transient Guest, and Other Episodes. Chicago, New York, and San Francisco: Belford, Clarke & Co. London: Henry J. Drane [cop. 1889]. 199 p.     AP, BU, CU, HEH, LC, N, UC, UP, UVB

*Also contains:* The Grand Duke's Rubies—A Maid of Modern Athens—Fausta. At head of title: "Edgar Saltus."
Verso of title page: "Press of E. B. Sheldon & Co., New Haven, Conn."
2nd issue omits "press" note on verso of title page.

4754 ——— The Truth about Tristrem Varick: A Novel ... Chicago and New York: Belford, Clarke & Company [cop. 1888]. 240 p.
AP, BU, CU, H, HEH, LC, N, UC, UM, UP, UVB, Y

4755 ——— When Dreams Come True: A Story of Emotional Life ... New York and London: The Transatlantic Publishing Company, 1895. 187 p.     BU, CU, N, UM, UP, Y

SAMPLETON, SAMUEL, *pseud.* *See* Monti, Luigi

SAMSON, *pseud.* *See* Clippinger, John Albert

4756 SANBORN, ALVAN FRANCIS. Meg McIntyre's Raffle, and Other Stories ... Boston: Copeland and Day, 1896. 209 p., 1 l.     H, HEH, LC, N, O

*Also contains:* Mrs. Molloy's Revenge—The Clinging Leaf—A Celebrated Case—Baucis and Philemon in Bigelow Street—Molly and Giuseppe—Trousers—Heroism Up to Date—Episodes in the Career of a Lodging-House Bum —De Mortuis Nil Nisi Bonum—Suffer Little Children.

4757 ——— Moody's Lodging House, and Other Tenement Sketches ... Boston: Copeland and Day, 1895. 175 p.     BA, CU, H, HEH, N, O, UV, Y

*Contents:* Becoming a Cheap Lodger—Moody's—A Free Breakfast—Riley's — The Bed I Earned—Joe Gunn's—Brewster's—Whiting's — The Fairmont House—Appreciation—A Tenement Street — A Tough Alley — Among the Sandwich Men.

4758 SANBORN, EDWIN WEBSTER. People at Pisgah ... New York: D. Appleton and Company, 1892. 185 p.     CU, H, HEH, LC, O, UM, Y
Vermont.

4759 SANBORN, KATHERINE ABBOTT. Abandoning an Adopted Farm ... New York: D. Appleton and Company, 1894. 185 p.
BA, BU, CU, H, HEH, LC, N, O, UC, Y

4760 ——— Adopting an Abandoned Farm ... New York: D. Appleton and Company, 1891. 171 p.     BA, BU, CU, H, HEH, LC, O, Y

4761 SANBORN, MARY FARLEY (SANBORN). It Came to Pass ... Boston: Lee and Shepard, 1892. 339 p.     BA

4762 ——— Paula Ferris ... Boston: Lee and Shepard, 1893. 276 p.
HEH, LC
Of a Boston society woman.

SANDA, *pseud. See* Stowers, Walter H.

4763 SANDERSON, JAMES GARDNER. Cornell Stories . . . New York: Charles
Scribner's Sons, 1898. 251 p.                        BU, CU, H, HEH, LC, UV, Y
*Contents:* The Wooing of Melville R. Corydon—Little Tyler—Company D's
Revenge—One Who Didn't—One Who Did—The Elder Miss Archlen.

SANDETTE, *pseud. See* Walsh, Marie A.

SANDYS, EDWYN WILLIAM. Moeran's Moose. *In* C. King, Rancho del
Muerto [cop. 1895], No. 3109.

4764 SANFORD, FREDERICK R. The Bursting of a Boom . . . Philadelphia: J. B.
Lippincott Company, 1889. 250 p.                                  AP, H, LC, O
Land boom in Ventura County, California.

4765 SANFORD, M. MALONIA (RAY). Berrisford . . . New York: The Authors'
Publishing Company, Bond Street [cop. 1879]. 442 p.                     HEH

SANGRÉE, *pseud. See* Allen, Linda Marguerite Sangrée

SANGSTER, MARGARET E. My Borrowing Neighbor. *In* L. C. H. Langford, *comp.,* The Woman's Story (1889), No. 3206.

SARGENT, JACOB LIVERMORE. El Christo. The Justice of John Fannin.
Nuggets. [Three stories.] *In* E. S. Wilson, Sugar-Pine Murmurings
(1899), No. 6012.

4766 SATTERTHWAIT, MRS. ELISABETH CARPENTER. A Son of the Carolinas: A
Story of the Hurricane upon the Sea Islands . . . Philadelphia: Henry
Altemus, 1898. 273 p.                                    CU, HEH, LC, UV, Y

4767 SAUBER, HALBERT H. Adventures of a Tenderfoot . . . San Francisco,
Cal.: Published for the author by the Whitaker & Ray Company, 1899.
154 p., illus.                                                      HEH, LC
*Contents:* Old Corkscrew—The Bronco—The Trail—The Night Guard—Mill
Creeks—A Midnight Mystery.

4768 [SAUNDERS, ANNA M.] Golden-Rod: A Story of the West. By a Daughter of Nebraska . . . Lincoln, Nebraska: Golden-Rod Publishing Company [cop. 1896]. 134 p., illus.                                        LC
Deposited Oct. 16, 1896.

4769 SAVAGE, MINOT JUDSON. Bluffton: A Story of To-Day . . . Boston: Lee
and Shepard. New York: Charles T. Dillingham, 1878. 248 p.
                                               BU, CU, H, HEH, LC, N, UC, Y
A minister's love story.

SAVAGE, RICHARD HENRY. [The Home Publishing Co. issued many of
Savage's novels in their paperbound subscription "Welcome Series" as

well as separately in cloth. It has not been determined whether all of the omitted series titles were published outside the series. The same unresolved question exists in regard to Savage's works in the Rand, Mc-Nally & Company "Rialto Series."]

4770 ——— The Anarchist: A Story of To-Day . . . Chicago, New York: F. Tennyson Neely, 1894. 399 p., front.        BU, HEH, LC

4771 ——— Brought to Bay: A Novel . . . New York: The Home Publishing Company [1900]. 290 p.
Advertised PW, May 12, 1900, p. 973, as "very shortly to be issued."
LC has copy in the omitted "Welcome Series," No. 56.

4772 ——— Captain Landon: A Story of Modern Rome . . . Chicago and New York: Rand, McNally & Company [cop. 1899]. 391 p., illus.
HEH, LC, O

4773 ——— Delilah of Harlem: A Story of the New York City of To-Day . . . New York: The American News Company, 1893. 329 p.
HEH, LC, UP, Y

4774 ——— An Exile from London: A Novel . . . New York: The Home Publishing Co., 3 East Fourteenth Street [cop. 1896]. 336 p.    H, LC, Y

4775 ——— A Fascinating Traitor: An Anglo-Indian Story . . . New York: The Home Publishing Co., 3 East Fourteenth Street [cop. 1897]. 333 p.
HEH

4776 ——— The Flying Halcyon: A Mystery of the Pacific Ocean . . . New Version. Chicago, New York: F. Tennyson Neely, 1894. 300 p.    LC

4777 ——— For Her Life: A Story of St. Petersburg . . . Chicago and New York: Rand, McNally & Company, 1897. 448 p.        HEH, Y

4778 ——— For Life and Love: A Story of the Rio Grande . . . Chicago and New York: F. Tennyson Neely [cop. 1893]. 448 p.    H, LC, Y

4779 ——— Her Foreign Conquest: A Novel . . . New York: The Home Publishing Company, 3 East Fourteenth Street [cop. 1896]. 308 p.
HEH, LC, UV

4780 ——— His Cuban Sweetheart: A Novel . . . New York: The Home Publishing Company [cop. 1895]. 255 p.        H, HEH, LC
Deposited Jan. 13, 1896.
Mrs. Archibald Clavering Gunter (i.e., Esther Lisbeth Burns Gunter), jt. au.

4781 ——— In the Shadow of the Pyramids: The Last Days of Ismail Khédive, 1879: A Novel . . . Chicago and New York: Rand, McNally & Co., 1898. 392 p.        HEH, O, Y

4782 ———— In the Swim: A Story of Currents and Under-Currents in Gayest New York . . . Chicago and New York: Rand, McNally & Company [cop. 1898]. 361 p. H, HEH

4783 ———— The King's Secret: A Novel . . . New York: The Home Publishing Company [cop. 1900]. 344 p. H

4784 ———— The Little Lady of Lagunitas: A Franco-Californian Romance . . . New York: The American News Company, 1892. 483 p.
AP, CU, HEH, LC, N, O, UC

4785 ———— Lost Countess Falka: A Story of the Orient . . . Chicago and New York: Rand, McNally & Company, 1896. 318 p., front.
H, HEH, UM, Y

4786 ———— The Masked Venus: A Story of Many Lands . . . New York: The American News Company, 1893. 284 p. HEH, LC, O, UP

4787 ———— Miss Devereux of the Mariquita: A Story of Bonanza Days in Nevada . . . Chicago, New York: F. Tennyson Neely [cop. 1895]. 482 p. HEH, N, O, UM

4788 ———— A Modern Corsair: A Story of the Levant . . . Chicago and New York: Rand, McNally & Company, 1897. 382 p., front. H, HEH, Y

4789 ———— My Official Wife: A Novel . . . New York: The Home Publishing Company, 1891. 231 p. HEH, LC, O

4790 ———— Our Mysterious Passenger, and Other Stories . . . New York: Street & Smith, 238 William Street [cop. 1899]. 238 p., illus. HEH, LC
*Also contains:* On the "Ecke"—A Waiting Game—For Pity and for Love—On the Vassily Ostrov—Love's Legacy—The Rigoletto Quartet.
Deposited Jan. 2, 1900.

4791 ———— The Passing Show . . . Chicago, New York: F. Tennyson Neely [cop. 1893]. 326 p. HEH

4792 ———— Prince Schamyl's Wooing: A Story of the Caucasus-Russo-Turkish War . . . New York: The American News Company, 1892. 346 p. H, HEH, O, UM, UV, Y

4793 ———— The Shield of His Honor: A Novel . . . New York: The Home Publishing Company, 1900. 279 p.
Listed PW, Apr. 21, 1900.
LC deposit copy, dated Jan. 18, 1900, is in the omitted "Welcome Series," No. 53.

4794 ———— The White Lady of Khaminavatka: A Story of the Ukraine . . . Chicago and New York: Rand, McNally & Company [cop. 1898]. 370 p. HEH

4795 A SAVAGE OF CIVILIZATION. [New York]: J. Selwin Tait & Sons, 1895. 405 p.    LC
Of industrial strife.

4796 SAVIDGE, EUGENE COLEMAN. The American in Paris: A Biographical Novel of the Franco-Prussian War. The Siege and Commune of Paris, from an American Stand-Point . . . Philadelphia: J. B. Lippincott Company, 1896. 273 p.    H, LC, UM, UV

4797 [———] Wallingford: A Story of American Life . . . Philadelphia: J. B. Lippincott Company, 1887. 308 p.    HEH, LC
New York.

4798 SAVILE, FRANK MACKENZIE. The Foray of the "Hendrik Hudson": A Tale of '54 . . . New York: Frederick A. Stokes Company [1898]. 146 p.    LC
Deposited Dec. 9, 1898.

4799 [———] John Ship, Mariner; or, By Dint of Valor. By Knarf Elivas [pseud.]. New York: Frederick A. Stokes Company [cop. 1898]. 304 p.    HEH

4800 SAWTELLE, MRS. MARY P. The Heroine of '49: A Story of the Pacific Coast . . . [San Francisco: Printed by Francis Valentine & Company], cop. 1891. 259 p.    CU, LC, UM, Y

4801 SAWYER, EDITH AUGUSTA. Mary Cameron: A Romance of Fisherman's Island . . . Boston, U.S.A.: Benj. H. Sanborn & Co., 1899. 220 p., front.    H, HEH, LC, O, UP, UVB
Off the Maine coast.

4802 SAWYER, WALTER LEON. A Local Habitation . . . Boston: Small, Maynard & Company, 1899. 313 p.    CU, HEH, LC, N, UC
Of a lodginghouse and the people who lived in it; Boston.

4803 ——— An Outland Journey . . . Boston: Copeland and Day, 1896. 135 p., 1 l., illus.    CU, H, HEH, LC, N
Satire on current reforms.

SAXON, VAN, pseud. See Simpson, Mrs. Evangeline M.

4804 SAYRE, THEODORE BURT. The Son of Carleycroft: A Dramatic Romance. Being the Memoirs Written by Lorrimer Weatherby, Sometime Captain in Prince Rupert's Horse, and Later Master of Fence in Loring's Cuirassiers . . . New York and London: Harper & Brothers, 1900. 344, [1] p.    H, HEH, LC, O

4805 ——— Two Summer Girls and I . . . New York: Godfrey A. S. Wieners, 1898. 255 p., illus.    HEH, LC, O

4806   SCAMMON, MRS. LAURA EVERINGHAM. Spoon-River Dan . . . Kansas
City [Mo.]: Hudson-Kimberly Publishing Co., 1894. 52 p., illus.
BU, LC, UC

4807   SCANLAN, ANNA C. Dervorgilla; or, The Downfall of Ireland . . . Com-
pleted and Revised with Preface, Map, Illustrations, and Notes by
Charles M. Scanlan. Milwaukee, Wis.: J. H. Yewdale & Sons Co.,
printers, 1895. 356 p., illus.                                HEH, LC

SCEETS, GEORGE N., *jt au. See* Armstrong, Minnie L. The Social Crime
[cop. 1896], No. 131.

4808   SCHAEFER, EDWARD P. The Hidden Voice; or, The Ghost of the Old
Genesee. An Interesting Story of Rochester, N.Y. A Novel . . .
Rochester, N.Y.: Press of Hervey H. Smith, printer and publisher, 1887.
134 p., front.                                               LC

4809   [SCHAEFER, KONRAD.] Agnes Goodmaid. A Mystery Explained. On
the Waves of Ether Sphere. [By] Grete Fischer [pseud.]. Chicago,
Ill., 1899. 450 p., illus.                                   LC

SCHALLENBERGER, V., *pseud? See* Simmons, Vesta S.

SCHAYER, JULIA (THOMPSON) VON STOSCH. The Story of Two Lives. *In*
Stories by American Authors, X (1885), No. 5276.

4810   ——— Tiger Lily, and Other Stories . . . New York: Charles Scribner's Sons, 1883. 227 p.                           BA, HEH, LC, O
*Also contains:* Thirza—Molly—A Summer's Diversion—My Friend Mrs. Angel.

SCHELLING, FELIX EMMANUEL. Villa Vielle's One Mystery. *In* The Septameron (1888), No. 4867.

4811   SCHERESCHEWSKY, SUSAN MARY (WARING). Miss Ruby's Novel . . . New
York: Thomas Whittaker, 1889. 69 p.                          LC

4812   SCHINDLER, SOLOMON. Young West: A Sequel to Edward Bellamy's Celebrated Novel Looking Backward . . . Boston: Arena Publishing Company, 1894. 283 p.        BA, BU, CU, H, HEH, N, UC, UM, UP, UVB, Y
HEH copy contains "Publishers' Notice" tipped in, stating that the book has
been printed with tinted margins, available in blue, green, or yellow.

4813   SCHLEY, JESSIE A. Fannie Davenport . . . St. Paul, Minn.: The Pioneer
Press Company, 1890. 119 p.                           CU, HEH, LC

4814   [SCHOEFFEL, FLORENCE BLACKBURN (WHITE).] The First or Second?
Or, a Mistaken Marriage: A Novel by Wenona Gilman [pseud.] . . .
New York: The American News Co., 1888. 223 p., front.        LC

4815 [————] Miss Davis of Brooklyn. By Wenona Gilman [pseud.] . . .
New York: Norman L. Munro, 1888. 224 p., front.          LC

4816 [————] Saddle and Sentiment. By Wenona Gilman [pseud.]. New
York, London: The Outing Company, Ltd. [cop. 1892]. 284 p., illus.
                                                        HEH, UP

4817 [————] A Wandering Beauty; or, The Temptations of a Great City.
By Wenona Gilman [pseud.] . . . New York: Munro's Publishing
House, 1891. 186 p.                                      LC

SCHOFIELD, MISS J. J. Wooing by Wire. *In* [W. J. Johnston] *comp.*,
Lightning Flashes and Electric Dashes (1877), No. 3023.

4818 SCHONACKER, HUBERT J. Musical Crotchets . . . Indianapolis: Cathcart,
Cleland & Co., 26 E. Washington St. [cop. 1887]. 259 p.      H, LC, Y
Deposited June 22, 1887.
The 1888 ed. adds subtitle *From Darkness to Light*. Deposited July 19,
1888.

SCHRIVER, ERNEST. Stealing Railroad Engines. *In* Tales from McClure's:
War (1898), No. 5364.

4819 SCHURMANN, HELEN. The Solitary Survivor, and Other Stories . . . Indianapolis, 1896.
Listed in Banta, p. 283.

4820 SCHUYLER, CHARLES E. "Jim": A Railroad Novel . . . Omaha: Henry
Gibson Co., printers and binders, 1891. 386 p., illus.          HEH

4821 SCHWAHN, JOHN GEORGE. The Tableau; or, Heaven as a Republic . . .
Los Angeles: Press of the Franklin Printing Company, 1892. 233 p.
                                                        HEH, LC

4822 SCHWARTZ, JULIA AUGUSTA. Vassar Studies . . . New York & London:
G. P. Putnam's Sons; the Knickerbocker Press, 1899. 290 p., illus.
                                      BA, BU, H, HEH, LC, O, UM, UP, Y
*Contents:* In Search of Experience—The History of an Ambition—The Gen-
ius—Heroic Treatment—The Career of a Radical—A Case of Incompatibility
—For the Honor of the Class—A Superior Young Woman—That Athletic
Girl—The Ghost of Her Senior Year—Danger—One of the Girls.

4823 SCOFIELD, CHARLES JOSIAH. A Subtle Adversary: A Tale of Callitso
County . . . First Thousand. [Cincinnati]: Published by the author,
1891. 640 p.                                            HEH, LC, N
Illinois in the 1870's.

SCOLLARD, CLINTON. At Sûk Wady Barada. *In* F. E. McKay, *ed.*, Vignettes [cop. 1890], No. 3523.

4824 ——— A Man-at-Arms: A Romance of the Days of Gian Galeazzo Visconti, the Great Viper . . . Boston, New York, and London: Lamson, Wolffe and Company, 1898. 362 p., illus. CU, H, HEH, LC, O, UVB, Y

4825 SCOTT, HARRIET. Henrietta: A Novel . . . Minneapolis, Minn., 1892. 280 p. HEH, LC, UM

4826 SCOTT, JOHN WALTER. Anita; or, The Spectre of a Snow-Storm. A Novel . . . New York: G. W. Dillingham, 1891. 282 p. LC

4827 SCOTT, MARY E. Keith; or, Righted at Last . . . Philadelphia: J. B. Lippincott & Co., 1881. 308 p. HEH, LC, UV
Southern scene and characters.

4828 SCOTT, MILTON ROBINSON. Ernest Marble, the Labor Agitator . . . Newark, Ohio, 1895. 275 p. LC

4829 ——— Henry Elwood: A Theological Novel . . . Newark, Ohio: Newark American Print, 1892. 324 p. LC, O, UC

4830 ——— Paul Vernon, Prisoner . . . Newark, Ohio, 1900. 248, [4] p. LC, O, Y

4831 SCOTT, SUTTON SELWYN. Southbooke . . . Columbus, Ga.: Thos. Gilbert, printer and bookbinder, 1880. 259 p. BU, LC, UC, Y
*Contains:* Theodoric Burnside: An Alabama Tale.

4832 SCRIBNER, FRANK KIMBALL. A Continental Cavalier: The Record of Some Incidents Pertaining to the Chevalier de Marc, Brevet Major in the Army of the Colonies, Aid-de-Camp to General, the Marquis Lafayette . . . New York: The Abbey Press, 114 Fifth Avenue [cop. 1899]. 258 p., illus. CU, HEH, LC, UM, UV

4833 ——— The Honor of a Princess: A Romance of the Time of "Good Queen Bess" . . . New York: F. Tennyson Neely, 1897. 260 p. HEH, UM

——— *jt. au. See* Bentley, C. S. The Fifth of November [cop. 1898], No. 493.

4834 SCRIBNER, HARVEY. My Mysterious Clients . . . Cincinnati: Robert Clarke Company, 1900. 276 p., front. LC, O, UC
*Contents:* My First Client—The Mystery of a Diamond Robbery—The Romance of a Stolen Will—The Silent Witness—Was It Forgery?—The Unexpected Witness—The Grooved Bullet—The Resurrected Witness—A Glimpse of Santa Claus—Santa Claus' Deputy—The Magic Whistle.

SCRIBNER, KIMBALL. *See* Scribner, Frank Kimball

4835 [SCRIMSHAW, F. C.] The Dogs and the Fleas. By One of the Dogs . . . Chicago, Ill.: Douglas McCallum, 1893. 273 p., illus.    HEH, UC
Marginal notes in HEH copy identify characters.

4836 SCUDDER, HORACE ELISHA. The Dwellers in Five-Sisters Court . . . New York: Hurd and Houghton. Cambridge: The Riverside Press, 1876. 282 p.    BA, BU, CU, H, HEH, LC, N, O, UVB, Y

4837 ———— The King and the Cowboy . . . Philadelphia: Franklin Printing Company, 1897. 27 p.    HEH

4838 ———— Stories and Romances . . . Boston: Houghton, Mifflin and Company. The Riverside Press, Cambridge, 1880. 298 p.
   AP, BA, CU, H, HEH, LC, O, UC, UVB, Y
*Contents:* Left Over from the Last Century—A House of Entertainment—Accidentally Overheard—A Hard Bargain—A Story of the Siege of Boston—Matthew, Mark, Luke, and John—Do Not Even the Publicans the Same?—Nobody's Business.

4839 SCUDDER, MOSES LEWIS. Almost an Englishman . . . New York: G. P. Putnam's Sons, 1878. 250 p.    H, HEH, LC, O

4840 [————] Brief Honors: A Romance of the Great Dividable. Chicago: Jansen, McClurg & Co., 1877. 218 p.    CU, HEH, LC, N, O, UM, UV
Of the "Dividable Life Insurance Co.," New York.

4841 [SEABROOK, WHITEMARSH B.] Saved by a Woman; or, The Hidden Romance. A Story of the Late War. By Strobhart [pseud.]. Atlanta, Ga.: James P. Harrison Co., printers and binders, 1884. 196 p.    LC

4842 SEARING, ANNE ELIZA (PIDGEON). A Social Experiment . . . New York & London: G. P. Putnam's Sons; the Knickerbocker Press, 1885. 182 p.
   AP, H, HEH, LC, UVB
New York.

4843 SEARLES, FLORA M. The Scarlet Ribbon . . . Boston: James H. Earle, 178 Washington Street [cop. 1900]. 332 p., illus.    LC
Deposited Sept. 17, 1900.

SEARS, HAMBLEN. *See* Sears, Joseph Hamblen

4844 SEARS, JOSEPH HAMBLEN. Fur and Feather Tales . . . New York and London: Harper & Brothers, 1899. 216, [1] p., illus.    LC, N, O, Y
*Contents:* Henry's Birds—The Marquis's Meet—William's Moose—Vigdal of the Jotunheim—A Little Upland Game.

4845 SEAWELL, MOLLY ELLIOT. The Berkeleys and Their Neighbors . . . New York: The American News Company [cop. 1888]. 232 p.    LC, UVB, Y
Virginia.

4846 ———— Children of Destiny . . . New York: D. Appleton and Company, 1893. 341 p. HEH

4847 ———— The History of the Lady Betty Stair . . . New York: Charles Scribner's Sons, 1897. 144 p., illus. HEH, LC, N, O, Y

4848 ———— The House of Egremont: A Novel . . . New York: Charles Scribner's Sons, 1900. 515 p., illus. CU, H, HEH, LC, N, O, UVB, Y

4849 ———— The Loves of the Lady Arabella . . . New York: The Macmillan Company. London: Macmillan & Co., Ltd., 1898. 244 p., illus. CU, H, LC, O, Y

4850 ———— Maid Marian, and Other Stories . . . New York: D. Appleton and Company, 1891. 237 p. HEH, O
*Also contains:* Little Missy—The Sea Fortunes of Dicky Carew—The Kourasoffs—A Virginia Colonel—The Valbella Brothers—Theodora—Tubal the Fiddler—Priscilla—Kaintuck.

4851 ———— The Sprightly Romance of Marsac . . . New York: Charles Scribner's Sons, 1896. 194 p., illus. HEH, LC, O, Y

4852 ———— A Strange, Sad Comedy . . . New York: The Century Co., 1896. 281 p., front. H, LC, O, UV, Y
Of a southern girl; Virginia and Newport.

4853 ———— Throckmorton: A Novel . . . New York: D. Appleton and Company, 1890. 304 p. AP, BA, HEH, N, O, Y
A southern family after the war.

4854 SEDGWICK, ANNE DOUGLAS. The Confounding of Camelia . . . New York: Charles Scribner's Sons, 1899. 309 p. BA, BU, H, HEH, LC, O, UP
Author later married Basil De Selincourt.

4855 ———— The Dull Miss Archinard . . . New York: Charles Scribner's Sons, 1898. 287 p. HEH, LC, O, UP

SEELEY, CHARLES SUMNER, *pseud. See* Munday, John William

SEELY, EDWARD HOWARD. *See* Seely, Howard

4856 SEELY, HOWARD. A Border Leander . . . New York: D. Appleton and Company, 1893. 168 p. CU, H, HEH, LC, N, O, UC, Y
Texas.

4857 ———— The Jonah of Lucky Valley, and Other Stories . . . New York: Harper & Brothers, 1892. 235 p., illus. HEH
*Also contains:* A Romance of the Big Horn—A Daphne of the Foot-Hills—The Sheriff of Oskaloo—"Yaller-Bird"—Yaller-Bird's Christmas Turkey.

4858 ———— A Lone Star Bo-Peep, and Other Tales of Texan Ranch Life . . . New York: W. L. Mershon & Co., 1885. 285 p.

BA, BU, CU, H, HEH, LC, N, O, Y

*Also contains:* The Mystery of San Saba—Three Strephons of Concho—An Episode of Paint Rock—A Stage-Coach Enchantress—A Wandering Meliboeus—A Frontier Bohemian—The Temperance Ball at Brady.

4859 ———— A Nymph of the West: A Novel . . . New York: D. Appleton and Company, 1888. 232 p. HEH, LC, N, O, Y

4860 ———— A Ranchman's Stories . . . New York: Dodd, Mead & Company, 1886. 356 p. CU, HEH, N, O, Y

Contains same stories as No. 4858, with the following additions: The Tiger Lily of Llano Post—Christmas at Centerfitt.

———— The Star of the Folies Bergères. *In* The First Book of the Authors Club (1893), No. 1868.

4861 SEIBERT, MARY FRANCES. "Zulma": A Story of the Old South . . . Natchez, Miss.: Natchez Printing and Stationery Co., 1897. 310 p. CU, LC

4862 SEIVER, MRS. JULIA A. B. Birkwood: A Novel . . . Boston: Arena Publishing Company, 1896. 344 p. H, HEH, LC

Women's rights; Florida.

4863 SELDEN, D. A. Joe Saxton in Japan: A Story of the East and the West . . . Baltimore: The Deutsch Company, printers, 1897. 183 p. LC

4864 [SELLERS, ELIZABETH JAUDON.] From 18 to 20: A Novel. Philadelphia: J. B. Lippincott Company, 1888. 195 p. AP, HEH, LC

4865 SELLINGHAM, ELLA J. H. The Hero of Carillon; or, Fort Ticonderoga in 1777 . . . Ticonderoga, N.Y.: W. T. Bryan, 1897. 171 p. LC, UC

4866 SELTZER, CHARLES A. The Council of Three . . . New York: The Abbey Press, 114 Fifth Avenue [cop. 1900]. 177 p., port. LC

Deposited Dec. 13, 1900.

4867 THE SEPTAMERON . . . Philadelphia: David McKay, 1888. 171 p. LC

*Contents:* Boscobel, by Francis Howard Williams—A Symphony, by Harrison Smith Morris—Hazard, by Samuel Williams Cooper—The Lost Elixir, by Charles Henry Lüders—Parthenope's Love, by Colin Campbell Cooper, Jr.—Villa Vielle's One Mystery, by Felix Emmanuel Schelling—An Old Town Tale, by William Henry Fox.

4868 SERENE, SAMUEL, *pseud?* The Story of a Day in London . . . New York: G. W. Dillingham, 1888. 99 p. LC

The experiences of an American couple.

4869 SERVISS, GARRETT PUTNAM. The Moon Metal . . . New York and London: Harper & Brothers, 1900. 163, [1] p. HEH

The metal becomes the coinage of the world.

4870 SEVERANCE, MARK SIBLEY. Hammersmith: His Harvard Days . . . Boston: Houghton, Osgood and Company. Cambridge: The Riverside Press, 1878. 524 p.   H, HEH, LC, O, UP, Y

SEVERANCE, MARY FRANCES (HARRIMAN). "Lib." *In* J. J. Conway, *ed.*, Stories (1893), No. 1172.

SEVERN, LAWRENCE, *pseud. See* Trotter, Ada M.

4871 SEVERY, MELVIN LINWOOD. Fleur-de-Lis, and Other Stories . . . Boston: The Esoteric Publishing Company, 1889. 150 p.   LC
*Contents:* Leonard Monroe—A Curious Manuscript—Beatrice—Fleur-de-Lis.

4872 SEYMOUR, CHARLES W. A College Widow: An Improbable Story . . . New York: G. W. Carleton & Co. London: S. Low, Son & Co., 1881. 432 p.   H, HEH, LC, Y

4873 SEYMOUR, MRS. H. M. "Fealty and Duty" (Foy pour Devoir); or, "The Snap Shot." A Society Narrative . . . Rome, N.Y.: Citizen Office, cop. 1898. 154, [1] p., illus.   LC

4874 [SEYMOUR, MARY ALICE (IVES).] Imperia: A Story from the Court of Austria. By Octavia Hensel [pseud.] . . . Buffalo: Charles Wells Moulton, 1892. 352 p.   LC, UC
Author's second husband was George A. Fonda.

SHACKELFORD, COLLINS. Neighbor King. *In* Tales from McClure's: Romance (1897), No. 5362.

4875 [SHACKELFORD, MISS E. A. B.] Virginia Dare: A Romance of the Sixteenth Century. By E. A. B. S. New York: Thomas Whittaker, 1892. 207 p., front.   LC

4876 SHACKLETON, ROBERT. Toomey and Others . . . New York: Charles Scribner's Sons, 1900. 254 p., illus.   CU, LC
*Contents:* How Toomey Willed His Government Job—A Burial by Friendless Post—Over the River from Blackwell's—A Police Court Episode—The Experiment of Frederica—The Misery in Mis' Randolph's Knee—Before the Archbishop—The Promotion of Berkwater—On Cherry Hill—A Proposal during Shiva.

4877 SHAFFER, FRED G. Knute Hellson's Hard Luck, Complicated by His Wife Hulda in the Merry-Go-Round of Married Life . . . Yuma, Colorado: The Pioneer Publishing House, 1895. 128 p.   LC

4878 [SHALER, SOPHIA PENN (PAGE).] The Prelude and the Play. By Rufus Mann [pseud.]. Boston and New York: Houghton, Mifflin and Company. The Riverside Press, Cambridge, 1900. 416 p., 1 l.   HEH, LC

4879 [SHAPLEY, RUFUS EDMONDS.] Solid for Mulhooly: A Sketch of Municipal Politics under the Leaders, the Ring, and the Boss. New York: G. W. Carleton & Co., 1881. 178 p. CU, HEH, LC, N, O, Y
At head of title: "I'm fur 'Im."

4880 SHARKEY, MRS. TALLULA K. Mate to Mate: A Novel ... New York: G. P. Putnam's Sons, 1879. 390 p. LC

SHARP, WILLIAM, jt. au. See Teuffel, B. W. H. A Fellowe and His Wife (1892), No. 5413.

4881 SHAW, EDWARD RICHARD. Legends of Fire Island Beach and the South Side ... New York: Lovell, Coryell & Company, 310-318 Sixth Avenue [cop. 1895]. 212 p., illus. BA, CU, H, HEH, LC, O, UM
Contents: The Pot of Gold—The Bogy of the Teach—The Mower's Phantom—Enchanted Treasure—The Money Ship—Widow Molly—The Mineral-Rod—Notes.

4882 ——— The Pot of Gold: A Story of Fire Island Beach ... Chicago, New York, and San Francisco: Belford, Clarke and Co. [cop. 1888]. 162 p., illus. AP, HEH, LC
Also contains: Widow Molly.
Both stories later printed in No. 4881.

4883 SHAW, MARIAN. Queen Bess; or, What's in a Name ... New York and London: G. P. Putnam's Sons; the Knickerbocker Press, 1885. 301 p.
AP, LC, O

4884 SHAW, W. J. Old Anthony's Secret: A Kentucky Love Tale Based on Our System of Judicial Robbery and a Crime Unparalleled ... Cincinnati, O.: Published by the author, 1888. 216 p. LC

4885 ——— Solomon's Story: A Novel ... Cincinnati: Peter G. Thomson, 1880. 415 p., illus. H, HEH, LC, UVB
Western life; St. Louis.

4886 [———] Under the Auroras: A Marvellous Tale of the Interior World ... New York: Excelsior Publishing House, 29 & 31 Beekman Street [cop. 1888]. 376 p., illus. LC
Deposited Apr. 9, 1888.
Also published as: Cresten, Queen of the Toltus; or, Under the Auroras. 3rd ed. New York: Excelsior Publishing House [cop. 1892]. LC, UM
Deposited June 20, 1892.

4887 SHEDD, HARRY GRAVES. Over Grass-Grown Trails ... Lincoln, Neb., U.S.A.: The Kiote Publishing Co., 1900. 174 p., 1 l. HEH, LC, N, Y
Contents: After Ten Years—The Coward—At Dawn of Day—The Blizzard—Ashley—His Love for the People—"Cherrybeak" Stewart, Barnacle.

SHEFFIELD, ALFRED DWIGHT. At "The Temple of Unending Peace." In New Stories from the Chap-Book (1898), No. 3949.

4888   SHELDON, CHARLES MONROE. Born to Serve ... Chicago: Advance Publishing Co. London, England: The Authors' Syndicate, 1900. 246 p.
LC

4889   ———— The Crucifixion of Philip Strong ... Chicago: A. C. McClurg and Company, 1894. 267 p.                HEH, LC, Y

4890   ———— Edward Blake, College Student ... Chicago: Advance Publishing Company, 1900. 281 p., front.        H, HEH, LC

4891   ———— For Christ and the Church ... Chicago, New York, Toronto: Fleming H. Revell Company, 1899. 42 p.      BU, HEH, LC, UV, Y

4892   ———— In His Steps: "What Would Jesus Do?" ... Chicago: Advance Publishing Co., 1897. 282 p.          H, N, UVB

4893   ———— John King's Question Class ... Chicago: Advance Publishing Co., 215 Madison Street [cop. 1899]. 283 p.      BU, HEH, LC

4894   ———— Malcom Kirk: A Tale of Moral Heroism Overcoming the World ... Chicago: Advance Publishing Co., 1900. 264 p., illus.   LC

4895   ———— The Miracle at Markham: How Twelve Churches Became One ... Chicago: Advance Publishing Co., 1900. 314, [2] p., illus.   LC

4896   ———— One of the Two ... Chicago, New York, Toronto: Fleming H. Revell Company [cop. 1898]. 50 p.      BU, LC, UM, Y

4897   ———— The Redemption of Freetown ... Chicago: Advance Publishing Co., 1899. 64 p., illus.        H, HEH, UM
First published by the United Society of Christian Endeavor [cop. 1898].
LC

4897a  ———— Robert Hardy's Seven Days: A Dream and Its Consequences ... Chicago: Advance Publishing Co., 1899. 238 p.           O
First published by the Congregational Sunday School, 1893.

SHELDON, MRS. GEORGIE, *pseud.* See Downs, Sarah Elizabeth (Forbush)

4898   SHELDON, LOUISE (VESCELIUS). An I. D. B. in South Africa ... New York: John W. Lovell Company, 14 and 16 Vesey Street [cop. 1888]. 206 p., illus.          BA, BU, LC, UM
Deposited Feb. 18, 1889.

4899   SHELDON, RUTH LOUISE. Flexible Morals ... New York: H. I. Kimball, 1898. 284, [1] p.                 LC
Of a woman.

4900   ———— Red, White, & Blue Days ... New York: H. Ingalls Kimball, 1898. 230 p., 1 l.              HEH, LC
One woman's life.

4901 SHELHAMER, MARY THERESA. Outside the Gates, and Other Tales and Sketches. By a Band of Spirit Intelligences, through the Mediumship of Mary Theresa Shelhamer ... Boston: Colby & Rich, 1887. 515 p.
HEH, LC

Contents: PART I: Thoughts from a Spirit's Standpoint—Outside the Gates—What I Found in Spirit Life. PART II: Morna's Story—Here and Beyond—Slippery Places—The Blind Clairvoyant.

4902 SHELLEY, MORTIMER M. Blobson's Dire Mishaps in a Barn Storming Company: This Story Deals with the Humorous as Well as the Serious Side of a Barn Storming Company on Its Travels ... New York: M. M. Shelley, cop. 1890. 186, 32, [3] p., illus.          BU, HEH, UC, UM, Y

Separately paged material at end gives excerpts from his proposed publication "Shelley's History of the American Stage ... 1750 to 1891."

SHELTON, HERBERT, pseud. See Black, Robert Lee

4903 SHELTON, KESIAH. Our Peggotties ... New York: The Authors' Publishing Company, Bond Street [cop. 1878]. 249 p.          HEH, LC

4904 SHELTON, WILLIAM HENRY. A Man without a Memory, and Other Stories ... New York: Charles Scribner's Sons, 1895. 330 p.
HEH, LC, O, Y

Also contains: The Wedding Journey of Mrs. Zaintree—Uncle Obadiah's Uncle Billy—The Missing Evidence in "The People vs. Dangerking"—"The Demented Ones"—The Horses That Responded—"Lights Out! 'Liz'-beth Rachael"—The Widow of the General—The Adventures of Certain Prisoners.

SHEPARD, CHARLES O. In a Bowery Regiment. War Tales. [Two stories.] In Tales from McClure's: War (1898), No. 5364.

4905 [SHEPHERD, ELIZABETH LEE (KIRKLAND).] Boss. By Odette Tyler [pseud.]. New York and London: The Transatlantic Publishing Company, 1896. 215 p.          H, LC

4906 SHEPPARD, ANTOINETTE. The Heroine of Santiago de Cuba (A Sequel); or, What Followed the Sinking of the Merrimac ... New York: The Abbey Press, 114 Fifth Avenue. London, Montreal [cop. 1900]. 260 p.
LC

4907 [SHEPPARD, MRS. LYDIA H.] Gold and Guilt; or, The Mystery at Norwood ... Philadelphia: James A. Moore, 1877. 288 p., illus.
HEH, LC, O

Blue Ridge Mountains of Virginia.

4908 SHEPPARD, NATHAN HOYT. The Christ Revenge: A Tale of Intemperance and Impurity ... South Bend, Indiana: N. H. Sheppard, 1897. 207 p., illus.          LC

SHERIDAN, EMMA V. A Choice. In F. E. McKay, ed., Vignettes [cop. 1890], No. 3523.

4909   [SHERIDAN, EUGENE.]   A False Couple: A Novelization of the Drama "A False Couple" . . . New York: Exchange Publishing Company, 54 Broad Street [cop. 1889].   227 p.                          LC

4910   [SHERMAN, CHARLES POMEROY.]   A Bachelor's Wedding Trip.   By Himself . . . Philadelphia: The Pen Publishing Company, 1888.   214, [4] p.
                                                                   LC, O
Designed as an advertisement of a New York insurance company.

        SHERMAN, FRANK DEMPSTER.   "Ise Gwine ter Puff Dem Weed."   In Stories from the Harvard Advocate (1896), No. 5277a.

4911   [SHERMAN, MISS FRANKIE B.]   For Him; or, A Promise Given and a Promise Kept.   By Gipsy [pseud.].   Chicago and New York: Brentano Bros., 1887.   265 p.                          LC

4911a  SHERMAN, HERBERT LEROY.   The King of Cuba . . . New York: F. Tennyson Neely, 114 Fifth Avenue.   Chicago, London [cop. 1899].   326 p.                                           HEH
Spanish-American War.

4912   [SHERMAN, MRS. MILLIE.]   Quizma.   [Milwaukee: Godfrey & Crandall, printers, 1878.]   355 p., front.                          LC

4913   [SHERWIN, MRS. D. S.]   Why? or, Tried in the Crucible.   By D. S. S. . . . Boston: James H. Earle, 178 Washington Street [cop. 1884].   321 p.                                           HEH, LC, O
Religious novel.

4914   [SHERWOOD, MARGARET POLLOCK.]   An Experiment in Altruism.   By Elizabeth Hastings [pseud.] . . . New York and London: Macmillan and Co., 1895.   215 p.                          BA, BU, HEH, LC
Of mission work in the slums.

4915   ———   Henry Worthington, Idealist . . . New York: The Macmillan Company.   London: Macmillan & Co., Ltd., 1899.   294 p.
                                           BU, CU, H, HEH, LC, O, UC, UV, Y
A study of business methods.

4916   ———   A Puritan Bohemia . . . New York: The Macmillan Company. London: Macmillan & Co., Ltd., 1896.   191 p.                          HEH, LC, O
Of New England artists.

4917   [SHERWOOD, MARY ELIZABETH (WILSON).]   The Sarcasm of Destiny; or, Nina's Experience.   A Novel.   By M. E. W. S. . . . New York: D. Appleton and Company, 1878.   389 p.                          CU, H, HEH, N, O, Y

4918   ———   Sweet-Brier . . . Boston: D. Lothrop Company, Washington Street opposite Bromfield [cop. 1889].   262 p., illus.                          CU, H, LC, O, UV

4919 [————] A Transplanted Rose: A Story of New York Society. New York: Harper & Brothers, 1882. 307 p.   AP, BA, BU, H, HEH, LC, O, UVB
A western girl in New York society.

SHERWOOD, S. V. The Claim of the Heathen. A Question of Science. A Smile of Fortune. [Three stories.] *In* At Wellesley (1896), No. 151.

SHEVITCH, S., *jt. au. See* Ventura, L. D. Misfits and Remnants (1886), No. 5670.

4920 SHIBLEY, FRED WARNER. A Bundle of Yarns . . . Providence: H. Gregory, 1899. 249, [1] p.   BU, CU, H, HEH, LC, N, O
*Contents:* Me an' Ed an' Jane—Goin' to Market—The Chivaree—The Schoolmarm—The Colt with the Tough Mouth—Scarin' the Duke—The Remarkable Taste of Ebenezer Brown—When Me an' Ed Got Religion—The Persuasive Eloquence of John Wesley Cuff—The Tale of a Strange Bed—The Cold Girl from Bald Mountain—The Calgary Poet—The Willipers at Newport—The Willipers at the Pier—The Willipers' Thanksgiving—The Wolf at the Door.

SHINN, MILICENT WASHBURN. Young Strong of "The Clarion." *In* Stories by American Authors, IX (1885), No. 5275.

4921 SHIPE, MRS. MARY MAGDALENE. Clinta; or, The Inside of Life . . . Baltimore: Wm. J. C. Dulany Company, 1899. 88 p.   LC

4922 SHIPMAN, LOUIS EVAN. D'Arcy of the Guards; or, The Fortunes of War . . . Chicago and New York: Herbert S. Stone and Company, 1899. 237, [1] p.   BA, CU, H, HEH, LC, N, UV, Y
Philadelphia during the American Revolution.

4923 ———— Predicaments . . . New York: Life Publishing Company, 1899. 152 p., illus.   H, HEH, LC, UP, Y

4924 ———— Urban Dialogues . . . New York: Stone & Kimball, 1896. 115 p., 1 l., illus.   BA, CU, H, HEH, LC, UC, Y

SHIPP, MAY LOUISE, *jt. au. See* Judah, Mrs. M. J. The Outcomings of Addisonville (1892), No. 3045.

4925 SHIPPEN, EDWARD. A Christmas at Sea . . . Philadelphia: L. R. Hamersly & Co., 1882. 204 p.   CU, LC

4926 ———— Thirty Years at Sea: The Story of a Sailor's Life . . . Philadelphia: J. B. Lippincott & Co., 1879. 380 p., illus.   AP, BA, HEH, LC, Y

SHIRLEY, PHILIP, *pseud. See* Townsend, Mrs. Anne Lake

4927 SHORES, HERMAN. The Keys of Fate: A Novel . . . Boston, Mass.: Arena Publishing Co., 1895. 345 p.   LC

4928 SHORT, WILLIAM F., JR. Costigan's Funeral, and Other Stories . . .Jacksonville, Ill.: Henderson & Depew, 1898. [123] p., illus.    LC

*Also contains:* The Young Assistant Rector Makes a Bid for a Church—A Case of Mistaken Identity; or, Terrible Tom's Last Raid—A Colossal Wolf Fight—Not Anxious about Mr. Champlin—Mr. Champlin Should Have Spoken—Mr. Champlin's Twin Calves.

4929 SHORT STORIES BY CALIFORNIA AUTHORS . . . San Francisco: Golden Era, 1885. 180 p.    CU, H, HEH, Y

*Contents:* Portrait of a California Girl, by Ella Sterling Cummins [i.e., Ella Sterling Clark Mighels]—Quartz, by J. W. Gally—Mea Culpa, by W. S. Green—Liz, by Mary Willis Glascock—Miranda Higgins, by William Atwell Cheney—The Marquis of Aguayo, by Henry B. McDowell—A Sensation in the Orange Groves, by Ben C. Truman—Nathan, the Jew, by Harr Wagner.

4930 SHORT STORIES FROM OUTING . . . New York and London: The Outing Publishing Company [cop. 1895]. 158, 189 p., illus.    HEH

*Contents:* PART I: Donald Grey (The Luck of a Good for Nothing), by A. B. Ward [i.e., Alice W. Bailey]—Rev. Dr. Black, by Alfred A. Gardner—Fidèle, by A. A. Gardner—Two Year Old Heroine, by Francis Trevelyan—Racing at Southern Fairs, by F. Trevelyan—Over a Cigar, by Fox Russell—Jack Lindsay, by F. Trevelyan. PART II: A Comedy of Counterplots, by Edgar Fawcett—Pastelle, by Clara Sprague Ross—A Medley of the Midway Plaisance, by A. B. Ward [i.e., Alice W. Bailey]—A Very Strange Case, by William Hinckley—The Flagelante's Sin, by Theresa M. Randall—The Letter of Credit, by Charles C. Nott, Jr.—The Ghost at White Bear, by Franklyn W. Lee.

4931 SHORT STORY MASTERPIECES. By the Best American Authors . . . Chicago: Daily Story Publishing Co., 1900. 325 p., illus.    LC, O

*Contents:* By Uncomprehended Ways, by Octave Thanet [i.e., Alice French]—Eliza Sam, by Mary E. Wilkins [Freeman]—Alouette's Warning, by Gen. Charles King—When Tom's Luck Changed, by Opie Read—A Held-Up Ball Gown, by Elizabeth Phipps Train—An Idyll of Mesquiteland, by H. S. Canfield—A Girl and a Copyright, by Stanley Waterloo—A Passage in the Life of an Honest Man, by Howard Fielding [i.e., Charles W. Hooke]—Shiner's Love-Making in a Crowd, by George Ade—Old Hank and His Money, by [Fred] Hayden Carruth—Old Clockwork, by Julia Truitt Bishop—As the Curtain Fell, by Mrs. Gen. George E. [i.e., La Salle Corbell] Pickett—The Atonement, by Garrard Harris—The Miracle of Love, by Elizabeth M. Gilmer—The Museme with the Silver Heart, by William Ray Gardiner—The Guidon of the Grays, by Gen. C. King—Why Judge Dutton Resigned, by Helen H. Gardener—Tongue of Flame, by Elizabeth Cherry Waltz—The Night of a Thousand Years, by Irving Bacheller—Where Love Was Blind, by John Habberton—The Princess Yepti, by O. Read—A Fair Exchange, by Martha McCulloch Williams—When the Chance God Slept, by H. S. Canfield—Their Lives and Letters, by Henry Gallup Paine—Old Majah Chaffee, by Elia W. Peattie—Debtors to Chance, by Elizabeth P. Train—A Glimpse of Bohemia, by Albert Bigelow Paine—Flora and Hannah, by Mary E. Wilkins [Freeman]—The Rose of Hell, by Mrs. Gen. George E. [i.e., La Salle Corbell] Pickett—Patty's First Call-Out, by Jeannette Hadermann Walworth—The General Hatred of Mr. Darby, by G. Ade—She Who Listened, by Mrs. Wade Hampton, Jr.—Half Devil, Half Child, by Octave Thanet [i.e., Alice French]—On the Woodbrook Accommodation, by Lynn Roby Meekins—

Between the Acts, by Walker Kennedy—Easter Day, by Elizabeth P. Train —A New Year's Resolution, by Mary E. Wilkins [Freeman]—The Sheridan Romance, by Gen. C. King.

*Also issued with imprint:* Chicago: Jamieson-Higgins Co., 1900.   H, HEH

SHORTCUT, DAISY, *pseud.*   *See* Cohen, David Solis

4932   [SHOVE, CARRIE L.]   Connubial Bliss: Passages in the Lives of Alice and Arthur . . .   Chicago: Rhodes & McClure, 1882.   191 p., illus.   LC

4933   [————]   Wedded and Saved! Spreading the Toils. Cruelly Wronged. The Sport of Fortune. Her Mistake. A Secret Engagement . . . Chicago: Rhodes & McClure, 1882.   450 p.
Information from LC card; no copy seen.

4934   SHREWDER, *Col.* H. CLAY, *pseud?*   The Carpet-Bagger: An Autobiography . . . Washington: R. O. Polkinhorn & Son, printers, 1884.   236 p.   Y
Burlesque account of life in Salt Lake City.

4935   SHRIVER, JOHN SHULTZ.   Almost: A Novel . . . Baltimore: Lombard, Druid & Co., 1888.   200 p., illus.   LC

4936   SHUEY, LILLIAN (HINMAN).   David of Juniper Gulch: A Story of the Placer Regions of California . . .   Chicago: Laird & Lee [cop. 1894]. 413 p., illus.   HEH

4937   ————   Don Luis' Wife: A Romance of the West Indies . . .   Boston, New York, and London: Lamson, Wolffe and Company, 1897.   235 p.
BU, H, HEH, LC, UM, Y

4938   SHUGERT, FANNY ALRICKS.   The Day Breaketh . . .   A Tale of Jerusalem and Rome in the Days of Christ . . .   Philadelphia: Henry Altemus, 1898. 291 p.   LC

4939   SHUMARD, JOHN H.   The Ford Policy; or, A True Life Insurance Story . . .   Cincinnati: Standard Publishing Company, 1890.   137 p.   LC

SIDNEY, *pseud.*   The Magic City.   *In* Mavericks (1892), No. 3663.

SIDNEY, MARGARET, *pseud.*   *See* Lothrop, Harriet Mulford (Stone)

SILVA, GORHAM, *pseud.*   *See* Lawrence, Elizabeth

4940   SIMMONDS, S. E.   Shifting Shadows: A Tale of Real Life . . .   Cincinnati: Standard Publishing Co., 1889.   276 p.   LC
Story opens at Miami College.

4941   [SIMMONS, VESTA S.]   Green Tea: A Love Story.   By V. Schallenberger [pseud.?].   New York: Cassell Publishing Company, 104 & 106 Fourth Avenue [cop. 1892].   187 p.   BA, H, LC

At head of title: "The 'Unknown' Library."

Deposited Oct. 22, 1892.

It has not been determined whether V. Schallenberger is pseud. or author's maiden name.

California ranch life.

4941a [————] ———— New York: Cassell Publishing Company, 104 & 106 Fourth Avenue [cop. 1892]. 190 p.     HEH
At head of title: "The 'Unknown' Library."
Cover imprint: New York: The Cassell Publishing Co., 31 East 17th St. (Union Square).
This ed. printed about 1895, adds chap. xix, "Will O'Halloran," pp. [188]-190.

4942 ———— A Village Drama ... New York: The Cassell Publishing Co., 31 East 17th St. (Union Square) [cop. 1896]. 199 p.     LC
At head of title: "The 'Unknown' Library."
Deposited Mar. 2, 1896.

4943 SIMMS, MARGARET D. What Will She Do? A Romance of Southern Life ... New York: The Abbey Press, 114 Fifth Avenue. London, Montreal [cop. 1900]. 216 p.     LC

4944 SIMONDS, WILLIAM EDWARD. The Home-Coming of Thorstein Ericsson ... Galesburg, Illinois: [Press of the Wagoner-Mehler Co.], 1897. Cover title, [12] p., 1 l., illus.     HEH
Page [1]: "A Little Story written at the bidding of a Friend and now reprinted in a 'Limited Edition' (twenty-five copies) ... [as a] Christmas Greeting. ..."

4945 SIMPLETON, *Major, pseud.* Civil-Service Reform; or, The Postmaster's Revenge. Written for the Half-Breeds at the Request of Some Stalwarts ... New York: Metropolitan Publishing Company, 1882. 106, [3] p.     O, UVB

4946 SIMPSON, CHARLES H. Life in the Far West; or, A Detective's Adventures among the Indians and Outlaws of Montana ... Chicago: Rhodes & McClure Publishing Company, 1896. 264 p., illus.     LC, Y

4947 ———— Life in the Mines; or, Crime Avenged. Including Thrilling Adventures among Miners and Outlaws ... Chicago: Rhodes & McClure Publishing Company, 1898. 343 p., illus.     LC, Y

4948 [SIMPSON, MRS. EVANGELINE M.] Marplot Cupid. By Van Saxon [pseud.] ... Boston, 1883. 276 p.     H, HEH
Summer resort on the Maine coast.

4949 [SIMPSON, WILLIAM.] The Man from Mars, His Morals, Politics, and Religion. By Thomas Blot [pseud.]. San Francisco: Bacon & Company, printers, 1891. 173 p.     HEH, LC

4950 SINCLAIR, ELLERY. Christie's Choice . . . New York: Thomas R. Knox & Co., successors to James Miller, 1886. 295 p.  HEH
Before and during the Civil War; Texas to Virginia.

4951 —— Victor . . . New York: Cassell & Company, Limited, 739 & 741 Broadway [cop. 1887]. 351 p.  AP, HEH, LC, O
Civil War background; the South.

4952 SISSON, S. ELIZABETH. Gathered Thistles; or, A Story of Two Households . . . Fremont, Neb.: Hammond Brothers, 1897. 275 p.  HEH
Covers 50 years in Illinois.

4953 SITES, I. A. Ned Hampden; or, The Ravages of Intemperance. With a Plea for Prohibition of the Liquor Traffic . . . Reading, Pa.: Daniel Miller, 1893. 274 p., front.  LC, UM

SKEEL, ADELAIDE. See Kelley, Adelaide (Skeel)

4953a SKILLMAN, PHIL. A Living Dead Man; or, The Strange Case of Moses Scott. An Accurate and Truthful Narration of the Complications Caused by a Litigant's Return from the Lethean Shore . . . By Phil. Skillman, Olympia, Wash. Albany, N.Y.: Albany Law Journal Co., 1897. 81 p.  HEH

SKINNER, CHARLES MONTGOMERY. A Deed with a Capital D. In Ten Notable Stories (1894), No. 5391.

4954 SKINNER, HENRIETTA CHANNING (DANA). Espíritu Santo: A Novel . . . New York and London: Harper & Brothers, 1899. 328, [1] p.
BA, H, HEH, LC, N, O, UM
SKINNER, MOSE, pseud. See Brown, James E.

4955 SLATER, CHARLES WILLIAM. A Modern Babylon: A Tale of the Metropolis . . . Poughkeepsie, N.Y.: Queen City Publishing Company, 1897. 189 p.  LC
Advertised in the above is his Saints or Sinners; not found.

4956 SLEE, RICHARD. Dr. Berkeley's Discovery. By Richard Slee and Cornelia Atwood Pratt. New York and London: George P. Putnam's Sons; the Knickerbocker Press, 1899. 219 p.  H, HEH, LC
Cornelia Atwood Pratt Comer, jt. au.
Science fiction.

4957 SLEIGHT, MARY BRECK. The Flag on the Mill . . . New York and London: Funk & Wagnalls, 1887. 455 p., illus.  LC

4958 —— The House at Crague; or, Her Own Way . . . New York: Thomas Y. Crowell & Co., 13 Astor Place [cop. 1886]. 362 p.
AP, H, HEH, LC, O

494

4959 ——— An Island Heroine: The Story of a Daughter of the Revolution
... Boston: Lothrop Publishing Company [cop. 1898]. 432 p., illus.

H, HEH, LC

Of the occupation of Long Island by the British.

4960 ——— Pulpit and Easel ... New York: Thomas Y. Crowell & Co., 13
Astor Place [cop. 1885]. 301 p., front.

Copy examined at Boston Public Library.

4961 SLENKER, ELMINA (DRAKE). The Darwins: A Domestic Radical Romance ... New York: D. M. Bennett, 1879. 257 p.         CU, HEH

4962 ——— John's Way: A Domestic Radical Story ... New York: Published at the Truth Seeker Office, 28 Lafayette Place [1884?]. 96 p.

CU, H

4963 SLOCOMB, CORA. An American Idyll ... Boston: Arena Publishing Co.,
1896. 244 p., illus.

Listed PW, Feb. 13, 1897.

Also published as: *Ampharita: An American Idyll. By the Countess di Braz-
zà (Cora Slocomb)*. New York City: Peace Bureau, 1897.    BU, HEH

SLOPER, JOEL, *pseud. See* Peters, William Andrew

4964 SLOSSON, ANNIE (TRUMBULL). Anna Malann . . . Hartford, Conn.:
Press of the Case, Lockwood, & Brainard Company, 1894. 40 p.

At head of title: "From Harper's Bazaar."

Copy examined at New York Public Library.

Later printed in No. 4966.

4965 ——— Aunt Liefy ... New York: Anson D. F. Randolph & Co. (Incorporated), 182 Fifth Avenue [cop. 1892]. 50 p., illus.

HEH, LC, UM, UP, Y

Later printed in No. 4966.

4966 ——— Dumb Foxglove, and Other Stories ... New York and London: Harper & Brothers, 1898. 217, [1] p., front.

BA, CU, H, HEH, LC, O, UP, Y

*Also contains:* Apple Jonathan—Anna Malann—Davy's Christmas—Clavis—A
Transient—Aunt Liefy.

4967 ——— Fishin' Jimmy ... New York: Anson D. F. Randolph & Co.,
182 Fifth Avenue [cop. 1889]. 53 p., illus.

CU, H, HEH, LC, UC, UP, UVB, Y

Deposited July 10, 1889.

BA, BU, O, Y have copies with publisher's address "38 West Twenty-Third
Street."

Later printed in No. 4969.

4968 —— The Heresy of Mehetabel Clark ... New York: Harper and Brothers, 1892. 103 p.    BA, CU, H, HEH, O, UM, UP, Y
White Mountains, New Hampshire.

4969 —— Seven Dreamers ... New York: Harper & Brothers, 1891. 281 p., front.    AP, CU, H, HEH, LC, N, O, UM, UP, UV, Y
*Contents:* How Faith Came and Went—Botany Bay—Aunt Randy—Fishin' Jimmy—Butterneggs—Deacon Pheby's Selfish Natur—A Speakin' Ghost.

—— A Speakin' Ghost. *In* C. C. Harrison, *ed.*, Short Stories (1893), No. 2514.
Printed earlier in No. 4969.

4970 —— Story-Tell Lib ... New York: Charles Scribner's Sons, 1900. 79 p., front.    BU, HEH, LC, UC
*Also contains:* The Shet-Up Posy—The Horse That B'leeved He'd Get There —The Plant That Lost Its Berry—The Stony Head—Diff'ent Kind o' Bundles —The Boy That Was Scaret o' Dyin'.

4971 SLUGGERVAN, JOHN L., *pseud.* De Recomembrances of a 19-Cent Scrapper ... New York: Athletic Publishing League, 1892. 109 p., illus.    LC

4972 [SMALL, GEORGE G.] A Bachelor's Love Scrapes. By "Bricktop" [pseud.] ... New York: Frank Tousey, 34 and 36 North Moore Street [cop. 1883]. 54 p., illus.    LC

4973 [——] The Bald-Headed Club; or, The Shining Lights of Society. By "Bricktop" [pseud] ... New York: Frank Tousey, 20 Rose Street, 1881. 58 p., illus.    H, LC
HEH has copy with publisher's address "34 and 36 North Moore Street."

4974 [——] A Bald-Headed History of America. By the Bald-Headed Historian "Bricktop" [pseud.] ... New York: Collin & Small, 1876. Cover title, 63 p., illus.    N, O
Also published as: *Bricktop's Comic History of America.* New York: J. B. Collin, 1884.    LC

4975 [——] Going to the Centennial, and a Guy to the Great Exhibition. By Bricktop [pseud.] ... New York: Collin & Small, 1876. 58 p., illus.    H, HEH, Y

4976 [——] Going to the Country; or, Smudge in Search of Comfort. By Bricktop [pseud.] ... New York: Tousey & Small, 1878. 60 p., illus.    LC

4977 [——] Good Templars Exposed. By Bricktop [pseud.] ... New York: Tousey & Small, 1878. 60 p., illus.    H, LC

4978 [———] Hell. By Bricktop [pseud.] . . . New York: Tousey & Small, 1878. 64 p., illus.                                    LC
H has copy with title *H–l.*

4979 ——— "I Told You So"; or, The Beats and Baits of Society . . . New York: Collin & Small [1876?]. 91 p.
Listed in *The American Catalogue . . . 1876* (New York, 1880).

4980 [———] Joining the Freemasons; or, Getting It All. By "Bricktop" [pseud.] . . . New York: Frank Tousey, 34 and 36 North Moore Street [cop. 1882]. 53 p., illus.                                    LC

4981 [———] Joining the Militia; or, Comic Adventures of a Recruit . . . New York: L. H. Halsey & Co., 1879. 62 p., illus.                                    LC

4982 [———] The Life of Hungry Joe, King of the Bunco Men . . . New York: Frank Tousey, 34 and 36 North Moore Street [cop. 1885]. 41 p., illus.                                    LC

4983 [———] My Birthday. By Bricktop [pseud.] . . . New York: Frank Tousey, 34 and 36 North Moore Street [cop. 1883]. 53 p., illus.    LC

4984 [———] My Wife's Mother. By "Bricktop" [pseud.] . . . New York: Frank Tousey, 1881. 59 p., illus.                                    LC

4985 [———] On a Jury. By "Bricktop" [pseud.] . . . New York: Frank Tousey, 1881. 61 p., illus.                                    H, LC

4986 [———] Our First Baby; or, Infelicities of Our Honeymoon . . . New York: M. J. Ivers & Co., 86 Nassau Street [cop. 1887]. 64 p., illus.    LC

4987 [———] Our Servant Girls. By "Bricktop" [pseud.] . . . New York: Frank Tousey, 34 and 36 North Moore Street [cop. 1882]. 53 p., illus.                                    LC

4988 [———] A Quiet Fourth of July. By "Bricktop" [pseud.] . . . New York: Tousey & Small, 1878. 60 p., illus.                                    LC

4989 [———] The Quiet Youth; or, Just Like His Uncle. By Bricktop [pseud.] . . . New York: J. B. Collin, 1881. 52 p., illus. Printed in double columns.                                    LC

4990 [———] Smith in Search of a Wife. By Bricktop [pseud.]. New York: Collin & Small, 1876. 59 p., illus.                                    UM

4991 [———] "Them Thar" Grasshoppers. By Bricktop [pseud.]. New York: Collin & Small [1876?]. Illus.
Listed in *The American Catalogue . . . 1876* (New York, 1880).

4992 [———] Trip to Niagara Falls. By Bricktop [pseud.]. New York: Collin & Small, 1876. 64 p., illus.
Listed in *The American Catalogue ... 1876* (New York, 1880).

4993 [———] The Troubles of Mr. and Mrs. Tumbleton. By "Bricktop" [pseud.] ... New York: F. Tousey [1894]. 48 p., illus.          LC

4994 [———] Where Are You Going? By "Bricktop" [pseud.] ... New York: Frank Tousey, 34 and 36 North Moore Street [cop. 1882]. 60 p., illus.          HEH

4995 SMALL, SAMUEL WHITE. Humorous Sketches of "Old Si" ... Written When He Was "A Wicked Newspaper Man." New York: Frank A. Small, 1886. 95, [1] p.          HEH, LC

4996 [SMILIE, ELTON R.] Investigations and Experience of M. Shawtinbach at Saar Soong, Sumatra ... San Francisco: Joseph Winterburn & Company, printers and electrotypers, 1879. 263 p.          LC, N

4997 ——— The Manatitlans; or, A Record of Recent Scientific Explorations in the Andean La Plata, S.A. .... Cambridge: Printed at the Riverside Press, 1877. 478 p.          LC

4998 SMITH, A. F. Ernest Leighton ... St. Louis: Christian Publishing Co., 1881. 336 p.          LC
New York, 1832-45.

4999 [SMITH, ANDREW MADSEN.] Luck of a Wandering Dane. By Hans Lykkejaeger [pseud.] ... Philadelphia: Matlack & Harvey, printers, cop. 1885. 130 p., illus.          H, LC, N, UM

5000 SMITH, ANN ELIZA (BRAINERD). Atla: A Story of the Lost Island. By Mrs. J. Gregory Smith ... New York: Harper & Brothers, 1886. 284 p.          BU, H, HEH, LC, O

5001 [———] Seola. Boston: Lee and Shepard. New York: Charles T. Dillingham, 1878. 251 p.          CU, HEH, LC, O

5002 SMITH, ARTHUR COSSLETT. The Monk and the Dancer ... New York: Charles Scribner's Sons, 1900. 241 p., 1 l.          BA, H, HEH, UP, UV, Y
*Also contains:* Trot, Trot to Market—The Peach—The Senior Reader—Some Old Families—The Eye of the Harem.

5003 SMITH, BENJAMIN GEORGE. From over the Border; or, Light on the Normal Life of Man ... Chicago: Charles H. Kerr & Company, 1890. 238 p.          LC
Of life after death.

SMITH, BRAINARD GARDNER. A Tragedy of High Explosives. *In* Eleven Possible Cases [cop. 1891], No. 1737.

5004 SMITH, CARRIE CLAY. Passing Shadows and a Life's Sorrow ... Macon, Missouri: The Times Publishing House, 1892. 234 p.     HEH, N

5005 [SMITH, CHARLES HENRY.] Bill Arp's [pseud.] Scrap Book: Humor and Philosophy. Letters "Pendente Lite," Letters Historic, Domestic, and Pastoral, with Some True Stories Added ... Atlanta, Georgia: Jas. P. Harrison & Co., 1884. 405 p., illus.     HEH, LC, N, UM, UV, Y

5006 ———— The Farm and the Fireside: Sketches of Domestic Life in War and in Peace ... Atlanta, Georgia: The Constitutional Publishing Company, 1891. 345 p., illus.     CU, LC, N

5007 SMITH, CHARLES SUMNER. Ten Years in Love ... Blocton, Alabama: The C. S. Smith Printing and Publishing Co., 1900. 163 p.     LC

5008 SMITH, EDWARD J. Jo: A Telegraphic Tale ... Fort Worth: Ed. J. Smith & Co., 1885. 211 p., front.     HEH, LC

5009 [SMITH, MRS. ELVIRA V.] Gretta Alone; or, The Environments of Life. By Dorathy Dott [pseud.]. Forest, Ohio: Published by Mrs. Josiah Smith [cop. 1890]. 226 p.     HEH, LC

5010 [SMITH, EMERY P.] The Triple Wedding; or, Secrets Revealed ... Chicago: Emery P. Smith & Co., 1892. 304 p.     LC
At head of title: "True Story by a Clergyman."

SMITH, EMMA POW. *See* Bauder, Emma Pow (Smith)

SMITH, ESTHER LOUISE, *jt. au. See* McCray, F. T. Wheels and Whims (1884), No. 3493.

SMITH, MRS. F. BURGE. *See* Griswold, Frances Irene (Burge) Smith

5011 [SMITH, FANNIE N.] Peace Pelican, Spinster: A Love Story. By Christabel Goldsmith [pseud.] ... New York: G. W. Carleton & Co. London: S. Low, Son & Co., 1881. 396 p.     LC, Y

5012 SMITH, FRANCIS HOPKINSON. Caleb West, Master Diver ... Boston and New York: Houghton, Mifflin and Company. The Riverside Press, Cambridge, 1898. 378 p., 1 l., illus.
AP, BA, BU, CU, H, HEH, LC, N, O, UM, UP, UVB, Y
The building of a lighthouse.

5013 ———— Colonel Carter of Cartersville ... Boston and New York: Houghton, Mifflin and Company. The Riverside Press, Cambridge, 1891. 208 p., illus.     CU, H, HEH, LC, N, O, UP, UVB, Y
2nd issue moves the staircase illus. from p. 1 to p. 3. Census of copies does not distinguish between issues.

499

5014 ——— A Day at Laguerre's, and Other Days: Being Nine Sketches . . . Boston and New York: Houghton, Mifflin and Company. The Riverside Press, Cambridge, 1892. 190, [2] p.

BA, CU, H, HEH, LC, N, O, UM, UP, UVB, Y

*Also contains:* Espero Gorgoni, Gondolier—Under the Minarets—An Escapade in Cordova—La Canal de la Viga—A Bulgarian Opera Bouffe— Captain Joe—Hutchins—Six Hours in Squantico.

Census of copies does not distinguish between trade and large-paper eds.

——— Espero Gorgoni, Gondolier. *In* Stories of Italy (1893), No. 5278.

Printed earlier in No. 5014.

5015 ——— A Gentleman Vagabond, and Some Others . . . Cambridge: Printed at the Riverside Press, 1895. 182 p.

AP, CU, H, HEH, LC, N, O, UM, UP, UVB

*Also contains:* A Knight of the Legion of Honor—John Sanders, Laborer— Bäader—The Lady of Lucerne—Jonathan—Along the Bronx—Another Dog— Brockway's Hulk.

Census of copies does not distinguish between trade and large-paper eds.

5016 ——— The Other Fellow . . . Boston and New York: Houghton, Mifflin and Company. The Riverside Press, Cambridge, 1899. 218 p., 1 l., illus.　　BA, CU, H, HEH, N, O, UM, UP, UVB, Y

*Contents:* Dick Sands, Convict—A Kentucky Cinderella—A Waterlogged Town—The Boy in the Cloth Cap—Between Showers in Dort—One of Bob's Tramps—According to the Law—"Never Had No Sleep"—The Man with the Empty Sleeve—"Tincter ov Iron"—"Five Meals for a Dollar."

*Also issued with imprint:* Cambridge: Printed at the Riverside Press, 1899.

H, HEH, UP

300 copies printed.

——— The Professor on "How to Train Our Wives and Children." *In* The First Book of the Authors Club (1893), No. 1868.

5017 ——— Tom Grogan . . . Boston and New York: Houghton, Mifflin and Company. The Riverside Press, Cambridge, 1896. 246, [1] p., illus.　　BA, CU, H, HEH, LC, O, UM, UP, UVB, Y

Census of copies does not distinguish between trade and large-paper eds.

Of labor interest.

5018 SMITH, GEORGE BYRNE. Noah's Confession . . . Jamestown, N.Y.: The Cicerone Publishing Company, 1898. 218 p., illus.　　LC

5019 SMITH, GERTRUDE. Dedora Heywood . . . New York: Dodd, Mead and Company, 1896. 151, [1] p.　　H, HEH, LC, UC, Y

Of a New England town.

——— A Game Postponed. *In* Tales from McClure's: Romance (1897), No. 5362.

5020 ———— The Rousing of Mrs. Potter, and Other Stories . . . Boston and New York: Houghton, Mifflin and Company. The Riverside Press, Cambridge, 1894. 232 p.      BA, H, HEH, LC, O

*Also contains:* A Lone Old Woman—Weighed in the Balance—A Theft Condoned—A Hope Deferred—On Pawnee Prairie—Colonel Paddington's Nurse—Dan's Little Girl—An Only Son—At the Spring—Gardi.

SMITH, H. D. Tamba. *In* C. King, *ed.,* By Land and Sea (1891), No. 3092.

Later printed in No. 3099.

5021 [SMITH, H. H.] Downfall of a Politician; or, Death or Destiny. A Story of Politics, Religion, and Society. By the Hon. Bell Eli [pseud.] . . . Louisville: John P. Morton and Company, printers, 1891. 216 p. LC, UC

5022 SMITH, HARRY B. The New Don Quixote: A Continuation of Cervantes' Faithful Relation of the Most Marvelous Adventures of the Gallant Knight . . . Buffalo, N.Y.: Made in the complete art-printing works of the Matthews-Northrup Co. [cop. 1891]. 67 p., illus.      LC

Deposited Jan. 23, 1892.

5023 [SMITH, HELEN BUTLER.] A Modern Jacob. By Hester Stuart [pseud.]. Boston: D. Lothrop Company, Franklin and Hawley Streets [cop. 1888]. 209 p., front.      BU, H, HEH, LC

From an eastern farm to life in the West.

SMITH, MRS. J GREGORY. *See* Smith, Ann Eliza (Brainerd)

5024 SMITH, JABEZ BURRITT. Barriers Broken; or, Right Makes Might . . . Madison, Wisconsin: The Busy World Publishing Co. [cop. 1897]. 240 p.      LC

5024a ———— "High Joe"; or, The Logger's Story . . . Madison, Wis.: The Busy World [cop. 1892]. 240 p.      O

Temperance story.

SMITH, JAMES HARVEY. Burglars Three. *In* Tales from McClure's: Humor (1897), No. 5361.

5025 SMITH, JEANIE OLIVER (DAVIDSON.) Donald Moncrieff . . . A Companion Book to "The Mayor of Kanemeta." Buffalo: Charles Wells Moulton, 1893. 184 p.      LC

5026 ———— The Mayor of Kanemeta . . . New York: The American News Company, 1891. 239 p.      LC

SMITH, JOHN, *pseud. See* Benedict, Roswell Alphonzo

SMITH, JOHN TALBOT. The Baron of Cherubusco. *In* A Round Table of the Representative American Catholic Novelists (1897), No. 4703.

Printed earlier in No. 5027.

5027    ———— His Honor, the Mayor, and Other Tales . . . New York: The Vatican Library, 1891. 258 p., illus.         LC

*Contents:* The Deacon of Lynn—The Four Sons of Jael—One of Many—A Novel Experiment—The Baron of Cherubusco—A Voice from the Wilderness—His Honor, the Mayor—How the McGuinness Saved His Pride.

Also published as: *His Honor, the Mayor: Tales of the Puritan and His Neighbors.* 3rd ed. New York: William H. Young & Company, 1897. HEH, Y

5028    ———— Solitary Island: A Novel . . . New York: P. J. Kenedy, 1888. 393 p.         HEH

On intermarriage of Catholics and Protestants.

SMITH, JOHNSTON, *pseud. See* Crane, Stephen

5029 SMITH, MRS. JULIE P.   Blossom-Bud and Her Genteel Friends: A Story . . . New York: G. W. Carleton & Co. London: S. Low & Co., 1883. 390 p.       CU, H, HEH, LC

5030    ———— Courting and Farming; or, Which Is the Gentleman? . . . New York: G. W. Carleton & Co. London: S. Low, Son & Co., 1876. 368 p.       CU, HEH, O

5031    ———— His Young Wife: A Novel . . . New York: G. W. Carleton & Co. London: S. Low & Co., 1877. 456 p.       HEH, LC, O

5032    ———— Kiss and Be Friends: A Novel . . . New York: G. W. Carleton & Co. London: S. Low, Son & Co., 1879. 396 p.       BU, HEH, LC, O

5033    ———— Lucy: A Novel . . . New York: G. W. Carleton & Co. London: S. Low, Son & Co., 1880. 382 p.       HEH, O

5034 SMITH, MARION COUTHOUY.   Dr. Marks, Socialist . . . Cincinnati: The Editor Publishing Co., 1897. 272 p.       HEH, LC, O

5035 [SMITH, MARY E.]   Ambition's Contest; or, Faith and Intellect. By Christine Faber [pseud.]. New York: P. J. Kenedy & Sons, 44 Barclay Street [cop. 1896]. 361 p.

Copy examined at Boston Public Library; probably printed after 1900. *The Guide to Catholic Literature* (Grosse Pointe [1940]), notes *Ambition's Conquest,* by this author, published in 1891.

5036 [————]   Carroll O'Donoghue: A Tale of the Irish Struggles of 1866, and of Recent Times. By Christine Faber [pseud.] . . . New York: P. J. Kennedy, 5 Barclay Street [1881]. 501 p.       HEH, UM, Y

Listed PW, June 11, 1881.

5037 [————]   A Chivalrous Deed and What Came of It. By Christine Faber [pseud.] . . . New York: P. J. Kenedy, 1891. 456 p.       LC

5038 [————] A Fatal Resemblance: A Novel. By Christine Faber [pseud.].
New York: P. J. Kenedy, 1900. 391 p., front.
Information supplied by Helen D. Baird, St. Benedict's College Library,
Atchison, Kansas. Copy lacks title page.

5039 [————] Fickle Fortune: A Story of Place La Grêve. By Christian
Faber [pseud.]. New York, Montreal: D. & J. Sadlier & Co., 1878.
146 p.                                                      LC, UV

5040 [————] The Guardian's Mystery; or, Rejected for Consciences' Sake.
By Christine Faber [pseud.] ... New York: P. J. Kenedy & Sons [cop.
1888]. 435 p.
Copy examined at New York Public Library.

5041 [————] A Mother's Sacrifice; or, Who Was Guilty. By Christine
Faber [pseud.]. New York: P. J. Kenedy, 1885. 516 p., illus.
Listed PW, Aug. 1, 1885.
Boston Public Library has: New York: P. J. Kenedy [cop. 1891]. 369 p.

5042 [————] An Ugly Heroine: A Novel of Domestic Life. By Christine
Faber [pseud.]. Philadelphia: J. B. Lippincott & Co., 1883. 336 p.
LC, O

5043 SMITH, MRS. MARY ELLIS. A Model Actress ... [Chicago: Vollrath &
Veronee, cop. 1892.] 240 p., illus.                         LC

5044 [————] The Prince of Mull; or, Glimpses of Royal Life. By an Alien
Subject of the Crown ... Chicago: A. N. Marquis & Company, 1884.
234 p.                                                      LC

5045 [SMITH, MARY PAULINE.] Guy's Fortune. By M. B. Eagan [pseud.].
St. Louis, Mo.: B. Herder, 1900. 361 p.
Information from LC card; no copy seen.

5046 SMITH, MARY STUART (HARRISON). Lang Syne; or, The Wards of Mount
Vernon. A Tale of the Revolutionary Era ... New York: John B.
Alden, 1889. 133 p.                          CU, HEH, LC, UV
*Also contains:* The Women of the Revolution.

5047 SMITH, MINNA CAROLINE. Mary Paget: A Romance of Old Bermuda ...
New York: The Macmillan Company. London: Macmillan & Co.,
Ltd., 1900. 326 p.                   BA, CU, H, HEH, LC, O, UV

5048 SMITH, MYRA MALINDA JOHONNOT. Demands of Society ... Boston,
Mass.: A. I. Bradley & Company [cop. 1899]. 219 p., front.    LC

5049 [SMITH, NINA LARRE.] Tales of St. Augustine. By N. L. S. [Cam-
bridge, Mass.: Printed by W. H. Wheeler, 1891.] 133 p.
CU, HEH, LC, UV

*Contents:* "It Might Have Been"—Julib's "Sea-Sarpen' "—The End of an Earl-dom—Prince Charming of New York—The Romance of a Pair of Shoes—Priscilla Alden.

5050 SMITH, NORA ARCHIBALD. Under the Cactus Flag: A Story of Life in Mexico ... Boston and New York: Houghton, Mifflin and Company. The Riverside Press, Cambridge, 1899. 281, [1] p., illus.

H, HEH, LC, O, Y

5051 SMITH, OREON (MANN). The Novice. By Mrs. Rufus W. Smith (Nee Oreon Mann). La Grange, Georgia: Press of the Graphic; Cox & Ward, publishers, 1894. 372 p.

LC

5052 [SMITH, PHILIP HENRY.] The Barn-Yard Statesmen; or, Rum and Dy-namite ... Pawling, N.Y.: Philip H. Smith, 1886. 74 p.

LC

5053 SMITH, MRS. POCA T. Margoleen ... Clarkeville, Tenn.: W. P. Titus, printer and binder, 1897. 248 p., front.

LC

5054 [SMITH, R. B.] Hugging to Music: A Story from Life. By an Ameri-can Observer ... New York: University Publishing Company, 1890. 253 p., illus.

LC

5055 SMITH, ROBERT J. A Divorce Contract ... Terre Haute, Ind.: C. W. Brown, 1898. 190 p.

LC

In a western city.

5056 SMITH, SAMUEL ROBERT. Daniel North of Wyoming Valley ... Wilkes-Barre, Pa., 1897. 144 p., illus.

HEH, LC, Y

From the American Revolution to about 1800.

5057 SMITH, SAQUI. Back from the Dead: A Story of the Stage ... New York: Cassell Publishing Company, 104 & 106 Fourth Avenue [cop. 1892]. 185 p.

BA, H, O, Y

At head of title: "The 'Unknown' Library."

5058 SMITH, SARA TRAINER. Old Charlmont's Seed-Bed ... New York, Cin-cinnati: Benziger Bros., 1900. 154 p., front.

Information from LC card; no copy seen.

5059 ——— The Room of the Rose, and Other Stories ... Philadelphia: John McVey, 1900. 266 p.

HEH, LC, UP

*Also contains:* My Old Gray Plaid—Strung on a Silver Chain—A Boy and a Balcony—The Story Told to Me—Father Patrick's Burden—"One Prayer"—"A Little Fair Soul"—Miss Maria's Little Maid—Three Generations—Prison Walls—Tessa's Blossom Time—By No Means an Average Woman—One of the Family.

5060 SMITH, THOMAS EDWIN. The Wizard of Conlin: A Tale of an Election, Telling of Woman's Devotion and Man's Credulity ... [Rock Island, Ill.: La Velle Publishing Co., cop. 1899.] 189 p., front.

LC

5061 SMITH, TITUS KEIPER. Altruria . . . New York: Altruria Publishing Company, 39 Cortlandt Street [cop. 1895]. 120 p. CU, HEH, LC, N, UP, Y
A western utopian settlement.

5062 SMITH, WILLIAM A. Who Is Responsible? A Story of American Western Life . . . Boston: D. Lothrop and Company, 32 Franklin Street [cop. 1883]. 270 p., front. HEH, LC

5063 [SMITH, WILLIAM B.] Egypt Ennis; or, Prisons without Walls. A Novel. By Kelsic Etheridge [pseud.]. New York: The Authors' Publishing Company, 1876. 97 p. LC

5064 SMITH, WILLIAM HAWLEY. The Evolution of "Dodd" in His Struggle for the Survival of the Fittest in Himself, Tracing His Chances, His Changes, and How He Came Out . . . Peoria, Illinois: William Hawley Smith, 1884. 153 p. H, LC, UC, UV
Also published as: *The Evolution of "Dodd": A Pedagogical Story.* Chicago and New York: Rand, McNally & Company [cop. 1884]. 245 p.
HEH, N, O, UM, Y

5065 SMITHSON, NOBLE. Judge Ladd: A Novel . . . Knoxville, Tenn.: Ogden Bros. & Co., printers, 1900. 319 p., illus. HEH, LC
Of divorce; Virginia.

5066 SNIDER, DENTON JACQUES. Castle Esperance: A Novel of Education. Edited from a Diary Containing the Confessions of Doctor Philo Newman . . . St. Louis, Mo.: Sigma Publishing Co., 215 Pine Street [1899]. 551 p. CU, HEH

5067 ———— The Freeburgers: A Novel . . . [St. Louis, Mo.: Press of Nixon-Jones Printing Co.]; Literary School Edition, 1889. 432 p.
CU, HEH, LC, N, O, UVB
The St. Louis, Sigma Publishing Co., 210 Pine St. [cop. 1889], ed. appears to be later.
Of the Fugitive Slave Law of 1850.

5068 SNOW, CHAUNCEY EDGAR. Sister Gratia: Satan's Simplicity . . . Chicago: Charles H. Kerr and Company, 1895. 212 p. LC, Y
Of Americans in Paris.

SNOW, KEL, *Esq., pseud.* *See* Knowles, James O.

5069 SNYDER, ANN E. (HILL). My Scrap-Book . . . Nashville, Tenn.: Printed for the author, 1884. 400 p., illus. BU, HEH
Quotation from Massinger at head of title.
Contains short stories, essays, etc.

SOLA, *pseud.* *See* Anderson, Olive Santa Louise

5070 SOME SHORT STORIES . . . New York: Impressionist Publishing Co., 24 & 26 Vandewater St. [cop. 1900]. 188 p.     CU, HEH, LC

*Contains:* Ambrose's Christmas Gift, by Octave Thanet [i.e., Alice French]—Redemption, by Julien Gordon [i.e., Julie G. S. Cruger]—A Change of Temperature, by John A'Becket—A Matter of Course, by Marguerite Merington.

5071 SOMETHING BETTER. Boston: Lee and Shepard. New York: Charles T. Dillingham, 1878. 232 p.     HEH, LC

Of home life.

5072 [SOMMER, DANIEL.] Hector among the Doctors; or, A Search for the True Church. A Volume of Thoughts for Thinkers. Indianapolis, Ind.: Daniel Sommer [cop. 1896]. 256 p.     LC

5073 [———] Jehenne Lefevre; or, A Miner's Daughter. Indianapolis, Ind.: Published by Daniel Sommer [19–?]. 84 p.     LC

5074 ——— Rachel Reasoner; or, A Scriptural Daughter, Wife, and Mother . . . Indianapolis, 1900.

Listed in Banta, p. 299.

SOMMER, H. B., *jt. au. See* [Cohen, D. S.] One Hundred Years a Republic (1876), No. 1137.

5075 SOMMERS, LILLIAN E. Jerome Leaster of Roderick, Leaster & Co. . . . Chicago: Charles H. Sergel & Co., 1890. 376 p., illus.     HEH, LC

Chicago.

5076 SOUTHGATE, HORATIO. The Cross above the Crescent: A Romance of Constantinople . . . Philadelphia, London: J. B. Lippincott & Co., 1878. 359 p.     BA, HEH, LC, O

5077 SOUTHWICK, ALBERT PLYMPTON. Bijou: The Foundling of Nag's Head . . . New York: The American News Company, 1889. 186 p.     LC

5078 ——— Brown, the Lawyer: A Novel . . . New York: Franklin Publishing Company, 1893. 249 p.     LC

5079 SOUTHWICK, E. B. The Better World . . . New York: The Truth Seeker Company, 28 Lafayette Place [1895]. 375 p.     LC

Deposited Jan. 2, 1895.

5080 SOUTHWICK, LELLIE C. A Neighborhood of Girls . . . Springfield, Mo.: Jewell Publishing Company, 1896. 355 p., front.     LC

SOUTHWORTH, EMMA DOROTHY ELIZA (NEVITTE). [Sixteen of the 24 titles by Southworth herein listed were published by Robert Bonner's Sons in its subscription "Ledger Library" and "Choice Series." Four of the 16 were found in separate cloth eds., and advertisements for others indicate that possibly all were so published. The series eds. are therefore included even though no hard-cover copies have been located. Regis L. Boyle's *Mrs. E. D. E. N. Southworth, Novelist* (Washington, D.C., 1939) is helpful in determining which stories first appeared in periodicals.]

5081 —— Brandon Coyle's Wife. A Sequel to "A Skeleton in the Closet" . . . New York: Robert Bonner's Sons, 1893. 411 p., illus.
LC has copy in the "Ledger Library," No. 93.

5082 —— Broken Pledges: A Story of Noir et Blanc . . . Philadelphia: T. B. Peterson & Brothers, 306 Chestnut Street [cop. 1891]. 266 p.  LC

5083 —— David Lindsay: A Sequel to "Gloria" . . . New York: Robert Bonner's Sons, 1891. 469 p., illus.
New York Public Library has copy in the "Ledger Library," No. 49.

5084 —— "Em": A Novel . . . New York: Robert Bonner's Sons, 1892. 368 p., illus.  HEH

5085 —— Em's Husband: A Novel . . . New York: Robert Bonner's Sons, 1892. 395 p., illus.
LC has copy in the "Ledger Library," No. 75.

5086 —— The Fatal Secret. By Mrs. Emma D. E. N. Southworth . . . And Other Stories by Her Sister, Mrs. Frances Henshaw Baden . . . Philadelphia: T. B. Peterson & Brothers, 306 Chestnut Street [cop. 1877]. 374 p.  BU, CU, HEH, LC, UVB

5087 —— For Woman's Love: A Novel . . . New York: Robert Bonner's Sons, 1890. 486 p., illus.
LC has copy in the "Ledger Library," No. 18.

5088 —— Gertrude Haddon: "Only a Girl's Heart." Third Series . . . New York: Robert Bonner's Sons, 1894. 416 p., illus.  HEH

5089 —— Gloria: A Novel . . . New York: Robert Bonner's Sons, 1891. 348 p., illus.  HEH

5090 —— The Hidden Hand; or, Capitola the Madcap . . . New York: G. W. Dillingham, successor to G. W. Carleton & Co., 1888. 600 p., front.  HEH, N, UM

5091 —— Ishmael; or, In the Depths . . . Philadelphia: T. B. Peterson & Brothers, 306 Chestnut Street [cop. 1876]. 718 p., front.  CU, HEH, UVB, Y

5092 —— A Leap in the Dark: A Novel . . . New York: Robert Bonner's Sons [cop. 1889]. 556 p., front.  HEH

5093 —— Lilith: A Sequel to "The Unloved Wife" . . . New York: Robert Bonner's Sons, 1891. 399 p., illus.
LC has copy in the "Ledger Library," No. 29.

5094 —————— The Lost Lady of Lone: A Novel ... New York: Robert Bonner's Sons, 1890. 561 p.
New York Public Library has copy in the "Ledger Library," No. 16.

5095 —————— Nearest and Dearest: A Novel ... New York: Robert Bonner's Sons, 1889. 572 p., front.
Listed PW, May 24, 1890, in both cloth and paper.

5096 —————— Only a Girl's Heart: A Novel ... New York: Robert Bonner's Sons, 1893. 453 p., illus.
Information from LC card for copy in the "Choice Series," No. 99; no copy seen.

5097 —————— The Phantom Wedding; or, The Fall of the House of Flint. By Mrs. Emma D. E. N. Southworth ... And Other Stories by Her Sister, Mrs. Frances Henshaw Baden ... Philadelphia: T. B. Peterson & Brothers, 306 Chestnut Street [cop. 1878]. 370 p.     HEH, LC, Y

5098 —————— The Red Hill Tragedy: A Novel ... Philadelphia: T. B. Peterson & Brothers, 306 Chestnut Street [cop. 1877]. 266 p.     HEH, LC

5099 —————— The Rejected Bride. "Only a Girl's Heart." Second Series ... New York: Robert Bonner's Sons, 1894. 445 p., illus.
LC has copy in the "Choice Series," No. 100.

5100 —————— Self-Raised; or, From the Depths. A Sequel to Ishmael; or, In the Depths ... Philadelphia: T. B. Peterson & Brothers, 306 Chestnut Street [cop. 1876]. 658 p., front.     HEH, N, UVB, Y

5101 —————— A Skeleton in the Closet: A Novel ... New York: Robert Bonner's Sons, 1893. 381 p., illus.
Information from LC card for copy in the "Ledger Library," No. 92; no copy seen.

5102 —————— Sybil Brotherton: A Novel ... Philadelphia: T. B. Peterson & Brothers, 306 Chestnut Street [cop. 1879]. 168 p.     HEH, LC

5103 —————— Unknown; or, The Mystery of Raven Rocks ... New York: Robert Bonner's Sons [cop. 1889]. 592 p., front.     UM

5104 —————— The Unloved Wife: A Novel ... New York: Robert Bonner's Sons, 1891. 374 p., illus.
Information from LC card for copy in the "Choice Series," No. 28; no copy seen.

5105 SOUTHWORTH, MRS. S. A. Gold and Dross; or, The False Life and the True ... Boston: James H. Earle, 178 Washington Street [cop. 1890]. 220 p., illus.     LC

5106 SPARHAWK, FRANCES CAMPBELL. A Chronicle of Conquest . . . Boston: D. Lothrop Company, Washington Street opposite Bromfield [cop. 1890]. 239 p.      H, HEH, LC, N, Y
Of the Carlisle school for Indians.

5107 ———— A Lazy Man's Work: A Novel . . . New York: Henry Holt and Company, 1881. 377 p.      AP, BA, H, HEH, LC, O, UC, Y
At head of title: "Leisure Hour Series—No. 122."

5108 ———— Onoqua . . . Boston: Lee and Shepard, 1892. 263 p.    HEH, N, O
Indians' problems; Montana.

5109 ———— Senator Intrigue and Inspector Noseby: A Tale of Spoils . . . Boston: Red-Letter Publishing Company, 1895. 162 p.
AP, BU, HEH, LC, N, O, UC, UM, Y

5110 ———— A Wedding Tangle . . . Boston: Arena Publishing Company, 1893. 341 p.      BA, CU, HEH

5111 SPARKS, ALICE WILKINSON. My Wife's Husband: A Touch of Nature . . . Chicago: Laird & Lee, 1897. 303 p., illus.      HEH, O, UM

5112 SPARROW, C. B. The Bane of Bendon: A Tale of New Hampshire in the Days of the Temperance Excitement . . . Knoxville, Tenn.: Ogden Bros. & Co., printers and binders, 1885. 150 p.      LC

SPEAR, ANNE B., *jt. au. See* [Morris, B.C.] The Lost Key (1879), No. 3839.

5113 SPEAR, JOHN W. Grace Winslow; or, Gold and Dross . . . New York: N. Tibbals & Sons, 1883. 429 p., illus.      HEH, LC
Vermont.

5114 ———— Out of the Toils . . . New York: Phillips & Hunt. Cincinnati: Cranston & Stowe, 1887. 389 p.      HEH, LC
Temperance novel.

5115 ———— Peg Bunson: A Domestic Story . . . New York: G. W. Dillingham Co., 1897. 271 p.      HEH, LC

5116 SPEARMAN, FRANK HAMILTON. The Nerve of Foley, and Other Railroad Stories . . . New York and London: Harper & Brothers, 1900. 234, [1] p., illus.      BA, HEH, O
*Also contains:* Second Seventy-Seven—The Kid Engineer—The Sky-Scraper—Soda-Water Sal—The McWilliams Special—The Million-Dollar Freight-Train—Bucks—Sankey's Double Header—Siclone Clark.

5117 SPEARS, JOHN RANDOLPH. The Fugitive: A Tale of Adventure in the Days of Clipper Ships and Slavers . . . New York: Charles Scribner's Sons, 1899. 325 p., illus.      H, HEH, LC, N, O

5118 —— The Port of Missing Ships, and Other Stories of the Sea . . .
New York: The Macmillan Company. London: Macmillan & Co.,
Ltd., 1897. 183 p.                                    BA, HEH, LC, N, Y
*Also contains:* Skipper of the Nancy C—Story of a Second Mate.
Title story printed earlier in No. 5282.

5119 SPECHT, EMMA E. H. Alfrieda: A Novel . . . St. Louis: Published by
the author, 1890. 614 p.                             BA, CU, HEH, LC
Of religious interest; St. Louis.

SPENCER, MRS. GEORGE E. *See* Spencer, William Loring (Nuñez)

5120 SPENCER, JOSEPHINE. The Senator from Utah, and Other Tales of the
Wasatch . . . Salt Lake City, Utah: Printed by George Q. Cannon &
Sons Company, 1895. 301 p.                                  H, HEH
*Also contains:* A Municipal Sensation—Finley Parke's Problem—Maridon's
Experiment—Letitia—Mariposa Lilies—Hester.

5121 SPENCER, LILLIAN. After All: A Novel . . . Chicago: S. C. Griggs and
Company, 1885. 150 p.                                      HEH, LC

5122 [——] Star-Crossed: The Life and Love of an Actress. By an Actress . . . New York: The Judge Publishing Company, 1888. 264 p.,
front.                                                         HEH

SPENCER, MAJA, *pseud. See* Spencer, William Loring (Nuñez)

5123 SPENCER, WILLIAM LORING (NUÑEZ). Calamity Jane: A Story of the
Black Hills. By Mrs. George E. Spencer . . . New York: Cassell &
Company, Limited, 739 & 741 Broadway [cop. 1887]. 172 p.        O

5124 [——] A Friend to the Widow. By Maja Spencer [pseud.] . . .
Chicago, New York, San Francisco: Belford, Clarke & Co., 1888. 244
p., front.                                                  LC, UM

5125 —— A Plucky One . . . New York: Cassell & Company, Limited,
739 & 741 Broadway [cop. 1886]. 353 p.                     HEH, LC, O
A Nevada mining camp.

5126 [——] Salt-Lake Fruit: A Latter-Day Romance. By an American.
Boston: Franklin Press; Rand, Avery and Company, 1884. 328 p., illus.
BU, HEH, LC, O, UC, UV, Y

5127 [——] The Story of Mary. By an American. New York. G. W.
Carleton & Co. London: S. Low, Son & Co., 1885. 391 p.        LC
PW, July 9, 1887, lists: *Dennis Day, Carpet-Bagger; or, The Story of Mary.*
New York: G. W. Dillingham, 1887. May be a later ed. with a new title;
not found.

5128 SPENSER, MARY CLARE. The Benefit of the Doubt . . . New York: G. P.
Putnam's Sons, 1883. 371 p.                            CU, H, HEH, LC

5129 ———— Brinka, an American Countess . . . New York: Spenser Publishing Company, 1888. 417 p.      CU, HEH, O, Y

5130 SPERRY, ARTHUR. Sperry Stories . . . Washington, D.C.: H. B. Sperry, 1894. 117 p., front.      N
*Contents:* Quong Tin—A Failure—The Inspector's Cat—The Jade Snake—Cox's Blunder—Said the Paretic—Meg and Ben—R. A. T. S.—The Hatchet Society for Fin Tien—A Woman Who Did Not—Saved by a Sphygmogram—Hop Wah, Philosopher.

SPOFFORD, HARRIET ELIZABETH (PRESCOTT). Captain Mallinger. *In* I. Bacheller, *ed.*, Best Things from American Literature (1899), No. 195.

5131 ———— An Inheritance . . . New York: Charles Scribner's Sons, 1897. 172 p.      CU, H, HEH, LC, N, O, UP, UVB, Y

5132 ———— The Maid He Married . . . Chicago and New York: Herbert S. Stone and Company, 1899. 201 p., 1 l., front.
     CU, H, HEH, LC, N, O, UM, UP, UVB, Y

5133 ———— The Marquis of Carabas . . . Boston: Roberts Brothers, 1882. 211 p.      BA, H, HEH, LC, N, O, UC, UP, UVB, Y

5134 ———— A Master Spirit . . . New York: Charles Scribner's Sons, 1896. 135 p.      BU, CU, H, HEH, LC, O, UM, UP, UVB, Y

———— A Moonlight Wreck. *In* [W. F. Gill] *ed.*, Laurel Leaves (1876), No. 2167.

———— The Mount of Sorrow. *In* Stories by American Authors, II (1884), No. 5268.

5135 ———— Old Madame, & Other Tragedies . . . Boston: Richard G. Badger & Co., 1900. 302 p., 1 l.
     BA, CU, H, HEH, LC, N, O, UC, UM, UP, UVB, Y
*Also contains:* Ordronnaux—The Wages of Sin—Her Story—A Lost Identity. Title story printed earlier in No. 3206.

5136 ———— Priscilla's Love-Story . . . Chicago & New York: Herbert S. Stone & Company, 1898. 129 p., 1 l.
     BA, CU, H, HEH, LC, N, O, UC, UM, UP, UVB, Y

———— Rougegorge. *In* W. F. Gill, *ed.*, Papyrus Leaves (1880), No. 2168.
Printed earlier in Wright II, No. 2130.

5137 ———— A Scarlet Poppy, and Other Stories . . . New York: Harper & Brothers, 1894. 283 p.      BA, CU, H, HEH, LC, N, O, UC, UM, UP, UVB, Y
*Also contains:* Best-Laid Schemes—An Ideal—Mrs. Claxton's Skeleton—The Tragic Story of Binns—The Composite Wife—Mrs. Van Nore's Daughter-in-Law.

5138 SPOLLON, JOHN. Adventures of a Tramp . . . Harrisville, N.H.: John
Spollon, 1897. 83 p.     LC

SPRAGUE, CARLETON. Confessions of a Frivolous Youth. *In* Stories from
the Harvard Advocate (1896), No. 5277a.

5139 [SPRAGUE, MARY APLIN.] An Earnest Trifler. Boston: Houghton, Osgood and Company. The Riverside Press, Cambridge, 1880. 249 p.
AP, BA, BU, HEH, N, O, UC, UM, UVB, Y

5140 SPRAGUE, WARD. The Way to Win . . . Syracuse, N.Y.: Published for
the author by Charles C. Hall & Co. [cop. 1885]. 471 p.     LC

5141 SPRATLEY, MARIENNE GAILLARD. Confessions of Two: A Novel . . .
New York: G. W. Dillingham. London: S. Low, Son & Co., 1886.
257 p.     HEH, LC
Elizabeth Octavia Willisson, jt. au.

5142 SPRINGER, MARY ELIZABETH. "Lady Hancock": A Story of the American Revolution . . . New York: Isaac H. Blanchard Co. [cop. 1900].
267 p.     BA, LC

5143 SPRINGER, NARCISSA SMITH. Cloudy Sky; or, The Unfortunate Children.
A True Tale . . . Cleveland, 1882. 479 p.     LC

5144 SPRINGER, REBECCA (RUTER). Self . . . Philadelphia: J. B. Lippincott &
Co., 1881. 290 p.     HEH, LC
Of married life.

5145 SPURR, GEORGE GRAHAM. A Fight with a Grizzly Bear: A Story of
Thrilling Interest . . . Boston: Published by George G. Spurr, 1886.
26 p.     H, HEH, Y
California.

5146 ——— The Land of Gold: A Tale of '49. Illustrative of Early Pioneer
Life in California and Founded upon Fact . . . Boston: A. Williams &
Company, 1881. 271 p., illus.     AP, BU, H, HEH, O, Y

STAATS, *pseud.* See Staats, William

STAATS, JOHANNA, *pseud.* See Meredith, Katherine Mary Cheever

5147 [STAATS, WILLIAM.] A Tight Squeeze; or, The Adventures of a Gentleman, Who, on a Wager of Ten Thousand Dollars, Undertook to Go
from New York to New Orleans in Three Weeks, without Money, as
a Professional Tramp. By "Staats" [pseud.]. Boston: Lee and Shepard. New York: Charles T. Dillingham, 1879. 282 p.
BA, CU, HEH, LC, O, UVB

5148 STACEY, ARTHUR MERRILL. Edward Earle: A Romance . . . Augusta, Me.: A. M. Hovey & Co., 1885. 327 p.
Listed in Williamson, No. 9442.

5149 STAFFORD, WILLIAM A. H. Broken Bonds: A Novel . . . New York: Andrew F. Underhill & Co., 1885. 258 p.     HEH, LC, O

STAMPER, MRS. FRANKIE, *pseud.* See Tompkins, Georgia H.

5150 STANDEN, WILLIAM THOMAS. A Bundle of Straws . . . New York: Theodore D. Rich, 1899. 291, [1] p., illus.     HEH, LC
*Contents:* My Inspiration—Childhood—Church Bells—About Idleness—Travel-ing—On Humor—Money, and the Lack of It—Out of Work—The End.

5151 [————] The Great Buxton Mystery: A Story. By an Author Un-known. New York, 1889. [52] p., illus.     LC

5152 STANLEY, MARY. Measure for Measure: A Novel . . . New York: G. W. Carleton & Co. London: S. Low, Son & Co., 1883. 420 p.     LC

5153 STANLEY, Z. L. The Mysterious Doctor: A Novel . . . New York: G. W. Dillingham. London: S. Low, Son & Co., 1888. 420 p.     LC
Texas and Kentucky before the Civil War.

STANTON, EDWARD, *pseud.* See Huntington, Edward Stanton

5154 STANTON, HENRY THOMPSON. A Graduate of Paris . . . Washington, D.C.: William H. Morrison [cop. 1889]. 166 p.     LC

5155 ———— Social Fetters; or, Within a Shadow . . . Washington, D.C.: W. H. Morrison, 1889. 100 p.     LC

5156 STANTON, PEYTON L. Love and War in Cuba, Including Many Thrilling Scenes of the Last Years of Spanish Rule . . . Atlanta, Ga.: The Foote & Davies Company, printers and binders, 1900. 312 p.     LC

5157 STANTON, WILLIAM H. The Morgue of the Wage-Earners; or, Jerry Sly's Republic . . . Scranton, Pa.: Published by the author, 1890. 167 p.     LC

5158 STAPLETON, PATIENCE (TUCKER). Babe Murphy . . . Chicago: Belford-Clarke Co., 1890. 280 p.     LC
From Colorado to Texas.

———— The Breaking of Winter. *In* C. King, Rancho del Muerto [cop. 1895], No. 3109.

5159 ———— Kady . . . [Chicago: Belford, Clarke & Co., cop. 1888.] 403 p.     LC
Deposited Jan. 2, 1889.
Rocky Mountains in Colorado.

5160 ——— The Major's Christmas, and Other Stories . . . Denver, Colo.: News Printing Company, 1886. 308 p. BA, LC

*Also contains:* Cindery Jane—The Oldest Inhabitant—Andrew Strong's Affinity—Bobby's Christmas—Jacob Kohler's Repentance—Christmas at Montsweag—The Modern Magician—Bija's Santa Claus—A Fairy Godmother—A Christmas Dinner Party—At Dresden by the Sea—The Madison Bowman—Miss Bean's Revenge.

5161 STARK, ERNEST. Ed. Sommer, the Pinkerton Detective; or, The Murdered Miser . . . New York: J. S. Ogilvie and Company, 31 Rose Street, cop. 1886. 160 p., illus. LC

5162 STARK, HARRIET. The Bacillus of Beauty: A Romance of To-Day . . . New York: Frederick A. Stokes Company [cop. 1900]. 340 p. CU, HEH, LC

Barnard College student is subject of a professor's experiment.

5163 STARK, JAMES HIRAM. Hugh Carlin; or, Truth's Triumph . . . St. Louis: Christian Publishing Company, 1896. 185 p. LC

5164 STARR, JULIAN. The Disagreeable Woman: A Social Mystery . . . New York: G. W. Dillingham, 1895. 190 p. LC
New York.

5165 [STEBBINS, SARAH (BRIDGES).] The Annals of a Baby: How It Was Named, How It Was Nursed, How It Was a Tyrant, How Its Nose Got Out of Joint. Also, a Few Words about Its Aunties, Its Grandfathers, Grandmothers, and Other Important Relations. By One of Its Slaves. New York: G. W. Carleton & Co. London: S. Low & Co., 1877. 226 p. BA, CU, H, HEH, LC, O, UC, UM, UP
At head of title: "A Companion to 'Helen's Babies'."

5166 [———] He and I; or, Was It He? . . . New York: G. W. Carleton & Co. London: S. Low, Son & Co., 1877. 198 p. HEH, LC, UM

5167 STEDMAN, S. O. Allen Bay: A Story . . . Philadelphia: J. B. Lippincott Co., 1876. 152 p. HEH

STEELE, CHRISTIE, *pseud. See* Bernard, Mary N.

5168 STEELE, JAMES WILLIAM. Frontier Army Sketches . . . Chicago: Jansen, McClurg & Company, 1883. 329 p.
BA, CU, H, HEH, LC, N, O, UC, UM, Y

This is Wright II, No. 2353, with a new title and seven stories added: Men of the Border—A Good Indian—A Guard-House Gentleman—A Fight between Buffaloes—Chicquita—Army Mules—A Lonesome Christian.

5169 ——— West of the Missouri . . . Chicago: Rand, McNally & Co., 1885. 313 p. HEH, LC, N, Y
Contains same stories as No. 5168 with one story, "Grimes's Girl," added and two, "Captain Jinks" and "A Lonesome Christian," omitted.

5170 STEELE, MRS. L. A. B. Rev. Adonijah and His Wife's Relations . . . New York: The Authors' Publishing Company, Bond Street [cop. 1879]. 267 p.    LC

5171 STEELE, ROWENA (GRANICE). Weak or Wicked? A Romance . . . Lodi, Cal.: Steele Publishing Co., 1893. 242 p.    HEH
Hinkel lists also *Blue-Eyed Mary* and *Victims of Fate,* books by this author that were privately printed without date.

5172 STEELL, WILLIS. Isidra . . . Boston: Ticknor and Company, 1888. 271 p.    HEH, LC, O
Deposited Apr. 11, 1888.
Imprint date easily misread as 1883.
Mexican politics in 1864.

5173 ——— The Whole Truth: A Story . . . New York: Hillier Murray & Co., 32 West 30th Street [cop. 1892]. 158 p.    LC

5174 STEFFENS, JOSEPHINE BONTECOU. Letitia Berkeley, A.M.: A Novel . . . New York: Frederick A. Stokes Company [cop. 1899]. 292 p.
   HEH, LC, Y
Heroine becomes a medical student in Paris.

5175 STELL, CHARLES. The Life of a Reprobate . . . New York: F. Tennyson Neely, 114 Fifth Avenue. Chicago, London [ cop. 1899]. 265 p.  HEH

5176 [STEMPEL, MARY GAILLARD (TOBIN) McCAN.] The Finished Web. New Orleans: Current Topics Publishing Co., 1892. 44 p.
Information from LC card; no copy seen.

5177 STEPHENS, ANN SOPHIA (WINTERBOTHAM). Norston's Rest . . . Philadelphia: T. B. Peterson & Brothers, 306 Chestnut Street [cop. 1877]. 441 p.    CU, H, HEH, LC

STEPHENS, C. A. Young Moll's Peevy. *In* Stories by American Authors, X (1885), No. 5276.

5178 STEPHENS, ROBERT NEILSON. The Continental Dragoon: A Love Story of Philipse Manor-House in 1778 . . . Boston: L. C. Page and Company (Incorporated), 1898. 299 p., illus.    AP, H, HEH, LC, UV

5179 ——— An Enemy to the King: From the Recently Discovered Memoirs of the Sieur de la Tournoire . . . Boston: L. C. Page and Company (Incorporated), 1897. 459 p., illus.    BA, HEH, O, UM
Henry IV and Henry of Navarre.

5180 ——— A Gentleman Player: His Adventures on a Secret Mission for Queen Elizabeth . . . Boston: L. C. Page and Company (Incorporated), 1899. 438 p., illus.    BA, H, HEH, LC, O, UM, Y
Story opens in the Globe Theatre, London, in 1601 at the first presentation of Hamlet.

5181 ———— The Life and Adventures of Steve Brodie ... New York: T. H. Davis, 1894. 57 p., illus.
Information from LC card; no copy seen.

5182 ———— Philip Winwood: A Sketch of the Domestic History of an American Captain in the War of Independence, Embracing Events That Occurred between and during the Years 1763 and 1786, in New York and London ... Boston: L. C. Page & Company (Incorporated), 1900. 412 p., illus. BA, BU, CU, H, HEH, LC, O, UC, UM, UV, Y

5183 ———— The Road to Paris: A Story of Adventure ... Boston: L. C. Page and Company (Incorporated), 1898. 552 p., illus.
AP, H, LC, O, UC
Colonial period.

5184 STEPHENSON, HENRY THEW. Patroon Van Volkenberg: A Tale of Old Manhattan in the Year Sixteen Hundred & Ninety-Nine ... Indianapolis: The Bowen-Merrill Company [cop. 1900]. 360 p., illus.
CU, H, HEH, LC, Y

STEPHENSON, NATHANIEL. The Tumbrils. *In* New Stories from the Chap-Book (1898), No. 3949.

STERNE, STUART, *pseud. See* Bloede, Gertrude

5185 [STERNS, E. E.] Eros; or, Miss Barbara's Escape. A Summer Story ... New York: G. W. Carleton & Co. London: S. Low & Co., 1878. 146 p.
Copy examined at New York Public Library.

STESH, FEWI, *pseud. See* Wood, Mrs. Seth S.

STETSON, CHARLOTTE (PERKINS). *See* Gilman, Charlotte (Perkins) Stetson

5186 STETSON, GRACE ELLERY (CHANNING). The Fortune of a Day ... Chicago: Herbert S. Stone & Company, 1900. 319 p. BU, HEH, LC, Y
*Also contains:* Ashes, Dust, and Nothing—The Feast of Bluebirds—The Uccelli with Golden Voices—The Bonselli's Daughter—Oreste's Patron—The Rise of the Vanni—A Wise Little Fool.

———— The House on the Hilltop, by Grace Ellery Channing. *In* Stories of Italy (1893), No. 5278.
Later printed in No. 5187.

———— Oreste's Patron. *In* Stories from the Chap-Book (1896), No. 5277.
Later printed in No. 5186.

5187 ———— The Sister of a Saint, and Other Stories . . . Chicago: Stone & Kimball, 1895. 261 p., 1 l.                BA, BU, H, HEH, LC, N, O, Y
*Also contains:* The House on the Hill-Top—The Lucky Number—Coleur de Rose—A Strange Dinner-Party—The Basket of Anita.
At head of title: "Carnation Series."

5188 [STEVENS, CHARLES McCLELLAN.] The Adventures of Uncle Jeremiah and Family at the Great Fair . . . By "Quondam" [pseud.] . . . Chicago: Laird & Lee, 1893. 237 p., illus.                CU, HEH
Columbian Exposition, Chicago.
Author's name frequently spelled "Stevans" on title pages.

5189 ———— Labor Is King: Relief from the Almighty Overlord of Imperialistic Wealth. A Story of the Final Civilization . . . Chicago: The Popular Publishing Company [cop. 1900]. 158 p.                LC

5190 ———— Lucky Ten Bar of Paradise Valley: His Humorous, Pathetic, and Tragic Adventures . . . Chicago: Rhodes & McClure Publishing Company, 1900. 279 p., illus.                LC

5191 STEVENS, IDA WOOD. Light Out of Darkness; or, The Blue and the Gray United . . . [King City, Mo.], 1887. 189 p.                CU, LC

5192 STEVENS, MARY FLETCHER. By Subtle Fragrance Held . . . Philadelphia: J. B. Lippincott Company, 1893. 206 p.                H, HEH, LC

5193 STEVENS, SUSAN SHEPPARD (PIERCE). I Am the King: Being the Account of Some Happenings in the Life of Godfrey de Bersac, Crusader-Knight . . . Boston: Little, Brown and Company, 1898. 213 p.
HEH, LC, O

5194 ———— The Sword of Justice . . . Boston: Little, Brown and Company, 1899. 275 p.                HEH, LC, N, O, UM
French and Spanish struggle for Florida.

5195 [STEVENS, T. HOOD.] Reveries of a Young Man in Quest of a Wife. By Frank M. Willoughby [pseud.] . . . Philadelphia: Sherman & Co., printers, 1888. 275 p., illus.                HEH, LC, Y

5196 STEVENSON, A. C. Unspotted from the World . . . New York: F. Tennyson Neely, 114 Fifth Avenue. Chicago, London [cop. 1899]. 362 p.                H, HEH, O
Southern California.

STEVENSON, EDWARD IRENAEUS PRIME. Madame Clerc. *In* F. E. McKay, *ed.*, Vignettes [cop. 1890], No. 3523.

5197 STEVENSON, ROBERT LOUIS. The Ebb Tide: A Trio & Quartette . . . Chicago & Cambridge: Stone & Kimball, 1894. 204 p., 1 l.
H, HEH, LC, N, O, Y
Lloyd Osbourne, jt. au., an American.

5198 —— The Wrecker . . . New York: Charles Scribner's Sons, 1892.
553 p., illus. AP, BA, CU, H, HEH, N, O, UP, Y
Lloyd Osbourne, jt. au., an American.

5199 —— The Wrong Box . . . New York: Charles Scribner's Sons, 1889.
244 p. AP, BA, H, HEH, LC, O, UC, UP, UV, Y
Lloyd Osbourne, jt. au., an American.

5200 STEWART, ELLA MAUDE. Majella; or, Nameless and Blind. A Story of
the Susquehanna . . . Philadelphia: Printed by J. B. Lippincott Company, 1893. 314 p. HEH, LC

5201 STEWART, ELWOOD STOKES. The Veiled Lady . . . Philadelphia, Pa.:
Holtz & Co., 19 South Ninth Street [cop. 1896]. 84 p. LC
*Also contains:* A Fortunate Meeting.

5202 STEWART, MRS. GEORGE ELIOT. The Burnhams; or, The Two Roads.
A Novel . . . New York: G. W. Carleton & Co. London: S. Low &
Co., 1884. 756 p. HEH, LC

5203 STEWART, MARY. Unspotted from the World . . . New York: Robert
Lewis Weed Company [cop. 1898]. 289 p. LC
Deposited Dec. 31, 1897.
From the Ozarks to St. Louis and Europe.

5204 [STEWART, MATILDA.] Lily's Lover; or, A Trip Out of Season . . . New
York: The Authors' Publishing Company, Bond Street [cop. 1878].
135 p. LC
Connecticut.

5205 STEWART, MERCH BRADT. The N'th Foot in War . . . New York: The
Abbey Press, 114 Fifth Avenue. London, Montreal [cop. 1900]. 175
p. LC
Deposited Dec. 19, 1900.
Cuba.

5206 STICKNEY, MARY ETTA (SMITH). Brown of Lost River: A Story of the
West . . . New York: D. Appleton and Company, 1900. 309 p.
HEH, LC, O, Y
Wyoming.

5207 [STILES, W. L., JR.] All Is Not Gold That Glistens: A Sketch. By Rae
[pseud.]. Philadelphia, 1887. 226 p. AP, LC, O

5208 STILES, WILLIAM CURTIS. Double Jeopardy! A Novel . . . New York:
The Home Publishing Company [cop. 1898]. 242 p. LC

5209 —— The Master's Mission; or, The Minister Who Dared . . . New
York: Street & Smith, 238 William Street [cop. 1900]. 213 p. LC

5210 ———— A Matter of Business, and Other Stories ... Chicago: Advance
Publishing Co., 1899. 246 p.      HEH, LC
*Also contains:* On the Whole—The Avenging Brook.

5211 [STILLMAN, ANNIE RAYMOND.] How They Kept the Faith: A Tale of
the Huguenots of Languedoc. By Grace Raymond [pseud.]. New
York: Anson D. F. Randolph & Company, 38 West Twenty-Third
Street [cop. 1889]. 389 p.      AP, CU, H, LC, Y

5212 STILLSON, FLORENCE GEORGEANNA MERCHANT. Doris: A Story of 1778
... Danbury [Conn.]: Published for private circulation, 1891. 96 p.,
front.      HEH
Connecticut.

5213 STIMPSON, HERBERT BAIRD. The Regeneration: A Novel . . . Washington, D.C.: Walter Neale, 1896. 181 p., illus.      LC, UV
Of the South and the Ku Klux Klan.

5214 ———— The Tory Maid: Being an Account of the Adventures of James
Frisby of Fairlee, in the County of Kent, on the Eastern Shore of the
State of Maryland, and Sometime an Officer in the Maryland Line of
the Continental Army during the War of the Revolution . . . New
York: Dodd, Mead and Company, 1899. 245 p.      CU, HEH, LC, N

5215 [STIMSON, FREDERIC JESUP.] The Crime of Henry Vane: A Study with
a Moral. By J. S. of Dale . . . New York: Charles Scribner's Sons,
1884. 206 p.      AP, BA, CU, H, HEH, LC, N, O, UM, UP, UV, Y
New York.

5216 ———— First Harvests: An Episode in the Life of Mrs. Levison Gower.
A Satire without a Moral . . . New York: Charles Scribner's Sons,
1888. 468 p.      AP, BA, BU, CU, H, HEH, LC, N, O, UM, UVB, Y
New York society.

5217 [————] Guerndale: An Old Story. By J. S. of Dale. New York:
Charles Scribner's Sons, 1882. 444 p.      AP, BA, CU, H, HEH, LC, N, O, UP, Y
College background.

5218 ———— In the Three Zones . . . New York: Charles Scribner's Sons,
1893. 204 p.      BA, BU, CU, H, HEH, LC, N, O, Y
*Contents:* Dr. Materialismus—An Alabama Courtship—Los Caraqueños.

5219 ———— King Noanett: A Story of Old Virginia and the Massachusetts
Bay . . . Boston and New York, London: Lamson, Wolffe and Company, 1896. 327 p., illus.      AP, BA, CU, H, HEH, LC, O, UM, UVB, Y

5220 ———— Mrs. Knollys, and Other Stories . . . New York: Charles Scrib-
ner's Sons, 1897. 207 p.      BA, CU, H, HEH, LC, N, O, UM, Y
*Also contains:* The Three Achievements of Eileen—Our Consul at Carlsruhe—
A First Love-Letter—In a Garret—A Daughter of Spain (Los Caraqueños)—
Dynevor.
Title story printed earlier in Nos. 5223 and 5268.

519

5221 —— Pirate Gold . . . Boston and New York: Houghton, Mifflin and Company. The Riverside Press, Cambridge, 1896. 209 p.

BA, CU, H, HEH, LC, N, O, UM, UP, Y

Boston in the early 1800's.

5222 —— The Residuary Legatee; or, The Posthumous Jest of the Late John Austin . . . New York: Charles Scribner's Sons, 1888. 142 p.

AP, BU, CU, H, HEH, LC, N, O, UM, Y

5223 [——] The Sentimental Calendar: Being Twelve Funny Stories. By J. S. of Dale . . . New York: Charles Scribner's Sons, 1886. 280 p., illus. AP, BA, BU, CU, H, HEH, LC, N, O, UM, UVB, Y

Contents: The Bells of Avalon—Mr. Pillian Wraye—The Seven Lights of Asia —A First Love-Letter—"Bill Shelby"—Two Passions and a Cardinal Virtue— Our Consul at Carlsruhe—Gloriana—Passages from the Diary of a Hong Kong Merchant—In a Garret—A Tale Unfolded—Mrs. Knollys.

—— jt. au. See Grant, R. The King's Men (1884), No. 2236.

5224 STINE, MILTON HENRY. The Niemans . . . York, Pa.: P. Anstadt & Sons, 1897. 388 p. HEH

STIRLING, A., pseud. See Kimball, Annie Lydia (McPhail)

5225 DELETED.

5226 STITZEL, MRS. H. V. What Came of It: A Novel . . . Portland, Oregon: Geo. H. Himes, 1878. 320 p., front. BU, CU, HEH, LC, UVB

Also contains: Waifs and Estrays.

5227 STOCKTON, FRANK RICHARD. The Adventures of Captain Horn . . . New York: Charles Scribner's Sons, 1895. 404 p.

AP, BA, BU, CU, H, HEH, N, O, UC, UVB, Y

5228 —— Afield and Afloat . . . New York: Charles Scribner's Sons, 1900. 422 p., illus. AP, BA, BU, CU, H, HEH, LC, N, O, UC, UVB, Y

Contents: The Buller-Podington Compact—The Romance of a Mule-Car— The Governor-General—Old Applejoy's Ghost—Struck by a Boomerang— The Skipper and El Capitan—Come In, New Year!—A Sailor's Knot—The Great Staircase at Landover Hall—The Ghosts in My Tower—The Landsman's Tale.

5229 —— Amos Kilbright, His Adscititious Experiences, with Other Stories . . . New York: Charles Scribner's Sons, 1888. 146 p.

AP, BA, CU, H, HEH, LC, N, O, UC, UM, UP, UVB, Y

Also contains: The Reversible Landscape—Dusky Philosophy, in Two Expositions—Plain Fishing.

5230 —— Ardis Claverden . . . New York: Dodd, Mead and Company [cop. 1890]. 498 p. AP, BA, CU, H, HEH, LC, O, UC, UM, UP, UVB, Y

Deposited Aug. 9, 1890.

5231 —— The Associate Hermits ... New York and London: Harper & Brothers, 1899. 256, [1] p., illus. BA, CU, H, HEH, LC, N, O, UC, UM, UVB, Y

5232 —— The Bee-Man of Orn, and Other Fanciful Tales ... New York: Charles Scribner's Sons, 1887. 193 p.

AP, BA, CU, H, HEH, LC, N, O, UC, UM, UP, UVB, Y

*Also contains:* The Griffin and the Minor Canon—Old Pipes and the Dryad—The Queen's Museum—Christmas before Last; or, The Island of the Fragile Palm—Prince Hassak's March—The Battle of the Third Cousins—The Banished King—The Philopena.

Early copies have "The Island" in table of contents; corrected to "The Fruit" in later copies.

5233 —— A Bicycle of Cathay: A Novel ... New York and London: Harper & Brothers, 1900. 239, [1] p., illus.

BA, CU, H, HEH, LC, N, O, UC, UM, UP, UVB, Y

5234 —— The Casting Away of Mrs. Lecks and Mrs. Aleshine ... New York: The Century Co. [cop. 1886]. 130 p.

AP, CU, H, HEH, LC, N, O, UC, UP, UVB, Y

5235 —— A Chosen Few Short Stories ... New York: Charles Scribner's Sons, 1895. 240 p., front. CU, H, HEH, LC, O, UC, UM, UV, Y

*Contents:* A Tale of Negative Gravity—Asaph—"His Wife's Deceased Sister"—The Lady or the Tiger?—The Remarkable Wreck of the "Thomas Hyke"—Old Pipes and the Dryad—The Transferred Ghost—"The Philosophy of Relative Existences"—A Place of Red Calico.

These stories were all published in earlier collections.

5236 —— The Dusantes: A Sequel to "The Casting Away of Mrs. Lecks and Mrs. Aleshine" ... New York: The Century Co. [cop. 1888]. 150 p. AP, BA, CU, H, HEH, LC, N, O, UC, UM, UP, UVB, Y

5237 —— The Girl at Cobhurst ... New York: Charles Scribner's Sons, 1898. 408 p. AP, BA, CU, H, HEH, LC, N, O, UC, UM, UP, UVB, Y

5238 —— The Great Stone of Sardis: A Novel ... New York and London: Harper & Brothers, 1898. 230 p., illus.

BA, CU, H, HEH, LC, N, O, UC, UVB

5239 —— The Great War Syndicate ... New York: P. F. Collier, 1889. 111 p., illus. H, HEH, O, UC, UVB, Y

5240 —— The House of Martha ... Boston and New York: Houghton, Mifflin and Company. The Riverside Press, Cambridge, 1891. 375 p.

AP, BA, CU, H, HEH, N, O, UM, UP, UVB, Y

5241 —— The Hundredth Man ... New York: The Century Co. [cop. 1887]. 432 p. AP, BA, CU, H, HEH, LC, N, O, UC, UM, UP, UVB, Y

5242 ——— The Lady or the Tiger? and Other Stories . . . New York: Charles Scribner's Sons, 1884. 201 p.
AP, BA, CU, H, HEH, LC, N, O, UC, UP, UVB, Y
*Also contains:* The Transferred Ghost—The Spectral Mortgage—Our Archery Club—That Same Old 'Coon—His Wife's Deceased Sister—Our Story—Mr. Tolman—On the Training of Parents—Our Fire-Screen—A Piece of Red Calico—Every Man His Own Letter-Writer.
Title story later printed in No. 5235.
Also published as: *Stockton's Stories: First Series.* New York: Charles Scribner's Sons, 1886. 201 p.    BA, BU, LC, UC, UVB
For "Second Series" see No. 5252.

5243 ——— The Late Mrs. Null . . . New York: Charles Scribner's Sons, 1886. 437 p.    AP, CU, H, HEH, LC, N, O, UC, UM, UP, UVB, Y

5244 ——— The Merry Chanter . . . New York: The Century Co. [cop. 1890]. 192 p., illus.    AP, BA, BU, CU, H, HEH, LC, N, O, UC, UM, UP, UVB, Y

5245 ——— Mrs. Cliff's Yacht . . . New York: Charles Scribner's Sons, 1896. 314 p., illus.    AP, BA, CU, H, HEH, LC, N, O, UC, UM, UVB, Y

5246 ——— My Terminal Moraine . . . Specially Written for "Once a Week Library" . . . New York: P. F. Collier, 1892. 96 p.    H, HEH, UVB

——— Pomona's Club. *In* The First Book of the Authors Club (1893), No. 1868.

5247 ——— Pomona's Travels . . . [New York]: Charles Scribner's Sons [cop. 1894]. 275 p., illus.    BA, BU, CU, H, HEH, LC, N, O, UM, UP, UVB, Y

5248 ——— Rudder Grange . . . New York: Charles Scribner's Sons, 1879. 270 p., illus.    AP, CU, H, HEH, LC, O, UC, UP, UVB, Y
This ed. contains 18 chapters.

5249 ——— ——— New York: Charles Scribner's Sons [1880]. 292 p.
BA, H, HEH, O, UM, UVB
This ed. contains 20 chapters.
Listed PW, May 29, 1880.

5250 ——— The Rudder Grangers Abroad, and Other Stories . . . New York: Charles Scribner's Sons, 1891. 195 p.
AP, BA, CU, H, HEH, LC, O, UM, UP, UVB, Y
*Contents:* Euphemia among the Pelicans—The Rudder Grangers in England—Pomona's Daughter—Derelict—The Baker of Barnbury—The Water-Devil.

5251 ——— The Squirrel Inn . . . New York: The Century Co., 1891. 222 p., illus.    BA, CU, H, HEH, LC, N, O, UC, UM, UVB, Y

5252 ——— Stockton's Stories: Second Series. The Christmas Wreck, and Other Stories . . . New York: Charles Scribner's Sons, 1886. 242 p.
AP, BU, CU, H, HEH, LC, N, UC, UM, UP, UVB, Y

*Also contains:* A Story of Assisted Fate—An Unhistoric Page—A Tale of Negative Gravity—The Cloverfields Carriage—The Remarkable Wreck of the "Thomas Hyke"—My Bull-Calf—The Discourager of Hesitancy—A Borrowed Month.

For "First Series" see No. 5242n.

5253 ———— The Stories of the Three Burglars ... New York: Dodd, Mead & Company [cop. 1889]. 159 p., front.

AP, CU, H, HEH, N, O, UC, UM, UVB, Y

5254 ———— A Story-Teller's Pack ... New York: Charles Scribner's Sons, 1897. 380 p., illus.      AP, BA, CU, H, HEH, LC, N, O, UC, UM, UP, UVB, Y

*Contents:* A Few Words to Begin With—The Magic Egg—The Staying Power of Sir Rohan—The Widow's Cruise—Love before Breakfast—The Bishop's Ghost and the Printer's Baby—Captain Eli's Best Ear—As One Woman to Another—My Well and What Came Out of It—Stephen Skarridge's Christmas—My Unwilling Neighbor.

———— A Thing That Glistened. *In* Eleven Possible Cases [cop. 1891], No. 1737.

———— The Transferred Ghost. *In* Stories by American Authors, II (1884), No. 5268.

Also included in No. 5242 and later printed in No. 5235.

5255 ———— The Vizier of the Two-Horned Alexander ... New York: The Century Co., 1899. 235 p., illus.

AP, BA, CU, H, HEH, LC, N, O, UC, UM, UP, UVB, Y

5256 ———— The Watchmaker's Wife, and Other Stories ... New York: Charles Scribner's Sons, 1893. 225 p.

AP, BA, CU, H, HEH, LC, N, O, UC, UM, UP, UVB, Y

*Also contains:* Asaph—My Terminal Moraine—The Philosophy of Relative Existences—The Knife That Killed Po Hancy—The Christmas Shadrach—The Reverend Ezekiel Crump.

5257 STOCKTON, JOHN P., JR. Zaphra: A Story of To-Day ... Boston, Mass.: Arena Publishing Company, 1894. 95 p., front.      H, HEH
New York's East Side.

5258 [STOCKTON, LOUISE.] Dorothea ... Boston: James R. Osgood and Company, 1882. 314 p.      AP, BA, H, HEH, LC
At head of title: "Round-Robin Series."
Centennial Exposition background, Philadelphia, 1876.

———— Kirby's Coals of Fire. *In* Stories by American Authors, VII (1884), No. 5273.

5259 STOCKWELL, GEORGE A. The Good-Bye Club ... Boston: George M. Whitaker [cop. 1888]. 38 p. Printed in double columns.      BU, LC
A group of easterners' experiences in the West.

STODDARD, CHARLES WARREN. Joe of Lahaina. *In* A Round Table of the Representative American Catholic Novelists (1897), No. 4703.

STODDARD, ELIZABETH DREW (BARSTOW). My Own Story. *In* C. C .Harrison, *ed.,* Short Stories (1893), No. 2514.

———— Osgood's Predicament. *In* Stories by American Authors, VIII (1884), No. 5274.

5260 STODDARD, WILLIAM OSBORN. Esau Hardery: A Novel of American Life ... New York: White & Stokes, 1881. 405 p.          HEH, LC, UM, UVB

5261 ———— The Heart of It: A Romance of East and West ... New York: G. P. Putnam's Sons, 1880. 438 p.          AP, HEH, LC, O

5262 ———— Wrecked? A Novel ... New York: White, Stokes, and Allen, 1883. 395 p.          AP, H

5263 STOKES, EDWARD ANSLEY. A Sinner in Orders . . . Somerville, N.J.: Press of the Unionist-Gazette Association [cop. 1895]. 178 p.          LC New York.

———— *jt. au. See* [Dickinson, E. M.] So Runs the World Away (1891), No. 1525.

5264 STONE, MRS. C. H. One of "Berrian's" Novels ... New York: Welch, Fracker Company, 1890. 210 p.          H, LC, UM
An answer to Bellamy's *Looking Backward.*

5265 STONE, CLARENCE E. The Phantom Horseman; or, Saved by a Spectre. A Story of the Dark Ages ... Amherst, Mass.: Robert A. Marsh, 1877. 47 p.          LC

STONE, MARY E. *See* Bassett, Mary E. (Stone)

5266 [STONER, LEROY.] The Adventures of a Rustic. By "Leroy" [pseud.]. Kansas City, Mo.: Press of Ramsey, Millett, & Hudson, 1888. 211 p. LC
Of an American abroad.

5267 STORIES BY AMERICAN AUTHORS. I ... New York:Charles Scribner's Sons, 1884. 177 p., illus.          AP, BA, BU, CU, H, HEH, O, UVB, Y
*Contents:* Who Was She? by Bayard Taylor—The Documents in the Case, by Brander Matthews and H. C. Bunner—One of the Thirty Pieces, by William Henry Bishop—Balacchi Brothers, by Rebecca Harding Davis—An Operation in Money, by Albert Webster.

5268 STORIES BY AMERICAN AUTHORS. II . . . New York: Charles Scribner's Sons, 1884. 198 p.          AP, BA, CU, H, O, UC, UVB, Y
*Contents:* The Transferred Ghost, by Frank R. Stockton—A Martyr to Science, by Mary Putnam Jacobi, M.D.—Mrs. Knollys, by J. S. of Dale [i.e., Frederic J. Stimson]—A Dinner-Party, by John Eddy—The Mount of Sorrow, by Harriet Prescott Spofford—Sister Silvia, by Mary Agnes Tincker.

5269 STORIES BY AMERICAN AUTHORS. III . . . New York: Charles Scribner's Sons, 1884. 198 p. AP, BA, CU, H, HEH, LC, O, UVB, Y
*Contents:* The Spider's Eye, by Fitz James O'Brien [actually by Lucretia P. Hale]—A Story of the Latin Quarter, by Frances Hodgson Burnett—Two Purse-Companions, by George Parsons Lathrop—Poor Ogla-Moga, by David D. Lloyd—A Memorable Murder, by Celia Thaxter—Venetian Glass, by Brander Matthews.

5270 STORIES BY AMERICAN AUTHORS. IV . . . New York: Charles Scribner's Sons, 1884. 186 p. AP, BA, CU, H, HEH, LC, O, UVB, Y
*Contents:* Miss Grief, by Constance Fenimore Woolson—Love in Old Cloathes, by H. C. Bunner—Two Buckets in a Well, by N. P. Willis—Friend Barton's Concern, by Mary Hallock Foote—An Inspired Lobbyist, by J. W. De Forest—Lost in the Fog, by Noah Brooks.

5271 STORIES BY AMERICAN AUTHORS. V . . . New York: Charles Scribner's Sons, 1884. 191 p. AP, BA, CU, H, HEH, LC, O, UVB, Y
*Contents:* A Light Man, by Henry James—Yatil, by F. D. Millet—The End of New York, by Park Benjamin—Why Thomas Was Discharged, by George Arnold—The Tachypomp, by E. P. Mitchell.

5272 STORIES BY AMERICAN AUTHORS. VI . . . New York: Charles Scribner's Sons, 1884. 164 p. AP, BA, CU, H, HEH, O, UVB, Y
*Contents:* The Village Convict, by C. H. White [i.e., Heman W. Chaplin]— The Denver Express, by A. A. Hayes—The Misfortunes of Bro' Thomas Wheatley, by Lina Redwood Fairfax—The Heartbreak Cameo, by L. W. Champney—Miss Eunice's Glove, by Albert Webster—Brother Sebastian's Friendship, by Harold Frederic.

5273 STORIES BY AMERICAN AUTHORS. VII . . . New York: Charles Scribner's Sons, 1884. 179 p. AP, BA, CU, H, HEH, O, UM, UVB, Y
*Contents:* The Bishop's Vagabond, by Octave Thanet [i.e., Alice French]— Lost, by Edward Bellamy—Kirby's Coals of Fire, by Louise Stockton— Passages from the Journal of a Social Wreck, by Margaret Floyd—Stella Grayland, by James T. McKay—The Image of San Donato, by Virginia W. Johnson.

5274 STORIES BY AMERICAN AUTHORS. VIII . . . New York: Charles Scribner's Sons, 1884. 206 p. AP, BA, CU, H, HEH, O, UM, UVB, Y
*Contents:* The Brigade Commander, by J. W. De Forest—Split Zephyr, by Henry A. Beers—Zerviah Hope, by Elizabeth Stuart Phelps [Ward]—The Life-Magnet, by Alvey A. Adee—Osgood's Predicament, by Elizabeth D. B. Stoddard.

5275 STORIES BY AMERICAN AUTHORS. IX . . . New York: Charles Scribner's Sons, 1885. 180 p. AP, BA, CU, H, HEH, O, UVB
*Contents:* Marse Chan, by Thomas Nelson Page—Mr. Bixby's Christmas Visitor, by Charles S. Gage—Eli, by C. H. White [i.e., Heman W. Chaplin] —Young Strong of "The Clarion," by Milicent Washburn Shinn—How Old Wiggins Wore Ship, by Captain Roland T. [i.e., Folger] Coffin—"——mas Has Come," by Leonard Kip.

5276 STORIES BY AMERICAN AUTHORS. X ... New York: Charles Scribner's Sons, 1885. 186 p., 3 l.          AP, BA, CU, H, HEH, O, UVB, Y

Contents: Pancha, by T. A. Janvier—The Ablest Man in the World, by E. P. Mitchell—Young Moll's Peevy, by C. A. Stephens—Manmat'ha, by Charles De Kay—A Daring Fiction, by H. H. Boyesen—The Story of Two Lives, by Julia Schayer.

STORIES FROM SCRIBNER. See Nos. 5278-83.

5277 STORIES FROM THE CHAP-BOOK: Being a Miscellany of Curious and Interesting Tales ... Chicago: Herbert S. Stone & Company, 1896. 241 p., 1 l.          CU, H, HEH, N, UM, Y

Contents: Whither Thou Goest, by Katharine Bates—An Impassable Gulf, by K. Bates—In a Garden, by Neith Boyce—Oreste's Patron, by Grace Ellery Channing [Stetson]—The Appeal to Anne, by Edward Cummings—The Dead Oak, by Anna Vernon Dorsey [Williams]—The Making of Monsieur Lescarbot's Ballad, by William Holloway, Jr.—On the Brink, by Edwin Lefevre—A Woman's Life, by Anthony Leland—"When the King Comes In," by A. Leland—Mandany's Fool, by Maria Louise Pool—The Way to Constantinople, by Clinton Ross—The Old Partisan, by Octave Thanet [i.e., Alice French]. For second series see No. 3949.

5277a STORIES FROM THE HARVARD ADVOCATE ... Cambridge, Mass.: Harvard University, 1896. 251 p.          HEH, LC

Contains: Confessions of a Frivolous Youth, by Carleton Sprague—An Indian Legend, by C. H. Grandgent—"Ise Gwine ter Puff Dem Weed," by F. D. Sherman—Phryne: A Phantasy, by L. McK. Garrison—Viola, by A. A. Gardner—A Hollow Sham, by Charles Warren—In the Redwoods, by Case Bull—A Streak of Crimson, by C. Bull—Goodale's Revival, by Kenneth Brown—For Unknown Reasons, by Arthur S. Pier—Mr. Thaddeus Almanac's Scientific Proposal: A Christmas Story, by Luther W. Mott and Louis How. HARVARD TYPES: I, The Moody Man, by Edward G. Knoblauch—II, The "Paper" Sport, by John Mack, Jr.—III, The College Belle, by C. M. Flandrau—IV, "Hollis Holworthy," by C. M. Flandrau. An Unconventional Detective Story, by L. W. Mott and L. How—On a Paris Omnibus, by John Allyne Gade—Notre Dame de Paris, by J. A. Gade—Little Sister: A Love Story, by L. How—The Wrong Scent: The True Story of a "Mauvais Quart d'Heure," by Arthur Cheney Train.

Of the many contributors to this collection, the above have been selected because they are recognized by standard biographical dictionaries.

5278 STORIES OF ITALY. New York: Charles Scribner's Sons, 1893. 208 p., illus.          BA, CU, H, HEH, O, UP, UV, Y

Contents: Espero Gorgoni, Gondolier, by F. Hopkinson Smith—The Anatomist of the Heart, by T. R. Sullivan—The Song of the Comforter, by John J. A'Becket—The House on the Hilltop, by Grace Ellery Channing [Stetson]. At head of title: "Stories from Scribner."

5279 STORIES OF NEW YORK. New York: Charles Scribner's Sons, 1893. 214 p., illus.          BA, BU, CU, H, HEH, N, O, UC, UM, UP, UV, Y

Contains: The Commonest Possible Story, by Bliss Perry—The End of the Beginning, by George A. Hibbard—A Puritan Ingénue, by John S. Wood—Mrs. Manstey's View, by Edith Wharton. "A Puritan Ingénue" included in No. 6070 as "A New England Ingénue." At head of title: "Stories from Scribner."

5280 STORIES OF THE ARMY. New York: Charles Scribner's Sons, 1893. 186 p., illus.         BA, CU, H, HEH, O, UC, UV, Y
*Contents:* Memories, by Brander Matthews—A Charge for France, by John Heard, Jr.—Sergeant Gore, by LeRoy Armstrong—The Tale of a Goblin Horse, by Charles C. Nott.
At head of title: "Stories from Scribner."

5281 STORIES OF THE RAILWAY. New York: Charles Scribner's Sons, 1893. 195, [1] p., illus.       BA, BU, H, HEH, LC, UV, Y
*Contents:* As the Sparks Fly Upward, by George A. Hibbard—How I Sent My Aunt to Baltimore, by C. S. Davison—Run to Seed, by Thomas Nelson Page—Flandroe's Mogul, by A. C. Gordon.
At head of title: "Stories from Scribner."

5282 STORIES OF THE SEA. New York: Charles Scribner's Sons, 1893. 256 p., illus.         BA, H, HEH, LC, UC, UV, Y
*Contents:* The Port of Missing Ships, by John R. Spears—The Fate of the Georgiana, by Maria Blunt—Captain Black, by Charles E. Carryl—The Last Slave-Ship, by George Howe, M.D.
At head of title: "Stories from Scribner."

5283 STORIES OF THE SOUTH. New York: Charles Scribner's Sons, 1893. 222 p., illus.         CU, HEH, O, UM, UV, Y
*Contents:* No Haid Pawn, by Thomas Nelson Page—How the Derby Was Won, by Harrison Robertson—Aunt Fountain's Prisoner, by Joel Chandler Harris—Tirar y Soult, by Rebecca Harding Davis.
At head of title: "Stories from Scribner."

5284 STORKE, FRANCIS EUGENE. Mr. De Lacy's Double . . . New York: Continental Publishing Co., 25 Park Place [cop. 1898]. 306 p.    LC, UV
Part of the action is on a Mississippi River steamboat.

5285 STORRS, LEWIS AUSTIN. Koheleth: A Novel . . . New York: G. W. Dillingham Co., 1897. 265 p.         HEH, LC
New London, Connecticut, during the whaling days.

5286 STORY, WILLIAM WETMORE. Fiammetta: A Summer Idyl . . . Boston and New York: Houghton, Mifflin and Company. The Riverside Press, Cambridge, 1886. 284 p.   BA, BU, H, HEH, N, O, UC, UM, UP, UVB, Y

5287 THE STORY OF A COUNTERFEIT DOLLAR: How It Passed from Hand to Hand and Reached Its Final Resting Place . . . Lowell, Mass.: C. I. Hood & Co., 1889. 23 p., illus.         HEH
Printed in the shape of a silver dollar.

5288 STOVALL, DENNIS H. "Heart of the Valley" . . . Corvallis, Oregon, 1899. 100 p., illus.         BU, HEH
*Contains:* The Spirit of the Haunted House—The Eyes of Caracalla—The Way of a Woman—The Dream City—A Patriot in Spain—Cowboy Tom—A Crime of Thirteen.

5289 [STOW, MARIETTA LOIS (BEERS).] Probate Chaff; or, Beautiful Probate; or Three Years Probating in San Francisco. A Modern Drama, Showing the Merry Side of a Dark Picture ... [Boston?]: Published by the author and sold by subscription, 1879. 307 p., illus. BU, CU, HEH, UM
Author's home was Boston but preface is signed New York.

5290 [STOWE, MRS. H. M.] The Elixir of Life; or, Robert's Pilgrimage. An Allegory. By Eleve [pseud.] ... Chicago, Ill.: Publisher of the Elixir of Life, 87 Washington St. [cop. 1890]. 124 p. LC

5291 STOWE, HARRIET ELIZABETH (BEECHER). Betty's Bright Idea. Also, Deacon Pitkin's Farm, and The First Christmas of New England ... New York: J. B. Ford & Company, 1876. 121 p., illus.
BA, BU, CU, H, HEH, LC, N, O, UC, UP, UVB, Y
The variant drops "The End" on p. 121. Census of copies does not distinguish between the two.

5292 ——— Poganuc People: Their Loves and Lives ... New York: Fords, Howard, & Hulbert [cop. 1878]. 375 p., illus.
CU, H, HEH, LC, N, O, UC, UP, UVB, Y

5293 ——— Sam Lawson's Oldtown Fireside Stories ... Boston: Houghton, Mifflin and Company. The Riverside Press, Cambridge, 1881. 287 p., illus. O, Y
This is Wright II, No. 2395, with a new title and five stories added: Laughin' in Meetin'—Tom Toothacre's Ghost Story—Parson's Horse-Race—Oldtown Fireside Talks of the Revolution—Students' Sea Story.

——— Uncle Lot. In L. C. H. Langford, comp., The Woman's Story (1889), No. 3206.

5294 [STOWERS, WALTER H.] Appointed: An American Novel. By Sanda [pseud. of W. H. Stowers and William H. Anderson]. Detroit: Detroit Law Printing Co., 1894. 371 p. LC

5295 STRATTON, MRS. JENNIE M. Cecil's Crown ... Cleveland, Ohio: The Williams Publishing Company, 1891. 266 p. LC

5296 STRAY, ERMINA C. The Golden Link; or, The Shadow of Sin. A Story of Our Times ... Almont, Mich.: Larger Hope Publishing Company, 1891. 418 p. HEH, LC

STREBOR, EIGGAM, pseud. See Roberts, Maggie

STREEBOR, E. S., pseud. See Roberts, Mrs. Elizabeth S.

5297 STRICKLAND, TERÉSA HAMMOND. Under the Ban: A South Carolina Romance ... Chicago and New York: Rand, McNally & Company [cop. 1898]. 225 p. HEH, UC
Ante bellum.

STROBHART, *pseud.* *See* Seabrook, Whitemarsh B.

5298 STRONG, EDMUND C. Manacle and Bracelet; or, The Dead Man's Secret. A Thrilling Detective Story . . . Chicago, Ills.: George W. Ogilvie, 216 Lake Street [cop. 1886]. 105 p., illus. Printed in double columns. LC

5299 [STRONG, ELIZABETH P.] Conquered: A Novel . . . New York: G. W. Carleton & Co. London: S. Low & Co., 1878. 315 p. HEH, LC

5300 STRONG, GRACE. The Worst Foe: A Temperance Novel . . . Columbus, Ohio: Wm. G. Hubbard & Co., 1885. 385 p. LC

5301 STRONG, MRS. MARY F. Margie's Mistake, and Other Stories . . . Chicago: W. B. Conkey Company, 1891. 286 p., front. LC
*Contains:* The Doctor's Second Love—Frank Leyton's Bride—Our Visitors—Washington Letters—Hot Springs Letters—Geneva to Rome.

STUART, ELEANOR, *pseud.* *See* Childs, Eleanor Stuart (Patterson)

STUART, HESTER, *pseud.* *See* Smith, Helen Butler

5302 [STUART, MISS M. B.] The Two Barbaras: A Novel. By Grace Mortimer [pseud.] . . . New York: G. W. Carleton & Co. London: S. Low & Co., 1876. 353 p. HEH, LC

5303 STUART, RUTH (MCENERY). Carlotta's Intended, and Other Tales . . . New York: Harper & Brothers, 1894. 277 p., illus. BA, H, HEH, LC, O, Y
*Contains:* Bud Zunts's Mail—"Christmas Geese"—Caesar—Aunt Delphi's Dilemma—Duke's Christmas.

5304 ———— A Golden Wedding, and Other Tales . . . New York: Harper & Brothers, 1893. 366 p., illus. CU, H, HEH, N, UVB, Y
*Contains:* Lamentations of Jeremiah Johnson—Uncle Mingo's "Speculatioms"—The Widder Johnsing—Christmas Gifts—"Blink"—Jessekiah Brown's Courtship—Crazy Abe—Queen Anne—Camelia Riccardo—The Woman's Exchange of Simpkinsville.

5305 ———— Holly and Pizen, and Other Stories . . . New York: The Century Co., 1899. 216 p., illus. CU, H, HEH, LC, N, O, UM, UV, Y
*Also contains:* Queen o' Sheba's Triumph—A Note of Scarlet—Uncle Still's Famous Weather Prediction—Picayune: A Child Story.

5306 ———— In Simpkinsville: Character Tales . . . New York: Harper & Brothers, 1897. 244 p., illus. BA, LC, O
*Contents:* An Arkansas Prophet—Weeds—The Unlived Life of Little Mary Ellen—The Dividing-Fence—The Middle Hall—Miss Jemima's Valentine—A Slender Romance.
Deposited July 9, 1897.
*Also issued with imprint:* New York and London: Harper & Brothers, 1897. CU, H, HEH, Y

5307 ——— Moriah's Mourning, and Other Half-Hour Sketches . . . New York and London: Harper & Brothers, 1898. 218, [1] p., illus.

BA, H, HEH, LC, O, Y

*Also contains:* An Optical Dilemma—The Second Mrs. Slimm—Apollo Belvedere: A Christmas Episode of the Plantation—Nearest of Kin (On the Plantation)—The Deacon's Medicine—Two Gentlemen of Leisure—The Rev. Jordan White's Three Glances—Lady: A Monologue of the Cow-Pen—A Pulpit Orator—An Easter Symbol: A Monologue of the Plantation—Christmas at the Trimbles'—A Minor Chord.

5308 ——— Sonny . . . New York: The Century Co., 1896. 135 p., front.

CU, H, LC, Y

*Contents:* A Christmas Guest—The Boy—Sonny's Christenin'—Sonny's Schoolin'—Sonny's Diploma—Sonny "Keepin' Company"—Weddin' Presents. Also published as: *Sonny, a Christmas Guest.* New York: The Century Co., 1898. BA, HEH

5309 ——— The Woman's Exchange of Simpkinsville . . . New York and London: Harper & Brothers, 1899. 74 p., front. CU, HEH, LC, O, Y First separate printing; printed earlier in No. 5304.

5310 STUMP, D. L. From World to World: A Novel . . . Asbury, Mo.: World to World Publishing Co., 1896. 125 p. LC

5311 [STURDY, WILLIAM ALLEN.] Shaking the Apple Tree; or, Education vs. Common Sense. A Novel. By Isaac Didwin [pseud.] . . . Boston: Published by the author; Horace Partridge & Co., printers, 1886. 380, [2] p., illus. CU, HEH, LC Civil War background.

5312 STURGES, JONATHAN. The First Supper, and Other Episodes: The Moonlighter of County Clare, The Brother, Three Forms, Koznuishef . . . New York: Dodd, Mead & Co., 1893. 176 p. BA, CU, HEH, Y

5313 STURGIS, REBECCA FORBES. The Price of a Life: A Novel . . . New York: G. W. Carleton & Co. London: S. Low, Son & Co., 1881. 372 p.

CU, LC

Life in a mill town.

5314 SUBDUED SOUTHERN NOBILITY: A Southern Ideal. By One of the Nobility. New York: Sharps Publishing Company [cop. 1882]. 392 p.

AP, BA, BU, CU, HEH, LC, N, O, UC, UM, UV

Prior to and during the Civil War.

SULE, LEON, *pseud. See* Fagan, T. A.

5315 SULLIVAN, MRS. A. SHACKELFORD. A Questionable Marriage . . . Chicago and New York: Rand, McNally & Company [cop. 1897]. 189 p. Copy examined at New York Public Library. Pertains to Oklahoma divorce laws.

5316 [SULLIVAN, HELEN.] How to Get Rich. By Zutana [pseud.]. Cincinnati, Ohio: Quinby Bros., print., 1884. 18 p.     LC

5317 SULLIVAN, JAMES WILLIAM. So the World Goes . . . Chicago: Charles H. Kerr & Company, 1898. 280 p.     BU, HEH, LC
Social reform.

5318 ———— Tenement Tales of New York . . . New York: Henry Holt and Company, 1895. 233 p., front.     CU, H, HEH, LC, UC, Y
*Contents:* Slob Murphy—Minnie Kelsey's Wedding—Cohen's Figure—Threw Himself Away—Luigi Barbieri—Leather's Banishment—Not Yet—A Young Desperado.

SULLIVAN, THOMAS RUSSELL. The Anatomist of the Heart. *In* Stories of Italy (1893), No. 5278.
Also included in No. 5321.

5319 ———— Ars et Vita, and Other Stories . . . New York: Charles Scribner's Sons, 1898. 302 p., illus.     BA, CU, H, HEH, LC, N, O, UV, Y
*Also contains:* The Phantom Governess—The Madonna That Is Childless—An Undiscovered Murder—The Whirligig of Fortune—Signor Lanzi—"Corraterie."

5320 ———— Day and Night Stories . . . New York: Charles Scribner's Sons, 1890. 253 p.     AP, BA, CU, H, HEH, LC, N, O, UV, Y
*Contents:* The Lost Rembrandt—Out of New England Granite—"Cordon!"—The Tincture of Success—The Rock of Béranger—Maestro Ambrogio—Through the Gate of Dreams.

5321 ———— ———— Second Series . . . New York: Charles Scribner's Sons, 1893. 249 p.     BA, CU, H, HEH, LC, Y
*Contents:* The Clerk of the Weather—A Toledo Blade—"To Her"—The Anatomist of the Heart—The Man in Red—Jack-in-the-Box—Under Cover of the Darkness.

5322 ———— Roses of Shadow: A Novel . . . New York: Charles Scribner's Sons, 1885. 270 p.     AP, BA, CU, H, HEH, LC, N, O, UVB, Y
Boston society.

5323 ———— Tom Sylvester: A Novel . . . New York: Charles Scribner's Sons, 1893. 428 p.     BA, CU, H, HEH, LC, N, O, UVB, Y
Of an American banking firm in Paris.

SUMICHRAST, FREDERICK CAESAR JOHN MARTIN SAMUEL ROUSSY DE. The Untold Word. *In* F. E. McKay, *ed.*, Vignettes [cop. 1890], No. 3523.

SUMMERDALE, *pseud. See* Young, Alexander

SUMNER, HELEN LAURA. *See* Woodbury, Helen Laura (Sumner)

5324  SUPER, MRS. EMMA LEFFERTS.  One Rich Man's Son . . .  Cincinnati: Cranston & Curts.  New York: Hunt & Eaton, 1895.  209 p., illus.
HEH, LC

5325  SURGHNOR, MRS. M. F.  Uncle Tom of the Old South: A Story of the South in Reconstruction Days . . .  New Orleans: L. Graham & Son, Ltd., 1897.  391 p.
CU, HEH, LC

5326  SUTHERLAND, HOWARD VIGNE.  The Legend of Love: A Tale Adapted to the Requirements of Children and Others . . .  San Francisco: Privately printed, 1893.  34 p.
HEH, LC

5327  [———]  The Old, Old Story (Only Differently Treated) . . .  Privately Printed.  San Francisco, 1893.  25 p.
LC

5328  SUTPHEN, ELEANOR AMERMAN.  Ye Nexte Thynge . . .  New York, Chicago, Toronto: Fleming H. Revell Company [cop. 1897].  57 p., front.
LC, UM, UV

SUTPHEN, VAN TASSEL.  See Sutphen, William Gilbert Van Tassel

5329  SUTPHEN, WILLIAM GILBERT VAN TASSEL.  The Cardinal's Rose: A Novel . . .  New York and London: Harper & Brothers, 1900.  270, [1] p., illus.
H, HEH, LC, UM, Y
Adventures of a New York newspaperman in Europe.

5330  ———  The Golficide, and Other Tales of the Fair Green . . .  New York and London: Harper & Brothers, 1898.  227, [1] p., illus.
H, HEH, LC, N, O, UM, Y
*Also contains:* The Hong-Kong Medal—The Obsession of Robinson Brown—The Peripatetic Hazard—The Lost Ball—The Prime Great Secret.

5331  SWAIN, CHARLES F.  Captain Waters and Bill His Bo'son: A Tale of the Ocean and the Farm . . .  New York: John P. Jewett, 1877.  297 p., illus.
CU, HEH, LC, Y

5332  [SWAN, ELIZA B.]  Once a Year; or, The Doctors' Puzzle.  By E. B. S. Cincinnati: Robert Clarke & Co., 1881.  244 p.
AP, CU
Of a fashionable spa in the Blue Ridge Mountains.

5333  ———  The Opal Queen . . .  Cincinnati: Robert Clarke & Co., 1892. 387 p.
HEH, LC

5334  SWAN, HERBERT E.  It Might Be: A Story of the Future Progress of the Sciences, the Wonderful Advancement in the Methods of Government . . .  Stafford, Kansas: H. E. Swan, 1896.  180 p., front.
H, LC, UM

5335  SWAN, MIRANDA ELIOT.  Daisy: The Autobiography of a Cat . . .  Boston: Noyes Brothers [cop. 1900].  268 p., front.
H, HEH, LC
Written to engender interest in humane societies.

5336 [SWAZEY, ARTHUR.] A Boston Girl: A Story of Boston, Bar Harbor, and Paris. Chicago and New York: Belford, Clarke & Co., 1886. 375 p.
HEH, LC, Y

5337 SWEET, ALEXANDER EDWIN. On a Mexican Mustang through Texas, from the Gulf to the Rio Grande . . . Hartford, Conn.: S. S. Scranton & Company, 1883. 672 p., illus. BA, LC, UM, Y
*Also issued with imprint:* Hartford, Conn.: S. S. Scranton & Company. Houston and St. Louis: T. N. James & Co. Syracuse: Watson Gill. Cleveland: C. C. Wick & Co. Cincinnati: The Cincinnati Book and Bible House. Chicago: C. B. Beach & Co. Philadelphia: Thayer, Merriam & Co. San Francisco: A. L. Bancroft & Co., 1883. H, Y
o, uv has copy which omits "Cleveland: C. C. Wick & Co." in imprint.
John Armoy Knox, jt. au.

5338 ———— Sketches from "Texas Siftings" . . . New York: Texas Siftings Publishing Company, 1882. 228 p., illus.
BU, CU, H, HEH, LC, N, O, UC, UM, UP, Y
John Armoy Knox, jt. au.

5339 A SWEETHEART FOR SOMEBODY: A Novel. By the Author of "Margaret's Engagement" . . . New York: G. W. Carleton & Co., 1878. 192 p. LC
This may be of English origin.

5340 SWEETSER, MOSES FOSTER. In Distance and in Dream . . . Boston: Joseph Knight Company, 1895. 43 p. LC
At head of title: "Cosy Corner Series."

5341 SWETT, SOPHIA MIRIAM. Pennyroyal and Mint . . . Boston: Estes and Lauriat [cop. 1896]. 446 p. CU, H, HEH, LC, N, O
*Contents:* The Conscience Case of Mrs. Roxy Pell—"Own Folks"—"Yender Grass"—Cap'n 'Sander's "Wrastle"—A Case of Incompatibility—Sar' Ann—Coals of Fire—David's Colt—The 'Piscopal Lot—The Little Rift within the Lute—A Pelican of the Wilderness—Grandma Baker's Thumb—A Stroke of Fortune—The Deceitfulness of Riches—A Courtship at Sedgecomb's Corner—Arctury Ann—Waitsill Peavy's "Conscience Spells"—Mrs. Prouty's Pension—The Topham Meadow Lot—The Schoolmistress on Barberry Island—'Squog. Deposited Aug. 20, 1896.
Also published as: *Sar' Ann; or, Pennyroyal and Mint.* New York and Boston: H. M. Caldwell Company [cop. 1896]. CU
Date of publication not determined.
Majority of her books were juveniles.

5342 SWETT, SUSAN HARTLEY. Field Clover and Beach Grass . . . Boston: Estes and Lauriat [cop. 1896]. 350 p. BU, HEH, LC, Y
*Contents:* Tom's Monument—Mis' David's Auction—A Difficulty in the Way—Swan's Island Folk—Mr. Snow and Miss Laura—An Affair at Sunday Cove—The Dressmaker at Green Harbour—A Floral Affinity—Mrs. Norton's Disappointment—A Desperate Case—Marthy Ellen—Luthery Ann's New Neighbour—Miss Matilda Jane and the Minister—A Happening in the Winter Mountains—"Meetin' Sunday"—The Wrong Card.

5343 SWIFT, AUGUSTUS M. Cupid, M.D.: A Story . . . New York: Charles
Scribner's Sons, 1882. 172 p.                AP, BU, CU, H, HEH, LC, O
Of the opium habit.

5344 SWING, DAVID. A True Love Story . . . [Chicago]: Chicago Literary
Club, 1894. 33, [2] p., illus.                          HEH, LC, N, Y
215 copies privately printed for the members.

5345 SWISHER, BELLA (FRENCH). Rocks and Shoals in the River of Life: A
Novel . . . New York: G. W. Dillingham, 1889. 379 p.        HEH, LC

5346 ——— Struggling Up to the Light: The Story of a Woman's Life. By
Bella French . . . Chicago: W. B. Keen, Cooke & Co., 1876. 221 p.
                                                            HEH, Y

5347 SWITZER, JENNIE (BARTLETT). Elder Northfield's Home; or, Sacrificed
on the Mormon Altar. A Story of the Blighting Curse of Polygamy.
By A. Jennie Bartlett. New York: The J. Howard Brown Company,
45 Centre Street [cop. 1882]. 319 p.                          HEH
Also published as: *Elder Northfield's Home . . . A Story of Territorial Days
in Utah.* 2nd ed. Boston: B. B. Russell Co., 57 Cornhill [cop. 1894]. 319 p.
H, LC
Also published as: *Elder Northfield's Home . . . A Story of Utah.* Boston:
B. B. Russell & Co., 57 Cornhill [cop. 1895]. 320 p.     H, HEH, LC, UM
Page 319 reset, and new material extends story to p. 320.

SYDENHAM, ALVIN H. Conyngham Foxe and the Charity Ball. The Lost
Pine Mine. Wauna, the Witch-Maiden. [Three stories.] *In* C. King,
*ed.,* An Initial Experience (1894), No. 3105.

——— The Ebb-Tide. The Story of Alcatraz. [Two stories.] *In*
C. King, *ed.,* Captain Dreams (1895), No. 3097.

5348 SYDNEY, JOSEPH. The American "L'Assommoir": A Parody on Zola's
"L'Assommoir" . . . Philadelphia: T. B. Peterson & Brothers, 306
Chestnut Street [cop. 1879]. 171 p.                          LC

5349 SYLVERAN, ANNA. Nancy's Eventful Christmas . . . [Lowell, Mass.,
1897.] 15 p., illus.                                         HEH

T., M. I. *See* Todd, Mary Van Lennup (Ives)

5350 TAGGART, MARION AMES. Aser, the Shepherd . . . New York, Cincinnati, Chicago: Benziger Brothers, 1897. 63 p., front.        LC

5351 ——— Bezaleel . . . New York, Cincinnati, Chicago: Benziger Brothers, 1897. 59 p., front.                                     LC

5352 TAINTER, HELEN (DAVIES). The Reveries of a Spinster. By Helen Davies. New York: F. Tennyson Neely, 1897. 216 p.              O, Y
Of a New York schoolteacher.

5353  TALBOT, ELLA GRAVES. Which? A Novel... Denver, Colo.: The Perry Publishing Company, 1888. 248 p.                                    HEH

5354  [TALBOT, HANNAH LINCOLN.] Not in the Prospectus. By Parke Danforth [pseud.]. Boston and New York: Houghton, Mifflin and Company, 1887. 302 p.                                                          H
First printed in the omitted "Riverside Paper Series," No. 23, 1886.
Experiences of a group of tourists in Europe.

5355  TALCOTT, HANNAH ELIZABETH (BRADBURY) GOODWIN. Christine's Fortune. By Mrs. H. B. Goodwin ... Boston: A. Williams and Company, 1881. 270 p.
Copy examined at New York Public Library.

5356  ——— Dorothy Gray: An Indian Summer Idyl... Boston: Damrell & Upham, 1891. 267 p.                                          H, HEH
New England characters.

5357  ——— The Fortunes of Miss Follen. By Mrs. Goodwin-Talcott ... New York: D. Appleton and Company, 1876. 270 p.          CU, H, HEH, O
German country life.

5358  ——— One among Many ... Boston: Cupples, Upham and Company, 1884. 312 p.                                                    H, HEH
Of a turbulent marriage.

5359  ——— Our Party of Four: A Story of Travel... Boston: Cupples and Hurd, 1887. 215 p.                                     H, HEH, LC

5360  TALES FROM McCLURE'S: Adventure ... New York: Doubleday & McClure Co., 1897. 192 p., illus.
*Contents:* The Mistress of the Foundry, by Earl Joslyn—Dreams Go by Contraries, by George H. Jessop—A Leap in the Dark, by James T. McKay—How Cassie Saved the Spoons, by Annie Howells Fréchette—A Strange Story: The Lost Years, by Lizzie Hyer Neff—Two Modern Prodigals, by J. T. McKay.
Listed PW, Dec. 4, 1897.

5361  TALES FROM McCLURE'S: Humor ... New York: Doubleday & McClure Co., 1897. 186 p., illus.                                        HEH
*Contents:* Burglars Three, by James Harvey Smith—The Joneses' Telephone, by Annie Howells Fréchette—A Yarn without a Moral, by Morgan Robertson—The King of Boyville, by William Allen White—The Merry Thanksgiving of the Burglar and Plumber, by Octave Thanet [i.e., Alice French]—The Romance of Dulltown, by James W. Temple—Fairy Gold, by Mary Stewart Cutting.

5362  TALES FROM McCLURE'S: Romance ... New York: Doubleday & McClure Co., 1897. 170 p., illus.                                      HEH
*Contents:* The Type-Written Letter, by Robert Barr—Rachel, by Mrs. E. V. Wilson—A Game Postponed, by Gertrude Smith—When She Was Thirty,

by Louise Chandler Moulton—Neighbor King, by Collins Shackelford—A Feline Fate, by Anna Robeson Brown [Burr]—The Whip-Hand, by Ann Devoore.

5363 TALES FROM MCCLURE'S: The West . . . New York: Doubleday & Mc-Clure Co., 1897. 195 p., illus.                                CU, HEH, Y

Contents: Town Lot No. 1303, by Octave Thanet [i.e., Alice French]—Barb'ry, by Mrs. E. V. Wilson—The Home-Coming of Colonel Hucks, by William Allen White—A Point of Knucklin' Down, by Ella Higginson—The Surgeon's Miracle, by Joseph Kirkland—Dikkon's Dog, by Dorothy Lundt —The Divided House, by Julia D. Whiting.

5364 TALES FROM MCCLURE'S: War, Being True Stories of Camp and Battle-field . . . New York: Doubleday & McClure Co., 1898. 193 p., illus.
                                                                CU, HEH, Y

Contains: In a Bowery Regiment, by Capt. Musgrove Davis (Charles O. Shep-ard)—The Bravest Deed of the War, by Capt. T. J. Mackey—The Men in the Ranks, by Major Philip Douglas—War Tales, by Capt. M. Davis (C. O. Shepard)—An Incident of Gettysburg, by Capt. T. J. Mackey—A Raid on the Wires, by Capt. George L. Kilmer—Stealing Railroad Engines, by Ernest Shriver—The Escape, by Major Alfred R. Calhoun.

5365 TALES OF OUR COAST . . . New York: Dodd, Mead and Company, 1896. 203 p., illus.                       BA, BU, CU, H, HEH, LC, N, O, UC, UV, Y
Contains: The Path of Murtogh, by Harold Frederic.

5366 TALLMAN, GEORGE DOUGLAS. Caught: A Romance of Three Days . . . New York: G. W. Dillingham, 1895. 284 p.                            LC
New Orleans.

5367 [———] Innocents from Abroad . . . New York: G. W. Carleton & Co. London: S. Low & Co., 1878. 252 p., illus.                   HEH, Y
Perils of a stranger in New York.

5368 [———] Tom's Wife! and How He Managed Her. By a Married Bachelor . . . New York: G. W. Carleton & Co. London: S. Low, Son & Co., 1877. 172 p.                                        HEH, LC
Also published as: Just Married; or, How Tom Managed His Wife. New York: G. W. Carleton & Co., 1878. Listed PW, July 6, 1878.

5369 TARKINGTON, BOOTH. The Gentleman from Indiana . . . New York: Doubleday & McClure Co., 1899. 384 p.    BA, H, HEH, LC, N, O, UP, UV, Y

5370 ——— Monsieur Beaucaire . . . New York: McClure, Phillips & Co., 1900. 127, [1] p., 1 l., illus.    BA, CU, H, HEH, LC, O, UC, UM, UP, UV, Y

5371 TASCHER, JULIA M. Arbutus and Dandelions: A Novel . . . New York: Press of J. J. Little & Co., 1883. 400 p.                     HEH, LC

TASSIN, ALGERNON DE VIVIER. The Return. In F. E. McKay, ed., Vignettes [cop. 1890], No. 3523.

5372 TATE, HENRY. Bicycle Yarns ... New York: F. Tennyson Neely, 114 Fifth Avenue. Chicago, London [cop. 1899]. 154 p., front. HEH

5373 TAYLOR, A. RYCROFT. Lally Letham's Will: A Tale of the Great City ... New York: Wilbur B. Ketcham [cop. 1896]. 96 p., illus.
Listed PW, Dec. 19, 1896.

TAYLOR, BAYARD. Who Was She? In Stories by American Authors, I (1884), No. 5267.

5374 TAYLOR, BELLE GRAY. The Sardonyx Seal: A Romance of Normandy ... New York, London: G. P. Putnam's Sons; the Knickerbocker Press, 1891. 316 p., front. LC, O, UM, Y

5375 TAYLOR, BENJAMIN FRANKLIN. Theophilus Trent: Old Times in the Oak Openings ... Chicago: S. C. Griggs and Company, 1887. 250 p.
AP, H, HEH, LC, N, UM, Y
A Michigan settlement.

5376 TAYLOR, BERT LESTON. Under Three Flags: A Story of Mystery ... Chicago and New York: Rand, McNally & Company, 1896. 343 p.
CU, HEH, LC
Alvin T. Thoits, jt. au.

TAYLOR, BRIDE NEILL. When Hester Came. In Ten Notable Stories (1894), No. 5391.

TAYLOR, BURPEE CALDWELL. An Experience with the Rho Kap's. The Undecided Bet. [Two stories.] In H. J. Hapgood, ed., Echoes from Dartmouth (1895), No. 2446.

TAYLOR, H. C. CHATFIELD. See Chatfield-Taylor, Hobart Chatfield

5377 TAYLOR, HENRY D. 16 Old Maids, and Other Stories ... Springfield, Mass.: The Phelps Publishing Co., 1888. 158 p., illus. H, HEH, LC
Also contains: A Fair Catch at First Base—A Queer Deed—Five Merry Girls —Edward Wilson's Holiday—Our Village Gossip—Two Christmases.

5378 TAYLOR, HENRY WILLIAM. The Romantic Story of Wickly's Woods ... Chicago: T. S. Denison, 163 Randolph Street [cop. 1888]. 142 p.
HEH, LC, UVB

TAYLOR, HOBART CHATFIELD. See Chatfield-Taylor, Hobart Chatfield

TAYLOR, JUDSON R., pseud. See Halsey, Harlan Page

5379 TAYLOR, MRS. MARY COLLIVER. The Divorce ... Columbus, Ohio, 1895. 130 p. LC

5380 TAYLOR, MARY IMLAY. The Cardinal's Musketeer ... Chicago: A. C. McClurg & Co., 1900. 357 p., front. BA, H, HEH, LC, N, O, UM
Cardinal Richelieu.

5381 ——— The Cobbler of Nîmes . . . Chicago: A. C. McClurg & Co., 1900. 277 p.  LC, O, UV
Reign of Louis XIV.

5382 ——— The House of the Wizard . . . Chicago: A. C. McClurg and Company, 1899. 340 p., front.  HEH, LC, N
Court of Henry VIII.

5383 ——— An Imperial Lover . . . Chicago: A. C. McClurg and Company, 1897. 377 p., front.  H, HEH, LC, O, UM
Peter the Great; Russia.

5384 ——— On the Red Staircase . . . Chicago: A. C. McClurg and Company, 1896. 352 p., front.  CU, HEH, LC, O
Peter the Great; Russia.

5385 ——— A Yankee Volunteer . . . Chicago: A. C. McClurg and Company, 1898. 383 p.  CU, HEH, LC, N, O
American Revolution.

5386 TAYLOR, WINNIE LOUISE. His Broken Sword . . . Chicago: A. C. McClurg and Company, 1888. 354 p.  AP, H, HEH, LC, UM
Of prison life.

5387 TEAL, ANGELINE (GRUEY). John Thorn's Folks: A Study of Western Life . . . Boston: Lee and Shepard. New York: Charles T. Dillingham, 1884. 187 p.  AP, CU, H, HEH

5388 ——— Muriel Howe . . . New York: Dodd, Mead & Company [cop. 1892]. 280 p.  HEH, LC
Deposited Aug. 25, 1892.

5389 ——— The Rose of Love . . . New York: Dodd, Mead & Company, 1893. 224 p.  HEH, LC

5390 TEETZEL, MRS. FRANCES GRANT. The Dynamite Cartridge . . . Boston: Cleaves, MacDonald & Co., 1885. 101 p.  CU, HEH, LC, UC, UM

TEMPLE, JAMES W. The Romance of Dulltown. *In* Tales from McClure's: Humor (1897), No. 5361.

TEMPLETON, FAITH, *pseud. See* Barber, Harriet Boomer

5391 TEN NOTABLE STORIES from Lippincott's Magazine. Philadelphia: J. B. Lippincott Company, 1894. 145 p.  CU, O
*Contents:* A Rose of the Mire, by Kate Jordan—Abraham's Mother, by Annie Flint—A Pastel, by Cornelia Kate Rathbone—The Philosophers, by Geraldine Bonner—The Reprieve of Capitalist Clyve, by Owen Wister—Jane's Holiday, by Valerie Hays Berry—The Cross-Roads Ghost, by Matt Crim—A Deed with a Capital D, by Charles M. Skinner—The Rustlers, by Alice MacGowan—When Hester Came, by Bride Neill Taylor.

5392　TENNEY, EDWARD PAYSON. Agamenticus . . . Boston: Lee and Shepard.
New York: Charles T. Dillingham, 1878. 267 p.
BA, BU, CU, H, HEH, LC, O, Y
Of Yorke, Maine.

5393　[————] Agatha and the Shadow: A Novel. Boston: Roberts Brothers, 1887. 321 p. AP, BA, HEH, LC
Puritans in colonial days.

5394　[————] Constance of Acadia: A Novel. Boston: Roberts Brothers,
1886. 368 p. AP, BA, CU, HEH, LC, O, Y
New France.

5395　———— Coronation: A Story of Forest and Sea . . . Boston: Noyes,
Snow and Company, 1877. 389 p. BA, H, HEH, Y

5396　[————] A Story of the Heavenly Camp-Fires. By One with a New
Name. New York: Harper & Brothers, 1896. 218, [1] p. BA, BU, LC

TERHUNE, MARY VIRGINIA (HAWES). A Confederate Idyl, by Marion
Harland [pseud.]. *In* L. C. H. Langford, *comp.*, The Woman's Story
(1889), No. 3206.

5397　[————] Dr. Dale: A Story without a Moral. By Marion Harland
[pseud.] and Albert Payson Terhune. New York: Dodd, Mead and
Company, 1900. 408 p. H, LC, O, UVB
Pennsylvania oil fields.

5398　[————] A Gallant Fight. By Marion Harland [pseud.] . . . New
York: Dodd, Mead & Company [cop. 1888]. 414 p.
AP, CU, HEH, LC, O, UM, Y
Deposited Nov. 1, 1888.

5399　[————] Handicapped. By Marion Harland [pseud.]. New York:
Charles Scribner's Sons, 1881. 391 p. AP, CU, HEH, O, UM, UP, Y
*Contents:* Two—The Heart of John Stewart—Wall-Flowers—Abigail's Wait-
ing—How "Mad Marcy" Was Tamed—Lois Grant and Her Reward—One
Old Maid—Nurse Brown's Story.

5400　[————] His Great Self. By Marion Harland [pseud.] . . . Philadelphia: J. B. Lippincott Company, 1892. 355 p. CU, H, HEH, LC, O, UV
Colonial Virginia.

5401　[————] Judith: A Chronicle of Old Virginia. By Marion Harland
[pseud.] . . . Philadelphia: Our Continent Publishing Co. New York:
Fords, Howard, & Hulbert, 1883. 391 p., illus.
AP, BA, CU, H, HEH, LC, O, UC, UM, UVB, Y
At head of title: " 'Our Continent' Library."

5402 ——— Mr. Wayt's Wife's Sister . . . New York: The Cassell Publishing Co., 31 East 17th St. [cop. 1894]. 314 p.     H, HEH, LC, O, UV, Y
*Also contains:* A Social Success—The Articles of Separation.

5403 [———] My Little Love. By Marion Harland [pseud.]. New York: G. W. Carleton & Co. London: S. Low & Co., 1876. 396 p.
BU, CU, HEH, LC, N, O, UM, UP, UV

5404 [———] Not Pretty, but Precious. By Marion Harland [pseud.]. Greenfield, Mass.: H. D. Watson Publishing Co., 1887. 308 p., front.
HEH

5405 [———] The Royal Road; or, Taking Him at His Word. By Marion Harland [pseud.] . . . New York: Anson D. F. Randolph and Company (Incorporated), 182 Fifth Avenue [cop. 1894]. 377 p.
H, HEH, LC, O, UC, UV

5406 [———] Ruth Bergen's Limitations: A Modern Auto-da-fe. By Marion Harland [pseud.]. New York, Chicago, Toronto: Fleming H. Revell Company, 1897. 123 p.     LC, UC, UM, UV

5407 [———] With the Best Intentions: A Midsummer Episode. By Marion Harland [pseud.]. New York: Charles Scribner's Sons, 1890. 303 p.     AP, BA, HEH, LC, O, UVB
Fort Mackinac, Michigan.

5408 TERRY, FREDERIC BATTELL. Stories . . . New York: The De Vinne Press, 1890. 77, [1] p.     HEH, N, Y

5409 TESTUT, CHARLES. Les Filles de Monte-Cristo . . . Nouvelle-Orléans: Imprimerie Cosmopolite, 1876. 507 p.
Edward L. Tinker, *Les Écrits de Langue Française en Louisiane au XIXe Siècle* (Paris, 1932), p. 462, locates a copy in the Howard-Tilton Memorial Library at Tulane University.

TETERS, WILBERTINE. *See* Worden, Wilbertine (Teters)

5410 TEUFFEL, BLANCHE WILLIS (HOWARD) VON. Aulnay Tower. By Blanche Willis Howard . . . Boston: Ticknor and Company, 1885. 343 p.
CU, H, HEH, LC, N, O, UC, UM, UP, Y

5411 ——— Aunt Serena . . . Boston: James R. Osgood and Company, 1881. 358 p.     BU, CU, H, HEH, LC, N, O, UM, UP, UV, Y

5412 ——— Dionysius the Weaver's Heart's Dearest . . . New York: Charles Scribner's Sons, 1899. 375 p.
BU, CU, H, HEH, LC, N, O, UC, UV, Y

5413 ——— A Fellowe and His Wife . . . Boston and New York: Houghton, Mifflin and Company. The Riverside Press, Cambridge, 1892. 255 p.     CU, H, HEH, LC, N, O, UP, UV, Y
William Sharp, jt. au.

5414 ———— The Garden of Eden ... New York: Charles Scribner's Sons, 1900. 444 p.  CU, H, HEH, LC, N, O, UP, Y

5415 ———— Guenn: A Wave on the Breton Coast . . . Boston: James R. Osgood and Company, 1884. 439 p., illus.  CU, H, HEH, LC, N, O, UV, Y
2nd issue changes "Soyez gentille" to "Voyons, voyons" on p. 283, next to last line; other minor variations. Census of copies does not distinguish between issues.

5416 ———— The Open Door ... Boston and New York: Houghton, Mifflin and Company. The Riverside Press, Cambridge, 1889. 436 p.
BU, CU, H, HEH, LC, N, O, UC, UM, UP, UV, Y

5417 ———— Seven on the Highway ... Boston and New York: Houghton, Mifflin and Company. The Riverside Press, Cambridge, 1897. 272 p., 1 l.  BA, CU, H, HEH, LC, N, O, UM, Y
*Contents:* Marigold-Michel—No Continuing City—Thalatta!—Puss-in-Boots —The Youth That Never Smiled—The Majesty of the Law—All Sails Spread for Monkeyland.

5418 ———— Tony, the Maid: A Novelette . . . New York: Harper & Brothers, 1887. 166 p., illus.  BA, CU, H, HEH, LC, N, O, UC, UP, Y

Tföffer, *pseud. See* Tupper, Henry Allen

Thanet, Octave, *pseud. See* French, Alice

5419 That Awful Boy! By the Author of "That Bridget of Ours" ... New York: G. W. Carleton & Co. London: S. Low, Son & Co., 1877. 142 p.  HEH, LC, UM

5420 That Bridget of Ours! By the Author of "That Awful Boy" ... New York: G. W. Carleton & Co. London: S. Low, Son & Co., 1877. 180 p.  LC, UM

5421 That Horrid Girl ... New York: G. W. Carleton & Co., 1877. 192 p.  LC, O

5421a That Young Man. Boston: N. H. Whitney & Co., 1878. 220 p.  HEH

Thaxter, Celia (Laighton). A Memorable Murder. *In* Stories by American Authors, III (1884), No. 5269.
Later printed in No. 3206.

5422 Thayer, Ella Cheever. Wired Love: A Romance of Dots and Dashes ... New York: G. W. Carleton & Co. London: S. Low, Son & Co., 1879. 256 p.  CU, HEH, LC

5423 Thayer, Emma (Homan). The English-American ... Chicago: Donohue, Henneberry & Co., 1890. 463 p., illus.  LC, UM
Colorado.

5424 ——— A Legend of Glenwood Springs . . . Chicago: Colvin Publishing Company, 1900. 37 p.    LC

5425 ——— Petronilla, the Sister . . . New York, London: F. Tennyson Neely [cop. 1897]. 408 p., illus.    LC
Deposited Dec. 20, 1897.
White Mountains, New Hampshire.

5426 THAYER, WILLIAM ROSCOE. In the Meshes; or, A Drop of Boston Blue Blood . . . From the Harvard Lampoon. Cambridge: Charles W. Sever, 1881. 62 p., illus.    BA, HEH, LC, O, Y

5427 THEBAUD, AUGUSTUS. Louisa Kirkbride: A Tale of New York . . . New York: Peter F. Collier, 1879. 528 p., illus.    CU, HEH, N, UM
Of Irish Catholics in America.

5428 THEODORA; or, Star by Star . . . Philadelphia: J. B. Lippincott & Co., 1880. 320 p.    H

THICKSTUN, FREDERICK, pseud. See Clark, Frederick Thickstun

5429 THIESING, WINFIELD W. Nineteen Hundred Years; or, The Power of Christ. A Narrative . . . Covington, Ky.: Winfield W. Thiesing [cop. 1898]. 611 p., illus.    LC
Deposited Aug. 8, 1898.

THIUSEN, ISMAR, pseud. See Macnie, John

THOITS, ALVIN T., jt. au. See Taylor, B. L. Under Three Flags (1896), No. 5376.

5430 THOMAS, CHAUNCEY. The Crystal Button; or, Adventures of Paul Prognosis in the Forty-Ninth Century . . . Edited by George Houghton. Boston and New York: Houghton, Mifflin and Company. The Riverside Press, Cambridge, 1891. 302 p.
   AP, BU, H, HEH, LC, N, O, UC, UM, UP, Y
Of airships and underground railroads.

5431 THOMAS, EDWARD A. At Swords' Points: A Novel . . . Philadelphia: Claxton, Remsen, & Haffelfinger, 1877. 325 p.    HEH, LC, O
Of lawyers and trials.

5432 THOMAS, HENRY WILTON. The Last Lady of Mulberry: A Story of Italian New York . . . New York: D. Appleton and Company, 1900. 330 p., illus.    H, HEH, LC, O, Y

THOMAS, KATE, pseud. See Bull, Katherine Thomas (Jarboe)

5433 THOMAS, KATHERINE ELWES. Not All the King's Horses: A Novel of Washington Society . . . New York: The Cassell Publishing Co., 31 East 17th St. [cop. 1896]. 210 p.    HEH, LC, O, UC
At head of title: "The 'Unknown' Library."

5434 THOMAS, MARY VON ERDEN. Winning the Battle; or, One Girl in Ten Thousand . . . Philadelphia: T. B. Peterson & Brothers, 306 Chestnut Street [cop. 1882]. 472 p.     HEH, LC
Ante bellum Baltimore and New Orleans.

5435 THOMAS, REUEN. Grafenburg People: Fiction but Fact . . . Boston: D. Lothrop & Company, Franklin & Hawley Streets [cop. 1886]. 291 p.
    HEH, LC

5436 ———— The Kinship of Souls: A Narrative . . . Boston: Little, Brown and Company, 1899. 295 p.     H, HEH, LC, N

5437 THOMES, WILLIAM HENRY. The Belle of Australia; or, Who Am I? . . . Boston: De Wolfe, Fiske & Company, 1883. 325 p., illus.     HEH, LC, Y

5438 ———— Lewey and I; or, Sailor Boys' Wanderings. A Sequel to "On Land and Sea". . . Boston: De Wolfe, Fiske & Company, 1885. 407 p., illus.     HEH

5439 ———— On Land and Sea; or, California in the Years 1843, '44 and '45 . . . Boston: De Wolfe, Fiske & Company, 1884. 351 p., illus.
    BU, CU, H, HEH, LC, Y

5440 [THOMPSON, ALFRED.] Society as It Found Me Out. By Steward McGuzzler [pseud.]. New York: Carlton-Regand, 1890. 115, [6] p.
    H, LC, Y

5441 THOMPSON, ANNIE E. Elsie: A Story for the Home . . . Boston: James H. Earle, 1892. 311 p.     HEH, LC

5442 THOMPSON, AUGUSTIN. A Waif in the Conflict of Two Civilizations: A Tale of the Great Civil War in America and the Last Days of Slavery . . . Boston: The Rapid Printing Co., 1892. 328 p.     H, HEH, LC

5443 THOMPSON, HELEN STUART. Windy Creek . . . New York: Charles Scribner's Sons, 1899. 356 p.     HEH, LC, O, Y
Contents: A Colorado Claim—A Campbellite Sermon—The Immersion—Spending the Day—Some Neighborly Gossip—Free Methodism versus Campbellitism—A Dance—Two Weddings—The Come-Outers—Rose Rooney's Error—Diantha.

5444 THOMPSON, M. AGNES. Metairie, and Other Old Aunt Tilda of New Orleans Sketches . . . New Orleans, La., cop. 1892. 94 p.     LC

5445 THOMPSON, MAURICE. Alice of Old Vincennes . . . Indianapolis: The Bowen-Merrill Company [cop. 1900]. 419 p., illus.
    AP, BA, BU, CU, H, HEH, LC, N, O, UC, UM, UP, UVB, Y
Running headlines in bold-faced capitals of 1st issue reset in light-faced upper and lower case letters in 2nd issue. Census of copies does not distinguish between issues.

5446 —— At Love's Extremes . . . New York: Cassell & Company, Limited, 1885. 266 p.     AP, CU, H, HEH, LC, N, O, UM, UP, UVB, Y

5447 —— A Banker of Bankersville: A Novel . . . New York: Cassell & Company, Limited, 739 & 741 Broadway [cop. 1886]. 323 p.
    AP, H, LC, UC, UP, UVB, Y
Deposited Nov. 30, 1886.

5448 —— A Fortnight of Folly . . . New York: John B. Alden, 1888. 140 p.     CU, HEH, LC, O, UC, UVB, Y

—— Gil Horne's Bergonzi. *In* New Stories from the Chap-Book (1898), No. 3949.

5449 [——] His Second Campaign . . . Boston: James R. Osgood and Company, 1883. 342 p.     AP, BA, CU, HEH, LC, N, O, UP, UVB, Y
At head of title: "Round-Robin Series."

5450 —— The King of Honey Island: A Novel . . . New York: Robert Bonner's Sons, 1893. 343 p., illus.     CU, LC, N, UVB, Y

—— The Mystic Krewe. *In* Eleven Possible Cases [cop. 1891], No. 1737.

—— Rudgis and Grim. *In* I. Bacheller, *ed.*, Best Things from American Literature (1899), No. 195.
Printed earlier in No. 5451.

5451 —— Stories of the Cherokee Hills . . . Boston and New York: Houghton, Mifflin and Company. The Riverside Press, Cambridge, 1898. 255, [1] p., illus.     BA, CU, H, HEH, LC, N, O, UM, UP, UVB, Y
*Contents:* Color-Line Jocundities—Ben and Judas—Hodson's Hide-Out—Rudgis and Grim—A Race Romance—A Dusky Genius—The Balance of Power.

5452 [——] A Tallahassee Girl . . . Boston: James R. Osgood and Company, 1882. 355 p.     AP, BA, CU, HEH, LC, N, O, UM, UVB, Y
At head of title: "Round-Robin Series."

5453 THOMPSON, RAY. A Respectable Family . . . Chicago: Donnelley, Gassette, & Loyd, 1880. 552 p.     HEH, LC, Y
Suburbs of New York.

5454 [THOMPSON, WILLIAM TAPPAN.] John's Alive; or, The Bride of a Ghost. And Other Sketches. By Major Jones [pseud.] . . . Philadelphia: David McKay, 1883. 264 p., illus.     BU, CU, H, LC, N, O, UC, UP, UV
Collected by the author's daughter, Mrs. May A. Wade.
Title story first published in 1846: Wright I, 2588.

5455 [————] Rancy Cottem's Courtship: Detailed, with Other Humourous Sketches and Adventures. By Major Joseph Jones [pseud.] ... Philadelphia: T. B. Peterson & Brothers, 306 Chestnut Street [cop. 1879]. 128 p., illus.       H, LC

THOMSON, MRS. L. NORTON. *See* Thomson, Priscilla (Norton)

5456 THOMSON, PRISCILLA (NORTON). Looking through the Mists; or, Every Heart Knoweth Its Own Sorrow ... New York: Neely Co. [cop. 1900]. 334 p.
Listed PW, Dec. 15, 1900.
Author also known as Mrs. L. Norton Thomson.

THORNET, TERESA A., *pseud. See* Holloway, Mrs. Anna

5457 THORNTON, HENRY. Silas Hood: A Novel ... Chicago, Ill.: Henry T. Jaynes & Company, 1898. 218 p., illus.       LC

5458 THORNTON, M. JACQUELINE. Di Cary: A Novel ... New York: D. Appleton and Company, 1879. 231 p. Printed in double columns.
      HEH, LC
Postwar Virginia.

THORPE, KAMBA, *pseud. See* Bellamy, Elizabeth Whitfield (Croom)

5459 A THRILLING INCIDENT. [Port Jervis, N.Y., 189-?] Cover title, 7 p.   HEH
Short story interspersed with advertisements for D. C. Hallock & Co.'s products.

5460 THROPP, CLARA. A Few Little Lives ... New York, 1896. 100 p., illus.
      LC

5461 THRUMSTON, CORA M. Polly and I ... Chicago: Donohue & Henneberry [cop. 1893]. 180 p.       LC
Deposited Jan. 8, 1894.
References to Columbian Exposition, Chicago.

5462 THURBER, ALWYN M. The Hidden Faith: An Occult Story of the Period ... Chicago: F. M. Harley Publishing Co., 87-89 Washington St. [cop. 1895]. 294 p.       CU, LC
Deposited Dec. 10, 1895.
Chicago.

5463 ———— Quaint Crippen, Commercial Traveler ... Chicago: A. C. Mc-Clurg and Company, 1896. 253 p.       H, HEH, LC, UM, Y
Of a Boston salesman.

5464 ———— Zelma, the Mystic; or, White Magic versus Black ... Chicago: Authors Publishing Co., 1897. 380 p., illus.       LC, Y

5465 [THURSTON, GEORGE T.] Forty Years a File-Closer. By Captain Minus Wonbar [pseud.]. Washington, D.C.: Chapman & Taylor, 1889. 40 p. LC

THURSTON, OLIVER, *pseud. See* Flanders, Henry

5466 TIBBLES, THOMAS HENRY. Hidden Power: A Secret History of the Indian Ring, Its Operations, Intrigues, and Machinations. Revealing the Manner in Which It Controls Three Important Departments of the United States Government. A Defense of the U.S. Army, and a Solution of the Indian Problem . . . New York: G. W. Carleton & Co. London: S. Low, Son & Co., 1881. 356 p.    CU, HEH, LC, N, O, UC, Y
At head of title: "'Law Is Liberty.' . . ."

5467 TICKNOR, CAROLINE. A Hypocritical Romance, and Other Stories . . . Boston: Joseph Knight Company, 1896. 244 p., illus.
BA, H, HEH, LC, N, O, UC, UP
*Also contains:* The Fate of Clyde Moorfield, Yachtsman—The Judgment of Paris Reversed—A Little Study in Common Sense—Mr. Hurd's Holiday—The Evolution of a Bonnet—Mrs. Hudson's Picnic—A Bag of Pop-Corn—The Romance of a Spoon—The History of a Happy Thought—A Furnished Cottage by the Sea—A Hallowe'en Party.

5468 ———— Miss Belladonna: A Child of To-Day . . . Boston: Little, Brown and Company, 1897. 236 p., illus.    BA, BU, HEH, LC, UV

5469 TIDBALL, MARY LANGDON. Barbara's Vagaries . . . New York: Harper & Brothers, 1886. 175 p.    AP, BU, H, HEH, LC, O, Y
"Unsophisticated North Carolina mountain girl is the brunt of the malicious wit of popular Washington hostess." Powell, No. 587.

5470 [TIERNAN, FRANCES CHRISTINE (FISHER).] After Many Days: A Novel. By Christian Reid [pseud.] . . . New York: D. Appleton and Company, 1877. 212 p. Printed in double columns.    HEH, LC, O, Y

5471 [————] Bonny Kate: A Novel. By Christian Reid [pseud.] . . . New York: D. Appleton and Company, 1878. 222 p. Printed in double columns.    HEH, LC, O

5472 [————] Carmela. By Christian Reid [pseud.] . . . Philadelphia: H. L. Kilner & Co. [cop. 1891]. 371 p.    CU, HEH, LC, UV

5473 [————] The Chase of an Heiress. By Christian Reid [pseud.]. New York & London: G. P. Putnam's Sons; the Knickerbocker Press, 1898. 261 p.    LC, O

5474 [————] A Child of Mary. By Christian Reid [pseud.]. Notre Dame, Ind.: Joseph A. Lyons, 1885. 352 p.
Powell, No. 590, locates four copies, including one in University of North Carolina Library.

5475 [————] A Comedy of Elopement. By Christian Reid [pseud.] . . . New York: D. Appleton and Company, 1893. 261 p.     HEH, LC, O

5476 [————] Fairy Gold. By Christian Reid [pseud.] . . . Notre Dame, Ind.: The Ave Maria [cop. 1897]. 357 p.     LC
Deposited Feb. 9, 1898.

5477 [————] A Gentle Belle: A Novel. By Christian Reid [pseud.] . . . New York: D. Appleton and Company, 1879. 142 p. Printed in double columns.     BU, HEH, LC, O, Y

5478 [————] Heart of Steel: A Novel. By Christian Reid [pseud.] . . . New York: D. Appleton and Company, 1883. 543 p.     HEH, LC, O, UV

5479 [————] His Victory. By Christian Reid [pseud.]. Notre Dame, Ind.: Ave Maria Press, 1887. 83 p.
Powell, No. 594, locates two copies, including one in University of North Carolina Library.

———— In the Quebrada, by Christian Reid [pseud.]. *In* A Round Table of the Representative American Catholic Novelists (1897), No. 4703.

5480 [————] "The Land of the Sky"; or, Adventures in Mountain By-Ways. By Christian Reid [pseud.] . . . New York: D. Appleton and Company, 1876. 130 p., illus. Printed in double columns.
    CU, HEH, LC, O, UV

5481 [————] The Land of the Sun: Vistas Mexicanas. By Christian Reid [pseud.] . . . New York: D. Appleton and Company, 1894. 355 p., illus.     HEH, LC, O, UV

5482 [————] A Little Maid of Arcady. By Christian Reid [pseud.] . . . Philadelphia: H. L. Kilner & Co. [cop. 1893]. 284 p.     HEH, LC

5483 [————] The Lost Lode. By Christian Reid [pseud.]. And Stella's Discipline. By F. X. L. [pseud.]. Philadelphia: H. L. Kilner & Co. [cop. 1892]. 278 p.     HEH, LC
"F. X. L." not identified.
Deposited Dec. 13, 1892.

5484 [————] The Man of the Family: A Novel. By Christian Reid [pseud.] . . . New York & London: G. P. Putnam's Sons; the Knickerbocker Press, 1897. 336 p.     LC, O

5485 [————] Miss Churchill: A Study. By Christian Reid [pseud.] . . . New York: D. Appleton and Company, 1887. 294 p.
    AP, BA, H, HEH, LC, O

5486 [————] The Picture of Las Cruces: A Romance of Mexico. By Christian Reid [pseud.] ... New York: D. Appleton and Company, 1896. 275 p.          AP, BU, CU, HEH, LC, O, UV

5487 [————] Roslyn's Fortune: A Novel. By Christian Reid [pseud.] ... New York: D. Appleton and Company, 1885. 288 p.
         AP, BA, CU, HEH, LC, N, O, UC

5488 [————] A Summer Idyl. By Christian Reid [pseud.] ... New York: D. Appleton and Company, 1878. 211 p.        O
At head of title: "Appletons' New Handy-Volume Series."
O copy lacks title page; copy examined at New York Public Library.

5489 [————] Weighed in the Balance. By Christian Reid [pseud.] ... Boston: Marlier, Callanan & Company, 1900. 500 p., illus.    HEH, O, UV

5490 [————] A Woman of Fortune: A Novel. By Christian Reid [pseud.] ... New York, Cincinnati, Chicago: Benziger Brothers, 1896. 285 p.
         BA, HEH, LC

5491 [TIERNAN, MARY SPEAR (NICHOLAS).] Homoselle ... Boston: James R. Osgood and Company, 1881. 367 p.    AP, H, HEH, LC, UV
At head of title: "Round-Robin Series."

5492 ———— Jack Horner: A Novel ... Boston and New York: Houghton, Mifflin and Company. The Riverside Press, Cambridge, 1890. 347 p.
         AP, BA, H, HEH, LC, O, UM

5493 ———— Suzette: A Novel ... New York: Henry Holt and Company, 1885. 306 p.      AP, HEH, LC, O, UV, Y
Ante bellum Richmond.

5494 TIERNEY, CATHERINE A. Paule ... Westfield, Mass.: C. A. Tierney [cop. 1897]. 47 p.          LC
Deposited July 22, 1897.

5495 TILDEN, JOHN HENRY. Cursed before Birth: A Few Straight Tips Regarding Our Social Condition ... Denver, Colo.: Published by the author [cop. 1895]. 314 p., illus.      HEH, LC
Deposited Aug. 7, 1896.

TIMSOL, ROBERT, pseud. See Bird, Frederic Mayer

5496 TINCKER, MARY AGNES. Aurora: A Novel ... Philadelphia: J. B. Lippincott Company, 1886. 315 p., front.      AP, BA, HEH, O, Y
Of Italian life.

5497 ———— Autumn Leaves: Verse and Story ... New York: William H. Young and Company, 1899. 291 p.          BU, HEH
*Contains:* Lolita—Two Little Roman Beggars—Palingenesis—A Gloria—From the Garden of a Friend—His Honor's Daughter—A Dove of St. Mark's—An Evening in Rome.

5498 [————] By the Tiber . . . Boston: Roberts Brothers, 1881. 390 p.
AP, BU, H, HEH, LC, UC, Y
Americans in Italy.

5499 ———— The Jewel in the Lotos: A Novel . . . Philadelphia: J. B. Lippincott & Co., 1884. 338 p., illus. AP, BA, BU, CU, H, HEH, LC, O, UP, Y
Of Italian life.

5500 ———— San Salvador . . . Boston and New York: Houghton, Mifflin and Company. The Riverside Press, Cambridge, 1892. 335 p.
BA, H, HEH, LC, N, O
A utopian community.

5501 [————] Signor Monaldini's Niece. Boston: Roberts Brothers, 1879.
334 p. AP, BA, CU, H, HEH, LC, N, O, UM, UP, UV, Y
At head of title: "No Name Series."

———— Sister Silvia. *In* Stories by American Authors, II (1884), No. 5268.

5502 ———— Two Coronets . . . Boston and New York: Houghton, Mifflin and Company. The Riverside Press, Cambridge, 1889. 523 p.
AP, BA, BU, CU, H, HEH, O, UC, Y

5503 [TIPPETTS, KATHERINE (BELL).] Prince Arengzeba: A Romance of Lake George. (By Jerome Cable [pseud.].) And Beautiful Lake George. Glens Falls, N.Y.: W. H. Tippetts, Star Publishing Company [cop. 1892]. 154 p., illus. LC
"Beautiful Lake George," nonfiction, by W. H. Tippetts.
Deposited Apr. 22, 1893.

TODD, IRVING. Our Twins. *In* J. J. Conway, *ed.*, Stories (1893), No. 1172.

5504 TODD, MABEL (LOOMIS) Footprints . . . Amherst, Massachusetts, 1883.
44 p. BA, CU, H, LC

5505 [TODD, MARY VAN LENNUP (IVES).] Deborah, the Advanced Woman. By M. I. T. . . . Boston: Arena Publishing Company, 1896. 233 p.
H, HEH, LC
Of the early Mormon years in Salt Lake City.

5506 ———— The Heterodox Marriage of a New Woman . . . New York: Robert Lewis Weed Co. [cop. 1898]. 207 p. LC
Chicago woman and Russian man originate a new wedding ceremony.

5507 ———— The New Adam and Eve: A Love Story . . . New York: G. W. Dillingham, 1890. 361 p. LC

TODKILL, ANAS, *pseud. See* Cooke, John Esten

5508 TOILE, GEORGE. The Boarder of Argyle Place . . . New York City: R. F. Fenno & Company, 1900. 241 p., illus. HEH, LC
New Jersey.

5509 TOMLINSON, EVERETT TITSWORTH. Exiled from Two Lands . . . Boston: Lee and Shepard, 1898. 119 p. HEH, LC
French family migrated to Canada; late 18th century.

5510 TOMPKINS, ELIZABETH KNIGHT. The Broken Ring: A Romance . . . New York, London: G. P. Putnam's Sons; the Knickerbocker Press, 1896. 277 p. H, HEH, LC, O
Laid in Germany.

5511 ——— Her Majesty: A Romance of To-Day . . . New York, London: G. P. Putnam's Sons; the Knickerbocker Press, 1895. 222 p.
BA, H, HEH, LC, N, O, UM, Y

5512 ——— Talks with Barbara: Being an Informal and Experimental Discussion, from the Point of View of a Young Woman of To-Morrow, of Certain of the Complexities of Life, Particularly in Regard to the Relations of Men and Women . . . New York and London: G. P. Putnam's Sons; the Knickerbocker Press, 1900. 279 p. HEH, LC, Y

5513 ——— The Things That Count . . . New York and London: G. P. Putnam's Sons, 1900. 383 p. LC

5514 [TOMPKINS, GEORGE H.] Why Become a Mother: A Novel. By Mrs. Frankie Stamper [pseud.] . . . New York: Stellar Publishing Company, 1180 Broadway [cop. 1893]. 134 p., illus. LC

TOODLES, TIMOTHY, *pseud. See* Parks, Mary Wonderly

TORRANCE, TALBOT. The Mystery of a Christmas Hunt. *In* C. King, Rancho del Muerto [cop. 1895], No. 3109.

5515 TOURGEE, ALBION WINEGAR. Black Ice . . . New York: Fords, Howard, & Hulbert, 1888. 435 p. AP, BA, CU, H, HEH, LC, N, O, UC, UM, UVB, Y

5516 ——— Bricks without Straw: A Novel . . . New York: Fords, Howard, & Hulbert. London: Sampson Low & Co. Montreal: Dawson Bros. [cop. 1880]. 521 p., front.
AP, BA, BU, CU, H, HEH, LC, N, O, UC, UM, UP, UVB, Y
Listed PW, Oct. 2, 1880.
Textual changes in 2nd issue include "the rich man's war and the poor man's fight" from "the poor man's war and the rich man's fight," p. 343, line 17. Census of copies does not distinguish between issues.

5517 ——— Button's Inn . . . Boston: Roberts Brothers, 1887. 418 p.
AP, BA, BU, CU, H, HEH, LC, N, O, UC, UM, UP, UVB, Y

5518   [————] "89. Edited from the Original Manuscript. By Edgar Henry [pseud.]. New York, London, Paris, and Melbourne: Cassell & Company, Limited, MDCCCXCI [i.e., 1888]. 498 p.

AP, H, HEH, LC, O

Listed PW, May 5, 1888, under pseud.

5519   ———— Figs and Thistles: A Western Story . . . New York: Fords, Howard, & Hulbert [cop. 1879]. 538 p.     BU, HEH, LC, UP, UV, Y

Verso of title page: "Electrotyped by Lovejoy, Son & Co., N.Y."

"New Books" opposite title page is a boxed list of four titles.

"Trade Publications" at end, dated "Sept. 1st, 1879," lists five authors.

Listed PW, Oct. 11, 1879.

Also published as: *Figs and Thistles: A Romance of the Western Reserve.* New York: Fords, Howard, & Hulbert [cop. 1879]. 538 p., front.   HEH

At head of title: "The Story of an Earnest Man."

Verso of title page: "Electrotyped by Lovejoy, Son & Co., N.Y."

"Trade Publications" tipped in at front replacing the excised "New Books" list.

O and H have copies with verso of title page: "Jenkins & Thomas, Printers, 8 Spruce St., N.Y. J. Fowler Trow, Jr., Bookbinder, 15 Vandewater St., N.Y." Published between Sept. and Dec. 1880.

5520   [————] A Fool's Errand. By One of the Fools . . . New York: Fords, Howard, & Hulbert, 1879. 361 p.

BA, BU, CU, HEH, LC, N, O, UC, UP, UVB

5521   ———— ———— By One of the Fools. The Famous Romance of American History. New, Enlarged, and Illustrated Edition. To Which Is Added, by the Same Author, Part II: The Invisible Empire, a Concise Review of the Epoch on Which the Tale Is Based . . . Sold Only by Subscription. New York: Fords, Howard, & Hulbert. Boston: W. H. Thompson & Co. St. Louis: Scammell & Co. Cleveland: H. M. Lochary & Co. Chicago: Weston Hulbert. Indianapolis: J. M. Olcott. Boston & Concord: D. L. Guernsey. New Orleans: Southern Publishing Co. [cop. 1880]. 521 p., illus.

AP, BU, H, HEH, LC, N, O, UC, UP, UV, Y

*Also issued with imprint:* Cincinnati: Forshee & McMakin, 1880.   O

Title page is a cancel.

Also published as: *The Invisible Empire. Part I: A New, Illustrated, and Enlarged Edition of A Fool's Errand . . . The Famous Historical Romance of Life in the South since the War. Part II: A Concise Review of Recent Events . . . Including . . . Deeds of the Mysterious Ku-Klux-Klan.* New York: Fords, Howard, & Hulbert. Boston: W. H. Thompson & Co. Chicago: Weston Hulbert. St. Louis: Scammell & Co. San Francisco: A. L. Bancroft & Co. [cop. 1880]. 521 p., illus.   BU, HEH, UC, UVB

5522   ———— Hot Plowshares: A Novel . . . New York: Fords, Howard, & Hulbert, 1883. 610 p., illus.

AP, BA, BU, CU, H, HEH, LC, N, O, UC, UM, UP, UV

5523 ——— John Eax, and Mamelon; or, The South without the Shadow . . . New York: Fords, Howard, & Hulbert [cop. 1882]. 300 p.
AP, BA, BU, CU, H, HEH, LC, N, O, UC, UM, UP, UV, Y

5524 ——— The Man Who Outlived Himself . . . New York: Fords, Howard, and Hulbert, 1898. 215 p. CU, H, HEH, N, O, UC, UM, UP, UVB, Y
*Also contains:* Poor Joel Pike—The Grave of Tante Angélique.

5525 ——— The Mortgage on the Hip-Roof House . . . Cincinnati: Curts & Jennings. New York: Eaton & Mains, 1896. 206 p., illus. LC, UM

5526 ——— Murvale Eastman, Christian Socialist . . . New York: Fords, Howard, & Hulbert. London: Sampson Low, Marston, Searle, & Rivington, Ld. [cop. 1890]. 545 p.
BA, BU, CU, H, HEH, LC, N, O, UC, UM, UVB, Y

5527 ——— Out of the Sunset Sea . . . New York: Merrill & Baker, 74 Fifth Avenue [cop. 1893]. 462 p., illus. CU, HEH, LC, N, O, UC, UM, UP, UVB

5528 ——— An Outing with the Queen of Hearts . . . New York: Merrill & Baker, 1894. 133 p., illus. BU, CU, H, HEH, LC, UC, UM, UVB

5529 ——— Pactolus Prime . . . New York: Cassell Publishing Company, 104 & 106 Fourth Avenue [cop. 1890]. 359 p.
AP, BU, CU, HEH, LC, N, O, UC, UM, UP, Y

5530 ——— A Royal Gentleman . . . And 'Zouri's Christmas . . . New York: Fords, Howard, & Hulbert [cop. 1881]. 529 p., illus. O
" 'Zouri's Christmas" added to this revised ed. of the title story, which was published earlier as *Toinette:* Wright II, No. 2523.
Verso of title page: "Manufactured by S. W. Green's Son, 74 & 76 Beekman St., New York."
*Also issued with imprint:* New York: Fords, Howard, & Hulbert. Boston and Concord: D. L. Guernsey [cop. 1881]. O
"Manufactured" note on verso of title page.
*Also issued with imprint:* New York: Fords, Howard, & Hulbert [cop. 1881]. O
No "manufactured" note on verso of title page.
*Also issued with imprint:* New York: Fords, Howard, & Hulbert. Cincinnati: Douglass Bros. & Payne [cop. 1881]. HEH
No "manufactured" note on verso of title page.

5531 ——— A Son of Old Harry: A Novel . . . New York: Robert Bonner's Sons, 1891. 438 p., illus. HEH, O, UM

5532 ——— With Gauge & Swallow, Attorneys . . . Philadelphia: J. B. Lippincott Company, 1889. 271 p. AP, HEH, LC, O, UC, UP, UVB, Y

TOWNE, BELLE KELLOGG. The Taking In of Martha Matilda. *In* F. V. Fisher, The Transformation of Job [cop. 1900], No. 1871.

5533 TOWNER, AUSBURN. Chedayne of Kotono: A Story of the Early Days of the Republic ... New York: Dodd, Mead & Company, 751 Broadway [cop. 1877]. 606 p.     CU, H, HEH, LC, N, O, UM, Y
LC copy has registration stamp dated 1877.
Also published as: *After Long Years; or, Chedayne of Kotono*. New York: Dodd, Mead & Company [cop. 1882].   LC
   Deposited Nov. 28, 1882.
Wyoming Valley, Pennsylvania.

5534 ——— Seven Days in a Pullman Car ... New York: J. S. Ogilvie & Company, 31 Rose Street [cop. 1883]. 247 p.     HEH, LC

5535 [TOWNSEND, MRS. ANNE LAKE.] On the Verge: A Romance of the Centennial. By Philip Shirley [pseud.] ... San Francisco: A. L. Bancroft & Company, 1879. 295 p.     HEH, LC

5536 TOWNSEND, EDWARD WATERMAN. "Chimmie Fadden," Major Max, and Other Stories ... New York: Lovell, Coryell & Company, 310-318 Sixth Avenue [cop. 1895]. 346 p., illus.
                    BU, CU, H, HEH, LC, N, UM, UP, UVB, Y
Contents made up of "Chimmie Fadden Stories," "Other Stories," "Major Max Stories," and "The New Editor" (single story).

5537 ——— A Daughter of the Tenements ... New York: Lovell, Coryell & Company, 310-318 Sixth Avenue [cop. 1895]. 4 p.l., [9]-301 p.
                    CU, LC, N, UC, UP, Y
Deposited Oct. 12, 1895.
2nd issue, deposited Oct. 18, 1895, collates 4 p.l., [7]-301 p., illus., and contains a dedication and table of contents.   HEH, LC, O

——— The Dog on the Roof. *In* I. Bacheller, *ed.*, Best Things from American Literature (1899), No. 195.
Printed earlier in No. 5538.

5538 ——— Near a Whole City Full ... New York: G. W. Dillingham Co., 1897. 260 p., illus.     BU, CU, H, HEH, LC, N, UM
*Contents:* Just across the Square—A Rose of the Tenderloin—Ann Eliza's Triumph—The Man Outside—The Dog on the Roof—Guardians of the Law—A Dinner of Regrets—The Night Elevator Man's Story—By Whom the Offence Cometh—The Reward of Merit—The House of Yellow Brick—The Little Life of Pietro—When a Man Judges—Polly Slanguer's Trousseau.

——— The Night Elevator Man's Story. *In* I. Bacheller, *ed.*, Best Things from American Literature (1899), No. 195.
Printed earlier in No. 5538.

5539 TOWNSEND, GEORGE ALFRED. Bohemian Days: Three American Tales ... New York City: The Author's Private Issue, 242 West 23rd Street [cop. 1880]. 280 p.     LC, Y
*Contains:* The Rebel Colony in Paris—Married Abroad—The Deaf Man of Kensington.
*Also issued with imprint:* New York: H. Campbell & Co., No. 21 Park Row [cop. 1880].   HEH, UVB, Y

5540 ———— The Entailed Hat; or, Patty Cannon's Times. A Romance . . .
New York: Harper & Brothers, 1884. 565 p.
AP, CU, H, HEH, LC, N, O, UC, UM, UVB
Of kidnaping free Negroes and selling them as slaves.

5541 ———— Katy of Catoctin; or, The Chain-Breakers. A National Romance . . . New York: D. Appleton and Company, 1886. 567 p.
AP, BA, CU, H, HEH, LC, O, UP, Y
From John Brown's raid to the assassination of Lincoln.

5542 ———— Mrs. Reynolds and Hamilton: A Romance . . . New York: E.
F. Bonaventure, 1890. 276 p. CU, HEH, LC, N, O, UM, UVB

5543 ———— Tales of the Chesapeake . . . New York: American News Company, 1880. 285 p., front. AP, CU, H, HEH, LC, N, O, UM, UP, UVB, Y
*Contains:* King of Chincoteague—Ticking Stone—Fall of Utie—Judge Whaley's Demon—Crutch, the Page—Kidnapped—Dominion over the Fish—The Big Idiot—Sir William Johnson's Night—The Lobby Brother—Tell-Tale Feet —Preachers' Sons in 1849—Old Washington Almshouse.

5544 TOWNSEND, VIRGINIA FRANCES. A Boston Girl's Ambitions . . . Boston:
Lee and Shepard. New York: Charles T. Dillingham, 1887. 395 p.
BA, BU, CU, HEH, LC, Y

5545 ———— But a Philistine . . . Boston: Lee and Shepard. New York:
Charles T. Dillingham, 1884. 328 p. AP, HEH, LC

5546 ———— Lenox Dare . . . Boston: Lee and Shepard. New York: Charles
T. Dillingham, 1881. 451 p. AP, HEH, LC, Y

5547 ———— Mostly Marjorie Day . . . Boston: Lee and Shepard. New
York: Chas. T. Dillingham, 1892. 383 p. H, HEH

5548 ———— A Woman's Word and How She Kept It . . . Boston: Lee and
Shepard. New York: Charles T. Dillingham, 1879. 270 p.
HEH, LC, O, Y

5549 TOWNSHEND, RICHARD BAXTER. Lone Pine: The Story of a Lost Mine . . .
New York and London: G. P. Putnam's Sons; the Knickerbocker Press,
1899. 400 p. H, HEH, LC
Pueblo Indians in the 1870's.

5550 [TRABUE, ISAAC HODGEN.] Black Wench. By General Puntagorda
[pseud.]. Puntagorda, Fla.: I. Trabue [cop. 1900]. 174 p., illus.
Information from LC card; no copy seen.

5551 [TRACEY, FRANCIS.] The Sensational Tragedy in the New Orleans Parish Prison: A Startling Confession of Henri Romani, the King of the
Mafia . . . Philadelphia: Barclay & Co., cop. 1891. 96 p., illus. LC
Deposited June 1, 1891.

TRACY, MARGUERITE, *jt. au. See* Earle, M. T. The Race of the Little Ships. The Fig-Trees of Old Jourdé. [Two stories.] *In* M. T. Earle, The Man Who Worked for Collister (1898), No. 1689.

TRAFTON, ADELINE. *See* Knox, Adeline (Trafton)

5552 TRAIL, FLORENCE. Under the Second Renaissance: A Novel . . . Buffalo: Charles Wells Moulton, 1894. 190 p.           H, LC

TRAIN, ARTHUR CHENEY. The Wrong Scent. *In* Stories from the Harvard Advocate (1896), No. 5277a.

5553 TRAIN, ELIZABETH PHIPPS. The Autobiography of a Professional Beauty . . . Philadelphia: J. B. Lippincott Company, 1896. 233 p., illus.
          BU, HEH, N, O, UV, Y

——— Debtors to Chance. *In* Short Story Masterpieces (1900), No. 4931.

5554 [———] Doctor Lamar . . . New York: Thomas Y. Crowell & Co., 46 East Fourteenth Street [cop. 1891]. 335 p.     AP, BA, HEH, LC, O
Deposited June 22, 1891.
2nd ed. gives author's name on title page.
Of a mercy killing; New York.

——— Easter Day. A Held-Up Ball Gown. [Two stories.] *In* Short Story Masterpieces (1900), No. 4931.

5555 ——— Madam of the Ivies . . . Philadelphia & London: J. B. Lippincott Company, 1898. 266 p.     BA, BU, H, HEH, LC, O

5556 ——— A Marital Liability . . . Philadelphia: J. B. Lippincott Company, 1897. 213 p., illus.     BU, H, HEH, LC, N
Husband serves ten years for crime his wife committed.

5557 ——— A Queen of Hearts . . . Philadelphia: J. B. Lippincott Company, 1898. 280 p.     BA, H, HEH, N, O
Of theatrical interest.

5558 ——— A Social Highwayman . . . Philadelphia: J. B. Lippincott Company, 1896. 196 p., illus.     CU, H, HEH, LC, N, O, UV, Y

5559 TRAIN, M. Ray Burton: A Chicago Tale . . . Chicago, 1895. 128 p.  LC

5560 TRASK, KATE (NICHOLS). John Leighton, Jr.: A Novel . . . New York and London: Harper & Brothers, 1898. 252 p.     HEH, LC, O, UV

5561 ——— Lessons in Love . . . New York and London: Harper & Brothers, 1900. 137, [1] p., front.     HEH, LC
*Contents:* A Just Man—After a Year—Acts and Entr'actes—The Hall-Mark—Beyond—After All—Evidence—S. P. Q. R.

5562 ———— White Satin and Homespun ... New York: Anson D. F. Randolph and Company, 91 and 93 Fifth Avenue [cop. 1896]. 139 p.

HEH, LC

Deposited May 6, 1896.
Social welfare work.

TREBOR, *pseud. See* Davis, Robert S.

TREBOR, SNIVIG C., *pseud. See* Givins, Robert Cartwright

5563 TREGO, BENJAMIN BROOKE THOMAS. The Life of Irene Hawthorne; or, The Struggle between Love and Honor ... Philadelphia: Barclay & Co., cop. 1888. 112 p., illus.

LC

TREVELYAN, FRANCIS. Jack Lindsay. Racing at Southern Fairs. Two Year Old Heroine. [Three stories.] *In* Short Stories from Outing [cop. 1895], No. 4930.

5564 TRIMMER, FREDERICK MORTIMER. The Golden Crocodile ... Boston: Roberts Brothers, 1897. 318 p.

HEH, LC, O

Western mining.

5565 [TRIPP, GEORGE HENRY.] Student-Life at Harvard ... Boston: Lockwood, Brooks & Company, 1876. 518 p. BA, H, HEH, LC, N, O, UC, UP, Y

5566 TROTTER, ADA M. Bledisloe; or, Aunt Pen's American Nieces. An International Story ... Boston: Cupples and Hurd, 1887. 324 p.

AP, BA, HEH, LC

5567 [————] Heaven's Gate: A Story of the Forest of Dean. By Lawrence Severn [pseud.]. Boston: D. Lothrop & Company, Franklin and Hawley Streets [cop. 1886]. 348 p. BA, H, HEH, LC

5568 TROUBETZKOY, AMÉLIE (RIVES) CHANLER. According to St. John. By Amélie Rives ... New York: John W. Lovell Company, 150 Worth St. [cop. 1891]. 352 p., illus. BU, CU, HEH, LC, N, O, UV, Y

Of second marriages.

5569 ———— Barbara Dering: A Sequel to The Quick or the Dead? ... Philadelphia: J. B. Lippincott Company, 1893. 285 p.

BA, CU, H, HEH, LC, N, O, UC, UM, UV, Y

5570 ———— A Brother to Dragons, and Other Old-Time Tales ... New York: Harper & Brothers, 1888. 230 p. CU, H, HEH, LC, N, O, UM, UV, Y

*Also contains:* The Farrier Lass o' Piping Pebworth—Nurse Crumpet Tells the Story.

5571 ———— A Damsel Errant ... Philadelphia: J. B. Lippincott Company, 1898. 211 p., illus. BA, CU, H, HEH, LC, N, O, UC, UV

5572 ———— The Quick or the Dead? A Study . . . Philadelphia: J. B. Lippincott Company, 1889. 255 p., front. HEH, N, O, UV

5573 ———— Tanis, the Sang-Digger . . . New York: Town Topics Publishing Co., 1893. 187 p. CU, H, HEH, LC, N, O, UC, UM, UV, Y

5574 ———— Virginia of Virginia: A Story . . . New York: Harper & Brothers, 1888. 222 p., illus. BA, BU, CU, HEH, LC, N, O, UM, UV, Y

5575 ———— The Witness of the Sun . . . Philadelphia: J. B. Lippincott Company, 1889. 248 p., front. BA, CU, H, HEH, LC, N, UM, UV, Y

5576 [TROWBRIDGE, JOHN.] The Great Match, and Other Matches. Boston: Roberts Brothers, 1877. 293 p., illus. BA, CU, H, HEH, LC, O, UM, UV
Entry from LC.
At head of title: "No Name Series."
Love and baseball.

5577 TROWBRIDGE, JOHN TOWNSEND. The Man Who Stole a Meeting-House, and Preaching for Selwyn . . . Boston: Lee & Shepard, 1897. 76 p.
H, HEH, LC, Y
Both stories printed earlier in Wright II, No. 2547.

5578 ———— A Question of Damages . . . Boston: Lee and Shepard, 1897. 78 p. BU, CU, H, LC, N, UP, Y

TRUEMAN, ANITA. *See* Pickett, Anita (Trueman)

5579 TRUESDELL, SENECA E. Snider's Wickedness, and Other Stories . . . St. Paul, Minn.: Pioneer Press Company, 1892. 193 p. LC
*Also contains:* Ingebret Olesdatter—Trapping for Bear—Eatin' B'iled Dog—Inkpadoota's Son—A Great Man's Divorcement—A Desperate Expedient—Loss of the Prudence Smith—A Tale of Two Oranges—The House of Bennett—Story of a Panic.

5580 THE TRULY REMARKABLE LIFE OF THE BEAUTIFUL HELEN JEWETT, Who Was So Mysteriously Murdered. The Strangest and Most Exciting Case . . . in the Great City of New York. Philadelphia: Barclay & Co., 21 North Seventh Street [cop. 1878]. 64 p., illus. N, Y

5581 TRUMAN, BENJAMIN CUMMINGS. Occidental Sketches . . . San Francisco: San Francisco News Company, 1881. 212 p.
BU, CU, H, HEH, LC, N, UM, Y
*Contents:* Hill Beechy's Dream—Divorced on the Desert—An Episode of Echo Cañon—An Hour with an Antediluvian—A Midnight Adventure in Nevada—A Summer in Alaska—Three Extinct Citizens—A Ramble with Flora—The Wickenburg Massacre—A Matchless Achievement—A Sensation in the Orange Groves—The Renaissance of Monterey.

———— A Sensation in the Orange Groves. *In* Short Stories by California Authors (1885), No. 4929.
Printed earlier in No. 5581.

TRUMAN, PERCIVAL HENRY. Poor Little Reginald. *In* [F. L. Knowles] *ed.*, Cap and Gown in Prose (1900), No. 3182.

———— *jt. au.* See Lehman, H. H., *ed.* Williams Sketches (1898), No. 3269.

5582 [TRUMBLE, ALFRED.] Coney Island Frolics: How New York's Gay Girls and Jolly Boys Enjoy Themselves by the Sea ... New York: Richard K. Fox [cop. 1881]. 67, [1] p., illus.
Information supplied by Clifford K. Shipton of American Antiquarian Society.

5583 [————] The Mott St. Poker Club: The Secretary's Minutes ... New York and London: White & Allen, 1889. 50 p., illus.
H, HEH, UC, UM, UV
Chinese quarter, New York.

5584 [————] New York by Day and Night: Life Scenes and Stirring Incidents. New York: Richard K. Fox [cop. 1881]. 63 p.
Listed PW, Aug. 13, 1881.

5585 [————] New York Tombs: Its History and Its Mysteries ... New York: Richard K. Fox [cop. 1881]. 52 p.
Y

5586 TRUMBULL, ANNIE ELIOT. A Cape Cod Week ... New York: A. S. Barnes and Company, 1898. 170 p.
BA, HEH, LC, O, Y

5587 ———— A Christmas Accident, and Other Stories ... New York: A. S. Barnes and Company, 1897. 234 p.
H, HEH, LC, N, O, UV, Y
*Also contains:* After the Deluge—Memoir of Mary Twining—A Postlude—The "Daily Morning Chronicle"—Hearts Unfortified—Her Neighbor's Landmark.

5588 ———— An Hour's Promise ... New York: A. S. Barnes & Co. [cop. 1889]. 265 p.
HEH, O, Y

5589 ———— Mistress Content Craddock ... New York: A. S. Barnes and Company, 1899. 306 p., illus.
BU, CU, HEH, LC, N, O, UP, Y
Colonial New England.

5590 ———— Rod's Salvation ... New York: A. S. Barnes and Company, 1898. 285 p., illus.
BA, HEH, LC, O, Y
*Also contains:* Decline and Fall—Uneffectual Fire—The Chevalier Saint Agar.

5591 [————] White Birches: A Novel. By Annie Eliot [pseud.]. New York: Harper & Brothers, 1893. 356 p.
AP, BA, BU, HEH, LC, O, Y

5592 TUCKER, GEORGE FOX. Mildred Marville ... Boston: George B. Reed, 1899. 283 p.
CU, H, HEH, LC, O

5593    ——— A Quaker Home ... Boston: George B. Reed, 1891. 426 p.

BA, BU, CU, H, HEH, LC, O, UM, Y

5594    ——— Uncle Calup's Christmas Dinner ... Boston: George B. Reed, 1892. 82 p.

HEH, LC, Y

5595    TUFTS, WILLIAM WHITTEMORE. A Market for an Impulse ... Boston: Arena Publishing Co., 1895. 234 p.

H, HEH, LC

5596    [TUNSTALL, NANNIE WHITMELL.] "No. 40": A Romance of Fortress Monroe and the Hygeia. Richmond, Va.: Carlton McCarthy & Co., 1884. 111 p., front.

AP, HEH, LC, O, UV

5597    TUPPER, MRS. EDITH SESSIONS. By a Hair's Breadth ... New York: Willard Fracker and Company, 1889. 135 p., illus.

HEH

At head of title: "Prize Story in the Chicago Tribune."

5598    ——— By Whose Hand? ... New York: Willard Fracker & Company, 1889. 187 p.

LC

5599    TUPPER, FREDERIC ALLISON. Moonshine: A Story of the Reconstruction Period ... Boston: Cupples, Upham and Company, 1884. 233 p.

BU, LC, O, Y

5600    [TUPPER, HENRY ALLEN.] The Truth in Romance: A German Story. By Tföffer [pseud.] ... Baltimore: H. M. Wharton and Company, 1887. 361 p.

LC

5601    TURNBULL, FRANCESE HUBBARD (LITCHFIELD). The Catholic Man: A Study. By Mrs. Lawrence Turnbull. Boston: D. Lothrop Company, Washington Street opposite Bromfield [cop. 1890]. 311 p.

HEH, LC, O, UV, Y

5602    ——— The Golden Book of Venice: A Historical Romance of the 16th Century ... New York: The Century Co., 1900. 399 p.

H, HEH, LC, O, Y

5603    ——— Val-Maria: A Romance of the Time of Napoleon I ... Philadelphia: J. B. Lippincott Company, 1893. 200 p., front.

H, HEH, LC, O, UC, Y

TURNBULL, MRS. LAWRENCE. *See* Turnbull, Francese Hubbard (Litchfield)

TURNER, ALICE. *See* Yardley, Alice Turner

5604    TURRILL, CHARLES B. Deuteronomy Brown: A Real Estate Transaction ... [San Diego, Calif.], 1888. 16 p.

H, HEH, LC, Y

5605    TUTTLE, HUDSON. Clair: A Tale of Mormon Perfidy ... Chicago, 1881. Listed in Coyle.

5606 ——— The Convent of the Sacred Heart . . . Philadelphia: Carter Publishing Company, 1892. 173 p.                                          Y

5607 ——— Heresy; or, Led to the Light . . . Chicago: Published by the author, 1895. 223 p.                                                  LC

5608 ——— Life in Two Spheres . . . Philadelphia: The Carter Publishing Company, 1892. 242 p.                                              BA

5609 ——— Secrets of the Convent . . . Philadelphia: The Carter Publishing Company, 1892. 173 p.                                            LC

TWAIN, MARK, *pseud.* *See* Clemens, Samuel Langhorne

5610 TWELLS, JULIA HELEN (WATTS). Souci: A Novel . . . Philadelphia, London: J. B. Lippincott & Co., 1878. 334 p.                HEH, LC, O

5611 ——— A Triumph of Destiny . . . Philadelphia: J. B. Lippincott Company, 1896. 281 p.                                        H, HEH, LC, O

5612 TWING, CAROLINN EDNA (SKINNER). 'Lisbeth: A Story of Two Worlds . . . Boston: Banner of Light Publishing Co., 1900. 354 p., front.
                                                                              HEH, LC

5613 TWO AMATEUR AUTHORS. By One of Them . . . St. Paul: Press of Wm. L. Banning, Jr., 1889. [138] p.                                  HEH

5613a TWO NEW STORIES: The Anglo-American Lady, and Two Waifs of the Maritime Alps. Written by a Lady. Syracuse, N.Y.: Masters & Stone, printers, 1892. 218 p.                                                HEH

5614 TWOMBLY, ALEXANDER STEVENSON. Kelea, the Surf-Rider: A Romance of Pagan Hawaii . . . New York: Fords, Howard, & Hulbert, 1900. 402 p., illus.                                              CU, H, HEH, LC

TYLER, ODETTE, *pseud.* *See* Shepherd, Elizabeth Lee (Kirkland)

5615 TYLER, RANDALL IRVING. The Blind Goddess: Being a Tale of To-Day, Showing Some of the Undercurrents of a Big City . . . New York: Stuyvesant Publishing Company, 253 Broadway [cop. 1899]. 253 p., illus.                                                              UV, Y
New York.

5616 ——— "Four Months after Date": A Business Romance . . . New York: Stuyvesant Publishing Company, 253 Broadway [cop. 1898]. 288 p., illus.                                                            LC

5617 TYLER, ROBERT LEE. A Yale Man: A Novel . . . New York: Street & Smith, 238 William Street [cop. 1896]. 303 p.              CU, HEH, Y

5618 TYNDALE, TROILUS HILGARD. Don Cosme: A Romance of the South . . . New York: G. W. Dillingham Co., 1899. 287 p.     HEH, LC

5619 TYNER, PAUL. Through the Invisible: A Love Story . . . New York and London: Continental Publishing Co., 1897. 196 p., illus.     LC, UV
Of theosophical interest.

5620 [ULMANN, ALBERT.] Chaperoned: A Brief Page from a Summer Romance. New York: The Cassell Publishing Co., 31 East 17th St. [cop. 1894]. 173 p.     HEH, LC, O
At head of title: "The 'Unknown' Library."
Told in a series of letters.

5621 ———— Frederick Struthers' Romance . . . New York: Brentano's, 1889. 195 p.     H
Told in a series of letters.

5622 UNCLE DANIEL'S STORY OF "TOM" ANDERSON and Twenty Great Battles. By an Officer of the Union Army. New York: A. R. Hart & Co., 1886. 435 p., illus.     BA, CU, HEH, LC, N, O, UV
Authorship not determined. It has been ascribed variously to John McElroy, Senator John Logan, and some member of Logan's household.

5623 UNDERWOOD, FRANCIS HENRY. Doctor Gray's Quest . . . Boston: Lee and Shepard, 1895. 406 p.     HEH, LC

5624 [————] Man Proposes: A Novel. Boston: Lee and Shepard. New York: Charles T. Dillingham, 1880. 344 p.     AP, CU, HEH, LC
Civil War novel.

5625 UNDERWOOD, MARY LANMAN. An American Mother, & Other Stories . . . Wausau, Wisconsin: VanVechten and Ellis, in January, 1898. 290 p.
    H, HEH, LC
*Also contains:* The Baby's Inheritance—Agatha Sage—A Common Ambition —An Unattractive Girl—Mr. Van Twiller's Strange Alibi—Miss Quinley's Story—The Christening of Janet Grace—A Seceding Puritan—Mrs. Barnaby —The Invasion of Michael—A Triumph of Mind.

UNKNOWN, *pseud. See* Bishop, William Henry

5626 AN UNLAID GHOST: A Study in Metempsychosis. New York: D. Appleton and Company, 1888. 178 p.     H, HEH, O

5627 UNVEILING A PARALLEL: A Romance. By Two Women of the West. Boston: Arena Publishing Co., 1893. 269 p.     HEH
The names "Jones (Alice Ilgenfritz)" and "Merchant (Ella)" are written on title page of HEH copy as though they were the authors.
On Mars, where women have equal rights.

5628 UPTON, LOUISE R. Castles in the Air . . . New York: G. P. Putnam's Sons, 1878. 311 p., front.     HEH

5629 URIE, MARY LE BARON (ANDREWS). The Villa Bohemia: No Man Permitted on These Premises under Penalty of the Law . . . New York: Kochendoerfer & Urie, 1882. 247 p. LC

5630 URNER, NATHAN DANE. Link by Link; or, The Chain of Evidence. A Great Detective Story . . . Chicago, Illinois: George W. Ogilvie, cop. 1886. 186 p. HEH

5631 [————] Naughty New York; or, The Apron-Strings Relaxed. A Novel of the Period. Being a Truthful Narrative of a Week's Jollification of Three Young Benedicts . . . By O. N. Looker [pseud.]. [New York]: The American News Company [cop. 1882]. 192 p. LC

5632 [VAHLE, JOSEPH.] The Irish Prince and the Hebrew Prophet: A Masonic Tale of the Captive Jews and the Ark of the Covenant . . . New York: Masonic Publishing Company, 1896. 200 p., illus. HEH, LC

5633 [————] The Jerico Papers: A Quaint and Amusing Side of Early New England Life . . . New York: The Jerico Papers, 1218 Broadway [cop. 1893]. 274 p. CU, HEH, LC, N, UC, UM

5634 VALENTINE, FERDINAND CHARLES. Gotham and the Gothamites. By Heinrich Oscar von Karlstein. Translated by F. C. Valentine . . . Chicago: Laird & Lee, 286 S. Water St., cop. 1886. 179 p. CU, HEH, LC
Also published as: Gotham and the Gothamites; or, The Gay Girls of New York. Chicago: Laird & Lee, Clark & Adams Sts. [1888?]. H

5635 ———— Horrors! Adapted from the French . . . New York: S. W. Green's Sons [cop. 1884]. 165 p., illus. LC
Deposited Feb. 3, 1884.

VALENTINE, JANE, pseud. See Meeker, Mrs. Nellie J.

VALLIÈRE, GEORGE DE, pseud. See Duysters, George F.

5636 VANAMEE, LIDA (OSTROM). An Adirondack Idyl . . . New York: Charles T. Dillingham & Co. [cop. 1893]. 152 p. H, HEH, LC, UC
Of summer residents.

5637 ———— Two Women; or, "Over the Hills and Far Away". . . New York: The Merriam Company, 67 Fifth Avenue [cop. 1895]. 234 p., front. HEH, LC
European vacation.

VAN-ANDERSON, HELEN. See Gordon, Helen (Van Metre) Van-Anderson

VAN ARKEL, GARRET, pseud. See Buffet, Edward Payson

5638 VANCE, ELMER ELLSWORTH. Nellie Harland: A Romance of Rail and Wire . . . New York: G. W. Dillingham, 1888. 214 p. LC

5639 VANCE, J. WILSON. God's War ... New York: 1889.
Listed in Coyle.
CU, HEH, LC have: London, New York: F. Tennyson Neely [cop. 1899]. 348 p.
Civil War.

5640 ———— Little Amy's Christmas ... New York: The American News
Company, 1880. 120 p., illus.                                      LC

5641 ———— Princes' Favors: A Story of Love, War, and Politics ... New
York: The American News Company, 1880. 266 p.              HEH, LC
Civil War.

5642 VANCE, SUSA S. Katherine: A Novel ... Philadelphia: J. B. Lippincott
& Co., 1885. 346 p.                                             LC, O
Of Unitarian interest.

5643 VAN DEVENTER, EMMA MURDOCH. Against Odds: A Romance of the
Midway Plaisance ... Chicago and New York: Rand, McNally &
Company [cop. 1894]. 272 p.                                    H, HEH

5644 [————] The Diamond Coterie. By Lawrence L. Lynch [pseud.]
... Chicago: R. R. Donnelley & Sons, 1884. 557 p., illus.    HEH, UM
At head of title: "The New Detective Story."

5645 [————] A Mountain Mystery; or, The Outlaws of the Rockies. By
Lawrence L. Lynch [pseud.] ... Chicago: Alex. T. Loyd & Co., 1887.
600 p., illus.                                                   HEH

5646 [————] Out of a Labyrinth. By Lawrence L. Lynch [pseud.] ...
Chicago: Alex. T. Loyd & Co., 1885. 471 p., illus.        CU, HEH, LC

5647 [————] Shadowed by Three. By Lawrence L. Lynch [pseud.] ...
Chicago: Donnelley, Gassette, & Loyd, Clark and Adam Streets [cop.
1879]. 738 p., illus.                                      CU, HEH, LC

5648 VANDIVER, JOHN S. The Boss of the Ward: A Story of Municipal Politics
... St. Paul: H. L. Collins Company, 1896. 118 p.                 LC

———— Private Potter. In J. J. Conway, ed., Stories (1893), No. 1172.

5649 VAN DYKE, CURTIS. A Daughter of the Prophets ... New York: The
Abbey Press, 114 Fifth Avenue. London, Montreal [cop. 1900]. 263
p.                                                            HEH, LC
Woman lawyer marries a minister.

5650 VAN DYKE, HENRY. The First Christmas-Tree ... New York: Charles
Scribner's Sons, 1897. 76 p., illus. BA, BU, CU, H, HEH, LC, O, UC, UM, UV, Y

5651 ———— The Lost Word: A Christmas Legend of Long Ago ... New
York: Charles Scribner's Sons, 1898. 71 p., illus.
                           BU, CU, H, HEH, LC, O, UM, UP, UV, Y

5652 ——— The Story of the Other Wise Man . . . New York: Harper & Brothers, 1896. 82, [3] p., illus.     BA, BU, H, HEH, LC, O, UV, Y

5653 VAN DYKE, THEODORE STRONG. Flirtation Camp; or, The Rifle, Rod, and Gun in California. A Sporting Romance . . . New York: Fords, Howard, & Hulbert, 1881. 299 p.     AP, CU, H, HEH, LC, O, Y
Also published as: *Rifle, Rod, and Gun in California* . . . 3rd ed. New York: Fords, Howard, & Hulbert, 1889.     H

5654 ——— Millionaires of a Day: An Inside History of the Great Southern California "Boom" . . . New York: Fords, Howard, & Hulbert, 1890. 208 p.     H, HEH, LC, UC, Y

5655 [VAN FOSSEN, LOO B.] Abandoned: A Romance. By Louis B. Zelcoe [pseud.]. New York, Chicago, London: F. T. Neely Co. [cop. 1900]. 186 p.     LC
Deposited Sept. 18, 1900.

VAN HOESEN, ANTOINETTE. *See* Wakeman, Antoinette Prudence (Van Hoesen)

VAN HOEVENBERGH, H. Into the Jaws of Death. *In* [W. J. Johnston] *comp.*, Lightning Flashes and Electric Dashes (1877), Nos. 3022, 3023.

5656 VAN LOON, MRS. ELIZABETH. A Heart Twice Won; or, Second Love . . . Philadelphia: T. B. Peterson & Brothers, 306 Chestnut Street [cop. 1878]. 349 p.     HEH, LC

5657 ——— The Mystery of Allanwold . . . Philadelphia: T. B. Peterson & Brothers, 306 Chestnut Street [cop. 1880]. 380 p.     LC

5658 ——— The Shadow of Hampton Mead . . . Philadelphia: T. B. Peterson & Brothers, 306 Chestnut Street [cop. 1878]. 281 p.     LC
Plantation in North Carolina.

5659 ——— Under the Willows; or, The Three Countesses . . . Philadelphia: T. B. Peterson & Brothers, 306 Chestnut Street [cop. 1879]. 296 p.     HEH, LC

5660 VAN RENSSELAER, MARIANA (GRISWOLD). One Man Who Was Content . . . By Mrs. Schuyler Van Rensselaer . . . New York: The Century Co., 1897. 127 p.     BA, CU, H, HEH, LC, O, Y
*Also contains:* "Mary"—The Lustigs—Corinna's Fiammetta.

VAN RENSSELAER, MRS. SCHUYLER. *See* Van Rensselaer, Mariana (Griswold)

5661 [VAN SLINGERLAND, MRS. NELLIE BINGHAM.] Love and Politics: A Social Romance of a Prominent Orator and a Society Queen . . . By Neile Bevans [pseud.] . . . [Jersey City, N.J.: Jersey City Printing Co., cop. 1899.] 356 p., illus.     BU

5662  VAN VORST, FREDERICK B.  Without a Compass: A Novel . . . New
York: D. Appleton and Company, 1885.  414 p.   AP, HEH, LC, O, UM, Y
Business, religion; New York.

5663  VAN ZILE, EDWARD SIMS.  Don Miguel, and Other Stories . . . New
York: Cassell Publishing Company, 104 & 106 Fourth Avenue [cop.
1891].  276 p.                                                      LC

5664  ———— Kings in Adversity . . . New York: F. Tennyson Neely, 1897.
232 p.                                                    HEH, N, O, UM, Y

5665  ———— The Manhattaners: A Story of the Hour . . . New York: Lovell, Coryell & Company, 1895.  257 p.                      BU, HEH, LC

5666  ———— With Sword and Crucifix: Being an Account of the Strange
Adventures of Count Louis de Sancerre, Companion of Sieur de La
Salle, on the Lower Mississippi in the Year of Grace 1682 . . . New
York and London: Harper & Brothers, 1900.  298, [1] p., illus.
                                                        HEH, LC, O, UP, Y

5667  VAUGHAN, FRANK.  Kate Weathers; or, Scattered by the Tempest. A
Novel . . .  Philadelphia: J. B. Lippincott & Co., 1878.  437 p.   LC, O

VAUGHN, HAMPDEN, pseud.  See Pusey, Pennock

5668  DELETED.

5669  VEEDER, EMILY ELIZABETH (FERRIS).  Her Brother Donnard . . . Philadelphia: J. B. Lippincott Company, 1890.  274 p., illus.   HEH, LC, N, O

VENTURA, LUIGI DONATO.  Mario.  In J. J. Conway, ed., Stories (1893),
No. 1172.

5670  ———— Misfits and Remnants . . .  Boston: Ticknor and Company, 1886.
235 p.                                                    AP, H, HEH, LC, UC
Contents: Peppino—Only a Dog—Beppo—The "Herr Baron"—Our Nihilist—
A Wrecked Life—The Stage Fiend—Graziella the Model—Who Was He?—
The Elf of Hohenheim.
S. Shevitch, jt. au.

5671  ———— Peppino . . .  New York: William R. Jenkins Company, 1885.
65 p.                                                                 H, O
Later printed in No. 5670.

5672  VERDENDORP, BASIL, pseud.  The Verdendorps: A Novel . . .  Chicago:
Charles M. Hertig, 1880.  376 p.                          H, HEH, LC, N
"Under fictitious names . . . the newspaper account of the Vanderbilt will
case is here given."  PW, May 22, 1880.

5673 VERDIER, MARGUERITE LOUISE. Two Little Maids: A Tale of South Florida; and Conchita: A Mexican Romance . . . New York: William L. Allison Company, 54 Warren Street [cop. 1894]. 143, 107 p.

CU, HEH, LC

VERMILYE, KATE (JORDAN). *See* Jordan, Kate

5674 VERNE, EDNA. Fidélité . . . San Francisco: A. L. Bancroft and Company, 1877. 125 p. HEH, LC

5675 VERNON, RAPHAEL. All in a Lifetime; or, Everything Goes . . . [N.p.]: Published for the author, 1894. 98 p. LC

5676 VERNON, SAMUEL MILTON. Lux Vitae as Seen in the Life of John Paulus . . . New York: Eaton & Mains. Cincinnati: Jennings & Pye [cop. 1900]. 463 p. LC
Of a Methodist clergyman; Mississippi.

5677 [VERNON, THOMAS R.] Twice Adopted: A Story of Delaware County. By En Quad [pseud.] . . . Media, Pa.: Cooper & Vernon, 1898. 224 p., illus. HEH

5678 VERY, LYDIA LOUISA ANNA. A Strange Discourse: A Tale of New England Life . . . Boston: James H. Earle, 178 Washington Street [cop. 1898]. 217 p. LC, Y

5679 ——— A Strange Recluse; or, Ye Did It unto Me . . . [Salem, Mass.: The Salem Press Co., 1899.] 143 p., illus. BU, LC
Deposited Nov. 17, 1899.

5680 ——— Sylph; or, The Organ-Grinder's Daughter . . . Boston: James H. Earle, 1898. 107 p., illus. HEH, LC

5681 VEYSEY, ARTHUR HENRY. A Cheque for Three Thousand . . . New York: G. W. Dillingham Co., 1897. 218 p. H, HEH, LC
Of a gift that must be spent in one year.

5682 ——— Hats Off! . . . New York: G. W. Dillingham Co., 1899. 225 p.
LC
Satire on American social life.

5683 ——— A Pedigree in Pawn . . . New York: G. W. Dillingham Co., 1898. 248 p., illus. HEH, LC

5684 ——— The Stateroom Opposite . . . New York: G. W. Dillingham Co., 1900. 234 p. HEH, LC
Detective story.

5685 ——— The Two White Elephants . . . New York: G. W. Dillingham Co., 1899. 234 p. HEH, LC

5686 VICKERS, ROBERT HENRY. Zawis and Kunigunde: A Bohemian Tale . . .
Chicago: C. H. Kerr & Company, 1895. 307 p. LC, N

5687 VICTOR, FRANCES (FULLER) BARRETT. The New Penelope, and Other
Stories . . . San Francisco: A. L. Bancroft & Company, printers, 1877.
349 p. BU, H, HEH, N, UC, Y
*Contains:* A Curious Interview—Mr. Ela's Story—On the Sands—An Old Fool
—How Jack Hastings Sold His Mine—What They Told Me at Wilson's Bar
—Miss Jorgensen—Sam Rice's Romance—El Tesoro.

5688 [VICTOR, METTA VICTORIA (FULLER).] Abijah Beanpole in New York:
Detailing the Misfortunes and Mishaps of a Country Storekeeper on a
Business Visit to the Great City of New York . . . New York: G. W.
Carleton & Co., 1884. 202 p., illus. LC

5689 [———] The Blunders of a Bashful Man . . . New York: J. S. Ogilvie
& Company, 25 Rose Street [cop. 1881]. 168 p., illus. H, HEH, UM, Y

5690 ——— Dora Elmyr's Worst Enemy; or, Guilty or Not Guilty . . .
New York: Street & Smith, 1878. 61, [3], 75-100 p. BU, CU, HEH, N, O
Story covers first 61 p. of text and is continued in Street & Smith's *New York
Weekly*, No. 51. Remaining pages devoted to an English author's story.

5691 [———] Miss Slimmens' Boarding House . . . New York: J. S. Ogilvie
& Company, 31 Rose Street, cop. 1882. 188 p., illus. LC

5692 [———] Mrs. Rasher's Curtain Lectures . . . New York: J. S. Ogilvie
& Company, 31 Rose Street [cop. 1884]. 288 p., illus. HEH, LC

5693 ——— Passing the Portal; or, A Girl's Struggle. An Autobiography
. . . New York: G. W. Carleton & Co. London: S. Low & Co., 1876.
408 p. CU, HEH, LC, O, UVB, Y

5694 VIELÉ, HERMAN KNICKERBOCKER. The Inn of the Silver Moon . . . Chicago: Herbert S. Stone & Company, 1900. 198 p. BU, CU, HEH, LC, O, Y

VIGILANS, *pseud. See* Hawkins, Thomas Hayden

5695 VILLARS, MRS. MARY H. Stories of Home and Home Folks; or, Leaves
from a Parsonage Portfolio . . . Volume I. Each Volume Complete
in Itself. Cincinnati: Printed by Walden & Stowe for the author, 1882.
334 p. HEH
No more published?

VILLENEUVE, LOUIS DE, *pseud. See* Gibbons, Louise Elise

5696 VINCENT, FRANK. The Lady of Cawnpore: A Romance . . . New York,
London, Toronto: Funk & Wagnalls, 1891. 420 p. LC, O, Y
Albert Edmund Lancaster, jt. au.

5697 VINTON, ARTHUR DUDLEY. Looking Further Backward: Being a Series of Lectures Delivered to the Freshman Class at Shawmut College, by Professor Wong Lung Li . . . Edited and Condensed by Arthur Dudley Vinton. Albany, N.Y.: Albany Book Company, 1890. 236 p.

CU, H, HEH, N, UM, UP, UV, Y

*Also contains:* The Dominant—An International Auction: A Story of Things to Be.

Lectures delivered in the year 2023.

5698 ———— The Pomfret Mystery: A Novel of Incident . . . New York: J. S. Ogilvie & Company, 31 Rose Street [cop. 1886]. 232 p., illus.

HEH, LC

Detective story.

5699 VISSCHER, WILLIAM LIGHTFOOT. 'Way Out Yonder: The Romance of a New City . . . Chicago: Laird & Lee, 1898. 236 p., illus.  HEH, N

Of a "boom" city.

5700 VIVIAN, THOMAS JONDRIE. Luther Strong: His Wooing and Madness . . . New York: R. F. Fenno & Company, 1899. 283 p.  BU, HEH, LC

5701 ———— Seven Smiles and a Few Fibs . . . New York City: R. F. Fenno & Company, 9 & 11 East Sixteenth Street [cop. 1900]. 195 p., illus.

HEH, LC

*Contents:* The Waiter Smiled—The Widow Smiled—The Broker Smiled—The Purser Smiled—The Grandma Smiled—The Lady Smiled—The Maiden Smiled. A FEW FIBS: The Protoplasmic Misadventure of Hans Jorgensen—Down to the Medulla—Taken under Advisement—Old Lick's Ghost—"If Thine Enemy Thirst"—He Kept the Engagement—The Magic Mirror—How I Had 'Em!—To Freeze Out England.

VOISIN, *pseud. See* Collins, Mrs. Clara

5702 VOORHEES, JAMES PAXTON. The Tale of Wealth: Being the Personal Narrative of Chambers Rundel . . . Washington, D. C.: Wm. H. Morrison, 1890. 213 p.  HEH, LC

5703 VORSE, ALBERT WHITE. Laughter of the Sphinx . . . Philadelphia: Drexel Biddle, 1900. 329 p., illus.

Listed PW, Aug. 25, 1900.

HEH, LC, o have: Toronto, London, New York, Philadelphia, San Francisco: Drexel Biddle, 1900.

VROOMAN, ISAAC H., JR., *jt. ed. See* Lehman, H. H., *ed.* Williams Sketches (1898), No. 3269.

5704 VYNNE, HAROLD RICHARD. Love Letters: A Romance in Correspondence . . . New York: Zimmerman's, 1898. 170 p., illus.  Y

At head of title: "Zimmerman's Pocket Library."

Letters between a New York lawyer and a Chicago girl.

5705 ——— The Woman That's Good: A Story of the Undoing of a Dreamer . . . Chicago and New York: Rand, McNally & Company [cop.
1900]. 473 p.                                                    HEH, LC, O, UM
Of married life.

W., A. B.  *See* Wood, Augustus B.

W., C. H.  *See* Chaplin, Heman White

W., L. C.  *See* Wood, Lydia Cope

WACK, HENRY WELLINGTON.  Mr. Wilkes of Harvard.  *In* J. J. Conway,
*ed.*, Stories (1893), No. 1172.
He is also jt. ed. of the collection.

5706 WADE, DECIUS SPEAR.  Clare Lincoln: A Novel . . . Cambridge: Printed
at the Riverside Press, 1876.  451 p.                            HEH, LC, N

5707 WADLEIGH, FRANCES ELLEN.  'Twixt Wave and Sky . . . New York: The
Authors' Publishing Company, Bond Street [cop. 1878].  261 p.    HEH

5708 WAGNALLS, MABEL.  Miserere (A Musical Story) . . . New York, London, Toronto: Funk & Wagnalls Company, 1892.  63 p., illus.
                                                                 HEH, LC, O

——— Selma the Soprano.  *In* J. Hawthorne, One of Those Coincidences (1899), No. 2596.

5709 WAGNER, MRS. BELLE M.  Within the Temple of Isis . . . Denver: Astro-
Philosophical Publishing Co., 1899.  156 p.
Information from LC card; no copy seen.

WAGNER, HARR.  Nathan, the Jew.  *In* Short Stories by California Authors (1885), No. 4929.
Author's full name James Harrison Wagner.

5710 ——— The Street and the Flower: A Novel . . . San Francisco, Cal.:
San Francisco News Company, 1883.  111 p.                        CU, HEH
E. T. Bunyan, jt. au.

WAIT, FRONA EUNICE, *pseud*.  *See* Colburn, Frona Eunice Wait (Smith)

5711 WAITE, CAMPBELL WALDO.  Among the Moonshiners . . . New York:
F. Tennyson Neely, 114 Fifth Avenue.  Chicago, London [cop. 1899].
289 p.                                                           HEH
Tennessee.

5712 WAITE, CARLTON.  A Silver Baron: A Novel . . . Boston: Arena Publishing Company, 1896.  325 p.                                   CU, HEH, LC
Colorado.

5713 [WAITE, LUCY.] Doctor Helen Rand. By Lois Wright [pseud.] . . . Chicago: The Physicians' Publishing Co., 1891. 117 p.    LC

5714 WAKEMAN, ANTOINETTE PRUDENCE (VAN HOESEN). Questions of Conscience: A Novel. By Antoinette Van Hoesen . . . Chicago, New York: George M. Hill Company [cop. 1900]. 499 p.    HEH, N

5715 WAKEMAN, JOEL. The Golden Horn; or, Fatal Exchange . . . Lewisburgh, Pa.: S. T. Buck, Son & Co., 1882. 457 p., illus.    LC

5716 [WALKER, SAMUEL.] The Reign of Selfishness: A Story of Concentrated Wealth. New York: M. K. Pelletreau, cop. 1891. 448 p.    LC
Deposited July 17, 1891.
Also published as: *Dry Bread; or, The Reign of Selfishness: A Novel for Men.* New York: G. W. Dillingham Co., 1899.    LC

5717 [WALKLEY, ALBERT.] Captain Israel, the Hopeful. Boston: Geo. H. Ellis, 1899. 56 p.    HEH, LC
Maine.

5718 ———— Theodore Parker: A Series of Letters . . . Boston: Neponset Press, 1900. 127 p.    H, Y
Imaginary letters dealing with facts in Parker's life.

5719 WALL, GEORGE A. Jacob Valmont, Manager . . . Chicago and New York: Rand, McNally & Company, 1889. 361 p., illus.    BU, LC
George B. Heckel, jt. au.
Vermont politics.

———— jt. au. See Robinson, E. A. The Disk (1884), No. 4587.

5720 WALLACE, LEWIS. Ben-Hur: A Tale of the Christ . . . New York: Harper & Brothers, 1880. 552 p.    BU, CU, HEH, N, UC, UP, UVB, Y
Dedication: "To the Wife of My Youth."

5721 ———— The First Christmas: From "Ben-Hur" . . . New York and London: Harper & Brothers, 1899. 139, [1] p., front.    LC, UM

5722 ———— The Prince of India; or, Why Constantinople Fell . . . New York: Harper & Brothers, 1893. 2 vols. (502, 578 p.)
   AP, BA, BU, CU, H, HEH, LC, N, O, UC, UP, UVB, Y
2nd printing adds dedication in Vol. I.

5723 WALLACE, WILLIAM DE WITT. Love's Ladder: A Novel . . . Chicago and New York: Belford, Clarke & Co., 1886. 253 p.    HEH, LC

5724 WALLBERG, ANNA CRONHJELM. The Romance of Swedenborg's Life . . . San Francisco: C. A. Murdock & Co., 1890. 67 p.    LC

5725 WALLER, MARY ELLA. The Rose-Bush of Hildesheim: A Cathedral Story . . . Boston: Estes and Lauriat [cop. 1889]. 36 p., illus.    HEH, LC

5726 WALLING, ELIZABETH (BACON). Phebe . . . [Wilmington, Del., cop. 1895.] 44 p., illus.                                            LC
Deposited Dec. 9, 1895.

5727 WALLIS, JOHN CALVIN. A Frolicsome Girl . . . Chicago, Illinois: George W. Ogilvie, cop. 1886. 149 p.                          LC
Deposited Aug. 28, 1886.

5728 ——— A Prodigious Fool . . . Philadelphia: J. B. Lippincott & Co., 1881. 216 p.                                           HEH, LC

5729 WALSH, ALEXANDER STEWART. Mary, the Queen of the House of David and Mother of Jesus: The Story of Her Life . . . New York: Henry S. Allen, 1886. 626 p., illus.                                       LC
*Also issued with imprint:* New York: Henry S. Allen. Indianapolis, Ind.: Robert Douglass, 1886.    HEH

5730 WALSH, MARIE. His Wife or Widow? A Novel . . . New York: G. W. Dillingham, 1889. 343 p.                                      LC
Civil War soldier, reported dead, returns to find his wife remarried.

5731 DELETED.

5732 [WALSH, MARIE A.] My Queen: A Romance of the Great Salt Lake. By "Sandette" [pseud.] . . . New York: G. W. Carleton & Co. London: S. Low, Son & Co., 1878. 384 p.                              H, LC

5733 WALSINGHAM, CHARLOTTE, *pseud?* O'er Moor and Fen: A Novel . . . Philadelphia: Claxton, Remsen, & Haffelfinger, 1876. 422 p.
                                                            HEH, LC, O, Y

5734 WALTER, CARRIE (STEVENS). An Idyl of Santa Barbara . . . San Francisco: Golden Era Company, 1886. 54 p., illus.             HEH

5735 WALTON, ELEANOR GOING. She Who Will Not When She May . . . Philadelphia: Henry Altemus, 1898. 140 p., illus.    HEH, LC, O, UP, UV
Told in a series of letters.
Of a society woman devoted to art.

WALTON, FRANCIS, *pseud. See* Hodder, Alfred

WALTZ, ELIZABETH CHERRY. Tongue of Flame. *In* Short Story Masterpieces (1900), No. 4931.

5736 WALWORTH, JEANNETTE RITCHIE (HADERMANN). Baldy's Point . . . New York: Cassell & Company, Limited, 104 & 106 Fourth Avenue [cop. 1889]. 276 p.                                             HEH, LC, Y
Deposited May 4, 1889.

5737 [————] The Bar-Sinister: A Social Study . . . New York: Cassell & Company, Limited, 1885. 354 p.     AP, BU, H, HEH, LC, UP
Also published as: *His Celestial Marriage; or, The Bar-Sinister. A Social Study*. By Mrs. Jeannette H. Walworth. New York: The Mershon Company [cop. 1899].   LC
Also published as: *His Three Wives; or, The Bar-Sinister. A Mormon Study*. By Mrs. Jeannette H. Walworth. New York: The Mershon Company [cop. 1900].   LC, UM

5738 ———— Fortune's Tangled Skein: A Novel . . . New York: The Baker and Taylor Company, 5 and 7 East Sixteenth Street [cop. 1898]. 286 p.
    LC, O
Rural district in Mississippi.

5739 ———— Heavy Yokes . . . Boston: William F. Gill and Company, 1876. 131 p. Printed in double columns.     BA

5740 ———— The New Man at Rossmere . . . New York: Cassell & Company, Limited, 739 & 741 Broadway [cop. 1886]. 359 p.   AP, H, HEH, LC
Carpetbaggers; Arkansas.

5741 ———— Nobody's Business. By Jeannette Hadermann . . . New York: The Authors' Publishing Company, Bond Street [cop. 1878]. 128 p.
    LC

5742 ———— An Old Fogy . . . New York: The Merriam Company, 67 Fifth Avenue [cop. 1895]. 292 p.     AP, HEH, LC
Deposited Nov. 25, 1895.
A southerner moves to New York.

5743 ———— Old Fulkerson's Clerk . . . New York: Cassell & Company, Limited, 739 & 741 Broadway [cop. 1886]. 171 p.     AP, HEH, LC

5744 ———— On the Winning Side: A Southern Story of Ante-Bellum Times . . . New York: R. F. Fenno & Company, 9 and 11 East 16th Street [cop. 1893]. 287 p., illus.     HEH, O
Listed PW, Feb. 5, 1898.
First published in the omitted "Once a Week Library," 1893.

———— Patty's First Call-Out. *In* Short Story Masterpieces (1900), No. 4931.

5745 ———— Scruples: A Novel . . . New York: Cassell & Company, Limited, 739 & 741 Broadway [cop. 1886]. 191 p.     AP, BA, LC
Deposited May 29, 1886,

5746 ———— The Silent Witness . . . New York: Cassell & Company, 104-106 Fourth Avenue [cop. 1888]. 208 p.     LC
Detective story.

5747 ———— A Strange Pilgrimage: A Novel . . . New York: A. L. Burt [cop. 1888]. 301 p.           H, HEH, UC

5748 ———— That Girl from Texas: A Novel . . . Chicago, New York, and San Francisco: Belford, Clarke & Co. [cop. 1888]. 256 p.    HEH, LC

5749 ———— True to Herself: A Novel . . . New York: A. L. Burt [cop. 1888]. 311 p.           HEH

5750 ———— Uncle Scipio: A Story of Uncertain Days in the South . . . New York: R. F. Fenno & Company, 112 Fifth Avenue [cop. 1896]. 310 p., front.           CU, HEH, LC, O, Y
Post Civil War.

5751 ———— Without Blemish: To-Day's Problem . . . New York: Cassell & Company, Limited, 1886. 381 p.    AP, CU, H, HEH, LC, O, UV, Y
Of the Negroes' future.

5752 WALWORTH, MANSFIELD TRACY. Married in Mask: A Novel . . . New York: A. L. Burt [cop. 1888]. 345 p.         H, HEH, UC

5753 ———— Zahara; or, A Leap for Empire. A Novel . . . New York: G. W. Dillingham, 1888. 376 p.         HEH, LC, N

5754 WANDER, WILL, *pseud.* Deacon Boggles' Struggle with a Liver Pad . . . New York: M. J. Ivers & Co., 86 Nassau Street [cop. 1886]. 64 p., illus.
        Y

WARD, A. B. *See* Bailey, Alice (Ward)

5755 WARD, ELIZABETH STUART (PHELPS). Beyond the Gates. By Elizabeth Stuart Phelps . . . Boston, New York: Houghton, Mifflin and Company. The Riverside Press, Cambridge, 1883. 196 p.
        BA, BU, CU, H, HEH, LC, N, O, UC, UP, UVB, Y

5756 ———— Burglars in Paradise . . . Boston and New York: Houghton, Mifflin and Company. The Riverside Press, Cambridge, 1886. 220 p.
        BA, CU, HEH, N, UP, UVB
Also published, perhaps simultaneously, in the omitted "Riverside Paper Series," No. 14.
Later printed in No. 5767.
Cape Ann.

5757 ———— Come Forth! . . . Boston and New York: Houghton, Mifflin and Company. The Riverside Press, Cambridge, 1891. 318 p.
        BA, BU, CU, H, HEH, LC, O, UC, UM, UVB, Y
Herbert D. Ward, jt. au.
At the time of Christ.

5758 ———— Doctor Zay . . . Boston, New York: Houghton, Mifflin and Company. The Riverside Press, Cambridge, 1882. 258 p.
        BA, BU, CU, HEH, LC, N, O, UV, Y
Beacon Street Bostonian restored to health by this woman doctor.

5759 ——— Donald Marcy ... Boston and New York: Houghton, Mifflin and Company. The Riverside Press, Cambridge, 1893. 242 p.

BA, CU, H, HEH, LC, N, O, UC, UP, UVB, Y

A college story.

5760 ——— Fourteen to One ... Boston and New York: Houghton, Mifflin and Company. The Riverside Press, Cambridge, 1891. 464 p.

BU, CU, H, HEH, LC, O, UM, UP, UVB, Y

*Also contains:* The Bell of St. Basil's—Shut In—Jack the Fisherman—The Madonna of the Tubs—A Brave Deed—The Sacrifice of Antigone—Sweet Home—Too Late—The Reverend Malachi Matthew—His Relict—Mary Elizabeth—Annie Laurie—The Law and the Gospel.

5761 ——— Friends: A Duet ... Boston: Houghton, Mifflin and Company. The Riverside Press, Cambridge, 1881. 255 p.

BA, CU, H, HEH, LC, N, O, UP, UVB, Y

5762 ——— The Gates Between ... Boston and New York: Houghton, Mifflin and Company. The Riverside Press, Cambridge, 1887. 222 p., 1 l.

BA, BU, CU, H, HEH, LC, N, O, UC, UM, UP, UVB, Y

A doctor's spirit wanders around before reaching heaven.

5763 ——— Jack the Fisherman ... Boston and New York: Houghton, Mifflin and Company. The Riverside Press, Cambridge, 1887. 59 p., illus.

BA, H, HEH, LC, N, O, UC, UP, Y

Later printed in No. 5760.

Of inherited intemperance.

5764 ——— The Lady of Shalott ... Boston and New York: Houghton, Mifflin & Co., 1892. 21 p.

Copy examined at New York Public Library.

Printed earlier in No. 5768.

5765 ——— The Madonna of the Tubs ... Boston and New York: Houghton, Mifflin and Company. The Riverside Press, Cambridge, 1887. 94 p., illus.

BA, CU, H, HEH, LC, N, O, UM, UVB, Y

Later printed in No. 5760.

The fishermen of Gloucester, Massachusetts.

5766 ——— The Master of the Magicians ... Boston and New York: Houghton, Mifflin and Company. The Riverside Press, Cambridge, 1890. 324 p.

BA, BU, CU, H, HEH, LC, N, O, UM, UP, UVB, Y

Herbert D. Ward, jt. au.

Babylon, 600 B.C.

5767 ——— Old Maids, and Burglars in Paradise ... Boston and New York: Houghton, Mifflin and Company. The Riverside Press, Cambridge, 1887. 195, 220 p.

CU, LC, O

"Old Maids" first published in the omitted "Riverside Paper Series," No. 9, 1885.

5768 ———— Sealed Orders . . . Boston: Houghton, Osgood and Company. The Riverside Press, Cambridge, 1879. 345 p.

BA, CU, H, HEH, LC, N, O, UC, UVB, Y

*Also contains:* Old Mother Goose—The Lady of Shalott—The True Story of Guenever—Doherty—The Voyage of the "America"—Wrecked in Port—Running the Risk—Long, Long Ago—Since I Died—A Woman's Pulpit—Number 13—Two Hundred and Two—Cloth of Gold—Saint Caligula—Miss Mildred's Friend—Neblitt.

5769 ———— A Singular Life . . . Boston and New York: Houghton, Mifflin and Company. The Riverside Press, Cambridge, 1895. 426 p.

BA, CU, H, HEH, LC, N, UC, UM, UP, UVB

Of a minister and his work.

5770 ———— The Story of Avis . . . Boston: James R. Osgood and Company (Late Ticknor & Fields, and Fields, Osgood & Co.), 1877. 457 p.

BA, BU, CU, H, HEH, LC, N, O, UC, UP, UVB, Y

5771 ———— The Supply at Saint Agatha's . . . Boston and New York: Houghton, Mifflin and Company. The Riverside Press, Cambridge, 1896. 38 p., illus.     BA, BU, CU, H, HEH, LC, N, O, UC, UP, UVB, Y

———— Zerviah Hope *In* Stories by American Authors, VIII (1884), No. 5274.

5772 WARD, HERBERT DICKINSON. The Burglar Who Moved Paradise . . . Boston and New York: Houghton, Mifflin and Company. The Riverside Press, Cambridge, 1897. 226 p., front.

AP, BA, BU, CU, H, HEH, LC, O, UP, UV, Y

5773 ———— A Republic without a President, and Other Stories . . . New York: Tait, Sons & Company, Union Square [cop. 1891]. 271 p.

HEH, LC, O, UVB

*Also contains:* The Lost City—A Terrible Evening—Scud—The Romance of a Mortgage—Colonel Oldminton: A Sequel to "A Republic without a President."

Deposited Jan. 17, 1893; listed PW, Feb. 4, 1893.

5774 ———— The White Crown, and Other Stories . . . Boston and New York: Houghton, Mifflin and Company. The Riverside Press, Cambridge, 1894. 336 p.     BA, H, HEH, LC, O, UC

*Also contains:* The Semaphore—The Value of a Cipher—A Romance of the Faith—Only an Incident—A Cast of the Net—The Equation of a Failure—The Missing Interpreter.

———— *jt. au. See* Ward, E. S. P. Come Forth! (1891), No. 5757; *and* The Master of the Magicians (1890), No. 5766.

5775 [WARD, MABEL HENSHAW.] The Diary of an Old Maid. [Washington, D.C.: Published by the author, Mabel Henshaw Ward, cop. 1895.] Cover title, [28] p.     LC

Deposited Dec. 5, 1895.

5776 WARDDEL, NORA HELEN. The Romance of a Quiet Watering-Place (Being the Unpremeditated Confessions of a Not Altogether Frivolous Girl): Extracted from the Private Correspondence of Miss Evelyn L. Dwyer . . . Chicago, New York, and San Francisco: Belford, Clarke & Co., 1888. 187 p., illus. CU, LC
"New Birmingham," Pennsylvania.

5777 WARE, EVELYN WOODFORD. The Islanders: A Romance of Martha's Vineyard . . . Boston: Press of A. Mudge & Son, 1892. 153 p. LC, Y

5778 WARFIELD, CATHERINE ANN (WARE). The Cardinal's Daughter: A Sequel to "Ferne Fleming" . . . Philadelphia: T. B. Peterson & Brothers, 306 Chestnut Street [cop. 1877]. 366 p. CU, H, HEH, LC, N, UP

5779 ——— Ferne Fleming: A Novel . . . Philadelphia: T. B. Peterson & Brothers, 306 Chestnut Street [cop. 1877]. 424 p.
H, HEH, LC, N, UC, UP, UVB

5780 ——— Lady Ernestine; or, The Absent Lord of Rocheforte . . . Philadelphia: T. B. Peterson & Brothers, 306 Chestnut Street [cop. 1876]. 528 p. CU, HEH, LC, N, O, UC, UVB, Y

5781 WARMAN, CY. The Express Messenger, and Other Tales of the Rail . . . New York: Charles Scribner's Sons, 1897. 238 p.
BA, CU, H, HEH, LC, N, Y
*Also contains:* The Locomotive That Lost Herself—A Wild Night at Wood River—Wakalona—A Locomotive as a War Chariot—A Ghost Train Illusion—The Story of Engine 107—Catching a Runaway Engine—A Railway Mail Clerk—The Mysterious Message—Scraptomania.

5782 ——— Frontier Stories . . . New York: Charles Scribner's Sons, 1898. 246 p. CU, H, HEH, O, Y
*Contents:* The Columbine of Cripple Creek—"Injun Fin' um Paper-Talk"—A Scalp for a Scalp—Slaying the Wild Bull—Valley Tan—In the Hospital—The Bishop of Price—A Quiet Day in Creede—A Cowboy's Funeral—Half-Breeds—The Seductive Six-Shooter—The Brakeman and the Squaw—Hoskaninni—Tickaboo—Little Cayuse—The Wahsatch Band of Bandits—Wantawanda—A Couple o' Captains.

5783 ——— Short Rails . . . New York: Charles Scribner's Sons, 1900. 310 p. HEH, LC, Y
*Contents:* The New Ticket Agent—Jack Farley's Flying Switch—Out on the Road—The Engineer's White Hair—A Running Switch—A Perpendicular Railroad—The Wreck at Roubideau—The Black Fliers—The Fighting Manager—The Passing of McIvor—A Sympathy Strike—A Railway Emergency—Railroading in France—"Ar' Ye Woth It?"—A Roumanian Romance—Opening of the Alpine Tunnel—On the Black-List—The First Train over the Bridge—Fanny and the Fireman.

5784 ——— Snow on the Headlight: A Story of the Great Burlington Strike . . . New York: D. Appleton and Company, 1899. 248, [1] p.
CU, HEH, LC, N, O, UM, Y

5785 ——— Tales of an Engineer, with Rhymes of the Rail ... New York: Charles Scribner's Sons, 1895. 242, [3] p.

AP, BU, CU, H, HEH, LC, O, UV, Y

*Contains:* A Thousand-Mile Ride on the Engine of a "Flyer"—The Death Run—Flying through Flames—A Novel Battle—On Board an Ocean Flyer—On an Iron Steed—Over an Earthquake—Through the Dardanelles—Jaffa to Jerusalem—Relations of the Employee to the Railroad—From the Cornfield to the Cab.

5786 ——— The White Mail ... New York: Charles Scribner's Sons, 1899. 197 p.

H, HEH, LC, N, O, Y

5787 WARNE, E. W. Queen Elfreda: A Historic Romance of British Life ... Nashville, Tenn.: Printed for the author, 1884. 240 p. LC

WARNEFORD, *Lieut., pseud. See* Gunter, Archibald Clavering

5788 WARNER, ANNA BARTLETT. Patience ... Philadelphia: J. B. Lippincott Company, 1891. 412 p. AP, CU, HEH, O, Y

——— *jt. au. See* Warner, S. B. The Gold of Chickaree (1876), No. 5798; *and* Wych Hazel (1876), No. 5803.

5789 WARNER, BEVERLY ELLISON. Troubled Waters: A Problem of Today ... Philadelphia: J. B. Lippincott Company, 1885. 327 p.

AP, BU, CU, H, HEH, LC, O, UC, Y

Of labor and capital.

5790 WARNER, CHARLES DUDLEY. The Golden House: A Novel ... New York: Harper & Brothers, 1895. 346 p., illus.

BA, CU, H, HEH, LC, N, O, UC, UM, UV, Y

Of rich and poor; New York.

5791 ——— A Little Journey in the World: A Novel ... New York: Harper & Brothers, 1889. 396 p.

AP, BA, CU, H, HEH, LC, N, O, UC, UM, UV, Y

New York society.

5792 ——— That Fortune: A Novel ... New York & London: Harper & Brothers, 1899. 393, [1] p. AP, BA, CU, H, HEH, LC, N, O, UC, UM, UV, Y

A fortune lost with beneficial results.

5793 ——— Their Pilgrimage ... New York: Harper & Brothers, 1887. 363 p., illus. AP, BA, BU, CU, H, HEH, LC, N, O, UVB, Y

Of American resorts.

5794 WARNER, ELLEN E. (KENYON). A Lucky Waif: A Story for Mothers, of Home and School Life. By Ellen E. Kenyon. New York: Fowler & Wells Co., 1885. 299 p. HEH

5795 [WARNER, SUSAN BOGERT.] Daisy Plains ... New York: Robert Carter
& Brothers, 530 Broadway [cop. 1885]. 609 p.
CU, H, HEH, LC, N, O, UC, Y

5796 ——— Diana ... New York: G. P. Putnam's Sons, 1877. 460 p.
BA, BU, HEH, LC, N, O, UC, UP, UVB, Y

5797 [———] The End of a Coil ... New York: Robert Carter and Brothers, 1880. 718 p. BA, CU, H, LC, O, UC

5798 ——— The Gold of Chickaree ... New York: G. P. Putnam's Sons,
1876. 426 p. BA, CU, HEH, LC, O, UVB, Y
Anna Warner, jt. au.

5799 [———] The Letter of Credit ... New York: Robert Carter and
Brothers, 1882. 733 p. AP, BA, CU, LC, O, UC, Y

5800 [———] My Desire ... New York: Robert Carter and Brothers, 1879.
629 p. BA, CU, HEH, LC, N, O, Y

5801 [———] Nobody ... New York: Robert Carter & Brothers, 1883.
695 p. BU, H, HEH, LC, N, O, UC, Y

5802 [———] A Red Wallflower ... New York: Robert Carter & Brothers, 1884. 650 p. HEH, LC, UC, Y

5803 ——— Wych Hazel ... New York: G. P. Putnam's Sons, 1876. 528 p.
CU, HEH, LC, N, O, UC, UM, Y
Anna Warner, jt. au.

5804 WARR, J. W. The Business House That Jack Built ... Moline, Illinois:
Plowman Publishing Company, 1896. 204 p., illus. LC, Y

5805 WARREN, B. C. Asareth: A Tale of the Luray Caverns ... New York:
A. Lovell & Co. [cop. 1893]. 273 p. H, LC, UV, Y

5806 WARREN, CHARLES. The Girl and the Governor ... New York: Charles
Scribner's Sons, 1900. 407 p., illus. H, HEH, LC, Y
Contents: The Amalgamated Bill—A Daughter of the State—A Copley Boy
—The Second Act of Carmen—The Rehearsal—The Colligo Club Theatricals
—A Small Girl's Letter—The Arrival of the Ahwahnee—The Girl and the
Boss.

——— A Hollow Sham. In Stories from the Harvard Advocate
(1896), No. 5277a.

5807 WARREN, CORNELIA. Miss Wilton ... Boston and New York: Houghton, Mifflin and Company. The Riverside Press, Cambridge, 1892.
583 p. BA, H, HEH, LC, O, UC

5808 WARREN, FRANCES. The Woman's Side . . . A Woman's Answer to the Kreutzer Sonata of Count Lyof Tolstoi . . . New York: The Manhattan Publishing Company, 1890. 84 p.     LC

5809 WARREN, MRS. MARY EVALIN. Compensation: A Tale of Temperance . . . New York: National Temperance Society [cop. 1887]. 275 p.
    H, LC, UM

5810 WARREN, THOMAS ROBINSON. Drifting on Sunny Seas: Detached Fragments Selected at Random from an Old Sailor's Journal . . . New York: G. W. Dillingham, 1893. 314 p., front.     LC

5811 ———— Juliette Irving and the Jesuit: A Novel . . . New Brunswick, N. J.: J. Heidingsfeld, 1895. 281 p.     HEH, LC

5812 WARREN, WILLIAM FAIRFIELD. The Story of Gottlieb . . . Meadville, Penn'a.: Flood and Vincent, 1892. 48 p., illus.     H, Y

WARTH, JULIAN, *pseud. See* Parsons, Julia (Warth)

5813 WASHBURN, WILLIAM TUCKER. The Unknown City: A Story of New York . . . New York: Jesse Haney & Company, 119 Nassau Street [cop. 1880]. 448 p.     CU, H, HEH

5814 WATERBURY, JENNIE BULLARD. A New Race Diplomatist: A Novel . . . Philadelphia & London: J. B. Lippincott Company, 1900. 367 p., illus.
    AP, HEH, LC, O, UV
Washington, New York, Paris.

5815 WATERLOO, STANLEY. Armageddon: A Tale of Love, War, and Invention . . . Chicago and New York: Rand, McNally & Company [cop. 1898]. 259 p., front.     HEH, LC, N, O
Projected into the twentieth century.

———— A Girl and a Copyright. *In* Short Story Masterpieces (1900), No. 4931.

5816 ———— The Launching of a Man . . . Chicago and New York: Rand, McNally & Company, 1899. 285 p.     H, HEH, LC, N, O, UM
Building railroads in the Southwest.

5817 ———— A Man and a Woman . . . Chicago: F. J. Schulte & Company; the Ariel Press, 298 Dearborn Street [cop. 1892]. 250 p.     CU, HEH
Wisconsin frontier.

5818 ———— The Seekers . . . Chicago & New York: Herbert S. Stone & Company, 1900. 257 p.     CU, HEH, LC, N, O, UM, Y
Of Christian Science.

5819 ——— The Story of Ab: A Tale of the Time of the Cave Men... Chicago: Way & Williams, 1897. 351, [1] p., front.

BA, HEH, LC, N, O, UC, UV

5820 ——— The Wolf's Long Howl... Chicago & New York: Herbert S. Stone & Company, 1899. 288 p. BU, H, HEH, LC, N, O, UM, UVB, Y
*Also contains:* An Ulm—The Hair of the Dog That Bit Him—The Man Who Fell in Love—A Tragedy of the Forest—The Parasangs—Love and a Triangle —An Easter Admission—Professor Morgan's Moon—Red Dog's Show Window—Markham's Experience—The Red Revenger—A Murderer's Accomplice—A Mid-Pacific Fourth—Love and a Latch-Key—Christmas 200,000 B.C.— The Child—The Baby and the Bear—At the Green Tree Club—The Rain-Maker—Within One Life's Span.

5821 WATERMAN, CHARLES ELMER. The Promised Land, and Other Tales... Mechanic Falls, Maine: Ledger Publishing Company, 1897. 84 p., front. Printed in double columns. LC
*Also contains:* Among the Dummies—The Interrupted Song—A Message from the Enemy—The Evolution of a Tramp—The Fanatic Herald—The Century-Clock—The Elwin Claim—Uriah Upton—A Blight in the Land of the Lotus —A Slave of Bacchus—Legend of Search-Acre.

5822 WATERS, CLARA (ERSKINE) CLEMENT. Eleanor Maitland: A Novel. By Clara Erskine Clement. Boston: James R. Osgood and Company, 1881. 365 p. BA, HEH, LC, O
Washington, D.C., and Berlin as background for romance.

5823 WATERS, GAY. Alma; or, Otonkah's Daughter. A Story of the 20,000 Sioux... Chicago: T. S. Denison, 163 Randolph Street [cop. 1888]. 170 p. LC, N

5824 [WATROUS, CHARLES.] Told at Tuxedo. By A. M. Emory [pseud.]. New York and London: G. P. Putnam's Sons; the Knickerbocker Press, 1887. 145 p., front. AP, HEH, LC, O, Y

5825 WATSON, AUGUSTA (CAMPBELL). Beyond the City Gate: A Romance of Old New York... New York: E. P. Dutton & Company, 1897. 324 p., front. HEH, LC, O, Y

5826 ——— Dorothy the Puritan: The Story of a Strange Delusion... New York: E. P. Dutton and Company, 1893. 341 p., front.
BU, HEH, LC, O, Y
Salem, Massachusetts, in 1691.

5827 ——— Off Lynnport Light: A Novel... New York: E. P. Dutton Company, 1895. 343, [1] p., front. HEH, LC, O, Y
New England fishing village.

5828 ——— The Old Harbor Town: A Novel... New York: G. W. Dillingham, 1892. 275 p., illus. HEH, LC

5829 WATSON, LEWIS H. Not to the Swift: A Tale of Two Continents . . . New York: Welch, Fracker Company, 1891. 399 p.    HEH, LC, O
At head of title: "By Lewis H. Watson (Lewis Harrison). . . ."

5830 [———] A Strange Infatuation. By Lewis Harrison [pseud.] . . . Chicago and New York: Rand, McNally & Company, 1890. 313 p., illus.
HEH

5831 WATSON, MARIE. The Two Paths . . . Chicago: Alfred C. Clark, 1897. 195 p.    LC

WATSON, MARY DEVEREUX. *See* Devereux, Mary

5832 WATTERS, AUGUSTUS. A Newark Knight: A Romance . . . Newark, N.J.: L. J. Hardham, printer and binder, 1888. 151 p.
Copy examined at New York Public Library.

5833 ——— The Puritans; or, Newark in the Olden Time. An Historical Romance . . . Newark, N.J., 1894. 107 p.    BU

5834 ——— The Vale of Rampo: A New Jersey Idyl . . . Newark, N.J.: L. J. Hardham, printer and bookbinder, 1886. 127 p.
Copy examined at New York Public Library.

5835 WATTS, WILLIAM COURTNEY. Chronicles of a Kentucky Settlement . . . New York, London: G. P. Putnam's Sons; the Knickerbocker Press, 1897. 490 p.    BU, CU, H, HEH, LC, N, UC, UM, Y
Before and after the Civil War.

WAYNE, CHARLES J., *pseud.* *See* Charles, James

5836 WAYNE, CHARLES STOKES. The Lady and Her Tree: A Story of Society . . . Philadelphia: The Vortex Company, 10 S. 18th St. [cop. 1895]. 221 p.    HEH, UP
Philadelphia and New York.

5837 ——— Mrs. Lord's Moonstone, and Other Stories . . . Philadelphia: Wynne & Wayne, 1888. 142 p.    LC
*Also contains:* How Belford Won—A Modern Miracle—A Trap of Cupid—The Wizard's Jar.

5838 A WAYWARD LIFE; or, A Girl's Destiny. A Novel. New York: G. W. Carleton & Co., 1886. 235 p.    BU, HEH, LC

5839 WE ARE ONE: A Story of American Life . . . Louisville: S. L. Ewing & Co., 1878. 361 p.    HEH, LC, N, UM

5840 WEAVER, ANNA D. Richards's Crown, How He Won and Wore It . . . Chicago, Ill., 1882. 304 p., illus.    LC

5841 WEBB, CHARLES HENRY. Sea-Weed and What We Seed: My Vacation at Long Branch and Saratoga . . . New York: G. W. Carleton & Co. London: Low & Co., 1876. 228 p.    BU, CU, H, HEH, N, O, UC, UM, UP, Y

5842 WEBB, FRANCES ISABEL (CURRIE). A Breath of Suspicion: A Novel . . . New York: F. I. Webb, 200 W. 52d St. [cop. 1895]. 288 p.
Listed PW, Feb. 16, 1895.

WEBSTER, ALBERT FALVEY. Miss Eunice's Glove. *In* Stories by American Authors, VI (1884), No. 5272.

———— An Operation in Money. *In* Stories by American Authors, I (1884), No. 5267.

5843 WEBSTER, HENRY KITCHELL. The Banker and the Bear: The Story of a Corner in Lard . . . New York: The Macmillan Company. London: Macmillan & Co., Ltd., 1900. 351 p.    AP, CU, HEH, LC, N, O, UM, UP, Y

———— *jt. au.* See Merwin, S. The Short Line War (1899), No. 3708.

5844 WEBSTER, JONATHAN VINTON. Two True California Stories: Augusta Dane; or, The Influence of Circumstances. Mary Morton; or, The Result of a Fashionable Education . . . San Francisco: P. J. Thomas, printer and publisher, 1883. 256 p.    HEH, LC

5845 WEED, MARIA. A Voice in the Wilderness . . . Chicago: Laird & Lee [cop. 1895]. 225 p., illus.
Listed PW, June 1, 1895.

5846 WEEKS, CLARA WINSLOW. Story of a China Plate . . . [New York: Press of Albert B. King, 19 Liberty St., cop. 1888.] [14] p., illus.    HEH
Text printed within circular border.

5847 WEEKS, HELEN MARIAN. The Sequel of a Wasted Life: Comprising a Story Founded on Facts . . . Girard, Pa.: Murphy & Nichols, printers, 1896. 159 p., illus.    LC

5848 WEEKS, J. HATTON. The Tin Kitchen . . . [Worcester, Mass.]: Published by the Westborough Historical Society, 1895. 90 p., illus.
BU, HEH, O, Y
Also contains: The Old Clock—The Teapot—The Satin Shoes.
LC has ed. with imprint: New York, Boston: T. Y. Crowell & Company [cop. 1896]. 92 p. Deposited Aug. 10, 1896.

5849 WEIR, A. M. Old Times in Georgia: Good Times and Bad Times . . . Atlanta, Ga.: Constitution Publishing Company, 1889. 199 p.    H, LC

5850 [WEITZEL, SOPHIE (WINTHROP).] Counter-Currents: A Story . . . Boston: Roberts Brothers, 1888. 303 p.    BA, H, HEH, UVB
Southern California.

5851   [————]  Justina.  Boston: Roberts Brothers, 1886.  249 p.
                                          AP, BA, H, HEH, O, UV
      At head of title: "No Name Series."
      New England.

5852   WELCH, ALFRED.  Extracts from the Diary of Moritz Svengali.  Translated and Edited by Alfred Welch . . . New York: Henry Holt and Company, 1897.  89 p.                         CU, H, Y

5853   WELCKER, ADAIR.  Snob Papers: A Humorous Novel . . . Philadelphia: T. B. Peterson & Brothers, 306 Chestnut Street [cop. 1885].  456 p.
                                          HEH, LC, UP, UV
      San Francisco society.

      WELLFORD, CLARENCE.  Her Last Love.  *In* New Stories from the Chap-Book (1898), No. 3949.

5854   WELLINGTON, MRS. A. A.  By a Way That They Knew Not . . . Chicago: Rand, McNally & Co., printers, 1885.  288 p.          LC
      Chicago society.

5855   WELLINGTON, COURTNEY.  Congressman Hardie, a Born Democrat . . . New York: G. W. Dillingham Co. [cop. 1900].  240 p.   H, HEH, LC, N

5856   WELLS, CATHERINE BOOTT (GANNETT).  Miss Curtis: A Sketch.  By Kate Gannett Wells . . . Boston: Ticknor and Company, 1888.  271 p.
                                  BU, CU, H, HEH, LC, O, UC, Y
      Of Bostonians.

5857   ———— Two Modern Women: A Novel . . . Philadelphia: J. B. Lippincott Company, 1890.  291 p.             H, HEH, LC, O, UP
      Campobello Island, Maine.

5858   WELLS, DAVID AMES.  Robinson Crusoe's Money; or, The Remarkable Financial Fortunes and Misfortunes of a Remote Island Community . . . New York: Harper & Brothers, 1876.  118 p., illus.
                                BA, BU, CU, HEH, N, O, UC, UP, Y

5859   WELLS, DAVID DWIGHT.  Her Ladyship's Elephant . . . New York: Henry Holt and Company, 1898.  234 p.       BA, H, HEH, LC, Y

5860   ———— His Lordship's Leopard: A Truthful Narration of Some Impossible Facts . . . New York: Henry Holt and Company, 1900.  301 p.                             AP, H, HEH, LC, O, Y
      Of a journalist.

5861   ———— Parlous Times: A Novel of Modern Diplomacy . . . New York: J. F. Taylor & Company, 1900.  439 p.     H, HEH, LC, O, UM

5862 [WELLS, ELEANOR P. BELL.] Madame Lucas ... Boston: James R. Osgood and Company, 1882. 347 p. AP, BA, CU, H, HEH, LC, O
At head of title: "Round-Robin Series."
French widow moves to western U.S. city of "St. Leon."

WELLS, KATE GANNETT. *See* Wells, Catherine Boott (Gannett)

5863 [WELLS, SAMUEL E.] In Spite of Integrity, Would You under These Circumstances Have Stolen One Hundred Thousand. By Junious Junior [pseud.]. New York: The American News Company, 1889. 211 p. LC

5864 [————] Valmond the Crank: The Forbidden Book. By "Nero" [pseud.]. Albany, N.Y.: The Original Publishing Company [cop. 1891]. 212 p. LC
Valmond is a socialist.

5865 WELSH, JAMES. A White Baby ... New York and London: Frederick A. Stokes Company [cop. 1895]. 190 p., front. H, HEH, LC
Written in Negro dialect.
Charleston.

5866 [WELTON, MISS A. E.] Cora: A Tale of Right and Wrong. A Novel of To-Day. New York: J. S. Ogilvie [cop. 1891]. 187 p. LC
Early Omaha.

5867 WENDELL, BARRETT. The Duchess Emilia: A Romance ... Boston: James R. Osgood and Company, 1885. 241 p.
AP, BA, CU, H, HEH, LC, N, O, UVB, Y
Rome.

5868 ———— Rankell's Remains: An American Novel ... Boston: Ticknor and Company, 1887. 316 p. BA, CU, H, HEH, LC, N, O, UVB, Y
Of business.

5869 WENDLER, EMMA. Peccavi: A Novel ... New York: G. W. Carleton & Co. London: S. Low & Co., 1878. 321 p. LC

5870 WENDT, FREDERICK W. Ocean Sketches ... New York: The Colonial Book Co., 52 Lafayette Place [cop. 1897]. 151 p., 1 l. CU, HEH, LC
*Contents:* Checkmate—Incognita—A Tale of Two—The Romance of a Stowaway—A Honeymoon at Sea—A Farmer in a Fog—A Sunrise.

5871 ———— Transatlantics ... New York: Brentano's, 1899. 219 p.
CU, HEH, LC, Y
*Contents:* A Problem—The Making of a Man—A Tale with a Moral—The Loss of the Microbes—A Quiet Trip for the Nerves—After Many Years—The "Yes" Flag—A Ghost-of-a-Ghost Story—Peter—"And While We Fret on Shore"—The Professor—Revery of a Bachelor Steamer Chair—Mr. and Mrs. Milford.

Wentworth, William, *pseud.* *See* Beckman, Edwin

5872 Wernberny, John. Love & Company, Limited. By John Wernberny and Another. New York: J. Selwin Tait & Sons, 1897. 113 p.
Copy examined at New York Public Library.

5873 Wertheimer, Louis. A Muramasa Blade: A Story of Feudalism in Old Japan ... Boston: Ticknor and Company, 1887. 118 p., illus.
AP, BA, LC, O, Y

5874 Westcott, Blanche. Jean; or, Clouds with a Silver Lining. A Story ... Philadelphia: J. B. Lippincott & Co., 1879. 255 p.          H, HEH
From Kentucky to California.

5875 Westcott, Edward Noyes. The Christmas Story from David Harum ... New York: D. Appleton and Company, 1900. 107 p., illus.
BU, H, HEH, O, UV, Y
At head of title: "Wm. H. Crane Edition."
Comprises chaps. xvii-xx, part of xxii, and xiii-xiv of *David Harum.*

5876 ——— David Harum: A Story of American Life ... New York: D. Appleton and Company, 1898. 392 p.          HEH, N, UC, UV, Y

5877 Westervelt, Leonidas. The Puppet-Show: A Sketch ... New York: F. Tennyson Neely, 114 Fifth Avenue. Chicago, London [cop. 1898]. 219 p., illus.          H, HEH, Y
New York society.

Wetherill, Julie K. *See* Baker, Julia Keim (Wetherill)

5878 Wetmore, Claude Hazeltine. Sweepers of the Sea: The Story of a Strange Navy ... Indianapolis: The Bowen-Merrill Company [cop. 1900]. 349 p., illus.          LC

Wetmore, Elizabeth (Bisland), *jt. au. See* Broughton, R. A Widower Indeed (1891), No. 694.

5879 [Wetmore, Mai M.] Wee Folk of No-Man's Land. By Oaks [pseud.] ... Chicago: Shepard & Johnston, printers, 1883. 336 p.          HEH

Wettleson, William. The Rev. Mr. Morrow. *In* J. J. Conway, *ed.,* Stories (1893), No. 1172.

5880 Wharton, Edith Newbold (Jones). The Greater Inclination ... New York: Charles Scribner's Sons, 1899. 254 p.
AP, BA, CU, HEH, N, O, UC, UP, UV, Y
*Contents:* The Muse's Tragedy—A Journey—The Pelican—Souls Belated—A Coward—The Twilight of the God—A Cup of Cold Water—The Portrait.

———— Mrs. Manstey's View. *In* Stories of New York (1893), No. 5279.

5881 ———— The Touchstone ... New York: Charles Scribner's Sons, 1900. 155, [1] p., 2 l. AP, BA, BU, CU, HEH, LC, N, O, UP, UV, Y

5882 [WHARTON, EDWARD CLIFTON.] The War of the Bachelors: A Story of the Crescent City at the Period of the Franco-German War. By "Orleanian" [pseud.]. New Orleans: Printed for the author, 1882. 406 p. LC

5883 WHARTON, THOMAS ISAAC. "Bobbo," and Other Fancies ... New York: Harper & Brothers, 1897. 182, [1] p., illus.

BA, BU, CU, H, HEH, LC, N, O, UC, Y

*Contains:* The Last Sonnet of Prinzivalle di Cembino—Ratu Tanito's Wooing —Old and New.

———— The Cashier and the Burglar. *In* Mavericks (1892), No. 3663.

5884 ———— Hannibal of New York: Some Account of the Financial Loves of Hannibal St. Joseph and Paul Cradge ... New York: Henry Holt and Company, 1886. 326 p. BA, CU, HEH, LC, O, UC, UM, Y
At head of title: "Leisure Hour Series—No. 193."

5885 [————] A Latter Day Saint: Being the Story of the Conversion of Ethel Jones. Related by Herself. New York: Henry Holt and Company, 1884. 200 p. AP, HEH, O, UVB, Y
At head of title: "American Novel Series—No. 1."

5886 WHEATLEY, LOUISE KNIGHT. Ashes of Roses . . . New York: Dodd, Mead & Company [cop. 1893]. 206 p. HEH, LC, O

[WHEELER, ANDREW CARPENTER.] The End of All, by Nym Crinkle [pseud.]. *In* Eleven Possible Cases [cop. 1891], No. 1737.

5887 ———— The Iron Trail: A Sketch . . . New York: F. B. Patterson, 1876. 46 p., illus. BA, CU, H, HEH, LC, N, O, UM, Y

5888 ———— The Toltec Cup: A Romance of Immediate Life in New York City . . . New York: Lew Vanderpoole Publishing Company, 1890. 333 p. Printed in double columns. LC

5889 WHEELER, CORA KELLEY. My Allegiance . . . Franklin, Ohio: The Editor Publishing Company, 1896. 120 p. LC
A romance of the French Revolution.

5890 WHEELER, ESTHER GRACIE (LAWRENCE). Stray Leaves from Newport . . . Boston: Cupples & Hurd, 1888. 195 p. AP, BA, BU, CU, HEH, LC, Y
*Contains:* Sentiment and Seaweed—My Wife, Where Is She? A Story of Newport Middy-evil Life—Our Boy: A Sketch of Newport Domestic Life.

5891 ———— A Washington Symphony. By Mrs. William Lamont Wheeler . . . New York, London: G. P. Putnam's Sons; the Knickerbocker Press, 1893. 194 p.     BA, CU, HEH, LC
Life in Washington, D.C.

WHEELER, HALLIE ERMINIE (RIVES). *See* Rives, Hallie Erminie

5892 WHEELER, IDA WORDEN. Siegfried the Mystic: A Novel . . . Boston: Arena Publishing Company, 1896. 295 p.     LC, UM
Psychic and occult phenomena.

5893 WHEELER, NELSON W. Old Thunderbolt in Justice Court . . . Baraboo, Wisconsin, 1883. 163 p., front.     CU, N

WHEELER, PRESERVED, *pseud.* *See* McDougall, Ella L. (Randall)

5894 WHEELER, SAMUEL WATSON. Count de Mornay; or, Back from the Dead. A Novel . . . [N.p.], cop. 1894. 186 p.     LC

WHEELER, MRS. WILLIAM LAMONT. *See* Wheeler, Esther Gracie (Lawrence)

5895 WHEELER, WILLIAM WALLACE. Life: A Novel . . . Meriden, Conn., 1890. 287 p.     LC
Of a visit to the spirit world.

5896 ———— Rest . . . Boston: Arena Publishing Company, 1894. 280 p.     HEH
A fantasy.

5897 [WHEELOCK, JOHN E.] In Search of Gold: The Story of a Liberal Life. By Don Juan [pseud.]. New York: H. W. Thompson, 1884. 392 p.     CU, HEH, LC, N, Y

5898 WHEELOCK, JULIA FLANDER. Annis Warden; or, A Story of Real Life . . . Hamilton, N.Y.: Republican Print, 1889. 295 p.     BU, HEH, LC
Upstate New York from 1813 to 1889.

5899 WHEELWRIGHT, JOHN TYLER. A Bad Penny . . . Boston and New York: Lamson, Wolffe and Company, 1896. 162 p., illus.     BA, H, HEH, LC, O
Massachusetts seacoast, early 1800's.

5900 ———— A Child of the Century . . . New York: Charles Scribner's Sons, 1887. 348 p.     AP, BA, BU, H, HEH, LC, O
A Boston lawyer goes to Washington.

5901 [————] Rollo's Journey to Cambridge . . . Boston: A. Williams and Company, 1880. 28 p., illus. Printed in double columns.     BA, CU, H, Y
Satire.

——— *jt. au. See* Grant, R.   The King's Men (1884), No. 2236.

5902   WHELESS, WILL J.   Yazoo: A Study . . .   Denison, Texas: Printed at Murray's Steam Printing House, 1889.   182 p.                                    LC

5903   WHITE, ALFRED LUDLOW.   Doctor Hildreth: A Romance . . .   Philadelphia: J. B. Lippincott & Co., 1880.   272 p.                          HEH, LC, O

5904   WHITE, MRS. BETSEY ANN.   Richmond and Way Stations: '61 and '64 . . . [Milford], Massachusetts: [Commercial Job Printing House], 1889. 54 p., 1 l.                                                                BU, HEH, N
A series of letters purporting to be from William G. Warren, a soldier in Co. A, 16th Massachusetts Volunteer Infantry.

5905   [———]   Three Holes in the Chimney; or, A Scattered Family.   By Didama [pseud.] . . .   Newton [Mass.]: B. A. White, 1886.   297 p., illus.                                                                        BU, HEH, LC
BU copy contains a broadside identifying the characters in this temperance story.

WHITE, C. H., *pseud. See* Chaplin, Heman White

5906   WHITE, CAROLINE (EARLE).   Love in the Tropics: A Romance of the South Seas . . .   Philadelphia: J. B. Lippincott Company, 1890.   150 p.
AP, HEH, LC, O, UP

5907   ———   A Modern Agrippa.   Patience Barker: A Tale of Old Nantucket . . .   Philadelphia: J. B. Lippincott Company, 1893.   285 p.
HEH, LC, O
First story laid in New York.

5908   WHITE, ELIZA ORNE.   A Browning Courtship, and Other Stories . . . Boston and New York: Houghton, Mifflin and Company.   The Riverside Press, Cambridge, 1897.   276 p., 1 l.   BA, BU, CU, H, HEH, LC, N, O
*Also contains:* Commonplace Carrie—A Bismarck Dinner—A Hamerton Type-Writer—A Faithful Failure—The Queen of Clubs—The Fatted Calf—Two Authors.

5909   ———   The Coming of Theodora . . .   Boston and New York: Houghton, Mifflin and Company.   The Riverside Press, Cambridge, 1895. 304 p.                                                        BA, H, HEH, LC, O, Y
Theodora, a teacher of political economy, visits her Bohemian brother.

5910   ———   A Lover of Truth . . .   Boston and New York: Houghton, Mifflin and Company.   The Riverside Press, Cambridge, 1898.   319, [1] p.                                                          BA, BU, CU, H, HEH, LC, O
Of life in a New England town.

5911   ———   Miss Brooks: A Story . . .   Boston: Roberts Brothers, 1890. 283 p.                                                  AP, BU, H, HEH, LC, O, UM, Y
Boston social life.

5912 ——— Winterborough ... Boston and New York: Houghton, Mifflin and Company. The Riverside Press, Cambridge, 1892. 350 p.

BA, HEH, LC, O

New Hampshire.

5913 WHITE, ELIZABETH STOUGHTON (GALE). Uno Who ... New York: The Abbey Press, 114 Fifth Avenue. London, Montreal [cop. 1900]. 245 p., front.

LC

5914 WHITE, ERNEST L. E. Sketches from the Sunset Land ... McMinnville, Or.: E. L. E. White, 1888. 44 p.

LC

Contents: "For His Sake"—Orna Lavoir—Sequel to Orna Lavoir.

5915 WHITE, HERVEY. Differences ... Boston: Small, Maynard & Company, 1899. 311 p.

CU, HEH, LC, O, Y

Of "settlement work" in Chicago.

5916 ——— Quicksand ... Boston: Small, Maynard & Company, 1900. 328 p.

H, HEH, LC, O, Y

New Hampshire.

5917 WHITE, MATTHEW. The Affair at Islington ... New York: Frank A. Munsey, 1897. 233 p.

H, HEH, LC, O

5918 ——— A Born Aristocrat: A Story of the Stage ... New York: Frank A. Munsey, 1898. 228 p.

H, LC, Y

New York.

——— A Quarter Past Six. In F. E. McKay, ed., Vignettes [cop. 1890], No. 3523.

5919 WHITE, RICHARD GRANT. The Fate of Mansfield Humphreys, with the Episode of Mr. Washington Adams in England, and an Apology ... Boston, New York: Houghton, Mifflin and Company. The Riverside Press, Cambridge, 1884. 446 p.

AP, BA, BU, CU, H, HEH, LC, N, O, UC, UM, UVB, Y

Opinions of Americans and Englishmen of each other.

5920 WHITE, TEN EYCK. The Lakeside Musings ... Chicago: Rand, McNally & Company, 1884. 283 p.

HEH, LC, N, Y

5921 WHITE, MRS. W. H. Jessica; or, A Diamond with a Blemish. A Novel ... New York: G. W. Carleton & Co. London: S. Low & Co., 1884. 417 p., illus.

AP, CU, LC

5922 [———] Some Women of To-Day. By One of Them ... New York: G. W. Carleton & Co. London: S. Low, Son & Co., 1880. 388 p.

HEH, LC

WHITE, WILLIAM ALLEN. The Home-Coming of Colonel Hucks. *In* Tales from McClure's: The West (1897), No. 5363.
Printed earlier in No. 5923.

——— The King of Boyville. *In* Tales from McClure's: Humor (1897), No. 5361.
Printed earlier in No. 5923.

5923 ——— The Real Issue ... Chicago: Way and Williams, 1896. 212 p., 1 l.         H, HEH, LC, N, O, UP, UVB, Y
*Also contains:* The Story of Aqua Pura—The Prodigal Daughter—The Record on the Blotter—The King of Boyville—A Story of the Highlands—The Fraud of Men—The Reading of the Riddle—The Chief Clerk's Christmas—The Story of a Grave—The Home-Coming of Colonel Hucks—The Regeneration of Colonel Hucks—The Undertaker's Trust—That's for Remembrance—A Nocturne.

5924 [WHITE, WILLIAM FRANCIS.] A Picture of Pioneer Times in California ... By William Grey [pseud.] ... San Francisco: Printed by W. M. Hinton & Co., 1881. 677 p.      BA, CU, H, HEH, UC, Y
*Contains:* Ellen Harvey; or, The Wife's Disappointment—Ada Allen; or, The Husband's Surprise—Minnie Wagner; or, The Forged Note.

5925 WHITELEY, ISABEL (NIXON). The Falcon of Langéac ... Boston: Copeland and Day, 1897. 227 p., 1 l.      BU, HEH, LC, N, O, Y

5926 ——— For the French Lilies (A.D. 1511-1512) ... St. Louis, Mo.: B. Herder, 1899. 241 p.      LC

5927 WHITELOCK, LOUISE (CLARKSON). How Hindsight Met Provincialatis ... Boston: Copeland and Day, 1898. 294 p., 1 l.
     CU, H, HEH, LC, N, O, UV, Y
Ante bellum South.

5928 ——— A Mad Madonna, and Other Stories ... Boston: Joseph Knight Company, 1895. 203 p., illus.      CU, HEH, LC, O
*Also contains:* A Bit of Delft—Ignoto—Love's House—Apollo—From Another Country.

5929 ——— The Shadow of John Wallace: A Novel. By L. Clarkson. New York: White, Stokes, & Allen, 1884. 417 p., 1 l.
     CU, HEH, LC, UM, UP, UV
Long Island.

WHITING, JULIA D. The Divided House. *In* Tales from McClure's: The West (1897), No. 5363.

[WHITMAN, MRS. HENRY] *attrib. au.* Happiness. *In* [Mrs. J. Lodge] *ed.*, A Week away from Time (1887), No. 3382.

5930 WHITNEY, ADELINE DUTTON (TRAIN). Ascutney Street: A Neighborhood Story . . . Boston and New York: Houghton, Mifflin and Company. The Riverside Press, Cambridge, 1890. 259 p.
AP, BA, H, HEH, LC, Y

5931 ―――― Bonnyborough . . . Boston and New York: Houghton, Mifflin and Company. The Riverside Press, Cambridge, 1886. 388 p.
AP, BA, BU, CU, H, HEH, LC, O, UM

5932 ―――― A Golden Gossip: Neighborhood Story Number Two . . . Boston and New York: Houghton, Mifflin and Company. The Riverside Press, Cambridge, 1892. 348 p. BA, BU, H, HEH, LC, N, O, UM, Y

5933 ―――― Homespun Yarns . . . Boston and New York: Houghton, Mifflin and Company. The Riverside Press, Cambridge, 1887. 394 p.
AP, BA, H, LC, Y
A collection of adult and juvenile tales.

5934 ―――― Sights and Insights: Patience Strong's Story of over the Way . . . Boston: James R. Osgood and Company, late Ticknor & Fields, and Fields, Osgood & Co., 1876. 2 vols. (677 p.)
BU, CU, H, HEH, LC, N, O, UM, UV, Y

5935 ―――― Square Pegs . . . Boston and New York: Houghton, Mifflin and Company. The Riverside Press, Cambridge, 1899. 507, [1] p.
BA, BU, CU, H, HEH, LC, N, O, UM, Y

5936 WHITNEY, ATWELL. Almond-Eyed: A Story of the Day . . . [San Francisco]: Printed for the author by A. L. Bancroft & Company, 1878. 168 p., illus. HEH, LC, O
Chinese in California.

5937 WHITSON, ROLLAND LEWIS. Rolinda: A Tale of the Mississinewa . . . Columbus, Ohio: The Champlin Press [cop. 1898]. 356 p., illus. LC
Deposited May 23, 1899.

5938 [WHITSON, THOMAS.] Walter Graham, Statesman: An American Romance. By an American, Who . . . Still Believes in America. Lancaster, Pa.: Fulton Publishing Company, 1891. 602 p. HEH, LC, UM, Y

5939 WHITTAKER, FREDERICK. The Cadet Button: A Novel of American Army Life . . . New York: Sheldon & Company, 1878. 354 p.
BU, CU, HEH, LC, O, Y

5940 WHITTLESEY, ELSIE LEIGH. Elyria . . . Philadelphia: Claxton, Remsen, & Haffelfinger, 1877. 335 p. HEH, LC, O

5941 WHYTE, JOHN H. New Orleans in 1950: Being a Story of the Carnival City from the Pen of a Descendant of Herodotus, Possessing the Gift of Prescience . . . New Orleans: A. W. Hyatt Co., 407 Camp Street [1899]. 167 p.
Information supplied by Ann R. Graves of Tulane University Library.

5942 WICKERSHAM, JAMES ALEXANDER. Enoch Willoughby: A Novel . . .
New York: Charles Scribner's Sons, 1900. 356 p.     HEH, LC, O
Pioneer Quakers of Ohio.

5943 WIDDEMER, IRENE. Daisy Brentwell . . . New York: G. P. Putnam's
Sons, 1876. 434 p.     HEH, LC, O

5944 WIGGIN, JAMES BARTLETT. The Wild Artist in Boston: A Story of Love
and Art in the Actual . . . Boston: Published by J. B. Wiggin, 1888.
407 p.     BU, HEH, LC, Y

5945 WIGGIN, KATE DOUGLAS (SMITH). A Cathedral Courtship, and Penelope's English Experiences . . . Boston and New York: Houghton,
Mifflin and Company, 1893. 164 p., illus.     CU, H, HEH, LC, N, UVB, Y

5946 —— Marm Lisa . . . Boston and New York: Houghton, Mifflin and
Company. The Riverside Press, Cambridge, 1896. 199 p.
AP, CU, H, HEH, LC, N, O, UC, UP, UVB, Y

5947 —— Penelope's English Experiences . . . Boston and New York:
Houghton, Mifflin & Company, 1900. 176 p., 1 l., illus.
CU, H, HEH, LC, UC, UP, UVB, Y

5948 —— Penelope's Progress: Being Such Extracts from the Common-
place Book of Penelope Hamilton as Relate to Her Experiences in
Scotland . . . Boston and New York: Houghton, Mifflin and Company.
The Riverside Press, Cambridge, 1898. 268 p., 1 l.
BA, CU, H, HEH, LC, N, O, UC, UM, UP, UVB, Y

5949 —— The Village Watch-Tower . . . Boston and New York:
Houghton, Mifflin and Company. The Riverside Press, Cambridge,
1895. 218 p.     BA, CU, H, HEH, LC, N, O, UC, UM, UP, UVB, Y
*Also contains:* Tom o' the Blueb'ry Plains—The Nooning Tree—The Fore-
Room Rug—A Village Stradivarius—The Eventful Trip of the Midnight Cry.

5950 WIGGS, ANNA OLDFIELD. Apple Blossoms: A Novel . . . Chicago: A. E.
Davis & Company, 1886. 391 p.     LC

5951 —— Hayne Home . . . Chicago and New York: Rand, McNally &
Company, 1890. 336 p.     HEH
Northern Kentucky.

5952 —— Kathie: A Novel . . . New York: G. W. Dillingham, 1889.
391 p.     LC

5953 WIGHT, EMMA HOWARD. The Little Maid of Israel . . . St. Louis, Mo.:
B. Herder, 1900. 96 p.     LC

5954 —— Passion Flowers and the Cross: A Novel . . . Baltimore, Md.:
Calendar Publishing Co., 1891. 247 p., front.     LC
Of a society woman's infatuation for a priest.

5955 WILBUR, MRS. C. E. The Thread of Gold . . . Cincinnati: Cranston & Stowe. New York: Phillips & Hunt, 1885. 172 p. HEH
Temperance novel.

5956 WILCOX, ELLA (WHEELER). An Ambitious Man . . . Chicago: W. B. Conkey Company [cop. 1896]. 197 p., front. BU, CU, H, HEH, LC, UM, Y
Of a loveless marriage.

——— Dave's Wife. In L. C. H. Langford, comp., The Woman's Story (1889), No. 3206.
Printed earlier in No. 5958.

5957 ——— Mal Moulée: A Novel . . . New York: G. W. Carleton & Co. London: S. Low, Son & Co., 1886. 296 p. CU, H, HEH, LC, N, O, UM, UVB, Y

5958 ——— Perdita, and Other Stories . . . New York: J. S. Ogilvie and Company, 31 Rose Street [cop. 1886]. 118 p. CU, LC, UVB
Also contains: Dave's Wife—Violet's Emancipation—A Mental Crime—John Smith.

5959 ——— Was It Suicide? . . . New York: F. Tennyson Neely, 1897. 164 p. BU, CU, UM, Y

5960 [WILCOX, HENRY S.] Flaws. By a Lawyer. Des Moines, Iowa: Geo. S. Cline, 1885. 217 p. LC

5961 ——— The Great Boo-Boo . . . A Tale of Fun and Fancy, Replete with Love, Wit, Sentiment, and Satire. Des Moines, Iowa: J. B. Swinburne, 1892. 285 p. LC

5962 WILCOX, MARRION. Real People . . . New York: White, Stokes, & Allen, 1886. 247 p. AP, CU, HEH, LC, O, Y
Contents: A Spanish-American Engagement—Bertram Born—Keepsakes—Parsifal, Paul, and Pauline—Good-Bye to Common Sense—Concha Casablanca.

5963 [———] Señora Villena; and Gray: An Oldhaven Romance. Two Volumes in One . . . New York: White, Stokes, & Allen, 1887. 179, 262 p. H, HEH, LC, O

5964 ——— Vengeance of the Female. Edited by Marrion Wilcox . . . Chicago & New York: Herbert S. Stone & Company, 1899. 318 p., 1 l., illus. H, HEH, LC, UP, Y

5965 THE WILD RANGER OF SANTA FÉ. [Philadelphia: J. H. Schenck & Son, 189-?] Cover title, 31 p., illus. HEH
The tale, written to promote Schenck's remedies, occupies first 17 p.

5966 WILDE, M. VAUGHAN. Juleps and Clover . . . New York: R. F. Fenno & Company, 9 and 11 East 16th Street [cop. 1898]. 215 p. BU, HEH, LC
North Carolina mountains.

5967 WILDE, WEIN. "Whatever Thou Art": A Novel . . . New York: G. W. Dillingham, 1892. 282 p. LC

5968 WILDENBRÜCK, ERNST VON. Noble Blood: A Prussian Cadet Story, Translated from the German . . . by Charles King, U.S. Army, and Anne Williston Ward. And A West Point Parallel: An American Cadet Story, by Captain Charles King . . . New York: F. Tennyson Neely, 1896. 211 p. HEH, O, UC, UM, Y
Book included because of second story.

5969 WILDMAN, ROUNSEVELLE. The Panglima Muda: A Romance of Malaya . . . San Francisco: Overland Monthly Publishing Company, 1894. 139 p., illus. HEH, LC, Y

5970 ———— Tales of the Malayan Coast: From Penang to the Philippines . . . Boston: Lothrop Publishing Company [cop. 1899]. 347 p., illus.
BA, CU, H, HEH, LC, O, UC, UP, Y
*Contents:* Baboo's Good Tiger—Baboo's Pirates—How We Played Robinson Crusoe—The Sarong—The Kris—The White Rajah of Borneo—Amok!—Lepas's Revenge—King Solomon's Mines—Busuk—A Crocodile Hunt—A New Year's Day in Malaya—In the Burst of the Southwest Monsoon—A Pig Hunt on Mount Ophir—In the Court of Johore—In the Golden Chersonese—A Fight with Illanum Pirates.

5971 WILDRICK, MRS. MARION WHITE. Lord Strahan: A Novel . . . Philadelphia: J. B. Lippincott & Co., 1879. 221 p. CU, H, HEH, LC, N, O

5972 ———— A Zealot in Tulle: A Novel . . . New York: D. Appleton and Company, 1887. 209 p. AP, BA, BU, HEH, LC, O, Y
Of Spanish treasure in Florida.

5973 WILKES, A. B. The Great Social Boycott; or, Society Readjusted and the Causes Leading to Its Establishment . . . Brownwood, Texas, 1895. 40 p. LC

WILKES, CLEMENT, *pseud. See* Goodwin, Henry Leavitt

5974 WILKIE, FRANC BANGS. The Gambler: A Story of Chicago Life . . . Chicago: T. S. Denison, 163 Randolph Street [cop. 1888]. 328 p.
LC, UM

WILKINS, MARY ELEANOR. *See* Freeman, Mary Eleanor (Wilkins)

5975 WILKINS, WILLIAM A. The Cleverdale Mystery; or, The Machine and Its Wheels. A Story of American Life . . . New York: Fords, Howard, & Hulbert, 1882. 287 p. CU, HEH, LC, N, O, UM, Y
Of political interest.

WILKINSON, FLORENCE. *See* Evans, Florence (Wilkinson)

5976 [WILKINSON, ROBERT CARLTON.] The Kingdom of Love: A Story Inter-
mingled with the Facts of the Gospels . . . Plymouth, Ind.: Marshall
County Independent Power Print, 1895. 216 p., front. LC

5977 WILLARD, CAROLINE McCOY (WHITE). Kin-da-Shon's Wife: An Alaskan
Story. By Mrs. Eugene S. Willard . . . New York, Chicago: Fleming
H. Revell Company [cop. 1892]. 281 p., illus. H, HEH, N, UM, Y

5978 [———] A Son of Israel: An Original Story. By "Rachel Penn"
[pseud.] . . . Philadelphia: J. B. Lippincott Company, 1898. 306 p.
BA, LC, O, UP, UV

WILLARD, MRS. EUGENE S. See Willard, Caroline McCoy (White)

5979 [WILLARD, JOSIAH FLYNT.] The Powers That Prey. By Josiah Flynt
and Francis Walton [pseuds.]. New York: McClure, Phillips & Co.,
1900. 259, [1] p. BU, CU, HEH, LC, N, O, UC, UM, UP, UV, Y
Contents: In the Matter of His Nibs—A Bill from Tiffany's—The Revenge of
the Four—The Order of the Penitents—The Prison Demon—The Great Idea—
Found Guilty—On Sentence Day—Peggie Niven—A Dead One.
Alfred Hodder, jt. au.

5980 WILLARD, KATE LIVINGSTON. A Colony of Girls: A Novel . . . New
York: Dodd, Mead & Company, 1892. 267 p. HEH, LC

5981 WILLCOX, GILES BUCKINGHAM. Beyond the Veil . . . New York: Anson
D. F. Randolph & Company, 182 Fifth Avenue [cop. 1894]. 207 p.
LC, Y
In the form of a diary.

5982 WILLETS, SARAH B. Married Too Early: A Story of More Than Twenty
Years Ago . . . New York: Brentano Brothers [cop. 1885]. 221 p.
Listed PW, Jan. 17, 1885.

WILLIAMS, ANNA VERNON (DORSEY). The Dead Oak, by Anna Vernon
Dorsey. In Stories from the Chap-Book (1896), No. 5277.

5983 WILLIAMS, CHARLES EVARTS. The Penalty of Recklessness; or, Virginia
Society Twenty Years Ago. A Thrilling Romance. A Tale of Love,
Duelling, and Death as Enacted among the F. F. V. . . . Boston: Frank-
lin Press; Rand, Avery & Co., 1884. 252 p. CU, HEH, LC, UV

5984 WILLIAMS, FLORA (McDONALD). Who's the Patriot? A Story of the
Southern Confederacy . . . Louisville, Ky.: Press of the Courier-
Journal Job Printing Company, 1886. 288 p., illus.
BU, CU, H, HEH, LC, N, UC, UM, UV

5985 WILLIAMS, FRANCIS HOWARD. Atman: The Documents in a Strange Case
. . . New York: Cassell Publishing Company, 104 & 106 Fourth Avenue [cop. 1891]. 303 p. AP, HEH, LC, O, Y

———— Boscobel. *In* The Septameron (1888), No. 4867.

5986 WILLIAMS, FRANK PURDY. Hallie Marshall, a True Daughter of the South ... New York: The Abbey Press, 114 Fifth Avenue. London, Montreal [cop. 1900]. 183 p., illus.                    HEH, LC
Deposited Nov. 5, 1900.

5987 ———— A True Son of Liberty ... New York: E. Scott, printer and publisher, 1892. 190 p.                    H

5988 WILLIAMS, GEORGE FORRESTER. Bullet and Shell: War as the Soldier Saw It ... New York: Fords, Howard, & Hulbert, 1883. 454 p., illus.
CU, H, HEH, LC, N, UC, Y
The 1895 ed. changed title to *Bullet and Shell: A Soldier's Romance.*

5989 [WILLIAMS, HAROLD.] Mr. and Mrs. Morton: A Novel. Boston: Cupples, Upham & Co., 1883. 292 p.          AP, BA, CU, H, HEH, LC, O
Miscegenation.

5990 [————] Silken Threads: A Detective Story. By George Afterem [pseud.]. Boston: Cupples, Upham and Company, 1885. 342 p.
BA, CU, H, HEH, LC

5991 WILLIAMS, JESSE LYNCH. The Adventures of a Freshman ... New York: Charles Scribner's Sons, 153-157 Fifth Avenue [cop. 1899]. 201 p., illus.                    H, LC, O, UVB, Y
Deposited Oct. 26, 1899.

5992 ———— Princeton Stories ... New York: Charles Scribner's Sons, 1895. 319 p.                    CU, HEH, LC, O, UP, Y
*Contents:* The Winning of the Cane—The Madness of Poler Stacy—The Hazing of Valliant—Hero Worship—The Responsibility of Lawrence—Fixing That Freshman—The Scrub Quarter-Back—When Girls Come to Princeton—The Little Tutor—College Men—The Man That Led the Class.

5993 ———— The Stolen Story, and Other Newspaper Stories ... New York: Charles Scribner's Sons, 1899. 291 p., front.
CU, H, HEH, LC, N, O, UM, UVB, Y
*Also contains:* The New Reporter—Mrs. H. Harrison Wells's Shoes—The Great Secretary-of-State Interview—The City Editor's Conscience—The Cub Reporter and the King of Spain—The Old Reporter.

5994 WILLIAMS, JOHN AUGUSTUS. Rosa Emerson; or, A Young Woman's Influence. A Story of the Lodge, the Church, and the School ... Saint Louis: Christian Publishing Company, 1897. 373 p.          LC, UC

5995 ———— Thornton: A Kentucky Story ... Cincinnati: F. L. Rowe, 1900. 304 p.
Listed in L. S. Thompson, p. 117.

5996 WILLIAMS, JOHN GRANDISON. The Adventures of a Seventeen-Year-Old Lad and the Fortunes He Might Have Won . . . Boston: Printed for the author by the Collins Press, 1894. 308 p., illus.

H, HEH, LC, N, UM, Y

Whaling and gold mining in California.

5997 ———— Invasion of the Moon; or, Something for Philanthropists to Do. Second Enlarged Edition . . . Charleston, S.C.: Edward Perry & Co., printers and stationers, No. 217 Meeting St. [1888]. 66 p.
Listed in Turnbull, Vol. IV, p. 261.

5998 ———— "De Ole Plantation". . . Charleston, S.C.: Walker, Evans, & Cogswell Co., printers, 1895. 67 p. Printed in double columns.  LC

WILLIAMS, MARTHA MCCULLOCH. A Fair Exchange. *In* Short Story Masterpieces (1900), No. 4931.

5999 WILLIAMS, MRS. RHOBY S. Alice Norwood; or, The Winter of the Heart . . . New York: N. Tibbals & Sons, 124 Nassau Street [cop. 1884]. 330 p.  LC
Deposited Jan. 9, 1885.

6000 ———— Not Like Other Men . . . New York: J. S. Ogilvie Publishing Company, 57 Rose Street [cop. 1896]. 147 p.  LC
Deposited Sept. 24, 1897.

6001 ———— Pearl Trevelyan; or, Virtue Reaps Its Own Reward . . . Quincy, Ill.: The Whig Book and Job Printing House, 1876. 148 p.  LC, N

WILLIAMS, ROBERT DOLLY, *pseud. See* Potter, Margaret Horton

6002 WILLIAMSON, EDWARD HAND. The Scout: A Legend of Old Thornbury Township . . . Philadelphia, 1886. 190, IV p.  LC

6003 [WILLIS, CHARLES W.] Not Before Marriage: A Novel. By Allan Eric [pseud.] . . . Chicago: The Twentieth Century Publishing Co. [cop. 1897]. 38, [1] p.  LC

6004 [————] A Yankee Crusoe; or, The Golden Treasure of the Virgin Islands. By Allan Eric [pseud.] . . . Boston: Henry A. Dickerman & Son, 1900. 262 p., illus.  HEH, LC

6005 WILLIS, J. S. John Martin, Jr.: A Story of "The Iron Mask". . . [N.p., cop. 1892.] 232 p.  HEH

WILLIS, NATHANIEL PARKER. Two Buckets in a Well. *In* Stories by American Authors, IV (1884), No. 5270.

WILLISSON, ELIZABETH OCTAVIA, *jt. au. See* Spratley, M. G. Confessions of Two (1886), No. 5141.

6006 WILLMOTT, NELLIE LOWE. A Dash of Red Paint . . . New Haven, Conn.: Press of the E. B. Sheldon Co., 1894. 86 p., illus. HEH, LC, Y

WILLOUGHBY, FRANK M., *pseud.* *See* Stevens, T. Hood

6007 WILLS, J. BAXTER. A Mystery Solved . . . Burlington, Vermont: Wells, Richardson & Co. [cop. 1897]. 28 p., illus. LC
A tale to promote publisher's "English Pills."

6008 WILLSON, THOMAS EDGAR. It Is the Law: A Story of Marriage and Divorce in New York . . . New York & Chicago: Belford, Clarke & Company [cop. 1887]. 218 p. AP, CU, HEH, LC
Deposited Mar. 3, 1888.

6009 WILSON, AUGUSTA JANE (EVANS). At the Mercy of Tiberius: A Novel . . . New York: G. W. Dillingham, successor to G. W. Carleton & Co. London: Chapman and Hall, 1887. 616 p. CU, HEH, N, UM, UVB, Y

6010 ———— Infelice: A Novel . . . New York: G. W. Carleton & Co. London: S. Low, Son & Co., 1876. 572 p. CU, H, HEH, O, UVB, Y
Of the theater.

———— The Trial of Beryl. *In* L. C. H. Langford, *comp.*, The Woman's Story (1889), No. 3206.

6011 [WILSON, DAVID.] Life in Whitehall during the Ship Fever Times. Whitehall, N.Y.: Inglee & Tefft, 1900. 76 p., illus. Printed in double columns. HEH, Y

WILSON, MRS. E. V. Barb'ry. *In* Tales from McClure's: The West (1897), No. 5363.

———— Rachel. *In* Tales from McClure's: Romance (1897), No. 5362.

6012 WILSON, ELIZABETH (SARGENT). Sugar-Pine Murmurings. By Elizabeth Sargent Wilson and J. L. Sargent. San Francisco, Cal.: Published for the authors by the Whitaker & Ray Company, Incorporated, 1899. 109 p., illus. HEH, LC
*Contents:* Tailings, by Elizabeth Sargent Wilson—Nuggets, by J. L. Sargent—A Digger Injun, by E. S. Wilson—El Christo, by J. L. Sargent—Majel, by E. S. Wilson—The Justice of John Fannin, by J. L. Sargent—The Colonel and Betty Ann, by E. S. Wilson—Squealing Alex, by E. S. Wilson—Prince of Orange, by E. S. Wilson.

6013 [WILSON, F. T.] Surf: A Summer Pilgrimage. By Saul Wright [pseud.]. New York: Fords, Howard, & Hulbert [cop. 1881]. 218 p. BU, HEH, LC
Newspapermen take a boat trip on the Potomac.

WILSON, HARRY LEON. The Story of William. *In* Hanks: Assorted Yarns from Puck (1893), No. 2444.

———— True Love's Triumph. *In* Mavericks (1892), No. 3663.

6014 ———— Zigzag Tales from the East to the West . . . New York: Keppler & Schwarzmann, 1894. 167 p., illus.   BA, HEH, UC, UP, UVB, Y
*Contents:* Bromley vs. Gilner—An Overland Journey—How a Good Man Went Wrong—Skinner's Awakening—Smith's Biography—The Defection of Maria Hepworth—A Old Clock—The Success of James Ferguson, M.D.—A Pan-American Romance—A Family Affair—A Western Man—An Amateur Lover—Father Cortland's Vacation.

6015 WILSON, HENRY R. The Russian Refugee: A Tale of the Blue Ridge . . . New York: Thomas R. Knox & Co., successors to James Miller, 1887. 610 p.   AP, BA, H, HEH, LC, O

6016 WILSON, MRS. LESTER S. Mrs. Sinclair's Experiments . . . Kansas City, Mo.: H. T. Wright, 1900. 238 p.
Listed PW, June 16, 1900.

6017 WILSON, MARIAN CALVERT. Guy Ormsby: A Romance . . . New York: Charles T. Dillingham, No. 718 Broadway [1889]. 208 p.   AP, HEH, LC
Deposited Dec. 2, 1889.
London and Rome.

6018 ———— Manuelita: The Story of San Xavier del Bac . . . New York: United States Book Company, 5 and 7 East Sixteenth Street. Chicago, 266 & 268 Wabash Ave. [cop. 1891]. 305 p., front.   HEH, LC, N
Deposited Jan. 17, 1892.
At the time of Father Kino.

6019 ———— Rénée: A Romance . . . New York: Charles T. Dillingham, 1888. 294 p.   HEH, LC, O
From the Cumberland Moutains to Europe.

6020 WILSON, ROBERT BURNS. Until the Day Break: A Novel . . . New York: Charles Scribner's Sons, 1900. 330 p.   LC, N, O

6021 WILSON, SYDNEY J. Stanley Huntingdon: A Novel . . . Philadelphia: J. B. Lippincott Company, 1886. 269 p.   HEH, LC
Of a southerner's move to San Francisco.

6022 WILSON, THEODORA B. After Many Days: An American Novel . . . New York: Lovell, Coryell & Company, 43, 45, and 47 East Tenth Street [cop. 1892]. 366 p.   HEH
James Clarence Harvey, jt. au.

WILSON, THOMAS H. The Senior Lieutenant's Story. *In* C. King, *ed.,* The Colonel's Christmas Dinner (1890), No. 3098.
Later printed in No. 3099.

6023   ——— A Soldier's Sweetheart, and Other Stories . . . Omaha, Neb.: Jno. L. Gideon & Co., 1894. 224 p.     HEH, LC
*Also contains:* My Bunkey—Biddy—A Sudden Impulse—A Bird of Honor—An Unfinished Romance—Mrs. Jack of "Ours"—Ringing of the Chimes.

6024   WILSON, WILLIAM HUNTINGTON. Rafnaland: The Strange Story of John Heath Howard . . . New York and London: Harper & Brothers, 1900. 352 p., illus.     LC, UV
Of an unknown country beyond the North Pole.

6025   WILSON, WILLIAM ROBERT ANTHONY. Good-for-Nuthin': The Tale of a Christmas Promise . . . Buffalo, N.Y.: Peter Paul Book Co., 1896. 52 p.
Listed PW, Mar. 7, 1896.

WINCHESTER, CARROLL, *pseud.* *See* Curtis, Caroline Gardiner (Cary)

6026   WINDSOR, WILLIAM. Loma: A Citizen of Venus . . . St. Paul, Minn.: The Windsor & Lewis Publishing Co., 1897. 429 p., front.     N
The citizen visits Chicago and expresses radical religious views.

6027   WINSLOW, HELEN MARIA. Salome Shepard, Reformer . . . Boston, Mass.: Arena Publishing Company, 1893. 256 p., front.     CU, HEH
New England tale.

6028   WINSLOW, WILLIAM. A Daughter of Neptune, and Other Stories . . . New York: Continental Publishing Co., 24 & 26 Murray Street [cop. 1899]. 229 p.     LC
*Also contains:* To the Death—A Wild Flower of Elkhorn—The Graven Image—The Rose of Princess Valley.

6029   WINSLOW, WILLIAM HENRY. Cruising and Blockading . . . Pittsburgh, Pa.: J. R. Weldin & Co., 1885. 207 p.     CU, H, LC, UM, UP, UV
At head of title: "A Naval Story of the Late War."

6030   WINSOR, JUSTIN. Was Shakespeare Shapleigh? A Correspondence in Two Entanglements. Edited by Justin Winsor. Boston and New York: Houghton, Mifflin and Company. The Riverside Press, Cambridge, 1887. 76 p.     AP, BA, BU, CU, H, HEH, LC, UP, Y

6031   WINSTOCK, MELVIN G. "A Modern Hercules": The Tale of a Sculptress . . . Leadville, Colo.: Herald Democrat Print, 1899. 112 p.     LC

WINSTON, NANNIE B. Miss Isabella. *In* [Mrs. K. P. Minor] *comp.,* From Dixie (1893), No. 3756.

6032   ——— Waters That Pass Away . . . New York: G. W. Dillingham Co., 1899. 322 p.     HEH, LC
Wife supports crippled artist husband by selling herself to obtain work in a newspaper office.

WINTER, MRS., *pseud.* *See* Griswold, Jane (Emmet)

6033 WINTERBURN, FLORENCE HULL. Southern Hearts ... New York: The F. M. Lupton Publishing Company, 1900. 406 p., front.
CU, HEH, LC, O, UV
*Contents:* When Love Enslaves—The Wife of Lothario—Peter Weaver—A Halt at Dawn—Pink and Black—Mrs. May's Private Income—The Laziest Girl in Virginia—An Awakening—Apple Blossoms.

6034 WISE, JOHN SERGEANT. Diomed: The Life, Travels, and Observations of a Dog ... Boston, London, and New York: Lamson, Wolffe and Company, 1897. 330 p., illus. BA, BU, H, HEH, LC, O, UV, Y
Autobiography of a hunting dog.

WISSER, JOHN PHILIP. A Pitiful Surrender. *In* C. King, *ed.*, An Initial Experience (1894), No. 3105.

———— The Warlock Fight. *In* C. King *ed.*, By Land and Sea (1891), No. 3092.
Later printed in No. 3099.

6035 WISTER, OWEN. The Jimmyjohn Boss, and Other Stories . . . New York and London: Harper & Brothers, 1900. 332, [1] p., illus.
AP, BA, H, HEH, LC, O, UC, UM, UP, UVB, Y
*Also contains:* A Kinsman of Red Cloud—Sharon's Choice—Napoleon Shave-Tail—Twenty Minutes for Refreshments—The Promised Land—Hank's Woman—Padre Ignazio.

6036 ———— Lin McLean ... New York and London: Harper & Brothers, 1898. 277, [1] p., illus. AP, BA, HEH, LC, UC, UP, UVB, Y

6037 ———— The New Swiss Family Robinson: A Tale for Children of All Ages ... Cambridge: Charles W. Sever, University Bookstore, 1882. 25 p., illus. Printed in double columns. BA, H, HEH, Y

[————] *attrib. au.* The Palace of the Closed Window. *In* [Mrs. J. Lodge] *ed.*, A Week away from Time (1887), No. 3382.

6038 ———— Red Men and White ... New York: Harper & Brothers, 1896. 280 p., illus. BA, CU, H, HEH, LC, UM, UVB
*Contents:* Little Big Horn Medicine—Specimen Jones—The Serenade at Siskiyou—The General's Bluff—Salvation—Gap—The Second Missouri Compromise—La Tinaja Bonita—A Pilgrim on the Gila.

———— The Reprieve of Capitalist Clyve. *In* Ten Notable Stories (1894), No. 5391.

6039 WITHERSPOON, MRS. ISABELLA M. Rita de Garthez, the Beautiful Reconcentrado: A Tale of the Hispano-American War ... Bellport, New York: Regent Publishing Company, 1898. 38 p.
Copy examined at New York Public Library.

6040 [WITHERSPOON, ORLANDO.] Doctor Ben: An Episode in the Life of a Fortunate Unfortunate ... Boston: James R. Osgood and Company, 1882. 382 p. AP, BA, LC, O
At head of title: "Round-Robin Series."
Of insanity.

WITTE, BEATRICE. A Little Boy of Dreams. *In* New Stories from the Chap-Book (1898), No. 3949.

6041 WIXON, SUSAN HELEN. All in a Lifetime: A Romance ... Fall River, Mass.: Published by the author, 1884. 397 p. HEH, Y

6042 WOERNER, JOHN GABRIEL. The Rebel's Daughter: A Story of Love, Politics, and War ... Boston, Mass.: Little, Brown & Co., 1899. 775 p., illus. CU, HEH, LC, N, O

6043 WOLF, ALICE S. A House of Cards ... Chicago: Stone & Kimball, 1896. 281 p., 1 l. CU, HEH, LC, O, UP, Y
San Francisco.

6044 WOLF, EMMA. Heirs of Yesterday ... Chicago: A. C. McClurg & Co., 1900. 287 p. CU, HEH, LC, O, Y
Social life of the Jews in San Francisco.

6045 ———— The Joy of Life ... Chicago: A. C. McClurg and Company, 1896. 253 p. HEH, LC, O

6046 ———— Other Things Being Equal ... Chicago: A. C. McClurg and Company, 1892. 275 p. CU, H, HEH, LC, UC, UV
San Francisco.

6047 ———— A Prodigal in Love: A Novel ... New York: Harper & Brothers, 1894. 258 p. HEH, LC, O
San Francisco to Europe.

6048 THE WOLF AT THE DOOR. Boston: Roberts Brothers, 1877. 242 p.
BA, H, HEH, LC, O, UV
At head of title: "No Name Series."
Boston heiress loses fortune.

6049 WOLTOR, ROBERT. A Short and Truthful History of the Taking of California and Oregon by the Chinese in the Year A.D. 1899 ... San Francisco: A. L. Bancroft and Company, 1882. 82 p. HEH, LC, O

6050 WOMBLE, WALTER L. Love in the Mists: A Novel ... Raleigh, N.C.: Presses of Edwards and Broughton, 1892. 141 p. LC
North Carolina moonshiners.

6051 WOMEN'S HUSBANDS. I, The Barber of Midas. II, The False Prince. III, Narcissus. Philadelphia: J. B. Lippincott & Co., 1880. 99 p. Printed in double columns.  LC, O

6052 WON BY LOVE: The Story of Irene Kendall. By the Author of "Bound-brook." Boston: Ira Bradley & Co., 1888. 257 p.
Listed PW, Mar. 3, 1888.

WONBAR, *Captain* MINUS, *pseud.* *See* Thurston, George T.

6053 THE WONDERFUL NARRATIVE OF MISS JULIA DEAN, the Only Survivor of the Steamship "City of Boston," Lost at Sea in 1870. Miss Dean Was Shipwrecked and Cast upon an Uninhabited Island Where She Remained for Over Nine Years! . . . Philadelphia, Pa.: Published for her by Barclay & Co., 21 North 7th Street, 1880. 64 p., illus.  HEH, LC
Signed at end: "Julia Dean (Mrs. Charles Vollar)."

6054 WOOD, AIMÉE M. Musical Romances . . . Kansas City, Mo.: The Life Publishing Co., 1898. 142 p.  LC

6055 [WOOD, ANNA COGSWELL.] Diana Fontaine: A Novel. By Algernon Ridgeway [pseud.]. Philadelphia: J. B. Lippincott Company, 1891. 306 p.  LC, O, UC, UV
The South after the Civil War.

6056 [WOOD, AUGUSTUS B.] Cupid on Crutches; or, One Summer at Narragansett Pier. By A. B. W. . . . New York: G. W. Carleton & Co. London: S. Low, Son & Co., 1879. 223 p., front.  BA, BU, HEH, LC, UM, Y

6057 [WOOD, CHARLOTTE DUNNING.] A Step Aside. By Charlotte Dunning [pseud.] . . . Boston and New York: Houghton, Mifflin and Company. The Riverside Press, Cambridge, 1886. 333 p.  AP, CU, HEH, LC, O

6058 [———] Upon a Cast. By Charlotte Dunning [pseud.] . . . New York: Harper & Brothers, 1885. 330 p.  AP, H, HEH, LC, O, UC
Village life and gossip on the Hudson River.

6059 WOOD, E. ALLEN. Tancredi: A Tale of the Opera. A Novel . . . New York: G. W. Dillingham, 1888. 363 p.  HEH, LC, UC

6060 WOOD, EDITH (ELMER). Her Provincial Cousin: A Story of Brittany . . . New York: The Cassell Publishing Co., 31 East 17th St. [cop. 1893]. 184 p.  LC, O, Y
At head of title: "The 'Unknown' Library."
Deposited Feb. 1, 1894.

6061 WOOD, FRANCES HARTSON. Warp and Woof; or, New Frames for Old Pictures . . . Boonton, New Jersey: F. H. Wood, 1890. 431 p. HEH, LC
Eva Paine Kitchel, jt. au.

6062 WOOD, HENRY. Edward Burton . . . Boston: Lee and Shepard. New York: Chas. T. Dillingham, 1890. 299 p.    AP, CU, H, HEH, LC, O, Y
Bar Harbor, Maine.

6063 ———— Victor Serenus: A Story of the Pauline Era . . . Boston, U.S.A.: Lee and Shepard, 1898. 502 p.    BU, H, HEH, LC, N, O, UM, UVB, Y

6064 [WOOD, MRS. J.] Pantaletta: A Romance of Sheheland . . . New York: The American News Company, 1882. 239 p.    LC
Satire on women's rights movement.

6065 WOOD, JEROME JAMES. The Wilderness and the Rose: A Story of Michigan . . . Hudson, Mich.: Wood Book Company, 1890. 133 p.
HEH, LC, N, UM

6066 WOOD, JOHN SEYMOUR. A Coign of Vantage . . . New York: Dodd, Mead & Company [cop. 1893]. 264 p., front.    BA, HEH, LC, O, Y
A New York couple in Switzerland.

6067 ———— College Days; or, Harry's Career at Yale . . . New York, London: The Outing Company, Limited, 1894. 429 p., illus.
H, HEH, LC, O, UM, UV, Y

6068 ———— A Daughter of Venice . . . New York: Cassell Publishing Company, Fourth Avenue, 1893. 189 p., illus.    HEH, O, UM, Y
Of an American in Venice.

6069 ———— Gramercy Park: A Story of New York . . . New York: D. Appleton and Company, 1892. 218 p.    CU, H, HEH, LC, N, O, Y

6070 ———— An Old Beau, and Other Stories . . . New York: Cassell Publishing Company, 104 & 106 Fourth Avenue [cop. 1892]. 314 p., illus.
HEH, LC, O
*Contents:* The Story of an Old Beau—A New England Ingénue—Patriotism—An Unworldling—How Amasa Snow Got on His Feet—Poor Cousin Parker!—A Street Car Adventure.
Deposited Feb. 4, 1893.

———— A Puritan Ingénue. In Stories of New York (1893), No. 5279.
Included in No. 6070 as "A New England Ingénue."

6071 ———— Yale Yarns: Sketches of Life at Yale University . . . New York, London: G. P. Putnam's Sons; the Knickerbocker Press, 1895. 307 p., illus.    BA, BU, CU, H, HEH, LC, N, O, UC, UM, UV, Y
*Contents:* One on the Governor—The Old Fence—In the Political Cauldron—"Little Jack" Horner's Pie—With the Dwight Hall Heelers—The "Dwarf's" Prom—The Last Cruise of the "Nancy Brig"—Old Sleuth's Level Head—Nate Hale, of '73—The Dawn Tea—The Great Springfield Games—In the Toils of the Enemy—An Hypnotic Seance—A Violent Remedy—"Chums over in Old South"—Commencement.

6072 [WOOD, JULIA AMANDA (SARGENT).] The Brown House at Duffield: A Story of Life without and within the Fold. By Minnie Mary Lee [pseud.] ... Baltimore: Kelly, Piet & Co., 1876. 234 p.                     LC

6073 [———] Strayed from the Fold: A Story of Life in the Northwest. Founded on Facts. By Minnie Mary Lee [pseud.] . . . Baltimore: Kelly, Piet and Company, 1878. 303 p.                     UM

WOOD, LOCK, *pseud. See* Lockwood, William Lewis

6074 [WOOD, LYDIA COPE.] The Haydocks' Testimony. By L. C. W. . . . Philadelphia: Christian Arbitration and Peace Society, 1890. 276 p.
                     BU, HEH, LC, O, UP
Of a Quaker family.

6075 WOOD, S. ELLA. Shibboleth: A Novel . . . Chicago: W. B. Conkey Company [cop. 1898]. 125 p.                     HEH, LC
New York.

6076 [WOOD, MRS. SETH S.] Doctor Phoenix Skelton; or, The Man with a Mystery. By Fewi Stesh [pseud.] . . . Fortress Monroe, Va.: S. S. Wood, cop. 1887. 176 p.                     LC

6077 [WOOD-SEYS, ROLAND ALEXANDER.] The Great Chin Episode. By Paul Cushing [pseud.] . . . New York and London: Macmillan and Co., 1893. 256 p.                     AP, HEH, LC

6078 WOODBRIDGE, H. HORATIO. Dig: Two Heads Wanted. A Novel . . . Jacksonville, Ill.: T. D. Price & Co., 1876. 362 p.     H, HEH, LC, Y
Murder mystery; England.

6079 WOODBURY, HELEN LAURA (SUMNER). The White Slave; or, "The Cross of Gold." By Helen L. Sumner. Chicago: Charles H. Kerr & Company, cop. 1896. Cover title, 34 p.                     CU, LC

6080 [WOODBURY, JOHN HUBBARD.] How I Found It, North and South. Together with Mary's Statement. Boston: Lee and Shepard. New York: Charles T. Dillingham, 1880. 295 p.                     LC, O, UC
Would seem to be an actual account.
Of a New England farm.

6081 WOODBURY, MARY C. Heredity; or, Harry Harwood's Inheritance . . . Boston: The McDonald & Gill Co., 1892. 285 p.                     LC

6082 [WOODRUFF, JULIA LOUISA MATILDA (CURTISS).] Bellerue; or, The Story of Rolf. By W. L. M. Jay [pseud.] . . . New York: E. P. Dutton & Company, 1891. 478 p.                     HEH, LC, O

6083 WOODS, KATE (TANNATT). A Fair Maid of Marblehead . . . New York: Frank F. Lovell & Company, 142 and 144 Worth Street [cop. 1889]. 243 p.                     HEH, UM
Artists at Marblehead, Massachusetts.

6084 ———— That Dreadful Boy: An American Novel . . . Boston: De Wolfe, Fiske and Company, 1886. 316 p.                    AP, H, LC, O

6085 WOODS, KATHARINE PEARSON. The Crowning of Candace . . . New York: Dodd, Mead and Company, 1896. 233 p.        H, HEH, LC, Y
Of a writer.

6086 ———— From Dusk to Dawn . . . New York: D. Appleton and Company, 1892. 310 p.                                        HEH, LC, O
Of a young clergyman.

6087 ———— John: A Tale of King Messiah . . . New York: Dodd, Mead and Company, 1896. 346 p.                          BU, HEH, LC

6088 ———— Metzerott, Shoemaker . . . New York: Thomas Y. Crowell & Co., 46 East Fourteenth St. [cop. 1889]. 373 p.    H, HEH, LC, O, UC
Of socialistic interest.

6089 ———— The Son of Ingar . . . New York: Dodd, Mead and Company, 1897. 315 p.                                        HEH, LC, O, Y
Jerusalem.

6090 ———— A Web of Gold . . . New York: Thomas Y. Crowell & Co., 46 East Fourteenth Street [cop. 1890]. 307 p.      AP, H, HEH, LC, O, Y
References to labor and Mafia.

6091 WOODS, VIRNA. An Elusive Lover . . . Boston and New York: Houghton, Mifflin and Company. The Riverside Press, Cambridge, 1898. 254 p., 1 l.                                                       BU, HEH, LC, O
Los Angeles.

6092 ———— A Modern Magdalene . . . Boston: Lee and Shepard, 1894. 346 p.                                                    HEH, LC
Girl runs off with a married man to San Francisco.

6093 WOODWARD, GEORGE AUSTIN. The Diary of a "Peculiar" Girl . . . Buffalo: The Peter Paul Book Company, 1896. 130 p.       LC

6094 WOODWARD, ROBERT PITCHER. Trains That Met in the Blizzard: A Composite Romance. Being a Chronicle of the Extraordinary Adventure of a Party of Twelve Men and One Woman in the Great American Blizzard March 12, 1888 . . . New York: Salmagundi Publishing Company, 1896. 396 p., illus.                                 CU, H, HEH, LC

6095 WOOLET, A. WELLINGTON, pseud. The Woolet Papers . . . New York, London: Trade-Mark Record Publishers, 1899. 231 p., front.
                                                                    HEH, LC, Y

6096 WOOLF, PHILIP. Who Is Guilty . . . New York: Cassell & Company, Limited, 739 & 741 Broadway [cop. 1886]. 247 p.    AP, BA, HEH, LC, O
Detective story.

6097 WOOLLEY, CELIA (PARKER). A Girl Graduate . . . Boston and New York: Houghton, Mifflin and Company. The Riverside Press, Cambridge, 1889. 459 p.     AP, BA, BU, H, HEH, O
Of a girl educated above her family.

6098 ——— Love and Theology: A Novel . . . Boston: Ticknor and Company, 1887. 439 p.     BA, H, HEH, LC, O
Also published as: *Rachel Armstrong; or, Love and Theology.* 5th ed. Boston: Ticknor and Company, 211 Tremont Street [cop. 1887].     AP, BU

6099 ——— Roger Hunt . . . Boston and New York: Houghton, Mifflin and Company. The Riverside Press, Cambridge, 1892. 370 p.
    BA, HEH, LC, O, UC, Y
Of matrimony.

WOOLSON, ABBA LOUISA (GOULD). An Evening's Adventure. *In* L. C. H. Langford, *comp.,* The Woman's Story (1889), No. 3206.

6100 WOOLSON, CONSTANCE FENIMORE. Anne: A Novel . . . New York: Harper & Brothers, 1882. 540 p., illus.     BA, CU, H, HEH, LC, N, O, UVB, Y
Great Lakes and Mackinac Island.

6101 ——— Dorothy, and Other Italian Stories . . . New York: Harper & Brothers, 1896. 287 p., illus.     AP, CU, HEH, LC, N, O, UC, UM, UVB, Y
*Also contains:* A Transplanted Boy—A Florentine Experiment—A Waitress—At the Château of Corinne.

6102 ——— East Angels: A Novel . . . New York: Harper & Brothers, 1886. 591 p.     AP, BA, CU, H, HEH, N, O, UC, UM, UP, UVB, Y

6103 ——— For the Major: A Novelette . . . New York: Harper & Brothers, 1883. 208 p., illus.     AP, BA, CU, H, HEH, LC, N, O, UC, UP, UVB
North Carolina town life.

6104 ——— The Front Yard, and Other Italian Stories . . . New York: Harper & Brothers, 1895. 272 p., illus.
    BA, BU, CU, H, HEH, LC, N, O, UC, UM, UP, UVB, Y
*Also contains:* Neptune's Shore—A Pink Villa—The Street of the Hyacinth—A Christmas Party—In Venice.

6105 ——— Horace Chase: A Novel . . . New York: Harper & Brothers, 1894. 419 p.     AP, BU, CU, H, HEH, LC, N, O, UC, UM, UP, UVB, Y

6106 ——— Jupiter Lights: A Novel . . . New York: Harper & Brothers, 1889. 347 p.     AP, BA, BU, CU, H, HEH, LC, N, O, UC, UP, UVB, Y
On the Florida coast.

——— Miss Grief. *In* Stories by American Authors, IV (1884), No. 5270.

6107 ——— Rodman the Keeper: Southern Sketches . . . New York: D. Appleton and Company, 1880. 339 p.

CU, H, HEH, LC, N, O, UC, UM, UVB, Y

*Also contains:* Sister St. Luke—Miss Elisabetha—Old Gardiston—The South Devil—In the Cotton Country—Felipa—"Bro."—King David—Up in the Blue Ridge.

WORDEN, A. T., *jt. au. See* Arkell, W. J. Napoleon Smith (1888), No. 127.

6108 WORDEN, MRS. HATTIE WELLER. Edna Lee: A Novel . . . Chicago: Scroll Publishing Company, 1900. 240 p. LC

6109 [WORDEN, WILBERTINE (TETERS).] The Snows of Yester-Year: A Novel. By Wilbertine Teters . . . Boston: Arena Publishing Company, 1895. 244 p. LC

A consumptive couple move to mountains of Colorado.

6110 THE WORLDLY TWIN: The Heavenly Twins "Not in It." New York: G. W. Dillingham, 1893. 232 p. LC

6111 [WORLEY, FREDERICK U.] Three Thousand Dollars a Year. Moving Forward; or, How We Got There. The Complete Liberation of All the People. Abridged from the Advance Sheets of a History of Industrial and Governmental Reforms in the United States, to Be Published in the Year 2001. By Benefice [pseud.]. [Washington, D.C.: J. P. Wright, printer, 1890.] 104 p. LC, N

6112 [WORRON, HARRIET B.] "Trustum" and His Grandchildren. By One of Them. Nantucket: Published by the author. Yarmouth Port, Mass: Printed at the "Register" Printing Office, 1881. 261 p.

BU, H, HEH, LC, N

WORTH, ELLIS, *pseud. See* Ellsworth, Mrs. Louise C.

6113 [WORTHINGTON, ELIZABETH STRONG.] The Biddy Club and How Its Members, Wise and Otherwise, Some Toughened and Some Tender-Footed in the Rugged Ways of Housekeeping, Grappled with the Troublous Servant Question . . . By Griffith A. Nicholas [pseud.]. Chicago: A. C. McClurg and Company, 1888. 308 p.

AP, BA, H, HEH, LC, O, UC, UM, Y

6114 ——— The Gentle Art of Cooking Wives . . . New York: Dodge Publishing Company, 150 Fifth Avenue [cop. 1900]. 247 p., front.

LC, UV, Y

Quotation at head of title.

6115 ——— How to Cook Husbands . . . New York: The Dodge Publishing Company, 1899. 190 p., illus. H, HEH, LC, UV, Y

At head of title: "They are really delicious—when properly treated."

6116 ———— The Little Brown Dog: A Tale of the Presidio . . . San Francisco: Cubery & Company, printers and publishers, 1898. 58 p.   HEH San Francisco.

6117 [————] When Peggy Smiled: A Love Story. By Griffith Nicholas [pseud.]. Chicago: Augustus J. Palmer & Co., 1888.
Listed PW, Aug. 25, 1888.

6118 WRAY, ANGELINA W. Tales and Poems . . . New Brunswick, N.J.: J. Heidingsfeld, 42 Albany Street [cop. 1890]. 251 p.   HEH, UVB, Y
Contains: Mark—In a Fool's Paradise—In Two Worlds—A Dead Sin.

6119 [WRIGHT, C. W.] Joe Cummings; or, The Story of the Son of a Squaw in Search of His Mother. Written by Himself. Boston: J. G. Cupples Co. [cop. 1890]. 329 p.   HEH, LC
Deposited Sept. 29, 1890.

6120 WRIGHT, CALEB EARL. Legend of Bucks County: A Novel . . . Doylestown, Pa.: B. McGinty, printer and publisher, 1887. 280 p.
CU, HEH, UP, UVB

6121 ———— On the Lackawanna: A Tale of Northern Pennsylvania . . . Doylestown, Pa.: McGinty, printer, 1886. 254 p.
HEH, LC, UC, UM, UP, Y

6122 ———— Rachel Craig: A Novel. Connected with the Valley of Wyoming . . . Wilkes-Barre, Pa.: Robt. Baur & Son, printers and publishers, 1888. 308 p.   HEH, LC, N, UP, Y

6123 [————] Two Years behind the Plough; or, The Experience of a Pennsylvania Farm-Boy. Giving a True and Faithful Account of Life on a Bucks County Farm as He Found It during an Apprenticeship of Two Years . . . Philadelphia: Claxton, Remsen, & Haffelfinger, 1878. 224 p.   HEH
Authorship not firmly established.

6124 WRIGHT, EDWARD E. Everard and Eulalia: A Novel . . . Council Bluffs, Ia.: Herald Printing, 1886.
Listed in Alice Marple, Iowa Authors and Their Works (Des Moines, Ia., 1918), p. 334.

6125 ———— The Lightning's Flash, an Unveiling of Mysteries: A Stenographic Episode . . . Council Bluffs, Ia.: A. R. Woodford, printer [cop. 1892]. 91 p.   LC
Deposited Sept. 27, 1892.

6126 WRIGHT, JULIA (McNAIR). The Captain's Bargain . . . New York: National Temperance Society [cop. 1889]. 340 p., front.   CU, HEH

6127 —— Circled by Fire: A True Story . . . New York: National Temperance Society, 1879. 91 p., front.　　HEH, LC

6128 —— The Curse and the Cup . . . New York: National Temperance Society, 1879. 96 p., front.　　HEH, LC

6129 —— Cynthia's Sons: A Commonplace Story . . . New York: National Temperance Society [cop. 1896]. 366 p., front.　　LC

6130 —— A Day with a Demon . . . New York: National Temperance Society, 1880. 95 p., front.　　LC

6131 —— The Dragon and the Tea-Kettle: An Experience; and The Doppelgänger . . . New York: National Temperance Society, 1885. 288 p., front.　　LC, Y

6132 —— Firebrands: A Temperance Tale . . . New York: National Temperance Society, 1879. 357 p., front.　　LC

6133 —— Hannah, One of the Strong Women . . . New York: National Temperance Society [cop. 1883]. 290 p., front.　　HEH, LC

6134 —— Her Ready-Made Family . . . New York: National Temperance Society [cop. 1895]. 352 p.　　H, LC

6135 —— A Made Man: A Sequel to "The Story of Rasmus; or, The Making of a Man". . . New York: National Temperance Society, 1887. 308 p., front.　　HEH, Y

6136 —— A Modern Prodigal . . . New York: National Temperance Society, 1892. 325 p., front.　　LC

6137 —— On London Bridge: A True Story . . . New York: National Temperance Society, 1879. 88 p., front.　　LC

6138 —— Step by Step . . . New York: National Temperance Society, 1880. 92 p., front.
Listed PW, May 1, 1880.

6139 —— A Wife Hard Won: A Love Story . . . Philadelphia: J. B. Lippincott & Co., 1884. 320 p.　　AP, H, HEH, O

WRIGHT, LOIS, *pseud. See* Waite, Lucy

6140 WRIGHT, MARY (TAPPAN). A Truce, and Other Stories . . . New York: Charles Scribner's Sons, 1895. 287 p.　　BA, H, HEH, LC, O
*Also contains:* "As Haggards of the Rock"—"A Portion of the Tempest"—From Macedonia—Deep as First Love—A Fragment of a Play, with a Chorus.

WRIGHT, MAY, *pseud. See* Grumbine, Jesse Charles Fremont

WRIGHT, SAUL, *pseud*. *See* Wilson, F. T.

6141 WUNDERLICH, JENNIE M. Sweet Blossoms 'neath Frosted Leaves . . .
York, Pa.: P. Anstadt & Sons, 1899. 64 p. LC

WYATT, EDITH FRANKLIN. The Wolf in Sheep's Clothing. *In* New
Stories from the Chap-Book (1898), No. 3949.

6142 WYATT, ROSA. James Latrew . . . New York: John B. Alden, 1890. 175
p., front. LC

6143 WYMAN, EDWIN ALLEN. Ships by Day: A Novel . . . Boston: James
H. Earle, 1895. 451 p., illus. CU, H, HEH, LC, N, Y

6144 WYMAN, LILLIE BUFFUM (CHACE). Poverty Grass . . . Boston and New
York: Houghton, Mifflin and Company. The Riverside Press, Cam-
bridge, 1886. 320 p. AP, BU, H, HEH, LC, O, UC, Y
*Contents:* Hester's Dower—Saint or Sinner—Luke Gardiner's Love—The
Child of the State—"A Stranger, yet at Home"—And Joe—Bridget's Story—
Valentine's Chance.

X., A., *pseud*. *See* Mathews, Frances Aymar

X., S. M. *See* Queen, *Sister* Mary Xavier

6145 YALE, WELLINGTON, *pseud?* Congressman John L.: A History of His
Trials and Triumphs in Washington . . . Louisville, Ky.: The St.
James Publishing House, 1892. 185 p., illus. LC

6146 YANDELL, ENID. Three Girls in a Flat . . . By Enid Yandell, of Kentucky, Jean Loughborough, of Arkansas, Laura Hayes, of Illinois.
[Chicago: Press of Knight, Leonard & Co., cop. 1892.] 154, [1] p.,
illus. CU, LC, UC

6147 ——— ——— [Chicago: Press of Knight, Leonard & Co., cop. 1892.]
163, [1] p., illus. CU, HEH
Jean Loughborough's name dropped from title page in this ed.; pp. 59-73 reset
and extended to p. 83 with subsequent pages renumbered; some illus. differ.

6148 YARDLEY, ALICE TURNER. Yarns. By Alice Turner. Baltimore: John
Murphy & Co., 1895. 149 p., front. LC
*Contents:* The Pocket of the Old Dutch Costume—Uncle Zeb—Madeline—
Romance of the Little Tin Tea Kettle—Hannah—Aunt Deborah Alliwater—
A Half-Dime—On the Trail—Birch Bark—A Dutch Tulip—A Ghost Story—
Twin Sabots.

6149 [YARDLEY, MRS. JANE WOOLSEY.] Little Sister. Boston: Roberts
Brothers, 1882. 286 p. AP, HEH, LC, O
At head of title: "No Name Series."

6150 [————] A Superior Woman. Boston: Roberts Brothers, 1885. 348
p.                                                    AP, BA, HEH, LC, O, UV
At head of title: "No Name Series."

6151 [YATES, FREDERIC B.] Glendover: A Novel. By Deane Roscoe [pseud.]
. . . New York: The Authors' Publishing Company, 27 Bond Street
[cop. 1880]. 286 p.                                                    LC

YECHTON, BARBARA, pseud. See Krausé, Lyda Farrington

YORKE, ANTHONY, pseud. See Reilly, Bernard James

6152 [YOUNG, ALEXANDER.] Why We Live. By Summerdale [pseud.] . . .
Chicago: Howard, White & Co., printers, 1880. 135 p.         HEH, LC
Imaginary conversations with angels and archangels.

YOUNG, E. H. A College Adhesion. In At Wellesley (1896), No. 151.

6153 YOUNG, ELEANOR DEY. Two Princetonians and Other Jerseyites . . .
Trenton, N.J.: MacCrellish & Quigley, printers, 1898. 206 p., illus.
                                                              HEH, LC

6154 [YOUNG, ERNEST A.] Abner Ferret, the Lawyer Detective. By Harry
Rockwood [pseud.] . . . New York: J. S. Ogilvie & Company, 31 Rose
Street [cop. 1883]. 131 p.                                            LC

6155 [————] Allan Keene, the War Detective. By Harry Rockwood
[pseud.] . . . New York: J. S. Ogilvie & Company, 31 Rose Street
[cop. 1884]. 132 p.
Information supplied by Earle E. Coleman of Princeton University Library.

6156 [————] Clarice Dyke, the Female Detective. By Harry Rockwood
[pseud.] . . . New York: J. S. Ogilvie & Company, 31 Rose Street [cop.
1883]. 133 p.                                                        HEH

6157 [————] File No. 114: A Sequel to File 113 by Emile Gaboriau . . .
Chicago: George W. Ogilvie, 216 Lake Street, cop. 1886. 155 p.    LC

6158 [————] Fred Danford, the Skillful Detective; or, The Watertown
Mystery. By Harry Rockwood [pseud.] . . . Chicago: Geo. W.
Ogilvie, 230 Lake Street [cop. 1885]. 125 p.                         HEH
At head of title: "A Thrilling Detective Story."

6159 [————] Luke Leighton, the Government Detective. By Harry Rockwood [pseud.] . . . New York: J. S. Ogilvie Company, 31 Rose Street
[cop. 1884]. 111 p.                                              H, HEH, UM

6160 [————] Nat Foster, the Boston Detective: A Thrilling Story of
Detective Life. By Harry Rockwood [pseud.] . . . New York: J. S.
Ogilvie & Company, 31 Rose Street [cop. 1883]. 126 p.                LC

6161 [————] Neil Nelson, the Veteran Detective; or, Tracking Mail Robbers. By Harry Rockwood [pseud.] ... Chicago: Geo. W. Ogilvie, 230 Lake Street [cop. 1885]. 126 p., front.                    LC

6162 ———— A Wife's Honor: A Novel ... Chicago: Geo. W. Ogilvie, 230 Lake Street [cop. 1885]. 152 p.                    HEH, LC, UM

6163 YOUNG, FRED GRANT. Day-Dreams and Night-Mares ... Groveland, Mass.: The Hermitage Publishing Co., 1894. 170 p.                    HEH, LC
Contents: A Modern Cain—The Scarf Pin—Her Wedding Day—A Dental Tragedy—The Black Poodle—Hobson's Blighted Hopes—The Whispering Gallery—Brown's Ghost Story—The Gordon Rubies.

YOUNG, HUGH CARLYLE, jt. au. See Mitchell, G. D. "1999" (1887), No. 3767.

6164 YOUNG, JAMES L. Helen Duval: A French Romance ... San Francisco: The Bancroft Company, 1891. 202 p.                    LC, Y

6165 YOUNG, JULIA EVELYN (DITTO). Adrift: A Story of Niagara ... Philadelphia: J. B. Lippincott Company, 1889. 275 p.          BA, HEH, LC, O, Y

6166 YOUNG, KENNETH. Selene ... [Spartansburg, S.C., cop. 1896.] 81 p.                    LC

6167 [YOUNG, VIRGINIA C.] Philip: The Story of a Boy Violinist. By T. W. O. [pseud. of Virginia Young and Mary C. Hungerford]. Boston, New York, and London: Lamson, Wolffe and Company, 1898. 295 p.                    LC, Y

6168 YOUNG, VIRGINIA (DURANT). "Beholding as in a Glass": A Novel ... Boston: Arena Publishing Company, 1895. 277 p.                    HEH, LC

6169 ———— A Tower in the Desert ... Boston: Arena Publishing Company, 1896. 321 p.                    LC

6170 YOURELL, AGNES BOND. A Manless World ... New York: G. W. Dillingham, 1891. 169 p.                    LC, O, UP

Z., Z., pseud. See Doissy, Louise

6171 ZANE, ELIZABETH Z. While the World Slept ... Philadelphia: J. E. Winner, cop. 1896. 213 p.                    LC

ZAROVITCH, Princess VERA, pseud. See Lane, Mary E. (Bradley)

6172 ZEARING, MARGUERITE. Hasta Luego, Amigo Mio; and Out of the Silent Forever ... Denver, Colo.: W. H. Kistler & Co., 1898. 38 p., illus.                    LC

6173 —————— Where Angels Fear to Tread: A Tale of Life on a Mexican Hacienda and Bits of Travel in Mexico . . . Denver, Colo.: W. F. Robinson & Co., 1895. 195 p.                    LC

6174 ZEIGLER, WILBUR GLEASON. It Was Marlowe: A Story of the Secret of Three Centuries . . . Chicago: Donohue, Henneberry & Co., 407-429 Dearborn St. [cop. 1895]. 310 p., front.                    H, LC
Deposited May 9, 1898; H copy contains author's autograph and date "June 8, 1898."

ZELCOE, LOUIS B., *pseud.* *See* Van Fossen, Loo B.

6175 ZIMMERMAN, L. M. Yvonne: A Romance . . . 2d. ed. Baltimore, Md.: Published by the author, 1900. 333 p.
Listed PW, Dec. 8, 1900.

ZUTANA, *pseud.* *See* Sullivan, Helen

TITLE INDEX

# TITLE INDEX

*Initial articles are usually omitted in this index.*
*Numbers refer to items.*
*An "n" after a number refers to the notes under the item.*

A.D. 2050, 194
Abandoned, 5655
Abandoned Claim, 3404
Abandoning an Adopted Farm, 4759
Abbie Saunders, 3859
Abduction of Princess Chriemhild, 2282
Abijah Beanpole, 5688
Ablest Man in the World, 5276n
Abner Ferret, 6154
Aboard "The American Duchess," 3931
About My Father's Business, 3724
Abraham's Mother, 5391n
Accidental Romance, 4697
According to St. John, 5568
Achsah, 4701
Across the Campus, 2070
Across the Chasm, 3569
Actaeon, 1371
Action and the Word, 3645
Active Service, 1250
Actress' Daughter, 1899
Ada Greenwood, 4001
Adam Floyd, 3206n
Adam Johnstone's Son, 1262
Ada's Trust, 1590
Added Upon, 110
Adeline Gray, 834
Adirondack Idyl, 5636
Adirondack Romance, 4602
Adirondack Stories, 1487
Adirondack Tales, 3904
Adjutant's Story, 3098n, 3099n
Administratrix, 1350
Adobeland Stories, 4492
Adopted, 3959
Adopted Daughter, 1806a
Adopting an Abandoned Farm, 4760
Adrienne de Portalis, 2314
Adrietta, 1378
Adrift, 1591
Adrift: A Story of Niagara, 6165
Adrift on the Black Wild Tide, 3052

Adventures of a Consul Abroad, 3802
Adventures of a Fair Rebel, 1297
Adventures of a Freshman, 5991
Adventures of a Naval Officer, 2315
Adventures of a Philosopher, 1990
Adventures of a Rustic, 5266
Adventures of a Seventeen-Year-Old Lad, 5996
Adventures of a Tenderfoot, 4767
Adventures of a Tramp, 5138
Adventures of a Virginian, 1892
Adventures of a Widow, 1807
Adventures of an Atom, 120
Adventures of an Old Maid, 2258
Adventures of Captain Horn, 5227
Adventures of Ferdinand Tomasso, 2745
Adventures of François, 3776
Adventures of Frank Friendless and Elder Webber, 2574
Adventures of Harry Marline, 4308
Adventures of Huckleberry Finn, 1087
Adventures of Jones, 921
Adventures of My Freshman, 1430
Adventures of Three Worthies, 4684
Adventures of Timias Terrystone, 773
Adventures of Tom Sawyer, 1088
Adventures of Uncle Jeremiah and Family, 5188
Affair at Islington, 5917
Affinities, 737
Afield and Afloat, 5228
After All, 5121
After Business Hours, 1868n
After His Kind, 4084
After Long Years, 5533n
After Many Days: A Novel, 5470
After Many Days: An American Novel, 6022
After Many Years, 1063
After the Freshet, 4422
Afterglow, 3219